COVENT

THE EL

– A Comple

Desert Island Football Histories

Aberdeen: A Centenary History 1903-2003	1-874287-57-0
Aberdeen: Champions of Scotland 1954-55	1-874287-65-1
Aberdeen: The European Era – A Complete Record	1-874287-11-2
Bristol City: The Modern Era – A Complete Record	1-874287-28-7
Bristol City: The Early Years 1894-1915	1-874287-74-0
Cambridge United: The League Era – A Complete Record	1-874287-32-5
Cambridge United: 101 Golden Greats	1-874287-58-9
The Story of the Celtic 1888-1938	1-874287-15-5
Chelsea: Champions of England 1954-55	1-874287-77-5
Colchester Utd: Graham to Whitton – A Complete Record	1-874287-27-9
Coventry City: The Elite Era – A Complete Record	1-874287-83-X
Coventry City: An Illustrated History	1-874287-59-7
Dundee: Champions of Scotland 1961-62	1-874287-86-4
Dundee United: Champions of Scotland 1982-83	1-874287-71-6
History of the Everton Football Club 1878-1928	1-874287-14-7
Halifax Town: From Ball to Lillis – A Complete Record	1-874287-26-0
Hereford United: The League Era – A Complete Record	1-874287-18-X
Huddersfield Town: Champions of England 1923-1926	1-874287-88-0
Ipswich Town: The Modern Era – A Complete Record	1-874287-43-0
Ipswich Town: Champions of England 1961-62	1-874287-63-5
Kilmarnock: Champions of Scotland 1964-65	1-874287-87-2
Luton Town: The Modern Era – A Complete Record	1-874287-05-8
Luton Town: An Illustrated History	1-874287-37-6
Manchester United's Golden Age 1903-1914	1-874287-80-5
The Matt Busby Chronicles: Manchester United 1946-69	1-874287-53-8
Motherwell: Champions of Scotland 1931-32	1-874287-73-2
Norwich City: The Modern Era – A Complete Record	1-874287-67-8
Peterborough Utd: The Modern Era – A Complete Record	1-874287-33-3
Peterborough United: Who's Who?	1-874287-48-1
Plymouth Argyle: The Modern Era – A Complete Record	1-874287-54-6
Plymouth Argyle: 101 Golden Greats	1-874287-64-3
Plymouth Argyle: Snakes & Ladders 1930-2004	1-874287-82-1
Portsmouth: From Tindall to Ball – A Complete Record	1-874287-25-2
Portsmouth: Champions of England – 1948-49 & 1949-50	1-874287-50-3
The Story of the Rangers 1873-1923	1-874287-16-3
The Romance of the Wednesday 1867-1926	1-874287-17-1
Stoke City: The Modern Era – A Complete Record	1-874287-76-7
Stoke City: 101 Golden Greats	1-874287-55-4
Potters at War: Stoke City 1939-47	1-874287-78-3
Tottenham Hotspur: Champions of England 1951 & 1961	1-874287-84-8
West Ham: From Greenwood to Redknapp	1-874287-19-8
West Ham: The Elite Era – A Complete Record	1-874287-31-7
Wimbledon: From Southern League to Premiership	1-874287-09-0
Wimbledon: From Wembley to Selhurst	1-874287-20-1
Wimbledon: The Premiership Years	1-874287-40-6
Wrexham: The European Era – A Complete Record	1-874287-52-X
World Cup Histories	
England's Quest for the World Cup – A Complete Record	1-874287-61-9
Scotland: The Quest for the World Cup – A Complete Record	1-897850-50-6
Ireland: The Quest for the World Cup – A Complete Record	1-897850-80-8
Miscellaneous	
Red Dragons in Europe – A Complete Record	1-874287-01-5
The Book of Football: A History to 1905-06	1-874287-13-9
Football's War & Peace: The Tumultuous Season of 1946-47	1-874287-70-8

COVENTRY CITY

THE ELITE ERA

— A Complete Record —

(Second Edition)

Series Editor: Clive Leatherdale
Series Consultant: Leigh Edwards

Jim Brown

Desert Island Books

First Paperback Edition 2004
First Edition (cased) published in 1998
Second Edition (cased) published in 2001

DESERT ISLAND BOOKS LIMITED
7 Clarence Road, Southend on Sea, Essex SS1 1AN
United Kingdom
www.desertislandbooks.com

British Library Cataloguing-in-Publication Data
A catalogue record for this book is available from the British Library

ISBN 1-874287-83-X

Printed in Great Britain
by
4Edge Ltd

The publishers acknowledge with thanks the following for provision of photographs for this book: *The Coventry Evening Telegraph*, Coventry City FC, Edna Davis, and Allsport

Contents

Preface

In my eight years as chairman of Coventry City FC, there has rarely been a dull moment at Highfield Road. Over that period and for most of the club's 34 years in the top flight, the national media have patronisingly tagged the club as eternal strugglers, living to survive. People who understand and follow the team know better. It has not just been a story of survival; it has been a roller-coaster adventure, sometimes frustrating, sometimes exhilarating, but never dull; it has been an adventure of which to be proud.

This book chronicles City's years at the English game's top table and is a fascinating story. In my time at the club I have had to endure a couple of nail-biting eleventh-hour reprieves, which in a way are as memorable as a Cup final, but there have been major highlights, such as the Cup win of 1987, the adventure in Europe, and famous victories over the glamour clubs such as Manchester United, Liverpool and Arsenal.

I believe that the club still has the spirit and the will that enabled it to survive the battles over the remarkable era. For that reason I am convinced that our stay outside of the Premier League will be a temporary one and that a collective determination will carry us back to the Premiership at the earliest opportunity.

Jim Brown's knowledge of the club and its history, together with his passion for it, have enabled him to produce this definitive book on the club's modern history. His attention to detail ensures that every match and statistical fact is recorded with accuracy and makes this an essential book for every Coventry City fan.

Bryan Richardson
Chairman
Coventry City FC

Author's Note

The decision to update and re-publish this book was made easy by the success of the first edition, which quickly went out of print, and by the Sky Blues' sad relegation from English football's top division. It also seems appropriate to provide a publication that includes the complete history of the last 34 tremendous years.

It is three years since the first edition was published. This new edition includes those three seasons and the statistical records of 131 extra matches, making a grand total of 1,602 games covered. These statistics now include a full record of all sendings off in the era. In addition, new photographs have been used and a new dust cover designed. Some readers may wonder why it graces an image of John Hartson, especially now that he has left the club. The reason is simple: Hartson for a brief time epitomised the club's fight against relegation and most fans would agree that – had he been signed earlier – relegation would have been avoided.

Thanks again to all those who have helped me with *The Elite Era* including Rod Dean, David Brassington, Don Chalk, Martin and Paul O'Connor, David Selby and Ian Chadband. Roger Draper and the *Coventry Evening Telegraph* sports desk continue to support and assist me, and I am indebted to all the newspapers' football writers back into the mists of time.

The majority of the photographs came from the collection of the late Trevor Davies and my thanks go to his mother Edna Davies for allowing me to use them. I am grateful to many others, including Graham Hover and Neil Bryson and the staff of Coventry City FC, friends from the Coventry City London Supporters Club, and many other club statisticians.

My faith in book publishing has been enhanced during my fruitful relationship with Desert Island Books. Its proprietor, Clive Leatherdale, has bullied and praised me, stroked and chided me, but overall has given me advice and guidance. My aim for excellence is more than matched by his. Finally thanks to my family. My wife Doreen and my children Lisa and Alastair have all given me wonderful support in this and my other writing projects.

Jim Brown

Publishers Note:
This book contains full details – line-ups of both sides, goalscorers and goal-times, referees, attendances, League positions after each game, cumulative points totals, plus a 50-word summary of the key moments – of every first-team competitive match Coventry City have played in the League, FA Cup, League Cup, and Europe from 1967 to 2001. Minor cup competitions have been excluded for reasons of space.

Introduction

The club which is the subject of this book was founded in 1883 by employees of Singers, the cycle firm, and was known as Singers until 1898 when the name was changed to Coventry City. Early matches were played at Dowells Field, off Binley Road, then at Stoke Road from 1887 until the move to the present Highfield Road site in 1899. The period between 1887 and 1892 was a golden one for the club, with the Birmingham Junior Cup being won in consecutive years, 1891 and 1892. Having been members of the Birmingham League since 1894, the club progressed to the Southern League in 1908, before being elected to Football League Division 2 immediately after World War I. In 1910 they enjoyed one of their finest moments when as a non-league club they reached the FA Cup quarter-finals, beating First Division Preston and Nottingham Forest en route.

City's first season in the league was a disaster. They lost their opening game, at home to Tottenham, 0-5 and did not win a match until Christmas Day. Setting the precedent for their later dramatic survival battles, they avoided relegation on the final day, but only after a bribery scandal had rocked the club. Throughout the 1920's City struggled, with managers coming and going, until relegation finally caught up with them in 1925. It was not until the arrival of manager Harry Storer in 1931 that fortunes improved and the 1930's were a golden period for the Bantams, as the club was nicknamed. Despite City being substantially in the red, Storer developed a side which scored 100 goals in four seasons out of five, with the club's greatest ever goalscorer Clarrie Bourton netting 49 goals in 1931-32 and 40 the following season. In 1936, City won promotion back to Division 2 with crowds averaging almost 20,000. The three seasons prior to World War II saw the club come close to promotion to Division 1. In 1938 they missed out by one point, and many observers believed that but for the war City would have achieved that target.

The post-war years brought troubled times. Storer left for Birmingham City in 1945 and returned in 1951, but his ageing side were relegated to Division Three South in 1952. That decade witnessed many false dawns before the team embarked on the slide which touched rock bottom in 1958 with membership of the newly formed Division 4. Fortunately, one season was enough to clamber out of the league's basement.

The 1960's was a boom time in Coventry, with car factories keeping pace with the consumer revolution in the nation at large. It was the arrival of Jimmy Hill as manager in 1961 which sparked revolution at the club. A new sky blue kit was unveiled, the nickname was changed to the Sky Blues, trains were laid on for travelling fans, the Sky Blue Song was composed (to the tune of the Eton Boating Song), and pre-match entertainment became commonplace. Most importantly, on the pitch the team delivered. In 1963, after a feverish FA Cup run, City lost out in the quarter-finals to Manchester United, but the following season they became champions of Division 3, boasting average home crowds of 26,000. The Highfield Road stadium was substantially rebuilt in the 1960's, with three new stands erected in four years. Hill, with the backing of chairman Derrick Robins, was the Pied Piper and after three seasons in Division 2 he steered the club to the promised land in 1967. In that promotion season, 1966-67, the team went 25 games unbeaten, and the campaign reached an exhilarating finale in what was dubbed the 'midlands match of the century', when nearest rivals Wolves were beaten 3-1 in front of a record 51,455 Highfield Road crowd to virtually clinch the Division 2 championship.

On the eve of their baptism in the top flight, Jimmy Hill announced that he was leaving the club to pursue a career in television a blow which many people – inside and outside Coventry – thought would sound the death knell for the club's ambitions.

One

The Cantwell Years 1967-1972

LEAGUE DIVISION 1	**1967-68**
Division 1	20th
League Cup	2nd Round
FA Cup	4th Round

It is a view widely held that, since the advent of a satellite-TV funded Premiership, survival in the top flight of English football has assumed greater importance than at any other time. But, like its partner shibboleth – that the English League is the greatest league in the world – it is far easier to state than to prove.

Certainly, it is difficult to imagine survival in England's top division meaning more to anyone than it did to Coventry City supporters back in 1968 when, had the club been relegated, it could easily have drifted back into the wilderness that it had occupied for much of the previous three quarters of a century.

At the time, City supporters were divided into two schools of thought. The optimistic felt that the club's march to the top was irresistible; the pessimistic argued that the combination of inspiration and perspiration that had got them there could not in itself be guaranteed to ensure survival. The latter opinion was closer to the truth, but three factors complicated the argument.

Firstly, two days before the opening match the club announced the resignation of manager Jimmy Hill, who wished to take up a media position with London Weekend Television. Secondly, five days later, in the course of a 3-3 draw at Nottingham Forest, skipper George Curtis broke his leg and would miss virtually the whole season. Finally, Ian Gibson, the one player most capable of bridging the gap in class between Second and First Division, was dogged by a knee injury which restricted him to just fourteen appearances.

The board had been grappling with the Hill issue throughout the summer. It is said that he had demanded a ten-year managerial contract, and, if true, Chairman Derrick Robins was not prepared to mortgage the club over such a length of time. Whatever the case, after five years of almost unbroken success Hill appeared willing to turn his back on the chance to test his managerial skills at the highest level. The news of his resignation, when it broke, carried sufficient weight to make the national television channels.

However, these considerations were pushed to the back of supporters' minds, such was their enthusiasm and appetite for First Division football. Some 7,000 of them trekked to Burnley for the curtain-raiser, with City seeking to extend their long unbeaten run to 26 games. Sadly, the bubble burst at once, City losing 1-2. Curtis's injury a few days later sparked a frantic search for a replacement. Tony Knapp was signed to fill the void, but the board was obviously inhibited from making further signings until the managerial issue was settled. Hill had declared his intention to stay on until a successor was appointed, but his day to day frustrations must have weighed heavily as the enormity of the task confronting City began to dawn.

The search for a fresh manager alighted on any number of top names. Brian Clough dillied and dallied too long, having been made what was described as an 'unbelievable offer'. He preferred instead to sign a new contract with Derby. Malcolm Allison, Manchester City's young coach, announced publicly that he had accepted the Coventry post, a mindless breach of confidence that cost him the job there and then. Finally, on 12 October, former Manchester United captain Noel Cantwell was appointed to take over. Two days later Jimmy Hill formally handed over the managerial reins, whereupon Coventry promptly lost 2-3 to Spurs. A 0-3 defeat at home to Fulham plunged City to the foot of the table, and it wasn't until his tenth game that Cantwell's team tasted victory, 5-1 over Burnley.

Cantwell began the task of rebuilding at once. The signing of ex-Old Trafford team-mate Maurice Setters from Stoke for £25,000 stiffened the centre of defence, Tony Knapp having ineffectively tried to plug the gap caused by Curtis's injury. Forwards Gerry Baker for £25,000 and Ernie Hannigan for £55,000 were signed from Ipswich and Preston respectively. In February 1968, the elegant striker Neil Martin arrived from Sunderland for £90,000, after the local boy-made-good, Bobby Gould, was sacrificed for a similar fee to Arsenal. Two other players were snapped up on transfer deadline day – Ernie Hunt, another forward, from Everton for £65,000, and full-back Chris Cattlin from Huddersfield for £70,000.

By the end of January the Sky Blues were still bottom, with just sixteen points from 25 games, but on 3 February victory at the Hawthorns signalled a turnaround, and wins over Chelsea and Sheffield Wednesday soon followed. Punctuating these victories was an ignominious FA Cup exit at Third Division Tranmere, which in other circumstances would have been calamitous. Now it came almost as a relief, for survival in the top division excluded all other considerations.

One crisis followed another. On 16 March Highfield Road's main stand was gutted by fire, leaving among the cinders a melted and twisted Second Division championship trophy and most of the club's archives. The stand was patched up sufficiently to enable the match of the season to go ahead ten days later. The opponents were European Champions-to-be Manchester United. The gate of 47,111 witnessed a famous City victory, secured by goals from Ernie Machin and new skipper Setters.

As the season neared its climax, the Sky Blues found themselves locked in their fight for survival with Fulham and Sheffield United, any two of whom would be doomed. Fulham were the first to perish. With two games left, City led the Blades by one point. Both of City's games were away, at West Ham and Southampton. They drew the first 0-0, but Sheffield won at Burnley, leaving the two clubs tied on points going into the final game. On a nerve-jangling occasion at the Dell, 7,000 City fans roared their team to another backs-to-the-wall goalless draw. When the final whistle blew, ecstatic supporters invaded the pitch, knowing that Chelsea had won at Sheffield to send the Blades down into Division Two.

Looking back, City's performances during 1967-68 were as heroic as any in the ensuing decades and it is testimony to the spirit of players and supporters alike that the average home gate of 34,715 has never been bettered.

Match of the Season 1967-68

Coventry 2 Manchester United 0

Division 1, 16 March 1968

Very occasionally a match is played that constitutes a watershed in a club's history. Such a game was City's Division One clash with Manchester United in March 1968 at Highfield Road.

City had struggled to find their feet. With just three league wins by the turn of the year, relegation stared the Sky Blues in the face. By the time of the Manchester United fixture, City lay twentieth, one place above the trap-door. Only the most blinkered supporters imagined that points might be easy to obtain from the defending champions, who topped the league once again, but who had just flown home from a tough midweek European Cup-tie in Poland.

United's ranks embraced Bobby Charlton, Denis Law, George Best and a host of other stars. But City also had other problems to contend with. Ten days before the game, just after George Curtis's return to action in the reserves, fire gutted the central section of Highfield Road's main stand. It required round-the-clock labour to erect temporary gantries in front of the charred remains to permit the game to take place. The rickety new stand enabled all season-ticket holders to be accommodated for a fixture they yearned to see.

On the eve of the match Cantwell signed Ernie Hunt and Chris Cattlin, who made their debuts in the most telling of circumstances. Gerry Baker had hamstring problems but Maurice Setters took up his usual position in defence, despite spending the previous weekend in hospital, concussed during the 1-3 defeat at Maine Road.

Turnstiles opened at 12.30 in an attempt to ease congestion, and by kick-off at 3.15, 47,111 bodies had crammed into the stadium – the second highest gate of all time at Highfield Road.

The atmosphere was, as they say, electric. Each and every City player did his job. Cattlin shackled George Best, who rarely escaped his attentions and was shunted mostly to the margins of the action. Newcomer Hunt slotted in well, whilst Willie Carr buzzed in his usual manner, and the ever dour, dependable and abrasive Setters took the eye for his positive as well as his negative contribution.

After 34 minutes Ernie Machin rocketed a 30-yard volley past Alex Stepney to open the scoring. United responded like a wounded tiger, and Glazier, Setters and the rest of the defence needed to batten down the hatches. But then, eight minutes after half-time, Setters headed a goal from Hannigan's corner.

Protected by a two-goal lead, City enjoyed some breathing space, but United hit back strongly. Setters was booked following one typical act of belligerence and Glazier's woodwork was struck twice in the closing quarter of the game, but that was as close as Matt Busby's team came. City's defence held out to earn a merited victory. United's defeat cost them dearly. Their Maine Road rivals pipped them to the league title by two points. They did, however, have the last laugh when winning the European Cup at Wembley.

As for City, they had picked up more than two precious points. They also benefited from a massive injection of confidence, which stood them well in the closing weeks of the season. The first, crucial battle against relegation had been won; a new main stand would shortly grace the most modern stadium in the country, and within two years City would be playing in Europe.

LEAGUE DIVISION 1 1968-69

Division 1	20th
League Cup	4th Round
FA Cup	4th Round

The supporters' cry went up 'Never again', which seems ironic in the light of events thirty years on. The logic behind the optimism in the summer of 1968 was grounded in the noticeable improvement exhibited in the second half of the previous season, which harvested 21 points (a point a game, mid-table form) as against a paltry twelve in the first half. Cantwell's new signings had also had time to be bedded in, and were expected to play even better next time round.

The optimists were fooled. In too many respects the new season was a carbon copy of the last. By the end of February 1969 City had earned a miserly fourteen points from 25 games, but to general astonishment they yet again staged a dramatic recovery, climaxing once more with a heroic win over Manchester United. In a further echo of 1967-68, the season concluded with three battling draws. In those days there was no rule obliging all teams to play their final game concurrently – which has put a thankful stop to tacit match-fixing – and City had to endure a tortuous wait as Leicester played out five outstanding fixtures, a product of inclement weather and a protracted FA Cup run, which carried Leicester to Wembley. They needed seven points to overhaul the Sky Blues' tally, but mustered just five, thereby finishing one point below the City.

But let us return to August. The close season had been quiet, with no major comings or goings. The energies of the club were concentrated on the speedy construction of a new main stand. As for the team, it had acquired a more settled look. Coop and Cattlin were established as regular full-backs, the latter playing himself into Alf Ramsey's England Under-23 squad. Curtis recovered from his broken leg to reclaim his stopper role, while young Jeff Blockley was introduced in mid-season as Curtis's defensive partner, at the expense of Brian Hill.

In the engine room, Willie Carr, Dave Clements and Ernie Machin were virtual ever-presents, with Carr playing even better in his second season than in his first. Injury again restricted Ian Gibson's appearances, but when he did play it emphasised just how much he was needed. To add to City's woes, Neil Martin was out until November, and in a desperate attempt to beef up his attack Cantwell bought Tony Hateley from Liverpool for £80,000.

DID YOU KNOW?

In the 1890s the club's nickname was the Little Blackbirds, because most of the players were small, and the team's colours were black and red.

But the well-travelled striker proved to be a spent force, and neither he, nor supporters would claim that his time at Highfield Road was a fruitful one. Once Martin regained fitness it became clear that the side could not accommodate both strikers, and it surprised no one when Hateley soon languished for long periods in the reserves before being off-loaded to Birmingham in September 1969. The foil for the strikers was the impish Ernie Hunt, who topped the goalscoring lists with thirteen.

There may have been other contributing factors, but in reality City were in trouble even before the season started. Building work on the new stand meant they kicked-off a week late, and opened with two away fixtures that yielded nothing. They lost their third match, too, so started off at the foot of the table looking forlornly up at the rest. Curtis had not yet dislodged Setters at the heart of defence, and with Martin injured Curtis played as a stop-gap striker, to little effect. Ian Gibson, the fans' hero, was omitted from the opening game and caused a stir when he suggested it might be in everyone's interests if he moved on. But Gibson returned with a bang for the home game with West Brom, being the architect of the 4-2 victory. Cantwell afterwards raved about Gibson's display, declaring it to be 'as good an inside-forward performance as I have ever seen. No club in the country would want to sell a man playing like this.' Gibson's return to form helped forge good results against Burnley, Newcastle and Portsmouth, Gibson scoring in each match. The West Brom game was also a personal triumph for Ernie Hunt, whose hat-trick vindicated Noel Cantwell's decision to play him up front.

Rearranged midweek games had a habit of turning sour on the Sky Blues. Over 36,000 turned out against Chelsea in atrocious weather as City ploughed through the puddles, only to lose to a soft goal after running the Londoners ragged. A week later, 40,000 packed in to witness a virtual replica: this time it was Spurs who snatched an undeserved win. Unmerited defeats have a way of draining the spirits, and in Coventry's case they set in train an eleven-match run without a league win. The signing of Hateley couldn't avert a miserable October. West Brom exacted handsome revenge for their earlier defeat, to the tune of 6-1, and Third Division Swindon added City's to their impressive collection of scalps on their march to the League Cup final.

The one glimmer of hope came when Martin and Hateley hit it off for the one and only time in a 3-0 win at Stoke, but three home defeats ensued, leaving City in the mire and at the mercy of a capricious winter that played havoc with the fixture list. Ten weeks passed without a home game, in which time the Sky Blues clocked up three more away defeats to leave them rock bottom. This was some achievement, since they were even beneath QPR, by common consent one of the worst teams Division One had ever seen. City settled that particular argument by thrashing Rangers 5-0. A win was a win, no matter the opposition, and now the confidence flowed. Two more victories helped persuade supporters that safety was attainable, even though the away form remained as wretched as ever. Everything boiled down to three vital evening matches, first the repeat win over Manchester United, then the crunch game with relegation rivals Leicester, the result of which, looking back, proved to be decisive. City's final game, an evening goal-less draw with Liverpool, was contested in an atmosphere the like of which Highfield Road has rarely seen.

With City's programme complete, all eyes turned to Leicester. First, they suffered the colossal disappointment of losing the Cup final to Manchester City, after which they had to pick themselves up to cram five league games into just two weeks. Their target to overhaul the Sky Blues was seven points. Home wins over Tottenham and Sunderland collected four of them. Leicester lost narrowly at Ipswich, then drew at home to Everton, leaving them needing to win at Manchester United – of all places – to ensure survival. In view of Noel Cantwell's Old Trafford connections, rumours of dirty deeds were rife. With three minutes gone Leicester were in front. They hit the woodwork twice, too, but United had reasons of their own to put on a show. It was Matt Busby's final game in charge, and his boys eventually triumphed 3-2. Leicester were down.

Match of the Season 1968-69

Coventry 1 Leicester 0

Division 1, 1 April 1969

Although this was by no means the most attractive of games, with hindsight it turned out to be the most significant result of the 1968-69 season. In the final reckoning City finished two points ahead of Leicester, and that was the difference between heaven and hell.

Leicester had been wobbling all season. Manager Matt Gillies was sacked just before Christmas and had been replaced by former

Torquay boss, Frank O'Farrell. He and Cantwell went back a long way; both were Irishmen who in the 1950's had played together for the Republic and for West Ham.

O'Farrell had instilled grit into Leicester, whose form of late suggested they might yet claw their way to safety. A narrow defeat at Southampton was their first reverse in twelve games, but they then toppled holders West Brom in an FA Cup semi-final, the perfect confidence-booster for the match with City three days later.

The Sky Blues, meanwhile, had dragged themselves off the foot of the table by virtue of their home form, which claimed nine points out of ten. They had lost their most recent match 0-2 at Newcastle, where Trevor Shepherd and Chris Cattlin returned in place of Ernie Hannigan and Jeff Blockley.

Leicester's injury worries meant they took the field without four key players – Lenny Glover, British record signing Allan Clarke, who had endured a miserable season, Scottish inside-forward Davie Gibson, and Welsh international full-back Peter Rodrigues.

History pointed to Leicester, Coventry having vanquished their opponents only twice at home in the league since World War II, the most recent occasion being in 1950. But in front of the largest gate of the season so far, 41,846, the Sky Blues started at a furious pace. Gaping holes were left at the back, and Leicester's Rodney Fern really should have capitalised. In the second half Coventry laid siege to young Peter Shilton's goal, but in a rare Leicester break-out Andy Lochhead breached the offside trap and Glazier had to make a superb block with his feet to prevent a goal. Mike Stringfellow then hit a screamer towards the top corner which Glazier fisted over.

The result hinged on an incident seven minutes from time. Leicester substitute Brian Greenhalgh raced into the penalty box and in the act of shooting had his legs whipped away by one of George Curtis's crunching tackles. It was an obvious penalty and the referee blew, then noticed a linesman's flag raised for offside. After a brief confab between the officials, Coventry restarted play not from the centre-circle – which they would have done had a penalty been converted – but with a free-kick instead.

Leicester were further aggrieved when in the 88th minute Mick Coop crossed to the far post. Shilton, for once, was caught in two minds whether to come or to stay and did neither. Martin hurled himself forward to volley the only goal. Its worth to Coventry was immeasurable.

The Sky Blues won just one more game that season, against Manchester United, taking five points from their last six games to finish with 31, two fewer than 1967-68, but – crucially – two more than Leicester could muster.

LEAGUE DIVISION 1	**1969-70**
Division 1	6th
League Cup	2nd Round
FA Cup	3rd Round

In the 1969 close-season City followers once more whispered 'never again', as they had done a year earlier, while those outside the city of spires took a more sceptical view. Not surprisingly, City were installed as bookmakers' favourites for the drop – a situation that supporters have since become accustomed to, and even – perversely – to relish, for there are few greater pleasures in life than thumbing your noses at those who are invariably proved wrong.

So what lay behind this widespread sense of optimism? For a start, two seasons of mostly desperate struggle had forged a gritty resolve within the club. Whilst it might grudgingly be confessed that the players were short on attacking plan and style, as a defensive unit the Sky Blues were usually adequate and occasionally impenetrable.

It should also be remembered that the 1960's and 70's was a time of brutal, no-nonsense football, of highly physical encounters, when scything tackles, which would be red-carded today, were regarded as part of the natural order of things. At the summit of this palace of cynicism lay Don Revie's Leeds United, and however much others bad-mouthed and outwardly reviled them, most clubs were trying hard to emulate them. City, it must be said, were no exception. An iron core ran through the side, so much so that few opponents relished a visit to Highfield Road. The side had acquired a solid, familiar look, with the highly respected Bill Glazier in goal, Setters and/or Curtis marshalling resistance at the heart of defence, Coop and Cattlin, the dependable full-backs, together with crowd favourite Ian Gibson in midfield, who supplied most of the chances for Neil Martin and Ernie Hunt up front.

For the first time since promotion, City's nursery players were beginning to bloom. The most prominent of these were Dennis Mortimer, Jeff Blockley, and the prodigy Willie Carr. Blockley and Carr would in time be capped for their respective countries. Noel Cantwell, whose tactics had been questioned and ridiculed in some quarters, had also learned lessons. He had entered management with no experience behind him and it was public knowledge that he was by no means the first choice for the job, but his forays into the transfer market had yielded more successes than failures – though Tony Hateley ranked high on the list of debits.

DID YOU KNOW?

On Christmas Day 1925, police were called to Highfield Road. Fans had snowballed the referee after he gave a penalty for Crewe. City won 2-1.

This time, City did not wait for the appearance of a league table to hammer home harsh truths; they set out from day one to avoid a relegation battle, grinding out a dreary 0-0 draw at Sunderland which won them few friends on Wearside. One point already in the bag – things were looking up. City battled their way through the first seven games and, when they came up for breath, were as surprised as anyone to find themselves in the top six with just one defeat. A double over West Brom and a win at Ipswich meant that the previous season's meagre total of two away wins was already equalled.

It soon became apparent that the seasons of struggle were over – at least for now. For many supporters 8 October 1969 announced the arrival of City as a *bona fide* member of the top flight. That was the day City took on Brian Clough's all-conquering Derby County at the Baseball Ground. Undefeated in 25 home games, Derby had conceded only five goals in thirteen matches, but City wrecked that proud sequence, running out 3-1 winners. It was the Sky Blues' finest away display for years and one which even Clough acknowledged as 'brilliant'.

Two more players were signed shortly afterwards, striker John O'Rourke from Ipswich for £80,000 and central defender Roy Barry from Dunfermline for half as much. Like Albert Lewis in 1906, Ernie Toseland in 1928 or perhaps Chris Marsden in 1993, Barry was one of those players whose historical significance is disproportionate to the number of games he played. Barry made only fourteen appearances in 1969-70 yet, as that rarity, a creative central defender, he became the fulcrum of the side and gave supporters the sight of a true great. Barry and O'Rourke made their home debuts in a 1-0 win over Newcastle at the end of November. This marked the beginning of a prodigious run of eight wins and a draw in ten games, at the end of which City occupied fourth place. Away wins at Palace, Hillsborough and Upton Park established City – for the time being – as a member of the First Division elite, but the finest result was a goal-less draw at Goodison Park, where the champions elect, boasting the much-vaunted Ball-Kendall-Harvey midfield, had hitherto proved invincible.

City suffered a dreadful blow in March, when Barry broke his leg against Sheffield Wednesday, but by that time they had a novel experience on their hands. They entered the final straight needing three points from three away games: this time the target was not survival, but a place in Europe.

In the first of the three they thrashed Nottingham Forest 4-1, O'Rourke grabbing a hat-trick. Three days later the dream was realised, and it was the old enemy Wolves who obliged. City won 1-0, their tenth away win of the season, witnessed by 7,000 celebrating fans. Brian Joicey, who had been signed from amateurs North Shields at the beginning of the season, scored the historic goal early in the game, and the wily old masters Gibson, Hunt and Martin used all their know-how to stifle Wolves for the rest of the game. City's final position of sixth guaranteed a place in the next season's European Fairs Cup.

It had been a long, hard road but after three seasons the Sky Blues had proved that the optimists knew best. Jimmy Hill's proud vision looked like materialising. Chairman Derrick Robins pronounced with justified pride: 'we can now look forward to a new era'.

Match of the Season 1969-70

Derby 1 Coventry 3

Division 1, 8 October 1969

The summer of 1969 saw Derby County preparing for their first season in the top flight since 1953. Their players had romped to promotion on the back of nine straight wins. Manager Brian Clough and his assistant Peter Taylor had constructed a well-balanced side, strong on experience and rich in youth. Former Spurs war-horse Dave Mackay and ex-Forest winger Alan Hinton represented the former, and young Roy McFarland and full-back John Robson the latter.

County then proceeded to storm the First Division, powering their way among the pacesetters. City, who also started brightly, had experienced a foretaste of the Rams in a tight draw at Highfield Road. Clough's team had subsequently beaten leaders and champions-to-be Everton and hammered Spurs 5-0 in front of a record 41,800 crowd. County's 22-match unbeaten run was finally ended at Hillsborough, ten days before City's visit, though they quickly shrugged it off to topple Manchester United 2-0.

City, meanwhile, had won at Arsenal, thanks to an Ernie Hunt goal, and were looking forward to renewing old rivalries with the Rams. Centre-forward Neil Martin was doubtful and summer signing Brian Joicey was included in the squad as substitute. Chris Cattlin was unfit, allowing Dietmar Bruck to continue at left-back.

DID YOU KNOW?

After a poor run in 1938, manager Harry Storer put the players on a course of monkey-gland treatment. They won their next four matches.

McFarland passed a fitness test for Derby but Ron Webster was not risked and Clough retained reserve Peter Daniel at right-back.

The attendance was almost 40,000, a sizeable contingent of which had travelled up from Coventry. The game had hardly started when the home crowd were almost silenced. Martin pierced the Derby defence with a long square pass. Carr pushed the ball on to Gibson, whose cunning shot bounced back off the post into the arms of the grateful Green.

City looked confident, and the ruthlessness of their play reflected their determination not to be overawed by the new wonder team of Division One.

Neil Martin put City ahead after seventeen minutes, rising above McFarland to meet Clements' free-kick and glance a header into the far corner of the net. The Sky Blues then had to soak up long bouts of pressure, but their resilience slowly drew the sting from Derby's players and supporters alike. City finished off the home side with two goals in the space of six second-half minutes. First McFarland, with not a Sky Blue shirt in sight, diverted Coop's low cross into the roof of the net. Bruck started the move that culminated in City's killer goal, finding Martin with a 35-yard crossfield pass. Over came Martin's short cross and Jeff Blockley, still lingering upfield from a corner, leaned forward to direct a close-range header into the net.

Alan Durban's consolation was an almost casually hit effort that raised barely a cheer from choked Derby fans, who knew that their team had been beaten fair and square. Brian Clough offered this cryptic word – 'brilliant', whilst Derek Henderson in the *Coventry Evening Telegraph* wrote: '... probably their finest show in recent years. Because of the fact that the victory was not really "on" it had the hallmark of greatness.'

LEAGUE DIVISION 1 **1970-71**

Division 1	10th
League Cup	Quarter-finals
FA Cup	3rd Round

The disappointment of 1970-71 was magnified by expectation. This was to have been the season City established themselves among the elite of the division and confirmed that 1969-70 had not been a flash in the pan. It might seem strange when recalled today, but in the summer of 1970 the talk in the pubs of Coventry was not merely of the thrill of being in Europe, but of the genuine probability of winning the Fairs Cup. Perhaps those expectations were unrealistic, for in the event City were shown to have made a rod for their own back.

Europe was almost a non-event. The fifty stalwarts who made the arduous trek to Bulgaria were rewarded with a 4-1 win over Trakia Plovdiv, but such a wide margin in the first leg had the inevitable consequence of reducing interest in the second. Highfield Road's European baptism was therefore an unexpectedly tepid occasion. The same could be said, though for different reasons, of the second round against Bayern Munich. Even if City fielded their strongest team, they faced an enormous task. Messrs Beckenbauer, Maier and Muller had been the backbone of the West Germany side which the previous summer made an impressive run to the Mexico World Cup semi-finals, and Bayern were on the verge of becoming one of the top European sides of the 1970's. But Coventry could not field their best eleven. Without the injured Glazier (he was replaced in goal by the unfortunate Eric McManus), City were thrashed 1-6 on a waterlogged pitch in Bavaria, so the home leg, originally earmarked as a potential 50,000 all-ticket extravaganza, was watched by barely half that number.

The new season had started ominously when City's return visit to Nottingham Forest – scene of a glorious 4-1 romp four months previously – ended in a 0-2 defeat, with the new £35,000 signing from Liverpool, Geoff Strong, failing to plug worrying holes in defence. Goals, or the lack of them, were also a problem – as City won only one of the first four home games. In the heady pre-Europe mood of the summer the fans' favourite, Ian Gibson, had quietly departed for Second Division Cardiff for £35,000, thereby terminating the player's three-year love-hate relationship with Cantwell. Wilf Smith's arrival for a sizeable fee briefly convinced supporters that the club weren't letting grass grow under their feet.

DID YOU KNOW?

The first overseas players to play for City were Emilio Aldecoa and Jose Bilbao between 1945 and 1947. Both were Basque refugees from the Spanish Civil War.

There were signs, however, that City's great tide of support was beginning to ebb, not least when the gate for the local derby with Wolves in August was 7,000 down on a similar game early in the previous season. Further statistics made grim reading. In 1970-71 City failed to score on nineteen occasions; their goal-tally of 37 was the lowest since 1919-20; the average gate was down 6,000. Looking back, it is therefore something of a relief to find that the Sky Blues finished a comfortable tenth.

Any thoughts of glory in the FA Cup were rudely quashed on a Monday afternoon in January at Spotland, home of Third Division Rochdale. After a postponement caused by snow, Cantwell, in an unfortunate display of condescension, refused to play under Rochdale's candle-powered floodlights. When the game did take place, City were extinguished in one of the great cup humiliations.

The defeat at Rochdale was something of a watershed. Up front, the Martin-O'Rourke combination had spluttered all season – the latter rarely lived up to expectations, while Martin was nearing the winter of his career and was soon on his way to Forest. O'Rourke, despite scoring a hat-trick in Plovdiv, had scored only two league goals and was rarely the first choice for his position. Even in a lean season, Ernie Hunt was still a force when employed to his best advantage – as a central front-runner, poaching goals with his own brand of shooting skill. Before the season was over, youngsters Brian Alderson, a Scots-born winger, and Billy Rafferty, a tall striker enjoyed try-outs in the first team. Willie Carr simply got better and better. From November he was partnered by Dennis Mortimer, destined to become one of the finest players the club ever produced.

The shortage of goals placed an intolerable burden on the defenders, who knew that one slip could mean two points lost. Mercifully, Munich apart, City's defence was as impregnable as ever. Bill Glazier seemed to touch new heights and, in the wake of the Rochdale fiasco, Strong was replaced by the outstanding prospect Bobby Parker, who quickly developed a sturdy partnership with the ever-improving Blockley.

Amid the general dross a number of memorable games stand out. The 4-3 win at Derby looks freakish in the wider context – and the 3-1 win over champions Everton warms the memory for one incredible moment. Long after other details of the season are forgotten, none who saw it will forget Willie Carr's legendary 'donkey-kick'. Awarded a free-kick, Carr pincered the ball between his heels, flicked it vertically up into the air, and as it fell Hunt, lurking behind him, executed a perfect dipping volley over Rankin. The goal was captured by BBC's Match of the Day cameras and remains one of the most remarkable goals ever seen at Highfield Road. Late season home victories over Liverpool and Manchester United were also reminders of how potent the side could be.

The bad days, however, outnumbered the good and the worst were epitomised by the single-goal defeats at Blackpool and Huddersfield – the two promoted teams, who were both woefully short of reasonable talent – and a home defeat by struggling West Ham, for whom Jimmy Greaves scored his obligatory goal to win the game.

In the League Cup, City had a faint whiff of Wembley in their nostrils after good home wins over West Ham and Derby, but were sunk on a wet night at White Hart Lane by a hat-trick from the striker of the season, Martin Chivers.

Away from the spotlight, City's youth policy was generating a wealth of talent under the tutelage of Ron Farmer, so it came as a major shock when the youth team were knocked out of the FA Youth Cup by Arsenal. City's young starlets, Mick McGuire and Alan Dugdale, joined Bobby Parker in England's winning team in the Little World Cup, whilst others – Jimmy Holmes, Colin Randell and Alan Green – all showed great potential for the future. Despite the bright future the fans were not prepared to sit idly by and wait for the youngsters to develop. They demanded jam today.

Match of the Season 1970-71

Derby 3 Coventry 4

Division 1, 2 September 1970

The previous season City finished sixth in Division One, thereby qualifying for Europe. Supporters anticipated a yet more successful season, and were correspondingly dejected when the opening five games brought two wins but only three goals scored.

Coventry fans ached for the Fairs Cup to come around. At the time, however, the *Evening Telegraph* letters column was bristling with heated debate. Many supporters were fed up with the lack of goals, blaming the ultra-defensive tactics expounded by Cantwell.

By the time City travelled to the Baseball Ground they were in thirteenth place and were about to tackle a Derby side which had amassed seven points out of a possible ten, scoring nine goals in the process – four of which had come against Wolves at Molineux. Derby had finished last season fourth in Division One, and like City were preparing for their European debuts. Derby's one team-change was enforced. Alan Durban was injured and would be replaced by former Forest striker Frank Wignall, the man blamed by many City fans for breaking George Curtis's leg in 1967.

Following an odd-goal defeat at Tottenham, Cantwell axed Hunt, O'Rourke and Ian Goodwin, and brought in Brian Joicey, Ernie Machin and one other new signing. With the fans crying out for money to be spent on a new forward, Cantwell bought another defender – Wilf Smith from Sheffield Wednesday, who at £100,000 was at the time the most expensive full-back in Britain.

The game kicked off in a torrential downpour and within five minutes new-boy Smith took a bad knock. Three minutes later, with Smith temporarily off the field and City down to ten men, Kevin Hector scored in off a post. Ernie Hunt came on as substitute and Cantwell reshuffled his side, but on thirteen minutes Alan Hinton slammed in a rebound after Bill Glazier had made a good save. City were two goals down. Game, set and match to Derby, surely.

However, striker Neil Martin, who relished his tussles with the much vaunted Roy McFarland, was winning their aerial battle and it was Martin who, after 28 minutes, reduced the deficit with a hooked shot from Hunt's cross. Three minutes later Dave Clements levelled the score with a daisy cutter. Against the odds, City were still alive and kicking.

The second half was nine minutes old when Martin headed City ahead for the first time. John McGovern levelled the scores again with a shot that flew in off Willie Carr; then Geoff Strong seemed to seal City's fate when elbowing Wignall off the ball in the penalty box. Penalty to Derby!

Alan Hinton, who boasted one of the most explosive shots in football, stepped up and fired to Glazier's right, but City's keeper made a prodigious leap to turn the ball aside. City were left hanging on grimly for a draw, and survived several stomach-churning moments. Two Derby 'goals' were disallowed for offside, Strong headed off the line, and Hector hit the bar.

It was still 3-3 when, with only two minutes remaining, City stunned the home crowd. Non-stop Willie Carr blasted the winner to gain a victory that Derek Henderson in the *Evening Telegraph* described as probably City's finest win in the First Division in the face of great adversity.

This was Coventry's second consecutive league win at Derby. For the statistically minded it was also City's 200th away win in the Football League since they were elected in 1919.

LEAGUE DIVISION 1	**1971-72**
Division 1	18th
League Cup	2nd Round
FA Cup	4th Round

From the very first match it was clear this would be Noel Cantwell's make or break season. Rumblings from terraces and boardroom were becoming louder, particularly as the side had a disjointed look about it from the beginning. A poor opening game clearly reinforced the need for a goalscorer, while a crowd of less than 21,000 illustrated the apathy that was pervading the club's previously loyal following. In August long-serving midfielder Dave Clements and promising striker Brian Joicey were sold to Sheffield Wednesday. The money funded the purchase of Chris Chilton, who was signed for £92,000 to beef up the forward line and score goals. Chilton had been a regular goal-getter for Hull City – 224 goals in twelve years – but he was not the first, nor the last to discover that the step up to Division One was a step too many. At least, that was the kindest conclusion one could reach based on his performances for City.

The defence remained Coventry's trump card. Wilf Smith performed stylishly at full-back and Roy Barry finally returned from his broken leg to lend his class to central defence, where he renewed his partnership with the blossoming Blockley – who became a regular in the England Under-23 side. In midfield, the Mortimer-Carr combination seemed to become stronger year by year. But the overall mix was wrong. Those players whom Coventry had brought up through the ranks invariably acquitted themselves well. It was by and large the imports who looked out of place. Too many signings appeared short-sighted or stop-gap, the veteran Ian St John being an obvious example. His short-lived partnership with Chilton impressed no one and after a flurry of good results in October the pair delivered only a sequence of damp squibs. New winger Quintin Young, a £40,000 summer purchase from Ayr United, dazzled in the autumn but by the spring had faded badly.

By late autumn it looked as though City were in for what is euphemistically called a 'transitional season', but then things began to deteriorate. From early November until April, City mustered only one win in nineteen games, and yet again they found themselves sucked into a relegation battle.

Perhaps the pressing needs of the league distracted City enough to make them fold like cardboard in the two cups. Ten years on and fans still became misty eyed at talk of the epic fifth round home win over Sunderland in 1963, but for Cantwell the FA Cup remained a disaster zone. Having experienced defeats at Tranmere and Rochdale, one might have thought it couldn't get any worse. At least those defeats were away from home. Now, just when a cup run might have saved him, City lost 0-1 at home to Second Division Hull City and from that moment there would be no way back for Cantwell. He lingered on, a lame-duck manager, for another month, and ironically the game which probably sealed his fate does not feature in official records. On 4 March Sheffield United were leading 2-0 at Highfield Road during a snow-storm when the referee controversially abandoned the game.

Cantwell's time had come, and gone, and he was sacked on Sunday, 12 March. The board's press statement was blunt and to the point: 'Results have not come up to the expectations or necessary standard required for Coventry City.' Curiously, in the light of recent trends to appoint a new manager even before the old one has cleared his desk, no successor had been lined up to take over. Bob Dennison, the club's chief scout, took charge as acting-manager until the end of the season. The pressures on Dennison were onerous: with no top flight managerial experience to call upon he was now given a few weeks to rescue City from the drop. The question on supporters' minds was, 'would Coventry be better without Cantwell or worse?' The answer was decisive. For the final month of the season it was as if a dead-weight had been lifted from the team. They responded with three wins, enough to ensure safety, restore some pride and hint at brighter prospects ahead.

After a faltering start by Dennison, including an abject 0-4 reverse at soon-to-be relegated Forest, City – with Hunt and Machin recalled – won their first match in twelve by thrashing Everton 4-1 over Easter. Hunt was inspirational in that victory and even Chris Chilton found the net.

The final verdict on Cantwell's five-year tenure is best summed up in his own words: 'the ghost of Jimmy Hill followed me around the dressing room.' Set in the context of Coventry City's history, he deserves a more favourable judgment than he enjoyed at the time. Circumstances, at times, dictated a functional, muscular and defensive approach, but that was in keeping with much of the football of the time. More to the point, any side put out by Cantwell carried greater threat to the opposition than those of some of his successors – Terry Butcher, Don Howe and Phil Neal for example. Cantwell also bore too much of the blame for the collapse in support after 1970. Viewed with hindsight, gates of 30,000 were improbably high, a quirk of history perhaps, and even a winning side would have struggled to maintain such a figure.

DID YOU KNOW?

Highfield Road's floodlights were officially switched on for the first time in 1953 for the visit of East Fife in a friendly.

Perhaps it was simply a matter of timing. To those familiar only with the self-deprecating, avuncular, quasi-comic figure of TV panels, it is hard to convey the awe in which Jimmy Hill was held. His hold over the club, the team and fans was absolute. Subsequent managers were doomed to unfavourable comparison and it would take a generation before that changed.

Match of the Season 1971-72

Coventry 3 Leeds 1

Division 1, 9 October 1971

City's poor start to the season – only one win in their first nine and a home League Cup defeat by Burnley to boot – seemed to indicate that darkness lay ahead. Then a brief ray of light: three new players sparked a revival. Chris Chilton, a prolific goalscorer for many years with Hull City was signed, the 33-year-old former Liverpool star Ian St John arrived from a sojourn in South Africa, and Quintin Young, a promising winger signed in the close season from Ayr United, forced his way into the side. City beat Tottenham 1-0, with Young bamboozling the normally elegant Cyril Knowles, then travelled to Everton and won 2-1, courtesy of goals from Young and St John. Ahead lay a visit from the team of the moment, Leeds United. Don Revie's team were still smarting from losing the 1970-71 championship by one point to Arsenal, though they had proceeded to defeat Juventus in the Fairs Cup final. They were the closest English soccer could come to a footballing machine and were renowned for their so-called 'professional' and excessively cynical and physical approach.

The Leeds side for this game was packed with famous players: Terry Cooper, Billy Bremner, Norman Hunter, Jackie Charlton and Johnny Giles. The names rolled off the tongue. Leeds were, however, without Allan Clarke, his striking partner Mick Jones, and the tricky Scottish winger Eddie Gray.

City's Chris Cattlin – who had been sent off the previous week at Everton in a case of mistaken identity – was injured, and Roy Barry came in as an auxiliary central defender. Wilf Smith continued as the midfield dynamo, in which position he had performed well in recent weeks.

DID YOU KNOW?

In 2000-01, Coventry City's total of just 19 home points and 14 home goals was the worst in the club's league history.

Since their elevation to the First Division, City had managed just one draw with Leeds, and that at Elland Road, which meant they had lost four out of four at Highfield Road. This time, however, City's tactics were spot on. They surrendered space in midfield, waiting for Leeds to lose possession, and then hit them to devastating effect on the counter-attack, taking three of the six good chances they created. Quintin Young was particularly effective against Terry Cooper, but the rest of the team also played their parts. After five minutes Chris Chilton scored his first goal for the Sky Blues, when Hunt and St John foxed the Leeds defence. Young, fast becoming one of City's most popular players since George Hudson, laid on St John's goal just after the half hour, at which point City fans were having to pinch themselves.

Willie Carr gave Scotland's new team manager Tommy Docherty a meaningful nudge with a fine display of aggressive attacking. On the evidence of this match he stood excellent midfield comparison with his fellow Scot, Billy Bremner, and superbly robbed the Leeds captain to set up the third goal for Hunt in the 54th minute.

City would dearly have loved to keep a clean sheet, just to rub it in, but it wasn't to be. Johnny Giles' hit-and-hope shot in the closing moments sliced off Bobby Parker to leave Glazier stranded.

Leeds recovered from this body-blow to lose only two of their next 26 league games. They won the FA Cup and missed out on a league and cup double by only one point.

Ernie Machin shoots for goal at Chelsea (September 1967)

Goalscorer Ernie Hunt is mobbed as City equalise at Sunderland (March 1968)

Newcastle's Bryan Robson beats Glazier from the spot (March 1969)

Neil Martin fires in a penalty against West Brom (December 1969)

John O'Rourke is poised to score at Nottingham Forest (April 1970)

Brian Joicey and Wolves keeper Oldfield race for a loose ball (August 1970)

Willie Carr climbs above Ernie Hunt to score the winner v Spurs (September 1971)

On-loan keeper Ron Healey safely catches against Southampton (January 1972)

Two

The 'M' Men 1972-1977

LEAGUE DIVISION 1	**1972-73**
Division 1	19th
League Cup	3rd Round
FA Cup	Quarter-finals

Following the dismissal of Noel Cantwell and the three-month hiatus during which Bob Dennison was caretaker manager, the club buzzed with anticipation as to who would take over the reins. The job, on paper, looked enticing. It offered a reasonable squad of players, a modern stadium with state-of-the-art training facilities, not to mention the backing of the Robins family's financial resources. Rumours spread like wildfire as many of the game's 'great and the good' were reputedly linked with the job. Brian Clough was approached, but decided to stay at the Baseball Ground. Much later Clough admitted that he had been very tempted by City's offer.

The search ended on 15 June 1972 with the announcement that Gordon Milne, non-league Wigan's player-manager, and Joe Mercer, Manchester City's general supremo, were to be jointly appointed. There would be no early splash into the transfer market, as the duo needed to take stock of the players available. But when the first six games came and went without a win, the stocktaking process had to be accelerated. After eleven games, by which time the Sky Blues had clocked up their first two wins – over a very poor Stoke and a fortuitous victory at Old Trafford – the dealing started in earnest. Jeff Blockley was sold to Arsenal for club record receipts of £200,000. Blockley deservedly won an England cap soon afterwards, but that was to mark the peak of a career that tailed off rather quickly, which meant that, with hindsight, the fee proved to be good business for City. The cash generated enabled the club to pull off two master strokes that would kick-start the season into life. Tommy Hutchison and Colin Stein, players of proven pedigree, were signed from Blackpool and Glasgow Rangers respectively. Fringe players Billy Rafferty and Quintin Young were the make-weights in the two deals. Evergreen midfielder, and Jimmy Hill's former blue-eyed-boy, Ernie Machin, left soon afterwards for Plymouth as the new team took shape. There were other changes too, as Bobby Parker and Brian Alderson finally established themselves as regular first-teamers. Both were to exert a beneficial influence on the season. Not only did an irresistible league run of eight unbeaten games banish thoughts of relegation, but the season also offered many individual highlights – Hutchison's goal at Highbury, for example, some sparkling home performances, and an FA Cup run which ended surprisingly and tamely at Molineux in the quarter-finals. Only twice before had Coventry progressed so far on the road to the Cup final, in 1910 and 1963.

All things considered, the transformation was remarkable. Earlier in the season it had been the old story, lack of goals, this time on account of the makeshift strike force of Bobby Graham and Ernie Hunt. The victory at Selhurst Park, habitually a lucky ground for the Sky Blues, turned things round and the transformation was complete the following week when a scintillating victory over Manchester City gave fans a taste of things to come. The sight of Hutchison running the opposing right-back ragged was a constant talking point among City fans for years to come. Some of Hutch's early performances were the stuff of legend. The ability to beat a man once, then again, and again, and then send an inch-perfect centre onto Stein's head will live with many City fans for a lifetime. Hutchison's early tussles with the likes of Billy Bonds and Mick Mills would sow the seeds for man-to-man confrontation that would last throughout the 1970's.

City's golden spell ended in unfortunate circumstances: a flood-light failure at Ipswich, with City in the lead and in total command, led to an abandonment. When the game was replayed a couple of weeks later an early injury to Roy Barry disrupted the team, contributing to defeat. A harsh loss at Derby also helped to knock the stuffing out of the players.

Still, the FA Cup kept interest going. This team seemed destined to enjoy a good cup run. An early demolition of Orient in Round 3 whetted appetites and good victories against Grimsby, in a cliff-hanger, and a thrashing of Hull City in Round 5 set up a 'clash of the titans' in the quarter-finals – that stage now being reached for only the third time in the club's history. With league form having recovered to such an extent that it warranted a top-ten position, the 15,000 City faithfuls who descended on Molineux for that mid-March appointment had every reason to be optimistic. Sad to say they were to be disappointed. City never really got going, giving one of their poorest displays for some months to exit the competition in deflated circumstances. Tactics may have played a part – Hutchison was assigned to the right flank instead of the left and produced one of his most ineffective games. The second goal by Richards, after an uncharacteristic howler by Bobby Parker, sent some City fans scurrying for the exits.

The aftermath was anti-climactic, and anyone surveying the season as a whole would have deduced that it was a poor season. It had not, however, been short on entertainment, and had given the fans something to cheer after years of dull defensive soccer. That said, the seven consecutive defeats to round off the season was unprecedented in the club's history, and an injury to Carr was a further blow to the longer-term prospects. No doubt the final fade-out would be forgotten come the new season in August, by which time the autopsy results on 1972-73 would have given Milne and Mercer the benefit of the doubt regarding the team's shortcomings.

Match of the Season 1972-73

Arsenal 0 Coventry 2

Division 1, 4 November 1972

Highbury had not been a happy hunting ground for the Sky Blues, and the victory in November 1972 will be treasured by those City fans present for one of the finest goals in the club's history. Scottish winger Tommy Hutchison, playing only his fourth game since signing from Blackpool for a Coventry record outlay of £140,000, scored at the Clock End to clinch a 2-0 win and inflict one of only two home defeats of that season on the Gunners.

Arsenal, whilst not of the calibre of the double side of 1971, were strong enough to occupy second place in the table. Most of the double-winning side were still in situ, although Jeff Blockley had been signed from City a month earlier to replace Peter Simpson, Geoff Barnett had temporarily taken over from Bob Wilson in goal, and Alan Ball had been signed from Everton.

Coventry were unbeaten for four games following the signing of Colin Stein. The match was only ten minutes old when City netted through Brian Alderson, their new goalscoring discovery. A sweet move involving Cattlin and Mortimer culminated with the nippy Scot heading in Stein's right-wing cross at the far post. Arsenal responded by exerting frenzied pressure, but City always looked the more poised side and capable of adding to their lead.

In the second half Alderson could have completed a hat-trick: he blazed over with only Barnett to beat, and then just failed to connect with a good cross. The nearest Arsenal came to scoring was when a Blockley header scraped the post from Ball's corner.

The decisive second goal came midway through the half, at a time when City's defence, admirably marshalled by Roy Barry, were under intense Arsenal pressure. Hutch intercepted a pass from Ball on the halfway line and set off on a mazy run. Ball tried to foul him but Hutchison kept his feet. Next man was Pat Rice, who was left floundering by a body swerve. On the edge of the box Hutchison somehow evaded McLintock's lunging body-check, side-stepped the oncoming Barnett, and kept his head to shoot into the net from a narrow angle. The pace of the shot beat two defenders desperately trying to intervene on the line.

Joe Mercer afterwards described it as one of the finest goals he had ever seen, Derek Henderson of the *Coventry Evening Telegraph* summed it up as 'sheer poetry' and said that if the TV cameras had been there the goal would have been drooled over by the whole country.

Incredibly, Hutchison almost repeated the punishment a minute later, but this time Barnett smothered the ball. Arsenal brought on substitute George Graham for what turned out to be his last appearance for the Gunners, but by that time City were taking the mickey out of the ragged home side.

Arsenal recovered well from the defeat, losing just one game in fourteen, finishing second in the league to Liverpool and reaching the FA Cup semi-final.

LEAGUE DIVISION 1 **1973-74**

Division 1	16th
League Cup	Quarter-finals
FA Cup	5th Round

Although the close season was relatively quiet as far as incoming transfers were concerned – the only significant acquisition being Gordon Milne's old Blackpool team-mate John Craven, who was signed from Crystal Palace for a modest fee of £42,500 – the fans had seen enough the previous season to feel more upbeat than usual. Craven was not the sort of signing to set the pulse racing, but he proved to be a useful utility player during the three and a half seasons he stayed with the club. Roy Barry moved on during the close season to Crystal Palace, having never re-established that eye-catching form he exhibited before breaking his leg in 1970. He was another case of 'if only'. Otherwise the squad was very much as before, though the best of the younger players were coming through. These included Jimmy Holmes, Alan Dugdale and Alan Green from the start, and Les Cartwright and Mick McGuire making their mark later on.

It was a shame that Bobby Parker failed to establish himself. From being tipped as the next Bobby Moore in early 1971, he was hardly ever in contention during 1973-74, and was on his way the following summer. Many supporters were of the opinion that Parker's mistake in the FA Cup-tie at Wolves the previous season badly eroded his confidence and although he played on for many years he was never the same force again. Willie Carr was another player whose golden years were behind him. We did not know it at the time, but the knee injury suffered at home to Liverpool in April 1973 prevented him scaling the heights he might otherwise have reached. Coventry surprisingly agreed to sell him to arch rivals Wolves in the middle of the 1973-74 season, with a fee of £240,000 agreed. However, Carr failed a medical on account of his knee and the deal was called off. Wolves got their man a year later for a vastly reduced fee and Willie played on for many years, plying his trade in West Midlands non-league soccer as late as 1987.

The autumn also bad farewell to that old warhorse Ernie Hunt. Always a crowd favourite, Ernie had been one of the team's few personalities and, more importantly, a regular goalscorer in an age of defensive football. He suffered from weight problems of late and was clearly finding the pace a bit hot. A transfer to second division Bristol City proved a good way of extending his playing career.

DID YOU KNOW?

City's oldest ever player was goalkeeper Alf Wood, who played his final game in December 1958 at the age of 43 years and 206 days.

The season started well and for the first ten games the City were handily placed in the top five, their unchanged team playing spirited attacking football. Of particular note were the home victories against Liverpool, Manchester City and Derby. Hutchison's dazzling form earned him a call-up for Scotland and, later, a place in Willie Ormond's squad for the 1974 World Cup finals in West Germany. Home crowds too, were up, averaging around 25,000, and a good season seemed to be in prospect. Even a place in Europe did not seem too fanciful. Away form, however, was patchy, the first victory coming in late September at local rivals Leicester, where on a rainy afternoon debutant substitute Les Cartwright curled a beauty around Peter Shilton.

As summer turned into autumn everything started to turn sour. A first home defeat by Everton started the rot, late goals from Lyons and Connolly spiking Coventry's early season sparkle. An injury to Craven, coupled with other enforced changes, disrupted the flow of the team. Goals, always a scarce commodity, dried up completely, and six successive goal-less league games expunged all hopes of a successful league season. It took a plunge into the transfer market to help arrest the slide. David Cross, the Norwich striker, was signed for £150,000. He would serve the Sky Blues' cause for three seasons and became a popular performer both on and off the pitch.

Football at large was heavily disrupted for three months by the miners' strike, which saw Ted Heath's government implement the 'three-day week'. These problems coincided with a potent run in the League Cup. Following victories over Darlington and Bristol City (Bobby Gould making a reappearance against his former club), the home tie with Stoke City in November went ahead only with the assistance of generators – only three floodlight towers were active. Even so, City were able to negotiate the gloom to progress to the next round. The national crisis deepened, so that after Christmas evening floodlight matches were banned. For the first time in twenty years football supporters experienced 2.15 kick-offs in mid-winter, and evening fixtures had to be played in the afternoons. Needless to say, all this had a deleterious effect on attendances, with cup replays attracting only half the usual gate.

Though the playing field was level for all clubs, City negotiated the twin roads to Wembley with admirable pluck, stumbling in unfortunate circumstances on both journeys. The League Cup quest ended in a replay at Manchester City, with Coventry cursing themselves for not having won the first game at Highfield Road, which they might have done but for the controversial dismissal of young full-back Jimmy Holmes. At Maine Road, City were ahead and cruising, but three late goals sealed their fate.

The FA Cup witnessed the first ever Sunday cup-tie involving the Sky Blues. The fourth round home game with Derby County attracted a crowd of over 41,000 – the last occasion such a figure would ever be associated with Highfield Road. Having surmounted Derby's challenge after a replay, City were destined for another late show in Round 5. The gates were closed at a packed Loftus Road for yet another replay, and at 2-2 City were seconds from extra-time when Stan Bowles' free-kick sent them out.

The rest of the league season was anti-climactic, with the final placing of sixteenth not really doing justice to some of the early season performances. But at least relegation was never a threat.

Match of the Season 1973-74

Manchester City 4 Coventry 2

League Cup, quarter-final replay, 16 January 1974

The winter of 1973 is remembered in political terms as the winter of discontent, a period when the Conservative Prime Minister Edward Heath took on the then mighty coal-miners in an industrial dispute that ended in defeat for the government in an early 1974 election. The impact on life in Britain that winter is still vividly recalled by those old enough to have lived through it.

City's League Cup march to the quarter-finals equalled their longest ever run in the competition, but sadly they failed to progress into the semi-finals for the first time. The reward for having beaten Stoke in Round 4 was a home tie with Manchester City in the quarter-finals. Power cuts necessitated that the match be played on a Wednesday afternoon in December, in front of a predictably low crowd of 12,000.

City held their opponents to a 2-2 draw, despite the normally placid Jimmy Holmes having been ordered off early in the game. Alderson was again the hero of the hour, scoring twice in reply to Tommy Booth and Dennis Leman.

The replay took place in mid-January, with both teams having the incentive of knowing their semi-final opponents would be Third Division Plymouth Argyle. Put simply, if Coventry could win at Maine Road they would have one and a half feet at Wembley.

DID YOU KNOW?

City were the first British club to relay a televised match back to their own ground. This happened v Cardiff in October 1965 for the benefit of 10,000 fans.

No side could have given more, short of dying in the attempt, than City's youngsters on an afternoon of mud, wind, rain and effervescent football.

Two more goals from Alderson had carried the team to within twelve minutes of that first elusive semi-final. Attempting to protect a 2-1 lead, City were cruelly struck down by three Manchester City goals in ten minutes. It was a finish that drained the Sky Blues of emotion and left 25,000 fans stunned and incredulous.

Apprehension filled the air from the start, when a bomb hoax threatened to delay the kick-off, but mercifully the only explosions were the sounds of the ball crashing into the net. Coventry weathered a difficult opening and looked the better team when taking the lead after 35 minutes. Hutchison cut in from the left, passed to Alderson and the striker jinked left and then right before shooting. The ball spun out of Keith MacRae's hands and over the line. The home side would have levelled almost at once, but for Bill Glazier's wonderful save from Colin Bell's header.

Three successive corners preceded an equaliser after 65 minutes. Dennis Law crossed and the veteran Mike Summerbee headed in. But two minutes later the Sky Blues were back in front with a stunning goal, Alderson exhibiting control, balance and speed, before finishing with aplomb.

Coventry then foolishly sat back, with the result that pressure on their goal built up until it became intolerable. Francis Lee equalised in the 78th minute, after Glazier strayed too far off his line. Three minutes later it was Lee again, this time from the penalty spot after Willie Carr manhandled Colin Bell off the ball. A fourth goal two minutes from time from Denis Law put the game out of Coventry's reach and inflicted a heavier defeat than they deserved.

Manchester City duly beat Plymouth Argyle but lost at Wembley to Wolves.

LEAGUE DIVISION 1 1974-75

Division 1	14th
League Cup	2nd Round
FA Cup	4th Round

The 1974 close season was dominated by the World Cup finals held in West Germany. With England missing out, the focus fell on Scotland and, for Coventry fans, on Tommy Hutchison. Sadly, Hutch was restricted to a cameo role, although when he came on in Scotland's third group game against Yugoslavia he almost turned the game around in Scotland's favour.

With England manager Alf Ramsey having been dethroned, and the blazers at Lancaster Gate not yet finalising the small print of his successor Don Revie's contract, the English spotlight fell for the moment on Coventry City and the club's general manager Joe Mercer. Joe agreed to be England's caretaker manager for what turned out to be seven internationals, winning three and losing just one. During those carefree few weeks England played soccer in the old way, eschewing the dull defensive tactics practised by Ramsey. Mercer even utilised some of the game's mavericks, such as Frank Worthington, whom Ramsey had spurned.

Back at Highfield Road, there were more pressing problems to contend with. The defence had sprung a few leaks in the past season. Bobby Parker had gone to Carlisle, and with Dugdale and Craven not quite shaping up, a dominant central defender was high on the shopping list. As ever, it seems, in the history of Coventry City, a financial crisis was brewing. The free-spending days were over and money to buy could only be acquired by agreeing to sell. Liverpool's Larry Lloyd was City's target, for whom a record fee of £240,000 was agreed. Lloyd duly signed, but the other half of the deal – the contingent sale of Mick McGuire and Jimmy Holmes to Tottenham for £200,000 – fell through when Spurs manager Bill Nicholson lost his job. Having in consequence gone substantially into the red, it would be some years before City would again be in a position to trade freely in the transfer market.

Once the curtain went up it was clear that this was going to be a long hard season. Attendances were falling and without a victory in the first nine matches the club quickly settled to the bottom of the pack. The one bright spot was the debut of a young right-back from Worcester, Graham Oakey, who quickly established himself in the first team and looked set for a long and successful career. Fate decreed otherwise – a badly twisted knee sustained three years later in a harmless-looking incident on a quagmire pitch at Villa Park truncated that career.

One familiar face missing from the early matches was goalkeeper Bill Glazier. A regular for over ten years, in November Glazier was granted a well-earned testimonial match against the England 1966 World Cup XI. He played just a handful of games for City after that, the last of which, at Wolves in December, bringing the curtain down on an outstanding career. Apart from Steve Ogrizovic, no other goalkeeper has played more games for the club. Neil Ramsbottom, a bargain-basement signing from Bury, took over for the rest of the season, an adequate if unspectacular stand in.

As was so often the case in the Milne era, the sun suddenly reappeared from behind a black cloud. A settled side, a few goals rattled in, and in the time it takes to say 'the M men' Coventry had soared into the top half of the table. There would be no cup runs this season: City were knocked out of the League Cup at the first hurdle at home to Ipswich, and out of the FA Cup at Arsenal in a fourth round replay, following a torrid draw at Highfield Road. The brightest memory of that short-lived cup campaign was Larry Lloyd's goal in the third round, when from deep in his own half he hoisted a sky-bound shot which swept over the outstretched arms of Norwich's astonished Kevin Keelan. For older supporters, that goal was reminiscent of a Roy Kirk strike at Northampton twenty years previously.

Overall, league form was too uneven to reveal any pattern, and although a final position of fourteenth may be considered satisfactory, the club's financial problems overshadowed everything else. Boot-sales were the order of the day as McGuire, Carr and Stein were sold for what the fans considered to be derisory fees. The three outgoing players brought in just over £200,000, but this did little to ease the pressure on the club's cashiers. Lloyd was not the player for Coventry that he had been for Liverpool, looking overweight, unfit and displaying an attitude that did not endear him to many supporters. It could hardly be said that he was over the hill: three years later he would help Nottingham Forest to a league championship and the European Cup. In Forest's shirt he even earned a recall to the England team.

Finances were not helped by the announcement in April that Derrick Robins, the club's main benefactor, was to settle in South Africa. Robins had been actively involved with the club for over twenty years, fourteen as chairman, and his wealth and generosity would be greatly missed. From the perspective of the boardroom, it was the end of an era. Sir Jack Scamp, more famous for his industrial relations expertise than anything else, was already chairman designate. Scamp had the advantage of being a local man, and had in the 1950's been chairman of the now defunct Rugby Town Football Club. But whatever his other qualities, Scamp's pockets could hardly be as deep as those of Derrick Robins, which told its own tale.

Another, even bigger bombshell came at the end of the season with the news that Jimmy Hill was returning in the capacity of managing director. Football was changing fast both on and off the pitch but it was not yet clear what function the 'bearded wonder' would perform. It had been eight years since his departure to the world of television. He was returning in a more cynical time – the 1960's were now a distant memory.

Match of the Season 1974-75

Middlesbrough 4 Coventry 4

Division 1, 19 October 1974

In 1973 England's World Cup-winning centre-half, Jack Charlton, was given his managerial baptism at Middlesbrough, who had been out of the top flight for almost twenty years. In Big Jack's first season in charge the Boro stormed to the Second Division title with 65 points and a 24-match unbeaten run.

Jack's Boro were as hard and uncompromising as they come. They needed the goals of Hickton, Foggon and Mills, otherwise almost every match they played was sure to end 0-0. Having been promoted, Charlton would demand even more from his midfield, whose mainstays were young Graeme Souness and former Celtic European Cup winner Bobby Murdoch. The defence sounded gruesome – Platt in goal, Craggs and Spraggon at full-back, and Boam and Maddren at its heart.

Critics said Boro hadn't the finesse to cope with Division One, but by the time Coventry arrived on Teesside the new boys were doing pretty nicely. They had lost only three league games and had laid the foundations of a good League Cup run by thrashing Spurs 4-0 at White Hart Lane. City, correspondingly, had started the season poorly, but had turned things round to the extent that they were unbeaten in five and unchanged for the fourth successive match. Few players, however could, with hand on heart, say they were looking forward to the trip to the Boro.

Against the odds the game was a sensation, leaving 25,000 fans hoarse and breathless after eight goals, though in time-honoured way both managers – Big Jack especially – bemoaned the defensive shortcomings.

DID YOU KNOW?

In season 1965-66, City had the unusual distinction of being knocked out of the League Cup and FA Cup by the eventual winners.

Boro started the strongest, and when Colin Stein collected a long pass from Larry Lloyd to hit a right-footer past Platt it was against the run of play. Stein had already taken a knock and immediately limped off to be replaced by Alderson. Souness's equaliser five minutes later screamed into the net from 25 yards. The fiery young Scot then put the home side ahead just before the break, his shot ricocheting off the unfortunate Graham Oakey. Two minutes after half-time it looked game over for Coventry after David Mills scored from close range.

It was when they were 1-3 down that City started to play. An intricate 56th-minute move was finished off by David Cross – having arguably his best game since joining City – leaping to head a memorable goal. Eight minutes later it was back to all-square as Jimmy Holmes' bullet shot rounded off another delightful build-up.

Middlesbrough struck back in the 72nd minute to make it 4-3, Alan Foggon pouncing after a fine save by Ramsbottom from John Hickton.

That had to be it, thought City's fans. But the brave, battling Sky Blues had other ideas and three minutes from time that golden left boot of Holmes struck again, this time volleying a dipper that beat Jim Platt all ends up. At the final whistle the whole ground stood to salute two teams who had placed such wholehearted emphasis on entertainment.

LEAGUE DIVISION 1 1975-76

Division 1	14th
League Cup	3rd Round
FA Cup	4th Round

The fanfare which signalled the second coming of Jimmy Hill was far less triumphal than that which greeted his original arrival in late 1961. Derrick Robins was no longer there to bear the burden of expenditure that was required if the club was to make further progress from a lower-middling first division side to the levels that would satisfy the raised aspirations of the average City fan. In fact, the selling that had begun the previous season continued as players were traded to balance the books. Out went two goalkeepers. The first was veteran Bill Glazier for a modest £12,500 to Brentford. An early injury with the Bees brought his career to a premature close and he became an hotelier in Brighton, his home town. The second was Glazier's expected successor, Neil Ramsbottom, on a free transfer to Sheffield Wednesday. The next player to depart was Brian Alderson, who made the short journey up the A46 to near-neighbours Leicester City, for a welcome £110,000.

The incoming signings were not those to set the pulse racing. In the close season veteran Celtic full-back Jim Brogan arrived on a free transfer, and Bryan King, the long-serving Millwall goalkeeper, finally escaped the lower divisions for a crack at the top flight. King cost £57,000. Soon after the season was underway, Barry Powell, Wolves' England Under-23 midfield player, was signed for a bargain £75,000. Of these three, only Powell would make any real impact at Highfield Road. General manager Joe Mercer was also appointed to the board, where his many years of experience in the game would supplement Scamp's undoubted business acumen.

All told, it was therefore a welcome surprise to the fans when the team started the season so well. The stunning opening day win at Goodison Park was followed by a pleasing draw at Old Trafford – against Tommy Docherty's exciting, newly promoted young side – and a home win over a star-studded Manchester City. Hostilities were also resumed with promoted Aston Villa, after a break of 37 years, and a Villa Park attendance of over 40,000 saw City go down to Ray Graydon's late goal, in what was the Sky Blues' only reverse in their first eight games.

A good season seemed in prospect, but the impressive early form was soon confined to memory, in the wake of consecutive home defeats by Stoke, Middlesbrough and Burnley. The slide accelerated with an early exit from the League Cup at Mansfield – another black cup exit to add to a long and growing list. Bryan King had struggled from the start of the season, and after a shambolic 0-5 thrashing at Highbury in October, when King's errors cost two goals, any hope of him rediscovering his confidence seemed forlorn. Previously rated as the best goalkeeper outside the first division, King sustained an injury in February that brought the curtain down on his City career after just 27 games. Having exceeded 350 consecutive appearances for Millwall, it seemed as though his move to Highfield Road had been jinxed. But some clouds have silver linings, and what was a personal disaster for King opened the door for young Scottish goalie Jim Blyth. He grabbed his chance with both hands, becoming a City stalwart, not to mention being capped by his country.

The fans might have ignored the club's finances but the directors could not, for the wolf was inching closer to the door. An injection of cash was paramount, and £175,000 was obtained by selling star player Dennis Mortimer to arch-rivals Aston Villa. The loss of such a jewel, not to mention the timing of the sale – a week before Christmas – stretched supporters' patience to breaking point. Mortimer had played over 200 games for City and had blossomed into a much-coveted England Under-23 performer who was strongly tipped to win full caps. But labouring under a £250,000 overdraft (puny by today's standards), City were hardly in a position to keep him, no matter how bitter a pill it was to swallow.

In the wider context, of course, Mortimer's sale provided further evidence of Coventry's parlous financial state and its inability to compete on a level playing field with bigger clubs. Jimmy Hill dressed up the sale 'as in the long term interests of the club and building a stronger position for the future'. But these words were to ring hollow when the Sky Blues were kicked out of the FA Cup, 0-5 at Newcastle. Ironically, that game marked Bryan King's last for City. Nor would it be the last hiding they ever received at St James' Park.

Mortimer's place in the side was taken by the inelegant John Craven who, despite scoring the winning goal at Molineux – in City's first match after Mortimer's departure – could never hope to fill the void. It was Powell who took up the mantle of becoming the side's principal playmaker. With a total of seven goals that season, he emerged as City's most prolific predator from midfield for some years.

Although still capable of fine performances – notably wins over West Ham, Norwich, and a draw with Manchester United, which kept City in the comfort zone – the season was hardly one to shout about. Following the sale of Mortimer, attendances dipped further, as low as 13,000 on a couple of occasions, the lowest for more than thirteen years. If ever City needed Jimmy Hill to weave his old magic, this was the time.

It had been a strange season in many ways. David Cross, who kicked-off with a hat-trick at Goodison, finished the season off with another at Turf Moor, albeit against a Burnley side already relegated. The previous week, Alan Green had notched a hat-trick as the old enemy Wolves were sent back down to Division Two, having accompanied City into the top flight nine years earlier. Tommy Hutchison was again an ever present (he had missed just one league match in four seasons with the club). Hutch was fast becoming a City institution, something of a legend in his own lifetime. Whenever the going got tough, he could always be relied upon to turn on a bit of magic, to bring a smile and a cheer to the fans.

Match of the Season 1975-76

Everton 1 Coventry 4

Division 1, 16 August 1975

The 1975-76 season began with City facing insolvency and, according to bookmakers, relegation. Their campaign could hardly have got off to a more demanding start, an away game at Goodison Park. Everton had finished fourth the previous season, losing only twice at home.

Billy Bingham's Everton contained a few old stagers whose careers were dimming towards the twilight stage. Former City player Dave Clements, who was also the manager of the Northern Ireland side, was coming to the end of his career, and John Hurst, an unsung hero in defence for many years, was close to retirement. The Toffees still boasted England squad players Martin Dobson and Bob Latchford, the latter having scored seventeen goals the previous season.

City, reverting to their popular green and black striped away kit, were without Larry Lloyd and Mick Ferguson, but Jimmy Holmes and Alan Dugdale performed a marvellous marking job on Everton's twin strikers, Latchford and Mick Lyons. Mick Coop also returned to the City side after almost twelve months out in the cold, playing in midfield. New signings Bryan King and Jim Brogan made their debuts, the latter in place of the popular Cattlin, who was suspended. Both debutants did well, though in the event King was rarely tested in goal.

DID YOU KNOW?

City's three largest home crowds came in a two-year period. The visitors were Wolves (April 1967) and Manchester United (March 1968 and April 1969).

City were two up after only sixteen minutes, with both goals stemming from moves obviously rehearsed on the training ground. On both occasions throw-ins were exploited, with players making space for themselves to receive the ball. First, Coop gathered a Graham Oakey throw and his first-time centre was headed home by David Cross. Ten minutes later Jim Brogan threw the ball to Tommy Hutchison, who cut in and let fly with a sizzling 30-yarder that Lawson failed to hold. Cross raced up to jab the ball over the line.

Kenyon pulled one back for Everton, when King failed to hold Smallman's shot, but Cross put the result beyond doubt when he seized on a back-pass from Hurst to dribble round Lawson. Alan Green completed the scoring from a Hutchison cross, a goal which signalled a mass exodus of disgruntled Evertonians.

Hutchison was inspired throughout, frequently bamboozling the home defence. Most fans nominated him as their man of the match, with hat-trick man Cross not far behind.

LEAGUE DIVISION 1 1976-77

Division 1	19th
League Cup	4th Round
FA Cup	4th Round

The close season of 1976 was unusually quiet, both on and off the field. With average home attendances the previous season down to 19,000 – the lowest for fourteen years – and fiscal reports making grim reading, the outlook was gloomy. There was only one incoming transfer, the QPR midfielder John Beck, and at just £40,000 he was a low-key signing. The bookmakers installed City as firm favourites for relegation, not the first nor the last time that they would occupy this unenviable position. But on this occasion that judgment also reflected the views of many supporters. The first two games did little to alleviate their pessimism, as Middlesbrough and Manchester United both recorded victories far more comfortable than the scorelines suggested – the latter match was also highlighted by the dismissal of Larry Lloyd for any number of nasty fouls. It was an indisciplined performance that would hasten his departure from the club; he was to play only three more matches for the Sky Blues.

Clearly drastic action was called for to stabilise the club, and it arrived quicker than expected. Out of the blue, on 27 August, three major signings were made – Terry Yorath from Leeds for £145,000, Ian Wallace a young striker from Dumbarton for £75,000, and Bobby McDonald, a full-back from Aston Villa for £40,000. All three were introduced to the crowd before the home game against Leeds United on a wet Saturday afternoon and their appearance seemed to spur the rest of the team to a much needed victory. That match also marked the coming of age of a young centre-forward from Newcastle, Mick Ferguson, who scored a splendid goal in a 4-2 home victory. The fortunes of the club took an upturn that afternoon and although there would be traumas to overcome in the second half of the season, these too heralded better times. This came at a price. The ritual 'balancing of the books' meant that David Cross was sold to West Brom, the silver lining being the good form of Mick Ferguson, which to some extent softened the blow of Cross's departure.

Better results and a brighter style of play went hand in hand. City enjoyed a small run in the League Cup and some heartening results in the league, with Ian Wallace finally seizing his chance and looking every bit a Division One player. City also put on a splendid display at Villa Park, where it needed a late Andy Gray goal to salvage a draw for the home team. Not for the first time, and just as the corner seemed to have turned, Lady Luck deserted the Sky Blues. Like buses, City's misfortunes all rolled up together. Mick Ferguson injured his ankle against Everton and was sidelined for the best part of two months. Soon afterwards Ian Wallace suffered facial injuries when his car careered out of control on an icy road, forcing him to miss the next six matches. Thirdly, a spell of harsh weather resulted in severe damage to the Highfield Road pitch which, coupled with FA Cup-ties, meant that the stadium saw not a single home league match between 22 January and 2 April. Another blow came with keeper Jim Blyth's serious knee injury, sustained in the Easter Saturday home match against West Ham. As a consequence, seventeen-year-old Les Sealey was thrown in at the deep end and quickly established himself as one for the future. For beleaguered City, after thirteen matches without a win, relegation was again staring them in the face. Although Jim Holton had been signed from Sunderland in March for £40,000, and brought some stability to the defence, he too was short of fitness.

Speculation about Gordon Milne's future was rife and, coupled with a dreaded vote of confidence from Jimmy Hill, his future looked bleak. Hope resided largely in the newly established strike-force of Ferguson and Wallace. The duo had been scoring quite freely, though without swinging matches City's way. Home victories over Derby and Stoke in April eased the situation, albeit temporarily, but two draws and two defeats left Coventry's First Division life hanging by a thread as they faced Bristol City at home in the final match of the season. The situation was finely balanced, with one or the other clearly favourites for the drop. The complicating factor was Sunderland, who would be sucked into the equation should they lose at Everton.

Match of the Season 1976-77

Coventry 2 Bristol City 2

Division 1, 19 May 1977

At kick-off time, the foot of Division One looked incredibly congested.

Pos		P	Goal-diff	Pts
18	Sunderland	41	-6	34
19	Bristol City	41	-10	34
20	COVENTRY	41	-11	34
21	Stoke	42	-23	34
22	Tottenham	42	-24	33

DID YOU KNOW?

City's 1-6 thrashing away to Bayern Munich in 1970 remains the heaviest defeat any English club has suffered in a European competition.

Spurs and Stoke had wound up their season and were down, leaving any one of the three clubs above them to join them in Division Two. A draw would suit Bristol City, since that would keep them above Coventry. Likewise a draw for Sunderland would keep them above at least one of the two clubs slugging it out beneath them. The Sky Blues could ensure safety only by winning. The only other combination of results that could rescue them was to draw with Bristol City while Sunderland lost at Goodison.

An ironic twist to the game was the fact that Bristol City – desperate not to make an immediate return to Division Two – were managed by Alan Dicks, previously assistant to Jimmy Hill at Highfield Road in the Sky Blues' Second Division days.

A huge, almost capacity crowd of 37,000 had assembled, but severe traffic congestion delayed large numbers of Bristol fans. Not for the last time, a late kick-off involving Coventry would incur allegations of gamesmanship. Whether responsibility for the delay fell at the feet of the club, the police, or the referee may never be known, but Jimmy Hill, in his book *The Jimmy Hill Story*, points the finger squarely at the referee. Whatever, the start was put back by five minutes. Any possible repercussions seemed academic as the Sky Blues took an early lead. John Shaw could only palm away a cross and Tommy Hutchison scored only his second goal of the season. Bristol, however, were matching Coventry for effort, and Bobby McDonald had to clear off his line. Sealey then saved Trevor Tainton's twenty-yard effort, but just before half-time he allowed a shot to slither through his hands. Luckily, the ball passed wide of the post.

In the second half Hutchison began to weave his magic, and on 52 minutes he put Coventry two up, shooting in off the bar after Powell's shot had hit a post. Within a minute, though, Bristol pulled one back, Gerry Gow netting with a low shot after combining neatly with Gillies. The visitors, roared on by their vocal fans, pressed hard, and with eleven minutes left scored a deserved equaliser. Gillies, overlapping on the right, squeezed in a shot at the near post.

A draw, of course, was all Bristol needed. Depending on what Sunderland were doing, Coventry might have just minutes in which to score again and ward off relegation. Whatever the logic of the situation, for the next five minutes the Sky Blues looked dead on their feet. Their composure vanished and they could do nothing more than boot the ball upfield in desperation. Bristol, meanwhile, coolly went for the jugular. It looked odds on relegation for Coventry, when a commotion in the directors box sparked news that the final whistle had blown at Goodison, and that Sunderland had lost 0-2. In less time than it takes to tell it, word had spread to the crowd and, more importantly, to the players. Provided there was no change to the score at Highfield Road, both teams were safe. Without going so far as to sign a truce on the pitch, both teams simply stopped playing. The remaining five minutes saw the ball tapped this way and that, aimlessly from one side of the field to the other and back again. It was an extraordinary sight for those who witnessed it, almost unprecedented in competitive English football. The referee was probably as embarrassed as anyone, and in the circumstances injury-time would have been an irrelevance. When he finally called a halt to the farce, both sets of supporters celebrated by embracing each other.

Sunderland were understandably aggrieved, and – according to Jimmy Hill – Alan Hardaker of the Football League reprimanded Coventry for their part in the unfortunate events of the evening. At a subsequent hearing the club were exonerated of all wrong-doing and the matter was buried.

Record signing Chris Chilton heads over the Wolves crossbar (February 1972)

Dennis Mortimer's belter earns a point against Manchester City (April 1972)

Colin Stein drives narrowly wide of the Sheffield United goal (November 1972)

Brian Alderson scores his second goal against Sheffield United (November 1972)

Mick Coop beats Spurs' Ralph Coates to score with a floating header (August 1973)

Jim Blyth punches clear in this Ipswich attack (January 1976)

Mick Ferguson challenges John Bird of Newcastle (March 1976)

Ian Wallace scores his second goal against Aston Villa (April 1977)

Three

Blue Skies, Dark Clouds 1977-1983

LEAGUE DIVISION 1	**1977-78**
Division 1	7th
League Cup	4th Round
FA Cup	3rd Round

In spite of the close shave at the end of the previous season, a relatively optimistic atmosphere pervaded the club and its supporters in the summer of 1977. The consensus was that the squad was better than the final position in May indicated, and that better times might be just around the corner.

Transfer activity was quiet, with the only notable signing being the Aston Villa right-winger Ray Graydon for a modest £40,000 fee. Graydon's arrival was, however, indicative of an attacking tactical emphasis. The team would line up 4-2-4 with two wingers to nourish the goalscoring potential of Wallace and Ferguson.

The pre-season friendlies gave little indication that things were improving, with heavy defeats at Brighton and Charlton. The first half of the opening match against Derby County was no better. The match was transformed via Wallace's boot and Ferguson's head, and that pattern was to be sustained more or less throughout the season – which turned out to be the most exciting since the Second Division championship year.

Goals flowed freely at both ends of the pitch, with dynamic duo Ferguson and Wallace quickly establishing themselves as one of the most feared strike-forces in the land. The midfield, comprising two players – Terry Yorath and Barry Powell – were called upon to work like Trojans to compensate for their numerical deficit.

The stay-away fans of recent years were lured back by the excitement of it all. Coventry netted 75 goals this season, their highest total since 1963-64, but more importantly, the team provided entertainment of the highest order. Some of the home matches this season would be contenders for the top ten thrillers of the club's elite era, notably those against Manchester City, Norwich, Chelsea and Everton.

Many City players were performing at their peak – Yorath and Powell certainly, Ferguson and Wallace probably, and Blyth and McDonald possibly. Full international honours were won by Wallace, Yorath, Nardiello and Blyth – the last-named was called up for Ally McLeod's ill-fated Argentina expedition – though the form of McDonald, Ferguson and Hutchison ought to have merited international recognition.

City's League Cup run acquired a head of steam with a win at Tottenham. This was followed by a breathtaking draw at Anfield, where it looked for long periods as if a famous first victory was on the cards, with 8,000 City fans shouting themselves hoarse. Given the fact that Coventry had been thrashed 0-6 at Goodison the previous Saturday, the draw at Anfield was some achievement.

In fact, the whole season was like that – unpredictable but exhilarating. The replay at Highfield Road had to be put back three weeks on account of Liverpool's other commitments. By that time, a run of five matches without a win had blunted City's edge, and they ended up well beaten by a totally professional Liverpool team. Many fans, with their heads in the clouds, had been convinced that City's name was on the cup that year. Their hopes crashed to earth with a bang.

It wasn't long before City entertained Liverpool again, this time in the league, but the 1-0 victory was scant revenge for the cup defeat. That league encounter is fondly remembered for a bruising battle between Yorath and Souness, and was part of a six-match winning streak at Highfield Road. Among City's other victims in that purple patch were Manchester United, beaten 3-0.

Away from home it was a different story. The FA Cup defeat at Middlesbrough was typical of City's spluttering away form. It was this travel sickness that finally put paid to hopes of qualifying for Europe. One win in the last eight league games was hardly European form, but had Ipswich not confounded expectations by beating Arsenal in the FA Cup final, Coventry would have claimed a UEFA Cup place.

On the transfer front, the mid-season signing of Keith Osgood from Tottenham bolstered the defence, at least for a time, before he faded. Graham Oakey had been badly hurt in the Boxing Day match at Villa Park – he would never play for the first team again – but this allowed Brian 'Harry' Roberts a chance to claim the right-back spot as his own. For a brief spell Donato Nardiello burst upon the scene in ways reminiscent of Ronnie Rees fifteen years previously. Unlike Rees, Nardiello's impact was far less enduring. A young Birmingham-born centre-forward, Garry Thompson, earned rave reviews near the end of the season, illustrating that competition for first-team places was hotting up.

Match of the Season 1977-78

Coventry 4 Manchester City 2

Division 1, 4 October 1977

Two matches stand out among many as contenders for match of the season. In terms of goal-avalanches, nothing could compare with the extraordinary happenings when Norwich City were beaten 5-4 on 27 December.

The Canaries were a team of journeymen, with the exception of England 1966 World Cup star Martin Peters, who was still scoring regularly from midfield with his famous ghosting runs. City led 2-0 after 26 minutes, thanks to a Barry Powell penalty (his first for the club and City's 500th goal in Division One) and a spectacular bicycle-kick from Wallace. However, three Norwich goals in the space of thirteen minutes brought City down to earth: a John Ryan penalty and two goals from future million-pound striker Kevin Reeves. In addition, Martin Peters had a goal disallowed for offside.

The second half saw no let up in the scoring. Gooding's thunderous shot, his first ever City goal, made it 3-3. Eleven minutes later, Bobby McDonald curled a shot around Keelan, and but for two disallowed Coventry goals the outcome would have been sealed. But Norwich bounced back again, Peters heading an equaliser and then hitting a post with a free-kick.

The ninth goal came after 82 minutes, when Graydon headed over Keelan, but Norwich had the chance to make it 5-5 when, with ninety seconds remaining, they were awarded the third penalty of the match. Blyth's save extended Norwich's dismal record at Highfield Road to seventeen successive defeats.

It takes something special to relegate such a goal-feast to the also-rans, but that is the case in 1977-78. In the second half of the game with Manchester City the Sky Blues touched heights never equalled before or since, scoring three times in the final seventeen minutes to turn probable defeat into exhilarating triumph.

During the 1960's and 70's the Maine Road club produced some dazzling teams, none better than that which descended on Highfield Road in October 1977 as unbeaten league leaders. Coventry, too, had started the season promisingly, and prior to a home defeat by West Brom on the previous Saturday had lost only at Old Trafford and Anfield. A settled side partly explained this string of results, helped by the blossoming partnership between Mick Ferguson and Ian Wallace. Wally had scored eight goals in nine games and was making everyone who saw him in action sit up and take notice.

For the match in question injuries forced manager Milne to make his first changes, bringing in young Les Sealey for Jim Blyth and John Beck for Ray Graydon. Sealey was called into action as early as the fourth minute, stooping to pick the ball out of the net after Dennis Tueart had scored from Joe Royle's headed pass.

The Manchester club, also playing 4-2-4, dominated the early stages. Wingers Peter Barnes and Tueart were in devastating form, giving Coventry's full-backs a torrid time. The Sky Blues were grateful not to fall further behind, but then stunned the visitors with an equaliser on the half hour. Wallace held the ball up, allowing Beck to overlap and centre for Ferguson to shoot home.

Ferguson's goal raised the temperature of the match. Manchester attacked incessantly and Barnes restored their lead on the stroke of half-time, latching onto a long punt over Coventry's static defence before shooting past Sealey.

Throughout the second half Coventry camped in the visitors' half, attacking relentlessly and creating chances galore. In the 73rd minute the dam broke: Beck flicked on Oakey's cross and Fergie lobbed Corrigan to make it 2-2. Six minutes later Yorath, architect of many City attacks, swung over a cross. Ferguson glided a header into Wallace's path and the Scotsman beat Corrigan with ease.

Manchester hit back. Barnes climaxed a dazzling run with a shot that flew narrowly wide, leaving Coventry fans baying for the final whistle. With a minute left Ferguson completed his hat-trick, putting the result beyond doubt with a classic goal. Hutchison crossed from the left and the big man took it on his chest and smote the dropping ball past Corrigan.

That goal brought the crowd to their feet, where they stayed to the final whistle. The Sky Blues trooped off to a standing ovation.

LEAGUE DIVISION 1	**1978-79**
Division 1	10th
League Cup	2nd Round
FA Cup	3rd Round

After the previous season's success, expectations were high that City could repeat and even improve upon their seventh place. They consistently failed, however, to recapture their goal touch. This was due in part to a run of injuries – Yorath only played in half the games and his leadership was sorely missed. Ferguson was also out for a long spell, and his replacement, Garry Thompson, having made a promising introduction, had the misfortune to break a leg in training. Ian Wallace was never likely to startle opposing defences second time round. It is to his credit that, though marked even more tightly, he still managed fifteen goals, including a hat-trick against Southampton. What consistency the side possessed was attributable to two players, Bobby McDonald and Tommy Hutchison, both of whom were ever present and earned consistently good reviews.

Two bargain buys were to prove excellent investments in the long term. The first of these was defender Gary Gillespie, who had been snapped up for £75,000 the previous March from Falkirk, where at eighteen he had become the youngest club captain in British football. He was destined to blossom into one of the finest defenders of the era. In the close season Steve Hunt had signed for £40,000 from New York Cosmos. Hunt, a former Villa player, was something of a star in America, where he had partnered Pele in two successive NASL Championships, but he was determined to succeed in the English League. He scored on his debut in a 2-0 win at Derby, as City opened their programme with nine points from five games. This meant that game number six, versus Liverpool, was contested by the country's top two clubs. But the position was misleading, at least in Coventry's case. The League Cup defeat at Third Division Chester was ominous enough, but the wheels stayed on until an apocalyptic trip to the Hawthorns in October. Ron Atkinson's West Brom, brimming with the talents of Regis, Cunningham and co, proved irresistible, breaching City's defence seven times. Rumours of dressing-room rancour after the game suggested that team-spirit was fast ebbing away; Yorath, noticeably, did not reappear in the first team until February. Away from home, City too often looked likely to capsize, and did so twice – 0-4 at the Dell and 0-5 at Ashton Gate.

DID YOU KNOW?

George Best scored his last goal for Manchester United in City's 3-2 league win at Old Trafford in December 1973.

At home, a thrilling victory over Derby and a pre-Christmas win to terminate Everton's long unbeaten run kept spirits up, but the big winter freeze then mothballed Highfield Road for seven weeks. When the snows finally melted, City's form melted with them. Having been impregnable at home for almost a year, City suffered three reverses in a row before regaining the plot with a thumping win over FA Cup finalists Manchester United. The win sparked a productive run-in, with City losing only one of their last nine games, and achieving commendable draws at Villa, Everton and Manchester United. The one blemish was an embarrassing 1-5 setback at Loftus Road, to a home side already condemned to relegation, and who therefore took the opportunity to introduce seventeen-year-old Clive Allen into the fray. Allen destroyed City's defence almost single-handedly and emerged with a hat-trick.

The FA Cup draw was harsh, pitching the Sky Blues against their bogeymen of West Brom. The Baggies had a potent side, had already handed out one seven-goal thumping to the Sky Blues, and were well in contention for the league title. City missed chances in the first cup-tie for which they were severely punished in the Hawthorns replay, their modest consolation being a share of the gate receipts over the two games – that from the 38,000 crowd at Highfield Road constituting a City record.

City's conveyor belt of gifted youngsters showed no signs of slackening. In Yorath's absence Andy Blair seized his chance well. Paul Dyson, Gary Bannister, Jim Hagan and Mark Hateley were others who made encouraging debuts at one time or other. But no matter how good they were, a team of kids needed experience to guide them, and if improvement was to be maintained two or three key signings were required, especially in defence.

Off the pitch, the season was dominated by a transfer that never was. Early in January the Sky Blues bid £1 million for the England striker Trevor Francis from Birmingham. For a club that had only recently been up to its eyes in debt, it seemed extraordinarily bold – or foolhardy – for low-lights like Coventry City to be the first British club to offer a million pounds for a player. Sadly, for City, Francis preferred the lure of joining Brian Clough at Nottingham Forest. City also made strenuous efforts to buy Kevin Beattie from Ipswich for £450,000, but fears about the player's underlying fitness proved well founded and the deal fell through.

DID YOU KNOW?

In September 1980, a 'goal' by Crystal Palace's Clive Allen came back off the stanchion and was disallowed. As a result, goal stanchions were redesigned.

Match of the Season 1978-79

Coventry 4 Manchester United 3

Division 1, 20 March 1979

Though City had gone exactly three months without a home win, they had somehow clung on to eighth place in the league. They had been handicapped by injury to the experienced Mick Ferguson, which forced Gordon Milne to bid for two players – an unnamed Yugoslavian and Charlton's Mike Flanagan. Charlton thought the offer derisory and rejected it.

Against Manchester United, Milne therefore had little choice but to name an unchanged side for the first time in six games. The promising Garry Thompson continued at centre-forward. He had been attracting admiring glances from Ron Greenwood and was pushing for inclusion in the England Under-21 side. Thompson used this game to further his international claims and lengthen his list of admirers.

United were having a bad time of it and were in the lower half of the league. What bullets they were able to fire were largely reserved for FA Cup opponents. They were already through to the semi-final and would shortly be booked to face Arsenal at Wembley.

United's defence on paper looked solid enough. Gary Bailey, in his first full season in goal, was already pushing for an England place, while central defenders Martin Buchan and Gordon McQueen carried over their Old Trafford partnership into the Scottish national team. Up front, Jimmy Greenhoff and Joe Jordan had few peers among Division One strikers. All in all, then, United's malaise was something of a mystery.

Under normal circumstances a heavyweight like Gordon McQueen would have been expected to teach the likes of Garry Thompson a lesson or two. But the normally dominating Scot found himself for once totally dominated, both in the air and on the ground as his opponent mercilessly exploited the centre-half's weaknesses.

The scoring began after eighty seconds, when Barry Powell fired home following a Tommy Hutchison cross. After eight minutes the lead was doubled when Thompson thumped the ball home after cushioning Don Nardiello's cross on his chest.

City continued to press. Nardiello had a goal disallowed after Thompson had headed down a cross, and Ian Wallace then had a shot kicked off the line.

With the home crowd roaring City to even greater exertions, United hit back. Jimmy Greenhoff set up the goal for Steve Coppell, whereupon Greenhoff himself nearly equalised. His near-miss proved costly. On the stroke of half-time Thompson dummied two defenders and left Hutchison to score with a right-footer. City led 3-1 at the break and soon after it was 4-1, when Hutchison set up Bobby McDonald to lash a shot inside Gary Bailey's near post. Nardiello then shot over the bar and sent over a cross from which Thompson was just inches away. United, who had tried to play a patient game, synonymous with Dave Sexton, their manager, now threw caution to the wind and pushed men forward in numbers.

They were rewarded with Sammy McIlroy's 20-yard free-kick, but it was not until the last minute that Coppell scored United's third with a fierce drive. Time ran out and City triumphed to a rapturous response from their supporters, evoking memories of the excitement generated the previous season.

Garry Thompson was undoubtedly the star of the show. But with England representative honours beckoning, his was the cruel misfortune to break his leg in two places in a practice game. He would be lost to the team for almost a year.

LEAGUE DIVISION 1 **1979-80**

Division 1	15th
League Cup	3rd Round
FA Cup	4th Round

1979-80 was a season of experiment and laying of foundations for the future, but supporters found themselves disappointed by the inconsistency of the side, impatient at its shortcomings, and by the end of the season disenchanted with everything. After five years of prudent forays into the transfer market, which unearthed cut-price gems like Wallace, Yorath, and McDonald, the club now decided to brandish the chequebook. Gary Collier was no more than an average centre-half with Bristol City but in June 1979 he became the first out-of-contract player to negotiate his own transfer when walking out on Ashton Gate to join Coventry. The fee of £325,000 was determined by a tribunal and, coupled with Everton's England Under-21 defender David Jones signing for £250,000, City announced their return to the big-spending league.

These two costly purchases were intended to complete the jigsaw and push City into contention for a European place. Both players showed up well in a pre-season Skol Trophy that saw City triumphant in a four-team tournament staged in Scotland. With Ian Wallace injured, youngsters Tom English and Mark Hateley earned an early opportunity to stake places in the side, English doing enough to make his full debut on the opening day at promoted Stoke.

That match proved disastrous. City's defence – including new men Collier and Jones – looked all at sea and shipped three goals within the first 55 minutes. Collier and Gooding were publicly blamed and were dropped forthwith. One week later the axe fell on Jones, following further humiliation at Nottingham Forest.

Milne's plans lay in tatters and it was clear to everyone that the season ahead would be long and arduous. The few bright spots in a depressing string of away results included a League Cup win at Ipswich and City's first win at the Dell for over forty years. Mercifully, the vultures were kept at bay by virtue of City's form at Highfield Road, which harvested eleven points from the first six games, and with Wallace returning in September the clouds began to lift. His return coincided with a comprehensive win over Bolton. It was the first time that he and Ferguson had played together since February. But a week later Ferguson was crocked again and sidelined for another six weeks.

DID YOU KNOW?

City's 5-5 draw with Southampton in 1981-82 was the first occasion that 10 goals had been scored in a top division match since 1966.

The latest Hawthorns hoodoo struck at the end of October with the Albion underlining their League Cup victory a month earlier by crushing the Sky Blues 4-1 in the league. A week later City surrendered their undefeated home record to Stoke. Coventry looked a shambles in that match, but were not helped by individual errors by David Jones which precipitated the end of his City career. He was pulled off at half-time and barely got another look in. Suddenly, everything about the club was put under the microscope – tactics, transfers, and ambition (or lack of it).

But football is as fickle as everything else in life. Within a week, with Ferguson back from injury, the team embarked on their most productive spell of the season. The next four games saw no defeats, ten goals scored, eight of them by the bearded striker. The Wallace-Ferguson partnership was re-established and 3-0 wins over Leeds and Wolves were followed by a 0-0 at high-flying Crystal Palace. A week later came Ferguson's crowning glory, a four-goal bonanza to demolish Bobby Robson's Ipswich, who had themselves tried to pick him up for a bargain fee just a week earlier. Ferguson was now a wanted man and within weeks he came close to making a £900,000 move to Nottingham Forest, with Martin O'Neill coming in part-exchange. Forest manager Brian Clough, however, had second thoughts.

City's inconsistency was amply demonstrated during a topsy-turvy Christmas programme. A 0-3 capitulation at Villa Park was hard for the fans to take, but City bounced back to win at the Baseball Ground, albeit against a dreary Derby side, only to suffer a relapse at home to Forest. The New Year brought an FA Cup win at Oldham, which promised a seemingly easy Fourth Round tie at Third Division Blackburn. Expectations were further raised with a stunning victory over the league leaders, Liverpool, in which several of City's kids came of age in front of the Match of the Day cameras. Perhaps the win went to their heads. A week later, at an icy Ewood Park, before a large and vociferous City following, the team bowed out of the FA Cup, miserably losing 0-1. Several of the youngsters froze in their minds as well as their boots. Wallace's wretched luck in front of goal continued and before many weeks had passed he was dropped and had slapped in a transfer request.

Milne went shopping abroad, paying FC Cologne £250,000 for 29-year-old Belgian winger Roger Van Gool. But Milne had to balance the books, and arranged a deal by which Ferguson would go to Villa Park for £750,000. The signing fell through when the Villa board blocked the move. With Bobby McDonald out of contract at the end of the season, and indicating that he planned to go elsewhere, the side of 1977-78 was breaking up. Nor did Van Gool's early games for the club suggest to the fans that here was a player of genuine international class.

Garry Thompson returned from his year out with a broken leg and made an immediate impact with two goals in a comfortable win over Southampton. But that was the only win in the seven games Wallace missed through being dropped. Following a disgraceful home defeat by Wolves, Milne was forced to recall the flame-haired Scotsman for the trip to Middlesbrough. By this time 'Milne out' chants were increasing in intensity, and Wallace responded by scoring both goals in a 2-1 win. His overall performance, however, did little to convince supporters that his heart was really with the club, and that unless he buckled down the sooner he was gone the better. Wallace at least brightened up the last few weeks of a dull season by getting sent off, along with Crystal Palace's Kenny Sansom. The following week at Old Trafford City seemed to be playing king-maker – United were vying with Liverpool for the title – until referee George Courtney inexplicably allowed McIlroy's goal, scored direct from an indirect free-kick.

After the season's end, chairman Phil Mead retired and Jimmy Hill, by now a major shareholder, took over. Almost Hill's first act was to sanction the sale of Wallace to Nottingham Forest for a huge £1,250,000. Hill's explanation to the largely resigned City fans was that: 'Ian Wallace doesn't own the word ambition, we are ambitious too.' The fee obtained went some way to financing the impressive 'Sky Blue Connexion' at the club's Ryton training ground. It also meant that in five years City had sold nearly £4 million worth of players while spending only half that sum on new ones.

Match of the Season 1979-80

Coventry 4 Ipswich Town 1

Division 1, 1 December 1979

Coming into this game City had kept a clean sheet in the previous three games for the first time in Division One and were in eleventh place in the league. Ipswich Town were in an unusual twentieth, having struggled to score goals all season.

To spice up his attack Bobby Robson, the Ipswich manager, had expressed interest in Coventry's centre-forward Mick Ferguson.

City's ace striker was in super form, having scored four goals in the three previous games after returning from injury. Robson made his bid two days prior to the game, adding: 'If Ferguson can play well against my defence it could open my eyes.' Not surprisingly, the Ipswich manager took some flak in Coventry quarters.

Mick Ferguson began his scoring spree with a right-foot shot which flashed into the net off the inside of the far post. Ipswich surged back and City had to battle to stay ahead. Ferguson gashed his knee late in the first half, which required stitches, leaving ten-man Coventry to see out the closing minutes of the half. City were indebted to Les Sealey's heroics in City's goal for retaining their lead.

Ferguson returned, his knee heavily strapped, after half-time. It took him only another seven minutes to score again when prodding home a Steve Hunt cross at the second attempt. Then, to the delight of the crowd as much as himself, he completed his hat-trick with a bullet header from another Hunt cross. Wark replied for Ipswich with a penalty, but within minutes it was that man Ferguson again, with a cute lob over the stranded Ipswich keeper, Cooper, to make it four.

Ferguson proudly claimed the match ball, saying: 'I was not motivated by Robson's comments because I don't feel I have anything to prove to anyone. I know I can score goals and I was thrilled to score four goals today.'

Gordon Milne's verdict was that Ferguson's performance was 'magic', despite his lack of match practice, which showed in the first half when he missed a couple of easy headers. Robson refused to comment, but later in the week withdrew his offer for Ferguson. His explanation was that Coventry were insisting on a player exchange deal, but he was not prepared to make any of his squad available, nor could he agree to Coventry's asking price.

Not that Robson's side needed strengthening. Coventry were the last team to beat them for 24 matches, Ipswich finishing the season in third place. The roles were reversed in Coventry's case. The win over Ipswich lifted them to sixth, but by season's end they had slumped to fifteenth. Christmas injuries to Ferguson and Holton deprived the Sky Blues of their services for the rest of the season.

LEAGUE DIVISION 1 **1980-81**

Division 1	16th
League Cup	Semi-final
FA Cup	5th Round

Despite the pressures on manager Gordon Milne to quit he started the new campaign in charge. Ian Wallace was not the only player to leave in the summer, Gary Collier having been transferred to Portland Timbers in the NASL for the astonishing fee of £365,000, more than he cost in the first place. Considering he only played two first-team games for Coventry, the club were fortunate to recoup the money. Bobby McDonald was still around, despite all the noises he had made about getting away. Five players – Tommy Hutchison, Jim Hagan, Mark Hateley, Jim Holton and Gary Bannister – missed the start of the season because they were playing in the NASL in America. The fee received from Forest for Wallace was still unspent, although many big names had been rumoured to be on the verge of signing. New chairman Hill negotiated the club's first sponsorship deal, with Coventry-based car manufacturer Talbot. This provided another welcome injection of cash, although the FA rejected an application to rename the club Coventry Talbot.

For the second season running the campaign opened with a depressing away defeat against a promoted side, in this instance Birmingham. The result prompted Milne to seek reinforcements and Derby's Republic of Ireland international midfielder Gerry Daly joined for £300,000. He signed just in time to make his debut in a goal-less home draw with Liverpool. The defeat at St Andrews also marked McDonald's last start, allowing 'Harry' Roberts to come in and make the left-back position his own. At centre-back, Paul Dyson was forming a strong partnership with Gary Gillespie, and another talented youngster, Andy Blair, secured his place in midfield alongside Steve Hunt, a winger converted into a midfield playmaker. Up front, Garry Thompson started the season alongside Tom English, though the latter was later replaced by Mark Hateley. The side showed undeniable promise but, with an average age of just 21, it lacked the necessary discipline that can only be gained with experience.

In the league it was to be an erratic season, and there seemed little hope of pleasant diversion in the League Cup when City were drawn against Manchester United at the first hurdle, but 1-0 wins home and away marked the beginning of one of the finest cup runs in the club's history. In the third round, they were drawn away to

Brighton and, with Hutchison returning from his summer sojourn in Seattle, Coventry's midfield glittered sufficiently to see them through 2-1. Four days later the roof fell in at Highfield Road. Everton inflicted Coventry's biggest home league defeat since 1919, winning 5-0 and wrecking City's goal-difference with a vengeance.

By the time the next round of the League Cup came around the storm clouds were gathering. Feeble Norwich had won at Highfield Road for the first time since 1933, and McDonald and Hutchison had been sold to Manchester City. Gates had slipped to less than 12,000 and when the team could only scrape a home draw against Second Division Cambridge the knives were out for Milne. Happily, a gritty display in the replay on a rain-swept pitch produced a 1-0 win. The quarter-finals paired City with Second Division Watford. In a tense game at Vicarage Road, and roared on by 9,500 travelling fans, City drew 2-2. But they made no mistake in the replay. On a night to remember, the Sky Blues ran out 5-0 winners, going through to a semi-final against FA Cup holders West Ham.

In the meantime, the good cup form spilled over into the league, at least at home. From mid-October to the end of February the only side to lower City's colours at Highfield Road were the old bogey side Aston Villa, who were destined to lift the league title. Away from home things weren't so rosy; in the same period City won just once on their travels – at struggling Leicester. By now an FA Cup run was starting to take shape, thanks to a hard-fought third round tie with Leeds, which was won after a replay, followed by a fourth round win over neighbours Birmingham.

Coventry's come-uppance was delivered in the space of four cruel days in mid-February, and this effectively terminated their season. Neighbour's late goal clinched a League Cup final place for the Hammers, and four days later Spurs ended City's FA Cup hopes, after errors – both tactical and individual – left the Sky Blues with a mountain to climb for the rest of the tie.

The effect of these twin blows on a young side was little short of catastrophic, and the team nose-dived into a run of seven defeats in eight games, the result of which was to pitch City once again into the jaws of relegation. Two wins and a draw in the last three games were enough to avert the danger; but it had been a close enough shave to convince some members of the board that the team needed a new steersman at the helm.

On 13 May 1981, after nine seasons in charge, Milne was shunted sideways to the post of general manager. A week later, Dave Sexton, recently sacked by Manchester United, took charge of Coventry's team affairs. His appointment was a break from City's tradition of going for young untried managers. Sexton was as experienced as they come, having guided Chelsea and Manchester United to FA Cup triumphs and taken unfashionable QPR to within a whisker of the league championship. He was also a member of Ron Greenwood's England coaching staff, with responsibility for the Under-21 side.

Milne's 'move' upstairs pacified many of the club's critics but Jimmy Hill's decision to convert Highfield Road into England's first all-seater stadium caused uproar. Not only did it take a knife to the whole concept of standing on terraces, upon which generations of football-goers had been reared, and from where most Coventry fans chose to watch their team, but it also reduced the ground's capacity to just 20,500. That figure was 15,000 below the gate for City's home semi-final with West Ham a few months earlier, and for that reason did not appear to make economic sense. Even more distressing to supporters was the way the decision had been reached, without warning and without consultation.

Match of the Season 1980-81

Coventry 3 West Ham 2

League Cup, semi-final, 1st leg, 27 January 1981

Coventry City reached their first major semi-final in 1980-81, when they progressed to the last four of the Football League Cup. The club had first entered the competition in its inaugural season, 1960-61, but had never previously gone further than the quarter-finals, which they had reached on three occasions. Leicester put paid to their hopes (1-8) in 1964-65, Tottenham (1-4) in 1970-71 and Manchester City (2-4 after a replay) in 1973-74.

City's route to the semi-final had its share of close shaves, not to mention some euphoric highs. The 5-0 quarter-final replay win over Graham Taylor's Watford sparked a wave of enthusiasm and talk of Wembley was on everyone's lips. Facing Coventry at the penultimate hurdle were Second Division West Ham, who were seeking to add to the FA Cup won in 1980 by winning the League Cup and Second Division championship. Their side had changed little in the three years out of the top flight. Trevor Brooking, Billy Bonds, Phil Parkes and Alvin Martin were the mainstays of the team, which in earlier rounds had seen off the challenges of Burnley, Charlton, Barnsley and Tottenham.

Both legs of the semi-final were enthralling. With eighteen minutes left in the first leg at Highfield Road, West Ham appeared to be cruising to their second successive Wembley final. They led by two soft goals given to them by City in a nightmare opening half.

DID YOU KNOW?

When City entertained Liverpool in December 1983, only one player remained from the team which hosted the Reds the previous season – 'Harry' Roberts.

First Sealey allowed Bonds' harmless header to squirm from his grasp and roll agonisingly over the line. Then Thompson, chasing back to dispossess Devonshire, won the ball and poked it back to Sealey, only for the goalkeeper and ball to pass each other like trains on different tracks. The big striker sank to the earth and had to be consoled by Steve Hunt before he could continue. Hunt raised a clenched fist to the West End, demanding that the fans get behind the team.

As the minutes ticked away it seemed that City's stirring riposte would come to nothing, blunted by Parkes' defiant goalkeeping. Then Thompson, put clear by Blair, steered the ball past the West Ham keeper, and five minutes later Gerry Daly equalised when Parkes could only parry Danny Thomas' fierce shot.

The game now reached a breathtaking climax. With five minutes to go David Cross met a low cross from Goddard. Cross's firm shot flew into the net, but Allen was given offside. In the 89th minute Thompson collected a short, square pass from Hunt, bamboozled Alvin Martin in the act of shooting and let fly for the left hand corner of the net. City now had a vital one-goal lead to take to Upton Park two weeks later.

Alas, Coventry's slim advantage was overturned at Upton Park. Few disputed that West Ham were the better side, though the tie was seconds from going into extra-time when substitute Jimmy Neighbour, perhaps offside, got on the end of a free-kick to put the Hammers through 4-3 on aggregate.

West Ham lost the League Cup to Liverpool in a replayed final.

LEAGUE DIVISION 1	**1981-82**
Division 1	14th
League Cup	2nd Round
FA Cup	Quarter-finals

The new season opened with the perfect test for new manager Sexton's young lions – his old club Manchester United. It was also the perfect curtain raiser for the club's new all-seater stadium. The long suffering fans had seen three more sales in the summer, to add to the growing exodus over the last few years. Injury-jinxed Mick Ferguson left for Everton for £280,000, promising winger Gary Bannister moved to Sheffield Wednesday for £100,000, and Scottish Under-21 midfielder Andy Blair was sold to Aston Villa for £300,000. Curiously, two of the three would return to Highfield Road later in their careers, and whilst Ferguson would cause some short-term embarrassment for City, only Bannister went on to greater things.

Several other players also left on free transfers – the veteran Mick Coop moved to Derby, Jim Holton followed Bannister to Hillsborough, and Roger Van Gool returned to Belgium to play for Antwerp in exchange for young Dutch winger Rudi Kaiser. Along with the lightweight David Bradford, bought for £60,000 from Washington Diplomats, Kaiser was City's only newcomer.

What puzzled supporters at this time was the apparent willingness of the board to invest in anything except new players. Many fans were at a loss to understand the direction the club was taking. This encouraged a sense of alienation on their part, as did the attempts to change the club's name, the introduction of a garish strip incorporating the Talbot logo, not to mention the all-seater stadium, tickets for which were expensive and had to be bought at least 48 hours before the game.

For their part, the board argued that they had taken account of the broader economic situation. Declining gates and escalating running costs had driven some clubs to the edge of bankruptcy, and many others were carrying huge overdrafts. The board did not want City to become a victim of soccer's recession, but in their efforts to anticipate the various pitfalls, they were caught in a downward spiral, which became increasingly difficult to reverse.

The club's finances were not helped by an ill-advised overseas investment. £500,000 was written off when the Washington Diplomats, owned by Jimmy Hill's World Soccer Academy, folded. It was within these tight financial constraints that Sexton began the task of bringing style and consistency to a talented young team.

DID YOU KNOW?

When Ipswich's Jason Dozell scored against City in February 1984, he became the league's youngest ever goalscorer – just 16 years and 57 days old.

For a while the side virtually picked itself, with another youngster, Steve Jacobs, in place of Blair and Jim Blyth back between the posts. In attack, Mark Hateley and Garry Thompson had Steve Whitton breathing down their necks, and it was Whitton, the young Londoner, who set up the opening day win against Manchester United, scoring in only his second full game. Within a week, however, all City's inconsistencies resurfaced, with defeats recorded at Stoke and Notts County. Mick Ferguson returned in an Everton shirt for a League Cup-tie and promptly quashed City's interest in the competition by scoring a late winner.

A safe mid-table course was steered until December, with only Liverpool lowering the flag at home, but a measly two points from eight away games told an age-old story. An unexpected 2-1 win at Tottenham, far from leading a charge towards the top six, precipitated a terrible slump. City picked up just three points, all from draws, in twelve games. The gloom was pierced only by a comfortable advance to the quarter-finals of the FA Cup, thanks to wins over Sheffield Wednesday, Manchester City and Oxford. But the Wembley train came to a shuddering halt at the Hawthorns, where Cyrille Regis's superb goal deserved to win any match.

This poor run, which included six home defeats in a row, saw crowds dip below 10,000 for the first time since 1962. Disenchanted Steve Hunt slapped in a transfer request. A woeful 1-5 home defeat by Notts County was for many City fans the last straw. However, just as things were at their blackest, and fans wondered where the next win was going to come from, City mounted a tremendous revival. Former England captain Gerry Francis had arrived for £145,000 from QPR in February, and his experience was a major factor in the team's resurgence. Sealey and Whitton were recalled and another youth product, defender Ian Butterworth, was given his chance. City's first win in more than three months arrived, of all places, at Old Trafford.

That win triggered a run of thirteen games with only one defeat. Highlights of those glorious weeks included a never-to-be-forgotten 5-5 draw at the Dell, the ending of the Hawthorns jinx, and City's biggest first division winning margin, 6-1 over Sunderland. Almost three years had elapsed since a Coventry player last claimed a hat-trick; now Mark Hateley and Steve Whitton notched one apiece in the space of four days, both away from Highfield Road.

DID YOU KNOW?

The fastest yellow card earned by a City player was shown to Steve Sedgley after 14 seconds against Villa in November 1988. He had fouled Gordon Cowans.

One other explanation for City's wonderful late surge was the solving of the problematical right-wing berth. The wayward Bodak started the season in that position, the popular Kaiser was next up but failed to impress, whilst Bradford looked like a fish out of water on the right flank. Eighteen-year-old John Hendrie caught the eye as one for the future and it fell to Whitton to fill the position for the final third of the season, allowing Thompson and Hateley to continue their prosperous England Under-21 striking partnership at club level.

Come the end of the season, the supporters felt more optimism than for some time. The younger players had responded well to Sexton's astute coaching, and the acquisition of the experienced Gerry Francis appeared to be a master stroke. He may have lost pace, but his was an inspiring on-field presence, and in this respect he succeeded where Gerry Daly had failed. Additionally, and crucially, Francis understood clearly what Sexton wanted and acted as his lieutenant on the pitch.

Sexton's coaching was already paying dividends. Thompson, Hateley and Danny Thomas were England Under-21 regulars, and within a few months Thomas would be called into the full England squad.

Match of the Season 1981-82

Southampton 5 Coventry 5

Division 1, 4 May 1982

The superlatives rolled off the pens of the press corps after this result at the Dell, only the second 5-5 draw in Coventry's history, the first having been registered in 1932 against Fulham. The Saints were pressing hard for a UEFA Cup place, their good form rooted in an outstanding home record, whilst City were prospering from a prodigious end-of-season run that saw Sunderland thrashed 6-1 the previous week.

Saints and City provided a feast of football, leaving the crowd in almost hysterical mood. The goals flew in so quickly that some spectators and players lost count. Southampton substitute Danny Wallace believed his side had lost 4-5 until his team-mates corrected him in the dressing-room afterwards.

Aside from the sheer volume of goals, it was their quality that took the breath away, not to mention the fact that Mark Hateley bagged his first senior hat-trick.

Steve Whitton started the feast in the eleventh minute, volleying in at the far post after Steve Hunt's looping cross had cut open the Saints' defence. Kevin Keegan equalised after 22 minutes, racing through to slide the ball past Sealey. A barren period of 21 minutes then ensued, barren only in the sense that no goals were scored, but Hateley then opened his account, with a little help from the butter-fingered Katalinic.

Southampton were level again two minutes into the second half, Cassells glancing in a header from a Williams free-kick, but two goals in ten minutes seemed to have won the game for City. Hateley beat Golac on the left and fired low past Katalinic. Then Whitton scored one of his finest goals for the club, outpacing Chris Nicholl before beating Katalinic for pace from a narrow angle. It was now 4-2 to City, but within seconds it was 4-3. The players were still mentally celebrating when Alan Ball sprinted through from the kick-off to fire past Sealey from thirty yards.

The Saints were buzzing, and their predictable equaliser arrived after 69 minutes, Cassells chipping into the top corner from the edge of the box. Seven minutes from time the Dell went wild as Keegan beat City's fragile offside trap to score his second and put Southampton ahead for the first time. City were not beaten, though, and Hateley levelled from a tight angle in the dying seconds.

Joe Mercer described the game as the best he had seen since the 1930s. But football is an escape from reality. The reality was that on that same night *HMS Sheffield* was sunk off the Falklands.

LEAGUE DIVISION 1 1982-83

Division 1	19th
Milk Cup	3rd Round
FA Cup	4th Round

If the form shown at the end of the 1981-82 season was meant to carry over into the new one, it was a forlorn hope. Sexton was given no money to enlarge what had become the smallest squad in the First Division. Jim Blyth – partly because of recurring back problems and partly because of Sealey's ascendancy – moved to Birmingham, while fringe players like Bodak, Hagan, Kaiser, Barnes and Gooding carried on their careers elsewhere for little or no fee. Early in the season, with goals scarce, Sexton was given licence to buy, snapping up Leicester's Scottish striker Jim Melrose, though he had to sacrifice Tom English in exchange. English thereby rejoined his former manager Gordon Milne, who after one season had tired of his position as City's general manager and been lured into the hot seat at Filbert Street.

The opening day fixture against unglamorous Southampton attracted only 10,000 spectators to Highfield Road, and neither the performance nor the result, a 1-0 win, encouraged stay-away fans to return to the fold. Gates quickly dropped to 8,000, and the entertainment on offer at some games could best be described as pitiful. Following the 2-0 home win over Norwich in October, the *Coventry Evening Telegraph* was stung into printing an editorial entitled 'a vision blurred', which described Highfield Road as a 'dreary and depressing place to be, with spiritless players failing to lift the crowd, and the crowd finding no encouragement to cheer on the players'. According to the editorial, the policies of the board were a clear demonstration that chairman Jimmy Hill was 'out of touch with the people who like to watch football'.

Matters got worse before they got better. City's latest nadir was a humiliating Milk Cup exit at home to lowly Second Division side Burnley. But then the storm clouds lifted. Eleven games with only two defeats hoisted the team to a heady fifth place in the table. The defence – with Paul Dyson and Gary Gillespie maturing, and Danny Thomas (now a full England squad member) bristling with confidence – was more than solid. Steve Hunt was by now also being touted as an England possible, while up front the goals flowed from Hateley and Melrose, with Whitton lending support.

But another, altogether larger storm was brewing. Following the FA Cup exit at lowly Norwich, the board decided to sell Garry

Thompson to West Brom for £225,000. Sexton did not want to lose the player, arguing that the motives were purely financial. Jimmy Hill responded by claiming that Hateley and Thompson were ill-matched. One consequence of Thompson's departure was that Sexton was left with only fourteen senior players. As for Gerry Daly, he and Sexton were chalk and cheese and the Irishman was soon loaned out to Leicester. For the fans, and no doubt for many of the players too, the loss of such players spoke volumes about the club's lack of ambition. All that mattered, apparently, was balancing the books and staying up.

Another problem was that the contracts of almost half the squad were due to expire at the end of the season. Not surprisingly, in the final gloomy weeks of the season, several players made their feelings plain – they had no intention of putting pen to paper. For its part, the club gave the impression of not wanting to even negotiate new deals. The whole sorry situation was one which guaranteed disaster. From the end of February team spirit evaporated and the side fell apart. In a thirteen-game run City failed to win at all, picked up only three points, scoring five goals. From being good outside bets for Europe, the team were on a helter-skelter slide that looked sure to end in relegation.

One fan was at the end of his tether. During the home game with Birmingham in April he dashed across the pitch, tore off his sky blue shirt and hurled it to the ground in front of the directors box. The police apprehended him but, significantly, the crowd loudly applauded his gesture.

One way or another the board got the message, and behind closed doors it was clear that harmony was in short supply. By early May the rest of the directors had joined ranks and – though the circumstances are unclear – Hill either volunteered, or was forced, to step down. Ian Jamieson took over as chairman. Hill's demise was largely unlamented among supporters at large, who felt that the man who had rebuilt the club as a manager was burying it as chairman. He had brought success to the city in the 1960's, but though the club was crying out for more of the same spirit, it appeared to have deserted him. Hill lost a fortune for himself and the club in America. He had invested in the Sky Blue Connexion rather than players. His dream all-seater stadium flopped and a misguided soccer tour to South Africa collapsed. No doubt the passage of time will encourage a more generous verdict on Hill's second coming, but it is fair to say that in May 1983 most fans greeted his departure enthusiastically.

The players, meanwhile, had more pressing concerns. The team put Hill's departure out of their minds and ended their horrific run with a 3-0 win at Stoke, which ensured their survival. The board responded on the last day of the season by sacking Sexton and appointing Bobby Gould, one of Hill's blue-eyed boys of the 1960's. For the disaffected players, the departure of their mentor and coach proved to be the final straw, and within days a trickle had turned into a flood. Mark Hateley signed for Second Division Portsmouth, who had the effrontery to offer just £50,000 for the player. The figure set by tribunal was little better, at £190,000, especially when one considers that within a year AC Milan would pay £1 million for the young striker. Danny Thomas went off on an England tour of Australia, becoming the first City player to be capped by England since Reg Matthews in 1956. Within days of his return he signed for Tottenham for £300,000. Whitton joined West Ham for £175,000 and Gerry Francis left to manage Exeter. With Sealey joining Luton for £80,000, Dyson moving to Stoke for £150,000, and Melrose transferred to Celtic for £100,000, the club's overdraft was slashed.

The saddest departure of all was that of Gary Gillespie, who appeared to be backing Gould's new regime, but when Liverpool came knocking the temptation was irresistible. Arguably City's best defender of the decade, he was sold for £325,000. Hateley, Sealey and Thomas all made parting side-swipes at the club, accusing it of parsimony and lack of ambition, and those fans with long memories would never forget their cruel taunts. As the *Evening Telegraph* pointed out: 'The determination of those players to go is emphasised by the status of the clubs some of them have joined. It is arguable whether their careers will blossom as freely.' Of the old team, only 'Harry' Roberts, Steve Hunt, and Steve Jacobs remained. One way or another, things would never be quite the same again.

Match of the Season 1982-83

Stoke 0 Coventry 3

Division 1, 7 May 1983

In the middle of February 1983 City beat Manchester City 4-0 at Highfield Road to return to fifth place in the league. Despite having the smallest and least experienced squad in Division One, City had risen to a position challenging for a place in the UEFA Cup, playing exciting and open football under Dave Sexton's tutelage. The dreadful run that followed – City gaining only three points out of a possible 39 – meant that it was a demoralised bunch of players who descended on the Victoria Ground on the penultimate Saturday of the season, knowing that another defeat could see the water rise over their heads.

DID YOU KNOW?

When Ogrizovic missed the match with Luton in September 1989, it ended his uninterrupted run of 241 league and cup games, a City record.

City went into the match with two games to play, fifth from bottom, one point above Birmingham and Manchester City. Paul Dyson, the first choice centre-half, was out injured, and Steve Jacobs was suspended. Stoke were having their best season for years and were comfortably in mid-table. With Jimmy Hill having been ousted on the Tuesday before the match, and the club seemingly disintegrating, few fans would have wagered on a Coventry victory, far less by three goals.

Young John Hendrie was brought into attack to make only his seventh start of the season and a tactical switch saw eighteen-year-old Ian Butterworth move into central defence. Against all expectations, City played positively from the outset, with vociferous backing from a large travelling support. Hendrie provided the cutting edge, setting up the first goal for Mark Hateley after twenty minutes, scoring the second four minutes after half-time, and laying on the pass for Danny Thomas to net the third, nine minutes from time. The City fans were jubilant, but safety was not guaranteed. Victories for Birmingham and Manchester City kept them one point behind Coventry, but Luton, crucially, had lost. The Hatters were still on 46 points, two behind City but with a game in hand.

It was Luton's defeat at Old Trafford the following Monday that secured Coventry's safety. The Hatters' final match was at Manchester City, and no matter the result one of those two teams would remain below Coventry. That final day will be remembered for Luton boss David Pleat's jig of delight at the final whistle. Coventry, meanwhile, lost 2-4 to West Ham, which showed how important the win at Stoke had been in ensuring that the Sky Blues would enter their centenary season still in Division One.

Ferguson and Wallace cause panic in the Middlesbrough defence (September 1977)

Roberts chases John Robertson as Forest take the title at Highfield Road (April 1978)

For once, Tommy Hutchison loses out. The opponents are West Brom (March 1980)

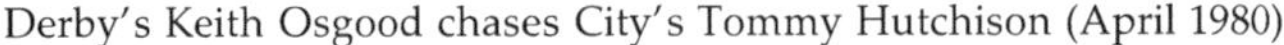
Derby's Keith Osgood chases City's Tommy Hutchison (April 1980)

Liverpool's Neal and Thompson watch Gary Thompson head for goal (August 1980)

Hutchison scores City's third goal in a 3-3 draw with Brighton (October 1980)

Peter Bodak takes on Manchester United's Arthur Albiston (August 1981)

Gerry Francis and Jim Melrose have Manchester City back-pedalling (February 1983)

Four

Three Close Shaves 1983-1986

LEAGUE DIVISION 1	**1983-84**
Division 1	19th
Milk Cup	3rd Round
FA Cup	4th Round

Bobby Gould arrived from Bristol Rovers as City's new manager and had no illusions about the task that faced him. It wasn't just a question of who would be in the team but whether there would be a team at all. The club was in a sorry state, and disaffected fans needed winning round and quickly. In Gould's own words: 'I have been thrown into the lion's den. At the moment this club is taking one hell of a battering and I've got one of the toughest battles of my life on my hands.'

Gould had two things going for him – an encyclopaedic knowledge of the lower divisions and a passionate commitment to Coventry City, his home town club. Whilst dealing with the problem of the club's disaffected out-of-contract players, he was also busy planning his side for the new season. In all he spent about £750,000 during the summer, buying players either with top division experience or who had impressed him in the lower leagues. In the former category were Ashley Grimes (£200,000 from Manchester United), Dave Bennett (£125,000 from Cardiff) and Terry Gibson (£100,000 from Tottenham). Amongst the latter were Trevor Peake (£100,000 from Lincoln), Michael Gynn (£60,000 from Peterborough), Dave Bamber (£50,000 from Blackpool) and Mickey Adams (£85,000 from Gillingham). Others who came on board included Sam Allardyce, Raddy Avramovic, Nicky Platnauer and Graham Withey. The final purchase, Stuart Pearce, didn't arrive until November, but would turn out, pound for pound, to be the best of them all. He cost just

£25,000 from non-league Wealdstone. With this band of footballing gypsies Gould faced up to the seemingly impossible task of keeping City in Division One. Predictably, bookies and the pundits made them favourites for the drop.

Financially, the club took another kick in the teeth on the eve of the season, when Talbot abruptly terminated their sponsorship. That meant another £100,000 annual income went by the wayside.

Gould's first game was at Watford, runners-up the previous season. He fielded just five of his summer purchases, preferring to give a few long-servers a chance to stake their claim. Any fears were quickly dispelled as City waltzed to victory. The first weeks of the season flew by in a blur as supporters got used to the new faces. Gould's influence ensured that any shortage of skill was made up for by an abundance of heart and guts. By December, City were fourth, following a nine-game unbeaten run highlighted by the 4-0 drubbing of champions Liverpool, their biggest defeat for a decade. Despite an unlucky Milk Cup exit at Everton, City's away form was exemplary, earning wins at Highbury, St Andrews, Luton and Stoke. By now, the likes of Gibson, Pearce, Bamber and Platnauer were genuine Sky Blue heroes.

Few could have predicted that City's win at home to Sunderland on 2 January would usher in a catastrophic run of results that was halted only after the previous season's sequence of thirteen winless games had been equalled. City dropped down the league like a stone. From gazing up at the ceiling they were left staring down at the floor. Confidence drained away, especially at home, where six out of seven games were lost and all the doomsday chickens seemed to be coming home to roost.

In an effort to pull the rip-cord Gould tried everything he could. He swapped the players around, played different tactics, fiddled with formations, all to no effect. On transfer deadline day the club had to cash in on its assets. The unsettled Steve Hunt went for a song to West Brom, skipper 'Harry' Roberts moved for £10,000 to Birmingham, and Bamber, who had faded badly after a bright start, signed for Walsall for £50,000.

December's confident team that had trounced Liverpool had collapsed to such an extent that relegation became possible, then probable. Two strikers came on loan in a last frantic effort to avoid the drop. Ex-Chelsea player Tommy Langley arrived after a sojourn in Greece, and on the evidence of his two games looked among the worst strikers ever to have worn a City shirt. For injury-prone Mick Ferguson, however, it was a sentimental return after four years away. His club, fellow strugglers Birmingham, incredibly saw no reason not to lend him back.

DID YOU KNOW?

In 1994-95, Gordon Strachan became City's oldest ever debutant, at the age of 38 years and 2 months. The previous record was set by Jim Sanders in 1958.

Ferguson scored in his first two games, helping defeat Wolves and Forest. But the upturn proved to be brief and illusory. There followed four games from which only one point was gained and nineteen goals conceded, eight of them during a nightmarish ninety minutes at the Dell.

The upshot was that Coventry had to win their final game to stay up. Mid-table Norwich were the visitors to Highfield Road and scored first, but the Sky Blues equalised a minute later and, with twenty minutes remaining, Bennett put them ahead, direct from a corner. In the dying minutes, Norwich striker Robert Rosario was presented with the easiest of chances. A deathly hush gripped the stadium as his header rebounded off the inside of a post into the arms of the petrified Perry Suckling in goal.

Twenty miles away at St Andrews, Birmingham were being denied victory over Southampton by the width of the post. Little more than a coat of paint caused them to be relegated. To add to the irony, Coventry's first goal against Norwich was scored by – guess who – Birmingham reject Mick Ferguson.

Gould had achieved his target. It was both modest and monumental – to keep City in Division One.

Match of the Season 1983-84

Coventry 4 Liverpool 0

Division 1, 10 December 1983

Bobby Gould's team, a combination of unknowns and disaffected Division One players, had strolled through the autumn thumbing their noses at all those who predicted imminent demotion.

The acid test, however, would be the visit of Liverpool, against whom all pretenders in the 1970's and 80's were judged. The reigning champions were once again out in front, having lost only two out of seventeen games and conceded only nine goals in the process. City, for their part, were unbeaten in six league games and fifth in the league, and were therefore worthy opponents for the mighty Reds, whose side glittered with magical players.

Liverpool were rocked onto their heels in the first minute. The ball was played into Liverpool's box, Bruce Grobbelaar failed to hold Gibson's shot, and Nicky Platnauer pounced from close range, sinking on his hands and knees to head the ball over the goal-line. What a start!

City continued to press and after nineteen minutes Gibson ran onto Bamber's knock-down to score. He happened to be wearing his lucky boots, even though one of them had split early in the match. He had refused to replace them and his decision was further justified shortly before half-time as he belted a half-chance from the edge of the box to make it 3-0.

Liverpool were the last side imaginable to lie down and die, but their efforts to claw their way back into the game were contemptuously rejected. Throughout the second half it was City who looked the more likely side to score, and but for Grobbelaar Liverpool's embarrassment might have been heightened. The icing was put on City's cake with six minutes remaining. Gibson chased a clearance that bounced wickedly, deceiving defender Phil Neal, leaving the striker to advance and lob the keeper. Gibson thereby became the first Coventry player ever to score a hat-trick against Liverpool, and the first opposing player to do such damage to the Reds for eleven years.

The standing ovation that greeted the final whistle was fitting reward for City's virile display, while Joe Fagan, the Liverpool boss, admitted that Coventry had outclassed his team in every department and tipped them as championship contenders.

For the next couple of weeks, City basked in the media spotlight but, sadly, the result was no better than a mirage. City soon went into a nose-dive, while Liverpool quickly recovered their winning ways, losing only three more games all season. They retained their league title with ease.

LEAGUE DIVISION 1	**1984-85**
Division 1	18th
Milk Cup	2nd Round
FA Cup	4th Round

Having had their nerves stretched to breaking point in 1983-84, the last thing supporters wanted was another relegation battle. Not only was that what they got, the battle pitched Coventry even closer to the brink of relegation. The circumstances of their eventual escape would cement the club's status as the 'Great Houdinis' of the First Division.

Gould had shuffled the pack vigorously in the summer. Six players came in, Steve Ogrizovic (from Shrewsbury for £72,500), Brian Kilcline (from Notts County for £60,000) and Kirk Stephens, who arrived from Luton in exchange for Ashley Grimes – City receiving an additional £50,000 from the deal. Three other players came on free transfers, Bob Latchford from Dutch club Breda, Martin Jol from West Brom, and Kenny Hibbitt from Wolves.

Six players left, Grimes and five others for small fees – Jacobs, Daly, Allardyce, John Hendrie and Avramovic, who was banished by Gould after a horrendous performance against Stoke. Hendrie blossomed to become an accomplished striker, and fourteen years after he left City he was still gracing the top division – in Barnsley's colours.

The boardroom was no more stable than the dressing room, with Jersey-based (but Coventry-born) John Poynton taking over the chairmanship from Ian Jamieson. The *Coventry Evening Telegraph* paid handsome tribute to the outgoing chairman: 'Most of all, Jamieson's one year reign will be remembered for bringing the club back to the supporters. Gone was the arrogance that distanced it from the people of the city – and in its place all the effort the new management team could muster to seek better relations with the local community. What was missing was the risk capital to invest in new players. By persuading John Poynton to return to his home town with some of the fortune he has made since leaving it, the management now have money to invest.'

A month into the season Gould appointed the Scot, Don Mackay, as his assistant, and by October the benefits of Poynton's involvement began to be felt. City had been linked with a variety of players, including Peter Withe, Graeme Sharp and Alan Brazil, but none of them signed. Instead, Gould swooped for Peter Barnes (£65,000 from Leeds), Cyrille Regis (from West Brom for £300,000), and – a month later – midfielder Dave Bowman (from Hearts for £160,000). Regis and Barnes were former internationals, keen to rebuild careers with a club prepared to assist them. To the ultra critical supporters, such buys showed that City meant business.

On the field, however, things were not going well. Successive home defeats by Manchester United and Arsenal were followed by a humbling Milk Cup exit at home to Third Division Walsall. A lack of goals and an embarrassing inability to hold onto a lead had become major problems, and in November alone the defence shipped fourteen goals in four games. Promoted Chelsea, for example, recovered from two down to beat City 6-2, and Regis's return to the Hawthorns heralded a miserable 2-5 defeat, notwithstanding his first goal in City colours. Hard-fought wins over Watford and Sheffield Wednesday were but glimpses of light in an ocean of gloom. By and large, City's new players were performing no better than the old.

Spineless Christmas defeats at Leicester and Luton sealed Gould's fate. At Filbert Street the irate manager strode on to the pitch during play, risking serious retribution from the FA. The calendar year 1984 had been a wretched twelve months for the Sky Blues, who had won only nine out of 42 games, and the buck stopped at Bobby Gould. The fans were largely sympathetic to the beleaguered manager, insisting that he deserved credit for keeping City up, and deserved more time in which to impose himself. Chairman Poynton thought otherwise: he was ambitious, impatient, and – after Gould's sacking – unrepentant.

Gould's number two, Don Mackay, took charge, with Frank Upton as his deputy. Without radically altering the side, Mackay initially did the trick. The defence stopped leaking goals and Terry Gibson kept scoring them. Five wins in eight games, including a headline-making victory at Old Trafford, ensured Mackay enjoyed his honeymoon period, but Easter brought him back to earth with a bump. A flu virus swept through the club, causing the postponement of three matches. By the time the players were fit to resume, the team's inactivity had seen them slide into the bottom three.

A home defeat by rivals Sunderland made matters worse. It was now a case of all hands on deck. City staggered through a tough closing programme, and after a goal-less draw at Ipswich the magnitude of the task confronting them was clear for all to see. Sunderland and Stoke were already relegated, leaving one other club to join them. Norwich had finished their programme with 49 points, eight more than City, who still had three games to play. Put simply, Coventry had to win all three of their final games. Anything less and, come August, they would be playing in Division Two.

DID YOU KNOW?

In 1992-93, Mick Quinn became the first player since George Hudson in 1963 to score more than one goal on his City debut.

The first game was at moribund Stoke. It should have been easy: it was anything but. City scraped home 1-0, thanks to a Stuart Pearce penalty, and only survived when Ian Painter, later to join the Sky Blues, hit the underside of the bar with a penalty in the dying minutes. In the second game Luton came to Highfield Road and fought as if their lives depended on it. The points were settled by a thunderous volley from Kilcline, which flew into the net with just six minutes remaining. All now rested on the visit of Everton, who happened to be champions of England.

Match of the Season 1984-85

Coventry 4 Everton 1

Division 1, 26 May 1985

It did not seem possible that City could come closer to relegation than in 1984, but their escape one year later was even more dramatic. With three games to play they looked dead and buried. Victories in the first two would count for nothing if they failed to defeat the newly crowned champions.

Howard Kendall had been given time to develop a fine side in true Goodison tradition. Everton's success was founded on a granite defence, with goalkeeper Neville Southall at the peak of his powers and voted Footballer of the Year. In front of him, Kevin Ratcliffe and Derek Mountfield were indomitable central defenders. Full-backs Gary Stevens and Pat van den Hauwe had contrasting styles, but were indicative of a side who were greater than the sum of the parts. The goals flowed from Graeme Sharp, who had scored 21 already, helped by excellent service from the flanks in the shape of Trevor Steven and Kevin Sheedy. Everton's pivot, however, was midfield dynamo Peter Reid, who – along with Stevens and Steven – was an England international.

In twenty league games since Christmas the Toffees had won seventeen, drawn two, and lost only once – the week before their ultimately disappointing FA Cup final defeat by Manchester United. Having been robbed of the double, it was not surprising that Everton were hardly fired up for their visit to Highfield Road. City's Easter virus meant that they would have to play almost into June to round off their league programme, while Everton, worthy but jaded champions, would doubtless have preferred to be on holiday. They were already incapacitated by injuries to four regulars – Reid, Stevens, Mountfield and former Villa striker Andy Gray – and had nothing to play for but pride.

An all-ticket crowd packed into Highfield Road for a match that, because of a Scotland v England international at Hampden Park, kicked off at 11.30 am on a sunny Sunday. For City's long-suffering fans, accustomed over the years to a diet of adrenalin, this would have been another occasion for watching a game through closed fingers, but they were rewarded with a goal inside four minutes, a powerful Regis header from a Kilcline flick-on. Regis was a constant thorn in Everton's side, playing his best game since arriving at Highfield Road the previous October, and after seventeen minutes he contributed to a second goal. He found Micky Adams with a superb pass inside the full-back, leaving the left-winger to beat Southall with a lovely ground shot.

Two goals dispelled the nerves, though City wasted chances to put the game out of Everton's reach and paid the price by falling to pieces during an inexplicable fifteen-minute spell late in the first half. During that time the champions pulled a goal back through Wilkinson and could have had more.

The half-time interval was therefore more nervy than it might have been, but Regis administered the tranquillisers just ninety seconds after the restart. Gibson swivelled and fired in a shot that Southall could only parry. For what seemed like an eternity, the ball bobbled in front of the big man before he prodded it home.

The fans duly let off steam, and their joy was unconstrained when, with twelve minutes left, Gibson capped a superb show by sprinting clear to beat Southall from the edge of the area for his nineteenth goal of the season. More chances went begging as City spurned the opportunity to score six or seven and turn a victory into a rout. At the final whistle, the jubilant crowd engulfed the pitch and enticed Don Mackay and his players out on the directors box, where they received a rousing ovation. Not so pleased were the players of Norwich City, many of whom were relaxing on a beach when they heard the final score. Norwich made obligatory protests about Everton fielding a weakened side, but all to no avail.

Neville Foulger, in his match report in the *Coventry Evening Telegraph* pleaded 'never again' but it is sad to record that twelve months hence, for the third successive season, City would also have to win their final game to stay up.

Two days after beating Everton, Pearce and Butterworth were sold to Forest. Regis was expected to leave too, after a poor season, but he stayed to become a Coventry hero.

CANON DIVISION 1	**1985-86**
Division 1	17th
Milk Cup	3rd Round
FA Cup	3rd Round

A season that offered so much began badly and grew steadily worse. Survival was once more the name of the game with City's Division One status preserved yet again only by victory in their final league match. It was a season in which the coach was sacked, the manager quit, and three different captains were appointed.

By City's standards, transfer activity in the summer had been quiet. Stuart Pearce and Ian Butterworth left to join Brian Clough at Nottingham Forest for a combined fee of £450,000. Mackay's replacement full-backs were destined to play a part in the club's FA Cup fantasy the following season. Brian Borrows had been an outstanding youngster at Everton, but found his opportunities limited by the form of Gary Stevens. Borrows moved to Bolton, took wing, and it wasn't long before City paid £80,000 to bring him back to Division One. As for Greg Downs, he had been a member of the Norwich side relegated by City's momentous run in the previous season. He was too good for Division Two, and a fee of £40,000 secured his transfer.

The captaincy issue blew up even before the season started. As part of their pre-season preparations, the City squad were taken for a week's stay at the Crystal Palace Sports Centre in London, which they used as a base for friendly matches against Reading, Crystal Palace and Millwall. But a simmering row developed about the quality of the accommodation and finally blew up into a confrontation between skipper Trevor Peake and manager Mackay. Following the match against Palace, Mackay imposed a curfew on the players. Heated words were exchanged, as a result of which Peake was sent home, missing the friendly with Millwall.

The incident sparked allegations of a behind-the-scenes revolt at the club, though this was vehemently denied by Mackay and most of the players. But Peake relinquished the captaincy by 'mutual agreement' and midfield man Wayne Turner, signed from Luton for £75,000 during the summer, was eventually handed the job. Injury, however, kept Turner out for the first five matches. He was on the outside looking in as City picked up just two points from a possible fifteen and found themselves one off the bottom of the table.

The home defeat by Newcastle on 26 August was to provide a foretaste of things to come. City were one up through Terry Gibson, but conceded two goals in the last five minutes. 'A disgrace,' fumed an irate Mackay: 'It was down to a lack of discipline – we just didn't do our job properly in the last five minutes.' Sadly, he was to say much the same many times during the season, with the Sky Blues proving to be particularly vulnerable in front of their own supporters.

Home form went from bad to worse, the total of ten defeats being the worst at Highfield Road in nineteen seasons of First Division football. At one stage Coventry went four and a half months between one home win and the next – they beat Leicester on 6 October but did not win again until the 3-2 victory over Southampton on 22 February. In between, City lost at home to Watford in Round 3 of the FA Cup. It was hardly surprising that gates fell to the second lowest average in their Division One history, just 11,638. Never was the ground full to its 22,500 capacity (the Kop having been restored to standing terraces) and the biggest gate – for the visit of Manchester United – failed to top 17,000. Two weeks after the Hornets knocked City out of the Cup, Watford returned in the league. This time the gate was a paltry 7,478, which still constitutes City's lowest ever top division crowd.

After their poor start, City stemmed the tide, helped by the return of Lloyd McGrath. A run of one defeat in nine games saw comprehensive home wins over West Brom and Leicester and an amazing Milk Cup-tie with Chester. Having brought back a one-goal lead from the first leg, City let rip in the second, winning 7-2, with Cyrille Regis setting a League Cup record of five goals – which equalled his total haul of the previous season. In the main, however, the goals continued to fall to his striking partner, Terry Gibson, with the result that City had to fend off numerous enquiries about the striker.

December was a shocking month, which saw City slip back to seventeenth, following a Boxing day home defeat by struggling Ipswich. Skipper Wayne Turner was substituted, and a few days later he handed the captaincy to Brian Kilcline. Continued bad form into January prompted more changes – on and off the field. Three new directors – Ted Stocker, John Reason and Derrick Richardson, all Poynton men – joined the board, which almost in the same breath opted to accept Manchester United's £650,000 bid for Gibson. Scottish international striker Alan Brazil arrived as part of the Gibson deal. Some of the balance was used to buy Nick Pickering from Sunderland and Jim McInally, a full-back cum midfielder, from Nottingham Forest.

The comings and goings freshened up the side for a while, and excellent wins at Oxford and Tottenham, plus a 4-4 draw with

Birmingham, and the long-awaited first home win for nineteen weeks, hinted at better times. It was not to be. After squandering a lead to lose at Leicester, City plummeted back into the red zone. Someone had to take the rap, and coach Upton was sacked the week after Easter.

Mackay stayed on – but not for long. Eight games without a win, culminating in an abject surrender at Anfield, saw him dramatically leave with just three matches to go, at which point City lay nineteenth. Perhaps Mackay jumped; more likely he was pushed.

Executive director George Curtis and youth-team coach John Sillett took temporary charge, and home wins over Luton and QPR proved enough to keep the Sky Blues in Division One for a twentieth successive season. On the brighter side, City's reserve team won promotion from Division Two of the Central League. The question on everyone's lips at the end of another relegation-haunted season was 'who would be the new manager?'

Match of the Season 1985-86

Coventry 2 QP Rangers 1

Division 1, 3 May 1986

For the third season in a row City's bid for safety went down to the last game. The Sky Blues had struggled all season but even at the beginning of March it seemed that a reasonable run would see them safe. But City proceeded to go eight games without victory, scoring only two goals in the process. The 0-5 drubbing at Anfield proved to be the straw that broke the camel's back. Don Mackay was out.

With three games to go, City were one point above the trap door, having played more games than all their rivals. The first task of old boys George Curtis and John Sillett was to boost spirits, particularly as the next two opponents, Luton and West Ham, were chasing a place in Europe.

Coventry beat Luton but lost to West Ham, both matches settled by the only goal. The upshot was that City entered their final game as one of four teams aiming to avoid joining Birmingham and West Brom in Division Two. City had a point more than Leicester and Oxford, who had a game in hand, and one point less than Ipswich.

The caretaker bosses made a number of team changes, and the atmosphere was tense and nervy as City took the field against QPR. As play unfolded, it was clear the players needed a goal to calm things down, but City were hit by a sucker punch after 28 minutes when QPR's John Byrne scored with a shot that took a critical deflection off Trevor Peake.

DID YOU KNOW?

Three players have been sent off TWICE at Highfield Road – Steve Hunt (for WBA and City), Chris Whyte (Arsenal and Leeds), and Paul Williams (twice for City).

City might have crumbled, but Curtis and Sillett were made of sterner stuff. Urging on their team from the sidelines, they were rewarded ten minutes later when City won a free-kick on the edge of the box. Up stepped Brian Kilcline to drill home a low shot to equalise. And there was better to come. Just before half-time Dave Bennett gathered possession and with a typical dribble carved out a shooting chance to fire City into the lead.

With Leicester winning and Oxford and Ipswich drawing it was imperative that City held on. The second half saw Rangers at their most menacing, playing like a side with nothing to lose, while City conspicuously played in the knowledge that they had everything to lose! Desperate defending kept Rangers at bay, but in the 77th minute only the crossbar saved them from a QPR equaliser. After the final whistle blew all ears turned towards other results. Ipswich had lost and so City were safe!

Curtis 'reluctantly' let City players celebrate with the crowd – 'reluctantly' because safety was no cause for celebration. The local press speculated about the sort of reaction there might be if City ever won anything. At the time, few thought this team could be something special.

Terry Gibson takes on the Watford defence (August 1983)

Gibson scores Coventry's second goal in a 3-1 win at Stoke (October 1983)

Dave Bamber shoots past Luton's Paul Elliott (December 1983)

Trevor Peake joins the attack against Stoke (February 1984)

Five

Wembley and Beyond 1986-1990

TODAY DIVISION 1	**1986-87**
Division 1	10th
Littlewoods Cup	4th Round
FA Cup	Winners

Coventry fans were fed up with the phrase 'never again', trotted out three seasons running after nail-biting relegation battles. The appointment as manager of George Curtis – who as a player had captained the side from Division 4 to Division One, before being sold to Villa in 1969 – backed up by the elevation of former player John Sillett to first-team coach, was seen by most supporters at the time as unadventurous and unambitious. Terry Yorath had been the name on many people's lips, but the City board veered away from the people's choice and plumped for the option that they believed offered stability.

Nor were supporters reassured by the club's summer transfers. Alan Brazil was jettisoned after only fifteen games, joining QPR for £200,000, at a net loss to City of £100,000. Suspicions that Brazil was not fit were confirmed soon afterwards when he was forced to retire with back problems. Scotsmen Jim McInally and Dave Bowman, bought by previous managers, were sold in a double package to Dundee United for £130,000. This also constituted a loss to City, particularly as both players gave excellent service to the Tannadice club for many years. Finally, early in the season, Wayne Turner left for Brentford for £35,000.

The net proceeds went towards the purchase of Scunthorpe striker Keith Houchen (for £60,000), Manchester City's Welsh midfielder David Phillips (£50,000, plus Perry Suckling), Stoke's Under-21 international Ian Painter (£80,000). Phillips and Houchen made their debuts in an opening day defeat at West Ham, replacing Adams and Brazil. Painter barely got a chance in the first team and was forced out of the game through injury the following summer.

The major difference from the previous season was the tactics. McGrath was the lynchpin in midfield, supported by Phillips and Pickering. Up front, Regis started the season alongside Houchen, but Dave Bennett soon established himself as Cyrille's preferred partner and dazzled in his new role. Sillett appears to have been the first City boss to consult Regis about his preferred style of play, and was told that the big man wanted the ball to his feet rather than in the air as a target man. High balls into the box would from now on be strictly rationed.

An unfortunate first-day defeat at West Ham was followed by an eight-game unbeaten run, the highlight of which was a 3-0 win against Newcastle in which Regis was outstanding. After so many false dawns, the fans were not likely to get carried away, and were certainly not returning in droves, as the 11,000 gate testified. The squad was so small that supporters dreaded the inevitable injury crisis that would scythe down the team.

The good run was ended, predictably, by Aston Villa, who were still able to win at Highfield Road despite having their worst season for years. But the snap purchase of Rotherham's midfield dynamo Dean Emerson, following an eye-catching display against City in the Littlewoods Cup, was the catalyst of another string of good results. The best of these was a superbly professional win over league leaders Nottingham Forest. A cruel Littlewoods Cup replay exit at Anfield, after City ought to have won the first tie, did little to dampen City's league form. By Christmas, not only had the Sky Blues rarely been out of the top eight, but they also boasted one of the best defensive records in the division.

The Christmas home win over Tottenham finally won over the doubting Thomas's. An epic encounter, described by some as the game of the decade, saw City twice come from behind, before Regis clinched a 4-3 win in injury-time. Gynn and Houchen were back in the side by this time, and Emerson's impact was arguably greater than Roy Barry's in 1969 and Stuart Pearce's in 1983.

The FA Cup run started inauspiciously at home to Phil Neal's Bolton Wanderers, who were sent packing 3-0 on an icy pitch. Next up were Manchester United, still finding their feet under new manager Alex Ferguson. Keith Houchen, the man destined to be dubbed 'Roy of the Rovers', snatched a goal, City soaked up the pressure and the first signs of Cup fever were in the air.

The Victoria Ground was the next stop and Michael Gynn scored the winner following a bout of intense Stoke pressure. 8,000 City fans made the trip, and were rewarded by seeing the Sky Blues through to only their fifth quarter-final in 104 years. The win over Stoke was the second in a run of six victories, which established a post-war club record. Sheffield Wednesday were City's victims in the quarter-finals, in what became known as 'Houchen's match'. Sillett had had to shuffle the side following Emerson's injury the previous week, and Bennett took his place to set up all three City goals.

Not surprisingly, the nearer City got to Wembley the more their league form suffered. Defeats at Wimbledon and Villa preceded the semi-final as Hillsborough, where City had overcome the Owls at the previous hurdle. This time their opponents were Second Division Leeds, and City needed extra-time to dispose of them. The league run-in to Wembley was largely carefree, with City for once safe from relegation. The Sky Blues played relaxed football, largely avoided the temptation of fielding weakened sides, and ended the league season unbeaten in seven games. Along the way, Liverpool's title hopes were buried, 1-0, before a gate of almost 27,000, City's biggest league crowd since 1981. Home gates, averaging 12,000 in February, rocketed in the final weeks when attendance at league games was needed to stand any hope of obtaining a Wembley ticket.

Sadly, Brian Borrows' knee injury in the final home game denied him a place in the greatest day in the club's history. He sat out Wembley, alongside the equally unfortunate Dean Emerson.

Match of the Season (1) 1986-87

Leeds 2 Coventry 3

FA Cup, semi-final, 12 April 1987

This semi-final was rated by David Miller in *The Times* as one of the best the competition had seen for the last twenty years, a match of rare drama and excitement. It was all those things and more.

City were returning to Hillsborough only four weeks after their epic quarter-final win, and this time more than 27,000 supporters made the journey to see the Sunday lunchtime confrontation with Leeds United.

Ground conditions were good on a bright, cool spring day, the pitch having been heavily watered. City were favourites against Billy Bremner's Second Division side but, in contrast to their cool confidence against Wednesday, City appeared to develop stage fright against Leeds, who enjoyed most of the opening exchanges. Ogrizovic had already saved from John Pearson before Leeds took the lead in the fourteenth minute, courtesy of Rennie's header.

> **DID YOU KNOW?**
>
> **Between 1976 and 1992, only twice did Liverpool ever lose a league fixture by four goals. On both occasions their conquerors were Coventry City.**

The Sky Blues at last started to rouse themselves. Regis missed three good chances. Indeed, it was one of those games where he did everything right until he saw the whites of the keeper's eyes.

City continued to press in the second half, leaving themselves exposed to a Leeds counter-punch. On the hour Coventry brought on Michael Gynn for the limping Nick Pickering, and this seemed to give them an extra dimension. Just when it seemed that Leeds had quelled the storm, City levelled. Bennett pressurised Ormsby into an error on his own bye-line and crossed. Lloyd McGrath missed his kick, but Gynn, lurking on the left-hand edge of the penalty area, fired inside the near post. The momentum was now clearly with City and it was no surprise when they scored a second. Houchen gathered a ricochet off Ormsby, calmly side-stepped Mervyn Day in the Leeds goal and slotted home.

Leeds brought on Keith Edwards and Haddock and the substitutions paid off. Seven minutes from time Andy Ritchie crossed and Edwards converted. Leeds looked to have the wind in their sails at the start of extra-time but it was City who scored. Bennett was fouled, Gynn floated across the free-kick, Regis headed back at the far post, Houchen shot against Day, Bennett pounced.

City's hearts were in their mouths with three minutes left when Aspin hoofed the ball down the middle and Edwards raced clear. Oggy deflected the ball to safety. Wembley beckoned.

Match of the Season (2) 1986-87

Tottenham 2 Coventry 3

FA Cup final, 16 May 1987

The dreams of all Coventry fans at last came true at Wembley in a fairy-tale game as City twice came from behind to win the FA Cup in their first final. In a classic contest, City's never-say-die attitude won the day over the superstars from north London.

Perhaps it was clear all along that this would be Coventry's day. John Sillett had been saying since February that City's name was on the cup and *Old Moore's Almanac* predicted that a team in blue stripes would win it. The bookies favoured logic to astrology, installing Tottenham as firm favourites. After all, Spurs had never lost in seven FA Cup finals.

> **DID YOU KNOW?**
>
> **In season 1993-94, City's Mick Quinn became the first opposing player to score a league hat-trick at Highbury since Chelsea's Bobby Tambling in 1964.**

After just two minutes it looked as though the bookies were right. Chris Waddle fleeced Greg Downs on the right and Clive Allen darted in front of Trevor Peake to score with a near-post header. But City were level seven minutes later. Downs crossed, Houchen flicked on, and Dave Bennett was there in a flash, guiding the ball past Spurs' hesitant 39-year-old keeper Ray Clemence.

Spurs took the honours in that breathless first half, in which Glenn Hoddle, despite the close marking of Lloyd McGrath, elegantly pulled the strings, and Waddle did more or less as he pleased against poor Downs. City might have gone ahead when Gynn burst clear, but he was foiled by Clemence. Spurs restored their advantage five minutes before the break, this time with a messy goal. Hoddle's teasing free-kick caught Ogrizovic in two minds, the ball bounced off Kilcline and ended up in the net. The FA later credited the goal to Spurs' Gary Mabbutt.

City began to show their true colours in the second half. After a quiet first period, Bennett started to see more of the ball and it was his delicate cross in the 63rd minute that eluded Gough for Houchen to equalise with a famous diving header. 'Roy of the Rovers' had struck again, with his fifth cup goal of the season.

It was now anyone's game, and although City had their tails up at the end of normal time few would have been so foolish as to predict the outcome as the match entered the extra thirty minutes. Only six had been consumed when Rodger, who had come on as substitute for the injured Kilcline, sent McGrath clear down the right and his cross-cum-shot was deflected off Mabbutt's knee over Clemence to give City the lead for the first time.

Doubts about City's ability to hold out and turn the tide of history proved unfounded. It was Spurs who were now on the back foot. City's midfielders had wings to their heels as they stifled every Spurs attack at birth. Gynn might have scored a fourth in the dying minutes but Clemence saved. By this time the 'Sky Blue Song' was echoing around Wembley and moments later the subbed Kilcline climbed the steps to receive the Cup.

City's fans gave a sporting ovation to Spurs, reserving their taunts for TV pundit Jimmy Greaves, who had predicted Coventry's demise at every hurdle in the competition. The media concurred that this had been one of the best FA Cup finals since the War and that the underdogs had merited their win.

TODAY DIVISION 1 **1987-88**

Division 1	10th
Littlewoods Cup	3rd Round
FA Cup	4th Round

Three months after the FA Cup triumph, 50,000 Coventry fans descended on Wembley for the Charity Shield fixture against league champions Everton. The size of the City support demonstrated the expectations of the Sky Blue Army; the Cup final victory was to be the launch-pad for an assault on the league and then, who knows, Europe. Some hopes. Within three months those dreams were shattered as City went through a disastrous ten-game run without a win and last season's heroes were shown to be mere mortals.

An uncharacteristic Trevor Peake error, which led to Wayne Clarke's goal, decided the Charity Shield, which enabled Everton to carve their name on the trophy for a record fourth time. The outing gave City fans a first look at new striker David Speedie, purchased from Chelsea for £780,000. During the summer John Sillett had stepped up from coach to manager, and as he unveiled his prize new signing he uttered the immortal words: 'for too long this club has shopped at Woolworth's, from now on we'll be shopping at Harrods.' The truth was that though the club's cup run had helped to pay off the overdraft, success would have to come knocking regularly for Sillett to return to the Knightsbridge emporium.

The fixture computer perversely sent Tottenham to Highfield Road on the opening day, and they lost again, Speedie scoring after 21 minutes of his league debut. Four days later a Kilcline penalty at Luton meant City had kicked off with two wins. Liverpool, however, were made of sterner stuff and would test the substance behind Sillett's pre-season boasts. Liverpool outclassed a slapdash and cocky Sky Blues to win 4-1. That result slammed the door on the Cup final party and brought City fans and players alike down to earth with a bump. Any pretensions to a major assault on the title were ruthlessly ended that afternoon.

The real problems, however, started in October, with two bad home defeats in four days. Southampton won at Highfield Road for the first time since 1949, coming back from a two-goal deficit, and Newcastle, with Gascoigne and Mirandinha in dazzling form, won with something to spare. Luton dashed City's League Cup hopes in a third round tie played at Filbert Street because of Luton's ban on away fans, and the large City following expressed their frustrations by chanting 'What a load of rubbish'. It seemed light years away from Wembley. As Christmas approached the side drew five games in a row, three of them without a goal, and doubts about the pairing of Regis and Speedie in attack intensified.

It was at home that City really suffered. The team went from early October until mid-February without a league win at Highfield Road. Fortunately the away form went some way to redress the balance, and wins at Everton, QPR and Sheffield Wednesday kept Sky Blue heads above the relegation waters. City began their defence of the FA Cup by making heavy weather of what should have been a straightforward home tie with Torquay, on a pitch that because of drainage problems resembled a beach. Three weeks later lowly Watford ended a feeble defence of the trophy, with the pitch again shouldering much of the blame.

It had been Coventry's misfortune to win the FA Cup during the five-year penance English clubs served following the tears of Heysel. Denied a place in the Cup-Winners' Cup, they sought consolation in the Simod Cup, a meaningless Mickey Mouse competition introduced by the English football authorities to compensate clubs for the lost revenues of competing in Europe. The two teams reaching the final would be granted a Wembley showcase. City defeated Ipswich and Wimbledon in front of small crowds to set up a semi-final at Second Division Reading. The thought of a third visit to the Twin Towers in a matter of months – no matter the reduced circumstances – was enough to entice thousands of City fans to queue for hours in the rain to buy tickets. Defeat in a penalty shoot-out, which was not concluded until 10.45 pm, denied them a further visit to the national stadium, which would have been their third in a year.

Paradoxically, it was as if Watford's FA Cup ambush lifted a weight from the City players' minds. Their form picked up, and a sixteen-game league run brought only two defeats, both at home. Away from Highfield Road the team went from strength to strength, notching wins at Watford – revenge for the Cup defeat – Southampton and Wimbledon. Injuries and vagaries of form meant that by the end of the season Sillett's preferred line-up contained only five of his Wembley heroes. Dave Bennett and Lloyd McGrath had suffered broken legs, the form of Phillips, Gynn and Downs had lost its cutting edge, while Houchen was picked only intermittently all season. Borrows, when fit, had regained his full-back place, and Dean Emerson and Steve Sedgley policed midfield. Gary Bannister had returned to the club for £300,000 from QPR, and young David Smith, on the verge of being freed the previous summer, had forced his way into the side in February and made a major impact on the left flank. Regis recovered from a poor autumn, ironically after he had been recalled to the England squad after a six-year break. But as ever, Regis seldom threatened to score, preferring to win the plaudits for leading the line with style and leave the goalscoring to others. One such 'other' should have been David Speedie, but despite playing in almost every game, he netted only six goals. The club already had one classy striker who did not score his quota, and could not afford two.

City finished tenth, which would have been creditable enough in an earlier era, but not now that Sillett had promised fans the moon. In fact, City had finished tenth the previous season, too, which meant there had been no improvement. The supporters, with their appetites whetted, looked upon the mid-table position not as a glass half-full but as half-empty, which confirmed the extent to which raised aspirations can affect fans' perceptions. Supporters no longer just hoped, they expected, and the attendances reflected the mood. Home gates were the best for seven years, the average of 17,530 being up ten per cent on the previous season

Match of the Season 1987-88

Coventry 2 Tottenham 1

Division 1, 15 August 1987

The city of Coventry was alive with anticipation as the new season kicked off. With David Pleat's Tottenham having to open their programme at Highfield Road, City fans were presented with the chance to cock a snook at opponents humbled at Wembley just three months previously.

City's pre-season form had been poor, evidenced less by the defeat by Everton in the FA Charity Shield than by the 1-2 embarrassment inflicted by the non-leaguers of Poole Town. Grumblings were already being aired that despite all Sillett's fancy talk of Harrods, the only summer signing had been David Speedie. But such misgivings were put aside as a crowd of almost 24,000 turned up on a sweltering afternoon to applaud the FA Cup holders.

As in the Cup final, City began shakily and would have conceded an early goal, but for Steve Ogrizovic's alertness, which enabled him to thwart Richard Gough. As was typical of matches against Spurs, the play slowly opened up. Before long Ray Clemence's goal was the one under greater threat. After 21 minutes Michael Gynn tore at the Spurs defence, passed to Speedie and dashed into the area for a return ball. The defence was wrong-footed, allowing Speedie to turn on the edge of the box and curl a beauty into the far corner. What a start for City's fiery striker!

DID YOU KNOW?

In season 1994-95, City's Peter Ndlovu became the first opposing player to score a hat-trick at Anfield since Norwich's Terry Allcock in 1962.

That goal might have opened the floodgates as City turned on the style. Dave Bennett caused mayhem on the right whilst Gynn and the remarkable Lloyd McGrath sewed up the midfield. Fine saves from Clemence prevented Pickering and Kilcline from scoring, whilst McGrath and Regis missed chances they would rather forget. It looked as if Spurs might be able to regroup after half-time, but a Coventry corner just before the break saw the ball played quickly to Greg Downs, who with the aid of a deflection buried the ball from 25 yards.

The second half had the air of a *fait accompli,* with City looking comfortably in control. The home crowd took the opportunity to taunt the unfortunate Gary Mabbutt, who had forever endeared himself to City fans for his own-goal at Wembley. On this day however, he repaid the jibes by scoring Spurs' goal with 21 minutes left to play.

But Spurs had nothing more to offer. The occasion was rounded off by Wembley hero Keith Houchen coming on as a 77th-minute substitute in place of Speedie, both of whom were given a rapturous ovation.

BARCLAYS DIVISION 1 **1988-89**

Division 1	7th
Littlewoods Cup	3rd Round
FA Cup	3rd Round

Looking back from today's vantage point, season 1988-89 was not so wretched as it seemed at the time. Back then, the defeat at Sutton blackened everything, hanging like a pall over the club, and it is arguable in retrospect to claim that the club's barren era of the early 1990's was set in train that awful day at Gander Green Lane. The other disappointment at the time was City's failure to clinch their first ever top four place, though by February that had been well within their gasp. Looking on the bright side, seventh place was a considerable achievement, City's highest for eleven years. The club was never out of the top eight all season and a handful more goals would have pushed them into a higher final position.

The season also had its share of gripping matches and memorable City performances – for example, defeating champions Arsenal and finally ending the Villa bogey after 51 years. City also did the double over title-chasing Norwich and Manchester United. On the other hand, City frustrated their fans by losing at home to two relegated teams – Newcastle and Middlesbrough – and succumbed early in both cup competitions. To sum up 1988-89 in one word – Sutton – is therefore to oversimplify.

There had been only two significant transfers in the summer. Nick Pickering, unhappy at playing out of position at left-back, moved to Derby for £300,000, and Celtic's reserve winger, Dougie McGuire, signed for £40,000. McGuire contracted glandular fever soon after coming down from Scotland and could not force his way into the first team all season.

For the second season running the Sky Blues were scheduled to open up against Tottenham, this time at White Hart Lane. But the fixture had to be postponed on the morning of the match when the local authority failed to grant a safety certificate for the new East Stand. Spurs were subsequently docked two points by the FA, later overturned on appeal. A week later, following Everton's win at Highfield Road, City, having played one game fewer than everyone else, found themselves in the bottom three. But four successive wins, three of them away from home, soon put a smile on everyone's faces. City continued their excellent recent winning ways at Hillsborough, newly crowned FA Cup holders Wimbledon were beaten at Plough Lane, and City took a big step towards the next round of the Littlewoods Cup with an easy win at Bournemouth. A key factor in the team's form was the conversion of David Speedie from striker to midfield, behind Regis and Bannister, and the little Scot's form was rewarded with a recall to the international scene after a two-year break.

A home defeat, albeit in a seven-goal thriller to promoted Middlesbrough with Speedie and Bernie Slaven trading hat-tricks, was a minor blip in City's ascendancy, as the following week they travelled to Newcastle and thumped the woeful Geordies. City were helped by steering clear of injuries: in fact, Sillett fielded an unchanged side for the first nine games, and the first change, after Kilcline was injured in training, was barely noticed during a brave goal-less draw at Anfield.

The Littlewoods Cup run was terminated at Forest, after City's first-half enterprise was erased by a second-half charge from Clough's team, who would go on to lift the trophy. As late summer turned to autumn, City's form stuttered. Phillips returned for the injured Gynn, and Houchen was recalled in place of the inconsistent Bannister. It was Houchen who scored the vital second goal to end the Villa jinx, to record the first win over the local rivals in 27 attempts since 1937. A dip in form at the end of the year, together with two out-of-character red cards for Peake and Bannister, saw Sillett shuffle the pack for the visit of Sheffield Wednesday. Bennett and McGrath returned after long injury lay-offs, Speedie reverted to his striking role at the expense of Houchen, and Downs was dropped in favour of Phillips. Speedie scored a spectacular headed hat-trick in a 5-0 win, nicely setting up the FA Cup-tie the following Saturday with non-league Sutton United, which looked a formality.

The one positive thing to come out of the Sutton debacle was that it inspired City to take out their frustrations on their league opponents. City picked up a cluster of points in the following weeks. They came from behind to snatch a win at Carrow Road, with Speedie scoring the spectacular late winner with a delicious chip over Gunn, and followed that up with a home win over Wimbledon. This time Speedie left the fans open-mouthed with a lobbed winner. The outstanding result, though, came at home to the league leaders Arsenal, who were destined to win the title in extraordinary circumstances at Anfield in May. City's hero against Arsenal was Brian Kilcline, who recovered from missing an early penalty to step up eight minutes from time to convert a second.

Post-Sutton, City had dragged themselves into being dark horses for the championship, lying third in the table and eleven points off the lead. Four days later Millwall punctured their hopes and a poor run of five games without a win let the bookies breathe more easily.

DID YOU KNOW?

In season 1997-98, Dion Dublin scored more goals than any other City player for 20 years, and was the Premiership's joint top league scorer.

On the transfer front, Sillett was already thinking long term. Cup final scorers Houchen and Bennett both left in March. Houchen had been out of sorts for a while and almost joined QPR, until a red card in a reserve game resulted in a suspension and the deal collapsing. Scottish club Hibernian eventually paid £300,000 for him, with Bennett signing for Ron Atkinson's Sheffield Wednesday in a £250,000 deal that came out of the blue. As for first-team regular Steve Sedgley, he looked set to move on in the summer, but ill-advisedly allowed his agent to pepper the press with a list of the player's grievances, which got everyone's backs up, whereupon Sedgley slapped in a transfer request.

The season petered out after Liverpool had come to Highfield Road and dished out a lesson in football's finer points. Although City were defeated in only two of their last nine games, too many were drawn to improve on seventh place. Highlights of those closing weeks were a win at Old Trafford, the form of Tony Dobson, who had made the left-back position his own, and the evergreen Cyrille Regis, who finished the season at his most impressive. Many City fans made the short trip to Villa Park on the final Saturday of the season, hoping that the Sky Blues would send their rivals down, but Villa grabbed the point they needed to survive.

Match of the Season 1988-89

Sutton United 2 Coventry 1

FA Cup, 3rd round, 7 January 1989

Sutton United from the Vauxhall Conference wrote a new chapter in football folklore with an epic FA Cup victory that sent a shockwave throughout English soccer. The unimaginable, the unthinkable, had happened. Just 21 months after they paraded the cherished trophy at Wembley, Coventry City were humiliated and humbled in front of 8,000 spectators at Gander Green Lane.

City fans old enough to remember the assassination of John F Kennedy or the moment Geoff Hurst rifled home the glorious fourth World Cup final goal in 1966 will probably in future years ask each other where they were when the final whistle blew on Saturday, 7 January 1989. This was the Sky Blue Titanic struck by the Gander Green iceberg.

DID YOU KNOW?

In season 1997-98, Dion Dublin set a City record of taking and scoring penalties in four successive home league games.

Five days before the Cup disaster, City thrashed Sheffield Wednesday 5-0 and, not surprisingly, John Sillett named the same side. In retrospect, the omens were not good. TV pundit Jimmy Greaves, who had consistently tipped the Sky Blues to lose during the 1987 Cup run, changed his tune in 1989 and said they'd go far. The players clowned their way through the pre-match warm-up. Yesteryear's heroes thought they were invincible.

When play got under way City carved out three chances in the first two minutes, but accepted none of them. That was the end of Coventry's ascendancy until their death throes in the closing ten minutes. Despite enjoying the bulk of possession, the midfield never had a firm grip. Nor was there any penetration down the flanks. City fans started feeling uneasy when the unmarked Kilcline headed straight at the keeper. Three minutes before the break unease turned to shock when Ogrizovic flailed at a near-post corner, was beaten by the flick on and the unmarked Tony Rains headed the non-leaguers in front.

The optimists among the City fans at half-time thought 'Sillett will sort them out now,' and seven minutes into the second half Phillips equalised from a through ball by Sedgley. This should have been the springboard for City to step up a gear and stamp down on these Conference upstarts. Instead, six minutes later, more dreadful marking on the edge of the box allowed Matthew Hanlon to volley home, with Ogrizovic flapping the air.

Panic set in. City threw everyone forward, even risking the loss of further goals. Regis missed a sitter, then trudged off to be replaced by the ultimate Cup talisman, Keith Houchen. As Sutton tired, City's desperate endeavours saw the woodwork intervene, but faced with a packed defence what they needed most was cool heads. It might be said that City enjoyed little luck, but a First Division side should not have to rely on luck against such modest opponents. At the close, the City fans sportingly applauded off the Sutton players, having nothing but contempt for their own.

Tony Rains put his finger on the root of the problem: 'I expected a bit more from Coventry, a bit more passion, more heart, more commitment, more determination.' None of these accusations could be made against Sutton's team of bricklayers, assistant bank managers and insurance clerks. In Round 4 Sutton travelled to Norwich and got thrashed 0-8, which only made the pain worse.

BARCLAYS DIVISION 1 **1989-90**

Division 1	12th
Littlewoods Cup	Semi-finals
FA Cup	3rd Round

The major problem in season 1989-90 was the lack of goals scored. In 38 league matches City only managed to score 39, the lowest total since 1970-71 when they scored only 37. Despite the presence in the squad of Cyrille Regis and David Speedie, and the record purchases of Kevin Drinkell and Kevin Gallacher, no player got into double figures, the first time this had occurred in fifteen years. Speedie ended the season as top scorer with only eight league goals, despite missing eight games through his appalling disciplinary record.

The defence, too, had an off season, conceding 59 goals, the worst record since 1985-86. If mitigating circumstances are sought, 38 of that total were crammed into just ten games. Liverpool hit City for six, and the Sky Blues were on the wrong end of a 1-4 scoreline on no less than five occasions. Yet they still managed to keep a clean sheet on thirteen occasions.

There was a considerable turnover of players in the summer. Peter Billing, a young centre-half from Crewe, joined for £120,000, and Kevin MacDonald arrived on a free from Liverpool. MacDonald had had his share of injury problems since joining the Reds from Leicester, and had played only forty games in five years at Anfield. The third newcomer provided goalkeeping cover for Oggy. Jake Findlay had not had a sniff of first-team action in three seasons at Highfield Road and sadly had to retire with a neck injury. His replacement was 33-year-old Keith Waugh, signed from Bristol City for £40,000, who, as luck would have it, had a first-team outing within a month.

David Phillips' contract had expired and he had joined Norwich for a tribunal-set fee of £550,000. Steve Sedgley's transfer request had been granted and he had signed for Tottenham, whom he had supported as a boy, for a fee of £750,000. Centre-back Graham Rodger had gone to Luton for £150,000. Transfer fees in general were escalating alarmingly, illustrated by Spurs' Chris Waddle signing for Marseille for £4.5 million. Sillett, with a net income of almost £1.3 million, thought the market was overheated and preferred to sit back and wait for quality players at affordable prices. When Chairman Poynton announced a profit of £770,000 – excluding the summer income – fans questioned the wisdom of waiting.

DID YOU KNOW?

During the Coca-Cola Cup-tie at Wolves in November 1995, Oggy became the first City keeper ever to be sent off, and Jonnie Gould City's first sub keeper.

The season started brightly, with three wins out of four lifting City to the top of the table. Everton and Manchester City were beaten at home and promoted Crystal Palace at Selhurst Park. With a free weekend in the fixture list on account of international duties, City's first ever occupation of pole position lasted ten days. In their first game as leaders they slumped 1-4 at Millwall, who took over the top spot themselves. That game saw Oggy injured, bringing an end to his long uninterrupted run of matches, leaving Waugh to make his debut.

Despite the promising start, Sillett had been trying to strengthen the attack and swooped for Kevin Drinkell, who was surplus to requirements at Glasgow Rangers. Drinkell cost £800,000. He had an impressive scoring record with Grimsby, Norwich and Rangers, and scored for City after only 23 minutes of his debut, a League Cup-tie against his old club Grimsby. His goal sparked a comeback after a first-leg defeat had rendered City vulnerable to another early cup exit. Four goals in his first six games suggested that he had settled quickly to City's style, but he too became a victim of the scoring drought, and by the end of the season many were doubting his value, monetarily and otherwise.

Two good away wins saw City through to the last eight of the Littlewoods Cup, where the kind draw sent the Sky Blues to Second Division Sunderland. Thoughts of Wembley were in the air again, but before the tie at Roker Park, City suffered another FA Cup embarrassment, this time at Third Division Northampton. On a miserably wet day the Cobblers made light of the glue-pot pitch and their solitary goal was enough against a sad City side which barely created a chance. The supporters vented their anger: nothing seemed to have been learned in the twelve months since Sutton and the pervading opinion was that action was necessary. But for City being through to the quarter-finals of the other cup, decisive action would surely have been forthcoming. But Sillett, off the hook, did nothing other than appoint a new coach, Dixie McNeil. Many supporters were of the opinion that the side had become sterile and boring, the exact antithesis of Sillett's principles, and that the man who had masterminded the heroics of 1987 had stayed loyal for too long to the under-achievers in his team.

The heated reaction to the Northampton defeat stirred up the players sufficiently to despatch Sunderland, after a replay, thereby setting up a potentially mouth-watering two-leg semi-final with Nottingham Forest. In the interim, Sillett broke the club's transfer record for the second time in four months when paying £900,000 for Dundee United's winger Kevin Gallacher. The lightweight Scottish international, having barely been introduced to his new team-mates, was thrown into the first leg at the City Ground, where he came face to face with Stuart Pearce in the first of many memorable duels between the two players. Forest came out narrowly on top that day, thanks to a debatable penalty and a Pearce 'special' from a free-kick, although TV replays exposed Forest's shenanigans in the defensive wall as the kick was taken. In the second leg, Forest battened down the hatches, securing the goal-less draw they sought, en route to a successful Wembley final against Oldham.

It was typical of Coventry City that a cup defeat should spark a rich vein of league form. An epic win over Aston Villa, with Drinkell coming off the bench to score, was trumped by an improbable 4-2 win at Forest, which saw City climb to fourth in the table with nine games remaining. The good form had shallow foundations, however, and one win out of the final nine saw City slip into the bottom half. Home defeats by Charlton and Sheffield Wednesday, both doomed, was an insult to City's pride, as was a final day hammering at home by the champions, Liverpool. Sillett did not help his cause afterwards by warmly applauding the Merseyside fans, while appearing to ignore City's own supporters.

Player-wise, Sillett finally took steps to address the left-back problem position by signing Crewe's Paul Edwards for £325,000, which signalled the end of Greg Downs' City career. His partner, Brian Borrows, was improving with age and he received overdue recognition when Graham Taylor selected him for the England B squad. Gallacher's early form looked promising, but the shortage of talent in midfield had been evident for some time. McGrath and Emerson missed large parts of the season through injury, and MacDonald's lack of pace limited his effectiveness. None of the youngsters breaking through looked to have what was required to be a success in the top division.

Match of the Season 1989-90

Coventry 5 Sunderland 0

Littlewoods Cup, quarter-final replay, 24 January 1990

City's best result of the season was undeniably the 1-0 win at Anfield, their first win there in 25 visits. But there are certain games when the stage is set for one player to take the spotlight, and under the Highfield Road floodlights against Sunderland Steve Livingstone stepped forward to give a virtuoso performance in front of a discerning and appreciative crowd.

City went into the game still reeling from their FA Cup defeat at Northampton, and faced elimination from both cups in a matter of weeks. The tension was evident, partly because a semi-final place was at stake and partly because City had come off worst from the goal-less draw at Roker and been grateful to hear the final whistle. David Speedie and Sunderland's Gary Bennett had also been sent off in the second half for an incident which resulted in Bennett grabbing Speedie round the throat and pinning him to an advertising hoarding.

It was clear from the outset that there were scores to settle and Speedie was singled out for harsh treatment. This resulted in two Sunderland players being booked and Gary Owers being sent off just before half-time for elbowing Speedie off the ball. The dismissal extinguished Sunderland's faint hope of salvaging the tie, for by then they were already trailing by two goals.

Steve Livingstone had yet to score for the first team and was only playing because injury ruled out Kevin Drinkell. Nevertheless, he staked a claim for a regular place by scoring in the fifteenth and nineteenth minutes. The first was a neat header from a Greg Downs free-kick, the second a rifled shot after Borrows and Regis had created the chance. Livingstone's hat-trick arrived six minutes into the second half, when Borrows and Regis combined again to give him the chance to hold off Bennett before volleying home.

Highfield Road was buzzing and Sunderland were reeling. City went for the kill and Livingstone struck again on 64 minutes. With his confidence sky high, he controlled Ogrizovic's clearance, shrugged off two defenders and rounded the keeper to score a memorable individual goal. Having scored four, Livingstone turned provider, heading on to Regis, who set up Michael Gynn.

City proceeded to miss several more glaring chances, notably Borrows, who could have crowned a towering performance but blazed his shot high and wide. City's 1-2 aggregate defeat by Nottingham Forest at the penultimate hurdle could take nothing away from a night Steve Livingstone could only have dreamt about.

Terry Gibson miskicks against Wolves (April 1984)

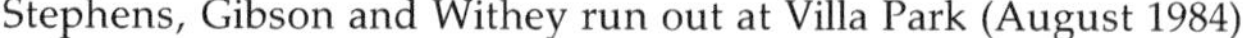

Stephens, Gibson and Withey run out at Villa Park (August 1984)

Dave Bennett goes for goal against Newcastle (October 1984)

Latchford and Pearce celebrate Terry Gibson's goal v Manchester City (January 1985)

Cyrille Regis on the attack at Oxford (October 1986)

Nick Pickering in the thick of the action at Oxford (October 1986)

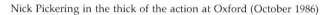

Six

The Merry-Go-Round 1990-1995

BARCLAYS DIVISION 1	**1990-91**
Division 1	16th
Rumbelows Cup	Quarter-final
FA Cup	4th Round

The season started with John Sillett talking of championships – and ended with him out of a job and City finishing in the bottom half of the table. It was an eventful season of sackings, controversial transfers, blazing rows, injuries, highs and lows, and an end-of-season thrashing.

Transfer activity in the close season was thin. Sillett ignored the cries to bring in a midfield general and bought central defender Andy Pearce from non-league Halesowen for £15,000. Long-serving defender Greg Downs moved on a free transfer to Birmingham. The manager was confident that his existing squad could arrest the slump of the last two months of the previous season and push for a top six finish.

That notion was shredded in the first weeks, with lacklustre performances at Old Trafford and Villa Park and an undistinguished win over a woeful Everton. Sillett turned to the Continent for inspiration, at a time when it was not yet fashionable to do so. Hungarian international winger Zoltan Czucsansky came over for a trial period, but was injured after seventeen minutes of a friendly. With Emerson and McGrath still unfit, Sillett borrowed the talents of Uruguayan captain, Jose Perdomo, on loan from Italian club Genoa. Just a few months previously, Perdomo had scored a spectacular winning goal against England at Wembley. There was no doubting his talent but his fitness was in doubt and he couldn't speak English. He showed a delightful touch, playing a deep, holding midfield role and on the six occasions he pulled on a Sky Blue shirt proved himself to be a superb passer of the ball. Sadly, Sillett was unsuccessful in his attempts to sign him permanently, and Perdomo returned to Italy, before signing for a minor Argentine club.

Controversy reared its head minutes after the home Rumbelows Cup-tie with Bolton in September. David Speedie, who after a poor start to the season had been axed from the side, clashed with a club vice-president with whom he had apparently been engaged in a long-running dispute. The Scot was fined two weeks wages. The tabloids got wind of the story, which hit the front pages of the *Sun*, and Speedie wisely went to ground as speculation over his future intensified.

Pressure on the beleaguered Sillett increased following home defeats by Southampton and Arsenal. Not even Speedie's return could prevent the side slumping to sixteenth. And then, all of a sudden, Sillett was gone. The club denied that he had been sacked, but intimated that he had offered to step down at the end of the season anyway. As the board were not prepared to wait, the unwell Sillett found himself out in the cold, learning of his dismissal from his sick-bed.

The signs were that the board had been scheming for Sillett's departure, for behind the scenes Poynton had been negotiating with the big-name manager he coveted, Rangers and England centre-half Terry Butcher. But Butcher had never managed anyone and was still a first-team regular at Ibrox. He therefore arrived at Highfield Road as a designated 'player-manager'. Nor did Butcher come cheap. Rangers demanded a fee of £400,000, not to mention the huge salary he commanded at his new club as both player and manager. Butcher's appointment was to prove an expensive mistake for Poynton and Coventry City.

Butcher's baptism was not the stuff of dreams, rather a home defeat by Liverpool, but the players looked fired up and Butcher lent a steadying influence to the defence, which was bereft of the hamstrung Kilcline. Eleven days later Butcher enjoyed the result of the season, a 5-4 victory over Forest in the Rumbelows Cup, in the wake of which Mick Mills, Butcher's former team-mate at Ipswich, joined City as assistant manager.

It would take another month before Butcher recorded his first league win, over Tottenham on Boxing Day, but by this time relegation clouds were hovering. The New Year was no time for celebration. Wigan forced a replay in the FA Cup, and another humiliation looked on the cards until City rolled up their sleeves and pulled through. Soon afterwards youngsters Steve Livingstone and Tony Dobson were controversially sold to Blackburn for a combined fee of

£750,000 to help fund the purchase of Ray Woods from Wigan for £200,000 and reduce the overdraft.

In one particularly memorable week, though for all the wrong reasons, Second Division Sheffield Wednesday ended City's run in the Rumbelows Cup, and with eight players on the injury list the Sky Blues' FA Cup campaign was brought to a shuddering halt at the Dell in a replay.

Speedie's season had staggered from bad to worse. He had been sent off at Crystal Palace in November. No pun is intended – given their respective heights – by disclosing that he and Butcher did not always see eye to eye. Speedie looked set to join Aston Villa, which galled many City fans, until Kenny Dalglish came in at the last minute and signed him for Liverpool for £675,000. Poynton later disclosed that Speedie had repeatedly asked for a move away from Highfield Road, and the club did not want to keep a player whose heart was not in the club.

With relegation looking probable rather than possible, Butcher rang the changes. Paul Edwards and Peter Billing were dropped, Kilcline was injured again, and Andy Pearce and Ray Woods came in. Butcher's former England team-mate, Kenny Sansom, arrived from Newcastle for £100,000, and midfielder Stewart Robson came on loan from West Ham, where he had been marooned in the reserves after a bad back injury. Suitably refreshed, City strung together a run of ten games with only two defeats, hauling themselves up to ninth place before sliding back to sixteenth by the close. Two defeats in the last three games was not a glorious finale, especially as City were reduced to being the sacrificial lambs in their final match, away to champions Arsenal.

Overall, City had remained unbeaten at home in fourteen games since Butcher's baptism against Liverpool. But this was offset by their abject away form, which earned just one win, and that before Butcher took over.

Of the players, Kevin Gallacher adjusted well to the switch from winger to central striker, scoring sixteen league and cup goals – the best haul by a City player since Terry Gibson in 1984-85 – and deserving his recall to the Scotland squad. Michael Gynn also chipped in with eleven goals. Cyrille Regis was again superb, and although he didn't score many goals supporters were aggrieved when Butcher announced he would be releasing Regis at the end of the season. Robert Rosario arrived from Norwich for £650,000 with the aim of replacing Regis, and he faced a tall order. Kilcline's days were also numbered; his contract was up at the end of the season. Injury restricted Butcher to just seven starts and many doubted whether he would ever wear a City shirt again.

DID YOU KNOW?

Michael Gynn became the first player to miss a penalty in the newly formed Premier League when he failed against Tottenham in August 1992.

Match of the Season 1990-91

Coventry 5 Nott'm Forest 4

Rumbelows Cup, fourth round, 28 November 1990

In terms of 'shock factor', this result probably ranks alongside the 4-0 thrashing of Liverpool in 1983. Brian Clough's Forest had won this particular competition for the past two seasons. Nor were Forest accustomed to conceding five goals in a match. That had not happened for two and a half years.

This was only Terry Butcher's third game in charge at City, and rarely in his playing career can he have experienced such emotions. He will surely remember this staggering match – his first managerial victory – throughout his life.

Revenge was in the air, Forest having knocked City out of the League Cup in both previous seasons, including a hotly debated semi-final. Kevin Gallacher now scored his first hat-trick in English football, although his achievement was overshadowed by a threesome for Forest's Nigel Clough, all scored in the space of seven minutes. Gallacher struck first from close range after Speedie's header had been blocked. A minute later, Regis passed to Gallacher, who chipped the badly-positioned Crossley. Livingstone scored City's third after Gallacher had attacked the Forest defence and the ball broke for the big striker. After 35 minutes it was 4-0, Gallacher completing his hat-trick with another close-range shot after Billing had won the ball in the air.

Forest fans could be seen pouring out of the ground, disgusted by their team's performance. But they were the foolish ones, as City pressed the self-destruct button and let Forest back into the game, Clough scoring from the edge of the area after being given acres of space. Forest looked a different side and Clough scored two more soft goals before half-time to make it 4-3.

It would be worth much to have been a fly on the wall during Butcher's half-time verbal blast. But upon the resumption Speedie dived in on Parker, who levelled the scores when turning to shoot past Ogrizovic. Just after the hour Livingstone scored what proved to be the winner after a terrific scramble in the Forest goal.

City fell at the next hurdle, at home to Sheffield Wednesday in what was Speedie's last game. The Owls went on to lift the Cup.

BARCLAYS DIVISION 1 1991-92

Division 1	19th
Rumbelows Cup	4th Round
FA Cup	3rd Round

Life in the top division has never been easy for Coventry City but the 1991-92 season will go down as one of the most turbulent in their history. Most of the drama took place off the field during twelve months that saw two chairmen, two managers and three assistant managers. Yet despite, or maybe because of, all the changes the team continued to struggle, and City fans were put through the sort of nail-biting final day of the season that they thought they had left behind in the mid-1980's.

Terry Butcher, at 32 the youngest manager in the First Division, started the season with just four additions to his squad. Stewart Robson, who in four loan appearances had become a crowd favourite, completed a free transfer. Enfield striker, Paul Furlong, who had been on QPR's books as a youngster, was bought for £100,000, primarily as cover for Rosario and Gallacher. The gifted Zimbabwean, Peter Ndlovu, first spotted by John Sillett and invited to Highfield Road for a trial, signed from Bulawayo Highlanders for £10,000. Ndlovu quickly proved that in terms of raw skill he was one of the best players the club had ever had, but Butcher, like his successors, never quite got the best out of him. Finally, Clive Baker arrived from Barnsley as goalkeeping cover for Oggy, but was destined to be another custodian who kicked his heels as the big man kept playing on and on.

Butcher jettisoned 1987 Wembley heroes Regis and Kilcline. Regis joined his old mentor Ron Atkinson at Villa Park on a free, while promoted Oldham paid a generous £400,000 for Kilcline.

Problems disrupted the camp even before the season started. A three-match tour of Scotland was overshadowed by the sending home of Kenny Sansom, Trevor Peake and Lloyd McGrath, who had been caught drinking in Troon less than 48 hours before a tournament in Kilmarnock. Butcher was determined to set an example of the miscreants, and each was heavily fined and put on the transfer list. Peake was soon on his way to Luton, signing for the Hatters the day after City had thumped them 5-0. The £100,000 fee paved the way for the signing of young Wigan defender Peter Atherton for £330,000.

After nine games City lay fourth, but it was a false picture. They had played six home games and only three away. Their form was patchy – Manchester City and Wimbledon had both won at Highfield Road – but an extraordinary win at defending champions Arsenal, inspired by Dixon's memorable own-goal and Ndlovu's first ever goal for City, showed that City could cause upsets.

It was not long before the Sky Blue vessel was rocking badly. Five league defeats in a row precipitated another crisis. On 9 November, amid rumours of serious financial problems and the impending sale of Gallacher, Poynton resigned. The new chairman was Peter Robins, son of 1960's benefactor Derrick. He was backed by Bryan Richardson, a publishing entrepreneur with a sporting background, and London lawyer Michael Jepson.

Within ten days of the palace coup Butcher was forced to sack his assistant Mick Mills and reserve team coach Brian Eastick, replacing them with the vastly experienced Don Howe. A Rumbelows Cup victory over Arsenal and a home win over Southampton provided the only respite for an increasingly beleaguered Butcher, who announced his retirement from playing following a rusty performance against Aston Villa in the Zenith Data Systems Cup that ended with a red card.

December was a bad month. Spurs grabbed a late victory to knock City out of the Rumbelows Cup, and defeats at Old Trafford and Luton saw City slide ever nearer the relegation zone. Another non-league striker, Sean Flynn from Halesowen, was thrown straight into the first team and scored at Sheffield United in a rare win. A New Year's day defeat by Tottenham and a home FA Cup draw with Cambridge, however, forced Robins' hand and Butcher was told he was no longer wanted.

Robins alluded in the press to Butcher's contract, and indicated that he had attempted to re-negotiate it to reflect the fact that Butcher had retired as a player. It was an issue that needed court action to resolve. With the birth of the Premier League just months away, with all its perceived crocks of gold, the board felt it necessary to make changes at the top sooner rather than later. Assistant Don Howe was invited to take over as caretaker manager, on the understanding that the kitty was empty and there was no money to spend.

Howe couldn't avert an FA Cup replay defeat at Cambridge, courtesy of a goal from their powerful striker, Dion Dublin, but took action to stiffen City's defence. This he was only able to do by depleting the team's attacking strength. Drab, dour football was the consequence, and although only one game in nine was lost, the run included four goal-less draws and saw only four goals scored. The slow accumulation of points was enough to keep the threat of relegation at bay until mid-March, when City were overtaken by

Sheffield United, Southampton and Tottenham, each of whom had put on a surge.

Successive defeats by Tottenham and Arsenal meant that City would have to scrap for everything to survive. Deflected goals then cost them the points against both Notts County and Everton. On Easter Monday Lloyd McGrath was sent off in the televised clash with champions elect Leeds for deliberate handball, although TV replays suggested the ball had struck his knee and not his hand.

The Sky Blues could afford to lose only so long as others beneath them were also losing. But Luton were stringing together a winning run, and beat Aston Villa in their penultimate game. It was just as well that City recorded their first home win since November, against doomed West Ham, for that set up a climactic final day at Villa Park. By that time Notts County and West Ham were already relegated, leaving Luton, who were two points behind City, to travel to Notts County. With the Sky Blues having a superior goal-difference, a draw was all they needed to survive.

Within twenty-one seconds City's hopes of even a point looked thin, as their former hero Cyrille Regis put Villa ahead. News that Luton were winning at Meadow Lane, coupled with a second Villa goal, scored by Dwight Yorke, put City in the bottom three for the first time all season. The fans were almost resigned to relegation. Salvation came, not through a City fight-back, but in the shape of Loughborough University student Rob Matthews, who scored twice for Notts County to send Luton down.

A champagne swilling Robins vowed that the club would not struggle again, and to that end £2-3 million would be invested in new players. Where did we hear that before?

Match of the Season 1991-92

Leeds 2 Coventry 0

Division 1, 20 April 1992

With three games of the season remaining, City were on the brink. West Ham were almost certainly down and Notts County were favourites to join them. A battle royal was taking place between Coventry and Luton to avoid the third relegation place. The reward for staying up was even greater this year than previously, for August would usher in the new FA Premier League, a revamped top division embellished with all the peripherals that the marketing men could conceive of, in an attempt to revitalise the English game. Leeds were aiming to become the last winners of the old style First Division, vying for the championship with Manchester United.

DID YOU KNOW?

Coventry City are the only club to play in seven divisions of the English League – Divisions 1 to 4, Third Division North and South, and the Premiership.

This Easter Monday fixture was televised live at 5 pm. Results earlier that afternoon had given encouragement to both sides. Manchester United had lost 1-2 at home to Nottingham Forest, keeping them two points ahead of Howard Wilkinson's Leeds but using up their game in hand. Should Leeds beat City, they would go top of the table. Luton, meanwhile had been defeated 1-2 by QPR, a result that would further depress the Hatters should City win at Elland Road. But that seemed improbable. City had scored in only five of their previous fourteen league games, while Leeds were unbeaten at home all season.

Leeds began confidently, their impressive midfield enlivened by future City stars Gordon Strachan and Gary McAllister. Peter Atherton and Andy Pearce took time to get to grips with the Leeds strike-force of Rod Wallace and Lee Chapman, but once they had done so Leeds became frustrated and were content to hear the half-time whistle in order to regroup.

Early in the second half City were forced back into desperate defence, but the dam was breached on 53 minutes. A needlessly conceded free-kick was punished as Brian Borrows failed to clear Strachan's chip, enabling Chris Fairclough to head past Ogrizovic. Leeds were rampant now, swarming forward to try to make victory certain.

They did so eleven minutes from time, but in controversial circumstances. French substitute Eric Cantona linked with Gary Speed and shot towards an empty net. Lloyd McGrath dived to get his body in the way and cleared the ball with his knee. Alas, the linesman believed he had deliberately handled and McGrath was sent off. Television replays conclusively showed the interception was legitimate, but that was no comfort to City as McAllister scored from the penalty to secure a 2-0 victory. Leeds went top, a position they held until the end of the season.

City survived on the final day, thanks to events elsewhere, though for the first time in all their relegation battles they lost their last match of the season.

FA PREMIER LEAGUE	**1992-93**
Premier League	15th
Coca-Cola Cup	2nd Round
FA Cup	3rd Round

After the trials and tribulations of the previous campaign, City's inaugural season in the Premier League had to be judged a success, with the proviso that some of their football was not pretty to watch. With Bobby Gould reinstalled as manager, the Sky Blues started with a bang and were the first leaders of the new league. When Mick Quinn signed, he accomplished City's best scoring sequence in 25 years of top flight football. The season tailed off badly, but it wasn't until 17 April that City drifted into the bottom half of the table, and that was far too late to generate fears of relegation.

Back in May, Bobby Gould had been sacked by West Brom and within days was ensconced at Highfield Road as the new joint manager with Don Howe. The idea was that Howe would retain responsibility for coaching and tactics. But his record and style – not to mention his decision to sign Les Sealey (who had bad-mouthed the club when leaving in 1983) on loan – had not endeared him to City fans. Howe, though, decided that the daily trip from his Hertfordshire home was too much, stepped down, and allowed Gould to recruit axed Bolton boss Phil Neal as his assistant.

Gould's familiarity with the lower divisions once again came in handy. Swansea's flying winger John Williams arrived for £250,000 and defender Phil Babb signed from Bradford City for £500,000. Gould's son Jonathan, a promising goalkeeper, also arrived for a small fee from West Brom. The outgoing players included Paul Furlong, originally bought as cover – but because of injuries pushed regularly into the team – who was sold for £250,000 to Watford. Kevin Drinkell and Dean Emerson also departed, to Falkirk and Hartlepool respectively, both players having kicked their heels for almost two years on the sidelines.

City made an impeccable start to their Premier League history. Wins over Middlesbrough, Tottenham and Wimbledon gave them a maximum nine-point haul. When they went on to win at Sheffield Wednesday and Oldham, the Sky Blues established a club record of four successive away wins.

But success on the field was accompanied by a backdrop of yet more financial pressures. There was a period when Kevin Gallacher seemed sure to sign for Manchester City any day, though in the event the only player to leave was full-back Paul Edwards, who never lived up to his reputation and signed for Wolverhampton for £75,000.

Williams, Gallacher and Hurst all played their part in City's early season promise, but the player to grab the headlines was the inimitable Ndlovu, who ran defences ragged with his speed and dexterity. Press interest in the player grew to fever pitch after he scored a superb individual goal against league leaders Norwich which was eulogised on Match of the Day. Coventry's success was rewarded in other ways, too. Gould earned the Bell's Manager of the Month award, while Phil Neal was invited into the England set up, becoming Graham Taylor's part-time assistant manager.

The first banana skin to trip up the Sky Blues was waiting in the Coca-Cola Cup. What should have been a routine trip to Scarborough, with two goals in the bank after the first leg, ended in a nightmare 0-3 defeat. In the past, Coventry had often responded to a cup upset with a good result in the league. This time their league form stuttered, and Gould introduced well-travelled striker Mick Quinn on loan from Newcastle. Quinn's impact was the stuff of fantasy. His ten goals in six games kick-started City's season. Christmas wins at home to Liverpool (5-1) and Aston Villa (3-0) were attributable in no small part to the stocky striker and his rejuvenated partner, Robert Rosario. City's financial situation was reported to be so serious – debts of £3 million were announced – that help was welcome wherever it could be found. Quinn's fee of £250,000, for example, was rumoured to have been paid by a wealthy supporter.

After Christmas the side was rarely out of the top six and two more away wins, at Middlesbrough and at title-chasing Blackburn, even had the more impressionable supporters talking about Europe. Financial pressures, however, could no longer be deflected or hidden under the carpet. Rosario was the first to go, much to Gould's chagrin, joining Forest for £500,000. Gallacher finally left for Blackburn in a part exchange deal that saw Gallacher valued at £1 million and Roy Wegerle at £500,000. Other buys concluded by the transfer deadline day included Leigh Jenkinson, who arrived from Hull for £250,000, and David Rennie, who came in a swap deal that took David Smith to Birmingham.

The season tailed away badly with just one win from the last eleven games. Even on the last day, a 3-1 lead over Leeds was squandered in the dying seconds, costing the club £250,000 in prize money, as the team slipped three places in the final table.

Some players had made the progress expected of them; others had not. Ogrizovic found himself experiencing healthy competition for his place, in the shape of Jonathan Gould. Pearce had lost his centre-half-position to another non-league recruit, Dave Busst, a £10,000 buy from Moor Green. Atherton enjoyed a marvellous season in defence, while Phil Babb, in the Republic of Ireland squad, had displaced Sansom, who had gone on a free to Everton. In midfield, Lee Hurst emerged as an outstanding prospect, despite losing his mentor, Robson, with more injury problems. Up front, Quinn's excellent start was not sustained, though he still finished with seventeen league goals, equalling Terry Gibson's league tally nine seasons earlier. Quinn missed playing alongside Rosario and looked ill at ease when partnered by Flynn or Wegerle. Ndlovu, predictably, faded in the mid-winter chill, although he seemed at one stage to be permanently in transit, either flying out to play for Zimbabwe or flying back again. He at least put on one of his special shows in the final game of the season against Leeds.

Chairman Peter Robins was not able to justify his pre-season boast about releasing large sums of money, though progress was made on improving the stadium. The Kop was officially closed at the end of the season to allow work to commence on a new East Stand, which would take the best part of a year to complete. The summer also witnessed more boardroom battles, with Robins standing down as chairman. Local businessman John Clarke looked set to take over, but his bid failed at the eleventh hour. Fellow director Bryan Richardson assumed the chairmanship and Clarke resigned.

Match of the Season 1992-93

Coventry 5 Liverpool 1

Premier League, 19 December 1992

During the build-up to this game many City fans looked for omens predicting victory. After all, Bobby Gould had led unfancied City into a pre-Christmas home game against Liverpool during his first managerial tenure, but not many believed that the 4-0 whitewash could be emulated.

New signing Mick Quinn was still scoring goals for fun, but the defence was leaking goals badly, with the result that City had gone eleven games without a win. Liverpool, meanwhile, were embarking on a transition period under Graeme Souness and found themselves in eighth position, just one place above City. Promising Anfield youngsters – McManaman, Redknapp and Rob Jones – were helping to maintain Liverpool's formidable standards, though journeymen like Paul Stewart and Mark Walters were not destined for lengthy careers on Merseyside.

DID YOU KNOW?

City had TWO players – Shaw and Williams – sent off at home to Wimbledon in November 1995. But nine-man City fought back from 1-3 down to draw 3-3.

City's preparations were upset by an injury to Ogrizovic, which allowed Jonathan Gould to make his debut. Summer signing Phil Babb was making only his second start at centre-half, and would have to mark Ian Rush, who made a nasty habit of scoring against City.

The first half was almost all Liverpool, with Babb and Atherton constantly stretched by Rush and Stewart, and John Barnes a majestic figure in the Reds' midfield. Despite this, City took the lead after 37 minutes, capitalising on Borrows' penalty-kick after Jamie Redknapp had checked Lee Hurst's run into the box, stumbled, and handled the ball.

The second half opened with Gould forced into making several fine saves, and it was once more against the run of play that City scored their second goal. A free-kick on the edge of the box was touched sideways for Borrows to smash home from twenty yards. It was now that City started to turn on the style. Hurst and McGrath were tigerish in midfield and Gould's bold tactics of playing four strikers – Quinn, Rosario, John Williams and Kevin Gallacher – were now paying off, exposing huge gaps in the Liverpool defence. It was Gallacher who calmly slotted home the third goal just after the hour, following a shrewd pass by Rosario.

Liverpool edged back into contention three minutes later when Redknapp beat Gould with a vicious 25-yarder, but Redknapp's was to be a chequered performance. No sooner had he scored than he was sent off for fouling Gallacher. There was no way back for ten-man Liverpool, and City's predatory striker Quinn sent the crowd home singing his praises following two poacher's goals late in the match. Even then, City had the chances to make the result even worse for Liverpool.

The score brought back memories of the 4-0 win in December 1983. This Liverpool side was not a patch on that earlier one, but it did not matter. City were once again grabbing the headlines, becoming the first side to put five goals past Liverpool since Aston Villa in 1976.

FA CARLING PREMIERSHIP 1993-94

Premiership	11th
Coca-Cola Cup	3rd Round
FA Cup	3rd Round

Phil Babb, City's latest full international, summed up 1993-94 perfectly: 'We did well at the start of the season and well at the end of the season – it's just the 25 games in between we struggled with.' It was a fair description of a season that once again saw Coventry City propelled onto the back pages of the tabloids as the club was shaken by further internal ructions.

Bobby Gould's October walkout, characteristically dramatic and unexpected, rocked the club to its foundations and might well have sent it tumbling out of the Premiership – now sponsored by Carling. The traditional players' numbers of one to eleven were replaced by a much-ridiculed squad numbering system. Perhaps the seeds of Gould's departure had been sown during the close season when Peter Robins, his friend and confidante, moved from club chairman to chief executive, which meant that Gould was now answerable to his successor, Bryan Richardson. The new chairman maintained that his relationship with Gould was cordial, though clearly, away from the public eye, the wheels on the City wagon were working loose.

After the hectic transfer activity of the past twelve months, the close season had been tranquil by comparison. Veteran striker Mick Harford was signed from Sunderland for £200,000, and promising Stockport full-back Paul R Williams arrived for £150,000. Gould sold Andy Pearce to Sheffield Wednesday for £500,000 in the knowledge that Babb was a more than adequate replacement. Michael Gynn was released after a ten-year career with the club.

Coventry had to start the season with a glut of injuries. Gould's pre-season jaunt to an army camp backfired when Lee Hurst tore knee ligaments on an assault course. At the time, the injury did not look too serious, but the promising local youngster would never play first-team football again. Ten minutes into the opening game, at Highbury, Stewart Robson also fell victim to knee trouble, and the heart of City's midfield had been ripped out. Like Hurst, Robson would never appear for City again. Robson's distress was largely ignored at the time, as Coventry had marked up an astonishing 3-0 triumph, with Mick Quinn scoring all three.

Four days later – with stadium improvements reducing Highfield Road's three-sided capacity to 17,000 – City enjoyed their first home victory, over Kevin Keegan's promoted Newcastle, new signing Harford coming off the bench to score the winning goal. Harford never turned out for the Sky Blues again, struck down by back problems. His Sky Blues career lasted just sixteen minutes.

In what proved to be their best start since 1937, City were unbeaten in their first eight league games, claiming Liverpool's scalp and drawing at Villa Park. But all was not rosy. Having piled up a three-goal advantage from the first leg of a Coca-Cola Cup-tie with Wycombe, the league's newest team destroyed City at Adams Park, took the game to extra-time and led 4-3 overall. Fortunately, two late goals saved City's bacon, but the fans were far from impressed.

Coventry City has seldom witnessed a day like 23 October, 1993. A 1-5 defeat at QPR was bad enough, but Gould stunned the post-match press conference by announcing his resignation. The reasons were hard to fathom. Gould appeared to accuse Richardson of forcing him to sell Peter Ndlovu, but the player was not sold and Richardson, one hears, later apologised to Gould for claiming that his resignation was 'stress related'. A week of claim and counter claim ensued, involving rumours of a Gould-backed consortium taking over. Gould turned up at Highfield Road as a Sky TV pundit for the home match with Sheffield United, an act which did little to help the team or enhance support for his own position. The match itself degenerated almost into a side-show, with the stadium reverberating to factional protests. The net result was that City earned yet more headlines of the wrong kind, losing a hometown manager who cared passionately for the club and the city. The whole story may never come out, and in any case truth is relative, but the general feeling is that, once Gould had resigned, Richardson made little effort to persuade him to reconsider. If true, that suggests the new chairman wanted his own man all along.

His own man, for the time being, was Gould's assistant, Phil Neal who, far from being forced to sell players, was encouraged to buy them. Lower division players Julian Darby (£150,000 from Neal's old club Bolton) and Ally Pickering (£85,000 from Rotherham) were signed, and Huddersfield midfielder Chris Marsden arrived on loan. Marsden looked the part from the outset, a ball-playing midfielder with a sweet left foot. His presence in the side over Christmas helped City look the genuine article. Roy Wegerle was playing his best football since arriving at the club, with Marsden the key man in the triangle with Ndlovu.

City, however, dithered when Marsden's loan period expired, and he slipped away to Wolves. The City board sounded unconvincing with its side of the story, and the fans were left feeling that someone had dropped a massive clanger. The club signed instead Sandy Robertson, another midfielder, this time from Glasgow Rangers for £250,000. It was quickly obvious to most supporters that Robertson was out of his depth in the Premiership.

Nor was Bobby Gould the only ex-manager causing waves at the club. The board also had to face legal action from Terry Butcher, who was claiming unfair dismissal. The case was settled out of court for a sum believed to be in the region of £240,000.

City's bubble burst during the first three months of 1994. This was in no small way due to Mick Quinn's goals drying up. City won just twice in that period, against Ipswich and Manchester City, and the slump sucked the Sky Blues perilously close to the relegation zone. Neal's response to the problem was to axe Quinn and John Williams, and play Ndlovu and Sean Flynn as his striking partnership. Ndlovu's brilliance, subdued for much of the season, suddenly erupted again, and he ended the campaign in devastating form proving to the doubters that he was a player of the highest class. Ndlovu's five goals in the final eight games sparked a defiant upturn of results, climaxed by out-battling and out-playing title-chasing Blackburn in front of a passionate Highfield Road crowd.

The early signs were that Neal and his new assistant, Mick Brown, had got the team playing adventurous football of a kind to lure back the stay-away supporters. In Phil Babb and Peter Ndlovu – who equalled the club's record as the most capped international player – they had two of the brightest stars of the Premiership, The duo were fit to grace the biggest clubs, who would undoubtedly soon be waving chequebooks to secure their services. Babb made his debut for the Republic of Ireland in the spring and was touted as a strong candidate for the 1994 World Cup finals, by which time City had rejected a £1.8 million bid for him from Newcastle.

Chairman Bryan Richardson faced the classic dilemma. By selling Ndlovu and Babb he could erase the club's debts at a stroke, but that would stir up the ire of supporters, understandably sceptical after so many years of seeing their top players moving on.

Match of the Season 1993-94

Arsenal 0 Coventry 3

Premiership, 14 August 1993

The omens for the 1993-94 season were not good. Economic necessity meant the club disposing if its major assets, and City were likely to be put through their paces when the fixture computer asked them to visit Highbury for the league curtain-raiser.

> **DID YOU KNOW?**
>
> **In three of City's seasons in the top division they have picked up more league points away than at home – 1969-70, 1987-88, and 1996-97.**

Having won both the FA Cup and Coca-Cola Cup the previous season, George Graham's team planned to parade the two trophies around the stadium at the final whistle, having seen off what they presumably thought would be an ineffective challenge from Bobby Gould's innocents. That feeling of expectation appears to have filtered through Highbury's marble halls to the Arsenal players, who never really knuckled down to the task in hand until it was too late.

Arsenal seemed to ignore two important facts. First, Bobby Gould's teams, however weak or strong, do not lie down and die; second, defenders took their eyes off Mick Quinn at their peril. Gould had experimented in the pre-season with a defensive formation that did away with full-backs. The system had proved entertaining but seemed far too risky to unleash on Arsenal's formidable organisation. But Gould kept his nerve, and his novel formation worked a treat.

For the first half an hour everything seemed to be going to form. Arsenal had City by the throat. Paul Merson and Tony Adams might have scored and Ian Wright threatened to explode into action at any moment. Added to which, the Sky Blues lost Stewart Robson after ten minutes when his knee gave in. Then, somewhat fortuitously, City were awarded a penalty when Peter Ndlovu was sent tumbling by Lee Dixon, and Mick Quinn give the visitors the lead from the spot.

Arsenal tried to regroup but the Londoners had suddenly gone off the boil. Their passing, which had previously been so crisp, was now wayward, with the ball played to a blue shirt as often as a red. The Gunners' mounting self-doubts were exploited by two excellent City goals in the second half, both manufactured by Roy Wegerle. The first came when he harried Andy Linighan deep into his own half. Having won possession, Wegerle back-heeled the ball to the lurking Quinn, who drove it cleanly past Seaman. Three minutes later Wegerle set up the chunky striker for another well-struck shot. The goals made a little piece of history: Quinn became the first City player to score an FA Carling Premiership hat-trick.

But the icing on the cake was still to come. As the large home crowd drifted silently away, Highbury's public address system announced that the cup parade had been cancelled for reasons beyond the club's control!

FA CARLING PREMIERSHIP 1994-95

Premiership	16th
Coca-Cola Cup	3rd Round
FA Cup	4th Round

A season which started with great optimism, with the new East Stand officially opened, quickly sunk into one of mounting despair as City plummeted ten places in two months. But this was a season of paradox, for rarely can a campaign of struggle – with City avoiding relegation by just five points – have ended with supporters so buoyant about the future. The reason for the optimism was the ebullient personality of the Sky Blues' new manager, Ron Atkinson.

The arrival in February of the much-travelled managerial legend revived a season that looked as though it might end in the duck-pond of the Endsleigh League. The threat was, on paper, that much greater this season. The Premiership was pledged to reduce its numbers from 22 to twenty teams, and to accomplish that end an extra club would be relegated – four in all, which spelled danger to all those clubs used to dwelling at the wrong end of the table.

Phil Neal had passed muster under Gould, and 1993-94's strong finish had raised expectations. But as the injuries mounted and the critics became increasingly vocal, it was clear that tinkering with the side would not be enough to ward off relegation. Drastic surgery was needed. Big Ron arrived in a blaze of glory, bought some new players, enticed an extra 5,000 spectators through the turnstiles for his first home game and, intriguingly, acquired Leeds midfielder Gordon Strachan, initially as assistant manager, but soon, when his experience was needed, as a reluctant player.

But let us return to the close season. Neal's transfer activity was minimal. Peter Atherton took advantage of freedom of contract to join Sheffield Wednesday for an insultingly low fee of £800,000, which was set by a tribunal. Paul Cook, a classy midfielder with a sweet left foot, arrived from Wolves for £600,000. Manager and chairman had surveyed the players on show at World Cup '94 with interest, and for a while coveted USA's central defender Alexei Lalas. When the red-headed Lalas signed for Italian club Padova, City's bosses turned to his team-mate Cobi Jones, a winger with a taste for dreadlocks. Work permit problems meant Jones did not make his City debut until mid-September, though that coincided with City's first win.

Phil Babb went into the World Cup with only five Republic of Ireland caps, but returned with an enhanced reputation as one of the stars of the tournament. It was therefore no surprise that bigger clubs came calling. He finally bade farewell to Highfield Road, en route to Anfield, following the home match with Aston Villa. City benefited from the sale to the tune of £3.75 million, which was more than double what Newcastle had been prepared to pay six months previously. The fee constituted a British record for a defender and Neal was entrusted with a large slice of it to strengthen the side. The £2 million he paid for Manchester United's reserve striker Dion Dublin seemed excessive at the time, though not in retrospect. He quickly proved to be a revelation, scoring sixteen goals in 38 games in his first season. Young central defender Steven Pressley, for whom Neal paid £630,000 to Glasgow Rangers, was not such an unqualified success. He collected seven bookings and a sending off in his first eleven games, and looked short of Premiership mettle. Pressley was the fourth player City had bought from the Scottish giants in recent years, and the fourth dud.

The arrival of Dublin and Jones enabled City to get their second wind, so that when Liverpool came to Highfield Road in early December the Sky Blues lay tenth. It was not long, however, before Dublin picked up an injury that kept him out of the side for six matches. With David Busst also missing a run of games, City's lack of strength in depth was rudely exposed. None of those six games was won, and only one goal scored. City plumbed the depths at Hillsborough, where they were thrashed 1-5, picking up more injuries in the process. Neal dived into the transfer market to sign West Ham midfielder Mike Marsh for £500,000, but that did not prevent City being on the receiving end of a four-goal blast from Tottenham on New Year's Eve.

Dublin returned for the visit to his old club in early January, but the first six weeks of 1995 were generally depressing, with only an FA Cup replay victory at the Hawthorns to keep fans' spirits up. The worse the results, the worse the mood of supporters became, and Bryan Richardson felt the need to publicly urge the fans to get behind the manager. In these brittle circumstances the FA Cup Fourth Round tie with Norwich assumed an importance far beyond it face value. The Sky Blues failed to capitalise upon home advantage, and lost the replay at Carrow Road to two Norwich goals in extra-time.

By now, the knives were out for Phil Neal. In other circumstances goals by Dublin and Jones at Crystal Palace might have brought breathing space to the embattled manager when they earned City their first league win in twelve games. But, ominously, that win arrived on the same day that Atkinson agreed his pay-off from Aston Villa, following his autumn sacking from the club.

Events now moved swiftly. The following Tuesday Neal was sacked, pausing only to deliver a broadside at the local media and some of the fans. Injuries and bad luck had conspired to dethrone an honest man who, in retrospect, was probably a useful assistant manager, but who never seemed to have the measure of the Premiership's top managers. The next day Ron Atkinson was confirmed in the job. The very fact of his arrival sent a shiver of excitement through the most sceptical of fans. Big Ron was among the half dozen or so genuine heavyweight managers in the country, a man who had won things and wanted to win more. At a stroke, his arrival elevated small-time Coventry City to the league of major players in the Premiership.

His first task, therefore, was to make sure City stayed up. He had only fourteen matches left and wasted no time bringing in reinforcements. Kevin Richardson, his former on-field general at Villa Park, arrived for £300,000, and two weeks later Everton full-back David Burrows joined the club for a massive £1 million.

Big Ron made an instant impact. Not only were 5,000 extra fans lured along for City's first home match under his charge, against West Ham, but City delivered his first win. Six games into his reign they were still unbeaten, had earned a precious point at Villa and demolished Liverpool at Anfield. Perched in ninth position City looked free from all worries, and Atkinson, unprecedentedly, was named Premiership manager of the month after his first full month in the job.

Then, somehow, it all started to go wrong. City lost five games out of six, the last an embarrassing defeat at already relegated Ipswich. Strong action was called for, and several players were axed for the penultimate game at Tottenham, including the unfortunate Pressley and Jonathan Gould, who had been standing in for broken-leg victim Ogrizovic. Filan took Gould's place. Inspired by Strachan, who had been press-ganged into service some weeks earlier, City won to guarantee Big Ron another season in the big time.

The season therefore ended on a high note, with strong hints that ahead lay a summer of rebuilding, and that at least one star performer could be on his way to Highfield Road.

Match of the Season 1994-95

Tottenham 1 Coventry 3

Premiership, 9 May 1995

Many City fans had predicted the early demise of Phil Neal since the infamous TV 'Cutting Edge' documentary had revealed him to be little more than a parrot to England manager Graham Taylor. Ron Atkinson may be described as many things, but 'parrot' is not one of them. His arrival as Coventry City manager in March 1995 extended City's unbeaten run to nine games, which seemed to dispel all thoughts of relegation. But the unexpected collapse in form, and confidence, which culminated with an abject 0-2 defeat at relegated Ipswich, meant that City needed points from their final matches against Tottenham and/or Everton.

Big Ron blew a fuse after the Ipswich performance, dropping Gould and Pressley, and shunting Brian Borrows – veteran of many relegation battles – across to central defence.

And would you believe it? City pulled it off again, and in style. The stars of the show were the little men. Peter Ndlovu's running, a mixture of the dogged and the dazzling, had the home side at sixes and sevens for much of the first half, while Gordon Strachan's contribution was simply immense. The 39-year-old Scot had insisted, when joining the club six weeks previously, that he would play only in an emergency. Atkinson reportedly had to beg him to pull on his boots for the cause, and on this night he played a major part in all three goals.

The first, a far-post diving header from Peter Ndlovu, stemmed from Strachan's cross. The second, a Ndlovu penalty, came after Strachan had taken apart full-back Justin Edinburgh, thirteen years his junior, and been chopped down. The third, five minutes later, was the fruit of an exchange of passes with Julian Darby, leaving Strachan to cross for Dublin to hook home.

Darren Anderton's lob over John Filan was more menacing in theory than in fact, for Coventry's goal was seldom threatened thereafter. At the final whistle the players stripped off their shirts to throw to the crowd and Atkinson led the fans in the Sky Blue Song. Minutes after the emotional finale the phone rang in a hotel room in Singapore, where the local time was 5am, alerting Bryan Richardson to the wonderful result. City's chairman had spent a largely sleepless night, hoping for the best but fearing the worst, but he could now rest easy in the knowledge that his team were safe for another year, and that his investment would probably pay dividends in seasons to come.

Brian Kilcline blasts a penalty home against Chelsea (February 1987)

Greg Downs in a snowstorm v Sheffield Wednesday (March 1987)

Bennett wins an aerial duel against Leeds in the FA Cup semi-final (April 1987)

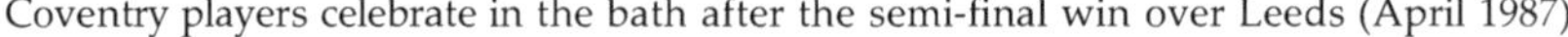
Coventry players celebrate in the bath after the semi-final win over Leeds (April 1987)

David Phillips scores the fourth goal in a 4-1 win over QPR (April 1987)

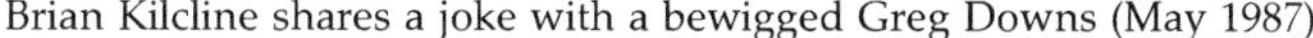

Brian Kilcline shares a joke with a bewigged Greg Downs (May 1987)

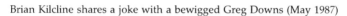

David Speedie scores one of a hat-trick of headers v Middlesbrough (October 1988)

Kevin Drinkell bustles his way through the Forest defence (September 1990)

Seven

Big Ron & Wee Gordon 1995-2001

FA CARLING PREMIERSHIP 1995-96

Premiership	16th
Coca-Cola Cup	4th Round
FA Cup	4th Round

A season which started with so much expectation, delivered mostly disappointment, and ended with City having to do the business on the final day of the season for the ninth time in 29 seasons. 1995-96 was not exactly a season to savour, but certainly one to remember.

In August, everything seemed right with the world. City had a manager more used to success than struggle, his assistant had been one of the Britain's finest players and Atkinson was being given serious money to spend by one of the most popular chairman in the club's history. What could go wrong?

The answer? Just about everything. The bullish talk this season had more substance than hitherto. City turned down offers totalling £10 million for Dublin and Ndlovu, signalling to the fans that the club had turned the corner and was now a buying, not a selling club. During the summer Atkinson had been liberally splashing the cash to bring in the calibre of player he wanted. At the time, few doubted his judgment. Having spent £1.5 million soon after his arrival, Ron bought a further six players – Brazilian midfielder Isaias from Benfica for £500,000, Portuguese youngster Carlita from Farense for £250,000, Luton midfielder Paul Telfer for £1.15 million, Crystal Palace winger John Salako for £1.5 million, Paul D Williams from Derby for £1 million, and Ghanaian prodigy Nii Lamptey from Anderlecht for £450,000. Out went Sean Flynn to Derby as part of the Williams deal, John Williams to Wycombe, Mike Marsh to Galatasaray of Turkey, Paul R Williams to Plymouth, and Steven

Pressley and Sandy Robertson to Dundee United. Ron's most audacious move – to try to sign Wolves striker Steve Bull – didn't come off. Despite the two clubs agreeing a fee, Bull decided to stay at Molineux and reap the rewards of a bumper testimonial.

The new signings seemed to offer a good blend of muscle and flair, but come May only Williams could be classified as a success. Carlita was never seen, Isaias shone brightly in the early weeks but faded after an injury, whilst Lamptey rarely got an opportunity to show his full potential. Salako and Telfer both held down regular places in the team, but after promising starts looked over-rated and struggled to meet expectations.

The season started well enough. City shrugged off an opening-day defeat at Newcastle to put Manchester City to the sword in the first home game. Creditable draws against Arsenal, Chelsea and Forest suggested relegation was not on the agenda this season. But City had a long habit of counting their chickens. A depressing autumn saw the team go fourteen league games without a win, City's worst sequence in the top flight. The only bright note was a 3-2 Coca-Cola Cup win over Spurs, the Sky Blues recovering from two goals down. Not only were the team losing matches, they were gathering red and yellow cards at an alarming rate. Five players were sent off in a nine-game spell, including Ogrizovic in a miserable Coca-Cola Cup defeat at Molineux.

Out came the chequebook again. Richard Shaw was signed from Crystal Palace for £1 million to bolster the suspect defence. He was quickly followed by Leeds starlet Noel Whelan, who cost a club record £2 million. Whelan made an instant impact with three goals in his first four games. The dreadful run was arrested at a snowbound Highfield Road with a 5-0 thumping of Blackburn. A prosperous Christmas saw City creep off the foot of the table.

The impetus given by Whelan's signing lasted well into the New Year, and relegation fears seemed to be receding until successive home draws were followed by a shocking home defeat at the hands of fellow strugglers Bolton. By this time, Big Ron had taken the spending to £13 million, with the addition of Eoin Jess, a £1.75 million signing from Aberdeen, and Liam Daish, yet another central defender, bought for £1.5 million from Birmingham to shore up the persistently leaking defence.

The week before Easter it looked all over for the Sky Blues, who had a testing run-in. They were in nineteenth place with only one win in twelve, and confidence had drained away. Defeats at the Dell, where Atkinson had an on-camera bust up with Sky TV pundit Andy Gray, who questioned the players' commitment, and at Spurs, where City threw away a lead, pushed them to the brink.

DID YOU KNOW?

In 34 seasons of top division league football, Coventry had 51 players sent off (24 in Premiership games). Only 40 opponents were dismissed (16 in the Premiership).

Those last weeks of 1995-96 were crammed with incident. Title-chasing Liverpool were beaten by another Whelan goal. Two days later City fell to the eventual champions, at Old Trafford, in a game marred by a tragic accident which left David Busst's leg and career shattered. A home win over rival strugglers QPR and a plucky draw at Forest eased the fingers from around City's throat, but the key result was a win at Wimbledon, inspired by Peter Ndlovu, which left Big Ron shaking like a jelly at the post-match press-conference. Now all that was needed was to beat Leeds at home on the final day. In the event a goal-less draw was enough, though the occasion was marred by mindless Leeds hooligans posing as fans. City survived on goal-difference, though the circumstances of that final day would merit a chapter on their own. Rivals Manchester City came back from two goals down at home to Liverpool, and at 2-2 there was general uncertainty among their players whether or not they had done enough to finish above Coventry or Southampton. They took their foot off the gas, which was just as well for the Sky Blues. Had both Manchester City and the Saints scored late winners, Coventry would have gone down.

It would have been ironic had City been relegated. Under the astute chairmanship of Bryan Richardson the club had shown more ambition than for many years. The vast sums put at the disposal of the manager to buy players was funded in part by the novel 'buy a player' scheme. This involved club benefactors funding the purchase of new players in return for a slice of any future transfer fee. In addition to the new players, investment in ground improvements had begun to convince the Coventry public that the club meant business. Gates were up almost forty per cent in two years.

Match of the Season 1995-96

Wimbledon 0 Coventry 2

Premiership, 27 April 1996

Wimbledon had had a strange season. In August the pundits tipped them more strongly than usual for relegation. Three wins in the first five games had quietened the sceptics, but a horrendous run of fourteen winless games saw the Dons plummet from third in the table to eighteenth at Christmas. Like City, their season was reduced to one of simple survival. Unlike City, Wimbledon came good with a late run of thirteen points from five games that seemed to have banished the shadow of relegation from Selhurst Park. What might have been a classic six-pointer was now a match that meant less to the Dons than to the Sky Blues, and that could make all the difference. With Bolton and QPR already down, the third relegation place seemed to lie between Coventry, Southampton and Manchester City.

Contrary to popular perception, Wimbledon have finished in the top half of the league more often than the bottom, and only rarely been sucked into a relegation dog-fight. The main cause of their poor season had been a succession of injuries to key players. The Crazy Gang tag lived on in spirit rather than fact, though the Dons were still formidable at set pieces.

As for City, their dreadful disciplinary record had caught up with them. Both Liam Daish and Brian Borrows were suspended. David Busst, David Rennie, Kevin Richardson and Paul Williams were all injured, and Atkinson was left with little choice but to 'pick and mix' to send out a defence. In the end he took the huge gamble of fielding three central defenders, Richard Shaw (who played with a face-mask), David Burrows (who hadn't kicked a ball for a month) and Dion Dublin (normally a centre-forward). Dublin's goalscoring touch had deserted him in recent months and some fans were asking questions about his commitment. Hence the gamble in playing him at the back.

Dublin looked a natural centre-back, Jess controlled the midfield, and Ndlovu tormented the Wimbledon defence mercilessly. The Zimbabwean squandered the best two chances in an even first half, putting one shamelessly over and the other against a post with keeper Sullivan transfixed.

Six minutes into the second half, Ndlovu was at the near post to connect with Pickering's cross and the ball flew past Sullivan. Wimbledon might have quickly levelled, but Andy Clarke fired over following Dublin's only mistake. A minute from time, with the Dons committed to attack, Ndlovu raced onto Jess's clever pass and put the result beyond doubt. Some of City's 7,000 travelling fans, who had roared on their heroes from the start, briefly invaded the pitch, saving their major invasion for the final whistle.

Results elsewhere did not go Coventry's way, for both Southampton and Manchester City also won, the latter at Villa Park. That meant all three clubs would go into the final game on 37 points, with the Sky Blues enjoying the superior goal-difference. All three teams drew on the final day, leaving Alan Ball's Manchester City, like the unlucky child in musical chairs, as the odd one out.

FA CARLING PREMIERSHIP 1996-97

Premiership	17th
Coca-Cola Cup	3rd Round
FA Cup	5th Round

Another year, another manager, another struggle. Having survived yet another close shave, the Sky Blues management were adamant that there would be no repeat. During the summer they pulled off the biggest signing in the club's history, not only for the size of the fee, but for the profile of the man. Gary McAllister, captain of Leeds and Scotland, would not have joined Coventry City were it not for the persuasive skills of Ron Atkinson and Gordon Strachan, and the fans greeted his arrival rapturously. Here, they thought, was the sort of playmaker the team had yearned for during their barren years. Sadly, McAllister did not live up to the hype.

McAllister's arrival for £3 million was not the only signing. Belgian international full-back Regis Genaux arrived from Standard Liege for £1 million, and Northern Ireland international winger Michael O'Neill signed from Hibernian for £500,000. Genaux was injured early on and stayed only a few months before moving to Udinese of Italy, muttering over his shoulder about Scottish bias. As for O'Neill, he was subbed after 45 minutes of his debut and never made the first team again this season. Several players signed by Gould and Neal also slipped away. Ally Pickering went to Stoke for £200,000, David Rennie to Northampton on a free, and Steve Morgan to Wigan, also on a free.

The signs were ominous in the pre-season, Benfica thrashing City 7-2 in a home friendly. A week later Forest won 3-0 at Highfield Road in the league, with a hat-trick from Kevin Campbell, a rare victory in a miserable season for Frank Clark's team. City's draw at West Ham was followed by a farcical game at Stamford Bridge when Petrescu's blatant handball was missed by the officials and Chelsea scored. Liam Daish was sent off in the ferocious aftermath and Strachan and Atkinson hit the roof. Their heat-of-the-moment words later cost them hefty fines for bringing the game into disrepute.

Ron Atkinson had boldly declared the previous season that if only City could stay up they would go places in 1996-97. But when November arrived with the Sky Blues having only one win under their belts, the only place they were going was 'down'. One sensed that Big Ron had tried all he knew, and that he had run out ideas and steam. Before crisis turned to tragedy, and following a draw at

Everton, he stepped 'upstairs' to take up a new role as Director of Football, a job which involved much scouting away from Highfield Road, leaving the 'hands on' work to his successor, Strachan. Atkinson was angered that a director at the club leaked the story to the press, but at least he had the good sense to know when it was time to step aside. Big Ron's overall record at City, having spent close on £17 million on new players, showed just fourteen wins from 64 games, and readers can draw their own conclusions.

There was never any doubt over who would succeed Big Ron, even though Gordon Strachan seemed rather taken aback by the speed of events. The timing seemed, at least, hardly ideal. City had netted just five league goals in twelve games, they were nineteenth in the table, and their only win had come against Leeds, City recovering from a first-minute deficit, thanks to Noel Whelan's first goal of the season, ironically against his old club. Dublin, who had forfeited the captaincy to McAllister, was having such a wretched time that he had been relegated to the subs' bench, a move that at last sparked him into life.

Strachan's first match in charge was a home replay with Gillingham in the Coca-Cola Cup, which was lost to a goal from Neil Smith. Strachan's response was typically forthright: 'if players listen and play to the standards I require then they should be all right. If not there will have to be changes. It's up to the players!' Believe it or not, rumours were rife of sloppy training sessions and general indiscipline under Atkinson, but somehow one could not imagine that state of affairs continuing under the fiery Scot who, after all, had been schooled at Aberdeen by the ultra-strict Alex Ferguson.

The players responded with a fighting comeback to draw at Wimbledon, only to lose their next three games. At this point Strachan appointed fellow Scot Alex Miller – Scottish manager Craig Brown's number two – as his assistant. Kevin Richardson had been the first to feel Strachan's axe, but the veteran midfielder was recalled to face Newcastle. Darren Huckerby, a victim of Kevin Keegan's strange decision to dispense with Newcastle's reserve team, had by this time signed for a £1 million fee, and the circumstance of facing his former club was tailor-made for him. City started the game in bottom place, but Huckerby netted after six minutes of a memorable match which saw Strachan earn his first win. Richardson looked superb in the anchor role and with Dublin playing in defence City won their next three games, earning Strachan the manager of the month award. The highlight was a 3-1 Boxing Day win at Leeds, which was marred only by Whelan's silly dismissal. In the 3-0 win over Middlesbrough, Oggy broke George Curtis's club appearance record by playing his 544th first-team game.

Now up to twelfth, City's visit to Blackburn, themselves struggling, should have held no fears. Strachan restored Dublin to his attacking slot after his sending off against Sunderland, but Dion suffered the ignominy of another red card for a dreadful challenge on Henning Berg. It meant Dublin would miss seven matches.

City prospered in the FA Cup without him, though they needed a replay to overcome plucky Woking, but won only one of the four league games that Dublin missed. With Daish suffering an injury in training, the need to strengthen central defence was imperative, and Strachan splashed out £2.5 million for Birmingham's Gary Breen and £800,000 for Ukrainian Alex Evtushok.

An impressive win at Ewood Park set up an FA Cup Fifth Round tie at Derby. Two early goals seemed to have secured a quarter-final place, only for the Rams to hit back and snatch a late winner. At least City were now free to focus on their relegation battle but, as with the previous season, they hit rock bottom in February and March. Eight games without a win left City with a mountain to climb. When rivals West Ham grabbed all three points at Highfield Road, bottom-of-the-table City faced a trip to Liverpool, who were hoping to go top.

That match at Anfield was painfully one-sided. City were overwhelmed but somehow won, courtesy of keeper David James' phobia of crosses. Whelan netted from McAllister's corner-kick, and Dublin repeated the medicine in injury-time.

For the third season running the officially-retired Strachan donned his boots, helping City to a stirring three points against FA Cup semi-finalists Chelsea. Draws against Southampton and Arsenal lifted City to fifteenth, at which point a win over Derby in the final home game would secure City's safety. But they blew it, and with all their relegation rivals winning it left them below the safety line, needing not only to win their last match but praying that *both* Middlesbrough and Sunderland tripped up. It was dubbed Super Sunday, and it was. City were closer to the precipice than ever before, carrying their fate to the last match for the tenth time in thirty years in the top flight.

Match of the Season 1996-97

Tottenham 1 Coventry 2

Premiership, 11 May 1997

Perhaps, as the years pass and this match recedes into the murky mists of time, it will be seen as just another typical end of season fixture. No matter that, at the time, it felt like the win of all wins.

DID YOU KNOW?

Until World Cup '98, when Viorel Moldovan did so for Romania, the last City player to score against England was Northern Ireland's Hugh Barr in 1962.

All but the insanely optimistic had written off City's chances a week earlier, when everything that could go wrong against Derby did go wrong. Logically, City were down, and as the fans trudged home after that awful Derby defeat they knew in their hearts that relegation was unavoidable. The great dream had ended.

For a professional like Gordon Strachan, his pressing need was to distract his players' minds from their plight and ensure that the team won. Only then should they listen out for results elsewhere.

The tension of the occasion was magnified by echoes of the past. Kick-off for the last day of the Premiership was 4 pm on Sunday, but traffic problems on the M1, which appeared to be clogged with Coventry supporters, necessitated a delay at White Hart Lane of fifteen minutes. This flouted the whole purpose of having crucial matches kick off simultaneously. The delay would not raise an eyebrow if City lost, but might if they won and survived.

It was clear from the opening exchanges that City were, in the vernacular, 'up for it'. Tackles flew in thick and fast, Burrows was booked inside two minutes, and Whelan – frankly – was lucky to stay on the field. But after thirteen minutes McAllister's cross found Dublin's head and the ball looped over Baardsen in the Spurs goal. On 39 minutes an apparently poor corner from McAllister was volleyed by Williams past Baardsen from twenty yards. Just before half-time Sheringham's free-kick came back off the crossbar but fell kindly for Paul McVeigh, following up, to pull one back for Spurs.

The second half was unbearably tense, the seconds seeming like minutes, 4,500 fraught City fans keeping their eyes on their watches as much as the pitch. Those with radios pressed to their ears kept up a constant commentary on affairs elsewhere. With a quarter of an hour to play, the other results staggered in. Middlesbrough had only drawn at Leeds; they were down. After a seemingly interminable wait, it was announced that Sunderland had lost at Wimbledon. Now all City had to do was to hold on to their 2-1 advantage.

Inevitably, City funneled back to protect their lead. Neale Fenn's header for Spurs looked goal-bound, but Ogrizovic was equal to it. Was there ever a longer fifteen minutes in the history of Coventry City? When the final whistle blew on the Sky Blues' 'Great Escape', there were tears amid the explosion of relief.

FA CARLING PREMIERSHIP 1997-98

Premiership	11th
Coca-Cola Cup	4th Round
FA Cup	Quarter-finals

It is not often that Coventry City fans can have ended a season feeling warm and satisfied, but that was the case after 1997-98. To finish eleventh in the Premiership – one year after the club had pulled back from the brink – and reach the FA Cup quarter-finals was more than most fans dared hope for.

City's success was fitting tribute to the managerial and coaching skills of Gordon Strachan, in his first full season of football management. With a little luck City might have sneaked into Europe, and Wembley was tantalisingly within reach at 9.45 pm on 17 March at Bramall Lane.

This season, moreover, Strachan was on his own. Atkinson's contract expired in June and he slipped quietly away, appearing regularly as a TV match summariser, before being recruited in November to manage Sheffield Wednesday.

Strachan's summer transfer targets were a mix of Scandinavians and lower division strikers. Trond-Egil Soltvedt, a midfielder, cost £500,000 from Rosenborg Trondheim, for whom he had scored against AC Milan and Juventus in the Champions League. Swedish goalkeeper Magnus Hedman cost £600,000 from AIK Stockholm and was expected to press hard for Oggy's place. Danish midfielder Martin Johansen arrived on a free transfer from FC Copenhagen, but alone of these he failed to win a place and left the following summer. City's buy of the season was Swedish international right-back Roland Nilsson, a snip at £200,000, who looked the part from day one, lending composure and style to the defence.

Kyle Lightbourne and Simon Haworth cost £500,000 apiece from Walsall and Cardiff respectively. Lightbourne failed to make an impact in several substitute appearances and left in the spring to join Stoke. Haworth was capped by Wales but his first-team opportunities at City were few and far between.

Leaving the club before the season started were Eoin Jess, who returned to Aberdeen for a cut-price £650,000, Oggy's understudy, the Australian John Filan, who joined Blackburn for £700,000 but broke an arm early on after wresting the goalkeeper's jersey from Tim Flowers, and Peter Ndlovu, the enigmatic Zimbabwean, who signed for Birmingham. The fee initially was £1.75 million, but a stringent medical raised complications, as a result of which the fee was slashed to £200,000, plus so much per game, which by the end of the season brought the total up close to the original fee. Shortly after the season started Kevin Richardson, feeling his years, joined Southampton for £200,000. His contribution to two seasons of war against relegation was largely undervalued, and a week before his departure he was the man of the match against West Ham.

The season started explosively with a Dion Dublin hat-trick to sink Chelsea after City had twice fallen behind. But – a 1-0 home win over Southampton apart – this was City's only league win until early November, by which time all the old ghosts were coming back to haunt the fans. What was different this time was that City were conspicuously better than in previous seasons. Of seven draws in the first twelve matches, City had chances to win them all, and had acquired a self-destructive habit of letting opponents off the hook.

The main problem was a lack of goals. Huckerby was not fully fit and Dublin's brain wasn't connecting with his boots. A one-sided Coca-Cola Cup defeat of lowly Everton, following on the heels of a first away league win, at Wimbledon, appeared to herald better things, but did not.

Following the departure of assistant manager Alex Miller, who took charge at Aberdeen, City suffered defeat in three successive midlands derbies, as a consequence of which they slid down to sixteenth. But several factors combined to suddenly turn the season into one of relative success. December alone witnessed five key changes. First, Gary McAllister suffered a bad injury in the Leicester home defeat and exacerbated it in the game against Tottenham. Second, City's £250,000 signing from Feyenoord, George Boateng, provided welcome bite to the midfield. Third, Romanian striker Viorel Moldovan arrived from Grasshoppers of Zurich for a record £3.25 million and many fans felt that his coming lit the fuse under the other strikers. Fourth, a couple of below-par performances from Ogrizovic opened the door for Hedman in goal. Finally, Noel Whelan made his long awaited return after serious injury.

It is difficult to know which of these was the most significant and which was the least, but the outcome was that champions Manchester United got stung in a classic Christmas match. That sparked a welcome unbeaten run which – other than a blip at Chelsea – extended all the way to Easter. City set a club record of seven straight wins in league and cup, part of a longer run of fourteen games without defeat.

The threat of Dublin and Huckerby sent shivers through opposing defences. Huckerby had won BBC's Match of the Day 'goal of the month' in December, for his sublime winner against Manchester United, and the following month his goal at Anfield was runner up in the same award. As for Dublin, his six January goals made him Carling's player of the month, although Huckerby's virtuoso FA Cup demolition of Liverpool might have pointed the judges his way. An objective measure of Dublin's form can be seen from the fact that he was called up by England that month, having never previously been in the frame for international honours. It was the fact that Dublin appeared equally comfortable at centre-forward or centre-half that attracted the admiration of Glenn Hoddle, who was on the lookout for adaptable players.

February was even better than January. City won five matches on the trot, including the momentous victory at Villa Park in the FA Cup. Not surprisingly, City's manager got his just desserts, Gordon Strachan winning the manager of the month award.

With old scores settled against Villa, Cup fever gripped the city of Coventry, with fans clamouring for tickets for the quarter-final home tie with Division 1 Sheffield United. The rudderless Yorkshire side had lost their manager, Nigel Spackman, just days before the tie but held out for a draw, thereby bringing to an unwelcome end City's seven-match winning run. But the Sky Blues were still overwhelming favourites for the replay, the more so when Paul Telfer gave them an early lead. City spurned chances to add a second goal, and were made to pay through Holdsworth's late, late equaliser. The team staggered through extra-time, only to lose a nerve-racking penalty shoot-out that swung first one way then the other. Even the reliable Dublin – with five penalty goals since Christmas – lost his nerve.

That was the worst moment of City's otherwise laudable season. They kept their good league run going, and only Villa lowered their colours in the remaining nine games, but the slim hopes of Europe were stymied by returning to an epidemic of draws – no fewer than six of those nine games ended all square. On the final day, with eleventh place assured, City enjoyed the quaint luxury of participating in a relegation battle involving somebody else. That trip to Goodison was not entirely meaningless for supporters of Coventry City, for Everton were one of only three clubs to have enjoyed a longer unbroken run in the top division than the Sky Blues. Beating them would reduce that list to just two, Arsenal and Liverpool.

It was not to be. Everton drew and survived on goal-difference. Their supporters responded to the final whistle with an outpouring of emotion that City fans, looking on in detached amusement, knew only too well from the past. Dublin's late equaliser, incidentally, gave him a share of the Premiership's Golden Boot, along with Michael Owen and Chris Sutton. Too bad Dublin was omitted from England's final 22 selected for France '98.

Match of the Season 1997-98

Aston Villa 0 Coventry 1

FA Cup, fifth round, 14 February 1998

Never in 26 matches at Villa Park, spanning 62 years of soccer combat, had City ever beaten the hosts. But Valentine's Day 1998 will be treasured by Sky Blues fans everywhere as the day they finally broke the hoodoo. The man accredited with the goal, Romanian Viorel Moldovan, had probably never heard of Coventry City six months previously, but in one of his rare appearances he popped up to score a priceless goal eighteen minutes from time.

Dion Dublin's first full cap, against Chile, coupled with an England 'B' cap for Darren Huckerby, meant that City's two brightest jewels were still on cloud nine. Strachan, though, had injuries and suspensions to contend with. Telfer and Whelan were in the sin-bin, and therefore ineligible, and hopes that Gary McAllister might return after two months out injured proved wildly optimistic. There was better news regarding George Boateng, who was passed fit after taking a knock in the previous game, with Sheffield Wednesday. He switched to right midfield, enabling Strachan to field his son, Gavin, making his full debut after five substitute appearances. Marcus Hall filled Whelan's left midfield position.

Villa had selection problems of their own. Ian Taylor was suspended, Dwight Yorke was missing through a calf injury, Milosevic was on strike, and Stan Collymore, though he played, might as well not have done.

Huckerby created the best chance of the first half, but City's Norwegian, Soltvedt – who had earlier come close with a bicycle kick – pulled his shot just wide of the far post.

Ten minutes into the second half Strachan withdrew the limping Shaw, pulled back Dublin into defence, and brought on Moldovan. Seventeen minutes later the tie was won. The Romanian had been champing at the bit to get a game and prove his mettle. He had promised to score goals, and now he proved he was a man of his word. Strachan junior found Boateng, who skipped past Wright, Southgate and Ehiogu in a mazy run. His left-foot shot was pushed out by Bosnich, but Moldovan stroked the loose ball into the net from four yards. After the match, City's Transylvanian hero admitted he could hardly believe the reaction to his goal, which among other things cost Villa manager Brian Little his job. Moldovan's memory will always be sacred among City fans for that goal alone. His other claim to fame is that his two goals for Romania in France '98 were the first scored by a City player in any World Cup finals.

FA CARLING PREMIERSHIP 1998-99

Premiership	15th
Worthington Cup	3rd Round
FA Cup	5th Round

After the comparative success of the previous season, 1998-99 was a major let-down. It started well enough with a thrilling win over the overseas all-stars of Chelsea, but four defeats in the next five games dumped them into the relegation zone. The rest of the season was spent trying to keep heads above water. Cup expectations were high but woeful displays at Luton and Everton dashed them. In all, 31 players were called upon by Gordon Strachan as the transfer merry-go-round continued.

An already sizable squad was enhanced by four new signings. Two were spotted by City's 'Euro-Scout' Ray Clarke. French central defender Jean-Guy Wallemme, 29, arrived from Lens for £700,000, and Belgium's 'Player of World Cup 98', Philippe Clement, a strong tackling midfielder, cost £625,000 from Genk. Jamaican international striker Paul Hall arrived from Portsmouth for £300,000, while Ian Brightwell came on a free transfer from Manchester City. None of the four could be called a success. Wallemme made only six starts before, in December, his son's schooling forced him back to France. He signed for Sochaux for £500,000. Clement's injury problems restricted him to eight starts and he signed for FC Bruges in the summer of 1999. Hall, given few chances, failed to make the grade and would later join Walsall, along with Brightwell, whose only appearance was in the Worthington Cup defeat at Luton.

The only significant summer departure was Viorel Moldovan, whose value had risen after scoring for Romania against England in the World Cup. He joined Fenerbahce of Turkey for £4 million, netting City a £750,000 profit in five months.

The most bizarre close season event was the Robert Jarni saga, which saw the wing-back sign for City for £2.6 million. Within days Real Madrid, desperate to sign one of Croatia's World Cup heroes, paid City £3.35 million for a player who never played in a City shirt.

The fans, meanwhile, were captivated by Dion Dublin's 'would he stay or would he go' contract talks. The club captain, unluckily omitted from Glen Hoddle's World Cup squad, boasted the Golden Boot as the Premiership's leading marksman. With only a year left on his contract and City fearing a walkout on a Bosman transfer, they agreed a £1 million per annum deal. But in October Dublin began attracting interest from struggling Blackburn. His advisers had inserted a clause that allowed him to talk to any club who offered a fee of £5 million.

With Dublin's form patchy in any case, City accepted Blackburn's bid of £6.75 million, seen by many to be excessive for a 30-year-old striker. But, once the clause became public, other clubs joined the hunt. Dublin snubbed Blackburn and after a week of impasse and legal threats he was given permission to talk to Aston Villa, who paid £5.75 million to get their man. The scars inflicted by the episode would sour relations between the two clubs for years.

On the pitch, lack of goals was the main problem, and in late September Strachan signed the man he thought could provide the service to hot-shots Dublin and Huckerby – Stephen Froggatt from Wolves for £1.9 million. Froggatt played only three games with the big striker before Dublin's move to Villa but he enjoyed a promising season with his positive wing play and teasing crosses.

The defence looked solid, with only Newcastle scoring more than two goals against City. Newcastle won 5-1 in a freak result at Highfield Road and 4-1 at St James', a traditional graveyard for the Sky Blues. Although City had a capable right-back in Nilsson, they purchased another in Marc Edworthy from relegated Crystal Palace. He cost £850,000 and filled in at left-back for the long-term injury victim Marcus Hall and the injury-plagued Burrows.

In the Worthington Cup, City made heavy weather of Southend at home but sunk the Shrimpers without trace in the second leg. A trip to Second Division Luton in the next round always looked ominous. Dublin, his transfer in the offing, refused to play. The rest of the team seemed numbed by his impending departure and gave up the ghost. Irate City fans booed the team off at the end, with McAllister, fresh from his long injury lay-off, receiving more than his share of abuse.

Strachan, the subject of speculation linking him with the vacant Leeds and Blackburn manager's jobs, steadied the ship. With City weighing the merits of signing Scandinavian strikers Andreas Lund and Rune Lange, Whelan and Huckerby did their best to convince the manager that they were the solution to Dublin's departure. Fine wins over lowly Blackburn and Everton eased the pressure, but the team earned just three points from the next seven games and did not win again until a new striker, John Aloisi, a bargain £650,000 from penurious Portsmouth, got his chance at Christmas.

January's form lifted everyone's spirits. Aloisi, even though he was often on the bench, spurred the whole team into action. It was the Moldovan effect all over again. In a turnaround not dissimilar to the previous campaign, following the Romanian's arrival, the side simply clicked. McAllister and Boateng, previously unimpressive in midfield, looked world-beaters. McAllister had been the target of City's boo-boys at West Ham at Christmas and he responded with a superb spell where he was at the heart of all City's moves. Seven goals were fired past Macclesfield in the FA Cup and four more past Forest a week later. Huckerby hit two successive hat-tricks, and he scored again at Chelsea where the Sky Blues lost in stoppage time. That game was marred by a touchline fracas involving up to twenty coaches and officials of the two clubs, as a result of which Strachan was banished to the stands and fined £1,000.

A 3-0 FA Cup win at Leicester was followed a week later by a grinding home win over Liverpool, and 8,000 City fans travelled to Goodison Park for the FA Cup fifth-round tie with hopes high. Whatever happened before kick-off is subject to rumour, but on the pitch the defence played like strangers. A feeble Everton side went through at City's expense.

Another foreign defender, Mohammed Konjic, a Bosnian, cost £2 million from Monaco in January and got a chance in the aftermath of Goodison. Like Wallemme in the home game with Newcastle, he was unable to cope with Alan Shearer at his peak and although the Bosnian got a couple of other outings he looked ill-equipped for the Premiership.

A run of six games with only one defeat effectively banished the relegation fears. The run included the club's first ever League win at Aston Villa, a thumping 4-1 victory that gave City and their fans even more pleasure in the light of the Dublin transfer wranglings. The crucial result, however, came the following week, at home to struggling Charlton. A goal and a man down, after Aloisi had been sent off, Strachan brought on Norwegian substitute Soltvedt, who hit the winner with five minutes remaining.

Strachan set a points target at 40 to avoid the drop, but the team dragged out the agony. With six games left they only needed three points to reach that target, but proceeded to lose three games in a row, at Everton and Leicester, and at home to Middlesbrough, who took advantage of an injured Hedman to score twice from 25 yards. The Swede appeared to want to come off before half-time but Strachan insisted that the keeper had wanted to stay on.

A home win over Wimbledon, which saw Huckerby score his first goal in fourteen games, brought the 40th point, although in the event the final margin of safety was six points. An emotional final game saw visitors Leeds play their part in a four-goal thriller, with City denied by a stoppage-time goal by David Hopkin. Roland Nilsson, who had fractured two ribs and suffered a punctured lung at Arsenal in March, returned for his final game before retiring from English football, and earned a tumultuous ovation from the fans.

DID YOU KNOW?

The 7-0 FA Cup win over Macclesfield in January 1999 equalled City's biggest ever win in the competition, set in 1934 versus Scunthorpe United.

The season ended with chairman Bryan Richardson spelling out that players who were not dedicated to the Sky Blues cause could leave. Speculation had linked Huckerby, Whelan and Breen to possible moves, whilst Boateng had been the subject of rumours linking him to Aston Villa ever since his outstanding performance at Villa Park in February. Bad blood had existed between the two West Midlands rivals since the Dublin transfer, and this had been aggravated in March when Richardson accused Villa of having made an illegal approach to Boateng. The Dutch player's form, which had been inconsistent all season, took another dip after this and the fans accepted that he would be on his way out of Highfield Road during the close season.

On a brighter note plans for a new stadium and retail complex at Foleshill were given approval by all the necessary parties, including the Government, and was expected to be ready for August 2001 at a cost of £135 million.

Match of the Season 1998-99

Aston Villa 1 Coventry 4

Premiership, 27 February 1999

'Dion, Dion, what's the score?' sang the Sky Blues fans at Villa Park as their former hero's new club were put to the sword to end 63 years of hurt. Although City had won at the ground in the FA Cup just last season, they had failed in 24 League visits stretching back to 1936.

It was a thoroughly deserved result against their local rivals who had been up in the title race at Christmas. For their chairman, Doug Ellis, and manager, John Gregory, the men who had so angered the Highfield Road hierarchy over their handling of the Dion Dublin transfer in November, it was just desserts.

City had striker Noel Whelan missing with a damaged collar bone, which left John Aloisi to deputise in only his third start since signing in December. Otherwise the Sky Blues were at full strength. For their part, Villa were without injured goalkeeper Mark Bosnich, the man who had broken City fans' hearts before with his agile skills, but Michael Oakes was a more than adequate deputy for a player who would later end up at Old Trafford.

The Sky Blues were fired up from the start and roared on by their large and vociferous following they dominated the early play. Midway through the first half Aloisi put City ahead, controlling Froggatt's cross before turning past Scimeca and hitting a left-foot shot past Oakes. The only other chance of a Coventry-dominated first period was a penalty claim after the pacy Huckerby – causing endless problems for Villa's rearguard – was wrestled to the ground by Scimeca. Referee Uriah Rennie waved play on.

Huckerby did, however, set up the second goal, five minutes into the second half. He beat Southgate for speed and fed an early ball to the near post, where Boateng lifted it over Scimeca and Oakes in the tightest of space, high into the roof of the net.

Four minutes later Villa hit back when Richard Shaw shoved Joachim in the box. Though Magnus Hedman had anticipated Dublin taking any penalties awarded, he failed to anticipate his former team-mate's shot, which flew high and hard into the net at the Holte End. The goal shook Villa into action and for ten minutes the pressure was firmly on the visitors. Hedman pulled off a fine save from Dublin, Villa's best player, and substitute Stan Collymore hit the post with the rebound. But with McAllister pulling the strings, Telfer winning the ball in midfield, and Huckerby running like a bat out of hell, Coventry steadied the ship.

With eighteen minutes left, City restored their two-goal cushion. Former Villa-man Froggatt crossed for Aloisi to volley home at the far post. That goal signalled a mass exodus of home fans, certain in the knowledge that any lingering title hopes were now gone, and it was left to Boateng to wrap up the victory with a fourth goal seven minutes from time. McAllister's through ball sprang Villa's offside trap and the Dutchman's cheeky lob sailed over Oakes into the net in front of City's travelling support. Sheer heaven.

Another little bit of history was made in the last minute when substitute Gary McSheffrey, at sixteen years 198 days the club's youngest ever player, entered the action but failed to touch the ball!

FA CARLING PREMIERSHIP 1999-2000

Premiership	14th
Worthington Cup	5th Round
FA Cup	2nd Round

In 1999-2000, the team's fine home form gained them the tag as the Premiership's 'Entertainers'. Twelve wins and 38 goals made it the best home season since the late 1970s. But the price was an awful away record, City failing to win a league game away for the first time in their history. The cups saw a thrashing at Tranmere and a two-goal home lead squandered against Charlton in the FA Cup.

The summer transfer saga brought in midfielder Youssef Chippo from Porto for £1 million, Moustapha Hadji, a star of the 1998 World Cup from Deportivo La Corunna for a club record £4 million, and a young Norwegian winger, Runnar Normann for £1 million. Following another media war of words, City and Aston Villa finally agreed a fee of £4.5 million for George Boateng.

Lack of goals was still perceived to be the problem. After a one-goal defeat on the opening day to Southampton Darren Huckerby was sold to Leeds for £5.5 million and Trond Soltvedt offloaded to Southampton for £300,000 to help raise £6 million to sign Wolves' Irish international striker Robbie Keane. It was a major gamble. Other top clubs had looked hard at the 19-year-old and decided not to take the risk, but on his Premiership debut against Derby the most expensive teenager in history scored two trademark poacher's goals to clinch City's first win. Another goal at Sunderland a week later meant Keane was the new Coventry hero and Carling's player of the month.

The next issue to be sorted was in midfield, where the combative Chippo, whilst skilful and with an eye for goal, was not giving McAllister the sort of protection offered by Boateng. The need for midfield steel was highlighted by a 3-4 home defeat by Leeds. The solution was to buy the old warhorse Carlton Palmer, a former colleague of Strachan's at Leeds, but a player who, according to Ron Atkinson, Strachan would find difficult to handle.

Palmer arrived from Nottingham Forest on loan, but signed for £500,000 after City went unbeaten for his first eight games. Home wins over West Ham, Newcastle, Watford and Aston Villa saw the team climb to eleventh. Keane and Hadji were on song, but when injuries to Noel Whelan and John Aloisi caused Strachan to seek a loan striker, his Euro-scout Ray Clarke came up with 21-year-old Belgian Cedric Roussel. Roussel shredded the Watford defence on his first start and in his second he scored a good goal against Villa. His partnership with Keane was a major factor in City's dominant home form, with his aerial prowess providing chances for the nippy young Irishman. In January Roussel rejected other Premiership clubs to sign permanently, the fee £1.2 million.

Another problem area was at full-back. Injuries and two red cards had hampered David Burrows, and Marcus Hall's comeback from injury had been abortive. Marc Edworthy had replaced Nilsson but was injured in October. All this meant that wingers Paul Telfer and Steven Froggatt had to play out of position, which appeared to work at home but not away. Swedish international right-back Tomas Gustafsson was signed from AIK Solna for £250,000 as cover.

In central defence Paul Williams and Richard Shaw started as first choices before Gary Breen took over from Shaw when he was injured. The Bosnian Konjic played just four games before injury struck him again. Williams' contract expired at the end of the season and for many months he looked set to move on a 'Bosman', with Wolves rumoured to be the destination. In March Strachan signed veteran Scottish international Colin Hendry from Rangers, but Hendry looked rusty and after nine unspectacular games he took a serious facial knock which ended his season.

Apart from a blip against Leicester, the impressive home form continued into 2000, bringing wins over Arsenal and Wimbledon and an exciting draw with Chelsea. January saw the loss of the two Moroccans on international duty at the African Nations Cup for the best part of the month, and they were missed. The FA Cup home defeat by First Division Charlton might have been avoided had they been available. That result was a watershed and hopes of European qualification were dashed by the away form, which collapsed in its wake. The last nine away games were lost, including a 0-5 drubbing at West Ham and a last-day defeat at relegated Watford. Only three goals were scored in this run, two of them by Roussel at Old Trafford. Fans became fed up with the regular chiding of players by Strachan in Monday's press.

Home performances kept the home fans happy though, and the first half against Sunderland was one of the finest in the modern era. That game witnessed a dreadful challenge on Froggatt by Nicky Summerbee that inflicted serious ankle damage. Froggatt's season had been patchy but his form had picked up after a surprise England call-up by Kevin Keegan in November. Froggatt was on the bench for England's European Championship play-off with Scotland and looked set to win a cap in the near future. He took the field several times after the Summerbee incident but by the end of the season he was in pain and forced to rest.

> **DID YOU KNOW?**
>
> **Coventry City's 34-year-run in the top division has only been bettered by 8 clubs in the League's 113-year history**

In March, Hedman was injured on international duty, so up stepped 42-year-old Steve Ogrizovic for his swansong. He played two blinders and could not be faulted for the defeats. He announced his retirement but returned for the final home game to a huge ovation and bowed out with 601 appearances to his name.

Speculation surrounded the future of Whelan and McAllister. Whelan, who had rejected new terms, returned from injury but rarely reached his potential. McAllister, on the other hand, now 35, had an outstanding season, being at the fulcrum of all of the team's moves, and even outscoring Robbie Keane. Rumours were rife of a move to Liverpool, and Coventry offered him substantial sums to re-sign. In the end it was his desire for medals, not money, that decided his future, and Anfield duly delivered.

For the second season running City's Under-18s reached the final of the FA Youth Cup, only to lose again. This time Arsenal beat the Sky Blues youngsters 5-1 on aggregate. Two of the side – Gary McSheffrey and Robert Betts – got first-team opportunities, whilst others like Craig Pead and Lee Fowler sat on the first-team bench. The club's investment in their academy began to pay off and in the future the vast sums spent in the transfer market should diminish. One previous youth-team player, John Eustace, established himself in the first team and looked an excellent midfield prospect. His gutsy displays against stars such as Paul Ince and Patrick Vieira won him a host of admirers.

Match of the Season 1999-00

Coventry 3 Arsenal 2

Premiership, 26 December 1999

The Sky pundits had viewed City three times during the autumn and raved about Gordon Strachan's team, even nicknaming them the Entertainers. The opportunity for Sky to screen this match was too good to miss. Coventry turned on the style yet again for the cameras and the display made the rest of the country take notice of a team on the up.

This game had everything, from spectacular goals to intriguing personal battles all over the pitch, and will be remembered for years to come. From the opening minutes it was clear that City were out to impose themselves on an Arsenal side whose stalwart back four was reunited for the first time in several weeks.

The Gunners had strengthened their squad with the acquisition of Brazilian Silvinho, French World Cup winner Thierry Henry, and Croatian striker Davor Suker. Ruled out through injury were Bergkamp and Parlour, whilst Patrick Vieira was suspended. For City, Gary Breen passed a late fitness test, but Edworthy, Hall and Burrows were all on the long-term injury list.

Cedric Roussel, back at the expense of Noel Whelan, started the fireworks, heading Telfer's cross into the path of Gary McAllister for the Coventry captain to score from 25 yards – aided by a deflection off Keown's backside. The first half provided a host of chances at both ends, with Hedman saving well from Overmars and Petit, and Keane creating opportunities that went begging. Just before the break, Hadji made it 2-0. The Moroccan was instrumental in much of Coventry's excellent build-up play and finally produced a goal to match. Receiving the ball from McAllister on the edge of the D, the midfielder lifted his shot between the closing Adams and Keown, directing it round Seaman and inside the right-hand post. Seconds before the half-time whistle, Hedman pulled off a one-handed save to keep out Henry's left-foot shot.

The Sky Blues came out for the second half looking to put the outcome beyond doubt, and nearly succeeded with two chances. First, the ubiquitous Keane controlled a Roussel flick-on but shot over, before the young Irishman returned the favour and set up a chance for Roussel, who drove the ball across the face of goal with Chippo sliding in at the far post.

Arsenal, however, began to assert themselves. Kanu's mazy dribbling caused more than one flutter. The breakthrough came when the lanky Nigerian fed Ljungberg, who scored a scrappy goal off the legs of Hedman and Breen. But City were soon back in the driving seat with a superb combination. Williams' angled free-kick was headed into the box by Palmer for Roussel to flick on to Keane. With the striker running away from goal and Tony Adams in close attendance, he cheekily hit the ball with the outside of his boot from the acutest of angles to beat both defender and keeper and put the ball in the opposite corner to the one they expected.

The crowd were loving every minute and substitute Noel Whelan almost grabbed a fourth with one of his trademark dribbles, but his shot went narrowly wide. Three minutes from time Suker scored again for Arsenal, forcing City to hang on for a few tense minutes of stoppage time to record a memorable victory.

FA CARLING PREMIERSHIP 2000-01

Premiership	19th (relegated)
Worthington Cup	4th Round
FA Cup	4th Round

By any criteria Coventry City in 2000-01 were one of the three worst sides in the Premiership: an avalanche of goals against, all too few scored. Result: an appalling goal-difference, only eight wins all season and relegation thoroughly deserved.

It is easy to blame the club's demise on the sales of Robbie Keane and Gary McAllister in the summer of 2000. It wasn't the first time, nor will it be the last, that the club have been forced to sell top players. Dennis Mortimer, Gary Thompson, Gary Gillespie, Ian Wallace all left Coventry at their peak. The difference between then and now is player-power. Those earlier players were sold to balance the books, but only sold when it suited the club. Today's stars decide when and to whom they will be sold. McAllister enjoyed a great season at Liverpool, but who is to say whether he would, at his age, have lasted another season of struggle at Highfield Road. Keane and his agent's ambitions were obviously whetted after his superb first season in the Premiership. City, amid rumours of the transfer system collapsing, made a sound decision to cash in their chips and sell Keane to Internazionale for £13 million.

The major factor in sliding from the Entertainers to relegation fodder was the inability to replace the two stars. McAllister had an excellent final season at Highfield Road, but it is easy to forget some of his lacklustre performances before he was protected by the combative Palmer; and that the successes of 1997-98 were achieved without Gary. In the club's defence McAllister, who was entitled to a free transfer, was virtually impossible to replace. Everton's Don Hutchison might have fitted the bill and looked set to sign until his childhood team, Sunderland joined the chase. City also lost out on Sheffield Wednesday's Niclas Alexandersson. David Thompson was signed from Liverpool for £3 million but he was a wide player as opposed to the playmaker Gary had been. Keane's replacement was the inexperienced Craig Bellamy, a £6 million buy from Norwich. His effort and endeavour was never in question but he was no Keane and his goals were sparse, although the service to him was poor. Add to this the poor form of Roussel, Chippo and Hadji, such hits the previous term, and you had the recipe for a nightmare.

Hadji was an enigma. Handed the captaincy he showed only glimpses of his past form and rarely looked capable of lifting spirits when things went awry on the pitch. He did, however, put club before country for the vital game at Villa Park.

Hard questions must be directed at the manager. Gordon had four years earlier in 1997 saved the club from the drop and avoided major relegation worries in the subsequent three seasons. Whilst he had to tolerate the loss of quality players it is debatable whether he got he best out of his squad. Additionally his transfer dealings saw a large number of foreign players fail to make an impact.

David Burrows and Ian Brightwell had also left in the summer, on free transfers to Birmingham and Walsall respectively, and Noel Whelan who refused a new contract was sold to Middlesbrough for £2 million. He was back at Highfield Road on the opening day as Boro ran City, and particularly Colin Hendry, ragged. The Scottish captain was booed off, dropped by Strachan and soon offloaded to Bolton. Some felt Strachan too hasty in jettisoning the Scot but it's hard to imagine Hendry altering the course of the season.

The defeat was forgotten as the away hoodoo ended with back-to-back wins at Southampton and Manchester City, but it proved to be a false dawn. No goals and only one point from the next three home games, culminating in a 3-0 stroll for West Ham, confirmed that it was going to be a tough season. Many fans called for Strachan's head after the West Ham debacle and rumours surfaced that he had offered to resign.

The left side of the team caused headaches. With Froggatt and Gustafsson ruled out for the season, an attempt was made to sign Rangers' stars Jorg Albertz and Neil McCann, but Rangers pulled out of the deal amid recriminations between the two clubs. Marcus Hall was injured in September and for several months Strachan was forced to play Edworthy or Quinn out of position – the Honduran Guerrero having been found wanting in the defensive department. A move for Hearts' Gary Naysmith failed when the young left-back joined Everton.

Injuries to Hedman and Roussel provided opportunities to goalkeeper Chris Kirkland and John Aloisi, whose five goals in three games raised spirits. The first home win came against Tottenham on the young keeper's debut, albeit at the cost of a red card to Carlton Palmer. A week later at Stamford Bridge Kirkland was sent off for appearing to topple Hasselbaink, a decision later overturned by the referee. Chelsea hit six, all of them past on-loan substitute keeper Alan Miller, who actually did quite well.

Palmer's relationship with Strachan was strained and following another collapse at Anfield the big man was dropped. Before long he was transfer listed and loaned out to Watford. His replacement as midfield enforcer was Blackburn's Lee Carsley, signed for £2.5

million in December. Carsley could not match Carlton's form of the previous season, and many felt that Palmer's experience was wasted. Rumours suggested that other players such as Edworthy, Konjic and Breen had fallen foul of Strachan, thereby limiting their first-team opportunities. In central defence the old guard of Shaw and Williams never looked as commanding as in the past and it took too long for the excellent Gary Breen to be reinstated.

Only one further game was won before Christmas, at home to Leicester, but defeats at home to Ipswich and at Bradford City had the fans seething. The team's passing was poor, they surrendered possession too easily, and too many late goals were being conceded. In total eighteen goals were conceded in the last quarter of an hour – these would prove crucial in the final reckoning and posed questions about the team's fitness.

Christmas was vital, but City missed the chance of putting space between themselves and their fellow strugglers by failing to beat Southampton and Manchester City at home. Chances were being created but none of the multitude of strike partnerships – five different permutations were used in ten games – could capitalise on them. Crying out for a proven goalscorer, the club tried to sign Wimbledon's John Hartson, but the deal snagged. First Cedric Roussel, who had to move the other way to make the deal viable, refused to join the Dons. Then Hartson's unconvincing medical meant the player was uninsurable.

The season's watershed came at home to lowly Everton, who were stricken with injuries and suspensions. City were 0-3 down after 31 minutes and by the end the ground was half empty, with those remaining booing players and management off the pitch.

The Hartson deal was resurrected, Roussel moved to Wolves for £1.5 million, and the Dons, desperate to reduce their wage bill, accepted a pay-per-play deal that gave them £15,000 for every match Hartson played, up to a maximum of £5 million. The big Welshman had an immediate impact, helping to win a point at West Ham, and scoring on his home debut in a 2-2 draw with Charlton. He demonstrated what had been lacking all season, an ability to hold the ball up – something that Aloisi and Roussel failed to do – and hurt opposing defenders. He also displayed leadership, something lacking on the pitch all season. It was, however, too little too late.

Only two of Hartson's first eight games were lost. He netted six goals, but home draws with Charlton and Chelsea were not enough; wins were needed. Successive victories over Derby and Leicester gave hope, but defeats at Manchester United, Ipswich and Liverpool opened the trap-door wide. The team travelled to Villa Park on 5 May needing not only a win to avoid the drop but others to lose.

DID YOU KNOW?

When Coventry played at Old Trafford in April 2001, the attendance of 67,637 was the largest league crowd in England since 1963 and the largest at Man U since 1936.

In a display which encapsulated the whole sad season, the Sky Blues, who led 2-0 at the break thanks to Hadji's goals (why didn't he score a few more), were beaten by two goals in the dying minutes. The defending was amateurish and the capitulation was embarrassing. Ironically, results elsewhere meant the result was immaterial: if City had won they would have still been relegated. There would be no opportunity to add to their ten last-day escapes. After 34 years in the top flight they were sent down at the one ground the fans would have chosen to avoid.

The future is uncertain. The new stadium, originally planned for 2001, has encountered numerous problems, but relegation has not dimmed the club's optimism over the project. The close season saw the departure of Hadji, Aloisi, Bellamy and, after protracted debate, Hartson. A total of £15 million was raised as the club faced a loss of £15 million in income in the Nationwide League. Wimbledon also had to be paid off for Hartson and £5 million went on West Brom striker Lee Hughes. Two weeks into the new season, with pressure from the bankers increasing, City sold Kirkland to Liverpool for a fee that may rise to £9 million. More players are likely to be sold to further trim the wage-bill. On the pitch, the losing habit could not be kicked and Strachan paid the ultimate price. Roland Nilsson took over as caretaker and quickly reversed the trend. At the time of writing, chairman Richardson is also under pressure. Nothing stays still for long in the turbulent world of Coventry City FC.

Match of the Season 2000-01

Aston Villa 3 Coventry 2

Premiership, 5 May 2001

Coventry's relegation battle came to an unhappy and unsatisfying end at Villa Park when the home side, still with an outside chance of Europe, sent City into the Nationwide League. This was despite the Sky Blues taking an early two-goal lead and controlling the game for over an hour.

Easter Saturday had proved critical, with City giving champions-elect Manchester United a massive fright in a noon kick-off, before succumbing to two late goals. Three hours later Middlesbrough, the side most likely to go down if Coventry were to survive, somehow won at Highbury thanks to two Brazilian's own-goals. Boro now had a five-point lead over City with only five games left.

Successive 0-2 defeats at Ipswich and at home to Liverpool meant that a win at Villa was not only essential but, as in 1997, others had to lose. Derby had slipped into the danger zone and faced a tough trip to champions Manchester United. If Derby lost their two final games and City won theirs, then City would stay up.

Coventry's recent record at Villa Park was good with two wins in the last three visits, but there was an underlying feeling of doom among the 4,500 City fans in the ground. Former Coventry stars Dublin and Boateng gave warning that no sympathy would be extended to their former team-mates.

Coventry started with gusto. In the first minute Villa's Vassell collapsed under Williams' challenge and the combative John Eustace then clattered Boateng like a pit-bull terrier. On seventeen minutes Eustace fed Paul Telfer on the right wing. Telfer's cross found Hadji, and the Moroccan's diving header flew out of David James' reach. Eight minutes later Hadji made it two, controlling Williams' hopeful ball on his chest before volleying into the far corner.

City were in control, Villa in tatters. Two significant events then changed the game. First Paul Telfer, enjoying a purple patch in midfield, fell awkwardly in a challenge and was carried off with a broken leg, then Villa boss John Gregory, pacing the touchline like a caged tiger, introduced David Ginola for Steve Staunton.

The second half, however, started as the first had ended with Carsley missing a chance to make it three. Ginola then started to weave his magic and City failed to counter the balance which now swung in Villa's favour. Poor defending on the left let Delaney get a cross in but there still seemed no danger until Williams inexplicably left the ball for Kirkland. The young keeper let the ball slip from his hands and Vassell prodded it home. The goal lifted the previously quiet home fans and one could almost sense what was to follow.

On came Angel, Villa's £9.5 million Columbian misfit, and nine minutes from time he scored his first Villa goal to make it 2-2. Again it stemmed from City's careless left flank. Southgate's cross clipped Quinn's head to fall perfectly for the South American to crash home a right-foot volley.

All that remained was the funeral rites, administered by the previously subdued Paul Merson, who struck a thunderous 25-yarder into the top corner. It was less than City deserved and more than Villa merited but the Villa fans gleefully danced on the grave. Coventry tears flowed on the pitch and on the terraces, and news that Derby had won at Old Trafford, meaning that the result at Villa Park had been meaningless, was ignored.

Gallacher completes his hat-trick in a 5-4 League Cup win v Forest (November 1990)

Cyrille Regis's diving header gives City the lead over Manchester City (March 1991)

John Williams scores City's first Premiership goal – v Middlesbrough (August 1992)

Andy Pearce thunders home a header against Crystal Palace (October 1992)

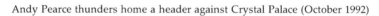

Mick Quinn is through, but blasts over the bar against Everton (November 1993)

Gordon Strachan and Arsenal's Paul Merson are booked at Highbury (February 1996)

Brian Hill (left) is no longer City's youngest player. It is now Gary McSheffrey (right)

Huckerby is applauded for his second successive hat-trick – v Forest (January 1999)

COVENTRY CITY'S SEASONAL RECORDS 1967-2001

				Home					Away					Total					
Season	Div	Pos	P	W	D	L	F	A	W	D	L	F	A	W	D	L	F	A	*Pts
1967-68	1	20	42	8	5	8	32	32	1	10	10	19	39	9	15	18	51	71	33
1968-69	1	20	42	8	6	7	32	22	2	5	14	14	42	10	11	21	46	64	31
1969-70	1	6	42	9	6	6	35	28	10	5	6	23	20	19	11	12	58	48	49
1970-71	1	10	42	12	4	5	24	12	4	6	11	13	26	16	10	16	37	38	42
1971-72	1	18	42	7	10	4	27	23	2	5	14	17	44	9	15	18	44	67	33
1972-73	1	19	42	9	5	7	27	24	4	4	13	13	31	13	9	20	40	55	35
1973-74	1	16	42	10	5	6	25	18	4	5	12	18	36	14	10	18	43	54	38
1974-75	1	14	42	8	9	4	31	27	4	6	11	20	35	12	15	15	51	62	39
1975-76	1	14	42	6	9	6	22	22	7	5	9	25	35	13	14	15	47	57	40
1976-77	1	19	42	7	9	5	34	26	3	6	12	14	33	10	15	17	48	59	35
1977-78	1	7	42	13	5	3	48	23	5	7	9	27	39	18	12	12	75	62	48
1978-79	1	10	42	11	7	3	41	29	3	9	9	17	39	14	16	12	58	68	44
1979-80	1	15	42	12	2	7	34	24	4	5	12	22	42	16	7	19	56	66	39
1980-81	1	16	42	9	6	6	31	30	4	4	13	17	39	13	10	19	48	69	36
1981-82	1	14	42	9	4	8	31	24	4	7	10	25	38	13	11	18	56	62	50
1982-83	1	19	42	10	5	6	29	17	3	4	14	19	42	13	9	20	48	59	48
1983-84	1	19	42	8	5	8	33	33	5	6	10	24	44	13	11	18	57	77	50
1984-85	1	19	42	11	3	7	29	22	4	2	15	18	42	15	5	22	47	64	50
1985-86	1	18	42	6	5	10	31	35	5	5	11	17	36	11	10	21	48	71	43
1986-87	1	10	42	14	4	3	35	17	3	8	10	15	28	17	12	13	50	45	63
1987-88	1	10	40	6	8	6	23	25	7	6	7	23	28	13	14	13	46	53	53
1988-89	1	7	38	9	4	6	28	23	5	9	5	19	19	14	13	11	47	42	55
1989-90	1	12	38	11	2	6	24	25	3	5	11	15	34	14	7	17	39	59	49
1990-91	1	16	38	10	6	3	30	16	1	5	13	12	33	11	11	16	42	49	44
1991-92	1	19	42	6	7	8	18	15	5	4	12	17	29	11	11	20	35	44	44
1992-93	P	15	42	7	4	10	29	28	6	9	6	23	29	13	13	16	52	57	52
1993-94	P	11	42	9	7	5	23	17	5	7	9	20	28	14	14	14	43	45	56
1994-95	P	16	42	7	7	7	23	25	5	7	9	21	37	12	14	16	44	62	50
1995-96	P	16	38	6	7	6	21	23	2	7	10	21	37	8	14	16	42	60	38
1996-97	P	17	38	4	8	7	19	23	5	6	8	19	31	9	14	15	38	54	41
1997-98	P	11	38	8	9	2	26	17	4	7	8	20	27	12	16	10	46	44	52
1998-99	P	15	38	8	6	5	26	21	3	3	13	13	30	11	9	18	39	51	42
1999-00	P	14	38	12	1	6	38	22	0	7	12	9	32	12	8	18	47	54	44
2000-01	P	19	38	4	7	8	14	23	4	3	12	22	40	8	10	20	36	63	34
Totals:			1390	294	197	204	973	791	136	199	360	631	1164	430	396	564	1604	1955	1500

* 3 points for a win from 1981-82

COVENTRY CITY'S COMPLETE LEAGUE RECORD 1967-2001

		Home					Away					Total					
	P	W	D	L	F	A	W	D	L	F	A	W	D	L	F	A	*Pts
Arsenal	68	8	9	17	31	43	5	9	20	25	59	13	18	37	56	102	57
Aston Villa	50	6	7	12	31	38	1	8	16	17	43	7	15	28	48	81	36
Barnsley	2	1	0	0	1	0	0	0	1	0	2	1	0	1	1	2	3
Birmingham	24	6	2	4	18	13	3	4	5	12	18	9	6	9	30	31	33
Blackburn	14	3	3	1	11	5	2	1	4	9	18	5	4	5	20	23	19
Blackpool	2	1	0	0	2	0	0	0	1	0	1	1	0	1	2	1	3
Bolton W	8	1	2	1	7	7	2	2	0	8	3	3	4	1	15	10	13
Bradford C	4	1	1	0	4	0	0	1	1	2	3	1	2	1	6	3	5
Brighton	8	2	1	1	7	5	0	2	2	4	8	2	3	3	11	13	9
Bristol C	8	2	2	0	9	6	0	2	2	1	7	2	4	2	10	13	10
Burnley	14	3	2	2	15	9	1	4	2	7	9	4	6	4	22	18	18
Carlisle	2	1	0	0	2	1	0	1	0	0	0	1	1	0	2	1	4
Charlton .	12	3	2	1	10	6	0	6	0	7	7	3	8	1	17	13	17
Chelsea	52	11	8	7	42	36	4	6	16	29	50	15	14	23	71	86	59
Crys Palace	24	6	4	2	21	16	8	3	1	19	5	14	7	3	40	21	49
Derby	40	10	6	4	28	19	4	5	11	19	31	14	11	15	47	50	53
Everton	68	16	7	11	52	43	5	12	17	30	58	21	19	28	82	101	82
Fulham	2	0	0	1	0	3	0	1	0	1	1	0	1	1	1	4	1
Huddersfield	4	1	1	0	2	1	1	0	1	1	1	2	1	1	3	2	7
Ipswich	44	8	7	7	28	27	3	7	12	12	32	11	14	19	40	59	47
Leeds	52	7	10	9	33	30	2	7	17	14	46	9	17	26	47	76	44
Leicester	40	10	5	5	28	19	7	7	6	25	22	17	12	11	53	41	63
Liverpool	68	10	11	13	29	40	3	5	26	16	73	13	16	39	45	113	55
Luton	22	9	1	1	23	7	5	1	5	15	15	14	2	6	38	22	44
Manchester C	52	12	8	6	43	30	4	4	18	21	52	16	12	24	64	82	60
Manchester U	66	10	7	16	39	51	5	7	21	20	62	15	14	37	59	113	59
Middlesbrough	30	7	3	5	21	18	4	5	6	15	22	11	8	11	36	40	41
Millwall	4	1	1	0	3	1	0	0	2	1	5	1	1	2	4	6	4
Newcastle	48	9	7	8	31	33	4	4	16	22	58	13	11	24	53	91	50
Norwich	40	15	4	1	33	12	3	9	8	19	26	18	13	9	52	38	67
Nott'm Forest	50	5	10	10	23	34	3	7	15	22	50	8	17	25	45	84	41
Notts Co	8	3	0	1	5	6	0	0	4	3	10	3	0	5	8	16	9
Oldham	6	1	2	0	5	2	1	1	1	5	5	2	3	1	10	7	9
Oxford	6	3	0	0	9	2	1	0	2	1	3	4	0	2	10	5	12
Portsmouth	2	1	0	0	1	0	0	1	0	0	0	1	1	0	1	0	4
QPR	40	10	5	5	31	16	3	5	12	19	40	13	10	17	50	56	49
Sheffield Utd	20	5	4	1	18	11	4	2	4	8	9	9	6	5	26	20	33
Sheffield Wed	36	11	4	3	28	9	5	8	5	19	25	16	12	8	47	34	60
Southampton	60	18	8	4	48	23	4	12	14	30	54	22	20	18	78	77	86
Stoke	32	9	3	4	30	19	5	2	9	20	28	14	5	13	50	47	47
Sunderland	26	7	4	2	24	14	1	6	6	4	13	8	10	8	28	27	34
Swansea	4	1	1	0	3	1	0	1	1	1	2	1	2	1	4	3	5
Swindon	2	0	1	0	1	1	0	0	1	1	3	0	1	1	2	4	1
Tottenham	66	10	11	12	42	45	8	8	17	43	63	18	19	29	85	108	73
West Brom	32	6	3	7	24	22	3	6	7	15	33	9	9	14	39	55	36
Watford	14	4	0	3	10	6	4	1	2	8	8	8	1	5	18	14	25
West Ham	56	7	11	10	29	34	7	6	15	31	53	14	17	25	60	87	59
Wimbledon	28	5	6	3	18	16	6	4	4	17	15	11	10	7	35	31	43
Wolves	30	8	3	4	20	11	5	6	4	13	13	13	9	8	33	24	48
76 opponents	1390	294	197	204	973	791	136	199	360	631	1164	430	396	564	1604	1955	

* 3 points given for a win throughout.

GUIDE TO SEASONAL SUMMARIES

Col 1: Match number (for league fixtures); Round (for cup-ties).
e.g. 2:1 means 'Second round; first leg.'
e.g. 4R means 'Fourth round replay.'

Col 2: Date of the fixture and whether Home (H), Away (A), or Neutral (N).

Col 3: Opposition.

Col 4: Attendances. Home gates appear in roman; Away gates in *italics*.
Figures in **bold** indicate the largest and smallest gates, at home and away.
Average home and away attendances appear after the final league match.
N.B. Home attendances are those registered with the Football League and should be taken as accurate.

Col 5: Respective league positions of Coventry and their opponents after the match.
Coventry's position appears on the top line in roman.
Their opponents' position appears on the second line in *italics*.
For cup-ties, the division and position of opponents is provided.
e.g. *2:12* means the opposition are twelfth in Division 2.

Col 6: The top line shows the result: W(in), D(raw), or L(ose).
The second line shows Coventry's cumulative points total.

Col 7: The match score, Coventry's given first.
Scores in **bold** indicate Coventry's biggest league win and heaviest defeat.

Col 8: The half-time score, Coventry's given first.

Col 9: The top line shows Coventry's scorers and times of goals in roman.
The second line shows opponents' scorers and times of goals in *italics*.
A 'p' after the time of a goal denotes a penalty; 'og' an own-goal.
The third line gives the name of the match referee.

Team line-ups: Coventry line-ups appear on the top line, irrespective of whether they are home or away. Opposition teams appear on the second line in *italics*.
Players of either side who are sent off are marked !
Coventry players making their league debuts are displayed in **bold**.
In the era of squad numbers, players' names are positioned as far as possible as if they were still wearing shirts 1 to 11.

Substitutes: Names of substitutes appear only if they actually took the field.
A player substituted is marked *
A second player substituted is marked ^
A third player substituted is marked "
These marks indicate the sequence of substitutions.

N.B. For clarity, all information appearing in *italics* relates to opposing teams.

No	Date		Att	Pos	Pt	F-A	H-T	Scorers, Times, and Referees	1	2	3	4	5	6	7	8	9	10	11	12 sub used
1	A	BURNLEY			L	1-2	0-1	Merrington 81 (og)	Glazier	Kearns	Bruck	Farmer	Curtis	Clements	Key	Machin	Tudor	Lewis	Rees	
	19/8		21,483		0			Casper 32, Irvine 62	Thomson	Angus	Latcham	O'Neill	Merrington	Todd	Morgan	Bellamy	Irvine	Harris	Casper	
								Ref: K Howley	7,000 City fans witness City's Division 1 debut and their first league defeat for nine months and 25 games. Manager Hill's resignation does not seem to affect the players, who appear in a strange all-white kit. Casper scores on his debut and Irvine nets when Glazier spills Morgan's shot.											
2	A	NOTT'M FOREST			D	3-3	3-2	Gould 19, 27, Machin 38	**Dickie**	Kearns	Bruck	Farmer	Curtis*	Clements	Key	Machin	Tudor	Lewis	Rees	Gould
	22/8		44,950		1			Baker 22, Wignall 36, Moore 53p	Grummitt	Hindley	Winfield	Hennessey	McKinlay	Newton	Lyons	Chapman	Baker	Wignall	Moore*	Hinton
								Ref: A Jones	The gates are locked. In a dramatic match with last season's runners up Curtis breaks a leg in the fourth minute in a tackle with Wignall. Bobby Gould makes his top flight bow as sub and scores twice. City lead three times but are pegged back by a deflected free-kick and a penalty.											
3	H	SHEFFIELD UTD		16	D	2-2	1-1	Key 19, Bruck 56	Glazier	Kearns	Bruck	Lewis	**Knapp**	Clements	Key*	Machin	Gould	Tudor	Rees	Morrissey
	26/8		33,328	17	2			Reece 7, Cliff 52	Hodgkinson	Badger	Shaw	Munks	Matthewson	Wagstaff	Cliff	Fenoughty	Jones	Birchenall	Reece	
								Ref: M Sinclair	The sapping heat, a Glazier 'howler' and the Blades intention on a draw all take the edge off City's first home Division 1 game. John Key's header from a Rees corner is the best goal of the game. Dietmar Bruck saves a point with a low deceptive shot following Machin's free-kick.											
4	H	NOTT'M FOREST		21	L	1-3	0-2	Rees 81	Glazier	Kearns	Bruck	Denton	Coop	Clements	Lewis	Machin	Gould	Tudor	Rees	
	29/8		41,212	2	2			Baker 5, 62, Moore 41	Grummitt	Hindley	Winfield	Hennessey	McKinlay	Newton	Lyons	Barnwell*	Baker	Wignall	Moore	Hinton
								Ref: W Gow	On paper, defeat is predictable. On the field a cruelly depleted City side strive with such gallantry that the score does them no justice. Kearns plays at centre-half for the injured Knapp. Glazier has a shaky game, parrying a cross to Baker for the first and missing a cross for the second.											
5	A	ARSENAL		19	D	1-1	1-0	Gould 29	Glazier	Kearns	Bruck	Farmer	Knapp	Clements	Lewis*	Machin	Gould	Tudor	Rees	**Carr**
	2/9		30,404	12	3			Graham 79	Furnell	Storey	McNab*	McLintock	Neill	Simpson	Johnston	Addison	Graham	Sammels	Armstrong	Court
								Ref: P Walters	First ever visit to Highbury. Arsenal miss chances before Graham gives them a well deserved point after a Glazier-Clements mix-up. Gould takes a superb Machin through-ball around Furnell before slotting home. 18-year-old Willie Carr catches the eye and Glazier is back to his best.											
6	H	SOUTHAMPTON		15	W	2-1	0-0	Tudor 59, Rees 64	Glazier	Kearns	Bruck	Lewis	Knapp	Clements	Carr	Machin	Gould	Tudor	Rees*	Morrissey
	5/9		32,986	8	5			Chivers 49	Forsyth	Webb	Hollywood	Fisher	Gabriel	Walker	Paine	Chivers	Davies*	Melia	Sydenham	Wimshurst
								Ref: J Warburton	The highly vaunted Davies-Chivers strikeforce is thwarted by Davies' back injury. City record their first win in a patchy, ill-tempered game with four bookings and 101 minutes played. Rees scores when the ref plays on after a bad tackle and Saints hesitate. City hang on desperately.											
7	H	MANCHESTER C		17	L	0-3	0-1		Glazier	Kearns	Bruck	Lewis	Knapp	Clements	Key	Carr	Gould	Tudor	Rees	
	9/9		34,578	5	5			Hince 37, Summerbee 61, Bell 70	Dowd	Book	Pardoe	Doyle	Heslop	Oakes	Hince	Bell	Summerbee	Young	Coleman	
								Ref: H New	The hunt for a new manager continues with Revie and Allison tipped. Mercer's men give Coventry a hiding but the resistance is puny. Colin Bell's goal is the best: he mesmerises the defence before firing home. Coventry's injury list grows longer; the stars of Division 2 are fading.											
8	A	NEWCASTLE		21	L	2-3	2-2	Rees 14, Gould 20	Glazier	Coop	Bruck	Lewis	Knapp	Clements	Carr	Machin	Gould	Gibson*	Rees	Farmer
	16/9		28,890	12	5			Davies 24, Iley 44, Bennett 72	McFaul	Craig	Guthrie	Elliott	McGrath	Moncur	Bennett	Scott	Davies	Iley	Robson	
								Ref: D Laing	Ian Gibson runs the game for 20 minutes, creates two goals from corners but then is injured. City fall to pieces and superb headers from Wyn Davies, the best header of a ball in Britain, and Albert Bennett, together with a Jim Iley goal right on half-time leave them in the bottom two.											
9	H	WEST BROM		17	W	4-2	2-1	Lewis 14, Rees 43, 77, Machin 58	Glazier	Coop	Bruck	Lewis	Knapp	Hill	Rees	Morrissey	Gould*	Machin	Clements	Tudor
	23/9		31,258	21	7			Astle 9, Clark 46	Osborne	Colquhoun	Williams	Collard*	Talbut	Campbell	Stephens	Kaye	Astle	Hope	Clark	Treacy
								Ref: J Finney	A convincing victory over Alan Ashman's struggling side after a run of bad results. Hill makes his Div 1 debut and shackles Kaye, Coop keeps a tight rein on Clark. City win it with a gritty display in the last 20 minutes when the points are in the balance. On a sore note, Gould is injured.											
10	A	CHELSEA		16	D	1-1	0-0	Clements 64	Glazier	Kearns	Bruck	Morrissey	Knapp	Hill	Rees	Machin	Tudor	Lewis	Clements	
	30/9		29,800	19	8			Boyle 78	Bonetti	Thomson	Butler	Hollins	Waldron	Harris	Cooke	Baldwin	Osgood	McCreadie	Tambling*	Boyle
								Ref: D Brady	Chelsea, with seven internationals, are going through a bad spell and don't have the stomach for a fight. But for Bonetti, City would have been easy winners before the late equaliser. Glazier saves Cooke's penalty two minutes from time after the same player is tripped by Mick Kearns.											

No/Date	H/A	Opponents/Att	Pos	Res/Pts	F-A	H-T	Scorers, Times, Referees	1	2	3	4	5	6	7	8	9	10	11	12 sub used
11	A	SHEFFIELD WED	18	L	**0-4**	0-3	*[Fantham 87]*	Glazier	Coop	Kearns	Morrissey	Knapp	Hill	Rees	Machin	Roberts	Lewis	Clements	
7/10		*33,360*	1	8			*McCalliog 2, Mobley 33, Eustace 41,*	*Springett*	*Quinn*	*Megson*	*Mobley*	*Ellis*	*Young*	*Usher*	*Fantham*	*Ritchie*	*McCalliog**	*Eustace*	*Branfoot*
							Ref: F Nicholson	The end of a week when veteran Ron Farmer moves to Notts County and Alan Dicks becomes Bristol City manager. Wednesday hammer City without breaking sweat. The game is over before half-time and but for Bill Glazier the scoreline could have been doubled. The Owls go top.											
12	H	TOTTENHAM	20	L	2-3	1-2	Rees 16, 47	Glazier	Coop	Hill	Morrissey	Knapp	Clements	Lewis*	Machin	Tudor	Gibson	Rees	Carr
14/10		38,008	*4*	8			*Jones 5, Greaves 10, 63*	*Jennings*	*Kinnear*	*Knowles*	*Mullery*	*England*	*Beal*	*Robertson*	*Greaves*	*Gilzean*	*Venables*	*Jones*	
							Ref: E Wallace	Hill hands over to Cantwell, whose baptism is ominous. City acquit themselves well and come back from an early two-goal deficit and deserve a point. The difference between the sides is Jimmy Greaves, whose dipping shot from the edge of the area is world-class and wins the points.											
13	A	MANCHESTER U	20	L	**0-4**	0-2		Glazier	Coop	Hill*	Kearns	Knapp	Clements	Lewis	Machin	Tudor	Gibson	Rees	Morrissey
25/10		***54,253***	*2*	8			*Aston 31, 58, Best 33, Charlton 68*	*Stepney*	*Dunne*	*Burns*	*Crerand*	*Sadler*	*Fitzpatrick*	*Best*	*Kidd*	*Charlton*	*Law*	*Aston*	
							Ref: J Carr	Despite being 0-2 down at the break, City had battled well. But in the second half United tear them apart. The best goal is Charlton's 30-yarder, which the crowd applauds for over two minutes. Glazier saves Law's late twice-taken penalty. City's highest away league crowd since 1949.											
14	H	SUNDERLAND	20	D	2-2	1-1	Tudor 12, Lewis 75p	Glazier	Coop	Kearns	Lewis	Knapp	Clements	Key	Shepherd	Tudor	Machin	Rees	
28/10		30,004	*16*	9			*Martin 19p, 60p*	*Montgomery*	*Irwin*	*Parke*	*Todd*	*Hurley*	*Heslop*	*Suggett*	*Kinnell**	*Martin*	*Herd*	*Hughes*	*Mulhall*
							Ref: A Darlington	Match of the Day sees City's early lead wiped out by two penalties, the first for a foul by Lewis on Kinnell, the second for Knapp's foul on Martin. City miss chances before deservedly equalising when Irwin brings down Rees. Pat Saward is appointed City's new assistant manager.											
15	A	WOLVES	20	L	0-2	0-2		Glazier	Coop	Kearns	Hill	Clements	Morrissey	Key	Carr	Tudor	Machin	Rees	
4/11		*38,659*	*10*	9			*Knowles 36, 43*	*Williams*	*Taylor*	*Thomson*	*Bailey*	*Woodfield*	*Holsgrove*	*Farrington*	*Evans*	*Dougan*	*Knowles*	*Wagstaffe**	*Hawkins*
							Ref: A Dimond	City's lack of class is becoming obvious and the battling character is temporarily gone. The old enemy win more easily than the score suggests, with City's defence caught watching Dougan and ignoring Knowles. Confusion reigns over Wagstaffe's reappearance after he'd been subbed.											
16	H	FULHAM	22	L	0-3	0-2		Glazier	Coop	Bruck	Hill	Clements	Morrissey	**Hannigan**	**Baker**	Tudor	Machin	Rees	
11/11		32,231	*21*	9			*Gilroy 28, Clarke 42, 85*	*Macedo*	*Cohen*	*Dempsey*	*Brown*	*Callaghan*	*Conway*	*Haynes*	*Earle**	*Clarke*	*Gilroy*	*Parmenter*	*Pearson*
							Ref: H Davies	The £75,000 new signings can't stop this demoralising defeat in a psychologically important game. Haynes, Cohen and record signing Clarke combine to demolish City with a swift-passing game and deadly finishing. The lack of a scorer and a leader in the Curtis mould is now critical.											
17	A	LEEDS	22	D	1-1	0-1	Hannigan 58	Glazier	Hill	Bruck	Lewis	**Setters**	Clements	Hannigan	Baker	Tudor	Machin	Rees	
18/11		*32,465*	*6*	10			*Lorimer 35*	*Sprake*	*Reaney*	*Cooper*	*Bremner*	*Madeley*	*Hunter*	*Greenhoff*	*Lorimer*	*Belfitt*	*Bates*	*Hibbitt*	
							Ref: P Partridge	A ray of hope shines through the Elland Road murk. A fighting rearguard action from a defence led by the veteran Maurice Setters, a £25,000 buy from Stoke, ends Leeds' run of seven straight home wins. Hannigan's volley cancels Lorimer's scrappy goal after a Glazier-Rees mix-up.											
18	H	EVERTON	22	L	0-2	0-0		Glazier	Coop	Bruck	Machin	Setters	Clements	Hannigan	Gibson	Tudor	Baker	Rees	
25/11		32,330	*7*	10			*Husband 69, Royle 88*	*West*	*Wright*	*Wilson*	*Kendall*	*Labone*	*Harvey*	*Young*	*Ball*	*Royle*	*Hurst*	*Husband*	
							Ref: P Bye	An improved display after a short break in Blackpool, but City still seek that elusive win. In wet conditions they pay for bad misses by Tudor and Baker but the scoreline flatters the Toffees. Alan Ball doesn't endear himself to City fans with two wild kicks which deserved a booking.											
19	A	LEICESTER	21	D	0-0	0-0		Glazier	Kearns	Bruck	Coop	Setters	Clements	Hannigan	Gibson*	Baker	Machin	Rees	Tudor
2/12		*30,102*	*18*	11				*Shilton*	*Rodrigues*	*Bell*	*Roberts*	*Sjoberg*	*Nish*	*Sinclair*	*Large*	*Stringfellow*	*Gibson*	*Tewley*	
							Ref: G McCabe	The first clean sheet of the season in the first visit to Filbert Street since 1952. Hannigan missed four chances, including one where he rounded Shilton only for Nish to clear. In an exciting game a 4-4 draw would have been a fair result. Sub Tudor, on for two minutes, didn't get a touch.											
20	H	WEST HAM	22	D	1-1	1-1	Baker 8	Glazier	Kearns	Bruck	Coop	Setters	Clements	Hannigan	Gibson	Baker	Machin	Rees	
8/12		**28,393**	*20*	12			*Hurst 30*	*Ferguson*	*Charles*	*Burkett*	*Peters*	*Bonds*	*Moore*	*Redknapp*	*Boyce*	*Brabrook*	*Hurst*	*Sissons*	
							Ref: J Osborne	An evening match on a snowbound pitch that deteriorated as the game went on. City looked easy winners early on but by the end were relieved not to lose. Baker headed in Gibson's sweet cross. Hurst scored after Peters flicked a free-kick over the wall. Eleven games now without a win.											
21	H	BURNLEY	21	W	**5-1**	2-0	Rees 11, Gould 44, 53, 63, Machin 88	Glazier	Kearns	Bruck	Machin	Setters	Clements	Hannigan	Baker	Gould	Gibson	Rees	
16/12		28,559	*14*	14			*Lochhead 76*	*Thomson*	*Smith**	*Latcham*	*O'Neill*	*Waldron*	*Merrington*	*Morgan*	*Lochhead*	*Irvine*	*Bellamy*	*Thomas*	*Casper*
							Ref: D Smith	Jimmy Andrews and Bob Dennison are installed as coach and scout respectively. Gould is back as City humiliate troubled Burnley, who had axed skipper Harris for disciplinary reasons. Gould's first was the best, a 25-yard blockbuster. The chant is 'we want six' as the bad run ends.											

No	Date	Att	Pos	Pt	F-A	H-T	Scorers, Times, and Referees	1	2	3	4	5	6	7	8	9	10	11	12 sub used
22	A SHEFFIELD UTD	22	L	0-2	0-1			Glazier	Kearns	Bruck	Machin	Setters	Clements	Lewis	Gibson	Gould	Baker	Rees	
	23/12	*17,631*	*21*	14			*Addison 13, Woodward 54*	*Hodgkinson*	*Badger*	*Shaw*	*Munks*	*Mallender*	*Wagstaff*	*Woodward*	*Carlin*	*Hill*	*Addison**	*Cliff*	*Matthewson*
							Ref: F Cowen	City never repeat the Burnley form in this relegation battle and are fortunate to lose only 0-2. Setters, recovering from a cold, is off-form and Glazier is in constant action. The first goal is headed in from a poor clearance from Glazier. Woodward then scored in a one on one situation.											
23	H LIVERPOOL	22	D	1-1	1-1		Baker 32	Glazier	Kearns	Bruck	Lewis	Setters	Clements	Baker*	Machin	Gould	Gibson	Rees	Coop
	26/12	42,207	*3*	15			*Hunt 13*	*Lawrence*	*Lawler*	*Byrne*	*Smith*	*Yeats*	*Hughes*	*Callaghan*	*Hunt**	*Hateley*	*St John !*	*Thompson*	*Strong*
							Ref: M Fussey	Liverpool's first visit to Highfield Road produces its sixth highest ever gate. Hunt scores from a Tony Hateley knockdown. St John fells Lewis with a right hook after 30 minutes and is ordered off. Although City quickly equalise, they fail to capitalise, despite several chances for Gould.											
24	A LIVERPOOL	22	L	0-1	0-1			Glazier	Clements	Bruck	Machin	Setters	Tudor	Coop	Baker	Gould	Gibson	Rees*	Carr
	30/12	*48,866*	*2*	15			*Callaghan 17*	*Lawrence*	*Lawler*	*Byrne*	*Smith*	*Yeats*	*Hughes*	*Callaghan*	*Strong*	*Hateley*	*St.John*	*Thompson*	
							Ref: P Baldwin	An improved display in a fierce match against the Red machine. Callaghan scores his first of the season after Bruck loses possession on the edge of the box. Both sides are guilty of spiteful tackles, with Tommy Smith and Setters to the fore. Clements blots out Thompson's threat.											
25	H ARSENAL	22	D	1-1	1-0		Gould 40	Glazier	Clements	Bruck	Machin	Setters	Tudor	Hannigan	Baker	Gould	Gibson	Rees	
	6/1	32,839	*8*	16			*Graham 76*	*Furnell*	*Storey*	*McNab*	*Simpson*	*Neill*	*Ure*	*Radford*	*Johnston*	*Graham*	*Sammels*	*Armstrong*	
							Ref: D Brady	The crowd generates a pressure-cooker atmosphere but City miss chances to climb off the bottom. Setters flicks on Machin's free-kick for Gould to score. George Graham finally beats the impressive Glazier from a corner. Either side could have won in a hectic last 15 minutes.											
26	H NEWCASTLE	22	L	1-4	1-1		Baker 37 *[Davies 80]*	Glazier	Hill	Bruck	Machin	Setters	Tudor	Hannigan	Baker	Gould	Gibson	Rees	
	20/1	33,760	*5*	16			*Scott 29, Sinclair 64, Robson T 67,*	*Marshall*	*Burton*	*Clark*	*Elliott*	*McNamee*	*Moncur*	*Sinclair*	*Bennett**	*Davies*	*Iley*	*Robson T*	*Scott*
							Ref: V Batty	A black result for the Sky Blues as Joe Harvey's men canter to their first away win. City were so busy watching Wyn Davies that they allowed his team-mates to have a field day. Ronnie Rees' form has become cause for concern. Baker's effort was a well-taken shot from 20 yards.											
27	A WEST BROM	21	W	1-0	0-0		Hannigan 58	Glazier	Bruck	Clements	Machin	Tudor	Hill	Hannigan	Carr	Baker	Gibson	Rees	
	3/2	*29,000*	*9*	18				*Sheppard*	*Colquhoun*	*Williams*	*Brown*	*Talbut*	*Fraser*	*Lovett**	*Kaye*	*Astle*	*Hope*	*Clark*	*Stephens*
							Ref: J Finney	Without Gould, transferred to Arsenal for £90,000, City achieve their first away win to give a ray of hope. Gibson is in brilliant form: his pass splits the Albion defence for Hannigan to score. Glazier and his defence - with emergency stopper Tudor outstanding - keep the Baggies out.											
28	H CHELSEA	21	W	2-1	0-1		Baker 47, Hannigan 69	Glazier	Hill	Bruck	Machin	Setters	Tudor	Hannigan	Baker*	**Martin**	Gibson	Carr	Clements
	10/2	36,542	*12*	20			*Tambling 23*	*Bonetti*	*Hollins*	*McCreadie*	*Boyle*	*Hinton*	*Harris*	*Cooke*	*Baldwin*	*Osgood*	*Tambling*	*Houseman**	*Kirkup*
							Ref: L Callaghan	Rees is dropped again as City play an all-Scottish forward line including £90,000 Neil Martin. Sexton's Chelsea dominate the first-half. After the break Gerry Baker heads in Gibson's pinpoint cross. Ernie Hannigan wins it with a searing shot. Chelsea fans then run rampage in the city.											
29	H SHEFFIELD WED	17	W	3-0	3-0		Martin 3p, 32, 39	Dickie	Bruck	Clements	Machin	Setters	Tudor	Hannigan	Baker	Martin	Carr	Rees	
	24/2	28,528	*13*	22				*Springett*	*Smith*	*Megson*	*Ellis*	*Mobley*	*Branfoot*	*Whitham*	*Symm*	*Ritchie*	*McCalliog*	*Usher**	*Woodall*
							Ref: A Jones	A good recovery after the Tranmere debacle. City gain two penalties for fouls on Rees by Sam Ellis and Vic Mobley but Martin blasts the second over the bar. It is the Owls seventh defeat in eight games and they look a shadow of the side that topped the table earlier in the season.											
30	A EVERTON	20	L	1-3	1-3		Hannigan 10	Glazier	Bruck	Clements	Machin	Setters	Tudor	Hannigan	Baker*	Martin	Carr	Rees	Gibson
	2/3	*38,804*	*7*	22			*Ball 3, Royle 18, 31*	*West*	*Wright*	*Brown*	*Kendall*	*Labone*	*Harvey**	*Husband*	*Ball*	*Royle*	*Hurst*	*Morrissey*	*Hunt*
							Ref: V James	The winning run is ended by slick Toffees, who took their foot off in the second half. 18-year-old Joe Royle should have scored a hat-trick, but Glazier looked impeded for his first. Hannigan's goal is created by Carr's through ball, and is the first scored by a visiting player in six games.											
31	A MANCHESTER C	20	L	1-3	0-1		Tudor 76	Glazier	Bruck !	Clements	Machin	Setters	Tudor	Hannigan	Baker*	Martin	Carr	Rees	Lewis
	9/3	*33,310*	*2*	22			*Summerbee 19, Bell 49, Young 80*	*Mulhearn*	*Book*	*Pardoe*	*Doyle*	*Heslop*	*Oakes**	*Lee*	*Bell*	*Summerbee*	*Young*	*Coleman !*	*Kennedy*
							Ref: R Tinkler	Relegation looks a probability after a poor performance against Joe Mercer's men. Bruck is perhaps unlucky to be sent off after Tony Coleman retaliates following his strong challenge. Glazier saves a late Lee penalty to spare the blushes. City's main stand was gutted by fire on 6 March.											

No	H/A	Opponent	Pos	Res	F-A	H-T	Scorers, Times, and Referees	1	2	3	4	5	6	7	8	9	10	11	12
32	H	MANCHESTER U	20	W	2-0	1-0	Machin 34, Setters 52	Glazier	Bruck	**Cattlin**	Machin	Setters	Clements	Hannigan	**Hunt**	Martin	Tudor	Carr	
	16/3	**47,111**	*2*	24				*Stepney*	*Brennan*	*Burns*	*Crerand*	*Sadler*	*Stiles*	*Fitzpatrick*	*Kidd**	*Charlton*	*Best*	*Herd*	*Aston*
							Ref: H New	Although the main stand is closed because of the fire, the gate is the second biggest ever. Two transfer deadline purchases help salvage some pride and knock United off the top. United claim tiredness after their European jaunt to Poland. Machin's 30-yard volley sparks a pitch invasion.											
33	A	SUNDERLAND	20	D	1-1	0-0	Hunt 73	Glazier	Bruck	Cattlin	Machin	Setters	Clements	Hannigan	Hunt	Martin	Tudor	Carr	
	23/3	*26,286*	*21*	25			*Moore 59*	*Montgomery*	*Irwin**	*Ashurst*	*Todd*	*Kinnell*	*Palmer*	*Herd*	*Suggett*	*Harris*	*Harvey*	*Mulhall*	*Moore*
							Ref: H Richards	The home side look doomed without a home win since November, despite new manager Alan Brown. Carr is dominant and Ernie Hunt earns a deserved draw with a cheeky goal. Martin looks to be fouled by Kinnell but the ref waves play on. Strong North Sea winds spoil the game.											
34	H	WOLVES	18	W	1-0	0-0	Martin 82p	Glazier	Bruck	Cattlin	Lewis	Setters	Clements	Hannigan*	Hunt	Martin	Tudor	Carr	Coop
	30/3	36,242	*20*	27				*Parkes*	*Parkin*	*Thomson*	*Munro*	*Woodfield*	*Holsgrove*	*Kenning*	*Knowles*	*Wignall*	*Bailey*	*Wagstaffe*	
							Ref: A Dimond	City leapfrog Wolves with two vital points in a dire relegation battle in which only the result matters. Martin slots home after Thomson handles Coop's goal-bound header. City fans give Wignall a torrid time over the Curtis incident earlier in the season. Setters takes no Wolves prisoners.											
35	A	FULHAM	19	D	1-1	0-0	Hill 86	Glazier	Bruck	Cattlin	Machin	Setters	Clements	Hannigan*	Hunt	Martin	Tudor	Carr	Hill
	6/4	*20,869*	*22*	28			*Earle 88*	*Macedo*	*Conway*	*Dempsey*	*Matthewson*	*Callaghan*	*Brown*	*Haynes*	*Earle*	*Byrne*	*Barratt*	*Salvage*	
							Ref: J Finney	Five points separate eleven teams at the foot of the table but Fulham are now six points adrift. City seem to have won it with Hill's first goal for four years. City relaxed and Earle headed home. Hunt's third game on the ground for different clubs this season. Gibson has knee operation.											
36	H	LEEDS	20	L	0-1	0-0		Glazier	Bruck	Cattlin	Machin	Setters	Clements	Baker	Hunt*	Martin	Tudor	Carr	Hill
	13/4	38,778	*2*	28			*Hibbitt 69*	*Harvey*	*Reaney*	*Cooper*	*Bremner*	*Charlton*	*Hunter*	*Lorimer*	*Madeley*	*Jones*	*Giles**	*Hibbitt*	*Belfitt*
							Ref: H Davey	Cool, clinical and lucky, Leeds plunder the points. A goal-less draw looks likely until Glazier mis-hits a clearance to Terry Hibbitt, who hits it into the top right corner. Baker misses City's best chance just before half-time. Leeds are a point off the leaders, Man U, with a game in hand.											
37	H	STOKE	18	W	2-0	0-0	Martin 69, Tudor 73	Glazier	Hill	Cattlin	Machin	Setters	Clements	Hannigan	Lewis	Martin*	Tudor	Carr	Curtis
	15/4	31,380	*21*	30				*Banks*	*Skeels*	*Bentley*	*Bernard*	*Moore*	*Allen*	*Bridgewood*	*Dobing*	*Hulse**	*Eastham*	*Burrows*	*Marsh*
							Ref: K Styles	Stoke's seventh defeat in a row. Martin's head beats Gordon Banks' fist to Cattlin's cross. Tudor hits home Hannigan's defence-splitting pass. A scrappy, niggly game with 42 infringements and Bentley booked. George Curtis makes his overdue comeback for the last eleven minutes.											
38	A	STOKE	19	D	3-3	1-0	Hannigan 24, Carr 58, Martin 63p	Glazier	Hill	Cattlin	Machin	Setters	Clements	Hannigan	Curtis*	Martin	Tudor	Carr	Baker
	16/4	*20,170*	*21*	31			*Mahoney 59, Bentley 78, Dobing 89*	*Banks*	*Skeels*	*Bentley*	*Allen*	*Moore*	*Stevenson*	*Mahoney*	*Vernon*	*Dobing*	*Eastham*	*Burrows*	
							Ref: J Finney	An away win looks certain until Bentley, with a 25-yard free-kick and Dobing in a goalmouth scramble, save a point and spark a pitch invasion. An enthralling match with a large and noisy City following. Martin's penalty came after Allen handles. Curtis takes a knock on his healed leg.											
39	A	TOTTENHAM	19	L	2-4	0-3	Martin 46, 80	Glazier	Hill	Cattlin	Machin	Setters	Clements	Hannigan	Baker*	Martin	Tudor	Carr	Lewis
	20/4	*36,175*	*6*	31			*Jones 6, Mackay 29, Greaves 39, 78*	*Jennings*	*Beal*	*Knowles*	*Mullery*	*Kinnear*	*Mackay*	*Robertson*	*Greaves*	*Chivers**	*Venables*	*Jones*	*Gilzean*
							Ref: R Spittle	Greaves does the damage again. Spurs let City off the hook in the second half and two Martin headers give the scoreline a better look. Spurs' second is controversial as Venables takes a free-kick while the ref is pacing out ten yards and Mackay scores. At 1-3 Carr misses a easy chance.											
40	H	LEICESTER	19	L	0-1	0-0		Glazier	Hill	Cattlin	Machin	Setters	Clements	Hannigan	Hunt*	Martin	Tudor	Carr	Bruck
	27/4	39,888	*14*	31			*Stringfellow 57*	*Shilton*	*Cross*	*Bell*	*Nish*	*Sjoberg*	*Manley*	*Fern*	*Roberts*	*Large*	*Gibson*	*Stringfellow*	
							Ref: S Kayley	A cruel blow in the relegation fight and an undeserved defeat. Brian Hill's fatal mistake lets in Stringfellow. City fail to capitalise on Martin's aerial domination and despite having the lion's share of possession are left rueing their misses. City's rivals also slip up at the foot of the table.											
41	A	WEST HAM	19	D	0-0	0-0		Glazier	Bruck	Cattlin	Hill	Setters	Clements	Hannigan	Machin	Martin	Tudor	Carr	
	4/5	*30,180*	*12*	32				*Ferguson*	*Bonds*	*Howe*	*Peters*	*Stephenson*	*Moore*	*Redknapp*	*Boyce*	*Dear*	*Hurst*	*Sissons*	
							Ref: W Gow	City, Sheff U and Stoke are all on 32 points, leaving fans working out the goal-averages. A gutsy display in which City create more chances than the Hammers but would have been lucky to win. Machin hits the bar near the end. Upton Park's Chicken Run is demolished after the game.											
42	A	SOUTHAMPTON	20	D	0-0	0-0		Glazier	Bruck	Cattlin	Lewis	Setters	Clements	Hannigan	Machin	Martin	Tudor	Carr*	Hunt
	11/5	*25,617*	*16*	33				*Martin*	*Kirkup*	*Hollywood*	*Fisher*	*McGrath*	*Gabriel*	*Thompson*	*Channon*	*Davies*	*Melia*	*Saul*	
	Home	Away					Ref: E Jennings	A muddy surface makes football difficult but City chase, work and harass. In a nail-biting final 20 minutes they slow it down as the players have heard that Chelsea are winning at Bramall Lane. Maurice Setters is the hero for marking the giant Ron Davies. City are safe once again.											
Average	34,715	31,965																	

League Cup								F-A	H-T	Scorers, Times, and Referees	1	2	3	4	5	6	7	8	9	10	11	12 sub used
2	H	ARSENAL		17	L			1-2	0-0	Machin 77	Glazier	Coop	Bruck*	Lewis	Knapp	Clements	Key	Machin	Gould	Gibson	Rees	Carr
	12/9		22,605	*1:6*						*Sammels 48, Graham 58*	*Furnell*	*Storey*	*Simpson*	*McLintock*	*Neill*	*Ure*	*Radford*	*Addison*	*Graham*	*Sammels*	*Armstrong*	
										Ref: V Batty	Even with the returning Gibson and Machin, City lack the subtlety to break down a compact Arsenal. City work hard but it is uphill after Jon Sammels' superb volley. Strong City penalty claims are turned down before Machin squeezes in a consolation, following good work by Gibson.											

FA Cup																					
3	H	CHARLTON		22	W	3-0	0-0	Baker 81, Carr 84, Hannigan 87	Glazier	Kearns	Bruck	Lewis	Setters*	Tudor	Hannigan	Gibson	Baker	Machin	Carr	Hill
	27/1		25,297	*2:18*					*Wright*	*Curtis*	*Kinsey*	*Booth*	*Went*	*Reeves*	*Campbell*	*Tees*	*Gregory*	*Bolland*	*Peacock*	
								Ref: T Dawes	A fumbling display with an unrealistic scoreline. Eddie Firmani's team are unlucky to lose to three late goals. Charlie Wright is at fault for two of them. Rees is dropped and Gould's absence fuels rumours that he might be on his way. Curtis is back in light training after his broken leg.											
4	H	TRANMERE		21	D	1-1	0-0	Rees 74	Glazier	Kearns	Bruck	Machin	Tudor	Hill	Hannigan	Gibson*	Baker	Carr	Rees	Coop
	17/2		32,831	*3:19*				*King A 87*	*Cumbes*	*Storton*	*Martin*	*King J*	*Pritchard*	*King A*	*McNamee*	*Stevens*	*Yardley*	*Hudson*	*Williams*	
								Ref: J Osborne	A sub-standard performance against average opponents. Martin is cup-tied. The unconvincing lead should have been retained. Williams looked to have run the ball out before his cross is headed in by King with Glazier impeded by a shoulder injury. George Hudson misses two chances.											
4R	A	TRANMERE		21	L	0-2	0-2		Dickie	Hill	Bruck	Machin	Setters	Tudor	Hannigan	Morrissey	Baker	Carr	Rees	
	21/2		*20,996*	*3:19*				*Hudson 30, Yardley 36*	*Cumbes*	*Storton*	*Martin*	*Stevens**	*Pritchard*	*A.King*	*McNamee*	*Sinclair*	*Yardley*	*Hudson*	*Williams*	*Casey*
								Ref: J Osborne	Hudson haunts City as the Merseysiders dominate the game and win more easily than the score suggests. Hudson's goal has a suspicion of off-side and Tudor's mistimed tackle leaves Yardley free to rifle home. The crowd is a near record and Dave Russell's team meet Everton in Rd 5.											

		Home					Away					
	P	W	D	L	F	A	W	D	L	F	A	Pts
1 Manchester C	42	17	2	2	52	16	9	4	8	34	27	58
2 Manchester U	42	15	2	4	49	21	9	6	6	40	34	56
3 Liverpool	42	17	2	2	51	17	5	9	7	20	23	55
4 Leeds	42	17	3	1	49	14	5	6	10	22	27	53
5 Everton	42	18	1	2	43	13	5	5	11	24	27	52
6 Chelsea	42	11	7	3	34	25	7	5	9	28	43	48
7 Tottenham	42	11	7	3	44	20	8	2	11	26	39	47
8 West Brom	42	12	4	5	45	25	5	8	8	30	37	46
9 Arsenal	42	12	6	3	37	23	5	4	12	23	33	44
10 Newcastle	42	12	7	2	38	20	1	8	12	16	47	41
11 Nott'm Forest	42	11	6	4	34	22	3	5	13	18	42	39
12 West Ham	42	8	5	8	43	30	6	5	10	30	39	38
13 Leicester	42	7	7	7	37	34	6	5	10	27	35	38
14 Burnley	42	12	7	2	38	16	2	3	16	26	55	38
15 Sunderland	42	8	7	6	28	28	5	4	12	23	33	37
16 Southampton	42	9	8	4	37	31	4	3	14	29	52	37
17 Wolves	42	10	4	7	45	36	4	4	13	21	39	36
18 Stoke	42	10	3	8	30	29	4	4	13	20	44	35
19 Sheffield Wed	42	6	10	5	32	24	5	2	14	19	39	34
20 COVENTRY	42	8	5	8	32	32	1	10	10	19	39	33
21 Sheffield Utd	42	7	4	10	25	31	4	6	11	24	39	32
22 Fulham	42	6	4	11	27	41	4	3	14	29	57	27
	924	244	111	107	850	548	107	111	244	548	850	924

Odds & ends.

Double wins: (1) West Brom.
Double losses: (4) Man City, Tottenham, Everton, Newcastle.

Won from behind: (3) Southampton (h), West Brom (h), Chelsea (h).
Lost from in front: (1) Newcastle.

High spots: Gould's hat-trick in 5-1 win over Burnley.
Beating champions and European champions-elect Man United.
Three successive wins in February after only three in 26 prior to that.

Low spots: Losing 25 match unbeaten run in opening game.
11 games without a win from September-December.
Losing in FA Cup to Tranmere.
George Curtis breaking leg at Nott'm Forest.

Red cards: City – Bruck (Manchester C a).
Red cards: Opponents – St John (Liverpool h), Coleman (Manchester C a).

Ever presents: (0).
Hat-tricks: (2) Bobby Gould, Neil Martin.
Opposing hat-tricks: (0).
Leading scorer: (9) Ronnie Rees.

	Appearances						Goals			
	Lge	*Sub*	LC	*Sub*	FAC	*Sub*	Lge	LC	FAC	Tot
Baker, Gerry	**18**	*1*			3		**4**		1	**5**
Bruck, Dietmar	**33**	*1*	1		3		**1**			**1**
Carr, Willie	**20**	*3*		*1*	3		**1**		1	**2**
Cattlin, Chris	**11**									
Clements, Dave	**40**	*1*	1				**1**			**1**
Coop, Mick	**13**	*2*	1			*1*				
Curtis, George	**3**	*1*								
Denton, Peter	**1**									
Dickie, Alan	**2**				1					
Farmer, Ron	**3**	*1*								
Gibson, Ian	**14**	*1*	1		2					
Glazier, Bill	**40**		1		2					
Gould, Bobby	**13**	*1*	1				**8**			**8**
Hannigan, Ernie	**23**				3		**5**		1	**6**
Hill, Brian	**16**	*2*			2		**1**			**1**
Hunt, Ernie	**6**	*1*					**1**			**1**
Kearns, Mick	**17**				2					
Key, John	**6**		1				**1**			**1**
Knapp, Tony	**11**		1							
Lewis, Brian	**20**	*2*	1		1		**2**			
Machin, Ernie	**40**		1		3		**4**	1		**5**
Martin, Neil	**15**						**8**			**8**
Morrissey, Pat	**6**	*3*			1					
Rees, Ronnie	**30**		1		2		**8**		**1**	**9**
Roberts, Dudley	**1**									
Setters, Maurice	**25**				2		**1**			**1**
Shepherd, Trevor	**1**									
Tudor, John	**34**	*2*			3		**4**			**4**
(own-goals)							**1**			
28 players used	**462**	***22***	**11**	***1***	**33**	***1***	**51**	**1**	**4**	**56**

No	Date	Att	Pos	Pt	F-A	H-T	Scorers, Times, and Referees	1	2	3	4	5	6	7	8	9	10	11	12 sub used
1	A SHEFFIELD WED		22	L	0-3	0-1		Glazier	Bruck*	Cattlin	Machin	Setters	Clements	Hannigan	Hunt	Curtis	Tudor	Carr	Baker
	17/8	*26,235*	*4*	0			*Fantham 22, 70, Ritchie 78*	*Springett*	*Smith*	*Megson*	*Ellis*	*Mobley*	*Eustace*	*Fantham*	*McCalliog*	*Ritchie*	*Ford*	*Pugh**	*Whitham*
							Ref: R Darlington	Building works on the new stand mean City start the season a week late. Gibson is dropped and Curtis up front doesn't work but the scoreline is a bit harsh on a reasonable City performance. Two set pieces are Coventry's downfall, Fantham scoring with a low ground shot and a tap in.											
2	A MANCHESTER U		22	L	0-1	0-1		Glazier	Bruck	Cattlin	Hill*	Setters	Clements	Hannigan	Hunt	Tudor	Machin	Carr	Gibson
	21/8	***51,201***	*8*	0			*Ryan 16*	*Stepney*	*Kopel*	*Dunne*	*Fitzpatrick*	*Sadler*	*Stiles*	*Ryan*	*Kidd*	*Charlton*	*Burns*	*Best*	
							Ref: K Walker	A dull game and a poor performance by the European champions. Coventry never threaten to pull back the deficit and Alex Stepney is under-employed. City's defence contains United's stars well and Glazier makes four outstanding saves. Ryan connects with a high-bouncing ball.											
3	H WEST HAM		22	L	1-2	1-1	Setters 31	Glazier	Bruck	Cattlin	Machin	Setters	Hill	Hannigan	Tudor	Baker	Gibson	Clements	
	24/8	33,575	*5*	0			*Peters 3, Brooking 58*	*Ferguson*	*Bonds*	*Charles*	*Peters*	*Stephenson*	*Moore*	*Redknapp*	*Boyce*	*Brooking*	*Hurst*	*Sissons*	
							Ref: A Jones	City dominate the first half after Martin Peters ghosts in to meet Redknapp's cross. Setters pulls them level and Gerry Baker hits a post. After the break West Ham take over. City's defence is in disarray but they miss a hatful of chances. Neil Martin and Willie Carr are badly missed.											
4	H WEST BROM		22	W	4-2	3-1	Hunt 2p, 15, 25, Machin 64	Glazier	Bruck	Cattlin	Machin	Setters	Hill	Hunt	Gibson	Baker	Tudor	Clements	
	27/8	36,678	*6*	2			*Rees 17, Brown 85*	*Sheppard*	*Clarke*	*Williams*	*Fraser*	*Talbut*	*Kaye*	*Krzywicki*	*Brown*	*Astle*	*Lovatt*	*Rees*	
							Ref: H New	A memorable night as Ernie Hunt and the unsettled Ian Gibson demolish Albion. Kaye makes an innocuous challenge on Baker for the penalty. Gibson places a 35-yard ball onto Hunt's head for the second and sets up the third with a jinking run. Sheppard can't hold Machin's fierce shot.											
5	A BURNLEY		21	D	1-1	1-0	Gibson 15	Glazier	Coop	Cattlin	Machin	Setters	Hill	Hunt	Tudor	Baker*	Gibson	Clements	Curtis
	31/8	***12,936***	*15*	3			*Waldron 60*	*Thomson*	*Angus*	*Latcham*	*O'Neill**	*Waldron*	*Merrington*	*Coates*	*Lochhead*	*Casper*	*Bellamy*	*Thomas*	*Blant*
							Ref: D Pugh	Gibson stars again. City dominate a bright first half and Gibson scores a super goal by rounding the keeper. After the break City let the home side back in, and Colin Waldron scores with a volley. Hunt is booked for not retreating at a free-kick. A new stand is being built at Turf Moor.											
6	H NEWCASTLE		19	W	2-1	1-1	Baker 23, Gibson 75	Glazier	Coop	Cattlin	Machin	Setters	Hill	Hunt	Tudor	Baker*	Gibson	Clements	Shepherd
	7/9	33,361	*11*	5			*Sinclair 8*	*McFaul*	*Craig**	*Clark*	*Gibb*	*McNamee*	*Burton*	*Sinclair*	*Robson B*	*Davies*	*Elliott*	*Allen*	*Iley*
							Ref: R Capey	Gibson enjoys a purple patch and his superb shot inflicts Newcastle's second defeat of the season. Baker's header had cancelled out Sinclair's soft opener. Press reports link Wyn Davies with a move to City and the fans show their respect for him. Cantwell resigns as Eire co-manager.											
7	H CHELSEA		19	L	0-1	0-1		Glazier	Coop	Cattlin	Machin	Setters	Hill	Hunt	Tudor	Baker*	Gibson	Clements	Carr
	10/9	36,217	*4*	5			*Osgood 18*	*Bonetti*	*Hinton*	*McCreadie*	*Hollins*	*Webb*	*Boyle*	*Baldwin*	*Tambling*	*Osgood*	*Birchenall*	*Cooke*	
							Ref: G Singleton	One of the great games of the era played in heavy rain on a quagmire. City paralyse Chelsea with flair and authority but can't retrieve Osgood's goal, when he pounced on Setters' back-pass that stuck in the mud. Chelsea defend in depth, but still allow City to muster 21 shots on target.											
8	A NOTT'M FOREST		19	D	0-0	0-0		Glazier	Coop	Cattlin	Machin	Setters	Hill	Hunt	Carr	Tudor	Gibson	Clements	
	14/9	*22,260*	*13*	6				*Williamson*	*Hindley*	*Winfield*	*Hennessey*	*McKinlay*	*Newton**	*Lyons*	*Barnwell*	*Baker*	*Chapman*	*Moore*	*Hilley*
							Ref: K Markham	A recent fire at the City Ground means this game is played at Meadow Lane. City's defence held firm. The best chance fell to Gibson, but Hindley clears off the line. Coop is hero - for a last-ditch tackle on Moore, and villain - with a wild challenge on Newton, who requires stitches.											
9	H TOTTENHAM		19	L	1-2	1-0	Tudor 17	Glazier	Coop	Cattlin	Machin	Setters	Hill	Hunt	Tudor	Baker*	Gibson	Clements	Carr
	17/9	40,950	*9*	6			*Chivers 54, Gilzean 78*	*Jennings*	*Kinnear*	*Knowles*	*Mullery*	*England*	*Beal*	*Jones*	*Greaves*	*Chivers*	*Venables*	*Gilzean*	
							Ref: D Brady	City let Spurs off the hook after dominating the first hour of another classic. Tudor hits a screamer from 25 yards. Chivers replies with a soft header and Glazier can only push Alan Gilzean's header into the net. Coventry have three goals disallowed. Eddie Plumley joins as secretary.											
10	H EVERTON		19	D	2-2	2-2	Setters 9, Gibson 41	Glazier	Coop	Cattlin	Machin	Setters	Hill	Hunt	Tudor	**Hateley**	Gibson*	Clements	Carr
	21/9	37,846	*7*	7			*Husband 23, Hurst 28*	*West*	*Wright*	*Brown*	*Kendall*	*Labone*	*Harvey*	*Husband*	*Ball*	*Royle*	*Hurst*	*Morrissey*	
							Ref: K Styles	The £80,000 striker signed from Liverpool is well shackled in a below par performance. Everton dominate for long periods with Royle superb but City have some luck at last. Setters' bullet header and Gibson's half-volley set up a keen second half. Everton are now unbeaten in nine.											

No	Date	Opponent	Att	Pos	Pt	F-A	H-T	Scorers, Times, and Referees	1	2	3	4	5	6	7	8	9	10	11	12 sub used
11	A	LEICESTER		15	D	1-1	1-0	Hunt 38	Glazier	Coop	Cattlin	Machin	Curtis	Hill	Hunt	Tudor	Hateley	Carr	Clements	
	28/9		*32,122*	*21*	8			*Fern 52*	*Shilton*	*Woolett*	*Bell*	*Nish*	*Manley*	*Cross*	*Glover*	*Clarke**	*Fern*	*Gibson*	*Stringfellow*	*Roberts*
								Ref: N Burtenshaw	Gibson, the recent hero, is missing injured. City erect a stern rearguard but Carr misses an open goal 19 minutes from end. Hunt hits a screamer from a narrow angle. City fail to clear a corner and Rodney Fern takes advantage. Many City fans make up Leicester's biggest gate of the season.											
12	H	WOLVES		20	L	0-1	0-0		Glazier	Coop	Bruck	Machin	Curtis	Hill	Hunt	Tudor	Hateley	Gibson	Clements	
	5/10		39,271	*15*	8			*Dougan 60*	*Boswell*	*Parkin*	*Thomson*	*Bailey*	*Woodfield*	*Holsgrove*	*Wilson*	*Knowles*	*Dougan*	*Wignall*	*Kenning*	
								Ref: A Dimond	Wolves lost 0-6 at home to Liverpool last week. They soak up City's pressure and snatch a fortuitous win through Derek Dougan's close-range header. Coventry look tired after their midweek win. Frank Wignall was constantly given the bird, yet had the temerity to charge into Glazier.											
13	A	WEST BROM		21	L	**1-6**	0-1	Hunt 64 *[Hartford 66, Tudor 81 (og)]*	Glazier	Coop	Bruck	Hill*	Curtis	Setters	Hunt	Machin	Hateley	Carr	Clements	Tudor
	9/10		*29,926*	*9*	8			*Rees 9, Brown 46p, Astle 51, 75,*	*Osborne*	*Fraser*	*Wilson*	*Brown*	*Talbut*	*Kaye*	*Rees*	*Collard*	*Astle*	*Hope*	*Hartford*	
								Ref: B Homewood	Albion gain revenge in magnificent manner and could easily have scored nine. Hill is injured fouling Jeff Astle for the penalty. Tudor is unable to master the lively Astle and deflects Brown's hard cross for the sixth. Hartford's screamer was the best. City's biggest defeat for three years.											
14	A	ARSENAL		22	L	1-2	1-0	Hunt 36	Glazier	Coop	Bruck	Machin	Setters	Hill	Hunt	Carr	Hateley	Clements	Gibson*	Tudor
	12/10		*35,240*	*3*	8			*Court 65, Radford 87*	*Wilson*	*Storey*	*McNab*	*Ure*	*Neill*	*Simpson*	*Radford*	*Armstrong*	*Gould*	*Court*	*Jenkins**	*Graham*
								Ref: C Thomas	City lose despite creating more chances. Hateley hasn't scored for five games. Hunt heads in Coop's cross. Sub Graham's entry turned the game. Glazier palms out a corner and Court fires in. Radford clinches it following a slick move from a free-kick. Bruck and Machin are both booked.											
15	H	MANCHESTER C		19	D	1-1	0-1	Hateley 54	Glazier	Bruck	Cattlin	Machin*	Setters	Hill	Hunt	Gibson	Hateley	Tudor	Clements	Coop
	19/10		30,670	*12*	9			*Bruck 29 (og)*	*Dowd*	*Connor*	*Pardoe*	*Doyle*	*Booth*	*Oakes*	*Lee*	*Bell*	*Summerbee*	*Young*	*Coleman*	
								Ref: J Osborne	Another lacklustre first-half show. Bruck diverts Lee's cross in. A better second half sees Hateley nudge home his first league goal to make up for a bad miss. Brian Hill marks Mike Summerbee out of the game. A fair result against the champions, wearing a new red and black away kit.											
16	A	SUNDERLAND		21	L	0-3	0-1		Glazier	Bruck	Cattlin	Machin	Curtis	Hill	Carr	Hunt	Hateley	Martin*	Gibson	Tudor
	26/10		*21,981*	*11*	9			*Harris 18p, 75, Mulhall 52*	*Montgomery*	*Irwin*	*Harvey**	*Hurley*	*Todd*	*Palmer*	*Herd*	*Harris*	*Hughes*	*Suggett*	*Mulhall*	*Porterfield*
								Ref: L Cussons	Roker's gate is down following Sunderland's 0-8 crushing at West Ham. Martin is captain for the day. Curtis lunges at Harris, Glazier saves the penalty, but a linesman says he moved. Harris scores at the second attempt. Mulhall heads in Hughes' cross and Harris scores from 15 yards.											
17	H	SOUTHAMPTON		20	D	1-1	0-1	Machin 84	Glazier	Coop	Clements	Machin	Curtis	Hill	Hunt	Gibson	Hateley	Martin	Carr	
	2/11		**24,126**	*15*	10			*Paine 24*	*Gurr*	*Kirkup*	*Jones*	*Kemp*	*McGrath*	*Byrne*	*Paine*	*Channon*	*Davies*	*Walker*	*Saul*	
								Ref: P Walters	A cold wintry day. City create endless chances and hit the woodwork four times. Ron Davies sets up Paine after a slick move. Machin drives in the equaliser from 18 yards, but it is now eleven games without a win. Lowest gate for two years. Gerry Baker is on World Cup duty for USA.											
18	A	STOKE		19	W	3-0	2-0	Hateley 7, 41, Martin 68	Glazier	Coop	Clements	Machin	Curtis	Hill	Hunt*	Gibson	Hateley	Martin	Carr	Tudor
	9/11		*16,117*	*17*	12				*Banks*	*Marsh*	*Elder*	*Skeels*	*Bloor*	*Bernard*	*Mahoney*	*Dobing*	*Herd*	*Stevenson*	*Burrows*	
								Ref: D Laing	First away win since February. The Hateley-Martin combo comes off. Hateley nets with a bullet header from Machin's cross and again with a hooked goal after Alan Bloor fails to clear from Hunt. Martin's looping header clinches it against England's keeper. City's fans are in ecstasy.											
19	H	LEEDS		19	L	0-1	0-1		Glazier	Coop	Clements	Machin	Curtis	Hill	Hunt	Gibson	Hateley	Martin	Carr	
	16/11		33,224	*3*	12			*Madeley 21*	*Sprake*	*Reaney*	*Cooper*	*Bremner*	*Charlton*	*Hunter*	*O'Grady*	*Madeley*	*Jones*	*Giles*	*Gray*	
								Ref: V Batty	Leeds are without a win for a month but once ahead are virtually unbeatable. Sprake is much the busier keeper and he keeps out two specials from Tony Hateley. Paul Madeley bends a fierce shot in after a corner isn't cleared. John Tudor transfers to Sheffield United for £65,000.											
20	A	LIVERPOOL		19	L	0-2	0-1		Glazier	Coop*	Clements	Machin	Curtis	Hill	Hannigan	Hunt	Hateley	Gibson	Carr	Cattlin
	23/11		*44,820*	*1*	12			*Strong 36, Callaghan 86*	*Lawrence*	*Lawler*	*Strong*	*Smith*	*Yeats*	*Hughes*	*Callaghan*	*Hunt*	*Evans*	*St.John*	*Thompson*	
								Ref: K Styles	A heroic performance, but City fail to turn their superiority into goals. Strong's long-range shot deceives Glazier and goes in off a post. St John makes Callaghan's goal. Ernie Hunt's 'goal' is ruled out, Hateley hits the bar, Lawrence saves from Gibson. Machin and Clements are booked.											
21	H	IPSWICH		19	L	0-2	0-1		Glazier	Coop	Clements	Machin	Curtis	Hill	Hunt	Gibson*	Hateley	Martin	Carr	Baker
	30/11		26,760	*17*	12			*O'Rourke 3, Hunt 49*	*Hancock*	*Mills*	*Houghton*	*Morris*	*Baxter*	*Jefferson*	*Hegan*	*Viljoen*	*Hunt*	*O'Rourke*	*Brogan*	
								Ref: A Morrissey	Modest opponents inflict City's sixth home defeat. O'Rourke's flicked header from a corner and Bobby Hunt's tap in from Morris's free-kick win the points. Keeper Hancock is in good form but City's attack is powder puff. Gibson injures knee ligaments and will be out for a while.											

No	Date	Opponent	Att	Pos	Pt	F-A	H-T	Scorers, Times, and Referees	1	2	3	4	5	6	7	8	9	10	11	12 sub used
22	A	QP RANGERS		19	W	1-0	1-0	Carr 3	Glazier	Coop	Cattlin	Machin	Curtis	Clements	Hannigan	Hunt	Hateley	Martin	Carr	
	7/12		*17,921*	*22*	14				*Springett*	*Clement*	*Harris*	*Sibley*	*Watson*	*Hazell*	*Morgan I*	*Wilks*	*Leach*	*Marsh*	*Morgan R*	
								Ref: T Dawes	A vital win in a poor quality, ugly, relegation clash. City dominate early on and deserve more than Carr's crisp shot. Then they sink to QPR's level. Marsh seems to make a meal of Martin's challenge but fires the spot-kick wide nine minutes from time. Martin and Hunt are booked.											
23	H	ARSENAL		21	L	0-1	0-0		Glazier	Coop	Cattlin	Machin	Curtis	Clements	Hannigan*	Hunt	Hateley	Martin	Carr	Shepherd
	14/12		27,332	*4*	14			*Gould 70*	*Wilson*	*Storey*	*McNab*	*McLintock*	*Ure*	*Simpson*	*Radford*	*Robertson*	*Court*	*Gould*	*Graham*	
								Ref: R Harper	A carbon copy of recent home games. Bags of enthusiasm and pressure in the first half but then tailing away and being punished by opponents. Gould converted Arsenal's only real chance, an acute angled shot after Radford's effort was blocked. Hateley won his aerial duel with Ian Ure.											
24	A	MANCHESTER C		21	L	2-4	1-2	Shepherd 5, Hateley 77	Glazier	Coop	Cattlin	Machin	Curtis	Clements	Shepherd	Hunt	Hateley	Martin	Carr	
	21/12		*27,700*	*15*	14			*Booth 16, Young 39, 48, Curtis 53 (og)*	*Dowd*	*Pardoe*	*Mann*	*Doyle*	*Booth*	*Oakes*	*Lee*	*Bell*	*Owen*	*Young*	*Coleman*	
								Ref: P Partridge	One blatant offside goal, two deflections and a Neil Young special from 30 yards sink City. They score first and last and create two good chances near the end but never deserved a draw. Curtis deflects Bell's shot for the fourth. Glazier and the defence are not in commanding form.											
25	A	SOUTHAMPTON		21	L	0-1	0-0		Glazier	Coop	Cattlin	Machin	Curtis	Hill	Hannigan	Carr	Hateley	Shepherd*	Clements	**Blockley**
	11/1		*19,616*	*8*	14			*Gabriel 89*	*Gurr*	*Kirkup*	*Hollywood*	*Kemp*	*McGrath*	*Gabriel*	*Paine*	*Saul*	*Davies*	*Walker*	*Sydenham*	
								Ref: D Smith	A ninth one-goal defeat in 15 and another unlucky loss to Ted Bates' men. Only 22 goals scored tells the story, and more chances are missed here. Jimmy Gabriel's header from an unnecessary corner, conceded by Mick Coop, wins it. Cattlin and Paine are booked on a sticky surface.											
26	A	LEEDS		21	L	0-3	0-1		Glazier	Coop	Cattlin	Machin	Curtis	Hill	Hannigan	Hunt	Martin	Carr	Clements	
	1/2		*32,590*	*2*	14			*O'Grady 4, Bremner 69, 89*	*Sprake*	*Reaney*	*Cooper*	*Bremner*	*Charlton*	*Hunter*	*Lorimer*	*Madeley**	*Jones*	*Gray*	*O'Grady*	*Hibbitt*
								Ref: S Kayley	City play well but Leeds are awesome, especially Bremner. He scores when Glazier, impeded by Charlton, partially clears a corner. He takes advantage of slack defence for the third. The situation is critical as City are losing touch with the safety zone. Will Malcolm Allison be coach?											
27	H	QP RANGERS		21	W	**5-0**	2-0	Machin 10, Hunt 29, Martin 58,	Glazier	Coop	Cattlin	Machin	Curtis	Hill	Shepherd*	Hunt	Martin	Carr	Clements	**Paddon**
	25/2		26,449	*22*	16			*[Clements 70, 80]*	*Kelly*	*Watson*	*Clement*	*Hazell*	*Hunt*	*Harris*	*Morgan I*	*Leach*	*Clarke*	*Marsh*	*Bridges*	
								Ref: G Kew	The first home game for ten weeks lifts City off the bottom. This is City's biggest Div 1 win to date, and their first home win since September. Machin's piledriver and Clements first, a superb move involving four players, are the best goals. QPR look doomed. The stadium clock stopped.											
28	H	SUNDERLAND		21	W	3-1	1-0	Martin 42, 57p, Carr 88	Glazier	Coop	Cattlin	Machin	Curtis	Hill*	Shepherd	Hunt	Martin	Carr	Clements	Hannigan
	4/3		29,546	*17*	18			*Moore 89*	*Montgomery*	*Irwin*	*Harvey*	*Todd*	*Pitt*	*Heslop*	*Harris*	*Palmer*	*Moore*	*Suggett*	*Hughes**	*Beesley*
								Ref: R Spittle	City get ruthless in front of goal. Martin stars against his old team. From a free-kick he forces in when Montgomery, called up for the England squad, parries. Irwin handles and Martin converts the penalty. Carr drives in a hard low cross and it defects off Harvey. City are back in touch.											
29	H	SHEFFIELD WED		20	W	3-0	2-0	Martin 8, Curtis 19, Hunt 61	Glazier	Coop	Cattlin	Machin	Curtis	Hill	Shepherd	Hunt	Martin	Carr	Clements	
	8/3		30,230	*10*	20				*Springett*	*Smith*	*Burton*	*Young*	*Mobley*	*Pugh**	*Irvine*	*McCalliog*	*Ritchie*	*Fantham*	*Ford*	*Branfoot*
								Ref: N Burtenshaw	Three wins in a row. Safety looks possible. Martin stars again and scores with a jack-knife header from Clements' corner. Curtis thunders in a header as Martin acts as decoy from a corner. Shepherd back-heels to Hunt, who drives in a low shot. Wednesday are anaemic and outfought.											
30	A	CHELSEA		20	L	1-2	0-2	Martin 66	Glazier	Coop	Cattlin	Machin	Curtis	Hill*	Shepherd	Hunt	Martin	Carr	Clements	Bruck
	10/3		*17,630*	*5*	20			*Hutchison 2, Tambling 28*	*Bonetti*	*Webb*	*McCreadie*	*Hollins*	*Dempsey*	*Harris*	*Boyle*	*Tambling*	*Hutchison*	*Birchenall*	*Houseman*	
								Ref: R Tinkler	Chelsea hang on for both points. New hero Hutchinson looks offside as he scores at the near post. Bobby Tambling's 200th goal for Chelsea is easy but Curtis is fouled by Hutchinson in the build up. Martin nets a sweet header from Clements' cross. Poor crowd for a Monday night game.											
31	A	WEST HAM		21	L	2-5	0-2	Machin 49, Hunt 73 *[Bonds 87]*	Glazier	Coop	Cattlin	Machin	Curtis	Blockley	Hannigan	Hunt	Martin	Carr	Clements	
	14/3		*29,053*	*6*	20			*Sissons 2, Peters 12, Hurst 59p, 81p,*	*Ferguson*	*Bonds*	*Howe*	*Peters*	*Stephenson*	*Moore*	*Redknapp*	*Boyce*	*Brooking*	*Hurst*	*Sissons*	
								Ref: R Johnson	Two late goals give the score a surreal look. Sissons' cross slices off Curtis and Glazier lets Peters' header through his hands. Two penalties, for Coop tripping Sissons, and, disputed, when the ball hits Coop's hand. City replied with Machin's deflected free-kick and Hunt's volley.											

No	Venue / Date	Opponent	Att	Pos	Res	Pts	F-A	H-T	Scorers, Times, Referees	1	2	3	4	5	6	7	8	9	10	11	12
32	H	STOKE		21	D		1-1	0-1	Carr 61	Glazier	Coop	Cattlin	Machin	Curtis	Blockley	Shepherd	Hunt	Martin	Carr	Clements	
	18/3		25,102	*18*		21			*Herd 29*	*Banks*	*Marsh*	*Elder*	*Skeels*	*Smith*	*Stevenson*	*Herd**	*Dobing*	*Conroy*	*Mahoney*	*Burrows*	*Lacey*
									Ref: E Wallace	Honours even in a tight relegation battle. Curtis' error lets in David Herd. Carr levels with a thunderous shot off the underside of the bar after Gordon Banks punches out Clements' corner. Martin was mastered by young Dennis Smith. Stoke withstood massive City pressure on Banks.											
33	H	BURNLEY		20	W		4-1	0-0	Clements 57, Martin 60, Hunt 77, [Machin 84]	Glazier	Coop	Cattlin	Machin	Curtis	Blockley	Shepherd	Hunt*	Martin	Carr	Clements	Baker
	22/3		26,584	*9*		23			*Collins 79*	*Jones**	*Murray*	*Latcham*	*Merrington*	*Waldron*	*Blant*	*Thomas*	*Coates*	*Casper*	*Dobson*	*Collins*	*Bellamy*
									Ref: K Walker	After a dour first half, City take control. Clements scores from Martin's skied centre, Martin from Coop's lob, Hunt with a banana-shot that looks to be going wide. Latcham goes in goal for the injured Jones. Collins scores after Waldron's bad miss, before Machin takes Baker's pass.											
34	A	IPSWICH		20	D		0-0	0-0		Glazier	Coop	Cattlin	Machin	Curtis	Blockley	Hannigan	Hill	Martin	Carr	Clements	
	25/3		*20,525*	*10*		24				*Best*	*Mills*	*Harper*	*Barnard*	*Baxter*	*Jefferson*	*Miller*	*Hegan*	*Brogan*	*O'Rourke*	*Lambert*	
									Ref: B Homewood	With several players down with flu Bobby Robson tries to get the game postponed. Miller and Lambert make their debuts. City fight rearguard action and congest midfield. Martin should have won it five minutes from time. Ipswich, having a good first season, don't get a shot on target.											
35	A	NEWCASTLE		20	L		0-2	0-0		Glazier	Coop	Hill	Machin	Curtis	Blockley	Hannigan	Hunt	Martin	Carr	Clements	
	29/3		*27,500*	*14*		24			*Robson B 63p, McNamee 71*	*McFaul*	*Craggs*	*Clark*	*Gibb*	*McNamee*	*Moncur*	*Sinclair*	*Robson B*	*Davies*	*Elliott*	*Foggon*	
									Ref: A Jones	Newcastle return from a tough Fairs Cup tie in Portugal to do just enough to win. City hold out for an hour with Curtis holding his old foe Wyn Davies, then Blockley handles. McNamee squeezes home a hook shot. The closest City get is when Craggs clears Martin's shot off the line.											
36	H	LEICESTER		20	W		1-0	0-0	Martin 88	Glazier	Coop	Cattlin	Machin	Curtis	Hill	Shepherd	Hunt	Martin	Carr	Clements	
	1/4		41,484	*21*		26				*Shilton*	*Woolett*	*Nish*	*Manley*	*Sjoberg*	*Cross*	*Fern*	*Roberts*	*Lochhead*	*Matthews*	*Stringfellow**	*Greenhalgh*
									Ref: A Dimond	A vital win in the definitive four pointer. Fern and Carr miss good chances before Martin volleys home Coop's cross at the death. Six minutes earlier the ref gives Leicester a penalty when Greenhalgh fell in the box under pressure from Curtis, but the linesman gives a foul the other way!											
37	A	TOTTENHAM		20	L		0-2	0-2		Glazier	Coop	Cattlin	Machin	Curtis	Hill	Shepherd	Hunt	Martin	Carr	Clements*	Blockley
	4/4		*35,034*	*8*		26			*Johnson 3, Pearce 44*	*Jennings*	*Evans*	*Knowles*	*Mullery*	*England*	*Beal*	*Johnson*	*Greaves*	*Pearce*	*Pratt*	*Morgan*	
									Ref: D Consell	Another sloppy away performance on a blustery day against disinterested Spurs. Johnson scores from a narrow angle. City miss three good chances and Evans hits his own post. Pearce capitalises on Curtis' indecision with a crisp drive. Clements slowed down and eventually subbed.											
38	H	MANCHESTER U		20	W		2-1	1-0	Curtis 3, Martin 48	Glazier	Coop	Cattlin	Machin	Curtis	Blockley	Baker*	Hunt	Martin	Carr	Hill	Hannigan
	8/4		**45,402**	*9*		28			*Fitzpatrick 69*	*Stepney*	*Fitzpatrick*	*Stiles*	*Crerand*	*James*	*Sadler*	*Morgan*	*Kidd*	*Best*	*Charlton*	*Aston*	
									Ref: H New	United have picked up 12 points out of 14 but City are good value for this win. Stepney can only parry Curtis' header over the line. Martin hits a post before half-time and fires home when Stepney drops the ball. John Fitzpatrick drives in after Kidd's run. United lay siege till the whistle.											
39	A	EVERTON		20	L		0-3	0-1		Glazier	Coop	Cattlin	Machin	Curtis	Blockley	Baker	Hunt	Martin	Carr	Setters	
	12/4		*36,165*	*4*		28			*Hurst 30, Husband 64, Royle 76*	*West*	*Wright*	*Brown*	*Jackson*	*Labone*	*Harvey*	*Husband*	*Whittle**	*Royle*	*Hurst*	*Morrissey*	*Kendall*
									Ref: N Graham	One away point since December tells the story. Setters plays his first game for seven months. City are never in it once Hurst takes advantage of indecision. Husband finishes off a fluent move. Royle nets a freakish third. All City's rivals lose. Everton look a good bet for next year's title.											
40	A	WOLVES		20	D		1-1	1-0	Hunt 30	Glazier	Coop	Cattlin	Machin	Setters	Bruck	Hannigan	Hunt	Martin	Carr	Blockley	
	15/4		*32,535*	*15*		29			*Knowles 71*	*Parkes*	*Taylor**	*Parkin*	*Wilson*	*Holsgrove*	*McAlle*	*Lutton*	*Knowles*	*Dougan*	*Curran*	*Wagstaffe*	*Munro*
									Ref: T Hill	City are vastly superior to a Wolves side with nothing to play for. Setters is back at centre-half and the defence looks tight. Cattlin's free-kick is headed on by Blockley and Hunt steers in from an acute angle. McGarry's men grab a point with a deflected free-kick off Machin's shoulder.											
41	H	NOTT'M FOREST		20	D		1-1	0-1	Hannigan 74	Glazier	Coop	Bruck	Machin	Setters	Blockley	Shepherd	Hunt	Martin	Carr	Clements*	Hannigan
	19/4		37,772	*19*		30			*Moore 9*	*Hill*	*Hindley*	*Winfield*	*Chapman*	*McKinlay*	*Newton*	*Lyons*	*Hilley*	*Baker*	*Baxter*	*Moore**	*Richardson*
									Ref: R Harper	A tense game with so much at stake. Moore scores a classy goal but goes off at half-time. Chairman Robins calls for more vocal support. Forest hang on until Ernie Hannigan hooks Coop's cross in. Martin's header shaves the bar. Leicester are five points behind with four games in hand.											
42	H	LIVERPOOL		20	D		0-0	0-0		Glazier	Coop	Cattlin*	Bruck	Setters !	Blockley	Hannigan	Hunt	Martin	Hateley	Carr	Curtis
	22/4		35,116	*2*		31				*Lawrence*	*Lawler*	*Strong*	*Smith*	*Yeats*	*Hughes*	*Callaghan*	*Graham*	*Evans !*	*St.John*	*Thompson*	
	Home		Away						Ref: V James	A cliff hanger for both teams. Liverpool must win to have any chance of catching Leeds. On the hour Alun Evans reacts to a late Setters tackle and they are both sent off. Leicester earn five points from their next four games but lose their final match at Old Trafford 2-3 and City are safe.											
Average	33,224		28,053																		

League Cup	F-A	H-T	Scorers, Times, and Referees	1	2	3	4	5	6	7	8	9	10	11	12 sub used
2 H PORTSMOUTH 21 W	2-0	0-0	Gibson 54, Hunt 80	Glazier	Coop	Cattlin	Machin	Setters	Hill	Hunt	Gibson	Martin	Tudor	Clements	
3/9 20,946 *2:17*				Milkins	Pack	Youlden	Smith	Tindall	Harris	Pointer	Travers	Brown	Hiron	Jennings	
			Ref: D Smith	City dominated and were never in danger. Bill Glazier is a spectator with barely a shot to save. Neil Martin returns, pulls a muscle but stays on. Ian Gibson scores with a crisp ground shot. Coop, Tudor and Clements go close before Machin finds Hunt, who easily sweeps the ball home.											
3 A WEST HAM 19 D	0-0	0-0		Glazier	Coop	Cattlin	Curtis	Setters	Hill	Hannigan	Machin	Hunt	Carr	Clements	
25/9 *27,594 5*				*Ferguson*	*Bonds*	*Charles*	*Peters*	*Stephenson*	*Moore*	*Redknapp*	*Boyce*	*Brooking*	*Hurst*	*Sissons*	
			Ref: R Johnson	West Ham had scored seven against Bolton in Round 2. Curtis returns to play double centre-half and, along with the defiant Glazier, thwarts the rampant Hammers. Cattlin's Under 23 call-up does him the power of good and Brian Hill man-marks Geoff Hurst. London jinx is checked.											
3R H WEST HAM 15 W	3-2	2-1	Hunt 42, Tudor 44, Clements 53	Glazier	Coop	Bruck	Machin	Curtis	Hill	Hunt	Carr	Tudor	Gibson*	Clements	Hannigan
1/10 26,896 *4*			*Hurst 45, Peters 86*	*Ferguson*	*Howe*	*Charles*	*Peters*	*Cushley*	*Moore*	*Redknapp*	*Boyce*	*Brooking*	*Hurst*	*Dear*	
			Ref: I Jones	This hard-fought win avenges the league defeat. Gibson is back and torments Moore. Hunt forces in Machin's free-kick. Minutes later Tudor looks offside as he nets. Hurst's instant volley sets up a keen second half. Tudor hits a post and Clements pokes it in. Hammers' late flurry fails.											
4 H SWINDON 22 D	2-2	0-1	Tudor 86, Hateley 88	Glazier	Coop	Bruck	Machin	Setters	Hill	Hunt	Gibson	Hateley	Martin*	Carr	Tudor
16/10 23,587 *3:4*			*Rogers 42, Smart 70*	*Downsboro'*	*Dawson*	*Thomas*	*Butler*	*Burrows*	*Harland*	*Heath*	*Smart*	*Smith*	*Noble*	*Rogers*	
			Ref: R Paine	Martin returns but limps off in the 13th minute. City are lucky to force a replay. Rogers races through the middle to fire home. Heath heads down for Smart to drive in a second. With the crowd pouring out, Tudor scores from close range then Hateley soars to head in Gibson's cross.											
4R A SWINDON 19 L	0-3	0-3		Glazier	Clements	Cattlin	Curtis	Setters	Hill	Hannigan*	Tudor	Hateley	Hunt	Gibson	Bruck
21/10 *23,828 3:1*			*Rogers 11, Smart 16, Penman 26*	*Downsboro'*	*Butler*	*Thomas*	*Penman*	*Burrows*	*Harland*	*Heath*	*Smart*	*Smith*	*Noble*	*Rogers*	
			Ref: K Walker	A great night for Swindon. They outclass and outfight Coventry. Bert Head's team are Wembley bound and City are brushed aside within 30 minutes. Ex-City man John Smith is the architect. Rogers goal comes from nothing as he unleashes a right footer, as he cuts in from the left.											

FA Cup															
3 H BLACKPOOL 21 W	3-1	0-0	Machin 83, Curtis 88, Shepherd 89	Glazier	Coop	Cattlin	Machin	Curtis	Hill	Hunt	Carr	Hateley	Martin*	Clements	Shepherd
4/1 28,223 *2:10*			*Brown 66*	*Thomas*	*Armfield*	*Thompson*	*Craven*	*James*	*McPhee*	*Brown*	*Green*	*Rowe*	*White**	*Suddick*	*Milne*
			Ref: P Baldwin	With seven minutes left it looked like another home defeat but for once City kept going. Machin equalises with a great shot from Carr's free-kick. Curtis bangs home the second and Shepherd latches on to a back-pass and gives the scoreline a surreal look. Curtis is at fault for the goal.											
4 A EVERTON 21 L	0-2	0-1		Glazier	Coop	Cattlin	Machin	Curtis	Hill	Shepherd*	Hunt	Martin	Carr	Clements	Hannigan
25/1 *53,289 3*			*Royle 28, Hurst 89*	*West*	*Wright*	*Wilson*	*Kendall*	*Labone*	*Brown*	*Husband*	*Ball*	*Royle*	*Hurst*	*Morrissey*	
			Ref: G McCabe	George Curtis' 500th game. Everton are largely contained but City never threaten West's goal. Royle rounds off a superb move by beating Glazier to Morrissey's cross. Glazier injures a shoulder but plays on. Coach Andrews leaves the club. Noel Cantwell is linked to Man Utd job.											

		Home						Away					
		P	W	D	L	F	A	W	D	L	F	A	Pts
1	Leeds	42	18	3	0	41	9	9	10	2	25	17	67
2	Liverpool	42	16	4	1	36	10	9	7	5	27	14	61
3	Everton	42	14	5	2	43	10	7	10	4	34	26	57
4	Arsenal	42	12	6	3	31	12	10	6	5	25	15	56
5	Chelsea	42	11	7	3	40	24	9	3	9	33	29	50
6	Tottenham	42	10	8	3	39	22	4	9	8	22	29	45
7	Southampton	42	13	5	3	41	21	3	8	10	16	27	45
8	West Ham	42	10	8	3	47	22	3	10	8	19	28	44
9	Newcastle	42	12	7	2	40	20	3	7	11	21	35	44
10	West Brom	42	11	7	3	43	26	5	4	12	21	41	43
11	Manchester U	42	13	5	3	38	18	2	7	12	19	35	42
12	Ipswich	42	10	4	7	32	26	5	7	9	27	34	41
13	Manchester C	42	13	6	2	49	20	2	4	15	15	35	40
14	Burnley	42	11	6	4	36	25	4	3	14	19	57	39
15	Sheffield Wed	42	7	9	5	27	26	3	7	11	14	28	36
16	Wolves	42	7	10	4	26	22	3	5	13	15	36	35
17	Sunderland	42	10	6	5	28	18	1	6	14	15	49	34
18	Nott'm Forest	42	6	6	9	17	22	4	7	10	28	35	33
19	Stoke	42	9	7	5	24	24	0	8	13	16	39	33
20	COVENTRY	42	8	6	7	32	22	2	5	14	14	42	31
21	Leicester	42	8	8	5	27	24	1	4	16	12	44	30
22	QP Rangers	42	4	7	10	20	33	0	3	18	19	62	18
		924	233	140	89	757	456	89	140	233	456	757	924

Odds & ends.

Double wins: (1) QPR.
Double losses: (4) West Ham, Tottenham, Leeds, Arsenal.

Won from behind: (2) Newcastle (h), Blackpool FAC (h).
Lost from in front:: (3) Tottenham (h), Arsenal (a), Man City (a).

High spots: Another home win over Man U.
Beating Leicester in vital relegation game.
The 5-0 drubbing of QPR to lift the Sky Blues off the bottom.
The Gibson wonder show in the 4-2 home win over West Brom.

Low spots: The 1-6 drubbing at West Brom.
11 games without a win in the autumn.
The League Cup exit at Third Division Swindon.

Red cards: City – Setters (Liverpool h).
Red cards: Opponents – Evans (Liverpool h).

Ever presents: (1) Bill Glazier.
Hat-tricks: (1) Ernie Hunt.
Opposing hat-tricks: (0).
Leading scorer: (13) Ernie Hunt.

	Appearances						Goals			
	Lge	*Sub*	LC	*Sub*	FAC	*Sub*	**Lge**	LC	FAC	**Tot**
Baker, Gerry	**8**	*3*					**1**			**1**
Blockley, Jeff	**10**	*2*								
Bruck, Dietmar	**12**	*1*	2	*1*						
Carr, Willie	**33**	*3*	3		2		**3**			**3**
Cattlin, Chris	**32**	*1*	3		2					
Clements, Dave	**37**		4		2		**3**	1		**4**
Coop, Mick	**36**	*1*	4		2					
Curtis, George	**28**	*2*	3		2		**2**		1	**3**
Gibson, Ian	**17**	*1*	4				**3**	1		**4**
Glazier, Bill	**42**		5		2					
Hannigan, Ernie	**13**	*3*	2	*1*		*1*	**1**			**1**
Hateley, Tony	**17**		2		1		**4**	1		**5**
Hill, Brian	**31**		5		2					
Hunt, Ernie	**39**		5		2		**11**	2		**13**
Machin, Ernie	**41**		4		2		**5**		1	**6**
Martin, Neil	**25**		2		2		**9**			**9**
Paddon, Graham		*1*								
Setters, Maurice	**17**		4				**2**			**2**
Shepherd, Trevor	**11**	*2*			1	*1*	**1**		1	**2**
Tudor, John	**13**	*4*	3	*1*			**1**	2		**3**
20 players used	**462**	***24***	**55**	***3***	**22**	***2***	**46**	**7**	**3**	**56**

No	Date	Opponent	Att	Pos	Pt	F-A	H-T	Scorers, Times, and Referees	1	2	3	4	5	6	7	8	9	10	11	12 sub used
1	A	SUNDERLAND			D	0-0	0-0		Glazier	Coop	Cattlin	Hill	Curtis	Blockley	Hannigan	Gibson	Martin	Carr	Clements	
	9/8		*20,974*		1			Ref: K Walker	*Montgomery*	*Harvey*	*Ashurst*	*Heslop*	*Pitt*	*McGiven*	*Harris*	*Tueart*	*Baker*	*Symm*	*Hughes**	*Palmer*
									A forgettable game against Alan Brown's team, who look relegation favourites. Willie Carr plays up front and Clements has City's best chance which Montgomery saves. Ashurst slices a header over his own bar. Glazier is mostly idle. Joe Baker and Harris look shadows of themselves.											
2	H	WEST BROM			W	3-1	3-1	Carr 13, 14, 39	Glazier	Coop	Cattlin	Hill	Curtis	Blockley	**Gould**	Gibson	Martin	Carr	Clements	
	12/8		37,025		3			*Krzywicki 15* Ref: I Jones	*Nisbet*	*Williams*	*Wilson**	*Brown*	*Talbut*	*Kaye*	*Hegan*	*Suggett*	*Astle*	*Hope*	*Krzywicki*	*Fraser*
									Albion have spent £250,000 on new players but are destroyed by 19-year-old Carr. Nisbet, later to be a full-back, has a nightmare debut in goal. The goals are a header from Clements' corner, a crisp shot at the end of a slick move and an opportunistic effort after Hegan fails to clear.											
3	H	DERBY		5	D	1-1	1-1	Martin 5	Glazier	Coop	Cattlin	Hill	Curtis	Blockley	Gould	Gibson	Martin	Carr	Clements	
	16/8		41,036	*8*	4			*McFarland 4* Ref: K Howley	*Green*	*Webster*	*Robson*	*Durban*	*McFarland*	*Mackay*	*McGovern*	*Carlin*	*O'Hare*	*Hector*	*Hinton*	
									A tight, keenly fought but uninspiring match. The goals are almost identical. McFarland heads in Hinton's free-kick, Martin heads in Gibson's. The ref rules out Hector's first-half effort for offside against Carlin and turns down strong penalty claims when Durban appears to handle.											
4	A	WEST BROM		5	W	1-0	0-0	Blockley 67	Glazier	Coop	Cattlin	Hill	Curtis	Blockley	Gould	Gibson	Martin	Carr	Clements	
	20/8		*34,815*	*18*	6			Ref: W Gow	*Cumbes*	*Fraser*	*Williams*	*Brown*	*Talbut*	*Kaye*	*Hegan*	*Suggett*	*Krzywicki*	*Hope*	*Hartford*	
									Five wins out of six against Albion. A disciplined performance in fetching green shirts and black shorts. Without Jeff Astle, Albion suffer their third defeat in a row. Jeff Blockley's first goal is a header from Clements' inswinging corner. Tony Hateley is set to join Div 2 Birmingham.											
5	A	IPSWICH		4	W	1-0	0-0	Carr 61	Glazier	Coop*	Cattlin	Hill	Curtis	Blockley	Gould	Gibson	Martin	Carr	Clements	Bruck
	23/8		*18,274*	*22*	8			Ref: L Callaghan	*Best*	*Carroll*	*Mills*	*Viljoen*	*Baxter*	*Jefferson*	*Woods*	*Collard*	*Wigg*	*O'Rourke*	*Brogan*	
									City sport green shirts again. Hero Glazier foils three Wigg efforts and a shot from O'Rourke, the striker whom City covet. Gould steps over the ball and Carr beats David Best with a zipping drive. The previously written-off Curtis is back to his best. Crowd trouble mars the game.											
6	A	STOKE		6	L	0-2	0-1		Glazier	Bruck	Cattlin	Machin	Curtis	Blockley	Gould*	Gibson	Martin	Carr	Clements	Hunt
	27/8		*25,507*	*9*	8			*Greenhoff 38, Conroy 53* Ref: G Kew	*Banks*	*Marsh*	*Elder*	*Skeels*	*Smith*	*Allen*	*Conroy*	*Greenhoff*	*Ritchie*	*Dobing*	*Eastham*	
									The unbeaten run of seven ends, but not without a fight. From a Dobing pass, Greenhoff scores the first away goal City have conceded in 308 minutes. Curtis fouls Ritchie but the ref ignores penalty claims. Glazier blocks but Conroy scores. City's large support goes home saddened.											
7	H	WOLVES		4	W	1-0	0-0	Hunt 54	Glazier	Coop	Cattlin	Machin	Curtis	Blockley	Hunt	Gibson	Martin	Carr	Clements	
	30/8		38,340	*5*	10			Ref: J Finney	*Parkes*	*Wilson*	*Parkin*	*Bailey*	*Holsgrove*	*Munro*	*McCalliog*	*Knowles*	*Dougan*	*Curran*	*Farrington**	*McAlle*
									A physical contest with many stoppages. Ernie Hunt ends Wolves unbeaten record when he controls Blockley's long ball, turns and volleys home. Curtis hits the bar and Phil Parkes saves Chris Cattlin's effort. Blockley, Gibson and Mike Bailey are booked. Sky Blue Sam launched.											
8	A	LIVERPOOL		6	L	1-2	1-1	Gibson 34	Glazier	Coop	Cattlin	Machin	Curtis	Blockley	Hunt*	Gibson	Martin	Hill	Clements	Paddon
	6/9		***48,337***	*1*	10			*St John 37, Strong 90* Ref: N Burtenshaw	*Lawrence*	*Lawler*	*Strong*	*Smith*	*Yeats*	*Hughes*	*Callaghan*	*Evans*	*Graham*	*St.John*	*Thompson*	
									Geoff Strong's winner comes from a free-kick four minutes into injury-time. The ref finally blows up after 95 minutes. A travesty of a result. Shankly says 'All the good teams have luck'. Gibson's fierce shot is cancelled out when Glazier deflects a cross into the path of Ian St John.											
9	H	CRYS PALACE		7	D	2-2	0-2	Martin 60p, 77p	Glazier	Coop	Cattlin	Bruck	Curtis	Blockley	Baker*	Gibson	Martin	Paddon	Clements	Hannigan
	13/9		29,310	*13*	11			*Queen 6, 45* Ref: P Partridge	*Jackson J*	*Sewell*	*Loughlan*	*Hoy*	*McCormick*	*Hynd*	*Lazaraus**	*Kember*	*Jackson C*	*Queen*	*Taylor T*	*Hoadley*
									Palace suffer like City last week. Coventry are woeful and get a point through two penalties, one of which was saved and retaken. The ref generously gave the first when Taylor 'nudged' Baker and John Sewell handled for the other. Curtis was at fault for both Gerry Queen goals.											
10	H	NOTT'M FOREST		5	W	3-2	1-1	Martin 41, Clements 52, Paddon 78	Glazier	Coop	Clements	Bruck	Curtis	Blockley	Hunt	Gibson	Martin	Setters	Paddon	
	16/9		26,038	*10*	13			*Collier 26, Rees 77* Ref: B Homewood	*Hill*	*Hindley*	*Winfield*	*Chapman*	*Hennessey*	*Newton*	*Rees*	*Hilley*	*Collier**	*Barnwell*	*Moore*	*O'Kane*
									City's first ever Div 1 win over Forest is well deserved. Collier scored his first League goal. Martin's flicked header from Bruck's cross and Clements' thunderous shot put City ahead. Rees fizzed one in, then immediately Hunt set up Graham Paddon for the 18-year-old's first goal.											

No	Venue / Date	Opponent / Att	Pos	Res / Pts	FT	HT	Scorers, Times, and Referees	1	2	3	4	5	6	7	8	9	10	11	12 sub used
11	A	MANCHESTER C	7	L	1-3	0-2	Hunt 79	Glazier	Coop	Clements	Bruck	Curtis	Blockley	Hunt	Gibson	Martin	Machin	Paddon	
	20/9	*34,230*	*9*	13			*Bell 1, 88, Lee 32p*	*Corrigan*	*Book*	*Pardoe*	*Doyle*	*Heslop*	*Oakes*	*Summerbee*	*Bell*	*Lee*	*Young*	*Bowyer*	
							Ref: M Fussey	City contain Man C's stars for long periods but fail through moments of aberration. Bad marking at a free-kick sees Bell have a clear shot for the first and Bruck waited in vain for the offside flag for the third. The penalty was given against Blockley for feet up and Lee blasted it in.											
12	H	LEEDS	7	L	1-2	1-2	Hunt 26	Glazier	Coop	Cattlin	Machin	Curtis	Blockley	Hunt	Gibson*	Martin	Carr	Clements	Bruck
	27/9	36,080	*5*	13			*Clarke 28, Gray 40*	*Sprake*	*Reaney*	*Cooper*	*Bremner*	*Madeley*	*Hunter*	*Lorimer*	*Clarke*	*Jones*	*Giles*	*Gray*	
							Ref: W Gow	City's run of 13 home league games without defeat is ended by the champions. In a good first half Clarke is given too much space for the first and crosses for Eddie Gray. In between, Hunt's spanking shot had raised hopes. Coventry tail off after the break and rarely threaten to pull level.											
13	A	ARSENAL	7	W	1-0	1-0	Hunt 30	Glazier	Coop	Bruck	Setters	Curtis	Blockley	Hunt	Gibson	Martin	Carr	Clements	
	4/10	*28,977*	*14*	15				*Barnett*	*Storey*	*McNab*	*McLintock*	*Roberts*	*Simpson*	*Robertson*	*Sammels*	*Court**	*Graham*	*Gould*	*George*
							Ref: T Dawes	A first ever win over Arsenal. Debutant Geoff Barnett looks dodgy and can't stop Ernie Hunt, who foxes Jon Sammels on the edge of the box. City don't press home their superiority in the first half. Despite four bookings - Curtis, Gibson, McLintock and Gould - it wasn't a dirty game.											
14	A	DERBY	5	W	3-1	1-0	Martin 17, McFarland 62 (og), [Blockley 68]	Glazier	Coop	Bruck	Setters	Curtis	Blockley	Hunt	Gibson	Martin	Carr*	Clements	**Joicey**
	8/10	*39,880*	*3*	17			*Durban 89*	*Green*	*Daniel*	*Robson*	*Durban*	*McFarland*	*Mackay*	*McGovern*	*Carlin*	*O'Hare*	*Hector*	*Hinton*	
							Ref: G Hill	Coventry end Derby's unbeaten run of 25 home games in spectacular fashion. This is one of City's best away performances ever. Martin beat McFarland all night and bagged the first goal from Clements' cross. The Derby man sliced one into his own net and Blockley nodded the third.											
15	H	WEST HAM	6	D	2-2	1-1	Joicey 31, Clements 54	Glazier	Coop	Bruck	Setters*	Curtis	Blockley	Hunt	Joicey	Martin	Carr	Clements	**Mortimer**
	11/10	34,279	*15*	18			*Brooking 30, Sissons 46*	*Ferguson*	*Bonds*	*Lampard*	*Howe*	*Stephenson*	*Moore*	*Redknapp*	*Lindsay*	*Brooking*	*Sissons*	*Best*	
							Ref: H New	The heroes' homecoming turns sour. Mediocre Hammers earn a point after twice leading. Glazier can't hold Redknapp's banana shot and Brooking scores. Joicey scores a debut goal from Clements' free-kick. Ferguson takes too many steps and Clements scores with a deflection.											
16	A	SOUTHAMPTON	6	D	0-0	0-0		Glazier	Coop	Bruck	Setters*	Curtis	Blockley	Hunt	Joicey	Martin	Carr	Clements	Machin
	18/10	*20,238*	*20*	19				*Martin*	*McCarthy*	*Hollywood*	*Kemp*	*McGrath*	*Gabriel*	*Paine*	*Stokes*	*Channon*	*Byrne*	*Sydenham*	
							Ref: P Oliver	City have the ascendancy in the first half but are unable to turn their domination into goals. Hunt has three chances, one of which forced Eric Martin into super a save. Setters was stretchered off but X-rays show no break. Saints finish strongly. After a good run, Fred Kemp blazes over.											
17	H	EVERTON	7	L	0-1	0-0		Glazier	Coop	Bruck	Machin*	Curtis	Blockley	Hunt	Gibson	Martin	Carr	Clements	Joicey
	25/10	37,816	*1*	19			*Royle 87*	*West*	*Wright*	*Brown*	*Kendall*	*Labone*	*Harvey*	*Husband*	*Ball*	*Royle*	*Hurst*	*Morrissey*	
							Ref: V James	Rough justice for a gritty team display which holds Everton until the late headed winner. The Toffees are heading for the title and are already six points clear at the top. This is described as an off day for them, but despite looking shaky they hold on and go for the kill late on.											
18	A	CHELSEA	9	L	0-1	0-0		Glazier	Coop	Cattlin	Machin	Curtis	Blockley	Hunt	Gibson*	Martin	Carr	Clements	**Barry**
	1/11	*38,899*	*7*	19			*Cooke 47*	*Bonetti*	*Harris*	*McCreadie*	*Hollins*	*Webb*	*Hinton*	*Boyle**	*Hudson*	*Osgood*	*Houseman*	*Cooke*	*Hutchinson*
							Ref: R Matthewson	City play well but lose again. Martin, Coop and Machin all hit the woodwork, but Cooke's volley steals the points after Glazier had punched out a corner under a strong challenge. Roy Barry makes his bow after a £40,000 move from Dunfermline and 'Chopper' Harris breaks his nose.											
19	H	MANCHESTER U	12	L	1-2	0-1	Hunt 85	Glazier	Coop	Cattlin	Machin	Curtis	Blockley	Hunt	Joicey*	Martin	Carr	Clements	Gibson
	8/11	**43,446**	*8*	19			*Aston 42, Law 72*	*Stepney*	*Brennan*	*Dunne*	*Burns*	*Ure*	*Sadler*	*Sartori*	*Best*	*Charlton*	*Law*	*Aston*	
							Ref: P Walters	Three easy chances go begging for the Sky Blues before United take the lead. Joicey, Martin and Curtis all miss, the latter from point blank range. Best sets up Aston and then, with a delicious ball, sets up Law to poach the second. Five games without a win and hopes of Europe fade.											
20	A	BURNLEY	12	D	0-0	0-0		Glazier	Coop	Cattlin	Machin	Barry	Blockley	Hunt	Carr	Martin*	Setters	Clements	Curtis
	15/11	***11,328***	*15*	20				*Mellor*	*Angus*	*Latcham*	*O'Neill*	*Waldron*	*Blant*	*Probert*	*Coates*	*Casper*	*Bellamy*	*Kindon**	*Thomas*
							Ref: P Baldwin	A depressing game in a drab ground. Burnley looked sharp early on but Casper's miss and Glazier's reflexes kept City in it. Curtis is dropped for the first time since 1958. Gibson also axed. Burnley make six changes and bring in Michael Docherty, son of Tommy. Cattlin was booked.											
21	H	NEWCASTLE	11	W	1-0	0-0	Hunt 80p	Glazier	Coop	Clements	Machin	Barry	Blockley	Hunt	Carr	Setters	**O'Rourke**	Gibson	
	22/11	31,824	*12*	22				*McFaul*	*Craig*	*Clark*	*Gibb*	*Burton*	*Moncur*	*Robson*	*Smith*	*Scott*	*Arentoft*	*Guthrie*	
							Ref: M Sinclair	Both sides have injuries. Wyn Davies and Keith Dyson are out for Magpies, Martin and Joicey for City. Setters plays up front with £80,000 buy O'Rourke. McFaul keeps a fumbling City out until Burton flattens Hunt, who scores from the spot. Carr is watched by a Scottish selector.											

No	Date		Att	Pos	Pt	F-A	H-T	Scorers, Times, and Referees	1	2	3	4	5	6	7	8	9	10	11	12 sub used
22	H	TOTTENHAM		8	W	3-2	2-1	Machin 12, O'Rourke 22, Gibson 51	Glazier	Coop	Clements	Machin	Barry	Blockley	Hunt	Carr*	Martin	O'Rourke	Gibson	Setters
	6/12		28,443	*12*	24			*England 35, Gilzean 60*	*Jennings*	*Want*	*Knowles*	*Mullery*	*England*	*Pratt*	*Johnson**	*Greaves*	*Gilzean*	*Chivers*	*Perryman*	*Collins*
								Ref: H Williams	An emphatic win. Martin is involved in all three goals. Jennings saves but Machin nets the rebound. A header from Clements' free-kick allows O'Rourke to head in. He jumps over Coop's cross to let Gibson score with ease. Spurs goals are headers. Curtis, Bruck and Hill are up for sale.											
23	A	CRYS PALACE		8	W	3-0	1-0	Hunt 42, Joicey 48, 73	Glazier	Coop	Clements	Machin	Barry	Blockley	Hunt*	Carr	Joicey	O'Rourke	Setters	Cattlin
	13/12		*16,763*	*20*	26				*Jackson J*	*Sewell*	*Hoadley*	*Payne*	*McCormick*	*Hynd*	*Dawkins*	*Kember*	*Bartram**	*Queen*	*Blyth*	*Vansittart*
								Ref: R Tinkler	A ruthlessly efficient performance against a poor Palace outfit provides a fifth away win. Injuries mean a weak side. Joicey is the star. The bargain buy from North Shields helps set up Hunt's opener, then hits a superb volley out of nothing before beating Jackson in a one on one.											
24	H	IPSWICH		9	W	3-1	2-0	Hunt 34, Harper 39 (og), Martin 73p	**McManus**	Coop	Cattlin	Clements	Barry	Blockley	Hunt	Carr	Martin	O'Rourke	Gibson*	Mortimer
	26/12		32,649	*18*	28			*Wigg 86*	*Best*	*Carroll*	*Harper*	*Morris*	*Baxter*	*McNeill*	*Woods*	*Wigg*	*Hill*	*Viljoen*	*Brogan*	
								Ref: I Jones	A makeshift City side inflict dispirited Ipswich's fourth defeat on the run. Martin sets up Hunt to score from close range, Harper mis-hits Clements' cross into his own net, and Baxter up-ends Hunt for the penalty. Gibson badly twists his knee. Curtis transfers to Villa for £30,000.											
25	H	MANCHESTER C		9	W	3-0	2-0	Martin 27, O'Rourke 41, 51	Glazier	Coop	Cattlin	Machin	Barry	Blockley	Hunt	Carr	Martin	O'Rourke	Clements	
	10/1		30,043	*8*	30				*Corrigan*	*Connor*	*Pardoe*	*Doyle*	*Booth*	*Oakes*	*Summerbee*	*Bell*	*Lee*	*Bowles*	*Bowyer*	
								Ref: B Homewood	This is one of the best results since promotion and confirms City's form as more than a flash in the pan. Three headers sink the FA Cup holders. Hunt crosses for Martin, then Machin lays on two for John O'Rourke. Roy Barry is the hero as Coventry make it five wins in a row.											
26	A	LEEDS		10	L	1-3	0-2	Madeley 64 (og)	Glazier	Coop	Cattlin	Machin	Barry	Clements	Hunt	Carr	Martin	O'Rourke	Joicey	
	17/1		*34,295*	*1*	30			*Clarke 31, 82, Charlton 31*	*Sprake*	*Reaney*	*Cooper*	*Bremner*	*Charlton**	*Hunter*	*Lorimer*	*Clarke*	*Jones*	*Giles*	*Madeley*	*Bates*
								Ref: R Matthewson	Leeds go top for the first time this season but the score flatters them. Martin's mistake lets in Lorimer to cross for Clarke to net. Charlton heads home unchallenged. Madeley deflects O'Rourke's cross-shot into his own net. Clarke looks offside for the third. City's winning run is over.											
27	A	SHEFFIELD WED		8	W	1-0	0-0	O'Rourke 57	Glazier	Coop	Cattlin	Clements	Barry	Blockley	Hunt	Carr	Martin	O'Rourke	Joicey	
	28/1		*18,149*	*22*	32				*Grummitt*	*Wilcockson*	*Burton*	*Smith*	*Prophett*	*Craig*	*Sinclair*	*Whitham*	*Downes*	*Pugh**	*Coleman*	*Warboys*
								Ref: D Pugh	City's first win at Hillsborough since 1911. Sad Wednesday look doomed with only one win in 15 but still trouble a hesitant Coventry defence. O'Rourke ends a five-man move with a rising left-foot shot. Ernie Machin is injured in a car crash. Maurice Setters is given a free transfer.											
28	H	ARSENAL		6	W	2-0	0-0	O'Rourke 58, Martin 73	Glazier	Coop	Cattlin	Hunt	Barry	Clements	Hannigan	Carr	Martin	O'Rourke	Mortimer	
	31/1		31,661	*14*	34				*Wilson*	*Storey*	*McNab*	*McLintock*	*Roberts*	*Simpson*	*Marinello*	*Sammels*	*Radford*	*Graham*	*Armstrong*	
								Ref: J Thacker	Arsenal are run ragged and are lucky not to lose by more. Roy Barry is a colossus. City are frustrated by dodgy refereeing and gamesmanship until O'Rourke scores from short range after Clements' corner. Martin's is a classic header with Wilson rooted. Several chances go begging.											
29	A	WEST HAM		4	W	2-1	1-1	Martin 23, 52	Glazier	Coop	Cattlin	Hunt	Barry	Clements*	Hannigan	Carr	Martin	O'Rourke	Mortimer	Hill
	11/2		*22,723*	*17*	36			*Hurst 10p*	*Grotier*	*Bonds*	*Howe*	*Peters*	*Stephenson*	*Moore*	*Brooking*	*Lindsay*	*Eustace*	*Hurst*	*Best*	
								Ref: G Hartley	First Div 1 win over West Ham. Hurst's penalty, for a push by Barry on Peters, is his 154th goal, a post-war West Ham record. Two goals from Martin – the second a strong header – take the deserved points. Eustace's late 'goal' was given as offside. Upton Park resorts to slow handclaps.											
30	A	EVERTON		4	D	0-0	0-0		Glazier	Coop	Cattlin	Hunt	Barry	Blockley	Hannigan	Carr	Martin	O'Rourke	Hill	
	21/2		*45,934*	*2*	37				*West*	*Wright*	*Newton*	*Kendall*	*Labone*	*Harvey*	*Husband*	*Ball*	*Royle*	*Hurst*	*Morrissey*	
								Ref: M Fussey	A marvellous result at a ground where only four sides have avoided defeat. Barry is again the star, along with Glazier. Brian Hill shackles Ball. Most of the play is in City's half and they survive some narrow squeaks. O'Rourke has City's best chance but hits West's legs when clear.											
31	H	CHELSEA		7	L	0-3	0-1		Glazier	Coop	Cattlin	Hunt	Barry	Blockley	Hannigan*	Carr	Martin	O'Rourke	Mortimer	Joicey
	28/2		37,454	*3*	37			*Baldwin 25, Webb 53, Hudson 83*	*Bonetti*	*Webb*	*Harris*	*Hollins*	*Dempsey*	*Mulligan*	*Cooke*	*Hudson*	*Osgood*	*Baldwin*	*Houseman*	
								Ref: D Pugh	Cantwell wins the Manager of Month award and it's the kiss of death. Chelsea are in dazzling form. 18-year-old Alan Hudson sets up Baldwin's goal. The dazzling Peter Osgood makes one for Webb. Hudson blasts home his first ever goal with aplomb. Chelsea are set to win the FA Cup.											

No	Venue	Opponent / Date	Att	Pos	Res / Pts	F-A	H-T	Scorers, Times, and Referees	1	2	3	4	5	6	7	8	9	10	11	12 sub used
32	H	LIVERPOOL		9	L	2-3	1-1	Hunt 32, O'Rourke 78	Glazier	Coop	Cattlin	Hunt	Barry	Blockley	Hannigan	Carr	Martin	O'Rourke	Hill	
		3/3	29,497	*5*	37			*Hughes 38, Evans 66, 72*	*Clemence*	*Lawler*	*Strong*	*Smith*	*Yeats*	*Hughes*	*Callaghan*	*Livermore*	*Evans*	*Lindsay*	*Graham*	
								Ref: J Finney	Liverpool are in change mode after a Cup defeat at Watford. Hunt's prodded goal is equalised by the unchallenged Emlyn Hughes. Liverpool made their advantage tell with two Alun Evans goals - the first a screamer. John O'Rourke's header from Coop's free-kick is too little too late.											
33	H	SHEFFIELD WED		7	D	1-1	1-1	Blockley 25	Glazier	Coop	Cattlin	Hunt	Barry*	Blockley	Hannigan	Carr	Martin	Joicey	Mortimer	Bruck
		14/3	25,473	*19*	38			*Whitham 10*	*Grummitt*	*Wilcockson*	*Smith*	*Ellis*	*Prophett*	*Craig*	*Sinclair*	*Young*	*Warboys*	*Whitham**	*Lawson*	*Downes*
								Ref: C Thomas	Fixtures are piling up because of the bad weather. Everything is overshadowed by Roy Barry's broken leg in a nasty challenge with Tommy Craig after 12 minutes. Jeff Blockley's header from Cattlin's cross earns a point for a shell-shocked team missing their inspirational leader.											
34	A	TOTTENHAM		7	W	2-1	0-1	Martin 60, O'Rourke 81	Glazier	Bruck	Cattlin	Gibson*	Blockley	Coop	Gould	Carr	Martin	O'Rourke	Mortimer	Joicey
		21/3	*34,942*	*14*	40			*Peters 13*	*Jennings*	*Evans*	*Want*	*Mullery*	*England*	*Beal*	*Jenkins**	*Peters*	*Gilzean*	*Bond*	*Morgan*	*Chivers*
								Ref: E Wallace	Spurs paid a British record £200,000 for debut boy Martin Peters and he headed them in front. City had their youngest Div 1 side on show but weren't overawed. Neil Martin headed in from Carr's corner and Brian Joicey lays on John O'Rourke's winner. Martin takes over captaincy.											
35	H	SUNDERLAND		7	D	1-1	0-1	Clements 73	Glazier	Coop	Cattlin	Bruck	Blockley	Clements	Gould	Carr	Martin	O'Rourke	Gibson*	Joicey
		24/3	**24,590**	*22*	41			*Hughes 2*	*Montgomery*	*Irwin*	*Ashurst*	*Todd*	*Heslop*	*McGiven*	*Park*	*Kerr*	*Hughes*	*Harris*	*Tueart*	
								Ref: R Darlington	Dave Clements rescues City against defensive Sunderland, who didn't trouble Glazier after Hughes' early header. Montgomery has a blinder but is beaten by Clements' powerful shot from Dietmar Bruck's pass. Joicey and Martin waste late chances in front of lowest crowd of season.											
36	H	BURNLEY		7	D	1-1	1-0	Martin 33p	Glazier	Coop	Cattlin	Mortimer*	Blockley	**Parker**	Gould	Carr	Martin	O'Rourke	Gibson	Joicey
		28/3	24,713	*14*	42			*Kindon 64*	*Mellor*	*Docherty*	*Thomson**	*O'Neill*	*Dobson*	*Waldron*	*Casper*	*Coates*	*Probert*	*Thomas*	*Kindon*	*Todd*
								Ref: L Callaghan	Both sides play four teenagers. Mellor has a shaky first half and brings down Martin who scores from the spot. Burnley improve and Kindon's 16th goal of the season, after Coop dithers, is just reward. England Youth captain Parker starts his career with a heavy challenge on O'Neill.											
37	A	MANCHESTER U		7	D	1-1	0-1	Martin 80	Glazier	Bruck	Cattlin	Coop	Blockley	Gould	Gibson*	O'Rourke	Martin	Joicey	Carr	Parker
		30/3	*41,335*	*11*	43			*Kidd 3*	*Stepney*	*Edwards*	*Dunne*	*Fitzpatrick*	*Ure*	*Sadler*	*Morgan*	*Best*	*Law*	*Kidd**	*Aston*	*Burns*
								Ref: D Smith	City's First Div 1 point at Old Trafford. They recovered from Kidd's goal - made by George Best - and could have won. O'Rourke had a goal disallowed, Joicey and Coop missed good chances. Martin, playing well in a midfield role, hits a well-placed shot to level. Blockley is the star.											
38	H	SOUTHAMPTON		6	W	**4-0**	3-0	Joicey 22, 74, O'Rourke 25, Martin 37	Glazier	Coop	Cattlin	Gibson	Blockley	Bruck	Hunt	Carr	Martin	O'Rourke	Joicey	
		31/3	25,431	*18*	45				*Martin*	*Kirkup*	*Byrne*	*Kemp*	*McGrath*	*Gabriel*	*Paine*	*Fisher*	*Davies*	*Walker*	*Channon*	
								Ref: M Kerkhof	The best home performance of the season keeps City on target for Europe. Joicey scores from a back-header, after his shot spun in the air, and then with a cheeky shot under Eric Martin. O'Rourke taps in Bruck's pull-back and Neil Martin buries a header from Coop's looping cross.											
39	H	STOKE		7	L	0-3	0-1		Glazier	Coop	Cattlin	Gibson*	Blockley	Bruck	Hunt	Carr	Martin	O'Rourke	Joicey	Mortimer
		4/4	27,754	*8*	45			*Ritchie 44, 74, Dobing 70*	*Banks*	*Marsh*	*Pejic*	*Bernard*	*Smith*	*Bloor*	*Conroy*	*Greenhoff*	*Ritchie*	*Dobing*	*Eastham*	
								Ref: R Tinkler	A sad end to a great season for home fans as Banks frustrates City with some great saves. Martin shoots wide with a penalty after he is fouled by Bloor. Eastham sets up Ritchie on the break, Conroy sets up Dobing and Ritchie heads in Bernard's cross. City reach FA Youth Cup final.											
40	A	NOTT'M FOREST		6	W	4-1	2-0	O'Rourke 4, 42, 54, Joicey 65	Glazier	Coop	Cattlin	Gibson	Blockley	Clements	Hunt	Carr	Martin	O'Rourke	Joicey	
		7/4	*15,569*	*17*	47			*Rees 89*	*Hollins*	*Hindley*	*Winfield*	*Chapman*	*O'Kane*	*Newton**	*Rees*	*Richardson*	*Ingram*	*Collier*	*Hilley*	*McCaffrey*
								Ref: N Burtenshaw	City bounce back in style with their biggest Div 1 away win. O'Rourke comes back to form with a hat-trick, two close in shots and a full-pelt header. Joicey's header from Gibson's cross emphasises the Sky Blues' superiority. Rees' 25-yarder is a token. Willie Carr is in Scotland squad.											
41	A	WOLVES		6	W	1-0	1-0	Joicey 8	Glazier	Coop	Cattlin	Gibson	Blockley	Clements	Hunt	Carr	Martin	O'Rourke	Joicey	
		10/4	*23,395*	*11*	49				*Oldfield*	*Taylor*	*Parkin*	*Bailey*	*Holsgrove*	*Munro*	*McCalliog*	*Wilson*	*Dougan*	*Curran*	*Lutton*	
								Ref: G Hill	Sixth place and a Fairs Cup place is secured with another Midland derby victory and a tenth away win. Brian Joicey's opportunism from Gerry Taylor's sloppy back-pass is enough against a barracked home team. Martin's shot hits Holsgrove on the line and Hunt shoots narrowly wide.											
42	A	NEWCASTLE		6	L	**0-4**	0-2	*[Foggon 88]*	McManus	Coop	Cattlin	Machin	Blockley	Clements	Gibson	Martin	**Rafferty**	Joicey	Carr	
		14/4	*32,840*	*7*	49			*Robson 34, Dyson 39, Gibb 65,*	*McFaul*	*Craig*	*Guthrie*	*Gibb*	*Burton*	*Moncur*	*Robson*	*Dyson*	*Davies*	*Smith*	*Foggon*	
	Home	Away						Ref: A Morrissey	A first defeat in eight trips since January. City's relaxed young side can't handle a Magpies side determined to qualify for Europe. Coop gifts the first to Bryan Robson, who sets up Dyson and then Gibb before Foggon fires in a suspiciously offside fourth. The end of a brilliant season.											
Average	32,031	28,903																		

LEAGUE DIVISION 1 (CUP-TIES)   Manager: Noel Cantwell   SEASON 1969-70

League Cup				F-A	H-T	Scorers, Times, and Referees	1	2	3	4	5	6	7	8	9	10	11	12 sub used
2 H CHELSEA		4	L	0-1	0-0		Glazier	Coop	Cattlin	Machin	Curtis	Blockley	Hunt	Gibson	Martin	Carr	Clements	
2/9	*24,672*	*15*				*Hutchinson 50*	*Bonetti*	*Webb*	*McCreadie*	*Hollins*	*Dempsey*	*Harris*	*Osgood*	*Hinton*	*Hutchinson*	*Houseman*	*Birchenall*	
						Ref: V Batty	Sexton's boys cruise into the next round against lacklustre Coventry, whose run of 13 unbeaten home league and cup games is ended. Chelsea defend in depth and break through when Ian Hutchinson heads home Peter Houseman's cross. Chelsea's bus catches fire on the way home.											

FA Cup				F-A	H-T	Scorers, Times, and Referees	1	2	3	4	5	6	7	8	9	10	11	12 sub used
3 H LIVERPOOL		9	D	1-1	1-1	Martin 27	Glazier	Coop	Clements	Machin	Barry	Blockley	Hunt	Carr	Martin	O'Rourke	Mortimer*	Setters
7/1	34,140	*3*				*Graham 31*	*Lawrence*	*Lawler*	*Wall*	*Strong*	*Yeats*	*Hughes*	*Callaghan*	*Ross*	*Thompson*	*St.John*	*Graham*	
						Ref: V James	This tie was postponed from Saturday because of snow. An enthralling tie with a fair result. Lawrence had more to do than Glazier. Martin's header from Clements' free-kick was equalised with a contested goal. Bobby Graham looked yards offside when receiving Callaghan's pass.											
3R A LIVERPOOL		9	L	0-3	0-1		Glazier	Coop	Cattlin	Machin	Barry	Setters	Hunt	Carr	Martin	O'Rourke	Clements	
12/1	*51,261*	*3*				*Ross 39, Thompson 54, Graham 72*	*Lawrence*	*Lawler*	*Wall*	*Strong*	*Yeats*	*Hughes*	*Callaghan*	*Ross*	*Thompson*	*St.John*	*Graham*	
						Ref: V James	4,000 City fans watch their team spanked in front of an exultant, roaring Kop. An even match until Thompson sets up a Ross header, then hits a brilliant second. Graham scores from an overhead kick. Liverpool meet Wrexham in Round 4. Jeff Blockley misses his first game of the season.											

		Home						Away					
		P	W	D	L	F	A	W	D	L	F	A	Pts
1	Everton	42	17	3	1	46	19	12	5	4	26	15	66
2	Leeds	42	15	4	2	50	19	6	11	4	34	30	57
3	Chelsea	42	13	7	1	36	18	8	6	7	34	32	55
4	Derby	42	15	3	3	45	14	7	6	8	19	23	53
5	Liverpool	42	10	7	4	34	20	10	4	7	31	22	51
6	COVENTRY	42	9	6	6	35	28	10	5	6	23	20	49
7	Newcastle	42	14	2	5	42	16	3	11	7	15	19	47
8	Manchester U	42	8	9	4	37	27	6	8	7	29	34	45
9	Stoke	42	10	7	4	31	23	5	8	8	25	29	45
10	Manchester C	42	8	6	7	25	22	8	5	8	30	26	43
11	Tottenham	42	11	2	8	27	21	6	7	8	27	34	43
12	Arsenal	42	7	10	4	29	23	5	8	8	22	26	42
13	Wolves	42	8	8	5	30	23	4	8	9	25	34	40
14	Burnley	42	7	7	7	33	29	5	8	8	23	32	39
15	Nott'm Forest	42	8	9	4	28	28	2	9	10	22	43	38
16	West Brom	42	10	6	5	39	25	4	3	14	19	41	37
17	West Ham	42	8	8	5	28	21	4	4	13	23	39	36
18	Ipswich	42	9	5	7	23	20	1	6	14	17	43	31
19	Southampton	42	3	12	6	24	27	3	5	13	22	40	29
20	Crys Palace	42	5	6	10	20	36	1	9	11	14	32	27
21	Sunderland	42	4	11	6	17	24	2	3	16	13	44	26
22	Sheffield Wed	42	6	5	10	23	27	2	4	15	17	44	25
		924	205	143	114	702	510	114	143	205	510	702	924

Odds & ends

Double wins: (6) West Brom, Ipswich, Wolves, Nott'm Forest, Arsenal, Tottenham.
Double losses: (3) Leeds, Stoke, Chelsea.

Won from behind: (3) Nott'm Forest (h), West Ham (a), Tottenham (a).
Lost from in front: (3) Liverpool (a), Leeds (h), Liverpool (h).

High spots: Five game unbeaten start to the season.
The win at Derby, who had just beaten Tottenham 5-0.
The 0-0 at champions-elect Everton.
The win at Wolves to clinch the Fairs Cup place.
10 away wins, a club record.

Low spots: Gibson's injury in the Ipswich game.
The FA Cup exit at Liverpool.
Roy Barry's broken leg in the Sheffield Wed home game.

Ever-presents: (0).
Hat-tricks: (2) Willie Carr and John O'Rourke.
Opposing hat-tricks: (0).
Leading scorer: (15) Neil Martin.

	Appearances						Goals			
	Lge	*Sub*	LC	*Sub*	FAC	*Sub*	**Lge**	LC	FAC	**Tot**
Baker, Gerry	**1**									
Barry, Roy	**14**	*1*			2					
Blockley, Jeff	**39**		1		1		**3**			**3**
Bruck, Dietmar	**14**	*3*								
Carr, Willie	**38**		1		2		**4**			**4**
Cattlin, Chris	**32**	*1*	1		1					
Clements, Dave	**33**		1		2		**3**			**3**
Coop, Mick	**41**		1		2					
Curtis, George	**19**	*1*	1							
Gibson, Ian	**28**	*1*	1				**2**			**2**
Glazier, Bill	**40**		1		2					
Gould, Trevor	**9**									
Hannigan, Ernie	**7**	*1*								
Hill, Brian	**8**	*1*								
Hunt, Ernie	**30**	*1*	1		2		**9**			**9**
Joicey, Brian	**13**	*6*					**7**			**7**
Machin, Ernie	**15**	*1*	1		2		**1**			**1**
Martin, Neil	**40**		1		2		**14**		1	**15**
McManus, Eric	**2**									
Mortimer, Dennis	**6**	*3*			1					
O'Rourke, John	**20**				2		**11**			**11**
Paddon, Graham	**3**	*1*					**1**			**1**
Parker, Bobby	**1**	*1*								
Rafferty, Billy	**1**									
Setters, Maurice	**8**	*1*			1	*1*				
(own-goals)							**3**			**3**
25 players used	**462**	***23***	**11**		**22**	***1***	**58**		**1**	**59**

No	Date		Att	Pos	Pt	F-A	H-T	Scorers, Times, and Referees	1	2	3	4	5	6	7	8	9	10	11	12 sub used
1	A	NOTT'M FOREST			L	0-2	0-2		Glazier	Coop	Bruck	Carr	Blockley	**Strong**	Hunt	Joicey	Martin	O'Rourke	Clements	
	15/8		*25,137*		0			*Cormack 17, Moore 29*	*Barron*	*Hindley*	*Winfield*	*Chapman*	*O'Kane*	*Newton*	*Lyons*	*Rees*	*Ingram**	*Cormack*	*Moore*	*Hilley*
								Ref: P Baldwin	Forest are favourites for relegation after one win in twelve to end last season, but they deserved this win. Cormack flicks in Lyon's free-kick. Glazier saves well from Rees' shot but Moore whips the ball in for the second. Joicey offers a brave header and Martin misses a good chance.											
2	A	IPSWICH			W	2-0	0-0	Martin 49, 52	Glazier	Coop	Clements	**Goodwin**	Blockley	Strong	Hunt	Carr	Martin	O'Rourke	Machin	
	18/8		*21,188*		2				*Best*	*Carroll**	*Harper*	*Morris*	*Baxter*	*Jefferson*	*Robertson*	*Mills*	*Clarke*	*Woods*	*Lambert*	*Whymark*
								Ref: B Homewood	City weather Ipswich's intense early pressure and Neil Martin snatches victory, first capitalising on David Best and Tommy Carroll's mix-up, then with a superb side-foot volley from Coop's cross. Confident City rarely look troubled again. John O'Rourke was baited by his old fans.											
3	H	SOUTHAMPTON		7	W	1-0	1-0	Hunt 17	Glazier	Coop	Clements	Goodwin	Blockley	Strong	Hunt	Carr	Martin	O'Rourke	Machin*	Joicey
	22/8		26,238	*20*	4				*Martin*	*Kirkup*	*Byrne*	*Fisher*	*Gabriel*	*Walker*	*Thompson*	*Channon*	*Davies*	*O'Neill*	*Jenkins*	
								Ref: T Reynolds	A struggle against an over-physical Southampton. Ernie Machin suffers ankle ligament damage in a late tackle by O'Neill. Hunt pounces on Byrne's back-header against the post, but City fail to make their superiority count. Bill Glazier saves from O'Neill during a frantic finale.											
4	H	WOLVES		7	L	0-1	0-0		Glazier	Coop	Clements	Goodwin	Blockley	Strong	Hunt	Carr	Martin	Joicey	Mortimer*	Cattlin
	25/8		31,160	*22*	4			*Curran 68*	*Oldfield*	*Taylor*	*Parkin*	*Bailey*	*Holsgrove*	*Munro*	*McCalliog*	*Wilson*	*Gould*	*Curran*	*Wagstaffe*	
								Ref: R Matthewson	Wolves arrive without a win in 16 games, with seven defeats in a row, but salvage some pride. In a tight game the first goal is vital and Bobby Gould chests down David Wagstaffe's cross for Hugh Curran to sweep home. Willie Carr blasts over City's best chance in the last minute.											
5	A	TOTTENHAM		13	L	0-1	0-1		Glazier	Coop	Cattlin	Goodwin	Blockley	Strong	Hunt	Carr	Martin	O'Rourke*	Clements	Parker
	29/8		*27,103*	*9*	4			*Chivers 12*	*Jennings*	*Kinnear*	*Knowles*	*Mullery*	*England*	*Collins*	*Gilzean*	*Perryman*	*Chivers*	*Peters*	*Morgan**	*Pearce*
								Ref: D Pugh	City don't deserve anything from this mediocre game. O'Rourke comes closest to scoring from a Knowles error. Martin Chivers scores with a powerful shot from the edge of the box. City are on the verge of signing Sheff Wed's Wilf Smith for a British full-back record fee of £100,000.											
6	A	DERBY		10	W	4-3	2-2	Martin 28, 54, Clements 31, Carr 88	Glazier	Coop	Cattlin	**Smith***	Blockley	Strong	Joicey	Carr	Martin	Machin	Clements	Hunt
	1/9		*31,621*	*8*	6			*Hector 8, Hinton 13, McGovern 62*	*Green*	*Webster*	*Robson*	*Wignall*	*McFarland*	*Mackay*	*McGovern*	*Carlin*	*O'Hare*	*Hector*	*Hinton*	
								Ref: R Capey	A tremendous match that swings several times and is decided by Carr's late winner. At 3-3 Glazier saves Hinton's penalty after Strong fouls Wignall. Martin destroys McFarland again and Glazier and Machin shine in a magnificent team performance. Smith was carried off on 5 mins.											
7	H	HUDDERSFIELD		10	D	0-0	0-0		Glazier	Coop	Cattlin	Machin	Blockley	Strong	Hunt	Carr	Martin	Joicey*	Clements	**Alderson**
	5/9		26,087	*11*	7				*Poole*	*Clarke*	*Hutt*	*Nicholson*	*Ellam*	*Cherry*	*Smith*	*Lawson*	*Worthington*	*McGill*	*Krzywicki**	*Dobson*
								Ref: C Nicholls	The returning heroes can't reproduce their away form at home in a drab game. Ian Greaves' newly promoted Terriers hadn't scored away from home and rarely look likely today. Their are chances for Martin, Clements and Joicey and a strong penalty appeal when Geoff Hutt handles.											
8	A	MANCHESTER U		16	L	0-2	0-0		Glazier	Coop	Smith	Machin	Blockley	Strong	Hunt	Carr	Martin	O'Rourke*	Clements	Bruck
	12/9		*48,939*	*10*	7			*Best 55, Charlton 60*	*Rimmer*	*Edwards*	*Dunne*	*Fitzpatrick*	*Ure*	*Sadler*	*Stiles*	*Law*	*Charlton*	*Kidd*	*Best*	
								Ref: H Davey	United are held for almost an hour before Best races onto Charlton's through ball, looking four yards offside, and scores. Glazier saves a Best free-kick only for Charlton to follow up and score easily. After that United find the gaps and could have had more. City's goals are drying up.											
9	H	CHELSEA		16	L	0-1	0-0		Glazier	Smith	Clements	Machin	Blockley	Strong	Hunt	Carr*	Martin	O'Rourke	Alderson	Bruck
	19/9		29,649	*7*	7			*Hollins 48*	*Bonetti*	*Mulligan*	*Harris*	*Hollins*	*Dempsey*	*Webb*	*Weller*	*Hudson*	*Osgood*	*Hutchinson*	*Cooke**	*Houseman*
								Ref: K Howley	Both sides return from European trips. Chelsea's sixth win in a row over City. Efficient Chelsea have only lost once this season. Glazier allows Hollins' shot to creep under his body. O'Rourke clips the post and Harris's foul on Hunt looks like a penalty. Exciting first start by Alderson.											
10	A	NEWCASTLE		17	D	0-0	0-0		Glazier	Coop	Clements	Machin !	Blockley	Strong	Hunt	Carr	Martin	O'Rourke	Alderson	
	26/9		*32,050*	*9*	8				*McFaul*	*Craig*	*Clark*	*Gibb*	*Burton*	*Moncur*	*Robson*	*Dyson**	*Davies*	*Arentoft*	*Young*	*Ford*
								Ref: R Nicholson	Machin is sent off 13 minutes from time by an officious referee for a lunging tackle at Davies. The repercussions will go to the High Court. Nicholson also booked Machin, Carr and Blockley in a dull match. Alderson scores but Carr is offside. Glazier saves from Young and Gibb.											

No	Venue	Opponent / Att	Pos	Res / Pts	F-A	H-T	Scorers, Times, and Referees	1	2	3	4	5	6	7	8	9	10	11	12 sub used
11	H	EVERTON	13	W	3-1	1-1	Martin 18, Hunt 58, 80	Glazier	Coop	Bruck	Clements	Blockley	Strong	Hunt	Carr	Martin	O'Rourke	Alderson	
3/10		29,212	*12*	10			*Hurst 26*	*Rankin*	*Wright**	*Newton K*	*Kendall*	*Kenyon*	*Harvey*	*Whittle*	*Ball*	*Royle*	*Hurst*	*Morrissey*	*Brown*
							Ref: T Dawes	Champions Everton had won six on the trot but are mesmerised by a super City show, topped by the famous donkey-kick goal. Carr flicks the free-kick up between his heels and Hunt volleys it over the wall and past Rankin. Alf Ramsey raves about Alderson but discovers he's a Scot.											
12	A	BURNLEY	13	D	0-0	0-0		Glazier	Coop	Bruck	Clements	Blockley	Strong	Hunt	Carr	Martin	O'Rourke*	Alderson	Joicey
10/10		*12,505*	*22*	11				*Waiters*	*Angus*	*Thomson*	*Docherty*	*Waldron*	*West*	*Thomas*	*Coates*	*Casper*	*Wilson*	*Bellamy*	
							Ref: N Burtenshaw	Burnley are without a win but give City a tough game. Glazier saves well from Alan West and Wilson hits the post. Ex-England goalie Waiters has come out of retirement and saves well from Hunt. David Thomas and Ralph Coates star for home team, who look too good to go down.											
13	H	NOTT'M FOREST	10	W	2-0	2-0	Martin 35, Hunt 39	Glazier	Coop	Cattlin	Clements	Blockley	Strong	Hunt	Carr	Martin	O'Rourke	Alderson	
17/10		25,418	*15*	13				*Barron*	*Hindley*	*Winfield*	*Chapman*	*O'Kane*	*Jackson**	*Lyons*	*Richardson*	*Ingram*	*Cormack*	*Rees*	*Collier*
							Ref: R Kirkpatrick	Hapless Forest are enduring a rough spell and if City did not have Bayern on their mind they might have scored more. City are now unbeaten in seven. Glazier suffers a groin injury and debutant Jackson limps off after Geoff Strong's tackle. Winfield and Hindley's errors lead to goals.											
14	H	ARSENAL	13	L	1-3	0-1	Martin 76	McManus	Coop	Smith	Machin	Blockley	Strong	Hunt	Carr	Martin	Joicey	Clements	
24/10		29,975	*2*	13			*Kennedy 11, Radford 47, Graham 86*	*Wilson*	*Rice*	*McNab*	*Kelly*	*McLintock*	*Roberts*	*Armstrong*	*Storey*	*Radford*	*Kennedy*	*Graham*	
							Ref: M Kerkhof	Solid Arsenal take advantage of City's Munich hangover. The Radford-Kennedy partnership is the key to the Gunners' title challenge and they both score from headers. Martin pulls one back with a header but George Graham seals it. McManus is one of few City men to play well.											
15	A	LEEDS	13	L	0-2	0-1		Glazier	Coop	Smith	Clements	Blockley	Strong	Hunt	Carr	Martin	O'Rourke	Mortimer	
31/10		*31,670*	*1*	13			*Glazier 2 (og), Giles 65*	*Sprake*	*Davey*	*Cooper*	*Bremner*	*Charlton*	*Hunter*	*Lorimer*	*Clarke*	*Jones*	*Giles*	*Madeley*	
							Ref: K Walker	Despite the early goal, City enjoy a big share of the first half without ever threatening. Johnny Giles, returning from injury, scores with a well-placed 30 yarder, and its game over. Bill Glazier misses a corner and Strong, attempting to clear, whacked the ball into Glazier and into the net.											
16	H	MANCHESTER C	12	W	2-1	2-0	Doyle 2 (og), Carr 19	Glazier	Coop	Smith	Mortimer	Blockley	Strong	Hunt	Carr	Martin	O'Rourke	Clements	
7/11		25,287	*6*	15			*Bell 76*	*Corrigan*	*Mann*	*Pardoe*	*Doyle*	*Heslop*	*Oakes*	*Bowyer*	*Bell*	*Lee*	*Hill*	*Towers*	
							Ref: M Sinclair	Mike Doyle's own-goal and Willie Carr's gem of a shot from Clements' pass give City a good start. In a red blooded encounter, O'Rourke misses two good chances and Joe Mercer's men come roaring back. Bell rifles in Oakes' cross but the Sky Blues survive a nail-biting finale.											
17	A	LIVERPOOL	12	D	0-0	0-0		Glazier	Coop	Smith	Mortimer	Blockley	Strong	Hill	Carr	Martin	O'Rourke	Clements	
14/11		***50,503***	*8*	16				*Clemence*	*Lawler*	*Lindsay*	*Smith*	*Lloyd*	*Hughes*	*Hall*	*McLaughlin*	*Heighway*	*Toshack*	*Thompson*	
							Ref: P Walters	Geoff Strong is given a great reception by the crowd as he captains City for the day. £100,000 buy Toshack has a quiet debut. City snatch their first ever point at Anfield. Brian Hill plays his first game of the season in a rearguard action. Glazier saves late efforts by Lawler and Lindsay.											
18	H	CRYS PALACE	10	W	2-1	1-0	Martin 27, Clements 72	Glazier	Coop	Smith	Mortimer	Blockley	Parker	Hill	Carr	Martin	O'Rourke	Clements	
21/11		23,074	*8*	18			*Kember 83*	*Jackson*	*Loughlan*	*Wall*	*Payne*	*McCormick*	*Blyth*	*Taylor*	*Kember*	*Queen*	*Hoadley*	*Scott*	
							Ref: D Laing	City again keep their fans on tender-hooks during the last few minutes. Martin heads home Clements' cross. Coop hits the post and Clements' mistimed shot rolls slowly in. Kember sweeps in Payne's cross. John O'Rourke has now gone 14 league games this season without a goal.											
19	A	WEST HAM	10	W	2-1	2-0	Clements 37, O'Rourke 40	Glazier	Coop	Smith	Mortimer	Blockley	Parker	Hill	Carr	Martin	O'Rourke	Clements	
28/11		*22,300*	*19*	20			*Best 57*	*Ferguson*	*McDowell*	*Lampard*	*Eustace*	*Taylor*	*Moore*	*Holland*	*Howe*	*Best*	*Hurst*	*Greaves*	
							Ref: L Callaghan	West Ham had won only two games all season and never looked in it. They got the slow handclap in the first half when Moore ducks under Carr's corner and Clements heads in. Ferguson claws at Mortimer's cross and O'Rourke breaks his duck. Alf Ramsey is impressed by City kids.											
20	H	STOKE	10	W	1-0	1-0	O'Rourke 19	Glazier	Coop	Smith	Mortimer	Blockley	Parker	Hill	Carr	Martin	O'Rourke	Clements	
5/12		23,785	*13*	22				*Banks*	*Marsh*	*Pejic*	*Bernard*	*Smith D*	*Bloor*	*Mahoney**	*Conroy*	*Greenhoff*	*Eastham*	*Burrows*	*Smith T*
							Ref: R Challis	Gordon Banks makes a rare mistake, allowing O'Rourke's routine header to get past him. City are again hanging on, despite having the lion's share of the match. Martin has two penalty claims turned down. Dennis Mortimer grows in stature with every game. Nine points out of ten.											
21	A	BLACKPOOL	10	L	0-1	0-1		Glazier	Coop	Smith	Mortimer	Blockley	Strong	Parker	Carr	Martin	O'Rourke	Clements	
12/12		***11,381***	*21*	22			*Craven 32*	*Taylor*	*Armfield*	*Mowbray*	*Kemp*	*Alcock*	*Hatton*	*Burns*	*Green*	*Craven*	*Coleman**	*Hutchison*	*Brown*
							Ref: V Batty	The managerless Seasiders earn their first win in 16 games against a lax and lazy Sky Blues. Indecision by Blockley lets in Craven, who buried his shot. City improve after a Cantwell blast at half-time, but they are not good enough. The home fans react as if they have won the FA Cup.											

No	Date		Att	Pos	Pt	F-A	H-T	Scorers, Times, and Referees	1	2	3	4	5	6	7	8	9	10	11	12 sub used
22	A	SOUTHAMPTON		11	L	0-3	0-1		Glazier	Coop	Smith	Hunt	Blockley	Strong	Parker	Carr	Martin	O'Rourke	Clements	
	19/12		*17,569*	*8*	22			*O'Neill 35, Channon 58, Davies 64*	*Martin*	*Kirkup*	*Byrne*	*Fisher*	*McGrath*	*Gabriel*	*Paine*	*Channon*	*Davies*	*O'Neill*	*Jenkins*	
								Ref: A Oliver	An improved display compared to Blackpool. Saints have lost only once at home. Three headers win the game: McGrath headed on for Brian O'Neill, Jenkins' long cross found Channon, Ron Davies beat Blockley in the air just once. O'Rourke had City's best effort, cleared by Kirkup.											
23	H	WEST BROM		10	D	1-1	1-0	Martin 32p	Glazier	Coop	Smith	Hill	Blockley	Strong	Hunt	Carr	Martin	O'Rourke	Clements	
	26/12		27,527	*12*	23			*Brown 52p*	*Cumbes*	*Lovett*	*Wilson*	*Brown*	*Wile*	*Merrick*	*McVitie*	*Suggett*	*Astle*	*Cantello*	*Hartford*	
								Ref: H New	Freezing temperatures and a snow bound pitch didn't make for a great spectacle. Albion earn their first Div 1 point at Highfield Road. Alan Merrick upends O'Rourke. Penalty! The ref is far away when Brian Hill lunges at Suggett but he gives a penalty. Brown's 15th goal of season.											
24	H	IPSWICH		9	W	1-0	1-0	Joicey 12	McManus	Smith	Clements	Machin	Blockley	Strong	Hunt	Mortimer	Martin	Joicey	Alderson	
	9/1		19,938	*17*	25				*Sivell*	*Hammond*	*Mills*	*Morris*	*Baxter*	*McNeill*	*Robertson*	*Viljoen*	*Clarke**	*Collard*	*Hill*	*Jefferson*
								Ref: J Lewis	The smallest home crowd since 1966 sees a deserved win. Brian Alderson and Brian Joicey are recalled and the latter wins it with a neat header from Martin's cross. Eric McManus, in for the injured Glazier, has little to do. Wilf Smith plays his first game in No 2 shirt and looks classy.											
25	A	WOLVES		11	D	0-0	0-0		Glazier	Smith	Clements	Machin	Blockley	Parker	Mortimer	Carr	Joicey	O'Rourke	Alderson	
	16/1		*27,441*	*5*	26				*Parkes*	*Shaw*	*Parkin*	*Bailey*	*Munro*	*McAlle*	*McCalliog*	*Hibbitt*	*Gould*	*Dougan*	*Wagstaffe**	*Curran*
								Ref: K Howley	21-year-old Jeff Blockley is captain, as Cantwell makes changes. Martin, Strong and Hunt are dropped and City's youngsters grab a hard won point in pouring rain. Joicey misses two good chances and Wolves look ragged. City are only the second team to stop Wolves scoring at home.											
26	A	STOKE		12	L	1-2	1-1	Alderson 39	Glazier	Smith	Clements	Machin	Blockley	Parker	Mortimer	Carr	Joicey	Hunt	Alderson	
	6/2		*17,208*	*10*	26			*Mortimer 45 (og), Greenhoff 50*	*Farmer*	*Marsh*	*Pejic*	*Skeels*	*Smith D*	*Jump*	*Haslegrave*	*Greenhoff*	*Conroy*	*Bernard*	*Eastham*	
								Ref: G Hartley	The lack of goals is a problem: only bottom club Burnley have scored fewer. Alderson nets his first ever goal but City are unhinged by the red-haired Terry Conroy. Mortimer diverts his shot in for the first, then he sets up Jimmy Greenhoff. Machin is linked to a move to West Ham.											
27	H	WEST HAM		11	L	0-1	0-1		Glazier	Coop	Smith	Mortimer	Blockley	Parker	Hunt	Carr	Martin	Joicey	Alderson	
	9/2		25,090	*20*	26			*Greaves 26*	*Ferguson*	*McDowell*	*Lampard*	*Bonds*	*Taylor*	*Moore*	*Redknapp*	*Boyce*	*Hurst*	*Eustace*	*Greaves**	*Lindsay*
								Ref: G Kew	Only West Ham's fourth win of the season. They are thankful that Burnley and Blackpool are so bad. Martin is recalled after scoring four in the reserves. Moore and Greaves are back after the Blackpool nightclub incident. Greaves' opportunism wins it after Glazier saves from Hurst.											
28	H	BLACKPOOL		11	W	2-0	0-0	O'Rourke 60, Carr 85	Glazier	Smith	Strong	Machin	Blockley	Parker	Mortimer	Carr	Martin	O'Rourke	Clements	
	13/2		**18,643**	*21*	28				*Thomson*	*Mowbray*	*Bentley*	*Suddaby*	*James*	*Hatton*	*Green*	*Kemp*	*Craven*	*Pickering**	*Coleman*	*Burns*
								Ref: I Jones	A disappointing crowd see a game played in blustery conditions. O'Rourke's 25-yarder went in off the post. Dave Hatton misses two golden chances before Carr clinches it with a rising drive. Blackpool have only won once in 23, against City, and look doomed. Hull want Clements.											
29	A	CRYS PALACE		9	W	2-1	0-0	Carr 47, 65	Glazier	Smith	Strong	Machin	Blockley	Parker	Mortimer	Carr	Joicey	O'Rourke	Clements	
	20/2		*24,114*	*10*	30			*Birchenall 72*	*Jackson*	*Sewell*	*Wall*	*Dawkins*	*Hoadley*	*Blyth*	*Wharton*	*Kember*	*Queen**	*Birchenall*	*Payne*	*Scott*
								Ref: A Morrissey	Martin has signed for Forest. Carr assumes his scoring mantle and punishes the Palace defence for lax marking. He connects with Smith's cross and then seizes on Kember's back-pass. Birchenall outwit's Parker for the home goal. Wilf Smith presses England claims and Strong is superb.											
30	H	LEEDS		11	L	0-1	0-0		Glazier	Smith	Strong	Machin*	Blockley	Parker	Mortimer	Carr	Joicey	O'Rourke	Clements	Alderson
	26/2		**40,022**	*1*	30			*Lorimer 48*	*Harvey*	*Reaney**	*Cooper*	*Bates*	*Charlton*	*Hunter*	*Lorimer*	*Clarke*	*Jones*	*Giles*	*Madeley*	*Belfitt*
								Ref: N Burtenshaw	Leeds' fourth win in a row at Coventry. Once Lorimer had forced a mistake out of Strong the leaders rarely looked troubled. A thoroughly professional performance by Leeds, even without Bremner and Sprake. Mick Coop is on the transfer list. Roy Barry has started his comeback											
31	H	LIVERPOOL		10	W	1-0	1-0	O'Rourke 9	Glazier	Smith	Strong	Machin	Blockley	Parker	Mortimer	Carr	Joicey	O'Rourke	Clements	
	13/3		27,731	*6*	32				*Clemence*	*Lawler*	*Lindsay*	*Smith*	*Lloyd*	*Hughes*	*Boersma**	*Evans*	*Heighway*	*Toshack*	*Hall*	*Callaghan*
								Ref: R Tinkler	Fresh from a Fairs Cup victory over Bayern, Liverpool suffer their first ever defeat against Coventry. Machin taps a free-kick to Clements, whose deflected shot is tipped onto the post by Clemence and O'Rourke hits it in. Alf Ramsey watches as Blockley and Parker stifle Liverpool.											

32	A	MANCHESTER C	11	D	1-1	1-0	O'Rourke 31	Glazier	Smith	Strong	Machin	Blockley	Parker	Mortimer	Carr	Joicey	O'Rourke	Clements	
	20/3	*22,120*	*8*	33			*Lee 85p*	*Healey*	*Connor*	*Towers*	*Doyle*	*Booth*	*Donachie*	*Jeffries*	*Bell*	*Lee*	*Young*	*Mellor*	
							Ref: G Hartley	Glazier, called into Football League side, saves Lee's penalty, only for the ref to order a re-take. Lee had run into Clements and fell. Clements has a dazzling game but City only take advantage after O'Rourke had headed home his cross. A draw was a fair result. Strong was booked.											
33	A	HUDDERSFIELD	11	L	0-1	0-1		Glazier	Cattlin	Strong	Machin	Blockley	Parker	Mortimer	Carr	Joicey*	O'Rourke	Clements	Hunt
	27/3	*15,141*	*15*	33			*Ellam 30*	*Lawson D*	*Clarke*	*Hutt*	*Nicholson*	*Ellam*	*Cherry*	*Smith*	*Mahoney*	*Worthington*	*McGill*	*Lawson J*	
							Ref: D Laing	City play in borrowed yellow shirts and play like strangers. This is their worst showing of the season against a side without a home win since January. Ian Greaves admits that Glazier is impeded at the in-swinging corner from which Ellam scores. City have just one shot in whole game.											
34	H	TOTTENHAM	11	D	0-0	0-0		Glazier	Strong	Cattlin	Machin	Blockley	Parker*	Mortimer	Carr	Rafferty	Hunt	Clements	Alderson
	3/4	22,947	*7*	34				*Jennings*	*Kinnear*	*Want*	*Mullery*	*Collins*	*Beal*	*Gilzean*	*Perryman*	*Chivers*	*Peters*	*Pearce*	
							Ref: C Nicholls	Lack of goals mean that the club lowest total of 35 goals in a season is under threat. Spurs employ negative tactics and chances are few. Hunt tries the donkey kick again and hits the angle. Rafferty on his home debut tried hard. Roy Barry played in a friendly during the week.											
35	A	ARSENAL	11	L	0-1	0-0		Glazier	Coop	Cattlin	Machin	Blockley	Strong	Mortimer	Carr	Rafferty	Hunt	Joicey	
	6/4	*37,029*	*2*	34			*Kennedy 52*	*Wilson*	*Rice*	*McNab*	*Storey*	*McLintock*	*Simpson*	*Armstrong*	*Graham*	*Radford*	*Kennedy*	*George*	
							Ref: D Smith	City perform with great credit against the Gunners, who are now four points behind Leeds with two games in hand. Carr and Hunt are unlucky not to score before Ray Kennedy chests down Armstrong's cross and volleys home. Coventry, inspired by Carr, fail to take more chances.											
36	A	WEST BROM	11	D	0-0	0-0		Glazier	Smith	Cattlin	Hunt	Blockley	Strong	Mortimer	Carr	Joicey*	Rafferty	Clements	O'Rourke
	10/4	*18,759*	*16*	35				*Cumbes*	*Hughes*	*Merrick*	*Cantello*	*Wile*	*Kaye*	*McVitie*	*Brown*	*Astle*	*Suggett*	*Hartford*	
							Ref: H Williams	Defences are on top in this mediocre Midlands derby. Rafferty is unlucky with an effort that strikes Kaye on the line. Glazier saves well from 26-goal Tony Brown but Strong shines in City's defensive display. Though WBA have the worst defence in Div 1, City rarely look like scoring.											
37	A	EVERTON	13	L	0-3	0-2		Glazier	Coop	Cattlin	O'Rourke	Blockley	Strong	Mortimer	Carr	Rafferty	Hunt	Clements	
	12/4	*24,371*	*10*	35			*Royle 12, 23, Ball 48*	*Rankin*	*Wright*	*Newton H*	*Darracott*	*Kenyon*	*Harvey*	*Johnson*	*Ball*	*Royle**	*Hurst*	*Jones*	*Lyons*
							Ref: K Howley	Everton are without a win in eight, City the same in five. Royle heads home Ball's free-kick. Glazier gets a hand to Royle's shot but it creeps in. Ball has two bites of the cherry from Tommy Wright's cross. City's defence was for once found wanting. Lowest Goodison gate since 1965.											
38	H	MANCHESTER U	10	W	2-1	1-0	Hunt 5, 49	Glazier	Smith	Cattlin	Machin	Blockley	Strong	Alderson*	Carr	Rafferty	Hunt	Clements	Mortimer
	13/4	33,849	*12*	37			*Best 60*	*Stepney*	*Dunne*	*Burns*	*Crerand*	*Edwards*	*Stiles*	*Best*	*Gowling*	*Charlton*	*Kidd*	*Morgan*	
							Ref: K Walker	Ernie Hunt ends City's five-game goal drought with a crisp shot after United fail to clear a corner. His second is an exquisite volley from 15 yards. Best then comes to life and ghosts in to volley home Crerand's cross. City deservedly survive, despite Best dominating the second half.											
39	H	BURNLEY	9	W	**3-0**	0-0	Hunt 53, 90, Rafferty 86	Glazier	Smith	Cattlin	Machin	Blockley	Parker	Alderson*	Carr	Rafferty	Hunt	Clements	Mortimer
	17/4	18,377	*21*	39				*Waiters*	*Angus*	*Latcham*	*Docherty*	*Dobson*	*Nulty*	*Casper**	*Coates*	*Fletcher*	*Bellamy*	*Collins*	*Probert*
							Ref: H New	Burnley are all but relegated after this defeat, before City's lowest crowd since 1963. Hunt cheekily lobs Waiters from 40 yards. Two late goals distort the scoreline. Hunt sets up Rafferty, who scores his first goal at the second attempt. Carr sets up Hunt for an explosive shot at the death.											
40	A	CHELSEA	12	L	1-2	0-0	Hunt 90	Glazier	Smith	Cattlin	Machin	Blockley	Parker	Mortimer	Carr	Rafferty	Hunt	Clements	
	24/4	*27,517*	*3*	39			*Smethurst 77, Feely 79*	*Bonetti*	*Boyle*	*Harris*	*Hollins**	*Dempsey*	*Webb*	*Weller*	*Smethurst*	*Feely*	*Hudson*	*Houseman*	*McCreadie*
							Ref: K Styles	Osgood and Hutchinson are rested by the Cup-Winners Cup finalists and both their replacements net. Smethurst heads in Boyle's cross. Feely's goal bounced off his shoulder after Glazier was impeded. Rafferty had a good 'goal' ruled out. Hunt's consolation was the best of the three.											
41	H	DERBY	12	D	0-0	0-0		Glazier	Smith	Cattlin	Machin	Blockley	Parker	Mortimer	Carr	Rafferty	Hunt	Clements	
	27/4	22,051	*8*	40				*Boulton*	*Todd*	*Robson*	*Durban*	*McFarland*	*Mackay*	*McGovern*	*Bourne**	*O'Hare*	*Hector*	*Hinton*	*Webster*
							Ref: B Homewood	Mackay's last away appearance for the Rams before joining Swindon. This is City's 21st game in which they fail to score this season. Defences dominate with Blockley and McFarland superb. Hunt misses two good chances and Durban hits a post. Derby have yet to beat City in Div 1.											
42	H	NEWCASTLE	10	W	2-0	1-0	Hunt 36, Blockley 66	Glazier	Smith	Cattlin	Machin	Blockley	Barry	Alderson	Carr	Rafferty*	Hunt	Clements	Mortimer
	1/5	20,781	*13*	42				*McFaul*	*Craig*	*Clark*	*Craggs*	*McNamee*	*Nattrass*	*Gibb*	*Davies*	*Dyson*	*Smith*	*Young*	
	Home	Away					Ref: M Sinclair	City avoid the lowest goals scored club record but set a new record for the least conceded. A good win to bring the curtain down. Chris Cattlin slipped the ball through for Hunt to score. The unmarked Jeff Blockley heads home Clements' corner. Roy Barry returns after his broken leg.											
Average	26,040	25,984																	

LEAGUE DIVISION 1 (CUP-TIES)

Manager: Noel Cantwell

SEASON 1970-71

League Cup			F-A	H-T	Scorers, Times, and Referees	1	2	3	4	5	6	7	8	9	10	11	12 sub used
2 A TRANMERE	12	D	1-1	1-0	Machin 40	Glazier	Coop	Bruck	Machin	Blockley	Strong	Hunt	Carr	Martin	Joicey	Clements	
9/9 *11,079*	*3:8*				*Yardley 84*	*Lane*	*Joy*	*Matthias*	*Moorcroft*	*Pointon*	*Brodie*	*Beamish*	*King A*	*Yardley*	*Hinch*	*Gill**	*Moore*
					Ref: M Fussey	Rovers have not lost for 21 games but City go close to winning. A howling wind spoils the game. Hunt craftily lays on Machin's goal. Yardley is credited with a flick on Brodie's free-kick but Glazier confirms later that Strong deflected it. Former City youth Brian Joy is in the home side.											
2R H TRANMERE	16	W	2-1	0-1	Hunt 54, Blockley 65	Glazier	Coop	Clements	Mortimer	Blockley	Strong	Hunt	Carr	Martin	O'Rourke	Alderson	
22/9 14,448	*3:11*				*Hinch 17*	*Lane*	*Joy*	*Matthias*	*Pointon*	*Knapp*	*Brodie*	*Moore*	*King A*	*Yardley*	*Hinch*	*Gill*	
					Ref: M Fussey	City have to work hard to beat plucky Rovers. Yardley sets up Jim Hinch and Frank Gill volleys over from 12 yards as Coventry are easily pulled apart in the first half. Hunt's 30-yarder levels the scores and Jeff Blockley's thunderous header from Brian Alderson's corner wins it.											
3 H WEST HAM	13	W	3-1	1-0	Martin 41p, O'Rourke 67, Carr 89	Glazier	Coop	Bruck	Clements	Blockley	Strong	Hunt	Carr	Martin	O'Rourke	Alderson	
6/10 19,793	*18*				*Hurst 86*	*Grotier*	*Bonds*	*Lampard*	*Lindsay*	*Stephenson*	*Moore*	*Ayris*	*Best*	*Hurst*	*Brooking*	*Eustace*	
					Ref: A Jones	West Ham have won only once in the League but give City a fright in an exciting game. Eustace fists over and Neil Martin scores from the spot. O'Rourke scores from 35 yards. After Hurst scores off a post from a Clyde Best pass to set up a nervy finish, Carr scores a brilliant solo goal.											
4 H DERBY	12	W	1-0	0-0	Martin 59	Glazier	Coop	Smith	Clements	Blockley	Strong	Hunt	Carr	Martin	O'Rourke	Alderson	
27/10 26,557	*18*					*Green*	*Webster*	*Robson*	*Hennessey*	*McFarland*	*Mackay*	*McGovern*	*Durban*	*O'Hare*	*Hector*	*Hinton*	
					Ref: C Thomas	Both sides are low in confidence but City win to achieve their best Cup run for five years. An uncompromising midlands derby is determined by Martin's far-post header from Alderson's cross. Clements deflected free-kick a minute later is ruled out. Glazier tips McFarland's header over.											
5 A TOTTENHAM	12	L	1-4	0-1	O'Rourke 69	Glazier	Coop	Smith	Mortimer	Blockley	Hill	Joicey	Carr	Martin	O'Rourke	Clements	
18/11 *31,864*	*2*				*Chivers 26, 62, 78, Gilzean 87*	*Jennings*	*Kinnear*	*Knowles*	*Mullery*	*England*	*Beal**	*Gilzean*	*Pratt*	*Chivers*	*Peters*	*Pearce*	*Neighbour*
					Ref: C Thomas	Spurs won it where it matters, in the penalty area. City matched them for most of the game but missed chances. Chivers' finishing power is deadly. He feeds on mistakes for the first two goals but plunders the third with a fierce shot. O'Rourke's header gives brief hope on a wet night.											

FA Cup			F-A	H-T	Scorers, Times, and Referees	1	2	3	4	5	6	7	8	9	10	11	12 sub used
3 A ROCHDALE	9	L	1-2	0-1	Hunt 51	Glazier	Smith	Clements	Machin	Blockley	Strong	Hunt	Carr	Martin	Joicey	Alderson	
11/1 *13,011*	*3:23*				*Cross 39, Butler 80*	*Tennant*	*Smith*	*Ryder*	*Riley*	*Parry*	*Ashworth*	*Whitehead*	*Buck*	*Cross*	*Downes*	*Butler*	
					Ref: J Thacker	This tie, played on Monday afternoon after a postponement, produces one of the biggest humiliations in City's history. David Cross heads in Whitehead's centre. Hunt's equaliser looks offside. Butler races clear for the winner. Blockley's last-gasp header hits the underside of the bar.											

European Fairs Cup			F-A	H-T	Scorers, Times, and Referees	1	2	3	4	5	6	7	8	9	10	11	12 sub used
1:1 A TRAKIA PLOVDIV	16	W	4-1	2-0	O'Rourke 39, 69, 89, Martin 43	Glazier	Coop	Smith	Machin	Blockley	Strong	Hunt	Carr	Martin	O'Rourke	Clements	
16/9 (Bulgaria) *15,000*					*Radkov 75*	*Karushkov**	*Deled*	*Gluhthev*	*Apostolov*	*Zagdouna*	*Marinov*	*Popov*	*Dermenjiev*	*Upinov*	*Stanoev*	*Radkov*	*Radenkov*
					Ref: C Naudi (Malta)	A fine European debut with O'Rourke's first goals of the season. 50 City fans watch their team survive early scares. Hunt's shot is parried for the first, then Martin hits a 25-yarder. The third comes from Gluhthev's error and the fourth a tap-in. The home keeper was subbed at half-time.											
1:2 H TRAKIA PLOVDIV	17	W	2-0	2-0	Joicey 30, Blockley 35	Glazier	Coop	Bruck	Clements	Blockley	Strong	Hunt	Carr	Joicey*	O'Rourke	Alderson	Rafferty
30/9 20,930						*Radenkov**	*Deled*	*Gluhthev*	*Apostolov*	*Zagdouna*	*Marinov*	*Popov*	*Dermenjiev*	*Nenov*	*Stanoev*	*Ubinov*	*Karushkov*
					Ref: F Rion (Belgium) (City win 6-1 on aggregate)	An easy passage for the Sky Blues as the Bulgarians flop again. Radenkov was carried off after a collision with Brian Joicey. Joicey chips the keeper before going off himself with bruised ribs after a clash with the sub keeper. Blockley's header from Brian Alderson's cross ends the tie.											

No	Date	Venue	Opponent	Att	Pos	Res	F-A	H-T	Scorers, Times, and Referees	1	2	3	4	5	6	7	8	9	10	11	12 sub used
2:1	20/10	A	BAYERN MUNICH (W Germ)	*12,548*	10	L	1-6	1-4	Hunt 10 *[Muller 19, 89, Roth 76] Schneider 4, 12, Schwarzenbeck 16,* Ref: Francescon (Italy)	McManus *Maier*	Coop *Hansen*	Cattlin *Koppenhofer*	Machin *Beckenbauer*	Blockley *Schwarz'beck*	Strong *Roth*	Hunt *Zobel*	Carr *Mrosko*	Martin *Schneider*	O'Rourke *Muller*	Clements *Brenninger*	
										Tragedy for rookie McManus - in for injured Glazier - at fault for at least three goals. On a wet night City are hammered, although at 1-4 they miss two good chances. Hunt's flying header gives them brief hope. Bayern parade three German World Cup players. 250 City fans travel.												
2:2	3/11	H	BAYERN MUNICH	26,033		W	2-1	1-0	Martin 35, O'Rourke 81 *Hoeness 63* Ref: A Rios (Spain) (City lose 3-7 on aggregate)	Glazier *Maier*	Coop *Hansen*	Smith *Koppenhofer*	Mortimer *Beckenbauer*	Blockley *Schwarz'beck*	Hill *Pumm*	Hunt * *Zobel*	Carr *Mrosko*	Martin *Hoeness*	O'Rourke *Muller*	Clements *Brenninger*	Joicey
										City regain some self-respect chasing a hopeless cause. Sepp Maier saves superbly from Clements and Carr in the opening spell. Blockley nods down Clements' cross for Martin to score and repeats the move for O'Rourke's winner. Bayern go on to face Sparta Rotterdam in Round 3.												

			Home					Away					
	P	W	D	L	F	A	W	D	L	F	A	Pts
1 Arsenal	42	18	3	0	41	6	11	4	6	30	23	65
2 Leeds	42	16	2	3	40	12	11	8	2	32	18	64
3 Tottenham	42	11	5	5	33	19	8	9	4	21	14	52
4 Wolves	42	13	3	5	33	22	9	5	7	31	32	52
5 Liverpool	42	11	10	0	30	10	6	7	8	12	14	51
6 Chelsea	42	12	6	3	34	21	6	9	6	18	21	51
7 Southampton	42	12	5	4	35	15	5	7	9	21	29	46
8 Manchester U	42	9	6	6	29	24	7	5	9	36	42	43
9 Derby	42	9	5	7	32	26	7	5	9	24	28	42
10 COVENTRY	42	12	4	5	24	12	4	6	11	13	26	42
11 Manchester C	42	7	9	5	30	22	5	8	8	17	20	41
12 Newcastle	42	9	9	3	27	16	5	4	12	17	30	41
13 Stoke	42	10	7	4	28	11	2	6	13	16	37	37
14 Everton	42	10	7	4	32	16	2	6	13	22	44	37
15 Huddersfield	42	7	8	6	19	16	4	6	11	21	33	36
16 Nott'm Forest	42	9	4	8	29	26	5	4	12	13	35	36
17 West Brom	42	9	8	4	34	25	1	7	13	24	50	35
18 Crys Palace	42	9	5	7	24	24	3	6	12	15	33	35
19 Ipswich	42	9	4	8	28	22	3	6	12	14	26	34
20 West Ham	42	6	8	7	28	30	4	6	11	19	30	34
21 Burnley	42	4	8	9	20	31	3	5	13	9	32	27
22 Blackpool	42	3	9	9	22	31	1	6	14	12	35	23
	924	215	135	112	652	437	112	135	215	437	652	924

Odds & ends

Double wins: (2) Ipswich, Crys Palace.
Double losses: (3) Chelsea, Arsenal, Leeds.

Won from behind: (2) Derby (a), Tranmere LC (h).
Lost from in front: (1) Stoke (a).

High spots: Win at Derby after being 0-2 down.
Ernie Hunt's donkey-kick goal against Everton.
League Cup run to the quarter-final.
Winning Fairs Cup debut in Plovdiv.
Revenge over Bayern in second leg.
Least goals conceded in club's league history.

Low spots: Fewest goals scored since 1919-20.
Dreadful performances at Blackpool and Huddersfield.
FA Cup embarrassment at Third Division Rochdale.
5 games (515 minutes) without a goal in April.

Red cards: City – Machin (Newcastle a).

Ever-presents: (1) Jeff Blockley
Hat-tricks: (1) John O'Rourke.
Opposing hat-tricks: (1) Martin Chivers (Spurs LC).
Leading scorer: (12) Ernie Hunt.

	Appearances						Goals			
	Lge	*Sub*	LC	*Sub*	FAC	*Sub*	Lge	LC	FAC	Tot
Alderson, Brian	**12**	*3*	3		1		**1**			**1**
Barry, Roy	**1**									
Blockley, Jeff	**42**		5		1		**1**	1		**2**
Bruck, Dietmar	**3**	*2*	2							
Carr, Willie	**41**		5		1		**5**	1		**6**
Cattlin, Chris	**14**	*1*								
Clements, Dave	**40**		5		1		**3**			**3**
Coop, Mick	**25**		5							
Glazier, Bill	**40**		5		1					
Goodwin, Ian	**4**									
Hill, Brian	**5**		1							
Hunt, Ernie	**29**	*2*	4		1		**10**	1	1	**12**
Joicey, Brian	**16**	*2*	2		1		**1**			**1**
Machin, Ernie	**24**		1		1			1		**1**
Martin, Neil	**26**		5		1		**9**	2		**11**
McManus, Eric	**2**									
Mortimer, Dennis	**24**	*3*	2							
O'Rourke, John	**27**	*1*	4				**5**	2		**7**
Parker, Bobby	**18**	*1*								
Rafferty, Billy	**9**						**1**			**1**
Smith, Wilf	**28**		2		1					
Strong, Geoff	**32**		4		1					
(own-goals)							**1**			**1**
22 players used	**462**	***15***	**55**		**11**		**37**	**8**	**1**	**46**

No	Date		Att	Pos	Pt	F-A	H-T	Scorers, Times, and Referees	1	2	3	4	5	6	7	8	9	10	11	12 sub used
1	H	STOKE			D	1-1	1-0	Hunt 44	Glazier	Smith	Cattlin	Machin	Blockley	Barry	Mortimer	Carr	Rafferty*	Hunt	Clements	Alderson
	14/8		20,894		1			Ritchie 49	Banks	Marsh	Pejic	Bernard	Smith	Bloor	Mahoney*	Greenhoff	Ritchie	Stevenson	Haslegrave	Skeels
								Ref: V James	Against last season's FA Cup semi finalists City are unable to press home their territorial advantage. A torrential rainstorm threatened to end the game in the first half. Hunt scored a header from Mortimer's cross. Ritchie's run beat Blockley and Barry and ended with a powerful shot.											
2	A	IPSWICH			L	1-3	1-2	Carr 35	Glazier	Smith	Cattlin	Machin*	Blockley	Barry	Mortimer	Carr	O'Rourke	Hunt	Parker	Coop
	17/8		18,921		1			Clarke 4, 50p, Hamilton 42	Best	Hammond	Harper	Morris	Bell	Jefferson	Robertson	Mills	Clarke	Hamilton	Miller	
								Ref: R Challis	The referee's new charter is applied by the book in a game with six bookings which was never dirty. Clements was dropped and Machin was stretchered off with a broken shin-bone. Ipswich won it with Frank Clarke's header, a penalty when Cattlin handles, and Hamilton's shot.											
3	A	WEST BROM		16	D	1-1	0-0	Hunt 58	Glazier	Smith	Cattlin	Mortimer	Blockley	Barry	**McGuire**	Carr	O'Rourke	Hunt	Joicey	
	21/8		25,449	2	2			Brown 66	Cumbes	Hughes	Wilson	Cantello	Wile	Kaye	Suggett	Brown	Astle	Hope	Hartford	
								Ref: P Walters	A clean, exciting derby. West Brom, under new boss Don Howe, have won their first two games. Hunt brilliantly volleys Carr's cross-field past Cumbes. Brown pounces onto the excellent Cattlin's back-header to equalise. An impressive debut by Sky Blues' 18-year-old Mick McGuire.											
4	H	DERBY		15	D	2-2	1-0	Joicey 39, Hunt 55p	Glazier	Smith	Cattlin	Mortimer	Blockley	Barry	**Young**	Carr	Joicey	Hunt	McGuire	
	24/8		27,759	3	3			O'Hare 53, Wignall 86	Boulton	Webster	Robson	McGovern	McFarland	Todd	Gemmill	Wignall	O'Hare	Hector	Hinton	
								Ref: J Taylor	Derby are unbeaten and Wignall's late header earns a point they deserve. McFarland lets in Joicey to score, then brings the same player down for the penalty. Good performances from Mortimer and Todd brighten a dull game. Dave Clements and Brian Joicey join Wednesday next day.											
5	H	NEWCASTLE		13	W	1-0	0-0	Blockley 57	Glazier	Smith	Cattlin	Mortimer	Blockley	Barry*	Young	Carr	O'Rourke	Hunt	McGuire	Alderson
	28/8		22,788	15	5				McFaul	Craig	Clark	Gibb	Burton	Moncur	Cassidy	Tudor	Macdonald	Young	Hibbitt	
								Ref: D Laing	The table and chairs are on the pitch for the signing of Hull's Chris Chilton, but he wants more time. Blockley's far-post header from Young's corner wins it but the Geordies are let off the hook and almost snatch a draw. Young has a superb second half. Alf Ramsey watches Mortimer.											
6	A	WEST HAM		15	L	**0-4**	0-2		Glazier	Smith	Cattlin	Mortimer	Blockley	Barry	Young	Carr	O'Rourke	Hunt	McGuire	
	30/8		28,176	10	5			Best 17, 53, Hurst 38, Robson 58	Ferguson	McDowell	Lampard	Bonds	Taylor	Moore	Ayris	Best	Hurst	Brooking	Robson	
								Ref: M Kerkhof	West Ham's poor start to the season is put behind them as they record their biggest win for 18 months. Brooking is the architect and Clyde Best's strength and powerful shooting earns him two goals. City need to buy a defender as well as striker Chilton, who signed today for £92,000.											
7	A	CHELSEA		15	D	3-3	3-3	Rafferty 4, O'Rourke 40, Mortimer 42	Glazier	Smith	Coop	Mortimer	Blockley	Parker	O'Rourke	Carr	Rafferty	Hunt	McGuire	
	4/9		35,459	14	6			Osgood 3, 17, Hollins 27	Phillips	Mulligan	Harris	Hollins	Dempsey	Webb	Cooke	Garland	Osgood	Boyle	Houseman	
								Ref: A Morrissey	Chelsea's six game winning run against City is ended in a goal-crazy first half. The irrepresible Hunt made all three, crossing for Rafferty's header, the free-kick for O'Rourke's great shot, and a clever pass for Dennis Mortimer's first ever goal. Bill Glazier at fault for Osgood's goals.											
8	H	NOTT'M FOREST		15	D	1-1	1-0	Hunt 4	Glazier	Coop	Smith	Mortimer	Blockley	Parker	Alderson	Carr	**Chilton***	Hunt	McGuire	O'Rourke
	11/9		20,380	21	7			Cormack 71	Barron	Hindley	Winfield	Chapman	O'Kane	Fraser	Jackson	McKenzie	Martin*	Cormack	Moore	Richardson
								Ref: K Styles	Forest have beaten Aldershot 5-1 in midweek but fall behind to Hunt's header. City fail to stamp their authority and Moore hauls the visitors back into the game. Cormack's header is ample reward. Richardson and Alderson hit the bar in search of the winner. Chilton off with cramp.											
9	A	SOUTHAMPTON		17	L	1-3	1-1	Hunt 27	Glazier	Coop	Smith	Mortimer	Blockley	Parker	Young	Carr	Chilton	Hunt	Cattlin	
	18/9		17,443	7	7			Fisher 22, Paine 66, Channon 73	Martin	Kirkup	Hollywood	Fisher	McGrath	Gabriel	Paine	Channon	Davies*	O'Neill	Jenkins	Stokes
								Ref: V Batty	City dominate for long periods but lose to two bad goals when Paine is allowed to turn and shoot and Channon surges from the halfway line. Coventry have not won in 19 visits to the Dell since the war. Saints are fresh from a UEFA Cup win over Bilbao. St John signs as player-coach.											
10	H	TOTTENHAM		14	W	1-0	0-0	Carr 82	Glazier	Coop	Cattlin	Smith	Blockley	Parker	Young	Carr	Chilton	Hunt	**St John**	
	25/9		26,517	9	9				Jennings	Kinnear	Knowles*	Mullery	England	Beal	Coates	Perryman	Chivers	Peters	Gilzean	Pearce
								Ref: J Thacker	Quintin Young is the star of an excellent win, roasting Knowles so much that he is subbed near the end. Young sets up Carr's headed winner and St John brings a cool head to bear. City are rarely in danger from feeble Spurs, who take their defeat in bad grace, refusing to talk to press.											

No	H/A	Opponent / Date	Att	Pos	Pts	F-A	H-T	Scorers, Times, Referees	1	2	3	4	5	6	7	8	9	10	11	12
11	A	EVERTON		12	W	2-1	1-0	Young 23, St John 68	Glazier	Coop	Cattlin !	Smith	Blockley	Parker	Young	Carr	Chilton	Hunt	St John	
		2/10	*36,882*	*17*	11			*Lyons 64*	*West*	*Scott*	*Newton K*	*Newton H*	*Kenyon*	*Harvey*	*Whittle*	*Wilson**	*Johnson*	*Hurst*	*Morrissey*	*Lyons*
								Ref: W Johnson	A fairy tale return to Merseyside for St John as he scores the winner. City lead through Young's explosive shot until Lyons header from Keith Newton's free-kick. Coventry's first ever win at Goodison. Blockley pushes Johnson but the ref sends off Cattlin. Royle out with a bad back.											
12	H	LEEDS		11	W	3-1	2-0	Chilton 5, St John 34, Hunt 54	Glazier	Coop	Barry	Smith	Blockley	Parker	Young	Carr	Chilton	Hunt	St John*	Mortimer
		9/10	32,108	*9*	13			*Parker 88 (og)*	*Sprake*	*Reaney*	*Cooper*	*Bremner*	*Charlton*	*Hunter*	*Lorimer*	*Yorath**	*Belfitt*	*Giles*	*Madeley*	*Jordan*
								Ref: C Nicholls	First Div 1 win over Leeds. Coventry outclass the best side in Britain in an outstanding team performance. Young fleeces Cooper. Hunt and St John set up Chilton's first City goal. Quintin Young makes St John's and Carr robs Bremner to create Hunt's. Parker deflects Giles shot.											
13	A	STOKE		12	L	0-1	0-0		Glazier	Coop	Barry	Smith	Blockley	Parker	Young*	Carr	Chilton	Hunt	St John	Alderson
		16/10	*20,540*	*9*	13			*Smith 82*	*Banks*	*Marsh*	*Pejic*	*Bernard*	*Smith*	*Bloor*	*Conroy*	*Greenhoff*	*Ritchie*	*Stevenson*	*Jump*	
								Ref: G Hill	A disappointing end to the mini-run. Stoke knocked Sheff United from the top of the league last week. City have few chances and Carr misses an easy header. Glazier keeps City in it but can't stop Smith's header from Conroy's corner. Brian Hill goes to Torquay and O'Rourke to QPR.											
14	H	CRYS PALACE		12	D	1-1	0-1	St John 68	Glazier	Coop	Barry	Smith	Blockley	Parker	Young	Carr	Chilton	Mortimer	St John	
		22/10	20,811	*20*	14			*Tambling 7*	*Jackson*	*Payne*	*Taylor*	*Blyth*	*McCormick*	*Pinkney*	*Tambling*	*Goodwin*	*Craven*	*Kellard*	*Hughes**	*Wallace*
								Ref: D Nippard	A rare Friday night game which City are always chasing, after Bobby Tambling punished an uncleared Kellard corner. Injured Ernie Hunt is sorely missed. Ex-Celtic debut boys John Hughes and Willie Wallace go close before St John scores from close range. Palace deserve a point.											
15	A	WOLVES		13	D	1-1	1-0	Carr 27	Glazier	Coop	Barry	Smith	Blockley	Parker	Young*	Carr	Chilton	Mortimer	St John	Hunt
		30/10	*25,841*	*11*	15			*Munro 88*	*Parkes*	*Shaw*	*Parkin*	*Bailey*	*Munro*	*McAlle*	*McCalliog*	*Daley*	*Richards*	*Dougan*	*Wagstaffe*	
								Ref: G Kew	A bright performance deserves two points against mediocre Wolves who scored from David Wagstaffe's corner. Carr's goal was swept in when Bernard Shaw only half cleared Chilton's cross. Wolves get the slow handclap. Opposition fans fight a battle on the pitch before the game.											
16	H	HUDDERSFIELD		11	W	2-1	1-0	Hunt 45, 51	Glazier	Coop	Barry	Smith	Blockley	Parker	Young	Carr	St John	Hunt	Alderson*	McGuire
		6/11	**16,309**	*19*	17			*Smith D 73*	*Lawson D*	*Clarke*	*Hutt*	*Jones*	*Ellam*	*Cherry*	*Smith D*	*Smith S*	*Worthington*	*Lawson J*	*Chapman*	
								Ref: C Fallon	The Terriers have lost four of the last five. Hunt flicks in from a corner and scores with a superb diving header from in-form midfield dynamo Wilf Smith's pass to Carr. Glazier's 250th League game is quiet until the goal, then he saves City. Ellam's late effort scrubbed out for offside.											
17	A	SHEFFIELD UTD		12	L	0-2	0-1		Glazier	Coop	Barry	Smith	Blockley	Parker	Young*	Carr	McGuire	Hunt	Alderson	Mortimer
		13/11	*32,630*	*4*	17			*Woodward 45, 87*	*Hope*	*Badger*	*Goulding*	*Flynn*	*Colquhoun*	*Hockey*	*Woodward*	*Salmons*	*Reece*	*Currie*	*Scullion*	
								Ref: B Homewood	In the three-sided stadium the promoted Blades show why they are league contenders. Woodward scores direct from a viciously bending corner on the stroke of half-time. The winger then has his penalty saved by Glazier when Blockley trips Reece, but makes amends six minutes later.											
18	H	LIVERPOOL		13	L	0-2	0-0		Glazier	Coop	Barry	Smith	Blockley	Parker	Young	Carr	Chilton	Hunt !	St John	
		20/11	25,452	*6*	17			*Whitham 80, 90*	*Clemence*	*Lawler*	*Lindsay*	*Smith*	*Ross*	*Hughes*	*Graham*	*Boersma*	*Heighway*	*Whitham*	*Callaghan*	
								Ref: T Reynolds	City's 14-game unbeaten home run is ended by Liverpool reserve Jack Whitham. His first goal looks offside and the second comes in the fifth minute of injury-time. Ernie Hunt is sent off for dissent after the second. The visitors defence, minus the injured Larry Lloyd, is little troubled.											
19	A	MANCHESTER C		14	L	**0-4**	0-2		Glazier	Coop	Strong	Smith	Blockley	Parker	McGuire	Carr	Chilton	Hunt	Rafferty	
		27/11	*31,003*	*2*	17			*Lee 26, 83 Bell 33, 77*	*Corrigan*	*Book*	*Donachie*	*Doyle*	*Booth*	*Oakes*	*Summerbee*	*Bell*	*Davies*	*Lee*	*Mellor*	
								Ref: K Walker	Before the pummeling starts Hunt and Chilton miss good chances. Lee pounces on Coop's back-pass. The defence are transfixed as Bell scores from Summerbee's corner. Bell scores from Davies' cross. Lee flicks Doyle's cross past Glazier. The ubiquitous Willie Carr gets scant support.											
20	H	LEICESTER		14	D	1-1	0-0	McGuire 90	Glazier	Smith	**Holmes**	St John	Blockley	Parker	Young	Carr	Rafferty	Mortimer	Alderson*	McGuire
		4/12	26,300	*16*	18			*Brown 57*	*Shilton*	*Whitworth*	*Nish*	*Cross*	*Sjoberg*	*Brown*	*Weller*	*Fern*	*Birchenall*	*Sammels*	*Glover*	
								Ref: E Jolly	Shilton performs heroics and keeps Coventry out until 92 minutes are on the clock, when McGuire slams home. Glazier can't hold Birchenall's stinging shot and Brown nets. Asprey and Farmer were sacked during the week and St John is made assistant, with Waiters coaching Director.											
21	A	ARSENAL		14	L	0-2	0-2		McManus	Smith	Holmes	St John*	Blockley	Parker	Young	Carr	Rafferty	Mortimer	Alderson	Coop
		11/12	*28,597*	*8*	18			*Radford 4, 45*	*Wilson*	*Rice*	*McNab*	*Storey*	*McLintock*	*Simpson**	*Armstrong*	*Kelly*	*Radford*	*Kennedy*	*Graham*	*Marinello*
								Ref: P Baldwin	The Double winners win easily. Fumbling City have one shot in the whole game. Radford heads home Armstrong's corner and pounces when McManus, in for the injured Glazier, can't hold Armstrong's fierce shot. Holmes looks cool in a shaky defence. Bid for Peter Thompson fails.											

LEAGUE DIVISION 1

Manager: Cantwell > Bob Dennison

SEASON 1971-72

No	Date		Att	Pos	Pt	F-A	H-T	Scorers, Times, and Referees	1	2	3	4	5	6	7	8	9	10	11	12 sub used
22	H	CHELSEA		15	D	1-1	0-0	Carr 62	McManus	Smith	Holmes	St John	Blockley	Parker	Young	Carr	Rafferty*	Chilton	Machin	Mortimer
	17/12		21,875	*9*	19			*Osgood 48*	*Bonetti**	*Mulligan*	*Harris*	*Hollins*	*Dempsey*	*Webb*	*Cooke*	*Kember*	*Osgood*	*Hudson*	*Houseman*	*Garland*
								Ref: W Hall	Bonetti is carried off with ankle damage after a 30th-minute clash with Young. Webb takes over and is well protected until Carr scores from Young's cross. Eric McManus, on his last appearance, lets Osgood's tame header in, but saves well from Garland. Chelsea unbeaten in nine.											
23	A	MANCHESTER U		15	D	2-2	1-0	Young 34, Carr 66	**Healey**	Smith	Cattlin	Machin*	Blockley	Parker	Young	Carr	Rafferty	Chilton	St John	Mortimer
	27/12		***52,117***	*1*	20			*Law 71, James 85*	*Stepney*	*Dunne*	*Burns*	*Gowling*	*James**	*Sadler*	*Morgan*	*Kidd*	*Charlton*	*Law*	*Best*	*McIlroy*
								Ref: D Turner	United had only dropped one point at home. Healey is on loan from Man City and gets stick from the home fans. Young scores from a 25-yard free kick. Carr pounces on Burns' error. Law and James head goals but United are lucky. A five-man City wall are booked for not retreating.											
24	H	SOUTHAMPTON		13	W	1-0	0-0	Mortimer 59	Healey	Smith	Cattlin	St John	Blockley	Parker	Young	Carr	Rafferty	Mortimer	Chilton	
	1/1		17,934	*14*	22				*Martin*	*McCarthy*	*Fry*	*Stokes*	*Gabriel*	*Byrne*	*Paine*	*Channon*	*Davies*	*O'Brien*	*Jenkins*	
								Ref: H Williams	High entertainment and it should have been a more resounding victory. A 25-yard drive is reward for the excellent Dennis Mortimer. Willie Carr hits the woodwork twice. Jeff Blockley masters Ron Davies. Quintin Young is electric on the wing. Chris Cattlin's 100th appearance.											
25	A	NEWCASTLE		13	L	2-4	1-2	Rafferty 5, Mortimer 67	Healey	Smith	Cattlin	Mortimer	Blockley	Parker	Young	Carr	Chilton	Rafferty	St John	
	8/1		*25,830*	*17*	22			*Hibbitt 6, Tudor 7, 57, Macdonald 47p*	*Burleigh*	*Craig*	*Clark*	*Nattrass**	*Burton*	*Howard*	*Barrowclough*	*Green*	*Macdonald*	*Tudor*	*Hibbitt*	*Reid*
								Ref: R Raby	Charitable City lost 1-5 here in the Texaco Cup. Tudor, against his old club, scores his first goals since September, a volley and a header from Green's cross. Reserve Burleigh is not tested enough. Supermac's penalty came when Blockley brought down Nattrass. Mortimer stars again.											
26	H	IPSWICH		15	D	1-1	1-0	Blockley 4p	Glazier	Smith	Cattlin	Machin	Blockley	Parker	Young	Carr	Chilton	Rafferty	Mortimer	
	22/1		18,183	*17*	23			*Hunter 66*	*Best*	*Mills*	*Harper*	*Morris*	*Hunter*	*Jefferson*	*Robertson*	*Viljoen*	*Belfitt*	*Hill*	*Miller**	*Woods*
								Ref: R Nicholson	A dour match on a gluey pitch which disappoints after the Cup win. Blockley scores after Jefferson handles but City never get out of second gear. Blockley is booked for the fourth time in a year. Hunter heads in from Robertson's corner which Coventry players insist was a goal-kick.											
27	A	DERBY		17	L	0-1	0-0		Glazier	Smith	Cattlin	Machin*	Blockley	Parker	Young	Carr	Chilton	Rafferty	Mortimer	McGuire
	29/1		*29,385*	*3*	23			*Robson 46*	*Boulton*	*Webster*	*Robson*	*Durban*	*McFarland*	*Todd*	*McGovern*	*Gemmill*	*O'Hare*	*Hector*	*Hinton*	
								Ref: H New	Derby break their City hoodoo and beat City for first time in Div 1. They are rarely troubled by an enfeebled away side who hardly get a shot on target. Gemmill seizes on Smith's poor clearance and feeds Robson, whose left foot shot fizzes in. Glazier fists away from Hector at the end.											
28	A	CRYS PALACE		17	D	2-2	2-1	Carr 24, Chilton 44	Glazier	Smith	Cattlin	Barry	Blockley	Parker	McGuire	Carr	Chilton	Rafferty	St John*	Mortimer
	12/2		*19,339*	*21*	24			*Craven 40, Queen 88*	*Jackson*	*Payne*	*Wall*	*Kellard*	*McCormick**	*Blyth*	*Craven*	*Queen*	*Wallace*	*Taylor*	*Tambling*	*Goodwin*
								Ref: P Partridge	Palace rampant for first 20 minutes, then they look relegation candidates. Chilton sets up Carr, then scores his second goal in 17 games with a header from St John's free-kick. With Palace at sea, City lack the killer punch and Queen grabs a point with a header from Tony Taylor's cross.											
29	H	WOLVES		17	D	0-0	0-0		Glazier	Smith	Cattlin	Parker	Blockley	Barry	McGuire	Carr	Rafferty	Chilton	St John	
	19/2		22,298	*6*	25				*Parkes*	*Shaw*	*Parkin*	*Taylor*	*Munro*	*McAlle*	*McCalliog*	*Hibbitt*	*Richards*	*Dougan*	*Wagstaffe*	
								Ref: R Tinkler	Wolves, with only one defeat in 12 games, are fortunate not to lose after a much improved City display. Chris Chilton is unlucky not to score a hat-trick and is given a standing ovation. The gluey surface doesn't help the skilful players in an exciting match. Phil Parkes' goal under siege.											
30	A	LEEDS		18	L	0-1	0-1		Glazier	Smith	Cattlin	Parker	Blockley	Barry	McGuire	Carr	Chilton	Graham	St John	
	11/3		*43,154*	*2*	25			*Charlton 11*	*Sprake*	*Reaney*	*Madeley*	*Bremner*	*Charlton*	*Hunter*	*Lorimer*	*Clarke*	*Jones*	*Giles*	*Gray*	
								Ref: R Challis	Jack Charlton's 600th league game and his header from Madeley's free-kick wins it. Leeds have scored 12 in their last two home games but City are made of sterner stuff. A draw would have been a fair result, but may not have saved Noel Cantwell, who is sacked the following day.											
31	H	WEST BROM		18	L	0-2	0-1		Glazier	Smith	Cattlin	Parker	Blockley	Barry	McGuire	Carr	Chilton	Graham	St John*	Mortimer
	17/3		22,887	*17*	25			*Wile 22, Brown A 80*	*Osborne*	*Nisbet*	*Wilson*	*Cantello*	*Wile*	*Robertson*	*Gould*	*Brown T*	*Suggett*	*Brown A*	*Hartford*	
								Ref: J Hunting	Despite their lowly position this is only City's second home league defeat. In a drab game Wile's deflection and Alistair Brown's twice-hit shot give Albion victory. Gould is clear through when Glazier races out of the area to save with his hands. Caretaker Dennison puts on a brave face.											

No	Venue	Opponent	Att	Pos	Res	FT	HT	Scorers, Times, and Referees	1	2	3	4	5	6	7	8	9	10	11	12
32	H	WEST HAM		18	D	1-1	1-1	Smith 13	Glazier	Smith	Cattlin	Machin*	Blockley	Barry	McGuire	Carr	Chilton	Graham	Hunt	Mortimer
	21/3		18,703	*12*	26			*Best 36*	*Ferguson*	*McDowell*	*Charles*	*Bonds*	*Taylor*	*Moore*	*Holland*	*Best*	*Hurst*	*Brooking*	*Robson*	
								Ref: R Lea	Wilf Smith scores his first City goal with a 25-yarder. Debut boy Charles and Holland set up Best for a ferocious shot. Hunt and Machin are back to their best in a much-improved performance. Ex-boss Jimmy Hill calls at half-time for vocal support. City have won once in 16 games.											
33	A	NOTT'M FOREST		18	L	**0-4**	0-1	*[Richardson 60, 83]*	Glazier	Smith	Cattlin	Machin	Blockley	Barry	McGuire	Carr	Chilton*	Graham	Hunt	Mortimer
	25/3		*12,205*	*22*	26			*Gemmell 44, McKenzie 48,*	*Barron*	*Hindley*	*Gemmell*	*Serella*	*Cottom*	*Robertson*	*McIntosh*	*Cormack*	*Buckley*	*Richardson*	*McKenzie*	
								Ref: G Hill	Forest are going down, but manage their biggest win of the season and humiliate City. It looked pretty even until Tommy Gemmill hit one from 35 yards. Then the roof fell in. Chilton went off for six stitches in eye wound. The relegation clouds are gathering after this abject display.											
34	A	TOTTENHAM		18	L	0-1	0-0		Glazier	Smith	Cattlin	Machin	Blockley	Barry	McGuire	Carr	Chilton	Graham	Mortimer	
	31/3		*32,542*	*5*	26			*Chivers 88*	*Jennings*	*Kinnear*	*Knowles*	*Coates*	*England*	*Beal**	*Gilzean*	*Pratt*	*Chivers*	*Peters*	*Morgan*	*Pearce*
								Ref: M Kerkhof	The best display since Xmas is cruelly rewarded with a late goal. Chilton misses two good chances, as did Carr. Spurs hit the woodwork three times but are denied until Martin Chivers makes a goal out of nothing, after Gilzean appeared to push Blockley going for Kinnear's free-kick.											
35	H	MANCHESTER U		18	L	2-3	1-3	Barry 45, Graham 53	Glazier	Smith	Cattlin	Mortimer	Blockley	Barry	McGuire	Carr	Chilton	Graham	Hunt	
	1/4		**37,798**	*6*	26			*Best 14, Moore 22, Charlton 44*	*Stepney*	*O'Neill*	*Dunne*	*Buchan*	*James*	*Gowling*	*Morgan*	*Best*	*Charlton*	*Law*	*Moore*	
								Ref: T Spencer	A magnificent spectacle. Barry's rare goal and Graham's flicked header enable City to recover from three down and give United a run for their money. United's goals are all classics, with Charlton's a thunderbolt. A thunderflash explodes in the West End. United had been top at Xmas.											
36	H	EVERTON		18	W	**4-1**	3-0	Hunt 23p, 44, Carr 36, Chilton 53	Glazier	Smith	Cattlin	Mortimer	Blockley	Barry	McGuire	Carr	Chilton	Graham	Hunt	
	4/4		22,129	*15*	28			*Johnson 84*	*West*	*Scott*	*McLaughlin*	*Kendall*	*Kenyon*	*Newton H*	*Johnson*	*Buckley*	*Wright B*	*Lyons*	*Morrissey*	
								Ref: N Burtenshaw	Both sides had gone eleven games without a win. Coventry click at last in this crucial evening game. Hunt scores after Lyons handles. Carr hits a stunning goal after two minutes of frenzied attacking. Lyons blunders for Hunt to slide the third in. Chilton heads in after Hunt hits the post.											
37	A	LIVERPOOL		18	L	1-3	0-1	Hunt 54	Glazier	Smith	Cattlin	Mortimer	Blockley	Barry	McGuire	Carr	Machin	Graham	Hunt	
	8/4		*50,628*	*2*	28			*Keegan 20, Smith 67p, Toshack 85*	*Clemence*	*Lawler*	*Lindsay*	*Smith*	*Lloyd*	*Hughes*	*Keegan*	*Hall*	*Heighway*	*Toshack*	*Callaghan*	
								Ref: H Hackney	A morning kick-off on Grand National Day. Liverpool have all the luck with a controversial penalty when Barry challenged Kevin Keegan, who fell to the floor dramatically. Hunt crowns a superb display with a goal. John Toshack's late effort gives the scoreline a distorted look.											
38	A	HUDDERSFIELD		18	W	1-0	0-0	Hunt 75	Glazier	Smith	Cattlin	Mortimer	Blockley	Barry	McGuire	Carr	Machin	Graham	Hunt	
	11/4		***11,782***	*21*	30				*Lawson D*	*Clarke*	*Hutt*	*Smith S*	*Ellam*	*Cherry*	*Hoy*	*Dolan*	*Worthington*	*Lawson J*	*Chapman*	
								Ref: B Homewood	City play some flowing football to ensure safety. Huddersfield look likely to go down and only have two shots all night. Machin put Hunt clear with a superb ball and the stocky striker picked his spot despite having three defenders around him. Willie Carr should have scored at the end.											
39	H	MANCHESTER C		18	D	1-1	0-0	Mortimer 80	Glazier	Smith	Cattlin	Mortimer	Blockley	Barry	McGuire	Carr	Machin	Graham	Hunt	
	15/4		34,302	*2*	31			*Towers 52*	*Healey*	*Book*	*Donachie*	*Doyle*	*Booth*	*Oakes*	*Summerbee*	*Bell*	*Davies*	*Lee*	*Towers*	
								Ref: E Wallace	Man City need a win to stay level with Derby at the top. Their title challenge has subsided since Rodney Marsh joined them a month ago, but he is on the bench today. Tony Towers scores from the edge of the box from a Davies pass. Mortimer ends a superb run with a searing shot.											
40	H	SHEFFIELD UTD		16	W	3-2	3-1	Graham 3, Carr 42, Machin 45	Glazier	Smith	Cattlin	Mortimer	Blockley	Barry	McGuire	Carr	Machin	Graham	Hunt*	Chilton
	18/4		19,220	*9*	33			*Currie 39, 60*	*McAllister*	*Badger*	*Hemsley*	*Mackenzie**	*Colquhoun*	*Flynn*	*Scullion*	*Staniforth*	*Dearden*	*Currie*	*Salmons*	*Woodward*
								Ref: P Walters	The original game was abandoned in a snow storm with City 0-2 down, and the Blades have little luck in the re-match. Graham breaks the offside trap. Hunt and Carr combine from a free-kick. Machin drives in from Blockley's free-kick. Currie scores two and has one disallowed.											
41	A	LEICESTER		17	L	0-1	0-1		Glazier	Smith	Cattlin	Mortimer	Blockley	Barry*	McGuire	Carr	Machin	Graham	Chilton	**Green**
	22/4		*24,254*	*11*	33			*Glover 2*	*Shilton*	*Whitworth*	*Nish**	*Manley*	*Woollett*	*Cross*	*Weller*	*Sammels*	*Partridge*	*Tomlin*	*Glover*	*Fern*
								Ref: I Smith	Leicester score early when Blockley fluffs David Nish's through ball and Len Glover pounces. Shilton keeps City at bay with some fine saves and City go home pointless. The match is spoiled by blustery winds. Mick McGuire and Dennis Mortimer star but the problem is lack of goals.											
42	H	ARSENAL		18	L	0-1	0-0		Glazier	Smith	Cattlin	Mortimer	Blockley	Parker	McGuire	Carr	Machin	Graham	Hunt	
	1/5		23,506	*5*	33			*Ball 75*	*Barnett*	*Rice*	*McNab*	*Storey*	*McLintock*	*Simpson*	*Armstrong*	*Ball*	*Radford*	*George*	*Graham*	
		Home	Away					Ref: A Morrissey	Coventry deserve something from this game after dominating for long periods. Armstrong set up Ball, whose shot hits Glazier's body and rolls in off the post. McLintock tries to claim it, but it's Ball's goal. Arsenal are ten games unbeaten and head for the FA Cup final in five days time.											
Average		23,721	28,674																	

LEAGUE DIVISION 1 (CUP-TIES)

Manager: Cantwell > Bob Dennison

SEASON 1971-72

League Cup					F-A	H-T	Scorers, Times, and Referees	1	2	3	4	5	6	7	8	9	10	11	12 sub used
2	H	BURNLEY	15	L	0-1	0-0		Glazier	Smith	Coop	Mortimer	Blockley	Parker	O'Rourke	Carr	Rafferty	Hunt	McGuire*	Young
	7/9	15,413	*2:7*				*Casper 53*	*Mellor*	*Docherty*	*Cliff*	*Bellamy*	*Waldron*	*Dobson*	*Thomas*	*West*	*Fletcher*	*Casper*	*James*	
							Ref: D Smith	This sad exit to lively Burnley earned slow handclaps and boos from an unhappy crowd. Chilton is still not fit but Billy Rafferty, O'Rourke and Hunt miss good chances. Following Frank Casper's superb goal, after Glazier parries Paul Fletcher's shot, City get desperate but all to no avail.											

FA Cup					F-A	H-T	Scorers, Times, and Referees	1	2	3	4	5	6	7	8	9	10	11	12 sub used
3	A	WEST BROM	13	W	2-1	1-0	Rafferty 42, Chilton 81	Glazier	Smith	Cattlin	Mortimer	Barry	Parker	Machin	Carr	Chilton	Rafferty	St John*	Hunt
	15/1	*26,472*	*21*				*Brown T 59*	*Osborne*	*Nisbet*	*Wilson*	*Cantello*	*Wile*	*Robertson*	*McVitie*	*Brown T*	*Gould*	*Suggett*	*Hartford*	
							Ref: K Styles	Bill Glazier and Roy Barry return and the Scot is colossal. After a dreadful autumn, WBA have beaten 'Pool and Ipswich over Xmas. Mortimer brilliantly sets up Rafferty. Chilton steers a great header past John Osborne from Carr's corner. First away Cup win over Div 1 side for 60 years.											
4	H	HULL	17	L	0-1	0-0		Glazier	Coop	Cattlin	Smith*	Blockley	Parker	Young	Carr	Chilton	Hunt	St John	Mortimer
	5/2	24,632	*2:20*				*Wagstaff 77*	*McKechnie*	*Banks*	*De Vries*	*Wilkinson*	*Neill*	*Baxter*	*McGill*	*Lord*	*Pearson*	*Wagstaff*	*Butler*	
							Ref: R Challis	Another Cup exit to a lower division club. Hull are nothing special but hold City's powder-puff attack and take their chance. Banks' shot from Glazier's punch hits the post and Wagstaffe pounces. Chilton is captain against his old club. Hunt, back after injury, has a goal disallowed.											

		Home					Away					
	P	W	D	L	F	A	W	D	L	F	A	Pts
1 Derby	42	16	4	1	43	10	8	6	7	26	23	58
2 Leeds	42	17	4	0	54	10	7	5	9	19	21	57
3 Liverpool	42	17	3	1	48	16	7	6	8	16	14	57
4 Manchester C	42	16	3	2	48	15	7	8	6	29	30	57
5 Arsenal	42	15	2	4	36	13	7	6	8	22	27	52
6 Tottenham	42	16	3	2	45	13	3	10	8	18	29	51
7 Chelsea	42	12	7	2	41	20	6	5	10	17	29	48
8 Manchester U	42	13	2	6	39	26	6	8	7	30	35	48
9 Wolves	42	10	7	4	35	23	8	4	9	30	34	47
10 Sheffield Utd	42	10	8	3	39	26	7	4	10	22	34	46
11 Newcastle	42	10	6	5	30	18	5	5	11	19	34	41
12 Leicester	42	9	6	6	18	11	4	7	10	23	35	39
13 Ipswich	42	7	8	6	19	19	4	8	9	20	34	38
14 West Ham	42	10	6	5	31	19	2	6	13	16	32	36
15 Everton	42	8	9	4	28	17	1	9	11	9	31	36
16 West Brom	42	6	7	8	22	23	6	4	11	20	31	35
17 Stoke	42	6	10	5	26	25	4	5	12	13	31	35
18 COVENTRY	42	7	10	4	27	23	2	5	14	17	44	33
19 Southampton	42	8	5	8	31	28	4	2	15	21	52	31
20 Crys Palace	42	4	8	9	26	31	4	5	12	13	34	29
21 Nott'm Forest	42	6	4	11	25	29	2	5	14	22	52	25
22 Huddersfield	42	4	7	10	12	22	2	6	13	15	37	25
	924	227	129	106	723	437	106	129	227	437	723	924

Odds & ends

Double wins: (2) Everton, Huddersfield.
Double losses: (2) Liverpool, Arsenal.

Won from behind: (0)
Lost from in front: (1) Newcastle (a).

High points: 2-2 draw at Old Trafford against the League leaders.
First ever First Division victory over Leeds.
FA Cup win at West Brom.

Low points: Slump in home attendances.
Burnley League Cup defeat.
11 League games without a win from January to April.
Abject display in 0-4 defeat at bottom of the table Nott'm Forest.

Red cards: City – Cattlin (Everton a), Hunt (Liverpool h).

Player of the Year: Ernie Hunt.
Ever-presents: (3) Jeff Blockley, Willie Carr, Wilf Smith.
Hat-tricks: (0).
Opposing hat-tricks: (0).
Leading scorer: (12) Ernie Hunt.

	Appearances						Goals			
	Lge	*Sub*	LC	*Sub*	FAC	*Sub*	**Lge**	LC	FAC	**Tot**
Alderson, Brian	**5**	*3*								
Barry, Roy	**27**				1		**1**			**1**
Blockley, Jeff	**42**		1		1		**2**			**2**
Carr, Willie	**42**		1		2		**8**			**8**
Cattlin, Chris	**29**				2					
Chilton, Chris	**26**	*1*			2		**3**		1	**4**
Clements, Dave	**1**									
Coop, Mick	**13**	*2*	1		1					
Glazier, Bill	**37**		1		2					
Graham, Bobby	**13**						**2**			**2**
Green, Alan		*1*								
Healey, Ron (loan)	**3**									
Holmes, Jimmy	**3**									
Hunt, Ernie	**26**	*1*	1		1	*1*	**12**			**12**
Joicey, Brian	**2**						**1**			**1**
Machin, Ernie	**15**				1		**1**			**1**
McGuire, Mick	**23**	*3*	1				**1**			**1**
McManus, Eric	**2**									
Mortimer, Dennis	**26**	*8*	1		1	*1*	**4**			**4**
O'Rourke, John	**5**	*1*	1				**1**			**1**
Parker, Bobby	**27**		1		2					
Rafferty, Billy	**13**		1		1		**2**		1	**3**
Smith, Wilf	**42**		1		2		**1**			**1**
St John, Ian	**18**				2		**3**			**3**
Strong, Geoff	**1**									
Young, Quinton	**21**				1		**2**			**2**
26 players used	**462**	*20*	**11**		**22**	*2*	**44**		**2**	**46**

No	Date		Att	Pos	Pt		F-A	H-T	Scorers, Times, and Referees	1	2	3	4	5	6	7	8	9	10	11	12 sub used
1	A	TOTTENHAM				L	1-2	0-1	Hunt 62	Glazier	Coop	Cattlin	Machin	Blockley	Barry	Mortimer	Graham	Hunt	Carr	Green	
	12/8		*33,884*		0				*Peters 6, 71*	*Jennings*	*Kinnear*	*Knowles*	*Pratt*	*England*	*Beal*	*Gilzean*	*Perryman*	*Chivers*	*Peters*	*Coates*	
									Ref: A Jones	New managers Joe Mercer and Gordon Milne watch Martin Peters score two headers. One from Gilzean's headed flick on from Perryman's corner, the other from Perryman's free-kick. Glazier is magnificent and saves Peters' penalty, given for Blockley's challenge on Gilzean.											
2	A	WEST HAM				L	0-1	0-0		Glazier	Coop	Cattlin	Machin	Blockley	Barry	Mortimer	Graham	Hunt	Carr	Smith	
	14/8		*27,435*		0				*Best 53*	*Ferguson*	*McDowell*	*Lampard*	*Bonds*	*Taylor*	*Moore*	*Tyler*	*Best*	*Coker*	*Brooking*	*Robson*	
									Ref: J Gow	Coventry's coach is delayed by heavy traffic and they cut things fine. Despite a spirited display City go down to Clyde Best's header, which Glazier scoops out but the linesman rules has crossed the goal-line. Barry, Cattlin and Carr are booked under new disciplinary points system.											
3	H	SOUTHAMPTON		19		D	1-1	1-1	Hunt 39p	Glazier	Coop	Cattlin	Machin	Blockley	Barry	Mortimer	Graham	Hunt	Carr	Smith	
	19/8		18,544	*7*	1				*Steele 44*	*Martin*	*McCarthy*	*Burns*	*Fisher*	*McGrath*	*Steele*	*O'Brien*	*Channon*	*Davies*	*O'Neill*	*Jenkins**	*Stokes*
									Ref: W Hall	Saints set out to defend in depth and are happy with a point. Coop is felled by McGrath for the penalty. Jim Steele equalises after finding a gap in defence. Two late Southampton moves would have snatched a win but for Glazier's reflexes. The lowest opening attendance for 11 years.											
4	H	ARSENAL		18		D	1-1	1-1	Graham 26	Glazier	Coop	Cattlin	Machin	Blockley	Barry	Mortimer	Graham	Hunt	Carr	Smith	
	22/8		24,670	*1*	2				*Rice 38*	*Barnett*	*Rice*	*McNab*	*Storey*	*McLintock*	*Simpson*	*Armstrong*	*Ball*	*Radford*	*Kennedy*	*Graham*	
									Ref: R Tinkler	Arsenal's 100% record goes after this entertaining tussle. Graham heads in Machin's cross. Rice cuts in from right and beats Glazier at his near post with an acute shot. Mortimer and Carr run Gunners ragged and Smith marks Ball closely. Storey is first Arsenal player booked this season.											
5	A	LEICESTER		17		D	0-0	0-0		Glazier	Coop	Cattlin	Machin	Blockley	Barry	Mortimer	Graham	Hunt	Carr	Smith	
	26/8		25,894	*18*	3					*Shilton*	*Whitworth*	*Rofe*	*Cross*	*Woollett*	*Farrington*	*Weller*	*Sammels*	*Worthington*	*Birchenall*	*Glover*	
									Ref: D Laing	Neither side have won yet and a draw is a fair result. Both sides have goals disallowed for offside, Farrington and Hunt the victims. Shilton, yet again, plays a blinder, saving twice when Mortimer looked like scoring. Rofe's debut after £112,000 move from Orient, a full-back record.											
6	H	WOLVES		18		L	0-1	0-0		Glazier	Coop	Cattlin	Machin	Blockley	Barry	Mortimer	Graham*	Hunt	Carr	Smith	Young
	29/8		24,569	*8*	3				*Richards 89*	*Parkes*	*Shaw*	*Taylor*	*Bailey*	*Munro*	*McAlle*	*McCalliog*	*Hibbitt*	*Richards*	*Dougan*	*Daley*	
									Ref: R Challis	City dominate for long periods but lose out to a sucker punch. Hunt has a good goal disallowed for offside against Carr. Shaw clears off the line from Mortimer. Parkes saves well from Carr's header. John Richards scores after long Parkes kick bounces over Barry and Glazier is stranded.											
7	H	STOKE		16		W	2-1	2-0	Carr 25, 43	Glazier	Coop	Cattlin	Machin	Blockley	Barry	Mortimer	Young	Hunt*	Carr	Smith	McGuire
	2/9		**16,391**	*20*	5				*Pejic 83*	*Banks*	*Marsh*	*Pejic*	*Lees*	*Smith*	*Skeels*	*Robertson*	*Greenhoff*	*Hurst*	*Conroy*	*Dobing**	*Jump*
									Ref: N Burtenshaw	A deserved first win of the season against lacklustre Stoke. Carr scores, first, after a ball slices off Dennis Smith's head and hits the post, and then gets a spectacular header on Coop's cross. Pejic's 35-yarder catches Glazier unawares and sparks a late flurry. Smith breaks Hunt's ankle.											
8	A	MANCHESTER U		14		W	1-0	0-0	Carr 55	Glazier	Coop	Cattlin	Machin	Blockley	Barry	Mortimer	Young	Rafferty	Carr	Smith	
	9/9		*37,073*	*22*	7					*Stepney*	*O'Neill*	*Buchan*	*Fitzpatrick*	*James*	*Sadler*	*McIlroy*	*Law**	*Charlton*	*Best*	*Moore*	*Young*
									Ref: V Batty	Match of the Day cameras see City gain their First Div 1 win at Old Trafford, leaving United still without a win. The impressive Cattlin overlaps and sends floating cross which Carr nods in at the far post. Some of Frank O'Farrell's stars look past it but Glazier still saves well from Best.											
9	H	NEWCASTLE		17		L	**0-3**	0-2		Glazier	Coop	Cattlin	Machin	Blockley	Barry	Mortimer	Young	Rafferty	Carr	Smith*	Alderson
	16/9		17,634	*11*	7				*Macdonald 27, 43, 61*	*McFaul*	*Craig*	*Clark*	*Young*	*Howard*	*Moncur*	*Barrowclough*	*Smith*	*Macdonald*	*Tudor*	*Hibbitt*	
									Ref: C Nicholls	Newcastle's £180,000 striker scores the first league hat-trick by a visiting player since John Galley in 1964. The first is a right-footer off the underside of the bar. The second is a blockbuster from an acute angle. The third is a header, after his own shot hit the post. A poor City display.											
10	A	WEST BROM		19		L	0-1	0-1		Glazier	Coop	Cattlin	Machin*	Blockley	Barry	Mortimer	Young	Rafferty	Carr	Alderson	McGuire
	23/9		*15,571*	*14*	7				*Suggett 34*	*Latchford*	*Nisbet*	*Merrick*	*Cantello*	*Wile*	*Robertson*	*Suggett*	*Brown T*	*Gould*	*Brown A*	*Hartford*	
									Ref: D Nippard	Suggett's header from Nisbet's cross is enough to beat a woeful City, who look like relegation candidates. Bobby Gould and Blockley have a lively encounter. Albion's third win in a row doesn't make them a good side. New blood is desperately needed by City, with goals the priority.											

11	H	CHELSEA		21	L	1-3	0-2	Alderson 51	Glazier	Coop	**Dugdale***	McGuire	Blockley	Barry	Mortimer	Green	Rafferty	Carr	Alderson	Smith
	30/9		20,295	*6*	7			*Garner 5, Blockley 37 (og), Houseman 83*	*Bonetti*	*Locke*	*McCreadie*	*Hollins*	*Webb*	*Harris*	*Garland*	*Kember*	*Osgood*	*Garner**	*Houseman*	*Hinton*
								Ref: I Smith	City, knocked out of the Texaco Cup in midweek by Motherwell, are plunged into the bottom two by defensive errors. Blockley's own-goal was farcical, lobbing Glazier when there was no danger. Brian Alderson's fierce shot gives some hope.Alan Dugdale damages ankle ligaments.											
12	A	CRYS PALACE		19	W	1-0	0-0	Mortimer 90	Glazier	Coop	Cattlin	Machin	Barry	Parker	Mortimer	Smith	**Stein**	Carr	Alderson	
	7/10		*22,229*	*20*	9				*Jackson*	*Mulligan*	*Hinshelw'd**	*Phillip*	*McCormick*	*Blyth*	*Cooke*	*Payne*	*Craven*	*Kellard*	*Taylor*	*Pinkney*
								Ref: S Kayley	Cooke and Mulligan make their Palace debuts but can't stop their fifth defeat in a row. City, rarely in danger, are not impressive. Colin Stein nods down Smith's cross for Mortimer to drive home after two minutes of injury-time. Blockley was sold to Arsenal for club record £200,000.											
13	H	MANCHESTER C		15	W	3-2	1-0	Carr 4, Stein 53, Alderson 77	Glazier	Coop	Cattlin	Smith	Barry	Parker	Mortimer	Alderson	Stein	Carr	**Hutchison**	
	14/10		24,541	*20*	11			*Marsh 59, Summerbee 70*	*Healey*	*Book*	*Donachie*	*Towers*	*Booth*	*Jeffries*	*Summerbee*	*Bell*	*Marsh*	*Lee*	*Hill**	*Doyle*
								Ref: M Sinclair	A rip-roaring game which City look to have thrown away. Stein sets up Carr then scores great header from Mortimer's cross. Sloppy defending let Man City score twice. Alderson wins it with a header from Coop's cross. Hutchison has super debut and Book is booked for fouling him.											
14	A	LEEDS		15	D	1-1	0-0	Carr 56	Glazier	Coop	Cattlin	Smith	Barry	Parker	Mortimer	Alderson	Stein	Carr	Hutchison	
	21/10		*36,240*	*4*	12			*Charlton 60*	*Harvey*	*Madeley*	*Cherry*	*Bremner*	*Charlton*	*Hunter*	*Lorimer*	*Clarke*	*Jones**	*Giles*	*Gray*	*Jordan*
								Ref: H Davey	City's first point at Leeds for five years after an admirable showing. City hit the bar twice before Stein sets up Carr. Charlton's header means he has scored four years running against City here. Tommy Hutchison sparkles and Cherry and the crude Hunter are booked for fouling him.											
15	H	BIRMINGHAM		15	D	0-0	0-0		**Ramsbottom**	Coop	Cattlin	Smith	Barry	Parker	Mortimer	Alderson	Stein	Carr	Hutchison	
	28/10		35,304	*19*	13				*Latchford D*	*Carroll*	*Pendrey*	*Page*	*Hynd*	*Harland*	*Hope*	*Francis*	*Latchford R*	*Hatton*	*Taylor*	
								Ref: H Williams	A full-blooded Midlands derby, played in front of a large and vociferous crowd. Blues had done their homework and stifled the threat of Carr and Stein. Similarly, Francis and Latchford are well handled by Barry and Parker. Hutch causes problems and Carroll is booked for fouling him.											
16	A	ARSENAL		14	W	2-0	1-0	Alderson 10, Hutchison 75	Glazier	Coop	Cattlin	Smith	Barry	Parker	Mortimer	Alderson	Stein	Carr	Hutchison	
	4/11		*33,699*	*2*	15				*Barnett*	*Rice*	*McNab*	*Storey*	*McLintock*	*Blockley*	*Marinello*	*Ball*	*Radford*	*George*	*Kelly**	*Graham*
								Ref: R Lee	Arsenal's unbeaten home record is smashed with a brilliant performance. Stein's cross is headed in by Alderson at the far post. Hutchison beats four men in a mazy dribble and scores the goal of the decade from a narrow angle. Scottish manager Docherty watches City's five Scots.											
17	H	WEST HAM		13	W	3-1	1-0	Hutchison 25, Stein 58, Alderson 85	Glazier	Coop	Cattlin	Smith	Barry	Parker	Mortimer	Alderson	Stein	Carr*	Hutchison	McGuire
	11/11		27,172	*9*	17			*McDowell 64*	*Ferguson*	*McDowell*	*Lampard*	*Bonds*	*Taylor*	*Moore*	*Tyler*	*Best*	*Holland*	*Brooking*	*Robson*	
								Ref: J Williams	A scintillating display and first home Div 1 win over Hammers. Hutchison hit one from the edge of the box. Colin Stein heads in from Coop's cross. Alderson robs Tommy Taylor and blasts in. McDowell's 30-yard bender briefly gives West Ham hope. Bobby Moore is magnificent.											
18	H	SHEFFIELD UTD		9	W	**3-0**	3-0	Alderson 15, 24, Mackenzie 33 (og)	Glazier	Coop	Cattlin	Smith	Barry	Parker	Mortimer	Alderson	Stein	Carr	Hutchison	
	18/11		22,079	*16*	19				*McAllister*	*Badger*	*Hemsley*	*Mackenzie*	*Colquhoun*	*Hockey*	*Woodward*	*Staniforth**	*Dearden*	*Currie*	*Ford*	*Holmes*
								Ref: C Thomas	Seven games unbeaten, a new Div 1 record for City. Another exhilarating display with non-stop attacking. Alderson pounces on Len Badger's uncertainty for the first and Hemsley's bad back-pass for the second. Mackenzie, under pressure, turns Alderson's cross in. Ramsey eyes City.											
19	H	EVERTON		9	W	1-0	0-0	Alderson 90	Ramsbottom	Coop	Cattlin	Smith	Barry	Parker	Mortimer	Alderson	Stein	Carr	Hutchison	
	2/12		22,774	*15*	21				*Lawson*	*Scott*	*Newton H*	*Kendall*	*Kenyon*	*McLaughlin**	*Wright B*	*Buckley*	*Belfitt*	*Hurst*	*Connolly*	*Harvey*
								Ref: K Styles	David Lawson stands between City and a cricket score. He is finally beaten in the third minute of injury-time after much Everton time-wasting. With Kendall starring in midfield, the Toffees had their chances, Wright and Belfitt missing. Scott booked after umpteen fouls on Hutchison.											
20	A	IPSWICH		9	L	0-2	0-1		Ramsbottom	Coop	Cattlin	Smith	Barry*	Parker	Mortimer	Alderson	Stein	Carr	Hutchison	Dugdale
	5/12		*17,809*	*4*	21			*Johnson 44, Whymark 71*	*Best*	*Mills*	*Harper*	*Morris*	*Hunter*	*Beattie*	*Hamilton*	*Viljoen*	*Johnson*	*Whymark*	*Lambert*	
								Ref: N Burtenshaw	Ten days ago the floodlights failed with City 1-0 up. Ipswich end their eight-game run. A shoddy performance after Barry goes off with a hip injury. Johnson heads in from Beattie's knock on. Whymark's overhead kick, after Hunter heads on at a corner. Mills booked for fouling Hutch.											
21	A	DERBY		12	L	0-2	0-0		Ramsbottom	Coop	Cattlin	Smith	Dugdale	Parker	Mortimer	Alderson	Stein	Carr	Hutchison	
	9/12		*31,002*	*7*	21			*Hinton 54p, Gemmill 69*	*Boulton*	*Webster*	*Nish*	*O'Hare*	*Daniel*	*Todd*	*McGovern*	*Gemmill*	*Davies*	*Hector*	*Hinton*	
								Ref: J Hunting	An unfair scoreline after City dominate the first half but miss chances. A free-kick is given for a foul on O'Hare, but the linesman signals a penalty. Gemmill's goal is a cross that catches Ramsbottom off his line. Webster is the seventh player in eight games booked for fouling Hutch.											

No	Date		Att	Pos	Pt	F-A	H-T	Scorers, Times, and Referees	1	2	3	4	5	6	7	8	9	10	11	12 sub used
22	H	NORWICH		10	W	3-1	1-0	Stein 13, 71, Alderson 47	Ramsbottom	Coop	Cattlin	Smith	Dugdale	Parker	Mortimer	Alderson	Stein	Carr	Hutchison	
	16/12		19,873	*13*	23			*Howard 63*	*Keelan*	*Butler*	*Black*	*Stringer*	*Govier*	*Briggs*	*Livermore*	*Bone*	*Cross*	*Paddon*	*Anderson**	*Howard*
								Ref: R Crabb	Another standing ovation for a sparkling display. The League Cup semi-finalists are destroyed by Stein's header from Alderson's corner and his pounce after Keelan saves Hutch's shot. Mortimer sets up Alderson's thunderous shot and also hits the post. Alderson has one disallowed.											
23	A	LIVERPOOL		11	L	0-2	0-2		Ramsbottom	Coop	Cattlin	Smith*	Barry	Parker	Mortimer	Alderson	Stein	Carr	Hutchison	McGuire
	23/12		***41,550***	*1*	23			*Toshack 6, 21*	*Clemence*	*Lawler*	*Lindsay*	*Thompson*	*Lloyd*	*Hughes*	*Keegan*	*Cormack*	*Heighway*	*Toshack*	*Callaghan*	
								Ref: A Morrissey	Liverpool's 20th home win on the run and 28 games unbeaten. City never threatened and were a shadow of their recent selves. Toshack was recalled and scored two headers, from a Callaghan cross and a Keegan flick. Ramsbottom keeps the score down and only Carr performs well.											
24	H	WEST BROM		11	D	0-0	0-0		Glazier	Coop	Cattlin	Smith	Barry	Parker	Mortimer	Alderson	Stein	Carr	Hutchison	
	26/12		31,545	*17*	24				*Latchford*	*Nisbet*	*Wilson*	*Cantello*	*Wile*	*Robertson*	*Merrick*	*Brown T*	*Brown A*	*Hartford*	*Johnston*	
								Ref: D Smith	Don Howe's Albion smother City in a poor spectacle for the Boxing Day crowd. Hartford and Tony Brown miss early chances but Albion went back into their shell. Stein heads Coventry's best chance straight at Latchford. Robertson is booked in his first game back after suspension.											
25	A	SOUTHAMPTON		11	L	1-2	1-0	Alderson 42	Glazier	Coop	Cattlin	Smith	Barry	Parker	Mortimer	Alderson	Stein	Carr	Hutchison	
	30/12		***15,261***	*12*	24			*Gilchrist 48, Parker 62 (og)*	*Martin*	*McCarthy*	*Kirkup*	*Fisher*	*Bennett*	*Steele*	*Paine*	*Channon !*	*Gilchrist*	*O'Neill*	*O'Brien*	
								Ref: B Daniels	Despite dominating the first half, City only have Alderson's goal, set up by Carr, to show. Gilchrist scores from Fisher's free-kick, then Saints cut up rough. There was no danger when a Jenkins shot deflected off Parker's leg. Three players booked and Channon off for striking Barry.											
26	H	LEICESTER		10	W	3-2	1-0	Stein 21, Woollett 46 (og), Carr 55	Glazier	Coop	Dugdale	Smith	Barry	Parker	Mortimer	Alderson	Stein	Carr	Hutchison	
	6/1		25,076	*18*	26			*Worthington 60, Weller 83*	*Shilton*	*Whitworth*	*Rofe*	*Woollett*	*Cross*	*Birchenall*	*Farrington*	*Stringfellow**	*Weller*	*Worthington*	*Glover*	*Tomlin*
								Ref: B Homewood	Leicester give City a fright with two late goals on a foggy afternoon. Peter Shilton is brilliant as City threaten a cricket score, at his best tipping Carr's header over. Colin Stein looks offside as he rounds Shilton. Woollett slices in Hutchison's cross. Hutch and Stein set up Carr's shot.											
27	H	MANCHESTER U		12	D	1-1	1-1	Alderson 36	Glazier	Coop	Dugdale	Smith	Barry	Parker	Mortimer	Alderson	Stein	McGuire	Hutchison	
	27/1		**42,911**	*19*	27			*Holton 34*	*Stepney*	*Young*	*Forsyth*	*Graham*	*Holton*	*Buchan*	*Morgan*	*McDougall*	*Charlton*	*Macari*	*Martin*	
								Ref: E Wallace	United lose a lot of admirers in a grim display but earn a point in their relegation battle. City stifled by a niggly defence, led by Holton, who heads home Morgan's free-kick. Alderson's fierce shot from Hutch's free-kick. Biggest crowd for three years. Graham lucky not to be sent off.											
28	A	NEWCASTLE		11	D	1-1	1-1	Stein 24	Glazier	Coop	Dugdale	McGuire	Barry	Parker	Mortimer	Alderson	Stein	Cattlin	Hutchison	
	10/2		*22,940*	*5*	28			*Barrowclough 25*	*McFaul*	*Craig*	*Clark*	*Nattrass*	*Howard*	*Moncur*	*Barrowclough*	*Smith*	*Macdonald*	*Tudor*	*Reid*	
								Ref: H Hackney	Wilf Smith is banned for two games. Newcastle have just lost to Luton in the Cup and the crowd are on their backs. A poor game with few chances is played in a blustery wind. Stein scores after Nattrass miskicks. Bill Glazier palms a cross into the air and Barrowclough is first to it.											
29	H	TOTTENHAM		13	L	0-1	0-0		Glazier	Dugdale	Cattlin	Coop	Barry	Parker	Mortimer	Alderson	Stein	McGuire	Hutchison	
	17/2		26,854	*9*	28			*Pratt 75*	*Jennings*	*Kinnear*	*Knowles*	*Pratt*	*England*	*Beal*	*Gilzean*	*Perryman*	*Chivers*	*Peters*	*Pearce*	
								Ref: J Wrennall	The main stand side of the pitch is frozen and both teams prefer the other side. City bombard Spurs in the second half with Stein at his best. Spurs have few chances and Pratt scores the winner with a speculative 25-yard lob. Coop goes close. City's first home defeat since September.											
30	H	CRYS PALACE		11	W	2-0	1-0	Stein 34, Alderson 52	Glazier	Coop	Cattlin	Smith	Barry	Parker	Mortimer	Alderson	Stein	Carr	Hutchison	
	2/3		25,194	*20*	30				*Hammond*	*Payne*	*Taylor*	*Phillip*	*Bell*	*Blyth*	*Possee*	*Hinshelw'd !*	*Whittle*	*Cooke*	*Rogers**	*Craven*
								Ref: R Raby	A one-sided game against a Palace side who don't manage a shot all night. Stein bundles in Carr's cross. Alderson volleys in after Stein heads down Coop's cross. Hinshelwood is sent off after an hour for foul language. Stein hits wood twice, Hammond saves from Carr and Mortimer.											
31	A	NORWICH		11	D	1-1	1-1	Carr 80	Glazier	Coop	Cattlin	Smith	Barry	Parker	McGuire	Alderson*	Stein	Carr	Hutchison	Dugdale
	7/3		*29,173*	*20*	31			*Cross 44*	*Keelan*	*Payne*	*Butler*	*Stringer*	*Forbes*	*Hockey*	*Livermore*	*Blair*	*Cross*	*Howard*	*Anderson*	
								Ref: T Oliver	Norwich have just lost the League Cup final and a draw is fair. Hutchison is back to form and Payne is booked for fouling him. David Cross scores when Cattlin's error lets in Livermore. Hutch ends a super run with a shot which Keelan saves but Carr follows up to score off the post.											

No/Date	Venue	Opponent / Att	Pos	Res / Pts	F-A	H-T	Scorers, Times, and Referees	1	2	3	4	5	6	7	8	9	10	11	12 sub used
32	A	MANCHESTER C	10	W	2-1	1-0	Carr 20, Stein 55	Glazier	Coop	Cattlin	Smith	Barry	Parker	Mortimer	Green	Stein	Carr	Hutchison	
10/3		*30,448*	*13*	33			*Booth 51*	*Corrigan*	*Pardoe*	*Donachie*	*Doyle**	*Booth*	*Jeffries*	*Summerbee*	*Bell*	*Marsh*	*Lee*	*Oakes*	*Carrodus*
							Ref: P Baldwin	First League win at Maine Road. Mercer is given a moving reception on his return. City weather the storm for 20 minutes. Jeffries boobs and Carr scores. Stein trips Bell but Glazier saves Lee's fierce spot-kick. Booth equalises from a corner. Stein wins it after Mortimer's fine run.											
33	A	BIRMINGHAM	11	L	0-3	0-2		Glazier	Coop	Cattlin	McGuire	Barry	Parker*	Mortimer	Alderson	Stein	Carr	Hutchison	Dugdale
24/3		*34,775*	*17*	33			*Hatton 29, Latchford R 42, Taylor 64*	*Latchford D*	*Martin*	*Pendrey*	*Page*	*Hynd*	*Roberts*	*Campbell*	*Francis*	*Latchford R*	*Hatton*	*Taylor*	
							Ref: R Crabb	Blues set out to contain Carr and the ploy worked. City have a Cup hangover and Birmingham, desperate for points, win easily. Hatton heads in Francis' cross. Latchford scores when Glazier parries Hatton's shot. Taylor drives home from Hatton's nod down. Hopes of Europe dwindle.											
34	A	STOKE	11	L	1-2	1-0	Stein 5	Glazier	Coop	Cattlin	McGuire	Barry	Dugdale	Mortimer	Alderson	Stein	Carr	Hutchison	
26/3		*20,218*	*18*	33			*Ritchie 47, Haslegrave 64*	*Farmer*	*Marsh*	*Pejic*	*Greenhoff*	*Smith*	*Skeels*	*Haslegrave*	*Hurst*	*Ritchie*	*Eastham*	*Conroy*	
							Ref: R Tinkler	Stoke City are desperate for points and have only lost two home games. Stein scores after Farmer fails to hold McGuire's fierce shot. City are denied a blatant penalty a minute before John Ritchie scores with a fortuitous header. Sean Haslegrave hits a low drive from 30 yards.											
35	H	IPSWICH	10	W	2-1	1-0	Alderson 36, Stein 86	Ramsbottom	Coop	Cattlin	McGuire*	Barry	Dugdale	Mortimer	Alderson	Stein	Carr	Hutchison	Smith
31/3		17,130	*4*	35			*Beattie 53*	*Best*	*Mills*	*Harper*	*Morris*	*Hunter*	*Beattie*	*Hamilton*	*Viljoen*	*Johnson*	*Whymark*	*Lambert*	
							Ref: A Hart	A much-improved performance and deseved victory. Stein heads down Hutch's cross and Alderson's fierce shot takes a deflection off Beattie. Beattie levels from a free-kick. Stein heads the winner from a Cattlin cross. Hutch back to his best. Bobby Robson's European hopes dented.											
36	H	LEEDS	10	L	0-1	0-1		Ramsbottom	Coop	Cattlin	McGuire	Barry	Dugdale	Green	Alderson	Stein	Carr	Hutchison	
2/4		24,435	*3*	35			*Reaney 40*	*Harvey*	*Reaney*	*Cherry*	*Bremner*	*Charlton*	*Yorath*	*Lorimer*	*Clarke*	*Jones*	*Giles*	*Madeley*	
							Ref: H New	A classic Leeds victory. Clarke's dazzling run ends with Reaney scoring on the overlap. The visitors then defend in depth, but City give them a second-half roasting. Harvey stars with saves from Green, Alderson twice. Hutch hits the bar and Leeds are still in with a chance of the title.											
37	A	EVERTON	11	L	0-2	0-1		Ramsbottom	Coop	Cattlin	McGuire	Barry	Dugdale	Green	Alderson	Stein	Carr	Hutchison	
7/4		*25,474*	*15*	35			*Harper 15, 75*	*Lawson*	*Wright T*	*Styles*	*Hurst*	*Kenyon*	*Bernard*	*Darracott*	*Kendall*	*Jones*	*Harper*	*Connolly*	
							Ref: V James	Everton need the points in their relegation battle. City dominate for 15 minutes then fall away badly. Harper pounces on Dugdale's block and then slides in Styles' cross. Stein misses two good chances and Ramsbottom keeps the score down and stops Harper's hat-trick with a fine save.											
38	H	DERBY	13	L	0-2	0-1		Ramsbottom	Coop	Cattlin	Smith	Barry	Dugdale	Mortimer	Alderson	Stein	Carr	Hutchison	
14/4		22,762	*9*	35			*O'Hare 13, Hector 79*	*Boulton*	*Webster*	*Nish*	*Durban**	*McFarland*	*Todd*	*McGovern*	*Gemmill*	*O'Hare*	*Hector*	*Powell*	*Parry*
							Ref: C Thomas	The Rams played Juventus in a European Cup semi-final in midweek and they look tired. They score from their only two chances. City back off O'Hare and he punishes them with a low shot. Hector loops a header over Neil Ramsbottom. Coventry look ready for the season to end.											
39	H	LIVERPOOL	13	L	1-2	0-1	Alderson 85	Ramsbottom	Coop	Cattlin	Smith	Barry	Dugdale	Mortimer	Alderson	Stein	Carr*	Hutchison	Green
17/4		27,334	*1*	35			*Boersma 38, 61*	*Clemence*	*Lawler*	*Thompson*	*Smith*	*Lloyd*	*Hughes*	*Keegan*	*Cormack*	*Hall*	*Boersma*	*Callaghan*	
							Ref: D Biddle	Liverpool edge closer to the title in a hard-fought game. Keegan latches on to a partially cleared corner and sets up Boersma. The otherwise excellent Ramsbottom drops a corner on to Phil Boersma's head. Alderson lashes a consolation goal. Lawler heads off the line from Cattlin.											
40	A	SHEFFIELD UTD	17	L	1-3	1-2	Barry 20	Ramsbottom	Coop	Dugdale	Smith	Barry	Parker	Mortimer	Alderson	Stein	McGuire	Hutchison	
21/4		*19,992*	*18*	35			*Coop 5 (og), Bone 18, Dearden 63*	*McAllister*	*Badger*	*Hemsley*	*Mackenzie*	*Colquhoun*	*Eddy*	*Scullion*	*Salmons*	*Dearden*	*Currie*	*Bone*	
							Ref: P Partridge	The slump continues. One win in nine. In heavy rain the Blades look keener to win. Coop tries to find Ramsbottom but lobs over him. Hutch heads an easy chance over. Dearden heads on for Bone to score and pounces after Currie's shot is palmed out. Barry cracks in a free-kick.											
41	A	CHELSEA	18	L	0-2	0-1		Ramsbottom	Coop	Dugdale	Smith	Barry	Parker	Mortimer	Alderson	Stein	McGuire*	Hutchison	Green
23/4		*18,279*	*12*	35			*Hinton 12, Hollins 65p*	*Bonetti*	*Harris*	*McCreadie*	*Hollins*	*Hinton*	*Droy*	*Britton*	*Baldwin*	*Osgood**	*Kember*	*Brolly*	*Garner*
							Ref: P Reeves	Lowest Chelsea crowd of the season with the new stand being built. A drab game and an easy win for the Blues. Hinton scored from a corner but Smith claimed it went in off him. Barry holds down Osgood and Hollins scores from the spot. Alderson and Stein both hit the woodwork.											
42	A	WOLVES	19	L	**0-3**	0-1		Ramsbottom	Coop	Holmes	Smith	Barry*	Dugdale	Mortimer	Alderson	Stein	McGuire	Hutchison	Green
28/4	Home	*21,520* Away	*5*	35			*Sunderland 31, Richards 59, Powell 77*	*Parkes*	*Taylor*	*Parkin*	*Bailey*	*Jefferson*	*McAlle*	*Powell*	*Sunderland*	*Richards*	*Dougan*	*Wagstaffe**	*Kindon*
Average	24,623	26,689					Ref: G Hill	Seven successive defeats, the worst run since 1924. Drab and lifeless end of season game. Barry off with a hamstring injury after 33 minutes and City never recover. Sunderland volley's in from a corner. John Richards taps in and Powell chests down before shooting past Ramsbottom.											

LEAGUE DIVISION 1 (CUP-TIES)

Manager: Joe Mercer & Gordon Milne

SEASON 1972-73

League Cup		F-A	H-T	Scorers, Times, and Referees	1	2	3	4	5	6	7	8	9	10	11	12 sub used
2 H HARTLEPOOL 16	W	1-0	1-0	Carr 33p	Glazier	Coop	Cattlin	Machin	Blockley	Barry	Mortimer	Young	Rafferty	Carr	Smith	
5/9 8,772 *4:12*					*Watling*	*Potter*	*Goad*	*Dawes*	*Green*	*Smith Rob*	*Waddell*	*Smith Bobby*	*Coyne*	*Spelman*	*Warnock*	
				Ref: H New	An unconvincing display against plucky opponents who cost £1,000. Alan Goad stretched a leg and Mortimer fell over it for a dubious penalty. Len Ashurst's men have Coyne's goal ruled out for offside. City's lowest League Cup gate since 1960. Wilf Smith and Quintin Young booked.											
3 A BIRMINGHAM 21	L	1-2	0-2	Alderson 65	Glazier	Coop	Cattlin	Machin	Barry	Parker	Mortimer	Smith	Rafferty	Carr	Alderson	
3/10 *27,803 17*				*Francis 2, Barry 33 (og)*	*Latchford D*	*Martin*	*Want*	*Campbell*	*Hynd*	*Page*	*Burns*	*Francis*	*Latchford R*	*Pendrey*	*Summerill*	
				Ref: R Matthewson	A fifth straight defeat but a remarkable transformation after the break deserves a draw. Roy Barry, captain in Blockley's absence, scores with a spectacular header. Mortimer gifts a goal to super-boy Francis. Alderson flicks a cross over Martin and hits a volley in. City twice hit the bar.											

FA Cup		F-A	H-T	Scorers, Times, and Referees	1	2	3	4	5	6	7	8	9	10	11	12 sub used
3 A ORIENT 10	W	4-1	3-1	Alderson 2, 87, Carr 4, Hutchison 24	Glazier	Coop	Dugdale	Smith	Barry	Parker	Mortimer	Alderson	Stein	Carr	Hutchison	
13/1 *12,272 2:20*				*Arber 21p*	*Goddard*	*Hoadley*	*Arber*	*Allen*	*Harris*	*Linton*	*Downing*	*Brisley*	*Bowyer*	*Queen*	*Heppolette*	
				Ref: V James	4,000 City fans and Match of the Day cameras see this comprehensive win. Alderson scored in the first attack from Coop's free-kick. Stein sets up Carr. Barry holds down Bowyer for the penalty. Goddard loses a Coop free-kick and Hutch chips in. Alderson rounds Goddard to seal it.											
4 H GRIMSBY 12	W	1-0	0-0	Coop 86p	Glazier	Coop	Dugdale	Smith	Barry	Parker	Mortimer	Alderson*	Stein	McGuire	Hutchison	Green
3/2 38,814 *3:4*					Wainman	Worthington	Booth	Chatterley	Wigginton	Gray	Brace	Hickman	Tees	Boylen	Gauden	
				Ref: A Hart	Grimsby commit 44 fouls, 12 by Hickman who amazingly stays on the field. Their over-physical approach is their downfall. Booth's foul on McGuire looks outside the box but the linesman gives it and Coop scores his first ever goal. 10,000 away fans expecting a replay cause trouble.											
5 H HULL 13	W	3-0	2-0	Alderson 17, Stein 25, 87	Glazier	Coop	Cattlin	Smith	Barry	Parker	Mortimer	Alderson	Stein	Carr	Hutchison	
24/2 31,724 *2:12*					*Wealands*	*Banks*	*Beardsley*	*Kaye*	*Neill*	*Knighton*	*McGill*	*Houghton**	*Pearson*	*Holme*	*Greenwood*	*Blampey*
				Ref: G Kew	Hull are never in it and City gain revenge for last season. Stein is the new king of Highfield Road as he has his best game yet. Alderson heads home Hutch's cross. Stein volleys in and heads home from Mortimer's cross. Carr and Mortimer shine. Ernie Hunt is loaned out to Doncaster.											
QF A WOLVES 10	L	0-2	0-1		Glazier	Coop	Cattlin	Smith*	Barry	Parker	Mortimer	Alderson	Stein	Carr	Hutchison	McGuire
17/3 *50,106 6*				*Richards 7, Hibbitt 49p*	*Parkes*	*Taylor*	*Parkin*	*Shaw*	*Munro*	*McAlle*	*McCalliog**	*Hibbitt*	*Richards*	*Dougan*	*Wagstaffe*	*Kindon*
				Ref: B Homewood	Only City's third ever quarter-final appearance, but Wolves are too good for them. Dougan heads down and Richards beats Parker to score. Cattlin and Coop bring down Richards and Hibbitt scores the penalty. Munro wraps up Stein. Wolves go on to lose to Leeds in the semi-final.											

		Home					Away					
	P	W	D	L	F	A	W	D	L	F	A	Pts
1 Liverpool	42	17	3	1	45	19	8	7	6	27	23	60
2 Arsenal	42	14	5	2	31	14	9	6	6	26	29	57
3 Leeds	42	15	4	2	45	13	6	7	8	26	32	53
4 Ipswich	42	10	7	4	34	20	7	7	7	21	25	48
5 Wolves	42	13	3	5	43	23	5	8	8	23	31	47
6 West Ham	42	12	5	4	45	25	5	7	9	22	28	46
7 Derby	42	15	3	3	43	18	4	5	12	13	36	46
8 Tottenham	42	10	5	6	33	23	6	8	7	25	25	45
9 Newcastle	42	12	6	3	35	19	4	7	10	25	32	45
10 Birmingham	42	11	7	3	39	22	4	5	12	14	32	42
11 Manchester C	42	12	4	5	36	20	3	7	11	21	40	41
12 Chelsea	42	9	6	6	30	22	4	8	9	19	29	40
13 Southampton	42	8	11	2	26	17	3	7	11	21	35	40
14 Sheffield Utd	42	11	4	6	28	18	4	6	11	23	41	40
15 Stoke	42	11	8	2	38	17	3	2	16	23	39	38
16 Leicester	42	7	9	5	23	18	3	8	10	17	28	37
17 Everton	42	9	5	7	27	21	4	6	11	14	28	37
18 Manchester U	42	9	7	5	24	19	3	6	12	20	41	37
19 COVENTRY	42	9	5	7	27	24	4	4	13	13	31	35
20 Norwich	42	7	9	5	22	19	4	1	16	14	44	32
21 Crys Palace	42	7	7	7	25	21	2	5	14	16	37	30
22 West Brom	42	8	7	6	25	24	1	3	17	13	38	28
	924	236	130	96	724	436	96	130	236	436	724	924

Odds & ends

Double wins: (2) Crys Palace, Manchester C.
Double losses: (5) Wolves, Chelsea, Tottenham, Derby, Liverpool.

Won from behind: (0)
Lost from in front: (2) Southampton (a), Stoke (a).

High spots: Arrival of Stein and Hutchison. Eight game unbeaten run.
Hutchison's goal at Highbury.
Reaching the FA Cup quarter-finals for only third time ever.

Low spots: Six games without a win at start of season.
Floodlight failure at Ipswich when leading 1-0.
Defeat in FA Cup quarter-final at Molineux.
A record seven straight defeats to end the season.

Red cards: Opponents – Channon (So'ton a), Hinshelwood (C Palace h).

Player of the Year: Willie Carr.
Ever-presents: (1) Mick Coop.
Hat-tricks: (0).
Opposing hat-tricks: (1) MacDonald (Newcastle).
Leading scorer: (17) Brian Alderson.

	Appearances						**Goals**			
	Lge	*Sub*	LC	*Sub*	FAC	*Sub*	**Lge**	LC	FAC	**Tot**
Alderson, Brian	**32**	*1*	1		4		**13**	1	3	**17**
Barry, Roy	**40**		2		4		**1**			**1**
Blockley, Jeff	**11**		1							
Carr, Willie	**36**		2		3		**8**	1	1	**10**
Cattlin, Chris	**36**		2		2					
Coop, Mick	**42**		2		4				1	**1**
Dugdale, Alan	**16**	*3*			2					
Glazier, Bill	**28**		2		4					
Graham, Bobby	**6**						**1**			**1**
Green, Alan	**5**	*3*				*1*				
Holmes, Jimmy	**1**									
Hunt, Ernie	**7**						**2**			**2**
Hutchison, Tommy	**30**				4		**2**		1	**3**
Machin, Ernie	**11**		2							
McGuire, Mick	**13**	*4*			1	*1*				
Mortimer, Dennis	**39**		2		4		**1**			**1**
Parker, Bobby	**24**		1		4					
Rafferty, Billy	**4**		2							
Ramsbottom, Neil	**14**									
Smith, Wilf	**32**	*2*	2		4					
Stein, Colin	**31**				4		**10**		2	**12**
Young, Quinton	**4**	*1*	1							
(own-goals)							**2**			**2**
22 players used	**462**	***14***	**22**		**44**	***2***	**40**	**2**	**8**	**50**

LEAGUE DIVISION 1 — Manager: Gordon Milne — SEASON 1973-74

No	Date	Att	Pos	Pt	F-A	H-T	Scorers, Times, and Referees	1	2	3	4	5	6	7	8	9	10	11	12 sub used
1	H TOTTENHAM			W	1-0	1-0	Coop 25	Glazier	Coop	Holmes	Mortimer	**Craven**	Dugdale	Smith	Alderson	Stein	Green	Hutchison	
	25/8	25,094		2				_Jennings_	_Evans_	_Knowles_	_Coates_	_Dillon_	_Beal_	_Gilzean_	_Perryman_	_Chivers_	_Peters_	_Neighbour*_	_Holder_
							Ref: P Partridge	City's first opening-day win since 1966. It's Glazier's 300th appearance. Sad Tottenham are outclassed. Coop's header from Hutchison's cross bobbled past Jennings, who had made several good saves to keep out Stein, Hutchison, Alderson and Green. John Craven blotted out Chivers.											
2	H LIVERPOOL			W	1-0	0-0	Hutchison 63	Glazier	Coop	Holmes	Mortimer	Craven	Dugdale	Smith	Alderson	Stein	Green*	Hutchison	Hunt
	28/8	29,364		4				_Clemence_	_Lawler_	_Lindsay_	_Thompson_	_Lloyd_	_Hughes_	_Keegan_	_Cormack_	_Heighway_	_Boersma_	_Callaghan_	
							Ref: A Hart	The champions are beaten in a scintillating display of skill and industry. Hutchison is the star, scoring a superb volley from the edge of the area after Stein heads back Alderson's cross. Keegan hits the post and Cormack goes close, but City deserve the win. Hunt's first game for a year.											
3	A BURNLEY		4	D	2-2	1-1	Green 35, 53	Glazier	Coop	Holmes	Mortimer	Craven	Dugdale	Smith	Alderson	Stein	Green*	Hutchison	Parker
	1/9	_20,711_	_3_	5			_Fletcher 31, Dobson 75_	_Stevenson_	_Noble_	_Newton_	_Dobson_	_Waldron_	_Thomson_	_Nulty_	_Casper_	_Fletcher*_	_Collins_	_James_	_Ingham_
							Ref: E Wallace	Jimmy Adamson's newly promoted Burnley are lucky to draw against solid City. Fletcher headed in James' cross. Mortimer crossed for Green to slot home. Green netted again following Craven's free-kick. Paul Fletcher headed back for Dobson. Alan Green could have scored four.											
4	A MANCHESTER C		6	L	0-1	0-0		Glazier	Coop	Holmes	Mortimer	Craven	Dugdale	Smith	Alderson	Stein	Green	Hutchison	
	5/9	_30,931_	_7_	5			_Marsh 70p_	_Corrigan_	_Pardoe_	_Donachie_	_Doyle_	_Booth_	_Oakes*_	_Summerbee_	_Bell_	_Law_	_Carrodus_	_Marsh_	_Lee_
							Ref: R Armstrong	City fight hard but can't match the smooth-flowing Manchester and lose their unbeaten record. A dubious penalty is given when Lee appears to dive, and Marsh scores. Soon after, Pardoe blatantly pushes Green over but nothing is given. Scottish boss Ormond watches Hutch and Stein.											
5	H SOUTHAMPTON		4	W	2-0	0-0	Coop 46p, Green 66	Glazier	Coop	Holmes	Mortimer	Craven	Dugdale	Smith	Alderson	Stein	Green	Hutchison	
	8/9	19,416	_9_	7				_Martin_	_McCarthy_	_Byrne_	_Fisher_	_McGrath*_	_Walker_	_Paine_	_Channon_	_Gilchrist_	_O'Neill_	_Stokes_	_Mills_
							Ref: E Jolly	City dominate after a dull first half. McCarthy topples Hutch and Coop scores. Alan Green latches on to Mortimer's through-ball and beats Martin low down. New Saints manager-designate McMenemy shoulders blame for his mean and boring team. Graham signs for Motherwell.											
6	H MANCHESTER C		3	W	2-1	1-0	Coop 8, Craven 70	Glazier	Coop	Holmes	Mortimer	Craven	Dugdale	Smith	Alderson	Stein	Green	Hutchison	
	11/9	27,491	_7_	9			_Marsh 90_	_Corrigan_	_Pardoe_	_Donachie_	_Doyle_	_Booth_	_Towers_	_Summerbee_	_Bell_	_Carrodus_	_Lee_	_Marsh_	
							Ref: R Capey	Another good performance against classy opponents. Coop hits a 20-yarder when Hutch's throw-in is not cleared. Craven takes advantage of Corrigan spilling Coop's free-kick by scoring from 18 yards. Marsh is left unmarked for the late consolation. Hutchison is in Scottish squad.											
7	A CHELSEA		6	L	0-1	0-1		Glazier	Coop	Holmes	Mortimer	Craven	Dugdale	Smith	Alderson	Stein	Green	Hutchison	
	15/9	_30,593_	_12_	9			_Osgood 11_	_Bonetti_	_Locke_	_Harris_	_Hollins_	_Droy_	_Webb_	_Kember_	_Hudson_	_Osgood_	_Baldwin_	_Garner_	
							Ref: R Crabbe	Chelsea are put under siege for long periods after Peter Osgood's tap-in but rarely look like scoring. Kember brings down Hutchison and Peter Bonetti saves Coop's penalty after 29 minutes. It's his first ever miss, Bonetti having seen him take a kick against Saints on Match of the Day.											
8	H DERBY		4	W	1-0	1-0	Stein 9	Glazier	Smith	Holmes	Mortimer	Craven	Dugdale	McGuire	Alderson	Stein	Hunt	Hutchison	
	18/9	26,511	_5_	11				_Boulton_	_Webster_	_Nish_	_Powell_	_McFarland_	_Todd_	_McGovern_	_Gemmill_	_Davies_	_Hector_	_Hinton_	
							Ref: J Williams	In a barn-storming finish, with both sides missing chances, City deservedly hold on to win. Stein beats the Derby offside trap to head in Wilf Smith's cross for his first goal of the season. Swirling wind and rain don't spoil a super game or prevent Coventry's fifth successive home win.											
9	H NEWCASTLE		3	D	2-2	2-1	Alderson 37, Stein 45	Glazier	Coop	Holmes	Mortimer	Craven	Dugdale	Smith	Alderson	Stein*	Hunt	Hutchison	McGuire
	22/9	25,556	_4_	12			_Macdonald 25, Tudor 78_	_McFaul_	_Nattrass_	_Clark_	_McDermott_	_Howard_	_Moncur_	_Cassidy_	_Smith_	_Macdonald_	_Tudor_	_Hibbitt_	
							Ref: D Nippard	The worst home display so far, but grit earns City their point. Supermac hits an explosive shot to impress the watching Alf Ramsey. Alderson bends home a free-kick. Stein injures his ankle but is able to score a superb header from Coop's cross. Supermac sets up Tudor in a tight finale.											
10	A LEICESTER		2	W	2-0	1-0	Alderson 15, Cartwright 70	Glazier	Coop	Holmes	Mortimer	Craven	Dugdale	Smith	Alderson	Hunt*	Green	Hutchison	**Cartwright**
	29/9	_29,317_	_6_	14				_Shilton_	_Whitworth_	_Rofe_	_Partridge_	_Munro_	_Cross_	_Weller_	_Sammels_	_Worthington_	_Birchenall_	_Glover_	
							Ref: H New	Leicester's unbeaten start is ended, leaving City in their highest ever position. Green replaces injured Stein. Birchenall's slip lets in Alderson for a strong cross shot. Cartwright's goal, deflected off Birchenall, is the first by a City debutant since 1965. Hutch has made his Scots debut.											

No	Venue	Opponent / Date	Att	Pos	Res / Pts	F-A	H-T	Scorers, Times, and Referees	1	2	3	4	5	6	7	8	9	10	11	12 sub used
11	H	EVERTON		3	L	1-2	1-0	Green 12	Glazier	Coop	Holmes	Mortimer	Craven	Dugdale	Smith	Alderson	Stein	Green	Hutchison	
		6/10	26,834	6	14			*Lyons 82, Connolly 88*	*Lawson*	*Darracott*	*McLaughlin*	*Clements*	*Kenyon*	*Hurst*	*Buckley*	*Husband**	*Lyons*	*Harper*	*Connolly*	*Bernard*
								Ref: H Williams	Everton extend their unbeaten run to five and end City's unbeaten home record with two late goals. Coventry look lethargic. Green heads home after Smith's shot hits the bar and Green then misses an easy chance. Lyons scores off the bar and Connolly off the post. Tempers fray late on.											
12	A	NORWICH		4	D	0-0	0-0		Glazier	Coop	Holmes	Mortimer	Craven	Dugdale	Smith	Alderson	Stein	Green	Hutchison	
		13/10	*22,841*	*20*	15				*Keelan*	*Prophett*	*Payne*	*Stringer*	*Forbes*	*Briggs*	*Livermore*	*Suggett*	*Cross*	*Paddon*	*Mellor*	
								Ref: I Smith	Struggling Norwich, with David Cross prominent, put City under plenty of pressure. The Sky Blues soak it up and look more likely winners at the end. Coop and Alderson miss good chances but a draw is fair. Roy Barry moves to Crystal Palace for £35,000. Carr is close to full fitness.											
13	H	WEST HAM		6	L	0-1	0-0		Glazier	Coop	Holmes	Mortimer	Craven*	Dugdale	Smith	Alderson	Stein	Green	Hutchison	Cartwright
		20/10	21,141	*21*	15			*McDowell 68*	*Day*	*Coleman*	*Lampard*	*Bonds*	*Taylor*	*Moore*	*Tyler*	*McDowell*	*Best*	*Brooking*	*Robson**	*Lock*
								Ref: I Jones	Inconsistent City enjoy most of the play but rarely trouble superb Moore and Co. Craven limps off after nine minutes with a hamstring injury. Hammers' first goal in five games earns their first win of the season. McDowell takes time off from marking Hutch to score with a left footer.											
14	A	STOKE		7	L	0-3	0-1		Glazier	Coop	Holmes	Mortimer	**Philpotts**	Dugdale	Smith	Alderson	Stein	Cartwright	Hutchison	
		27/10	*17,421*	*18*	15			*Greenhoff 6, 75, Hurst 72p*	*Farmer*	*Marsh*	*Pejic*	*Mahoney*	*Smith*	*Dodd*	*Robertson*	*Greenhoff*	*Ritchie*	*Hurst*	*Haselgrave*	
								Ref: P Baldwin	Coop is captain in Craven's absence, but City are hammered. Greenhoff scores from close range after a corner. The unsure David Philpotts fouls John Mahoney, but Robertson's penalty hits the bar. Holmes handles and Hurst doesn't miss. Jimmy Greenhoff scores from a rebound.											
15	H	IPSWICH		10	L	0-1	0-0		Glazier	Coop	Holmes	Mortimer	Philpotts	Dugdale	Cartwright	Alderson	Stein	McGuire	Hutchison	
		3/11	18,733	*7*	15			*Whymark 69*	*Best*	*Mills*	*Harper*	*Morris*	*Hunter*	*Beattie*	*Hamilton*	*Viljoen*	*Woods*	*Whymark*	*Lambert*	
								Ref: R Lee	City's defence always looks suspect against workmanlike Ipswich, who dominate the early play. Just as the Sky Blues start to look dangerous Whymark clinches it with a leaping header from Woods' cross. Stein and Hunter have a physical tussle. Craven, Smith and Carr are missed.											
16	A	QP RANGERS		11	L	0-3	0-1		Glazier	Coop	Holmes	Mortimer	Philpotts*	Dugdale	Cartwright	Alderson	Stein	McGuire	Hutchison	Smith
		10/11	*20,416*	*7*	15			*Bowles 6, Francis 57, Venables 61*	*Parkes*	*Clement*	*Hazell*	*Venables*	*Mancini*	*McLintock*	*Thomas*	*Francis*	*Leach**	*Bowles*	*Givens*	*Delve*
								Ref: P Walters	Newly promoted QPR notch their fifth successive win. They scored eight against Wednesday in midweek and look superb. Bowles side-foots the first. Free-kicks bring two more goals. Francis scores after Venables' cheeky chip over the wall. Glazier palms in Terry Venables' effort,											
17	A	LEEDS		15	L	0-3	0-1		Glazier	Coop	Holmes	Mortimer*	Parker	Dugdale	**Cross**	Alderson	Stein	McGuire	Hutchison	Cartwright
		17/11	***35,552***	*1*	15			*Clarke 10, Jordan 69, Bremner 73*	*Harvey*	*Reaney*	*Cherry*	*Bremner*	*McQueen*	*Hunter*	*Lorimer*	*Clarke*	*Jordan*	*Bates*	*Madeley*	
								Ref: A Morrissey	Cross, signed from Norwich for £150,000 can't stop the fifth defeat in a row. The early season euphoria has worn off and a relegation battle looms. Leeds barely need to get out of first gear but score three stunning goals. For the best, Bremner set up Bates to cross for Jordan's header.											
18	H	SHEFFIELD UTD		12	W	3-1	1-1	Stein 27, Cross 75, 89	Glazier	Coop	Holmes	Cartwright	Dugdale*	Parker	McGuire	Alderson	Stein	Cross	Hutchison	Green
		24/11	17,918	*14*	17			*Woodward 45*	*Connaughton*	*Badger*	*Hemsley*	*Flynn*	*Colquhoun*	*Speight*	*Woodward*	*Salmons*	*Dearden*	*Currie*	*Bone*	
								Ref: J Bent	A 2 pm start because of the power crisis. A win at last for City and a first League goal for 645 minutes. Cross and Stein combine well to upset Blades. Woodward scores direct from a free-kick. Currie copies him but a player is offside. Dugdale's injury means Coop plays at centre-half.											
19	A	ARSENAL		12	D	2-2	2-1	Alderson 22, Cross 26	Glazier	Coop	Holmes	Cartwright	Dugdale	Parker	McGuire	Alderson	Stein	Cross	Hutchison	
		1/12	*22,340*	*11*	18			*Hornsby 31, Nelson 66*	*Wilson*	*Rice*	*McNab*	*Storey*	*Simpson*	*Kelly**	*Ball*	*George*	*Hornsby*	*Kennedy*	*Armstrong*	*Nelson*
								Ref: R Matthewson	An enthralling match for Match of the Day on an ice-rink of a pitch. Alderson rammed in a right footer, Cross bundled a second after Stein nodded on Hutch's corner. Hornsby headed in before Sammy Nelson's screamer. It is Nelson's first match of the season. Stein back to his best.											
20	H	WOLVES		11	W	1-0	0-0	Stein 84	Ramsbottom	Coop	Holmes	Cartwright	Dugdale	Parker	McGuire	Alderson	Stein	Cross	Hutchison	
		8/12	20,770	*19*	20				*Parkes*	*Palmer*	*Parkin*	*Bailey*	*Munro**	*McAlle*	*Hibbitt*	*Powell*	*Richards*	*Dougan*	*Wagstaffe*	*Sunderland*
								Ref: H Hackney	Another early kick-off and Xmas shopping keeps the crowd down. Stein is pushing for a Scottish World Cup place and his form is hot. His lethal finish after Cartwright's mis-hit wins it. Cross should have scored when rounding Phil Parkes, who also makes a fine save from Stein.											
21	A	MANCHESTER U		8	W	3-2	1-0	Stein 44, Alderson 63, Cross 76	Glazier	Coop	Holmes	McGuire	Cattlin	Parker	Cartwright	Alderson	Stein	Cross	Hutchison	
		15/12	*28,589*	*19*	22			*Best 47, Morgan 66*	*Stepney*	*Buchan*	*Forsyth*	*Greenhoff B*	*James**	*Griffiths*	*Morgan*	*Macari*	*McIlroy*	*Young*	*Best*	*Martin*
								Ref: G Kew	United are without a win in seven and City's extra power up front wins before United's lowest crowd of the season. Stein's header from Les Cartwright's cross is deflected by Buchan. Best scores what will be his last ever United goal. Alderson blazes a goal and Cross heads another.											

LEAGUE DIVISION 1

Manager: Gordon Milne

SEASON 1973-74

No	Date		Att	Pos	Pt	F-A	H-T	Scorers, Times, and Referees	1	2	3	4	5	6	7	8	9	10	11	12 sub used
22	H	LEICESTER		12	L	1-2	1-1	Cartwright 10	Glazier	Coop	Holmes	McGuire	Dugdale	Parker	Cartwright	Alderson	Stein	Cross	Hutchison	
	22/12		23,413	*5*	22			*Glover 44, Worthington 88*	*Shilton*	*Whitworth*	*Rofe*	*Earle*	*Munro*	*Cross*	*Weller*	*Sammels*	*Worthington*	*Birchenall*	*Glover*	
								Ref: B Homewood	Leicester are having their best season for years and end City's six match unbeaten run. An entertaining game where Shilton is the difference. His two first-half saves from Stein and Cross are world class. Les Cartwright's goal is deflected. Worthington heads in from Glover's centre.											
23	A	BIRMINGHAM		13	L	0-1	0-1		Glazier	Coop	Holmes	McGuire	Craven	Dugdale	Cartwright	Alderson	Stein	Cross*	Hutchison	Carr
	26/12		*33,423*	*19*	22			*Latchford 18*	*Sprake*	*Martin*	*Gallagher*	*Pendrey*	*Roberts*	*Burns*	*Campbell*	*Francis*	*Latchford R*	*Hatton*	*Taylor*	
								Ref: D Biddle	City's injury crisis is easing. Craven and Carr return. Freddie Goodwin's team are desperate for points and win a poor game on a muddy pitch. Craven is left standing as Hatton sets up Latchford to score easily from 18 yards. Gary Pendrey marks Hutch well and City create few chances.											
24	A	SOUTHAMPTON		12	D	1-1	0-1	Craven 78	Glazier	Coop	Holmes	McGuire	Craven	Dugdale	Cartwright*	Alderson	Stein	Cross	Carr	Green
	29/12		*18,345*	*8*	23			*Channon 29p*	*Martin*	*McCarthy*	*Mills*	*Fisher*	*Bennett*	*Steele*	*Paine*	*Channon*	*Gilchrist*	*O'Neill*	*Stokes*	
								Ref: A Lees	Just when it looked like City had soaked up the early pressure Channon tumbles in a challenge with Dugdale. Channon nets from the spot, but City's fight-back is rewarded when Craven heads in McGuire's cross. Saints slump will end in relegation, having been fifth in December.											
25	H	BURNLEY		11	D	1-1	1-1	Cross 26	Glazier	Coop	Holmes	Carr	Craven	Dugdale	Cartwright	Alderson	Stein	Cross	Hutchison*	McGuire
	1/1		24,876	*3*	24			*Nulty 18*	*Stevenson*	*Noble*	*Newton*	*Dobson*	*Waldron*	*Ingham*	*Nulty*	*Hankin*	*Fletcher*	*Collins*	*James*	
								Ref: W Gow	Burnley have only lost four games all season and play their part in a sparkling game. Nulty heads in after Dobson wins the ball from Collins' corner. Cross heads in Stein's cross after Cartwright's shot is saved by Stevenson's legs. Fletcher's shot after the break almost snaps the bar.											
26	H	CHELSEA		12	D	2-2	0-1	Coop 50p, 83p	Glazier	Coop	Holmes	Carr	Craven	Dugdale	Cartwright	McGuire*	Stein	Cross	Hutchison	Green
	12/1		20,920	*18*	25			*Harris 32, Garland 82*	*Phillips*	*Locke*	*Harris*	*Hollins*	*Droy*	*Webb*	*Britton*	*Kember*	*Baldwin*	*Garland*	*Brolly*	
								Ref: I Jones	It's now 13 matches without a win against Chelsea. City do most of the attacking. Harris scores a rare goal after Glazier saves his shot. Hutch is fouled and Coop makes up for his penalty miss earlier in the season. Garland's diving header and Harris's handball make an exciting finale.											
27	A	TOTTENHAM		14	L	1-2	0-2	Alderson 73	Glazier	Coop	Holmes*	Carr	Craven	Dugdale	Mortimer	Alderson	Stein	Cross	Hutchison	Cattlin
	19/1		*20,985*	*16*	25			*Peters 29, 39*	*Jennings*	*Evans*	*Naylor*	*Pratt*	*England*	*Beal*	*McGrath*	*Perryman*	*Chivers*	*Peters*	*Coates*	
								Ref: E Jolly	City suffer from a League Cup hangover and Spurs win without fuss. Stein wasted three chances in the first twenty minutes. Alan Dugdale's mistake lets in Peters to chip Glazier. Poor marking allows Peters get a far-post header in. Alderson crashes in a consolation but it's too late.											
28	H	MANCHESTER U		11	W	1-0	0-0	Alderson 75	Glazier	Coop	Holmes	Mortimer	Craven	Dugdale	Cartwright	Alderson	Cross	Cattlin	Hutchison	
	2/2		25,407	*21*	27				*Stepney*	*Buchan*	*Houston*	*Greenhoff B*	*Holton*	*James*	*Morgan*	*Macari*	*McIlroy**	*Kidd*	*Young*	*Forsyth*
								Ref: T Spencer	United's magic is waning. Docherty's team have won just once in 14 and resort to strong-arm tactics. City look tired after playing extra-time in midweek but Alderson's blast sends Stepney the wrong way. Substitute Alex Forsyth hits the post in the 90th minute. Mortimer looks supreme.											
29	A	LIVERPOOL		11	L	1-2	0-1	Holmes 84	Glazier	Coop	Holmes	Mortimer	Craven	Dugdale	Cartwright	Alderson	Cross	Cattlin*	Hutchison	McGuire
	5/2		*21,106*	*2*	27			*Lindsay 28p, Keegan 57*	*Clemence*	*Smith*	*Lindsay*	*Thompson*	*Cormack*	*Hughes*	*Keegan*	*Hall*	*Boersma*	*Waddle*	*Callaghan*	
								Ref: P Partridge	This Tuesday afternoon fixture sees Anfield's lowest gate since 1961. Chris Cattlin fouls Waddle for the penalty. Keegan fires the second goal. City only looked dangerous in the last ten minutes. Holmes scores with a 25-yard free-kick. Cross's 88th minute header is ruled out for a foul.											
30	A	NEWCASTLE		15	L	1-5	0-1	Alderson 84 *[Tudor 80, Macdonald 83]*	Glazier	**Hindley**	Holmes	Mortimer	Craven*	Dugdale	Cartwright	Alderson	Cross	Carr	Hutchison	McGuire
	9/2		*26,247*	*9*	27			*Craven 43 (og), Bruce 48, Dugdale 71 (og),*	*McFaul*	*Craig*	*Clark*	*Gibb*	*Howard*	*Moncur*	*Bruce**	*Cassidy*	*Macdonald*	*Tudor*	*Hibbitt*	*Barrowclough*
								Ref: V James	A freak result with City the better side for 40 minutes as Alderson and Cross waste chances. Then the farce begins. Craven deflects Howard's speculative shot in. Dugdale turns Barrowclough's cross in for a second own-goal. Tudor heads No 4. Glazier drops a shot at Supermac's feet.											
31	A	EVERTON		17	L	0-1	0-1		Glazier	Hindley	Holmes	Mortimer	Craven	Dugdale	Cartwright	Alderson	Cross	Carr	Hutchison	
	23/2		*34,762*	*5*	27			*Hurst 18*	*Lawson*	*Darracott*	*McLaughlin*	*Bernard*	*Kenyon*	*Hurst*	*Buckley**	*Harvey*	*Latchford*	*Jones*	*Connolly*	*Lyons*
								Ref: M Lowe	Bob Latchford makes his Everton debut after a record £350,000 transfer from Birmingham. City appear to suffer a Cup hangover. Glazier loses Jones' corner and Hurst nods the goal. Latchford and Gary Jones should have extended the lead. Ernie Hunt has joined Bristol City for £7,500.											

32	H	NORWICH		14	W	1-0	1-0	Mortimer 20	Glazier	Coop	Holmes	Mortimer	Craven	Dugdale	Green*	Alderson	Cross	Carr	Hutchison	McGuire
	26/2		**16,457**	*22*	29				*Keelan*	*Machin*	*Benson*	*Stringer*	*Forbes*	*Howard*	*Prophett*	*MacDougall*	*Suggett*	*Boyer*	*Sissons*	
								Ref: R Capey	Norwich look doomed and contribute to a poor game. Despite being constantly man-handled by Forbes, David Cross is given the bird by the fans. Mortimer hits the post and Carr and Alderson waste chances. Dennis Mortimer lightens the gloom after Hutch's run and Cross's lay-off.											
33	H	BIRMINGHAM		15	L	0-1	0-1		Glazier	Coop	Holmes	Mortimer	Hindley	Dugdale	Green	Alderson	Cross	Carr	Hutchison	
	2/3		27,863	*20*	29			*Hatton 42*	*Latchford D*	*Martin*	*Pendrey*	*Kendall*	*Gallagher*	*Hynd*	*Campbell*	*Francis*	*Burns*	*Hatton*	*Taylor*	
								Ref: R Crabb	Jaded City cannot reproduce their Cup form and are sliding towards the relegation area. Blues look the more committed team and fully deserve their first away win. Kenny Burns heads on Francis' cross and Hatton snaps up the half-chance. Gordon Taylor and Green are both booked.											
34	H	STOKE		10	W	2-0	0-0	Hutchison 49, Cross 74	Glazier	Smith	Holmes	Mortimer	Cattlin	Dugdale	Green	Alderson*	Cross	Carr	Hutchison	Cartwright
	9/3		17,037	*15*	31				*McDonald*	*Marsh*	*Pejic*	*Dodd*	*Smith*	*Mahoney*	*Robertson*	*Greenhoff*	*Hurst*	*Ritchie*	*Hudson*	
								Ref: L Hayes	After a midweek blasting from manager Milne, City end Stoke's eleven-game unbeaten run. Carr and Hutchison are back in form. Hutch hits the bar, then scores after Carr's run. Cross chases Dodd's back-pass and robs McDonald to score. Stoke's £240,000 signing Hudson is quiet.											
35	A	WEST HAM		9	W	3-2	2-1	Cross 1, Alderson 35, Carr 86	Glazier	Smith	Holmes	Mortimer	Craven	Dugdale	McGuire	Alderson	Cross	Carr	Hutchison	
	16/3		*26,502*	*18*	33			*Bonds 27p, 75*	*Day*	*Coleman*	*Lampard*	*Bonds*	*Taylor*	*McGiven*	*Holland*	*Paddon*	*Robson*	*Brooking*	*Best*	
								Ref: H New	City end the Irons' ten game unbeaten run as Bobby Moore says farewell to the home fans. Bonds, a hat-trick hero in the last home game, nets after Smith's handball and hits a 25-yarder. Cross profits when Day drops the ball. Alderson flicks over Day. Hammers back off to let in Carr.											
36	H	QP RANGERS		12	L	0-1	0-1		Glazier	Smith	Holmes	Mortimer	Craven	Dugdale	McGuire	Alderson	Cross	Carr	Hutchison	
	23/3		18,825	*4*	33			*Francis 24*	*Parkes*	*Clement*	*Gillard*	*Busby*	*Mancini*	*McLintock*	*Thomas*	*Francis*	*Leach*	*Bowles*	*Givens**	*Abbott*
								Ref: J Williams	Inconsistent City are undone by slack defending, which leaves Francis unmarked to score. Parkes pulls off a great save from Alderson and the Coventry man also goes close with a scissors-kick. A disappointing match, interrupted by too many free-kicks. Mick Coop on the transfer list.											
37	A	IPSWICH		14	L	0-3	0-1		Ramsbottom	Smith	Holmes	Mortimer	Craven	Hindley	Cartwright	Alderson	Cross	Carr	Hutchison	
	30/3		*17,393*	*4*	33			*Johnson 33, Talbot 72, 83*	*Sivell*	*Burley*	*Mills*	*Morris*	*Peddelty*	*Beattie*	*Hamilton*	*Talbot*	*Johnson*	*Whymark*	*Woods*	
								Ref: E Wallace	A dreadful City display, but Ipswich fail to capitalise until late on. Glazier is injured and Dugdale is suspended. Holmes dithers and Johnson scores at the second attempt. Talbot races through to score after another blunder. Talbot heads in Woods' cross. Sivell has just one shot to save.											
38	A	SHEFFIELD UTD		12	W	1-0	1-0	Hutchison 15	Glazier	Smith	Cattlin	Mortimer	Craven	Hindley	Parker*	Alderson	Cross	McGuire	Hutchison	Cartwright
	6/4		***16,568***	*14*	35				*Brown*	*Badger*	*Hemsley*	*Eddy*	*Colquhoun*	*Salmons*	*Woodward*	*Garbett*	*Nicholl**	*Speight*	*Field*	*Cammack*
								Ref: K McNally	A match to forget, played in a swirling wind. City are probably safe. Parker limps off with an ankle injury in what will be his final game for the club. Hutch scores with a looping back-header from McGuire's flick. The Blades get stick from their fans and, minus Currie, they look poor.											
39	H	LEEDS		16	D	0-0	0-0		Glazier	Smith	Holmes	Mortimer	Hindley	Dugdale	Craven	Alderson	Cross	McGuire	Hutchison	
	13/4		**35,206**	*1*	36				*Harvey*	*Reaney*	*Cherry*	*Bremner*	*McQueen*	*Hunter*	*Lorimer*	*Yorath*	*Jordan*	*Giles*	*Madeley*	
								Ref: D Smith	Leeds are three points clear of Liverpool with four games left. This point is vital for them, but David Cross blasted wide with 20 minutes to go. The leaders look nervous and not prepared to gamble. Seven teams now have 36 points. Mick McGuire is City's star, outshining Johnny Giles.											
40	A	DERBY		17	L	0-1	0-1		Glazier	Smith	Holmes	Mortimer	Hindley	Dugdale	Craven	Alderson	Cross	McGuire*	Hutchison	Cartwright
	15/4		*23,348*	*4*	36			*Hector 40*	*Boulton*	*Webster*	*Nish*	*Rioch*	*McFarland*	*Todd*	*Powell*	*Gemmill*	*Davies*	*Hector*	*Bourne*	
								Ref: A Hart	A drab end-of-season game. City have two seemingly 'good' goals ruled out. Mortimer rifles in from 20 yards, only for a team-mate to be ruled offside. Cross beats McFarland in the air but the ref gives a foul. Dugdale fouls Hector, Glazier saves Rioch's penalty but Hector follows up.											
41	A	WOLVES		17	D	1-1	0-1	Craven 49	Glazier	Smith	Holmes	Mortimer	Hindley	Dugdale	Craven	McGuire	Stein	Cross	Hutchison	
	20/4		*24,902*	*10*	37			*Cross 38 (og)*	*Parkes*	*Palmer*	*Parkin*	*Bailey*	*Munro*	*McAlle*	*Hibbitt*	*Powell**	*Kindon*	*Sunderland*	*Daley*	*Dougan*
								Ref: B Daniels	Stein returns from a 17-game injury absence and makes a difference. Cross boobs, trying to clear a long throw flicked on by Kindon. Craven levels with a fine header from McGuire's corner. Craven picks up his second suspension of the season. City are still not mathematically safe.											
42	H	ARSENAL		16	D	3-3	2-0	Alderson 30, Stein 40, Cross 49	Glazier	Smith	Holmes	Mortimer	Hindley	Dugdale	McGuire	Alderson	Stein	Cross	Hutchison	
	27/4		20,049	*10*	38			*Rice 56, Kennedy 64, Radford 82*	*Wilson*	*Rice*	*McNab*	*Storey*	*Simpson*	*Kelly*	*Armstrong*	*Ball*	*Radford*	*Kennedy*	*George*	
		Home	Away					Ref: A Morrissey	Both sides throw caution to the wind in this goal-feast. Alderson and Stein take advantage of slack marking and Alderson sets up Cross's goal. Pat Rice volleys home Alan Ball's pass. Kennedy and Radford pull the Gunners level as City ease off. Bob Wilson plays his penultimate game.											
Average		23,280	24,951																	

League Cup					F-A	H-T	Scorers, Times, and Referees	1	2	3	4	5	6	7	8	9	10	11	12 sub used
2	H	DARLINGTON	3	W	5-1	3-1	Stein 12, 60, 84, Coop 25, Green 28	Glazier	Coop	Holmes	Mortimer	Craven	Dugdale	Smith	Alderson	Stein	Green	Hutchison	
8/10		8,769	*4:24*				*Cattrell 13*	*Morritt*	*Horner*	*Jones*	*Cattrell*	*Barker*	*Nattress*	*Burluraux*	*Sinclair*	*Yeats*	*Duffy**	*Sproates*	*McMahon*
							Ref: J Wrennall	An emphatic victory against chivalrous opponents. Stein's hat-trick are scored at close-range against an iffy defence. Coop heads home Hutch's cross. Stein sets up Green. Cattrell's is the pick of the bunch, a 30-yarder which Glazier barely saw. McMahon is a former City youth player.											
3	A	BRISTOL CITY	7	D	2-2	1-1	Smith 22, Cartwright 69	Glazier	Coop	Holmes	Mortimer	Parker	Dugdale	Smith	Alderson	Stein	Cartwright	Hutchison	
30/10		*19,129*	*2:4*				*Gould 10, 52*	*Bond*	*Sweeney*	*Drysdale*	*Emmanuel*	*Rodgers*	*Merrick*	*Tainton*	*Ritchie*	*Gould*	*Gow*	*Fear*	
							Ref: A Oliver	The Sky Blues only just survive as Bobby Gould haunts his old club. His first goal is a superb turn and volley, and then he wriggles through to poach a second. Wilf Smith scores with a great header from Coop's cross. Cartwright saves the day with a stooping header from Hutch's cross.											
3R	H	BRISTOL CITY	10	W	2-1	2-1	Alderson 20, 31	Glazier	Coop	Holmes	Mortimer	Philpotts	Dugdale	Cartwright	Alderson	Stein	McGuire	Hutchison	
6/11		13,127	*2:5*				*Whitehead 43*	*Bond*	*Tainton*	*Drysdale*	*Sweeney*	*Rodgers*	*Merrick*	*Whitehead*	*Ritchie*	*Gould*	*Gow*	*Gillies**	*Fear*
							Ref: A Oliver	Alan Dicks' aggressive Bristol lose a memorable tie as Alderson breaks his scoring drought. He volleys home from Stein's flick and heads in a left-wing cross. Dugdale keeps tight control on Bobby Gould this time and Philpotts has a much better game, going close with two headers.											
4	H	STOKE	15	W	2-1	1-1	Green 41, Stein 68	Glazier	Coop	Holmes	McGuire	Parker	Dugdale	Cartwright	Alderson	Stein	Green	Hutchison	
20/11		17,434	*17*				*Hurst 35*	*Farmer*	*Marsh*	*Pejic*	*Mahoney*	*Dodd*	*Jump*	*Robertson*	*Greenhoff*	*Ritchie*	*Hurst*	*Haselgrave*	
							Ref: R Challis	City borrow generators to power the floodlights because of the power crisis. A great comeback by City after going behind to Hurst's super goal means their poor League form is forgotten. Green headed in Hutch's cross. Colin Stein scores the winner after Green and Alderson miss chances.											
QF	H	MANCHESTER C	8	D	2-2	1-1	Alderson 22, 56	Glazier	Coop	Holmes !	McGuire	Dugdale	Parker	Cartwright	Alderson	Stein	Green*	Hutchison	Cattlin
19/12		12,491	*15*				*Booth 19, Leman 61*	*MacRae*	*Pardoe*	*Donachie*	*Doyle*	*Booth*	*Towers*	*Summerbee*	*Bell*	*Marsh*	*Lee*	*Leman*	
							Ref: M Sinclair	A midweek afternoon kick-off because of the power crisis. A gutsy performance earns City a replay. Jimmy Holmes is sent off after 18 minutes for allegedly retaliating on Lee by lifting his knee. Brian Alderson swerved in a free-kick and hit a screamer after a great run by Cartwright.											
QF	A	MANCHESTER C	12	L	2-4	1-0	Alderson 35, 67	Glazier	Coop	Holmes	McGuire	Craven	Dugdale	Cartwright	Alderson	Stein	Carr	Hutchison	
R 16/1		*25,409*	*13*				*Summerbee 65, Lee 78, 81p, Law 88*	*MacRae*	*Barrett*	*Donachie*	*Doyle*	*Booth*	*Towers*	*Summerbee*	*Bell*	*Lee*	*Law*	*Marsh*	
							Ref: P Partridge	A hoax bomb scare precedes an explosive match that has the crowd roaring. MacRae fails to hold Alderson's shot and is then beaten by power of the second. Summerbee heads in. Glazier boobs. Carr fouls Bell for the penalty. Law gives the score a false look. Man City meet Plymouth.											

FA Cup								1	2	3	4	5	6	7	8	9	10	11	12 sub used
3	A	SHEFFIELD WED	11	D	0-0	0-0		Glazier	Coop	Holmes	Carr	Craven	Dugdale	McGuire	Alderson	Stein	Cross	Hutchison*	Cartwright
5/1		*16,799*	*2:20*					*Springett*	*Cameron*	*Knighton*	*Thompson*	*Eustace*	*Shaw*	*Potts*	*Coyle*	*Sunley*	*Craig*	*Prendergast**	*Joicey*
							Ref: R Matthewson	A poor game on a disgraceful muddy pitch. Wednesday are managerless after Derek Dooley's Xmas Eve sacking. Few chances with defences on top. Glazier saves well from Prendergast and Coyle. Springett saves from Stein and Cross, and Thompson clears off the line from Stein..											
3R	H	SHEFFIELD WED	11	W	3-1	1-0	Cross 6, Hutchison 55, Coop 85p	Glazier	Coop	Holmes	McGuire	Craven	Dugdale	Carr	Alderson*	Stein	Cross	Hutchison	Cartwright
8/1		13,824	*2:20*				*Sunley 48*	*Springett*	*Cameron*	*Knighton*	*Thompson*	*Eustace*	*Mullen*	*Potts*	*Coyle*	*Sunley**	*Joicey*	*Henderson*	*Prudham*
							Ref: R Matthewson	Kick-off is at 1.30 p.m. The power crisis means a single sheet programme. City are rarely in trouble and miss a hatful of chances. Cross scores a classic header. Hutch scores with a superb right-footer. Coop scores after Knighton fouls Stein. Former City man Brian Joicey sets up Sunley.											
4	H	DERBY	14	D	0-0	0-0		Glazier	Coop	Holmes	McGuire	Craven	Dugdale	Cartwright	Alderson	Cross	Carr	Hutchison	
27/1		41,281	*5*					*Boulton*	*Webster*	*Nish*	*Newton*	*McFarland*	*Todd*	*Powell*	*Gemmill*	*Bourne*	*Hector*	*Hinton*	
							Ref: B Homewood	City's first ever Sunday game with a 2.15 kick-off. Biggest Cup crowd since 1963. Defences on top and few chances for below-par home side. Dugdale and Cartwright hit the post. Bill Glazier saves well from Henry Newton. Ref turns down strong City penalty appeals in 90th minute.											

Rd	Venue	Opponent	Pos	Res	Score	HT	Scorers, Times, Referees	1	2	3	4	5	6	7	8	9	10	11	12 sub used
4R	A	DERBY	14	W	1-0	0-0	Cross 95	Glazier	Coop	Holmes	Mortimer	Craven	Dugdale	Cartwright	Alderson	Cross	Cattlin	Hutchison	
30/1		*31,907*	*5*		*aet*			*Boulton*	*Webster*	*Nish*	*Newton*	*McFarland*	*Todd*	*Powell**	*Gemmill*	*Bourne*	*Hector*	*Hinton*	*Davies*
							Ref: B Homewood	Another great team performance at Derby. Bookies offer 5-1 against City. The Rams have the wind in the first half and Glazier saves well from Hector, Newton and Nish. Cross torments McFarland, heads in Cartwright's cross and has two disallowed. City's stamina sees them through.											
5	H	QP RANGERS	15	D	0-0	0-0		Glazier	Smith	Holmes	Mortimer	Craven	Dugdale	Cartwright	Alderson	Cross	Carr	Hutchison	
16/2		30,310	*8*					*Parkes*	*Hazell*	*Gillard*	*Venables*	*Mancini*	*McLintock*	*Thomas*	*Francis*	*Leach*	*Bowles*	*Givens*	
							Ref: T Reynolds	A classic cup-tie which had everything but goals. Non-stop action with two strong City penalty appeals turned down. Francis holds back Carr and Hazell handles. Glazier and Parkes are the heroes, the latter with a world-class save from Carr and a last-minute stop from Les Cartwright.											
5R	A	QP RANGERS	15	L	2-3	1-1	Cross 21, 60	Glazier	Smith	Holmes	Mortimer	Craven	Dugdale	Cartwright	Alderson	Cross	Carr	Hutchison	
19/2		*28,010*	*8*				*Givens 23, Thomas 61, Bowles 90*	*Parkes*	*Hazell*	*Gillard*	*Venables*	*Mancini*	*McLintock*	*Thomas*	*Francis*	*Leach*	*Bowles*	*Givens*	
							Ref: T Reynolds	In a pulsating and dramatic tie QPR reach the quarter-finals for first time. Twice Cross heads City ahead. Givens, with a header from Venables' chip and Dave Thomas from Givens' cross, set up the finale. City are unlucky as Bowles bends a free-kick round the wall with the last kick.											

			Home					Away					
		P	W	D	L	F	A	W	D	L	F	A	Pts
1	Leeds	42	12	8	1	38	18	12	6	3	28	13	62
2	Liverpool	42	18	2	1	34	11	4	11	6	18	20	57
3	Derby	42	13	7	1	40	16	4	7	10	12	26	48
4	Ipswich	42	10	7	4	38	21	8	4	9	29	37	47
5	Stoke	42	13	6	2	39	15	2	10	9	15	27	46
6	Burnley	42	10	9	2	29	16	6	5	10	27	37	46
7	Everton	42	12	7	2	29	14	4	5	12	21	34	44
8	QP Rangers	42	8	10	3	30	17	5	7	9	26	35	43
9	Leicester	42	10	7	4	35	17	3	9	9	16	24	42
10	Arsenal	42	9	7	5	23	16	5	7	9	26	35	42
11	Tottenham	42	9	4	8	26	27	5	10	6	19	23	42
12	Wolves	42	11	6	4	30	18	2	9	10	19	31	41
13	Sheffield Utd	42	7	7	7	25	22	7	5	9	19	27	40
14	Manchester C	42	10	7	4	25	17	4	5	12	14	29	40
15	Newcastle	42	9	6	6	28	21	4	6	11	21	27	38
16	COVENTRY	42	10	5	6	25	18	4	5	12	18	36	38
17	Chelsea	42	9	4	8	36	29	3	9	9	20	31	37
18	West Ham	42	7	7	7	36	32	4	8	9	19	28	37
19	Birmingham	42	10	7	4	30	21	2	6	13	22	43	37
20	Southampton	42	8	10	3	30	20	3	4	14	17	48	36
21	Manchester U	42	7	7	7	23	20	3	5	13	15	28	32
22	Norwich	42	6	9	6	25	27	1	6	14	12	35	29
		924	218	149	95	674	433	95	149	218	433	674	924

Odds & ends

Double wins: (2) Manchester U, Sheffield Utd.
Double losses: (4) Everton, Ipswich, Birmingham, QP Rangers.

Won from behind: (1) Stoke LC (h).
Lost from in front: (4) Everton (h), Leicester (h), Manchester C LC (a), QP Rangers FAC (a).

High spots: The excellent start which saw the team reach their highest position (2nd) in their history at the end of September.
The biggest home Cup crowd for 11 years watched the Derby tie.
Reaching the last eight of the League Cup.

Low spots: Losing in both cups after leading.
Six defeats in seven League games in the autumn.

Red cards: City – Holmes (Manchester City LC h).

Player of the Year: Bill Glazier.
Ever-presents: (0).
Hat-tricks: (1) Colin Stein.
Opposing hat-tricks: (0).
Leading scorer: (15) Brian Alderson.

	Appearances						Goals			
	Lge	*Sub*	LC	*Sub*	FAC	*Sub*	**Lge**	LC	FAC	**Tot**
Alderson, Brian	**40**		6		6		**9**	6		**15**
Carr, Willie	**12**	*1*	1		5		**1**			**1**
Cartwright, Les	**17**	*6*	5		4	*2*	**2**	1		**3**
Cattlin, Chris	**5**	*1*		*1*	1					
Coop, Mick	**30**		6		4		**5**	1	1	**7**
Craven, John	**30**		2		6		**3**			**3**
Cross, David	**26**				6		**8**		4	**12**
Dugdale, Alan	**39**		6		6					
Glazier, Bill	**40**		6		6					
Green, Alan	**14**	*3*	3				**4**	2		**6**
Hindley, Peter	**9**									
Holmes, Jimmy	**41**		6		6		**1**			**1**
Hunt, Ernie	**3**	*1*								
Hutchison, Tommy	**41**		6		6		**3**		1	**4**
McGuire, Mick	**19**	*5*	4		3					
Mortimer, Dennis	**33**		3		3		**1**			**1**
Parker, Bobby	**7**	*1*	3							
Philpotts, David	**3**		1							
Ramsbottom, Neil	**2**									
Smith, Wilf	**23**	*1*	2		2			1		**1**
Stein, Colin	**28**		6		2		**6**	4		**10**
21 players used	**462**	*19*	66	*1*	66		**43**	15	6	**64**

No	Date		Att	Pos	Pt	F-A	H-T	Scorers, Times, and Referees	1	2	3	4	5	6	7	8	9	10	11	12 sub used
1	A	NEWCASTLE			L	2-3	0-1	Alderson 81, Hutchison 86	Ramsbottom	Smith	Cattlin	Mortimer	Hindley	Dugdale	Coop	Alderson	Stein	Carr	Hutchison	
	17/8		*35,938*		0			*Kennedy 16, Macdonald 58, Howard 82*	*McFaul*	*Nattrass*	*Kennedy**	*Smith*	*Keeley*	*Howard*	*Burns*	*Cassidy*	*Macdonald*	*Tudor*	*Hibbitt*	*Craig*
								Ref: H Williams	City start as relegation favourites. The defence shows why Larry Lloyd has been bought from Liverpool for £240,000. Kennedy's deflected shot and Macdonald's screamer look enough. A late flurry with two City headers and Howard's effort from a narrow angle. Craven suspended.											
2	A	DERBY			D	1-1	1-0	Mortimer 21	Ramsbottom	Hindley	Cattlin	Mortimer	**Lloyd**	Dugdale	Craven*	Alderson	Stein	Cross	Hutchison	Coop
	21/8		*25,717*		1			*Lee 68*	*Boulton*	*Webster*	*Nish*	*Rioch*	*Daniel*	*Todd*	*Powell*	*Gemmill*	*Davies*	*Hector**	*Lee*	*Bourne*
								Ref: R Capel	A new away kit of red shirts and blue shorts proves lucky. Lloyd looks solid at the back and stand-in Ramsbottom has a blinder, making seven second-half saves. Craven's cross is buried from 25 yards by Mortimer. Francis Lee scores on his home debut after Powell's shot is blocked.											
3	H	CHELSEA		19	L	1-3	0-1	Cross 68	Ramsbottom	Hindley	Cattlin	Mortimer	Lloyd	Dugdale	McGuire	Alderson	Stein	Cross	Hutchison	
	24/8		21,246	*11*	1			*Cooke 44, Garner 60, Locke 66*	*Bonetti*	*Locke*	*Houseman*	*Hollins*	*Droy*	*Harris*	*Kember*	*Hay*	*Cooke*	*Garner*	*Sissons*	
								Ref: M Lowe	Lethargic City lose to three soft goals. With no Coventry ball winner, Chelsea have it all their own way. Ramsbottom allows Cooke's 25-yarder to creep in. He also leaves his line too soon for Garner's goal. Locke heads in Cattlin's sliced clearance. Cross nets after the ball has gone out.											
4	H	DERBY		19	D	1-1	0-1	Carr 77	Ramsbottom	Hindley	Cattlin	Mortimer	Lloyd	Dugdale	Carr	Alderson	Stein	McGuire	Hutchison	
	27/8		18,659	*7*	2			*Davies 20*	*Boulton*	*Webster*	*Nish*	*Rioch*	*Thomas*	*Todd*	*Powell*	*Gemmill*	*Davies*	*Hector*	*Lee*	
								Ref: J Williams	Never a classic, but an exciting finish with City going for a win that would have been undeserved. Todd's 40-yard pass finds Davies clear. Carr, back to form, sends Todd the wrong way and jabs past Boulton. Hutchison sparkles and Nish is booked for fouling him. Derby are unbeaten.											
5	A	BURNLEY		22	L	0-3	0-1		Glazier	Hindley	Cattlin	Mortimer	Lloyd	Dugdale	McGuire	Alderson	Stein	Carr	Hutchison	
	31/8		*14,619*	*16*	2			*Hankin 6, Noble 50, James 89*	*Stevenson*	*Newton*	*Brennan*	*Ingham*	*Waldron*	*Rodaway*	*Noble*	*Hankin*	*Fletcher*	*Collins*	*James*	
								Ref: P Partridge	City are in control for long spells but are let down by defensive errors. Burnley gain their first win. Hankin heads in unmarked. Dugdale and Lloyd are pulled apart as Noble heads in. James scores from 25 yards. Stevenson makes three good saves, the best from Stein's six-yard volley.											
6	H	MANCHESTER C		20	D	2-2	1-0	Alderson 19, Stein 53	Glazier	**Oakey**	Cattlin	Mortimer	Lloyd	Dugdale	McGuire	Alderson	Stein	Carr	Hutchison	
	7/9		15,555	*3*	3			*Marsh 70, Oakes 84*	*MacRae*	*Barrett*	*Donachie*	*Doyle*	*Booth*	*Oakes*	*Summerbee*	*Bell*	*Marsh*	*Hartford*	*Tueart*	
								Ref: T Spencer	Two spectacular goals in a gale-force wind deny City their first win. Alderson's back-header and Stein's shot from a rebound look enough. Captain Marsh scores with a left-footer. Oakes blasts in a 35-yarder but Marsh looks offside. Oakey impresses on debut. Milne away scouting.											
7	A	STOKE		21	L	0-2	0-0		Ramsbottom	Oakey	Cattlin	Mortimer	Lloyd	Hindley	McGuire	Alderson	Cross	Holmes	Hutchison	
	14/9		*22,842*	*4*	3			*Mahoney 59, Ritchie 84*	*Farmer*	*Marsh*	*Pejic*	*Mahoney*	*Smith*	*Dodd*	*Haselgrave*	*Greenhoff*	*Ritchie*	*Hudson*	*Salmons**	*Conroy*
								Ref: H Hackney	Injury-hit Sky Blues are benevolent to the Potters, missing five chances before Stoke score. Greenhoff sets up Mahoney after a fast break and poor defending by Lloyd. John Ritchie's unstoppable volley clinches it. Consistent Mortimer is invited to Don Revie's England get-together.											
8	H	EVERTON		22	D	1-1	0-0	Holmes 52p	Ramsbottom	Oakey	Cattlin	Mortimer	Lloyd	Hindley	Cartwright	Alderson	Cross	Holmes	Hutchison	
	21/9		**15,217**	*5*	4			*Latchford 59*	*Davies*	*Bernard*	*Seargeant*	*Lyons*	*Kenyon*	*Buckley*	*Kenny**	*Dobson*	*Pearson*	*Latchford*	*Clements*	*Connolly*
								Ref: B Daniels	Coventry's smallest gate since 1963. Nervous Coventry are riddled with tension and throw away Holmes' penalty lead after Lyons fouls Cross. Latchford looks offside as he runs on to Lyons' through-ball to equalise. Alderson hits the post ten minutes from time. Larry Lloyd looks unfit.											
9	H	LUTON		19	W	2-1	2-0	Stein 8, Cross 39	Ramsbottom	Oakey	Cattlin	Mortimer	Lloyd	Hindley	Holmes	Alderson	Stein	Cross	Hutchison	
	24/9		15,643	*21*	6			*Jim Ryan 83p*	*Barber*	*Shanks*	*Thomson*	*Anderson*	*Faulkner*	*John Ryan*	*Hindson*	*Jim Ryan*	*Butlin*	*West*	*Alston*	
								Ref: E Jolly	A sparkling display earns the first win. Hutchison and Mortimer are devastating and set up Oakey to cross for Stein's header. City waste three chances before Cross pounces on John Ryan's back-pass. Luton are outclassed but Jim Ryan is sent sprawling by Lloyd. Luton are still winless.											
10	A	LEICESTER		15	W	1-0	0-0	Holmes 86	Ramsbottom	Oakey	Cattlin	Mortimer	Lloyd	Hindley	Holmes	Alderson	Stein	Cross	Hutchison	
	28/9		*21,354*	*16*	8				*Shilton*	*Whitworth*	*Rofe*	*Sammels*	*Munro*	*Cross*	*Weller*	*Earle*	*Worthington*	*Woollett*	*Glover*	
								Ref: H New	Transfer-listed Shilton is booed as he makes his first appearance of the season. A determined performance from the Sky Blues. Mortimer touches a free-kick to Holmes who scores with a slight deflection from 25 yards. Hutchison hits the bar. Ramsbottom saves from Sammels.											

No	Venue	Opponent / Date	Att	Pos	Res	F-A	H-T	Scorers, Times, and Referees	1	2	3	4	5	6	7	8	9	10	11	12 sub used
11	A	BIRMINGHAM		14	W	2-1	1-0	Lloyd 20, Holmes 75	Ramsbottom	Oakey	Cattlin	Mortimer	Lloyd	Hindley	Holmes	Alderson	Stein	Cross	Hutchison	
		5/10	*30,282*	19	10			*Francis 50p*	*Latchford*	*Martin*	*Bryant*	*Kendall*	*Gallagher*	*Pendrey*	*Campbell*	*Francis*	*Burns*	*Hatton*	*Taylor*	
								Ref: K Styles	Another fighting performance earns a merited win. Lloyd heads home after a corner. Cattlin handles and Francis scores a disputed penalty. Holmes beats Latchford from 20 yards with a shot which hits both posts and rolls in. City miss more chances. Lloyd and Hindley are majestic.											
12	H	WEST HAM		13	D	1-1	0-0	Hutchison 70	Ramsbottom	Oakey	Cattlin	Mortimer	Lloyd	Hindley	Holmes	Alderson	Stein	Cross	Hutchison	
		12/10	22,556	*12*	11			*Gould 77*	*Day*	*Coleman*	*Lampard*	*Bonds*	*Taylor*	*Lock*	*Jennings*	*Paddon*	*Gould*	*Brooking*	*Robson*	
								Ref: L Hayes	A disappointing match with the stars outshone by others. Day lets Hutchison's corner slip through his hands. Gould volleyed home a 20-yard dipping shot after Lloyd's header out. West Ham are unlucky with a late penalty appeal as Hindley appeared to handle. Gould booed as usual.											
13	A	MIDDLESBROUGH		15	D	4-4	1-2	Stein 21, Cross 56, Holmes 64, 87	Ramsbottom	Oakey	Cattlin	Mortimer	Lloyd	Hindley	Holmes	Craven	Stein*	Cross	Hutchison	Alderson
		19/10	*25,499*	*5*	12			*Souness 26, 44, Mills 47, Foggon 72*	*Platt*	*Craggs*	*Spraggon*	*Souness*	*Boam*	*Maddren*	*Murdoch*	*Mills*	*Hickton**	*Foggon*	*Armstrong*	*Willey*
								Ref: J Rice	A humdinger. Stein is injured but scores. Souness hits a scorcher, then a deflected free-kick. Mills nets from close range, Cross with a header, Holmes with two 20-yarders. Foggon pounces after Hickton's shot is saved. Willie Carr fails a medical and his £240,000 move to Wolves is off.											
14	H	CARLISLE		14	W	2-1	1-1	Lloyd 15, 64	Ramsbottom	Oakey	Cattlin	Mortimer	Lloyd	Hindley	Holmes	Craven	Stein	Cross*	Hutchison	Alderson
		26/10	16,970	*15*	14			*Clarke F 20*	*Clarke T*	*Carr*	*Gorman*	*Balderstone*	*Green*	*Parker*	*Martin*	*Train*	*Clarke F**	*Owen*	*Barry*	*McIlmoyle*
								Ref: M Sinclair	A poor game, but City are seven games unbeaten. Carlisle, captained by Bobby Parker, beat Derby 3-0 last week but are finding Div 1 tough. Lloyd turns in an uncleared corner and heads in from Mortimer's cross. Ramsbottom drops Martin's cross and Frank Clarke nips in to score.											
15	A	QP RANGERS		15	L	0-2	0-1		Ramsbottom	Oakey	Cattlin	Mortimer	Lloyd	Hindley	Holmes	Craven*	Cross	Carr	Hutchison	Green
		2/11	*17,256*	*16*	14			*Bowles 41, Givens 81*	*Parkes*	*Clement*	*Gillard*	*Hazell*	*McLintock*	*Webb*	*Thomas*	*Rogers*	*Leach**	*Bowles*	*Givens*	*Beck*
								Ref: P Partridge	New England cap Gerry Francis has flu. Norway's King Olaf sees lop-sided City lose the first game in eight. There seems no danger as Bowles nets from 20 yards. Don Givens' goal is his sixth in eight days, after a hat-trick for Eire in midweek. City rarely threaten with just one striker.											
16	H	LEEDS		15	L	1-3	0-2	Cross 89	Ramsbottom	Oakey	Cattlin	Mortimer	Craven	Hindley	Holmes	Carr	Stein	Cross	Hutchison	
		9/11	**25,460**	*16*	14			*O'Hare 24, Hindley 26 (og), Bremner 71*	*Harvey*	*Reaney*	*Cooper*	*Yorath*	*McQueen*	*Cherry*	*Lorimer*	*Clarke*	*O'Hare*	*Bremner*	*Madeley*	
								Ref: D Nippard	Under Jimmy Armfield Leeds are recovering from the brief Brian Clough era. They still have too much for a poor City who make errors galore. Craven allows a cross to reach John O'Hare. Ramsbottom is lobbed by Hindley from 30 yards and lets Billy Bremner's shot through his hands.											
17	A	CHELSEA		14	D	3-3	2-2	Cross 4, Craven 44, Hutchison 84	Glazier	Oakey*	Cattlin	Mortimer	Craven	Hindley	Holmes	Carr	Stein	Cross	Hutchison	Green
		13/11	*11,048*	*19*	15			*Garner 27, Garland 40, Cooke 60*	*Bonetti*	*Locke*	*Harris*	*Hay*	*Droy*	*Hinton**	*Kember*	*Garner*	*Garland*	*Houseman*	*Cooke*	*Britton*
								Ref: R Challis	Chelsea's lowest crowd of the season. The rain lashes down and the quagmire pitch causes mistakes galore. Ron Suart is the new Chelsea boss. Cross scores with a header, Craven from 25 yards, Hutch near the end from Stein's pass. Cooke spots Glazier off his line to score the best goal.											
18	A	IPSWICH		16	L	**0-4**	0-0		Glazier	Smith	Cattlin	Mortimer	Lloyd	Hindley	Holmes	Carr	Stein	Cross	Hutchison	
		16/11	*21,172*	*1*	15			*Johnson 47, 60, 72, Talbot 64*	*Sivell*	*Mills*	*Harper*	*Talbot*	*Hunter*	*Beattie*	*Hamilton**	*Viljoen*	*Johnson*	*Whymark*	*Woods*	*Lambert*
								Ref: P Walters	A controversial first goal as David Johnson looks offside, but it opens the floodgates. Glazier saves Talbot's first-half penalty for accidental handball. Johnson scores from ten yards and gets his 'trick' with a header. Talbot's is a header. Lloyd upsets the crowd by dropping his shorts.											
19	H	ARSENAL		15	W	**3-0**	1-0	Mortimer 5, Stein 52p, Carr 73p	Glazier	Smith	Cattlin	Mortimer	Lloyd*	Hindley	Green	Carr	Stein	Cross	Hutchison	Cartwright
		23/11	16,095	*19*	17				*Rimmer*	*Rice*	*McNab*	*Kelly*	*Simpson*	*Powling*	*Armstrong*	*Ball*	*Radford*	*Kidd*	*Brady**	*George*
								Ref: W Gow	Security is high after recent Midland bombings, but the second half hoax doesn't dampen City's fervour. Mortimer sends Rimmer the wrong way from 25 yards. Brady trips Green for the first spot-kick. Powling fouls Stein for the other. Coventry look well-balanced. Arsenal are poor.											
20	H	LIVERPOOL		15	D	1-1	1-0	Stein 19p	Glazier	Smith	Cattlin	Mortimer	Craven	Hindley	Green	Carr	Stein	Cross	Hutchison	
		30/11	22,778	*3*	18			*Keegan 48*	*Clemence*	*Smith*	*Lindsay*	*Thompson*	*Cormack*	*Hughes*	*Keegan*	*McDermott*	*Heighway*	*Kennedy*	*Callaghan*	
								Ref: A Morrissey	Toshack is rested after his move to Leicester falls through for medical reasons. In a thrilling match Lindsay fouls Green for the penalty. Kevin Keegan's back-header squares matters. Cross's 77th-minute effort is ruled out for offside. Glazier, fresh from his testimonial, is in superb form.											
21	A	WOLVES		16	L	0-2	0-0		Glazier	Oakey	Cattlin	Mortimer	Craven	Hindley	Green	Carr	Stein	Cross	Hutchison	
		7/12	*20,002*	*14*	18			*Kindon 61, 64*	*Parkes*	*Palmer*	*Parkin*	*Bailey*	*Munro*	*McAlle*	*Hibbitt*	*Powell*	*Richards*	*Kindon*	*Wagstaffe*	
								Ref: R Matthewson	City more than match Wolves for an hour but are let down by more errors. Craven gives Richards too much space and his header is parried to Steve Kindon. Kindon capitalises again on more defensive frailties. Willie Carr shows that his fitness is not a problem with a fine performance.											

No	Date		Att	Pos	Pt	F-A	H-T	Scorers, Times, and Referees	1	2	3	4	5	6	7	8	9	10	11	12 sub used
22	H	NEWCASTLE		15	W	2-0	2-0	Cross 11, Lloyd 40	Ramsbottom	Oakey*	Cattlin	Mortimer	Lloyd	Hindley	Green	Carr	Stein	Cross	Hutchison	Craven
	14/12		15,585	*12*	20				*McFaul*	*Nattrass*	*Clark*	*Cannell*	*Keeley*	*Howard*	*Burns*	*Kennedy*	*Macdonald*	*Tudor*	*Bruce**	*Barrowclough*
								Ref: K McNally	City deserve a much bigger win in front of Match of the Day cameras. Hutchison sets up Cross's shot and Lloyd lashes home Stein's header. Cross limps throughout and Oakey has a severe cut on his head after a clash with Tudor. Four Newcastle players are booked in frustration.											
23	A	SHEFFIELD UTD		16	L	0-1	0-1		Ramsbottom	Smith	Cattlin	Mortimer	Lloyd	Hindley*	Cartwright	Green	Stein	Carr	Hutchison	Holmes
	20/12		*14,694*	*12*	20			*Dearden 42*	*Brown*	*Badger*	*Hemsley*	*Eddy*	*Colquhoun*	*Franks*	*Woodward*	*Bradford*	*Dearden**	*Currie*	*Field*	*Cammack*
								Ref: R Lee	A Friday night game to avoid Xmas shopping but still the lowest home crowd of the season. A tedious game won by Billy Dearden's flick from Tony Field's header. City's injury worries mount as Hindley limps off. City's board announce that players must be sold to balance the books.											
24	H	STOKE		16	W	2-0	0-0	Cross 65, Hutchison 73	Ramsbottom	Smith	Cattlin	Mortimer	Lloyd	Dugdale	Carr	Alderson	Stein	Cross	Hutchison	
	26/12		22,380	*7*	22				*Shilton*	*Dodd*	*Pejic*	*Mahoney*	*Smith*	*Skeels*	*Robertson**	*Greenhoff*	*Hurst*	*Hudson*	*Salmons*	*Marsh*
								Ref: R Crabb	Title pretenders Stoke have lost three in a row since going top. Their scrooge-like performance deserves nothing. Cross beats the offside trap from Stein's pass. Hutch hits a thunderbolt from 25 yards after Stein's cross isn't cleared. Robertson breaks a leg in first min clash with Cattlin.											
25	A	TOTTENHAM		15	D	1-1	1-0	Stein 7	Ramsbottom	Smith	Cattlin	Craven *	Lloyd	Dugdale	Carr	Alderson	Stein	Cross	Hutchison	Holmes
	28/12		*20,307*	*17*	23			*Smith 75 (og)*	*Jennings*	*Kinnear*	*Knowles*	*Pratt*	*England*	*Naylor*	*Coates*	*Perryman*	*Chivers**	*Peters*	*Duncan*	*Neighbour*
								Ref: A Lees	A charitable display by the Sky Blues as they let Spurs off the hook. Mortimer is going to be out for three months with knee ligament problems and Ramsbottom hurts his back when pushed over a wall by Pratt. Stein buries Craven's through-ball. Smith, trying to clear, nudges the ball in.											
26	H	WOLVES		15	W	2-1	1-1	Carr 14, Lloyd 47	Ramsbottom	Oakey	Cattlin	Craven	Lloyd	Dugdale	Carr	Alderson	Stein	Cross	Hutchison	
	11/1		20,271	*14*	25			*Kindon 24*	*Parkes*	*Palmer*	*Parkin*	*Bailey*	*Munro*	*McAlle*	*Hibbitt*	*Powell**	*Richards*	*Kindon*	*Wagstaffe*	*Daley*
								Ref: K Styles	A lively, entertaining game and opportunity again for Carr to demonstrate his fitness. He is first to the ball after Brian Alderson's shot is half-cleared to head home. Steve Kindon is gifted a goal. Lloyd scores a glorious header from Carr's cross, but earns his third caution of the season.											
27	A	LIVERPOOL		15	L	1-2	0-1	Alderson 90	Ramsbottom	Oakey	Cattlin	Craven	Lloyd	Holmes	Carr	Alderson	Stein	Cross	Hutchison	
	18/1		***43,668***	*4*	25			*Heighway 34, Keegan 89*	*Clemence*	*Neal*	*Lindsay*	*Thompson*	*Cormack*	*Hughes*	*Keegan*	*Hall*	*Heighway**	*Toshack*	*Callaghan*	*Boersma*
								Ref: G Kew	Lloyd captains City on his Anfield return, but it's a seventh defeat at Anfield in eight seasons for City. Heighway nets from Thompson's header. Stein and John Toshack have goals ruled out. Kevin Keegan's late effort looks offside, but Brian Alderson scores directly from the re-start											
28	A	LEEDS		14	D	0-0	0-0		Ramsbottom	Oakey	Cattlin	Craven	Lloyd	Dugdale	Carr	Alderson	**Ferguson**	Green	Hutchison	
	1/2		*33,901*	*10*	26				*Harvey*	*Reaney*	*Gray F*	*Bremner*	*McQueen*	*Madeley*	*McKenzie*	*Clarke*	*Lorimer*	*Yorath*	*Gray E*	
								Ref: T Reynolds	A fine performance after City's Cup exit. Ferguson has an outstanding debut and almost scores. Leeds have only lost twice in 15 games since Clough left, but they now face a Cup replay with non-league Wimbledon. McGuire goes to Norwich for cut-price £65,000. More sales follow.											
29	H	QP RANGERS		15	D	1-1	1-1	Green 27	Ramsbottom	Oakey	Holmes	Craven	Lloyd	Dugdale	Carr	Alderson	Ferguson	Green	Hutchison	
	8/2		18,830	*12*	27			*Leach 44*	*Parkes*	*Clement*	*Gillard*	*Masson*	*McLintock*	*Webb*	*Thomas*	*Francis**	*Beck*	*Bowles*	*Givens*	*Leach*
								Ref: E Wallace	A dismal game which Rangers should have won. They have two goals disallowed and two good penalty appeals rejected. Carr and Ferguson create Green's super-strike. Leach flicks in Clements' cross. Recent signing Don Masson shines through the gloom. Chris Cattlin is suspended.											
30	H	TOTTENHAM		15	D	1-1	1-1	Alderson 43	Ramsbottom	Oakey	Holmes	Craven	Hindley	Dugdale	Carr	Alderson	Ferguson	Green*	Hutchison	Cartwright
	15/2		15,227	*18*	28			*Duncan 11*	*Jennings*	*Kinnear*	*Knowles*	*McAllister*	*England*	*Naylor*	*Conn*	*Perryman*	*Chivers*	*Peters*	*Duncan*	
								Ref: W Johnson	A lottery of a game played on a waterlogged pitch. Struggling Spurs have only won one in nine. Duncan scores after defensive errors. Alderson scores his 'best goal of the season' with a cannonball shot. Oakey sparkles as he has done for most of the season. Spurs look relegation certs.											
31	H	IPSWICH		15	W	3-1	0-0	Ferguson 72, Green 84, 89	Ramsbottom	Oakey	Cattlin	Cartwright	Lloyd	Dugdale	Carr	Alderson	Ferguson	Green	Hutchison	
	22/2		16,973	*6*	30			*Hunter 87*	*Sivell*	*Burley*	*Mills*	*Talbot*	*Hunter*	*Beattie*	*Hamilton*	*Viljoen*	*Johnson**	*Whymark*	*Lambert*	*Woods*
								Ref: P Willis	Lloyd is skipper in Craven's absence on a heavily sanded pitch. This is an easy victory over the title challengers. Ipswich hold out until the last 20 minutes. Ferguson nets from Green's cross. Green scores a tap-in, then outpaces defenders before finishing clinically. A standing ovation.											

No	H/A	Opponent	Att	Pos	Res/Pts	F-A	H-T	Scorers, Times, and Referees	1	2	3	4	5	6	7	8	9	10	11	12 sub used
32	H	BURNLEY		15	L	0-3	0-1		Ramsbottom	Oakey	Cattlin	Cartwright	Craven	Dugdale	Carr	Alderson	Ferguson	Green	Hutchison	
	1/3		17,358	*2*	30			*James 38, Noble 51, Fletcher 88*	*Stevenson*	*Newton*	*Flynn*	*Noble*	*Waldron*	*Thomson*	*Ingham*	*Hankin*	*Fletcher*	*Collins*	*James*	
								Ref: B Homewood	With only one defeat in ten, Burnley have joined the title hunt. They end City's ten-game unbeaten home run with ruthless finishing. City were on top for 20 minutes, but outplayed after the break. Lloyd is suspended. Coach Tom Casey goes to Grimsby as boss. Match of the Day on TV.											
33	A	LUTON		14	W	3-1	2-0	Alderson 9, 25, Green 79	Ramsbottom	Oakey	Cattlin	Cartwright	Craven	Dugdale*	Carr	Alderson	Ferguson	Green	Hutchison	Holmes
	8/3		*14,423*	*21*	32			*Aston 55*	*Horne*	*John Ryan*	*Buckley*	*Anderson*	*Faulkner*	*Futcher P*	*Jim Ryan*	*Alston*	*Futcher R*	*West*	*Aston*	
								Ref: H Davey	City plough through the mud and puddles for a comfortable victory, which leaves Luton in dire relegation trouble. Alderson nets from Green's run and cross, and from Cartwright's cross. Aston's prodded goal from Jim Ryan sparks Luton's revival, but Green nets with a clinical finish.											
34	H	LEICESTER		14	D	2-2	1-2	Green 9, Ferguson 48	Ramsbottom	Oakey	Cattlin	Craven	Lloyd	Dugdale	Cartwright	Alderson	Ferguson	Green	Hutchison	
	15/3		23,160	*19*	33			*Worthington 24, Lee 25*	*Wallington*	*Whitworth*	*Rofe*	*Lee*	*Blockley*	*Cross*	*Weller*	*Sammels*	*Worthington*	*Birchenall*	*Garland*	
								Ref: D Richardson	The sale of Carr and Stein raises £185,000 to balance the books. Leicester have the better of a muddy battle. Green scores from Alderson's cross. Worthington slams an equaliser and debut boy Garland sets up Lee's shot. Mick Ferguson heads home superbly from Hutch's cross.											
35	A	MANCHESTER C		14	L	0-1	0-0		Ramsbottom	Oakey	Cattlin	Craven	Lloyd	Dugdale	Cartwright	Alderson	Ferguson*	Green	Hutchison	Holmes
	22/3		*25,903*	*10*	33			*Tueart 61p*	*Corrigan*	*Hammond*	*Donachie*	*Doyle*	*Booth*	*Oakes*	*Summerbee*	*Bell*	*Royle*	*Keegan*	*Tueart*	
								Ref: K McNally	An uninspiring fixture, won with a dubious penalty for the second year running. The ref alleged Lloyd pushed Joe Royle, and Dennis Tueart scored. Both sides miss chances but City lose Ferguson after 29 minutes and struggle. Coventry deserve a draw. Rodney Marsh is suspended.											
36	H	SHEFFIELD UTD		13	D	2-2	0-0	Craven 67, Cross 71	Ramsbottom	Oakey*	Cattlin	Craven	Lloyd	Dugdale	Cartwright	Alderson	Cross	Green	Hutchison	Coop
	28/3		18,857	*8*	34			*Speight 51, Woodward 90*	*Brown*	*Badger*	*Bradford*	*Eddy*	*Colquhoun*	*Flynn*	*Woodward*	*Speight*	*Cammck**	*Currie*	*Field*	*Nicholl*
								Ref: C White	The Blades have only lost one in twelve and still have a title chance. A Good Friday night thriller. Speight scores from Bradford's cross. The dominant Craven scores a stunning volley. Cross dives amongst the boots to meet Hutch's cross. Woodward chips an equaliser at the death.											
37	A	EVERTON		16	L	0-1	0-1		Ramsbottom	Oakey	Cattlin	Craven	Lloyd	Dugdale	Cartwright	Alderson*	Cross	Green	Hutchison	Coop
	31/3		*39,770*	*1*	34			*Dobson 45*	*Davies*	*Bernard*	*Seargeant*	*Buckley*	*Kenyon*	*Hurst*	*Jones*	*Dobson*	*Lyons*	*Latchford*	*Telfer**	*Pearson*
								Ref: R Capey	Everton wear the leaders crown uneasily in a mediocre game on a cold Easter Monday. Martin Dobson, a £300,000 signing from Burnley, scores an unstoppable shot from Telfer's cross. Dai Davies has no shots to save. Graham Oakey outshines everyone again. Cattlin is booked.											
38	A	CARLISLE		15	D	0-0	0-0		Ramsbottom	Coop	Cattlin	Craven	Lloyd	Dugdale	Mortimer	Oakey	Cross	Green	Hutchison	
	5/4		***10,857***	*21*	35				*Clarke T*	*Carr*	*Gorman*	*Balderstone*	*Green*	*Parker*	*Martin*	*Train*	*Owen*	*Laidlaw*	*Clarke F**	*Prudham*
								Ref: A Porter	Carlisle are relegated today, despite beating title challengers Everton and Burnley over Easter. An uninspiring game but a well-won point for City. Dennis Mortimer returns from injury and shows skill. Hutch has a good penalty appeal rejected. The lowest Div 1 gate ever to watch City.											
39	A	ARSENAL		15	L	0-2	0-1		Ramsbottom	Oakey*	Cattlin	Craven	Lloyd	Dugdale	Mortimer	Holmes	Ferguson	Green	Hutchison	Alderson
	8/4		*17,291*	*17*	35			*Kidd 37, 60*	*Rimmer*	*Rice*	*Nelson*	*Storey*	*Mancini*	*Simpson*	*Matthews*	*Kelly*	*Hornsby*	*Kidd*	*Armstrong*	
								Ref: M Lowe	Arsenal are desperate for points in the relegation battle. City put on a much-improved display but still lack punch up front. Ferguson and Craven miss chances. Rimmer saves well from Mortimer. Kidd's shot skids under Ramsbottom but he and Hornsby look offside for the second.											
40	H	BIRMINGHAM		14	W	1-0	1-0	Green 27	Ramsbottom	Oakey	Cattlin	Craven	Lloyd	Dugdale	Mortimer	Alderson*	Ferguson	Green	Hutchison	Coop
	12/4		24,163	*18*	37				*Latchford*	*Page*	*Bryant*	*Kendall*	*Gallagher*	*Pendrey*	*Hendrie**	*Francis*	*Burns*	*Hatton*	*Taylor*	*Smith*
								Ref: R Matthewson	Blues have lost an FA Cup semi-final replay in midweek but fight hard. Both teams wear black armbands and stand to a minute's silence in memory of former player Peter Murphy. Oakey's 40-yard run creates the space for Green to power in a great shot. City squander more chances.											
41	A	WEST HAM		12	W	2-1	2-1	Green 3, Mortimer 45	Ramsbottom	Oakey	Cattlin !	Craven	Lloyd	Dugdale	Mortimer	Holmes	Ferguson	Green	Hutchison	
	19/4		*27,431*	*14*	39			*Holland 44*	*Day*	*Coleman*	*Lampard*	*Holland*	*McDowell*	*Lock*	*Jennings*	*Paddon**	*Taylor A*	*Brooking*	*Gould*	*Curbishley*
								Ref: R Tinkler	The Hammers have gone seven league games without a win but have reached Wembley. City play 82 minutes with ten men after Cattlin is sent off for retaliating to Gould's tackle. Green prodded in after a long ball caused panic. Pat Holland heads in. Mortimer scores from a free-kick.											
42	H	MIDDLESBROUGH		14	L	0-2	0-1		Ramsbottom	Oakey	Cattlin	Craven	Lloyd	Dugdale	Mortimer	Holmes*	Ferguson	Green	Hutchison	Alderson
	26/4		18,121	*7*	39			*Foggon 41, Hickton 65*	*Platt*	*Craggs*	*Cooper*	*Souness*	*Boam*	*Maddren*	*Murdoch*	*Mills*	*Hickton*	*Foggon*	*Armstrong*	
		Home	Away					Ref: A Robinson	Jack Charlton's men end a great first season back up with an easy win. Foggon and Hickton's headers are enough to beat lacklustre City. Jimmy Hill becomes managing director. Ron Wylie is new coach. Sir Jack Scamp replaces Peter Robins as chairman. Joe Mercer is on the board.											
Average		19,053	23,523																	

LEAGUE DIVISION 1 (CUP-TIES)

Manager: Gordon Milne

SEASON 1974-75

League Cup						F-A	H-T	Scorers, Times, and Referees	1	2	3	4	5	6	7	8	9	10	11	12 sub used
2	H	IPSWICH		20	L	1-2	1-0	Stein 19	Glazier	Oakey	Cattlin	Mortimer	Lloyd	Dugdale	McGuire*	Alderson	Stein	Carr	Hutchison	Craven
	10/9		*13,211*	*2*				*Whymark 58, Hamilton 68*	*Sivell*	*Burley*	*Mills*	*Talbot*	*Peddelty*	*Beattie*	*Hamilton*	*Viljoen*	*Woods*	*Whymark*	*Lambert*	
								Ref: R Matthewson												

A Jekyll and Hyde performance by City. After dominating the first half they fall apart once Ipswich levelled. Mortimer crosses for Stein to nod in. Hutchison and Alderson go close. Glazier misses a cross and Trevor Whymark heads in. Kevin Beattie chests down for Hamilton to score.

FA Cup						F-A	H-T	Scorers, Times, and Referees	1	2	3	4	5	6	7	8	9	10	11	12 sub used
3	H	NORWICH		15	W	2-0	2-0	Alderson 25, Lloyd 39	Ramsbottom	Oakey	Cattlin	Craven	Lloyd	Dugdale	Carr	Alderson*	Stein	Cross	Hutchison	Holmes
	4/1		19,265	*2:3*					*Keelan*	*Machin*	*Sullivan*	*Morris*	*Forbes*	*Stringer*	*Benson*	*McDougall*	*Boyer*	*Suggett*	*Livermore*	
								Ref: P Partridge												
4	H	ARSENAL		15	D	1-1	0-0	Alderson 57	Ramsbottom	Oakey	Cattlin	Craven	Lloyd	Dugdale	Carr	Alderson	Stein	Cross	Hutchison	
	25/1		31,239	*16*				*Ball 59*	*Rimmer*	*Rice*	*McNab*	*Storey*	*Mancini*	*Simpson*	*Armstrong*	*Ball*	*Radford*	*Kidd*	*George**	*Matthews*
								Ref: I Jones												
4R	A	ARSENAL		15	L	0-3	0-2		Ramsbottom	Oakey	Cattlin	Craven*	Lloyd	Dugdale	Carr	Alderson	Cross	Holmes	Hutchison	Cartwright
	29/1		*30,867*	*16*				*Armstrong 2, 41, Matthews 75*	*Rimmer*	*Rice*	*McNab*	*Matthews*	*Mancini*	*Simpson*	*Armstrong*	*Ball*	*Radford**	*Kidd*	*Storey*	*Brady*
								Ref: I Jones												

3 (Norwich): Norwich fall at the third round for seventh year in a row. City deserve bigger victory. Alderson scores his first goal since September with a first time shot. Lloyd's freak effort from 50 yards sails over Keelan without a bounce. The much vaunted McDougall and Boyer are well marked.

4 (Arsenal): A marvellous tie, played in wind, rain and sleet on a glue-pot pitch. Both sides responded to the super-charged atmosphere. Alderson nets left-footed from 18 yards. Ball scores easily after Dugdale and Ramsbottom get into a tizzy. Both sides have chances in a pulsating last half hour.

4R (Arsenal): City are outclassed after a bright first half. Armstrong's goals were his first for two years. He slid in Rice's low cross and headed in Matthews' deflected centre. In between City looked threatening, with Cross twice going close. Ball and Kidd set up Matthews. Arsenal now meet Leicester.

		Home						Away					
	P	W	D	L	F	A	W	D	L	F	A	Pts
1 Derby	42	14	4	3	41	18	7	7	7	26	31	53
2 Liverpool	42	14	5	2	44	17	6	6	9	16	22	51
3 Ipswich	42	17	2	2	47	14	6	3	12	19	30	51
4 Everton	42	10	9	2	33	19	6	9	6	23	23	50
5 Stoke	42	12	7	2	40	18	5	8	8	24	30	49
6 Sheffield Utd	42	12	7	2	35	20	6	6	9	23	31	49
7 Middlesbro	42	11	7	3	33	14	7	5	9	21	26	48
8 Manchester C	42	16	3	2	40	15	2	7	12	14	39	46
9 Leeds	42	10	8	3	34	20	6	5	10	23	29	45
10 Burnley	42	11	6	4	40	29	6	5	10	28	38	45
11 QP Rangers	42	10	4	7	25	17	6	6	9	29	37	42
12 Wolves	42	12	5	4	43	21	2	6	13	14	33	39
13 West Ham	42	10	6	5	38	22	3	7	11	20	37	39
14 COVENTRY	42	8	9	4	31	27	4	6	11	20	35	39
15 Newcastle	42	12	4	5	39	23	3	5	13	20	49	39
16 Arsenal	42	10	6	5	31	16	3	5	13	16	33	37
17 Birmingham	42	10	4	7	34	28	4	5	12	19	33	37
18 Leicester	42	8	7	6	25	17	4	5	12	21	43	36
19 Tottenham	42	8	4	9	29	27	5	4	12	23	36	34
20 Luton	42	8	6	7	27	26	3	5	13	20	39	33
21 Chelsea	42	4	9	8	22	31	5	6	10	20	41	33
22 Carlisle	42	8	2	11	22	21	4	3	14	21	38	29
	924	235	124	103	753	460	103	124	235	460	753	924

Odds & ends

Double wins: (2) Birmingham, Luton.
Double losses: (1) Burnley.

Won from behind: (0)
Lost from in front: (1) Ipswich LC (h).

High spots: Seven game unbeaten run in autumn.
4-4 at Middlesbrough.

Low spots: Eight games without a win, the worst start since 1919.
Defeat at Arsenal in an FA Cup replay, after leading in the first game.
Cut price sale of Willie Carr to Wolves for £80,000.

Red cards: City – Cattlin (West Ham a).

Player of the Year: Graham Oakey.
Ever-presents: (1) Tommy Hutchison.
Hat-tricks: (0).
Opposing hat-tricks: (1) Johnson (Ipswich).
Leading scorer: (8) Brian Alderson and David Cross.

	Appearances						Goals			
	Lge	*Sub*	LC	*Sub*	FAC	*Sub*	**Lge**	LC	FAC	**Tot**
Alderson, Brian	**27**	*4*	1		3		**6**		2	**8**
Carr, Willie	**23**		1		3		**3**			**3**
Cartwright, Les	**9**	*2*				*1*				
Cattlin, Chris	**40**		1		3					
Coop, Mick	**2**	*4*								
Craven, John	**25**	*1*		*1*	3		**2**			**2**
Cross, David	**25**				3		**8**			**8**
Dugdale, Alan	**24**		1		3					
Ferguson, Mick,	**12**						**2**			**2**
Glazier, Bill	**7**		1							
Green, Alan	**20**	*2*					**7**			**7**
Hindley, Peter	**23**									
Holmes, Jimmy	**18**	*4*			1	*1*	**5**			**5**
Hutchison, Tommy	**42**		1		3		**4**			**4**
Lloyd, Larry	**34**		1		3		**5**		1	**6**
McGuire, Mick	**5**		1							
Mortimer, Dennis	**29**		1				**3**			**3**
Oakey, Graham	**31**		1		3					
Ramsbottom, Neil	**35**				3					
Smith, Wilf	**7**									
Stein, Colin	**24**		1		2		**6**	1		**7**
21 players used	**462**						**51**	**1**	**3**	**55**

No	Date		Att	Pos	Pt		F-A	H-T	Scorers, Times, and Referees	1	2	3	4	5	6	7	8	9	10	11	12 sub used
1	A	EVERTON				W	**4-1**	2-1	Cross 6, 16, 72, Green 78	**King**	Oakey	**Brogan**	Craven	Holmes	Dugdale	Coop	Mortimer	Green	Cross	Hutchison	
	16/8		*32,343*		2				*Kenyon 29*	*Lawson*	*Bernard*	*Seargeant*	*Clements*	*Kenyon*	*Hurst*	*Lyons*	*Dobson*	*Latchford*	*Smallman*	*Pearson*	
									Ref: M Lowe	A stunning display which defies the bookies who tip City for relegation. Cross scores twice before Everton are awake, a header from Oakey's cross and a pounce after Lawson parries Hutch's stinging shot. Hurst's back-pass lets Cross in for his hat-trick. Green heads the fourth goal.											
2	H	DERBY				D	1-1	0-0	Coop 69	King	Oakey	Brogan	Craven	Dugdale	Holmes	Coop	Mortimer	Cross	Green	Hutchison	
	19/8		24,209		3				*McFarland 49*	*Boulton*	*Thomas*	*Nish*	*Rioch*	*McFarland*	*Todd*	*Newton*	*Gemmill*	*Lee*	*Bourne*	*George*	
									Ref: T Reynolds	The champions are lucky to get a point after Craven twice hits the post. McFarland scores after Bryan King is caught in two minds at David Nish's corner. Coop scores at the second attempt after Hutch's deflected shot found him in space. Free transfer man Jim Brogan looks a 'steal'.											
3	H	MANCHESTER C		4		W	2-0	1-0	Green 22, 87	King	Oakey	Brogan	Craven	Lloyd	Holmes	Coop	Mortimer	Cross	Green	Hutchison	
	23/8		21,115	*8*	5					*Corrigan*	*Hammond*	*Donachie*	*Doyle*	*Watson*	*Oakes*	*Hartford*	*Bell*	*Marsh*	*Royle**	*Tueart*	*Telford*
									Ref: C Thomas	A hard won victory over classy Manchester. Cross has a battle royal with England centre-half Dave Watson and sets up Green for the second. The tiny striker shows lethal finishing after taking Brogan's header for the first. Craven is booked for the third game in a row by fussy Thomas.											
4	A	MANCHESTER U		3		D	1-1	0-1	Green 68	King	Oakey	Brogan	Craven	Lloyd*	Holmes	Coop	Mortimer	Cross	Green	Hutchison	Ferguson
	27/8		***52,169***	*1*	6				*Pearson 23*	*Stepney*	*Forsyth*	*Houston*	*Jackson*	*Greenhoff B*	*Buchan*	*Coppell*	*McIlroy*	*Pearson*	*Macari*	*Daly*	
									Ref: P Partridge	Ice cool City end newly promoted United's 100% record and almost snatch a win. Lloyd limps off early on and Stuart Pearson's stunning shot makes it an uphill struggle in a red-hot atmosphere. Green fires wide. Mortimer hits the bar. Green scores after Cross intercepts a back-pass.											
5	A	ASTON VILLA		6		L	0-1	0-0		King	Oakey	Brogan	Craven	Dugdale	Holmes	Coop	Mortimer	Cross	Green	Hutchison	
	30/8		*41,026*	*12*	6				*Graydon 68*	*Cumbes*	*Robson*	*Aitken*	*Ross*	*Nicholl*	*Phillips*	*Graydon*	*Little*	*Leonard*	*Hamilton*	*Carrodus*	
									Ref: A Morrissey	City's first ever Div 1 game with Villa and the first league meeting since 1938. City seem to have extended their unbeaten run until an error by Oakey lets in Chico Hamilton, whose cross is spilled by King and Ray Graydon pounces. Brogan and transfer-listed Alan Dugdale are superb.											
6	H	IPSWICH		6		D	0-0	0-0		King	Oakey	Brogan	Craven	Dugdale	Holmes	Coop	Mortimer	Cross	Green	Hutchison	
	6/9		17,563	*15*	7					*Cooper*	*Burley*	*Mills*	*Talbot*	*Hunter*	*Beattie*	*Hamilton*	*Osborne*	*Johnson*	*Whymark**	*Lambert*	*Woods*
									Ref: R Tinkler	The low crowd reflects the fact that few fans are convinced by the good start. This is a boring game with few chances. City twice cleared Town efforts off the line. Mortimer's 20-yarder was the best home effort: it was well saved by Cooper. Barry Powell signs from Wolves for £75,000.											
7	A	SHEFFIELD UTD		4		W	1-0	1-0	Ferguson 31	King	Holmes	Brogan	Craven	Dugdale	**Powell**	Coop	Mortimer	Cross	Ferguson	Hutchison	
	13/9		*20,153*	*22*	9					*Brown*	*Badger*	*Hemsley*	*Eddy**	*Colquhoun*	*Franks*	*Woodward*	*Garbett*	*Guthrie*	*Currie*	*Speight*	*Irving*
									Ref: G Kew	The Blades have lost six out of seven and look doomed for the drop. The Sky Blues soak up pressure and catch them on the break. Ferguson scores after Powell heads down Coop's tantalising centre. Sheffield only create one real chance and King saves well from Guthrie's header.											
8	H	STOKE		9		L	0-3	0-1		King	Coop	Brogan	Craven	Dugdale	Holmes	Powell*	Mortimer	Cross	Green	Hutchison	Ferguson
	20/9		19,113	*12*	9				*Greenhoff 44, Moores 47, 77*	*Shilton*	*Marsh*	*Pejic*	*Mahoney*	*Dodd*	*Bloor*	*Haselgrave*	*Greenhoff*	*Moores*	*Hudson*	*Salmons*	
									Ref: H Hackney	Slick Stoke bring City down to earth after luckily surviving a first-half battering. City's lack of goal power is worrying and the defence was found wanting. The unmarked Greenhoff heads the first. Salmons' corner is touched in by Moores and Holmes' error lets in Moores again.											
9	H	MIDDLESBROUGH		10		L	0-1	0-1		King	Oakey	Brogan	Craven	Dugdale	Holmes	Coop	Mortimer	Cross	Green	Hutchison	
	23/9		15,132	*8*	9				*Mills 22*	*Platt*	*Craggs*	*Spraggon*	*Souness*	*Boam*	*Maddren*	*Brine*	*Mills*	*Hickton*	*Foggon*	*Armstrong*	
									Ref: A Morrissey	City fail to break down Jack Charlton's cynical eight-man Boro' defence. Despite being well in control, City create very few chances. King is at fault for the goal, misjudging a centre and allowing Foggon to head against the bar for David Mills to swoop. City deserve the slow handclap.											
10	A	LEICESTER		7		W	3-0	1-0	Craven 21, Cross 52, 56	King	Oakey	Brogan	Craven	Dugdale	Holmes	Coop	Mortimer	Cross	Green*	Hutchison	Powell
	27/9		*20,411*	*20*	11					*Wallington*	*Whitworth*	*Rofe*	*Kember*	*Sims*	*Birchenall*	*Weller*	*Alderson*	*Worthington*	*Sammels*	*Garland*	
									Ref: B Homewood	Leicester arrive without a win and after the first ten minutes are never in it. Cross is deadly, heading in Hutchison's crosses at the near post and the far. Craven swept in the first goal from a Hutch corner. King, away from the home critics, makes good saves from Alderson and Kember.											

No	H/A	Opponent	Att	Pos	Res/Pts	Score	H-T	Scorers, Times, and Referees	1	2	3	4	5	6	7	8	9	10	11	12
11	H	BURNLEY		11	L	1-2	0-0	Cross 67	King	Oakey	Brogan	Craven	Dugdale	Holmes	Mortimer	Coop	Cross	Ferguson	Hutchison	
4/10			15,471	18	11			*Hankin 56, James 90*	*Stevenson*	*Docherty*	*Newton*	*Morgan*	*Waldron*	*Thomson*	*Flynn*	*Hankin**	*Summerbee*	*Noble*	*James*	*Ingham*
								Ref: E Wallace	Burnley win a scrappy match in the second minute of injury-time. King is penalised for stepping out of the area. Newton touches a free-kick to James, whose shot finds a gap in the wall. Five bookings including Craven's fifth, and Docherty for a foul on Hutch which requires six stitches.											
12	A	ARSENAL		14	L	**0-5**	0-4		King	Coop	Brogan	Craven	Lloyd	Holmes	Powell	Mortimer	Cross	Green	Hutchison	
11/10			*19,234*	*13*	11			*Cropley 13, 30, Ball 26, Kidd 45, 71*	*Rimmer*	*Rice*	*Nelson*	*Powling*	*Simpson*	*O'Leary*	*Ball*	*Cropley**	*Stapleton*	*Kidd*	*Brady*	*Rostron*
								Ref: T Spencer	Arsenal end a run of eight games without a win by humiliating the Sky Blues. King has a nightmare but his cover is poor. City are overrun in all departments. Cropley scores two good goals but King is at fault for Ball's 30-yarder, Kidd's lob and Brady's shot which Kidd pounced on.											
13	H	LIVERPOOL		14	D	0-0	0-0		King	Coop	Brogan	Dugdale	Lloyd	Holmes	Powell	Mortimer	Cross	Green	Hutchison	
18/10			20,919	*5*	12				*Clemence*	*Neal*	*Lindsay*	*Thompson*	*Case**	*Hughes*	*Keegan*	*Hall*	*Heighway*	*Toshack*	*Callaghan*	*Cormack*
								Ref: M Sinclair	After recent results this is a minor triumph over the Reds. City are the better side in the first half but lack finishing power. Liverpool finish stronger and King becomes the hero, tipping over Heighway's deflected shot. Lloyd and Toshack have a rare tussle. BBC's Match of the Day.											
14	A	LEEDS		16	L	0-2	0-0		King	Coop	Brogan	Dugdale	Lloyd	Holmes	Powell	Mortimer	Cross	Green	Hutchison	
25/10			*25,956*	*6*	12			*Yorath 60, Clarke 68*	*Harvey*	*Reaney*	*Gray F*	*Bremner*	*Madeley*	*Hunter*	*Lorimer*	*Clarke*	*McKenzie*	*Yorath*	*Cherry*	
								Ref: R Capey	Leeds are an ageing side but still have enough power to end City's stubborn resistance. The Sky Blues miss plenty of chances created by lively midfield play. Yorath breaks through with a header from Lorimer's free-kick. Lloyd slips and Clarke races 40 yards to slip one past King.											
15	H	QP RANGERS		16	D	1-1	0-0	Cross 59	King	Coop	Brogan	Dugdale	Lloyd	Holmes	Powell	Mortimer	Cross	Green	Hutchison	
1/11			18,047	*3*	13			*Givens 49*	*Parkes*	*Clement*	*Gillard*	*Leach*	*McLintock*	*Webb*	*Thomas*	*Francis*	*Masson*	*Bowles*	*Givens*	
								Ref: P Willis	The league leaders are given a roasting by City and get a point courtesy of a dubious goal which looks offside. In driving rain City pull level with Cross's shot from Mortimer's through-ball. It's their first goal for 442 minutes. Several players return to form, including Lloyd and Coop.											
16	A	WEST HAM		16	D	1-1	0-0	Powell 67	King	Coop	Brogan	Dugdale	Lloyd	Holmes	Powell	Mortimer	Cross	**Murphy**	Hutchison	
8/11			*29,501*	*1*	14			*Robson 48*	*Day*	*McDowell*	*Lock*	*Bonds**	*Taylor T*	*Coleman*	*Taylor A*	*Paddon*	*Holland*	*Brooking*	*Robson*	*Gould*
								Ref: K Styles	A splendid match full of incidents, which City could have won. The brilliant Mortimer hits the woodwork twice before Keith Robson scores from a narrow angle. Powell scores a cannonball after Cross nods down Coop's free-kick. Only one other side has left Upton Park unbeaten.											
17	H	NORWICH		12	W	1-0	1-0	Mortimer 18	King	Coop	Brogan	Dugdale	Lloyd	Holmes	Powell	Mortimer	Cross	Murphy	Hutchison	
15/11			14,906	*16*	16				*Keelan*	*Jones*	*Sullivan*	*Morris*	*Forbes*	*Powell*	*Miller*	*McDougall*	*Boyer*	*Suggett*	*Peters*	
								Ref: W Johnson	City win at home for the first time since August in appalling rain which turns the pitch into a quagmire. It makes 16 successive home wins over the Canaries going back to 1937. City deserve more than Mortimer's left-foot goal, though Boyer and Forbes go close, as does Donal Murphy.											
18	A	LIVERPOOL		13	D	1-1	0-1	Powell 63	King	Coop	Brogan	Dugdale	Lloyd	Holmes	Powell	Mortimer	Cross	Murphy	Hutchison	
22/11			*36,929*	*3*	17			*Toshack 28*	*Clemence*	*Neal*	*Jones*	*Thompson*	*Kennedy*	*Hughes*	*Case*	*Hall*	*Heighway*	*Toshack*	*Callaghan*	
								Ref: H Davey	Liverpool are ten games unbeaten, but are run close by an outstanding City performance. Toshack's simple header looks to have broken City's defensive curtain. Coventry, inspired by Mortimer and Powell, create seven clear chances. Clemence drops a Hutch cross and Powell pounces.											
19	H	BIRMINGHAM		10	W	3-2	3-1	Powell 12, Cross 30, Murphy 32	King	Coop	Brogan	Dugdale	Lloyd	Holmes	Powell	Mortimer	Cross	Murphy !	Hutchison	
29/11			21,800	*21*	19			*Burns 35, Kendall 67p*	*Latchford*	*Martin*	*Want*	*Kendall*	*Gallagher*	*Burns*	*Calderwood*	*Bryant*	*Withe*	*Hatton*	*Hibbitt*	
								Ref: B Daniels	Ten-men City hang on for a good win. Donal Murphy is sent off after kicking Burns right on half-time. Powell with a free-kick, Cross after Burns' error, and Murphy with a header all score. Burns replies with a header and Kendall with a twice-taken penalty after Coop fouls Hatton.											
20	A	NEWCASTLE		15	L	0-4	0-2		King	Coop	Brogan	Dugdale*	Hindley	Holmes	Powell	Mortimer	Cross	Green	Hutchison	Ferguson
6/12			*26,372*	*11*	19			*Craig D 17, Craig T 29, 68p, Burns 51*	*Mahoney*	*Nattrass*	*Kennedy*	*Nulty*	*Craig D*	*Howard*	*Burns*	*Barrowclough*	*Macdonald*	*Gowling*	*Craig T*	
								Ref: J Rice	City have now conceded eleven goals in three visits to Newcastle. The two Craigs have a field day. Macdonald creates confusion for David to head in. Tommy scores from Supermac's long throw. Burns capitalises upon errors. Coop obstructs Tommy, who slots home the spot-kick.											
21	A	MANCHESTER C		16	L	2-4	0-1	Cross 85, Ferguson 89 *[Tueart 90]*	King*	Coop	Brogan	Dugdale	Ferguson	Holmes	Powell	Mortimer	Cross	Murphy	Hutchison	Craven
13/12			*27,256*	*5*	19			*Oakes 43, Barnes 48, Booth 59,*	*Corrigan*	*Hammond*	*Donachie*	*Doyle*	*Watson*	*Oakes*	*Barnes*	*Booth**	*Royle*	*Hartford*	*Tueart*	*Power*
								Ref: T Reynolds	Courageous Coventry come close to a shock result against Manchester, 13 games unbeaten. King is dazed in 14 mins and staggers off after 69 mins with John Craven going in goal. The injury had a big influence on the result, but City were careless in defence and missed chances at 0-0.											

No	Date		Att	Pos	Pt	F-A	H-T	Scorers, Times, and Referees	1	2	3	4	5	6	7	8	9	10	11	12 sub used
22	H	EVERTON		17	L	1-2	0-0	Coop 83p	**Blyth**	Coop	Brogan	Mortimer	Lloyd	Holmes	Powell	Murphy	Cross	Ferguson	Hutchison	
	19/12		14,419	*9*	19			*Jones G 67p, Latchford 69*	*Davies*	*Bernard*	*Darracott*	*Hamilton*	*Kenyon*	*Lyons*	*Buckley*	*Dobson*	*Latchford*	*Telfer**	*Jones G*	*Hurst*
								Ref: C White	Everton win against the run of play. Jones is brought down by Coop and scores from the spot. Latchford scores from close range from Jones' cross. Kenyon handles Murphy's shot and Coop scores. City go close in the last 15 minutes and Davies seems to scoop out Mortimer's shot.											
23	A	WOLVES		15	W	1-0	1-0	Craven 25	King	Coop	Brogan	Craven	Dugdale	Holmes	Cartwright	Powell	Cross	Murphy*	Hutchison	Green
	26/12		*21,224*	*21*	21				*Parkes*	*Palmer*	*Parkin*	*Bailey*	*Munro*	*McAlle*	*Hibbitt*	*Daley*	*Kindon*	*Richards*	*Sunderland*	
								Ref: A Morrissey	Fans are up in arms at the sale of Mortimer to Villa. Craven replaces him and nets the winner in a scrappy match from Coop's cross. Dugdale takes over from Lloyd, victim of a back injury. Wolves stage a late rally without ever threatening. They are in deep trouble with fans in revolt.											
24	H	TOTTENHAM		14	D	2-2	1-1	Cross 26, Hutchison 76	King	Coop	Brogan	Craven	Dugdale	Holmes	Cartwright	Powell	Cross	Green	Hutchison	
	27/12		21,125	*16*	22			*Duncan 43, 70*	*Jennings*	*Naylor*	*McAllister*	*Pratt*	*Young*	*Osgood*	*McGrath**	*Perryman*	*Chivers*	*Duncan*	*Neighbour*	*Jones*
								Ref: P Partridge	A bright if error-strewn game dominated by the entertaining Hutch. He was in mesmeric form and deserved his first goal for a year. Jennings made the save of the season from Cross's volley before big David beat him with a header. Duncan's goals stemmed from sloppy City play.											
25	H	SHEFFIELD UTD		14	W	1-0	0-0	Green 76	Blyth	Coop	Brogan	Craven	Dugdale	Holmes	Cartwright*	Green	Cross	Murphy	Hutchison	Powell
	10/1		**13,777**	*22*	24				*Brown*	*Franks*	*Garner*	*Eddy*	*Colquhoun*	*Ludlam*	*McGeady*	*Bradford*	*Guthrie*	*Currie*	*Woodward*	
								Ref: P Walters	City's lowest Div 1 home crowd. A forgettable game with crucial points at stake. Green wins them with a near-post header from Barry Powell's corner. Dugdale shines in the gloom and keeps a weak United attack at bay. Brogan saves City with a last-minute clearance from Chris Guthrie.											
26	A	IPSWICH		14	D	1-1	1-1	Murphy 12	Blyth	Coop	Brogan	Craven	Dugdale	Holmes	Powell*	Green	Cross	Murphy	Hutchison	Oakey
	17/1		*23,516*	*10*	25			*Osborne 13*	*Cooper*	*Burley*	*Tibbott*	*Talbot*	*Hunter*	*Beattie*	*Osborne*	*Mills*	*Johnson*	*Whymark*	*Lambert**	*Gates*
								Ref: L Hayes	City's first point at Ipswich for five years, after a gutsy, red-blooded clash that saw 38 fouls. Powell is stretchered off after a gruesome Hunter tackle. Murphy hits a sweet half-volley, to which Cooper doesn't even move. Osborne beats a hesitant Blyth to a through-ball and slides it in.											
27	A	DERBY		17	L	0-2	0-0		Blyth	Coop	Brogan	Powell	Dugdale	Holmes	Cartwright	Green	Cross	Murphy	Hutchison	
	31/1		*24,253*	*3*	25			*George 62p, 83*	*Moseley*	*Thomas*	*Newton*	*Rioch*	*Mcfarland*	*Todd*	*Newton*	*Gemmill*	*Lee**	*George*	*James*	*Davies*
								Ref: R Matthewson	City's goal-shy attack lets them down again in front of Match of the Day cameras. Cross and Murphy miss good chances and Moseley saves well from Cross. Sub Roger Davies turns the game when Brogan handles his cross for the penalty. Thomas's free-kick is glanced in by George.											
28	H	MANCHESTER U		16	D	1-1	1-0	Cartwright 40	Blyth	Coop	Brogan*	Craven	Dugdale	Holmes	Powell	Green	Cross	Murphy	Hutchison	Cartwright
	7/2		**33,922**	*2*	26			*Macari 79*	*Stepney*	*Forsyth*	*Houston*	*Daly*	*Greenhoff B*	*Buchan*	*Coppell*	*McIlroy*	*Pearson**	*Macari*	*Hill*	*McCreery*
								Ref: A Grey	Slick United honour their pledge to attack and both teams contribute to a classic match. Cartwright scores a super 20-yarder two minutes after coming on as sub. City have chances to extend their lead and Blyth performs heroics at the other end. Lou Macari heads home Hill's corner.											
29	H	WEST HAM		14	W	2-0	1-0	Powell 44, Coop 54	Blyth	Oakey	Cattlin	Craven	Dugdale	Coop	Cartwright	Powell	Cross	Murphy	Hutchison	
	14/2		16,156	*6*	28				*Day*	*McDowell*	*Lampard*	*Holland*	*Taylor T*	*McGiven*	*Taylor A*	*Paddon*	*Jennings*	*Brooking*	*Robson*	
								Ref: N Ashley	An easy victory over the disappointing Londoners. Hutchison makes both goals, setting up Powell for a blistering shot and Coop for a cross which swerves into the top corner, leaving prodigy Day flapping. Chris Cattlin returns for his first game of the season, his 200th league game.											
30	A	NORWICH		10	W	3-0	1-0	Ferguson 29, Craven 50, Cross 78	Blyth	Oakey	Cattlin	Craven	Dugdale	Coop	Cartwright*	Powell	Cross	Ferguson	Hutchison	Holmes
	21/2		*20,798*	*16*	30				*Keelan*	*Jones*	*Sullivan*	*McGuire*	*Forbes*	*Stringer*	*Machin*	*McDougall*	*Boyer*	*Suggett*	*Peters*	
								Ref: A Robinson	Norwich's five-match unbeaten run is ended by a super Sky Blues show. 'They could have had six' says former City man Mick McGuire. Mick Ferguson superbly heads in Hutch's cross. Cross hits the post for Craven to follow up, then scores himself from Hutch's pass. A fifth away win.											
31	A	MIDDLESBROUGH		11	L	0-2	0-0		Blyth	Oakey	Cattlin	Craven	Dugdale	Coop	Holmes	Powell	Cross	Ferguson	Hutchison*	Murphy
	24/2		*18,279*	*6*	30			*Boam 60, Souness 80*	*Platt*	*Craggs*	*Cooper*	*Souness*	*Boam*	*McAndrew*	*Boersma**	*Mills*	*Hickton*	*Maddren*	*Armstrong*	*Woof*
								Ref: D Richardson	Boro's defence has conceded only six goals at home. Platt doesn't need to make a save. Fierce tackles abound and Hutch is carried off. Cattlin concedes a harsh penalty for fouling Cooper. Blyth saves Hickton's first kick, but is adjudged to have moved. The re-take goes over the bar.											

No	Venue	Date	Opponent	Att	Pos	Pts	Result	HT	Scorers, Times, Referees	1	2	3	4	5	6	7	8	9	10	11	12
32	H		LEEDS		13	L	0-1	0-0		Blyth	Oakey	Cattlin	Craven	Dugdale	Coop	Murphy	Powell	Cross	Ferguson*	Hutchison	Green
		28/2		25,597	*5*	30			*Gray F 49*	*Harvey*	*Reaney*	*Gray F*	*Bates*	*Madeley*	*Hunter*	*Cherry*	*Yorath*	*Jordan*	*McKenzie*	*Gray E**	*Clarke*
									Ref: R Challis	Leeds are on the fringe of the title race but have reverted to their old frustrating tactics. Trevor Cherry's indirect free-kick in the area is charged down but Frank Gray hits a 25 yarder past the unsighted Blyth. Ferguson is jeered, then substituted, only for Cross to be injured within minutes.											
33	A		QP RANGERS		16	L	1-4	0-1	Powell 82 *[Masson 74]*	Blyth	Oakey	Cattlin	Craven*	Dugdale	Coop	Murphy	Powell	Ferguson	Green	Hutchison	Cartwright
		6/3		*19,731*	*1*	30			*Thomas 6, Francis 61, Givens 71,*	*Parkes*	*Clement*	*Gillard*	*Hollins*	*McLintock*	*Webb*	*Thomas*	*Francis*	*Masson*	*Bowles*	*Givens*	
									Ref: H Robinson	QPR have won six out of seven and look championship material. After an even first half, Rangers, with the wind behind them, tear into City. Francis and Masson are in control against a shaky defence. Clement's 60-yard run to set up Francis is the highlight, but Powell's goal is a gem.											
34	H		ARSENAL		15	D	1-1	0-1	Green 56	Blyth	Oakey	Cattlin	Craven	Dugdale	Coop*	Murphy	Powell	Cartwright	Green	Hutchison	Ferguson
		13/3		13,912	*17*	31			*Powling 17*	*Rimmer*	*Rice*	*Nelson*	*Ross*	*Mancini*	*Powling*	*Armstrong*	*Ball*	*Radford*	*Kidd*	*Brady*	
									Ref: I Smith	Bertie Mee's Gunners have won three 1-0's in a row to pull away from the drop zone. They frustrate City and the fans with a blanket defence. Richie Powling rifles home after John Radford's nod down. Murphy sets up Green to head in. Ferguson hits the underside of the bar late on.											
35	A		BIRMINGHAM		16	D	1-1	1-0	Powell 12	Blyth	Oakey	Cattlin	Craven	Cross	Coop	Murphy	Powell	Cartwright	Green	Hutchison	
		20/3		*22,956*	*19*	32			*Francis 56p*	*Smith*	*Martin*	*Styles*	*Kendall*	*Gallagher*	*Pendrey*	*Page*	*Francis*	*Needham*	*Hatton*	*Hibbitt*	
									Ref: A Lees	A tale of two penalties. The referee misses Craven's blatant first-half handball but gives Blues a spot-kick for a foul outside the box. Willie Bell's men are desperate and City have to weather a late onslaught with Blyth outstanding. Powell's 25-yard drive leaves rookie Smith rooted.											
36	H		NEWCASTLE		17	D	1-1	1-1	Murphy 45	Blyth	Oakey	Cattlin	Ferguson	Dugdale	Coop	Cartwright	Green	Murphy	Powell	Hutchison	
		27/3		14,140	*13*	33			*Bird 42*	*Mahoney*	*Nattrass*	*Kennedy*	*Barrowclough*	*Bird*	*Howard**	*Burns*	*Oates*	*Macdonald*	*Gowling*	*Craig T*	*Hudson*
									Ref: M Taylor	The hardcore home following is down to about 13,000 and it's no wonder with such poor quality fare. Newcastle suffer a Cup hangover after losing in the quarter-finals to Derby, but City haven't beaten them in four games this season. Blyth is impeded as Bird scores. Murphy levels.											
37	H		LEICESTER		17	L	0-2	0-1		Blyth	Oakey	Cattlin	Cartwright	Dugdale	Coop	Murphy	Green	Ferguson*	Powell	Hutchison	Cross
		3/4		18,018	*8*	33			*Weller 1, Lee 81*	*Wallington*	*Whitworth*	*Rofe*	*Kember*	*Blockley*	*Woollett*	*Weller*	*Lee*	*Worthington*	*Alderson*	*Sammels*	
									Ref: W Gow	Jimmy Bloomfield's men have recovered from their poor start and are in with a chance of Europe. Weller volleys in after 45 seconds, when Blyth fails to cut out a cross. Ex-City man, Jeff Blockley, sets up Bob Lee's goal with a long free-kick. Ferguson is jeered and subbed again.											
38	A		STOKE		15	W	1-0	0-0	Powell 53	Blyth	Oakey	Cattlin	Craven	Holmes	Coop	Cartwright	Green	Ferguson	Powell	Hutchison	
		10/4		*16,059*	*12*	35				*Shilton*	*Lumsden*	*Pejic*	*Mahoney*	*Smith**	*Bloor*	*Conroy*	*Greenhoff*	*Crooks*	*Haslegrave*	*Salmons*	*Dodd*
									Ref: R Tinkler	The home team are barracked as City notch their first win in eight and ensure safety. Debut-boy Garth Crooks comes closest for big-spending Stoke but Jim Blyth saves his two efforts. Barry Powell scores his seventh goal of the season, and his sixth from a distance of 20 yards or more.											
39	H		ASTON VILLA		15	D	1-1	1-0	Coop 33p	Blyth	Oakey	Cattlin	Craven	Holmes	Coop	Cartwright	Green	Cross	Powell	Hutchison	
		13/4		27,569	*18*	36			*Nicholl 70*	*Burridge*	*Gidman*	*Robson*	*Phillips*	*Nicholl*	*Mortimer*	*Graydon*	*McDonald*	*Gray**	*Hunt*	*Carrodus*	*Masefield*
									Ref: R Capey	Villa have won only once in 16 games but this point ensures their safety. Phillips brings down Hutch and Coop scores from the spot. Cattlin is penalised harshly for fouling Graydon, who gets up and puts the penalty wide. Nicholl heads home Steve Hunt's corner and honours are even.											
40	H		WOLVES		12	W	3-1	1-1	Green 20, 53, 86	Blyth	Oakey	Cattlin	Craven*	Holmes	Coop	Cartwright	Green	Cross	Powell	Hutchison	Murphy
		17/4		19,957	*20*	38			*Bell 26*	*Parkes*	*Palmer*	*Parkin*	*Daley*	*Munro*	*McAlle*	*Carr*	*Hibbitt*	*Bell*	*Richards*	*Farley**	*Gould*
									Ref: H Davey	The dreadful home season ends with City scoring more than two for only the second time, which sends Wolves down. Bill McGarry is set to be sacked after seven years as boss. Green bags a hat-trick, thanks to some dreadful defending and Carr, captain for the day, will regret his move.											
41	A		TOTTENHAM		15	L	1-4	0-2	Murphy 64 *[Duncan 73]*	Blyth	Oakey	Cattlin*	Holmes	Dugdale	Coop	**Roberts**	Green	Cross	Powell	Hutchison	Murphy
		19/4		*21,107*	*7*	38			*Osgood 5, Neighbour 16, Pratt 59,*	*Jennings*	*Naylor*	*McAllister*	*Pratt*	*Young*	*Osgood*	*Coates*	*Perryman*	*Chivers**	*Duncan*	*Neighbour*	*Jones*
									Ref: R Crabb	Spurs are finishing the season with a flourish, one defeat in eight games, and have adopted a shoot-on-sight policy. Osgood's 30-yard screamer sets the tone and Spurs canter home. Harry Roberts in a No 7 shirt makes his debut at full-back and Donal Murphy smacks in a left-foot volley.											
42	A		BURNLEY		14	W	3-1	0-1	Cross 48, 86, 87	Blyth	Roberts	Cattlin	Holmes	Dugdale	Coop	Murphy	Green	Cross	Powell	Hutchison	
		24/4		***11,636***	*21*	40			*Parker 6*	*Peyton*	*Scott*	*Newton*	*Summerbee*	*Thomson*	*Rodaway*	*Ingham*	*Jakub*	*Noble*	*Morley*	*Parker*	
		Home		Away					Ref: P Partridge	Burnley are already relegated and field four teenagers in an experimental side. Cross repeats his opening day hat-trick feat and City win at Turf Moor for the first time ever. A mediocre game, drifting to a draw, comes to life in the final minutes with a stunning drive and a perfect header.											
Average		19,288		25,282																	

League Cup

Rd			Pos	Res	F-A	H-T	Scorers, Times, and Referees	1	2	3	4	5	6	7	8	9	10	11	12 sub used
2	A	BOLTON	6	W	3-1	2-1	Cross 6, Green 36, Ferguson 61	King	Oakey	Brogan	Craven	Dugdale	Powell	Coop	Mortimer	Cross	Green*	Hutchison	Ferguson
	10/9	*12,743*	*2:10*				*Byrom 28*	*Siddall*	*Ritson*	*Dunne*	*Greaves*	*Jones P*	*Allardyce*	*Byrom*	*Curran*	*Jones G*	*Reid*	*Thompson*	
							Ref: R Lee	A superb win in a thunderstorm sparked by a great debut from Powell. City's fluent football and lethal finishing wins plenty of admirers. Cross ghosts in to volley home Craven's cross. Bolton play their part in a gripping match. John Craven is booked for fouling 19-year-old Peter Reid.											
3	A	MANSFIELD	11	L	0-2	0-2		King	Oakey*	Brogan	Craven	Dugdale	Holmes	Coop	Mortimer	Cross	Green	Hutchison	Ferguson
	8/10	*10,027*	*3:23*				*Clarke 2, Eccles 35*	*Arnold*	*Pate*	*Foster B*	*Laverick*	*Mackenzie**	*Bird*	*Matthews*	*Eccles*	*Clarke*	*Hodgson*	*McDonald*	*Foster C*
							Ref: R Matthewson	Last season's Div 4 champions outfight City and deservedly go through to play Wolves. Clarke scores after 70 seconds when King drops a corner. Clarke heads down Hodgson's corner and the unmarked Eccles scores. City have only two chances and the home fans chant 'Easy'.											

FA Cup

Rd			Pos	Res	F-A	H-T	Scorers, Times, and Referees	1	2	3	4	5	6	7	8	9	10	11	12 sub used
3	H	BRISTOL CITY	14	W	2-1	1-0	Cross 14, Merrick 75 (og)	Blyth	Coop	Brogan	Craven	Dugdale	Holmes	Cartwright	Green*	Cross	Murphy	Hutchison	Oakey
	3/1	15,489	*2:3*				*Brolly 78*	*Cashley*	*Sweeney*	*Drysdale*	*Gow*	*Collier*	*Merrick*	*Tainton*	*Ritchie*	*Mann*	*Fear*	*Brolly*	
							Ref: A Robinson	Battling Bristol are let off the hook by a profligate Sky Blues. All City have to show for a strong first half is Cross's run and shot from the edge of the box. As Bristol press, a break by Cartwright ends with Merrick heading in under pressure from Green. Brolly's sizzling shot is too late.											
4	H	NEWCASTLE	14	D	1-1	0-1	Murphy 68	King	Coop	Brogan	Craven*	Dugdale	Holmes	Cartwright	Green	Cross	Murphy	Hutchison	Powell
	24/1	32,206	*12*				*Gowling 29*	*Mahoney*	*Nattrass*	*Kennedy*	*Nulty*	*Keeley*	*Howard*	*Burns*	*Cassidy*	*Macdonald*	*Gowling*	*Craig T*	
							Ref: D Nippard	The League Cup finalists only just survive a Sky Blue battering in a pulsating cup-tie. 19-goal Gowling finishes clinically from Cassidy's deft pass. City miss chances and Murphy hits the bar before the Irishman glances a header past Mahoney. Newcastle hang on in a frantic finale.											
4R	A	NEWCASTLE	14	L	0-5	0-2	*[Cassidy 90]*	King	Coop	Brogan	Powell	Dugdale	Holmes	Cartwright	Green	Cross	Murphy	Hutchison	
	28/1	*44,676*	*12*				*Burns 23, Gowling 38, Macdonald 70,75,*	*Mahoney*	*Nattrass*	*Kennedy*	*Nulty*	*Keeley*	*Howard*	*Burns*	*Cassidy*	*Macdonald*	*Gowling*	*Craig T*	
							Ref: E Wallace	Once the first goal went in it was a question of how many. On a slippery rock-hard surface the aggressive Magpies humiliate City. Supermac is the hero with his first goal since December, a wicked shot from an acute angle which brings the house down. King struggles with a groin injury.											

		Home					Away					
	P	W	D	L	F	A	W	D	L	F	A	Pts
1 Liverpool	42	14	5	2	41	21	9	9	3	25	10	60
2 QP Rangers	42	17	4	0	42	13	7	7	7	25	20	59
3 Manchester U	42	16	4	1	40	13	7	6	8	28	29	56
4 Derby	42	15	3	3	45	30	6	8	7	30	28	53
5 Leeds	42	13	3	5	37	19	8	6	7	28	27	51
6 Ipswich	42	11	6	4	36	23	5	8	8	18	25	46
7 Leicester	42	9	9	3	29	24	4	10	7	19	27	45
8 Manchester C	42	14	5	2	46	18	2	6	13	18	28	43
9 Tottenham	42	6	10	5	33	32	8	5	8	30	31	43
10 Norwich	42	10	5	6	33	26	6	5	10	25	32	42
11 Everton	42	10	7	4	37	24	5	5	11	23	42	42
12 Stoke	42	8	5	8	25	24	7	6	8	23	26	41
13 Middlesbro	42	9	7	5	23	11	6	3	12	23	34	40
14 COVENTRY	42	6	9	6	22	22	7	5	9	25	35	40
15 Newcastle	42	11	4	6	51	26	4	5	12	20	36	39
16 Aston Villa	42	11	8	2	32	17	0	9	12	19	42	39
17 Arsenal	42	11	4	6	33	19	2	6	13	14	34	36
18 West Ham	42	10	5	6	26	23	3	5	13	22	48	36
19 Birmingham	42	11	5	5	36	26	2	2	17	21	49	33
20 Wolves	42	7	6	8	27	25	3	4	14	24	43	30
21 Burnley	42	6	6	9	23	26	3	4	14	20	40	28
22 Sheffield Utd	42	4	7	10	19	32	2	3	16	14	50	22
	924	229	127	106	736	494	106	127	229	494	736	924

Odds & ends

Double wins: (3) Sheffield Utd, Wolves, Norwich.
Double losses: (2) Middlesbrough, Leeds.

Won from behind: (1) Burnley (a).
Lost from in front: (0)

High spots: 4-1 opening day win at Everton.
Cross hat-tricks on first and last days of the season.
Outstanding away draws at Manchester U and West Ham.

Low spots: Sale of Mortimer to arch rivals Villa.
League Cup embarrassment at Mansfield.
FA Cup disaster at Newcastle.

Red cards: City – Murphy (Birmingham h).

Player of the Year: Tommy Hutchison.
Ever-presents: (2) Mick Coop, Tommy Hutchison.
Hat-tricks: (3) David Cross (2), Alan Green (1).
Opposing hat-tricks: (0).
Leading scorer: (16) David Cross.

	Appearances						Goals			
	Lge	*Sub*	LC	*Sub*	FAC	*Sub*	Lge	LC	FAC	Tot
Blyth, Jim	**19**				1					
Brogan, Jim	**28**		2		3					
Cartwright, Les	**13**	*2*			3		**1**			**1**
Cattlin, Chris	**14**									
Coop, Mick	**42**		2		3		**4**			**4**
Craven, John	**27**	*1*	2		2		**3**			**3**
Cross, David	**37**	*1*	2		3		**14**	1	1	**16**
Dugdale, Alan	**34**		2		3					
Ferguson, Mick	**11**	*4*		*2*			**3**	1		**4**
Green, Alan	**29**	*2*	2		3		**9**	1		**10**
Hindley, Peter	**1**									
Holmes, Jimmy	**34**	*1*	1		3					
Hutchison, Tommy	**42**		2		3		**1**			**1**
King, Bryan	**23**		2		2					
Lloyd, Larry	**11**									
Mortimer, Dennis	**22**		2				**1**			**1**
Murphy, Donal	**19**	*3*			3		**4**		1	**5**
Oakey, Graham	**22**	*1*	2			*1*				
Powell, Barry	**32**	*2*	1		1	*1*	**7**			**7**
Roberts, Brian	**2**									
(own-goals)									1	**1**
20 players used	**462**	***17***	**22**	***2***	**33**	***2***	**47**	**3**	**3**	**53**

No	Date		Att	Pos	Pt	F-A	H-T	Scorers, Times, and Referees	1	2	3	4	5	6	7	8	9	10	11	12 sub used
1	A	MIDDLESBROUGH			L	0-1	0-0		Blyth	Coop	Holmes	Craven	Lloyd	Dugdale	Cartwright	Green	Cross*	**Beck**	Powell	Murphy
	21/8		*17,694*		0			*McAndrew 53*	*Platt*	*Craggs*	*Cooper*	*Souness*	*Boam*	*Maddren*	*McAndrew*	*Mills*	*Hedley*	*Boersma*	*Armstrong*	
								Ref: C Seel	Tony McAndrew jetted in from the USA yesterday and scores. Blyth saves Souness' penalty when Boersma is fouled. Dreary Boro have most of the play on a humid afternoon. Lloyd plays his first game for nine months and debutant John Beck, a £40,000 signing from QPR, is booked.											
2	H	MANCHESTER U			L	0-2	0-1		Blyth	Coop	Holmes	Craven	Lloyd !	Dugdale	Powell	Green	Murphy	Beck	Oakey	
	24/8		26,775		0			*Macari 18, Hill 61*	*Stepney*	*Nicholl*	*Houston*	*Daly*	*Greenhoff B*	*Buchan*	*Coppell*	*McIlroy*	*Pearson*	*Macari*	*Hill**	*McCreery*
								Ref: C Thomas	A one-sided game is turned into a procession after Lloyds 51st-minute dismissal for persistent fouling, having being booked. Mercifully United only add one more, thanks to Blyth's brilliant keeping. City's makeshift side have plenty of spirit but look out of their depth. Cheque book out!											
3	H	LEEDS		18	W	4-2	1-1	Beck 34, Ferguson 53, Murphy 76,	Blyth	Coop	Holmes	Craven	Murphy	Dugdale	Cartwright	Powell	Ferguson	Beck	Oakey	
	28/8		18,205	*19*	2			*Gray F 21, Currie 85* [Cartwright 77]	*Harvey*	*Reaney*	*Gray F*	*Bremner*	*Madeley*	*Hunter*	*Cherry*	*Clarke*	*Jordan*	*Currie*	*Gray E*	
								Ref: C White	Lloyd is axed and new signings McDonald (£40,000), Yorath (£135,000) and Wallace (£75,000) watch from the stand as City's bogey side Leeds are hammered in a great performance in the rain. Beck hits a screamer, Ferguson heads in Powell's delicate free-kick and City sail home.											
4	A	LIVERPOOL		21	L	1-3	1-0	Ferguson 1	Blyth	Coop	**McDonald**	Oakey	Holmes	Dugdale	Cartwright	**Yorath**	Ferguson	Beck	Green	
	4/9		*40,371*	*3*	2			*Keegan 56, Johnson 73, Toshack 80*	*Clemence*	*Neal*	*Jones*	*Thompson*	*Kennedy*	*Hughes*	*Keegan*	*Johnson*	*Heighway*	*Toshack*	*Callaghan*	
								Ref: M Lowe	City are unlucky to lose after taking a 59-second lead and having a McDonald effort disallowed at 1-1. The goal looked good and the ref gives no explanation. The champions come to life after this and two late goals give the scoreline a false look. Terry Yorath looks cool under pressure.											
5	H	NORWICH		16	W	2-0	1-0	Ferguson 30, Forbes 67 (og)	Blyth	Coop	McDonald	Powell	Holmes	Dugdale	Cartwright	Yorath	Ferguson	Beck	Green	
	11/9		13,459	*22*	4				*Keelan*	*Ryan*	*Sullivan*	*Steele*	*Forbes*	*Powell*	*Grapes*	*McDougall*	*Boyer*	*Suggett*	*Peters*	
								Ref: J Hough	City's lowest ever Div 1 crowd see a below-par display. Mick Ferguson scores for the fourth consecutive game with another header from Barry Powell's cross, but the entertainment level is low. Veteran Duncan Forbes heads into his own net from a Beck cross. Milne shuffles the squad.											
6	A	WEST BROM		15	D	1-1	1-0	Ferguson 19	Blyth	Coop	McDonald	Craven	Holmes	Dugdale	Cartwright	Yorath	Ferguson	Beck	Cross	
	17/9		*24,323*	*11*	5			*Wile 87*	*Osborne*	*Mulligan*	*Robson*	*Brown T*	*Wile*	*Robertson*	*Martin*	*Edwards*	*Mayo*	*Giles*	*Johnston*	
								Ref: D Biddle	Newly promoted Albion grab a late deserved equaliser after putting the Sky Blues under pressure in the second half. City lead for most of the game, thanks to Ferguson's header from Cartwright's cross. Beck keeps tabs on Johnny Giles and a young Bryan Robson plays at left-back.											
7	H	BIRMINGHAM		12	W	2-1	1-1	Green 23, Yorath 86	Blyth	Coop	McDonald	Yorath	Holmes	Dugdale	Beck	Green*	Ferguson	Powell	Hutchison	Murphy
	25/9		26,371	*15*	7			*Burns 32*	*Latchford*	*Page*	*Styles*	*Hibbitt*	*Gallagher*	*Want*	*Calderwood*	*Francis*	*Burns*	*Jones*	*Connolly*	
								Ref: D Lloyd	The Blues are fresh from a win at Villa Park and give Coventry a hard game. Ferguson gets the upper hand over Gallagher and sets up Green's goal. Hutch returns after pre-season injury. The winner would need to be something special, and Yorath's 30-yarder brings the house down.											
8	H	LEICESTER		14	D	1-1	1-0	Ferguson 1	Blyth	Coop	McDonald	Yorath	Holmes	Dugdale	Cartwright	Green	Ferguson	Powell	Hutchison	
	2/10		21,018	*9*	8			*Worthington 77*	*Wallington*	*Whitworth*	*Rofe*	*Kember*	*Blockley*	*Woollett*	*Weller*	*Sammels*	*Worthington*	*Birchenall**	*Garland*	*Earle*
								Ref: R Toseland	Leicester get their seventh draw in eight games with Frank Worthington's late scrambled equaliser. Ferguson puts City ahead in 57 seconds and dominate a breathtaking first half, but the visitors fight back well. Woollett receives the first ever yellow card while McDonald gets City's first.											
9	H	NEWCASTLE		13	D	1-1	0-0	Powell 71	Blyth	Coop	McDonald	Yorath	Dugdale	Holmes	Cartwright	Green*	Ferguson	Powell	Beck	Murphy
	16/10		18,114	*9*	9			*Gowling 81*	*Mahoney*	*Nattrass*	*Kennedy*	*Cassidy*	*McCaffrey*	*Nulty*	*Barrowclough*	*Cannell*	*Burns*	*Gowling*	*Craig*	
								Ref: T Spencer	Supermac has moved to Arsenal, but his partner Alan Gowling still haunts City and scores soon after having a good-looking 'goal' disallowed. Cartwright lays on Powell's goal and scrapes the post minutes later but the Magpies deserve their point. Lloyd joins Forest on a month's loan.											
10	A	TOTTENHAM		12	W	1-0	1-0	Murphy 19	Blyth	Coop	McDonald	Yorath	Dugdale	Holmes	Cartwright	Murphy	Ferguson	Powell	Beck	
	23/10		*21,877*	*18*	11				*Jennings*	*Keeley*	*McAllister*	*Hoddle*	*Young*	*Osgood*	*Coates*	*Perryman*	*Moores**	*Jones*	*Taylor*	*McNab*
								Ref: A Glasson	Spurs are reeling from a 2-8 hammering at Derby, while City are seven games unbeaten. Murphy returns to score a superb 30-yard shot but the superior Sky Blues can't score more. Spurs have a Moores 'goal' disallowed but don't test Blyth. Only City's second win at White Hart Lane.											

No	Venue	Opponent	Pos	Res	FT	HT	Scorers, Times, and Referees	1	2	3	4	5	6	7	8	9	10	11	12
11	H	SUNDERLAND	14	L	1-2	0-1	Ferguson 84	Blyth	Coop	McDonald	Yorath	Dugdale	Holmes*	Beck	Murphy	Ferguson	Powell	Hutchison	**Wallace**
	30/10	17,181	*21*	11			*Lee 14, Hughes 47*	*Siddall*	*Malone*	*Bolton*	*Towers*	*Clarke*	*Holton*	*Foggon*	*Hughes**	*Lee*	*Train*	*Greenwood*	*Kerr*
							Ref: R Capey	Sunderland clock up their first win of the season, a week after Bob Stokoe resigns. Former City schoolboy Ray Train is the architect, marking Yorath out of the game and setting up both goals. Wallace appears at half-time and goes close with two headers. The Sky Blues were unlucky.											
12	A	BRISTOL CITY	15	D	0-0	0-0		Blyth	Coop	McDonald	Yorath	Lloyd	Holmes	Beck	Murphy	Ferguson	Powell	Hutchison	
	6/11	*17,172*	*20*	12				*Shaw*	*Gillies*	*Merrick*	*Sweeney*	*Collier*	*Hunter*	*Tainton*	*Ritchie*	*Mann*	*Fear*	*Whitehead*	
							Ref: C Thomas	Larry Lloyd returns from his Forest loan in top form and plays a big part in this point in his home town. Newly promoted Bristol had lost four in a row but have bought ex-Leeds Norman Hunter to tighten the back. Despite the scoreline it is an exciting game but the defences are on top.											
13	H	QP RANGERS	11	W	2-0	1-0	Powell 16, Murphy 87	Blyth	Coop	McDonald	Yorath	Lloyd	Holmes	Beck	Murphy	Ferguson	Powell	Wallace	
	9/11	16,184	*16*	14				*Parkes*	*Clement*	*Gillard*	*Hollins*	*McLintock*	*Webb*	*Thomas*	*Leach*	*Masson*	*Bowles*	*Givens*	
							Ref: A Lees	An intriguing match which City dominated for all but 20 minutes in the second half. Powell gets on the end of a super move, started by Blyth. Wallace, starting for the first time, sets up Murphy to kill off the Bowles-inspired Rangers revival. Ian Wallace is given a standing ovation.											
14	A	ASTON VILLA	11	D	2-2	0-1	Ferguson 48, 53	Blyth	Coop	McDonald	Yorath	Lloyd	Holmes	Beck !	Murphy*	Ferguson	Powell	Wallace	Hutchison
	20/11	*40,047*	*3*	15			*Gidman 45, Gray 74*	*Findlay*	*Gidman*	*Smith*	*Phillips*	*Nicholl*	*Mortimer*	*Deehan*	*Little*	*Gray*	*Cropley*	*Carrodus*	
							Ref: J Yates	A well-earned point against City's local rivals, thanks to two super strikes from Fergie; the second a breathtaking volley from a dipping Mick Coop centre. John Beck is sent off twelve minutes from time for two bookable offences. David Cross has moved to West Brom for £130,000.											
15	H	ARSENAL	12	L	1-2	1-2	McDonald 18	Blyth	Coop	McDonald	Yorath	Dugdale	Holmes	Beck	Murphy*	Ferguson	Powell	Wallace	Hutchison
	27/11	18,313	*7*	15			*Macdonald 1, Stapleton 16*	*Rimmer*	*Rice*	*Nelson*	*Ross*	*O'Leary*	*Simpson*	*Ball*	*Brady*	*Macdonald*	*Stapleton*	*Armstrong*	
							Ref: B Newsome	The best side lost this game because of two moments of defensive madness. Supermac scores after 40 seconds without a City outfield player touching the ball. The Sky Blues pile on the pressure and waste good chances, while Rimmer saves from Wallace. Larry Lloyd signs for Forest.											
16	H	EVERTON	10	W	4-2	1-1	Beck 38, Coop 62p, Wallace 63, [Murphy 89]	Blyth	Coop	McDonald	Yorath	Dugdale	Holmes	Beck	Wallace	Ferguson*	Powell	Hutchison	Murphy
	11/12	18,977	*13*	17			*King 14, Kenyon 82*	*Davies*	*Darracott*	*Jones*	*Rioch*	*McNaught*	*Kenyon*	*King*	*Dobson*	*Latchford*	*McKenzie*	*Goodlass*	
							Ref: A Turvey	Wallace captures the headlines for scoring his first goal, making another for Beck, and earning the penalty. On a frosty pitch Everton, with new £200,000 signings Rioch and McKenzie, dominate the first 20 minutes. But once Beck equalises there is only one winner, despite the late goal.											
17	A	MANCHESTER C	11	L	0-2	0-1		Blyth	Coop	McDonald	Yorath	Dugdale	Holmes	Beck	Wallace	Murphy	Powell	Hutchison	
	18/12	*32,527*	*4*	17			*Kidd 20, Tueart 84*	*Corrigan*	*Clements*	*Donachie*	*Doyle*	*Watson*	*Power*	*Owen*	*Kidd*	*Royle*	*Hartford*	*Tueart*	
							Ref: H Hackney	Only Man United have won at Maine Road this season and although City hold them to 0-1 until near the end they are outclassed. Dennis Tueart is in Don Revie's England plans and plays a blinder, but hits the bar with a penalty in the 70th minute after Holmes brings down Gary Owen.											
18	H	IPSWICH	11	D	1-1	1-1	Green 20	Blyth	Coop	McDonald	Yorath	Dugdale	Holmes	Beck*	Green	Murphy	Powell	Hutchison	Cartwright
	27/12	28,283	*2*	18			*Bertschin 31*	*Cooper*	*Burley*	*Mills*	*Talbot*	*Roberts*	*Beattie*	*Osborne*	*Wark*	*Bertschin*	*Whymark*	*Woods*	
							Ref: W Gow	Bobby Robson's title chasers have won ten out of 12 but are knocked off top spot by a lively City side missing Ferguson and Wallace, the latter involved in a car crash. Green heads in Coop's cross and Bertschin, standing in for the injured Mariner, beats Blyth with a superb ground shot.											
19	A	SUNDERLAND	11	W	1-0	0-0	Murphy 90	Blyth	Coop	McDonald	Yorath	Dugdale	Holmes*	Beck	Green	Murphy	Powell	Hutchison	Craven
	3/1	*24,942*	*22*	20				*Siddall*	*Docherty*	*Bolton*	*Rowell*	*Clarke*	*Ashurst*	*Kerr*	*Train*	*Holden*	*Brown*	*Greenwood**	*Hughes*
							Ref: T Mills	Sunderland's new boss Jimmy Adamson is unable to stop the dreadful run; now eight defeats in a row with only one goal. City's first ever win at Roker is gained on an icy pitch with a late Murphy goal. Blyth plays a blinder as Sunderland turn up the heat with massive vocal support.											
20	A	MANCHESTER U	12	L	0-2	0-2		Blyth	Coop	McDonald	Yorath	Dugdale	Holmes	Beck	Green	Murphy	Powell	Hutchison	
	15/1	***46,567***	*11*	20			*Macari 6, 19*	*Stepney*	*Nicholl*	*Houston*	*McIlroy*	*Greenhoff B*	*Buchan*	*Coppell*	*Greenhoff J*	*Pearson*	*Macari*	*Hill*	
							Ref: G Courtney	After their great start, United have been stuttering for a while and are there for the taking. City don't take advantage, lacking penetration up front. Dugdale's clearing header is deflected in off Macari for the first goal. Martin Buchan cuffs team-mate Hill around the ear for not trying.											
21	H	MIDDLESBROUGH	13	D	1-1	0-0	Green 86	Blyth	Coop	McDonald	Yorath	Dugdale	Holmes	Beck*	Green	Murphy	Powell	Hutchison	Cartwright
	22/1	**12,893**	*6*	21			*Mills 72*	*Cuff*	*Craggs*	*Cooper*	*Souness*	*Boam*	*Maddren*	*Boersma*	*Mills*	*Brine*	*Wood*	*Armstrong*	
							Ref: N Ashley	The thought of Boro's traditional spoiling tactics keeps the fans away, producing another Div 1 lowest gate. David Mills' goal looks to have won the games until City gel for the last 15 minutes, Green scoring after a hectic scramble. Jack Charlton won't apologise for his negative side.											

No	Date		Att	Pos	Pt	F-A	H-T	Scorers, Times, and Referees	1	2	3	4	5	6	7	8	9	10	11	12 sub used
22	A	LEEDS		12	W	2-1	1-1	Green 16, Murphy 88	Blyth	Coop	McDonald	Yorath	Dugdale	Holmes	Beck	Green	Roberts	Powell*	Hutchison	Murphy
	5/2		*26,058*	*10*	23			*Jordan 18*	*Harvey*	*Reaney*	*Hampton**	*Cherry*	*McQueen*	*Madeley*	*Gray F*	*Clarke*	*Jordan*	*Lorimer*	*Gray E*	*Harris*
								Ref: A Jones	Murphy's late winner gives City their first ever win at Leeds. With Coop playing sweeper, Leeds' attack is smothered in a defensive triumph. Despite still missing the injured Wallace and Ferguson, Terry Yorath's celebratory return to Elland Road is captured by Match of the Day.											
23	A	STOKE		14	L	0-2	0-1		Blyth	Coop	McDonald	Yorath	Dugdale*	Holmes	Beck	Green	Roberts	Powell	Hutchison	Wallace
	16/2		***12,255***	*15*	23			*Conroy 1, 55p*	*Shilton*	*Dodd*	*Bowers*	*Mahoney*	*Smith*	*Bloor*	*Tudor*	*Suddick*	*Goodwin*	*Conroy*	*Salmons*	
								Ref: J Taylor	City slump pitifully to a side who have not won for nine games and had scored once in 810 minutes. Blyth's rare mistake causes the 55-second first goal, and Dugdale's foul on Conroy is punished with a spot-kick. The Sky Blues squander four good chances and are denied by Shilton.											
24	A	NORWICH		14	L	0-3	0-2		Blyth	Coop	McDonald	Yorath	Dugdale	Roberts	Beck	Wallace*	Ferguson	Powell	Hutchison	Holmes
	19/2		*17,900*	*11*	23			*Busby 20, 77, Reeves 22*	*Keelan*	*Ryan*	*Sullivan*	*Machin**	*Jones*	*Powell*	*Neighbour*	*Reeves*	*Busby*	*Steele*	*Peters*	*Evans*
								Ref: M Sinclair	Wallace and Ferguson are paired together for twelve minutes before Ian Wallace is hit in the eye with the ball and goes to hospital. City, with Mick Coop also limping, commit defensive blunders to ensure it's a stroll for John Bond's Canaries, who are unbeaten in eight home games.											
25	A	BIRMINGHAM		16	L	1-3	0-1	Powell 50	Blyth	Oakey*	McDonald	Yorath	Dugdale	Holmes	Roberts	Wallace	Ferguson	Powell	Hutchison	Cartwright
	5/3		*22,607*	*12*	23			*Francis 15, Connolly 64, Emmanuel 88*	*Latchford*	*Page*	*Rathbone*	*Calderwood*	*Gallagher**	*Want*	*Jones*	*Francis*	*Burns*	*Hibbitt*	*Connolly*	*Emmanuel*
								Ref: K McNally	The severe winter means City have 17 games to play in just over two months. Jim Holton, a £40,000 signing from Sunderland, is not fit, but Wallace's eye has healed. A pathetic Coventry display against poor opponents, for whom Francis shines like a jewel. Powell's goal is a gem.											
26	A	DERBY		15	D	1-1	1-0	Wallace 12	Blyth	Roberts	McDonald	Yorath	Dugdale	Holmes	Beck	Wallace	Ferguson	Powell	Hutchison	
	9/3		*22,808*	*21*	24			*Daniel 80*	*Boulton*	*Langan*	*Thomas*	*Daly*	*McFarland**	*Todd*	*Hector*	*Macken*	*Hales*	*George*	*James*	*Daniel*
								Ref: P Reeves	Honours are even between these two out-of-form sides. Derby end a run of five defeats under new manager Colin Murphy with £175,000 debut boy Gerry Daly promising. Wallace's spectacular overhead kick looks to be enough until sub Peter Daniel heads in after good work by Hector.											
27	A	LEICESTER		16	L	1-3	0-2	Ferguson 89	Blyth	Oakey	McDonald	Beck	Yorath	Roberts	Green*	Wallace	Ferguson	Powell	Hutchison	Cartwright
	12/3		*16,766*	*7*	24			*Alderson 25, Earle 37, Worthington 85*	*Wallington*	*Whitworth*	*Rofe*	*Kember*	*Woollett*	*Sims*	*Weller*	*Birchenall*	*Worthington*	*Alderson*	*Earle*	
								Ref: K Burns	Holmes has gone to Spurs for £130,000 and Brogan to Ayr on a free, which means a makeshift defence and a rare defeat at Filbert Street. The referee ignores his linesman as Alderson scores against his old club and Blyth makes a stunning save, only for Earle to score from the rebound.											
28	A	NEWCASTLE		17	L	0-1	0-1		Blyth	Coop	McDonald	Beck	Yorath	Roberts	**Gooding**	Wallace	Ferguson	Powell	Hutchison	
	23/3		*23,287*	*5*	24			*Burns 15*	*Mahoney*	*Nattrass*	*Kennedy*	*Cassidy*	*McCaffrey*	*Nulty*	*Barrowclough*	*Cannell*	*Burns*	*Gowling**	*Craig*	*Blackhall*
								Ref: D Richardson	City's seventh away game running leaves City in the bottom six. Wallace misses a hat-trick of chances against their bogey side. Burns scores an opportunist goal for the Europe-bound Magpies under caretaker boss Richard Dinnis. Gooding enjoys a solid debut in his native North East.											
29	H	TOTTENHAM		17	D	1-1	1-1	Wallace 21	Blyth	Roberts	McDonald	Yorath	Gooding	Coop	Beck	Wallace	Ferguson	Powell	Hutchison	
	2/4		16,210	*18*	25			*Taylor 18*	*Daines*	*Naylor*	*Holmes*	*Pratt*	*Osgood*	*Perryman*	*Jones*	*Hoddle*	*Armstrong*	*Coates*	*Taylor*	
								Ref: K Walmsley	The first home game for ten weeks enables Roberts to make his home debut after ten away appearances. After the goals, the game disintegrates into a tedious, mistake-ridden affair with a draw the fair result. Ian Wallace's 20-yarder is a cracker and McDonald hits the post near the end.											
30	A	IPSWICH		17	L	1-2	1-1	Ferguson 41	Blyth	Roberts	McDonald	Yorath	Gooding	Coop	Beck	Wallace	Ferguson	Powell	Hutchison	
	5/4		*23,633*	*1*	25			*Mariner 11, Burley 46*	*Cooper*	*Burley*	*Tibbott*	*Talbot*	*Hunter*	*Beattie*	*Lambert*	*Mills*	*Mariner**	*Whymark*	*Woods*	*Bertschin*
								Ref: T Bune	Ipswich go top on goal-difference, but City make them work hard for the win. Mariner's goal looks offside and Burley's takes a deflection off Yorath's heel. Blyth is again in sparkling form as Ipswich pile on the pressure. Gooding deserves a penalty and Yorath gets his sixth booking.											
31	H	WEST HAM		19	D	1-1	0-0	Ferguson 75	Blyth*	Roberts	McDonald	Beck	Yorath	Coop	Gooding	Wallace	Ferguson	Powell	Hutchison	Green
	9/4		15,755	*21*	26			*Robson B 85*	*Day*	*Bonds*	*Lampard*	*Pike*	*Taylor T*	*McGiven*	*Taylor A*	*Devonshire*	*Jennings*	*Brooking*	*Robson B*	
								Ref: T Reynolds	Jim Blyth seriously damages knee ligaments and will be out for the season as City's plight becomes desperate. McDonald takes over in goal for the last half hour but can't stop Pop Robson's header. Ferguson heads in from Yorath's free-kick but this is another disappointing performance.											

No	Venue / Date	Opponent / Att	Pos	Res / Pts	F-A	H-T	Scorers, Times, and Referees	1	2	3	4	5	6	7	8	9	10	11	12 sub used
32	A	QP RANGERS	19	D	1-1	0-1	Wallace 60	**Sealey**	Roberts	McDonald	Yorath	Dugdale*	Coop	Beck	Wallace	Ferguson	Powell	Hutchison	Green
	11/4	*15,445*	*18*	27			*Masson 23p*	*Parkes*	*Shanks*	*Gillard*	*Kelly*	*Abbott*	*Webb*	*Thomas**	*Leach*	*Masson*	*Eastoe*	*Givens*	*Cunningham*
							Ref: L Shapter	Rangers seem a shadow of last season's side and have already used their sub when Leach breaks a cheek-bone in a clash with Dugdale. City finally score against the ten men with a Wallace header from Yorath's cross. Dugdale is harshly penalised for tackling Eastoe. Masson scores.											
33	H	ASTON VILLA	20	L	2-3	2-1	Wallace 30, 41	Sealey	Roberts	McDonald	Yorath	Dugdale !	Coop	Beck	Wallace	Ferguson	Powell	Hutchison	
	16/4	31,288	*6*	27			*Cowans 40, Deehan 79, Little 83*	*Burridge*	*Smith*	*Robson*	*Phillips*	*Nicholl*	*Mortimer*	*Graydon*	*Little*	*Deehan*	*Cropley*	*Cowans*	
							Ref: D Lloyd	Villa are applauded on to the pitch by City's players in recognition of their midweek League Cup Final victory, and their match-winner Little does it again. Coventry lead 2-1 when Dugdale walks for tripping Mortimer after 53 mins and Villa run City off their feet to grab a lucky win.											
34	H	WEST BROM	19	D	1-1	0-0	Ferguson 74	Sealey	Oakey	McDonald	Yorath	**Holton***	Coop	Beck	Wallace	Ferguson	Powell	Hutchison	Cartwright
	19/4	19,136	*7*	28			*Wile 68*	*Osborne*	*Mulligan*	*Statham*	*Brown T*	*Wile*	*Robertson*	*Martin*	*Cunningham*	*Brown A*	*Giles*	*Johnston*	
							Ref: J Worrall	Albion boss Johnny Giles says he will be quitting management at the end of the season. Milne is given a new two-year contract as Bryan King retires through injury. In a tense game, negative West Brom score with their first shot but Ferguson then heads past the veteran John Osborne.											
35	A	ARSENAL	20	L	0-2	0-0		Sealey	Oakey	McDonald	Yorath	Holton	Coop	Beck*	Wallace	Ferguson	Powell	Hutchison	Cartwright
	23/4	*22,790*	*9*	28			*Stapleton 73, Macdonald 79*	*Rimmer*	*Rice*	*Matthews*	*Ross**	*O'Leary*	*Young*	*Brady*	*Hudson*	*Macdonald*	*Stapleton*	*Armstrong*	*Rix*
							Ref: H Robinson	A lapse of concentration lets City down and increases the pressure on themselves. Les Sealey is brilliant in goal and Holton pockets Supermac until a late lapse lets the striker in for his 27th goal of the season, from Rix's cross. Holton and Sealey's mix-up lets in Stapleton for the first.											
36	H	DERBY	18	W	2-0	1-0	Coop 42p, Ferguson 82	Sealey	Oakey	McDonald	Yorath	Cartwright	Coop	Beck	Wallace	Ferguson	Powell	Hutchison	
	25/4	15,788	*17*	30				*Moseley*	*Langan*	*Webster*	*Daly*	*McFarland**	*Todd*	*Daniel*	*Powell*	*Hector*	*Gemmill*	*James*	
							Ref: C Thomas	A vital victory in the relegation fight and City's best performance for weeks. Mick Coop's penalty, after McFarland climbs over Ferguson for the umpteenth time, is reward for a sparkling first half. Ferguson's header from John Beck's cross seals it against Colin Murphy's strugglers.											
37	H	STOKE	16	W	5-2	4-1	Beck 5, Wallace 7, 10, 85, Powell 29	Sealey	Oakey	McDonald	Beck	Holton	Coop	Cartwright	Wallace	Ferguson	Powell	Hutchison	
	30/4	15,719	*17*	32			*Ruggiero 40, 66p*	*Shilton*	*Dodd*	*Marsh*	*Mahoney*	*Smith !*	*Bloor*	*Conroy*	*Salmons*	*Tudor*	*Crooks*	*Ruggiero*	
							Ref: C White	Stoke are going down and Wallace's hat-trick, aided by Ferguson's aerial power, helps them on their way. They have Smith sent off for fouling Hutch with 24 mins left and Conroy misses from the spot after Sealey fouls Garth Crooks. Ruggiero atones when Coop brings down Salmons.											
38	A	WEST HAM	16	L	0-2	0-1		Sealey	Cartwright	McDonald	Yorath	Holton	Coop	Beck	Wallace	Ferguson	Powell	Hutchison	
	4/5	*25,461*	*18*	32			*Robson B 19, Pike 50p*	*Day*	*Bonds*	*Lampard*	*Pike*	*Taylor T*	*McGiven*	*Radford*	*Robson B*	*Devonshire*	*Brooking*	*Taylor A*	
							Ref: R Lewis	West Ham gain their first win in five games and survival is now possible for them. Brooking is in a class of his own at a wet and muddy Upton Park. Robson needs three attempts at scoring the first goal, and Yorath, back from suspension, handles Bonds' free-kick for Pike's penalty.											
39	A	EVERTON	17	D	1-1	0-1	Hutchison 89	Sealey	Oakey	McDonald	Yorath	Holton	Coop	Beck	Wallace	Gooding*	Powell	Hutchison	Green
	7/5	*24,569*	*13*	33			*Rioch 13*	*Davies*	*Darracott*	*Pejic*	*Lyons*	*McNaught*	*Rioch*	*Buckley*	*Dobson*	*Pearson*	*McKenzie*	*King*	
							Ref: N Ashley	A last-gasp goal from Hutchison gives City a valuable point in the relegation fight. Everton have only lost twice in 13 games since Gordon Lee took over and they enjoy the lion's share of the game. They miss good chances, but so do Coventry. Spurs are the first team to be relegated.											
40	H	LIVERPOOL	16	D	0-0	0-0		Sealey	Oakey	McDonald	Yorath	Holton	Coop	Beck*	Wallace	Ferguson	Powell	Hutchison	Cartwright
	10/5	**38,160**	*1*	34				*Clemence*	*Neal*	*Jones*	*Smith*	*Kennedy*	*Hughes*	*Keegan*	*Case*	*Heighway*	*Johnson*	*McDermott*	
							Ref: D Richardson	Liverpool are almost certain to win the title, and are in the FA and European Cup finals, yet City match them in a keen match. Holton marshals City's defence, while at the other end Clemence makes superb saves from Wallace and Ferguson. City's best league attendance for six years.											
41	H	MANCHESTER C	18	L	0-1	0-0		Sealey	Oakey	McDonald	Yorath	Holton*	Coop	Beck	Wallace	Ferguson	Powell	Hutchison	Cartwright
	14/5	21,370	*2*	34			*Conway 52*	*Corrigan*	*Clements*	*Donachie*	*Booth*	*Watson*	*Owen*	*Conway*	*Power*	*Royle*	*Hartford*	*Barnes*	
							Ref: J Bent	An unlucky defeat to the league runners-up means that City might need to win their final game. Wallace hits the post, Ferguson squanders two easy chances, Corrigan makes two world-class saves and a good penalty appeal is turned down. Jim Conway scores his first goal for Man City.											
42	H	BRISTOL CITY	19	D	2-2	1-0	Hutchison 15,51	Sealey	Oakey	McDonald	Yorath	Holton*	Coop	Beck	Wallace	Ferguson	Powell	Hutchison	
	19/5	36,892	*18*	35			*Gow 52, Gillies 79*	*Shaw*	*Gillies*	*Sweeney*	*Gow*	*Collier*	*Hunter*	*Tainton*	*Ritchie*	*Garland*	*Mann*	*Whitehead**	*Cormack*
	Home	Away					Ref: R Challis	The game is delayed for traffic reasons and City put their fans through it by losing a 2-0 lead. With five minutes left Sunderland's defeat is flashed on the scoreboard. Both sides are safe, if the score stays at 2-2, so a truce is declared. Bristol players pass the ball among themselves.											
Average	21,206	24,719																	

LEAGUE DIVISION 1 (CUP-TIES) Manager: Gordon Milne SEASON 1976-77

League Cup				F-A	H-T	Scorers, Times, and Referees	1	2	3	4	5	6	7	8	9	10	11	12 sub used
2 A BRISTOL CITY	18	W		1-0	1-0	Ferguson 41	Blyth	Coop	McDonald	Craven	Holmes	Dugdale	Cartwright	Yorath	Ferguson	Beck	Murphy	
31/8	*13,878*	*7*					*Cashley*	*Sweeney*	*Drysdale*	*Gow*	*Collier*	*Merrick*	*Tainton*	*Ritchie*	*Mann*	*Gillies*	*Whitehead*	
						Ref: D Reeves	Bristol are unbeaten in their first season in the top flight since 1911. Yorath is made captain on his debut and almost throws the game away with a 35-yard back-pass straight to Gillies. Ferguson's rocket header wins the tie. The Coventry team-coach breaks down to spoil a good night.											
3 A NOTT'M FOREST	15	W		3-0	3-0	Ferguson 23, Coop 30p, Cartwright 39	Blyth	Coop	McDonald	Craven	Holmes	Dugdale	Cartwright*	Yorath	Ferguson	Beck	Green	Cross
21/9	*15,969*	*2:12*					*Middleton*	*Barrett*	*Clark*	*McGovern*	*Chapman*	*Bowyer*	*Curran*	*O'Neill*	*O'Hare*	*Butlin*	*Robertson*	
						Ref: T Bosi	A comprehensive victory over Brian Clough's side, who will go on to win promotion. Ferguson scores yet again, the sixth game in a row. Coop scores from the spot after Alan Green is fouled by John McGovern and Green ends an superb 60-yard run with a cross for Cartwright to score.											
4 A EVERTON	12	L		0-3	0-1		Blyth	Coop	McDonald	Yorath	Dugdale	Holmes	Cartwright	Murphy	Ferguson	Powell*	Beck	Green
26/10	*21,572*	*4*				*King 18,78, Lyons 54*	*Davies*	*Bernard*	*Jones*	*Lyons*	*McNaught*	*Hamilton*	*King*	*Dobson*	*Latchford*	*Goodlass*	*Telfer*	
						Ref: N Ashley	City's worst performance since August sees Everton through to meet Man United in the quarter-finals and ultimately to Wembley. It takes a scrambled goal, a freak goal and a lucky goal for the Toffees to beat Coventry's frail challenge. Jim Blyth's brilliance avoids a heavier defeat.											

FA Cup				F-A	H-T	Scorers, Times, and Referees	1	2	3	4	5	6	7	8	9	10	11	12 sub used
3 H MILLWALL	11	W		1-0	0-0	McDonald 66	Blyth	Coop	McDonald	Yorath	Dugdale	Craven*	Beck	Green	Murphy	Powell	Hutchison	Cartwright
8/1	17,634	*2:6*					*Goddard*	*Evans*	*Donaldson*	*Brisley*	*Kitchener**	*Hazell*	*Lee*	*Seasman*	*Fairbrother*	*Moore*	*Walker*	*Shanahan*
						Ref: A Grey	Gordon Jago's Millwall give City a fright in a grim battle in the mud. Jim Blyth makes a string of fine saves to avoid the replay, but without Ferguson there is little oomph up front. McDonald scores the winner from a tight angle from Beck's cross. Coventry play in a red change strip.											
4 A ARSENAL	13	L		1-3	0-2	Hutchison 55	Blyth	Coop	McDonald	Roberts	Dugdale	Holmes	Beck	Green	Murphy	Powell	Hutchison	
29/1	*41,078*	*5*				*Stapleton 25, Macdonald 40, 56*	*Rimmer*	*Rice*	*Nelson*	*Ross*	*O'Leary*	*Simpson*	*Hudson*	*Brady*	*Macdonald**	*Stapleton*	*Rostron*	*Storey*
						Ref: K Styles	Key players are missing from the City line-up and the Gunners coast home in a predictable outcome. Terry Neill's men look a good bet for the Cup as Stapleton and Macdonald shoot on sight. Hutchison scores with a rare header to raise hopes, but Supermac's reply ends the contest.											

		Home					Away					
	P	W	D	L	F	A	W	D	L	F	A	Pts
1 Liverpool	42	18	3	0	47	11	5	8	8	15	22	57
2 Manchester C	42	15	5	1	38	13	6	9	6	22	21	56
3 Ipswich	42	15	4	2	41	11	7	4	10	25	28	52
4 Aston Villa	42	17	3	1	55	17	5	4	12	21	33	51
5 Newcastle	42	14	6	1	40	15	4	7	10	24	34	49
6 Manchester U	42	12	6	3	41	22	6	5	10	30	40	47
7 West Brom	42	10	6	5	38	22	6	7	8	24	34	45
8 Arsenal	42	11	6	4	37	20	5	5	11	27	39	43
9 Everton	42	9	7	5	35	24	5	7	9	27	40	42
10 Leeds	42	8	8	5	28	26	7	4	10	20	25	42
11 Leicester	42	8	9	4	30	28	4	9	8	17	32	42
12 Middlesbro	42	11	6	4	25	14	3	7	11	15	31	41
13 Birmingham	42	10	6	5	38	25	3	6	12	25	36	38
14 QP Rangers	42	10	7	4	31	21	3	5	13	16	31	38
15 Derby	42	9	9	3	36	18	0	10	11	14	37	37
16 Norwich	42	12	4	5	30	23	2	5	14	17	41	37
17 West Ham	42	9	6	6	28	23	2	8	11	18	42	36
18 Bristol City	42	8	7	6	25	19	3	6	12	13	29	35
19 COVENTRY	42	7	9	5	34	26	3	6	12	14	33	35
20 Sunderland	42	9	5	7	29	16	2	7	12	17	38	34
21 Stoke	42	9	8	4	21	16	1	6	14	7	35	34
22 Tottenham	42	9	7	5	26	20	3	2	16	22	52	33
	924	240	137	85	753	430	85	137	240	430	753	924

Odds & ends

Double wins: (1) Leeds.
Double losses: (3) Manchester U, Arsenal, Manchester C.

Won from behind: (2) Leeds (h), Everton (h).
Lost from in front: (2) Liverpool (a), Aston Villa (h).

High spots: Triple signing of Yorath, Wallace and McDonald in August.
Six-game unbeaten run in Autumn.
Home victory over Everton.
Stoke home win, with Wallace scoring a hat-trick against Shilton.
Bristol City game, which resulted in City staying up.

Low spots: 13 games without a win in the spring.
Losing at home to Villa after twice leading.

Red cards: City – Lloyd (Man U h), Dugdale (A Villa h), Beck (A Villa a).
Red cards: Opponents – Smith (Stoke h).

Player of the Year: Jim Blyth.
Ever-presents: (0).
Hat-tricks: (1) Ian Wallace.
Opposing hat-tricks: (0).
Leading scorer: (15) Mick Ferguson.

	Appearances						Goals			
	Lge	*Sub*	LC	*Sub*	FAC	*Sub*	Lge	LC	FAC	Tot
Beck, John	**40**		3		2		**3**			**3**
Blyth, Jim	**31**		3		2					
Cartwright, Les	**11**	*8*	3			*1*	**1**	1		**2**
Coop, Mick	**39**		3		2		**2**	1		**3**
Craven, John	**4**	*1*	2		1					
Cross, David	**2**		0	*1*						
Dugdale, Alan	**25**		3		2					
Ferguson, Mick	**32**		3				**13**	2		**15**
Gooding, Ray	**5**		0							
Green, Alan	**14**	*3*	1	*1*	2		**4**			**4**
Holmes, Jin	**25**	*1*	3		1					
Holton, Jim	**8**		0							
Hutchison, Tommy	**31**	*2*	0		2		**3**		1	**4**
Lloyd, Larry	**5**		0							
McDonald, Bobby	**39**		3		2		**1**		1	**2**
Murphy, Donal	**13**	*5*	2		2		**6**			**6**
Oakey, Graham	**13**		0							
Powell, Barry	**40**		1		2		**4**			**4**
Roberts, Brian	**12**		0		1					
Sealey, Les	**11**		0							
Wallace, Ian	**24**	*2*	0				**9**			**9**
Yorath, Terry	**38**		3		1		**1**			**1**
(own-goals)							**1**			**1**
22 players used	**462**	***22***	**33**	***2***	**22**	***1***	**48**	**4**	**2**	**54**

No	Date		Att	Pos	Pt	F-A	H-T	Scorers, Times, and Referees	1	2	3	4	5	6	7	8	9	10	11	12 sub used
1	H	DERBY			W	3-1	0-1	Ferguson 50, 89, Wallace 86	Blyth	Oakey	McDonald	Yorath	Holton	Coop	**Graydon**	Wallace	Ferguson	Powell	Hutchison	
	20/8		17,938		2			*Nish 14*	*Boulton*	*Langan*	*Nish*	*Daly*	*McFarland*	*Todd*	*O'Riordan*	*King*	*Hales*	*Hector*	*Hughes*	
								Ref: W Gow	Derby dominate the first half against a mediocre City and David Nish scores in his first game for a year. The home side wake up and take the direct route with two wingers. Ray Graydon sets up two goals on his debut after signing from Villa for £35,000. 14 arrests after crowd trouble.											
2	A	MANCHESTER U			L	1-2	1-1	Wallace 28	Blyth	Oakey	McDonald	Yorath	Holton	Coop	Graydon	Wallace	Ferguson	Powell	Hutchison	
	24/8		**55,726**		2			*Hill 7p, McCreery 72*	*Stepney*	*Nicholl*	*Albiston*	*McIlroy*	*Greenhoff B*	*Buchan*	*Coppell*	*McCreery*	*Pearson*	*Macari*	*Hill*	
								Ref: M Lowe	Before kick-off United parade both the FA Cup and their new manager, Dave Sexton. City spoil the party with a superb attacking display. Hill nets a twice-taken penalty after Pearson 'falls over' and McCreery's shot is deflected. Otherwise its all City. City's biggest away gate in Div 1.											
3	A	CHELSEA		6	W	2-1	2-0	Wallace 24, 40	Blyth	Oakey	McDonald	Yorath	Holton	Coop	Graydon	Wallace	Ferguson	Powell	Hutchison	
	27/8		*25,432*	*14*	4			*Langley 77*	*Phillips*	*Locke*	*Sparrow*	*Stanley*	*Wicks*	*Harris*	*Britton*	*Wilkins R*	*Finnieston*	*Lewington*	*Langley*	
								Ref: D Nippard	The Sky Blues' 4-2-4 system wins friends and matches, and newly promoted Chelsea are dispatched more easily than the scoreline suggests. Wallace deflects Powell's shot to claim the first goal. The second comes out of nothing as Wallace turns and rifles home. Holton is supreme.											
4	H	LEEDS		8	D	2-2	1-2	Ferguson 30, Wallace 49	Blyth	Oakey	McDonald	Yorath	Holton	Coop	Graydon	Wallace	Ferguson	Powell	Hutchison	
	3/9		21,312	*11*	5			*Hankin 10, McQueen 17*	*Stewart*	*Reaney**	*Cherry*	*Lorimer*	*McQueen*	*Madeley*	*Gray F*	*Hankin*	*Jordan*	*Currie*	*Graham*	*Harris*
								Ref: J Bent	City's attacking policy receives its first big test as Leeds take a two-goal lead with their own brand of attack. Mick Ferguson's glorious header from Hutch's cross, and Wallace's opportunism, earns City a point. Frank Gray brings Wallace down in the area late on, but the ref ignores it.											
5	A	LIVERPOOL		12	L	0-2	0-0		Blyth	Oakey	McDonald	Yorath	Holton	Coop	Graydon	Wallace	Ferguson	Powell	Hutchison	
	10/9		*45,574*	*2*	5			*Fairclough 64, Dalglish 66*	*Clemence*	*Neal*	*Jones*	*Smith*	*Kennedy*	*Hughes*	*Dalglish*	*Case*	*Fairclough*	*McDermott*	*Callaghan*	
								Ref: T Farley	Kenny Dalglish has replaced Keegan as the King with four goals in five games since joining Liverpool. Former boss Shankly says of City 'I've never seen a side create as many chances at Anfield'. But City's poor finishing is their undoing. Wallace's loud penalty appeal is rejected.											
6	H	MIDDLESBROUGH		9	W	2-1	0-0	Graydon 65, 81	Blyth	Oakey	McDonald	Yorath	Holton	Coop	Graydon	Wallace	Ferguson	Powell	Hutchison	
	17/9		**13,910**	*16*	7			*Mills 89*	*Platt*	*Craggs*	*Bailey*	*Souness*	*Boam*	*Ramage*	*Mahoney*	*Mills*	*Ashcroft*	*McAndrew*	*Armstrong*	
								Ref: T Reynolds	Jack Charlton has left but John Neal hasn't changed Boro's tactics - they are still mean and spoiling. City dominate a poor game and Ray Graydon finally gets the breakthrough. It gives City their first win in seven over the Ayresome Park men since Boro won promotion in 1974.											
7	A	NEWCASTLE		5	W	2-1	1-1	Wallace 37, 65	Blyth	Oakey	McDonald	Yorath	Beck	Coop	Graydon	Wallace	Ferguson	Powell	Hutchison	
	24/9		*22,482*	*22*	9			*Gowling 42*	*Mahoney*	*Craig D*	*Kennedy*	*McLean**	*McCaffery*	*Nattrass*	*Barrowclough*	*Callachan*	*Burns*	*Gowling*	*Craig T*	*Oates*
								Ref: J Worrall	Newcastle's sixth defeat on the run, and their fans are getting restless. In a wind-spoiled match City soak up plenty of Newcastle pressure but always look in control and snatch their first win at St James' since 1939. Jim Blyth's long kick catches out Mahoney. Wallace lobs the winner.											
8	H	WEST BROM		11	L	1-2	1-0	Wile 17 (og)	Blyth	Oakey	McDonald	Yorath	Holton	Coop	Graydon	Wallace	Ferguson	Powell	Hutchison	
	1/10		25,707	*3*	9			*Holton 65 (og), Brown T 84*	*Godden*	*Mulligan*	*Statham*	*Brown T*	*Wile*	*Robertson*	*Cantello**	*Brown A*	*Regis*	*Robson*	*Johnston*	*Martin*
								Ref: D Lloyd	Albion have only lost once and near the end of a super Midlands derby punish City's lack of caution. Goal-a-game Cyrille Regis is shackled by Holton and Wallace is subdued. Wile's header from Coop's cross, and the deflection of Tony Brown's shot off Holton's knee, are own-goals.											
9	H	MANCHESTER C		6	W	4-2	1-2	Ferguson 30, 73, 89, Wallace 79	Sealey	Oakey	McDonald	Yorath	Holton	Coop	Beck	Wallace	Ferguson	Powell	Hutchison	
	4/10		19,650	*2*	11			*Tueart 4, Barnes 45*	*Corrigan*	*Clements*	*Donachie*	*Kidd*	*Watson*	*Booth*	*Barnes*	*Power*	*Royle*	*Hartford*	*Tueart*	
								Ref: B Martin	City put paid to Manchester City's unbeaten record with a scintillating display, culminating in three goals in 16 minutes. The visitors, despite being under non-stop pressure, led 2-1 at half-time. Mick Ferguson is the star of the show with his hat-trick but all contribute to a super victory.											
10	A	BIRMINGHAM		7	D	1-1	0-1	Ferguson 59	Sealey	Oakey	McDonald	Yorath	Holton	Coop	Beck	Wallace	Ferguson	Powell	Hutchison	
	8/10		*27,414*	*16*	12			*Francis 44p*	*Montgomery*	*Calderwood*	*Pendrey*	*Page**	*Howard*	*Want*	*Connolly*	*Francis*	*Bertschin*	*Hibbitt*	*Emmanuel*	*Jones*
								Ref: K McNally	Blues caretaker manager Sir Alf Ramsey praises the 'new' City but they are not at their best. The penalty is controversially given when Beck and Connolly clash but City turn the heat up in heavy rain and are rewarded with Fergie's left-foot shot. Holton is booked and almost sent off.											

No	H/A	Opponent / Date	Att	Pos	Res / Pts	FT	HT	Scorers, Times, and Referees	1	2	3	4	5	6	7	8	9	10	11	12 sub used
11	A	LEICESTER		6	W	2-1	1-1	Coop 10p, 76p	Blyth	Oakey	McDonald	Yorath	Holton	Coop	Graydon	Wallace	Ferguson	Powell	Hutchison	
		15/10	*20,205*	*21*	14			*Sammels 23p*	*Wallington*	*Whitworth*	*Rofe*	*Kember*	*Williams*	*Webb*	*Weller*	*Kelly**	*Salmons*	*Alderson*	*Armstrong*	*Sammels*
								Ref: C Thomas	A tale of two City's and four penalties. Coop scores after Webb's handball. Blyth saves Rofe's 12th-minute effort after Holton shoves Weller. Sammels'shirt is pulled and he scores himself. Finally Webb handles again. Frank McLintock's Leicester have now lost four in a row at home.											
12	H	IPSWICH		6	D	1-1	0-0	Hutchison 58	Blyth	Oakey	McDonald	Yorath*	Dugdale	Coop	Nardiello	Wallace	Ferguson	Powell	Hutchison	Graydon
		22/10	20,176	*10*	15			*Mariner 47*	*Cooper*	*Burley**	*Roberts*	*Talbot*	*Hunter*	*Osman*	*Mills*	*Gates*	*Mariner*	*Whymark*	*Osborne*	*Geddis*
								Ref: R Lewis	Dugdale, about to move to Charlton for £50,000, comes in for the injured Holton. Ipswich show respect by adopting a five-man defence and it pays off. Mariner's header is cancelled out by Hutch's first goal of the season as Yorath limps off. Blyth keeps Ipswich at bay with fine saves.											
13	A	WOLVES		6	W	3-1	0-1	Ferguson 58, 68, 75	Blyth	Oakey	McDonald	Yorath	Beck	Coop	Nardiello	Wallace	Ferguson	Powell	Hutchison	
		29/10	*23,796*	*11*	17			*Hibbitt 3*	*Bradshaw*	*Palmer*	*Parkin*	*Patching*	*Brazier*	*McAlle*	*Hibbitt**	*Carr*	*Richards*	*Bell*	*Sunderland*	*Farley*
								Ref: D Richardson	'Fergie for England' chant the fans as he scores a 17-minute hat-trick to sink Wolves. He and Wallace have now scored 19 goals between them. Another superb display earns praise from Wolves boss Chung and Welsh boss Smith, 'the most exciting performance I've seen this season'.											
14	H	WEST HAM		4	W	1-0	1-0	Wallace 42	Blyth	Oakey	McDonald	Yorath	Beck	Coop	Nardiello	Wallace	Ferguson*	Powell	Hutchison	Graydon
		5/11	23,268	*19*	19				*Day*	*Lampard*	*Brush*	*Bonds*	*Taylor T*	*Pike*	*Devonshire*	*Robson B*	*Radford*	*Brooking*	*Hales*	
								Ref: E Hughes	There is a minute's silence for former chairman Jack Scamp, who died in the week. West Ham won at Ipswich last week but take a first-half pounding. Lampard handles in the 19th minute but Coop puts his penalty wide for his first miss in four years. Wallace back-heads the winner.											
15	A	ARSENAL		4	D	1-1	1-1	Green 3	Blyth	Oakey	McDonald	Yorath	Roberts	Coop	Nardiello	Wallace	Green	Powell	Hutchison	
		12/11	*31,653*	*5*	20			*Coop 34 (og)*	*Jennings*	*Rice*	*Nelson*	*Price*	*O'Leary*	*Young*	*Brady*	*Sunderland*	*Macdonald !*	*Stapleton*	*Rix*	
								Ref: A Robinson	Arsenal are behind after three minutes and reduced to ten men five minutes later. Green scores in his first game of the season and Supermac punches Yorath and is sent off. Mick Coop - in his 300th game and in his testimonial week - scores in his own net. Nardiello is in Wales' team.											
16	H	QP RANGERS		3	W	4-1	3-0	Wallace 2, 41, Yorath 33, Coop 73p	Blyth	Oakey	McDonald	Yorath	Roberts	Coop	Nardiello	Wallace	Green*	Powell	Hutchison	Beck
		19/11	20,390	*18*	22			*Givens 51*	*Richardson*	*Shanks*	*Gillard*	*Hollins*	*Needham*	*Busby*	*McGee**	*James*	*Givens*	*Bowles*	*Williams*	*Abbott*
								Ref: A Hughes	Nine games without defeat and the super Sky Blues lay siege to Rangers' goal, earning a standing ovation. QPR boss Frank Sibley says 'they are the best side we have met all season'. Yorath is awesome and chips the wall for his goal. Ian Wallace scores two and has one disallowed.											
17	A	EVERTON		4	L	**0-6**	0-3	*[Pearson 66, King 71]*	Blyth	Oakey	McDonald	Yorath	Roberts	Coop	Nardiello	Wallace	Graydon*	Powell	Hutchison	Murphy
		26/11	*43,309*	*2*	22			*Dobson 8, Latchford 41, 43, 89,*	*Wood*	*Jones*	*Pejic*	*Lyons*	*Higgins*	*Buckley*	*King*	*Dobson*	*Latchford*	*Pearson*	*Thomas*	
								Ref: N Ashley	The Toffees end City's unbeaten run and extend theirs to 18 games. Everything Everton try comes off, resulting in City's heaviest league defeat since 1958. Yet City are the better side until the 40th minute and have a blatant penalty turned down. Latchford scores three but does little else.											
18	H	BRISTOL CITY		5	D	1-1	1-0	Ferguson 29	Blyth	Oakey	McDonald	Yorath	Holton	Coop	Nardiello	Wallace	Ferguson	Powell	Hutchison	
		3/12	22,307	*17*	23			*Ritchie 78*	*Shaw*	*Sweeney*	*Merrick*	*Cormack*	*Collier*	*Hunter*	*Tainton*	*Ritchie*	*Royle*	*Gillies*	*Whitehead*	
								Ref: K Salmon	Despite not hitting their recent heights the Sky Blues are well on top in the first half. After the break the exertions of Anfield begin to take their toll and Bristol fight their way into the game. Jim Blyth makes two fine saves but fails to hold Joe Royle's shot and Ritchie nets the rebound.											
19	A	NOTT'M FOREST		6	L	1-2	1-2	Wallace 41	Blyth	Oakey	McDonald	Yorath	Holton	Coop	Nardiello	Wallace	Ferguson	Powell	Hutchison	
		10/12	*29,823*	*1*	23			*O'Neill 40, McGovern 45*	*Shilton*	*Anderson*	*Barrett*	*McGovern*	*Lloyd*	*Burns*	*O'Neill*	*Gemmill*	*Withe*	*Woodcock*	*Robertson*	
								Ref: J Hough	Forest, unbeaten at home, are lucky to survive a golden first 20 minutes from City on a heavy pitch. City are unlucky to lose a pulsating match and Forest assistant Peter Taylor describes the Sky Blues as 'easily the best side we've played this season'. Shilton and Blyth are both superb.											
20	H	ARSENAL		8	L	1-2	0-1	Coop 81p	Blyth	Oakey	McDonald	Yorath	Roberts	Coop	Nardiello*	Wallace	Ferguson	Powell	Hutchison	Graydon
		17/12	20,993	*5*	23			*Stapleton 33, 51*	*Jennings*	*Rice*	*Nelson*	*Price*	*O'Leary*	*Young*	*Brady*	*Sunderland*	*Macdonald*	*Stapleton*	*Rix*	
								Ref: D Biddle	Jim Holton pulls out before the kick-off and City's makeshift defence can't stop Stapleton's two headers. Inspired by Brady, Arsenal seal their fifth away win on the trot, catching the Sky Blues on an off day. Coop scores after Nelson trips Graydon. Blyth is set for a Scotland call-up.											
21	A	ASTON VILLA		8	D	1-1	0-0	Wallace 72	Blyth	Oakey*	McDonald	Yorath	Roberts	Coop	Graydon	Wallace	Ferguson	Powell	Hutchison	Beck
		26/12	*43,571*	*11*	24			*Deehan 73*	*Rimmer*	*Gregory*	*Smith*	*Phillips*	*McNaught*	*Mortimer*	*Deehan*	*Little*	*Gray*	*Cowans*	*Carrodus*	
								Ref: D Shaw	Jim Holton's absence is vital again, as Deehan heads home Mortimer's free-kick to give Ron Saunders' Villa a point. Graham Oakey is carried off after 21 minutes with a knee injury and Beck plays at right-back. The pitch resembles a beach but doesn't inhibit City's attacking football.											

No	Date		Att	Pos	Pt	F-A	H-T	Scorers, Times, and Referees	1	2	3	4	5	6	7	8	9	10	11	12 sub used
22	H	NORWICH		7	W	5-4	2-3	Po 12p, W 26, Good 56, Mc 67, Gra 82	Blyth	Beck	McDonald	Yorath	Roberts	Gooding	Graydon	Wallace	Ferguson	Powell	Hutchison	
	27/12		21,609	*8*	26			*Ryan 32p, Reeves 36, 44, Peters 75*	*Keelan*	*Bond*	*Sullivan*	*Ryan*	*Jones*	*Powell*	*Neighbour*	*Suggett*	*Gibbins*	*Reeves*	*Peters*	
								Ref: L Shapter	Sensational, breathtaking, unbelievable! One of the greatest games ever seen at Highfield Road, with Blyth saving Ryan's last-minute penalty to clinch the win. Wallace's bicycle-kick goal is out of this world and Peters hits the post at 5-4. Powell takes the penalty in Coop's absence.											
23	H	MANCHESTER U		6	W	3-0	2-0	Ferguson 8, Wallace 34, Yorath 83	Blyth	Beck	McDonald	Yorath	Roberts	Gooding	Graydon	Wallace	Ferguson	Powell	Hutchison	
	31/12		24,706	*13*	28				*Roche*	*Nicholl*	*Houston**	*McIlroy*	*Greenhoff B*	*Buchan*	*Coppell*	*Greenhoff J*	*Ritchie*	*Macari*	*Hill*	*McGrath*
								Ref: T Morris	City see the year out by demolishing United, who had won 6-2 at Everton on Boxing Day. All three goals are headers, the best coming from Yorath, who galloped the length of the pitch to connect with Wallace's cross. Despite a makeshift defence, the Sky Blues are rarely troubled.											
24	A	DERBY		7	L	2-4	0-2	Ferguson 75, Powell 86	Blyth	Beck	McDonald	Yorath	Roberts	Gooding	Graydon	Wallace	Ferguson	Powell	Hutchison	
	2/1		*25,929*	*10*	28			*George 9, 16p, 73, Daly 60*	*Middleton*	*Langan*	*Daniel*	*Daly*	*Hunt*	*Todd*	*Curran*	*Powell*	*Masson*	*George**	*Bartlett*	*Chesters*
								Ref: K Hackett	The makeshift defence crumbles under Charlie George's pressure. Yorath makes a hash of a back-pass for the first goal and Langan falls over Blyth for a crazy penalty. Another iffy decision allows the offside Daly to score a third. City rouse themselves at 0-4 but it is too little, too late.											
25	H	CHELSEA		6	W	**5-1**	2-0	McDonald 1, Wallace 31, Coop 60p,	Blyth	Roberts	McDonald	Yorath	Osgood	Coop	Graydon	Wallace	Ferguson	Powell	Hutchison	
	14/1		21,047	*13*	30			*Wilkins R 51* [Graydon 77, 86]	*Bonetti*	*Wilkins G*	*Sparrow*	*Britton*	*Harris*	*Wicks*	*Garner*	*Lewington*	*Langley*	*Wilkins R*	*Walker*	
								Ref: C Newsome	City's impressive home form continues against a Chelsea side which had beaten Liverpool 4-2 last week. The Londoners are demoralised by a devastating display from the Sky Blues. Harris fouls Wallace for the penalty and Graydon hits his best form of the season and scores two.											
26	A	LEEDS		7	L	0-2	0-2		Blyth	Roberts	McDonald	Yorath	Osgood	Coop	Graydon	Wallace	Ferguson	Powell*	Hutchison	Beck
	21/1		*27,062*	*6*	30			*Hankin 31, Harris 45*	*Harvey*	*Reaney*	*Gray F*	*Lorimer*	*Parkinson*	*Madeley*	*Cherry*	*Hankin*	*Currie*	*Gray E*	*Harris**	*Flynn*
								Ref: A Porter	Three away defeats running is not European form and City's attack is for once found wanting. Hankin scores his 16th goal of the season with a header and Harris looks to hand the ball in for the second. Leeds are poor with the exception of Tony Currie. Powell limps off after 36 minutes.											
27	H	LIVERPOOL		7	W	1-0	0-0	Ferguson 65	Blyth	Roberts*	McDonald	Gooding	Osgood	Coop	Graydon	Wallace	Ferguson	Powell	Hutchison	Nardiello
	4/2		28,474	*4*	32				*Clemence*	*Neal*	*Hansen*	*Thompson*	*Kennedy*	*Hughes*	*Dalglish*	*Case*	*Fairclough*	*Souness*	*Callaghan*	
								Ref: C White	England boss Ron Greenwood watches City snatch a hard won win, with England hopeful Ferguson lobbing the winner over Ray Clemence. Souness crunches Roberts on 30 minutes to add to the injury list. Hero Blyth saves Phil Neal's 61st-minute penalty after Coop fouls Fairclough.											
28	A	WEST BROM		7	D	3-3	1-1	Coop 35p, Wallace 50, Beck 84	Blyth	Roberts	McDonald	Gooding*	Osgood	Coop	Nardiello	Wallace	Ferguson	Powell	Hutchison	Beck
	25/2		*25,300*	*8*	33			*Trewick 19, 71, Wile 77*	*Godden*	*Robson**	*Statham*	*Brown T*	*Wile*	*Robertson*	*Martin*	*Brown A*	*Regis*	*Trewick*	*Johnston*	*Cunningham*
								Ref: J Worrall	Blyth and Wallace return from their Scottish debuts to a thrilling Midlands derby. City look set to win, thanks to Coop's penalty, for Statham's foul on Nardiello, followed by Wallace's tap-in. Trewick's two screamers require a goal from Beck's first touch to hold Big Ron's Albion.											
29	H	BIRMINGHAM		7	W	4-0	3-0	Ferguson 1, 34, 77, Beck 44	Blyth	Roberts	McDonald	Yorath	Holton	Coop	Green*	Wallace	Ferguson	Powell	Hutchison	Beck
	4/3		22,925	*18*	35				*Montgomery*	*Calderwood*	*Styles*	*Towers*	*Gallagher*	*Howard**	*Broadhurst*	*Francis*	*Bertschin*	*Hibbitt*	*Dillon*	*Fox*
								Ref: A Grey	In the week that Gary Gillespie signs from Falkirk for £75,000, Birmingham are given the treatment. Fergie scores from Green's cross in 25 seconds and proceeds to bag his third hat-trick of the season. Blues boss Alf Ramsey criticises his players and decides to quit St Andrews.											
30	H	LEICESTER		6	W	1-0	1-0	Nardiello 20	Blyth	Roberts	McDonald	Yorath	Holton	Coop	Nardiello	Wallace	Ferguson*	Powell	Hutchison	Beck
	11/3		24,214	*21*	37				*Wallington*	*Whitworth*	*Rofe*	*Williams*	*Sims*	*Woollett*	*Weller**	*Hughes*	*Christie*	*Salmons*	*Kelly*	*Webb*
								Ref: T Morris	Leicester are going down but put up stout resistance with their negative offside trap. Donato Nardiello heads his first goal from Hutch's corner before Ferguson limps off with ankle problems. Leicester are lightweight up front. Argentina-bound Blyth saves anything they have to offer.											
31	A	IPSWICH		7	D	1-1	0-0	Osgood 66	Blyth	Roberts	McDonald	Yorath	Holton	Coop	Nardiello*	Wallace	Osgood	Powell	Hutchison	Beck
	18/3		*21,110*	*17*	38			*Woods 61*	*Cooper*	*Burley*	*Mills*	*Talbot*	*Hunter*	*Beattie*	*Osborne*	*Wark*	*Mariner**	*Turner*	*Woods*	*Lambert*
								Ref: D Reeves	Despite reaching the FA Cup semi-finals the East Anglians are having an unexpected poor league season. Whilst Nardiello is being helped off with a broken collar bone Woods scores from Turner's cross. City bounce back with Osgood's fierce shot from Powell's back-heeled free-kick.											

No	H/A Date	Opponent	Att	Pos	Res Pts	F-A	H-T	Scorers, Times, and Referees	1	2	3	4	5	6	7	8	9	10	11	12
32	H	ASTON VILLA		7	L	2-3	0-2	McDonald 72, 83	Blyth	Roberts	McDonald	Yorath	Holton	Coop	Beck	Murphy	**Thompson**	Powell	Hutchison	
	21/3		30,920	*10*	38			*Little 36, McNaught 40, Gray 68*	*Rimmer*	*Gidman*	*Smith*	*Phillips*	*McNaught*	*Mortimer*	*Gregory*	*Little*	*Gray*	*Cowans*	*Carrodus*	
								Ref: A Robinson	The absence of Wallace and Ferguson is too much, and Villa's smash-and-grab style catches City out. Defensive blunders let in Little and McNaught and Gray scores with a diving header. McDonald leads the fightback, and Gray heads his shot off the line to prevent the equaliser.											
33	A	NORWICH		6	W	2-1	0-1	Powell 66p, Wallace 89	Blyth	Roberts	McDonald	Yorath	Holton	Osgood	Beck	Wallace	Thompson	Powell	Hutchison	
	25/3		*20,732*	*9*	40			*Reeves 4*	*Hansbury*	*Ryan*	*Sullivan*	*McGuire*	*Jones*	*Powell*	*Robson*	*Suggett*	*Paddon*	*Reeves*	*Peters**	*Bond*
								Ref: M Peck	A half-fit Wallace scores the winner and inflicts Norwich's second home defeat of the season. City fight back after Reeves' early header and Powell scores from the penalty spot after Ryan brings down Hutchison. Europe is still on the cards and City impress Norwich boss John Bond.											
34	H	WOLVES		5	W	4-0	2-0	T'mpson 37, Hutch'n 44, 67, Wallace 58	Blyth	Roberts	McDonald	Yorath	Holton	Osgood	Beck	Wallace	Thompson*	Powell	Hutchison	Murphy
	28/3		25,673	*18*	42				*Bradshaw*	*Palmer*	*Parkin*	*Daley*	*Hazell*	*McAlle*	*Patching*	*Carr*	*Eves*	*Brazier*	*Daly*	
								Ref: D Nippard	Tommy Hutchison dazzles as Wolves are steamrollered by City's attacking power. He scores two and creates one of the goals of the season by beating five Wolves men in a superb dribble, then crossing for Wallace to head home. Garry Thompson scores his first ever goal but limps off.											
35	A	WEST HAM		6	L	1-2	0-1	McDonald 61	Blyth	Roberts	McDonald	Yorath	Holton	Osgood	Beck	Wallace	Thompson*	Powell	Hutchison	Coop
	1/4		*19,260*	*19*	42			*Taylor T 19, Holland 59*	*Ferguson*	*Bonds*	*Lampard*	*Curbishley*	*Taylor T*	*Green*	*Pike**	*Holland*	*Hales*	*Brooking*	*Robson B*	*Martin*
								Ref: R Challis	West Ham, desperate for points, find City in a hesitant mood, sporting white shirts and red shorts. Taylor heads in before City have woken up. City's best forward is McDonald, who scores and has one disallowed. The late rally almost saves a point, but the Irons' win will not save them.											
36	H	NEWCASTLE		5	D	0-0	0-0		Blyth	Roberts	McDonald	Yorath	Holton	Osgood	Beck	Wallace	Green	Powell	Hutchison	
	4/4		22,196	*21*	43				*Mahoney*	*Blackhall*	*Kennedy*	*Barton*	*Nattrass*	*Nulty*	*Barrowclough*	*Burns*	*McGhee*	*Callachan*	*Scott*	
								Ref: S Bates	The Magpies have gone 12 games without a win, but this point lifts them off the bottom. Bill McGarry's team come with a blanket defence and are the first side to stop City scoring at home. Mahoney has a busy night, but so does Blyth as the home fans chant 'what a load of rubbish'.											
37	H	EVERTON		6	W	3-2	1-1	Thompson 43, Wallace 49, Green 80	Blyth	Roberts	McDonald	Yorath	Holton	Coop	Green	Wallace	Thompson*	Powell	Hutchison	Osgood
	8/4		26,008	*2*	45			*Latchford 18, Lyons 51*	*Wood*	*Darracott**	*Pejic*	*Lyons*	*Jones*	*Ross*	*King*	*Dobson*	*Latchford*	*McKenzie*	*Thomas*	*Telfer*
								Ref: T Bune	Another rip-roaring game with Green snatching a late winner as Wood collides with his own defender. Everton boss Gordon Lee accuses City of kicking Wood and is unhappy generally with the ref. All this overshadowed a fine game, which saw Latchford's 28th goal and Wallace's 21st.											
38	A	MIDDLESBROUGH		6	D	1-1	1-1	Green 20	Blyth	Roberts	McDonald	Yorath	Holton	Coop	Green	Wallace	Osgood	Powell	Hutchison	
	11/4		***14,184***	*11*	46			*Armstrong 5*	*Brown*	*Craggs*	*Bailey*	*Mahoney*	*Boam*	*Ramage*	*Johnston*	*Cummins*	*Shearer*	*McAndrew*	*Armstrong*	
								Ref: N Glover	Boro have sold Souness and are languishing in mid-table. It looks a foul when Shearer knocks it out of Blyth's grasp for David Armstrong to score. Alan Green equalises with what looks an offside goal and City play safety first in the second half to ease closer to a European place.											
39	A	QP RANGERS		6	L	1-2	1-1	Green 26	Blyth	Roberts	McDonald	Yorath	Holton	Coop	Green	Wallace	Osgood	Powell	Hutchison	
	15/4		*17,062*	*20*	46			*Goddard 33, James 75*	*Parkes*	*Clement*	*Gillard*	*Hollins*	*Howe*	*Shanks*	*McGee*	*Busby**	*James*	*Bowles*	*Goddard*	*Williams*
								Ref: M Taylor	For the second time in a month City lose to a relegation-threatened London team. Despite taking an early lead, City don't show enough determination to contain a desperate but ordinary QPR. Rangers' win is their second in a week and Paul Goddard scores his first ever goal.											
40	H	NOTT'M FOREST		6	D	0-0	0-0		Blyth	Roberts	McDonald	Yorath	Holton	Coop	Green	Wallace	Ferguson	Powell	Beck	
	22/4		**36,894**	*1*	47				*Shilton*	*Anderson*	*Barrett*	*O'Hare*	*Needham*	*Burns*	*O'Neill*	*Bowyer*	*With*	*Gemmill*	*Robertson*	
								Ref: J Bent	Forest clinch the title with a super rearguard action. Clough becomes only the second man to achieve the feat with two clubs. Footballer of the Year Burns is immaculate, as is PFA player of the Year Shilton, who makes the save of the century to keep out Ferguson's goal-bound header.											
41	A	MANCHESTER C		7	L	1-3	0-2	Green 61	Blyth	Roberts	McDonald	Yorath	Holton*	Osgood	Green	Wallace	Ferguson	Powell	Beck	Thompson
	25/4		*32,412*	*5*	47			*Kidd 5, Hartford 15, Owen 50p*	*Corrigan*	*Clements*	*Donachie*	*Booth*	*Watson*	*Owen*	*Channon*	*Bell*	*Kidd*	*Hartford*	*Power*	
								Ref: C Seel	The Maine Road hoodoo strikes again, and although Manchester deserve the win the penalty award for Channon's fall is ludicrous. City got to grips after a poor first-half display, but Europe looks out of the question. Alan Green pulled one back, but the mountain was too high to climb.											
42	A	BRISTOL CITY		7	D	1-1	0-0	Wallace 61	Blyth	Roberts	McDonald	Yorath	Osgood	Coop	Green*	Wallace	Ferguson	Powell	Hutchison	Beck
	29/4		*21,045*	*15*	48			*Royle 60*	*Shaw*	*Sweeney*	*Merrick*	*Gow*	*Rodgers*	*Hunter*	*Tainton*	*Ritchie*	*Royle*	*Mann*	*Whitehead**	*Mabbutt*
	Home		Away					Ref: A Gunn	If Arsenal win the FA Cup final and Liverpool win the European Cup, City will be in Europe. In a tepid game the City create a lot of chances but Shaw denies them. Wallace's 23rd goal of the season cancels out Royle's scrambled effort. Blyth is picked for Scotland's World Cup squad.											
Average	23,368		28,205																	

League Cup							F-A	H-T	Scorers, Times, and Referees	1	2	3	4	5	6	7	8	9	10	11	12 sub used
2	A	HUDDERSFIELD		6	W		2-0	0-0	Wallace 63, Holton 75	Blyth	Oakey	McDonald	Yorath	Holton	Coop	Graydon	Wallace	Ferguson	Powell	Hutchison	
30/8			*8,577*	*4:21*						*Starling*	*Brown*	*Baines !*	*Hart*	*Sandercock*	*Gray*	*Howey*	*Johnson*	*Eccles*	*Butler*	*McCaffrey*	
									Ref: P Willis	The Terriers have dropped from Div 1 to Div 4 in five years and despite a brave showe rarely look like creating a shock. Steve Baines is sent off after 24 minutes for two bookings, and it is an uphill task for the home team. Ian Wallace scores again and Holton's is his first for the club.											
3	A	TOTTENHAM		6	W		3-2	1-1	Hutchison 7, Powell 70, Graydon 81	Blyth	Oakey	McDonald	Beck	Holton*	Coop	Nardiello	Wallace	Ferguson	Powell	Hutchison	Graydon
26/10			*35,099*	*2:2*					*Pratt 39, Armstrong 90*	*Daines*	*Naylor*	*Holmes*	*Hoddle*	*McAllister*	*Perryman*	*Pratt*	*McNab*	*Moores*	*Armstrong*	*Taylor*	
									Ref: T Spencer	The Division 2 high fliers are brought down to earth after their 9-0 record win over Bristol Rovers. The Londoners are outclassed despite City losing Holton injured just after half-time and should have had more in a red-hot period after the break. City's eighth successive away cup draw.											
4	A	LIVERPOOL		4	D		2-2	1-2	Wallace 34, Powell 75	Blyth	Oakey*	McDonald	Yorath	Holton	Coop	Nardiello	Wallace	Ferguson	Powell	Hutchison	Roberts
29/11			*33,817*	*5*					*Fairclough 41, Neal 43p*	*Clemence*	*Neal*	*Smith*	*Thompson*	*Kennedy*	*Hughes*	*Dalglish*	*McDermott*	*Heighway*	*Fairclough*	*Callaghan*	
									Ref: G Courtney	Pride is restored after the Goodison mauling in a spell-binding match. Powell sends 10,000 City fans wild when he hits the second goal, and Bolton boss Ian Greaves says 'his pass for the first goal was the best I've seen in years'. Coop fouls Fairclough for the penalty. Wembley dreams.											
4R	H	LIVERPOOL		8	L		0-2	0-1		Blyth	Oakey	McDonald	Yorath	Roberts	Coop	Graydon	Wallace	Ferguson	Powell	Hutchison	
20/12			36,105	*3*					*Case 5, Dalglish 77*	*Clemence*	*Neal*	*Hansen*	*Thompson*	*Kennedy*	*Hughes*	*Dalglish*	*McDermott*	*Heighway*	*Fairclough*	*Case*	
									Ref: C Thomas	Record receipts are paid to see Liverpool call on all their European experience and grind out the win after Case's early thunderbolt. Wallace and Ferguson both miss chances before Pool put up the shutters. Then Dalglish, superbly marked by Roberts throughout, threaded in a second.											

FA Cup																					
3	A	MIDDLEBROUGH		7	L		0-3	0-2		Sealey	Coop	McDonald	Yorath	Roberts	Gooding	Beck*	Wallace	Ferguson	Powell	Hutchison	Graydon
7/1			*18,505*	*17*					*Mills 6, 22, McAndrew 72*	*Platt*	*Craggs*	*Bailey*	*Mahoney*	*Boam*	*Ramage*	*Mills*	*Cummins*	*Ashcroft*	*McAndrew*	*Armstrong*	
									Ref: T Morris	Even with Boro's star Souness suspended by the club, pending a £350,000 move to Liverpool, City are never in it. Mills inflicts the damage to a hesitant defence. Sealey enjoys a rare game in place of the injured Blyth. Keith Osgood has signed from Spurs for £125,000 to shore things up.											

		Home						Away					
	P	W	D	L	F	A	W	D	L	F	A	Pts
1 Nott'm Forest	42	15	6	0	37	8	10	8	3	32	16	64
2 Liverpool	42	15	4	2	37	11	9	5	7	28	23	57
3 Everton	42	14	4	3	47	22	8	7	6	29	23	55
4 Manchester C	42	14	4	3	46	21	6	8	7	28	30	52
5 Arsenal	42	14	5	2	38	12	7	5	9	22	25	52
6 West Brom	42	13	5	3	35	18	5	9	7	27	35	50
7 COVENTRY	42	13	5	3	48	23	5	7	9	27	39	48
8 Aston Villa	42	11	4	6	33	18	7	6	8	24	24	46
9 Leeds	42	12	4	5	39	21	6	6	9	24	32	46
10 Manchester U	42	9	6	6	32	23	7	4	10	35	40	42
11 Birmingham	42	8	5	8	32	30	8	4	9	23	30	41
12 Derby	42	10	7	4	37	24	4	6	11	17	35	41
13 Norwich	42	10	8	3	28	20	1	10	10	24	46	40
14 Middlesbro	42	8	8	5	25	19	4	7	10	17	35	39
15 Wolves	42	7	8	6	30	27	5	4	12	21	37	36
16 Chelsea	42	7	11	3	28	20	4	3	14	18	49	36
17 Bristol City	42	9	6	6	37	26	2	7	12	12	27	35
18 Ipswich	42	10	5	6	32	24	1	8	12	15	37	35
19 QP Rangers	42	8	8	5	27	26	1	7	13	20	38	33
20 West Ham	42	8	6	7	31	28	4	2	15	21	41	32
21 Newcastle	42	4	6	11	26	37	2	4	15	16	41	22
22 Leicester	42	4	7	10	16	32	1	5	15	10	38	22
	924	223	132	107	741	490	107	132	223	490	741	924

Odds & ends

Double wins: (4) Chelsea, Leicester, Wolves, Norwich.
Double losses: (0).

Won from behind: (6) Derby (h), Manchester C (h), Wolves (a), Norwich (h), Everton (h), Norwich (a).
Lost from in front: (2) West Brom (h), QP Rangers (a).

High spots: 75 League goals, the most in a season since 1963-64.
Eight-game unbeaten run in October and November.
International recognition for Blyth, Wallace, Nardiello, Hutch' & Yorath.
League Cup draw at Anfield.
Norwich, Man United, Man City, Everton and Chelsea home games.

Low spots: Missing out on UEFA Cup place.
League Cup exit versus Liverpool after drawn game at Anfield.

Red cards: Opponents – Macdonald (Arsenal a), Baines (Hudd'ld LC a).

Player of the Year: Ian Wallace.
Ever-presents: (2) Bobby McDonald, Barry Powell.
Hat-tricks: (3) Mick Ferguson.
Opposing hat-tricks: (2) Latchford (Everton), George (Derby).
Leading scorer: (23) Ian Wallace.

	Appearances						Goals			
	Lge	*Sub*	LC	*Sub*	FAC	*Sub*	**Lge**	LC	FAC	**Tot**
Beck, John	**15**	*8*	1		1		**2**			**2**
Blyth, Jim	**40**		4							
Coop, Mick	**34**	*1*	4		1		**6**			**6**
Dugdale, Alan	**1**									
Ferguson, Mick	**30**		4		1		**17**			**17**
Gooding, Ray	**5**				1		**1**			**1**
Graydon, Ray	**17**	*3*	2	*1*		*1*	**5**	1		**6**
Green, Alan	**10**						**5**			**5**
Holton, Jim	**25**		3					1		**1**
Hutchison, Tommy	**40**		4		1		**3**	1		**4**
McDonald, Bobby	**42**		4		1		**5**			**5**
Murphy, Donal	**1**	*2*								
Nardiello, Donato	**12**	*1*	2				**1**			**1**
Oakey, Graham	**21**		4							
Osgood, Keith	**13**						**1**			**1**
Powell, Barry	**42**		4		1		**3**	2		**5**
Roberts, Brian	**26**		1	*1*	1					
Sealey, Les	**2**				1					
Thompson, Garry	**5**	*1*					**2**			**2**
Wallace, Ian	**41**		4		1		**21**	2		**23**
Yorath, Terry	**40**		3		1		**2**			**2**
(own-goals)							**1**			**1**
21 players used	**462**	*16*	**44**	*2*	**11**	*1*	**75**	**7**		**82**

LEAGUE DIVISION 1

Manager: Gordon Milne

SEASON 1978-79

No	Date	Opponent	Att	Pos	Pt	F-A	H-T	Scorers, Times, and Referees	1	2	3	4	5	6	7	8	9	10	11	12 sub used
1	A	MIDDLESBROUGH			W	2-1	0-1	Powell 60, Ferguson 88	Sealey	Osgood	McDonald	Yorath*	Holton	**Gillespie**	Nardiello	Wallace	Ferguson	Powell	Hutchison	Green
	19/8		*17,956*		2			*Woof 4*	*Stewart*	*Craggs*	*Bailey*	*Mahoney*	*Boam*	*Ramage*	*McAndrew*	*Mills*	*Ashcroft*	*Woof*	*Armstrong**	*Hedley*
								Ref: K Walmsley	A goal down in four minutes, City bounce back to win with a late headed goal from Ferguson. Sealey makes a rare appearance due to Blyth's injury and shines. City's first win at Ayresome since 1965 is achieved with a battling performance and teenager Gary Gillespie looks confident.											
2	H	NOTT'M FOREST			D	0-0	0-0		Sealey	Osgood	McDonald	Beck	Holton	Gillespie*	Nardiello	Wallace	Ferguson	Powell	Hutchison	Green
	22/8		**28,585**		3				*Shilton*	*Anderson*	*Barrett*	*McGovern*	*Needham*	*Burns*	*O'Neill*	*Gemmill*	*Elliott*	*Woodcock*	*Robertson*	
								Ref: J Hunting	The transfer-listed Beck comes in for the injured Yorath and Gillespie shines on his home debut against Tony Woodcock. City are on top in the first half but Forest look stronger after the break. Forest are now unbeaten in 28 games. Steve Hunt has signed from New York Cosmos.											
3	H	NORWICH		4	W	4-1	2-0	Beck 12, Powell 45, Wallace 51, [Ferguson 77]	Sealey	Osgood	McDonald	Beck	Holton	Gillespie	Nardiello*	Wallace	Ferguson	Powell	Hutchison	**Bannister**
	26/8		20,377	*11*	5			*Peters 86*	*Keelan*	*Bond*	*Sullivan*	*Ryan*	*Hoadley*	*Powell*	*Neighbour*	*Reeves*	*Chivers*	*Robson*	*Peters*	
								Ref: J Hough	Last season's form is repeated as City, after a languid first half, turn up the heat and punish a woeful Norwich. Kevin Keelan keeps the score down but is helpless as Wallace and Ferguson score with headers. Teenager Gary Bannister comes on after 40 minutes and almost scores twice.											
4	A	DERBY		2	W	2-0	0-0	Hunt 55, Wallace 76	Sealey	Roberts	McDonald	Beck	Holton	Gillespie	Hutchison	Wallace	Ferguson	Powell	**Hunt**	
	2/9		*21,435*	*18*	7				*Middleton*	*Langan*	*Buckley*	*Daly*	*McFarland*	*Todd*	*Powell*	*Nish**	*Ryan*	*George*	*Carter*	*Daniel*
								Ref: A Hamil	Steve Hunt enjoys a dream start after signing from New York Cosmos for £40,000. He scores a superb left-foot drive after Ferguson touches on Hutch's cross. Wallace adds an easy second and the new chocolate brown kit gets a winning start. Tommy Docherty's men have yet to win.											
5	H	CHELSEA		2	W	3-2	1-2	Wallace 24, McDonald 50, Ferguson 60	Sealey	Roberts	McDonald	Beck	Holton	Gillespie	Hutchison	Wallace	Ferguson	Powell	Hunt	
	9/9		24,618	*18*	9			*Langley 17, McKenzie 31*	*Bonetti*	*Locke*	*Harris*	*Lewington*	*Hay*	*Wicks*	*Swain*	*Wilkins R*	*Langley*	*Stanley**	*McKenzie*	*Britton*
								Ref: J Worrall	For 25 minutes in the second half City play like world beaters and could easily have scored more than the two. McDonald ran from the halfway line to score a superb individual effort. Chelsea looked good early on, and McKenzie scores after signing from Everton for £165,000.											
6	A	LIVERPOOL		3	L	0-1	0-1		Sealey	Roberts	McDonald	Beck	Holton	Gillespie	Hutchison	Wallace	Ferguson	Powell	Hunt	
	16/9		***51,130***	*1*	9			*Souness 26*	*Clemence*	*Neal*	*Kennedy A*	*Thompson*	*Kennedy R*	*Hughes*	*Dalglish*	*Case*	*Heighway*	*McDermott*	*Souness*	
								Ref: D Richardson	The gates are locked. Can Liverpool repeat their 7-0 thrashing of Spurs, though they lost to Forest in the European Cup in midweek? Sealey performs heroics but can't stop Souness's stunning shot. City rarely worry the Reds. Alan Green turns down a £90,000 move to Swindon.											
7	H	LEEDS		3	D	0-0	0-0		Sealey	Coop	McDonald	Yorath	Holton	Gillespie	Hutchison	Wallace	Ferguson	Powell	Hunt	
	23/9		27,355	*12*	10				*Harvey*	*Stevenson*	*Gray F*	*Flynn*	*Hart*	*Madeley*	*Harris*	*Hankin*	*Lorimer*	*Cherry*	*Graham*	
								Ref: R Lewis	The players wear 'hand of peace' wrist bands in an anti-hooligan campaign as Match of the Day sees a rare poor game at Highfield Road. New manager Jock Stein adopts the Leeds style of old, frustrating City's golden attack with a packed defence. Ferguson injures his eye but stays on.											
8	A	TOTTENHAM		4	D	1-1	0-0	Ferguson 84	Sealey	Coop	McDonald	Yorath	Holton	Gillespie	Hunt	Wallace	Ferguson	Powell*	Hutchison	Beck
	30/9		*35,806*	*14*	11			*Hoddle 80*	*Daines*	*McAllister*	*Gorman*	*Holmes*	*Lacey*	*Perryman*	*Armstrong**	*Ardiles*	*Lee*	*Pratt*	*Taylor*	*Hoddle*
								Ref: H Robinson	Ricky Villa is injured but Ossie Ardiles' presence means a ticker tape welcome for the teams. After Spurs fans demand it, Hoddle comes off the bench and scores after a mazy run. Ferguson's riposte is a great header from Coop's cross. Gillespie is already in the Scottish Under-21 side.											
9	H	IPSWICH		3	D	2-2	0-2	Green 67, Thompson 70	Sealey	Coop	McDonald	Yorath	Holton	**Hagan**	Hutchison	Wallace	Thompson	Powell*	Hunt	Green
	7/10		21,776	*14*	12			*Osman 35, Woods 43*	*Cooper*	*Burley*	*Mills*	*Osman*	*Hunter*	*Beattie*	*Wark*	*Talbot*	*Mariner*	*Muhren*	*Woods*	
								Ref: A Challinor	With five men up front for the last 40 minutes, City come back from 0-2 down and deserve to win. The admiring Bobby Robson can't believe it and the fans go wild. Alan Green volleys home and Garry Thompson scores on his 19th birthday. Jim Blyth is still out with a back problem.											
10	A	MANCHESTER C		7	L	0-2	0-0		Sealey	Coop	McDonald	Yorath	Holton	Gillespie	Hutchison	Wallace	Thompson	Powell	Hunt	
	14/10		*36,723*	*5*	12			*Owen 66p, 89p*	*Corrigan*	*Clements*	*Donachie*	*Booth*	*Watson*	*Kidd*	*Palmer*	*Owen*	*Futcher R*	*Hartford*	*Barnes*	
								Ref: K Hackett	City have now conceded eleven penalties in eleven seasons at Maine Road. Holton and Gillespie are the culprits, fouling Futcher and Barnes respectively, although the first looks dodgy. The Sky Blues fight hard, but lack firepower up front. John Beck signs for Fulham for £80,000.											

No / Date	Venue	Opponent / Att	Pos	Res / Pts	F-A	H-T	Scorers, Times, Referees	1	2	3	4	5	6	7	8	9	10	11	12
11	A	WEST BROM	10	L	**1-7**	0-3	Ferguson 69 *[Brown T 75, Statham 89]*	Sealey	Coop	McDonald	Yorath	Holton*	Gillespie	Hutchison	Wallace	Ferguson	Powell	Hunt	Green
21/10		*27,381*	4	12			*Cantello 14, C'ham 28, 61, Regis 35, 81,*	*Godden*	*Batson*	*Statham*	*Cunningham*	*Wile*	*Robertson*	*Robson*	*Brown A*	*Regis*	*Cantello**	*Brown T*	*Johnston*
							Ref: C White	Big Ron's Albion record their biggest win for 11 years and inflict City's worst league defeat since 1958. It is a humiliation and the only crumb of comfort is that West Brom would have murdered anyone. Holton and Gillespie both fatally play with knocks. Brown scores his 210th goal.												
12	H	BIRMINGHAM	8	W	2-1	1-0	Hutchison 30, 48	Sealey	Roberts	McDonald	**Blair**	Osgood	Coop	Green	Wallace	Ferguson	Gooding	Hutchison	
28/10		25,429	*22*	14			*Givens 80*	*Freeman*	*Calderwood*	*Dennis*	*Towers*	*Gallagher*	*Pendrey !*	*Page*	*Buckley*	*Givens*	*Emmanuel*	*Barrowclough*	
							Ref: C Thomas	Blues, without a win all season, are just the side to meet after a 1-7 mauling and Hutchison reverts to his favourite left wing to torment them. He scores both goals as City recover some pride. Gary Pendrey gets his second red card of the season for fouling Green 23 minutes from time.												
13	A	BOLTON	8	D	0-0	0-0		Sealey	Coop	McDonald	Blair	Osgood	Gillespie	Green	Wallace	Ferguson	Powell	Hutchison	
4/11		*22,379*	*19*	15				*McDonagh*	*Nicholson*	*Dunne*	*Greaves*	*Walsh*	*Jones P*	*Morgan*	*Reid*	*Worthington*	*Gowling*	*McNab*	
							Ref: J Butcher	Newly promoted Bolton are struggling, but Frank Worthington is Div 1's top scorer. City's defensive display earns a point and Wallace almost wins it near the end. £250,000 signing McNab is outshone by Powell and young Andy Blair. Sealey pulls off a miracle save to deny Gowling.												
14	H	MIDDLESBROUGH	6	W	2-1	1-0	Wallace 28, Thompson 88	Sealey	Coop	McDonald	Blair	Osgood	Gillespie	Green	Wallace	Thompson	Powell	Hutchison	
11/11		18,636	*15*	17			*Burns 78*	*Stewart*	*Craggs*	*Bailey*	*Mahoney*	*Boam*	*McAndrew*	*Cochrane*	*Mills*	*Ashcroft**	*Burns*	*Armstrong*	
							Ref: D Hutchinson	An orange ball is used in the heavy mist and assists in an entertaining game. Boro look to have won a hard-earned point with Burns' goal until Thompson pops up for the headed winner. Wallace ends his goal drought. Jim Blyth is on his way to Man United for British record £440,000.												
15	A	NORWICH	8	L	0-1	0-0		Sealey	Coop	McDonald	Blair	Osgood	Gillespie	Bannister	Wallace	Thompson	Powell	Hutchison	
18/11		*17,696*	*11*	17			*Bond 73*	*Keelan*	*Bond*	*Davies*	*Ryan*	*Hoadley*	*Powell*	*Neighbour*	*Peters*	*Reeves*	*Symonds*	*Mendham*	
							Ref: B Homewood	Manager John Bond's son, Kevin, scores his first goal for Norwich when he pounces on a rebound. City, playing four teenagers who appear far from overawed, have most of the attacking play but lack punch. Blyth's move to Man United is called off because of his back 'injury'.												
16	H	DERBY	6	W	4-2	1-2	Wallace 21, 84, McDonald 79, Powell 87	Sealey	Roberts	McDonald	Blair	Osgood	Coop	Bannister*	Wallace	Thompson	Powell	Hutchison	Hunt
21/11		21,766	*13*	19			*Daly 1p, Caskey 41*	*Middleton*	*Langan*	*Buckley*	*Daly*	*Daniel*	*Moreland*	*Carter*	*Powell*	*Caskey**	*Clarke*	*Hill*	*Nish*
							Ref: D Turner	Derby are seeking their fourth win in a row and lead until eleven minutes from time. Wallace is back to his best and scores two, has three disallowed and makes the fourth for Powell in a fantastic eight minutes. It's twelve unbeaten home games for City and the injuries are clearing.												
17	H	ARSENAL	6	D	1-1	0-0	Hunt 80	Sealey	Roberts	McDonald	Blair	Osgood	Coop	Hunt	Wallace	Thompson	Powell	Hutchison	
25/11		26,674	*5*	20			*Stapleton 52*	*Jennings*	*Rice*	*Nelson*	*Price**	*O'Leary*	*Young*	*Brady*	*Sunderland*	*Stapleton*	*Walford*	*Rix*	*Heeley*
							Ref: K McNally	Terry Neill's Arsenal are in superb form, with Liam Brady the best midfield player in Britain. They look to have ended City's unbeaten record with Stapleton's goal and a strong defensive performance. Steve Hunt deservedly scores with a powerful left-footer and City almost grab a win.												
18	H	QP RANGERS	6	W	1-0	0-0	Thompson 59	Sealey	Coop	McDonald	Blair	Holton	Gillespie*	Hunt	Wallace	Thompson	Powell	Hutchison	Ferguson
9/12		18,693	*19*	22				*Parkes*	*Clement*	*Gillard**	*Hollins*	*Howe*	*Shanks*	*Eastoe*	*Roeder*	*Hamilton*	*Busby*	*Harkouk*	*Goddard*
							Ref: R Perkin	The Match of the Day editor cut most of this match out as Rangers come to frustrate with a five man defence. Milne brings on sub Ferguson for a five-man attack and Garry Thompson scores after Hutch's shot rebounds from the bar. City's defence is lucky to survive QPR's late flurry.												
19	A	SOUTHAMPTON	7	L	0-4	0-2	*[Baker 65]*	Sealey	Coop	McDonald	Blair	Holton	Ferguson	Hunt	Wallace*	Thompson	Powell	Hutchison	Gillespie
16/12		*19,102*	*12*	22			*Waldron 10, Hebberd 14, Boyer 52,*	*Gennoe*	*Golac*	*Peach*	*Williams S**	*Nicholl*	*Waldron*	*Ball*	*Boyer*	*Hebberd*	*Holmes*	*Baker*	*Sealy*
							Ref: T Reynolds	Milne's gamble of playing five attackers and three defenders backfires and Saints, with Yugoslav Golac menacing, expose City's frailties. Six City players are rescued by the fire brigade after getting stuck in a hotel lift an hour before kick-off. Gennoe saves Coop's 69th-minute penalty.												
20	H	EVERTON	6	W	3-2	0-0	Wallace 50, Thompson 68, Hunt 74	Sealey	Coop	McDonald	Blair	Holton	**Dyson**	Hunt	Wallace	Thompson	Powell	Hutchison	
23/12		22,778	*2*	24			*Lyons 81, Latchford 83*	*Wood*	*Todd*	*Jones*	*Lyons*	*Wright*	*Nulty*	*King*	*Dobson*	*Latchford*	*Higgins*	*Thomas*	
							Ref: M Peck	City smash Everton's 20-match unbeaten run on a pitch, a third of which is snow-covered. Everton boss Gordon Lee believes the pitch wasn't playable. The Sky Blues adapt more easily and look home and dry until a late rally ensures a cliff-hanging finale. Ian Wallace's goal is a gem.												
21	A	BRISTOL CITY	9	L	0-5	0-2	*[Cormack 72]*	Sealey	Coop	McDonald	Blair	Holton	Osgood	Hunt	Wallace	Thompson	Powell	Hutchison	
26/12		*22,324*	*7*	24			*Royle 16, 21, 50, Ritchie 52,*	*Shaw*	*Sweeney*	*Gillies*	*Gow*	*Rodgers*	*Hunter*	*Tainton*	*Ritchie*	*Royle*	*Cormack*	*Whitehead*	
							Ref: A Glasson	Bristol, under former City assistant Alan Dicks, are having their best season and are unbeaten in six. Defensive errors are the root of City's downfall and the sixth away defeat in seven. The second half is a formality as the home side find acres of space to rip through a flimsy defence.												

No	Date		Att	Pos	Pt	F-A	H-T	Scorers, Times, and Referees	1	2	3	4	5	6	7	8	9	10	11	12 sub used
22	A	WOLVES		8	D	1-1	0-1	Hutchison 65	Blyth	Osgood	McDonald	Blair	Holton	Coop	Nardiello	Wallace	Thompson*	Powell	Hutchison	Ferguson
	30/12		*21,514*	*20*	25			*Daley 11*	*Bradshaw*	*Palmer*	*Parkin*	*Daniel*	*McAlle*	*Berry*	*Hibbitt*	*Daley*	*Bell*	*Eves*	*Carr*	
								Ref: A Porter	Wolves are desperate for points in their relegation battle, whilst City lack confidence. Blyth makes his first appearance of the season in place of the axed Sealey, and an even game is brightened by two spectacular goals. Milne's offer of £450,000 for Ipswich's Kevin Beattie is rejected.											
23	A	LEEDS		8	L	0-1	0-1		Blyth	Coop	McDonald	Blair	Holton	Hagan	Yorath	Wallace	Ferguson	Powell*	Hutchison	Hunt
	3/2		*22,928*	*5*	25			*Currie 26*	*Harvey*	*Cherry*	*Gray F*	*Flynn*	*Parkinson*	*Madeley*	*Harris*	*Hankin*	*Stevenson*	*Currie*	*Graham*	
								Ref: A Saunders	City emerge from their enforced lay-off caused by the cold weather, with Yorath back for the first time since the WBA hammering in October. They are unlucky to lose their first League game in five weeks as Wallace and Ferguson waste good chances, and Tony Currie punishes them.											
24	H	TOTTENHAM		10	L	1-3	1-2	McDonald 35	Blyth	Coop	McDonald	Blair	Holton *	Hagan	Yorath	Wallace	Ferguson	Powell	Hutchison	Hunt
	10/2		25,071	*8*	25			*Taylor 14, 42, Lee 47*	*Kendall*	*Naylor*	*Holmes*	*Hoddle*	*Lacey*	*Perryman*	*Pratt*	*Ardiles**	*Lee*	*Gorman*	*Taylor*	*Armstrong*
								Ref: T Morris	City's eagerness to play on an icy pitch backfires, as reluctant Spurs deservedly end their 16-game unbeaten home run. The visitors, without a win in seven games, adapt to the treacherous conditions with the right footwear. Hutchison makes his 250th league appearance for Coventry.											
25	A	CHELSEA		8	W	3-1	3-1	Wallace 35, Ferguson 39, 40	Blyth	Coop	McDonald	Blair	Holton	Hagan	Yorath	Wallace	Ferguson	Powell	Hutchison	
	21/2		*15,282*	*21*	27			*Langley 30*	*Bonetti*	*Wilkins G*	*Stride*	*Bannon*	*Harris**	*Nutton*	*Stanley*	*Wilkins R*	*Aylott*	*Langley*	*Walker*	*Sitton*
								Ref: M Taylor	New Chelsea boss Danny Blanchflower can't prevent their eighth home defeat. City come from behind to bag their first away win since September. Barry Powell's header hits the bar and Ferguson touches it in. Birmingham's £1 million Trevor Francis chooses Forest, not City.											
26	H	MANCHESTER C		11	L	0-3	0-1		Blyth	Coop	McDonald	Blair	Holton*	Hagan	Yorath	Wallace	Ferguson	Powell	Hutchison	Thompson
	24/2		20,043	*15*	27			*Channon 35, 60, Kidd 63*	*Corrigan*	*Donachie*	*Power*	*Owen*	*Booth*	*Futcher P*	*Channon*	*Viljoen*	*Kidd*	*Hartford*	*Barnes*	
								Ref: B Homewood	Jim Blyth fails to hold shots for the second and third goals, as Manchester easily win a mediocre game for only their second win in 16 games. Andy Blair, after some good games, is beginning to wilt. Milne's half-time substitution fails. Sealey and Thompson are in the Under-21 squad.											
27	H	WEST BROM		13	L	1-3	0-1	Thompson 61	Sealey	Coop	McDonald	Blair	Holton	Hagan	Green	Wallace	Thompson	Powell	Hutchison	
	3/3		25,676	*3*	27			*Robson 11, Brown A 50, Mills 63*	*Godden*	*Batson*	*Statham*	*Trewick*	*Wile*	*Robertson*	*Robson*	*Brown A*	*Regis*	*Mills*	*Brown T*	
								Ref: J Hunting	Milne rings the changes with Blyth, Yorath and Ferguson axed. Albion, after two defeats, bounce back to form and beat an out of sorts City for the third time this season. David Mills starts his first game after his £500,000 move from Boro and wraps the game up after Tony Brown's run.											
28	H	LIVERPOOL		13	D	0-0	0-0		Sealey	Coop	McDonald	Yorath	Holton	Hagan	Green	Wallace	Thompson	Powell	Hutchison	
	6/3		26,638	*1*	28				*Clemence*	*Neal*	*Hughes*	*Thompson*	*Kennedy R*	*Hansen*	*Dalglish*	*Johnson*	*Case*	*McDermott*	*Souness*	
								Ref: R Toseland	City forsake their adventurous approach and tighten up midfield and defence to thwart the runaway leaders. Yorath returns to give midfield bite and Jim Holton and Jim Hagan keep tabs on Dalglish and Johnson. The poor home run is ended and, in a game of few chances, a draw is fair.											
29	A	BIRMINGHAM		11	D	0-0	0-0		Sealey	Coop	McDonald	Yorath	Holton	Hagan	Green	Wallace	Thompson	Blair	Hutchison	
	10/3		*17,311*	*22*	29				*Freeman*	*Page*	*Calderwood*	*Towers*	*Gallagher*	*Tarantini*	*Ainscow*	*Buckley*	*Givens*	*Dillon*	*Barrowclough*	
								Ref: N Ashley	Despite manager Jim Smith importing Argentina World Cup star Alberto Tarantini, Blues are anchored to the foot of the table. They can't find a way through City's new 4-3-3 system. In a dour derby game, the best chance falls to Thompson, but his header is cleared off the line by Page.											
30	A	IPSWICH		10	D	1-1	0-1	Thompson 73	Sealey	Coop	McDonald*	Yorath	Holton	Hagan	Roberts	Wallace	Thompson	Blair	Hutchison	Green
	13/3		*16,095*	*11*	30			*Muhren 35*	*Cooper*	*Burley*	*Mills*	*Thijssen*	*Osman*	*Butcher*	*Wark*	*Muhren*	*Mariner*	*Gates*	*Woods*	
								Ref: K Salmon	With the introduction of the Dutchmen, Muhren and Thijssen, Ipswich are enjoying an excellent second half to the season. Muhren puts them ahead, but some resolute defending keeps City in the game. Muhren's glorious goal direct from a free-kick is ruled out as the kick was indirect.											
31	H	BOLTON		8	D	2-2	2-2	Wallace 22, Powell 43p	Sealey	Coop	McDonald	Yorath	Holton	Hagan	Nardiello	Wallace	Thompson	Powell	Hutchison	
	17/3		**15,083**	*18*	31			*Worthington 28, McNab 35*	*McDonagh*	*Nicholson*	*Dunne**	*Greaves*	*Jones P*	*Walsh*	*Morgan*	*Allardyce*	*Gowling*	*Worthington*	*McNab*	*Burke*
								Ref: B Newsome	The morning's snow-clearing exercise is worthwhile as the game goes ahead. City revert to two wingers and entertain the small crowd. After heavy pressure Wallace breaks the offside trap to score, and, after a Bolton flurry, Powell nets a twice-taken penalty after Greaves fouls Hutch.											

No	Date	Opponent / Att	Pos	Res / Pts	F-A	H-T	Scorers, Times, and Referees	1	2	3	4	5	6	7	8	9	10	11	subs used
32	H	MANCHESTER U	7	W	4-3	3-1	Powell 2, T'son 8, Hutch'n 45, McD'd 51	Sealey	Coop	McDonald	Yorath	Holton	Hagan	Nardiello	Wallace	Thompson	Powell	Hutchison	
	20/3	25,382	*8*	33			*Coppell 36, 90, McIlroy 64*	*Bailey*	*Nicholl*	*Albiston*	*McIlroy*	*McQueen*	*Buchan*	*Coppell*	*Greenhoff J*	*Jordan*	*Greenhoff B*	*Thomas*	
							Ref: M Sinclair	A memorable, breathtaking match which could have ended 10-6. Garry Thompson destroyed £500,000 centre-half McQueen, Hutchison scored the goal of the season, and Ian Wallace is back to his best. United give as good as they get, though two late goals give the scoreline a false look.											
33	A	NOTT'M FOREST	8	L	0-3	0-1		Sealey	Coop	McDonald	Yorath	Roberts	Hagan	Nardiello	Blair	Thompson	Powell	Hutchison*	Hunt
	24/3	*29,706*	*6*	33			*Woodcock 25, Birtles 64, Needham 82*	*Shilton*	*Anderson*	*Barrett*	*McGovern*	*Lloyd*	*Needham*	*O'Neill*	*Francis*	*Birtles*	*Woodcock*	*Robertson*	
							Ref: D Shaw	Forest won the League Cup last week and have only lost twice all season. They play £1 million signing Trevor Francis and his shot bounces off a defender for Birtles to score the second goal. Harry Roberts keeps the dangerous John Robertson in his pocket. Holton is on the transfer list.											
34	A	ASTON VILLA	8	D	1-1	0-0	Thompson 72	Sealey	Roberts	McDonald	Yorath	Holton	Coop	Nardiello	Wallace	Thompson	Powell	Hutchison	
	28/3	*25,670*	*11*	34			*Evans 49*	*Rimmer*	*Linton*	*Williams*	*Gregory*	*Evans*	*Mortimer*	*Craig*	*Little*	*Gray*	*Cowans*	*Swain*	
							Ref: G Nolan	Villa are let off the hook in the lashing rain after being run ragged in the second half . Evans is unmarked for his headed goal and Thompson's adds a bullet-like header from Bobby McDonald's cross. Both sides seem to have missed out on a European place and it's not hard to see why.											
35	A	ARSENAL	8	D	1-1	1-0	Hunt 34	Sealey	Roberts	McDonald	Yorath	Holton	Coop	Nardiello	Blair	Hunt	Powell	Hutchison	
	3/4	*30,091*	*5*	35			*Nelson 76*	*Jennings*	*Rice*	*Nelson*	*Talbot*	*O'Leary*	*Young*	*Heeley**	*Sunderland*	*Stapleton*	*Gatting*	*Rix*	*Walford*
							Ref: C Thomas	Arsenal have just reached Wembley. City play with three wingers up front because of Thompson's broken leg. Ian Wallace and Liam Brady are both out injured. An away win looks likely until Sammy Nelson's blockbuster. Nelson will faces charges after naughtily dropping his shorts.											
36	H	ASTON VILLA	7	D	1-1	1-0	Hutchison 21	Sealey	Roberts	McDonald	Yorath	Holton	Coop	Nardiello	Wallace	Hunt	Powell	Hutchison	
	7/4	23,668	*12*	36			*Deehan 75*	*Rimmer*	*Gidman*	*Gregory*	*Evans !*	*McNaught*	*Mortimer*	*Cowans*	*Little*	*Deehan*	*Cropley*	*Swain*	
							Ref: A Glasson	In a poor derby match, the highlights are few. Evans is sent off after 42 minutes for head-butting Hutchison, who had earlier scored a dipping screamer. Rimmer brilliantly saved McDonald's header before Deehan's weak shot sneaks in for an undeserved point for Ron Saunders' men.											
37	A	EVERTON	8	D	3-3	3-1	Wallace 9, 34, Hunt 44	Sealey	Roberts	McDonald	Yorath	Holton	Coop	Nardiello*	Wallace	Hunt	Powell	Hutchison	Blair
	10/4	25,302	*3*	37			*Ross 21, Latchford 64, Kidd 85*	*Wood*	*Barton*	*Jones*	*Lyons*	*Wright*	*Ross*	*King*	*Dobson*	*Latchford**	*Kidd*	*Eastoe*	*Telfer*
							Ref: M Lowe	Everton's title hopes have disappeared after seven games without a win. Eastoe and Kidd have arrived to bolster their attack but City look more potent. Wallace and Hunt are deadly and the Toffees are booed off at the break. They revert to the long ball and Kidd saves a point at the death.											
38	H	BRISTOL CITY	7	W	3-2	3-0	Powell 5p, Hutchison 7, Hunt 39	Sealey	Roberts	McDonald	Yorath*	Holton	Coop	Nardiello	Blair	Hunt	Powell	Hutchison	Hagan
	14/4	17,681	*8*	39			*Mabbutt 75, Gow 86*	*Shaw*	*Sweeney*	*Cooper*	*Gow*	*Rodgers**	*Hunter*	*Mann*	*Ritchie*	*Royle*	*Mabbutt*	*Meyer*	*Whitehead*
							Ref: K Hackett	In the bright sunshine City roar into a three-goal lead and look set to avenge that 0-5 defeat. Powell scores from the spot after Cooper fouls Roberts and Hunt scores with an overhead kick. Yorath limps off and Bristol, who have won four on the trot, fight back. A cliff-hanging finish.											
39	A	MANCHESTER U	8	D	0-0	0-0		Sealey	Roberts	McDonald	Blair	Holton	Coop	Nardiello	Wallace	Hunt	Powell	Hutchison	
	16/4	*43,075*	*13*	40				*Bailey*	*Nicholl*	*Albiston*	*McIlroy*	*McQueen*	*Buchan*	*Coppell*	*Ritchie**	*Jordan*	*Greenhoff B*	*Thomas*	*McCreery*
							Ref: G Courtney	The FA Cup finalists haven't won since the semi-final and create only one chance in this end-of-season game. A shirt-sleeved crowd see City cope easily with United and restore respectability to their season. Nicholl fouls Nardiello but amazingly no penalty is given. United are booed.											
40	H	SOUTHAMPTON	8	W	**4-0**	1-0	Wallace 35, 84, 87, Blair 56	Sealey	Roberts	McDonald	Blair	Holton	Coop	Nardiello	Wallace	Hunt	Gooding	Hutchison	
	21/4	17,707	*13*	42				*Wells*	*Golac*	*Peach*	*Williams S*	*Nicholl*	*Waldron*	*Ball*	*Boyer*	*Hayes*	*Holmes*	*Baker*	
							Ref: K Walmsley	Alan Ball makes his 100th league appearance for the Saints, the first player to achieve that feat with four clubs. Wallace is the hero, grabbing a hat-trick and making Andy Blair's goal. His third is a superbly bent shot in a one-to-one with Peter Wells. Saints' unbeaten run of six is over.											
41	A	QP RANGERS	9	L	1-5	1-1	Wallace 8	Sealey	Roberts	McDonald	Blair	Holton	Coop	Nardiello*	Wallace	Hunt	Powell	Hutchison	Gooding
	28/4	***10,951***	*20*	42			*Allen 19, 46, 60, Shanks 52, Walsh 65p,*	*Richardson*	*Clement*	*Gillard*	*Hollins*	*Howe*	*Roeder*	*Busby*	*Shanks*	*Walsh*	*Goddard*	*Allen*	
							Ref: A Grey	17-year-old Clive Allen scores a hat-trick in his first full game, as QPR win their first home game since December. But it won't stop them from being relegated. 20 minutes of defensive madness cost City the game after Wallace scores first. Only Chelsea have conceded more goals.											
42	H	WOLVES	9	W	3-0	2-0	Powell 23, 47p, Bannister 38	Blyth	Roberts	McDonald	Blair	Dyson	Coop	Nardiello*	Bannister	Hateley	Powell	Hutchison	Gooding
	5/5	21,742	*18*	44				*Bradshaw*	*Palmer*	*Parkin*	*Daniel**	*McAlle*	*Brazier*	*Hibbitt*	*Daley*	*Rafferty*	*Richards*	*Carr*	*Hazell*
	Home	Away					Ref: E Read	Teenagers Hateley, Dyson and Bannister all get to play in a match affected by a snowstorm. Hateley's pace causes Wolves problems and he sets up Powell's first goal. Bannister heads the second. Powell's penalty is for handball by Parkin. Wolves are safe after arriving unbeaten in six.											
Average	22.693	25,231																	

LEAGUE DIVISION 1 (CUP-TIES) Manager: Gordon Milne SEASON 1978-79

League Cup					F-A	H-T	Scorers, Times, and Referees	1	2	3	4	5	6	7	8	9	10	11	12 sub used
2	A	CHESTER	4	L	1-2	0-1	Thompson 84	Sealey	Osgood	McDonald	Beck*	Holton	Yorath	Bannister	Powell	Ferguson	Wallace	Hutchison	Thompson
	30/8	*8,598*	*3:1*				*Edwards 35, Mellor 69*	*Lloyd*	*Raynor*	*Walker*	*Storton*	*Jeffries*	*Oakes*	*Delgado*	*Livermore*	*Edwards*	*Mellor*	*Phillips*	
							Ref: P Willis	Chester thoroughly deserve this famous victory as they outfight and outrun lazy City. Ex-WBA man Ian Edwards heads home from a free-kick and ex-Man City winger Ian Mellor wraps it up as Sealey hesitates. Thompson's goal is too little, too late, and the Seals go on to meet Norwich.											

FA Cup					F-A	H-T	Scorers, Times, and Referees	1	2	3	4	5	6	7	8	9	10	11	12 sub used
3	H	WEST BROM	8	D	2-2	1-1	Blair 17, Green 86	Blyth	Hagan	McDonald	Blair	Holton	Coop	Nardiello*	Wallace	Thompson	Powell	Hutchison	Green
	9/1	37,928	*2*				*Cunningham 20, Brown A 60*	*Godden*	*Batson*	*Statham*	*Brown T*	*Wile*	*Robertson*	*Robson*	*Brown A*	*Regis*	*Trewick*	*Cunningham*	
							Ref: C Thomas	A nerve-tingling cup-tie played in skating-rink conditions on a freezing night. Albion are the top side in the country and are unbeaten for 17 games, a club record. An entertaining match swings one way then the other with chances galore. Green grabs the equaliser and almost wins it.											
3R	A	WEST BROM	8	L	0-4	0-2	*[Brown A 85]*	Blyth	Hagan	McDonald	Blair	Holton	Coop	Nardiello*	Wallace	Thompson	Powell	Hutchison	Green
	15/1	*36,262*	*1*				*Brown T 16, 80, Batson 20,*	*Godden*	*Batson*	*Statham*	*Brown T*	*Wile*	*Robertson*	*Robson**	*Brown A*	*Regis*	*Cantello*	*Cunningham*	*Johnston*
							Ref: K Styles	The scoreline does not do justice to City's performance. They miss two good chances before WBA score and Thompson has a good goal disallowed with the score at 0-2. Albion's ability to break quickly from defence and finish clinically has made them possible title challengers.											

		Home					Away					
	P	W	D	L	F	A	W	D	L	F	A	Pts
1 Liverpool	42	19	2	0	51	4	11	6	4	34	12	68
2 Nott'm Forest	42	11	10	0	34	10	10	8	3	27	16	60
3 West Brom	42	13	5	3	38	15	11	6	4	34	20	59
4 Everton	42	12	7	2	32	17	5	10	6	20	23	51
5 Leeds	42	11	4	6	41	25	7	10	4	29	27	50
6 Ipswich	42	11	4	6	34	21	9	5	7	29	28	49
7 Arsenal	42	11	8	2	37	18	6	6	9	24	30	48
8 Aston Villa	42	8	9	4	37	26	7	7	7	22	23	46
9 Manchester U	42	9	7	5	29	25	6	8	7	31	38	45
10 COVENTRY	42	11	7	3	41	29	3	9	9	17	39	44
11 Tottenham	42	7	8	6	19	25	6	7	8	29	36	41
12 Middlesbro	42	10	5	6	33	21	5	5	11	24	29	40
13 Bristol City	42	11	6	4	34	19	4	4	13	13	32	40
14 Southampton	42	9	10	2	35	20	3	6	12	12	33	40
15 Manchester C	42	9	5	7	34	28	4	8	9	24	28	39
16 Norwich	42	7	10	4	29	19	0	13	8	22	38	37
17 Bolton	42	10	5	6	36	28	2	6	13	18	47	35
18 Wolves	42	10	4	7	26	26	3	4	14	18	42	34
19 Derby	42	8	5	8	25	25	2	6	13	19	46	31
20 QP Rangers	42	4	9	8	24	33	2	4	15	21	40	25
21 Birmingham	42	5	9	7	24	25	1	1	19	13	39	22
22 Chelsea	42	3	5	13	23	42	2	5	14	21	50	20
	924	209	144	109	716	501	109	144	209	501	716	924

Odds & ends

Double wins: (3) Middlesbrough, Chelsea, Derby.
Double losses: (2) Manchester C, West Brom.

Won from behind: (4) Middlesbrough (A), Chelsea (H&A), Derby (H).
Lost from in front: (1) QP Rangers (A).

High spots: 15 home games unbeaten before 1-3 Spurs defeat.
Scoring three goals in last 11 minutes to beat Derby.
Ending Everton's 19-game unbeaten run.
The 4-3 home win over Man United.

Low spots: The 1-7 defeat at West Brom and subsequent Cup defeat.
The 0-5 embarrassment at Bristol City.
The Chester League Cup debacle.
The 1-5 defeat at already relegated QP Rangers.

Red cards: Opponents – Pendrey (Birmingham h), Evans (A Villa h).

Player of the Year: Bobby McDonald.
Ever-presents: (2) Bobby McDonald, Tommy Hutchison.
Hat-tricks: (1) Ian Wallace.
Opposing hat-tricks: (2) Royle (Bristol C), Allen (QPR).
Leading scorer: (15) Ian Wallace.

	Appearances						Goals			
	Lge	*Sub*	LC	*Sub*	FAC	*Sub*	**Lge**	LC	FAC	**Tot**
Bannister, Gary	**3**	*1*	1				**1**			**1**
Beck, John	**5**	*1*	1				**1**			**1**
Blair, Andy	**25**	*1*			2		**1**		1	**2**
Blyth, Jim	**6**				2					
Coop, Mick	**36**				2					
Dyson, Paul	**2**									
Ferguson, Mick	**16**	*2*	1				**7**			**7**
Gillespie, Gary	**14**	*1*	1							
Gooding, Ray	**2**	*2*								
Green, Alan	**6**	*5*				*2*	**1**		1	**2**
Hagan, Jim	**12**	*1*			2					
Hateley, Mark	**1**									
Holton, Jim	**34**		1		2					
Hunt, Steve	**20**	*4*					**6**			**6**
Hutchison, Tommy	**42**		1		2		**6**			**6**
McDonald, Bobby	**42**		1		2		**4**			**4**
Nardiello, Donato	**16**				2					
Osgood, Keith	**11**		1							
Powell, Barry	**38**		1		2		**8**			**8**
Roberts, Brian	**17**									
Sealey, Les	**36**		1							
Thompson, Garry	**19**	*1*		*1*	2		**8**	1		**9**
Wallace, Ian	**38**		1		2		**15**			**15**
Yorath, Terry	**21**									
(own-goals)										
24 players used	**462**	***19***	**11**	***1***	**22**	***2***	**58**	**1**	**2**	**61**

No	Date		Att	Pos	Pt	F-A	H-T	Scorers, Times, and Referees	1	2	3	4	5	6	7	8	9	10	11	12 sub used
1	A	STOKE			L	2-3	0-1	Powell 63p, 70	Blyth	**Jones**	McDonald	Gooding	Holton	**Collier**	Hutchison	**English**	Ferguson	Powell	Hunt	
	18/8		*23,151*		0			*Busby 35, Crooks 50, 55*	*Jones*	*Evans*	*Scott*	*Irvine*	*Smith*	*Doyle*	*Busby*	*Heath*	*O'Callaghan*	*Crooks*	*Ursem**	*Richardson*
								Ref: D Richardson	Newly promoted Stoke rip City's new-look defence apart inside an hour, though two Powell goals raise hopes. Yorath has departed to Spurs and Gooding struggles as his replacement. Tommy English tries hard and is shoved for the penalty. Gary Collier and David Jones look rusty.											
2	H	BRISTOL CITY			W	3-1	1-1	English 24, Powell 63p, Hutchison 83	Blyth	Jones	McDonald	Blair	Holton	Gillespie	Hutchison	English	Ferguson	Powell	Hunt*	Hateley
	21/8		19,208		2			*Ritchie 37p*	*Shaw*	*Sweeney*	*Whitehead*	*Gow*	*Rodgers**	*Merrick*	*Fitzpatrick*	*Ritchie*	*Mabbutt*	*Jantunen*	*Meyer*	*Tainton*
								Ref: N Ashley	English scores his first City goal as they make hard work of resolute Bristol. £350,000 Collier is axed after one game and other new-boy Jones fouls Gow for the penalty. Justice is done with Powell's penalty for Merrick's handball and new skipper Hutch's goal direct from a corner.											
3	A	NOTT'M FOREST		16	L	1-4	0-2	English 48 *[Robertson 68p]*	Blyth	Jones*	McDonald	Blair	Holton	Gillespie	Hutchison	English	Ferguson	Powell	Hunt	Roberts
	25/8		*23,025*	*2*	2			*Woodcock 18, McGovern 39, 64,*	*Shilton*	*Anderson*	*Gray*	*McGovern*	*Lloyd*	*Burns*	*O'Neill*	*Hartford*	*Birtles*	*Woodcock*	*Robertson*	
								Ref: D Webb	Forest, unbeaten in their first three, steam-roll City's midfield. English's goal gives some fleeting hope before McGovern and Robertson, after Jones pulled him down, wrap it up. Hartford plays his third and final game for Clough before being sold on to Everton. Wallace is still injured.											
4	H	NORWICH		10	W	2-0	0-0	McDonald 50, Ferguson 63	**Murcott**	Roberts	McDonald	Blair	Holton	Gillespie	Hutchison	English*	Ferguson	Powell	Hunt	Hateley
	1/9		18,684	*2*	4				*Keelan*	*Bond*	*McDowell**	*McGuire*	*Hoadley*	*Brown*	*Neighbour*	*Reeves*	*Fashanu*	*Paddon*	*Peters*	*Ryan*
								Ref: D Reeves	Jim Blyth hurts his back in the warm-up and youth team keeper Steve Murcott is called in for his one and only game. He keeps a clean sheet as City end Norwich's 100% winning record. After a dull first half, when the team seemed more anxious than Murcott, they step up a gear to win.											
5	A	LIVERPOOL		16	L	**0-4**	0-1		Sealey	Roberts	McDonald	Collier	Holton	Gillespie	Hutchison	English	Ferguson*	Powell	Hunt	Blair
	8/9		*39,926*	*8*	4			*Johnson 29, 90, Case 57, Dalglish 64*	*Clemence*	*Neal*	*Kennedy A*	*Thompson*	*Kennedy R*	*Irwin*	*Dalglish*	*Case*	*Johnson*	*McDermott*	*Souness*	
								Ref: J Hough	Match of the Day sees City trampled underfoot by the rampant champions. Pool control the game so much that Clemence is a virtual spectator and the score could have been worse. Collier returns to play as the third centre-back, but to no avail. Mick Coop returns from summer in USA.											
6	H	BOLTON		13	W	3-1	1-0	Wallace 9, 61, Powell 48p	Sealey	Roberts	McDonald	Blair	Holton	Gillespie	Hutchison	Wallace	Ferguson	Powell	Hunt	
	15/9		15,268	*16*	6			*Morgan 81*	*McDonagh*	*Clement*	*Nicholson**	*Greaves*	*Jones*	*Walsh*	*Morgan*	*Whatmore*	*Gowling*	*Cantello*	*Burke*	*Thompson*
								Ref: S Bates	Wallace and Ferguson play together for the first time since February and the Scot scores two, misses a sitter, and has a shot handled for the penalty. Bolton are a poor side who rely heavily on an offside trap and look good bets for relegation. Walsh limps off, leaving Bolton with ten.											
7	A	MANCHESTER C		15	L	0-3	0-3		Sealey	Roberts	McDonald	Blair	Holton	Gillespie	Hutchison	Wallace	Ferguson	Powell	Hunt	
	22/9		*30,869*	*19*	6			*Robinson 3, 19, MacKenzie 42*	*Corrigan*	*Ranson*	*Donachie*	*Stepanovic*	*Caton*	*Futcher*	*MacKenzie*	*Daley*	*Robinson*	*Power*	*Bennett*	
								Ref: A Saunders	Manchester, with £1.4 million signing Daley, make a mockery of their position and notch their first win of the season. It's all over by half-time as City's midfield is overrun and the man-for-man marking system is ripped apart. It's the seventh straight defeat for Coventry at Maine Road.											
8	H	TOTTENHAM		15	D	1-1	1-0	Wallace 37	Sealey	Roberts	McDonald	**Whitton***	Holton	Gillespie	Hutchison	Wallace	English	Powell	Hunt	**Thomas**
	29/9		20,085	*20*	7			*Jones 60*	*Daines*	*Hughton*	*McAllister*	*Yorath*	*Miller*	*Perryman*	*Ardiles*	*Jones*	*Armstrong*	*Hoddle*	*Villa*	
								Ref: B Newsome	Spurs arrive bottom of the league and organise a defensive trap masterminded by Yorath. City breach it twice, first by Wallace, then, with 13 minutes left, when Steve Hunt went clean through to shot at Daines. In a match of five bookings, Coventry's midfield failings are highlighted.											
9	H	EVERTON		10	W	2-1	1-0	Wallace 34, 48	Sealey	Coop	McDonald	Gooding	Holton	Gillespie	Hutchison	Wallace	English*	Powell	Hunt	Thomas
	6/10		17,205	*15*	9			*King 79*	*Wood*	*Barton*	*Bailey*	*Lyons*	*Higgins*	*Nulty*	*Hartford*	*Stanley*	*Latchford**	*Kidd*	*King*	*Varadi*
								Ref: G Flint	Latchford is off the transfer list and plays his first game of the season. City win comfortably but have to survive a few late scares after King's blistering shot. Thomas is an early sub for the injured English, and will surely have impressed the watching England boss Ron Greenwood.											
10	A	BRISTOL CITY		13	L	0-1	0-0		Sealey	Coop	McDonald	Gooding	Holton	Gillespie	Nardiello	Wallace	Hutchison	Powell	Hunt	
	9/10		*14,853*	*11*	9			*Ritchie 58*	*Shaw*	*Sweeney*	*Whitehead*	*Gow*	*Rodgers*	*Merrick*	*Fitzpatrick*	*Ritchie*	*Royle*	*Mann*	*Tainton*	
								Ref: A Cox	13 away games without a win for City, but this should have ended the run. Bristol are overrun, but the killer punch is missing. Wallace hits the bar with a spectacular volley and three minutes later Ritchie scores. Osgood has moved to Derby for £150,000 and John Sillett is coaching .											

11	A	SOUTHAMPTON		12	W	3-2	0-0	Wallace 56, 62, Gooding 84	Sealey	Coop	McDonald	Gooding	Holton	Gillespie	Hutchison	Wallace	Nardiello	Blair	Hunt	
	13/10		*22,986*	*4*	11			*Boyer 46, George 71*	*Gennoe*	*Hebberd*	*Peach*	*Williams*	*Andruszewski*	*Waldron*	*Ball*	*Boyer*	*Channon*	*George*	*Holmes*	
								Ref: W Bombroff	A battling performance ends City's dreadful away run. It is Saints' first home defeat and City's first win at the Dell since 1939. Wallace shows why he is one of the most lethal finishers in the game with two opportunist goals. He also sets up Ray Gooding for a beautiful chipped winner.											
12	H	BRIGHTON		10	W	2-1	1-1	McDonald 20, English 82	Sealey	Jones	McDonald	Gooding	Holton	Coop	Hutchison	Wallace	English	Blair	Hunt	
	20/10		17,294	*21*	13			*Rollings 16*	*Moseley*	*Rollings*	*Williams*	*Horton*	*Foster*	*Stevens*	*Ryan*	*Ward**	*Maybank*	*Sayer*	*O'Sullivan*	*Chivers*
								Ref: D Hutchinson	Newly promoted Brighton are having a tough time of it, but look good for a point until Tommy English, celebrating his England Youth call up, scores. Veteran striker Martin Chivers has a shot well saved by Les Sealey. Out of form Barry Powell joins Derby County for £350,000.											
13	A	WEST BROM		12	L	1-4	0-2	Coop 62p	Sealey	Jones	McDonald	Gooding	Holton	Coop	Hutchison	Wallace	English	Blair	Hunt	
	27/10		*22,721*	*9*	13			*Brown A 15, 37, Brown T 86p, 88*	*Godden*	*Batson*	*Statham*	*Mills*	*Wile*	*Robertson*	*Robson*	*Brown A*	*Deehan*	*Owen*	*Brown T*	
								Ref: R Lewis	The Albion hoodoo continues but this is a cruel scoreline. Brown's two late goals don't reflect City's second-half fightback. Coop scores after Statham brings down Jones, but Holton fouls Deehan at a corner for a penalty and Tony Brown scores his 218th and final goal for the Baggies.											
14	H	STOKE		15	L	1-3	1-2	McDonald 42	Sealey	Jones*	McDonald	Gooding	Holton	Coop	Hutchison	Wallace	English	Blair	Hunt	Whitton
	3/11		16,719	*14*	13			*Jones 24 (og), Heath 26, Crooks 75*	*Jones*	*Evans*	*Scott*	*Johnson*	*Smith*	*Dodd*	*Heath*	*Irvine*	*O'Callaghan*	*Crooks*	*Richardson*	
								Ref: J Martin	Stoke's first away win and City's first home defeat. City never recover from two minutes of madness, when Jones' pass-back beats Sealey and Heath heads home. McDonald bends in a superb free-kick, and Jones is substituted at half-time, but Garth Crooks seals it. A dreadful display.											
15	H	LEEDS		13	W	3-0	1-0	Ferguson 38, 78, Wallace 68	Sealey	Coop	McDonald	Gooding	Holton	Gillespie	Hutchison	Wallace	Ferguson*	Blair	Hunt	Whitton
	10/11		19,329	*18*	15				*Lukic*	*Cherry*	*Stevenson*	*Flynn**	*Hart*	*Madeley*	*Hird*	*Greenhoff*	*Hankin*	*Curtis*	*Gray F*	*Entwistle*
								Ref: C Thomas	Leeds fans chant 'Adamson out' as their side collapses. The recalled Mick Ferguson and Gary Gillespie give City a better balance and disperse some of the storm clouds over Highfield Road. The tall striker scores two and Ian Wallace nets with a shot that John Lukic should have held.											
16	A	WOLVES		11	W	3-0	1-0	Wallace 8, Ferguson 55, 75	Sealey	Coop	McDonald	Gooding	Holton	Gillespie	Hutchison	Wallace	Ferguson	Blair	Hunt	
	17/11		*22,805*	*10*	17				*Bradshaw*	*Palmer*	*Parkin*	*Daniel**	*McAlle*	*Berry*	*Hibbitt*	*Carr*	*Gray*	*Richards*	*Eves*	*Hughes*
								Ref: K Walmsley	Ferguson and Wallace combine again to outclass Wolves, previously unbeaten at home. £1.4 million striker Andy Gray doesn't get a sniff out of Jim Holton. Steve Hunt is City's architect, setting up all three goals. A male streaker dashes on in the first half, wearing a shirt and jumper.											
17	A	CRYS PALACE		11	D	0-0	0-0		Sealey	Coop	McDonald	Gooding	Holton	Gillespie	Hutchison	Wallace	Ferguson	Blair	Hunt	
	24/11		*26,209*	*3*	18				*Burridge*	*Hinshelwood*	*Sansom*	*Nicholas*	*Cannon*	*Gilbert*	*Murphy*	*Francis*	*Flanagan*	*Swindlehurst*	*Hilaire**	*Walsh*
								Ref: B Stevens	Newly promoted Palace miss the chance to go top, but manager Venables is upset by City's defensive approach. A highly professional display, with Sealey in defiant mood, earns a point. Three clean sheets in a row for City, a Div 1 club record. Thompson and Oakey are still out injured.											
18	H	IPSWICH		6	W	**4-1**	1-0	Ferguson 10, 52, 60, 70	Sealey	Coop	McDonald	Gooding	Holton	Gillespie	Hutchison	Wallace	Ferguson	Blair	Hunt	
	1/12		16,411	*20*	20			*Wark 68p*	*Cooper*	*Burley*	*Butcher*	*Mills*	*Osman*	*Beattie*	*Wark*	*Muhren*	*D'Avray*	*Mariner*	*Gates*	
								Ref: D Shaw	The Ipswich boss jibbed at City's £750,000 valuation of Ferguson last week and the big man gives the perfect answer with City's first four-goal haul since 1959. He does it despite a damaged knee, which is strapped after half time. Wark gets a consolation penalty after Mariner is fouled.											
19	A	ARSENAL		9	L	1-3	1-2	Gooding 27	Sealey	Coop	McDonald	Gooding	Holton	Gillespie	Hutchison	Wallace	Ferguson	Blair	Bannister	
	8/12		*27,563*	*4*	20			*Stapleton 22, Sunderl'd 26, O'Leary 69*	*Jennings*	*Devine*	*Nelson**	*Talbot*	*O'Leary*	*Walford*	*Brady*	*Sunderland*	*Stapleton*	*Hollins*	*Rix*	*Gatting*
								Ref: T Spencer	Arsenal win comfortably as City suffer a relapse of form. They never recover from two quick goals, and after the break, with Brady pulling the strings, they are outclassed. Only poor finishing prevents it being a rout. Stapleton is very impressive, scoring the first and making the second.											
20	H	MANCHESTER U		11	L	1-2	0-0	Ferguson 82	Sealey	Coop*	McDonald	Gooding	Holton	Gillespie	Hutchison	Wallace	Ferguson	Blair	Hunt	Whitton
	15/12		25,541	*2*	20			*McQueen 58, Macari 70*	*Bailey*	*Nicholl*	*Houston*	*McIlroy*	*McQueen*	*Buchan*	*Coppell*	*Wilkins*	*Jordan*	*Macari*	*Thomas*	
								Ref: R Robinson	Despite the cold wind and rain this is a classic. United are neck and neck with Liverpool at the top of the table and give City a tough time. United deserve to win, thanks to two goals from right-wing crosses. Mick Ferguson headed Hutchison's corner in to set up a thrilling finale.											
21	A	ASTON VILLA		11	L	0-3	0-1		Sealey	Roberts	McDonald	Gooding	Holton	Gillespie	Hutchison	Wallace	Ferguson*	Blair	Hunt	Whitton
	19/12		*24,446*	*6*	20			*Donovan 8, Little 51, 60*	*Rimmer*	*Swain*	*Gibson*	*Ormsby*	*McNaught*	*Bullivant*	*Bremner*	*Little*	*Donovan*	*Cowans*	*Shaw*	
								Ref: J Worrall	A tiny City following see an embarrassing annihilation on a bitterly cold night. Terry Donovan scores on his debut and Little could have had a hatful as Villa extend their run to one defeat in 14. City make one chance all game, and Jim Holton's sixth booking completes a miserable night.											

No	Date		Att	Pos	Pt	F-A	H-T	Scorers, Times, and Referees	1	2	3	4	5	6	7	8	9	10	11	12 sub used
22	A	DERBY		12	W	2-1	0-1	McDonald 57, English 81	Sealey	Roberts	McDonald	Gooding !	Holton	Gillespie	Hutchison	Wallace	Ferguson	Blair	English	
	26/12		*15,531*	*21*	22			*Clark 20*	*McKellar*	*Langan*	*Buckley*	*Daly*	*Webb*	*Osgood*	*Clark*	*Powell B*	*Whymark**	*Davies*	*Emson*	*Emery*
								Ref: N Glover	Tom English's super winning goal brightens up a dull game and dumps Derby in deep relegation trouble. A minute later Gooding becomes the first City player to be sent off for over two years, for two bookable offences. City keep their head after Clark's goal and fully deserve the win.											
23	H	NOTT'M FOREST		14	L	0-3	0-0		Sealey	Roberts	McDonald	Coop	Holton	Gillespie	Hutchison	English	Ferguson	Blair	Hunt*	Whitton
	29/12		24,722	*8*	22			*Robertson 50p, 67, Bowles 70*	*Shilton*	*Anderson*	*Gray*	*McGovern*	*Lloyd*	*Burns*	*Francis*	*Bowles*	*Birtles*	*Bowyer*	*Robertson*	
								Ref: C White	Match of the Day viewers see Forest end a run of six away defeats with an easy win in a low-entertainment game. The penalty, given for a foul by Holton on Birtles, looks harsh but City's heads drop after it. The other goals are gifts for Robertson and Bowles. Ray Gooding is suspended.											
24	H	MIDDLESBROUGH		12	W	2-0	2-0	Blair 12, Gillespie 35	Sealey	Roberts	McDonald	Gooding	Holton	Gillespie	Nardiello	English	Ferguson	Blair	Hutchison	
	1/1		17,081	*8*	24				*Platt*	*Craggs*	*Johnson*	*Hedley*	*Ashcroft*	*McAndrew*	*Woof**	*Procter*	*Hodgson*	*Jankovic*	*Armstrong*	*Ramage*
								Ref: D Richardson	Workmanlike Boro rarely trouble City after the early goal, but despite lots of chances the Sky Blues have to rely on Blair's header after Platt's punch out and Gillespie's first ever goal; a great shot after a one-two with Gooding. The new undersoil heating allows the game to go ahead.											
25	A	NORWICH		13	L	0-1	0-1		Blyth	Coop	McDonald	Gooding	Dyson	Gillespie	Nardiello*	English	Hateley	Blair	Hutchison	Whitton
	12/1		*16,467*	*4*	24			*Robson 45*	*Keelan*	*Bond*	*Downs*	*Ryan*	*Brown*	*Powell*	*Mendham*	*Reeves*	*Robson**	*Paddon*	*Peters*	*Fashanu*
								Ref: D Vickers	Keith Robson's angled shot is deflected off Gooding past Blyth to preserve the Canaries' unbeaten home record. Coventry field seven players under 21 and they all work hard. Steadier finishing from Mark Hateley would have earned a point. Ferguson is set for £900,000 move to Forest.											
26	H	LIVERPOOL		13	W	1-0	1-0	Dyson 6	Blyth	Coop	McDonald	Gooding	Dyson	Gillespie	English*	Wallace	Hateley	Blair	Hutchison	Thompson
	19/1		**31,644**	*1*	26				*Clemence*	*Neal*	*Kennedy A*	*Thompson*	*Kennedy R*	*Hansen*	*Dalglish*	*Case**	*Johnson*	*McDermott*	*Souness*	*Heighway*
								Ref: K Salmon	The Reds' 19-match unbeaten run is ended by the magnificent Sky Blue babes in front of Match of the Day cameras. The game is won in midfield where Hutch, Blair and Gooding squeeze the life out of Souness and co. Paul Dyson's glances a header from McDonald's free-kick.											
27	H	MANCHESTER C		13	D	0-0	0-0		Blyth	Coop	McDonald	Gooding	Dyson	Gillespie	English	Wallace*	Thompson	Blair	Hutchison	Bannister
	9/2		17,185	*18*	27				*Corrigan*	*Ranson*	*Donachie*	*Henry*	*Caton*	*Booth*	*MacKenzie*	*Daley*	*Robinson*	*Power*	*Bennett*	
								Ref: R Challis	This bore-draw has the fans slow handclapping. The gluepot conditions don't help, neither does a Manchester side bereft of confidence after an FA Cup defeat at Halifax. Thompson returns from injury, Wallace is subbed, and it's City's youngest ever Div 1 side that finishes the game.											
28	H	SOUTHAMPTON		12	W	3-0	2-0	Thompson 24, 53, English 26	Blyth	Coop	McDonald	Gooding	Dyson	Gillespie	Hutchison	English	Thompson	Blair	Hunt	
	23/2		17,996	*5*	29				*Wells*	*Golac*	*Waldron*	*Baker*	*Watson*	*Peach*	*Ball*	*Boyer*	*Channon*	*Holmes*	*George*	
								Ref: A Banks	McMenemy's Saints have only lost one in twelve and await the arrival of Kevin Keegan in the summer. City's record against them, having not lost at home since 1949, is extended. Thompson scores two and gives England's Dave Watson a hard time. Belgian Van Gool looks set to sign.											
29	A	TOTTENHAM		12	L	3-4	2-2	Dyson 30, English 32, 90	Blyth	Coop	McDonald	Gooding*	Dyson	Gillespie	Hutchison	English	Thompson	Blair	Hunt	Roberts
	27/2		*22,536*	*13*	29			*Hoddle 15p, 18p, 81, Falco 90*	*Kendall*	*Hughton*	*Miller*	*Pratt*	*McAllister*	*Perryman*	*Ardiles*	*Falco*	*Armstrong*	*Hoddle*	*Yorath*	
								Ref: C Thomas	City's battling comeback is in vain as the referee adds on five minutes injury-time and Falco nabs the winner with the last kick. Both penalties are dubious; Hunt for a foul on Armstrong, and Thompson for a push on the same player. Superb Dyson's only mistake gives Hoddle his third.											
30	A	BRIGHTON		13	D	1-1	1-1	English 34	Blyth	Coop	McDonald	**Phillips**	Dyson	Gillespie	Hutchison	English	Thompson	Blair	Hunt	
	1/3		*21,605*	*18*	30			*Clarke 31*	*Moseley*	*Gregory*	*Williams*	*Horton*	*Foster*	*Suddaby*	*McNab*	*Ward*	*Clarke*	*Lawrenson**	*O'Sullivan*	*Ryan*
								Ref: L Burden	Brighton are barely keeping their head above the relegation mire and give City a hard battle on a sandy pitch. Tom English's stunning 25-yarder cancels out future City scout, Ray Clarke's, header. Nicky Phillips enjoys a promising debut. Ian Wallace is on the transfer list for £1 million.											
31	H	WEST BROM		14	L	0-2	0-1		Blyth	Coop	McDonald	Phillips	Dyson	Gillespie	**Van Gool**	English	Thompson	Blair*	Hutchison	Hunt
	8/3		23,251	*15*	30			*Barnes 21, 86p*	*Godden*	*Batson*	*Pendrey*	*Moses*	*Wile*	*Robertson*	*Robson*	*Deehan*	*Regis*	*Owen*	*Barnes*	
								Ref: T Bune	Roger Van Gool, a £250,000 signing from Cologne, can't banish the Albion jinx. City are pathetic and the Baggies should have sealed it well before the end. Barnes scores an overhead kick and a penalty when Gillespie fouls Deehan. Gary Collier joins Portland Timbers for £365,000.											

No	Venue / Date	Opponent / Att	Pos	Pts	Res	F-A	H-T	Scorers, Times, and Referees	1	2	3	4	5	6	7	8	9	10	11	12
32	A	EVERTON	14		D	1-1	1-1	Thompson 27	Blyth	Coop	McDonald	Phillips	Dyson	Gillespie	Van Gool	English	Thompson	Blair	Bannister	
	15/3	*25,970*	*19*	31				*Eastoe 8*	*Hodge*	*Gidman*	*Bailey*	*Wright*	*Lyons*	*Eastoe*	*Megson*	*King*	*Latchford*	*Hartford*	*McBride*	
								Ref: T Farley	Gordon Lee's Everton have won through to the FA Cup semi finals but have won only one league game in twelve. The City babes recover from Eastoe's goal to give Everton a scare but are let down by inexperience. Mick Ferguson's £750,000 move to Villa collapses due to lack of funds.											
33	A	LEEDS	14		D	0-0	0-0		Blyth	Coop	McDonald	Phillips	Dyson	Gillespie	Bannister*	English	Thompson	Hunt	Hutchison	Roberts
	22/3	*14,967*	*11*	32					*Lukic*	*Hird*	*Parkinson*	*Chandler*	*Hart*	*Madeley*	*Hamson*	*Cherry*	*Connor*	*Parlane*	*Graham*	
								Ref: P Richardson	A dire game watched by Leeds' lowest Div 1 crowd for 20 years. Steve Hunt plays his first game as a midfielder and looks excellent. The home side rarely trouble City and with a bit more composure City might have secured an away win. Bobby McDonald indicates that he wants a move.											
34	H	WOLVES	14		L	1-3	0-2	English 55	Blyth	Coop	McDonald	Hutchison	Dyson	Gillespie	Van Gool	English	Thompson	Hunt	Bannister*	Blair
	29/3	19,450	*6*	32				*Atkinson 13, Richards 28, 72*	*Bradshaw*	*Palmer*	*Parkin*	*Atkinson*	*Hughes*	*Berry*	*Brazier*	*Carr*	*Gray*	*Richards*	*Eves*	
								Ref: B Martin	Wolves have won seven out of eight, including the League Cup final. They're well worth this win despite Bradshaw's fine save from Thompson at 2-1. Atkinson scores his first ever goal as Wolves earn their first win at Highfield Road since 1972. The 'Milne out' chants grow ever louder.											
35	A	MIDDLESBROUGH	12		W	2-1	1-1	Wallace 15, 84	Blyth	Coop	McDonald	Blair	Dyson	Gillespie	Wallace	English	Thompson	Hunt	Hutchison	
	5/4	*15,398*	*9*	34				*Hodgson 2*	*Platt*	*Craggs*	*Johnson*	*Johnston*	*Ramage*	*Nattrass*	*Cochrane*	*Procter*	*Hodgson*	*Ashcroft**	*Armstrong*	*Jankovic*
								Ref: P Tyldesley	Transfer-listed Ian Wallace returns after two months out and wins the game with a tap-in, added to one of his specials. Boro are pushing for a European place but are lacklustre. David Hodgson looks to have fouled Jim Blyth as he touches in David Armstrong's inswinging corner.											
36	H	DERBY	12		W	2-1	1-0	Wallace 27, Hunt 83	Blyth	Coop	McDonald	Blair*	Dyson	Gillespie	Hutchison	Wallace	Thompson	English	Hunt	Roberts
	7/4	19,519	*20*	36				*McCaffery 72*	*McKellar*	*Langan*	*Buckley*	*McCaffery*	*McFarland*	*Osgood*	*Emery*	*Powell B**	*Biley*	*Swindlehurst*	*Emson*	*Clark*
								Ref: A Hamil	Gallant Derby are as good as relegated by Steve Hunt's volley, his first goal for a year, in this Easter Monday game. Derby control the second half after Wallace's acrobatic header, and get their reward with McCaffrey's goal. Former City players Powell and Osgood look pale shadows.											
37	A	IPSWICH	14		L	0-3	0-3		Blyth	Coop	McDonald	Roberts	Dyson	Gillespie	Wallace*	English	Thompson	Hunt	Hutchison	Gooding
	12/4	*20,502*	*3*	36				*Butcher 11, Mariner 16, Brazil 30*	*Cooper*	*Burley*	*Butcher*	*Thijssen*	*Hunter*	*Osman*	*Wark*	*Muhren**	*Mariner*	*Brazil*	*Gates*	*McCall*
								Ref: A Gunn	The inconsistent Sky Blues are ruthlessly punished in a torrid first-half hour. Ipswich have not lost in the league since their defeat at Coventry, 21 matches ago. This is City's worst game of the season and they never threaten Cooper's goal. Mercifully, Ipswich's finishing lets them down.											
38	A	BOLTON	13		D	1-1	1-1	Thompson 22	Blyth	Coop	**Barnes**	Gooding	Dyson	Gillespie	Van Gool	English	Thompson	Hunt	Hutchison	
	15/4	***8,995***	*22*	37				*Wilson 14*	*McDonagh*	*Graham*	*Bennett*	*Hoggan*	*Jones*	*Walsh*	*Nowak*	*Whatmore*	*Carter*	*Wilson*	*Reid*	
								Ref: J Lovatt	Bolton are already relegated and the crowd is the lowest to watch a City Div 1 game. Polish Tad Nowak sets up 18-year-old Wilson for his first goal, before Thompson scores at the second attempt. Bobby McDonald is dropped after 178 consecutive games, allowing Barnes a run out.											
39	H	CRYS PALACE	12		W	2-1	2-1	English 4, Thompson 19	Blyth	Coop	Barnes	Van Gool*	Dyson	Gillespie	Hutchison	Wallace !	Thompson	English	Hunt	Phillips
	19/4	**14,310**	*11*	39				*Hilaire 5*	*Burridge*	*Hinshelwood*	*Sansom !*	*Nicholas*	*Cannon*	*Boyle*	*Murphy*	*Francis*	*Flanagan*	*Smillie*	*Hilaire*	
								Ref: G Nolan	An exciting first half was followed by a dull second, enlivened by the double sending off ten minutes from time. Wallace and Sansom exchange punches which fail to connect, and the pair are unfortunate to be sent off. City are worth their win as Crystal Palace's good season tails off.											
40	A	MANCHESTER U	12		L	1-2	0-1	Thompson 53	Blyth	Coop	Jones	Blair	Dyson	Gillespie	Van Gool	English*	Thompson	Hunt	Hutchison	Bannister
	26/4	***52,154***	*2*	39				*McIlroy 5p, 69*	*Bailey*	*Nicholl*	*Albiston*	*McIlroy*	*Moran*	*Buchan*	*Coppell*	*Greenhoff**	*Jordan*	*Macari*	*Thomas*	*Sloan*
								Ref: G Courtney	Though Cup Final ref Courtney signals an indirect free-kick, McIlroy's kick curls into the net for the winner. The goals stands, even though Hutch was yanked out of the wall by Greenhoff. Gillespie fouls Coppell for the penalty. United pull level on points at the top with Liverpool.											
41	H	ASTON VILLA			L	1-2	0-1	Wallace	Blyth	Coop	Barnes	Hunt	Dyson	Gillespie	Van Gool	Wallace	Thompson	English*	Hutchison	Thomas
	29/4	*17,932*		39				*Gibson, Cowans p*	*Rimmer*	*Swain*	*Gibson*	*Blake*	*Ormsby*	*Heard*	*Bremner*	*Shaw*	*Geddis*	*Cowans*	*Linton*	
								Ref: K Hackett	In an uninspiring end-of-season game Ian Wallace scores his final goal for the club. Steve Hunt impresses everyone in his new midfield role, but cannot stop his former club snatching both points in their vain quest for a European place. One season later they will be league champions.											
42	H	ARSENAL	15		L	0-1	0-0		Blyth	Coop	**Jacobs**	Hunt	Dyson	Gillespie	Van Gool	Wallace	Thompson	Gooding	Bannister	
	3/5	16,782	*4*	39				*Vaessen 88*	*Barron*	*Rice*	*Nelson*	*Talbot*	*Walford*	*Young*	*Gatting*	*Sunderland*	*Vaessen*	*Price**	*Hollins*	*Davis*
Average	Home 19,323	Away 23,461						Ref: D Lloyd	Arsenal return to Highfield Road three days after beating Liverpool in the FA Cup semi-final third replay. Terry Neill rests six of his heroes, so this is almost Arsenal's reserves. Paul Vaessen's winner comes after Coventry miss a hatful of chances. Jimmy Hill is the new City chairman.											

League Cup

Rd		Opponent	Pos	Res	F-A	H-T	Scorers, Times, and Referees	1	2	3	4	5	6	7	8	9	10	11	12 sub used
2:1	A	IPSWICH	16	W	1-0	1-0	English 18	Blyth	Roberts	McDonald	Blair	Holton	Gillespie	Hutchison	English	Ferguson	Gooding*	Hunt	Coop
29/8		*13,217*	*17*					*Cooper*	*Burley*	*Mills*	*Thijssen*	*Butcher*	*Osman*	*Wark*	*Muhren*	*Mariner*	*Brazil*	*Gates*	
							Ref: P Richardson	A fine performance against one of the favourites for honours. English makes it three goals in three games after Steve Hunt and Andy Blair have shots saved by Cooper. City tighten up with the wingers withdrawn and Roberts in for Jones. Blyth saves brilliantly from Osman and Brazil.											
2:2	H	IPSWICH	10	D	0-0	0-0		Sealey	Roberts	McDonald	Blair	Holton	Gillespie	Hutchison	English	Ferguson	Powell	Hunt	
4/9		16,616	*12*					*Cooper*	*Burley*	*Mills*	*Thijssen*	*Osman*	*Butcher*	*Wark*	*Muhren*	*Mariner*	*Brazil**	*Woods*	*Gates*
							Ref: J Sewell (City win 1-0 on aggregate)	Sealey is the third keeper used in three games as City go through after an unimpressive second leg. City's defence was on top form with Holton and Gillespie holding the much-vaunted Mariner and Brazil combo. English misses City's best chance when he shot over from Hutch's cross.											
3	A	WEST BROM	15	L	1-2	1-2	English 10	Sealey	Coop	McDonald	Thomas*	Holton	Gillespie	Hutchison	Wallace	English	Powell	Hunt	Roberts
26/9		*18,069*	*18*				*Wile 16, Brown T 22p*	*Godden*	*Batson*	*Statham*	*Trewick*	*Wile*	*Robertson*	*Robson*	*Brown T*	*Mills*	*Owen*	*Barnes*	
							Ref: J Hunting	A disappointing exit for the Sky Blues after their best performance at the Hawthorns for a long time. Danny Thomas has an impressive debut and English leaves Wile on the ground to score superbly. Wile heads in and Robson wins a controversial penalty when Sealey dives at his feet.											

FA Cup

Rd		Opponent	Pos	Res	F-A	H-T	Scorers, Times, and Referees	1	2	3	4	5	6	7	8	9	10	11	12 sub used
3	A	OLDHAM	12	W	1-0	1-0	Hutchison 16	Sealey	Coop	McDonald	Gooding	Dyson	Gillespie	Nardiello	English	Ferguson	Blair	Hutchison	
5/1		*12,151*	*2:16*					*Platt*	*Wood*	*Holt*	*Kowenicki*	*Clements*	*Hurst*	*Valentine*	*Halom*	*Steel*	*Stainrod*	*Atkinson*	
							Ref: G Owen	A brilliant last-minute save by Les Sealey from Wood ensures City go through. Hutchison, rejected by Oldham as a teenager, scores from the edge of the box when Platt throws the ball straight to him. On a bitterly cold day Coventry soak up enormous pressure from an eager Oldham.											
4	A	BLACKBURN	13	L	0-1	0-1		Blyth	Coop	McDonald	Gooding	Dyson	Gillespie	English	Wallace	Hateley	Blair	Hutchison	
26/1		*20,785*	*3:11*				*Crawford 29*	*Arnold*	*Branagan*	*Rathbone*	*Kendall*	*Keeley*	*Fazackerley*	*Brotherston*	*Crawford*	*Garner*	*McKenzie*	*Parkes*	
							Ref: K McNally	City's nervous kids, who struggle on the partially frozen pitch, are dumped out by Howard Kendall's experienced Rovers team. Crawford keeps up his record of scoring in every round by steering a header in after Jim Blyth comes off his line. Blackburn meet Villa in Round 5.											

		Home						Away					
	P	W	D	L	F	A	W	D	L	F	A	Pts
1 Liverpool	42	15	6	0	46	8	10	4	7	35	22	60
2 Manchester U	42	17	3	1	43	8	7	7	7	22	27	58
3 Ipswich	42	14	4	3	43	13	8	5	8	25	26	53
4 Arsenal	42	8	10	3	24	12	10	6	5	28	24	52
5 Nott'm Forest	42	16	4	1	44	11	4	4	13	19	32	48
6 Wolves	42	9	6	6	29	20	10	3	8	29	27	47
7 Aston Villa	42	11	5	5	29	22	5	9	7	22	28	46
8 Southampton	42	14	2	5	53	24	4	7	10	12	29	45
9 Middlesbro	42	11	7	3	31	14	5	5	11	19	30	44
10 West Brom	42	9	8	4	37	23	2	11	8	17	27	41
11 Leeds	42	10	7	4	30	17	3	7	11	16	33	40
12 Norwich	42	10	8	3	38	30	3	6	12	20	36	40
13 Crys Palace	42	9	9	3	26	13	3	7	11	15	37	40
14 Tottenham	42	11	5	5	30	22	4	5	12	22	40	40
15 COVENTRY	42	12	2	7	34	24	4	5	12	22	42	39
16 Brighton	42	8	8	5	25	20	3	7	11	22	37	37
17 Manchester C	42	8	8	5	28	25	4	5	12	15	41	37
18 Stoke	42	9	4	8	27	26	4	6	11	17	32	36
19 Everton	42	7	7	7	28	25	2	10	9	15	26	35
20 Bristol City	42	6	6	9	22	30	3	7	11	15	36	31
21 Derby	42	9	4	8	36	29	2	4	15	11	38	30
22 Bolton	42	5	11	5	19	21	0	4	17	19	52	25
	924	228	134	100	722	437	100	134	228	437	722	924

Odds & ends

Double wins: (3) Southampton, Derby, Middlesbrough.
Double losses: (6) Stoke, Manchester U, Nott'm Forest, West Brom, Aston Villa, Arsenal.

Won from behind: (4) Southampton (a), Brighton (h), Derby (a), Middlesbrough (a).
Lost from in front: (1) West Brom LC (a).

High spots: Ferguson's eight goals in four games in the autumn.
4-1 victory over Ipswich.
Home victory over League leaders Liverpool with a youthful side.
Seven-goal thriller at Tottenham.
First win at the Dell since 1939.

Low spots: FA Cup exit at Third Division Blackburn.
Three more defeats at the hands of West Brom.
Disappointing form of big signings, Collier and Jones.

Red cards: City – Gooding (Derby a), Wallace (C Palace h).
Red cards: Opponents – Sansom (C Palace h).

Player of the Year: Gary Gillespie.
Ever-presents: (0).
Hat-tricks: (1) Mick Ferguson.
Opposing hat-tricks: (1) Hoddle (Tottenham).
Leading scorer: (13) Ian Wallace.

	Appearances						Goals			
	Lge	*Sub*	LC	*Sub*	FAC	*Sub*	**Lge**	LC	FAC	**Tot**
Bannister, Gary	**5**	*2*								
Barnes, David	**3**									
Blair, Andy	**30**	*2*	2		2		**1**			**1**
Blyth, Jim	**21**		1		1					
Collier, Gary	**2**									
Coop, Mick	**31**		1	*1*	2		**1**			**1**
Dyson, Paul	**18**				2		**2**			**2**
English, Tom	**30**		3		2		**10**	2		**12**
Ferguson, Mick	**17**		2		1		**10**			**10**
Gillespie, Gary	**38**		3		2		**1**			**1**
Gooding, Ray	**23**	*1*	1		2		**2**			**2**
Hateley, Mark	**2**	*2*			1					
Holton, Jim	**24**		3							
Hunt, Steve	**34**	*1*	3				**1**			**1**
Hutchison, Tommy	**40**		3		2		**1**		1	**2**
Jacobs, Steve	**1**									
Jones, David	**7**									
McDonald, Bobby	**37**		3		2		**4**			**4**
Murcott, Steve	**1**									
Nardiello, Donato	**4**				1					
Phillips, Nicky	**4**	*1*								
Powell, Barry	**10**		2				**4**			**4**
Roberts, Brian	**10**	*4*	2	*1*						
Sealey, Les	**20**		2		1					
Thomas, Danny	**0**	*3*	1							
Thompson, Garry	**16**	*1*					**6**			**6**
Van Gool, Roger	**8**									
Wallace, Ian	**25**		1		1		**13**			**13**
Whitton, Steve	**1**	*6*								
29 players used	**462**	*23*	**33**	*2*	**22**		**56**	**2**	**1**	**59**

No	Date		Att	Pos	Pt	F-A	H-T	Scorers, Times, and Referees	1	2	3	4	5	6	7	8	9	10	11	12 sub used
1	A	BIRMINGHAM			L	1-3	0-2	Blair 76	Blyth	Coop	McDonald	Blair	Dyson	Gillespie	Van Gool*	English	Thompson	Gooding !	Hunt	Roberts
	16/8		*21,907*		0			*Curbishley 20, 53, Dillon 27*	*Wealands*	*Langan*	*Dennis*	*Curbishley*	*Gallagher*	*Givens*	*Ainscow*	*Bertschin*	*Worthington*	*Gemmill*	*Dillon*	
								Ref: J Martin	In hot sunshine Coventry are outclassed by newly promoted Blues and have Gooding sent off after 50 mins for hitting Gemmill. It's the home side's first opening-day win for ten years and is fully deserved. Wallace has gone and Coventry haven't been strengthened. Relegation looms.											
2	H	LIVERPOOL			D	0-0	0-0		Blyth	Coop	Roberts	Blair	Dyson	Gillespie	Van Gool*	**Daly**	Thompson	English	Hunt	Jones
	19/8		22,852		1				*Ogrizovic*	*Neal*	*Kennedy A*	*Thompson*	*Kennedy R*	*Hansen*	*Dalglish*	*Case**	*Johnson*	*McDermott*	*Souness*	*Fairclough*
								Ref: M Lowe	Champions Liverpool tarnish their image by playing keep-ball in their own half for the last ten minutes. £300,000 Daly makes his City debut after his move from Derby and peps up midfield. City create only three chances in a boring game. Future City man Oggy makes a rare start.											
3	H	ARSENAL		10	W	3-1	0-0	Thompson 51, English 67, Gillespie 76	Blyth	Coop	Roberts	Blair	Dyson	Gillespie	Van Gool	Daly	Thompson	English	Hunt	
	23/8		15,333	*11*	3			*Stapleton 86*	*Jennings*	*Devine*	*Sansom*	*Talbot*	*O'Leary*	*Young*	*Hollins*	*Sunderland*	*Stapleton*	*Price*	*Rix*	
								Ref: D Owen	Arsenal are destroyed by a super second-half display of attacking, inspired by Steve Hunt. Thompson heads the first, Hunt's delicious ball sets up English, and Gary Gillespie races 40 yards, takes a pass from Van Gool, and dummies Jennings before scoring. Coop's 400th League game.											
4	A	ASTON VILLA		15	L	0-1	0-0		Blyth	Coop	Roberts	Blair	Dyson	Gillespie*	**Haywood**	Daly	Hateley	English	Hunt	Thomas
	30/8		*20,050*	*3*	3			*Shaw 65*	*Rimmer*	*Swain*	*Gibson*	*Evans*	*McNaught*	*Mortimer*	*Bremner*	*Shaw*	*Withe*	*Cowans*	*Morley*	
								Ref: A Porter	Hateley and others have played the summer in the USA and he returns for a good performance which deserves a point. Gillespie limps off after six minutes and sub Thomas plays a blinder at right-back. Shaw's header wins it in a rain-affected game, and Hunt stars against his old club.											
5	H	CRYS PALACE		11	W	3-1	0-0	Daly 49, 53, Blair 73	Blyth	Coop	Roberts	Blair	Dyson	Jones	**Bodak**	Daly	Thompson*	English	Hunt	Hateley
	6/9		13,001	*21*	5			*Allen 47*	*Barron*	*Hinshelwood*	*Fenwick*	*Murphy*	*Cannon*	*Gilbert*	*Smillie*	*Francis*	*Allen*	*Flanagan*	*Hilaire*	
								Ref: D Webb	Match of the Day cameras show that Clive Allen's 55th-minute shot went into the net and bounced out. The ref disallows it and fuming Palace end up beaten. Bodak sets up the third goal and is the fifteenth player under 21 to play for City this year. Allen is the first £1 million teenager.											
6	A	WOLVES		8	W	1-0	1-0	Bodak 3	Blyth	Coop	Roberts	Blair	Dyson	**Jacobs**	Bodak	Daly	Hateley	English	Hunt	
	13/9		*18,115*	*15*	7				*Bradshaw*	*Palmer*	*Parkin*	*Daniel**	*Hughes*	*Berry*	*Clarke*	*Carr*	*Gray*	*Richards*	*Eves*	*Villazan*
								Ref: N Glover	Wolves' veteran home defence is in disarray after their League Cup exit to Cambridge Utd, and City should have won comfortably. Hunt's 40-yard pass and Hateley's lay-off leave Bodak to finish coolly. Molineux's impressive new stand is half empty. Jacobs is the latest City teenager.											
7	A	IPSWICH		12	L	0-2	0-0		Sealey	Coop	Roberts	Blair	Dyson	Jacobs	Bodak*	Daly	Hateley	Hutchison	Hunt	English
	20/9		*20,507*	*1*	7			*Wark 57, 63*	*Cooper*	*Burley*	*Mills*	*Thijssen*	*Osman*	*Butcher*	*Wark*	*Muhren*	*Mariner*	*Brazil**	*Gates*	*O'Callaghan*
								Ref: D Letts	33-year-old Tommy Hutchison returns from Seattle to play against the league pacemakers. City squander too many chances when they are in the ascendancy for the first hour. John Wark beats the poor offside trap and scores his seventh goal of the week and eleventh of the season.											
8	H	EVERTON		15	L	**0-5**	0-3	*[McBride 30, 62]*	Blyth	Coop	Roberts	Blair	Dyson	Jacobs	Hutchison*	Daly	Hateley	English	Hunt	Bodak
	27/9		15,001	*3*	7			*Eastoe 6, Latchford 26, 70,*	*McDonagh*	*Gidman*	*Bailey*	*Wright*	*Lyons*	*Stanley*	*McMahon*	*Eastoe*	*Latchford*	*Hartford**	*McBride*	*O'Keefe*
								Ref: B Newsome	City's midweek League Cup heroes are slaughtered as the Toffees hit five for the second week running. Everton are good but City's defence is dire. Blyth boobs for two goals and Roberts gifts McBride the fourth. Hutch is carried off concussed. City equal their worst ever home score.											
9	H	BRIGHTON		13	D	3-3	2-0	Dyson 25, Thompson 44, Hutchison 64	Sealey	Coop	Roberts	Blair	Dyson	Jacobs	Hutchison	Daly	Thompson	Hateley	Hunt	
	4/10		**11,521**	*16*	8			*Smith 68, 83, 87*	*Moseley*	*Gregory*	*Williams*	*Horton*	*Foster*	*Lawrenson*	*Stevens**	*Ward*	*Robinson*	*Smith*	*McNab*	*McHale*
								Ref: N Ashley	With the recession exacerbating City's poor form, a new Div 1 low crowd watches City throw away a three-goal lead as Gordon Smith scores a hat-trick for Alan Mullery's side. All three goals stem from careless errors and the fans are stunned in disbelief. Thompson and Sealey return.											
10	A	WEST BROM		14	L	0-1	0-0		Sealey	Coop	Roberts	Blair*	Dyson	Gillespie	Hutchison	Daly	Thompson	English	Hunt	Jacobs
	8/10		*16,377*	*7*	8			*Barnes 80*	*Godden*	*Batson*	*Statham*	*Moses*	*Wile*	*Robertson*	*Robson*	*Brown*	*Monaghan*	*Owen*	*Barnes*	
								Ref: J Hough	Yet again City lose at the Hawthorns; it is eleven years since they won there. They deserve a point against Ron Atkinson's men, especially as Thompson has what looks a good headed goal disallowed. Bryan Robson's thunderous shot comes back off the cross-bar and Barnes scores.											

No	Venue	Opponent / Date	Att	Pos	Pts	F-A	H-T	Scorers, Times, and Referees	1	2	3	4	5	6	7	8	9	10	11	12 sub used
11	A	LEICESTER		14	W	3-1	1-1	Dyson 34, Gooding 48, English 88	Sealey	Coop	Roberts	Gooding	Dyson	Gillespie	Van Gool	Daly	Thompson	English	Hunt	
		11/10	*17,104*	*19*	10			*Lineker 44*	*Wallington*	*Williams*	*Gibson*	*Goodwin*	*May*	*Scott*	*Lineker*	*Buchanan**	*Henderson*	*Wilson*	*Smith*	*Young*
								Ref: T Mills	Steve Hunt inspires a comfortable victory in this local derby. He crosses for Dyson's awesome header and finds Gooding with a delicious ball for the second. Leicester have little to offer and look relegation certs. Hutch is dropped. Graham Oakey retires from football through injury.											
12	H	NORWICH		15	L	0-1	0-1		Sealey	Coop	Roberts	Gooding*	Dyson	Gillespie	Van Gool	Daly	Thompson	English	Hunt	Bannister
		18/10	11,984	*19*	10			*Downs 25*	*Hansbury*	*Bond*	*Downs*	*McGuire*	*Hoadley*	*Nightingale*	*Barham*	*Fashanu*	*Royle*	*Paddon*	*Goble*	
								Ref: K McNally	Norwich, deserted by manager John Bond, had not won an away point until today. Greg Downs' stunning 25-yard volley secures it. City scorn chances galore before half-time but deteriorate afterwards. Not even the unemployed, paying only 50p to get in, probably think it's worth it.											
13	H	SUNDERLAND		15	W	2-1	1-0	Hunt 1, Thompson 69	Sealey	Coop	Roberts	Gooding	Dyson	Gillespie	Bodak	Daly	Thompson	Van Gool*	Hunt	Jacobs
		21/10	13,112	*8*	12			*Cummins 50*	*Turner*	*Whitworth*	*Bolton*	*Allardyce*	*Elliott*	*Chisholm*	*Arnott*	*Rowell*	*Cooke*	*Brown*	*Cummins*	
								Ref: D Richardson	Ken Knighton's newly promoted team have only lost one away game in 15 and outplay City for long periods. Thompson's header from Bodak's cross gives the Sky Blues their first home win in four. Hutch and McDonald are on their way to Maine Road to sign for John Bond.											
14	A	TOTTENHAM		15	L	1-4	0-1	Gooding 68	Sealey	Coop	Roberts	Gooding	Dyson	Gillespie	Bodak	Blair	Thompson	Bannister*	Hunt	English
		25/10	*25,484*	*10*	12			*Hoddle 24, 73, Archibald 51, 72*	*Daines*	*Smith*	*Hughton*	*Miller*	*Lacy*	*Perryman*	*Ardiles*	*Archibald*	*Villa*	*Hoddle*	*Crooks*	
								Ref: T Bune	Goal-hungry Spurs take apart a shaky City defence with ease. Blair returns but Daly is injured and the attack is short of ideas and strength. City appeal that both Archibald's goals are offside but Hoddle's chip and 25-yard left-footer are sublime. Ray Gooding sparks a short-lived revival.											
15	H	LEEDS		12	W	2-1	2-0	Hunt 5, Bodak 24	Sealey	Coop	Roberts	Gooding*	Dyson	Gillespie	Bodak	Blair	Hateley	Van Gool	Hunt	Thomas
		1/11	13,949	*17*	14			*Connor 65*	*Lukic*	*Greenhoff*	*Madeley*	*Flynn*	*Hart*	*Cherry*	*Harris*	*Hird*	*Connor*	*Gray*	*Graham*	
								Ref: B Hill	Allan Clarke has replaced Jimmy Adamson as manager of Leeds but he fails to get a result here. Hunt again pulls the strings and heads the first goal. Bodak collects a superb 50-yard ball inside Madeley to chip Lukic. Leeds, outclassed in the first half, dominate later and deserve a point.											
16	A	MANCHESTER U		13	D	0-0	0-0		Sealey	Coop	Roberts	Blair	Dyson	Gillespie	Bodak	Van Gool*	Hateley	Thomas	Hunt	English
		8/11	***42,794***	*7*	15				*Bailey*	*Nicholl*	*Albiston*	*McIlroy*	*Jovanovic**	*Moran*	*Coppell*	*Birtles*	*Jordan*	*Macari*	*Thomas*	*Sloan*
								Ref: K Hackett	City are the only side to have won at Old Trafford this season and they frustrate United again. The Reds' recent £1.25 million signing Birtles is anonymous and the crowd are restless. Former United fan Harry Roberts has another blinder against Coppell. Steve Hunt is again inspirational.											
17	A	LIVERPOOL		14	L	1-2	0-1	Thomas 83	Sealey	Coop	Roberts	Blair	Dyson	Gillespie	Bodak	Van Gool*	Hateley	Thomas	Hunt	English
		11/11	*26,744*	*2*	15			*Johnson 27, 80*	*Clemence*	*Neal*	*Money*	*Thompson*	*Kennedy R*	*Hansen*	*Dalglish*	*Lee*	*Johnson*	*McDermott*	*Souness*	
								Ref: K Redfearn	Pool's lowest league crowd for seven years sees them equal Millwall's record of 59 home games without defeat. The Kop are unimpressed with their team, who need mistakes from Sealey and Gillespie to win. Clemence saves brilliantly from Hateley, who has still to score after 17 games.											
18	H	BIRMINGHAM		13	W	2-1	1-1	Blair 41, Hunt 80	Sealey	Coop	Roberts	Thomas	Dyson	Gillespie	Bodak	Blair	Hateley	Thompson	Hunt	
		15/11	18,429	*10*	17			*Curbishley 36*	*Wealands*	*Langan*	*Hawker*	*Curbishley*	*Gallagher*	*Todd*	*Ainscow*	*Bertschin*	*Worthington*	*Gemmill*	*Dillon**	*Lynex*
								Ref: G Flint	24 hours of rain have made the pitch a quagmire but adds to the excitement with mistakes galore. City end Blues' seven-match unbeaten run with Hunt's magnificent run and curled shot after a one-two with Thompson. Blues boss Jim Smith thinks they should have had a late penalty.											
19	A	MANCHESTER C		15	L	0-3	0-2		Sealey	Jacobs	Roberts	Blair	Dyson	Gillespie*	Bodak	Thompson	Hateley	Thomas	Hunt	Daly
		22/11	*30,047*	*16*	17			*Reeves 3, Power 7, Bennett 57*	*Corrigan*	*Ranson*	*McDonald*	*Reid*	*Power*	*Booth*	*Bennett**	*Gow*	*MacKenzie*	*Hutchison*	*Reeves*	*Henry*
								Ref: P Willis	City's youngest ever side, average age 20, crash to the eighth successive defeat at Maine Road. Hunt is captain in Coop's absence as old boys Hutch and Bobby McDonald lead the charge. Coventry are lucky not to be five down at the break as Manchester win their sixth game in nine.											
20	H	NOTT'M FOREST		15	D	1-1	0-1	Daly 51p	Sealey	Thomas	Roberts	Blair	Dyson	Gillespie	Bodak	Daly	Ferguson	English*	Hunt	Thompson
		29/11	15,151	*8*	18			*Wallace 26*	*Shilton*	*Anderson*	*Gray F*	*Ponte*	*Lloyd*	*Gunn*	*Mills*	*Bowyer*	*Ward*	*Wallace*	*Robertson**	*Walsh*
								Ref: G Owen	Ferguson makes his first appearance for eleven months against the European champions. Ian Wallace returns to score with a header against the run of play and captain Daly's penalty equaliser comes when Gunn handles on the line. City have yet to beat Forest since they came up in 1977.											
21	A	SOUTHAMPTON		16	L	0-1	0-1		Sealey	Thomas	Roberts	Blair	Dyson	Gillespie	Bodak	Daly	Thompson	Hateley	Hunt	
		6/12	*18,847*	*9*	18			*Holmes 44*	*Wells*	*Golac*	*McCartney*	*Agboola*	*Waldron*	*Nicholl*	*Wallace*	*Channon*	*Moran*	*Holmes*	*Baker*	
								Ref: R Challis	A low-quality match which Match of the Day edited heavily. Channon blasts over a 76th-minute penalty after Dyson had fouled him. The ref had turned down an identical claim when Waldron fouled Hateley. Holmes scores in a scramble after Baker had sprung Sky Blues' offside trap.											

No	Date		Att	Pos	Pt	F-A	H-T	Scorers, Times, and Referees	1	2	3	4	5	6	7	8	9	10	11	12 sub used
22	H	WEST BROM		15	W	3-0	1-0	Blair 4, Daly 67p, Hunt 81	Sealey	Thomas	Roberts	Blair	Dyson	Gillespie	Bodak	Daly	Thompson	Hateley	Hunt	
	13/12		16,034	*7*	20				*Godden*	*Batson*	*Cowdrill*	*Moses*	*Wile*	*Robertson !*	*Robson*	*Brown*	*Regis*	*Owen*	*Barnes**	*Deehan*
								Ref: D Shaw	The Albion jinx is ended after 18 games without a win over eleven years. City are cocky after their League Cup exploits and Danny Thomas has a stormer. Blair and Hunt hit superb goals, Daly scores from the spot after John Wile handles, and Ally Robertson walks for two bookings.											
23	A	NORWICH		16	L	0-2	0-2		Sealey	Thomas	Roberts	Blair	Dyson	Gillespie	Bodak	Gooding*	Thompson	Hateley	Hunt	Jones
	20/12		*12,630*	*19*	20			*Royle 23, Paddon 34*	*Baker*	*Bond*	*Muzinic**	*McGuire*	*Hoadley*	*McDowell*	*Mendham*	*Fashanu*	*Royle*	*Paddon*	*Goble*	*Powell*
								Ref: D Hutchinson	The Canaries have just lost 1-4 to fellow strugglers Palace and are revved up for this one. Leading scorer Fashanu is well marked but Royle and ex-City man Paddon expose City's defence. There is a big improvement after the break but despite a host of chances City can't rescue it.											
24	H	MIDDLESBROUGH		15	W	1-0	1-0	Daly 20	Sealey	Thomas	Roberts	Blair	Dyson	Gillespie	Bodak	Daly	Thompson	Hateley	Hunt	
	26/12		16,106	*12*	22				*Platt*	*Craggs*	*Bailey*	*Johnston**	*Ashcroft*	*Nattrass*	*Cochrane*	*Procter*	*Hodgson*	*Shearer*	*Armstrong*	*McAndrew*
								Ref: D Vickers	Gerry Daly returned with the ideal Xmas present, a superb left-footer from Thompson's flick on. City have to work hard to extend their unbeaten run over Boro to eight games. Blair stars and has a shot well saved by Platt. Entertaining Boro go close with Hodgson and Cochrane.											
25	A	STOKE		15	D	2-2	1-0	Hateley 41, Thompson 82	Sealey	Thomas	Roberts	Blair	Dyson	Gillespie	Bannister	Daly	Thompson	Hateley	Hunt	
	27/12		*17,765*	*8*	23			*Doyle 52, Griffiths 69*	*Fox*	*Evans*	*Munro*	*Dodd*	*O'Callaghan*	*Doyle*	*Ursem**	*Heath*	*Griffiths*	*Bracewell*	*Richardson*	*Thorley*
								Ref: J Worrall	An exciting game on a muddy pitch ends all square. Mark Hateley scores his first League goal with a classic header from Thomas' cross and Thompson misses a good chance before Stoke run City ragged for 20 minutes. Garry Thompson's diving header earns fighting City a point.											
26	H	MANCHESTER C		15	D	1-1	0-0	Hunt 52	Sealey	Coop	Roberts	Blair	Dyson	Gillespie	Thomas	Daly	Thompson	Ferguson	Hunt*	Bodak
	10/1		18,257	*3*	24			*MacKenzie 67*	*Corrigan*	*Ranson*	*McDonald*	*Reid*	*Power*	*Caton*	*Boyer*	*Gow*	*MacKenzie*	*Hutchison*	*Reeves*	
								Ref: B Daniels	A patchy game in an icy wind sees the League's most improved side held by a determined City performance. Hunt is weak after the flu, but hits another screamer from 25 yards. MacKenzie equalises with a low shot from Hutchison's corner. Thomas slides into and snaps a corner flag.											
27	H	ASTON VILLA		16	L	1-2	0-0	Hateley 70	Sealey	Coop	Roberts	Blair	Dyson	Gillespie	Thomas	Daly	Thompson	Ferguson*	Hunt	Hateley
	17/1		**27,094**	*2*	24			*Morley 56, Withe 65*	*Rimmer*	*Swain*	*Gibson*	*Evans*	*McNaught*	*Mortimer*	*Bremner*	*Shaw*	*Withe*	*Cowans*	*Morley*	
								Ref: K Salmon	Title-chasing Villa show their pedigree with 20 glorious minutes in the second half. In a fierce game with lots of petty, niggling fouls, Morley races from the halfway line to score. Peter Withe adds a header. Mark Hateley heads in and sparks a revival but he misses a chance to level it.											
28	A	ARSENAL		15	D	2-2	1-1	Bodak 45, Daly 65	Sealey	Thomas	Roberts	Blair	Dyson	Gillespie	Bodak*	Daly	Thompson	Hateley	Hunt	Jacobs
	31/1		*24,876*	*6*	25			*Talbot 37, Stapleton 57*	*Jennings*	*Hollins*	*Sansom*	*Talbot*	*Walford*	*Young*	*McDermott*	*Sunderland*	*Stapleton*	*Gatting*	*Rix*	
								Ref: A Grey	Terry Neill's Arsenal are on the fringe of the title race but are twice pegged back by a fighting performance by the Sky Blues. The midweek efforts against West Ham show in the later stages as tiredness creeps in. Walford is at fault for City's goals and Les Sealey does well in goal.											
29	H	WOLVES		15	D	2-2	2-0	Hunt 29, Hateley 35	Sealey	Thomas	Roberts	Blair	Dyson	Gillespie	Bodak	Daly	Thompson	Hateley	Hunt	
	7/2		18,242	*17*	26			*Richards 46, Gray 84*	*Bradshaw*	*Palmer*	*Parkin*	*Clarke*	*McAlle*	*Berry*	*Hibbitt*	*Atkinson*	*Gray*	*Richards*	*Eves**	*Bell*
								Ref: A Challinor	Sky Blues have one eye on the semi final second leg and let Wolves come back from two down and extend their unbeaten run to eight. John Barnwell's boys can't believe they are two down after bossing the first half but get their reward with goals from John Richards and Andy Gray.											
30	A	CRYS PALACE		13	W	3-0	3-0	Bannister 4, English 29, 44	Sealey	Thomas	Roberts	Blair	Gillespie	Jacobs	Bannister	Daly	Thompson	English	Hunt	
	17/2		*12,868*	*22*	28				*Fry*	*Hinshelwood*	*Dare*	*Nicholas*	*Boyle*	*Brooks*	*Smillie*	*Murphy**	*Allen*	*Hilaire*	*Walsh*	*Banfield*
								Ref: M Taylor	Palace, with one win in 15 games, look doomed. Ron Noades is their new chairman and Dario Gradi the fourth manager of the season, but they are a poor side and are watched by their lowest ever Div 1 crowd. An important psychological win for City after the disappointing cup defeats.											
31	A	EVERTON		16	L	0-3	0-1		Sealey	Thomas	Roberts	Jacobs	Dyson	Gillespie*	Bannister	Daly	Thompson	English	Hunt	Jones
	21/2		*26,741*	*12*	28			*Ross 25, McMahon 55, Eastoe 71*	*McDonagh*	*Gidman**	*Ratcliffe*	*Wright*	*Lyons*	*Ross*	*McMahon*	*Eastoe*	*Varadi*	*Hartford*	*O'Keefe*	*Lodge*
								Ref: M Peck	Everton gain their first league of the year as the cup defeats catch up with City. Sealey is brilliant and stops a rout but has no chance with the goals. Asa Hartford runs the game and Everton old boy David Jones has a nightmare 45 minutes. It will be Jones' last appearance for the club.											

No/Date	Venue	Opponent/Att	Pos	Res/Pts	F-A	H-T	Scorers, Times, and Referees	1	2	3	4	5	6	7	8	9	10	11	12 sub used
32	H	IPSWICH	16	L	0-4	0-1		Sealey	Thomas	Roberts	Jacobs	Dyson	Gillespie	Bodak	Daly	Thompson	English	Hunt	
28/2		17,596	*1*	28			*Brazil 32, Gates 46, McCall 80, [Osman 86]*	*Cooper*	*Mills*	*Butcher*	*Thijssen*	*Osman*	*Beattie*	*McCall*	*Muhren*	*Mariner*	*Brazil*	*Gates*	
							Ref: T Spencer	Championship chasing Ipswich make it nine wins in eleven and can afford to leave out 29-goal John Wark. Gillespie has a goal disallowed early on but Ipswich are awesome after the break, with Franz Thijssen superb. The final score on a muddy pitch flatters Bobby Robson's men.											
33	A	BRIGHTON	16	L	1-4	1-2	Bannister 32	Sealey	Thomas	Roberts	Blair	Dyson	Gillespie	Bodak	Daly	Thompson	English	Bannister	
7/3		*14,063*	*19*	28			*Robinson 20, 85, Stille 27, Smith 86*	*Digweed*	*Williams*	*Stevens*	*Horton*	*Foster*	*Lawrenson*	*McNab*	*Stille*	*Robinson*	*Smith*	*Vessey**	*Ryan*
							Ref: C Maskell	Having pulled a goal back after a disastrous start and dominated the second half, the Sky Blues commit suicide in the last few minutes. 19-goal Robinson eases the relegation fears in an important win. Thompson is 'Young Player of the Month' and Thomas plays for England Under-21's.											
34	H	LEICESTER	16	W	**4-1**	2-1	English 24, 41, 83, Thompson 62	Sealey	Thomas	Roberts	Blair	Dyson	Gillespie	Bodak	Daly	Thompson	English	Bannister	
14/3		21,427	*20*	30			*Young 19*	*Wallington*	*Williams*	*Friar*	*Peake*	*May*	*O'Neill*	*Lynex*	*Melrose*	*Young*	*Wilson*	*Macdonald*	
							Ref: A Robinson	Leicester's mini recovery is ended with a Tom English hat-trick on a sandy pitch, and they are destined for the drop. City concede an early goal but once level never look in danger. Thomas is again superb. City announce plans to turn Highfield Road into England's first all-seater stadium.											
35	A	SUNDERLAND	18	L	0-3	0-1		Sealey	Thomas	Roberts	Blair	Dyson	Gillespie	Bannister	Daly	Thompson	English	Hunt	
21/3		*20,622*	*14*	30			*Hinnigan 6, 86, Cummins 53p*	*Siddall*	*Hinnigan*	*Bolton*	*Elliott*	*Hindmarch*	*Buckley*	*Arnott*	*Cooke*	*Ritchie*	*Chisholm*	*Cummins*	
							Ref: R Banks	With four defeats in five City are sliding towards the relegation zone and on this performance safety is not certain. Sunderland are a mediocre side but they swat the Sky Blues aside. But for Les Sealey they might have scored six. Danny Thomas fouls Mick Buckley for the penalty.											
36	H	TOTTENHAM	18	L	0-1	0-1		Sealey	Thomas	Roberts	Blair*	Dyson	Gillespie	Coop	Daly	Thompson	English	Hunt	Whitton
28/3		18,654	*8*	30			*Roberts 28 (og)*	*Aleksic*	*Hughton*	*Miller*	*Roberts*	*Brooke**	*Perryman*	*Ardiles*	*Archibald*	*Galvin*	*Hoddle*	*Crooks*	*Smith*
							Ref: R Bridges	The younger players look drained of confidence and their heads went down once Harry Roberts had sliced in Crooks' cross. Garry Thompson misses two good chances and City have two good penalty appeals waved away. Veteran Mick Coop and Danny Thomas have excellent games.											
37	A	LEEDS	18	L	0-3	0-1		Sealey	Coop	Roberts	Thomas	Dyson	Gillespie	Bodak*	Daly	Thompson	English	Hunt	Bannister
4/4		*15,882*	*10*	30			*Stevenson 23, Parlane 64, Flynn 71*	*Lukic*	*Greenhoff*	*Gray*	*Flynn*	*Hart*	*Firm*	*Harris*	*Hird*	*Parlane**	*Stevenson*	*Graham*	*Butterworth*
							Ref: D Allison	Six wins in seven for Leeds, six defeats in seven for City. The pressure is on as their relegation rivals win and Leeds don't even have to get out of first gear. The Sky Blues tamely surrender after Byron Stevenson's swerving shot from an uncleared corner. City's lack of spirit is alarming.											
38	H	MANCHESTER U	18	L	0-2	0-2		Sealey	Coop	Roberts	Thomas	Dyson	Gillespie	Bannister	Daly	Thompson	English	Hunt	
11/4		20,201	*8*	30			*Jordan 35, 45*	*Bailey*	*Duxbury*	*Albiston*	*Moran*	*McQueen*	*Buchan*	*Coppell*	*Birtles*	*Jordan*	*Macari*	*Wilkins*	
							Ref: S Bates	Another defeat, but City show a bit more fight. The lowest crowd to watch United at Highfield Road sees Jordan head two goals. He is having to make up for poor Birtles who has yet to score in 22 league games since signing from Forest. United's fourth win in a row won't save Sexton.											
39	H	STOKE	20	D	2-2	2-0	Daly 25, Thompson 45	Sealey	Coop	Roberts	Blair	Dyson	Gillespie	Bannister	Daly	Thompson	English	Hunt	
18/4		12,800	*12*	31			*Chapman 50, Maguire 71p*	*Fox*	*Evans*	*Munro*	*Dodd*	*O'Callaghan*	*Doyle*	*Hampton*	*Bracewell*	*Chapman*	*Heath*	*Maguire*	
							Ref: M Bidmead	City throw away a 2-0 lead and are now in real trouble. A small crowd see Daly latch onto Dodd's back-pass and English set up Thompson. Stoke's penalty is for Roberts' innocuous challenge on Maguire, who had lost possession. Protests are heard against planned stadium changes.											
40	A	MIDDLESBROUGH	17	W	1-0	0-0	Daly 71	Sealey	Coop	Roberts	Blair	Dyson	Gillespie	Gooding	Daly	Thompson	English	Hunt	
21/4		***11,371***	*14*	33				*Platt*	*Nobbs*	*Bailey*	*Bell*	*Angus*	*McAndrew*	*Cochrane*	*Procter*	*Burns**	*Shearer*	*Armstrong*	*Askew*
							Ref: C Seel	Boro had won nine in a row at home, and lost only once, but City upset the odds with a vital win. They miss several chances and are also foiled by Platt before Dyson creates Gerry Daly's goal. The desperation and tension of the last few weeks disappears and the team show real fight.											
41	H	SOUTHAMPTON	15	W	1-0	0-0	Thompson 54	Sealey	Coop	Roberts	Blair	Dyson	Gillespie	Gooding	Daly	Thompson	English	Hunt	
25/4		18,242	*6*	35				*Wells*	*Golac*	*Holmes*	*McCartney**	*Waldron*	*Nicholl*	*Williams*	*Channon*	*Baker G*	*Moran*	*Ball*	*Puckett*
							Ref: M Heath	Even with five points out of six, City are not totally safe and any one of seven can still go down with Palace and Leicester. On the last day of terracing the fans turn out in numbers, despite the rain and cold. Thompson scores the goal after good work by Ray Gooding and Tom English.											
42	A	NOTT'M FOREST	15	D	1-1	1-1	Thompson 25	Sealey	Coop	Roberts	Blair	Dyson	Gillespie	Gooding	Daly	Thompson	English	Hunt	
2/5		*21,511*	*5*	36			*Robertson 42p*	*Shilton*	*Gunn*	*Gray F*	*McGovern*	*Burns*	*Aas*	*Mills*	*Wallace*	*Francis*	*Gray S*	*Robertson*	
Average	Home 16,916	Away 21,055					Ref: P Partridge	Thompson's goal means City are safe by three points, after Norwich lose at home to Leicester and are relegated. The Sky Blues suffer a few narrow squeaks but deserve their point. Dyson fouls Francis for the penalty and Robertson scores. This will be Milne's last match in charge.											

League Cup					F-A	H-T	Scorers, Times, and Referees	1	2	3	4	5	6	7	8	9	10	11	12 sub used
2:1	A	MANCHESTER U	10	W	1-0	0-0	English 67	Blyth	Coop	Roberts	Blair	Dyson	Gillespie	Van Gool	Daly	Thompson*	English	Hunt	McDonald
	27/8	*31,656*	*7*					*Bailey*	*Nicholl*	*Albiston*	*McIlroy*	*Jovanovic*	*Buchan*	*Coppell*	*Greenhoff**	*Ritchie*	*Macari*	*Thomas*	*Sloan*
							Ref: P Partridge	A professional if unspectacular first leg performance against Daly's old team, who lack penetration up front. The honours are won in defence, with Dyson and Gillespie supreme and Roberts shackling England winger Steve Coppell. Garry Thompson is given a rough time and limps off.											
2:2	H	MANCHESTER U	15	W	1-0	0-0	Blair 46	Blyth	Coop	Roberts	Blair	Dyson	Jones	Bannister	Daly	Thompson*	English	Hunt	Thomas
	2/9	18,946	*10*					*Bailey*	*Nicholl*	*Albiston*	*McIlroy*	*Jovanovic*	*Buchan*	*Coppell*	*Greenhoff*	*Ritchie*	*Macari*	*Thomas*	
							Ref: B Stevens (City win 2-0 on aggregate)	Blair and Dyson celebrate their international call-ups with excellent games in another professional team performance. Despite plenty of United pressure, City defend their first-leg lead and once ahead on the night they look safe. United have several stars injured, but look a mediocre side.											
3	A	BRIGHTON	12	W	2-1	1-1	English 44, Hutchison 88	Blyth	Coop	Roberts	Blair	Dyson	Jacobs	Hutchison	Daly	Hateley	English	Hunt	
	23/9	*14,426*	*14*				*Ryan 13*	*Moseley*	*Gregory*	*Williams*	*Horton*	*Foster*	*Lawrenson*	*Stevens*	*Ward*	*Robinson*	*Smith*	*Ryan*	
							Ref: C White	An outstanding performance in a blood and thunder cup-tie which City deserve to win. Blyth lets Ryan's shot slip through his hands. It takes City until half-time to equalise, English pouncing on Lawrenson's slip. Hutch wins it, chesting down Coop's cross and rifling in a right-footer.											
4	H	CAMBRIDGE	15	D	1-1	1-0	Thompson 2	Sealey	Coop	Roberts	Gooding	Dyson	Gillespie	Bodak	Blair	Thompson	English	Hunt	
	28/10	17,076	*2:11*				*Taylor 50*	*Key*	*Donaldson*	*Murray*	*Smith*	*Fallon*	*Gibbins*	*O'Neill*	*Spriggs*	*Reilly*	*Taylor*	*Christie*	
							Ref: E Read	City's first ever meeting with Cambridge U ends in a frustrating stalemate with the crowd baying for Milne's head. The U's have already k.o'd Wolves and Villa, and only a goal-post stops Christie from winning it. Tommo scores and former Hammer Alan Taylor scores on his U's debut.											
4R	A	CAMBRIDGE	12	W	1-0	1-0	Hunt 39	Sealey	Coop	Roberts	Blair	Dyson	Gillespie	Bodak	Van Gool	Hateley	Thomas	Hunt	
	4/11	*10,171*	*2:14*					*Key*	*Donaldson**	*Murray*	*Smith*	*Fallon*	*Gibbins*	*O'Neill*	*Spriggs*	*Reilly*	*Finney*	*Christie*	*Taylor*
							Ref: D Reeves	Sealey stars at the Abbey Stadium, saving Spriggs' 64th-minute penalty given for Thomas' foul on Tommy O'Neill. City reach the quarter-finals for the first time in seven years, thanks to a battling display by the kids, aided by veterans Coop and Van Gool. Dyson is awesome.											
5	A	WATFORD	15	D	2-2	2-2	Thompson 14, 39	Sealey	Thomas	Roberts	Blair	Dyson	Gillespie	Bodak	Daly	Thompson	Hateley	Hunt	
	2/12	*27,542*	*2:19*				*Poskett 22, 25*	*Steele*	*Rice*	*Sims*	*Jackett*	*Harrison*	*Blissett*	*Train*	*Rostron*	*Poskett*	*Armstrong*	*Jenkins*	
							Ref: L Shapter	9,500 supporters roar City to a deserved replay after a thrilling but nail-biting tie. Watford have already knocked Southampton and Forest out of the competition, but the Sky Blues dominate the second half. It's a tense last ten minutes, with penalty appeals when Blair appears to handle.											
5R	H	WATFORD	16	W	5-0	3-0	Bodak 7, Hateley 30, 84, Thompson 35, [Hunt 80]	Sealey	Thomas	Roberts	Blair	Dyson	Gillespie	Bodak	Daly*	Thompson	Hateley	Hunt	Jacobs
	9/12	*30,389*	*2:19*					*Sherwood*	*Rice*	*Harrison*	*Blissett*	*Terry*	*Jackett*	*Callaghan*	*Armstrong*	*Jenkins**	*Train*	*Poskett*	*Henderson*
							Ref: K Walmsley	City reach their first semi-final in 97 years on an emotional night of drama. Graham Taylor's side are demolished by the Coventry kids, with Mark Hateley finally scoring after Peter Bodak had netted a stunning early goal. Les Sealey gets concussed but has only one save to make.											
SF 1	H	WEST HAM	15	W	3-2	0-2	Thompson 71, 89, Daly 76	Sealey	Thomas	Roberts	Blair	Dyson	Gillespie	Bodak	Daly*	Thompson	Hateley	Hunt	Jacobs
	27/1	35,411	*2:1*				*Bonds 27, Thompson 35 (og)*	*Parkes*	*Stewart*	*Brush*	*Bonds*	*Martin*	*Devonshire*	*Allen*	*Goddard*	*Cross*	*Brooking*	*Pike*	
							Ref: G Courtney	One of the finest nights in the club's history sees City come back from the dead to give themselves hope for the second leg. Sealey's boob and Thompson's bad back-pass give West Ham the lead, but in 19 incredible minutes Tommo atones and Daly scores after Thomas' shot is saved.											
SF 2	A	WEST HAM	15	L	0-2	0-0		Sealey	Thomas	Roberts	Blair	Dyson	Gillespie	Bodak*	Daly	Thompson	Hateley	Hunt	Jacobs
	10/2	*36,551*	*2:1*				*Goddard 61, Neighbour 89*	*Parkes*	*Stewart*	*Lampard*	*Bonds*	*Martin*	*Devonshire*	*Neighbour*	*Goddard*	*Cross*	*Brooking*	*Pike*	
							Ref: K Hackett (City lose 3-4 on aggregate)	A cruel defeat for City's tense and nervous kids. Hateley misses a great chance after nine minutes and from then its all West Ham. Goddard's goal makes extra-time look certain until Jimmy Neighbour pops up, looking offside, to score the late winner and set up a final with Liverpool.											

FA Cup

Rd		Opponent	Att	Pos	Res	F-A	H-T	Scorers, Times, and Referees											
3	A	LEEDS		15	D	1-1	1-0	Thomas 30	Sealey	Thomas !	Roberts	Blair	Dyson	Gillespie	Bannister*	Daly	Thompson	Hateley	Hunt	Jacobs
	3/1		*24,523*	*16*				*Hird 82p*	*Lukic*	*Greenhoff**	*Gray*	*Flynn*	*Hart*	*Cherry*	*Parlane*	*Hird*	*Connor*	*Sabella*	*Graham*	*Hamson*
								Ref: P Partridge	City are down to ten men for the last 20 minutes after Thomas is sent off for two fouls on Hamson. The same player wins a controversial spot-kick after he falls under Jacobs' challenge. Lukic is at fault in a full-blooded cup-tie, allowing Thomas's 25-yard effort to spin from his hands.											
3R	H	LEEDS		15	W	1-0	0-0	Thompson 89	Sealey	Coop	Roberts	Blair	Dyson	Gillespie	Bodak	Daly	Thompson	Hateley	Bannister	
	6/1		22,051	*16*					*Lukic*	*Hird*	*Gray*	*Flynn*	*Hart*	*Cherry*	*Parlane*	*Chandler*	*Hamson*	*Sabella*	*Graham*	
								Ref: P Partridge	A pulsating cup-tie is decided by a scrambled goal from Andy Blair's free-kick a minute after Parlane looked certain to score at the other end. There are chances galore and Les Sealey makes three brilliant saves in the first half. Thomas is suspended and Hunt has flu, but Leeds go out.											
4	H	BIRMINGHAM		15	W	3-2	2-0	Daly 29, 63p, Blair 44	Sealey	Coop	Roberts	Blair	Dyson	Gillespie	Bodak*	Daly	Thompson	Ferguson	Hunt	Thomas
	24/1		29,639	*14*				*Worthington 52p, Ainscow 61*	*Coton*	*Langan*	*Lees*	*Curbishley*	*Gallagher*	*Todd*	*Ainscow*	*Bertschin*	*Worthington*	*Gemmill*	*Dillon*	
								Ref: K Hackett	In a thrilling cup-tie City go through to the fifth round for the first time in seven years, thanks to Daly's debatable penalty. Blues boss Jim Smith, elated after his teams fightback, thinks Hunt dives under Todd's tackle. Gary Gillespie fouls Frank Worthington for the other penalty.											
5	A	TOTTENHAM		15	L	1-3	1-2	English 41	Sealey	Thomas	Roberts	Blair	Dyson*	Gillespie	Jacobs	Daly	Thompson	English	Hunt	Hateley
	14/2		*36,688*	*7*				*Ardiles 16, Archibald 33, Hughton 77*	*Daines*	*Hughton*	*Miller*	*Roberts*	*Lacy*	*Perryman*	*Ardiles**	*Archibald*	*Galvin*	*Hoddle*	*Crooks*	*Brooke*
								Ref: J Worrall	Spurs have a three-sided stadium while the main stand is being rebuilt. City's defensive strategy, with Steve Jacobs as sweeper, backfires with two errors. A brave second half comeback, playing three strikers, is in vain. Spurs meet Exeter in the quarter-finals and go on to lift the Cup.											

			Home					Away					
		P	W	D	L	F	A	W	D	L	F	A	Pts
1	Aston Villa	42	16	3	2	40	13	10	5	6	32	27	60
2	Ipswich	42	15	4	2	45	14	8	6	7	32	29	56
3	Arsenal	42	13	8	0	36	17	6	7	8	25	28	53
4	West Brom	42	15	4	2	40	15	5	8	8	20	27	52
5	Liverpool	42	13	5	3	38	15	4	12	5	24	27	51
6	Southampton	42	15	4	2	47	22	5	6	10	29	34	50
7	Nott'm Forest	42	15	3	3	44	20	4	9	8	18	24	50
8	Manchester U	42	9	11	1	30	14	6	7	8	21	22	48
9	Leeds	42	10	5	6	19	19	7	5	9	20	28	44
10	Tottenham	42	9	9	3	44	31	5	6	10	26	37	43
11	Stoke	42	8	9	4	31	23	4	9	8	20	37	42
12	Manchester C	42	10	7	4	35	25	4	4	13	21	34	39
13	Birmingham	42	11	5	5	32	23	2	7	12	18	38	38
14	Middlesboro	42	14	4	3	38	16	2	1	18	15	45	37
15	Everton	42	8	6	7	32	25	5	4	12	23	33	36
16	COVENTRY	42	9	6	6	31	30	4	4	13	17	38	36
17	Sunderland	42	10	4	7	32	19	4	3	14	20	34	35
18	Wolves	42	11	2	8	26	20	2	7	12	17	35	35
19	Brighton	42	10	3	8	30	26	4	4	13	24	41	35
20	Norwich	42	9	7	5	34	25	4	0	17	15	48	33
21	Leicester	42	7	5	9	20	23	6	1	14	20	44	32
22	Crys Palace	42	6	4	11	32	37	0	3	18	15	46	19
		924	243	118	101	756	472	101	118	243	472	756	924

Odds & ends

Double wins: (3) Leicester, Crys Palace, Middlesbrough.
Double losses: (5) Everton, Norwich, Aston Villa, Ipswich, Tottenham.

Won from behind: (5) Crys Palace (h), Birmingham (h), Leicester (h), Brighton LC (a), West Ham LC (h).
Lost from in front: (0).

High spots: Reaching the semi-final of a major competition for the first time.
Dramatic 1st leg victory over West Ham.
The emergence of an outstanding crop of young players.

Low spots:
The Everton home thrashing - the biggest home defeat since 1919.
Departure of Hutchison and McDonald to Manchester C.

Red cards: City – Gooding (Birmingham a), Thomas (Leeds FAC a).
Red cards: Opponents – Robertson (West Brom h).

Player of the Year: Danny Thomas.
Ever-presents: (0).
Hat-tricks: (1) Tom English.
Opposing hat-tricks: (1) Smith (Brighton).
Leading scorer: (15) Garry Thompson.

	Appearances						Goals			
	Lge	*Sub*	LC	*Sub*	FAC	*Sub*	Lge	LC	FAC	Tot
Bannister, Gary	**9**	*2*	1		2		**2**			**2**
Blair, Andy	**35**		9		4		**4**	1	1	**6**
Blyth, Jim	**7**		3							
Bodak, Peter	**21**	*2*	6		2		**3**	1		**4**
Coop, Mick	**27**		5		2					
Daly, Gerry	**34**	*1*	7		4		**8**	1	2	**11**
Dyson, Paul	**41**		9		4		**2**			**2**
English, Tom	**24**	*4*	4		1		**7**	2	1	**10**
Ferguson, Mick	**3**				1					
Gillespie, Gary	**37**		7		4		**1**			**1**
Gooding, Ray	**10**		1				**2**			**2**
Hateley, Mark	**17**	*2*	6		2	*1*	**3**	2		**5**
Haywood, Clive	**1**									
Hunt, Steve	**40**		9		3		**6**	2		**8**
Hutchison, Tommy	**4**		1				**1**	1		**2**
Jacobs, Steve	**8**	*3*	1	*3*	1	*1*				
Jones, David	**1**	*3*	1							
McDonald, Bobby	**1**			*1*						
Roberts, Brian	**41**	*1*	9		4					
Sealey, Les	**35**		6		4					
Thomas, Danny	**23**	*2*	5	*1*	2	*1*	**1**		1	**2**
Thompson, Garry	**34**	*1*	7		4		**8**	6	1	**15**
Van Gool, Roger	**9**		2							
Whitton, Steve		*1*								
24 players used	**462**	*22*	**99**	*5*	**44**	*3*	**48**	**16**	**6**	**70**

No	Date		Att	Pos	Pt	F-A	H-T	Scorers, Times, and Referees	1	2	3	4	5	6	7	8	9	10	11	12 sub used
1	H	MANCHESTER U			W	2-1	1-1	Whitton 11, Bodak 48	Blyth	Thomas	Roberts	Jacobs	Dyson	Gillespie	Bodak	Daly	Thompson	Whitton	Hunt	
	29/8		**19,329**		3			*Macari 43*	*Bailey*	*Gidman*	*Albiston*	*Wilkins*	*McQueen*	*Buchan*	*Coppell*	*Birtles*	*Stapleton*	*Macari*	*McIlroy*	
								Ref: D Reeves	Dave Sexton starts his City career with a three-point win over the club that sacked him in the summer. Ron Atkinson's side, with £1 million debut boy Stapleton, are chasing the game after Whitton's goal. Bodak stars and Blyth makes two good saves in the capacity all-seater ground.											
2	A	STOKE			L	0-4	0-2		Blyth	Thomas	Roberts	Jacobs	Dyson	Gillespie	Bodak*	Daly	Thompson	Whitton	Hunt	**Kaiser**
	2/9		*13,914*		3			*Chapman 5, 77, Heath 13, 54*	*Fox*	*Evans*	*Hampton*	*Dodd*	*O'Callaghan*	*Doyle*	*Griffiths*	*Heath*	*Chapman*	*Bracewell*	*Maguire*	
								Ref: D Richardson	Adventurous City are given a lesson in finishing by the Potters and are left rueing missed chances in the first half. Two early headers from corners against the run of play put Stoke in control. Heath outpaces Jacobs for the third and Lee Chapman's header seals it. Kaiser looks lively.											
3	A	NOTTS CO		19	L	1-2	0-1	Daly 86	Blyth	Thomas	Roberts	Jacobs	Dyson	Gillespie	Kaiser	Daly	Thompson	Whitton	Hunt	
	5/9		***10,889***	*3*	3			*Christie 4, Hunt 52*	*Avramovic*	*Benjamin*	*O'Brien*	*Goodwin*	*Kilcline*	*Richards*	*Chiedozie*	*McCulloch*	*Christie*	*Hunt*	*Hooks*	
								Ref: C Thomas	City's first meeting with County since 1963 ends in an embarrassing defeat in the sunshine. Daly squanders a twice-taken penalty after 28 minutes and Hunt's easy goal seals a win for a very average-looking home side. Kaiser looks good on his full debut, but the defence is abject.											
4	H	LEEDS		8	W	4-0	2-0	Kaiser 8, Thompson 12, 77, Whitton 51	Blyth	Thomas	Roberts	Jacobs	Dyson	Gillespie	Kaiser	Daly	Thompson	Whitton	Hunt	
	12/9		13,452	*20*	6				*Lukic*	*Greenhoff*	*Gray E*	*Flynn*	*Firm*	*Cherry*	*Harris**	*Graham*	*Connor*	*Stevenson*	*Barnes*	*Hird*
								Ref: H King	Leeds fans disgrace themselves by ripping out seats and fighting as their poor team is demolished by the lively Sky Blues. Steve Hunt is the provider for Garry Thompson, who is deprived of a hat-trick by a post. Whitton's goal is created by a mammoth long throw from Paul Dyson.											
5	A	BRIGHTON		9	D	2-2	1-1	Kaiser 34, Hunt 56	Blyth	Thomas	Roberts	Jacobs	Dyson	Gillespie	Kaiser	Daly	Thompson	Whitton	Hunt	
	19/9		*15,262*	*12*	7			*Robinson 22, McNab 60p*	*Moseley*	*Shanks*	*Williams*	*Grealish*	*Foster*	*Gatting*	*Case*	*Ritchie**	*Robinson*	*McNab*	*Smith*	*Stevens*
								Ref: B Daniels	City's Talbot motif on their shirts keep the cameras away. They miss Hunt's contender for goal of the season. A swerving 25-yarder puts the Sky Blues ahead before McNab's penalty, a harsh decision for a Jacobs sliding tackle on Williams, gives the Seagulls a slightly lucky point.											
6	H	LIVERPOOL		9	L	1-2	1-2	Daly 1	Blyth	Thomas	Roberts	Jacobs	Dyson	Gillespie	Kaiser	Daly	Thompson	Whitton*	Hunt	Hateley
	22/9		16,738	*14*	7			*Kennedy A 2, McDermott 26p*	*Grobbelaar*	*Neal*	*Kennedy A*	*Thompson*	*Kennedy R*	*Hansen*	*Dalglish*	*Lee*	*Johnson**	*McDermott*	*Souness*	*Lawrenson*
								Ref: J Deakin	The Reds have won only one game in five but win at City for the first time in eight years. Daly scores after 35 seconds when Grobbelaar boobs but Kennedy is unmarked a minute later. McDermott's winner comes when Roberts brings down Johnson. City fail to turn pressure into goals.											
7	H	SOUTHAMPTON		8	W	4-2	1-1	Hunt 28, 85, Thompson 60, 69	Blyth	Thomas	Roberts	Jacobs	Dyson	Gillespie	Kaiser	Daly	Thompson	Whitton	Hunt	
	26/9		12,611	*9*	10			*Keegan 20, 77p*	*Wells*	*Golac*	*Holmes*	*Baker**	*Watson*	*Waldron*	*Keegan*	*Channon*	*Moran*	*Armstrong*	*Ball*	*Puckett*
								Ref: B Newsome	There are lots of attacking options for the Sky Blues and they ruthlessly expose Saints' weaknesses. Danny Thomas and Rudi Kaiser set up Thompson's goals and Hunt scores one snapshot and one individual effort after a great run. Keegan's penalty is harsh for Hunt's handball.											
8	A	SUNDERLAND		9	D	0-0	0-0		Blyth	Thomas	Roberts	Jacobs	Dyson	Gillespie	Kaiser	Daly*	Thompson	Whitton	Hunt	Hateley
	3/10		*19,269*	*19*	11				*Siddall*	*Hinnigan*	*Munro !*	*Buckley*	*Clarke*	*Hindmarch*	*Elliott*	*McCoist*	*Ritchie*	*Rowell*	*Cummins*	
								Ref: R Chadwick	Injuries are incurred in a battling performance on Wearside. Daly collides with Siddall and damages ribs, whilst Hunt injures his collarbone after a fearful tackle from Munro which earned him a red card 15 minutes from time. Sunderland have not won in six, and not scored in four.											
9	H	ASTON VILLA		12	D	1-1	1-1	Hateley 44	Blyth	Thomas	Roberts	Jacobs	Dyson	Gillespie	Kaiser	Whitton	Thompson	Hateley	Hunt	
	10/10		16,306	*16*	12			*Shaw 21*	*Rimmer*	*Swain*	*Gibson*	*Evans*	*Ormsby*	*Mortimer*	*Bremner*	*Shaw*	*Geddis*	*Cowans*	*Morley*	
								Ref: D Vickers	The defending champions have won only one in nine but keep up their long unbeaten record at Highfield Road. Jimmy Rimmer plays with pain-killing injections and keeps Villa in the game. Hateley beats him with a looping far-post header but City let the Brummies off the hook.											
10	A	NOTT'M FOREST		14	L	1-2	1-0	Hunt 44	Blyth	Thomas	Roberts	Jacobs	Dyson	Gillespie	Kaiser	Whitton	Thompson	Hateley	Hunt	
	17/10		*20,101*	*4*	12			*Wallace 66, 79*	*Shilton*	*Anderson*	*Gunn*	*McGovern**	*Needham*	*Aas*	*Gray*	*Wallace*	*Fashanu*	*Procter*	*Robertson*	*Walsh*
								Ref: M Heath	After a poor first season at Forest, Ian Wallace is in better form and his goals against his former club make it nine for the season. Both are close range efforts, but classy City should have been home and dry well before he pounces. Steve Hunt scores from Rudi Kaiser's swerving corner.											

No	Venue	Opponent / Date	Att	Pos	Res / Pts	FT	HT	Scorers, Times, Referees	1	2	3	4	5	6	7	8	9	10	11	12 sub used
11	H	SWANSEA		11	W	3-1	2-0	Hateley 37, 53, Kaiser 39	Blyth	Thomas	Roberts	Jacobs	Dyson	Gillespie	Kaiser	Whitton	Thompson	Hateley	Hunt	
		24/10	14,033	3	15			Curtis 75	Davies	Robinson	Stanley	Rajkovic	Irwin	Mahoney	Curtis	James R	James L	Thompson*	Latchford	Marustik
								Ref: M Lowe	Swansea are setting Div 1 alight in their first season in the top flight but are knocked off top spot by a classy City display. Hateley strikes again with two close-range finishes after good work by Whitton and Hunt. The attendances in the all-seater are disappointingly low. Daly is still out.											
12	A	ARSENAL		13	L	0-1	0-0		Blyth	Thomas	Roberts	Jacobs	Dyson	Gillespie	Kaiser	Hateley	Thompson	Gooding	Hunt	
		31/10	23,102	14	15			Thomas 62 (og)	Jennings	Hollins	Sansom	Talbot	O'Leary	Whyte	McDermott	Vaessen	Hawley	Nicholas	Rix	
								Ref: T Spencer	Arsenal look a very average side but City are poor and never threaten. Thompson, a transfer target of the Gunners recently, has lost his touch and not scored in seven. Thomas decides the dreadful game when, under pressure from Rix, he deliciously lobs over his keeper, Jim Blyth.											
13	A	WOLVES		15	L	0-1	0-0		Blyth	Thomas	Roberts	Jacobs	Dyson	Gillespie	Kaiser	Daly	Thompson	Whitton	Hunt	
		7/11	13,193	20	15			Eves 88	Bradshaw	Palmer	Parkin	Matthews	Berry	Brazier	Birch	Daniel	Eves	Richards	Atkinson	
								Ref: D Scott	John Barnwell is under pressure as Wolves have gone five games without a win and look relegation favourites. Mel Eves scores their first goal in six to win a dire game. City have sold ten players in 13 months and bought two. The selling policy is beginning to backfire on chairman Hill.											
14	A	WEST HAM		17	L	2-5	1-2	Hunt 6, 61 [Stewart 87p]	Blyth	Thomas	Roberts	Jacobs	Dyson	Gillespie	**Bradford**	Daly	Thompson	Hateley	Hunt	
		21/11	26,065	5	15			Brooking 22, Neighb'r 37, Martin 49, 54,	Parkes	Stewart	Lampard	Bonds	Martin	Devonshire	Neighbour	Goddard	Cross	Brooking	Pike	
								Ref: A Glasson	The Hammers have lost only once all season and win a thriller delayed 20 minutes through a floodlight failure. Brooking and Martin have just helped England to the World Cup finals and Martin wants to take the penalty to complete his hat-trick. Manager Lyall orders him to leave it.											
15	H	STOKE		14	W	3-0	2-0	Daly 1, Thompson 4, Bradford 49	Blyth	Thomas	Roberts	Jacobs	Dyson	Gillespie	Bradford	Daly	Thompson	Hateley	Hunt	
		24/11	10,260	12	18				Fox	Evans	Hampton	Dodd	O'Callaghan	Smith	Griffiths	Heath*	Chapman	Bracewell	Johnson	Maguire
								Ref: C Downey	A pitiful crowd, the lowest since 1962, on a bitter night sees Daly score after 27 seconds and it's as good as over three minutes later. Bradford, a £60,000 signing from Washington, scores with a bender from the edge of the box. City announce that their US investment has lost £500,000.											
16	H	MIDDLESBROUGH		14	D	1-1	1-0	Hateley 10	Blyth	Thomas	Roberts	Jacobs	Dyson	Gillespie	Bradford*	Daly	Thompson	Hateley	Hunt	Kaiser
		28/11	10,403	21	19			Woof 68	Platt	Nattrass	Bolton	Ross	Baxter	McAndrew	Cochrane	Otto	Woof*	Hodgson	Shearer	Ashcroft
								Ref: M Dimblebee	In a boring game on a bitterly cold day City to beat a woeful Boro side who haven't won in ten games. The early season stars Hunt and Thompson look jaded and a long way from England form. Woof is substituted immediately after scoring and warning bells are ringing.											
17	A	TOTTENHAM		12	W	2-1	1-1	Hunt 41, Gillespie 69	Blyth	Thomas	Roberts	Jacobs	Dyson	Gillespie	**Hendrie**	Daly*	Thompson	Hateley	Hunt	Kaiser
		5/12	28,073	5	22			Hazard 21	Clemence	Hughton*	Miller	Roberts	Hazard	Perryman	Ardiles	Archibald	Galvin	Hoddle	Crooks	Villa
								Ref: M Taylor	Unpredictable but fighting Coventry beat unpredictable Spurs. City win the game in the air with two headed goals. John Hendrie, on his debut, almost scores a spectacular goal after a 40-yard run. Gary Gillespie has another goal disallowed for offside as the confidence floods back.											
18	H	MANCHESTER C		12	L	0-1	0-1		Blyth	Thomas	Roberts*	Jacobs	Dyson	Gillespie	Hendrie	Daly	Thompson	Hateley	Hunt	Kaiser
		12/12	12,420	7	22			Tueart 9	Corrigan	Ranson	McDonald	Reid	Bond	Caton	Tueart	Reeves	Francis	Hartford	Hutchison	
								Ref: S Bates	Tommy Hutchison returns to torment his old team and set up Tueart's headed winner. City fight back but despite having the major share of the play can't score. Hunt is having a poor spell, but Hendrie gives McDonald a testing time. The club fall out with the local paper and ban photos.											
19	H	WEST BROM		14	L	0-2	0-1		Blyth	Thomas	Roberts	Jacobs	Dyson	Gillespie	Hendrie	Daly	Thompson	Hateley*	Hunt	Whitton
		26/12	15,215	15	22			Owen 4, Regis 53	Grew	Batson	Bennett	King	Wile	Robertson	Whitehead	Monagahn	Regis	Owen	MacKenzie	
								Ref: K Salmon	City appear on TV for the first time this season, but only after new shirts are made removing the Talbot 'T'. The under-soil heating saves the game despite snow and frost, but City wish it hadn't. Owen scores from a free-kick and Regis scores his 18th of the season but does little else.											
20	A	EVERTON		15	L	2-3	2-3	Thomas 20, Bodak 44	Blyth	Thomas	Roberts	Jacobs !	Dyson	Gillespie	Bodak	Daly	Thompson	English*	Hunt	Kaiser
		28/12	23,888	8	22			Higgins 12, 23, Sharp 38	Southall	Stevens	Ratcliffe	Higgins	Lyons	Kendall	McMahon	Ross	Sharp	Eastoe	Irvine	
								Ref: T Mills	Sexton recalls Bodak and English from the cold. Bodak scores a super goal from a narrow angle but it can't stop another defeat. The defence are charitable to the Toffees, who have manager Kendall making a rare appearance. Steve Jacobs gets a red card after an incident with Sharp.											
21	H	IPSWICH		16	L	2-4	1-1	Hunt 38, Daly 60 [Brazil 87]	Blyth	Thomas	Barnes	**Francis***	Dyson	Gillespie	Bodak	Daly	Hateley	Hendrie	Hunt	**H'mantsch'k**
		16/1	11,758	1	22			Wark 20, Muhren 80, Mariner 83,	Cooper	Burley	McCall	Mills	Osman	Butcher	Wark	Muhren	Mariner	Brazil	Gates	
								Ref: J Hough	Former England captain Gerry Francis is on loan, and impresses until he limps off with ten minutes left. City press the self-destruct button and in seven horrible minutes concede three goals to let the leaders off the hook. Daly juggles the ball brilliantly before volleying the second goal.											

No	Date		Att	Pos	Pt	F-A	H-T	Scorers, Times, and Referees	1	2	3	4	5	6	7	8	9	10	11	12 sub used
22	A	BIRMINGHAM		15	D	3-3	2-1	Hunt 10, Hateley 33, Thompson 80	Blyth	Thomas	Barnes	Francis	Dyson	Gillespie	Bodak	Daly*	Hateley	Thompson	Hunt	Jacobs
	26/1		*13,023*	*20*	23			*Broadhurst 13, Evans 64, 76*	*Coton*	*Langan*	*Gemmill*	*Dillon*	*v d Hauwe*	*Todd*	*Broadhurst*	*Evans*	*Worthington*	*Curbishley*	*Van Mierlo*	
								Ref: N Midgley	Blues have only won once since October but look to have ended that run when they come from behind to lead 3-2. Thompson has different ideas, and Hateley should have won it, but Tony Coton makes a superb arching save to tip over. £1 million valued Steve Hunt is unsettled.											
23	H	BRIGHTON		15	L	0-1	0-1		Blyth	Thomas	Barnes	Francis	Dyson	Gillespie	Bodak	Daly*	Hateley	Thompson	Hunt	Jacobs
	30/1		11,014	*7*	23			*Ritchie 36*	*Moseley*	*Shanks*	*Nelson*	*Grealish*	*Stevens*	*Gatting*	*Ryan*	*Ritchie*	*Smith*	*McNab*	*Thomas*	
								Ref: N Ashley	Mike Bailey's Brighton are winning few friends with their negative approach but City can't break them down and slump to their fourth home defeat in a row. Ritchie scores a breakaway goal and the defensive blanket gets thicker. Gerry Daly and Steve Hunt look woefully out of touch.											
24	A	LEEDS		17	D	0-0	0-0		Blyth	Thomas	Barnes	Jacobs	Hagan	Gillespie	Bodak	Bradford	Hateley	Thompson	Hunt	
	6/2		*16,385*	*18*	24				*Lukic*	*Cherry*	*Gray F*	*Flynn*	*Hart*	*Firm*	*Gray E*	*Graham*	*Parlane*	*Hamson*	*Hird*	
								Ref: G Courtney	Leeds are unbeaten at home but City have chances to win. Daly is dropped, Francis and Dyson are injured, and Hagan is back in the side after three years. Hunt, Bradford and Gillespie are foiled by the superb Lukic. Amazingly, Leeds will win only one more home game and go down.											
25	H	NOTTS CO		18	L	**1-5**	1-2	Hateley 40 *[Christie 84, Chiedozie 85]*	Blyth	Thomas	Barnes	Francis	Dyson	Gillespie	Bodak	Bradford	Hateley	Thompson	Hunt	
	16/2		10,237	*10*	24			*Goodwin 10, Harkouk 22, Mair 60,*	*Avramovic*	*Benjamin*	*O'Brien*	*Goodwin*	*Kilcline*	*Richards*	*Chiedozie*	*Harkouk**	*McCulloch*	*Hooks*	*Mair*	*Christie*
								Ref: R Lewis	County have already won at Villa, Forest and Ipswich but they really turn on the style to embarrass City. They have three more goals disallowed against a woeful City defence. Hunt reacts badly to the board's rejection of his transfer request, and Mark Hateley's form is the one bright spot.											
26	A	LIVERPOOL		18	L	0-4	0-3	*[McDermott 64p]*	Blyth	Thomas	Roberts	Francis	Dyson	Hagan	Bradford	Jacobs	Hateley	Thompson	Hunt	
	20/2		*28,286*	*6*	24			*Souness 5, Lee 13, Rush 34,*	*Grobbelar*	*Neal*	*Lawrenson*	*Kennedy A*	*Whelan*	*Hansen*	*Dalglish*	*Lee*	*Rush*	*McDermott*	*Souness*	
								Ref: G Owen	It's men against boys at Anfield as Liverpool score at will and Blyth's saves prevents the score from being an embarrassment. Ian Rush scores his 21st goal of the season. McDermott's penalty comes from Jim Hagan's foul on the troublesome Dalglish. Certain players are just not trying.											
27	A	ASTON VILLA		18	L	1-2	1-2	Thompson 2	Blyth	Roberts	Barnes	Francis	Gillespie	Hagan	Bodak	Thomas	Hateley	Thompson !	Hunt	
	27/2		*24,474*	*13*	24			*Cowans 5p, Shaw 19*	*Rimmer*	*Jones*	*Williams*	*Evans**	*McNaught*	*Mortimer*	*Bremner*	*Shaw*	*With*	*Cowans*	*Morley*	*Blair*
								Ref: D Owen	Sexton is fuming at the penalty decision - Shaw falling after little or no contact from Hagan. This is City's best display for weeks and after an excellent first half they are unlucky to be losing. The game then turns ugly and after 65 minutes Thompson is sent off for lashing out at Evans.											
28	H	NOTT'M FOREST		18	L	0-1	0-1		Sealey	Thomas	Roberts	Jacobs	Dyson	Gillespie	Hendrie	Francis	Hateley	English	Hunt*	Whitton
	9/3		**9,677**	*10*	24			*Rober 13*	*Shilton*	*Anderson*	*Bowyer*	*McGovern*	*Young*	*Gunn*	*Rober*	*Wallace*	*Ward*	*Procter*	*Gray*	
								Ref: J Worrall	The sixth home defeat in a row. A mere two points from eleven games push City closer to the trapdoor. German Jurgen Rober's first goal for Forest is enough to win an awful game played in wind and rain and watched by a new low Div 1 crowd at Highfield Rd. Sexton makes changes.											
29	A	SWANSEA		18	D	0-0	0-0		Sealey	Thomas	Roberts	Jacobs	Dyson	Gillespie	Hendrie*	Francis	Hateley	English	Whitton	**Butterworth**
	13/3		*16,425*	*2*	25				*Davies*	*Robinson*	*Marustik*	*Irwin*	*Kennedy*	*Rajkovic*	*Curtis*	*James R*	*James L*	*Thompson*	*Charles**	*Stanley*
								Ref: T Spencer	Swansea, in their first ever season in Div 1, are enjoying themselves with six wins out of seven. City take the wind out of their sails and almost get three points with a determined display. Gillespie, Dyson and Sealey are commanding and Steve Whitton twice hits the underside of the bar.											
30	A	MANCHESTER U		17	W	1-0	1-0	Whitton 39	Sealey	Thomas	Roberts	Jacobs	Dyson	Gillespie	Whitton	Francis	Hateley	English	Butterworth	
	17/3		***34,499***	*3*	28				*Bailey*	*Gidman*	*Albiston*	*Wilkins*	*Moran*	*Buchan*	*Robson**	*Birtles*	*Stapleton*	*Moses*	*Coppell*	*Duxbury*
								Ref: G Tyson	United have £1.5 million record signing Bryan Robson in their side, but he can't stop City's kids making this a winning return for Sexton with their first win in 13. Atkinson's team's title hopes are dented with a well-drilled, defensive display that restricted the home side to long shots.											
31	H	ARSENAL		17	W	1-0	0-0	Hateley 60	Sealey	Thomas	Roberts	Jacobs	Dyson	Gillespie	Whitton	Francis	Hateley	English	Butterworth	
	20/3		11,993	*6*	31				*Wood*	*Hollins*	*Sansom*	*Talbot*	*Devine*	*Whyte*	*Gorman**	*Sunderland*	*Davis*	*Robson*	*Rix*	*Meade*
								Ref: J Key	City's gung-ho attacking style has been jettisoned for a more defensive approach. The Arsenal pressure is soaked up and then Hateley heads home from English's cross. After that Hateley could have scored two more, Whitton should have had a penalty and Butterworth misses a sitter.											

No	Venue	Opponent	Att	Pos	Pts	Res	F-A	H-T	Scorers, Times, and Referees	1	2	3	4	5	6	7	8	9	10	11	subs used
32	H	WOLVES		18		D	0-0	0-0		Sealey	Thomas	Roberts	Jacobs	Dyson	Gillespie	Whitton	Francis	Hateley	English	Butterworth	
	27/3		11,734	*20*	32					*Bradshaw*	*Humphrey*	*Palmer*	*Matthews*	*Pender*	*Coy*	*Hibbitt*	*Carr*	*Gray*	*Eves*	*Kernan*	
									Ref: J Martin	Former Bolton boss Ian Greaves has taken over the poison chalice at Wolves but they have scored only 19 goals all season. Bradshaw rescues them against a quiet City as Sealey keeps a fourth clean sheet in a row. Bradford and Barnes are released, the latter for off-the field antics.											
33	A	IPSWICH		18		L	0-1	0-1		Sealey	Thomas*	Roberts	Jacobs	Dyson	Gillespie	Whitton	Francis	Hateley	English	Butterworth	Thompson
	3/4		*20,411*	*2*	32				*Wark 32*	*Cooper*	*Burley*	*McCall*	*Mills*	*Osman*	*Gernon*	*Wark*	*Muhren*	*D'Avray*	*Brazil*	*Gates*	
									Ref: D Vickers	John Wark scores his 18th of the season as Ipswich win their fourth in a row and pull level with Liverpool. There seems a lack of inspiration from City, who lose Thomas early on with an injury. Thompson and Francis almost leave on deadline day, to Arsenal and Palace respectively.											
34	A	WEST BROM		16		W	2-1	1-1	Thompson 2, Whitton 87	Sealey	Butterworth	Roberts	Jacobs	Dyson	Gillespie	Whitton	Francis	Hateley	Thompson	Hunt	
	10/4		*12,718*	*15*	35				*Mackenzie 44*	*Grew*	*Batson*	*Statham*	*Bennett*	*Wile*	*Robertson*	*Zondervan*	*Cross**	*Regis*	*Owen*	*MacKenzie*	*Brown*
									Ref: D Shaw	The 13-year Hawthorns jinx is broken by a workmanlike performance on Easter Saturday as Albion, with just one win in eleven, are dragged into the relegation mire. Hateley scored twice on his Under-21 debut and causes the Baggies problems. Allen's one year reign is soon to end.											
35	H	EVERTON		15		W	1-0	1-0	Singleton 36	Sealey	Butterworth	Roberts	Jacobs	Dyson	Gillespie	Whitton	**Singleton***	Hateley	Thompson	Hunt	H'rmantsch'k
	13/4		11,838	*11*	38					*Southall*	*Borrows*	*Ratcliffe*	*Higgins*	*Lyons*	*McMahon*	*Irvine*	*Heath*	*Sharp*	*Ainscow*	*Ross*	
									Ref: D Reeves	A debut goal from Martin Singleton, superbly struck from Thompson's lay-off, is all City have to show from a commanding display against Europe-bound Everton. Chances go begging and even Roberts goes close. The Toffees rally and in a nail-biting finish Adrian Heath goes close.											
36	H	WEST HAM		15		W	1-0	1-0	Hateley 44	Sealey	Thomas	Roberts	Butterworth	Dyson	Gillespie	Whitton*	Jacobs	Hateley	Thompson	Hunt	H'rmantsch'k
	17/4		13,446	*8*	41					*Parkes*	*Stewart*	*Cowie*	*Orr*	*Martin**	*Devonshire*	*Van der Elst*	*Goddard*	*Cross*	*Brooking*	*Allen*	*La Ronde*
									Ref: L Shapter	A vibrant game is decided by Hateley's opportunism, but Whitton misses three golden chances to bury his local team. Alvin Martin breaks a collarbone in a challenge on Thompson and may miss the World Cup. Acting skipper Dyson is dominant. Brooking inspires West Ham in vain.											
37	A	MIDDLESBROUGH		15		D	0-0	0-0		Sealey	Thomas	Jacobs	Butterworth	Dyson	Gillespie	Whitton	Francis	Hateley	Thompson	Hunt	
	24/4		*10,968*	*22*	42					*Platt*	*Craggs*	*Bailey*	*McAndrew*	*Baxter*	*Nattrass*	*Ross*	*Otto*	*Hodgson*	*Shearer*	*Thomas**	*Macdonald*
									Ref: D Allison	Dave Sexton plays three central defenders in his efforts to keep City unbeaten, and Boro, on the brink of relegation, are enmeshed in the web. McAndrew, Shearer and Hodgson all have efforts saved by the dazzling Les Sealey and Mark Hateley, twice and Steve Hunt go close for City.											
38	H	SUNDERLAND		15		W	**6-1**	2-1	Gillespie 23, T'pson 36, 54, Francis 69,	Sealey	Thomas	Jacobs	Butterworth	Dyson	Gillespie	Whitton	Francis	Hateley	Thompson	Hunt	
	27/4		11,282	*16*	45				*Cummins 40* [Hateley 75, 88]	*Turner*	*Hinnigan*	*Munro*	*Hindmarch*	*Chisholm*	*Elliott*	*Buckley*	*West*	*Rowell*	*Pickering**	*Cummins*	*McCoist*
									Ref: R Milford	The biggest City win since 1963 is just reward for an outstanding attacking rout. The finishing is deadly and City could have had nine. The Wearsiders get the hiding that's been on the cards for a few games. Thompson and Hateley are awesome and Gerry Francis bosses midfield.											
39	H	TOTTENHAM		15		D	0-0	0-0		Sealey	Thomas	Jacobs	Butterworth	Dyson	Gillespie	Whitton	Francis	Hateley	Thompson	Hunt*	Roberts
	1/5		15,468	*5*	46					*Clemence*	*Hughton*	*O'Reilly*	*Roberts*	*Lacy*	*Perryman*	*Villa*	*Archibald*	*Galvin**	*Falco*	*Brooke*	*Crook*
									Ref: L Burden	It's a case of after the Lord Mayor's show in a poor, niggly game. Spurs have just lost a Cup Winners' Cup semi-final to Barcelona but are back at Wembley for another FA Cup final. The Falklands War has meant that Ardiles has left. Ricky Villa has stayed and takes stick from the fans.											
40	A	SOUTHAMPTON		15		D	5-5	2-1	Whitton 11, 60, Hateley 43, 50, 90	Sealey	Thomas	Jacobs	Butterworth	Dyson	Gillespie	Whitton	Francis	Hateley	Thompson	Hunt	
	4/5		*18,522*	*6*	47				*Keegan 22, 83, Cassells 47, 69, Ball 61*	*Katalinic*	*Golac*	*Holmes*	*Williams*	*Nicholl*	*Whitlock**	*Keegan*	*Channon*	*Cassells*	*Armstrong*	*Ball*	*Wallace*
									Ref: T Bune	Another midweek goals-feast sees City lose a 4-2 lead and equalise through Hateley in the last minute. This match has everything and the fans go hysterical as the goals keep coming. Saints have scored 48 home goals and are into Europe. Kevin Keegan is the league's top scorer with 28.											
41	A	MANCHESTER C		14		W	3-1	2-0	Whitton 5, 6, 70	Sealey	Jacobs	Roberts	Butterworth	Dyson	Gillespie	Whitton	Singleton	Hateley*	Thompson	Hunt	H'rmantsch'k
	8/5		*27,580*	*9*	50				*Francis 78*	*Williams*	*May*	*McDonald*	*Reid*	*Bond*	*Caton*	*Boyer*	*Reeves*	*Francis*	*Hartford*	*Power*	
									Ref: C Seel	The Cannonball Kid makes it five goals in two games as City end the season with panache, one defeat in 13. Whitton's finishing is deadly as the Maine Road hoodoo, eight league defeats in a row, is broken. John Bond's influence is wearing off and only Trevor Francis looks up for it.											
42	H	BIRMINGHAM		14		L	0-1	0-0		Sealey	Thomas	Roberts	Butterworth*	Dyson	Jacobs	Whitton	Francis	English	Thompson	Singleton	H'rmantsch'k
	15/5		15,925	*16*	50				*Harford 86*	*Coton*	*Langan*	*Hawker*	*Stevenson*	*v d Hauwe*	*Curbishley*	*Van Mierlo*	*Dillon*	*Harford*	*Phillips*	*Evans**	*Handysides*
		Home	Away						Ref: C Maskell	Mick Harford has scored nine goals in 12 games since signing from struggling Bristol City and bags the goal that ensures safety. Ron Saunders was winning the league with Villa last year, but is now the Blues' boss. Their fans invade the pitch with relief as City's fantastic run ends.											
Average		13,132	19,860																		

League Cup					F-A	H-T	Scorers, Times, and Referees	1	2	3	4	5	6	7	8	9	10	11	12 sub used
2:1	A	EVERTON	9	D	1-1	0-0	Hateley 82	Blyth	Thomas	Roberts	Jacobs	Dyson	Gillespie	Kaiser	Whitton	Thompson	Gooding	Hateley	
	6/10	*17,228*	*11*				*Ferguson 49*	*Arnold*	*Stevens*	*Bailey*	*Walsh*	*Lyons*	*Thomas*	*McMahon*	*O'Keefe*	*Ferguson*	*Ross*	*McBride*	
							Ref: T Morris	Mick Ferguson left City for Everton for £300,000 in the summer and scores on his home debut. Mark Hateley scores a late equaliser on his first appearance of the season, having had a seventh-minute goal ruled out for no apparent reason. City are without he injured Steve Hunt and Daly.											
2:2	H	EVERTON	11	L	0-1	0-0		Blyth	Thomas	Roberts	Jacobs	Dyson	Gillespie	Kaiser	Whitton	Thompson	Hateley	Hunt	
	27/10	13,717	*7*				*Ferguson 85*	*Arnold*	*Stevens*	*Bailey*	*Higgins*	*Lyons*	*Lodge*	*McMahon*	*O'Keefe*	*Ferguson*	*Ainscow*	*McBride*	
							Ref: M Scott (City lose 1-2 on aggregate)	Ferguson grabs the late winner ten minutes after Thompson misses City's best chance, when he hits the post with the goal gaping. The Sky Blues fail to score at home for the first time, but Whitton and Kaiser also hit the wood. Howard Kendall's team meet Oxford in the next round.											

FA Cup																			
3	H	SHEFFIELD WED	15	W	3-1	2-1	Hunt 36, 43, Hateley 78	Blyth	Thomas	Barnes	Jacobs	Dyson	Gillespie	Bodak	Daly	Hateley	Kaiser*	Hunt	H'rmantsch'k
	2/1	14,231	*2:8*				*McCulloch 22*	*Bolder*	*Sterland*	*Williamson*	*Smith*	*Shirtliff*	*Taylor**	*Megson*	*Milocevic*	*Bannister*	*McCulloch*	*Curran*	*Mellor*
							Ref: J Worrall	Curfew breaking Thompson and English are dropped, but City recover their form after McCulloch's early setback. Steve Hunt is the star. He delicately chips the first and races on to Mark Hateley's flick for the second. The home crowd is sparked into life by 4,000 Wednesday fans.											
4	A	MANCHESTER C	17	W	3-1	2-0	Hunt 2, Hateley 22, Bodak 90	Blyth	H'rmantsch'k	Barnes	Thomas*	Dyson	Gillespie	Bodak	Daly	Thompson	Hateley	Hunt	Butterworth
	23/1	*31,276*	*4*				*Bond 75p*	*Corrigan*	*Gow**	*McDonald*	*Reid*	*Bond*	*Caton*	*Hutchison*	*Reeves*	*Francis*	*Hartford !*	*Power*	*Kinsey*
							Ref: G Courtney	City's kids ram Hutch's 'they'll be frightened out of their skins' jibe down his throat with a fearless display. Hartford is off for hacking down his marker Thomas after 70 minutes. Bond scores after Hormantschuk hauls Francis down and Bodak chips Corrigan for the goal of the month.											
5	H	OXFORD	17	W	4-0	1-0	Thompson 45, 50, Hateley 47, 83	Blyth	Thomas	Barnes	Francis*	Dyson	Gillespie	Bodak	Bradford	Hateley	Thompson	Hunt	Jacobs
	13/2	20,264	*3:9*					*Burton*	*Doyle*	*Fogg*	*Jeffrey*	*Briggs*	*Wright*	*Brock**	*Foley*	*Cassells*	*Thomas*	*Smithers*	*Kearns*
							Ref: C White	Francis has signed for £145,000 after turning down an offer to be Pompey's boss. City are in the last eight for the first time in nine years, courtesy of this thrashing of giant-killers Oxford U, who have ex-City man Roy Barry as caretaker boss. Thompson and Hateley are the heroes.											
QF	A	WEST BROM	18	L	0-2	0-1		Blyth	Roberts	Barnes	Francis	Gillespie	Hagan	Bodak	Thomas	Hateley	Thompson	Hunt	
	6/3	*27,825*	*16*				*Regis 18, Owen 65*	*Grew*	*Batson*	*Statham*	*Bennett*	*Wile*	*Robertson*	*Brown*	*King*	*Regis*	*Owen*	*MacKenzie*	
							Ref: P Willis	Playing in their red and white strip, City battle hard but are no match for the Albion. There seems to be no danger when Regis takes a pass from Brown, but he hits a sizzling 25-yarder past Blyth. Owen's chip deflects off Barnes and the Baggies are through to a semi final with QPR.											

	Home P	W	D	L	F	A	Away W	D	L	F	A	Pts
1 Liverpool	42	14	3	4	39	14	12	6	3	41	18	87
2 Ipswich	42	17	1	3	47	25	9	4	8	28	28	83
3 Manchester U	42	12	6	3	27	9	10	6	5	32	20	78
4 Tottenham	42	12	4	5	41	26	8	7	6	26	22	71
5 Arsenal	42	13	5	3	27	15	7	6	8	21	22	71
6 Swansea	42	13	3	5	34	16	8	3	10	24	35	69
7 Southampton	42	15	2	4	49	30	4	7	10	23	37	66
8 Everton	42	11	7	3	33	21	6	6	9	23	29	64
9 West Ham	42	9	10	2	42	29	5	6	10	24	28	58
10 Manchester C	42	9	7	5	32	23	6	6	9	17	27	58
11 Aston Villa	42	9	6	6	28	24	6	6	9	27	29	57
12 Nott'm Forest	42	7	7	7	19	20	8	5	8	23	28	57
13 Brighton	42	8	7	6	30	24	5	6	10	13	28	52
14 COVENTRY	42	9	4	8	31	24	4	7	10	25	38	50
15 Notts Co	42	8	5	8	32	33	5	3	13	29	36	47
16 Birmingham	42	8	6	7	29	25	2	8	11	24	36	44
17 West Brom	42	6	6	9	24	25	5	5	11	22	32	44
18 Stoke	42	9	2	10	27	28	3	6	12	17	35	44
19 Sunderland	42	6	5	10	19	26	5	6	10	19	32	44
20 Leeds	42	6	11	4	23	20	4	1	16	16	41	42
21 Wolves	42	8	5	8	19	20	2	5	14	13	43	40
22 Middlesbro	42	5	9	7	20	24	3	6	12	14	28	39
	924	214	121	127	672	501	127	121	214	501	672	1265

Odds & ends

Double wins: (1) Manchester U.
Double losses: (4) Liverpool, Ipswich, Notts County, Nott'm Forest.

Won from behind: (3) Southampton (h), Tottenham (a), Sheff W FAC (h).
Lost from in front: (5) Liverpool (h), Nott'm Forest (a), West Ham (a), Ipswich (h), Aston Villa (a).

High spots: Reaching the FA Cup quarter-finals.
Run of 13 games with only one defeat in the spring.
6-1 thrashing of Sunderland
5-5 draw at the Dell.
Sealey's four successive clean sheets, the best for almost 20 years.

Low spots: Lowest average attendance since 1961-62.
12 games without a win between December and March.
Six consecutive home defeats, the worst run in the club's history.

Red cards: City – Jacobs (Everton a), Thompson (A Villa a).
Red cards: Opponents – Munro (Sunderland a), Hartford (Man C FAC a).

Player of the Year: Danny Thomas.
Ever-presents: (0).
Hat-tricks: (2) Mark Hateley, Steve Whitton.
Opposing hat-tricks: (0).
Leading scorer: (18) Mark Hateley.

	Appearances Lge	*Sub*	LC	*Sub*	FAC	*Sub*	Goals Lge	LC	FAC	Tot
Barnes, David	**6**				4					
Blyth, Jim	**27**		2		4					
Bodak, Peter	**9**				4		**2**		1	**3**
Bradford, David	**6**				1		**1**			**1**
Butterworth, Ian	**13**	*1*				*1*				
Daly, Gerry	**19**				2		**4**			**4**
Dyson, Paul	**40**		2		3					
English, Tom	**8**									
Francis, Gerry	**18**				2		**1**			**1**
Gillespie, Gary	**40**		2		4		**2**			**2**
Gooding, Ray	**1**		1							
Hagan, Jim	**3**				1					
Hateley, Mark	**31**	*2*	2		4		**13**	1	4	**18**
Hendrie, John	**6**									
Hormantschuk, Peter		*5*			1	*1*				
Hunt, Steve	**36**		1		4		**9**		3	**12**
Jacobs, Steve	**37**	*2*	2		1	*1*				
Kaiser, Rudi	**11**	*5*	2		1		**3**			**3**
Roberts, Brian	**33**	*1*	2		1					
Sealey, Les	**15**									
Singleton, Martin	**3**						**1**			**1**
Thomas, Danny	**39**		2		4		**1**			**1**
Thompson, Garry	**35**	*1*	2		3		**10**		2	**12**
Whitton, Steve	**26**	*2*	2				**9**			**9**
24 players used	**462**	***19***	**22**		**44**	***3***	**56**	**1**	**10**	**67**

No	Date		Att	Pos	Pt	F-A	H-T	Scorers, Times, and Referees	1	2	3	4	5	6	7	8	9	10	11	12 sub used
1	H	SOUTHAMPTON			W	1-0	0-0	Whitton 68	**Suckling**	Thomas	Roberts	Jacobs	Dyson	Gillespie	Singleton	Francis	Hateley	Thompson G	Whitton	
	28/8		10,304		3				*Shilton*	*Baker*	*Rofe*	*Agboola*	*Nicholl*	*Wright*	*Ball*	*Holmes**	*Fashanu*	*Armstrong*	*Puckett*	*Cassells*
								Ref: N Midgley	16-year-old debutant Perry Suckling is the second youngest City player ever. He stars in an unexciting game. Blyth has moved to Brum, so the youngster, with only one reserve game to his name, is in for the injured Sealey. Ball plays his 1,000th game and Shilton makes his Saints' debut.											
2	A	SWANSEA			L	1-2	1-0	Whitton 13	Suckling	Thomas !	Roberts	Jacobs	Dyson	Gillespie	Singleton*	Francis	Hateley	Thompson G	Whitton	H'mantsch'k
	31/8		*11,712*		3			*James R 59p, Latchford 64*	*Davies*	*Marustik**	*Hadziabdic*	*Irwin*	*Mahoney*	*Rajkovic*	*James L*	*James R*	*Charles*	*Stevenson*	*Latchford*	*Charles*
								Ref: D Letts	Thomas is sent off after 51 minutes for two fouls on Leighton James. After looking comfortable, the pressure on City's ten men is too much and Whitton concedes a debatable penalty for pushing Charles. Latchford scores the winner from Rajkovic's cross. Suckling plays well again.											
3	A	IPSWICH		12	D	1-1	0-0	Thomas 86	Sealey	Thomas	Roberts	Jacobs	Dyson	Gillespie	H'mantsch'k	Francis	Hateley	Thompson G	Whitton	
	4/9		*16,662*	*16*	4			*Mariner 72*	*Cooper*	*Burley*	*Mills*	*Thijssen*	*Osman*	*Butcher*	*Wark*	*McCall*	*Mariner*	*Brazil*	*Gates*	
								Ref: M James	Bobby Robson has been appointed England boss, and Bobby Ferguson has taken over. But with Muhren also leaving, Town are reduced to the long ball. Sealey, rusty after his knee infection, makes several good saves until Mariner sweeps home Gates' cross. Thomas' 25-yarder is a gem.											
4	H	SUNDERLAND		6	W	1-0	1-0	Thompson G 7	Sealey	Thomas	Roberts	Jacobs	Dyson	Gillespie	H'mantsch'k	Francis	Hateley*	Thompson G	Whitton	Singleton
	7/9		8,910	*5*	7				*Turner*	*Venison*	*Munro*	*Atkins*	*Hindmarch*	*Elliott**	*Buckley*	*Rowell*	*McCoist*	*Pickering*	*Cummins*	*Cooke*
								Ref: J Hough	Sunderland's unbeaten start is ended by an early goal in front of a new low Div 1 crowd. City totally dominate and should have scored several more with Thompson, Dyson and Whitton guilty of misses. Hateley limps off and Jacobs breaks his nose but a pedantic referee ruins the game.											
5	H	ARSENAL		12	L	0-2	0-1		Sealey	Thomas	Roberts	Jacobs	Dyson	Gillespie	H'mantsch'k	Francis	Daly *	Thompson G	Whitton	Singleton
	11/9		10,192	*19*	7			*Chapman 40, Woodcock 58*	*Wood*	*Hollins*	*Sansom*	*Talbot*	*O'Leary*	*Whyte*	*Davis*	*Robson*	*Chapman*	*Woodcock*	*Rix*	
								Ref: R Nixon	The dispirited Sky Blues are woeful and collapse to an average Arsenal side who win for the first time this season. The Gunners' new £500,000 strikers both score their first goals from headers. The last half-hour is embarrassing and painful, and with gates already at a low a crisis looms.											
6	A	BIRMINGHAM		17	L	0-1	0-1		Sealey	H'mantsch'k	Roberts	Jacobs	Dyson	Gillespie	**Melrose**	Francis	Whitton	**Hall**	**Thompson K**	
	18/9		*11,681*	*21*	7			*Evans 45*	*Blyth*	*Langan*	*Dennis**	*Stevenson*	*Blake*	*Hagan*	*Phillips*	*Evans*	*Whatmore*	*Curbishley*	*Handysides*	*Francis*
								Ref: D Richardson	Jim Melrose has joined from Leicester, with Tom English going in exchange. With two other debutants, City look like strangers and a poor Blues side gain their first win of the season. Keith Thompson, in for his injured brother, has a useful game. Derek Hall will never be seen again.											
7	H	EVERTON		10	W	4-2	1-1	Melrose 21, 53, 67, Hunt 50	Sealey	Thomas	Roberts	Jacobs	Dyson	Gillespie	Whitton	Francis	Melrose	Thompson G	Hunt*	Thompson K
	25/9		9,297	*16*	10			*Heath 26, King 69*	*Southall*	*Richardson*	*Walsh*	*Higgins*	*Wright*	*McMahon*	*Ross**	*Heath*	*Sharp*	*King*	*Sheedy*	*Irvine*
								Ref: J Key	After the goal drought City fans see their share of the 50 goals scored in Div 1 today. Melrose has a dream home debut, thanks to Thompson's total domination in the air and Hunt's late return from America. The Thompsons are the first brothers to play together for City since the 1920s.											
8	A	MANCHESTER C		13	L	2-3	1-1	Melrose 8, Thompson G 77	Sealey	Thomas	Roberts	Jacobs	Dyson	Gillespie	Whitton	Daly*	Melrose	Thompson G	Hunt	Butterworth
	2/10		*25,105*	*6*	10			*Baker 38, Caton 49, Cross 70*	*Williams*	*Ranson*	*Power*	*Baker*	*Bond*	*Caton*	*Tueart*	*Reeves*	*Cross*	*Hartford*	*Simpson*	
								Ref: K Hackett	The referee controversially awards Manchester a free-kick for Sealey's five steps, and Caton blasts it home in the game's turning point. City were on top for most of the first half but old boy David Cross seals the win. Gerry Daly makes a rare appearance after being out of favour.											
9	A	TOTTENHAM		18	L	0-4	0-1		Sealey	Thomas	Roberts	Butterworth	Dyson	Gillespie	Whitton	Jacobs	Melrose	Thompson G	Hunt	
	9/10		*25,188*	*6*	10			*Crooks 13, Brooke 49, 50, 55p*	*Parks*	*Hughton*	*Lacy*	*Miller*	*Brooke*	*O'Reilly*	*Mabbutt*	*Archibald**	*Hazard*	*Villa*	*Crooks*	*Falco*
								Ref: M Taylor	The over-worked Les Sealey saves woeful City from a massacre but can't stop understudy Gary Brooke scoring a six-minute hat-trick. The penalty, for a push on Gary Mabbutt by Thompson, is debatable and Sealey saves Brooke's first effort. Sexton fumes 'we were soft touches'.											
10	H	NOTTS CO		14	W	1-0	0-0	Francis 74	Sealey	Thomas	Roberts	Butterworth	Dyson	Gillespie	Jacobs	Francis	Melrose	Thompson G	Hunt	
	16/10		8,314	*18*	13				*Avramovic*	*Benjamin**	*Worthington*	*Hunt*	*Kilcline*	*Richards*	*Chiedozie*	*Christie*	*McCulloch*	*Clarke*	*Mair*	*Lahtinen*
								Ref: C Downey	County are fresh from a 4-1 win over Villa, but can't extend their run against Francis-inspired City. Returning after a head injury sustained when falling off his garage roof, and wearing a protective plaster, he scores with a delightful chip to decide a mediocre, wind-affected game.											

No	Date	Venue	Opponent	Att	Pos	Pts	Res	F-A	H-T	Scorers, Times, Referees	1	2	3	4	5	6	7	8	9	10	11	12 sub
11		A	WATFORD		16		D	0-0	0-0		Sealey	Thomas	Roberts	Butterworth	Dyson	Gillespie	Jacobs	Francis	Melrose	Thompson G	Hunt	
	23/10			17,334	6	14					Sherwood	Rice	Rostron	Taylor	Sims	Jackett	Callaghan	Blissett	Armstrong*	Lohman	Barnes	Jenkins
										Ref: D Axcell	Match of the Day cameras are present to see newly promoted Watford continue their goalscoring exploits, they had scored 17 in five home games. City's defensive action frustrates Graham Taylor's boys, with Dyson especially good. Hunt and Thompson hit the bar, as does Blissett.											
12		H	NORWICH		12		W	2-0	0-0	Hateley 75, Thompson G 85	Sealey	Thomas	Roberts	Butterworth	Dyson	Gillespie	Hendrie*	Jacobs	Hateley	Thompson G	Hunt	Whitton
	30/10			8,210	21	17					Woods	Haylock	Walsh	Barham	Walford	Watson	Van Wyk	O'Neill	Deehan	Bertschin	Bennett	
										Ref: L Shapter	Norwich, after one season down, are back in the top flight, but are a poor side. A dire game comes to life with Hateley's header, his first goal of an injury-affected season. Beforehand, City, low on confidence, were given the slow handclap and jeered for their sad efforts. Dyson shines.											
13		H	ASTON VILLA		11		D	0-0	0-0		Sealey	Thomas	Roberts	Butterworth	Dyson	Gillespie	Hendrie	Francis*	Hateley	Thompson G	Hunt	Jacobs
	6/11			12,199	10	18					Rimmer	Deacy	Williams	Evans	McNaught	Mortimer	Bremner	Shaw	Withe	Cowans	Morley	
										Ref: J Deakin	20-year-old Danny Thomas is in the England squad and emerges from his shell for his best game for weeks. The entertainment level is much higher with back-to-form Hunt shining against his old club. Thompson hits the bar near the end but the European champions deserve a point.											
14		A	LIVERPOOL		13		L	0-4	0-2		Suckling	Thomas	Roberts	Butterworth	Dyson	Gillespie	Whitton	Jacobs	Hateley	Thompson G	Hunt	
	13/11			27,870	1	18				Dalglish 8, Rush 24, 72, 82	Grobbelaar	Neal	Kennedy A	Thompson	Johnston	Hansen	Dalglish	Lee	Rush	Lawrenson	Souness	
										Ref: P Tydesley	Rush scored four at Goodison last week in the 5-0 derby win. The Reds have scored 33 in 14 games and look odds-on favourites for the title. Anfield is not a place to restore pride and the closest City get is when Grobbelaar fouls Hateley, but saves the same players kick after 70 mins.											
15		H	LUTON		11		W	4-2	0-0	Dyson 58, Whitton 63, 82, Thompson 84	Sealey	Thomas	Roberts	Jacobs	Dyson	Gillespie	Whitton	Francis*	Hateley	Thompson G	Hunt	Butterworth
	20/11			9,670	18	21				Horton 64, Stein 79	Findlay	Stephens	Money	Horton	Goodyear	Turner	Hill	Stein	Walsh	Antic	Moss	
										Ref: H King	Newly promoted Luton are finding life in the top division hard, but play their part in a stunning second half which has the fans on their feet. City throw away a two-goal lead, the second a thunderous shot from Whitton, and then snatch victory as Jake Findlay makes two mistakes.											
16		H	IPSWICH		10		D	1-1	0-0	Thomas 69	Sealey	Thomas	Roberts	Butterworth	Dyson	Gillespie	Whitton	Jacobs	Hateley	Thompson G	Hunt	
	23/11			9,599	11	22				Brazil 75	Cooper	Burley	Gernon	Thijssen	Osman*	Butcher	Wark	McCall	Mariner	Brazil	Gates	D'Avray
										Ref: R Chadwick	Want-away striker Alan Brazil snatches an undeserved equaliser with Ipswich's only chance of the night. Six minutes earlier Thomas had scored after a slick move involving Hunt, Roberts and Hateley. Ferguson's team are lethargic and don't look interested in playing for him.											
17		A	WEST BROM		11		L	0-2	0-1		Sealey	Thomas	Roberts	Butterworth	Dyson	Gillespie	Whitton	Jacobs	Hateley*	Thompson G	Hunt	Melrose
	27/11			12,115	7	22				Robertson 37, Regis 88	Godden	Whitehead	Statham	Zondervan	Wile	Robertson	Jol	Cross	Regis	Owen	Eastoe	
										Ref: A Robinson	Former City number two Ron Wylie masterminds City's undoing as Albion totally dominate the game. But for Les Sealey and the defence the winning margin would have been greater. The Sky Blues have yet to win away, and they are afterwards treated to a verbal lashing from Sexton.											
18		H	BRIGHTON		10		W	2-0	2-0	Hunt 8, Whitton 20	Sealey	Thomas	Roberts	Butterworth	Dyson	Gillespie	Whitton	Jacobs	Hateley	Thompson G	Hunt	
	4/12			**8,035**	18	25					Digweed	Shanks	Nelson	Grealish	Foster	Stevens	Case	McNab*	Robinson	Ward	Gatting	Ryan
										Ref: M Heath	Brighton's fourth defeat in a row will mean boss Mike Bailey is sacked on Monday. Low gates are prevalent in Div 1 and Everton, Swansea and City all have record Div 1 lows. Steve Whitton scores another superb long-range goal but Brighton, with lots of possession, have no ideas.											
19		A	WEST HAM		8		W	3-0	3-0	Hateley 37, Roberts 43, Whitton 45	Sealey	Thomas	Roberts	Butterworth	Dyson	Gillespie	Whitton	Jacobs	Hateley	Melrose	Hunt	
	11/12			19,321	7	28					Parkes	Stewart	Lampard	Orr	Gallagher	Devonshire*	Van der Elst	Goddard	Brush	Allen	Pike	Morgan
										Ref: A Grey	After 192 first-team games Harry Roberts scores his first goal, as City inflict West Ham's first home defeat since the opening day with an eight-minute blast. Van der Elst, a hat-trick hero against Notts County in mid-week, looks out of touch. Joe Gallagher plays on loan for the Hammers.											
20		H	STOKE		7		W	2-0	1-0	Hateley 23, 50	Sealey	Thomas	Roberts	Jacobs	Dyson	Gillespie	Whitton	Francis*	Hateley	Melrose	Hunt	Butterworth
	18/12			10,052	14	31					Fox	Parkin D	Hampton	Maskery	Watson	Berry	Maguire*	McIlroy	Callaghan	Thomas	Chamberlain	Ursem
										Ref: B Stevens	Stoke are as inconsistent as City and rarely trouble the Sky Blues on a frosty pitch. Hateley scores two, the second from a dreadful Parkin back-pass, and misses an easy chance for his hat-trick. Thompson is suspended and Francis limps off with back problems. City continue their climb.											
21		A	NOTT'M FOREST		8		L	2-4	2-2	Whitton 31, Melrose 42 [Procter 85]	Sealey	Thomas	Jacobs*	Butterworth	Dyson	Gillespie	Whitton	Francis	Hateley	Melrose	Hunt	Hendrie
	27/12			24,487	2	31				Young 39, Robertson 45p, Birtles 80,	Sutton	Swain	Gunn	Todd*	Young	Bowyer	Procter	Wallace	Birtles	Hodge	Robertson	Walsh
										Ref: N Glover	Forest's biggest crowd of the season sees their eighth win in ten, thanks to two late goals and a harsh penalty. City are twice ahead in an excellent game, although they fade in the last 20 minutes. Wallace is fouled by Gillespie for the spot-kick but fails to get his customary goal.											

No	Date		Att	Pos	Pt	F-A	H-T	Scorers, Times, and Referees	1	2	3	4	5	6	7	8	9	10	11	12 sub used
22	H	MANCHESTER U		5	W	3-0	2-0	H'mantsch'k 25, Hateley 42, Melrose 70	Sealey	Thomas	H'mantsch'k	Butterworth	Dyson	Gillespie	Whitton	Francis	Hateley	Melrose	Hunt	
	28/12		**18,945**	*3*	34				*Bailey*	*Duxbury*	*Albiston*	*Moses*	*Moran*	*McQueen*	*Robson*	*Wilkins*	*Stapleton*	*McGarvey*	*Grimes*	
								Ref: B Daniels	The tightest defence in Div 1 is breached for the first time in six games and Ron Atkinson's title chasers are buried by an exhilarating Sky Blues performance. Hormantschuk scores his first ever goal with a 35-yarder which skids through Bailey's arms. Francis is superb against Wilkins.											
23	A	LUTON		6	W	2-1	2-0	Whitton 10, Melrose 15	Sealey	Thomas	H'mantsch'k	Butterworth	Dyson	Gillespie	Whitton	Francis	Hateley	Melrose	Hunt	
	1/1		*13,072*	*18*	37			*Donaghy 60*	*Findlay*	*Stephens*	*Money*	*Horton*	*Goodyear*	*Donaghy*	*Hill*	*Geddis*	*Walsh*	*Fuccillo**	*Moss*	*Antic*
								Ref: D Vickers	Sexton returns to his first club for the first time as a manager and the kids give a super first-half display. It's five wins out of six and European talk is in the air. Whitton scores with a looping header and Melrose finishes a Hunt-inspired move clinically. David Pleat's Luton are in trouble.											
24	A	SOUTHAMPTON		5	D	1-1	1-1	Hateley 1	Sealey	Thomas	H'mantsch'k	Butterworth	Dyson	Gillespie	Whitton	Francis	Hateley	Melrose	Hunt	
	15/1		*17,145*	*15*	38			*Armstrong 38*	*Shilton*	*Agboola*	*Mills*	*Williams*	*Nicholl*	*Wright*	*Holmes*	*Foyle*	*Moran*	*Armstrong*	*Wallace*	
								Ref: J Moules	Hateley's 14 second goal is the fastest ever at the Dell, and conjures up visions of last years 5-5 draw. This is a niggly, physical game on a rough pitch in a blustery wind. A draw is a fair result. Shilton makes three outstanding saves, although Danny Wallace misses a good chance											
25	H	SWANSEA		5	D	0-0	0-0		Sealey	Thomas	Roberts	Butterworth	Dyson	Gillespie	Whitton	Francis	Hateley	Melrose*	Hunt	Thompson G
	22/1		9,984	*18*	39				*Davies*	*Robinson*	*Marustik*	*Charles*	*Stevenson*	*Rajkovic*	*Gale*	*James R*	*Mahoney*	*Stanley*	*Latchford*	
								Ref: A Robinson	Swansea are sliding towards relegation and have not won away all season. The public address announcer is correct when he says Swansea have not won any friends. They come to frustrate and achieve their objective with eight men behind the ball. Dai Davies has barely a shot to save.											
26	A	SUNDERLAND		7	L	1-2	0-1	Whitton 50	Sealey	Thomas	Roberts	Butterworth	Dyson	Gillespie	Whitton	Francis	Hateley	Melrose*	Hunt	Thompson G
	5/2		*14,356*	*19*	39			*Cummins 36, Rowell 57*	*Turner*	*Nicholl*	*Munro**	*Atkins*	*Chisholm*	*Pickering*	*Venison*	*Rowell*	*Worthington*	*James*	*Cummins*	*Buckley*
								Ref: N Midgley	A freezing day on Wearside gives City a reminder of the thin dividing line between success and failure. In the second half they have the icy wind behind them and Whitton equalises with a stunning volley, but City make mistakes and pay dearly. Sunderland are unbeaten in eight.											
27	H	MANCHESTER C		5	W	**4-0**	2-0	Melrose 30, Hateley 38, Gillespie 56, [Hunt 72]	Sealey	Thomas	Roberts	Butterworth	Dyson	Gillespie	Whitton	Jacobs	Hateley*	Thompson G	Hunt	Melrose
	12/2		9,604	*11*	42				*Williams*	*Ranson*	*McDonald**	*Reid*	*Bond*	*Caton*	*May*	*Reeves*	*Cross*	*Hartford*	*Bodak*	*Park*
								Ref: M Dimblebee	Bond has resigned after a dreadful cup defeat at Brighton and Man City are on a slide to relegation. Thompson is dropped to allow a more subtle approach. Hunt and Francis hit form to lift confidence and provide an easy win. The ex-City men Cross, Bodak and McDonald are poor.											
28	A	NOTTS CO		6	L	**1-5**	0-2	Gillespie 79 *[Hooks 77]*	Sealey	Thomas	Roberts	Butterworth	Dyson	Gillespie	Whitton*	Francis	Hateley	Melrose	Hunt	Thompson K
	26/2		***8,689***	*16*	42			*Fash' 11, 75, Lahtinen 42, McCull'ch 68,*	*Leonard*	*Goodwin*	*Worthington*	*Hunt*	*Lahtinen**	*Richards*	*Chiedozie*	*Fashanu*	*McCulloch*	*O'Brien*	*Hooks*	*McParland*
								Ref: J Hough	Thompson has been sold to WBA for £225,000 for financial reasons and this is a disastrous result. Talk of Europe is crazy. On this form City wouldn't make it to the Isle of Wight. Sealey has a nightmare game and is at fault for three goals, but every player has to take some blame.											
29	H	WATFORD		7	L	0-1	0-1		Sealey	Thomas	Roberts	Butterworth	Dyson	Gillespie	Whitton	Francis	Hateley	Melrose	Hunt*	Jacobs
	5/3		11,254	*3*	42			*Taylor 44*	*Sherwood*	*Rice*	*Rostron*	*Taylor*	*Sims*	*Bolton*	*Callaghan*	*Blissett*	*Barnes*	*Jackett*	*Jobson*	
								Ref: T Mills	The first home defeat since early September, by the surprise side of the season. Watford's style is not one for the purists and City adopt it after the break. Hunt and Sexton have a bust up at half-time and the player is subbed. Sims' foul on Hateley is a penalty but the ref gives a free-kick.											
30	H	TOTTENHAM		7	D	1-1	1-0	Hunt 24p	Sealey	Thomas	Roberts	Butterworth	Dyson	Gillespie	Thompson K	Francis	Hateley	Melrose	Hunt	
	12/3		11,027	*12*	43			*Miller 80*	*Clemence*	*Hughton*	*O'Reilly*	*Roberts*	*Miller*	*Perryman*	*Galvin*	*Mabbutt*	*Gibson*	*Falco*	*Crook**	*Webster*
								Ref: K Cooper	Spurs have lost their footballing style and reverted to a niggly, aggravating style. Four of them are booked, yet unbelievably Roberts - when on a yellow card - stays on the pitch after clattering Melrose. Clemence brings down Melrose for Hunt's penalty. Miller scores with a deflection.											
31	A	ASTON VILLA		12	L	0-4	0-3		Sealey	Thomas	Roberts	Butterworth*	Dyson	Gillespie	Whitton	Francis	Hateley	Melrose	Hunt	Thompson K
	19/3		*20,509*	*4*	43			*Shaw 24, Withe 29, 70, Evans 38*	*Spink*	*Williams*	*Gibson*	*Evans*	*McNaught*	*Mortimer*	*Bremner*	*Shaw**	*Withe*	*Cowans*	*Walters*	*Morley*
								Ref: T Spencer	City are on top for 20 minutes but can't manage the goal they deserve. Once behind, they capitulate and this stands as their biggest ever defeat against Villa. Rumours are rife that the Thompson transfer has created unrest amongst the players. Judging by this, those stories must be true.											

No	Venue	Opponent / Date	Att	Pos	Res	F-A	H-T	Scorers, Times, and Referees	1	2	3	4	5	6	7	8	9	10	11	12
32	A	NORWICH		12	D	1-1	0-0	Whitton 68	Sealey	Thomas	Roberts	Jacobs	Dyson	Gillespie	Whitton	Francis	Hateley	Hunt	Hendrie	
		23/3	*13,944*	*20*	44			*Walford 79*	*Woods*	*Haylock*	*Downs*	*Mendham*	*Walford*	*Watson*	*Barham*	*O'Neill**	*Deehan*	*Bertschin*	*Bennett*	*Channon*
								Ref: J Scales	On a wet and windy night in Norfolk the Canaries grab a vital point with Walford's 20-yard net burster. City get a welcome point with a much better performance, despite being under the cosh in the first half. Norwich's finishing is poor and Whitton's far-post effort looks to be enough.											
33	A	MANCHESTER U		14	L	0-3	0-2		Sealey	Thomas	Roberts	Jacobs	Dyson	Gillespie	Whitton*	Francis	Hateley	Hunt	Hendrie	Butterworth
		2/4	***36,814***	*2*	44			*Stapleton 27, Gillespie 30 (og), [Macari 58]*	*Wealands*	*Duxbury*	*Albiston*	*Moses*	*McGrath*	*McQueen*	*Wilkins*	*Muhren*	*Stapleton**	*McGarvey*	*Coppell*	*Macari*
								Ref: N Ashley	United lost to Liverpool in last week's Milk Cup final and are well adrift in the title race, but have no problems winning this game. Wilkins is the architect, setting up Stapleton and crossing for Gillespie to score. Jeff Wealands, on loan from Birmingham, does not have a shot to save.											
34	H	NOTT'M FOREST		14	L	1-2	1-0	Whitton 2	Sealey	Thomas	Roberts	Jacobs	Dyson	Gillespie	Whitton	Francis	Hateley	Melrose	Hunt	
		5/4	9,760	*6*	44			*Wallace 56, Robertson 89p*	*v Breukelen*	*Anderson*	*Swain*	*Fairclough*	*Young*	*Bowyer*	*Wilson**	*Wallace*	*Davenport*	*Hodge*	*Robertson*	*Walsh*
								Ref: D Shaw	A travesty of a result, decided by the late penalty when Davenport appeared to fall over Dyson's leg. City fail to kill off feeble Forest when they had them on the ropes in the first half, with Melrose and Hateley especially guilty. Wallace's equaliser is his first goal for eleven games.											
35	A	ARSENAL		15	L	1-2	0-2	Hateley 82	Sealey	Thomas	Roberts	Jacobs	Dyson	Gillespie	Whitton	Francis	Hateley	Melrose*	Hunt	Hendrie
		9/4	*19,152*	*12*	44			*Rix 4, Woodcock 37*	*Wood*	*Robson*	*Sansom*	*Whyte*	*Kay*	*Nicholas**	*Talbot*	*Davis*	*Petrovic*	*Woodcock*	*Rix*	*Chapman*
								Ref: A Glasson	Arsenal have one eye on next week's FA semi final with Man United, and do just enough to win. They are helped by poor goalkeeping from Sealey for both goals. City need to make changes, but there is no one left to come in as the squad is so bare. Mark Hateley is the lone success.											
36	H	LIVERPOOL		15	D	0-0	0-0		Sealey	Thomas	Roberts	Jacobs	Dyson	Gillespie	Hendrie	Francis	Hateley	Whitton	Hunt	
		12/4	15,340	*1*	45				*Grobbelaar*	*Neal*	*Kennedy A*	*Lawrenson*	*Whelan*	*Hansen*	*Dalglish*	*Lee*	*Rush*	*Johnston*	*Souness*	
								Ref: T Ward	The Reds are 17 points clear and as good as champions, but they don't abandon their principles and squeeze the life out of the game. Whitton has three chances to win it, but fails and City have strong penalty appeals for Lee's handball rejected. Dyson marks 30-goal Ian Rush superbly.											
37	H	BIRMINGHAM		15	L	0-1	0-0		Sealey	Thomas	Roberts	Jacobs	Dyson	Gillespie	Hendrie	Francis	Hateley	Whitton	Hunt	
		16/4	10,221	*21*	45			*Phillips 88*	*Coton*	*v d Hauwe*	*Dennis*	*Hagan*	*Blake*	*Phillips*	*Gayle*	*Ferguson**	*Hartford*	*Halsall*	*Hopkins*	*Handysides*
								Ref: J Martin	Birmingham are the worst side in the league but gain their first away win against woeful City. It is a depressing game and near the end a fan on the pitch throws down his shirt in disgust. When Les Phillips scores the ground is almost half-empty and the fans seem resigned to relegation.											
38	A	BRIGHTON		16	L	0-1	0-0		Sealey	Thomas	Roberts	Butterworth	Dyson	Gillespie	Whitton*	Francis	Hateley	Jacobs !	Hunt	Hendrie
		23/4	*14,676*	*21*	45			*Connor 81*	*Moseley*	*Ramsey !*	*Gatting*	*Grealish*	*Foster*	*Stevens*	*Case**	*Howlett*	*Robinson*	*Smith*	*Smillie*	*Connor*
								Ref: E Read	Brighton reached their first FA Cup final last week but are still favourites for the drop. It is a ten-man game from the 37th minute, when Jacobs and Ramsey scuffled and were expelled. City are better but lack punch. Former City man Gary Howlett plays well for Jimmy Melia's team.											
39	H	WEST BROM		16	L	0-1	0-1		Sealey	Thomas	Roberts	Butterworth	Dyson*	Gillespie	Whitton	Francis	Hateley	Jacobs	Hunt	Melrose
		30/4	9,457	*13*	45			*Gillespie 18 (og)*	*Barron*	*Webb*	*Statham*	*Whitehead*	*Wile*	*Robertson*	*Jol**	*Thompson*	*Perry*	*Owen*	*Cross*	*Zondervan*
								Ref: D Scott	Jimmy Hill says he will stand down if someone wants to put capital into the club. The rumour-mill says that eight first-teamers have yet to sign contracts. Another depressing home defeat as Gary Thompson's header flies in off Gary Gillespie's shoulder. Twelve games without a win.											
40	A	EVERTON		18	L	0-1	0-0		Sealey	Thomas	Roberts	Butterworth	Gillespie	Jacobs	Whitton	Francis	Hateley	H'mantsch'k	Melrose*	Hendrie
		2/5	*12,986*	*6*	45			*Sharp 76p*	*Southall*	*Stevens*	*Bailey*	*Ratcliffe*	*Higgins*	*Richardson*	*McMahon*	*Johnson**	*Sharp*	*Heath*	*Sheedy*	*Irvine*
								Ref: A Challinor	Thirteen games without a win is City's worst run in Div 1 and Thomas' 25-yarder - which Southall tips over - is their only shot. The penalty is rough luck as the ball bounces up and hits Butterworth on the arm. Everton's lowest ever Division 1 crowd is proof of the sport's problems.											
41	A	STOKE		17	W	3-0	1-0	Hateley 20, Hendrie 49, Thomas 81	Sealey	Thomas	Roberts	H'mantsch'k	Butterworth	Gillespie	Whitton	Francis	Hateley	Hendrie	Hunt	
		7/5	*12,048*	*11*	48				*Fox*	*Bould*	*Hampton*	*Bracewell*	*O'Callaghan**	*Maguire*	*Painter*	*McIlroy*	*Griffiths*	*Thomas*	*Chamberl'n M*	*Heath P*
								Ref: E Chadwick	Hill has resigned and Jamieson is the new chairman. The first win in fourteen ensures safety and a massive following of fans roars City home. Hendrie's enthusiasm peps City's attack and he sets up Hateley before scoring himself. Thomas clinches it as injury-hit Stoke go for broke.											
42	H	WEST HAM		19	L	2-4	0-1	Hendrie 55, Whitton 75	Sealey	Thomas	Roberts	H'mantsch'k	Butterworth	Gillespie	Whitton	Singleton	Hateley	Hendrie	Hunt	
		14/5	11,214	*8*	48			*Goddard 8, Cottee 54, 88, Swind' 60*	*Parkes*	*Stewart*	*Lampard*	*Bonds*	*Orr*	*Devonshire*	*Van der Elst*	*Goddard*	*Swindlehurst*	*Allen*	*Pike**	*Cottee*
		Home / Away						Ref: B Newsome	Sexton's reign ends as rumours fly that Gould will take over. In an open game City leave themselves vulnerable at the back and Les Sealey's display is unsatisfactory. West Ham's finishing is ruthless, especially substitute Tony Cottee, who scores his second as City look like saving it.											
		Average 10,479	17,850																	

Milk Cup						F-A	H-T	Scorers, Times, and Referees	1	2	3	4	5	6	7	8	9	10	11	12 sub used
2:1	A	FULHAM		13	D	2-2	2-2	Melrose 9, 32	Sealey	Thomas	H'mantsch'k	Butterworth	Dyson	Gillespie	Whitton	Jacobs	Melrose	Thompson G	Hunt	
5/10			*6,237*	*2:5*				*Gale 39, Brown 43*	*Peyton*	*Hopkins*	*Lock*	*O'Driscoll*	*Brown*	*Gale*	*Davies*	*Wilson*	*Coney*	*Houghton*	*Lewington*	
								Ref: M Bodenham	Malcolm Macdonald's Fulham are setting Division Two alight after last season's promotion and have some outstanding kids. They fight back with goals from Gale and former AP Leamington defender Brown. Thompson is booked for the fifth time and Jim Melrose continues to score.											
2:2	H	FULHAM		16	D	0-0	0-0		Sealey	Thomas	Roberts	Butterworth	Dyson	Gillespie	Jacobs	Francis*	Melrose	Thompson G	Hunt	Whitton
26/10			8,249	*2:1*		*aet*			*Peyton*	*Hopkins*	*Parker*	*O'Driscoll*	*Brown*	*Gale*	*Reeves**	*Carr*	*Coney*	*Houghton*	*Lewington*	*Scott*
								Ref: R Milford (City win on away-goals rule)	Fulham look good bets for promotion and City and their fans are relieved at the end. Les Sealey, Gerry Francis and Jim Melrose are casualties in an endurance test. The Sky Blues can't turn their domination into goals in normal time but just survive as Fulham dominate extra-time.											
3	H	BURNLEY		11	L	1-2	1-1	Hunt 5	Suckling	Thomas	Roberts	Butterworth	Dyson	Gillespie	Hendrie*	Singleton	Melrose	Thompson G	Hunt	Whitton
9/11			7,437	*2:20*				*McGee 43, 69*	*Stevenson*	*Laws*	*Cassidy*	*Phelan*	*Holt*	*Scott*	*Dobson*	*Steven*	*Taylor*	*McGee*	*Young*	
								Ref: T Bune	Burnley have lost nine out of ten but take advantage of a disgraceful display from the Sky Blues. It is arguably the worst since promotion and in the last 20 minutes Burnley could have scored another three. Trevor Stevens is Burnley's inspiration, along with an overweight Cassidy.											

FA Cup						F-A	H-T	Scorers, Times, and Referees	1	2	3	4	5	6	7	8	9	10	11	12 sub used
3	H	WORCESTER		6	W	3-1	2-1	Whitton 30p, 85, Hateley 36	Sealey	Thomas	H'mantsch'k	Butterworth	Dyson	Gillespie	Whitton	Francis	Hateley	Melrose	Hunt	
8/1			11,881	*AP:17*				*Moss 18p*	*Parkes*	*Selby*	*Hunt*	*Phelps*	*Tudor**	*Hughes*	*Williams B*	*Williams J*	*Tuohy*	*Crompton*	*Moss*	*Brown*
								Ref: C Downey	The first non-league visitors since Kings Lynn in 1961 and City make heavy weather of the Alliance Premier side, managed by Nobby Clark. Sealey pushes Jimmy Williams and Malcolm Phelps handles for the penalties. Steve Whitton makes sure of victory with a right-foot volley.											
4	H	NORWICH		5	D	2-2	1-0	Thompson G 40, Roberts 65	Sealey	Thomas	Roberts	H'mantsch'k	Dyson	Gillespie	Whitton	Francis	Hateley	Thompson G	Hunt	
29/1			13,083	*20*				*Hareide 70, Barham 87*	*Woods*	*Hareide*	*Downs*	*Mendham*	*Walford*	*Watson*	*Barham*	*O'Neill*	*Deehan*	*Bertschin*	*Van Wyk*	
								Ref: B Hill	The never-say-die Canaries come back from the grave to snatch a replay. On-loan Aage Hareide's looks offside and Mark Barham pounces on Francis's mistake. Thompson had scored from Whitton's cross and Roberts scores again. Thomas plays in midfield and Hunt has lost his fizz.											
4R	A	NORWICH		5	L	1-2	1-0	Hateley 3	Sealey	Thomas	Roberts	Butterworth	Dyson	Gillespie	Whitton	Jacobs	Hateley	Thompson G !	Hunt*	Melrose
2/2			*18,625*	*20*		*aet*		*Bertschin 50, Roberts 98 (og)*	*Woods*	*Hareide*	*Downs*	*Mendham*	*Walford*	*Watson*	*Barham*	*O'Neill**	*Deehan*	*Bertschin*	*Van Wyk*	*Haylock*
								Ref: B Hill	City throw it away in extra-time after being in control for most of the game. Sealey can't hold Hareide's shot and Bertschin scores. Roberts' own-goal seals City's fate, although he believes Barham handles. Thompson is sent off in the 95th minute for fouls on Hareide and Downs.											

		P	Home W	D	L	F	A	Away W	D	L	F	A	Pts
1	Liverpool	42	16	4	1	55	16	8	6	7	32	21	82
2	Watford	42	16	2	3	49	20	6	3	12	25	37	71
3	Manchester U	42	14	7	0	39	10	5	6	10	17	28	70
4	Tottenham	42	15	4	2	50	15	5	5	11	15	35	69
5	Nott'm Forest	42	12	5	4	34	18	8	4	9	28	32	69
6	Aston Villa	42	17	2	2	47	15	4	3	14	15	35	68
7	Everton	42	13	6	2	43	19	5	4	12	23	29	64
8	West Ham	42	13	3	5	41	23	7	1	13	27	39	64
9	Ipswich	42	11	3	7	39	23	4	10	7	25	27	58
10	Arsenal	42	11	6	4	36	19	5	4	12	22	37	58
11	West Brom	42	11	5	5	35	20	4	7	10	16	29	57
12	Southampton	42	11	5	5	36	22	4	7	10	18	36	57
13	Stoke	42	13	4	4	34	21	3	5	13	19	43	57
14	Norwich	42	10	6	5	30	18	4	6	11	22	40	54
15	Notts Co	42	12	4	5	37	25	3	3	15	18	46	52
16	Sunderland	42	7	10	4	30	22	5	4	12	18	39	50
17	Birmingham	42	9	7	5	29	24	3	7	11	11	31	50
18	Luton	42	7	7	7	34	33	5	6	10	31	51	49
19	COVENTRY	42	10	5	6	29	17	3	4	14	19	42	48
20	Manchester C	42	9	5	7	26	23	4	3	14	21	47	47
21	Swansea	42	10	4	7	32	29	0	7	14	19	40	41
22	Brighton	42	8	7	6	25	22	1	6	14	13	46	40
			255	111	96	810	454	96	111	255	454	810	1275

Odds & ends

Double wins: (2) Luton, Stoke.
Double losses: (4) Arsenal, Nott'm Forest, Birmingham, West Brom.

Won from behind: (1) Worcester (FAC).
Lost from in front: (6) Swansea (a), Manchester C (a), Nott'm F (h&a). Burnley (LC), Norwich (FAC).

High spots: Christmas victory over Manchester U.
Danny Thomas becomes first England international since Reg Matthews.

Low spots: Milk Cup defeat by Third Division Burnley.
13 games without a win in spring - equals worst spell since the War.
Realisation that eight first team players were out of contract.
Average attendance falls by another 2,500.

Red cards: City – Thomas (Swansea a), Thompson (Norwich FAC a), Jacobs (Brighton a).
Red cards: Opponents – Ramsey (Brighton a).
Player of the Year: Gary Gillespie.
Ever-presents: (1) Gary Gillespie.
Hat-tricks: (1) Jim Melrose.
Opposing hat-tricks: (2) Brooke (Tottenham), Rush (Liverpool).
Leading scorer: (14) Steve Whitton.

	Appearances Lge	*Sub*	LC	*Sub*	FAC	*Sub*	Goals Lge	LC	FAC	Tot
Butterworth, Ian	**26**	*4*	3		2					
Daly, Gerry	**2**									
Dyson, Paul	**39**		3		3		**1**			**1**
Francis, Gerry	**32**		1		2		**1**			**1**
Gillespie, Gary	**42**		3		3		**2**			**2**
Hall, Derek	**1**									
Hateley, Mark	**35**				3		**9**		2	**11**
Hendrie, John	**8**	*4*	1				**2**			**2**
H'mantsch'k, Peter	**10**	*1*	1		2		**1**			**1**
Hunt, Steve	**35**		3		3		**4**	1		**5**
Jacobs, Steve	**30**	*2*	2		1					
Melrose, Jim	**21**	*3*	3		1	*1*	**8**	2		**10**
Roberts, Brian	**38**		2		2		**1**		1	**2**
Sealey, Les	**39**		2		3					
Singleton, Martin	**3**	*2*	1							
Suckling, Perry	**3**		1							
Thomas, Danny	**41**		3		3		**3**			**3**
Thompson, Garry	**18**	*2*	3		2		**4**		1	**5**
Thompson, Keith	**2**	*3*								
Whitton, Steve	**37**	*1*	1	*2*	3		**12**		2	**14**
20 players used	**462**	***22***	**33**	***2***	**33**	***1***	**48**	**3**	**6**	**57**

No	Date		Att	Pos	Pt	F-A	H-T	Scorers, Times, and Referees	1	2	3	4	5	6	7	8	9	10	11	12 sub used
1	A	WATFORD			W	3-2	1-0	Bolton 9 (og), Rice 56 (og), Gibson 65	Suckling	H'mantschuk	Roberts	**Grimes**	Butterworth	Jacobs	**Gynn***	Daly	**Bamber**	**Gibson**	Thompson	**Platnauer**
	27/8		*15,533*		3			*Barnes 57, Jobson 90*	*Sherwood*	*Rice*	*Rostron*	*Taylor*	*Sims**	*Bolton*	*Callaghan*	*Gilligan*	*Terry*	*Lohman*	*Barnes*	*Jobson*
								Ref: M Taylor	Eight players have left and eleven joined in a summer clear-out. City are relegation favourites. On a hot afternoon, victory over last year's runners-up wins the Fiat performance of the week. Bolton turns in Gibson's cross, Rice chips Sherwood and Gibson scores sitting on his bum.											
2	A	TOTTENHAM			D	1-1	0-1	Withey 87	Suckling	H'mantschuk	Roberts	Singleton*	**Peake**	Jacobs	Grimes	Platnauer	Bamber	Gibson	**Adams**	**Withey**
	29/8		*35,854*		4			*Hoddle 27p*	*Clemence*	*Bowen*	*Thomas*	*Roberts*	*Stevens*	*Perryman*	*Mabbutt*	*Archibald*	*Galvin*	*Hoddle*	*Brazil**	*Falco*
								Ref: I Borrett	Injuries mean more new faces and a debut goal from Graham Withey, 24 minutes after coming on as sub. New skipper Harry Roberts is full of admiration for Gould, who keeps silent. Ashley Grimes handles for the penalty and City dominate the last 20 minutes and deserve the point.											
3	H	EVERTON		10	D	1-1	1-1	Adams 13	Suckling	H'mantschuk	Roberts	Grimes	Peake	Jacobs	Singleton*	Daly	Platnauer	Gibson	Adams	Withey
	3/9		12,229	*12*	5			*Sheedy 27*	*Arnold*	*Harper*	*Bailey*	*Ratcliffe*	*Higgins*	*Richardson*	*Steven*	*Heath**	*Sharp*	*King*	*Sheedy*	*Johnson*
								Ref: D Axcell	Who would have thought that Gould's team of misfits would be unbeaten after three games? In a battling display, City have chances to win after Sheedy's sensational 30-yard equaliser, but so do Everton, Adams clears off the line. Ex-Spurs man Gibson causes problems with his pace.											
4	H	NOTTS CO		4	W	2-1	0-1	Gibson 68, Platnauer 81	Suckling	H'mantschuk	Roberts	Grimes	Peake	Jacobs	Singleton*	Daly	Platnauer	Gibson	Adams	Withey
	6/9		11,016	*8*	8			*Fashanu 30*	*McDonagh*	*Lahtinen*	*Worthington*	*Goodwin*	*Kilcline*	*Hunt*	*Chiedozie*	*Fashanu*	*McCulloch*	*Harkouk*	*O'Neill*	
								Ref: T Bune	Larry Lloyd's County have already won 4-0 at Leicester and take the lead here. A gutsy fight-back has the crowd on their feet and Platnauer gets the winner off his knee after Gibson hammers in Micky Adams' cross. Former Man United midfielder Grimes runs midfield with panache.											
5	A	WEST HAM		7	L	2-5	2-3	Peake 10, Platnauer 15	Suckling	H'mantsc'k*	Roberts	Grimes	Peake	Jacobs	Butterworth	Withey	Platnauer	Gibson	Adams	Singleton
	10/9		*22,195*	*1*	8			*Swindleh'st 29, 32, 68, Whitton 30, 60*	*Parkes*	*Stewart*	*Walford*	*Bonds*	*Martin*	*Devonshire*	*Whitton*	*Cottee*	*Swindlehurst*	*Brooking*	*Pike*	
								Ref: A Crickmore	The Hammers maintain their 100% record and end City's run. Suckling saves Stewart's seventh minute penalty after Grimes handles. Old Boy Whitton scores twice and sets up one of Dave Swindlehurst's hat-trick. West Ham look worthy leaders, but City's defence has a lot to learn.											
6	H	LEICESTER		6	W	2-1	1-0	Platnauer 45, Gibson 68	**Avramovic**	H'mantschuk	Roberts	Butterworth	Peake	Jacobs	Withey	Daly	Platnauer	Gibson	Thompson*	**Bennett**
	17/9		12,771	*22*	11			*Lineker 89*	*Wallington*	*Ramsey*	*Smith B*	*MacDonald*	*O'Neill*	*Rennie*	*Jones*	*Lineker*	*Smith A*	*Peake**	*Wilson*	*Williams*
								Ref: D Reeves	Milne's newly promoted Leicester have lost six in a row but almost salvage a point. New keeper Yugoslav Raddy Avramovic makes an injury-time point-blank save. Former Bristol Rover Nicky Platnauer slams one home and Terry Gibson takes advantage of David Rennie's mistake.											
7	A	SUNDERLAND		11	L	0-1	0-0		Avramovic	H'mantschuk	Roberts	Butterworth	Peake	**Allardyce**	Withey	Daly	Platnauer	Gibson	Thompson*	Bennett
	24/9		*11,612*	*17*	11			*West 53*	*Turner*	*Venison*	*Hindmarch*	*Atkins*	*Chisholm*	*Procter*	*Bracewell*	*Rowell*	*West*	*Pickering*	*James**	*Cooke*
								Ref: C Seel	Former Sunderland star Allardyce makes a rusty debut, alongside the impressive Trevor Peake, but City lack ideas up front. Sunderland are no great shakes but win an uninteresting game after Rowell heads back James' free-kick for West to score. Turner makes a brave save from Daly.											
8	H	IPSWICH		14	L	1-2	0-2	Gibson 63	Avramovic	H'mantsch'k*	Roberts	Grimes	Peake	Allardyce	Withey	Daly	Platnauer	Gibson	Bennett	Hendrie
	1/10		10,477	*3*	11			*Mariner 33, O'Callaghan 35*	*Cooper*	*Burley*	*Gernon*	*Putney*	*Osman*	*Butcher*	*Wark*	*McCall*	*Mariner**	*Gates*	*O'Callaghan*	*D'Avray*
								Ref: N Glover	Allardyce is City's man of the match, despite a crunching early tackle on Mariner, which upsets Ipswich boss Ferguson. The England man gets up to squeeze in a header and Hormantschuk's mistake lets in O'Callaghan. Gibson scores after Withey hits the bar, as City steadily improve.											
9	A	ARSENAL		10	W	1-0	0-0	Bamber 47	Avramovic	Butterworth	Roberts	Singleton	Peake	Allardyce*	Bamber	Gibson	Platnauer	Grimes	Bennett	Withey
	15/10		*20,290*	*14*	14				*Jennings*	*Robson*	*Sansom*	*Whyte**	*O'Leary*	*Hill*	*Sunderland*	*Davis*	*Chapman*	*Nicholas*	*Rix*	*McDermott*
								Ref: A Gunn	City's first win in 13 visits to Highbury over ten years is a credit to Bamber. The ex-Blackpool man returns after a virus to play his first game since August and looks rusty. He scores the goal, volleying in Grimes' cross. £650,000 signing from Celtic, Charlie Nicholas, looks forlorn.											
10	H	WEST BROM		14	L	1-2	0-1	Withey 62	Avramovic	Roberts	Butterworth	Grimes	Peake	Allardyce	Gynn	Singleton*	Bamber	Gibson	Platnauer	Withey
	22/10		13,321	*9*	14			*Regis 36, Perry 68*	*Barron*	*Whitehead*	*Cowdrill*	*Lewis*	*McNaught*	*Bennett*	*Zondervan*	*Thompson*	*Regis**	*Owen*	*Perry*	*Robson*
								Ref: E Read	Albion win at Highfield Road for the third year running, thanks to a dreadful error by Avramovic, who lets Perry's shot through his legs. Regis earlier scored a beauty, before Withey scores two minutes after coming on. In his first start since the opening day, Michael Gynn is impressive.											

11	A	STOKE	10	W	3-1	2-1	Bennett 32, Gibson 36, Bamber 78	Avramovic	Roberts	Singleton	Grimes	Peake	Allardyce	Bennett	Gynn	Bamber	Gibson	Platnauer	
	29/10	*11,836*	*19*	17			*Thomas 41*	*Fox*	*Berry*	*Hampton*	*James*	*Dyson*	*McAughtrie*	*Tueart*	*McIlroy*	*O'Callaghan*	*Thomas*	*Chamberlain*	
							Ref: D Scott	Stoke have won only one in nine and are in for a long relegation battle. Bamber seals the win by foxing ex-City man Dyson on the touch line, beating two players and hitting a stunning left-footer. Dyson faulted for the second. The referee pulls a muscle after 10 mins, D Crone subs.											
12	A	BIRMINGHAM	9	W	2-1	1-1	Gibson 30, Bennett 60	Avramovic	Roberts	Platnauer	Singleton	Peake	Allardyce	Bennett	Gynn	Bamber	Gibson*	Grimes	Hunt
	5/11	*16,169*	*14*	20			*Blake 18*	*Coton*	*Hagan*	*v d Hauwe*	*Blake*	*Wright*	*Stevenson*	*Gayle*	*Phillips*	*Harford**	*Halsall*	*Hopkins*	*Rogers*
							Ref: J Lovatt	A courageous performance in a deserved win as City come from behind. Mick Harford is taken to hospital with facial injuries after a clash with Sam Allardyce. Steve Hunt makes his first appearance of the season, and two minutes later has a hand in Bennett's far-post volleyed winner.											
13	H	QP RANGERS	6	W	1-0	1-0	Bamber 11	Suckling	Roberts	**Pearce**	Grimes	Peake	Allardyce	Bennett	Gynn	Bamber	Hendrie*	Hunt	Platnauer
	12/11	11,796	*9*	23				*Hucker*	*Neill*	*Dawes*	*Waddock**	*McDonald*	*Fenwick*	*Micklewhite*	*Stewart*	*Sealy*	*Stainrod*	*Gregory*	*Flanagan*
							Ref: R Guy	The crowd are buzzing at the exciting debut of Stuart Pearce a £25,000 signing from Wealdstone. City deserve to win a superb match by more than Bamber's header from Hunt's corner. Peter Hucker makes a string of saves and Grimes hits the post as QPR's run of three away wins ends.											
14	A	WOLVES	5	D	0-0	0-0		Suckling	Roberts	Pearce	Grimes	Peake	Allardyce	Bennett	Gynn	Bamber	Gibson*	Hunt	Platnauer
	19/11	*11,419*	*22*	24				*Bradshaw*	*Humphrey*	*Rudge*	*Blair*	*Pender*	*Dodd*	*Hibbitt*	*Clarke*	*Cartwright*	*Mardenboro'*	*Crainie*	
							Ref: R Nixon	Wolves have yet to win and have picked up only four points, but stop City from getting a record fourth away win in a row. Gibson returns from suspension, but the attack is patchy against poor Wolves. Ex-City youth Steve Mardenborough almost snatches it for Graham Hawkins' men.											
15	H	SOUTHAMPTON	6	D	0-0	0-0		Suckling	Roberts	Pearce	Grimes	Peake	Allardyce	Bennett	Gynn	Bamber	Gibson*	Hunt !	Platnauer
	26/11	11,601	*8*	25				*Shilton*	*Rofe*	*Baker*	*Williams**	*Armstrong K*	*Whitlock*	*Holmes*	*Moran*	*Worthington*	*Armstrong D*	*Wallace*	*Juryeff*
							Ref: D Owen	In a sickening incident after 77 minutes Steve Williams kicks out at Steve Hunt, who head-butts the Saint and is ordered off with Williams on a stretcher. It had been a good 0-0 draw and Gould drools over Trevor Peake and Gynn. Shilton saves well from Hunt, and Williams hits the bar.											
16	A	LUTON	5	W	4-2	2-0	Gibson 35, 36, Gynn 67, Bennett 73	Suckling	Roberts	Pearce	Platnauer	Peake	Allardyce	Bennett	Gynn	Bamber	Gibson	Hunt	
	3/12	*10,698*	*10*	28			*Pearce 50 (og), Aylott 69*	*Sealey*	*Stephens*	*Turner*	*Horton*	*Elliott*	*Donaghy*	*Hill*	*Stein*	*Walsh*	*Aylott*	*Bunn**	*Antic*
							Ref: B Hill	Les Sealey is taunted by City's travelling army as he lets in four. Luton claw their way back, only to be caught by slick counter-punches and Gynn and Bennett score good goals. Pearce's goal is a powerful header from Turner's cross. Hunt is fined £750 and banned for two games.											
17	H	LIVERPOOL	4	W	**4-0**	3-0	Platnauer 1, Gibson 19, 45, 84	Avramovic	Roberts	Pearce	Platnauer	Peake	Allardyce	Bennett	Gynn	Bamber*	Gibson	Daly	Withey
	10/12	20,649	*1*	31				*Grobbelaar*	*Neal*	*Kennedy*	*Lawrenson*	*Nicol*	*Hansen*	*Dalglish*	*Lee*	*Rush*	*Whelan*	*Souness*	
							Ref: D Letts	The champions are humiliated by City's best display for years. Platnauer nets after 45 seconds, then Gibson scores his first ever hat-trick, the first conceded by Pool since Keith Weller in 1972. Reds boss Joe Fagan says City are title contenders on this form. Match of the Day sees it all.											
18	A	NORWICH	5	D	0-0	0-0		Avramovic	Roberts	Pearce	Daly	Peake	Allardyce	Bennett	Gynn	Bamber	Gibson	Platnauer	
	17/12	*16,646*	*9*	32				*Woods*	*Haylock*	*Downs*	*Mendham*	*Deehan*	*Watson*	*Donowa*	*Channon*	*Hareide**	*Bertschin*	*Van Wyk*	*Clayton*
							Ref: M James	City are unbeaten in eight, Norwich have won six in a row, and a storming games ends predictably goalless. The gritty Sky Blues hang on after Watson hits the bar with one header and Avramovic saves another. Canaries boss Ken Brown receives his Manager of the Month award.											
19	H	MANCHESTER U	7	D	1-1	1-1	Gibson 45p	Avramovic	Roberts	Pearce	Platnauer*	Peake	Allardyce	Bennett	Gynn	Bamber	Gibson	Daly	Grimes
	26/12	**21,553**	*2*	33			*Muhren 21p*	*Wealands*	*Duxbury*	*Albiston*	*Wilkins*	*Moran*	*McQueen*	*Moses*	*Muhren*	*Stapleton*	*Crooks*	*Graham*	
							Ref: R Milford	Allardyce is judged to have high-kicked dangerously on Moses, and Muhren nets from the spot. Wealands fouls Bamber and Gibson scores his first senior penalty. Bamber and Gibson are denied by Wealands as City dominate the second half. Gerry Daly plays well against his old club.											
20	A	NOTT'M FOREST	7	L	0-3	0-1		Avramovic	Roberts	Pearce	Daly	Peake	Allardyce	Bennett	Gynn	Withey*	Grimes	Platnauer	Butterworth
	28/12	*22,169*	*5*	33			*Davenport 26, Birtles 53, 84*	*v Breukelen*	*Anderson*	*Swain*	*Gunn*	*Fairclough*	*Bowyer*	*Wigley**	*Davenport*	*Birtles*	*Hodge*	*Walsh*	*Wallace*
							Ref: T Jones	Forest inflict City's first defeat in ten games with a superb display of finishing from Gary Birtles. Forest look title contenders. The Sky Blues badly miss the injured Gibson and the ill Bamber, but still have chances and the scoreline flatters Forest who are pinned back for long periods.											
21	A	EVERTON	8	D	0-0	0-0		Avramovic	Roberts	Pearce	Daly	Peake	Allardyce	Bennett	Hunt	Withey	Grimes	Platnauer	
	31/12	*13,659*	*16*	34				*Southall*	*Stevens*	*Bailey*	*Ratcliffe*	*Mountfield*	*Reid*	*Irvine*	*Heath**	*Gray*	*King*	*Sheedy*	*Richardson*
							Ref: K Hackett	Finding the highlights of this drab game could not have been an easy task for the Match of the Day editors. In 18 months time Everton fans will look back at this period and define it as a watershed in their club's history, but right now the supporters are upset and the crowd figure shows it.											

LEAGUE DIVISION 1 — Manager: Bobby Gould — SEASON 1983-84

No	Date			Att	Pos	Pt	F-A	H-T	Scorers, Times, and Referees	1	2	3	4	5	6	7	8	9	10	11	12 sub used
22		H	SUNDERLAND		6	W	2-1	2-0	Withey 20, Daly 27	Avramovic	Roberts	Pearce	Platnauer	Butterworth	Jacobs	Bennett	Daly	Withey	Grimes*	Hunt	Gynn
	2/1			13,157	*13*	37			*West 50*	*Turner*	*Munro*	*Pickering*	*Atkins*	*Chisholm*	*Elliott*	*Bracewell*	*Chapman*	*West*	*Procter**	*Rowell*	*Robson*
									Ref: E Scales	An exciting match played in driving wind and rain on a pitch Sunderland boss Alan Durban calls a farce. City make the most of the wind in the first half, when Withey heads in and Daly nets his first goal for two years. West's goal looks ominous, but City's makeshift defence holds out.											
23		H	WATFORD		6	L	1-2	1-1	Peake 42	Avramovic	Roberts	Pearce	Gynn	Peake	Butterworth	Bennett	Hunt	Platnauer	Gibson*	Adams	Daly
	14/1			12,422	*16*	37			*Sherwood 12, Reilly 90*	*Sherwood*	*Bardsley*	*Rostron*	*Taylor*	*Sims*	*Franklin*	*Callaghan*	*Johnston*	*Reilly*	*Jackett*	*Barnes*	
									Ref: L Shapter	City are blown off course at windswept Highfield Road by Steve Sherwood's freak goal. Callaghan and Avramovic both jump at his mighty kick but Raddy misses his punch and the ball sails in. Raddy is also caught in two minds with the cross that earns Watford's undeserved winner.											
24		A	LEICESTER		8	D	1-1	1-0	Daly 10	Avramovic	Roberts	Pearce	Bennett	Peake	Butterworth	Daly	Hunt	Withey	Adams	Platnauer	
	21/1			*16,262*	*18*	38			*Lineker 79*	*Wallington*	*Smith B*	*Wilson*	*MacDonald*	*Hazell*	*O'Neill*	*Lynex*	*Lineker*	*Smith A*	*Ramsey*	*Banks*	
									Ref: J Worrall	A fair result from a match played on a frost-bound pitch. City deserve their early lead when Daly hits a dipping volley from 20-yards. Leicester come back strongly after the break, but the defence, with Peake and Stuart Pearce supreme, hold out after Gary Lineker's scrambled goal.											
25		A	IPSWICH		8	L	1-3	0-2	Gibson 71	Avramovic	Roberts	Adams	Gynn*	Peake	Butterworth	Bennett	Gibson	Bamber	Hunt	Pearce	Platnauer
	4/2			*13,406*	*15*	38			*Mariner 13, Brennan 16, Dozzell 89*	*Cooper*	*Burley*	*McCall*	*Putney*	*Osman*	*Butcher*	*Wark*	*Brennan*	*Mariner*	*Gates**	*O'Callaghan*	*Dozzell*
									Ref: K Salmon	It's 13 years since the Sky Blues won at Portman Road and current form suggested the run might end. Despite Gates going off injured and Paul Mariner a passenger from the half hour Ipswich coast home. Gibson offers hope but 16-year-old Dozzell is the youngest ever Division 1 scorer.											
26		H	WEST HAM		10	L	1-2	0-1	Hunt 90	Avramovic	Roberts	Pearce	Daly	Peake	Allardyce	Bennett	Hunt	Bamber	Gibson	Grimes	
	11/2			13,290	*3*	38			*Bamber 19 (og), Cottee 75*	*Parkes*	*Stewart*	*Lampard*	*Walford*	*Orr*	*Brush*	*Barnes*	*Cottee*	*Swindlehurst*	*Allen*	*Dickins*	
									Ref: L Burden	City's post-Xmas slump is gathering speed, with one win in nine since the Liverpool win. Bamber can't get out the way of Cottee's header and Cottee breaks clear at the height of City's brave fightback. Phil Parkes makes some stunning saves before Hunt hits a 25-yarder in injury-time.											
27		H	STOKE		10	L	2-3	1-1	Bennett 8, Gibson 58	Avramovic	Roberts	Pearce*	Gynn	Peake	Allardyce	Bennett	Hunt	Thompson	Gibson	Grimes	Withey
	18/2			9,756	*20*	38			*Hampton 42, Chamb' 67, O'Callag' 81*	*Fox*	*Bould*	*Hampton*	*James**	*Dyson*	*O'Callaghan*	*Maskery*	*McIlroy*	*Maguire*	*Hudson*	*Chamberlain*	*Painter*
									Ref: J Martin	Struggling Stoke, managed by former City coach Bill Asprey, are handed the points by dreadful errors from Avramovic. Gould publicly blames his keeper. It is Stoke's first away win for a year and the rogue ref upsets City and Allardyce in particular. Pearce limps off after 35 minutes.											
28		A	WEST BROM		12	D	1-1	0-0	Gibson 69	Suckling	Roberts	Adams	Gynn*	Peake	Allardyce	Grimes	Hunt	Bennett	Gibson	Singleton	Withey
	25/2			*10,900*	*19*	39			*Cross 47*	*Barron*	*Ebbanks*	*Statham*	*Zondervan*	*McNaught*	*Bennett*	*Jol*	*Thompson*	*Cross*	*MacKenzie*	*Morley*	
									Ref: P Tyldesley	Gould has sacked Avramovic after last week. Suckling faces Albion under boss Johnny Giles, who has replaced Ron Wylie. City come from behind to gain a valuable point with Gibson's 17th of the season in a drab game. The striker is given a rough ride by McNaught and Bennett.											
29		H	BIRMINGHAM		13	L	0-1	0-1		Suckling	Roberts	Adams	Withey	Peake	Butterworth	Grimes	Hunt	Bennett	Gibson	Singleton*	Bamber
	3/3			13,696	*14*	39			*Gayle 26*	*Coton*	*McCarrick*	*v d Hauwe**	*Blake*	*Wright*	*Broadhurst*	*Gayle*	*Kuhl*	*Harford*	*Stevenson*	*Hopkins*	*Hagan*
									Ref: C Downey	Ron Saunders' Blues are unbeaten in twelve and pulling out of trouble. They outclass and outfight an abject City, who lose their fourth home game in a row. Howard Gayle wins it with a swerving rocket after an Adams and Bennett mix-up. Suckling saves City from a bigger defeat.											
30		A	QP RANGERS		13	L	1-2	1-0	Daly 41p	Suckling	Roberts	Adams	Daly	Peake	Butterworth	Grimes	Bamber	Bennett	Gibson*	Singleton	Withey
	10/3			*10,284*	*6*	39			*Stainrod 78, Allen 84*	*Hucker*	*Neill*	*Dawes*	*Waddock*	*McDonald*	*Fenwick*	*Micklewhite*	*Stewart*	*Allen*	*Stainrod*	*Gregory*	
									Ref: A Gunn	QPR are back in Div 1 with their synthetic pitch, having lost only two games on it all season. Steve Hunt is rested as a transfer looms. Fenwick brings down Gibson for the penalty before Rangers' second half pressure pays off. The bounce beats Suckling for the first, but Allen's is a gem.											
31		H	ASTON VILLA		13	D	3-3	2-2	Daly 12, Allardyce 37, Gibson 76	Suckling	Jacobs	Adams	Daly	Peake	Allardyce	Bennett	Thompson*	Bamber	Gibson	Grimes	Hunt
	13/3			11,106	*12*	40			*Evans 17p, Withe 23, Rideout 46*	*Spink**	*Williams*	*Gibson*	*Evans*	*Ormsby*	*Curbishley*	*Birch*	*Walters*	*Withe*	*McMahon*	*Rideout*	*Walker*
									Ref: D Vickers	The match has everything. Walters torments City. He is fouled by Jacobs for the Villa penalty and denied another when tripped by Allardyce. In a frenzied finish Withe, in goal for the last 22 minutes for Nigel Spink, who was knocked out by Bennett, fails to keep out Gibson's shot.											

No	Venue	Opponent / Att	Pos	Res / Pts	FT	HT	Scorers, Times, and Referees	1	2	3	4	5	6	7	8	9	10	11	12 sub used
32	A	NOTTS COUNTY	13	L	1-2	0-0	Peake 86	Suckling	Jacobs	Adams	Daly*	Peake	Allardyce	Bennett	Grimes	Bamber	Gibson	Thompson	Butterworth
17/3		***6,564***	*21*	40			*O'Neill 65, Christie 81p*	*Leonard*	*Hodson*	*Clarke*	*Richards*	*Armstrong*	*Hunt*	*O'Neill*	*McCulloch*	*Christie*	*Mair*	*Chiedozie*	
							Ref: K Redfern	County are going down and this is their first home win since December. City play well but the finishing is woeful. The Magpies take advantage with an O'Neill volley and a penalty, when Christie is felled by Peake. Hunt has transferred to WBA and Harry Roberts to Birmingham City.											
33	H	TOTTENHAM	16	L	2-4	0-2	Withey 46, Daly 76p	Suckling	Jacobs	Pearce	Daly	Peake	Allardyce	Bennett	Grimes*	Withey	**Langley**	Butterworth	Adams
24/3		12,847	*9*	40			*Brazil 30p, 44, Roberts 50, Hazard 79*	*Clemence*	*Thomas*	*Hughton*	*Roberts*	*Miller*	*Perryman*	*Hazard*	*Archibald*	*Brazil*	*Stevens*	*Galvin*	
							Ref: R Dilkes	City are sliding towards the drop-zone. Without a win in eleven they are outclassed by Spurs. The old boy Thomas plays well but Brazil is the hero, scoring from the spot after Grimes fouls Perryman, then pouncing on Grimes' weak header. City's penalty is for Roberts' foul on Bennett.											
34	H	ARSENAL	17	L	1-4	1-1	Bennett 32 *[Mariner 86]*	Suckling	Butterworth	Pearce	Daly	Peake	Allardyce	Bennett	Singleton*	Platnauer	Gibson	Adams	Withey
31/3		10,533	*8*	40			*Whyte 39, Robson 49, Talbot 69,*	*Jennings**	*Hill*	*Sparrow*	*Talbot*	*O'Leary*	*Whyte !*	*Robson*	*Nicholas*	*Mariner*	*Woodcock*	*Rix*	*Kay*
							Ref: D Shaw	After 57 minutes, with Arsenal leading 2-1, Jennings goes off with a face injury inflicted by Bennett's challenge. Stewart Robson goes in goal. Arsenal score two more and have Chris Whyte sent off for retaliating to Withey. City are only four points off the danger area and it looks grim.											
35	A	ASTON VILLA	17	L	0-2	0-1		Suckling	Butterworth	Pearce	Daly	Peake*	Jacobs	Bennett	Singleton	Platnauer	Gibson	Langley	Grimes
7/4		*15,318*	*9*	40			*Ormsby 34, Birch 46*	*Day*	*Williams*	*Deacy*	*Evans*	*Ormsby*	*Mortimer*	*Bremner*	*Birch*	*Blair*	*McMahon*	*Walters*	
							Ref: B Stevens	It's 13 games without a win, equalling the City's Div 1 record, and a super-human effort is needed to pull out of this nose-dive. Peake captains in Allardyce's absence. It is Villa's lowest crowd since they were promoted in 1975. On-loan striker Langley is dire, so Ferguson joins on loan.											
36	H	WOLVES	16	W	2-1	1-1	Daly 6p, Ferguson 86	Suckling	Butterworth	Pearce	Daly	Allardyce	Jacobs	Adams	Grimes	Ferguson	Gibson	Platnauer	
14/4		**8,433**	*22*	43			*Livingstone 40*	*Burridge*	*Buckland*	*Palmer*	*Cartwright*	*Pender*	*Dodd*	*Hibbitt*	*Clarke**	*Livingstone*	*Rudge*	*Crainie*	*Towner*
							Ref: M Dimblebee	Ferguson hasn't played in Division 1 for over a year but pops up with the headed winner to end City's bad run and almost consign Wolves to the drop. Daly scores from the spot after Dodd handles but Coventry-born Billy Livingstone snatches a scrappy goal. A pitifully low crowd.											
37	H	NOTT'M FOREST	14	W	2-1	1-0	Ferguson 8, Platnauer 79	Suckling	Butterworth	Adams	Daly	Allardyce	Jacobs	Grimes	Platnauer	Ferguson	Gibson*	Bennett	Gynn
17/4		9,816	*3*	46			*Walsh 85*	*v Breukelen*	*Anderson*	*Swain*	*Fairclough*	*Hart*	*Bowyer*	*Wigley*	*Mills*	*Davenport*	*Hodge*	*Walsh*	
							Ref: T Ward	Another header from Ferguson sets City up for the second win in four days, and the relegation fears subside. Forest's title hopes are as good as finished although they push City hard and Walsh scores from Wigley's cross. It is a hard-won victory and the best performance since Xmas.											
38	A	MANCHESTER U	15	L	1-4	0-1	Daly 74	Suckling	Butterworth	Adams*	Daly	Allardyce	Jacobs	Bennett	Grimes	Ferguson	Gynn	Platnauer	Gibson
21/4		***38,524***	*2*	46			*Hughes 41, 77, McGrath 51, Wilkins 60*	*Bailey*	*Duxbury*	*Albiston*	*Wilkins**	*Moran*	*Hogg*	*McGrath*	*Moses*	*Stapleton*	*Hughes*	*Graham*	*Whiteside*
							Ref: D Hutchinson	Utd keep the pressure on Liverpool in the title race; they are two points behind with five games to play. The Sky Blues keep the deficit down to one at the break but, attacking the Stretford End in the second half, Ray Wilkins inspires United to a convincing victory. City appear to cave in.											
39	A	SOUTHAMPTON	17	L	**2-8**	0-2	Grimes 66, Gynn 87 *[Worth' 69]*	Suckling	Butterworth	Pearce	Daly	**McGrath***	Jacobs	Gibson	Grimes	Ferguson	Gynn	Platnauer	Hendrie
28/4		*16,746*	*4*	46			*Arm' 28, Wal' 36, 64, 85, Mor' 57, 75, 81,*	*Shilton*	*Mills*	*Golac*	*Curtis**	*Whitlock*	*Wright*	*Holmes*	*Moran*	*Worthington*	*Armstrong D*	*Wallace*	*Puckett*
							Ref: H King	Saints inflict City's biggest defeat since 1930, with six goals coming in the second half. Gibson and Ferguson hit the post, Gibson before Saints have scored, but the Sky Blues are annihilated and could have let in ten. Lloyd McGrath has a nightmare debut as the rookie defence collapses.											
40	H	LUTON	18	D	2-2	1-0	Platnauer 4, Gibson 79	Suckling	Butterworth	Pearce	Daly	Allardyce	Jacobs	Bennett	Grimes*	Ferguson	Gibson	Platnauer	Gynn
5/5		9,647	*13*	47			*Antic 62, Stein 75*	*Sealey*	*Stephens*	*Thomas*	*Horton*	*Goodyear*	*Donaghy*	*Parker*	*Stein*	*Walsh*	*Bunn*	*Antic*	
							Ref: R Bridges	Gibson hadn't netted for six games but scores a vital equaliser, which could be the most precious goal he's scored for the club. With a trip to Anfield to come, and likely to be pointless, this was a 'must win' game. Antic, direct from a free-kick, and Stein look to have doomed City.											
41	A	LIVERPOOL	19	L	0-5	0-2		Suckling	Butterworth	Pearce	Daly	Allardyce	Jacobs	Bennett	Platnauer	Ferguson*	Gibson	Gynn	**Spring**
7/5		*33,393*	*1*	47			*Rush 43, 45, 57p, 82, Hansen 71*	*Grobbelaar*	*Neal*	*Kennedy*	*Lawrenson*	*Whelan*	*Hansen*	*Dalglish*	*Lee*	*Rush*	*Wark*	*Souness*	
							Ref: A Challinor	A predictable result as Ian Rush follows his hat-trick last year with four, including a penalty when Suckling brings him down, taking Rush's total for the season to 47. City have conceded 17 in the last three away games and look ready to go down. The Reds need one point for the title.											
42	H	NORWICH	19	W	2-1	1-1	Ferguson 37, Bennett 70	Suckling	Butterworth	Pearce	Daly*	Allardyce	Jacobs	Bennett	Gynn	Ferguson	Gibson	Platnauer	Grimes
12/5		13,892	*17*	50			*Deehan 35p*	*Woods*	*Haylock*	*Spearing*	*Mendham*	*Downs*	*Watson*	*Devine*	*Farrington*	*Deehan**	*Rosario*	*Van Wyk*	*Goss*
	Home	Away					Ref: N Ashley	City, Blues and Stoke start level, with Blues having the best goal-difference. Until Bennett's winner, direct from a corner, City were down. Birmingham draw 0-0 with Saints, though a late goal from them would have sent City down. In the 86th minute Rosario's header hits the bar.											
Average	12,587	17,594																	

LEAGUE DIVISION 1 (CUP-TIES)

Manager: Bobby Gould

SEASON 1983-84

Milk Cup					F-A	H-T	Scorers, Times, and Referees	1	2	3	4	5	6	7	8	9	10	11	12 sub used
2:1	A	GRIMSBY	14	D	0-0	0-0		Avramovic	Allardyce	Roberts	Singleton	Peake	Jacobs	Platnauer	Withey	Grimes	Gibson	Bennett	
	4/10	*6,088*	*2:14*					*Batch*	*Cumming*	*Crombie*	*Waters*	*Nicholl*	*Moore*	*Ford*	*Wilkinson*	*Drinkell*	*Henshaw*	*Emson*	
							Ref: D Hutchinson	A scrappy game, lacking class at a blustery Blundell Park, ends in a tame draw. Sam Allardyce and ex-Lincoln man Peake snuff out the much vaunted Kevin Drinkell. At the other end Gibson struggles against the big ex-Villa man Nicholl. City sign Wealdstone full-back Stuart Pearce.											
2:2	H	GRIMSBY	14	W	2-1	1-0	Bennett 9, Grimes 84	Avramovic	Roberts	Platnauer	Gynn	Peake	Allardyce	Bennett	Singleton	Bamber	Gibson !	Grimes	
	25/10	8,652	*2:8*				*Wilkinson 55*	*Batch*	*Cumming*	*Crombie*	*Waters*	*Nicholl !*	*Moore*	*Ford*	*Wilkinson*	*Drinkell*	*Bonnyman*	*Emson*	
							Ref: J Hough (City win 2-1 on aggregate)	With extra-time looming, there is a dramatic finish. Grimes scores from Bennett's low centre and several other chances are missed before the last minute red cards. Gibson retaliates to Nicholl's elbow to the head, and Nicholl gets a second yellow card for a foul on Martin Singleton.											
3	A	EVERTON	9	L	1-2	0-0	Bamber 50	Suckling	Roberts	Platnauer	Gynn	Peake	Allardyce	Bennett	Hunt	Bamber	Grimes	Hendrie*	Singleton
	9/11	*9,080*	*17*				*Heath 77, Sharp 90*	*Southall*	*Harper*	*Bailey*	*Ratcliffe*	*Higgins*	*Stevens**	*Irvine*	*Heath*	*Sharp*	*King*	*Sheedy*	*Reid*
							Ref: A Challinor	Beleagured Howard Kendall is probably 13 minutes away from the sack when Everton's second-half pressure finally pays. Two minutes injury-time have been played when the winner arrives. City dominate the first half and deserve more than Dave Bamber's header from Hunt's cross.											

FA Cup																			
3	H	WOLVES	6	D	1-1	1-1	Withey 6	Avramovic	Roberts*	Adams	Daly	Peake	Allardyce	Bennett	Hunt	Withey	Gibson	Platnauer	Gynn
	7/1	15,986	*22*				*Clarke 17*	*Burridge*	*Humphrey*	*Palmer*	*Daniel*	*Pender*	*Dodd*	*Towner*	*Clarke*	*Troughton*	*Eves*	*Crainie*	
							Ref: J Martin	City make heavy weather of struggling Wolves, but unlike Man United, Forest and Arsenal, they are still in the Cup. They have Raddy Avramovic to thank, he saves Wayne Clarke's 77th-minute penalty, controversially awarded when Allardyce is adjudged to have fouled Clarke.											
3R	A	WOLVES	6	D	1-1	0-0	Peake 85	Avramovic	Roberts	Adams	Gynn	Butterworth	Peake	Bennett	Hunt	Withey*	Platnauer	Gibson	Daly
	10/1	*19,204*	*22*		*aet*		*Eves 69*	*Burridge*	*Humphrey*	*Palmer*	*Daniel*	*Pender*	*Dodd*	*Towner*	*Clarke*	*Troughton*	*Eves*	*Crainie*	
							Ref: J Martin	No result after 210 minutes of disappointing play, although City leave it late to equalise. Peake drives in at the far post from a Platnauer corner after Mel Eves had taken advantage of Roberts' mistake. City dominate extra-time and Bobby Gould wins the toss to decide the next venue.											
3R R	H	WOLVES	6	W	3-0	2-0	Withey 25, 67, Hunt 43	Avramovic	Roberts	Adams	Gynn	Peake	Butterworth	Daly	Hunt	Withey	Thompson	Platnauer	
	16/1	17,482	*22*					*Burridge*	*Humphrey*	*Palmer*	*Daniel*	*Pender*	*Dodd*	*Towner*	*Clarke**	*Troughton*	*Eves*	*Crainie*	*Mardenboro'*
							Ref: D Shaw	Amazingly, Wolves won at Anfield on Saturday, but they make no impression on Hunt-inspired City. Graham Withey is the hero, scoring a header from Roberts' cross and a tap-in when Burridge fails to hold Steve Hunt's shot. Burridge doesn't move for Hunt's goal from 25 yards.											
4	A	SHEFFIELD WED	8	L	2-3	2-1	Gibson 18, 25	Avramovic	Roberts	Adams	Butterworth	Peake	Hunt	Bennett	Daly	Withey*	Platnauer	Gibson	Bamber
	30/1	*26,154*	*2:2*				*Shirtliff 22, Bannister 76, Sterland 80p*	*Hodge*	*Sterland*	*Shirtliff**	*Smith*	*Lyons*	*Madden*	*Megson*	*Bannister*	*Varadi*	*Pearson*	*Shelton*	*Cunningham*
							Ref: D Hutchinson	City protest that the referee is Yorkshire-based, for his penalty decision is dubious. The ball hits Butterworth's arm but he says he was pushed. City lead until 14 minutes from time and are unlucky to go out to the Second Division pacemakers. Ex-City man Bannister scores for the Owls.											

		P	W	D	L	F	A	W	D	L	F	A	Pts
			Home					Away					
1	Liverpool	42	14	5	2	50	12	8	9	4	23	20	80
2	Southampton	42	15	4	2	44	17	7	7	7	22	21	77
3	Nott'm Forest	42	14	4	3	47	17	8	4	9	29	28	74
4	Manchester U	42	14	3	4	43	18	6	11	4	28	23	74
5	QP Rangers	42	14	4	3	37	12	8	3	10	30	25	73
6	Arsenal	42	10	5	6	41	29	8	4	9	33	31	63
7	Everton	42	9	9	3	21	12	7	5	9	23	30	62
8	Tottenham	42	11	4	6	31	24	6	6	9	33	41	61
9	West Ham	42	10	4	7	39	24	7	5	9	21	31	60
10	Aston Villa	42	14	3	4	34	22	3	6	12	25	39	60
11	Watford	42	9	7	5	36	31	7	2	12	32	46	57
12	Ipswich	42	11	4	6	34	23	4	4	13	21	34	53
13	Sunderland	42	8	9	4	26	18	5	4	12	16	35	52
14	Norwich	42	9	8	4	34	20	3	7	11	14	29	51
15	Leicester	42	11	5	5	40	30	2	7	12	25	38	51
16	Luton	42	7	5	9	30	33	7	4	10	23	33	51
17	West Brom	42	10	4	7	30	25	4	5	12	18	37	51
18	Stoke	42	11	4	6	30	23	2	7	12	14	40	50
19	COVENTRY	42	8	5	8	33	33	5	6	10	24	44	50
20	Birmingham	42	7	7	7	19	18	5	5	11	20	32	48
21	Notts Co	42	6	7	8	31	36	4	4	13	19	36	41
22	Wolves	42	4	8	9	15	28	2	3	16	12	52	29
		924	226	118	118	745	505	118	118	226	505	745	1268

Odds & ends

Double wins: (0).
Double losses: (2) Ipswich, West Ham.

Won from behind: (3) Notts County (h), Birmingham (a), Norwich (h).
Lost from in front: (6) West Ham (a), Stoke (h), QPR (a), Arsenal (h), Everton LC (a), Sheffield Wed FAC (a).

High spots: Nine games without defeat in autumn - longest since 1967.
Freakish last day of the season.
Stuart Pearce's debut v QP Rangers.
Liverpool 4-0 home win.
Six away games without defeat.

Low spots: 13 games without a win in Spring.
Southampton & Liverpool maulings.
Seven home games without a win in Spring.

Red cards: City – Gibson (Grimsby LC h), Hunt (Southampton h).
Red cards: Opponents – Whyte (Arsenal h), Nicholl (Grimsby LC h).

Player of the Year: Nicky Platnauer.
Ever-presents: (0).
Hat-tricks: (1) Terry Gibson.
Opposing hat-tricks: (4) Swindlehurst (W Ham), Moran (Southampton) Wallace (Southampton), Rush (Liverpool).
Leading scorer: (19) Terry Gibson.

	Appearances						Goals			
	Lge	*Sub*	LC	*Sub*	FAC	*Sub*	**Lge**	LC	FAC	**Tot**
Adams, Micky	**16**	*1*			4		**1**			**1**
Allardyce, Sam	**28**		3		1		**1**			**1**
Avramovic, Raddy	**18**		2		4					
Bamber, Dave	**18**	*1*	2			*1*	**3**	1		**4**
Bennett, Dave	**32**	*2*	3		3		**6**	1		**7**
Butterworth, Ian	**22**	*2*			3					
Daly, Gerry	**27**	*1*			3	*1*	**7**			**7**
Ferguson, Mick (loan)	**7**						**3**			**3**
Gibson, Terry	**35**	*1*	2		3		**17**		2	**19**
Grimes, Ashley	**29**	*3*	3				**1**	1		**2**
Gynn, Michael	**20**	*3*	2		2	*1*	**2**			**2**
Hendrie, John	**1**	*2*	1							
Hormantschuk, Peter	**8**									
Hunt, Steve	**13**	*2*	1		4		**1**		1	**2**
Jacobs, Steve	**18**		1							
Langley, Tommy	**2**									
McGrath, Lloyd	**1**									
Peake, Trevor	**33**		3		4		**3**		1	**4**
Pearce, Stuart	**23**									
Platnauer, Nicky	**29**	*5*	3		4		**6**			**6**
Roberts, Brian	**30**		3		4					
Singleton, Martin	**12**	*1*	2	*1*						
Spring, Andy		*1*								
Suckling, Perry	**24**		1							
Thompson, Keith	**6**				1					
Withey, Graham	**10**	*10*	1		4		**4**		3	**7**
(own-goals)							**2**			
26 players used	**462**	***35***	**33**				**57**	**3**	**7**	**67**

No		Date		Att	Pos	Pt	F-A	H-T	Scorers, Times, and Referees	1	2	3	4	5	6	7	8	9	10	11	12 sub used
1	A		ASTON VILLA			L	0-1	0-0		**Ogrizovic**	**Stephens**	Pearce	**Jol**	**Kilcline**	Peake	Bennett	Platnauer	Withey*	Gibson	Gynn	**Hibbitt**
		25/8		*20,970*		0			*Bremner 53*	*Day*	*Williams*	*Gibson*	*Evans*	*Foster*	*McMahon*	*Bremner*	*Walters*	*Withe*	*Cowans*	*Mortimer*	
									Ref: K Hackett	City are relegation favourites but perform well without looking likely to break the Villa hoodoo. Ogrizovic, a £72,000 signing from Shrewsbury, is outstanding, as is Kilcline, but Coventry-born Kirk Stephens looks nervous after his move from Luton. Allardyce, Jacobs and Daly have left.											
2	H		NORWICH			D	0-0	0-0		Ogrizovic	Stephens	Pearce	Jol	Kilcline	Peake	Bennett	Gynn	**Latchford**	Gibson	Platnauer	
		28/8		10,670		1				*Woods*	*Haylock*	*Van Wyk*	*Mendham*	*Watson*	*Bruce*	*Devine*	*Channon*	*Deehan*	*Bertschin*	*Gordon*	
									Ref: R Nixon	The Canaries are lucky to gain a point as City miss a hatful of chances and Chris Woods performs heroics. Dutchman Martin Jol, signed from WBA stars in midfield, and Brian Kilcline looks solid at the back. Coventry have a new chairman, 39-year-old Coventry-born John Poynton.											
3	H		LEICESTER		8	W	2-0	0-0	Latchford 53, Bennett 71	Ogrizovic	Stephens*	Pearce	Jol	Kilcline	Peake	Bennett	Gynn	Latchford	Gibson	Platnauer	Hibbitt
		1/9		13,322	*21*	4				*Wallington*	*Feeley*	*Smith B*	*MacDonald**	*Hazell*	*O'Neill*	*Lynex*	*Lineker*	*Smith A*	*Ramsey*	*Peake*	*Banks*
									Ref: T Ward	The referee takes the players off after one minute, as fans stage an horrendous pitched battle on the pitch. They return after 11 minutes and City win in handsome form, with Bob Latchford and Dave Bennett scoring. The unsettled Gibson is awesome and should have bagged a hat-trick.											
4	A		WEST HAM		14	L	1-3	0-2	Pearce 82	Ogrizovic	Gynn	Pearce	Jol	Kilcline	Peake	Bennett	Hibbitt	Latchford	Gibson	Platnauer	
		4/9		*14,949*	*5*	4			*Stewart 25p, 67p, Cottee 33*	*McAlister*	*Stewart*	*Walford*	*Allen*	*Martin*	*Gale*	*Barnes**	*Campbell*	*Cottee*	*Dickins*	*Pike*	*Bonds*
									Ref: A Robinson	Out-of-sorts City don't deserve anything, but in a barn-storming finish they almost snatch a point. The two penalties are debatable. Cottee's header hits Hibbitt's hand and Cottee falls over Oggy. Ray Stewart misses the second, but a City player encroached, and he scores the retake.											
5	A		EVERTON		19	L	1-2	1-0	Gibson 35	Ogrizovic	Gynn	Pearce	Jol	Kilcline	Peake	Bennett	Platnauer	Latchford	Gibson	Hibbitt	
		8/9		*20,026*	*13*	4			*Steven 71, Sharp 82*	*Southall*	*Stevens*	*Bailey*	*Ratcliffe*	*Mountfield*	*Reid*	*Steven*	*Heath*	*Sharp*	*Bracewell*	*Richardson**	*Curran*
									Ref: J Hough	Even Everton players accept that Derek Mountfield brought down Bennett after 65 minutes, but City are denied a penalty. They tenaciously hold a 1-0 lead but six minutes later Trevor Steven equalises and Sharp produces the winner. Gould says it's City's worst display of the season.											
6	H		MANCHESTER U		22	L	0-3	0-2		Ogrizovic	Gynn	Pearce	Jol	Kilcline !	Peake	Bennett	Thompson	Latchford*	Gibson	Platnauer	Butterworth
		15/9		18,312	*3*	4			*Robson 40, Whiteside 43, 64*	*Bailey*	*Duxbury*	*Albiston*	*Moses*	*Moran*	*Hogg*	*Robson*	*Strachan*	*Hughes*	*Whiteside*	*Olsen*	
									Ref: D Reeves	United are unbeaten and coast to an easy victory after Kilcline is sent off in the 36th minute for two yellow cards. United score two quick goals before half-time and Whiteside's lethal finish wraps up the points for the Reds. Butterworth comes on, but without Latchford the attack is poor.											
7	A		SUNDERLAND		21	D	0-0	0-0		Ogrizovic	Spring	Adams	Hibbitt*	Kilcline	Peake	Bennett	Gynn	Latchford	Gibson	Platnauer	Butterworth
		22/9		*16,308*	*13*	5				*Turner*	*Venison*	*Pickering**	*Bennett*	*Chisholm*	*Elliott*	*Daniel*	*Gayle*	*West*	*Procter*	*Walker*	*Wylde*
									Ref: I Hendrick	New assistant manager Don Mackay takes charge, with Gould scouting. City gain their first away point since February after nine defeats in a row. Adams returns for his first game of the season, alongside 18-year-old Geordie Spring. With a bit more sharpness, City could have won.											
8	H		ARSENAL		21	L	1-2	0-0	Gibson 50	Ogrizovic	Spring	Adams	Hibbitt	Butterworth	Peake	Singleton	Gynn	Jol*	Gibson	Platnauer	Withey
		29/9		14,353	*3*	5			*Woodcock 85, Mariner 90*	*Jennings*	*Anderson*	*Sansom*	*Talbot**	*O'Leary*	*Caton*	*Robson*	*Rix*	*Mariner*	*Woodcock*	*Nicholas*	*Davis*
									Ref: A Banks	Arsenal outclass an injury-hit City, but only win the game in the third minute of injury-time after coming from behind. Jennings saved Hibbitt's 54th-minute penalty when £650,000 Charlie Nicholas fouls Gibson. Bennett, the normal penalty taker is injured. The fences are going back up.											
9	A		WATFORD		20	W	1-0	0-0	Gibson 87	Ogrizovic	Spring	Adams	Hibbitt	Butterworth	Peake	Bennett	Gynn	Platnauer	Gibson	**Barnes**	
		6/10		*15,184*	*22*	8				*Coton*	*Bardsley*	*Jackett*	*Taylor*	*Terry*	*Sinnott*	*Callaghan*	*Johnston*	*Reilly*	*Porter**	*Barnes*	*Blissett*
									Ref: D Axcell	City's first away league win for ten months comes at bottom of the table Watford. Ogrizovic is a rock and is beaten only by Barnes' shot which hits the bar. Gibson snatches the winner after a mix-up between Terry and Sinnott, and Barnes looks good after his £65,000 move from WBA.											
10	H		NEWCASTLE		20	D	1-1	0-0	Hibbitt 75	Ogrizovic	Stephens	Adams	Hibbitt	Butterworth	Peake	Bennett	Gynn	**Regis**	Gibson	Barnes	
		13/10		14,030	*7*	9			*Beardsley 60p*	*Carr*	*Brown*	*Saunders*	*Heard*	*Anderson*	*Roeder*	*McDonald*	*Wharton*	*Waddle*	*Beardsley*	*McCreery*	
									Ref: M Heath	City recover their pride after the Walsall fiasco with a much-improved display against Newcastle's strong-arm tactics. Beardsley scores after Hibbitt is adjudged to have handled but the City player replies with a swerving free-kick. New man Regis is impressed by his new team-mates.											

No	Date	Opponent	Att	Pos	Pts	F-A	H-T	Scorers, Times, and Referees	1	2	3	4	5	6	7	8	9	10	11	12
11 A		QP RANGERS		20	L	1-2	1-0	Gynn 33	Ogrizovic	Stephens	Adams	Hibbitt	Butterworth	Peake	Bennett	Gynn	Regis	Jol	Barnes	
	20/10		*10,427*	*10*	9			*Stainrod 63, 83*	*Hucker*	*Neill*	*Dawes*	*Fereday*	*Wicks*	*Fenwick*	*Micklewhite**	*Fillery*	*Bannister*	*Stainrod*	*Gregory*	*Stewart*
								Ref: T Bune	City's habit of throwing way leads is repeated on QPR's plastic pitch. Tons of sand have been laid under the Loftus Road pitch, but the surface is still poor. Gynn is one who relishs the surface and he scores his first of the season before Stainrod punishes Coventry's retreating defence.											
12 H		SHEFFIELD WED		18	W	1-0	1-0	Gibson 26	Ogrizovic	Stephens	Adams	Hibbitt	McGrath	Peake	Bennett	Gynn	Regis	Gibson	Barnes	
	27/10		14,309	*4*	12				*Hodge*	*Sterland*	*Shirtliff*	*Smith*	*Lyons*	*Worthington*	*Marwood*	*Blair*	*Varadi*	*Chapman*	*Shelton*	
								Ref: L Shapter	McGrath plays his first game since the Dell disaster last season. He looks composed but fouls Varadi for a 75th-minute penalty. Oggy saves Sterland's spot-kick and newly promoted Owls suffer their first defeat in nine league games. Gibson pounces on a rebound from Barnes' cross.											
13 A		CHELSEA		18	L	**2-6**	2-2	Gynn 22, Latchford 26 *[Speedie 69]*	Ogrizovic	Stephens	Adams	Jol	McGrath	Peake	Latchford	Gynn	Regis*	Gibson	Barnes	Spring
	3/11		*17,306*	*9*	12			*Dixon 30, 70, 80, Jones K 45, 84,*	*Niedzwiecki*	*Lee*	*Rougvie*	*Pates*	*McLaughlin*	*Jones K*	*Nevin*	*Spackman*	*Dixon*	*Speedie*	*Canoville*	
								Ref: I Borrett	Newly promoted Chelsea are run ragged for 30 minutes, but by half-time are level. The second half is one way traffic but City hold out until David Speedie scores the third, then the floodgates open. Hat-trick hero Kerry Dixon and Nevin are superb and Oggy stops Chelsea scoring ten.											
14 H		IPSWICH		18	W	1-0	0-0	Adams 72	Ogrizovic	Stephens	Adams	Hibbitt	Butterworth	Peake	Bennett	Gynn	Latchford	Gibson	Jol	
	10/11		**8,807**	*16*	15				*Cooper*	*Burley*	*McCall*	*Zondervan*	*Cranson*	*Butcher*	*O'Callaghan*	*Brennan*	*Putney**	*Sunderland*	*Gates*	*Dozzell*
								Ref: R Guy	After the Chelsea slaughter, the result is more important than the performance and Adams seals the win with a fierce left-footer. The game is drab and without the injured Regis and Barnes the Sky Blues lack penetration. Their lowest gate of the season is 6,000 below break-even level.											
15 H		NOTT'M FOREST		19	L	1-3	0-1	Gibson 56p	Ogrizovic	Stephens	Adams	Hibbitt	Butterworth	Peake	Jol	Gynn	Regis	Gibson	Singleton	
	17/11		9,840	*9*	15			*Adams 42 (og), Walsh 77, Riley 90*	*Segers*	*Mills*	*Swain*	*Metgod*	*Fairclough*	*Bowyer*	*Wigley*	*Hodge*	*Raynor**	*Davenport*	*Walsh*	*Riley*
								Ref: K Walmsley	Debutant Hans Segers saves brilliantly from Singleton in the 89th minute and Forest race to the other end to net their third goal. A travesty of a scoreline, but City have only themselves to blame. Adams turns an innocent cross into his own goal. Gibson is fouled by Segers for the penalty.											
16 A		WEST BROM		20	L	2-5	1-2	Barnes 1, Regis 64 *[Statham 89]*	Ogrizovic	Stephens	Adams	Hibbitt	Butterworth	Peake	Jol	Gynn	Regis	Gibson !	Barnes	
	24/11		*12,742*	*13*	15			*T'son 14, V'tine 26, Mac 62, Grealish 65,*	*Godden*	*Nicholl*	*Statham*	*Hunt*	*Bennett*	*Robertson*	*Grealish*	*Thompson*	*MacKenzie*	*Cross D**	*Valentine*	*Cross N*
								Ref: D Shaw	Ex-City players Hunt, Thompson and Cross help the Baggies to a comfortable win, after Gibson is sent off for retaliating to Jimmy Nicholl's hair pulling after 29 minutes. City's ex-Albion men score their first goals for City, but the defence crumbles again and relegation fears mount.											
17 H		TOTTENHAM		20	D	1-1	0-1	Regis 90	Ogrizovic	Stephens	Adams	Hibbitt*	Kilcline	Peake	Bennett	Gynn	Regis	Gibson	Barnes	Butterworth
	1/12		14,474	*4*	16			*Falco 34*	*Clemence*	*Stevens*	*Hughton*	*Roberts*	*Miller*	*Perryman*	*Chiedozie*	*Falco*	*Allen*	*Hoddle*	*Galvin**	*Mabbutt*
								Ref: P Tyldesley	Cyrille Regis scores an injury-time winner to thwart Spurs and earn a deserved point. Glen Hoddle, dominant in the first half, is marked out of it by Ian Butterworth in the second half as Tottenham go off the boil. Mark Falco almost scores a second after the equaliser, but hits the post.											
18 A		LIVERPOOL		20	L	1-3	0-2	Hansen 75 (og)	Ogrizovic	Stephens	Adams	Butterworth*	Kilcline	Peake	Bennett	Gynn	Regis	Gibson	Barnes	Platnauer
	4/12		*27,237*	*6*	16			*Wark 8, 90, Rush 25p*	*Grobbelaar*	*Neal*	*Kennedy*	*Lawrenson**	*Nicol*	*Hansen*	*Dalglish*	*Molby*	*Rush*	*Johnston*	*Wark*	*Whelan*
								Ref: K Redfern	The Reds are already a goal up when they are awarded a penalty, as Peake is harshly adjudged to have handled a cross. City could have had two penalties when Regis was brought down by Grobbelaar and Lawrenson. Wark nets his second at the death, after Oggy had thwarted Pool.											
19 H		SOUTHAMPTON		20	W	2-1	0-0	Peake 52, Shilton 58 (og)	Ogrizovic	Stephens	Adams	Jol	Kilcline	Peake	Gynn	**Bowman**	Regis	Bennett	Barnes	
	15/12		10,366	*5*	19			*Jordan 70*	*Shilton*	*Mills*	*Dennis*	*Curtis*	*Agboola*	*Bond*	*Holmes*	*Moran**	*Jordan*	*Armstrong*	*Wallace*	*Puckett*
								Ref: R Bridges	Saints' club record unbeaten run of 14 games is ended: they haven't won at Coventry for 35 years. With the fog threatening a postponement, Peake's header and a Barnes corner that bounces off Shilton's knee give City a deserved win. £160,000 Scot Bowman makes a useful debut.											
20 A		LEICESTER		20	L	1-5	1-3	Gynn 18 *[Smith A 87]*	Ogrizovic	Stephens	Adams	Jol	Kilcline	Pearce	Gynn	Bowman	Regis	Bennett	Barnes	
	23/12		*18,016*	*14*	19			*Lynex 22p, Rennie 42, Lineker 45, 85,*	*Andrews*	*Feeley*	*Wilson*	*Smith B*	*Williams*	*O'Neill*	*Lynex*	*Lineker*	*Smith A*	*Rennie*	*Banks*	
								Ref: C Downey	A disastrous defeat for Coventry, who predictably take the lead only to toss it away. City criticise the referee over the penalty for Peter Barnes' 'foul' on Ian Banks. Six City players are booked and Gould courts trouble by remonstrating on the pitch. Leicester look weak but win with ease.											
21 A		LUTON		21	L	0-2	0-1		Ogrizovic	Stephens	Adams	Jol*	Kilcline	Pearce	Gynn	Bowman	Regis	Gibson	Barnes	Bennett
	26/12		*9,237*	*19*	19			*Stein B 15, Daniel 87*	*Sealey*	*Breaker*	*Thomas*	*Turner*	*Foster*	*Donaghy*	*Hill*	*Stein*	*Harford*	*Daniel*	*Nwajiobi**	*Bunn*
								Ref: M James	Gould is sacked after this spineless display against relegation rivals. City have won only nine games out of 42 in 1984 and are rarely in this game. Assistant Mackay takes over but has a massive task. A crisp shot from Brian Stein and the habitual late goal by Daniel seals Gould's fate.											

CANON LEAGUE DIVISION 1

Manager: Gould > Don Mackay

SEASON 1984-85

No	Date		Att	Pos	Pt	F-A	H-T	Scorers, Times, and Referees	1	2	3	4	5	6	7	8	9	10	11	12 sub used
22	H	WEST HAM		21	L	1-2	0-0	Stephens 62	Ogrizovic	Stephens	Pearce	Bowman	Kilcline	McGrath	Hibbitt	Gynn*	Regis	Gibson	Barnes	Adams
	29/12		10,732	*12*	19			*Cottee 56, 87*	*McAlister*	*Allen*	*Brush*	*Dickins*	*Martin*	*Gale*	*Orr*	*Hilton**	*Goddard*	*Cottee*	*Pike*	*Whitton*
								Ref: N Ashley	Cottee's winner is City's twelfth goal conceded in the last ten minutes this season. Kirk Stephens had appeared to have earned City a point with a deflected shot, but this is an unhappy start for Mackay despite a better performance. Gould wins Mercia's sports personality of the year poll.											
23	H	STOKE		20	W	**4-0**	3-0	Gibson 12, 53, Stephens 30, Hibbitt 33	Ogrizovic	Stephens	Pearce	Bowman	Kilcline	McGrath	Hibbitt*	Gynn	Latchford	Gibson	Adams	Bennett
	1/1		9,785	*22*	22				*Roberts*	*Bould*	*Spearing*	*Maskery*	*O'Callaghan*	*Berry*	*Parkin*	*McIlroy*	*Heath*	*Bertschin*	*Chamberlain*	
								Ref: D Hedges	Not too much should be read into this score, as Stoke have lost 13 out of 15 and are the worst Div 1 side for years. 17-year-old keeper Stuart Roberts is at fault for the first three, as City notch their biggest win for over a year. Mackay says a lot of hard work is needed to avoid the drop.											
24	A	MANCHESTER U		19	W	1-0	0-0	Gibson 70	Ogrizovic	Stephens	Pearce	Bowman	Kilcline	Peake	Bennett	McGrath	Latchford*	Gibson	Adams	Regis
	12/1		***35,992***	*3*	25				*Pears*	*Duxbury*	*Albiston*	*Moses*	*McQueen*	*McGrath*	*Robson**	*Strachan*	*Stapleton*	*Hughes*	*Muhren*	*Brazil*
								Ref: C Seel	City will return to Old Trafford for the cup-tie in high spirits after denting United's title hopes with their second home defeat in a row. Gibson nets his fifth goal in three games. A bigger blow to Utd is the loss of Bryan Robson, who crashes into the hoardings and damages a shoulder.											
25	H	ASTON VILLA		19	L	0-3	0-1		Ogrizovic	Stephens	Pearce	Bowman	Kilcline	Peake	Bennett*	McGrath	Regis	Gibson	Adams	Latchford
	19/1		15,290	*13*	25			*Walters 32, 70, Rideout 66*	*Spink*	*Norton*	*Dorigo*	*Glover*	*Ormsby*	*McMahon*	*Birch*	*Rideout*	*Withe*	*Gibson*	*Walters*	
								Ref: D Hutchinson	Villa grab their first away win since August with embarrassing ease. The game is won in midfield, where City's two king-pins have no attacking ideas and are overrun by McMahon and Co. Regis, shackled by Ormsby, struggles with this playing style and has scored only two in 15 games.											
26	A	ARSENAL		19	L	1-2	0-1	Pearce 47	Ogrizovic	Stephens	Pearce	Hibbitt	Kilcline	Peake	McGrath	Gynn	Regis	Gibson	Barnes	
	2/2		*21,791*	*4*	25			*Meade 44, Allinson 74*	*Lukic*	*Anderson*	*Sansom*	*Talbot*	*O'Leary*	*Caton**	*Robson*	*Williams*	*Mariner*	*Meade*	*Allinson*	*Nicholas*
								Ref: D Letts	Charlie Nicholas and Tony Woodcock are dropped after Arsenal's Cup disaster at York City, and their replacements score both goals. It was sub Nicholas who sparks the Gunners after Pearce's bent free-kick. City play well, but as Mackay says 'Good performances don't win things'.											
27	H	CHELSEA		19	W	1-0	1-0	Gibson 2	Ogrizovic	Stephens	Pearce	Hibbitt	Kilcline	Peake	McGrath	Gynn	Regis	Gibson*	Barnes	Bennett
	23/2		11,421	*9*	28				*Niedzwiecki*	*Wood*	*Jones J*	*Jasper*	*Droy*	*Jones K**	*Nevin*	*Spackman*	*Dixon*	*Speedie*	*Bumstead*	*Canoville*
								Ref: K Cooper	In order to avoid crowd trouble it is an all-ticket match with an 11.30 kick-off. City haven't played for three weeks and look rusty, but they catch Chelsea cold when Regis sets up Gibson. It is Mickey Droy's final game for the Pensioners. Playing Stephens in midfield does not work.											
28	A	SHEFFIELD WED		19	L	0-1	0-1		Ogrizovic	Stephens	Pearce	Hibbitt	Kilcline	McGrath	Bowman*	Gynn	Regis	Gibson	Adams	Bennett
	2/3		*20,422*	*4*	28			*Pearson 36*	*Hodge*	*Sterland*	*Madden*	*Smith*	*Lyons*	*Worthington*	*Marwood*	*Blair*	*Varadi*	*Pearson*	*Shelton*	
								Ref: D Richardson	Sheffield Wednesday's long-ball game and offside trap loses friends but wins matches. City are battered into submission. Pearson, standing in for the injured Lee Chapman, heads the winner from Andy Blair's free-kick. Peter Barnes is axed, and his short City career may be terminated.											
29	H	QP RANGERS		17	W	3-0	2-0	Gibson 14, 33, Kilcline 65	Ogrizovic	Stephens	Pearce	Hibbitt	Kilcline	McGrath	Bennett	Gynn	Regis	Gibson	Adams	
	9/3		8,914	*16*	31				*Hucker*	*Fereday*	*Dawes*	*Waddock*	*Wicks*	*Fenwick*	*Robinson**	*Fillery*	*Bannister*	*Byrne*	*Gregory*	*Chivers*
								Ref: R Gifford	The 'acting' title is removed from Mackay's job description. Pearce is captain. City produce their best display of the season against shaky QPR. Gibson takes his tally to 15 goals and Kilcline scores his first with a header. The press link Regis to an exchange deal with Wolves' Humphries.											
30	H	WATFORD		18	W	3-1	3-0	Gibson 8, 32, Adams 42	Ogrizovic	Stephens	Pearce	Hibbitt	Kilcline	McGrath	Bennett	Gynn	Regis	Gibson	Adams	
	23/3		9,679	*19*	34			*Blissett 86*	*Coton*	*Bardsley**	*Rostron*	*Taylor*	*Terry*	*McClelland*	*Callaghan*	*Blissett*	*Gilligan*	*Jackett*	*Barnes*	*Porter*
								Ref: R Dilkes	With Mackay absent with flu, assistant Frank Upton takes charge. The manager misses a vintage Regis performance after a poor spell. He does everything but score, though Gibson delivers again and it's all over by half-time. As Pearce and Adams' contracts end in June, talks have started.											
31	A	NORWICH		19	L	1-2	1-2	Gynn 45	Ogrizovic	Stephens	Pearce	Hibbitt	Kilcline	McGrath	Bennett	Gynn	Regis*	Gibson	Adams	Peake
	30/3		*14,067*	*10*	34			*Channon 28, 39*	*Woods*	*Haylock*	*Van Wyk*	*Bruce*	*Mendham*	*Watson*	*Barham*	*Channon*	*Deehan*	*Hartford*	*Donowa*	
								Ref: N Butler	The Canaries parade the Milk Cup they won last week at Wembley, and they put City under constant pressure. 36-year-old Mike Channon nets both goals after mistakes from McGrath and Ken Hibbitt. Chris Woods injures a hip, but the Sky Blues fail to capitalise and lose vital points.											

No	Venue	Opponent	Pos	Res	F-A	H-T	Scorers, Times, and Referees	1	2	3	4	5	6	7	8	9	10	11	12 sub used
32	H	SUNDERLAND	21	L	0-1	0-1		Ogrizovic	Stephens	Pearce	Hibbitt	Butterworth	McGrath	Bennett	Gynn	Regis	Gibson	Adams*	Bowman
13/4		9,609	*18*	34			*Moore 11*	*Turner*	*Venison*	*Pickering*	*Bennett*	*Chisholm*	*Elliott*	*Lemon*	*Wallace*	*Moore**	*Berry*	*Walker*	*Cummins*
							Ref: A Robinson	A flu epidemic forced City to postpone their Easter games and they have slipped into the relegation frame. City look lethargic, but should have won this vital game. Gibson has a 47th-minute penalty saved by Turner, after Elliott brings down Stephens. John Moore scores and is subbed.											
33	A	NEWCASTLE	20	W	1-0	1-0	Bennett 3	Ogrizovic	Stephens	Pearce	Hibbitt*	Butterworth	Peake	Bennett	McGrath	Regis	Gibson	Barnes	Gynn
17/4		*19,578*	*12*	37				*Thomas*	*Brown*	*Wharton*	*McCreery*	*Anderson*	*Roeder*	*Megson*	*Cunningham**	*Reilly*	*Beardsley*	*Heard*	*McDonald*
							Ref: G Aplin	A rare win on Tyneside helps compensate for the Sunderland defeat. Bennett's early lead, from a deflected Hibbitt shot, is grimly defended. The win is City's first at St James' Park since 1977 and momentarily eases their relegation worries. Jack Charlton's side look unimpressive.											
34	A	NOTT'M FOREST	21	L	0-2	0-2		Ogrizovic	Stephens	Pearce	Hibbitt	Butterworth	Peake	Bennett*	McGrath	Regis	Latchford	Barnes	Gynn
20/4		*12,990*	*7*	37			*Mills 26, Hibbitt 40 (og)*	*Segers*	*Fleming*	*McInally*	*Fairclough*	*Hart*	*Bowyer*	*Wigley*	*Metgod*	*Davenport*	*Hodge**	*Mills*	*Clough*
							Ref: J Lovat	17-goal Gibson is injured and missing against Brian Clough's team and is sorely missed by City. Two first-half goals flatter Forest, Mills scoring from 30 yards and Hibbitt turning Wigley's cross into his own net. Latchford struggles up front and Segers saves well from Regis and McGrath.											
35	H	WEST BROM	19	W	2-1	1-1	Barnes 32, Hibbitt 67	Ogrizovic	Stephens	Pearce	Hibbitt	Butterworth	Peake	Bowman*	McGrath	Regis	Gibson	Barnes	Gynn
27/4		10,329	*13*	40			*MacKenzie 18*	*Godden*	*Nicholl*	*Cowdrill*	*MacKenzie*	*Bennett*	*Robertson*	*Owen*	*Thompson*	*Whitehead**	*Cross N*	*Valentine*	*Grealish*
							Ref: T Spencer	This vital win is inspired by former Albion men Regis and Barnes. Oggy lets Steve MacKenzie's shot squeeze under his body before Barnes blasts in Stephens' cross. Hibbitt puts in the rebound after Regis' run and powerful shot. Under Johnny Giles, Albion are becalmed in mid-table.											
36	A	TOTTENHAM	20	L	2-4	0-1	Pearce 61p, Gibson 71	Ogrizovic	Stephens	Pearce	Hibbitt	Butterworth	Peake	Adams	McGrath	Regis	Gibson	Barnes*	Gynn
4/5		*16,711*	*3*	40			*Falco 20, 89, Hoddle 55, Hughton 72*	*Clemence*	*Thomas*	*Hughton*	*Roberts*	*Miller*	*Perryman*	*Ardiles*	*Falco*	*Leworthy*	*Hoddle*	*Galvin*	
							Ref: T Bune	City fall apart, having come from behind against a side who have lost four in a row at home. Pearce scores from the spot after Ray Clemence fouls Gibson. Gibson, Midland player of the Year, pounces when Clemence drops Pearce's long throw. Danny Thomas heads off the line at 3-2.											
37	H	LIVERPOOL	20	L	0-2	0-1		Ogrizovic	Stephens	Pearce	Hibbitt	Butterworth	Peake	McGrath*	Gynn	Regis	Gibson	Adams	Bennett
6/5		19,136	*2*	40			*Walsh 45, 58*	*Grobbelaar*	*Neal*	*Beglin*	*Lawrenson*	*Nicol*	*Hansen*	*Lee*	*Whelan*	*Rush*	*Walsh*	*Wark*	
							Ref: J Key	With their rivals winning, City are deep in the mire and the drop looms closer. Liverpool for once aren't in the title hunt but have one eye on their date with Juventus at the Heysel Stadium. Paul Walsh profits from Pearce's dreadful back-pass and Oggy's failure to hold Wark's effort.											
38	A	SOUTHAMPTON	20	L	1-2	1-1	Regis 42	Ogrizovic	Stephens*	Pearce	Hibbitt	Butterworth	Peake	Bennett	McGrath	Regis	Gibson	Adams	Gynn
11/5		*15,735*	*5*	40			*Stephens 6 (og), Moran 75*	*Shilton*	*Mills*	*Golac**	*Case*	*Wright*	*Bond*	*Holmes*	*Moran*	*Jordan*	*Armstrong*	*Lawrence*	*Whitlock*
							Ref: M Dimblebee	City's First Division future hangs by a thread after this unlucky defeat. Match of the Day cameras see luckless Stephens head in trying to clear Case's corner. Regis gets his first goal in 20 games when the otherwise superb Shilton fumbles Bennett's shot. The unmarked Moran wins it.											
39	A	IPSWICH	20	D	0-0	0-0		Ogrizovic	Butterworth	Pearce	Hibbitt*	Kilcline	Peake	Bennett	Gynn	Regis	Gibson	Adams	McGrath
14/5		*14,038*	*18*	41				*Cooper*	*Burley*	*Yallop*	*Zondervan*	*Cranson*	*Butcher*	*Parkin*	*Brennan*	*Dozzell*	*Wilson*	*Gates*	
							Ref: M Bodenham	In lashing rain City put up a gutsy display, despite Hibbitt limping off after 30 minutes. Cooper saves well from Bennett and Pearce as the Sky Blues push for the winner and Kilcline hits the bar. West Ham and Norwich both win, leaving City to win all their final three games to stay up.											
40	A	STOKE	20	W	1-0	0-0	Pearce 66p	Ogrizovic	Butterworth	Pearce	Hibbitt*	Kilcline	Peake	Bennett	McGrath	Regis	Gibson	Adams	Gynn
17/5		***6,930***	*22*	44				*Fox*	*Bould*	*Hemming*	*Maskery*	*Dyson*	*Berry*	*Heath*	*McIlroy*	*Painter*	*Saunders**	*Beeston*	*Chamberlain*
							Ref: N Midgley	Stoke are down with the lowest points total ever. This is their 31st defeat. With six minutes to go Regis is adjudged to have fouled Paul Dyson, but Painter hits the underside of the bar and City live to fight another day. Coventry's penalty is also harsh, as Regis' header hits Berry's hand.											
41	H	LUTON	20	W	1-0	0-0	Kilcline 84	Ogrizovic	Butterworth	Pearce	Hibbitt*	Kilcline	Peake	Bennett	McGrath	Regis	Gibson	Adams	Gynn
23/5		14,834	*15*	47				*Sealey*	*Breaker*	*Thomas*	*Nicholas*	*Foster*	*Donaghy*	*Hill*	*Stein*	*Harford*	*Nwajiobi*	*Preece**	*Daniel*
							Ref: B Stevens	City's First Division life is ebbing away when Luton only half-clear a corner and Brian Kilcline volleys in from the edge of the box. Nervous Norwich can have no complaints about Luton's gritty display. City are no less nervous, but they must now beat the new champions to stay up.											
42	H	EVERTON	18	W	4-1	2-1	Regis 4, 46, Adams 17, Gibson 78	Ogrizovic	Butterworth	Pearce	Hibbitt	Kilcline	Peake	Bennett	McGrath	Regis	Gibson	Adams	
26/5		**21,596**	*1*	50			*Wilkinson 40*	*Southall*	*Harper*	*v d Hauwe*	*Ratcliffe*	*Hughes*	*Richardson*	*Steven*	*Wilkinson*	*Sharp*	*Bracewell*	*Sheedy*	
	Home	Away					Ref: R Lewis	Everton are without four of their Cup-Winners' Cup winning side and are blown away. Two early goals don't settle City, and Wilkinson pulls one back. Regis' second eases the tension and Gibson wraps it up. Three wins in a row for the first time in three years sends Norwich down.											
Average	12,862	17,173																	

Milk Cup					F-A	H-T	Scorers, Times, and Referees	1	2	3	4	5	6	7	8	9	10	11	12 sub used
2:1	A	WALSALL	21	W	2-1	1-0	Singleton 33, Gibson 70	Ogrizovic	Spring	Adams	Butterworth	Kilcline	Peake	Bennett*	Gynn	Singleton	Gibson	Platnauer	Thompson
	25/9	*8,399*	*3:17*				*Shakespeare 63*	*Cherry*	*Caswell*	*Mower*	*Shakespeare*	*Brazier*	*Hart*	*Handyside*	*Bamber*	*O'Kelly*	*Preece**	*Childs*	*Buckley*
							Ref: T Fitzharris	This away win against last season's semi-finalists was earned by a battling performance from an injury-hit side. Ex-City man Dave Bamber makes no headway against Kilcline. Martin Singleton and Gibson score with headers and Gibson misses an open goal ten minutes from time.											
2:2	H	WALSALL	20	L	0-3	0-0		Ogrizovic	Spring	Adams	Hibbitt	Butterworth	Peake	Bennett	Gynn	Platnauer	Gibson	Barnes*	Kilcline
	9/10	9,197	*3:11*				*Kelly 53, 81, O'Kelly 65*	*Cherry*	*Jones*	*Mower*	*Shakespeare*	*Brazier*	*Hart*	*Handyside*	*Kelly*	*O'Kelly*	*Preece*	*Childs*	
							Ref: A Buksh (City lose 2-4 on aggregate)	Gould locks the players in the dressing room for 40 minutes after this embarrassing defeat. City are outfought and outclassed by the Saddlers. New £300,000 signing Cyrille Regis watches as the Sky Blues' 4-2-4 is exposed as naive. The fences are back up after incidents at Leicester.											
FA Cup																			
3	H	MANCHESTER C	20	W	2-1	2-0	Gibson 25, 28	Ogrizovic	Stephens	Pearce	Bowman	Kilcline	McGrath	Hibbitt	Gynn	Latchford	Gibson	Adams	
	5/1	15,643	*2:5*				*Power 85*	*Williams*	*Lomax*	*Power*	*May*	*McCarthy*	*Phillips*	*Smith**	*Baker*	*Melrose*	*Wilson*	*Kinsey*	*Cunningham*
							Ref: R Milford	Man City have lost one in twelve and start as favourites. They are unlucky to lose to a much more disciplined City team. Gibson's second goal is superb, he spins on the frosty pitch to volley past Williams. Power's goal creates a nervous finale. City keep possession by the corner flags.											
4	A	MANCHESTER U	19	L	1-2	1-2	Gibson 41	Ogrizovic	Stephens	Pearce	Hibbitt	Kilcline	Peake	McGrath	Gynn*	Regis	Gibson	Adams	Latchford
	26/1	*38,039*	*3*				*Hughes 20, McGrath 25*	*Pears*	*Gidman*	*Albiston*	*Moses*	*Moran*	*Hogg*	*McGrath*	*Strachan*	*Hughes**	*Whiteside*	*Olsen*	*Brazil*
							Ref: G Tyson	Lightening fails to strike twice and plucky, fighting City go out to the eventual winners, despite playing better than in the League win. Five minutes of indiscipline cost them two goals and the tie. Pears saves Gibson's 38th-minute penalty, awarded for a foul by Moran on Pearce.											

		P	W	D	L	F	A	W	D	L	F	A	Pts
			Home					Away					
1	Everton	42	16	3	2	58	17	12	3	6	30	26	90
2	Liverpool	42	12	4	5	36	19	10	7	4	32	16	77
3	Tottenham	42	11	3	7	46	31	12	5	4	32	20	77
4	Manchester U	42	13	6	2	47	13	9	4	8	30	34	76
5	Southampton	42	13	4	4	29	18	6	7	8	27	29	68
6	Chelsea	42	13	3	5	38	20	5	9	7	25	28	66
7	Arsenal	42	14	5	2	37	14	5	4	12	24	35	66
8	Sheffield Wed	42	12	7	2	39	21	5	7	9	19	24	65
9	Nott'm Forest	42	13	4	4	35	18	6	3	12	21	30	64
10	Aston Villa	42	10	7	4	34	20	5	4	12	26	40	56
11	Watford	42	10	5	6	48	30	4	8	9	33	41	55
12	West Brom	42	11	4	6	36	23	5	3	13	22	39	55
13	Luton	42	12	5	4	40	22	3	4	14	17	39	54
14	Newcastle	42	11	4	6	33	26	2	9	10	22	44	52
15	Leicester	42	10	4	7	39	25	5	2	14	26	48	51
16	West Ham	42	7	8	6	27	23	6	4	11	24	45	51
17	Ipswich	42	8	7	6	27	20	5	4	12	19	37	50
18	COVENTRY	42	11	3	7	29	22	4	2	15	18	42	50
19	QP Rangers	42	11	6	4	41	30	2	5	14	12	42	50
20	Norwich	42	9	6	6	28	24	4	4	13	18	40	49
21	Sunderland	42	7	6	8	20	26	3	4	14	20	36	40
22	Stoke	42	3	3	15	18	41	0	5	16	6	50	17
		924	237	107	118	785	503	118	107	237	503	785	1279

Odds & ends

Double wins: (2) Watford, Stoke.
Double losses: (5) Arsenal, Nott'm Forest, West Ham, Aston Villa, Liverpool.

Won from behind: (1) West Brom (h).
Lost from in front: (6) Everton (a), Arsenal (h), QP Rangers (a), Chelsea (a), West Brom (a), Leicester (a).

High spots: Winning last three games to avoid relegation.
The outstanding form of Stuart Pearce.
A rare win at Old Trafford.

Low Spots: Capitulations at Chelsea, West Brom and Leicester.
The Milk Cup exit to Walsall.
A miserable start - one win in eight games.

Red cards: City – Gibson (West Brom a), Kilcline (Manchester U h).

Player of the Year: Terry Gibson.
Ever-presents: (1) Steve Ogrizovic.
Hat-tricks: (0).
Opposing hat-tricks: (1) Dixon (Chelsea).
Leading scorer: (19) Terry Gibson.

	Appearances						Goals			
	Lge	*Sub*	LC	*Sub*	FAC	*Sub*	Lge	LC	FAC	Tot
Adams, Micky	**30**	*1*	2		2		**3**			**3**
Barnes, Peter	**18**		1				**2**			**2**
Bennett, Dave	**29**	*5*	2				**2**			**2**
Bowman, David	**9**	*1*			1					
Butterworth, Ian	**19**	*3*	2							
Gibson, Terry	**38**		2		2		**15**	1	3	**19**
Gynn, Michael	**32**	*7*	2		2		**4**			**4**
Hibbitt, Kenny	**31**	*2*	1		2		**3**			**3**
Jol, Martin	**15**									
Kilcline, Brian	**26**		1	*1*	2		**2**			**2**
Latchford, Bob	**11**	*1*			1	*1*	**2**			**2**
McGrath, Lloyd	**22**	*1*			2					
Ogrizovic, Steve	**42**		2		2					
Peake, Trevor	**33**	*1*	2		1		**1**			**1**
Pearce, Stuart	**29**				2		**4**			**4**
Platnauer, Nicky	**9**	*1*	2							
Regis, Cyrille	**30**	*1*			1		**5**			**5**
Singleton, Martin	**2**		1					1		**1**
Spring, Andy	**3**	*1*	2							
Stephens, Kirk	**32**				2		**2**			**2**
Thompson, Keith	**1**			*1*						
Withey, Graham	**1**	*1*								
(own-goals)							**2**			**2**
22 players used	**462**	***26***	**22**	***2***	**22**	***1***	**47**	**2**	**3**	**52**

No	Date		Att	Pos	Pt	F-A	H-T	Scorers, Times, and Referees	1	2	3	4	5	6	7	8	9	10	11	12 sub used
1	H	MANCHESTER C			D	1-1	1-1	McNab 22 (og)	Ogrizovic	**Borrows**	**Downs**	Bowman	Kilcline	Peake	Bennett	Gynn*	Regis	Gibson	Adams	Hibbitt
	17/8		14,521		1			*McIlroy 10*	*Williams*	*Phillips*	*Power*	*Clements*	*Johnson*	*Wilson*	*Lillis*	*McNab*	*Kinsey*	*McIlroy*	*Simpson*	
								Ref: A Buksh	Promoted Man C grab a deserved point in the sun. Coventry sport new full-backs, Borrows £80,000 from Bolton and Greg Downs, £40,000 from Norwich, though new skipper Wayne Turner from Luton is unfit. Free transfer McIlroy hits a 20-yarder; McNab heads an own-goal.											
2	A	CHELSEA			L	0-1	0-0		Ogrizovic	Borrows	Downs	Bowman	Kilcline	Peake	Bennett	Hibbitt*	Regis	Gibson	Adams	Gynn
	20/8		*15,679*		1			*Speedie 76*	*Niedzwiecki*	*Lee*	*Rougvie*	*Pates*	*McLaughlin*	*Bumstead*	*Nevin*	*Jones*	*Dixon*	*Speedie*	*Murphy*	
								Ref: A Robinson	A wet and miserable night and a late unlucky defeat for the Sky Blues. They seem to have weathered the storm until Nevin beats Downs for the only time and Speedie heads in. Oggy looks unbeatable and makes an acrobatic save from Kerry Dixon. Niedzwiecki has only one shot to save.											
3	A	EVERTON		18	D	1-1	1-0	Gibson 42	Ogrizovic	Borrows	Downs	Bowman	Kilcline	Peake	Bennett	Hibbitt*	Regis	Gibson	Adams	Gynn
	24/8		*27,673*	*11*	2			*Sharp 84*	*Southall*	*Stevens*	*v d Hauwe*	*Harper*	*Marshall*	*Heath*	*Steven*	*Lineker*	*Sharp*	*Bracewell*	*Sheedy**	*Atkins*
								Ref: F Roberts	An inspirational performance from Regis almost earns a surprise win over the champions. Sharp's late header saves the Toffees' blushes after Gibson had headed in Bennett's cross. £50,000 signing from Nuneaton, Paul Culpin, nets three for the reserves; he is close to a first-team debut.											
4	H	NEWCASTLE		19	L	1-2	0-0	Gibson 80	Ogrizovic	Borrows	Downs	Bowman*	Kilcline	Peake	Bennett	Hibbitt	Regis	Gibson	Adams	Gynn
	26/8		12,085	*3*	2			*Reilly 85, Stewart 89*	*Thomas*	*Anderson*	*Wharton*	*Gascoigne*	*Clarke*	*Roeder*	*McDonald*	*McCreery*	*Reilly*	*Beardsley*	*Stewart*	
								Ref: R Dilkes	The seats have been removed from the Spion Kop, increasing capacity to 22,500. A bad game, apart from the end, with City's defensive frailties exposed. The Magpies, with McFaul as acting manager after Jack Charlton's departure, snatch it with Reilly's volley and Stewart's low shot.											
5	A	WATFORD		21	L	0-3	0-2		Ogrizovic	Borrows	Downs	Bowman	Kilcline	Peake	Bennett	Hibbitt*	Regis	Gibson	Adams	Gynn
	31/8		*13,835*	*6*	2			*Rostron 4, West 43, Smillie 65*	*Coton*	*Gibbs*	*Rostron*	*Talbot*	*Terry*	*McClelland*	*Callaghan*	*Blissett**	*West*	*Jackett*	*Barnes*	*Smillie*
								Ref: I Borrett	Watford hit West Brom for five last week and carry on against City. All three goals come from near-post headers flicked on by John Barnes. Neil Smillie's is his debut goal. The warning bells are ringing already for the Sky Blues - no punch up front and being outfought in midfield.											
6	H	OXFORD		18	W	**5-2**	2-2	Bennett 19, Hibbitt 22, Briggs 60 (og),	Ogrizovic	Borrows	Downs	**Turner**	Kilcline	Peake	Bennett	Hibbitt	Regis	Gibson*	Gynn	**Culpin**
	3/9		10,233		5			*McDonald 2, 36* [Gynn 65, Kilcline 74p]	*Hardwick*	*Langan*	*McDonald*	*Trewick*	*Briggs*	*Shotton*	*McDermott*	*Aldridge**	*Charles*	*Hebberd*	*Brock*	*Barnett*
								Ref: T Ward	Oxford are playing in the top flight for the first time, and play a brave part in a magnificent error-strewn game. Bobby McDonald scores two on his return and former City youth Gary Barnett comes on as sub. Regis is involved in four goals and Gynn is fouled by Hebberd for the penalty.											
7	H	ARSENAL		20	L	0-2	0-1		Ogrizovic	Borrows	Downs	Turner	Kilcline	Peake	Adams	Hibbitt	Regis*	Gibson	Gynn	Culpin
	7/9		11,962	*5*	5			*Woodcock 27, Nicholas 89*	*Lukic*	*Anderson*	*Sansom*	*Davis*	*O'Leary*	*Caton*	*Robson*	*Allinson*	*Nicholas*	*Woodcock*	*Rix*	
								Ref: I Hendrick	Negative Arsenal strangle the life out of the game against ten-men City. Turner is stretchered off after 33 minutes, just four minutes after Paul Culpin came on for Regis. The Sky Blues are never in it against the over-physical Gunners. Terry Gibson is rumoured to be unsettled again.											
8	A	ASTON VILLA		20	D	1-1	1-1	Culpin 5	Ogrizovic	Borrows	Downs	Bowman	Kilcline	Peake	Adams	McGrath	Culpin	Gibson	Gynn*	Bennett
	14/9		*12,198*	*12*	6			*Hodge 10*	*Spink*	*Williams*	*Dorigo*	*Evans*	*Ormsby*	*Gibson*	*Birch*	*Walters*	*Gray*	*Hodge*	*Daley*	
								Ref: R Nixon	A minority of fans of both teams show disrespect for the minute's silence for Jock Stein. City come as close as ever to winning at Villa Park when Hodge fouls Bennett in the 87th minute. The ref waves play on and Villa are unbeaten in five. Culpin intercepted Williams' back-pass.											
9	A	SOUTHAMPTON		18	D	1-1	0-0	Gibson 60	Ogrizovic	Borrows	Downs	Bowman	Kilcline	Peake	Adams	McGrath	Culpin*	Gibson	Gynn	Bennett
	21/9		*12,576*	*17*	7			*Armstrong 70*	*Shilton*	*Golac**	*Dennis*	*Curtis*	*Wright*	*Bond*	*Townsend*	*Moran*	*Jordan*	*Armstrong*	*Wallace*	*Lawrence*
								Ref: N Butler	Five bookings for City in a game of 40 fouls and a welcome point at a bogey ground. Shilton makes a rare mistake when allowing Gibson's shot to go in but Armstrong's header levels. Bennett celebrates his new contract with a good half hour, soured by a flare-up with Mark Wright.											
10	H	WEST BROM		14	W	3-0	1-0	Adams 17p, Gibson 47, Peake 57	Ogrizovic	Borrows	Downs	Bowman	Stephens	Peake	Adams*	McGrath	Regis	Gibson	Bennett	Hibbitt
	28/9		10,270	*22*	10				*Godden*	*Nicholl*	*Statham*	*Hunt !*	*Bennett*	*Robertson*	*Valentine*	*Varadi*	*MacKenzie**	*Thomas*	*Crooks*	*Grealish*
								Ref: M Dimblebee	Albion are awful and it's their ninth defeat in a row. Manager Johnny Giles resigns after the game. Steve Hunt should have had a red card for a foul on Borrows but soon after lashes out at Bennett and is off. Debutant Mickey Thomas handles for the penalty. Stephens is back after injury.											

No	H/A	Opponent	Att / Pos	Res / Pts	F-A	H-T	Scorers, Times, and Referees	1	2	3	4	5	6	7	8	9	10	11	12 sub used
11	H	LEICESTER	16	W	3-0	1-0	Bowman 18, Gibson 47, Regis 50	Ogrizovic	Borrows	Downs	Bowman	Kilcline	Peake	Adams	McGrath	Regis*	Gibson	Bennett	Stephens
	6/10	10,956	*19*	13				*Andrews*	*Feeley*	*Morgan*	*McAllister*	*Rennie*	*Osman*	*Lynex*	*Bright*	*Smith A*	*Ramsey*	*Wilson*	
							Ref: K Cooper	Sunday morning games suit Cyrille Regis. He scores his first goal since the Everton game last season to seal an easy win against a struggling Leicester side. Gary Lineker has gone to Everton, but new signings Gary McAllister from Motherwell and Mark Bright look good prospects.											
12	A	SHEFFIELD WED	15	D	2-2	0-2	Adams 52, Gibson 78	Ogrizovic	Borrows	Downs	Bowman	Kilcline	Peake	Adams	McGrath	Regis	Gibson	Bennett	
	12/10	*19,132*	*5*	14			*Chapman 20, Shutt 44*	*Hodge*	*Sterland*	*Morris*	*Smith*	*Hart*	*Shirtliff*	*Chamberlain*	*Blair*	*Chapman*	*Shutt*	*Shelton*	
							Ref: A Robinson	The Owls take first-half advantage of a sloppy City performance with a Chapman header and a debut goal from Carl Shutt. After the break the tables are turned and Shirtliff's back-pass is pounced on by Adams and Gibson sets a Div 1 club record by scoring for the sixth game in a row.											
13	H	TOTTENHAM	15	L	2-3	2-1	Bennett 17, Kilcline 24p	Ogrizovic	Borrows	Downs	Bowman*	Kilcline	Peake	Adams	McGrath	Regis	Gibson	Bennett	Gynn
	20/10	13,578	*9*	14			*Hoddle 3p, Falco 54, Chiedozie 60*	*Clemence*	*Stevens*	*Hughton*	*Roberts*	*Miller*	*Perryman*	*Ardiles**	*Falco*	*Galvin*	*Hoddle*	*Waddle*	*Chiedozie*
							Ref: M Heath	Gibson has been up all night at the birth of his child and plays poorly. Keeper Clemence boobs for the first goal and can't stop Killer's penalty when Gibson is fouled. Spurs have two penalties. Hoddle scores as Downs fouls Waddle, but Oggy saves Graham Roberts 78th-minute kick.											
14	A	BIRMINGHAM	14	W	1-0	1-0	Gibson 16	Ogrizovic	Borrows	Downs	Bowman	Kilcline	Peake	Adams	McGrath	Regis	Gibson	Bennett	
	26/10	*9,267*	*15*	17				*Seaman*	*Ranson*	*Jones*	*Wright*	*Armstrong**	*Kuhl*	*Roberts*	*Hagan*	*Kennedy*	*Geddis*	*Hopkins*	*Platnauer*
							Ref: K Hackett	A low-quality derby match in front of a pitifully low crowd. Ron Saunders' team look a poor outfit and City scrape home. Gibson scores his 48th goal in his 100th game, fastening on to a long kick from Oggy, eluding two defenders and scoring coolly. Fans rampage after the game.											
15	A	MANCHESTER U	14	L	0-2	0-2		Ogrizovic	Borrows	Downs	Bowman	Kilcline	Peake	Adams	McGrath	**Evans**	Turner*	Bennett	Gynn
	2/11	***46,748***	*1*	17			*Olsen 18, 41*	*Bailey*	*Garton*	*Albiston*	*Whiteside*	*Moran*	*Hogg*	*McGrath*	*Olsen*	*Hughes*	*Stapleton*	*Barnes*	
							Ref: J McAuley	Big Ron's United are ten points clear and unbeaten after 15 games. The biggest crowd to watch City play since 1980 see a weakened City team fight hard but lose when errors by Turner and Bowman let in Olsen. United paid City £50,000 for Peter Barnes and he has a new lease of life.											
16	H	LIVERPOOL	16	L	0-3	0-1		Ogrizovic	Borrows	Downs*	Bowman	**Rodger**	Peake	Adams	McGrath	Evans	Gibson	Bennett	**Williams**
	9/11	16,648	*2*	17			*Beglin 5, Walsh 48, Rush 82*	*Grobbelaar*	*Nicol*	*Beglin*	*Lawrenson*	*Whelan*	*Hansen*	*Walsh*	*Johnston*	*Rush*	*Molby*	*McMahon**	*Neal*
							Ref: D Vickers	Liverpool under new player-manager Dalglish are stung by United's wonder start but are ignored at one's peril. They dominate an injury-hit City but require errors from Oggy and Peake to give them the points. Greg Downs is barracked by City fans, who have little to cheer about.											
17	A	LUTON	15	W	1-0	1-0	Bowman 35	Ogrizovic	Borrows	Adams	Bowman	Rodger	Peake	Gynn*	McGrath	Evans	Gibson	Bennett	Downs
	16/11	*9,607*	*11*	20				*Sealey*	*Breaker**	*Thomas*	*Nicholas*	*Foster*	*Donaghy*	*Hill*	*Stein*	*Harford*	*Nwajiobi*	*Preece*	*Parker*
							Ref: J Moules	City are the first team to beat Luton on their plastic pitch, but they upset the home fans with negative tactics. Davie Bowman's shot squirms through Les Sealey's hands to the delight of City fans. Five Coventry players are booked and Greg Downs comes on for ten seconds at the end.											
18	H	WEST HAM	15	L	0-1	0-0		Ogrizovic	Borrows	Downs	Bowman	Rodger	Peake	Adams	McGrath	Evans*	Gibson	Bennett	Turner
	23/11	11,027	*4*	20			*McAvennie 55*	*Parkes*	*Stewart*	*Walford*	*Gale*	*Martin*	*Devonshire*	*Ward*	*McAvennie*	*Dickens*	*Cottee*	*Orr*	
							Ref: J Worrall	High flying Hammers have won six in a row and are unbeaten in 14. Their latest scoring sensation, Frank McAvennie, scores his 17th goal of the season to win it. Downs silences his critics with a stormer. Ted Stocker joins the City board. Terry Gibson enters protracted contract talks.											
19	A	QP RANGERS	14	W	2-0	0-0	Gibson 77, Byrne 88 (og)	Ogrizovic	Borrows	Downs	Bowman	Rodger	Peake	Adams	Turner	Regis	Gibson	Bennett	
	30/11	*11,101*	*10*	23				*Barron*	*McDonald*	*Dawes*	*Robinson*	*Wicks*	*Fenwick*	*James*	*Fillery*	*Bannister*	*Byrne*	*Allen*	
							Ref: B Stevens	City win again on plastic and are only the second team to win at QPR this season. Gibson, cheered by Regis' return from injury, scores when Paul Barron fails to hold Brian Borrows' shot. Byrne heads in, trying to clear his lines, and Oggy has a blinder to keep Jim Smith's team at bay.											
20	H	CHELSEA	14	D	1-1	1-1	Gibson 7	Ogrizovic	Borrows	Downs	Bowman	Rodger	McGrath	Adams	Turner	Regis	Gibson	Bennett	
	7/12	8,439	*4*	24			*Murphy 30*	*Niedzwiecki*	*Wood*	*Dublin*	*Pates*	*McLaughlin*	*Jones*	*Nevin*	*Spackman*	*Dixon*	*Speedie*	*Murphy**	*McAllister*
							Ref: T Jones	The all-ticket morning kick-off keeps the crowd down as City gain a good point against John Hollins' team, who are unbeaten in six. Speedie has returned from playing for Scotland in Australia and his much-vaunted partnership with Dixon is well held by rookies Rodger and McGrath.											
21	A	MANCHESTER C	15	L	1-5	0-2	Gibson 72 *[Simpson 85]*	Ogrizovic	Borrows	Downs	Bowman	Rodger	McGrath*	Adams	Turner	Regis	Gibson	Bennett	Hibbitt
	14/12	*20,075*	*16*	24			*Davies 18, 55, Rodger 44 (og), Lillis 75,*	*Nixon*	*Reid*	*Power*	*Clements*	*McCarthy**	*Phillips*	*Lillis*	*May*	*Davies*	*McNab*	*Simpson*	*Melrose*
							Ref: D Hutchinson	Man City win in a canter against a poor Coventry team without regular defenders Kilcline and Peake. Three goals come after McGrath limps off, with Davies and Lillis scoring headers and Simpson lashing one in. The club are £800,000 in debt and quoted Luton £600,000 for Gibson.											

No	Date	Att	Pos	Pt	F-A	H-T	Scorers, Times, and Referees	1	2	3	4	5	6	7	8	9	10	11	12 sub used
22	H EVERTON		15	L	1-3	0-0	Gibson 60	Ogrizovic	Borrows	Downs	Bowman	Kilcline	Rodger	Adams	Turner	Regis	Gibson	Bennett	
	21/12	10,518	*6*	24			*Lineker 50,86, Sharp 62*	*Southall*	*Stevens*	*Pointon*	*Ratcliffe*	*v d Hauwe*	*Heath*	*Steven*	*Lineker*	*Sharp*	*Bracewell*	*Sheedy*	
							Ref: M Scott	Lineker is on his way to 30 league goals and he now has 13. He scores with an overhead kick after Rodger fails to clear and heads in after Oggy misses a cross. Gibson scores his 14th but City are powerless to stop Everton's victory. One point from five home games is relegation form.											
23	H IPSWICH		17	L	0-1	0-0		Ogrizovic	Borrows	Downs	Bowman	Kilcline	Rodger	Adams	Turner*	Regis	Gibson	McGrath	Bennett
	26/12	9,350	*20*	24			*D'Avray 88*	*Cooper*	*Yallop*	*McCall*	*Gleghorn*	*Cranson*	*Butcher*	*Stockwell**	*Brennan*	*D'Avray*	*Wilson*	*Dozzell*	*Sunderland*
							Ref: N Midgley	A heavy pitch and an icy wind make it hard work for both teams but Ipswich adapt better and snatch the late winner with Mitch D'Avray's shot off the underside of the bar. City fans boo the team off at the end after another awful home display, as City slip closer to the relegation zone.											
24	A NOTT'M FOREST		17	L	2-5	2-1	Regis 18, Adams 20	Ogrizovic	Borrows	Downs	Bowman	Kilcline	McGrath	Adams	Turner	Regis	Gibson	Bennett	
	1/1	*13,860*	*9*	24			*Webb 40, 52, 75, Metgod 79, D'port 84*	*Sutton*	*Mills*	*Williams*	*Walker*	*Birtles*	*Bowyer*	*Metgod*	*Webb*	*Clough*	*Davenport*	*Robertson*	
							Ref: M Cotton	By their high standards, Forest are having a poor season but they put on a super second-half display to consign City to their fourth defeat in a row. A two-goal lead on an icy pitch is wiped out by a super show by Neil Webb, who scores a hat-trick. Regis nets his first goal since October.											
25	H ASTON VILLA		16	D	3-3	3-1	Regis 22, Kilcline 41, 44p	Ogrizovic	Borrows	Downs	McGrath	Kilcline*	Peake	Hibbitt	Turner	Regis	Gibson	Williams	Bowman
	11/1	10,326	*18*	25			*Stainrod 2, Gray 61, Elliott 79*	*Spink*	*Norton*	*Dorigo*	*Evans*	*Elliott*	*Birch*	*Kerr*	*Stainrod*	*Gray*	*Hodge*	*Walters*	
							Ref: D Shaw	City haven't beaten Villa in 24 games since 1937 and let slip a 3-1 lead. Debut-boy Andy Williams sets up Regis' goal, then fouls Dorigo to give away a penalty at 3-2. Happily, Oggy saves Evans' kick. Kilcline scored earlier when Elliott felled Gibson. Stainrod nets after 73 seconds.											
26	H WATFORD		17	L	0-2	0-1		Ogrizovic	Borrows	Downs	McGrath	Rodger	Peake	Hibbitt	Turner	Regis	Evans*	Bennett	Williams
	18/1	**7,478**	*10*	25			*Barnes 22, 61*	*Coton*	*Gibbs*	*Rostron*	*Talbot*	*Terry*	*McClelland*	*Sterling*	*Callaghan**	*West*	*Jackett*	*Barnes*	*Lohman*
							Ref: K Hackett	Coventry's lowest league crowd since 1962 sees Watford win again. City create several chances but a combination of poor finishing and Coton saves keep them out. England man Barnes scores a tap in and a left-foot cracker after the defence opens like the Red Sea. It's getting desperate.											
27	A OXFORD		16	W	1-0	0-0	Turner 64	Ogrizovic	Borrows	Downs	McGrath	Rodger	Peake	Hibbitt*	Turner	Regis	Culpin	Williams	Evans
	25/1	*9,383*	*19*	28				*Judge*	*Trewick*	*Slatter*	*Phillips*	*Briggs*	*Shotton*	*Houghton*	*Aldridge*	*Leworthy*	*Hebberd*	*Brock**	*Jones*
							Ref: E Scales	City's first win in eight comes courtesy of Wayne Turner's first goal, a looping volley. Paul Culpin gets a game after 14 goals in 14 reserve games but £80,000 signing from Forest, Jim McInally, is out injured. The game is a dour relegation battle but City's defence keeps things tight.											
28	A NEWCASTLE		16	L	2-3	1-2	Regis 42, Brazil 63	Ogrizovic	Borrows	Downs	Bowman	McGrath	Peake	**Pickering**	Turner	Regis	**Brazil**	Williams*	Bennett
	1/2	*16,637*	*11*	28			*Beardsley 14, Allon 36, Wharton 79*	*Thomas*	*Anderson*	*Bailey*	*McCreery*	*Clarke*	*Roeder*	*Stephenson*	*Gascoigne**	*Allon*	*Beardsley*	*Wharton*	*McDonald*
							Ref: R Dilkes	City have been wheeling and dealing to avoid the drop. Gibson has gone to Man United for £650,000 with Alan Brazil coming the other way. Pickering has also arrived, from Sunderland. City pull back from 0-2, only to lose to a disputed goal which didn't look to have crossed the line.											
29	A TOTTENHAM		16	W	1-0	0-0	Regis 80	Ogrizovic	Borrows	Downs	Bowman	Kilcline	Peake	Bennett	McGrath	Regis	Brazil	Pickering	
	8/2	*13,155*	*13*	31				*Clemence*	*Stevens*	*Roberts**	*Mabbutt*	*Miller*	*Perryman*	*Chiedozie*	*Allen P*	*Dick*	*Hoddle*	*Waddle*	*Cooke*
							Ref: I Borrett	Spurs' second lowest crowd since the War, partially caused by a snowstorm, sees the home side beaten by a solid team performance. Clemence saves Spurs from a heavier defeat and manager Peter Shreeve find himself under pressure. Brazil has a good game against one of his old clubs.											
30	H BIRMINGHAM		16	D	4-4	0-2	Bennett 51, 73, Kilcline 58p, 88p	Ogrizovic	Borrows	Downs	Bowman	Kilcline	Peake	Bennett	Turner	Regis	Brazil	Pickering	
	16/2	14,353	*21*	32			*Kennedy 2, 81, Whitton 18, Kuhl 59*	*Seaman*	*Ranson*	*Roberts*	*Hagan*	*Whitton*	*Kuhl*	*Bremner*	*Clarke*	*Kennedy*	*Geddis*	*Hopkins*	
							Ref: K Lupton	Blues have won once in the last 20 games and John Bond is now in charge. They should have led 4-0 at half-time but City draw level as Roberts trips Bennett for a penalty. The game swings like a pendulum, with goals and misses galore, until Ranson fouls Pickering for a harsh penalty.											
31	H SOUTHAMPTON		14	W	3-2	0-2	Brazil 55, Pickering 58, Bennett 79	Ogrizovic	Borrows	Downs	Bowman	Kilcline	Peake	Bennett	McGrath	Regis	Brazil	Pickering	
	22/2	10,897	*15*	35			*Wright 17, Cockerill 38p*	*Shilton*	*Forrest*	*Holmes*	*Case*	*Wright*	*Bond*	*Lawrence*	*Cockerill*	*Moran*	*Armstrong*	*Wallace*	
							Ref: C Trussell	City come back again from 0-2 down, and this time earn their first home victory since October. Cockerill scores when Bowman fouls Wallace. Then Bennett takes over, setting up Brazil's header and scoring the third. In between, Pickering scores after Regis flicks on Borrows' free-kick.											

No	Venue	Opponent	Pos	Res	F-A	H-T	Scorers, Times, and Referees	1	2	3	4	5	6	7	8	9	10	11	12 sub used
32	A	LEICESTER	15	L	1-2	1-0	Pickering 27	Ogrizovic	Borrows	Downs	Bowman	Kilcline	Peake	Bennett	McGrath	Regis	Brazil	Pickering	
8/3		10,744	17	35			McAllister 80, Smith 87	Andrews	Feeley	Morgan	McAllister	Osman	O'Neill	Lynex	Sealey	Smith A	Mauchlan	Banks*	Cunningham
							Ref: G Courtney	On-loan substitute Laurie Cunningham turns the game after coming on in the 63rd minute. Leicester haven't played a league fixture for five weeks because of the weather but grab the points with McAllister's volley and Smith's pounce after Oggy fails to hold Cunningham's shot.											
33	H	SHEFFIELD WED	16	L	0-1	0-0		Ogrizovic	Borrows	Downs	Adams	Kilcline	Peake	Bennett*	McGrath	Regis	Brazil	Pickering	Williams
15/3		10,162	6	35			Sterland 63	Hodge	Sterland	Morris	Hart	Shirtliff	Worthington	Marwood	Megson	Chapman	Shutt	Snodin	
							Ref: A Gunn	Wednesday are FA Cup semi-finalists, but they are a boring team to watch. City lack the invention to break them down in a drab game on a muddy pitch. Sterland's header wins the points. Pickering, Suckling and McGrath play for England Under-21's, Pickering scoring the winner.											
34	A	WEST BROM	16	D	0-0	0-0		Ogrizovic	Borrows	Downs	McGrath	Kilcline	Peake	**McInally***	Brazil	Regis	Pickering	Adams	Williams
19/3		**8,831**	22	36				Naylor	Whitehead	Statham	Palmer	Dyson	Dickinson	Thompson	Varadi	Reilly	MacKenzie	Bradley	
							Ref: A Ward	Albion have had a dreadful season and are almost doomed. City also desperately need the points. Regis is shackled by new boy Carlton Palmer, who looks one for the future. Jim McInally finally makes his bow, but tires after an hour. The game offers lots of effort but little entertainment.											
35	A	ARSENAL	16	L	0-3	0-1	[Hayes 89]	Ogrizovic	Borrows	McInally	Adams*	Kilcline	Peake	Bennett	McGrath	Culpin	Brazil	Pickering	Williams
22/3		17,189	5	36			McInally 30 (og), Woodcock 51,	Lukic	Adams	Sansom	Williams	O'Leary	Keown	Hayes	Rocastle	Nicholas	Woodcock	Rix	
							Ref: L Shapter	McInally scores the 'own-goal of the season' with a header from Rix's cross as City are outclassed. Despite four wins in a row, Don Howe is sacked as stories circulate that Terry Venables is bound for Highbury. The new boss will inherit fine youngsters like Tony Adams and Rocastle.											
36	H	NOTT'M FOREST	16	D	0-0	0-0		Ogrizovic	Borrows	Downs	McGrath	Kilcline	Peake	Bennett	McInally*	Hibbitt	Brazil	Pickering	Culpin
29/3		9,447	10	37				Sutton	Fleming	Williams	Walker	Metgod	Bowyer	Carr	Campbell	Clough	Birtles	Rice	
							Ref: C Downey	A much-improved display by the Sky Blues but no victory. Brazil has a hat-trick of headed chances. One is cleared off the line, another saved by Steve Sutton, and the third hits the post. Des Walker handles two minutes from time but the ref waves play on. Hibbitt has a good game.											
37	A	IPSWICH	16	L	0-1	0-0		Ogrizovic	Borrows	Downs	McGrath	Kilcline	Peake	McInally*	Brazil	Regis	Pickering	Hibbitt	Bennett
31/3		13,485	17	37			Brennan 78	Hallworth	Parkin	McCall	Atkins	Cranson	Butcher	Cleghorn	Brennan	Cole	Wilson	Dozzell*	D'Avray
							Ref: J Key	A massive six-pointer on Easter Monday and City blow it. In a dreadful game, Ipswich just about deserve to win as the Sky Blues, without a goal for eight and a half hours, fail to muster a shot on target and Brazil is baited. Brennan's 30-yard screamer wins it for an enthusiastic Town.											
38	H	MANCHESTER U	17	L	1-3	0-2	Pickering 52	Ogrizovic	McInally	Downs*	Bowman	Kilcline	Peake	Bennett	McGrath	Regis	Brazil	Pickering	Adams
5/4		**16,898**	3	37			Gibson C 13, Robson 28, Strachan 83	Turner	Gidman	Albiston	Whiteside	McGrath	Higgins	Robson	Strachan	Hughes	Davenport	Gibson C*	Stapleton
							Ref: R Groves	United have thrown away their massive lead in the title race but still take City apart in the first half, with Strachan and Bryan Robson awesome. Pickering pulls one back before Strachan wraps it up from a tight angle. City assistant Frank Upton is sacked but Poynton says 'Mackay is safe'.											
39	A	LIVERPOOL	19	L	**0-5**	0-2		Ogrizovic	Borrows	Downs	Bowman*	Kilcline	Peake	Bennett	McGrath	Regis	Brazil	Pickering	Adams
12/4		42,729	1	37			Whelan 20, 25, 83, Molby 46, Rush 78	Grobbelaar	Gillespie	Beglin	Nicol	Whelan	Hansen	Dalglish	Johnston	Rush*	Molby	Wark	MacDonald
							Ref: D Hutchinson	Liverpool are in staggering form as they strive for the double and City are trampled underfoot. Whelan is the tormentor with a classy hat-trick and Rush scores his inevitable goal. City have not won in 19 visits to Anfield. Mackay resigns after the game and Curtis and Sillett take over.											
40	H	LUTON	17	W	1-0	0-0	Pickering 47	Ogrizovic	Borrows	Downs	Adams	Kilcline	Peake	Bennett	McGrath	Regis	Brazil	Pickering	
19/4		10,161	8	40				Sealey	Johnson*	Thomas	Nicholas	Foster	Donaghy	Hill	Breaker	Harford	Newell	Preece	Stein
							Ref: D Phillips	The Hatters are having their best season ever but are no match for a Curtis-Sillett inspired City, who attack non-stop for 90 minutes. The players look reborn and Nick Pickering seals it after several chances are missed. Ipswich lose to ease the Sky Blues relegation fears a bit more.											
41	A	WEST HAM	18	L	0-1	0-0		Ogrizovic	Borrows	Downs	Adams	Kilcline	Peake	Bennett	McGrath	Regis	Brazil	Pickering	
26/4		27,251	4	40			Cottee 62	Parkes	Stewart	Parris	Gale	Martin	Devonshire	Ward	McAvennie	Dickens	Cottee	Orr	
							Ref: I Hemley	West Ham hit Newcastle for eight in midweek and with games in hand they can still win the title. But City are made of sterner stuff and merited a point after a proud performance. Cottee's 24th goal of the season clinches it. For the third year running City need to win their final game.											
42	H	QP RANGERS	17	W	2-1	2-1	Kilcline 37, Bennett 44	Ogrizovic	Borrows	Downs	Adams	Kilcline	Peake	Bennett	McGrath	Regis	Brazil	Pickering	
3/5		14,080	13	43			Byrne 28	Barron	McDonald	Dawes	Neill	Wicks	Fenwick*	Kerslake	James	Rosenior	Byrne	Fereday	Chivers
	Home	Away					Ref: N Wilson	City fans have to live on their nerves as QPR take the lead. By half-time Coventry are ahead, thanks to Brian Kilcline's thunderous free-kick and Dave Bennett's cool finish. With 12 minutes left Kerslake hits the bar, but City hang on and, with Ipswich and Oxford losing, they are safe.											
Average	11,590	17,673																	

Milk Cup					F-A	H-T	Scorers, Times, and Referees	1	2	3	4	5	6	7	8	9	10	11	12 sub used
2:1	A	CHESTER	18	W	2-1	0-0	Gibson 53, Bowman 86	Ogrizovic	Borrows	Downs	Bowman	Kilcline*	Peake	Adams	McGrath	Bennett	Gibson	Gynn	Hibbitt
	25/9	*4,836*	*4:5*				*Rimmer 57p*	*Butcher*	*Glenn*	*Lane*	*Holden*	*Gage*	*Coy*	*Kelly*	*Graham*	*Rimmer*	*Houghton*	*Bennett*	
							Ref: T Mills	Lowly Chester, with four wins in a row behind them, match City until Bowman's Brazilian-style goal. His right-footer from 30 yards bends and dips and beats Butcher all ends up. Rimmer's twice-taken penalty is awarded for McGrath's foul on him. Gibson heads in from Gynn's cross.											
2:2	H	CHESTER	16	W	7-2	4-2	Regis 2, 18, 30, 43, 88, Gib' 52, Kil' 76	Ogrizovic	Borrows	Downs	Bowman	Kilcline	Peake	Adams	McGrath*	Regis	Gibson	Bennett	Stephens
	9/10	5,519	*4:3*				*Murray 20, Rimmer 35p*	*Butcher*	*Glenn*	*Lane*	*Speight*	*Greenhough*	*Coy*	*Kelly*	*Graham*	*Rimmer*	*Murray*	*Brett*	
							Ref: R Lewis (City win 9-3 on aggregate)	Regis equals the League Cup record and becomes the first City player to score five in a game since 1934. He bags a hat-trick inside 30 minutes but Rimmer scores from the spot after Regis fouls Greenhough to make it 3-2. Kilcline blasts home a free-kick before Cyrille gets his fifth.											
3	H	WEST BROM	14	D	0-0	0-0		Ogrizovic	Borrows	Downs	Bowman*	Kilcline	Peake	Adams	McGrath	Regis	Gibson	Bennett	Gynn
	29/10	9,814	*22*					*Bradshaw*	*Nicholl*	*Statham*	*Hunt*	*Bennett*	*Robertson*	*Valentine*	*Grealish*	*Varadi*	*Thomas*	*Crooks*	
							Ref: C Downey	The gate for this blood and thunder cup-tie is healthy, considering there is a bus strike. Under new boss Nobby Stiles, Albion are physical and have three men booked. City let the Baggies off the hook after a second-half onslaught and Paul Bradshaw saves two screamers from Regis.											
3R	A	WEST BROM	14	L	3-4	2-3	Evans 2, Bennett 21, 48	Ogrizovic	Borrows	Downs	Bowman	Kilcline*	Peake	Culpin	McGrath	Evans	Turner	Bennett	Rodger
	6/11	*8,987*	*22*				*Varadi 3, 19, Crooks 10, Hunt 66*	*Bradshaw*	*Nicholl*	*Statham*	*Hunt*	*Bennett*	*Robertson**	*Valentine*	*Grealish*	*Varadi*	*Thomas*	*Crooks*	*Whitehead*
							Ref: D Scott	City bow out to the worst side in the top division in a cracking cup-tie. In the first half both defences compete to see who can make the most mistakes. Bennett's goal brings City level, until man-of-the-match Steve Hunt's winner. Rodger makes his debut. WBA meet Villa in Round 4.											

FA Cup																			
3	H	WATFORD	17	L	1-3	0-0	Kilcline 58	Ogrizovic	Borrows	Rodger*	McGrath	Kilcline	Peake	Adams	Turner	Regis	Gibson	Bennett	Bowman
	4/1	10,498	*12*				*West 61, 71, Jackett 72*	*Coton*	*Gibbs*	*Rostron*	*Talbot*	*Terry*	*McClelland*	*Sterling*	*Callaghan*	*West*	*Jackett*	*Barnes*	
							Ref: J Martin	Three Watford goals in eleven minutes dump City out in a snow-affected game. Its a depressing performance and City lack confidence even when they are ahead. Big Colin West does the damage as the Hornets record their first away win since September. Peake is back after injury.											

		Home					Away					
	P	W	D	L	F	A	W	D	L	F	A	Pts
1 Liverpool	42	16	4	1	58	14	10	6	5	31	23	88
2 Everton	42	16	3	2	54	18	10	5	6	33	23	86
3 WestHam	42	17	2	2	48	16	9	4	8	26	24	84
4 Manchester U	42	12	5	4	35	12	10	5	6	35	24	76
5 Sheffield Wed	42	13	6	2	36	23	8	4	9	27	31	73
6 Chelsea	42	12	4	5	32	27	8	7	6	25	29	71
7 Arsenal	42	13	5	3	29	15	7	4	10	20	32	69
8 Nott'm Forest	42	11	5	5	38	25	8	6	7	31	28	68
9 Luton	42	12	6	3	37	15	6	6	9	24	29	66
10 Tottenham	42	12	2	7	47	25	7	6	8	27	27	65
11 Newcastle	42	12	5	4	46	31	5	7	9	21	41	63
12 Watford	42	11	6	4	40	22	5	5	11	29	40	59
13 QP Rangers	42	12	3	6	33	20	3	4	14	20	44	52
14 Southampton	42	10	6	5	32	18	2	4	15	19	44	46
15 Manchester C	42	7	7	7	25	26	4	5	12	18	31	45
16 Aston Villa	42	7	6	8	27	28	3	8	10	24	39	44
17 COVENTRY	42	6	5	10	31	35	5	5	11	17	36	43
18 Oxford	42	7	7	7	34	27	3	5	13	28	53	42
19 Leicester	42	7	8	6	35	35	3	4	14	19	41	42
20 Ipswich	42	8	5	8	20	24	3	3	15	12	31	41
21 Birmingham	42	5	2	14	13	25	3	3	15	17	48	29
22 West Brom	42	3	8	10	21	36	1	4	16	14	53	24
	924	229	110	123	771	517	123	110	229	517	771	1276

Odds & ends

Double wins: (3) Luton, QP Rangers, Oxford.
Double losses: (7) Newcastle, Liverpool, Arsenal, West Ham, Ipswich, Watford, Manchester U.

Won from behind: (3) Oxford (h), Southampton (h), QP Rangers (h).
Lost from in front: (6) Newcastle (h), Tottenham (h), Nott'm Forest (a), Leicester (a), West Brom (LC), Watfod (FAC).

High spots: Coming from 0-2 down to beat Southampton.
Gibson scoring in seven successive games.
Curtis and Sillett taking over from Mackay after Anfield debacle.
Winning on the last day of the season to guarantee safety.

Low spots: Losing at Forest after leading 2-0.
Only one win in first nine games.
Seven games without a win in December and January.
Five games without a goal in March.

Red cards: Opponents – Hunt (West Brom h).
Player of the Year: Trevor Peake.
Ever-presents: (1) Steve Ogrizovic.
Hat-tricks: (1) Cyrille Regis.
Opposing hat-tricks: (2) Webb (Nott'm Forest), Whelan (Liverpool).
Leading scorer: (13) Terry Gibson.

	Appearances						Goals			
	Lge	*Sub*	LC	*Sub*	FAC	*Sub*	Lge	LC	FAC	Tot
Adams, Micky	**29**	*2*	3		1		**3**			**3**
Bennett, Dave	**33**	*5*	4		1		**6**	2		**8**
Borrows, Brian	**41**		4		1					
Bowman, David	**29**	*1*	4			*1*	**2**	1		**3**
Brazil, Alan	**15**						**2**			**2**
Culpin, Paul	**4**	*3*	1				**1**			**1**
Downs, Greg	**40**	*1*	4							
Evans, Gareth	**5**	*1*	1					1		**1**
Gibson, Terry	**24**		3		1		**11**	2		**13**
Gynn, Michael	**6**	*6*	1	*1*			**1**			**1**
Hibbitt, Kenny	**11**	*3*		*1*			**1**			**1**
Kilcline, Brian	**32**		4		1		**7**	1	1	**9**
McGrath, Lloyd	**32**		4		1					
McInally, Jim	**5**									
Ogrizovic, Steve	**42**		4		1					
Peake, Trevor	**37**		4		1		**1**			**1**
Pickering, Nick	**15**						**4**			**4**
Regis, Cyrille	**34**		2		1		**5**	5		**10**
Rodger, Graham	**10**			*1*	1					
Stephens, Kirk	**1**	*1*		*1*						
Turner, Wayne	**14**	*1*	1		1		**1**			**1**
Williams, Andy	**3**	*5*								
(own-goals)							**3**			**3**
22 players used	**462**	***29***	**44**	***4***	**11**	***1***	**48**	**12**	**1**	**61**

TODAY LEAGUE DIVISION 1 — Manager: George Curtis — SEASON 1986-87

No	Date	Opponent	Att	Pos	Pt	F-A	H-T	Scorers, Times, and Referees	1	2	3	4	5	6	7	8	9	10	11	12 sub used
1	A	WEST HAM			L	0-1	0-0		Ogrizovic	Borrows	Downs	McGrath	Kilcline	Peake	**Phillips**	Bennett*	Regis	**Houchen**	Pickering	Adams
	23/8		*21,368*		0			*Gale 84*	*Parkes*	*Stewart*	*Parris*	*Gale*	*Martin*	*Devonshire*	*Ward*	*McAvennie*	*Dickens*	*Cottee*	*Orr*	
								Ref: L Shapter	Tony Gale scores his first goal for West Ham in his 94th match, a beautifully flighted free-kick that gave Oggy no chance. Phillips, Painter and Houchen have come, Brazil, Bowman, Suckling and McInally gone. With their new striped shirts, City defend well but lack punch up front.											
2	H	ARSENAL			W	2-1	1-0	Regis 20, Pickering 85	Ogrizovic	Borrows	Downs	McGrath	Kilcline	Peake	**Sedgley**	Phillips	Regis	Houchen	Pickering	
	26/8		11,370		3			*Anderson 48*	*Lukic*	*Anderson*	*Sansom*	*Robson*	*O'Leary*	*Adams*	*Rocastle*	*Davis*	*Quinn*	*Nicholas*	*Rix**	*Hayes*
								Ref: K Breen	With severe competition for places, Painter can't get a game and Regis is kept on his toes. Cyrille scores a special from 25-yards and Pickering grabs the win after Lukic fails to hold Houchen's header. Arsenal's new boss, George Graham, can't follow his winning start over Man United.											
3	H	EVERTON		13	D	1-1	1-0	Pickering 23	Ogrizovic	Borrows	Downs	McGrath	Kilcline	Peake	Sedgley	Phillips	Regis	Houchen	Pickering	
	30/8		13,662	*6*	4			*Marshall 78*	*Mimms*	*Harper*	*Power*	*Ratcliffe*	*Watson*	*Langley**	*Steven*	*Heath*	*Sharp*	*Adams*	*Sheedy*	*Marshall*
								Ref: J Deakin	City lead an under-strength Everton for almost an hour before Ian Marshall equalises three minutes after coming on. Pickering netted after fine work by Regis and Downs, as City dominated the first half with 18-year-old Sedgley superb. The Toffees fight back and come close to a win.											
4	A	CHELSEA		14	D	0-0	0-0		Ogrizovic	Borrows	Downs	McGrath	Kilcline	Peake	Bennett	Phillips	Regis	Sedgley	Pickering	
	2/9		*11,839*	*18*	5				*Godden*	*Wood*	*Millar*	*Pates*	*McLaughlin*	*Bumstead*	*Nevin*	*Spackman*	*Dixon*	*Speedie*	*Murphy*	
								Ref: G Napthine	Chelsea are having problems and their fans are baying for blood. They muster only one shot on goal and the Speedie-Dixon combo looks rusty. Cyrille Regis has City's best chances but is brought down in full flight by Tony Godden and is tackled by John Bumstead when about to score.											
5	A	MANCHESTER C		10	W	1-0	1-0	Regis 37	Ogrizovic	Borrows	Downs	McGrath	Kilcline	Peake	Bennett	Phillips	Regis	Sedgley	Pickering	
	6/9		*18,320*	*14*	8				*Suckling*	*Clements*	*May*	*Baker*	*McCarthy*	*Redmond*	*Hopkins*	*McNab*	*Christie*	*Davies**	*Wilson*	*Brightwell I*
								Ref: N Ashley	An impressive all-round performance, highlighted by Regis's goal from Borrows' cross. Bennett is the real architect against his old club and he could have netted twice. David Phillips has a goal from a free-kick ruled out for no good reason. Wayne Turner moves to Brentford for £30,000.											
6	H	NEWCASTLE		5	W	3-0	1-0	Kilcline 15, Bennett 48, Adams 60	Ogrizovic	Borrows	Downs	McGrath	Kilcline	Peake	Bennett	Adams	Regis	Sedgley	Pickering	
	13/9		11,439	*22*	11				*Thomas*	*McDonald*	*Bailey*	*McCreery*	*Clarke*	*Anderson*	*Davies*	*Gascoigne*	*Whitehurst*	*Cunningham*	*Stewart*	
								Ref: J Worrall	The Regis-Bennett partnership looks sharp and Cyrille is unlucky not to score. City shake off their Houdini tag and give bottom of the table Newcastle a good hiding. Brian Kilcline hits a free-kick special, Bennett coolly finishes, and Adams hits a volley after a long punt from Oggy.											
7	A	CHARLTON		6	D	1-1	0-0	Aizlewood 88(og)	Ogrizovic	Borrows	Downs	McGrath	Kilcline	Phillips*	Bennett	Adams	Regis	Sedgley	Pickering	Evans
	20/9		*5,527*	*19*	12			*Shirtliff 54*	*Johns*	*Humphrey*	*Reid*	*Peake*	*Thompson*	*Shirtliff*	*Lee*	*Stuart*	*Melrose*	*Aizlewood*	*Walsh*	
								Ref: A Gunn	Charlton celebrated their move from the Valley to Selhurst Park with promotion to Div 1 after a 30-year absence. But their gates are low and this is the lowest crowd to watch City in Div 1. City's good run continues with a lucky goal; the ball balloons off Aizlewood and past Johns.											
8	H	WATFORD		4	W	1-0	0-0	Bennett 56	Ogrizovic	Borrows	Downs	McGrath	Kilcline	Peake	Bennett	Phillips	Regis	Adams	Pickering	
	27/9		11,074	*12*	15				*Coton*	*Bardsley*	*Rostron*	*Richardson*	*Terry*	*McClelland*	*Callaghan*	*Blissett**	*Barnes*	*Jackett*	*Sterling*	*Talbot*
								Ref: R Milford	City's confidence is flowing again but the fans are only trickling back. Another entertaining game, with City well on top, but they are unable to turn their dominance into goals. Bennett breaks the deadlock with some magical individualism. City's new sponsors are Granada Social Clubs.											
9	H	ASTON VILLA		6	L	0-1	0-0		Ogrizovic	Borrows	Downs	McGrath	Kilcline	Peake	Bennett	Phillips*	Regis	Adams	Pickering	Gynn
	4/10		19,047	*20*	15			*Thompson 53*	*Spink*	*Norton*	*Dorigo*	*Evans*	*Elliott*	*Keown*	*Birch*	*Stainrod**	*Thompson*	*Hodge*	*Hunt*	*Gray*
								Ref: K Walmsley	Villa end City's unbeaten run by employing no-nonsense tactics on Regis and Bennett. Billy McNeill is Villa's new boss and this win lifts them off the bottom. City create plenty of chances, with Regis, Gynn and Kilcline all going close. Gary Thompson's headed goal looks offside.											
10	A	OXFORD		10	L	0-2	0-0		Ogrizovic	Borrows	Adams	Gynn*	Rodger	Peake	Bennett	Phillips	Regis	Sedgley	Pickering	Williams
	11/10		*9,530*	*15*	15			*Aldridge 46, 78p*	*Parks*	*Langan*	*Slatter*	*Trewick*	*Briggs*	*Dreyer*	*Houghton*	*Aldridge*	*Hamilton*	*Hebberd*	*Perryman*	
								Ref: B Hill (D Morgan)	Referee Hill went off with a pulled muscle after 27 minutes and his replacement, Don Morgan, infuriates Regis by disallowing two 'goals' and awarding a penalty against him for a dubious handball. John Aldridge slots it home to add to his earlier goal, which was against the run of play.											

No	Venue / Date	Opponent / Att	Pos	Res / Pts	F-A	H-T	Scorers, Times, and Referees	1	2	3	4	5	6	7	8	9	10	11	12
11	H	WIMBLEDON	8	W	1-0	0-0	Bennett 58	Ogrizovic	Borrows	Downs	**Emerson**	Kilcline*	Peake	Bennett	Phillips	Regis	Adams	Pickering	**Painter**
	19/10	11,068	*16*	18				*Beasant*	*Thorn*	*Winterburn*	*Downes*	*Morris*	*Gayle*	*Sanchez*	*Gannon*	*Fashanu*	*Sayer**	*Fairweather*	*Cork*
							Ref: N Midgley	Wimbledon have only been in the League for nine years and their kick and rush style belongs to the nether regions. They catch City offside 22 times and have no concern for the entertainment level. The first half is dreadful but things improve after the break. Emerson signs for £40,000.											
12	A	SHEFFIELD WED	6	D	2-2	1-1	Regis 35, Ogrizovic 63	Ogrizovic	Borrows	Downs	Emerson	Rodger*	Peake	Bennett	Phillips	Regis	Adams	Pickering	Painter
	25/10	*20,035*	*9*	19			*Chapman 43, 75*	*Hodge*	*Sterland*	*Worthington*	*Hart*	*Knight*	*Chamberlain*	*Marwood*	*Megson*	*Chapman*	*Walker*	*Gregory*	
							Ref: G Courtney	Hillsborough is wet and windy but both sides put on a great display of football with lots of goalmouth action. Oggy scores with a massive punt which bounces once and clears Owls' Martin Hodge. Lee Chapman equalises with his second headed goal. Emerson looks the part in midfield.											
13	A	MANCHESTER U	8	D	1-1	0-1	Phillips 51	Ogrizovic	Borrows	Downs	McGrath	Sedgley	Peake	Bennett	Phillips	Regis	Emerson	Pickering	
	1/11	***36,946***	*19*	20			*Davenport 31*	*Turner*	*Sivebaek*	*Albiston*	*Whiteside*	*McGrath*	*Hogg*	*Robson**	*Strachan*	*Stapleton*	*Davenport*	*Olsen*	*Moses*
							Ref: M Heath	United are having a rough patch and Ron Atkinson will be sacked after this result. That shouldn't detract from a fine City display that deserved all three points. Dean Emerson, the former Stretford-ender, looks brilliant and David Phillips caps a good display with the left-footed equaliser.											
14	H	NOTT'M FOREST	6	W	1-0	0-0	Pickering 55	Ogrizovic	Borrows	Downs	McGrath	Sedgley	Peake	Bennett	Phillips	Regis	Emerson	Pickering	
	8/11	16,306	*2*	23				*Segers*	*Butterworth*	*Pearce*	*Walker*	*Metgod*	*Bowyer*	*Carr*	*Webb*	*Clough*	*Birtles*	*Mills*	
							Ref: M Peck	A perfect City performance earns the points against the table-toppers. City are tight at the back, tigerish in midfield, dangerous up front. Forest never give up though, and could have snatched a point. Brooking raves about City on the radio but Curtis refuses to talk about a title challenge.											
15	A	TOTTENHAM	8	L	0-1	0-1		Ogrizovic	Borrows	Downs	McGrath	Sedgley	Peake	Bennett	Phillips	Regis	Emerson	Pickering	
	15/11	*20,255*	*9*	23			*Allen C 22*	*Clemence*	*Hughton**	*Thomas*	*Polston*	*Gough*	*Mabbutt*	*Allen C*	*Claessen*	*Waddle*	*Hoddle*	*Allen P*	*Ardiles*
							Ref: D Hedges	Spurs bounce back from three defeats to claim the points against a disappointing City. This is Clive Allen's season. His winning goal is his 16th of the season. Hoddle, with a white headband to protect a wound, is the inspiration in a star-studded team for whom Polston makes his debut.											
16	H	NORWICH	7	W	2-1	1-1	Phillips 7, 56	Ogrizovic	Borrows	Downs	McGrath	Sedgley	Peake	Bennett	Phillips	Regis	Emerson	Pickering	
	22/11	**11,029**	*8*	26			*Biggins 19*	*Gunn*	*Culverhouse*	*Seagraves*	*Bruce*	*Phelan**	*Elliott*	*Crook*	*Drinkell*	*Biggins*	*Putney*	*Gordon*	*Barham*
							Ref: D Hutchinson	Norwich topped the table a month ago and are stubborn opponents. Phillips hits two excellent strikes and has a third disallowed for an obscure infringement. The talented Gordon almost snatches a point before Regis and Emerson miss chances. The lack of goals from strikers is a worry.											
17	A	LIVERPOOL	9	L	0-2	0-1		Ogrizovic	Borrows	Downs	McGrath	Sedgley	Peake	Bennett	Phillips	Regis	Emerson	Pickering	
	29/11	*31,614*	*3*	26			*Molby 24p, Wark 90*	*Grobbelaar*	*Gillespie*	*Beglin*	*Lawrenson*	*Whelan*	*Hansen*	*Walsh*	*Nicol*	*Rush*	*Molby**	*McMahon*	*Wark*
							Ref: J Lovat	A return to Anfield four days after the Milk Cup exit. Another penalty is conceded when Oggy brings down Rush, but it looked outside the box. Pool fans are campaigning to stop Rush being sold to Juventus next summer. They were silenced when City were on top. Emerson shines.											
18	H	LEICESTER	8	W	1-0	0-0	Regis 72	Ogrizovic	Borrows	Downs	McGrath*	Sedgley	Peake	Bennett	Phillips	Regis	Emerson	Pickering	Culpin
	6/12	12,318	*20*	29				*Andrews*	*Morgan*	*Venus !*	*Osman*	*Walsh**	*McAllister*	*Mauchlen*	*Feeley*	*Smith*	*Wilson*	*Sealy*	*Moran*
							Ref: K Lupton	City's winning reputation goes before them. Leicester play a sweeper and thwart them until the last quarter. The Foxes have gone eight without a win and their one chance is when McAllister's free-kick beats Oggy but hits a post. Mark Venus walks for two yellow card fouls on Bennett.											
19	H	MANCHESTER C	10	D	2-2	2-1	Culpin 2, Adams 40	Ogrizovic	Borrows	Downs	Emerson	Sedgley	Peake	Bennett	Phillips	Regis	Culpin	Adams	
	21/12	12,689	*21*	30			*Redmond 5, 62*	*Suckling*	*Reid*	*Wilson*	*Clements*	*McCarthy*	*Redmond*	*White*	*McNab*	*Varadi*	*Moulden*	*McIlroy*	
							Ref: J Ashworth	Jimmy Frizzell has replaced Billy McNeill at Maine Road but can't keep Man City out of the relegation zone. They deserve their draw after twice coming from behind on a cold and windy Sunday morning. Varadi and Moulden cause City problems. Oggy is lucky not to be sent off.											
20	A	QP RANGERS	10	L	**1-3**	0-1	Gynn 69	Ogrizovic	Borrows	Downs	Emerson	Sedgley	Peake	Bennett	Phillips	Regis	Gynn	Adams	
	26/12	*10,053*	*15*	30			*Byrne 36, Bannister 54, Allen 85*	*Seaman*	*James*	*Dawes*	*Allen*	*McDonald*	*Fenwick*	*Lee*	*Robinson*	*Bannister*	*Byrne*	*Peacock**	*Rosenior*
							Ref: M Bodenham	QPR's plastic pitch doesn't make for an exciting morning match, as City are punished for defensive errors. Ex-City man Bannister scores when Oggy drops a cross and Allen catches the big man off his line with a floater. David Seaman is superb, making three great saves from Bennett.											
21	H	TOTTENHAM	7	W	4-3	1-2	Houchen 42, Bennett 59, 62, Regis 90	Ogrizovic	Phillips	Downs*	Emerson	Sedgley	Peake	Bennett	Houchen	Regis	Gynn	Adams	Pickering
	27/12	22,175	*6*	33			*Allen C 38, 45, Claessen 84*	*Clemence*	*Thomas*	*Ardiles**	*Hodge*	*Gough*	*Mabbutt*	*Allen C*	*Allen P*	*Waddle*	*Hoddle*	*Galvin*	*Claessen*
							Ref: J Lloyd	This first home win over Spurs for 13 years is a thriller, decided by Regis's header in the last minute after his first header hit the bar. Allen has now scored 28 times but Bennett's brace are better. Spurs wear City's yellow away shirts in front of City's biggest league crowd for six years.											

No	Date		Att	Pos	Pt	F-A	H-T	Scorers, Times, and Referees	1	2	3	4	5	6	7	8	9	10	11	12 sub used
22	H	LUTON		11	L	0-1	0-1		Ogrizovic	Borrows	Pickering	Emerson	Sedgley	Kilcline	Bennett	Phillips	Regis	Gynn	Houchen	
	1/1		16,667	7	33			Stein B 41	Sealey	Breaker	Johnson	Nicholas	Foster	Donaghy	Wilson	Stein B	Newell	Harford	Grimes	
								Ref: F Roberts	John Moore is having a good first season in charge at Luton, and Town win despite being outplayed. City's attack stutters again and when they get a shot on target Les Sealey defies them. The ex-City keeper is baited and does cartwheels at the final whistle. Kilcline returns after injury.											
23	A	NEWCASTLE		8	W	2-1	1-0	Bennett 1, Regis 57	Ogrizovic	Borrows	Downs	Emerson	Kilcline	Peake	Bennett	Phillips	Regis	Sedgley	Pickering	
	3/1		22,366	22	36			McDonald 85	Thomas M	Davies*	Wharton	McCreery	Jackson P	Roeder	McDonald	Thomas A	Goddard	Jackson D	Wrightson	Stewart
								Ref: A Flood	Iam McFaul's Newcastle have slipped into the relegation zone with five defeats in a row. They miss the injured Beardsley. City's second away win is sparked by Bennett scoring after 42 seconds. Brian Kilcline leads the players out of the wrong dressing room door and into the car park.											
24	A	ARSENAL		8	D	0-0	0-0		Ogrizovic	Borrows	Downs	Emerson	Kilcline	Peake	McGrath	Houchen	Regis	Gynn	Pickering	
	18/1		17,561	1	37				Lukic	Anderson	Sansom	Williams	O'Leary	Adams	Rocastle	Davis	Quinn	Nicholas	Hayes*	Rix
								Ref: K Hackett	This is City's first ever 'live' TV game. They appear to disappoint the TV men by refusing to lie down and allow Arsenal to walk all over them. It is an impressive defensive display and Arsenal don't have the guile to break them down. Arsenal are unbeaten in 21 games and top the table.											
25	H	WEST HAM		8	L	**1-3**	0-2	Borrows 87p	Ogrizovic	Borrows	Downs	Emerson	Kilcline*	Peake	McGrath	Houchen	Regis	Gynn	Phillips	Painter
	24/1		14,170	9	37			Cottee 15, 44, 58	Parkes	Walford	Parris	Hilton	Martin	Devonshire	Ward	McAvennie	Dickens	Cottee	Robson	
								Ref: D Allison	Cottee's razor-sharp finishing is the difference between two well matched sides. He has now scored ten goals in nine games against City and West Ham have won nine in a row against City. Hammers' £700,000 signing from Arsenal, Stewart Robson, is impressive and sets up the third.											
26	A	SOUTHAMPTON		8	L	0-2	0-0		Ogrizovic	Borrows*	Downs	Emerson	Kilcline	Peake	McGrath	Phillips	Regis	Houchen	Pickering	Gynn
	3/2		11,508	18	37			Cockerill 46, 67	Shilton	Forrest	Dennis	Case	Wright	Bond	Holmes	Cockerill*	Clarke	Armstrong	Hobson	Townsend
								Ref: D Vickers	A damp misty Dell pulls in its lowest crowd of the season. The Saints notch their first win in eight games. City don't perform until the last ten minutes when Shilton has to save from Peake, and Regis hits the bar. Dean Emerson is booked and now misses the Cup 5th round tie at Stoke.											
27	A	EVERTON		10	L	1-3	1-1	Regis 14	Ogrizovic	Borrows	Downs	Emerson	Kilcline	Peake	McGrath*	Phillips	Regis	Houchen	Pickering	Gynn
	7/2		30,408	1	37			Stevens 44, Steven 55p, Heath 70	Southall	Stevens	v d Hauwe	Ratcliffe	Watson	Reid	Steven	Heath	Sharp*	Snodin	Power	Harper
								Ref: J Key	Dejected City are hit by the Merseyside penalty hoodoo when Peter Reid's cross hits McGrath's hand. Until then, City were more than holding the prospective champions. Adrian Heath's header from a quickly taken free-kick clinches it. McGrath is booked and misses the Stoke cup-tie.											
28	H	CHELSEA		8	W	3-0	2-0	Kilcline 13p, McGrath 42, Pickering 63	Ogrizovic	Borrows	Downs	Emerson	Kilcline	Peake	McGrath	Phillips	Regis	Houchen	Pickering	
	14/2		12,906	16	40				Godden	Clarke	Dublin	Pates	Wicks	Bumstead*	Nevin	Hazard	Durie	Dixon	McNaught	Wood
								Ref: R Bridges	Troubled Pensioners, with nine players demanding transfers, are cannon fodder for City's Cup squad. Kilcline starts the rout after Dublin felled Houchen. McGrath provokes a massive roar as he scores his first ever goal and Pickering scores a sweet left-footer. City waste many chances.											
29	H	CHARLTON		8	W	2-1	0-0	Downs 48, Regis 69	Ogrizovic	Borrows	Downs	Gynn	Kilcline	Peake	Sedgley	Phillips	Regis	Houchen	Pickering	
	28/2		12,253	20	43			Melrose 54	Bolder	Humphrey	Reid	Peake	Thompson	Miller	Stuart	Lee	Melrose	Shipley	Walsh	
								Ref: M Peck	Long-serving manager Lennie Lawrence is struggling to keep the Robins up. Charlton have won once in 17 games. This is a poor game where City struggled. Ex-City man Melrose scores after sloppy errors. Charlton think Robert Lee's shot off the underside of the bar crossed the line.											
30	H	SHEFFIELD WED		8	W	1-0	0-0	McGrath 59	Ogrizovic	Borrows	Downs	Emerson*	Kilcline	Peake	McGrath	Phillips	Regis	Houchen	Pickering	Gynn
	7/3		12,846	15	46				Hodge	Sterland	Madden	Smith	May	Worthington	Marwood	Megson	Chapman	Bradshaw*	Shelton	Hirst
								Ref: D Hedges	A glue-pot of a pitch, near-blizzard conditions and an icy wind rule out inventive football in this FA Cup rehearsal. Regis makes the goal for McGrath, who is making a habit of scoring. City pass this test of strength and stamina, despite losing Emerson after Megson's bad tackle.											
31	H	OXFORD		8	W	3-0	0-0	Bennett 46, Regis 63, 69	Ogrizovic	Borrows	Downs	Gynn	Kilcline*	Peake	Bennett	Phillips	Regis	Houchen	Pickering	Sedgley
	20/3		23,924	16	49				Hardwick	Langan	Trewick	Phillips	Briggs	Caton	Houghton	Saunders	Whitehurst	Hebberd	Brock	
								Ref: D Phillips	The sixth successive win is a post-war record for Coventry, and is watched by their biggest league gate for six years, lured by hopes of semi-final vouchers. City produce champagne soccer after the break with three super goals after a dull first half. Maurice Evans' Oxford battle hard.											

No	Venue	Opponent	Pos	Res	FT	HT	Scorers, Times, Referees	1	2	3	4	5	6	7	8	9	10	11	12 sub used
32	A	WIMBLEDON	8	L	1-2	1-2	Gynn 5	Ogrizovic	Borrows	Downs	Gynn	Sedgley	Peake	Bennett	Phillips	Regis	Houchen*	Pickering	Rodger
	24/3	***4,370***	*9*	49			*Fashanu 28, Fairweather 41*	*Beasant*	*Gage*	*Winterburn*	*Jones*	*Gayle*	*Thorn*	*Fairweather*	*Sayer*	*Fashanu*	*Downes*	*Hodges*	
							Ref: K Cooper	City's first visit to Plough Lane is watched by the second smallest Div 1 crowd since the War. The fans see plenty of action but little quality play. City's winning run is ended. They could have been five up when they were on top, but they fall apart after John Fashanu's equaliser.											
33	A	ASTON VILLA	9	L	0-1	0-0		Ogrizovic	Borrows	**Dobson***	McGrath	Kilcline	Peake	Bennett	Phillips	Regis	Houchen	Pickering	Gynn
	28/3	*18,689*	*19*	49			*Birch 61*	*Spink*	*Williams*	*Dorigo*	*Keown*	*Elliott*	*Cooper*	*Birch*	*Stainrod**	*Gray*	*Hunt*	*Walters*	*Thompson*
							Ref: K Burge	With Villa in the bottom three and without a win since Boxing Day, here was City's chance to break the hoodoo. Their finishing against the worst defence in the league is dreadful and Birch's opportunist goal is enough for Billy McNeill's team to jump two places. Villa still go down.											
34	A	NOTT'M FOREST	9	D	0-0	0-0		Ogrizovic	Borrows	Downs	McGrath	Kilcline	Peake	Bennett	Phillips	Regis	Houchen	Pickering	
	4/4	*13,507*	*6*	50				*Sutton*	*Fleming*	*Pearce*	*Walker*	*Fairclough*	*Bowyer*	*Mills*	*Metgod*	*Clough*	*Birtles*	*Rice*	
							Ref: G Tyson	A near gale-force wind makes good football impossible, so the draw is fair. Both keepers are superb. Sutton prevents two certain goals and Oggy saves well from Metgod and Birtles. Most importantly, City have no injuries for next week. City's babes reach the FA Youth Cup final.											
35	A	LUTON	10	L	0-2	0-1		Ogrizovic	Borrows	Downs*	McGrath	Kilcline	Peake	Bennett	Phillips	Houchen	Gynn	Sedgley	**Livingstone**
	18/4	*9,380*	*4*	50			*Stein B 9, Newell 88*	*Sealey*	*Breacker*	*Grimes**	*Nicholas*	*North S*	*Donaghy*	*Wilson*	*Stein B*	*Newell*	*Harford*	*Preece*	*McDonough*
							Ref: H Taylor	The Youth team's scoring hero Livingstone almost makes a scoring debut, but this is an anti-climax for City. They can't reproduce their FA Cup semi- final form. Stein's header from Breacker's cross and Newell's volley win it. Luton's ban on away fans mean few Coventry get in.											
36	H	QP RANGERS	10	W	**4-1**	1-0	Gynn 45, Regis 67, 72, Phillips 87	Ogrizovic	Borrows	Downs	McGrath	Rodger	Peake	Bennett	Phillips	Regis	Gynn	Sedgley*	Livingstone
	20/4	20,926	*12*	53			*Bannister 48*	*Seaman*	*Neill*	*Channing*	*Lee*	*McDonald*	*Maguire*	*Rosenior*	*Fillery**	*Bannister*	*Peacock*	*Fereday*	*Ferdinand*
							Ref: D Allison	There is a carnival atmosphere with a Mexican wave, but the game doesn't get off the ground until the last half-hour. Regis then hits two and Bennett wraps it up with a searing 30-yard volley. Rangers' debutant sub, Les Ferdinand, is destined for higher things but makes little impact.											
37	A	NORWICH	10	D	1-1	0-1	Butterworth 81 (og)	Ogrizovic	Borrows*	Downs	McGrath	Kilcline	Peake	Bennett	Phillips	Regis	Houchen	Gynn	Rodger
	25/4	*14,610*	*6*	54			*Drinkell 26*	*Gunn*	*Brown*	*Spearing*	*Bruce*	*Phelan*	*Butterworth*	*Crook**	*Drinkell*	*Rosario*	*Putney*	*Gordon*	*Biggins*
							Ref: T Ward	The Canaries are having their best ever season and haven't lost at home since September. Drinkell's goal looks enough until City's rousing second-half rally yields an own-goal from Regis's cross. With steadier finishing, City might have won as Houchen and Phillips waste chances.											
38	A	WATFORD	8	W	3-2	2-1	Downs 11, Houchen 18, McGrath 67	Ogrizovic	Borrows	Downs	McGrath	Kilcline	Peake	Sedgley	Gynn	Regis	Houchen	Pickering	
	30/4	*11,590*	*7*	57			*Falco 40, 51*	*Sherwood*	*Gibbs*	*Rostron*	*Richardson*	*Bardsley*	*McClelland*	*Sterling*	*Blissett*	*Falco*	*Porter*	*Barnes*	
							Ref: J Martin	Graham Taylor's Watford have won four in a row since their disappointing semi final exit to Spurs, but are no match for City, who win without ever hitting top gear. City lose a two-goal lead to Falco's deadly finishing, but up the tempo again for Regis to back-heel the ball to McGrath.											
39	H	LIVERPOOL	9	W	1-0	0-0	Pickering 50	Ogrizovic	Borrows	Downs	McGrath	Kilcline	Peake	Bennett	Phillips	Regis	Houchen*	Pickering	Gynn
	2/5	**26,657**	*2*	60				*Hooper*	*Gillespie*	*Venison*	*Spackman*	*Whelan*	*Hansen*	*Ablett**	*Johnston*	*Rush*	*Molby*	*McMahon*	*Aldridge*
							Ref: A Buksh	The biggest home gate since 1981 watches City virtually end Liverpool's title hopes with a masterful display. It's City's first win over the Reds since 1983 and but for Mike Hooper's defiance the winning margin would have been bigger. It's City's 14th home win, a Div 1 club record.											
40	A	LEICESTER	8	D	1-1	0-0	Gynn 74	Ogrizovic	Borrows	Downs	Gynn	Kilcline	Rodger	Bennett	Phillips	Regis	Sedgley	Pickering	
	4/5	*14,903*	*20*	61			*Ramsey 84*	*Andrews*	*Morgan*	*Venus*	*Osman*	*O'Neill*	*Mauchlen*	*Russell**	*Moran*	*Smith*	*Ramsey*	*Wilson*	*Buckley*
							Ref: R Groves	Leicester are on the brink of relegation after this result, with City showing no mercy to their neighbours. Coventry have to defend for long periods and are inspired by Oggy's 76th-minute save from Wilson. Gynn pounces on Osman's error before Ramsey equalises from close range.											
41	H	MANCHESTER U	9	D	1-1	0-1	Gynn 80	Ogrizovic	Borrows	Downs	McGrath	Kilcline	Peake	Bennett	Phillips	Regis	Gynn	Pickering	
	6/5	23,407	*11*	62			*Whiteside 25*	*Walsh*	*Garton*	*Albiston*	*Duxbury*	*McGrath*	*Moran*	*Robson*	*Strachan**	*Whiteside*	*Davenport*	*Gibson C*	*Blackmore*
							Ref: H King	United's revolution under Alex Ferguson is just starting and they are seeking pride after a 0-4 drubbing at Spurs. City are tired in their fourth game in seven days but raise enough steam to put United under pressure in the second half. The noisy crowd get their reward with Gynn's goal.											
42	H	SOUTHAMPTON	10	D	1-1	1-1	Kilcline 29	Ogrizovic	Borrows	Downs	McGrath	Kilcline	Peake	Sedgley	Phillips	Livingstone	Gynn	Pickering*	**Lane**
	9/5	22,620	*12*	63			*Lawrence 38*	*Shilton*	*Forrest*	*Armstrong*	*Case**	*Wright*	*Bond*	*Lawrence*	*Cockerill*	*Clarke*	*Hobson*	*Townsend*	*Baker*
	Home	Away					Ref: J Worrall	It's carnival time in the sun as City sign off after a great season. The fans give them a Wembley send off. Borrows tragically injures his knee and will miss the final. Two spectacular goals are almost ignored in the explosion of joy and the pitch invasion at the end is a true celebration.											
Average	16,060	16,875																	

TODAY DIVISION 1 (CUP-TIES) Manager: George Curtis SEASON 1986-87

Littlewoods Cup					F-A	H-T	Scorers, Times, and Referees	1	2	3	4	5	6	7	8	9	10	11	subs used
2:1	H	ROTHERHAM	6	W	3-2	2-1	Bennett 31, Adams 40, Regis 65	Ogrizovic	Borrows	Downs	McGrath	Kilcline	Adams	Bennett	Phillips	Regis	Sedgley*	Pickering	Gynn
	23/9	6,573 *3:19*					*Dungworth 36, Douglas 48*	*O'Hanlon*	*Ash*	*Crosby*	*Gooding*	*Smith*	*Slack*	*Pugh*	*Emerson*	*Dungworth*	*Douglas*	*Campbell*	
							Ref: C Trussell	Trevor Peake is injured and is missed in defence against Norman Hunter's battlers. The Millers twice pull level, but are beaten when sub Gynn makes a darting run, only to be upended by O'Hanlon. The ball runs loose to Regis, who hammers it home. A tough trip to Millmoor beckons.											
2:2	A	ROTHERHAM	6	W	1-0	1-0	Kilcline 22	Ogrizovic	Borrows	Downs	McGrath*	Kilcline	Peake	Bennett	Phillips	Regis	Adams	Pickering	Gynn
	7/10	*4,694 3:23*						*O'Hanlon*	*Ash*	*Crosby*	*Gooding*	*Smith**	*Dungworth*	*Pugh*	*Emerson*	*Trusson*	*Douglas^*	*Campbell*	*Slack/Morris*
							Ref: P Tyldesley (City win 4-2 on aggregate)	1,500 City fans roar City through after a difficult first 20 minutes. Once Kilcline beats O'Hanlon to head home Adams' corner the tie is won. The Sky Blues defend well and catch the Millers on the break. Dean Emerson and Kevan Smith impress Sillett and will join City in the future.											
3	H	OLDHAM	6	W	2-1	1-0	Regis 43, Sedgley 84p	Ogrizovic	Borrows	Downs	McGrath	Sedgley	Peake	Bennett	Phillips	Regis	Adams*	Pickering	Gynn
	28/10	8,583 *2:2*					*Hoolickin 69*	*Goram*	*Irwin*	*Donachie*	*Jones**	*Linighan*	*Hoolickin*	*Palmer*	*Williams*	*Henry*	*Futcher*	*Milligan*	*Atkinson*
							Ref: R Lewis	Joe Royle's Latics have lost only two games all season and give City a fright. It takes a Steve Sedgley penalty, awarded when Hoolickin fouls Regis, to clinch the tie despite long spells of City domination which should have reaped more goals, with Dave Bennett particularly profligate.											
4	H	LIVERPOOL	8	D	0-0	0-0		Ogrizovic	Borrows	Downs	McGrath	Sedgley	Peake	Bennett	Phillips	Regis	Painter	Pickering	
	19/11	26,440 *2*						*Grobbelaar*	*Gillespie*	*Beglin*	*Lawrenson*	*Whelan*	*Hansen*	*Walsh*	*Nicol*	*Rush*	*Molby*	*McMahon*	
							Ref: A Gunn	The largest crowd for nearly six years see the Liverpool 'killjoys' pay City a major compliment by playing a sweeper to counter Regis. Painter comes in for the cup-tied Emerson but fades after a lively start. Grobbelaar tips City's best effort, Phillips' 25-yard free-kick, over the bar.											
4R	A	LIVERPOOL	6	L	1-3	0-2	Bennett 60	Ogrizovic	Borrows	Downs	McGrath	Sedgley	Peake	Bennett	Phillips	Regis	Adams*	Pickering	Painter
	26/11	*19,179 3*					*Molby 4p, 40p, 72p*	*Grobbelaar*	*Gillespie*	*Beglin*	*Lawrenson*	*Whelan*	*Hansen*	*Dalglish*	*Nicol*	*Rush*	*Molby**	*McMahon*	*Wark*
							Ref: G Tyson	City lose their way again at Anfield, despite an improved display in the second half. Dane Jan Molby achieves a hat-trick of penalties all placed in the same spot. Sedgley fouls Rush for numbers one and three, McGrath fouls Molby for the second. Liverpool meet Everton in next round.											

FA Cup																			
3	H	BOLTON	8	W	3-0	3-0	Downs 15, Regis 18, Bennett 45	Ogrizovic	Borrows	Downs	Emerson	Kilcline	Peake	Phillips	Bennett	Regis	Gynn	Pickering	
	10/1	12,051 *3:19*						*Salmon*	*Scott*	*Phillips*	*Joyce*	*Came*	*Sutton*	*Caldwell*	*Thompson*	*Darby*	*Hartford**	*Gavin*	*Oghani*
							Ref: M Scott	Bolton manager Phil Neal drops himself and castigates Mike Salmon for costing his team three goals. It is bitterly cold and the pitch freezes during play, making Gynn City's star player because of his size. Greg Downs scores his first goal from a back-heeled free-kick from Borrows.											
4	A	MANCHESTER U	8	W	1-0	1-0	Houchen 20	Ogrizovic	Borrows	Downs	Emerson	Kilcline	Peake	McGrath	Phillips	Regis	Houchen	Pickering	
	31/1	*49,082 13*						*Turner*	*Sivebaek*	*Duxbury*	*Whiteside*	*Garton*	*Moran*	*Blackmore^*	*Strachan*	*Stapleton**	*Gibson T*	*Olsen*	*Davenport/McGrath*
							Ref: R Lewis	On a frosty, bone-hard pitch City win a famous victory. Houchen, conqueror of Arsenal two years ago with York, scores the vital goal and the lead is defended well. United's new boss, Ferguson, blames the pitch. Adams has moved to Leeds and Martin Lane has signed from Chester.											
5	A	STOKE	8	W	1-0	0-0	Gynn 71	Ogrizovic	Borrows	Downs	Gynn	Kilcline	Peake	Bennett*	Phillips	Regis	Houchen	Pickering	Sedgley
	21/2	*31,255 2:6*						*Fox*	*Dixon*	*Parkin*	*Talbot*	*Bould*	*Berry*	*Ford*	*Kelly*	*Morgan**	*Saunders*	*Heath*	*Bertschin*
							Ref: R Nixon	Bennett and Gynn replace the suspended McGrath and Emerson. Gynn wins the tie after City had soaked up plenty of pressure by Brian Talbot in particular. Stoke have a case for a penalty, when Dixon falls down. 8,000 fans roar on Coventry in Stoke's biggest crowd for seven years.											
QF	A	SHEFFIELD WED	8	W	3-1	1-0	Regis 16, Houchen 78, 83	Ogrizovic	Borrows	Downs	McGrath*	Kilcline	Peake	Bennett	Phillips	Regis	Houchen	Pickering	Sedgley
	14/3	*48,005 15*					*Megson 66*	*Hodge*	*Sterland**	*Snodin*	*Smith*	*Madden*	*Worthington*	*Marwood*	*Megson*	*Chapman*	*Bradshaw^*	*Shelton*	*Morris/Hirst*
							Ref: A Gunn	A day of jubilation in Sheffield as Houchen scores two late goals to end Wednesday's 23-game unbeaten FA cup record at Hillsborough. City soak up enormous pressure after Regis's brilliant goal, and Gary Megson's equaliser looks ominous. 15,000 City fans can't believe their eyes.											

SF	N	LEEDS	9	W	3-2	0-1	Gynn 68, Houchen 77, Bennett 99	Ogrizovic	Borrows	Downs	McGrath	Kilcline	Peake	Bennett	Phillips	Regis	Houchen	Pickering*	Gynn
	12/4	*51,372*	*2:7*		*aet*		*Rennie 14, Edwards 83*	*Day*	*Aspin*	*Adams*	*Stiles^*	*Ashurst*	*Ormsby*	*Ritchie*	*Sheridan*	*Pearson**	*Baird*	*Rennie*	*Edwards/Haddock*
		(at Hillsborough)					Ref: R Milford	27,000 City fans see their team withstand stout resistance by Billy Bremner's team. Leeds' control the early play and Oggy keeps City alive until the power shifts on the hour. Coventry's two goals look to be enough until Edwards scores with his first touch. Bennett grabs the clincher.											
F	N	TOTTENHAM	10	W	3-2	1-2	Bennett 9, Houchen 63, Mabbutt 96 (og)	Ogrizovic	Phillips	Downs	McGrath	Kilcline*	Peake	Bennett	Gynn	Regis	Houchen	Pickering	Rodger
	16/5	*98,000*	*3*		*aet*		*Allen C 2, Mabbutt 42*	*Clemence*	*Hughton^*	*Thomas*	*Hodge*	*Gough*	*Mabbutt*	*Allen C*	*Allen P*	*Waddle*	*Hoddle*	*Ardiles**	*Stevens/Claessen*
		(at Wembley)					Ref: N Midgley	City add the FA Cup to the Youth Cup won earlier in the week on the club's greatest day in 104 years. This is a classic final, Spurs losing for the first time in seven finals. Allen's 49th goal of the season puts Spurs ahead, but in extra-time City's character and passion deserve the win.											

		Home					Away					
	P	W	D	L	F	A	W	D	L	F	A	Pts
1 Everton	42	16	4	1	49	11	10	4	7	27	20	86
2 Liverpool	42	15	3	3	43	16	8	5	8	29	26	77
3 Tottenham	42	14	3	4	40	14	7	5	9	28	29	71
4 Arsenal	42	12	5	4	31	12	8	5	8	27	23	70
5 Norwich	42	9	10	2	27	20	8	7	6	26	31	68
6 Wimbledon	42	11	5	5	32	22	8	4	9	25	28	66
7 Luton	42	14	5	2	29	13	4	7	10	18	32	66
8 Nott'm Forest	42	12	8	1	36	14	6	3	12	28	37	65
9 Watford	42	12	5	4	38	20	6	4	11	29	34	63
10 COVENTRY	42	14	4	3	35	17	3	8	10	15	28	63
11 Manchester U	42	13	3	5	38	18	1	11	9	14	27	56
12 Southampton	42	11	5	5	44	24	3	5	13	25	44	52
13 Sheffield Wed	42	9	7	5	39	24	4	6	11	19	35	52
14 Chelsea	42	8	6	7	30	30	5	7	9	23	34	52
15 West Ham	42	10	4	7	33	28	4	6	11	19	39	52
16 QP Rangers	42	9	7	5	31	27	4	4	13	17	37	50
17 Newcastle	42	10	4	7	33	29	2	7	12	14	36	47
18 Oxford	42	8	8	5	30	25	3	5	13	14	44	46
19 Charlton*	42	7	7	7	26	22	4	4	13	19	33	44
20 Leicester	42	9	7	5	39	24	2	2	17	15	52	42
21 Manchester C	42	8	6	7	28	24	0	9	12	8	33	39
22 Aston Villa	42	7	7	7	25	25	1	5	15	20	54	36
	924	238	123	101	756	459	101	123	238	459	756	1263

* Stayed up after play-off

Odds & ends

Double wins: (2) Newcastle, Watford.
Double losses: (3) Aston Villa, Luton, West Ham.

Won from behind: (3) Tottenham (h), Leeds FAC (n), Tottenham FAC (n).
Lost from in front: (2) Everton (a), Wimbledon (a).

High spots: First major trophy in 104 years.
Six consecutive League and Cup wins in spring (a record).
Seven games unbeaten at end of season.
4-3 Christmas classic with Spurs.
14 home wins - club record in Division One.

Low spots: Triple penalty in Littlewoods Cup exit at Anfield.
Villa hoodoo continues (now 26 games without a win).

Red cards: Opponents – Venus (Leicester h).

Player of the Year: Steve Ogrizovic.
Ever-presents: (1) Steve Ogrizovic.
Hat-tricks: (0).
Opposing hat-tricks: (2) Cottee (West Ham), Molby (Liverpool).
Leading scorer: (16) Cyrille Regis.

	Appearances						Goals			
	Lge	*Sub*	LC	*Sub*	FAC	*Sub*	Lge	LC	FAC	Tot
Adams, Micky	**10**	*1*	4				**2**	1		**3**
Bennett, Dave	**31**		5		5		**7**	2	3	**12**
Borrows, Brian	**41**		5		5		**1**			**1**
Culpin, Paul	**1**	*1*					**1**			**1**
Dobson, Tony	**1**									
Downs, Greg	**39**		5		6		**2**		1	**3**
Emerson, Dean	**19**				2					
Evans, Gareth		*1*								
Gynn, Michael	**16**	*6*		*3*	3	*1*	**5**		2	**7**
Houchen, Keith	**20**				5		**2**		5	**7**
Kilcline, Brian	**29**		2		6		**3**	1		**4**
Lane, Martin		*1*								
Livingstone, Steve	**1**	*2*								
McGrath, Lloyd	**30**		5		4		**3**			**3**
Ogrizovic, Steve	**42**		5		6		**1**			**1**
Painter, Ian		*3*	1	*1*						
Peake, Trevor	**39**		4		6					
Phillips, David	**39**		5		6		**4**			**4**
Pickering, Nick	**35**	*1*	5		6		**5**			**5**
Regis, Cyrille	**40**		5		6		**12**	2	2	**16**
Rodger, Graham	**4**	*2*				*1*				
Sedgley, Steve	**25**	*1*	4			*2*		1		**1**
Williams, Andy		*1*								
(own-goals)										
23 players used	**462**	*20*	**55**	*4*	**66**	*4*	**48**	**7**	**13**	**68**

No	Date		Att	Pos	Pt	F-A	H-T	Scorers, Times, and Referees	1	2	3	4	5	6	7	8	9	10	11	subs used
1	H	TOTTENHAM			W	2-1	2-0	Speedie 21, Downs 45	Ogrizovic	Borrows	Downs	McGrath	Kilcline	Peake	Bennett	Gynn	Regis	**Speedie***	Pickering	Houchen
	15/8		24,681		3			*Mabbutt 69*	*Clemence*	*Stevens*	*Thomas*	*Gough*	*Fairclough*	*Mabbutt*	*Allen C*	*Allen P**	*Waddle*	*Hodge*	*Claessen^*	*Metgod/Ardiles*
								Ref: B Hill	There is no revenge for Spurs as City turn in a marvellous first-half display which should have yielded five goals. After a poor pre-season preparation they show no mercy and Spurs' new man Chris Fairclough can't handle David Speedie, who scores a superb curler on his debut.											
2	A	LUTON			W	1-0	0-0	Kilcline 66p	Ogrizovic	Borrows	Downs	McGrath	Kilcline	Peake	Bennett	Gynn	Houchen	Speedie	Pickering	
	18/8		*7,506*		6				*Sealey*	*Breacker*	*Grimes*	*Hill*	*Foster*	*McDonough*	*Wilson D*	*Newell*	*Harford*	*Wilson R**	*Preece*	*Nwajiobi*
								Ref: D Hedges	City are unbeaten for ten games stretching back to April, a club Div 1 record. They win on Luton's plastic pitch, where only two sides won last season. There are 58 fouls in a petty, disjointed game, but one of them, McDonough's on Speedie, gives Kilcline his first penalty of the season.											
3	A	NORWICH		5	L	1-3	0-1	Kilcline 58p	Ogrizovic	Borrows^	Downs	McGrath	Kilcline	Peake	Bennett	Gynn	Regis*	Speedie	Pickering	Houchen/Phillips
	22/8		*13,726*	*12*	6			*Bruce 20, Drinkell 54, 84*	*Gunn*	*Culverhouse*	*Spearing*	*Bruce*	*Phelan*	*Butterworth*	*Fox*	*Drinkell*	*Biggins*	*Crook*	*Bowen*	
								Ref: A Buksh	The unbeaten run is over, thanks to three headed goals and a poor display. 2,000 City fans feel let down. Despite Kilcline making it 1-2 with a penalty when Bruce handles, Drinkell scores his second to clinch the points. Regis struggles and is pulled off. Sillett becomes a grand-daddy.											
4	H	LIVERPOOL		8	L	1-4	0-1	Regis 89	Ogrizovic	Borrows	Downs^	McGrath	Kilcline	Peake	Bennett	Gynn*	Regis	Speedie	Pickering	Houchen/Phillips
	29/8		**27,509**	*7*	6			*Nicol 19, 49, Aldridge 52p, Beardsley 82*	*Grobbelaar*	*Gillespie*	*Venison*	*Nicol*	*Whelan*	*Hansen*	*Beardsley*	*Aldridge**	*Johnston*	*Barnes*	*McMahon*	*Walsh*
								Ref: K Cooper	Sillett demanded a yard-stick to measure City's potential and got it loud and clear. Liverpool show real pedigree and destroy City. Beardsley scores his first goal since his record £1.9 million move, Nicol grabs two and Aldridge scores after Borrows fouls other new man, John Barnes.											
5	A	SHEFFIELD WED		5	W	3-0	2-0	Speedie 7, Sedgley 37, Rodger 82	Ogrizovic	Phillips	Downs	McGrath	Rodger	Peake	Bennett	Sedgley	Houchen	Speedie	Pickering	
	31/8		*17,171*	*19*	9				*Hodge*	*Sterland*	*McCall**	*Madden*	*May*	*Worthington*	*Hazel*	*Megson*	*Chapman*	*Hirst*	*Galvin*	*Bradshaw*
								Ref: D Scott	Four defeats out of five for the Owls means that boss Howard Wilkinson is under pressure. A shuffled City take advantage. Kilcline, Borrows, Gynn and Regis are dropped and stand-in centre-half Graham Rodger plays well. McCall breaks his leg in an innocuous clash with Bennett.											
6	H	MANCHESTER U		7	D	0-0	0-0		Ogrizovic	Phillips	Downs	McGrath	Rodger	Peake	Bennett	Sedgley	Houchen	Speedie*	Pickering !	Regis
	5/9		26,849	*2*	10				*Walsh*	*Anderson*	*Albiston*	*Moses*	*McGrath*	*Moran*	*Duxbury*	*Strachan*	*McClair*	*Whiteside*	*Olsen**	*Davenport*
								Ref: J Martin	United retain their unbeaten record in a game marred by pedantic refereeing. Ref Martin awards 63 free-kicks, books five players and sends off Pickering for his first offence, a foul on Anderson. He is booed off by both sets of players and given a police escort away from the ground.											
7	H	NOTT'M FOREST		10	L	0-3	0-1		Ogrizovic	Phillips	Downs*	McGrath	Rodger	Peake	Speedie	Sedgley	Regis	Houchen	Dobson^	Borrows/Gynn
	19/9		17,517	*5*	10			*Wilson 19, Carr 71, Pearce 73p*	*Sutton*	*Fleming**	*Pearce*	*Walker*	*Foster*	*Wilson*	*Carr*	*Webb*	*Clough*	*Wilkinson*	*Rice*	*Campbell*
								Ref: R Bridges	With Bennett out with flu, City play three front men but no one wide to provide service. Clough's kids are too good for City, who lack vision in midfield. Terry Wilson scores on his debut, Carr is unmarked from Rice's cross and Pearce converts penalty when Clough is tripped by Peake.											
8	A	EVERTON		8	W	2-1	2-1	Regis 37, Phillips 44	Ogrizovic	Borrows	Pickering	McGrath	Sedgley	Peake	Bennett	Phillips	Regis	Speedie*	Gynn	Houchen
	26/9		*28,161*	*9*	13			*Clarke 45*	*Southall*	*v d Hauwe**	*Pointon*	*Ratcliffe*	*Watson*	*Harper^*	*Steven*	*Clarke*	*Sharp*	*Snodin*	*Wilson*	*Heath/Mountfield*
								Ref: J Lloyd	Three away wins out of four. City's first win at Goodison for 12 seasons and Everton's first home defeat for a year. Superb goals from Regis and Phillips grab the headlines but McGrath gives a heroic, battling display, even heading the ball off Adrian Heath's toe in the dying minutes.											
9	H	WATFORD		8	W	1-0	1-0	Houchen 43	Ogrizovic	Borrows	Pickering	McGrath	Sedgley	Peake	Bennett	Phillips	Regis	Houchen	Gynn	
	3/10		16,094	*15*	16				*Coton*	*Gibbs*	*Rostron*	*Morris*	*Terry*	*McClelland*	*Sterling*	*Agana*	*Senior**	*Porter*	*Hodges*	*Roberts*
								Ref: J Deakin	Dave Bassett has taken some of his Wimbledon tactics to Vicarage Road. City are caught offside 13 times in the first half and Regis has two goals ruled out for offside. Speedie is out with a septic toe and Tony Coton makes good saves from Regis and Gynn to keep the score down.											
10	A	CHELSEA		9	L	0-1	0-0		Ogrizovic	Borrows	Pickering	McGrath	Rodger	Sedgley	Bennett	Phillips	Regis	Houchen*	Gynn	Speedie
	17/10		*16,699*	*5*	16			*Dixon 72*	*Niedzwiecki*	*Clarke*	*Dorigo*	*Pates*	*McLaughlin*	*Wood*	*Nevin*	*Hazard*	*Dixon**	*Wilson K*	*Wilson C*	*West*
								Ref: J Ashworth	The south-east was ravaged by gales yesterday but the game goes on. City miss many chances, including a Gynn shot which looks a goal before Pates clears. New England cap Regis misses a good chance. Kerry Dixon then loops a shot over Oggy following a fine ball from Micky Hazard.											

No	Venue / Date	Opponent / Att	Pos	Res	FT	HT	Scorers, Times, Referees	1	2	3	4	5	6	7	8	9	10	11	subs used
11	H	SOUTHAMPTON	9	L	2-3	2-1	Gynn 16, Bennett 19	Ogrizovic	Borrows	Pickering	McGrath	Rodger	Sedgley	Bennett	Phillips	Speedie	Houchen	Gynn	
	20/10	14,508	11	16			Bond 34, Baker G 48, Wallace D 77	Burridge	Forrest	Statham	Case	Moore	Bond	Le Tissier*	Cockerill	Clarke	Baker G	Wallace D	Baker S
							Ref: B Stevens	Chris Nicholl is the first Saints boss to win at Coventry since 1949 as City throw away a two-goal lead. The original game was controversially called off after heavy rain ten days earlier. David Speedie misses two sitters and the jury is still out on him. Matthew Le Tissier takes the eye.											
12	H	NEWCASTLE	11	L	1-3	1-2	Regis 25	Ogrizovic	Borrows	Downs	McGrath	Rodger*	Gynn	Bennett	Phillips	Regis	Speedie	Pickering	Sedgley
	24/10	18,596	12	16			Goddard 24, Gascoigne 37, Jackson D 67	Kelly	McDonald	Tinnion	McCreery	Jackson P	Roeder	Jackson D	Gascoigne	Goddard	Mirandinha*	Cornwell^	Anderson/Wharton
							Ref: L Shapter	Newcastle steal the points as City miss chances galore. This is their fourth home defeat and they've conceded 14 goals and are missing the injured Peake and Kilcline. The Brazilian, Mirandinha, usually grabs the headlines but he is well marked by McGrath. Paul Gascoigne shines.											
13	A	DERBY	12	L	0-2	0-0		Ogrizovic	Borrows	Downs	Emerson	Rodger	Gynn	Bennett	Phillips	Regis	Speedie*	Houchen	Lane
	31/10	15,738	11	16			Garner 69, 80	Shilton	MacLaren	Forsyth	Williams	Wright	Blades	Callaghan	Garner	Davison	Gregory	Cross	
							Ref: N Midgley	Emerson returns after two operations and countless weeks at Lilleshall recuperating. Newly promoted Derby win their first home game since the opening day, while City have lost five in a row. Two Callaghan-led counter-attacks create Garner's goals, the second after a 70-yard run.											
14	A	OXFORD	13	L	0-1	0-0		Ogrizovic	Borrows	Downs	Emerson	Kilcline	**Smith K**	Bennett	Phillips^	Regis	Speedie	Houchen*	Sedgley/Gynn
	7/11	7,856	9	16			Saunders 81p	Hucker	Bardsley	Dreyer	Shelton	Slatter*	Caton	Hebberd	Whitehurst	Saunders	Phillips	Rh--Brown	Mustoe
							Ref: K Hackett	Kevan Smith has waited a year to make his debut and is grief-stricken to bring down Saunders for the late winner. City have lost six in a row, their worst run since 1973. Regis is denied when Hackett doesn't allow the advantage. Oxford will not win again this season and will go down.											
15	H	WIMBLEDON	14	D	3-3	1-0	Kilcline 39p, Speedie 84, Gynn 90	Ogrizovic	Borrows	Downs	Emerson	Kilcline	Smith K	Bennett	McGrath*	Regis^	Speedie	Pickering	Phillips/Gynn
	14/11	13,945	9	17			Fashanu 62, 72, Wise 65	Beasant	Goodyear	Bedford*	Hazel	Gayle	Thorn	Gannon^	Wise	Fashanu	Sanchez	Fairweather	Scales/Cork
							Ref: G Tyson	The Dons, managed by Bobby Gould, are unhappy with the penalty when Thorn handles. They also have four players booked in ten minutes. They score three in ten second-half minutes with Fashanu the star. Speedie and Gynn goals bring City back from the grave to snatch a point.											
16	A	CHARLTON	15	D	2-2	0-1	Downs 47p, Gynn 88	Ogrizovic	Borrows	Downs	Emerson	Smith K	Gynn	Bennett	Phillips	Livingstone*	Speedie	Pickering	Lane
	21/11	**4,936**	21	18			Jones 41, Stuart 74	Bolder	Humphrey	Reid	Gritt	Shirtliff	Thompson	Bennett	Campbell*	Jones	Walsh	MacKenzie^	Crooks/Stuart
							Ref: A Gunn	Gynn scores another late equaliser for a deserved point against bottom club Charlton, who fight for their lives. Greg Downs, City's sixth captain of the season, scores with a poorly taken spot-kick when Speedie is fouled by Peter Shirtliff. Oggy looks to be fouled for the Valiants' second.											
17	H	WEST HAM	15	D	0-0	0-0		Ogrizovic	Borrows	Downs	Emerson	Smith K	Gynn	Bennett	Phillips	Houchen	Speedie	Pickering	
	28/11	16,754	14	19				McAllister	Bonds	Parris	Hilton	Stewart	Keen	Ward	Dickins	Ince	Cottee	Robson	
							Ref: R Nixon	Fog shrouds the stadium on a cold afternoon and the game is lucky to be finished. 34-year-old Tom McAllister is Hammers' hero, saving well from Phillips, Speedie and Kevan Smith. Ray Stewart should have been sent off for a professional foul on Houchen, who was through on goal.											
18	A	PORTSMOUTH	16	D	0-0	0-0		Ogrizovic	Borrows	Downs	Emerson	Kilcline	Peake	Bennett	Phillips	Houchen	Speedie*	Pickering	Gynn
	5/12	13,002	18	20				Knight	Swain	Hardyman	Fillery	Ball	Whitehead	Horne	Connor	Baird	Quinn	Hilaire	
							Ref: D Reeves	Peake and Kilcline return from injury but Speedie limps off with a hamstring pull after 41 minutes. Alan Ball's side, back in Division 1 after 30 years, rarely trouble City. For Coventry, Speedie hits the bar and Keith Houchen's goal is ruled out. Sillett blames the ball for the poor game.											
19	H	ARSENAL	16	D	0-0	0-0		Ogrizovic	Borrows	Downs	Emerson	Kilcline	Peake	Bennett	Phillips	Regis	Livingstone	Gynn	
	13/12	17,398	2	21				Lukic	Thomas	Sansom	Williams	O'Leary	Adams	Rocastle	Hayes*	Smith	Groves	Richardson	Merson
							Ref: T Mills	Arsenal's recent ten-match winning run is over and they are lucky to get a point on Sunday's Big Match after City miss chances galore. City's are without a win in eleven though they are unbeaten in five. A strong City claim for a penalty is turned down when Adams brings down Gynn.											
20	A	QP RANGERS	14	W	2-1	0-1	Houchen 82, Regis 86	Ogrizovic	Borrows	Downs	Emerson^	Kilcline	Peake	Bennett*	Phillips	Regis	Livingstone	Gynn	Houchen/Rodger
	18/12	7,299	5	24			Falco 30	Roberts	Fereday	Dennis	Parker	McDonald	Fenwick	Allen	Falco	Bannister*	Byrne	Brock	Coney
							Ref: L Shapter	The win-less run is ended on Friday night on plastic. Sillett gambles with 15 minutes left and throws on giant subs Houchen and Rodger for an aerial assault on Rangers' defence. It pays off with two superb headers past 17-year-old debutant Tony Roberts. 1,500 City fans go berserk.											
21	A	NOTT'M FOREST	16	L	1-4	1-1	Regis 25	Ogrizovic	Borrows	Downs	McGrath	Kilcline	Peake	Bennett	Phillips	Regis	Speedie	Gynn	
	28/12	31,061	2	24			Gaynor 30, 72, Borrows 77 (og), [Wilson 81]	Sutton	Chettle^	Pearce	Walker	Foster	Wilson	Plummer*	Webb	Glover	Gaynor	Rice	Starbuck/Fleming
							Ref: B Hill	Nine minutes of madness costs City a game they should have won by half-time. Forest have won four in a row and are serious title contenders and they benefit from two rare Peake mistakes. His back-header is intercepted by Gaynor, whose header loops in. Peake is at fault for the third.											

BARCLAYS LEAGUE DIVISION 1

Manager: John Sillett

SEASON 1987-88

No	Date		Att	Pos	Pt	F-A	H-T	Scorers, Times, and Referees	1	2	3	4	5	6	7	8	9	10	11	subs used
22	A	LIVERPOOL		17	L	**0-4**	0-1	*[Houghton 75]*	Ogrizovic	Borrows	Downs	McGrath	Kilcline	Smith K	Bennett*	Phillips	Regis	Speedie	Gynn^	Livingstone/Rodger
	1/1		***38,790***	*1*	24			*Beardsley 22, 82, Aldridge 53,*	*Grobbelaar*	*Gillespie*	*Venison**	*Nicol*	*Whelan*	*Hansen*	*Beardsley*	*Aldridge*	*Houghton*	*Barnes*	*McMahon^*	*Ablett/Spackman*
								Ref: D Phillips	Liverpool extend their unbeaten start to 22 games and their lead to 13 points with this easy win. Rush has gone to Juventus but his replacement, Aldridge, scores his 18th goal of the season and Beardsley scores two superb strikes. Speedie is anonymous and is booked for the seventh time.											
23	A	TOTTENHAM		15	D	2-2	0-1	Regis 53, Bennett 82	Ogrizovic	Borrows	Downs	McGrath	Kilcline	Peake	Bennett	Phillips	Regis	Sedgley	Gynn	
	16/1		*25,650*	*10*	25			*Allen C 36, 75*	*Parks*	*Hughton*	*Thomas*	*Fenwick*	*Fairclough*	*Mabbutt*	*Allen C*	*Allen P*	*Waddle*	*Ardiles**	*Moran^*	*Statham/Howells*
								Ref: J Carter	City grab a late equaliser after a stunning second half reminiscent of Wembley. They run Spurs ragged in the last 20 minutes and Bennett, Gynn and Regis spurn glorious chances. Bennett plays up front for the first time this season and Allen, a shadow of last season's player, nets twice.											
24	A	MANCHESTER U		17	L	0-1	0-1		Ogrizovic	Borrows	Downs	McGrath	Kilcline	Peake	Sedgley	Phillips*	Regis	Speedie	Gynn	**Smith D**
	6/2		*37,144*	*3*	25			*O'Brien 4*	*Turner*	*Anderson*	*Duxbury*	*Bruce*	*O'Brien**	*Hogg*	*Robson*	*Strachan*	*McClair*	*Whiteside*	*Olsen*	*Albiston*
								Ref: D Shaw	The 30th anniversary of the Munich air disaster and City fans respect the minute's silence. Liam O'Brien's goal, eerily, is scored at the exact time of the crash. Oggy is in super form but Gynn almost grabs a point with a shot which looked over the line when Graeme Hogg hooks it out.											
25	H	SHEFFIELD WED		17	W	3-0	1-0	Phillips 34, Bennett 55, 60	Ogrizovic	Borrows	Downs	Sedgley	Kilcline	Peake	Bennett	Phillips	Gynn*	Speedie	Smith D	Houchen
	13/2		14,407	*9*	28				*Hodge*	*Sterland*	*Worthington*	*Fee*	*May*	*Procter*	*Marwood*	*Megson*	*Chapman*	*West*	*Owen*	
								Ref: R Milford	City's injury jinx continues when McGrath breaks a leg in a Simod Cup game with Ipswich. Regis is not missed. Bennett dazzles the Owls and David Smith enjoys a dazzling first full game. Phillips, however, is the man of the match with a blistering goal. He also sets up Bennett's.											
26	H	NORWICH		17	D	0-0	0-0		Ogrizovic	Borrows	Downs	Sedgley	Kilcline	Peake^	Bennett	Phillips	Emerson*	Speedie	Smith D	Houchen/Smith K
	20/2		15,624	*15*	29				*Gunn*	*Culverhouse*	*Bowen*	*Goss*	*Phelan*	*Butterworth*	*Fox**	*Drinkell*	*Fleck*	*Elliott !*	*Gordon*	*Crook*
								Ref: E Parker	Norwich hang on for a point after Shaun Elliott is sent off for elbowing the petulant Speedie a minute into the second half. The sanded pitch is again City's worst enemy and they play badly. Fleck's shot hits the underside of the bar. Borrows hooks away, but the ball looks over the line.											
27	A	WATFORD		14	W	1-0	1-0	Speedie 23	Ogrizovic	Borrows	Downs	Sedgley	Kilcline	Peake	Bennett	Phillips	Regis	Speedie	Pickering	
	27/2		*12,052*	*21*	32				*Coton*	*Gibbs*	*Rostron*	*Jackett*	*Morris*	*McClelland*	*Sterling*	*Allen**	*Senior*	*Porter*	*Kuhl*	*Blissett*
								Ref: G Ashby	City's Cup conquerors have won only one in eleven and this is their eighth home defeat. City's injuries are clearing up and Regis and Pickering are welcomed back. Speedie's winner, a pirouette and a curling shot, is his first league goal for three months. Wembley beckons in the Simod.											
28	H	CHELSEA		15	D	3-3	2-3	Kilcline 18, Speedie 34, Smith D 59	Ogrizovic	Rodger	Downs	Sedgley	Kilcline	Peake	Bennett	Phillips	Regis	Speedie	Pickering*	Smith D
	5/3		16,801	*16*	33			*Wilson K 10, 40, Nevin 16*	*Digweed*	*Hall*	*Dorigo*	*Pates*	*Clarke*	*Bodley*	*Nevin*	*Hazard*	*Dixon*	*Wilson K*	*Bumstead*	
								Ref: A Gunn	The Bees' speedway team parade the British League trophy at the start. Chelsea haven't won for 16 games. They are relegation-bound but take a two-goal lead. City roar back, Speedie scores against his old club, Smith nets his first goal and Rodger hits the bar. Hollins looks set to leave.											
29	A	SOUTHAMPTON		14	W	2-1	0-1	Smith D 65, Kilcline 78	Ogrizovic	Phillips	Downs	Sedgley	Kilcline	Peake	Bennett*	Bannister	Regis	Speedie	Smith D	Emerson
	12/3		*12,914*	*10*	36			*Wallace D 28*	*Burridge*	*Forrest*	*Statham*	*Case*	*Moore**	*Bond*	*Le Tissier*	*Cockerill*	*Clarke*	*Townsend^*	*Wallace D*	*Baker G/Wallace R*
								Ref: L Shapter	The second win in thirty visits to the Dell is a fortuitous one. Oggy saves Clarke's early penalty, after Peake brings down Danny Wallace, who then puts Saints ahead. Bannister has been bought back for £300,000 after seven years away. Smith scores again after Speedie's good build-up.											
30	H	LUTON		9	W	**4-0**	2-0	Sedgley 35, Bannister 38, Kilcline 60p,	Ogrizovic	Phillips	Downs	Sedgley	Kilcline*	Peake	Emerson	Bannister	Regis	Speedie	Smith D	Rodger
	15/3		**13,711**	*10*	39			[Regis 64]	*Sealey*	*Breacker*	*Grimes*	*McDonough*	*Foster*	*Donaghy*	*Wilson D*	*Johnson R^*	*Harford*	*Stein*	*Allinson**	*Black/Cobb*
								Ref: D Allison	Luton are Littlewoods Cup finalists and FA Cup semi-finalists but are ripped apart on the sands of Coventry. Emerson, fouled by Hartford for the penalty, is the star for rampant City, for whom Bannister scores his first. Regis' goal is the best, a dummy, a power run and a shot to match.											
31	H	DERBY		11	L	0-3	0-2		Ogrizovic	Phillips	Downs	Sedgley^	Rodger*	Peake	Emerson	Bannister	Regis	Speedie	Smith D	Pickering/Bennett
	19/3		19,871	*16*	39			*Forsyth 12, Gee 44, Williams 54*	*Shilton*	*Blades*	*Forsyth*	*Williams*	*Wright*	*Hindmarch*	*Stapleton**	*Lewis*	*Gee*	*Gregory*	*Callaghan^*	*Mic'white/MacLaren*
								Ref: J Key	City's six-match unbeaten run is ended by the relegation haunted Rams. Sillett is angry at a below-par display and Dave Bennett breaks his leg in a clash with Peter Shilton. Derby's on-loan striker Frank Stapleton, borrowed from Ajax, causes havoc in the Sky Blues' makeshift defence.											

No	Venue	Opponent / Date	Att	Pos	Res / Pts	F-A	H-T	Scorers, Times, and Referees	1	2	3	4	5	6	7	8	9	10	11	12 sub used
32	A	NEWCASTLE		11	D	2-2	0-0	Smith D 48, Speedie 75	Ogrizovic	Phillips	Pickering	Sedgley	Kilcline	Peake	Emerson	Bannister*	Regis	Speedie	Smith D	Gynn
		26/3	*19,050*	*12*	40			*O'Neill 56, 71*	*Kelly*	*McDonald*	*Tinnion*	*McCreery*	*Anderson*	*Roeder*	*Stephenson**	*Gascoigne*	*Goddard*	*Jackson D*	*O'Neill*	*Bogie*
								Ref: I Hendrick	David Smith is one of the finds of the season and scores another super goal in a poor game at gale-lashed St James' Park. 18-year-old Michael O'Neill scores twice and looks a great prospect. Speedie scores too, and is booked for the eighth time before Emerson misses a sitter at the end.											
33	H	OXFORD		9	W	1-0	0-0	Regis 89	Ogrizovic	Borrows	Pickering	Sedgley	Kilcline	Peake	Emerson	Phillips	Regis	Speedie	Smith D*	Gynn
		2/4	15,745	*20*	43				*Hucker*	*Bardsley*	*Hill*	*Shelton*	*Briggs*	*Greenall*	*Hebberd*	*Foyle**	*Saunders*	*Rh-Brown*	*Mustoe*	*Nogan*
								Ref: K Walmsley	Oxford are without a win in 10 games and their new manager Mark Lawrenson has not had much impact. Hucker keeps them in this bore with a string of fine saves but is finally beaten in the last minute by Regis's header from Dean Emerson's quickly taken free-kick and Phillips' cross.											
34	A	WIMBLEDON		9	W	2-1	2-1	Kilcline 27p, Houchen 28	Ogrizovic	Borrows	Pickering	Sedgley	Kilcline	Peake	Emerson	Phillips	Houchen	Speedie	Smith D	
		5/4	*5,920*	*7*	46			*Young 38*	*Beasant*	*Scales*	*Phelan*	*Jones*	*Young*	*Thorn*	*Clement^*	*Ryan*	*Fashanu**	*Miller*	*Wise*	*Sayer/Gayle*
								Ref: R Groves	The Dons will play Luton in the FA Cup semi-final four days later and don't want a hard game. When Fashanu limps off after five minutes they lose their aerial power. Kilcline fires home after Phelan handles Phillips' shot. Houchen, on his return from injury, slides home the second.											
35	H	CHARLTON		8	D	0-0	0-0		Ogrizovic	Borrows	Pickering	Sedgley	Kilcline	Peake	Houchen*	Phillips	Regis	Speedie	Smith D	Bannister
		9/4	14,306	*18*	47				*Bolder*	*Humphrey*	*Reid*	*MacKenzie*	*Shirtliff*	*Miller*	*Stuart*	*Leaburn*	*Gritt*	*Lee*	*Crooks*	
								Ref: N Midgley (sub A Smith 46)	In a poor home season this earns Sillett's vote as the worst performance. Charlton, almost safe from the drop, wonder how they didn't win this game. They create the best chances and are the better side, with Stuart and Robert Lee going close and Houchen almost scoring an own-goal.											
36	H	EVERTON		10	L	1-2	1-0	Regis 25	Ogrizovic	Borrows	Pickering	Sedgley	Kilcline	Peake	Emerson	Phillips	Regis	Speedie	Smith D	
		19/4	15,629	*3*	47			*Sharp 85, Heath 87*	*Southall*	*Stevens*	*Pointon*	*v d Hauwe*	*Watson*	*Reid*	*Steven*	*Clarke*	*Sharp*	*Snodin**	*Wilson*	*Heath*
								Ref: K Morton	No side has done the double over Everton since 1985, but City are five minutes away when they hit the suicide button. The Toffees rarely threaten until Sharp's far post header and Heath's 18-yard shot from Clarke's lay-off. Regis's left-foot screamer gave the Sky Blues the lead.											
37	A	WEST HAM		9	D	1-1	0-0	Regis 56	Ogrizovic	Borrows	Pickering	Sedgley	Kilcline	Peake	Emerson	Phillips	Regis	Speedie	Smith D	
		23/4	*17,733*	*17*	48			*Cottee 78*	*McAllister*	*Parris*	*Dicks*	*Keen^*	*Strodder*	*Gale*	*Ward*	*Dickins*	*Ince**	*Cottee*	*Robson*	*Hilton/Slater*
								Ref: M James	Despite a blustery wind and a bone-hard pitch City deserve to win after Regis swivels to score. Speedie and Phillips have shots saved before Cottee nets after hesitation between Oggy and Peake. Stewart Robson almost wins both points. West Ham are one place above the play-offs.											
38	H	PORTSMOUTH		9	W	1-0	1-0	Kilcline 19p	Ogrizovic	Borrows	Pickering	Sedgley	Kilcline	Peake	Emerson	Bannister	Regis	Speedie	Smith D	
		30/4	14,288	*19*	51				*Gosney*	*Swain*	*Sandford*	*Dillon*	*Blake*	*Ball*	*Horne*	*Whitehead*	*Mariner*	*Quinn**	*Hilaire*	*Perry*
								Ref: F Roberts	Pompey boss Alan Ball is distraught as this defeat almost certainly confirms his team's relegation. The penalty is a travesty as Cyrille Regis's thunderbolt shot hits Kevin Ball's arm. Portsmouth fight to the end but don't trouble City, who are happy to soak things up and hit on the break.											
39	A	ARSENAL		9	D	1-1	1-1	Smith D 45	Ogrizovic	Borrows	Pickering	Sedgley	Kilcline	Peake	Emerson	Bannister*	Regis	Speedie	Smith D	Houchen
		2/5	*16,963*	*6*	52			*Marwood 40p*	*Lukic*	*Dixon*	*Sansom*	*Thomas*	*Caesar*	*Adams*	*Rocastle*	*Richardson^*	*Smith*	*Merson**	*Marwood*	*Hayes/Groves*
								Ref: I Borrett	A dull end-of-season game is highlighted by Kilcline's two thunderbolt free-kicks which Lukic does well to save. Kilcline concedes the penalty when he leans on Adams at a corner. Smith replies quickly after a one-two with Kilcline. City's travels conclude with a six-game unbeaten run.											
40	H	QP RANGERS		9	D	0-0	0-0		Ogrizovic	Borrows	Pickering	Sedgley	Kilcline	Peake	Emerson	Bannister	Regis	Speedie	Smith D	
		7/5	15,951	*5*	53				*Seaman*	*Neill**	*Dawes*	*Parker*	*McDonald*	*Pizanti^*	*Allen*	*Kerslake*	*Coney*	*Fereday*	*Francis*	*Falco/Channing*
		Home / Away						Ref: B Stevens	Jim Smith has steered Rangers into the top six. The highlight of this tame affair is the tussle between Speedie, who picks up his tenth booking, and Paul Parker, who looks a fine prospect. Seaman saves City's best effort, a Speedie header. New Ranger Trevor Francis has a quiet game.											
Average		17,530 / 17,468																		

BARCLAYS DIVISION 1 (CUP-TIES)

Manager: John Sillett

SEASON 1987-88

Charity Shield			F-A	H-T	Scorers, Times, and Referees	1	2	3	4	5	6	7	8	9	10	11	subs used
N EVERTON		L	0-1	0-1		Ogrizovic	Phillips	Downs	McGrath*	Kilcline	Peake	Bennett	Gynn^	Speedie	Houchen	Pickering	Sedgley/Borrows
1/8	*88,000*				*Clarke 44*	*Mimms*	*Harper*	*Power*	*Ratcliffe*	*Watson*	*Reid*	*Steven*	*Clarke*	*Sharp*	*Heath*	*Sheedy**	*Pointon*
(at Wembley)					Ref: R Lewis	50,000 City fans make the return trip to Wembley 78 days after the first one. The league champions, in their first game under new boss Colin Harvey, win the trophy for the fourth successive year. Clarke's volley after Peake's error is enough. Speedie's debut after his £750,000 move.											

League Cup																	
2:1 A CAMBRIDGE		10 W	1-0	1-0	Gynn 11	Ogrizovic	Borrows	Downs	McGrath	Rodger	Peake	Bennett	Phillips	Regis	Speedie	Gynn	
22/9	*5,166*	*4:13*				*Branagan*	*Poole*	*Kimble A*	*Beattie*	*Smith*	*Brattan**	*Butler*	*Clayton*	*Horwood^*	*Crown*	*Kimble G*	*Turner/Williams*
					Ref: T Simpson	Sillett's misgivings bring the Fleet Street vultures to the Abbey Stadium but they go home with no pickings. City are well in control during the first half and once Gynn's cross to the far post eludes everyone and goes in create many more chances. United waste their three good openings.											
2:2 H CAMBRIDGE		8 W	2-1	0-0	Gynn 71, Regis 73	Ogrizovic	Borrows	Pickering	McGrath	Sedgley	Peake*	Bennett	Phillips	Regis	Houchen^	Gynn	Downs/Livingstone
6/10	10,297	*4:12*			*Crown 86*	*Branagan*	*Poole*	*Kimble A*	*Beattie*	*Smith*	*Brattan*	*Butler*	*Clayton*	*Rigby**	*Crown*	*Kimble G*	*Horwood*
					Ref: R Dilkes (City win 3-1 on aggregate)	Trevor Peake, called up for England B this week, limped off after 13 minutes with a hamstring tear. City never look in danger, having a patient, cautious approach. A golden period just after the hour culminates in both their goals. Regis, back in the England squad, heads the second.											
3 A LUTON		11 L	1-3	0-1	Pickering 69	Ogrizovic	Borrows	Downs	McGrath*	Rodger	Sedgley	Bennett	Gynn	Houchen	Speedie	Pickering	**Cook**
27/10	*8,113*	*16*			*Harford 30, 51, Weir 55*	*Sealey*	*Breacker*	*Grimes*	*McDonough*	*Foster*	*Donaghy*	*Wilson D*	*Stein B*	*Harford*	*Johnson M*	*Weir*	
(at Leicester)					Ref: T Ward	This tie was played at Filbert Street because of Luton's away-fan ban. City's injury problems worsen when acting skipper McGrath goes off with a gashed eye after 20 minutes. Rodger and Sedgley have a nightmare at the back and 5,000 fans sing 'we're even worse than the Villa'.											

FA Cup																	
3 H TORQUAY		17 W	2-0	0-0	Kilcline 59p, Regis 60	Ogrizovic	Borrows	Downs	McGrath	Kilcline	Smith K	Bennett	Phillips	Regis	Speedie	Gynn	
9/1	16,967	*4:6*				*Allen*	*McNichol*	*Kelly*	*Haslegrave*	*Cole*	*Impey**	*Dawkins*	*Lloyd*	*Caldwell*	*Loram*	*Musker^*	*Pearce/Gardiner*
					Ref: N Butler	Torquay boss Cyril Knowles thinks his team should have had a replay. They could even have won but for Oggy's 58th-minute save from Dave Caldwell. But within two minutes City were home and dry, thanks to a penalty after John Impey's foul on Phillips and Regis's close-range goal.											
4 H WATFORD		15 L	0-1	0-0		Ogrizovic	Borrows	Downs	McGrath	Kilcline	Peake	Bennett	Phillips	Regis	Sedgley*	Gynn	Speedie
30/1	22,366	*20*			*Senior 55*	*Coton*	*Chivers^*	*Rostron*	*Jackett*	*Morris*	*McClelland*	*Sterling*	*Allen*	*Blissett**	*Porter*	*Hodges*	*Senior/Gibbs*
					Ref: R Nixon	The sanded pitch is like a beach and the holders slide out of the Cup despite having 17 goal attempts to Watford's two. Senior is the assassin, scoring ten minutes after coming on as sub, when City failed to clear a free-kick. Steve Harrison is the new boss at Watford, replacing Bassett.											

		Home					Away					
	P	W	D	L	F	A	W	D	L	F	A	Pts
1 Liverpool	40	15	5	0	49	9	11	7	2	38	15	90
2 Manchester U	40	14	5	1	41	17	9	7	4	30	21	81
3 Nott'm Forest	40	11	7	2	40	17	9	6	5	27	22	73
4 Everton	40	14	4	2	34	11	5	9	6	19	16	70
5 QP Rangers	40	12	4	4	30	14	7	6	7	18	24	67
6 Arsenal	40	11	4	5	35	16	7	8	5	23	23	66
7 Wimbledon	40	8	9	3	32	20	6	6	8	26	27	57
8 Newcastle	40	9	6	5	32	23	5	8	7	23	30	56
9 Luton	40	11	6	3	40	21	3	5	12	17	37	53
10 COVENTRY	40	6	8	6	23	25	7	6	7	23	28	53
11 Sheffield Wed	40	10	2	8	27	30	5	6	9	25	36	53
12 Southampton	40	6	8	6	27	26	6	6	8	22	27	50
13 Tottenham	40	9	5	6	26	23	3	6	11	12	25	47
14 Norwich	40	7	5	8	26	26	5	4	11	14	26	45
15 Derby	40	6	7	7	18	17	4	6	10	17	28	43
16 West Ham	40	6	9	5	23	21	3	6	11	17	31	42
17 Charlton	40	7	7	6	23	21	2	8	10	15	31	42
18 Chelsea*	40	7	11	2	24	17	2	4	14	26	51	42
19 Portsmouth	40	4	8	8	21	27	3	6	11	15	39	35
20 Watford	40	4	5	11	15	24	3	6	11	12	27	32
21 Oxford	40	5	7	8	24	34	1	6	13	20	46	31
	840	182	132	106	610	439	106	132	182	439	610	1128

* relegated after play-offs

Odds & ends

Double wins: (3) Luton, Sheffield Wed, Watford.
Double losses: (3) Liverpool, Nott'm Forest, Derby.

Won from behind: (2) QP Rangers (a), Southampton (a).
Lost from in front: (3) Southampton (h), Everton (h), Nott'm Forest (a).

High spots: 10 game unbeaten run - following on from last season.
6 away games without defeat from February to the end of the season.
Defeating League champions Everton at Goodison Park.
Highest average attendance for eight years.
Cyrille Regis getting England call up.

Low spots: 11 League and Cup games without a win in the autumn, including six successive defeats.
The poor home form.
The FA Cup exit to struggling Watford.

Red cards: City – Pickering (Manchester U h).
Red cards: Opponents – Elliott (Norwich h).
Player of the year: David Speedie.
Ever-presents: (1) Steve Ogrizovic.
Hat-tricks: (0).
Opposing hat-tricks: (0).
Leading scorer: (12) Cyrille Regis.

	Appearances						Goals			
	Lge	*Sub*	LC	*Sub*	FAC	*Sub*	Lge	LC	FAC	Tot
Bannister, Gary	**7**	*1*					**1**			**1**
Bennett, Dave	**27**	*1*	3		2		**4**			**4**
Borrows, Brian	**32**	*1*	3		2					
Cook, Michael				*1*						
Dobson, Tony	**1**									
Downs, Greg	**27**		2	*1*	2		**2**			**2**
Emerson, Dean	**19**	*1*								
Gynn, Michael	**19**	*6*	3		2		**3**	2		**5**
Houchen, Keith	**13**	*8*	2				**3**			**3**
Kilcline, Brian	**28**				2		**8**		1	**9**
Lane, Martin		*2*								
Livingstone, Steve	**3**	*1*		*1*						
McGrath, Lloyd	**17**		3		2					
Ogrizovic, Steve	**40**		3		2					
Peake, Trevor	**31**		2		1					
Phillips, David	**32**	*3*	2		2		**2**			**2**
Pickering, Nick	**26**	*1*	2					1		**1**
Regis, Cyrille	**30**	*1*	2		2		**10**	1	1	**12**
Rodger, Graham	**9**	*3*	2				**1**			**1**
Sedgley, Steve	**25**	*2*	2		1		**2**			**2**
Smith, David	**14**	*2*					**4**			**4**
Smith, Kevan	**5**	*1*			1					
Speedie, David	**35**	*1*	2		1	*1*	**6**			**6**
23 players used	**440**	***35***	**33**	***3***	**22**	***1***	**46**	**4**	**2**	**52**

BARCLAYS LEAGUE DIVISION 1

Manager: John Sillett

SEASON 1988-89

No	Date		Att	Pos	Pt	F-A	H-T	Scorers, Times, and Referees	1	2	3	4	5	6	7	8	9	10	11	subs used
1	H	EVERTON		18	L	0-1	0-1		Ogrizovic	Borrows	Downs	Sedgley	Kilcline	Peake	Gynn*	Speedie	Regis	Bannister	Smith D	Phillips
	3/9		18,239	*1*	0			*Cottee 44*	*Southall*	*McDonald*	*Pointon*	*Snodin*	*Watson*	*Reid*	*Nevin*	*McCall*	*Sharp*	*Cottee*	*Sheedy*	
								Ref: A Ward	City's opening day game is postponed because Spurs' new stand is not ready. Kilcline misses a penalty for the first time, Southall saving after Watson brings down Smith. Southall is awesome and makes a string of fine saves. Speedie plays in midfield. Pickering has signed for Derby.											
2	A	SHEFFIELD WED		11	W	2-1	0-0	Regis 77, Speedie 80	Ogrizovic	Borrows	Downs	Sedgley	Kilcline	Peake	Gynn	Speedie	Regis	Bannister	Smith D	
	10/9		*15,635*	*9*	3			*Hirst 81*	*Pressman*	*Sterland*	*Worthington*	*Pearson*	*Madden*	*Harper**	*Megson*	*Hirst*	*West*	*Jonsson*	*Galvin^*	*Bradshaw/Cranson*
								Ref: R Dilkes	Four wins in a row makes Hillsborough a lucky ground. Three goals are disallowed before Regis glances in a header and Speedie volleys home Smith's cross. Icelander Jonsson's effort looks good and the Owls celebrate for some time before reality dawns. Regis's effort also goes close.											
3	H	CHARLTON		9	W	3-0	0-0	Smith D 57, 75, Bannister 71	Ogrizovic	Borrows	Downs	Sedgley	Kilcline	Peake	Gynn	Speedie	Regis	Bannister	Smith D	
	17/9		11,859	*16*	6				*Bolder**	*Humphrey*	*Reid*	*MacKenzie*	*Shirtliff*	*Miller*	*Lee*	*Williams*	*Gritt*	*Leaburn*	*Stuart^*	*Peake/Campbell*
								Ref: D Allinson	The fans become impatient when City fail to capitalise on Bolder's injured finger, forcing Steve Gritt into goal. A Sillett rollicking at half-time does the trick and it is one-way traffic afterwards. Speedie relishes his new role and Regis looks more comfortable, too, setting up two goals.											
4	A	WIMBLEDON		6	W	1-0	1-0	Bannister 38	Ogrizovic	Borrows	Downs	Sedgley	Kilcline	Peake	Gynn	Speedie	Regis	Bannister	Smith D	
	24/9		***4,474***	*20*	9				*Green*	*Joseph*	*Clement*	*Jones*	*Young*	*Scales*	*Gibson**	*Fairweath'r^*	*Fashanu*	*Sanchez*	*Wise*	*Cork/Turner*
								Ref: G Ashby	City beat the FA Cup holders in a drab rain-swept game at Plough Lane. Gary Bannister wins both points with a diving header from Speedie's flick-on. Kilcline is inspirational as Fashanu and co pile on the pressure. The Dons are struggling and Dave Beasant has signed for Newcastle.											
5	H	MIDDLESBROUGH		8	L	3-4	1-3	Speedie 7, 60, 73	Ogrizovic	Borrows	Downs	Sedgley	Kilcline*	Peake	Gynn	Speedie	Regis	Bannister	Smith D	Phillips
	1/10		14,521	*15*	9			*Slaven 8, 24, 36, Burke 56*	*Pears*	*Parkinson*	*Cooper*	*Kernaghan*	*Hamilton*	*Pallister*	*Slaven*	*Brennan*	*Burke*	*Kerr*	*Ripley*	
								Ref: R Nixon	Boro are back and manager Bruce Rioch has built a very attractive side who for long periods play City off the park. David Speedie is in superb form and scores a hat-trick of headers. Ripley provides Bernie Slaven with a hat-trick of his own. Fighting Coventry almost snatch a draw.											
6	A	NEWCASTLE		3	W	3-0	3-0	Regis 15, Speedie 35, Gynn 45	Ogrizovic	Borrows	Downs	Sedgley	Kilcline	Peake	Gynn	Speedie	Regis	Bannister	Smith D	
	8/10		*22,896*	*19*	12				*Beasant*	*Anderson*	*Wharton*	*McCreery*	*Scott*	*Thorn^*	*Hendrie*	*Jackson*	*Mirandinha*	*O'Neill**	*Stephenson*	*Robertson/Cornwell*
								Ref: S Lodge	With Gascoigne gone to Spurs the Magpies are struggling, despite winning at Anfield last week. They are booed off at half-time and the post-match protest against the board means McFaul will be sacked on Monday. City are buzzing and extend their away unbeaten run to ten games.											
7	H	MILLWALL		3	D	0-0	0-0		Ogrizovic	Borrows	Downs	Sedgley	Kilcline	Peake	Gynn	Speedie	Regis	Bannister	Smith D	
	15/10		19,321	*2*	13				*Horne*	*Stevens*	*Dawes*	*Hurlock*	*Wood*	*McLeary*	*Salman*	*Morgan*	*Sheringham*	*Cascarino*	*O'Callaghan*	
								Ref: M Peck	Newly promoted and unbeaten Millwall are knocked off the top of the league in a game dominated by both defences. Regis and Bannister struggle to break down the Lions' rearguard. Greg Downs' shirt turns a vivid red after a clash of heads with Cascarino gives him a nosebleed.											
8	A	LIVERPOOL		3	D	0-0	0-0		Ogrizovic	Borrows	Downs	Sedgley	Rodger	Peake	Gynn*	Speedie	Regis	Bannister	Smith D	Phillips
	22/10		***38,742***	*6*	14				*Hooper*	*Ablett*	*Venison*	*Nicol*	*Whelan*	*Burrows*	*Beardsley*	*Houghton*	*Rush*	*Barnes*	*MacDonald**	*Aldridge*
								Ref: G Aplin	With Kilcline injured, City change their line up for the first time. Rodger deputises and helps a five-man defence keep the Reds out. Rush is back from Italy but yet to score in four home games. New signing David Burrows makes his debut. For once, Pool penalty appeals are rejected.											
9	A	ARSENAL		8	L	0-2	0-1		Ogrizovic	Borrows	Downs	Sedgley	Rodger	Peake	Phillips	Speedie	Regis	Bannister	Houchen	
	29/10		*31,273*	*2*	14			*Thomas 17, Adams 82*	*Lukic*	*Dixon*	*Winterburn*	*Thomas*	*Bould*	*Adams*	*Rocastle**	*Richardson*	*Smith*	*Merson^*	*Marwood*	*Hayes/Groves*
								Ref: G Tyson	The Gunners are settling into a groove and win easily. 13-goal Alan Smith peppers the City goal but cannot score and the new England squad member, Michael Thomas, scores a bending 30-yarder. Speedie gets his fifth booking of the season as City's unbeaten away record is ended.											
10	H	WEST HAM		7	D	1-1	0-1	Thompson 82	Ogrizovic	Borrows	Downs	Sedgley	Emerson^	Rodger	**Clark**	Speedie	Regis	Bannister*	Smith D	Houchen/Thompson
	5/11		14,618	*19*	15			*Kelly 33*	*McKnight*	*Potts*	*Dicks*	*Gale*	*Martin*	*Keen*	*Ward*	*Kelly*	*Rosenior*	*Dickens*	*Ince*	
								Ref: E Parker	Keith Thompson, the lesser-known brother of Garry, bought out his contract from Real Oviedo of Spain and returns to Coventry. He scores seven minutes after coming on as sub. Up to that point the inspired Allen McNight looks unbeatable. Coventry kid Howard Clark impresses.											

No	Venue	Opponent / Date	Att	Pos	Pts	F-A	H-T	Scorers, Times, Referees	1	2	3	4	5	6	7	8	9	10	11	12 sub used
11	H	LUTON		6	W	1-0	1-0	Rodger 37	Ogrizovic	Borrows	Downs	Sedgley	Kilcline	Rodger	Clark	Speedie	Regis	Bannister	Smith D	
		12/11	12,625	*16*	18			Ref: K Burge	*Sealey*	*Johnson R*	*Grimes*	*Williams**	*Foster*	*Johnson M*	*Wilson*	*Wegerle*	*Harford*	*Hill*	*Black*	*Oldfield*
									Sinner Sealey won't admit that he dragged out two headers from behind the goal-line. Rodgers' header from Smith's cross does hit the net. An uninspiring performance by City, who need the points. City unveil a new scoreboard but have a power problem which blows one floodlight.											
12	A	NOTT'M FOREST		6	D	0-0	0-0		Ogrizovic	Borrows	Downs	Sedgley	Kilcline	Peake	Clark*	Speedie	Regis	Houchen	Smith D	Phillips
		19/11	*17,250*	*9*	19			Ref: M Bailey	*Sutton*	*Chettle*	*Pearce*	*Walker*	*Foster*	*Hodge*	*Crosby**	*Webb*	*Clough*	*Chapman*	*Rice*	*Wilson*
									Coventry become only the second side to stop Forest scoring in this exciting and competitive draw. City have four players booked by a fussy referee, Kilcline for complaining that Forest's wall was not ten yards back. Crosby hits a post and David Smith misses a sitter near the end.											
13	A	TOTTENHAM		6	D	1-1	0-1	Houchen 73	Ogrizovic	Borrows	Downs	Sedgley	Kilcline	Peake	Phillips	Speedie	Regis	Houchen	Smith D	
		23/11	*21,961*	*17*	20			*Stewart 11* Ref: A Gunn	*Mimms*	*Butters*	*Thomas*	*Fenwick*	*Fairclough*	*Mabbutt*	*Moran**	*Gascoigne*	*Waddle*	*Stewart*	*Samways^*	*Walsh/Allen P*
									Spurs have been docked two points for failing to fulfil the opening day game and almost lose three more. They haven't beaten City since before the 1987 Cup final, though Sedgley almost wins this game, a free-flowing affair with much goalmouth action. £2 million Gascoigne is quiet.											
14	H	ASTON VILLA		5	W	2-1	1-0	Regis 11, Houchen 61	Ogrizovic	Borrows	Downs	Sedgley	Kilcline	Peake	Phillips	Speedie	Regis*	Houchen	Smith D	McGrath
		26/11	19,880	*14*	23			*McInally 74* Ref: J Deakin	*Spink*	*Price*	*Gray S*	*Gage*	*Mountfield*	*Keown*	*Gray A*	*Platt*	*McInally*	*Cowans*	*Daley**	*Birch*
									Villa are beaten at last, after 51 years and 26 league meetings. Regis and Houchen give their defence a chasing and Sillett says 'this is the best Coventry team ever'. Gray's mesmeric dribble sets ups Villa's consolation goal. Villa boss Graham Taylor is a good loser of a 'superb contest'.											
15	A	QP RANGERS		6	L	1-2	0-1	Speedie 78	Ogrizovic	Borrows	Downs*	Sedgley	Kilcline	Peake !	Phillips	Speedie	Regis	Houchen	Rodger	McGrath
		3/12	*9,853*	*13*	23			*Francis 42, Falco 59* Ref: R Hamer	*Seaman*	*Coney*	*Allen*	*Parker**	*Maguire*	*Maddix*	*Falco*	*Francis*	*Fereday*	*Pizanti*	*Brock*	*Dennis*
									Trevor Peake is controversially sent off for fouling Fereday in the centre circle. There are plenty of worse tackles in a physical match, not least Brock's foul on Houchen. A poor game is won by Francis's superb volley and Falco's close-range effort. Jim Smith resigns to join Newcastle.											
16	H	MANCHESTER U		3	W	1-0	0-0	Regis 81	Ogrizovic	Borrows	Downs	Sedgley	Kilcline	Peake	Phillips	Speedie	Regis	Houchen	Smith D	
		10/12	19,948	*10*	26			Ref: P Foakes	*Leighton*	*Garton**	*Martin*	*Bruce*	*Blackmore*	*Donaghy*	*Robson*	*Strachan*	*McClair*	*Hughes*	*Sharpe*	*Gill^/Milne*
									An uninspiring match but a crucial win, City's first home win over United since 1982. United are draw specialists, having tied nine out of 15, but are beaten by Regis's late header. Kilcline loses the captaincy to Speedie after his drink driving charge. City draw Sutton United in FA Cup.											
17	H	DERBY		5	L	0-2	0-0		Ogrizovic	Borrows	Downs	Sedgley	Kilcline*	Rodger	Phillips^	Speedie	Regis	Houchen	Smith D	Bannister/Thompson
		17/12	17,227	*4*	26			*Saunders 54, McMinn 66* Ref: J Martin	*Shilton*	*Blades*	*Forsyth*	*Williams*	*Wright*	*Hindmarch*	*McMinn*	*Saunders*	*Goddard*	*Hebberd*	*Callaghan*	
									Controversial referee Martin is at it again. He penalises Houchen for handball after five minutes but Oggy saves Callaghan's penalty. He then ignores Saunders' handball as he scores. Peake-less City struggle but hit Shilton's woodwork three times. The floodlights fail for 19 minutes.											
18	A	SOUTHAMPTON		6	D	2-2	2-0	Phillips 8, Bannister 26	Ogrizovic	Borrows	Downs	Sedgley	Kilcline	Emerson	Phillips	Speedie	Thompson	Bannister !	Houchen	
		26/12	*16,008*	*8*	27			*Wallace R 60, Moore 90* Ref: L Shapter	*Flowers*	*Wallace Ray*	*Statham*	*Case*	*Moore*	*Osman !*	*Wallace Rod*	*Cockerill**	*Le Tissier*	*Baker*	*Wallace D*	*Rideout*
									The second half lasts for 51 minutes. Moore equalises after 46 minutes and Bannister and Osman are sent off after 50 minutes for a silly clash. City get too defensive after the break and concede possession too easily. Five foot four inch Wallace beats Kilcline in the air for his goal.											
19	A	EVERTON		6	L	1-3	1-2	Bannister 25	Ogrizovic	Borrows	Downs*	Sedgley	Kilcline	Emerson	Phillips	Speedie	Thompson	Bannister^	Houchen	Bennett/Smith D
		31/12	*30,778*	*4*	27			*Sheedy 8, 39, Bracewell 65* Ref: R Hart	*Southall*	*Snodin*	*v d Hauwe**	*Ratcliffe*	*Watson*	*Bracewell*	*Steven*	*Reid*	*Nevin*	*Cottee*	*Sheedy*	*Pointon*
									John Sillett introduced Kevin Sheedy to league football at Hereford, and his prodigy scores his first goals of the season to sink lacklustre City. The Toffees are unbeaten in ten and have climbed into the title race. Cottee has scored 12 goals in total against City but can't extend his record.											
20	H	SHEFFIELD WED		4	W	5-0	2-0	Sedgley 38, Speedie 41, 46, 77, [Kilcline 88p]	Ogrizovic	Borrows	Phillips	Sedgley	Kilcline	Peake	Bennett	Speedie	Regis	McGrath	Smith D	
		2/1	15,174	*17*	30			Ref: T West	*Turner*	*Harper*	*Procter*	*Knight*	*Pearson**	*Madden*	*Megson*	*Hodgson*	*Varadi^*	*West*	*Jonsson !*	*Gregory/Galvin*
									The Three Musketeers - Regis, Bennett and McGrath are back - and Jonsson is sent off for fouling Lloyd twice. Speedie scores three headers, whilst Kilcline celebrates being reinstated as skipper with a thumping spot-kick when Megson handles. More floodlight problems near the end.											
21	A	NORWICH		3	W	2-1	0-0	Speedie 65, 88	Ogrizovic	Borrows	Phillips	Sedgley	Kilcline	Peake	Emerson	Speedie	Regis	McGrath*	Smith D	Clark
		14/1	*14,399*	*2*	33			*Gordon 56* Ref: P Alcock	*Gunn*	*Culverhouse*	*Bowen*	*Butterworth*	*Linighan*	*Townsend*	*Gordon*	*Fleck*	*Rosario*	*Phelan*	*Putney*	
									City restore some pride with an excellent performance and Norwich are beaten for only the third time this season. Kilcline is awesome as the Canaries pile on the pressure. Speedie fittingly wins the game with a fine goal as Regis sends him clear and he deliciously chips Bryan Gunn.											

No	Date	Att	Pos	Pt	F-A	H-T	Scorers, Times, and Referees	1	2	3	4	5	6	7	8	9	10	11	subs used
22	H WIMBLEDON		3	W	2-1	1-1	Kilcline 25, Speedie 66	Ogrizovic	Borrows	Phillips	Sedgley	Kilcline	Peake	Emerson	Speedie	Regis	McGrath	Smith D	
	21/1	12,471	*11*	36			*Scales 27*	*Segers*	*Scales*	*Phelan*	*Jones*	*Young*	*Curle*	*Fairweather*	*Gibson*	*Miller*	*Sanchez*	*Wise*	
							Ref: J Worrall	The Dons run of five wins is ended by a determined performance from City. Speedie's chip from the edge of the box has the crowd on it's feet and is one of the finest in years. Kilcline's penalty, after Segers brings down Smith, is saved but he follows up to score. Peake masters Gibson.											
23	A MIDDLESBROUGH		3	D	1-1	1-1	Regis 34	Ogrizovic	Borrows	Dobson	Sedgley	Kilcline	Peake	Emerson	Bannister	Regis	McGrath	Smith D	
	4/2	*17,352*	*10*	37			*Slaven 45*	*Poole*	*Mohan*	*Cooper*	*Mowbray*	*Hamilton*	*Pallister*	*Slaven*	*Brennan*	*Burke*	*Kerr**	*Ripley*	*Gill*
							Ref: K Redfearn	Boro's early season form has faded and debutant keeper Kevin Poole saves them with several vital saves. Sillett is angry that Slaven scores in the fourth minute of injury time when a trainer hasn't been seen. Tony Dobson is in for the transfer-listed Downs and Speedie is suspended.											
24	H NEWCASTLE		5	L	1-2	0-0	Pingel 52 (og)	Ogrizovic	Borrows	Dobson	Sedgley	Kilcline^	Peake	Emerson	Bannister	Regis	McGrath*	Smith D	Bennett/Thompson
	11/2	16,578	*19*	37			*Hendrie 50, Mirandinha 63p*	*Wright*	*Scott*	*Sansom*	*McCreery*	*Anderson*	*Roeder*	*Hendrie*	*Pingel*	*Mirandinha**	*O'Brien*	*Brazil*	*O'Neill*
							Ref: P Tyldesley	City reject John Hendrie returns to haunt them and score the first goal. The Magpies are tight at the back and don't look relegation favourites but this is their first win in six. Dane Frank Pingel glances a header in before Mirandinha seals the win with a penalty when Kilcline handles.											
25	H ARSENAL		3	W	1-0	0-0	Kilcline 82p	Ogrizovic	Borrows	Dobson	Sedgley	Kilcline	Peake	Emerson	Speedie	Regis	Bennett	Smith D	
	21/2	21,429	*1*	40				*Lukic*	*O'Leary*	*Winterburn*	*Thomas*	*Bould*	*Adams*	*Rocastle*	*Richardson*	*Smith*	*Merson*	*Marwood**	*Hayes*
							Ref: H Taylor	Gunners boss George Graham admits that dazzling City are one of the best sides Arsenal have met. They inflict their first league defeat since November. Kilcline's 90-second penalty miss, for Winterburn's foul on Speedie, doesn't prevent him taking the second, after Bould's handball.											
26	A MILLWALL		4	L	0-1	0-0		Ogrizovic	Borrows	Dobson	Sedgley	Kilcline	Peake	Emerson	Speedie	Regis	Bennett	Smith D	
	25/2	*13,021*	*3*	40			*Cascarino 84*	*Horne*	*Thompson*	*Sparham*	*Morgan**	*Wood*	*McLeary*	*Carter*	*Briley*	*Sheringham*	*Cascarino*	*O'Callaghan*	*Salman*
							Ref: I Hemley	City's first visit to the Den for over 20 years is a turgid affair on a mud-heap. The Lions are enjoying a fine first season in the top flight and win with Cascarino's drive, after Peake and Kilcline miss Kevin O'Callaghan's free-kick. Coventry show little ambition and rarely trouble Horne.											
27	A WEST HAM		6	D	1-1	1-0	Kilcline 13p	Ogrizovic	Borrows	Dobson	Phillips	Kilcline	Peake	Bennett	Speedie	Regis*	Bannister	Smith D	Clark
	11/3	*15,205*	*20*	41			*Ince 81*	*Parkes*	*Potts*	*Dicks*	*Gale*	*Martin*	*Devonshire*	*Kelly*	*Dickens*	*Slater*	*Brady*	*Ince*	
							Ref: B Stevens	The Hammers have won only one home game and City let them off the hook with a poor second-half display. Ince equalises when Peake errs. Oggy has to save well from Dicks with West Ham threatening. Recalled 38-year-old keeper Phil Parkes brings down Bennett for the penalty.											
28	H TOTTENHAM		6	D	1-1	1-0	Bannister 18	Ogrizovic	Borrows	Dobson	Phillips	Kilcline	Peake	Bennett	Speedie	Bannister	McGrath*	Smith D	Clark
	18/3	17,280	*9*	42			*Waddle 67*	*Thorstvedt*	*Butters*	*Hughton*	*Fenwick*	*Nayim*	*Mabbutt*	*Walsh*	*Gascoigne**	*Waddle*	*Stewart*	*Allen P*	*Howells*
							Ref: P Harrison	A draw is a fair result from an entertaining game played in wind and drizzle. Waddle is the outstanding player and scores a delicious lobbed goal from Nayim's pass. McGrath and Gascoigne have an intriguing tussle with Lloyd booked for a rugby tackle and Gazza retiring at half-time.											
29	H LIVERPOOL		6	L	1-3	1-2	Bannister 42	Ogrizovic	Borrows	Dobson	Phillips^	Kilcline	Peake	Emerson	Speedie	Regis	Bannister	Smith D*	Houchen/Thompson
	22/3	**23,880**	*4*	42			*Barnes 11, Aldridge 28, Whelan 52*	*Grobbelaar*	*Ablett*	*Staunton*	*Nicol*	*Whelan*	*Gillespie*	*Beardsley*	*Aldridge*	*Houghton*	*Barnes*	*McMahon*	
							Ref: D Axcell	Liverpool are charging in pursuit of Arsenal and are unbeaten in twelve. Kilcline passes straight to Barnes on the edge of the box for the first and Oggy fails to hold Staunton's shot for the second. It is an uphill battle after that and City are lucky not to lose by more to a super Pool.											
30	A CHARLTON		7	D	0-0	0-0		Ogrizovic	Borrows	Dobson	Phillips^	Kilcline	Peake	Emerson	Speedie	Regis*	Bannister	Smith D	Houchen/Clark
	25/3	*6,728*	*15*	43				*Bolder*	*Humphrey*	*Reid*	*Shirtliff*	*Pates*	*Peake**	*Lee*	*Williams^*	*MacKenzie*	*Mortimer*	*Leaburn*	*Walsh/Crooks*
							Ref: M Bodenham	Cup Final hero Bennett has moved to Sheffield Wed for £220,000. City should have won the game in the first half when Bannister misses four good chances. They are denied a penalty in the 57th minute when Shirtliff up-ends Houchen as he rounds Bolder. Oggy keeps the Addicks out.											
31	H SOUTHAMPTON		6	W	2-1	1-1	*Borrows 28, Speedie 71*	Ogrizovic	Borrows	Dobson	Sedgley	Kilcline	Peake	Emerson	Speedie	Houchen	Clark*	Smith D	Thompson
	27/3	11,735	*18*	46			*Wallace D 14*	*Flowers*	*Wallace Ray*	*Adams*	*Case*	*Ruddock*	*Moore*	*Wallace Rod*	*Cockerill*	*Shearer*	*Horne*	*Wallace D*	
							Ref: R Hart	The Saints are in dire straits, without a win in 20 games and heading for the drop. They dominate this game against lethargic City but fail to capitalise on Danny Wallace's goal from Peake's short back-pass. David Speedie superbly chips Tim Flowers to win it against the run of play.											

No	Venue / Date	Opponent	Att	Pos	Res / Pts	F-A	H-T	Scorers, Times, Referees	1	2	3	4	5	6	7	8	9	10	11	12
32	A	DERBY		7	L	0-1	0-0		Ogrizovic	Borrows	Dobson	Emerson	Kilcline	Peake	Phillips	Speedie	Regis	Sedgley	Smith D*	Thompson
	1/4		*15,175*	*9*	46			*Blades 85*	*Shilton*	*Blades*	*Forsyth*	*Williams*	*Wright*	*Hindmarch*	*McMinn*	*Saunders*	*Goddard*	*Hebberd*	*Micklewhite*	
								Ref: D Reeves	A disappointing result gives Derby the double. Paul Blades' thunderous shot from a free-kick on the edge of the area is his first in 160 games and sends City to a deserved defeat. Shilton has an easy afternoon with only two efforts of note. Keith Houchen moves to Hibs for £300,000.											
33	H	NORWICH		6	W	2-1	1-1	Phillips 24, Speedie 67	Ogrizovic	Borrows	Dobson	Emerson	Kilcline	Peake	Phillips	Speedie	Regis	Sedgley	Smith D	
	8/4		12,725	*3*	49			*Fleck 14*	*Gunn !*	*Culverhouse*	*Bowen*	*Butterworth*	*Linighan*	*Townsend*	*Gordon*	*Coney*	*Fleck*	*Phelan**	*Putney*	*Crook*
								Ref: D Elleray	Norwich have a chance of the double but this defeat is a blow. Speedie is back to his best, making one, scoring one and winning a penalty when fouled by Bryan Gunn. Gunn's dissent gets him sent off for foul language but Kilcline blasts the spot-kick wide, his fourth miss of the season.											
34	A	LUTON		7	D	2-2	0-0	Regis 70, Smith D 80	Ogrizovic	Borrows	Dobson	Emerson*	Rodger	Downs	Phillips	Speedie	Regis	Sedgley	Smith D	Bannister
	15/4		*8,610*	*18*	50			*Dreyer 55, Wilson 75*	*Chamberlain*	*Breacker*	*Dreyer*	*Preece*	*Foster*	*Beaumont*	*Wilson*	*Wegerle*	*Meade**	*Hill*	*Black*	*Cooke*
								Ref: D Hedges	The tragic events at Hillsborough overshadowed everything today. The draw is a fair result although both sides ride their luck. Luton's comes when Wilson follows up Oggy's penalty save, after Dobson handles. City's when Chamberlain and Beaumont collide and David Smith scores.											
35	H	QP RANGERS		8	L	0-3	0-2		Ogrizovic	Borrows	Dobson	Sedgley^	Rodger	Peake	Phillips	Speedie	Regis	Bannister	Smith D*	Thompson/Downs
	22/4		**11,246**	*11*	50			*Channing 13, Clarke 32, 60*	*Seaman*	*Channing*	*Fereday*	*Parker*	*Maddix*	*Spackman*	*Gray**	*Kerslake*	*Clarke*	*Reid*	*Sinton*	*Allen M*
								Ref: R Groves	Trevor Francis's appointment as boss has rejuvenated QPR and they win comprehensively as City slip a bit further down the table. The key is QPR's sweeper system and close marking by Parker and Maddix. Colin Clarke scores two, makes the other, and gives Rodger the run-around.											
36	A	MANCHESTER U		6	W	1-0	0-0	Bannister 72	Ogrizovic	Borrows	Dobson	Emerson	Kilcline	Peake	Phillips	Speedie	Regis	Bannister	Smith D	
	29/4		*29,799*	*11*	53				*Leighton*	*Duxbury*	*Donaghy*	*Bruce*	*McGrath*	*Whiteside*	*Robson*	*Beardsmore*	*McClair*	*Hughes*	*Martin**	*Robins*
								Ref: R Milford	Bannister escapes McGrath's clutches to give City a rare but deserved double over the Reds. United have scored just three goals in nine games and never threaten after Robson hits the bar just after the break. Alex Ferguson is under pressure as United end another season without a trophy.											
37	A	ASTON VILLA		7	D	1-1	0-1	Bannister 67	Ogrizovic	Borrows	Dobson	Emerson	Kilcline	Peake	Phillips	Speedie	Regis	Bannister	Smith D	
	13/5		*29,906*	*17*	54			*Platt 18*	*Spink*	*Price*	*Gray S*	*Evans*	*Sims*	*Keown*	*Birch*	*Platt*	*McInally**	*Cowans*	*Callaghan*	*Olney*
								Ref: R Bridges	Villa must now wait ten days to see if West Ham win their final two games and send them down. Villa could have been safe at half-time but Oggy repels desperate Villa, aside from David Platt's superb volley. Bannister heads the equaliser and almost wins the game as Villa wilt.											
38	H	NOTT'M FOREST		7	D	2-2	0-0	Clark 72, Regis 82	Ogrizovic	Borrows	Dobson	Emerson	Kilcline	Peake^	Phillips*	Speedie	Regis	Livingstone	Smith D	Clark/Downs
	15/5		14,011	*3*	55			*Webb 79, Clough 88*	*Sutton*	*Laws*	*Pearce*	*Walker*	*Wilson*	*Rice*	*Carr*	*Webb*	*Clough*	*Chapman*	*Parker*	
		Home	Away					Ref: T Holbrook	A late flurry of goals sends the fans home happy after an open, lively game. Clark scores his first ever goal from a tight angle and Regis powers in a header. Neil Webb is moving to Old Trafford this summer and he scores with a long-range effort and sets up Nigel Clough's late equaliser.											
Average		16,040	18,899																	

Littlewoods Cup				F-A	H-T	Scorers, Times, and Referees	1	2	3	4	5	6	7	8	9	10	11	subs used
2:1 A 27/9	BOURNEMOUTH *6,453*	6 *2:7*	W	4-0	2-0	Downs 10, Gynn 30, 65, Bannister 63	Ogrizovic	Borrows	Downs	Sedgley	Kilcline	Peake	Gynn	Speedie	Regis	Bannister	Smith D	
							Peyton	*Newson*	*Morrell*	*Bond*	*Williams*	*Whitlock**	*Cooke*	*Brooks^*	*Aylott*	*Bishop*	*Close*	*Richards/O'Driscoll*
						Ref: K Cooper	A comprehensive victory over Harry Redknapp's side, which has only lost once this season, makes the second leg a formality. Two first-half goals from outside the area by Downs and Gynn and two howlers by the Cherries' defence in the second half clinch it. A polished performance.											
2:2 H 11/10	BOURNEMOUTH *7,212*	3 *2:15*	W	3-1	1-0	Sedgley 28, Speedie 50, Gynn 75	Ogrizovic	Borrows	Downs*	Sedgley	Kilcline	Peake	Gynn	Speedie^	Regis	Bannister	Smith D	Dobson/Thompson
						Cooke 77	*Peyton*	*O'Driscoll*	*Morrell*	*Bond*	*Williams*	*Pulis*	*Close*	*Brooks*	*Puckett**	*Bishop^*	*Coleman*	*O'Connor/Cooke*
						Ref: A Flood (City win 7-1 on aggregate)	When Cooke's consolation goes in, the 41 Cherries fans chant 'we want seven'. A slick, professional City performance with three super goals. Speedie celebrates his recall to the Scotland squad by scoring the second from Borrows' cross and is given a standing ovation when subbed.											
3 A 2/11	NOTT'M FOREST *21,201*	8 *5*	L	2-3	2-1	Bannister 33, Kilcline 40p	Ogrizovic	Borrows	Downs	Sedgley	Kilcline*	Rodger	Phillips^	Speedie	Regis	Bannister	Smith D	Houchen/Emerson
						Foster 39, Hodge 51, Clough 70	*Crossley*	*Chettle*	*Pearce*	*Walker*	*Foster*	*Hodge*	*Charles*	*Wilson*	*Clough*	*Chapman*	*Rice*	
						Ref: R Milford	A superb first-half display is rewarded by Bannister from a brilliantly worked free-kick and Kilcline scoring after Regis is fouled by Crossley. Nigel Clough silences 5,000 away fans from a corner-kick as City try and substitute the limping David Phillips. Forest go on to win the trophy.											

FA Cup																		
3 A 7/1	SUTTON UNITED *8,000*	4 *VC:13*	L	1-2	0-1	Phillips 52	Ogrizovic	Borrows	Phillips	Sedgley	Kilcline	Peake	Bennett	Speedie	Regis*	McGrath	Smith D	Houchen
						Rains 42, Hanlan 58	*Roffey*	*Jones*	*Rains*	*Golley*	*Pratt*	*Rogers*	*Stephens*	*Dawson*	*Dennis*	*McKinnon*	*Hanlan*	
						Ref: A Buksh	City are humbled at Gander Green Lane in their worst ever result. They become only the fourth Div 1 side beaten by a non-league side since the War, and the highest placed one too. Barry Williams, the Kipling-quoting Sutton boss, is ecstatic and 2,300 City fans bravely clap his team.											

			Home					Away					
		P	W	D	L	F	A	W	D	L	F	A	Pts
1	Arsenal	38	10	6	3	35	19	12	4	3	38	17	76
2	Liverpool	38	11	5	3	33	11	11	5	3	32	17	76
3	Nott'm Forest	38	8	7	4	31	16	9	6	4	33	27	64
4	Norwich	38	8	7	4	23	20	9	4	6	25	25	62
5	Derby	38	9	3	7	23	18	8	4	7	17	20	58
6	Tottenham	38	8	6	5	31	24	7	6	6	29	22	57
7	COVENTRY	38	9	4	6	28	23	5	9	5	19	19	55
8	Everton	38	10	7	2	33	18	4	5	10	17	27	54
9	QP Rangers	38	9	5	5	23	16	5	6	8	20	21	53
10	Millwall	38	10	3	6	27	21	4	8	7	20	31	53
11	Manchester U	38	10	5	4	27	13	3	7	9	18	22	51
12	Wimbledon	38	10	3	6	30	19	4	6	9	20	27	51
13	Southampton	38	6	7	6	25	26	4	8	7	27	40	45
14	Charlton	38	6	7	6	25	24	4	5	10	19	34	42
15	Sheffield Wed	38	6	6	7	21	25	4	6	9	13	26	42
16	Luton	38	8	6	5	32	21	2	5	12	10	31	41
17	Aston Villa	38	7	6	6	25	22	2	7	10	20	34	40
18	Middlesbro	38	6	7	6	28	30	3	5	11	16	31	39
19	West Ham	38	3	6	10	19	30	7	2	10	18	32	38
20	Newcastle	38	3	6	10	19	28	4	4	11	13	35	31
		760	157	112	111	538	424	111	112	157	424	538	1028

Odds & ends

Double wins: (4) Sheffield Wed, Wimbledon, Norwich, Manchester U.
Double losses: (3) Everton, Derby, QP Rangers.

Won from behind: (3) Norwich (a), Southampton (h), Norwich (h).
Lost from in front: (2) Middlesbrough (h), Nott'm Forest LC (a).

High spots: Winning first three away games.
Beating Aston Villa for the first time since 1937.
Winning at 2nd placed Norwich in January.
Beating Champions elect, Arsenal, to go third in table.
Highest final place for 11 years.

Low spots: FA Cup embarrassment at Sutton.
Fade out after lying third with 13 games remaining.

Red cards: City – Peake (QP Rangers a), Bannister (Southampton a).
Red cards: Opponents – Osman (So'ton a), Jonsson (Sheffield Wed h), Gunn (Norwich h).
Player of the year: David Speedie.
Ever-presents: (2) Steve Ogrizovic, Brian Borrows.
Hat-tricks: (2) David Speedie.
Opposing hat-tricks: (1) Slaven (Middlesbrough).
Leading scorer: (15) David Speedie.

	Appearances						Goals			
	Lge	*Sub*	LC	*Sub*	FAC	*Sub*	**Lge**	LC	FAC	**Tot**
Bannister, Gary	**22**	*2*	3				**8**	2		**10**
Bennett, Dave	**5**	*2*			1					
Borrows, Brian	**38**		3		1		**1**			**1**
Clark, Howard	**4**	*5*					**1**			**1**
Dobson, Tony	**16**			*1*						
Downs, Greg	**20**	*2*	3					1		**1**
Emerson, Dean	**18**			*1*						
Gynn, Michael	**8**		2				**1**	3		**4**
Houchen, Keith	**10**	*3*		*1*		*1*	**2**			**2**
Kilcline, Brian	**33**		3		1		**4**	1		**5**
Livingstone, Steve	**1**									
McGrath, Lloyd	**6**	*2*			1					
Ogrizovic, Steve	**38**		3		1					
Peake, Trevor	**32**		2		1					
Phillips, David	**22**	*4*	1		1		**2**		1	**3**
Regis, Cyrille	**34**		3		1		**7**			**7**
Rodger, Graham	**8**		1				**1**			**1**
Sedgley, Steve	**31**		3		1		**1**	1		**2**
Smith, David	**34**	*1*	3		1		**3**			**3**
Speedie, David	**36**		3		1		**14**	1		**15**
Thompson, Keith	**2**	*7*					**1**			**1**
(own-goals)							**1**			**1**
21 players used	**418**	***28***	**33**	***3***	**11**	***1***	**47**	**9**	**1**	**57**

No	Date		Att	Pos	Pt	F-A	H-T	Scorers, Times, and Referees	1	2	3	4	5	6	7	8	9	10	11	subs used
1	H	EVERTON			W	2-0	0-0	Bannister 67, Speedie 90	Ogrizovic	Borrows	Dobson	Emerson	Kilcline	Peake	Gynn	Speedie	Regis	Bannister	Smith D	
	19/8		18,172		3				*Southall*	*Snodin*	*Pointon*	*Ratcliffe*	*Watson*	*Whiteside*	*Nevin*	*McCall*	*Sharp*	*Newell**	*Sheedy*	*Cottee*
								Ref: R Wiseman	Everton's expensive aristocrats are mugged by a City side which leads a charmed life. Everton, with new signings Newell and Whiteside, have the lion's share of chances but City, with no new signings, have only three chances. Speedie's jack-knife header from Borrows' cross is special.											
2	A	ARSENAL			L	0-2	0-0		Ogrizovic	Borrows	Dobson	Emerson	Kilcline	Peake	Gynn	Speedie	Regis	Bannister*	Smith D	**McGuire**
	22/8		*33,886*		3			*Marwood 49, Thomas 85*	*Lukic*	*Dixon*	*Winterburn*	*Thomas*	*O'Leary*	*Adams*	*Rocastle**	*Richardson*	*Smith*	*Merson*	*Marwood*	*Groves*
								Ref: B Stevens	The champions receive their trophy before the game and get over their opening day defeat at Old Trafford. City almost spoil the party but are finally breached by Marwood's header. Thomas swivels and hammers in the second. Golden boot winner Alan Smith is well held by Kilcline.											
3	A	CRYS PALACE		4	W	1-0	1-0	Kilcline 24	Ogrizovic	Borrows	Dobson	Emerson	Kilcline	Peake	Gynn	Speedie	Regis	Bannister	Smith D	
	26/8		*11,122*	*19*	6				*Suckling*	*Pemberton*	*Burke*	*Gray*	*Hopkins*	*O'Reilly*	*McGoldrick*	*Thomas*	*Bright*	*Wright*	*Dyer*	
								Ref: B Hill	The rain pours down and newly promoted Palace can find no way through City's experienced defence. The Wright-Bright combo which scored 58 goals last term doesn't get a single chance and Brian Kilcline's direct free-kick, which skids past ex-City keeper Perry Suckling, is enough.											
4	H	MANCHESTER C		1	W	2-1	0-1	Gynn 55, Smith 90	Ogrizovic	Borrows	Dobson	Emerson	Kilcline	Peake	Gynn	Speedie	Regis	Bannister	Smith D	
	30/8		16,129	*19*	9			*White 19*	*Cooper*	*Fleming*	*Hinchcliffe*	*Bishop*	*Gayle*	*Redmond*	*White*	*Morley*	*Allen*	*McNab*	*Brightwell I*	
								Ref: R Nixon	Michael Gynn missed most of last season with injury but is back to his best and scores a vital equaliser to help City go top of Div 1 for the first time ever. Mel Machin's newly promoted young team are unlucky to lose to David Smith's late winner. City's title odds are halved to 100-1.											
5	A	MILLWALL		4	L	1-4	0-3	Smith 65 *[Dawes 90]*	Ogrizovic^	Borrows	Dobson	Emerson	Kilcline	Peake	Gynn*	Speedie	Regis	Bannister	Smith D	McGuire/**MacDon'ld**
	9/9		*12,062*	*1*	9			*Sheringham 1, 13, Anthrobus 44,*	*Horne*	*Stevens*	*Dawes*	*Hurlock*	*Thompson*	*Wood*	*Carter*	*Briley*	*Sheringham*	*Cascarino*	*Anthrobus*	
								Ref: B Redfern	It took 106 years to get to the top and 44 seconds to slide off the summit. That's how long it took for Sheringham to score his first. City are a shambles in the first half and injured Oggy is replaced in goal by Speedie at half-time. City improve and Speedie holds out until near the end.											
6	H	LUTON		3	W	1-0	1-0	Bannister 17	**Waugh**	Borrows	Dobson	Emerson	Kilcline	Peake	Gynn	Speedie	Regis^	Bannister	McGuire*	MacD'ld/Livingstone
	16/9		11,207	*8*	12				*Chamberlain*	*Breacker*	*Dreyer*	*Wilson*	*McDono'gh**	*Beaumont*	*Kennedy^*	*Wegerle*	*Elstrup*	*Preece*	*Black*	*Harvey/Cooke*
								Ref: J Ashworth	A shoulder injury makes Oggy miss his first game in 241 since joining City. Dougie McGuire makes his full debut after a year on the injury list. Wilson shoots wide from the spot after Wegerle is fouled by Peake in the 66th minute. It's a poor game and City are happy to get the win.											
7	A	CHELSEA		6	L	0-1	0-1		Ogrizovic	Borrows	Dobson	Emerson*	Clark	Peake	Gynn	Speedie	MacDonald	Bannister	Smith	**Middleton L**
	23/9		*18,247*	*2*	12			*Wilson K 5*	*Beasant*	*Clarke**	*Dorigo*	*Roberts*	*Lee*	*Monkou*	*Dickens*	*Nicholas*	*Dixon*	*Wilson K*	*Hazard*	*Bumstead*
								Ref: A Gunn	Shot-shy City suffer another disappointing defeat and Emerson gets his fourth booking and faces suspension. Ex-Banbury man Wilson scores after Dobson's clearance is charged down. Coventry make no impact against the giant Lee and Monkou, while Clark misses two good chances.											
8	A	SHEFFIELD WED		7	D	0-0	0-0		Ogrizovic	Borrows	Dobson	MacDonald	Downs	Peake	Gynn^	Speedie*	Livingstone	Bannister	Smith	Middleton L/Th'pson
	30/9		*15,054*	*20*	13				*Pressman*	*Newsome**	*Worthington*	*Palmer*	*Shirtliff*	*Madden*	*Taylor*	*Whitton*	*Atkinson*	*Hirst*	*Shakespeare*	*Harper*
								Ref: N Midgley	City have agreed a club record £800,000 for Rangers' striker Kevin Drinkell and on this showing need him. Without the injured Regis, Kilcline and Emerson they need Oggy in top form to continue their run at Hillsborough. Big Ron's Wednesday have only scored two in nine games.											
9	H	NOTT'M FOREST		8	L	0-2	0-1		Ogrizovic	Borrows	Dobson^	MacDonald	Kilcline	Peake	McGrath	Speedie	Regis	Bannister*	Smith	Gynn/Downs
	14/10		15,852	*9*	13			*Crosby 36, Rice 52*	*Sutton*	*Laws*	*Pearce*	*Walker*	*Wilson*	*Hodge*	*Crosby*	*Parker*	*Clough*	*Chapman*	*Rice*	
								Ref: D Elleray	Former Grantham winger Gary Crosby stars as Forest continue to be a jinx. He hits a scorcher after Lee Chapman knocks down Sutton's huge clearance. Brian Rice, who almost joined City in the summer, wraps it up. Cyrille Regis goes close with two efforts but cannot break his duck.											
10	H	MANCHESTER U		11	L	1-4	0-2	Drinkell 79	Ogrizovic	Borrows	Downs	MacDonald*	Kilcline	Peake	McGrath	Speedie	Regis	**Drinkell**	Smith^	Gynn/Clark
	21/10		19,647	*14*	13			*Bruce 6, Hughes 29, 69, Phelan 65*	*Leighton*	*Donaghy*	*Martin*	*Bruce*	*Phelan*	*Pallister*	*Robson*	*Ince^*	*McClair*	*Hughes*	*Sharpe**	*Maiorana/Duxbury*
								Ref: T Ward	United's first away win for nine months is a romp for Ferguson's rebuilt side thanks to some dire defending by City. Bryan Robson is dominant but should have had a red card for a vicious tackle on City's man of the match Speedie. Drinkell's super goal is too late to influence the game.											

No/Date	H/A	Opponent/Att	Pos	Res/Pts	FT	HT	Scorers, Times, and Referees	1	2	3	4	5	6	7	8	9	10	11	subs used
11	A	CHARLTON	12	D	1-1	0-1	Speedie 64	Ogrizovic	Borrows	Downs	MacDonald*	**Billing**	Peake	McGrath !	Speedie	Regis	Drinkell	Smith	Gynn
28/10		*6,149*	*19*	14			*Mortimer 22*	*Bolder*	*Humphrey*	*Reid*	*Peake^*	*McLaughlin*	*Pates*	*Lee*	*Williams*	*Leaburn**	*Walsh*	*Mortimer*	*Achampng/M'Kenzie*
							Ref: K Morton	It's four draws in a row at Selhurst Park for City in a poor game spoilt by a gale-force wind. Borrows and Billing make late tackles to stop the Addicks adding to Mortimer's tap-in. Speedie equalises with a deflection off Pates before McGrath is harshly sent off for a tackle on Williams.											
12	A	LIVERPOOL	9	W	1-0	0-0	Regis 47	Ogrizovic	Borrows	Downs	MacDonald	Billing	Peake	McGrath	Speedie	Regis	Drinkell	Smith	
4/11		*36,433*	*2*	17				*Grobbelaar*	*Hysen*	*Burrows*	*Ablett*	*Whelan*	*Hansen*	*Beardsley*	*Houghton*	*Rush*	*Barnes*	*McMahon**	*Molby*
							Ref: T Simpson	City's first win in 25 visits to Anfield earns the Barclays performance of the week and is Sillett's finest League win ever. The Reds are knocked off the top of the table with their only home defeat of the season. Cyrille Regis's goal is his first of the season and his 50th for the Sky Blues.											
13	H	SOUTHAMPTON	7	W	1-0	0-0	Drinkell 75	Ogrizovic	Borrows	Downs	MacDonald*	Billing	Peake	Gynn	Speedie	Regis	Drinkell	Smith	Clark
11/11		12,171	*8*	20				*Flowers*	*Dodd*	*Benali*	*Case*	*Ruddock*	*Osman*	*Le Tissier*	*Cockerill*	*Shearer*	*Rideout*	*Wallace Rod*	
							Ref: D Allison	Kevin MacDonald puts an eighth-minute penalty wide after Neil Ruddock fouls Speedie. Drinkell pounces to win a hard-won victory with a superb volley after Tim Flowers appears to bring down Regis. Chris Nicholl's battling Saints had lost only one game in twelve before today.											
14	A	ASTON VILLA	10	L	1-4	1-2	Gynn 26 *[Platt 75p]*	Ogrizovic	Borrows	Dobson	MacDonald	Billing	Peake	Gynn	Speedie	Regis*	Drinkell	Smith^	Bannister/Livingst'ne
18/11		*22,803*	*3*	20			*Ormondroyd 10, 53, Peake 20 (og),*	*Spink*	*Price*	*Gray*	*McGrath*	*Mountfield*	*Neilson*	*Daley*	*Platt*	*Olney**	*Cowans*	*Ormondroyd*	*Williams*
							Ref: G Tyson	Daley's speed and Ormondroyd's height make it the biggest away defeat for two years and extends the jinx. City are in it until the lanky striker heads in off the bar and Platt clinches it for Graham Taylor's team after Peake's foul on him. Speedie gets his seventh booking of the season.											
15	H	NORWICH	6	W	1-0	0-0	Regis 84	Ogrizovic	Borrows	Downs	MacDonald	Billing	Peake	Gynn	Speedie	Regis	Drinkell	Smith	
25/11		11,996	*8*	23				*Gunn*	*Culverhouse*	*Bowen*	*Butterworth*	*Linighan*	*Townsend*	*Gordon*	*Allen*	*Rosario*	*Sherwood*	*Phillips*	
							Ref: R Dilkes	Regis nets his second winner in four days as brave Norwich lose for only the third time this season. He is enjoying a golden period and scores from Drinkell's flick on. 'Drinks' misses three good chances against his old club and Oggy saves well from Linighan, Gordon and Rosario.											
16	A	EVERTON	9	L	0-2	0-1		Ogrizovic	Borrows	Downs	MacDonald*	Billing	Kilcline	Gynn	Emerson	Regis	Drinkell	Smith^	McGrath/Livingstone
2/12		*21,127*	*8*	23			*McCall 22, Watson 50*	*Southall*	*Atteveld*	*McDonald*	*Ratcliffe*	*Watson*	*Ebbrell*	*Beagrie*	*McCall*	*Sharp*	*Cottee*	*Sheedy*	
							Ref: J Watson	Peter Billing makes up for his red card in midweek in the Zenith Data Cup against the Dons with the man-of-the-match award against his first club. City can't repeat their Anfield win and the Toffees arrest their slide with an easy win, despite Kilcline and Emerson returning after injury.											
17	H	ARSENAL	10	L	0-1	0-0		Ogrizovic	Borrows	Downs	MacDonald	Billing	Dobson	McGrath	Emerson	Regis	Drinkell	Smith	
9/12		16,152	*1*	23			*Merson 89*	*Lukic*	*Dixon*	*Winterburn*	*Thomas*	*O'Leary*	*Adams*	*Rocastle*	*Richardson*	*Smith*	*Groves*	*Marwood**	*Merson*
							Ref: J Worrall	Injuries to Gynn, Peake and Kilcline and Speedie's suspension hinder City badly, but they almost grab a point with a gritty display. Substitute Paul Merson, subject of tabloid stories about off the field misbehaviour, chips Oggy and takes the champions back to the top of the division.											
18	H	WIMBLEDON	8	W	2-1	1-1	Borrows 18p, Curle 90 (og)	Ogrizovic	Borrows	Downs	MacDonald	Gynn	Dobson	McGrath	Emerson	Regis	Drinkell	Smith	
16/12		**8,294**	*16*	26			*Young 45*	*Segers*	*Joseph*	*Phelan*	*Scales*	*Young*	*Curle*	*Fairweath'r**	*Cork*	*Gibson*	*Ryan*	*Wise*	*Brooke*
							Ref: N Midgley	The dreadful wind and rain keeps the gate down to the lowest for four years but can't stop City getting revenge for the Zenith Data defeat three weeks ago. Curle has a nightmare, fouling Drinkell for Borrows to score his third goal in five years, and deflecting Smith's cross in at the end.											
19	A	QP RANGERS	9	D	1-1	0-1	Speedie 64	Ogrizovic	Borrows	Downs	MacDonald	Gynn	Dobson	McGrath	Emerson	Speedie	Drinkell	Smith	
26/12		*9,889*	*14*	27			*Falco 42*	*Seaman*	*Bardsley*	*Sansom*	*Parker*	*McDonald*	*Maddix*	*Wilkins*	*Barker*	*Falco*	*Wegerle*	*Sinton*	
							Ref: I Hemley	The seventh Boxing Day game without a win since 1980 on QPR's new grass pitch. Speedie returns from suspension to grab the point with a delicious lob over Seaman. Don Howe has recently replaced Trevor Francis as manager. Wegerle makes his full debut after a £1 million move.											
20	A	DERBY	11	L	1-4	0-2	Speedie 56 *[Ramage 89]*	Ogrizovic	Borrows	Downs	MacDonald^	Gynn	Dobson	Drinkell	Speedie	McGrath	Emerson*	Smith	Regis/McGuire
30/12		*17,011*	*9*	27			*Pickering 16, Hebberd 26, 78,*	*Shilton*	*Sage*	*Forsyth*	*Williams G*	*Wright**	*Blades*	*Pickering*	*Saunders*	*Ramage*	*Hebberd*	*McCord*	*Cross*
							Ref: D Hedges	City's final game of the decade is the fifth defeat in a row against Derby, despite a positive attacking display. Pickering heads his first goal for Derby and sets up the second. Speedie's unstoppable header gives the Sky Blues some hope, but the makeshift defence finally collapses.											
21	H	TOTTENHAM	11	D	0-0	0-0		Ogrizovic	Borrows	Downs	MacDonald	Billing	Peake	Drinkell*	Speedie	McGrath	Gynn	Smith	Regis
1/1		19,631	*5*	28				*Mimms*	*Bergsson*	*v d Hauwe*	*Allen*	*Howells*	*Mabbutt*	*Samways*	*Gascoigne**	*Stewart*	*Lineker*	*Sedgley*	*Polston*
							Ref: R Hamer	An adventurous City, almost back to full strength, give Spurs a run for their money in the best game of the season. The McGrath-Gascoigne tussle ends after 12 minutes when Gazza lashes out at marker McGrath and breaks his fore-arm. Spurs finish stronger and Lineker goes close.											

No	Date	Att	Pos	Pt	F-A	H-T	Scorers, Times, and Referees	1	2	3	4	5	6	7	8	9	10	11	subs used
22	H CRYS PALACE		11	W	1-0	0-0	Speedie 85	Ogrizovic	Borrows	Downs	McGrath	Billing	Peake	Gynn	Speedie	Regis	Bannister*	Smith	Clark
	13/1	10,839	*14*	31				*Martyn*	*Pemberton*	*Burke*	*O'Reilly**	*Hopkins*	*Thorn*	*Barber*	*Thomas*	*Bright*	*Wright*	*Pardew*	*McGoldrick*
							Ref: R Gifford	Dixie McNeil is City's new coach and Speedie saves his blushes against a negative Palace with a late goal. Their defence move out to catch the Scot offside from Oggy's mighty kick but Gary O'Reilly is sluggish and Speedie shoots past Nigel Martyn. Kevin Drinkell has a back injury.											
23	A MANCHESTER C		12	L	0-1	0-0		Ogrizovic	Borrows	Dobson	McGrath*	Billing	Peake	Gynn	Speedie	Regis	Livingstone	Smith	Clark
	20/1	*24,345*	*14*	31			*White 83*	*Dibble*	*Harper**	*Hinchcliffe*	*Reid*	*Hendry*	*Redmond*	*White*	*Ward*	*Clarke*	*Megson^*	*Lake*	*Beckford/Brightwell I*
							Ref: L Shapter	A dire game which leaves City with the joint worst goalscoring record in Div 1. Speedie angrily kicks the ball against the ref but immediately flings an arm around the official to avoid a caution. Andy Hinchcliffe scores from a 40-yard free-kick but the ref had signalled it as indirect.											
24	H CHELSEA		9	W	3-2	2-1	Livingstone 1, McAllister 3 (og), [Regis 70]	Ogrizovic	Borrows	Downs	MacDonald*	Billing	Peake	**Gallacher**	Gynn	Regis	Livingstone	Smith	Dobson
	3/2	15,295	*6*	34			*Dorigo 37, Dixon 48*	*Beasant*	*Clarke*	*Dorigo*	*Roberts*	*Johnsen*	*Bumstead*	*McAllister*	*Dickens**	*Dixon*	*Wilson K*	*Wilson C*	*Lee*
							Ref: T Holbrook	£900,000 Kevin Gallacher's signing inspires City's attack to score three for the first time in the league this season. Norwich's Ian Crook is also set to sign. Livingstone scores after 28 seconds and it should have been wrapped up before the break. Chelsea fight back until Regis pounces.											
25	H MILLWALL		7	W	3-1	2-1	Smith 13, Livingstone 23, 50	Ogrizovic	Borrows	Downs	Dobson	Kilcline	Peake	Gallacher	Gynn	Regis	Livingstone	Smith	
	17/2	10,812	*19*	37			*Cascarino 5*	*Branagan*	*Dawes*	*Coleman*	*Treacy*	*Thompson*	*McLeary*	*Goddard*	*Hurlock*	*Sheringham**	*Cascarino*	*Stephenson*	*Carter*
							Ref: J Lloyd	One win in 19 league games have seen Millwall slump from 1st to 19th and got John Docherty the sack. Bob Pearson's managerial career enjoys a flying start with Tony Cascarino's header, but Livingstone's eighth goal in four games alerts England B boss Sexton to his talents.											
26	H ASTON VILLA		6	W	2-0	0-0	Drinkell 51, Smith 52	Ogrizovic	Borrows	Dobson	Gynn	Kilcline	Peake	Gallacher	Speedie	Regis	Livingstone*	Smith	Drinkell
	4/3	18,012	*2*	40				*Spink*	*Price*	*Gage*	*McGrath*	*Mountfield**	*Neilson*	*Daley*	*Platt*	*Olney*	*Cowans*	*Ormondr'yd^*	*Gray/Birch*
							Ref: G Courtney	An emphatic home win denies Villa the top spot and takes City into the top six. The TV cameras see City dominate the first half without reward but punish Villa with two excellent goals. Drinkell scores with his first touch and Smith curls a right-footer past the superb Spink.											
27	A LUTON		6	L	2-3	0-1	Drinkell 48, Regis 80	Ogrizovic	Borrows	Downs	Gynn	Dobson*	Peake	Gallacher	Speedie	Regis	Drinkell	Smith	Billing
	7/3	*8,244*	*19*	40			*Black 20, Gray 81, Dowie 86*	*Chamberlain*	*Breacker*	*Harvey**	*Rees*	*James*	*Dreyer*	*Wilson*	*Nogan*	*Dowie*	*Preece**	*Black*	*Johnson/Gray*
							Ref: K Cooper	When Regis scores a superb goal City look set for their first away win since November but relegation-threatened Hatters snatch their first home win in four months. Luton are on top for long periods on the plastic pitch against uncertain Sky Blues, who come to life with Drinkell's goal.											
28	A NOTT'M FOREST		6	W	**4-2**	2-0	Gallacher 2, Speedie 13, 75, Drinkell 68	Ogrizovic	Borrows	Dobson	Gynn	Billing	Peake	Gallacher	Speedie	Regis	Drinkell	Smith	
	10/3	*18,750*	*4*	43			*Currie 78, Laws 82*	*Sutton*	*Laws*	*Pearce*	*Walker*	*Wilson*	*Rice*	*Crosby*	*Parker^*	*Clough*	*Currie*	*Orlygsson**	*Jemson/Gaynor*
							Ref: P Harrison	Revenge for the semi-final defeat is sweet and comprehensive as City win at Forest for the first time since Clough took over in 1975. City slice through Forest's defence, Walker included, at will and only two late consolation goals save Forest from their biggest home defeat since 1966.											
29	A NORWICH		4	D	0-0	0-0		Ogrizovic	Borrows	Dobson	Gynn	Billing	Peake	Gallacher	Speedie	Regis	Drinkell	Smith	
	14/3	*13,673*	*9*	44				*Gunn*	*Culverhouse*	*Bowen*	*Tanner*	*Linighan*	*Townsend*	*Allen*	*Fleck*	*Rosario**	*Crook*	*Phillips*	*Mortensen*
							Ref: J Moules	Norwich have only lost once at home this season, but their lowest gate so far sees their third home 0-0 in a row. Oggy plays most of the game with a broken nose after a clash with Rosario but is the star with three excellent saves. Drinkell misses a sitter near the end against his old club.											
30	H SHEFFIELD WED		6	L	1-4	1-1	Gynn 28 *[Atkinson 72]*	Ogrizovic	Borrows	Dobson*	Gynn	Billing	Peake	Gallacher	Speedie	Regis^	Drinkell	Smith	**Edwards**/Livingst'ne
	17/3	13,321	*14*	44			*Hirst 16, Worthington 48, Sheridan 63,*	*Turner*	*Nilsson*	*King**	*Palmer*	*Shirtliff*	*Pearson*	*Carr*	*Sheridan*	*Hirst^*	*Atkinson*	*Worthington*	*Madden/Bennett*
							Ref: K Burge	The Owls are pulling away from the drop zone and give Big Ron, tanned from his honeymoon in Barbados, the perfect wedding present. Sheridan and Palmer rule the match for dazzling Wednesday against a lethargic City. Dave Bennett gets a standing emotional welcome back.											
31	H CHARLTON		8	L	1-2	1-0	*Gallacher 32*	Ogrizovic	Borrows	Dobson*	Gynn	Billing	Peake	Gallacher	Speedie	Regis	Drinkell	Smith^	Edwards/Livingstone
	24/3	10,037	*19*	44			*Minto 65, Drinkell 81 (og)*	*Bolder*	*Humphrey*	*Reid*	*Peake*	*McLaughlin*	*Caton*	*Lee*	*Watson**	*Williams*	*Minto*	*Mortimer*	*Jones*
							Ref: J Martin	Bottom of the table Charlton gain their first victory over City since 1966. It's a dire display from a top six team which badly lack a ball-winning midfielder. Greg Downs has been freed and Paul Edwards signed from Crewe for £300,000. Dobson is having a miserable time at left-back.											

No	Date	Venue	Opponent	Att	Pos	Pts	Res	F-A	H-T	Scorers, Times, and Referees	1	2	3	4	5	6	7	8	9	10	11	subs used
32		A	MANCHESTER U		9		L	0-3	0-2		Ogrizovic	Borrows	Edwards	Gynn	Billing*	Peake	Gallacher	Speedie	Regis	Drinkell^	Smith	Dobson/Livingstone
	31/3			***39,172***	*16*	44				*Hughes 27, 36, Robins 87*	*Leighton*	*Donaghy**	*Gibson*	*Bruce*	*Phelan*	*Pallister*	*Webb*	*Ince*	*McClair*	*Hughes*	*Wallace^*	*Martin/Robins*
										Ref: R Milford	City's players have had blood tests to see what is causing a lack of energy in recent matches. This is a better display in bright sunshine against the relegation haunted FA Cup semi-finalists. Mark Hughes looks deadly, although his second looks like handball. City's third defeat in a row.											
33		H	DERBY		8		W	1-0	0-0	Wright 49 (og)	Ogrizovic	Borrows	Edwards	Gynn	Dobson	Peake	Gallacher	Speedie	Regis	Livingstone	Smith	
	7/4			11,144	*13*	47					*Taylor*	*Sage*	*Forsyth*	*Williams G*	*Wright*	*Hindmarch*	*Williams P**	*Saunders*	*Harford*	*Hayward^*	*Briscoe*	*Davidson/Francis*
										Ref: D Phillips	The Derby jinx is put to rest and means Sillett has beaten every Division 1 side since he became City boss. It's a much improved display, with Gallacher's skill and pace causing problems and Edwards looking classy. Injury-hit Rams are beaten when Wright turns Smith's cross in.											
34		A	TOTTENHAM		9		L	2-3	2-1	Smith 18, Speedie 32	Ogrizovic	Borrows	Edwards	Gynn*	Dobson	Peake	Gallacher	Speedie	Regis	Clark	Smith	**Middleton C**
	14/4			*23,917*	*5*	47				*Lineker 38, 69, Stewart 46*	*Thorstvedt*	*Bergsson*	*v d Hauwe*	*Sedgley*	*Thomas*	*Mabbutt*	*Stewart*	*Gascoigne*	*Nayim*	*Lineker*	*Allen*	
										Ref: M James	Spurs come from two goals down to gain their first victory in eight over the Sky Blues. Erik Thorstvedt is all at sea for City's goals but Lineker and Stewart save his blushes, the latter bamboozling Dobson before volleying in. Speedie almost grabs a point but Erik comes good and saves.											
35		H	QP RANGERS		10		D	1-1	1-1	Smith 9	Ogrizovic	Borrows	Edwards	MacDonald	Dobson	Peake	Gallacher	Speedie	Regis*	Clark	Smith	Livingstone
	16/4			10,012	*11*	48				*Maddix 45*	*Seaman*	*Bardsley*	*Sansom**	*Parker*	*McDonald*	*Maddix*	*Wilkins*	*Channing*	*Clarke*	*Ferdinand*	*Sinton*	*Falco*
										Ref: T Mills	Brian Borrows and Gallacher get B international call-ups and are outsiders for the World Cup. Don Howe's team grab an equaliser well into first-half injury-time and then shut up shop with ten men behind the ball. Regis and Speedie set up David Smith's sixth goal of the season.											
36		A	WIMBLEDON		10		D	0-0	0-0		Ogrizovic	Borrows	Edwards	MacDonald	Dobson	Peake	Gallacher	Clark	Regis	Drinkell	Smith	
	21/4			***4,086***	*11*	49					*Segers*	*Goodyear*	*Phelan*	*Ryan*	*Young*	*Curle*	*Bennett^*	*Miller*	*Fashanu**	*Kruszynski*	*Wise*	*Cork/Joseph*
										Ref: S Lodge	After nine yellows and one red card, Speedie misses his seventh game through suspension, though Drinkell returns. The crowd is the lowest to watch a City game since 1963. It's dire stuff and Gould calls the Dons in for Sunday training. Segers tips over the best chance, a Regis header.											
37		A	SOUTHAMPTON		11		L	0-3	0-2		Ogrizovic	Borrows	Edwards*	Gynn	Dobson	Peake	Gallacher	Speedie	MacDonald	Drinkell	Smith	Billing
	28/4			*16,359*	*7*	49				*Le Tissier 36p, Horne 43, Osman 85*	*Flowers*	*Cherednik^*	*Adams*	*Case*	*Ruddock*	*Osman*	*Wallace Rod*	*Cockerill*	*Rideout*	*Horne*	*Le Tissier**	*Shearer/Dodd*
										Ref: G Tyson	Saints make it 40 home goals with a rampaging performance against a meek City who surrender without a fight. Le Tissier scores his 24th of the season after Peake is adjudged to have pushed the same player. Only Oggy, with six great saves, stands between City and a Dell drubbing.											
38		H	LIVERPOOL		12		L	**1-6**	1-3	Gallacher 2	Ogrizovic	Clark	Dobson^	Gynn	McGrath	Peake	Gallacher	Speedie	Regis	Drinkell*	Smith	Macdon'ld/**Titterton**
	5/5			**23,204**	*1*	49				*Rush 16, Barnes 37, 40, 61, [Rosenthal 50, 69]*	*Grobbelaar*	*Hysen*	*Venison*	*Ablett*	*Gillespie*	*Staunton*	*Molby*	*Rosenthal*	*Rush*	*Barnes*	*McMahon*	
Average		Home 14,292	Away 18,544							Ref: F Roberts	Liverpool, champions for the eighteenth time, run riot and inflict City's heaviest ever home league defeat. A makeshift defence with McGrath returning after injury at centre-back, is totally mesmerised as the Reds assume arrogant control. It could have been double figures in the heat.											

Littlewoods Cup					F-A	H-T	Scorers, Times, and Referees	1	2	3	4	5	6	7	8	9	10	11	subs used
2:1	A	GRIMSBY	3	L	1-3	0-1	Kilcline 64p	Waugh	Borrows	Dobson	Emerson*	Kilcline	Peake	Gynn^	Speedie	MacDonald	Bannister	Smith D	Liv'stone/Thompson
19/9		*10,150*	*4:7*				*Gilbert 10, Watson 51, Birtles 69*	*Sherwood*	*McDermott*	*Stephenson*	*Tillson*	*Lever*	*Cunnington*	*Childs*	*Gilbert*	*Rees*	*Watson*	*Birtles*	
							Ref: W Burns	Kevin MacDonald and Keith Waugh are unfamiliar faces. MacDonald, a free transfer from Liverpool, makes his first start in an embarrassing defeat which could have been a lot worse. Waugh, a summer buy from Bristol City, is at fault for the first goal. Gary Birtles scores a cracker.											
2:2	H	GRIMSBY	7	W	3-0	2-0	Drinkell 23, Speedie 44, MacDonald 71	Ogrizovic	Borrows	Dobson	MacDonald	Downs	Peake	Drinkell	Speedie	Regis	Bannister	Smith D	
4/10		15,346	*4:11*					*Sherwood*	*McDermott*	*Jobling**	*Tillson*	*Lever*	*Cunnington*	*Childs*	*Gilbert*	*Rees !*	*Cockerill*	*Alexander*	*Willis*
							Ref: D Axcell (City win 4-3 on aggregate)	Drinkell makes a dream debut with a superb overhead kick against his former team after Tony Rees is sent off in the third minute for stamping on Greg Downs. Speedie scores a first-timer from David Smith's cross and Kevin MacDonald clinches it with a 25-yarder into the top corner.											
3	A	QP RANGERS	11	W	2-1	1-0	Downs 30, Drinkell 62	Ogrizovic	Borrows	Downs	MacDonald	Kilcline*	Peake	McGrath	Speedie	Regis	Drinkell	Smith D	Billing
25/10		*9,277*	*17*				*Wright 80p*	*Seaman*	*Channing*	*Sansom*	*Maddix*	*McDonald*	*Barker*	*Wright*	*Reid*	*Clarke*	*Francis**	*Sinton*	*Rutherford*
							Ref: K Cooper	England hopeful David Seaman takes his eye off Greg Downs' 25-yarder and lets it through his hands to set City on the winning trail against Rangers' veterans. Drinkell makes it three in three before McGrath, who had dominated Reid, heads against his own arm. Peter Billing debut.											
4	A	MANCHESTER C	10	W	1-0	1-0	Regis 16	Ogrizovic	Borrows	Dobson	Clark	Billing	Peake	Gynn	Speedie*	Regis	Drinkell	Smith D	MacDonald
22/11		*23,355*	*19*					*Dibble*	*Fleming**	*Hinchcliffe*	*Bishop*	*Hendry*	*Redmond*	*White*	*Gayle*	*Allen*	*McNab*	*Lake^*	*Brightwell I/Oldfield*
							Ref: P Don	City go through to the last eight for the first time in eight years but it's not pretty. Lady Luck helps them to survive after Regis chests down Smith's cross and drives in the winner. Manchester's failure to press home their advantage leaves manager Machin on the verge of the sack.											
QF	A	SUNDERLAND	11	D	0-0	0-0		Ogrizovic	Borrows	Dobson	McGrath	Billing	Peake	Gynn	Speedie !	Regis	Livingstone	Smith D	
17/1		*27,218*	*2:3*					*Carter*	*Kay*	*Hardyman*	*Bennett !*	*McPhail*	*Owers*	*Bracewell*	*Armstrong*	*Gates**	*Gabbiadini^*	*Pascoe*	*Agboola/Hauser*
							Ref: D Allison	A superb fighting display at a freezing Roker earns a replay. The simmering game boils over in the 65th minute when Gary Bennett, brother of Dave, and Speedie, are ordered off when the Sunderland man retaliates to a high boot. Gynn and Gabbiadini have the best chances of the tie.											
QF R	H	SUNDERLAND	12	W	5-0	2-0	Livingstone 15, 19, 51, 64, Gynn 72	Ogrizovic	Borrows	Downs	Gynn	Billing*	Peake	MacDonald	Speedie	Regis	Livingstone	Smith D	Dobson
24/1		20,959	*2:5*					*Carter*	*Kay*	*Hardyman*	*Bennett^*	*Ord*	*Owers !*	*Bracewell*	*Armstrong*	*Gates**	*Gabbiadini*	*Lemon*	*Hauser/Agboola*
							Ref: J Martin	Livingstone destroys Dennis Smith's Roker men. He scores his first senior goal and then lashes in another three. Sunderland are intent on retribution against Speedie. Armstrong and Lemon are booked and Owers is sent off just before half-time for an unprovoked elbow in his face.											
SF 1	A	NOTT'M FOREST	9	L	1-2	0-1	Livingstone 72	Ogrizovic	Borrows	Downs	Dobson	Kilcline	Peake	Gallacher	Gynn	Regis	Livingstone	Smith D	
11/2		*26,153*	*4*				*Clough 37p, Pearce 79*	*Sutton*	*Laws*	*Pearce*	*Walker*	*Chettle*	*Hodge*	*Crosby*	*Parker*	*Clough*	*Jemson*	*Orlygsson**	*Starbuck*
							Ref: K Redfern	Unlucky City lose the televised first leg when the referee says Regis handles, though the ball hit his leg. 7,000 fans brave the rain and see Steve Livingstone nip in to score. Pearce wins it with a brilliant free-kick as the ref misses Hodge push Gynn out of the wall. Speedie is suspended.											
SF 2	H	NOTT'M FOREST	7	D	0-0	0-0		Ogrizovic	Borrows	Downs	Speedie	Kilcline*	Peake	Gallacher^	Gynn	Regis	Livingstone	Smith D	Dobson/Drinkell
25/2		25,500	*4*					*Sutton*	*Laws*	*Pearce*	*Walker*	*Chettle*	*Hodge*	*Crosby*	*Parker*	*Clough*	*Jemson*	*Wilson*	
							Ref: A Gunn (City lose 1-2 on aggregate)	'You'll never beat Des Walker' is the cry as Forest go through to meet Oldham in the final. A sell-out crowd with the fences down sees Regis only escape his clutches once and hit the bar. Pearce hits the bar and Drinkell goes close, but City lack the guile to break down Clough's team.											

FA Cup																			
3	A	NORTHAMPTON	11	L	0-1	0-1		Ogrizovic	Borrows	Downs	MacDonald	Billing	Peake	Drinkell	Speedie	McGrath	Gynn*	Smith D	Regis
6/1		*11,648*	*3:11*				*Berry 42*	*Gleasure*	*Chard*	*Gernon*	*Thomas*	*Wilcox*	*McPherson*	*Berry*	*Quow*	*Collins*	*Barnes*	*Brown*	
							Ref: K Morton	Another depressing cup defeat at the hands of Graham Carr's team, who are rarely troubled by a disappointing City. Bobby Barnes, who had earlier hit a post, sends a skidding cross across the quagmire and Berry nips ahead of Downs to score. Cobblers will not win again until April.											

		Home					Away					
	P	W	D	L	F	A	W	D	L	F	A	Pts
1 Liverpool	38	13	5	1	38	15	10	5	4	40	22	79
2 Aston Villa	38	13	3	3	36	20	8	4	7	21	18	70
3 Tottenham	38	12	1	6	35	24	7	5	7	24	23	63
4 Arsenal	38	14	3	2	38	11	4	5	10	16	27	62
5 Chelsea	38	8	7	4	31	24	8	5	6	27	26	60
6 Everton	38	14	3	2	40	16	3	5	11	17	30	59
7 Southampton	38	10	5	4	40	27	5	5	9	31	36	55
8 Wimbledon	38	5	8	6	22	23	8	8	3	25	17	55
9 Nott'm Forest	38	9	4	6	31	21	6	5	8	24	26	54
10 Norwich	38	7	10	2	24	14	6	4	9	20	28	53
11 QP Rangers	38	9	4	6	27	22	4	7	8	18	22	50
12 COVENTRY	38	11	2	6	24	25	3	5	11	15	34	49
13 Manchester U	38	8	6	5	26	14	5	3	11	20	33	48
14 Manchester C	38	9	4	6	26	21	3	8	8	17	31	48
15 Crys Palace	38	8	7	4	27	23	5	2	12	15	43	48
16 Derby	38	9	1	9	29	21	4	6	9	14	19	46
17 Luton	38	8	8	3	24	18	2	5	12	19	39	43
18 Sheffield Wed	38	8	6	5	21	17	3	4	12	14	34	43
19 Charlton	38	4	6	9	18	25	3	3	13	13	32	30
20 Millwall	38	4	6	9	23	25	1	5	13	16	40	26
	760	183	99	98	580	406	98	99	183	406	580	1041

Odds & ends

Double wins: (1) Crys Palace.
Double losses: (2) Manchester U, Arsenal.

Won from behind: (2) Manchester C (h), Millwall (h).
Lost from in front: (4) Charlton (h), Spurs (a), Liverpool (h), Luton (a).

High spots: Topping Division 1 for first time albeit after four games.
First ever win at Anfield at 23rd attempt.
First win at Forest since 1970.
Exciting Littlewoods Cup run.

Low spots: Embarrassing FA Cup exit at Northampton.
Losing at Tottenham after leading 2-0.
Annihilation by Liverpool in final game · City's biggest home defeat ever.

Red cards: City – McGrath (Charlton a), Speedie (Sunderland LC a).
Red cards: Opponents – Rees (Grimsby LC h), Bennett (Sunderland LC a), Owers (Sunderland LC h).

Player of the Year: Brian Borrows.
Ever-presents: (0).
Hat-tricks: (1) Steve Livingstone.
Opposing hat-tricks: (1) Barnes (Liverpool).
Leading scorer: (9) David Speedie.

	Appearances						Goals			
	Lge	*Sub*	LC	*Sub*	FAC	*Sub*	Lge	LC	FAC	Tot
Bannister, Gary	**10**	*1*	2				**2**			**2**
Billing, Peter	**16**	*2*	3	*1*	1					
Borrows, Brian	**37**		8		1		**1**			**1**
Clark, Howard	**5**	*4*	1							
Dobson, Tony	**28**	*2*	5	*2*						
Downs, Greg	**16**	*1*	5		1			1		**1**
Drinkell, Kevin	**21**	*1*	3	*1*	1		**5**	2		**7**
Edwards, Paul	**6**	*2*								
Emerson, Dean	**12**		1							
Gallacher, Kevin	**15**		2				**3**			**3**
Gynn, Michael	**31**	*3*	6		1		**3**	1		**4**
Kilcline, Brian	**11**		4				**1**	1		**2**
Livingstone, Steve	**6**	*7*	4	*1*			**3**	5		**8**
MacDonald, Kevin	**19**	*3*	4	*1*	1			1		**1**
McGrath, Lloyd	**12**	*1*	2		1					
McGuire, Dougie	**1**	*3*								
Middleton, Craig		*1*								
Middleton, Lee		*2*								
Ogrizovic, Steve	**37**		7		1					
Peake, Trevor	**33**		8		1					
Regis, Cyrille	**32**	*2*	7			*1*	**4**	1		**5**
Smith, David	**37**		8		1		**6**			**6**
Speedie, David	**32**		7		1		**8**	1		**9**
Thompson, Keith		*1*		*1*						
Titterton, David		*1*								
Waugh, Keith	**1**		1							
(own-goals)							**3**			**3**
26 players used	**418**	*37*	**88**	*7*	**11**	*1*	**39**	**13**		**52**

No	Date		Att	Pos	Pt	F-A	H-T	Scorers, Times, and Referees	1	2	3	4	5	6	7	8	9	10	11	subs used
1	A	MANCHESTER U			L	0-2	0-0		Ogrizovic	Borrows	Edwards*	McGrath	Kilcline	Peake	Gallacher	Dobson^	Speedie	Drinkell	Smith	Regis/MacDonald
	25/8		**46,715**		0			*Bruce 57, Webb 70*	*Sealey*	*Irwin*	*Donaghy*	*Bruce*	*Phelan*	*Pallister*	*Webb*	*Ince*	*McClair*	*Hughes*	*Blackmore*	
								Ref: R Nixon	An Old Trafford full house see City fail to convert their first-half superiority into goals. Irwin makes both goals, Bruce heading home a corner and Webb's diving header. Regis is given ten minutes to save the game. Speedie is roughed up by Blackmore and Donaghy, who are booked.											
2	H	EVERTON			W	3-1	2-0	Speedie 16, Gallacher 20, Dobson 70	Ogrizovic	Borrows	Edwards	McGrath	Kilcline	Peake	Gallacher	Dobson	Speedie	Drinkell	Smith*	Clark
	29/8		13,063		3			*Nevin 55*	*Southall*	*McDonald^*	*Hinchcliffe*	*Keown*	*Watson*	*Milligan*	*Atteveld**	*Ebbrell*	*Sharp*	*Newell*	*Nevin*	*Whiteside/Ratcliffe*
								Ref: J Moules	Southall staged a sit-in protest at half-time in Everton's previous game, but there is little he can do behind a dodgy Toffees defence against a lively City attack. Speedie scores a soft goal from Hinchcliffe's back-pass. Gallacher volleys No 2 and Dobson nets his first ever with a drive.											
3	H	NOTT'M FOREST		7	D	2-2	0-0	Kilcline 48p, Borrows 88p	Ogrizovic	Borrows	Edwards	McGrath^	Kilcline	Peake	Gallacher	Gynn	Speedie	Drinkell	Dobson*	Thompson/Regis
	1/9		12,622	*17*	4			*Jemson 50p, 72*	*Crossley*	*Laws*	*Williams*	*Walker*	*Chettle*	*Hodge**	*Keane*	*Parker*	*Clough*	*Jemson*	*Carr*	*Wilson*
								Ref: D Axcell	An exciting match of four penalties which City almost throw away after controlling the first half. Kilcline scores one when Gallacher is tripped, misses one when Wilson handles, and hands over to Borrows to score the third when Walker handles. Edwards handles for Forest's spot-kick.											
4	A	ASTON VILLA		11	L	1-2	0-1	Borrows 50	Ogrizovic	Borrows	Edwards	McGrath^	Kilcline	Peake	Gallacher	Gynn	Speedie	Drinkell*	**Perdomo**	Regis/Dobson
	8/9		*27,001*	*13*	4			*Platt 39p, Cascarino 78*	*Spink*	*Price*	*Gallacher*	*McGrath*	*Mountfield*	*Nielson*	*Daley*	*Platt*	*Olney**	*Cowans*	*Cascarino*	*Yorke*
								Ref: G Ashby	Uruguayan debutant Perdomo shows some delicious touches but can't stop Villa under Jozef Venglos continuing their jinx. McGrath fouls Platt and the star of Italia 90 scores from the penalty. Borrows bends a 20-yarder round Spink before Cascarino taps in after Yorke mis-hits his shot.											
5	H	WIMBLEDON		15	D	0-0	0-0		Ogrizovic	Borrows	Edwards	Perdomo*	Kilcline	Peake	Gallacher	Gynn	Speedie	Drinkell	Smith^	MacD'ld/Livingstone
	15/9		**8,875**	*16*	5				*Segers*	*Joseph*	*Phelan*	*Barton*	*Scales !*	*Curle*	*Gayle*	*Kruszynski*	*Fashanu**	*Sanchez*	*Cotterill*	*Cork*
								Ref: I Borrett	There is a minute's silence for the York player David Longhurst who died last week. Scales is sent off after nine minutes for a professional foul on Speedie. Perdomo almost scores from the resulting free-kick but later limps off. It's a dreadful bore-draw and won't entice the fans back.											
6	A	LUTON		17	L	0-1	0-1		Ogrizovic	Borrows	Edwards*	MacDonald	Kilcline	Peake	Gallacher	Gynn	Speedie	Drinkell^	Smith	Titterton/Livingstone
	22/9		*8,336*	*7*	5			*Dowie 2*	*Chamberlain*	*Breacker*	*Harvey*	*Rees*	*Beaumont*	*Dreyer*	*Elstrup**	*Preece*	*Dowie*	*Hughes*	*Black*	*James*
								Ref: J Rushden	Luton lost 1-6 to QPR last week but are too good for a punchless City. Dowie's early header after an untypical Kilcline slip is enough to win. The nearest City come is a deflected Kilcline free-kick, which Alec Chamberlain saves well. Keith Waugh is freed after two games in a year.											
7	H	QP RANGERS		12	W	3-1	2-0	Livingstone 2, 65, Gynn 16	Ogrizovic	Borrows	Edwards	MacDonald	Kilcline	Peake	Gallacher	Gynn	Regis	Livingstone	Perdomo*	Smith
	29/9		9,897	*10*	8			*Ferdinand 78*	*Roberts*	*Bardsley**	*Sansom^*	*Parker*	*McDonald*	*Maddix*	*Wilkins*	*Wilson*	*Ferdinand*	*Wegerle*	*Sinton*	*Channing/Barker*
								Ref: T Fitzharris	Regis, MacDonald and Livingstone are in for Smith, Drinkell and Speedie, the focus of an off-the-field incident, and Rangers are sent packing with a solid win. Perdomo looks unfit but sprays the ball about. Livingstone sets up Gynn, scores two and is top scorer after one full game.											
8	A	MANCHESTER C		14	L	0-2	0-0		Ogrizovic	Borrows	Edwards	Gynn	Kilcline	Peake	Gallacher	MacDonald*	Regis	Livingstone	Perdomo^	Smith/Emerson
	6/10		*26,918*	*5*	8			*Harper 51, Quinn 89*	*Coton*	*Brightwell I*	*Pointon*	*Reid^*	*Hendry*	*Redmond*	*White**	*Heath*	*Quinn*	*Harper*	*Ward*	*Allen/Brennan*
								Ref: A Bennett	Speedie is close to a move after hitting the front page of the *Sun* after an unsavoury incident following the Bolton game but he is sorely missed. City lose their fifth away game in a row to Howard Kendall's rejuvenated team, starring veteran Peter Reid, who should have won more easily.											
9	H	SOUTHAMPTON		16	L	1-2	1-1	Borrows 39p	Ogrizovic	Borrows	Dobson^	Speedie	Billing	Peake	Gallacher	Gynn	Regis	Livingstone	MacDonald*	Smith/Emerson
	20/10		10,048	*13*	8			*Billing 4 (og), Le Tissier 49*	*Flowers*	*Dodd*	*Benali*	*Case*	*Ruddock*	*Osman*	*Le Tissier*	*Horne*	*Shearer*	*Cook**	*Wallace Rod*	*Adams*
								Ref: I Hendrick	Speedie's comeback is overshadowed by a magical display by Le Tissier whose cross is headed in by Billing and who wins it with a curler from Horne's free-kick. Speedie 'scores' after 24 seconds but it is ruled out, and City only manage a penalty when Ruddock is forced to foul Regis.											
10	A	SHEFFIELD UTD		12	W	1-0	0-0	Borrows 80p	Ogrizovic	Borrows	Edwards	Gynn	Billing	Peake	Gallacher	Speedie	Regis	Emerson	Smith	
	27/10		*17,978*	*20*	11				*Tracey*	*Pemberton*	*Barnes*	*Jones*	*Morris*	*Beesley*	*Marwood*	*Todd**	*Agana^*	*Deane*	*Bryson*	*Hoyland/Bradshaw*
								Ref: K Breen	Perdomo's move looks in doubt, but the first away win is notched against the bottom club who have yet to win. It relieves some of the pressure on Sillett but City are lucky. Peake's tackle on Agana looks a penalty. Near the end Tracey fouls Regis and Borrows slots home from the spot.											

No	Venue	Opponent	Att	Pos	Res	F-A	H-T	Scorers, Times, Referees	1	2	3	4	5	6	7	8	9	10	11	Subs used
11	H	ARSENAL		16	L	0-2	0-0		Ogrizovic	Borrows	Edwards	Emerson	Billing	Peake	Livingstone	Gynn	Regis	Speedie	Smith	
	3/11		15,283	*2*	11			*Limpar 82, 87*	*Seaman*	*Dixon*	*Winterburn*	*Thomas*	*Bould*	*Adams*	*Groves^*	*Davis*	*Smith**	*Merson*	*Limpar*	*Campbell/O'Leary*
								Ref: P Durkin	Swedish international Limpar's two late goals are rough justice on City, who play their best football of the season. The Gunners are unbeaten and strong title contenders but are lucky to survive a goalmouth melee seconds before the first goal. Drinkell and Gallacher are under treatment.											
12	A	SUNDERLAND		14	D	0-0	0-0		Ogrizovic	Borrows	Edwards	Emerson	Billing	Peake	Livingstone	Gynn	Regis	Speedie	Smith	
	10/11		*20,101*	*18*	12				*Carter*	*Kay*	*Hardyman*	*Bennett*	*Ball*	*Owers*	*Bracewell*	*Armstrong*	*Davenport*	*Gabbiadini*	*Pascoe*	
								Ref: J Worrall	Missed opportunities mean City are hovering just above the relegation area. Their tight defence is rarely troubled by promoted Sunderland and Regis misses the best chance. Owers and Speedie continue their feud from last season. Sillett is sacked four days later and Butcher installed.											
13	H	LIVERPOOL		15	L	0-1	0-0		Ogrizovic	Borrows	Edwards	**Butcher**	Billing	Peake	McGrath	Speedie*	Regis	Gynn	Gallacher	Smith
	17/11		22,496	*1*	12			*Beardsley 73*	*Grobbelaar*	*Hysen*	*Burrows*	*Nicol*	*Whelan*	*Gillespie*	*Beardsley*	*Houghton*	*Rush*	*Ablett*	*McMahon*	
								Ref: K Redfern	A challenging first game for new player-boss Butcher who picks himself as a third centre-half. If Gallacher's second-minute shot had gone in instead of hitting the post the outcome may have been different. Beardsley snatches it when Terry and Oggy hesitate, but it's a fighting display.											
14	H	LEEDS		16	D	1-1	0-1	Gallacher 61	Ogrizovic	Borrows	Edwards	Butcher	Billing	Peake	McGrath*	Gynn	Regis	Speedie	Gallacher^	Smith/Livingstone
	24/11		16,184	*5*	13			*Chapman 23*	*Lukic*	*Sterland*	*Kamara**	*Batty*	*Fairclough*	*Whyte*	*Strachan*	*Shutt^*	*Chapman*	*McAllister*	*Speed*	*Haddock/Pearson*
								Ref: N Midgley	Leeds are back in the top flight and causing a few shocks. Chapman scores for the fifth game in a row from a Strachan cross and Gallacher equalises after a lot of pressure. Livingstone goes close in an end-to-end climax. City's commitment is obvious but they lack true creativity.											
15	A	CRYS PALACE		17	L	1-2	0-1	Regis 89	Ogrizovic	Borrows	Edwards	Butcher^	Billing	Peake	Gallacher	Speedie !	Regis	Livingstone	Gynn*	McGrath/Smith
	1/12		*16,562*	*3*	13			*Bright 18, Gray 86*	*Martyn*	*Humphrey*	*Shaw*	*Gray*	*Young*	*Hodges**	*Salako*	*Thomas*	*Bright*	*Wright*	*McGoldrick*	*Pardew*
								Ref: K Hackett	Speedie grabs the headlines for the wrong reasons after verbally abusing referee Hackett ten minutes from time. Despite Palace dominating, City have their chances: Regis hits the woodwork and Speedie has a goal disallowed. Gray's excellent display is rewarded with a fine goal.											
16	A	EVERTON		18	L	0-1	0-0		Ogrizovic	Borrows	Edwards	Emerson	Billing	Peake	Gallacher	Speedie	Drinkell	McGrath	Smith	
	8/12		*17,567*	*15*	13			*McCall 75*	*Southall*	*McDonald^*	*Keown*	*Ratcliffe*	*Watson*	*Milligan*	*Nevin*	*McCall*	*Newell*	*Cottee**	*Sheedy^*	*Sharp/Ebbrell*
								Ref: R Lewis	Kendall is back at Everton and gets his first win, albeit a lucky one. McCall, who had badly fouled McGrath, hits a 30-yarder after Speedie has a 'goal' ruled out and Drinkell hit a post. Mick Mills takes over from McNeil as assistant. City's team coach gets snowbound on the way home.											
17	H	MANCHESTER U		18	D	2-2	1-1	Gallacher 39, Regis 58	Ogrizovic	Borrows	Edwards	McGrath*	Billing	Peake	Gallacher	Gynn	Regis	Drinkell	Smith	Emerson
	15/12		16,256	*9*	14			*Hughes 5, Wallace 90*	*Sealey*	*Blackmore*	*Sharpe**	*Bruce*	*Phelan*	*Pallister*	*Webb*	*Ince^*	*McClair*	*Hughes*	*Wallace*	*Robson/Irwin*
								Ref: K Burge	United have lost one in eleven and boss the first half, with City lucky to be level at half-time. Regis crowns a super display with a header from Smith's cross. Wallace grabs a point in injury-time after a frantic last 20 minutes, with Bryan Robson on as sub. Brian Kilcline is up for sale.											
18	A	CHELSEA		18	L	1-2	0-0	Gallacher 59	Ogrizovic	Borrows	Edwards	Emerson	Billing	Peake	Gallacher	Gynn	Regis	Speedie	Smith*	Drinkell
	22/12		*16,317*	*6*	14			*Townsend 78, Wise 81*	*Beasant*	*Hall*	*Dorigo*	*Townsend*	*Cundy*	*Monkou**	*Le Saux*	*Lee*	*Dixon*	*Durie*	*Wise*	*Stuart*
								Ref: L Shapter	Chelsea record their seventh win in a row but leave it late against the unlucky Sky Blues. Kevin Gallacher scores with a bicycle kick. City continue to attack but are caught by the swift breaking Londoners, who are inspired by substitute Graeme Stuart. Kevin Drinkell is axed.											
19	H	TOTTENHAM		16	W	2-0	0-0	Gallacher 46, Gynn 51	Ogrizovic	Borrows	Edwards	Emerson	Butcher	Peake	Gallacher	Gynn	Regis	Speedie	Smith	
	26/12		**22,549**	*5*	17				*Thorstvedt*	*Thomas*	*v d Hauwe*	*Sedgley**	*Howells*	*Mabbutt*	*Stewart*	*Gascoigne*	*Allen*	*Lineker*	*Walsh^*	*Samways/Nayim*
								Ref: T Holbrook	City's desire to win is far greater than Spurs' and Butcher chalks up his first league win. Gallacher's goal comes from the second-half kick-off without an opponent touching the ball. Gallacher makes Gynn's goal, too. Tottenham's final charge never happens. Gazza is subdued by Gynn.											
20	H	NORWICH		16	W	2-0	0-0	Borrows 56p, Speedie 58	Ogrizovic	Borrows	Edwards	Emerson	Butcher	Peake	Gallacher	Gynn	Regis	Speedie*	Smith	Drinkell
	29/12		12,043	*9*	20				*Gunn*	*Culverhouse*	*Bowen*	*Butterworth*	*Polston*	*Crook*	*Gordon*	*Rosario*	*Sherwood*	*Fox**	*Phillips*	*Sutch*
								Ref: M Peck	Butcher again has to read the riot act at half-time. Transfer rumours surround Speedie, but he is the star of this emphatic win in driving rain. Polston brings him down for the penalty and after scoring the second he limps off to a standing ovation. Ex-Canary sub Drinkell almost scores.											
21	A	DERBY		16	D	1-1	1-1	Regis 33	Ogrizovic	Borrows	Edwards	Billing	Kilcline	Peake	Gallacher	Gynn	Regis	Emerson	Smith	
	1/1		*15,741*	*18*	21			*Harford 6*	*Taylor*	*Sage*	*Pickering*	*Williams P**	*Wright*	*Forsyth*	*Kavanagh*	*Saunders*	*Harford*	*Ramage*	*Cross*	*Davidson*
								Ref: M Bodenham	Butcher is injured and sits out his first away point. Kilcline plays his first game since Sillett left. The keepers are at fault for both goals, Oggy misjudging Harford's speculative shot and Martin Taylor palming Smith's cross to Regis. A mistake-ridden game in miserable rain and wind.											

No	Date		Att	Pos	Pt	F-A	H-T	Scorers, Times, and Referees	1	2	3	4	5	6	7	8	9	10	11	subs used
22	A	NOTT'M FOREST		16	L	0-3	0-0		Ogrizovic	Borrows	Dobson	Billing	Kilcline	Peake	Drinkell	Gynn	Regis	Emerson	Smith*	Livingstone
	12/1		*18,344*	*9*	21			*Pearce 63, Clough 78, Keane 90*	*Crossley*	*Laws*	*Pearce*	*Walker*	*Chettle*	*Keane*	*Carr**	*Wilson^*	*Clough*	*Crosby*	*Parker*	*Wassall/Starbuck*
								Ref: K Lupton	Oggy is back to his best and saves Pearce's first penalty since his World Cup miss. Clough had fired the first penalty wide. Forest then run City ragged with Pearce scoring and making one and Keane grabbing the best one. Gallacher has a cartilage operation and Speedie is linked to Villa.											
23	H	ASTON VILLA		15	W	2-1	0-0	Gynn 54, Speedie 80	Ogrizovic	Borrows	Edwards	McGrath	Butcher	Peake	MacDonald	Gynn	Regis	Speedie	Smith	
	19/1		15,696	*14*	24			*Platt 52*	*Spink*	*Price*	*Gray*	*McGrath*	*Comyn^*	*Nielson*	*Birch*	*Platt*	*Cascarino*	*Cowans*	*Gage**	*Yorke/Ormondroyd*
								Ref: B Hill	Speedie shows that he is indispensable by netting a superb headed winner. After a poor first half two quick goals liven things up and it looks like a draw until the little man pounces. Livingstone and Dobson go to Blackburn for a joint £750,000. £250,000 Woods signs from Wigan.											
24	A	WIMBLEDON		15	L	0-1	0-0		**Sutton**	Borrows	**Hurst**	Billing	Kilcline	Emerson	MacDonald*	Gynn	Regis	Smith	Drinkell	**Fleming**
	2/2		***4,061***	*7*	24			*Gibson 66*	*Segers*	*Joseph*	*Phelan*	*Barton*	*Blackwell*	*Curle*	*McGee*	*Kruszynski*	*Fashanu*	*Scales*	*Gibson*	
								Ref: A Gunn	Speedie has gone to Liverpool for £675,000 after six transfer requests in a month. It's a makeshift side with Steve Sutton on loan from Forest and Hurst and YTS youngster Fleming making their debuts in a dreadful game. The Fashanu-Kilcline duel livens up things with honours even.											
25	H	SUNDERLAND		16	D	0-0	0-0		Ogrizovic	Borrows	Edwards	Billing	Kilcline	Peake	MacDonald*	Gynn	Regis	Drinkell^	Smith	Hurst/Fleming
	23/2		10,449	*17*	25				*Norman*	*Owers*	*Smith*	*Bennett*	*Ball*	*Mooney*	*Bracewell*	*Armstrong*	*Davenport*	*Gabbiadini*	*Pascoe*	
								Ref: P Alcock	Another dire game and but for Gabbiadini's poor finishing it would have been an embarrassing defeat. The team are booed off and poor Kevin Drinkell who hasn't scored in 19 appearances this season limps off. Butcher, who has had a knee operation, needs to get the cheque book out.											
26	H	CRYS PALACE		16	W	3-1	1-0	Peake 36, Kilcline 48, 67	Ogrizovic	Borrows	Hurst	Emerson	Kilcline	Peake	**Woods**	Gynn	Regis	Gallacher*	Smith	Clark
	2/3		10,225	*3*	28			*Wright 86*	*Martyn*	*Humphrey*	*Shaw*	*Gray*	*Young*	*Thorn*	*Salako*	*Thomas*	*Bright*	*Wright*	*McGoldrick**	*Barber*
								Ref: R Groves	Palace, under Steve Coppell, are having their best season ever, but with Gallacher back City hit their best form for weeks. Peake scores his first for five years and Kilcline scores two, the first a searing free-kick into the top corner. Woods' debut is impressive and his cross makes the third.											
27	A	LEEDS		17	L	0-2	0-1		Ogrizovic	Borrows	Hurst	Emerson	Kilcline*	**Pearce**	Woods	Gynn	Regis^	Gallacher	Smith	McGrath/**Robson**
	9/3		*28,880*	*4*	28			*Davison 29, Whyte 87*	*Lukic*	*Sterland*	*Whitlow*	*Batty*	*Fairclough*	*Whyte*	*Strachan*	*Davison**	*Chapman*	*McAllister*	*Speed*	*Shutt*
								Ref: K Breen	City are disrupted by an early injury to Kilcline and are always under pressure in a scrappy match. Their hopes are not finally dashed until the late Chris Whyte goal. Davidson scores when Oggy can only palm out McAllister's drive. Andy Pearce, signed from Halesowen, does well.											
28	H	LUTON		14	W	2-1	0-1	Borrows 61p, Pearce 83	Ogrizovic	Borrows	McGrath	Emerson	Pearce	Peake	Woods	Gynn	Regis	Gallacher	Smith	
	13/3		9,725	*13*	31			*Rodger 10*	*Chamberlain*	*Johnson*	*McDonough*	*Beaumont**	*Rodger*	*Dreyer*	*Elstrup*	*Preece*	*Dowie*	*Pembridge*	*Black*	*Farrell*
								Ref: P Jones	After another grim first half City are losing to Graham Rodger's knee deflection. Butcher's motivational words seem to work and they bounce back to win, secured by a penalty after Chamberlain fouls Gallacher and a late diving header from Pearce. Stewart Robson joins City on loan.											
29	A	QP RANGERS		16	L	0-1	0-1		Ogrizovic	Borrows	McGrath	**Robson**	Pearce	Peake	Woods	Gynn	Regis	Gallacher	Smith	
	16/3		*9,510*	*17*	31			*Ferdinand 36*	*Stejskal*	*Bardsley*	*Sansom*	*Tilson*	*Peacock*	*Maddix*	*Wilkins*	*Barker*	*Ferdinand**	*Wegerle*	*Sinton*	*Iorfa*
								Ref: P Foakes	An impressive debut by Robson, who hasn't played in the top flight for three years. Very little to chose between the two sides but Stejskal is the busier keeper and City are punished for their failure to score. The winner is a soft header from Wilkins' cross. Seven away defeats in eight.											
30	H	MANCHESTER C		15	W	3-1	2-0	Regis 6, Gynn 27, Gallacher 69	Ogrizovic	Borrows	**Sansom**	Robson	Pearce	Peake	Woods	Gynn	Regis	Gallacher	Smith	
	23/3		13,195	*7*	34			*Allen 46*	*Coton*	*Brightwell I*	*Brennan*	*Reid*	*Heath*	*Redmond*	*White*	*Allen*	*Quinn*	*Harper*	*Ward*	
								Ref: R Lewis	The changes continue with ex-England full-back Kenny Sansom signing for £100,000 and Rosario set to join for £650,000. This is an excellent performance and Sansom has a hand in all three goals. City haven't lost at home since Butcher's first game and relegation now seems unlikely.											
31	A	TOTTENHAM		15	D	2-2	2-1	Smith 9, Gallacher 20	Ogrizovic	Borrows	Sansom	Robson*	Pearce	Peake	Woods	Gynn	Regis^	Gallacher	Smith	Emerson/Drinkell
	30/3		*29,033*	*8*	35			*Nayim 43, 77*	*Thorstvedt*	*Edinburgh*	*v d Hauwe*	*Sedgley^*	*Nayim*	*Mabbutt*	*Stewart*	*Samways*	*Gray**	*Walsh*	*Allen*	*Thomas/Moncur*
								Ref: B Stevens	City let a two-goal lead slip at Spurs for the second year in a row but gain a rare away point. Tottenham have their minds on their FA Cup semi-final and are without Lineker and Gascoigne. They should have been buried by City's best 45 minutes of the season, but Nayim grabs a point.											

No	Venue	Opponent / Date	Att	Pos	Pt	Res	F-A	H-T	Scorers, Times, and Referees	1	2	3	4	5	6	7	8	9	10	11	subs used
32	H	CHELSEA		12		W	**1-0**	0-0	Gynn 61	Ogrizovic	Borrows	Sansom	Emerson	Pearce	Peake	Woods	Gynn	Regis	Gallacher	Smith	
		1/4	14,279	*10*	38					*Beasant*	*Clarke*	*Dorigo*	*Townsend*	*Cundy*	*Monkou*	*Le Saux*	*Dickens*	*Dixon*	*Durie*	*Wise*	
									Ref: D Allison	Butcher's decision to free Cyrille Regis is very unpopular with the fans and Rosario has a lot to live up to. This is a disappointing game which looks like a draw until Gynn beats Beasant with a low shot from 20 yards. Stewart Robson is injured and will probably return to West Ham.											
33	A	NORWICH		11		D	2-2	1-1	Gallacher 29, Gynn 60	Ogrizovic	Borrows	Sansom	Emerson	Pearce	Peake	McGrath*	Gynn	Regis^	Gallacher	Smith	**Rosario**/Drinkell
		6/4	*11,550*	*13*	39				*Sherwood 40, Fleck 49*	*Gunn*	*Culverhouse*	*Bowen*	*Butterworth*	*Polston*	*Goss*	*Gordon*	*Fleck*	*Sherwood*	*Power**	*Phillips*	*Fox*
									Ref: A Buksh	City miss the injured Robson but Rosario finally makes his bow at half-time. He sets up Michael Gynn's equaliser after Norwich had nosed undeservedly in front, City having dominated the first half. Oggy has signed a new three-year deal and Cyrille Regis may yet sign for Villa.											
34	A	LIVERPOOL		11		D	1-1	1-1	Gynn 34	Ogrizovic	Borrows	Sansom	Emerson	Pearce	Peake	Woods	Gynn	Regis*	Gallacher	Smith	Rosario
		9/4	*31,063*	*2*	40				*Rush 20*	*Hooper*	*Hysen*	*Staunton**	*Nicol*	*Molby*	*Ablett*	*Beardsley*	*Houghton^*	*Rush*	*Barnes*	*Gillespie*	*Speedie/Carter*
									Ref: D Elleray	Dalglish resigned in February and Ronnie Moran is managing Liverpool. City put a spoke in the wheel of the Reds' title hopes, despite Rush's 13th league goal against City. Gynn continues his scoring run with his 10th of the season before Speedie comes on to a warm City welcome.											
35	H	DERBY		9		W	**3-0**	0-0	Gallacher 53, 59, Woods 72	Ogrizovic	Borrows	Sansom	Emerson	Pearce	Peake	Woods	Gynn	Regis	Gallacher	Smith	
		13/4	11,951	*20*	43					*Shilton*	*Sage*	*Cross*	*Williams G*	*Wright*	*Forsyth*	*Micklewhite*	*Saunders*	*Harford*	*Wilson*	*McMinn*	
									Ref: J Worrall	Almost relegated Derby hold out for almost an hour until Gallacher hits form for the watching Scottish boss, Andy Roxburgh. City are now mathematically safe after five home wins in a row. Gallacher has 15 goals, lobbing Shilton for the first and setting up Woods' first for City.											
36	A	SOUTHAMPTON		14		L	1-2	0-2	Gynn 73	Ogrizovic	Borrows	Sansom	Emerson	Billing	Peake	Woods	Gynn	Regis	Gallacher	Smith	
		20/4	*15,465*	*12*	43				*Wallace Rod 27, 30*	*Flowers*	*Horne*	*Adams*	*Cockerill*	*Ruddock*	*Gittens*	*Gotsmanov*	*Le Tissier**	*Shearer*	*McLoughlin*	*Wallace Rod*	*Banger*
									Ref: H King	City's mini-run is over at a familiar graveyard. It is not a good performance and Saints could have thrashed them but for Oggy. Billing and Le Tissier have a dust-up and the Saint clearly kicks Billing, but they amazingly stay on. Thirteen away games without a win is not good enough.											
37	H	SHEFFIELD UTD		14		D	0-0	0-0		Ogrizovic	Borrows	Sansom	Emerson	Pearce	Peake	Woods	Gynn	Regis	Gallacher	Smith	
		4/5	17,254	*16*	44					*Tracey*	*Wilder**	*Barnes*	*Jones*	*Beesley*	*Booker*	*Marwood^*	*Lucas*	*Agana*	*Deane*	*Hoyland*	*Lake/Whitehouse*
									Ref: T Ward	The Blades call upon a 5,000 strong following, who turn City's final home game into a carnival atmosphere. Cyrille Regis can't score on his farewell to City's home fans, though not through lack of effort. It's an instantly forgettable game. Robert Rosario has had a stomach operation.											
38	A	ARSENAL		16		L	**1-6**	1-2	Gallacher 34 *[Smith 76, Groves 86]*	Ogrizovic	Borrows	Sansom*	Emerson	Pearce	Peake	Woods	Gynn	Regis	Gallacher	Smith	Edwards
		11/5	*41,039*	*1*	44				*Peake 13 (og), Limpar 31, 78, 85,*	*Seaman*	*Dixon*	*Winterburn*	*Hillier*	*Bould*	*Adams*	*Campbell^*	*Davis*	*Smith*	*Merson**	*Limpar*	*Linighan/Groves*
		Home	Away						Ref: J Martin	With fifteen minutes left the nervous home fans are screaming for the whistle, then the champions let loose and hit four in eleven minutes with some ruthless finishing. Limpar adds a hat-trick to the two he scored at City and the celebrations start. Adams picks up the trophy at the end.											
Average		13,887	21,154																		

Rumbelows Cup					F-A	H-T	Scorers, Times, and Referees	1	2	3	4	5	6	7	8	9	10	11	subs used
2:1	H	BOLTON	12	W	4-2	1-1	Gynn 36, Gallacher 65, Liv'stone 79, 90	Ogrizovic	Borrows	Titterton*	Perdomo	Kilcline	Peake	Gallacher	Gynn	Regis	Livingstone	Smith	MacDonald
	26/9	6,146	*3:18*				*Philliskirk 31, 54*	*Felgate*	*Brown*	*Burke*	*Green*	*Crombie !*	*Seagraves*	*Storer*	*Thompson*	*Reeves*	*Philliskirk*	*Darby*	
							Ref: J Deakin	Phil Neal's Bolton side lead twice and are only beaten after Crombie's red card for a professional foul after 77 minutes. Titterton limps off after 14 minutes of his debut and MacDonald is at sea at left-back against the speedy Storer. Livingstone scores his second in the 92nd minute.											
2:2	A	BOLTON	14	W	3-2	1-1	Regis 14, 86, Gallacher 49	Ogrizovic	Borrows	Edwards	Perdomo^	Kilcline*	Peake	Gallacher	Gynn	Regis	Livingstone	Smith	MacDonald/Emerson
	9/10	*5,222*	*3:23*				*Philliskirk 45, 90p*	*Felgate*	*Brown*	*Cowdrill*	*Green**	*Stubbs*	*Winstanley*	*Lee*	*Thompson*	*Stevens*	*Philliskirk*	*Darby*	*Storer*
							Ref: J Watson (City win 7-4 on aggregate)	City start like a train and Regis' early goal, made by Perdomo, effectively ends the tie. Philliskirk has another good game and his swerving free-kick is worthy of Perdomo. MacDonald replaces the limping Kilcline and copes well at centre-back, but fouls Philliskirk for the late penalty.											
3	H	HULL	12	W	3-0	0-0	Speedie 47, Livingstone 66, Regis 84	Ogrizovic	Borrows	Edwards	Speedie	Billing	Peake	Emerson*	Gynn	Regis	Livingstone	MacDonald^	Drinkell/Thompson
	31/10	7,698	*2:21*					*Hesford*	*Hockaday*	*Jacobs*	*Buckley*	*Shotton*	*Doyle^*	*Finnigan*	*Payton*	*Bamber**	*Palin*	*McParland*	*Swan/Ngata*
							Ref: J Martin	Hull put up a brave fight and dominate the first half. Once ex-City man Bamber limps off and Sillett has his half-time gee-up they fall apart and Gynn and Regis inspire City to a good win. Perdomo has rejected City and looks set to move to Spain. Dougie McGuire's contract is ended.											
4	H	NOTT'M FOREST	16	W	5-4	4-3	Gallacher 14, 15, 35, Livingstone 29, 62	Ogrizovic	Borrows	Edwards	Gynn	Billing	Peake	Gallacher	Speedie	Regis	Livingstone	Smith	
	28/11	16,342	*10*				*Clough 36, 42, 43, Parker 53*	*Crossley*	*Laws*	*Pearce*	*Walker*	*Chettle*	*Hodge*	*Crosby*	*Keane*	*Clough*	*Jemson*	*Parker*	
							Ref: R Pawley	City are four up after 35 minutes and Forest fans are exiting the ground. Clough scores a seven-minute hat-trick and it's anyone's game. At 4-4 City lift themselves again and Livingstone pounces to defeat the holders of the last two years and give Butcher his first win. Breathtaking stuff.											
QF	H	SHEFFIELD WED	15	L	0-1	0-1		Ogrizovic	Borrows	Edwards^	McGrath	Butcher	Peake	MacDonald*	Gynn	Regis	Speedie	Smith	Emerson/Drinkell
	23/1	20,689	*2:3*				*Pearson 9*	*Turner*	*King*	*Worthington*	*Palmer*	*Shirtliff*	*Pearson*	*Wilson*	*Sheridan*	*Hirst*	*Williams*	*McCall*	
							Ref: T Holbrook	Second Division Wednesday, who are unbeaten in 14 games, deservedly go through thanks to Pearson's goal from Sheridan's free-kick. City create few chances and the Owls could have won by more. Butcher is injured again and looks a liability. Speedie looks strangely subdued.											

FA Cup																			
3	H	WIGAN	16	D	1-1	0-0	Gynn 66	Ogrizovic	Borrows	Edwards	Emerson*	Billing	Peake	Gallacher	Gynn	Regis	Drinkell	Smith	MacDonald
	5/1	10,777	*3:17*				*Patterson 90*	*Pennock*	*Parkinson*	*Tankard*	*Atherton*	*Johnson*	*Langley*	*Woods*	*Rimmer*	*Fairclough^*	*Page*	*Griffiths**	*Carberry/Patterson*
							Ref: C Trussell	19-year-old Tony Pennock is on loan from Stockport and makes his professional debut. He looks composed and unbeatable until Gynn scores from a well worked free-kick. It looks to be enough until Ray Woods, Wigan's best player, finds Darren Patterson unmarked to head home.											
3R	A	WIGAN	16	W	1-0	1-0	Gynn 12	Ogrizovic	Borrows	Edwards^	Billing	Kilcline	Peake	Gallacher*	Gynn	Regis	Emerson	Smith	Drinkell/MacDonald
	9/1	*7,429*	*3:17*					*Pennock*	*Parkinson*	*Tankard*	*Atherton*	*Johnson*	*Langley*	*Woods*	*Rimmer*	*Fairclough^*	*Page*	*Griffiths**	*Carberry/Patterson*
							Ref: C Trussell	A rip-roaring cup-tie is not one for the purist but City go through by the skin of their teeth. Saturday's hero Pennock drops Gallacher's cross and Gynn pounces. Wigan put City under relentless pressure with Woods at the heart of it all. Page blasts the best chance over from ten yards.											
4	H	SOUTHAMPTON	15	D	1-1	1-0	Kilcline 44	Ogrizovic	Borrows	McGrath	Billing	Kilcline	Emerson	MacDonald	Gynn	Regis	Smith	Drinkell	
	26/1	14,112	*13*				*Shearer 50p*	*Flowers*	*Dodd*	*Adams*	*Case*	*Moore*	*Osman*	*Gotsmanov*	*Horne*	*Shearer*	*McLoughlin*	*Wallace Rod*	
							Ref: M Bodenham	Kilcline - in the shop window but reinstated as captain because of injuries - heads the goal. City are much improved from the Sheff Wed game and deserve their lead until Oggy brings down the lively Shearer, who gets up to blast in the spot-kick. Time is running out for some players.											
4R	A	SOUTHAMPTON	15	L	0-2	0-1		Ogrizovic	Borrows	McGrath*	Billing	Kilcline	Emerson	MacDonald	Gynn^	Regis	Thompson	Drinkell	Hurst/Clark
	29/1	*17,001*	*13*				*Case 38, Wallace Rod 77*	*Flowers*	*Dodd*	*Cook*	*Case*	*Moore*	*Osman*	*Gotsmanov*	*Horne*	*Shearer*	*McLoughlin*	*Wallace Rod*	
							Ref: M Bodenham	The injury problems mount up with five more players hurt to add to the six who missed this pathetic loss. Oggy limps from the 24th minute and it's amazing that Saints take 38 minutes to score. Rod Wallace wraps it up after a glorious 40-yard pass from the veteran Jimmy Case.											

		Home					Away					
	P	W	D	L	F	A	W	D	L	F	A	Pts
1 Arsenal *	38	15	4	0	51	10	9	9	1	23	8	83
2 Liverpool	38	14	3	2	42	13	9	4	6	35	27	76
3 Crys Palace	38	11	6	2	26	17	9	3	7	24	24	69
4 Leeds	38	12	2	5	46	23	7	5	7	19	24	64
5 Manchester C	38	12	3	4	35	25	5	8	6	29	28	62
6 Manch U **	38	11	4	4	34	17	5	8	6	24	28	54
7 Wimbledon	38	8	6	5	28	22	6	8	5	25	24	56
8 Nott'm Forest	38	11	4	4	42	21	3	8	8	23	29	54
9 Everton	38	9	5	5	26	15	4	7	8	24	31	51
10 Tottenham	36	8	9	2	35	22	3	7	9	16	28	49
11 Chelsea	38	10	6	3	33	25	3	4	12	25	44	49
12 QP Rangers	38	8	5	6	27	22	4	5	10	17	31	46
13 Sheffield Utd	38	9	3	7	23	23	4	4	11	13	32	46
14 Southampton	38	9	6	4	33	22	3	3	13	25	47	45
15 Norwich	38	9	3	7	27	32	4	3	12	14	32	45
16 COVENTRY	38	10	6	3	30	16	1	5	13	12	33	44
17 Aston Villa	38	7	9	3	29	25	2	5	12	17	33	44
18 Luton	38	7	5	7	22	18	3	2	14	20	43	37
19 Sunderland	38	6	6	7	15	16	2	4	13	23	44	34
20 Derby	38	3	8	8	25	36	2	1	16	12	39	24
	758	189	103	88	629	420	88	103	189	420	629	1032

* 1 pt deducted
** 2 pts deducted

Odds & ends

Double wins: (0).
Double losses: (2) Southampton, Arsenal.

Won from behind: (3) Aston Villa (h), Luton (h), Bolton LC (h).
Lost from in front: (1) Chelsea (a).

High spots: The 5-4 Rumbelows Cup thriller with Forest.
14 home League and Cup wins unbeaten.
The brief appearance of Uruguayan international Perdomo.

Low spots: Another miserable FA Cup exit at Southampton.
Only one away win all season.
The premature departure of Cyrille Regis.
Eight games without a win in the autumn.

Red cards: City – Speedie (C Palace a).
Red cards: Opponents – Scales (Wimbledon h), Crombie (Bolton LC h).

Player of the Year: Kevin Gallacher.
Ever-presents: (1) Brian Borrows.
Hat-tricks: (1) Kevin Gallacher.
Opposing hat-tricks: (2) Clough (Forest LC (h), Limpar (Arsenal).
Leading scorer: (16) Kevin Gallacher.

	Appearances						Goals			
	Lge	*Sub*	LC	*Sub*	FAC	*Sub*	Lge	LC	FAC	Tot
Billing, Peter	15		2		4					
Borrows, Brian	38		5		4		6			6
Butcher, Terry	6		1							
Clark, Howard		*2*				*1*				
Dobson, Tony	5	*1*					1			1
Drinkell, Kevin	11	*4*		*2*	3	*1*				
Edwards, Paul	22	*1*	4		2					
Emerson, Dean	20	*4*	1	*2*	4					
Fleming, Terry		*2*								
Gallacher, Kevin	32		3		2		11	5		16
Gynn, Michael	35		5		4		8	1	2	11
Hurst, Lee	3	*1*				*1*				
Kilcline, Brian	14		2		3		3		1	4
Livingstone, Steve	6	*4*	4				2	5		7
MacDonald, Kevin	7	*2*	2	*2*	2	*2*				
McGrath, Lloyd	12	*2*	1		2					
Ogrizovic, Steve	37		5		4					
Peake, Trevor	36		5		2		1			1
Pearce, Andy	11						1			1
Perdomo, Jose (loan)	4		2							
Regis, Cyrille	31	*3*	5		4		4	3		7
Robson, Stewart (loan)	3	*1*								
Rosario, Robert		*2*								
Sansom, Kenny	9									
Smith, David	30	*6*	4		3		1			1
Speedie, David	18		3				3	1		4
Sutton, Steve (loan)	1									
Thompson, Keith		*1*		*1*	1					
Titterton, David		*1*	1							
Woods, Ray	12						1			1
30 players used	**418**	***37***	**55**	***7***	**44**		**42**	**15**	**3**	**60**

No	Date		Att	Pos	Pt	F-A	H-T	Scorers, Times, and Referees	1	2	3	4	5	6	7	8	9	10	11	subs used
1	H	MANCHESTER C			L	0-1	0-1		Ogrizovic	Borrows	McGrath	Robson	Pearce	Peake	Woods	Gynn	Rosario	Gallacher	Smith*	**Furlong**
	17/8		17,946		0			*Quinn 16*	*Margetson*	*Hill*	*Pointon*	*Reid**	*Curle*	*Redmond*	*White*	*Brightwell I*	*Quinn*	*Megson*	*Brennan*	*Heath*
								Ref: D Elleray	An average game brings Coventry's first opening day defeat at home since 1953. Niall Quinn's looping header wins it for Peter Reid's team who could have scored more. Keith Curle makes an impressive debut, while £100,000 buy from Enfield, Paul Furlong, looks lively for 15 mins.											
2	H	LUTON			W	**5-0**	3-0	Gallacher 7, 38, Rosario 45, Smith 68, [Furlong 71]	Ogrizovic	Borrows	McGrath	Robson	Pearce	Peake	Woods	Gynn	Rosario	Gallacher*	Smith	Furlong
	20/8		9,848		3				*Chamberlain*	*Beaumont*	*Harvey*	*McDonough*	*Rodger*	*Dreyer*	*Farrell !*	*Preece*	*Stein B**	*Pembridge*	*Black*	*Gray*
								Ref: M Bailey	City bounce back from their opening day defeat and hammer relegation favourites Luton. Sean Farrell is sent off in the 18th minute for belting Peake, playing his final game for City, with an elbow. Gallacher is deadly with a toe to Dreyer's back-pass, followed by an overhead kick.											
3	A	QP RANGERS		6	D	1-1	0-0	Gynn 46	Ogrizovic	McGrath	Edwards	Robson	Pearce	**Atherton**	Woods	Gynn*	Rosario^	Furlong	Smith	Billing/**Ndlovu**
	24/8		*9,393*	*17*	4			*Wegerle 69*	*Stejskal*	*Bardsley*	*Wilson*	*Holloway*	*Peacock*	*Maddix*	*Bailey*	*Barker*	*Ferdinand**	*Wegerle*	*Sinton*	*Thompson*
								Ref: K Morton	Peake has gone to Luton for £100,000 and been replaced by Wigan defender Atherton for £330,000. Ndlovu, the Bulawayo Bullet, makes his debut and looks skilful. City are lucky to survive in the first half but slowly improve. Gary Thompson is given a great reception by City's fans.											
4	H	SHEFFIELD UTD		3	W	3-1	3-1	Smith 8p, Furlong 18, Rosario 35	Ogrizovic	Borrows	Edwards*	Robson	Pearce	Atherton	Woods	McGrath	Rosario	Furlong	Smith^	Billing/Ndlovu
	28/8		12,594	*21*	7			*Bryson 15*	*Tracey*	*Pemberton*	*Cowan**	*Jones*	*Beesley*	*Hill*	*Hoyland*	*Wood^*	*Agana*	*Booker*	*Bryson*	*Mendonca/Whiteh'se*
								Ref: R Groves	David Smith takes over the penalty role from the transfer-listed Borrows, after the impressive Furlong is fouled by Pemberton. New skipper Robson, signed on a free transfer, creates Furlong's goal. Rosario's strength earns him the third. United come back well without testing City.											
5	H	WIMBLEDON		8	L	0-1	0-1		Ogrizovic	Borrows	Billing	Robson	Pearce	Atherton	McGrath	Furlong	Rosario*	Gallacher	Smith	Ndlovu
	31/8		9,345	*10*	7			*Cork 30*	*Segers*	*Joseph*	*Phelan*	*Barton**	*Scales*	*Fitzgerald*	*Cork*	*Earle*	*Fashanu^*	*Ryan*	*Fairweather*	*Clarke/Newhouse*
								Ref: R Dilkes	Wimbledon achieve their first ever league victory at Highfield Road, thanks to veteran Cork's downward header. The entertainment is poor and the brightest incident came when Segers flattened Robson 45 yards out of his goal, but only received a yellow card. Rosario went off injured.											
6	A	OLDHAM		8	L	1-2	0-1	Furlong 73	Ogrizovic	Borrows	Billing	Robson	Pearce	Atherton	Woods	McGrath	Furlong	Gallacher	Smith*	Ndlovu
	3/9		*12,996*	*15*	7			*Adams 31, Henry 63*	*Hallworth*	*Halle*	*Snodin*	*Henry*	*Barrett*	*Kilcline*	*Adams*	*Marshall*	*Sharp*	*Milligan*	*Holden*	
								Ref: J Lloyd	Sansom is out till Xmas and Smith joins the lengthy injury list after 25 minutes. Newly promoted Oldham haven't played in the top flight since 1923 and have signed Kilcline for £400,000. City's comeback starts too late, but Robson almost snatches a late equaliser after Furlong's goal.											
7	A	ARSENAL		6	W	2-1	1-0	Dixon 1 (og), Ndlovu 85	Ogrizovic	Borrows	Billing	Robson	Pearce	Atherton	Woods*	McGrath	Furlong	Gallacher	Drinkell^	Emerson/Ndlovu
	7/9		*28,142*	*15*	10			*Adams 89*	*Seaman*	*Dixon*	*Winterburn*	*Campbell*	*Linighan*	*Adams*	*Rocastle*	*Davis^*	*Smith*	*Merson*	*Limpar**	*O'Leary/Thomas*
								Ref: R Gifford	The league champions suffer their first home defeat for 18 months in this shock result of the season. England full-back Dixon lobs Seaman after 56 seconds and Arsenal dominate until Ndlovu wraps it up by robbing Linighan and firing under Seaman. Transfer-listed McGrath is superb.											
8	H	NOTTS COUNTY		4	W	1-0	0-0	Furlong 47	Ogrizovic	Borrows	Billing	Robson	Pearce	Atherton	McGrath	Gynn^	Furlong	Gallacher	Edwards*	Ndlovu/Emerson
	14/9		10,624	*15*	13				*Cherry*	*Palmer**	*Paris^*	*Short Craig*	*Yates*	*Draper*	*Thomas*	*Turner*	*Dryden*	*Bartlett*	*Johnson*	*Short Chris/Regis*
								Ref: J Worrall	County are back in the top flight after seven years and despite being favourites for the drop have some useful players. They easily contain a poor City until Ndlovu comes on at half-time. The African's pace and skill leave the Magpies breathless and he helps set up Furlong's winner.											
9	H	LEEDS		4	D	0-0	0-0		Ogrizovic	Borrows	Billing	Robson	Pearce	Atherton	McGrath	Gynn	Rosario	Gallacher*	Furlong	Ndlovu
	18/9		15,483	*2*	14				*Lukic*	*Sterland*	*Dorigo*	*Batty*	*McClelland*	*Whyte*	*Stachan*	*Shutt**	*Chapman*	*McAllister*	*Speed*	*Hodge*
								Ref: D Axcell	Leeds are unbeaten and look like title contenders but City match them with this gritty display. It's a fast and furious game and Rosario has a good header brilliantly saved by Lukic. Chapman misses an easy header in the second half and Gallacher is stretchered off with a knee injury.											
10	A	EVERTON		8	L	0-3	0-1		Ogrizovic	Borrows	Billing^	Robson	Pearce	Atherton	McGrath	Gynn*	Rosario	Ndlovu	Furlong	Emerson/Edwards
	21/9		*20,541*	*14*	14			*Beardsley 40, 62, 75p*	*Southall*	*Atteveld*	*Hinchcliffe*	*Ebbrell*	*Watson*	*Keown*	*Warzycha*	*Beardsley*	*Newell*	*Sheedy**	*Ward*	*McDonald*
								Ref: A Flood	The game is even until the first goal, with Gynn hitting the post, but after that City are outclassed. Peter Beardsley, signed from Liverpool, makes it six goals in his last four games, though the penalty is dubious. Ward looked a yard outside the area when Borrows clipped his heel.											

No	Venue	Opponent / Date	Att	Pos	Pt	Res	F-A	H-T	Scorers, Times, and Referees	1	2	3	4	5	6	7	8	9	10	11	subs used
11	H	ASTON VILLA		6		W	1-0	1-0	Ndlovu 40	Ogrizovic	Borrows	Edwards*	Billing	Pearce	Atherton	McGrath	Gynn	Furlong	Gallacher	Ndlovu	Emerson
		28/9	17,831	*16*	17					*Spink*	*Kubicki*	*Staunton*	*Teale*	*McGrath*	*Richardson*	*Yorke*	*Nielson*	*Regis*	*Penrice*	*Mortimer**	*Cowans*
									Ref: P Alcock	Injury-hit City keep up their good home sequence against Villa with a stunning Ndlovu goal. A dazzling, teasing run ended with a left-foot shot which left Spink for dead. Regis is back in a Villa shirt, but he has no luck against Andy Pearce and Villa's second-half siege comes to nothing.											
12	A	WEST HAM		5		W	1-0	0-0	Gallacher 81	Ogrizovic	Borrows	Billing	Robson	Pearce	Atherton	McGrath	Gynn	Furlong*	Gallacher	Ndlovu^	Rosario/Emerson
		5/10	*21,817*	*18*	20					*Miklosko*	*Breacker*	*Thomas^*	*Gale*	*Brown*	*Parris*	*Bishop*	*Slater*	*Small*	*Potts*	*Morley**	*Keen/Allen*
									Ref: P Foakes	Ndlovu has been voted Zimbabwean Footballer of theYear and he sets up Gallacher's winner against lacklustre Hammers, who look good bets to go straight back down to Division Two. Billy Bond's team are embarrassed by their freed former player, Robson, who stars with Pearce.											
13	H	CRYS PALACE		6		L	1-2	0-1	Gynn 69p	Ogrizovic	Borrows	**Greenman**	Robson	Pearce	Atherton^	McGrath	Gynn	Rosario	Gallacher	Ndlovu*	Furlong/Emerson
		19/10	10,540	*7*	20				*Bright 45, Gabbiadini 80*	*Martyn*	*Southgate*	*Sinnott*	*Gray*	*Young*	*Thorn*	*Mortimer**	*Thomas*	*Bright*	*Gabbiadini*	*McGoldrick*	*Shaw*
									Ref: G Ashby	Palace have sold Ian Wright to Arsenal and replaced him with £1.8 million Marco Gabbiadini, who wins the game with his first goal for the club. Ndlovu and new England Under-21 cap Atherton limped off, but Gynn's penalty - after Greenman is fouled by Young - injects hope.											
14	A	LIVERPOOL		9		L	0-1	0-1		Ogrizovic	Borrows*	McGrath	Robson	Pearce	Greenman	Woods	Gynn	Furlong^	Gallacher	Smith	Emerson/Rosario
		26/10	*33,339*	*8*	20				*Houghton 35*	*Grobbelaar*	*Jones*	*Burrows*	*Hysen*	*Molby**	*Tanner*	*Saunders^*	*Houghton*	*Rush*	*Walters*	*McMahon*	*Harkness/Rosenthal*
									Ref: R Milford	Liverpool are shadows of the great Anfield teams and City should have left with a point. Souness is changing things and gives Rob Jones a home debut. Butcher's long-ball style is not suited to Furlong up front, and the ex-non league player needs a rest. Drinkell is on loan at Brum.											
15	H	CHELSEA		10		L	0-1	0-1		Ogrizovic	**Booty**	Hurst	Robson	Pearce	Billing	Woods*	McGrath	Furlong	Gallacher	Smith	Ndlovu
		2/11	11,304	*8*	20				*Le Saux 18*	*Beasant*	*Clarke*	*Boyd*	*Jones*	*Elliott*	*Cundy*	*Le Saux*	*Matthew*	*Dixon*	*Wilson*	*Wise*	
									Ref: K Lupton	An early kick-off to avoid the Rugby World Cup final. City fail to repeat their midweek cup triumph over Arsenal. They waste chances and concede a soft goal when Oggy drops a cross. Terry Butcher's playing days look over when he is sent off in a Zenith Data Cup defeat by Villa.											
16	A	NOTT'M FOREST		14		L	0-1	0-1		Ogrizovic	Borrows	Hurst	Robson	Pearce	Atherton	Woods	Gynn	Furlong*	Gallacher	Ndlovu	McGrath
		16/11	*21,154*	*13*	20				*Sheringham 20*	*Crossley*	*Charles*	*Pearce*	*Walker*	*Chettle*	*Keane*	*Crosby*	*Gemmill*	*Glover*	*Sheringham*	*Woan*	
									Ref: G Courtney	Forest are ripped to shreds by a rejuvenated Forest and are lucky to keep the score respectable. £20,000 buy Roy Keane is their star in a strong midfield. Oggy brings down Sheringham five minutes from the end but then saves the striker's penalty. Butcher has retired from playing.											
17	A	NORWICH		14		L	2-3	1-0	Gallacher 29, 47	Ogrizovic	Booty	Hurst	Robson*	Pearce	Greenman	McGrath	Gynn	Furlong	Gallacher	Emerson	Ndlovu
		23/11	*12,056*	*8*	20				*Bowen 46, Fleck 85, Sutton 90*	*Gunn*	*Phillips*	*Bowen*	*Butterworth*	*Blades*	*Goss*	*Ullathorne*	*Fleck*	*Newman*	*Sherwood**	*Beckford^*	*Sutton/Crook*
									Ref: R Lewis	Five defeats in a row and relegation clouds darken the horizon. Coach Mills has been replaced by Don Howe as the new regime led by Peter Robins imposes cost cuts. Norwich come back from the dead, helped by inspired substitutions and by City's injury-hit team fatally relaxing.											
18	H	SOUTHAMPTON		13		W	2-0	1-0	Gallacher 23, Pearce 70	Ogrizovic	Borrows	Hurst	Emerson	Pearce	Atherton	McGrath	Gynn*	Rosario	Gallacher	Furlong	Booty
		30/11	8,582	*21*	23					*Flowers*	*Dodd*	*Adams*	*Hurlock*	*Gittens*	*Ruddock**	*Le Tissier*	*Cockerill*	*Shearer*	*Horne*	*Wood*	*Lee*
									Ref: P Taylor	Desperate City win at last, but only after a poor start against physical Saints. Gallacher heads home against the run of play and stand-in captain Pearce seals it with a diving header. Stewart Robson is out injured for three weeks whilst Sean Flynn has signed from Halesowen for £15,000.											
19	A	MANCHESTER U		16		L	**0-4**	0-3	*[Hughes 80]*	Ogrizovic	Borrows	Hurst	Emerson	Pearce	Atherton	McGrath	Middleton C	Rosario*	Gallacher	Furlong^	Ndlovu/Billing
		7/12	***42,549***	*2*	23				*Bruce 14, Webb 20, McClair 27,*	*Schmeichel*	*Parker**	*Irwin*	*Bruce*	*Webb*	*Pallister*	*Kanchelskis*	*Ince*	*McClair*	*Hughes*	*Giggs*	*Blackmore*
									Ref: P Wright	United have lost one in 22 and are in a two-horse race with Leeds for the title. They swat City aside without really breaking sweat and could have scored more. Butcher has crisis talks with his players, many of whom are just not good enough. Kanchelskis beats City defenders at will.											
20	A	LUTON		17		L	0-1	0-0		Ogrizovic	Borrows	Hurst	Emerson	Pearce	Atherton	McGrath	Ndlovu*	Furlong	Gallacher	Smith	Rosario
		20/12	*7,533*	*22*	23				*Harford 55*	*Sutton*	*James*	*Harvey*	*Kamara*	*Dreyer*	*Peake*	*Telfer*	*Stein B*	*Harford*	*Pembridge*	*Oakes**	*Preece*
									Ref: K Cooper	Luton clock their first win in 14 games in a dire Friday night game. City have only one shot on target and Mick Harford wins it with a scrappy goal when three defenders fail to clear. The confidence has gone but Butcher, threatened with a pay-cut, vows to revert to the long-ball game.											
21	A	SHEFFIELD U		14		W	3-0	0-0	Robson 49, Flynn 57, Billing 66	Ogrizovic	Borrows	Sansom	Robson	Billing	Atherton	McGrath	**Flynn**	Rosario*	Gallacher	Smith	Furlong
		26/12	*19,638*	*20*	26					*Tracey*	*Gage*	*Cowan*	*Gannon**	*Gayle*	*Beesley*	*Hodges*	*Hoyland*	*Littlejohn*	*Deane*	*Whitehouse*	*Lake*
									Ref: T Fitzharris	A forgettable first half is marred by Robson's challenge on Tracey, which sparks a spell of turbulence. City dominate the second half and three City players score their first ever goals, Flynn on his debut. Rosario, despite a broken nose, looks a different player as his confidence rises.											

No	Date	Opponent	Att	Pos	Pt	F-A	H-T	Scorers, Times, and Referees	1	2	3	4	5	6	7	8	9	10	11	subs used
22	A	WIMBLEDON		13	D	1-1	1-0	Robson 38	Ogrizovic	Borrows	Sansom	Robson	Billing	Atherton	McGrath	Flynn	Rosario*	Gallacher	Smith	Furlong
	28/12		*3,270*	*17*	27			*Earle 52*	*Segers*	*Joseph*	*Phelan*	*Barton*	*Scales*	*Fitzgerald*	*Elkins*	*Earle*	*Fashanu*	*Miller**	*Anthrobus*	*Newhouse*
								Ref: B Hill	Unchanged City look a different proposition with Robson and Sansom, and their commitment is much higher. Robson's delightful chip is cancelled out by Earle's crisp finish after a rare mistake. The Dons have moved to Selhurst. This is the lowest crowd to watch City since 1963.											
23	H	TOTTENHAM		15	L	1-2	1-1	Rosario 11	Ogrizovic	Borrows	Sansom	Robson	Pearce	Billing	McGrath	Flynn	Rosario	Gallacher	Smith*	Furlong
	1/1		19,609	*8*	27			*Lineker 39, Stewart 66*	*Thorstvedt*	*Fenwick*	*v d Hauwe*	*Sedgley*	*Howells*	*Mabbutt*	*Stewart*	*Walsh**	*Samways^*	*Lineker*	*Allen*	*Houghton/Edinburgh*
								Ref: J Key	Another defeat leaves Butcher under pressure as City wilt after an excellent first period. Rosario snatches a good goal before Lineker poaches his 19th of the season. From then it is a matter of time before Spurs win it, although Flynn almost grabs a point when Thorstvedt drops a cross.											
24	H	QP RANGERS		16	D	2-2	1-0	Gallacher 9, Rosario 65	Ogrizovic	Borrows	Sansom	Robson	Pearce	Billing	McGrath	Flynn	Rosario	Gallacher	Gynn*	Hurst
	11/1		12,003	*13*	28			*Penrice 76, 84*	*Stejskal*	*Bardsley*	*Wilson*	*Wilkins*	*Peacock*	*McDonald*	*Holloway*	*Barker*	*Bailey*	*Wegerle**	*Impey*	*Penrice*
								Ref: D Gallagher	Butcher has been sacked, to be replaced by Howe, and there is immediate improvement. Gallacher scores for the first time since November but a two-goal lead over Gerry Francis' Rangers is overturned by two stunning strikes from sub Penrice, his first goals since signing from Villa.											
25	A	MANCHESTER C		16	L	0-1	0-0		Ogrizovic	Borrows*	Sansom	Robson	Pearce	Atherton	Flynn	Gynn^	Rosario	Gallacher	Hurst	Emerson/Furlong
	18/1		*23,005*	*4*	28			*White 51*	*Coton*	*Hill*	*Pointon**	*Reid*	*Curle*	*Redmond*	*White*	*Brightwell I*	*Sheron*	*McMahon*	*Hughes*	*Quigley*
								Ref: M Peck	A disappointing game is decided by David White's well-taken goal after a seven-man move. Robert Rosario is unlucky not to equalise with a header well saved by Tony Coton. Brian Borrows, off the transfer list, limps off injured and Don Howe refuses to use the word 'relegation'.											
26	A	CRYS PALACE		15	W	1-0	1-0	Smith 30	Ogrizovic	Hurst	Sansom	Robson	Greenman	Atherton	Flynn	Emerson	Rosario	Gallacher	Smith	
	1/2		*13,818*	*9*	31				*Martyn*	*Humphrey*	*Sinnott*	*Gray^*	*Southgate*	*Thorn*	*Mortimer*	*Thomas*	*Bright*	*Whyte**	*McGoldrick*	*Moralee/Osborn*
								Ref: D Axcell	City are unbeaten in five visits to the capital and have lost only once in 16 at Palace. Gabbiadini has been sold to Derby after only 15 games, and Whyte makes his full debut. Smith's goal from Rosario's nod on wins it, but four minutes later Oggy saves Gray's penalty after a handball.											
27	H	LIVERPOOL		17	D	0-0	0-0		Ogrizovic	McGrath	Sansom	Robson	Billing	Atherton	Flynn	Emerson	Rosario	Gallacher	Smith	
	8/2		21,547	*3*	32				*Grobbelaar*	*Jones*	*Burrows*	*Marsh*	*Wright*	*Tanner**	*Saunders*	*Houghton*	*Walters^*	*Redknapp*	*McManam'n*	*Harkness/Rosenthal*
								Ref: R Hart	Kevin Gallacher has signed a new three-year contract and gives the Reds an uncomfortable afternoon, but wastes his best chance ten minutes from time. Grobbelaar makes three fantastic saves and Liverpool make it one defeat in fifteen league games. Howe's training regime is working.											
28	A	SOUTHAMPTON		17	D	0-0	0-0		Ogrizovic	McGrath	Sansom	Robson	Billing	Atherton	Flynn*	Emerson	Rosario !	Gallacher	Pearce	Furlong
	22/2		*13,719*	*22*	33				*Flowers*	*Kenna*	*Benali*	*Horne*	*Hall*	*Ruddock*	*Le Tissier*	*Hurlock*	*Shearer*	*Gray**	*Lee^*	*Dowie/Dodd*
								Ref: M Bodenham	Any chance of a City victory disappears when Rosario is sent off after 42 minutes for two late tackles. The Saints, though bottom of the table, are always hard to beat at home. There is little entertainment and even Shearer, fresh from his scoring England debut, makes little impression.											
29	H	MANCHESTER U		17	D	0-0	0-0		Ogrizovic	McGrath	Sansom	Robson	Pearce	Atherton	Flynn	Emerson	Rosario	Gallacher	Furlong	
	29/2		**23,962**	*1*	34				*Walsh*	*Parker*	*Irwin*	*Donaghy*	*Webb*	*Pallister*	*Kanch'lskis**	*Ince*	*McClair*	*Hughes*	*Giggs*	*Blackmore*
								Ref: R Hamer	Howe is happy with a point against the leaders and a fourth clean sheet in a row. United have lost only two games all season and Giggs and Kanchelskis are buzzing. Few chances are made in this entertaining game. Billing is suspended for three games after his outburst at Cambridge.											
30	H	NORWICH		17	D	0-0	0-0		Ogrizovic	Borrows	Sansom	Robson	Pearce	Atherton	Flynn	Emerson^	Rosario*	Gallacher	Furlong	Drinkell/McGrath
	4/3		**8,454**	*10*	35				*Walton*	*Culverhouse*	*Woodthorpe*	*Butterworth*	*Polston*	*Goss*	*Fox**	*Sutch*	*Newman*	*Sutton^*	*Phillips*	*Fleck/Ball*
								Ref: C Trussell	Four goalless draws in a row is a club record, but this one is awful. Coventry's scoring drought is causing concern and they show few signs of ending it. Jeremy Goss has the best chance, but blasts over from 18 yards. Kevin Drinkell gets a rare run, his first appearance since September.											
31	A	SHEFFIELD WED		15	D	1-1	0-0	*Gallacher 66*	Ogrizovic	Borrows	Sansom	Robson	Pearce	Atherton	Flynn	McGrath	Furlong	Gallacher	Smith	
	7/3		*23,959*	*3*	36			*Anderson 83*	*Woods*	*Nilsson*	*King*	*Palmer*	*Anderson*	*Shirtliff*	*Wilson*	*Bart-W'ms^*	*Hirst*	*Williams*	*Worthingt'n**	*Jemson/Warhurst*
								Ref: W Burns	A draw is a fair result against Trevor Francis's Wednesday, who have not been out of the top six all season. Gallacher's diving header, City's first goal in 486 minutes, comes against the run of play and Anderson's late effort is just reward. Paul Furlong is struggling and deserves a rest.											

No	Ven	Date	Opponent	Att	Pos	Res / Pts	F-A	H-T	Scorers, Times, and Referees	1	2	3	4	5	6	7	8	9	10	11	subs used
32	H		NOTT'M FOREST		18	L	0-2	0-2		Ogrizovic	Borrows	Sansom	Robson	Pearce	Atherton	Flynn	McGrath	Rosario^	Gallacher*	Smith	Furlong/Emerson
		11/3		11,258	*13*	36			*Smith 11 (og), Sheringham 40*	*Crossley*	*Charles*	*Pearce*	*Walker*	*Wassall*	*Keane*	*Crosby*	*Gemmill*	*Clough*	*Sheringham*	*Glover*	
									Ref: P Durkin	Forest make City suffer for their FA Cup exit at Portsmouth by catching City with two soft goals. City's mini-run ends as Forest bag their first win in eight to lift the relegation cloud for Brian Clough. Defeat is bad enough, but Kevin Gallacher limps off with a serious hamstring injury.											
33	A		CHELSEA		16	W	1-0	0-0	Robson 68	Ogrizovic	Borrows	Sansom	Robson^	Pearce	Atherton	Flynn	McGrath	Rosario	Furlong*	Smith	Drinkell/Emerson
		14/3		*10,962*	*9*	39				*Beasant*	*Clarke*	*Sinclair*	*Jones*	*Elliott^*	*Monkou*	*Le Saux*	*Townsend !*	*Dixon**	*Cascarino*	*Stewart*	*Wise/Allen !*
									Ref: J Martin	A low-key scrappy first half gives way to high drama and fierce controversy as ref Martin upsets the opposition, for once. Chelsea with a big replay at Roker looming, have Andy Townsend sent off after 64 minutes, followed by sub Clive Allen in the last minute, both for foul language.											
34	H		OLDHAM		16	D	1-1	1-1	Pearce 10	**Heald**	Borrows	Sansom	Robson	Pearce	Atherton	Flynn	Drinkell	Rosario	McGrath	Smith*	Gynn
		21/3		13,042	*15*	40			*Henry 29*	*Hallworth*	*Fleming*	*Barlow*	*Henry*	*Jobson*	*Marshall*	*Adams*	*Ritchie**	*Sharp*	*Milligan*	*Holden*	*Palmer*
									Ref: P Don	On loan keeper Paul Heald of Leyton Orient stands in for Oggy, who was injured in a training incident. A high wind and two desperate sides mean that the club's first Ladies Day is hardly a thriller. 3-4,000 females take advantage of the free entry but it's doubtful if many will return.											
35	A		TOTTENHAM		17	L	3-4	1-3	Flynn 24, Smith 78, McGrath 85	Heald	Borrows	Sansom*	Emerson	Pearce	Atherton	Flynn	Furlong	Rosario	McGrath	Smith	Billing
		28/3		*22,744*	*18*	40			*Durie 8, 45, 80, Lineker 32*	*Thorstvedt*	*v d Hauwe*	*Edinburgh*	*Gray**	*Cundy*	*Mabbutt*	*Stewart*	*Durie*	*Nayim*	*Lineker^*	*Allen*	*Walsh/Sedgley*
									Ref: G Courtney	An exciting game littered by goals and mistakes sees City lose for the first time in London. Spurs haven't won for eleven games since they won at Highfield Road and Lineker hasn't scored since then. Durie is unstoppable against an unusually poor defence and doubles his season's tally.											
36	H		ARSENAL		19	L	0-1	0-1		Sealey	Borrows	Sansom	Robson	Pearce	Atherton	Flynn^	McGrath*	Ndlovu	Furlong	Smith	Gynn/Billing
		4/4		14,119	*4*	40			*Campbell 28*	*Seaman*	*Dixon*	*Winterburn**	*Hillier*	*Bould*	*Adams*	*Lyderson*	*Wright*	*Campbell*	*Merson*	*Limpar^*	*Rocastle/Smith*
									Ref: R Gifford	***Les Sealey returns on loan*** to a muted reception but is left unprotected as Campbell powers through to score. City have the better chances but lack any power up front. Robson enjoys another impressive game and Howe tells Graham Taylor 'pick him'. The gap closes behind Coventry.											
37	H		SHEFFIELD WED		19	D	0-0	0-0		Sealey	Borrows	Sansom	Robson	Pearce	Atherton	McGrath	Gynn	Rosario	Furlong^	Smith*	Flynn/Ndlovu
		8/4		13,268	*3*	41				*Woods*	*Nilsson*	*King*	*Palmer*	*Pearson*	*Shirtliff**	*Wilson*	*Sheridan*	*Hirst*	*Williams^*	*Worthington*	*Harkes/Francis*
									Ref: A Buksh	City create far more chances than the visitors but once again fail to find the net to pull themselves away from the relegation zone. Atherton is outstanding and Gynn, on his return from injury, plays well and almost scores with a header. England failure Hirst causes lots of problems.											
38	A		NOTTS COUNTY		19	L	0-1	0-0		Ogrizovic	Borrows	Sansom	Robson	Pearce	Atherton	McGrath	Gynn	Rosario*	Furlong	Flynn	Ndlovu
		11/4		*6,655*	*21*	41			*Sansom 88(og)*	*Cherry*	*Palmer*	*Dryden*	*Short Craig*	*Johnson*	*Draper*	*Williams*	*Harding^*	*Devlin**	*Bartlett*	*Wilson*	*Matthews/Thomas*
									Ref: K Burge	County win their first game of the year with a cruel late goal, as City fan Dean Thomas' shot deflects off Sansom's face past Oggy. The stories of City domination are getting hackneyed and relegation looms. Rosario limps off after 24 minutes to be replaced by the more mobile Ndlovu.											
39	H		EVERTON		19	L	0-1	0-0		Ogrizovic	Borrows	Sansom	Robson	Pearce	Atherton	Flynn	Gynn	Furlong*	McGrath^	Gallacher	Ndlovu/Smith
		18/4		14,657	*13*	41			*Beagrie 76*	*Southall*	*Jackson*	*Ablett*	*Ward*	*Watson*	*Keown*	*Nevin*	*Beardsley*	*Johnston**	*Harper*	*Beagrie*	*Barlow*
									Ref: C Wilkes	Another cruel deflection, by Borrows on Beagrie's shot, has the vultures hovering over Highfield Road. Everton rarely escape their own half but City fail to turn their efforts into goals. Gallacher returns from injury and deserves a 53rd-minute penalty when he is upended by Southall.											
40	A		LEEDS		19	L	0-2	0-0		Ogrizovic	Borrows	Sansom	Robson	Pearce	Atherton	Flynn	Gynn	Furlong*	Gallacher^	McGrath !	Ndlovu/Emerson
		20/4		*26,582*	*1*	41			*Fairclough 53, McAllister 79p*	*Lukic*	*Newsome*	*Dorigo*	*Batty*	*Fairclough*	*Whyte*	*Strachan^*	*Wallace**	*Chapman*	*McAllister*	*Speed*	*Cantona/Shutt*
									Ref: R Nixon	The game is televised live at 5 pm and Leeds know a win will put them top of the table. They are unbeaten at home and City are only able to frustrate them. Leeds' controversial penalty sees McGrath clear the line with his knee but he is adjudged to have handled, and is sent off.											
41	H		WEST HAM		19	W	1-0	1-0	Gynn 44	Ogrizovic	McGrath	Sansom*	Robson	Billing	Atherton	Flynn	Gynn	Ndlovu	Gallacher	Smith	Borrows
		25/4		15,380	*22*	44				*Miklosko*	*Potts*	*Dicks*	*Gale*	*Martin*	*Thomas*	*Bishop**	*Keen*	*Small*	*Brown^*	*Slater*	*Morley/Martin*
									Ref: P Wright	At last a home victory, the first since November, and it might keep City up. Gynn has had a frustrating season with injuries and loss of form but scores a scrappy goal to keep City's noses in front of Luton. A poor West Ham side are relegated with little fight in a tense and nervous match.											
42	A		ASTON VILLA		19	L	0-2	0-2		Ogrizovic	Borrows	McGrath	Robson	Billing	Atherton	Flynn	Gynn	Ndlovu*	Gallacher	Smith^	Furlong/Hurst
		2/5		*31,984*	*7*	44			*Regis 1, Yorke 36*	*Spink*	*Barrett*	*Staunton*	*Teale*	*McGrath*	*Richardson*	*Daley*	*Parker*	*Regis*	*Yorke**	*Small*	*Olney*
		Home		Away					Ref: T Ward	If Luton win at relegated Notts County then City will need to beat Villa. After half an hour City look doomed as Luton lead. Regis does City no favours with a 21-second header and Yorke wraps it up. The attention switches to radios as County come back to beat Luton and City are safe.											
Average		13,876		19,327																	

Rumbelows Cup					F-A	H-T	Scorers, Times, and Referees	1	2	3	4	5	6	7	8	9	10	11	subs used
2:1	H	ROCHDALE	8	W	4-0	2-0	Rosario 2, 23, Gallacher 74, McGrath 90	Ogrizovic	Borrows	Edwards	Emerson	Pearce	Billing	McGrath	Ndlovu	Rosario*	Gallacher	Furlong	Hurst
	25/9	5,980	4:3					Williams	Payne	Ryan	Brown T	Reeves	Jones	Graham	Doyle	Flounders^	Milner*	Halpin	Whitehall/Butler
							Ref: M Brandwood	Gallacher's injury is not serious and he returns to score and hit the woodwork twice in a one-sided game. Rosario powers in a Ndlovu cross and chips the keeper before McGrath's speculative chip gets a deflection and loops in for a rare goal. Ex-Arsenal man Hayes is on loan to City.											
2:2	A	ROCHDALE	5	L	0-1	0-0		Baker	Borrows	Edwards	Robson*	Pearce	Billing	McGrath	Gynn	Furlong^	Gallacher	Ndlovu	Emerson/Rosario
	8/10	2,288	4:4				Milner 88	Gray	Brown M	Ryan*	Brown T	Reeves	Jones	Graham	Doyle	Flounders	Milner	Butler^	Payne/Whitehall
							Ref: C Trussell (City win 4-1 on aggregate)	City go through after a non-event which they should have strolled. Rochdale, unbeaten in the league, win after a moment of slackness. Clive Baker makes his one and only appearance as stand in for the injured Oggy. The former Man City player, Andy Milner, heads the late goal.											
3	H	ARSENAL	9	W	1-0	1-0	Gallacher 32	Ogrizovic	Booty	Hurst	Robson	Pearce	Billing	Woods	McGrath	Furlong	Gallacher	Smith	
	30/10	15,339	4					Seaman	Dixon	Winterburn	Davis	Pates^	Adams	Rocastle	Wright	Smith	Merson	Limpar*	Groves/Linighan
							Ref: M Bodenham	Arsenal come looking for revenge for the home defeat with £2.5 million striker Ian Wright but are outfought and outclassed by a makeshift City team for whom Gallacher is outstanding. His goal is a classic poach, after Seaman palms away Furlong's shot. Booty looks a star of tomorrow.											
4	H	TOTTENHAM	13	L	1-2	0-1	Furlong 66	Ogrizovic	Borrows	Hurst	Emerson	Pearce	Billing	McGrath	Middleton C	Rosario	Gallacher	Furlong	
	4/12	20,053	14				Allen 43, Durie 84	Thorstvedt	Fenwick	v d Hauwe	Bergsson	Howells	Mabbutt	Stewart	Durie	Samways*	Walsh^	Allen	Sedgley/Nayim
							Ref: R Gifford	Paul Allen scores a superb curler into the top corner and despite City having the greater share of an exciting second half Durie wins the tie for Lineker-less Spurs following Pearce's rare error. Thorstvedt makes dazzling saves from Gallacher's header and Middleton's thunderous shot.											

FA Cup																			
3	H	CAMBRIDGE	15	D	1-1	0-1	Borrows 77p	Ogrizovic	Borrows	Sansom	Robson	Pearce	Billing	McGrath	Booty*	Rosario	Gallacher	Smith	Furlong
	4/1	11,431	2:5				Dublin 30	Vaughan	Fensome	Kimble	Dennis	Chapple*	Daish	Rowett	Wilkins	Dublin	Taylor	Philpott	Heathcote
							Ref: T Ward	John Beck's Cambridge are in the Second Division promotion race and look set to knock City out until Borrows' late penalty after David Smith was brought down by Andy Fensome. The supposedly one-dimensional Dion Dublin leaves Pearce for dead and scores at the second attempt.											
3R	A	CAMBRIDGE	16	L	0-1	0-0		Ogrizovic	Borrows	Sansom	Booty*	Pearce	Billing	McGrath	Gynn	Rosario	Furlong	Hurst	Woods
	14/1	9,864	2:4				Dublin 90	Vaughan	Fensome	Kimble	Bailie	Chapple	O'Shea	Rowett*	Wilkins	Dublin	Taylor	Philpott	Heathcote^/Dennis
							Ref: T Ward	City's solid defensive performance easily copes with Cambridge's aerial bombardment but hardly create a scoring chance. The 92nd-minute winner comes after Dublin's penalty, for Pearce's innocuous handball, is saved, but Lee Hurst seems to get the last touch as Dublin follows up.											

		Home						Away					
		P	W	D	L	F	A	W	D	L	F	A	Pts
1	Leeds	42	13	8	0	38	13	9	8	4	36	24	82
2	Manchester U	42	12	7	2	34	13	9	8	4	29	20	78
3	Sheffield Wed	42	13	5	3	39	24	8	7	6	23	25	75
4	Arsenal	42	12	7	2	51	22	7	8	6	30	24	72
5	Manchester C	42	13	4	4	32	14	7	6	8	29	34	70
6	Liverpool	42	13	5	3	34	17	3	11	7	13	23	64
7	Aston Villa	42	13	3	5	31	16	4	6	11	17	28	60
8	Nott'm Forest	42	10	7	4	36	27	6	4	11	24	31	59
9	Sheffield Utd	42	9	6	6	29	23	7	3	11	36	40	57
10	Crys Palace	42	7	8	6	24	25	7	7	7	29	36	57
11	QP Rangers	42	6	10	5	25	21	6	8	7	23	26	54
12	Everton	42	8	8	5	28	19	5	6	10	24	32	53
13	Wimbledon	42	10	5	6	32	20	3	9	9	21	33	53
14	Chelsea	42	7	8	6	31	30	6	6	9	19	30	53
15	Tottenham	42	7	3	11	33	35	8	4	9	25	28	52
16	Southampton	42	7	5	9	17	28	7	5	9	22	27	52
17	Oldham	42	11	5	5	46	36	3	4	14	17	31	51
18	Norwich	42	8	6	7	29	28	3	6	12	18	35	45
19	COVENTRY	42	6	7	8	18	15	5	4	12	17	29	44
20	Luton	42	10	7	4	25	17	0	5	16	13	54	42
21	Notts Co	42	7	5	9	24	29	3	5	13	16	33	40
22	West Ham	42	6	6	9	22	24	3	5	13	15	35	38
		924	208	135	119	678	496	119	135	208	496	678	1251

Odds & ends

Double wins: (2) West Ham, Sheffield U.
Double losses: (4) Manchester C, Tottenham, Nott'm Forest, Everton.

Won from behind: (0).
Lost from in front: (2) Norwich (a), Tottenham (h).

High spots: Good early season form.
Two autumn wins over League champions, Arsenal.
Staying up on the final day, thanks to Notts County.

Low spots: Barren goal period under Howe including four 0-0s in a row.
FA Cup exit at Cambridge United.
Miserable defeat at Notts County.

Red cards: City – Rosario (Southampton a), McGrath (Leeds a).
Red cards: Opponents – Farrell (Luton h), Townsend and Allen (Chelsea a).

Player of the Year: Stewart Robson.
Ever-presents: (0).
Hat-tricks: (0).
Opposing hat-tricks: (2) Beardsley (Everton), Durie (Tottenham).
Leading scorer: (10) Kevin Gallacher.

	Appearances						Goals			
	Lge	*Sub*	LC	*Sub*	FAC	*Sub*	**Lge**	LC	FAC	**Tot**
Atherton, Peter	**35**									
Baker, Clive			1							
Billing, Peter	**17**	*5*	4		2		**1**			**1**
Booty, Martyn	**2**	*1*	1		2					
Borrows, Brian	**34**	*1*	3		2				1	**1**
Drinkell, Kevin	**2**	*2*								
Edwards, Paul	**4**	*1*	2							
Emerson, Dean	**10**	*11*	2	*1*						
Flynn, Sean	**21**	*1*					**2**			**2**
Furlong, Paul	**27**	*10*	4		1	*1*	**4**	1		**5**
Gallacher, Kevin	**33**		4		1		**8**	2		**10**
Greenman, Chris	**4**									
Gynn, Michael	**21**	*2*	1		1		**3**			**3**
Heald, Paul (loan)	**2**									
Hurst, Lee	**8**	*2*	2	*1*	1					
McGrath, Lloyd	**38**	*2*	4		2		**1**	1		**2**
Middleton, Craig	**1**		1							
Ndlovu, Peter	**9**	*14*	2				**2**			**2**
Ogrizovic, Steve	**38**		3		2					
Peake, Trevor	**2**									
Pearce, Andy	**36**		4		2		**2**			**2**
Robson, Stewart	**37**		2		1		**3**			**3**
Rosario, Robert	**26**	*3*	2	*1*	2		**4**	2		**6**
Sansom, Kenny	**21**				2					
Sealey, Les (loan)	**2**									
Smith, David	**23**	*1*	1		1		**4**			**4**
Woods, Ray	**9**		1			*1*				
(own-goals)							**1**			**1**
27 players used	**462**	***56***	**44**	***3***	**22**	***2***	**35**	**6**	**1**	**42**

No	Date		Att	Pos	Pt	F-A	H-T	Scorers, Times, and Referees	1	2	3	4	5	6	7	8	9	10	11	subs used
1	H	MIDDLESBROUGH			W	2-1	1-0	Williams 9, Smith 50	Ogrizovic	Fleming	Sansom	Robson	Pearce	Atherton	Gynn	Hurst^	Rosario	**Williams J**	Smith*	Flynn/**Babb**
	15/8		12,345		3			*Wilkinson 63*	*Pears*	*Morris*	*Phillips*	*Kernaghan*	*Whyte*	*Peake*	*Wright*	*Mustoe**	*Wilkinson*	*Hendrie*	*Falconer*	*Slaven*
								Ref: H King	Gould is back at the helm as the Premier League starts and has signed the ex-postman Williams for £250,000. The ex-Swansea man scores the second Premier League goal and the fastest City debut goal for 30 years. Lennie Lawrence's men fight back but City hang on for a vital win.											
2	A	TOTTENHAM		2	W	2-0	2-0	Williams 4, 30	Ogrizovic	Fleming	Sansom	Robson	Pearce	Atherton	Gynn	Hurst	Rosario	Williams J*	Smith	Ndlovu
	19/8		*24,388*	*19*	6				*Walker^*	*Fenwick*	*Edinburgh*	*Howells*	*Cundy**	*Ruddock*	*Turner*	*Durie*	*Samways*	*Anderton*	*Allen*	*Gray/Thorstvedt*
								Ref: D Gallagher	A deserved win as City create chances galore and have a striker capable of taking them. Cundy goes off with a split head in the first minute and the Spurs defence struggles. Williams is like grease lightning for the second and Gynn misses the first Premiership penalty in the 72nd minute.											
3	A	WIMBLEDON		1	W	2-1	1-0	Gynn 13, Rosario 46	Ogrizovic	Fleming	Sansom	Robson	Pearce	Atherton	Gynn^	Hurst	Rosario	Williams J*	Smith	Ndlovu/McGrath
	22/8		***3,759***	*22*	9			*Holdsworth 76*	*Segers*	*Joseph*	*Elkins*	*Barton*	*Blackwell*	*Fitzgerald**	*Dobbs^*	*Earle*	*Holdsworth*	*Sanchez*	*Anthrobus*	*Clarke/Miller*
								Ref: I Borrett	City are the first outright leaders of the new Premier League and keep up their welcome winning run . Segers lets in the second goal through his legs but Holdsworth sparks a dramatic last 15 minutes with his first goal for the Dons. Rosario is outstanding in City's team-performance.											
4	H	QP RANGERS		2	L	0-1	0-1		Ogrizovic	Fleming	Sansom	Robson	Pearce	Atherton	Gynn	Hurst^	Rosario	Williams J*	Smith	Ndlovu/McGrath
	26/8		13,437	*1*	9			*Impey 45*	*Stejskal*	*Bardsley*	*Wilson*	*Wilkins*	*Peacock*	*McDonald*	*Impey*	*Barker*	*Ferdinand**	*Bailey*	*Sinton*	*Penrice*
								Ref: S Lodge	City have no complaints after a slick Rangers end their winning streak with some dazzling football and a superb goal, made by Ferdinand for Impey. City livened up when Ndlovu came on for the second half but had used both subs when Gynn was carried off 15 minutes from time.											
5	H	BLACKBURN		6	L	0-2	0-0		Ogrizovic	Fleming	Sansom	Flynn*	Pearce	Borrows	McGrath	Hurst	Rosario	Gallacher	Smith^	Williams J/Babb
	29/8		14,496	*1*	9			*Shearer 69p, Atkins 78*	*Mimms*	*May*	*Dobson*	*Sherwood*	*Hendry*	*Moran*	*Ripley*	*Atkins*	*Shearer**	*Newell*	*Wright*	*Wegerle*
								Ref: R Lewis	Gallacher is back, but Robson, Atherton and Gynn are injured and big-spending Blackburn win to maintain their unbeaten start to their first season in the top flight since 1966. McGrath makes his first start and does a marking job on £3.4 million Shearer, but trips him for the penalty.											
6	A	SHEFFIELD WED		2	W	2-1	1-0	Ndlovu 42, Hurst 48	Ogrizovic	Fleming^	Sansom	Robson	Pearce	Ndlovu	McGrath	Hurst*	Rosario	Gallacher	Williams J	Babb/Borrows
	2/9		*22,874*	*14*	12			*Bart-Williams 62*	*Woods*	*Nilsson*	*Warhurst^*	*Palmer*	*Pearson*	*Shirtliff*	*Jemson**	*Bart-W'iams*	*Waddle*	*Williams*	*Worthington*	*Francis/Wilson*
								Ref: R Gifford	The ghastly new red away kit is proving to be lucky as City remain unbeaten at Hillsborough since 1985. The Owls dominate the first half until Ndlovu's flying header beats Woods. Stewart Robson outplays England midfielder Carlton Palmer in an attacking City formation with four up.											
7	A	OLDHAM		2	W	1-0	0-0	Gallacher 56	Ogrizovic	Borrows	Sansom	Robson	Pearce	Ndlovu	McGrath	Hurst	Rosario*	Gallacher^	Williams J	Babb/Fleming
	5/9		*11,254*	*16*	15				*Hallworth*	*Redmond*	*Pointon*	*Henry**	*Jobson*	*Marshall*	*Halle^*	*Olney*	*Sharp*	*Milligan*	*Bernard*	*Adams/Palmer*
								Ref: D Allison	This deserved win over the Latics is City's fourth away, equalling City's club record. Gallacher's first goal of the campaign is well taken from Rosario's nod down. Rosario is lucky to stay on after kneeing Richard Jobson. Bobby Gould's assistant Phil Neal joins the England set-up.											
8	H	TOTTENHAM		2	W	1-0	0-0	Williams 61	Ogrizovic	Borrows	Sansom	Atherton	Pearce	Ndlovu	McGrath	Hurst	Rosario	Gallacher	Williams J	
	14/9		15,293	*16*	18				*Walker*	*Austin*	*v d Hauwe*	*Gray*	*Cundy*	*Ruddock*	*Anderton**	*Durie*	*Samways^*	*Sheringham*	*Allen*	*Turner/Sedgley*
								Ref: M Bodenham	The club's first Sky TV game, but the first half doesn't live up to the hype. City win it with speed and spirit, plus Williams' looping header, which finds Ian Walker off his line. Sheringham almost scores with a deft chip and a diving header. New Spurs signing Anderton struggles.											
9	A	NOTT'M FOREST		2	D	1-1	1-0	Rosario 45	Ogrizovic	Borrows	Sansom	Atherton	Pearce	Ndlovu	McGrath	Hurst	Rosario	Gallacher	Williams J	
	21/9		*17,359*	*22*	19			*Clough 68*	*Crossley*	*Laws*	*Pearce*	*McKinnon*	*Tiler*	*Keane*	*Crosby*	*Gemmill*	*Clough*	*Bannister*	*Orlygsson*	
								Ref: K Morton	Forest end a run of six defeats by fighting back after Rosario deflected in Andy Pearce's indirect free-kick from the edge of the box. Forest miss the departed Des Walker and Sheringham. City miss late chances, spurned by Ndlovu and Gallacher, and leave disappointed with a draw.											
10	H	NORWICH		3	D	1-1	1-1	Ndlovu 37	Ogrizovic	Borrows	Sansom*	Atherton	Pearce	Ndlovu	McGrath	Hurst	Rosario	Gallacher	Williams J	Babb
	26/9		16,425	*1*	20			*Crook 13*	*Gunn*	*Culverhouse*	*Bowen*	*Polston*	*Sutton*	*Sutch*	*Crook*	*Newman*	*Robins*	*Goss*	*Phillips*	
								Ref: A Buksh	The top of the table clash fails to live up to the hype, apart from Ndlovu's spectacular goal, when he beats three defenders and dummies Gunn. Loose defending had given Ian Crook a good early goal, and Norwich's slick passing style unnerves the Sky Blues. A draw is a fair result.											

No	Date	Opponent / Att	Pos	Res / Pts	F-A	H-T	Scorers, Times, and Referees	1	2	3	4	5	6	7	8	9	10	11	12
11	H	CRYS PALACE	3	D	2-2	2-2	Pearce 6, Gallacher 17	Ogrizovic	Borrows	Sansom	Atherton	Pearce	Ndlovu	McGrath	Hurst	Rosario*	Gallacher	Williams J	Fleming
	3/10	11,833	*20*	21			*Coleman 7, McGoldrick 37*	*Martyn*	*Shaw*	*Sinnott*	*Southgate*	*Young*	*Osborn*	*Williams*	*Coleman*	*Armstrong*	*Salako*	*McGoldrick*	
							Ref: G Ashby	The pitch is sodden after 24 hours of rain and contributes to an entertaining first half. Graham Taylor watches Salako, who is recalled to the England squad and sets up the second equaliser. Headers by Pearce and Gallacher should have earned Gould, manager of the month, a win.											
12	A	EVERTON	3	D	1-1	1-1	Ndlovu 44	Ogrizovic	Borrows	Sansom	Atherton	Pearce	Ndlovu	McGrath	Hurst	Fleming	Robson	Williams J	
	17/10	*17,627*	*15*	22			*Beagrie 28*	*Southall*	*Warzycha**	*Hinchcliffe*	*Keown*	*Watson^*	*Ablett*	*Kenny*	*Beardsley*	*Cottee*	*Horne*	*Beagrie*	*Precki/Snodin*
							Ref: R Hamer	Everton start at a blistering pace and Beagrie's 20-yard free-kick gives them a well-deserved lead. Ndlovu hauls City back with a blistering 60-yard run which ends with a deflected shot off Horne's heel. Match of the Day cameras show that Pearce's late header is in before Horne clears.											
13	H	CHELSEA	5	L	1-2	0-1	Rosario 58	Ogrizovic	Borrows	Sansom	Atherton	Pearce	Ndlovu	McGrath*	Hurst	Rosario	Robson	Williams J	**Williams PA**
	24/10	15,553	*8*	22			*Harford 34, Stuart 70*	*Hitchcock*	*Hall*	*Sinclair*	*Townsend*	*Lee*	*Donaghy*	*Stuart*	*Fleck*	*Harford*	*Newton*	*Barnard**	*Le Saux*
							Ref: M Peck	City have lost four out of the last five on this Saturday, and their best start to a top flight season ends. Harford heads his seventh of the season before Rosario offers hope, but an awful Atherton mistake lets Stuart in. Gallacher is injured again and Paul Williams is on loan from WBA.											
14	A	LEEDS	5	D	2-2	1-0	McAllister 12 (og), Ndlovu 78	Ogrizovic	Borrows	Sansom	Atherton	Billing	Ndlovu	**Sheridan***	Hurst	Williams PA	Robson	Williams J	Babb
	31/10	*28,018*	*12*	23			*Chapman 70, Fairclough 90*	*Lukic*	*Newsome*	*Dorigo*	*Batty**	*Fairclough*	*Whyte*	*Strachan*	*Wallace R'd^*	*Chapman*	*McAllister*	*Speed*	*Rocastle/Cantona*
							Ref: B Hill	The champions save their 29-match unbeaten home run with a 91st-minute header. City defend well and thwart Leeds. McAllister glances a header in from Hurst's corner and Ndlovu hammers in after Babb hits a post. Robson puts David Batty on a stretcher and angers the home fans.											
15	A	ARSENAL	6	L	0-3	0-3		Ogrizovic	Borrows*	Sansom	Atherton	Billing	Ndlovu	Middleton C	Hurst	Rosario	Babb	Williams J	Fleming
	7/11	*27,693*	*1*	23			*Smith 7, Wright 30, Campbell 45*	*Seaman*	*Dixon*	*Morrow*	*Hillier*	*Bould*	*Adams*	*Jensen*	*Wright*	*Smith*	*Merson*	*Campbell**	*Limpar*
							Ref: J Worrall	The superb away run is ended within the first half by George Graham's title contenders. Without Robson, Pearce and Gallacher, City struggle to contain the Gunners' attack. Dixon creates the first with a superb cross and Wright's finishing is deadly for the second. Ndlovu is a lone star.											
16	H	MANCHESTER C	9	L	2-3	1-0	Quinn 12, 49	Ogrizovic	Borrows	Sansom	Atherton	Pearce	Ndlovu	Robson	Hurst	Rosario	**Quinn**	Williams J*	Babb
	21/11	14,556	*6*	23			*Sheron 56, Simpson 67, Curle 78p*	*Coton*	*Brightwell I**	*Phelan*	*McMahon*	*Curle*	*Hill*	*White*	*Sheron*	*Quinn*	*Simpson*	*Holden*	*Brightwell D*
							Ref: P Durkin	Mick Quinn, on loan from Newcastle, scores twice on his debut, but Man City come back to win with Curle's penalty after the England man is fouled by Pearce. City lose their grip and finally crack under a barrage of attacks in a torrid second half in which McMahon and Holden rule.											
17	A	SHEFFIELD UTD	11	D	1-1	1-1	Quinn 7	Ogrizovic	Borrows	Babb	Atherton	Pearce	Ndlovu	Robson	Hurst	Rosario	Quinn	Gallacher*	Williams J
	28/11	*15,625*	*18*	24			*Pearce 37 (og)*	*Kelly*	*Bradshaw !*	*Cowan*	*Gannon^*	*Pemberton*	*Beesley*	*Ward*	*Rogers*	*Cork**	*Deane*	*Hodges*	*Littlejohn/Kamara*
							Ref: P Don	City's accounts reveal they are £2 million in debt and rumours link Ndlovu with Leeds. This boring game turns nasty in the last quarter as Bradshaw is sent off for two yellow cards. Quinn scores an opportunist goal but Pearce lashes in Rogers' cross. Deane is the Blades' only hope.											
18	H	IPSWICH	11	D	2-2	1-1	Gallacher 16, Quinn 51	Ogrizovic	Borrows	Babb	Atherton	Pearce*	Ndlovu	Robson^	Hurst	Rosario	Quinn	Gallacher	McGrath/Williams J
	5/12	11,281	*8*	25			*Kiwomya 13, Whitton 69p*	*Baker*	*Whelan^*	*Thompson*	*Stockwell*	*Wark*	*Linighan*	*Johnson*	*Goddard**	*Whitton*	*Dozzell*	*Kiwomya*	*Youds/Bozinoski*
							Ref: K Hackett	City should have won this entertaining game. Demon referee Keith Hackett is at it again, deferring to his linesman over McGrath's challenge on Kiwomya, when he was closer. Quinn scores one and makes one but Ndlovu is the star. Macedonian Bozinoski makes his Ipwich debut.											
19	A	SOUTHAMPTON	9	D	2-2	2-1	Quinn 6, 25	Ogrizovic	Borrows	Babb	Atherton	Sansom	Ndlovu	McGrath	Hurst	Rosario	Quinn	Gallacher	
	12/12	*12,306*	*15*	26			*Maddison 9, Dowie 60*	*Flowers*	*Kenna*	*Adams*	*Hurlock*	*Hall*	*Wood*	*Le Tissier*	*Groves*	*Dowie*	*Maddison*	*Benali*	
							Ref: R Nixon	City are eleven games without a win and Saints are unbeaten in six so a draw is predictable in an exciting match. Quinn scores twice to clinch a permanent move but Oggy drops Le Tissier's corner to Maddison and City fail to clear, allowing Dowie to equalise. Babb begins to look good.											
20	H	LIVERPOOL	8	W	**5-1**	1-0	Borrows 37p, 54, Gallacher 61, [Quinn 71, 74]	**Gould**	Borrows	Babb	Atherton	Sansom	Williams J	McGrath	Hurst	Rosario	Quinn	Gallacher	
	19/12	19,847	*10*	29			*Redknapp 64*	*Hooper*	*Marsh*	*Jones**	*Bjornebye*	*Piechnik*	*Wright*	*Stewart*	*Redknapp !*	*Rush*	*Barnes*	*Walters*	*Hutchison*
							Ref: K Morton	A sensational result after the Reds had bossed the first half. Arguably the best 45 minutes of the decade. City run riot with Redknapp sent off for two bookings after 68 mins. Redknapp fouls Hurst for the penalty and hits a screaming free-kick. Jonathan, son of Bobby, makes his debut.											
21	H	ASTON VILLA	7	W	3-0	0-0	Quinn 52, 55, Rosario 59	Gould	Borrows	Babb	Atherton	Sansom	Williams J	McGrath	Hurst	Rosario	Quinn^	Gallacher*	Ndlovu/Pearce
	26/12	24,135	*4*	32				*Spink*	*Barrett*	*Staunton*	*Teale*	*McGrath*	*Richardson*	*Houghton*	*Parker^*	*Saunders*	*Regis**	*Small*	*Beinlich/Cox*
							Ref: R Dilkes	Gould gives the team Xmas Day off and then gets them running round the city to warm up. Villa are title contenders but off colour and Quinn and Rosario destroy them in an eight-minute spell before the fog comes down and threatens the game. Quinn has now scored ten in six games.											

No	Date			Att	Pos	Pt	F-A	H-T	Scorers, Times, and Referees	1	2	3	4	5	6	7	8	9	10	11	subs used
22		A	MANCHESTER U		8	L	**0-5**	0-2	*[Sharpe 71, Irwin 83]*	Gould	Borrows	Babb	Atherton	Sansom	Williams J*	McGrath	Hurst	Rosario	Quinn	Gallacher	Ndlovu
	28/12			*36,025*	*2*	32			*Giggs 6, Hughes 41, Cantona 64p,*	*Schmeichel*	*Parker*	*Irwin*	*Bruce**	*Sharpe*	*Pallister*	*Cantona*	*Ince*	*McClair*	*Hughes*	*Giggs^*	*Phelan/Kanchelskis*
									Ref: R Groves	A totally one-sided game that United could have won by more. They had some luck but dominated throughout and were the best side City have faced this season. Cantona looks a bargain at £1.2 million and he scores his third goal in four starts when Parker's cross hits Babb's hand.											
23		H	NOTT'M FOREST		10	L	0-1	0-0		Ogrizovic	Borrows	Babb	Atherton	Sansom*	Williams J	McGrath	Hurst	Rosario	Quinn	Gallacher	Pearce
	9/1			15,254	*22*	32			*Woan 65*	*Crossley*	*Laws*	*Pearce*	*Chettle*	*Tiler*	*Keane*	*Bannister*	*Gemmill*	*Clough*	*Webb*	*Woan*	
									Ref: M Bodenham	After excellent recent results at Highfield Road the Sky Blues spoil it by losing to the bottom club. Kevin Gallacher looks to have scored in 14 minutes but the referee rules that he has fouled Crossley. Ian Woan grabs Forest's third win of the season with a soft goal. Oggy is back.											
24		A	NORWICH		11	D	1-1	0-1	Quinn 57	Ogrizovic	Borrows	Babb	Atherton	**Busst**	Williams J	Greenman*	Gynn	Rosario	Quinn	Gallacher	**Rowland**
	16/1			*13,613*	*1*	33			*Sutton 13*	*Gunn*	*Culverhouse*	*Bowen*	*Butterworth*	*Polston^*	*Goss*	*Crook**	*Beckford*	*Sutton*	*Fox*	*Phillips*	*Sutch/Woodthorpe*
									Ref: A Gunn	Gunn saves Borrows' penalty after he had brought down Williams. Quinn hit the bar with the rebound but atoned two minutes later by drilling home a cross from on-loan full back Keith Rowland. City had the chances to win after that, but Norwich hang on. Busst makes a useful debut.											
25		H	OLDHAM		6	W	3-0	3-0	Gallacher 6, 19, Ndlovu 13	Ogrizovic	Borrows	Babb	Atherton	Busst	Williams J	Ndlovu	Gynn	Rosario	Quinn	Gallacher*	Rowland
	23/1			10,515	*21*	36				*Gerrard*	*Halle*	*Pointon**	*Bernard*	*Jobson*	*Fleming*	*Palmer*	*Olney*	*Marshall*	*Milligan*	*Redmond*	*Adams*
									Ref: R Lewis	Sky TV viewers get 20 minutes of excitement and goals and then the entertainment tails off against the worst side to visit Coventry this season. Gallacher, Quinn and Ndlovu rip the Latics apart with their pace and skill, but Kevin Gallacher limps off with a hamstring before half-time.											
26		A	BLACKBURN		5	W	5-2	2-1	Hendry 20 (og), Hurst 45, Williams 48,	Ogrizovic	Borrows	Babb	Atherton	Busst	Williams J	Ndlovu	Gynn	Rosario	Quinn	Hurst	
	26/1			*15,215*	*4*	39			*Newell 13, Hendry 72* [Quinn 85, 88]	*Mimms*	*May*	*Wright**	*Sherwood*	*Hendry*	*Marker*	*Ripley*	*Cowans^*	*Wegerle*	*Newell*	*Wilcox*	*Atkins/Andersson*
									Ref: K Redfern	City are expected to let Blackburn win and go top of the league but Gould's men turn in the performance of the season and are leading scorers in the Premiership. 16-goal Shearer is injured but then so is Gallacher and Robson. At 3-2 an equaliser looks inevitable until Quinn takes over.											
27		H	WIMBLEDON		8	L	0-2	0-1		Ogrizovic	Borrows	Babb	Atherton	Busst	Williams J	Billing*	Gynn	Rosario	Quinn	Hurst	Flynn
	30/1			11,657	*18*	39			*Holdsworth 4, Clarke 55*	*Segers*	*Joseph*	*McAllister*	*Jones*	*Scales*	*Blackwell*	*Ardley*	*Earle*	*Fashanu*	*Holdsworth*	*Clarke**	*Dobbs*
									Ref: R Gifford	Gould's old boys wreck the party after the Ewood result with a typical smash and grab raid against a poor City. Injuries force Gould to play Billing in midfield and shuffle his formation. Williams misses a great chance from the kick-off, then Dean Holdsworth scores a brilliant goal.											
28		A	MIDDLESBROUGH		4	W	2-0	0-0	Ndlovu 68, Quinn 79	Ogrizovic	Borrows	Babb	Atherton	Pearce	Williams J	Ndlovu	Gynn	Rosario	Quinn	Hurst	
	6/2			*14,008*	*18*	42				*Pears*	*Morris^*	*Phillips*	*Mohan*	*Gittens*	*Falconer*	*Slaven*	*Hignett*	*Wilkinson*	*Peake*	*Hendrie**	*Wright/Pollock*
									Ref: I Borrett	Europe is being mentioned as City win their sixth away game. After a thrilling first half Ndlovu, back from his travels with Zimbabwe, takes control. He plays a superb one-two with Hurst before chipping in beautifully, then hammers a volley which Pears can't hold and Quinn scores.											
29		A	QP RANGERS		7	L	0-2	0-2		Ogrizovic	Borrows	Babb	Atherton	Pearce	Williams J	Ndlovu	Gynn*	Rosario	Quinn	Hurst	Robson
	20/2			*12,453*	*4*	42			*Pearce 33 (og), Peacock 41*	*Roberts*	*Bardsley*	*Brevett*	*Barker*	*Peacock*	*Ready*	*Wilson*	*Impey*	*Ferdinand*	*Allen*	*Sinton*	
									Ref: P Durkin	This poor performance is a let-down for City's big away following. City are punished for a woeful first half with Andy Pearce's unnecessary clearance spinning past Oggy. The long-haired Darren Peacock looks guilty of handball before driving in the second. Robson returns as sub.											
30		A	CRYS PALACE		10	D	0-0	0-0		Ogrizovic	Borrows	Babb	Atherton	Pearce	Williams J	Robson	Gynn*	Rosario	Quinn	Smith	Flynn
	27/2			*12,248*	*17*	43				*Martyn*	*Humphrey*	*Shaw**	*Coleman*	*Young*	*Thorn*	*Bowry*	*Thomas*	*Armstrong*	*Rodger*	*McGoldrick*	*Ndah*
									Ref: P Foakes	City's record at Selhurst is excellent and they maintain it in a dire game almost devoid of chances. .Perennial yo-yos Palace are heading for the drop, due to their young, inexperienced attack. The raw Williams, played as a central striker, needs a rest. A minute's silence for Bobby Moore.											
31		H	SHEFFIELD WED		5	W	1-0	1-0	Gynn 44	Ogrizovic	Borrows	Babb	Atherton	Pearce	Williams J	Ndlovu	Gynn	McGrath	Quinn	Robson	
	3/3			13,192	*4*	46				*Woods*	*King*	*Worthington*	*Palmer*	*Jones**	*Anderson*	*Hyde^*	*Waddle*	*Warhurst*	*Bright*	*Sheridan*	*Watts/Jemson*
									Ref: K Cooper	The Owls are still in both cups and are unbeaten in 16 games but City run out deserved winners in an average game. John Williams exasperates and excites in equal measure, but today he makes Gynn's goal with a diagonal run. Robson is back to his best, nullifying the threat of Waddle.											

No	Date	Opponent	Att	Pos	Res / Pts	F-A	H-T	Scorers, Times, and Referees	1	2	3	4	5	6	7	8	9	10	11	12
32	H	EVERTON		6	L	0-1	0-1		Ogrizovic	Borrows	Babb	Atherton	Pearce	Williams J	Ndlovu	Gynn*	McGrath	Quinn	Flynn	Gallacher
	7/3		11,273	*15*	46			*Ward 8*	*Southall*	*Jackson*	*Sansom*	*Snodin**	*Watson*	*Ablett*	*Ward*	*Beardsley*	*Cottee*	*Horne*	*Ebbrell*	*Precki*
								Ref: D Elleray	Robson has more eye problems. With Hurst injured and Gallacher on the bench, City have little quality. Sansom has gone to Everton on a free and plays one of only seven games for the Toffees. Mark Ward's early volley wins a drab game with City rarely threatening despite possession.											
33	A	MANCHESTER C		8	L	0-1	0-1		Ogrizovic	Borrows	Babb	Atherton	Busst	Williams J	Ndlovu	Gallacher	McGrath	Quinn*	Flynn	Greenman
	10/3		*20,092*	*7*	46			*Flitcroft 33*	*Coton*	*Hill*	*Phelan*	*Simpson*	*Curle*	*Vonk*	*White*	*Sheron*	*Quinn*	*Flitcroft*	*Holden*	
								Ref: P Durkin	Another poor performance and the agile Ogrizovic keeps City in the game in a one-sided first half. Flitcroft breaks the tedium with an angled shot before Gould makes changes at half-time. Quinn comes off and Williams, playing centrally, misses a one-on-one. Rosario is badly missed.											
34	H	ARSENAL		8	L	0-2	0-2		Ogrizovic	Borrows	Babb	Atherton	Busst	Williams J	Ndlovu	Gallacher	**Rennie**	**Jenkinson**^	Flynn*	Gynn/McGrath
	13/3		15,419	*12*	46			*Campbell 28, Wright 29*	*Seaman*	*Dixon*	*Keown*	*Davis*	*Linighan*	*Adams*	*Parlour*	*Wright**	*Campbell*	*Merson^*	*Morrow*	*Limpar/Hillier*
								Ref: D Allison	Arsenal are chasing two cups and tiredness is creeping into their game. City have bought Rennie and Jenkinson to supplement their tired limbs but it is a poor performance with a worrying lack of poise and penetration. Oggy and Atherton err to give Ian Wright the easiest of his 26 goals.											
35	A	IPSWICH		8	D	0-0	0-0		Ogrizovic	Borrows	Babb	Atherton	Busst	Williams J	Ndlovu	Gallacher	Rennie	Quinn	Hurst	
	20/3		*16,698*	*14*	47				*Baker*	*Johnson*	*Whelan*	*Stockwell*	*Wark*	*Linighan*	*Williams*	*Guentchev*	*Goddard**	*Dozzell*	*Kiwomya*	*Whitton*
								Ref: J Worrall	After being fifth in January, Ipswich are on a depressing slide, but do enough to earn a point in a poor game on a rock-hard pitch. All talk of Europe has gone and Gould even mentions relegation. Lee Hurst's return bolsters midfield and Busst looks good. Ref Worrall has a nose-bleed.											
36	H	SHEFFIELD UTD		10	L	1-3	1-0	Williams 17	Ogrizovic	Borrows	Babb	Atherton	Busst	Rennie	Ndlovu	Hurst	Quinn	Gynn	Williams J	
	24/3		13,016	*19*	47			*Whitehouse 69, Deane 75, Littlejohn 86*	*Kelly*	*Gage*	*Cowan**	*Gannon*	*Gayle*	*Pemberton*	*Carr^*	*Whitehouse*	*Cork*	*Deane*	*Ward*	*Littlejohn/Hoyland*
								Ref: P Wright	Gallacher's move to Blackburn for £1 million plus £500,000-rated Wegerle is on ice but Kevin is rested. The Blades get their second away win of the season courtesy of a shoddy second-half display. Borrows misses his second penalty in a row in the 80th minute, after Gynn was fouled.											
37	H	SOUTHAMPTON		7	W	2-0	1-0	Quinn 7p, Williams 80	Gould	Borrows	Babb	Atherton	Busst	Rennie*	Ndlovu	Hurst	Quinn	**Wegerle**^	Williams J	McGrath/Gynn
	3/4		**10,455**	*14*	50				*Flowers*	*Kenna*	*Adams*	*Hurlock*	*Hall*	*Moore*	*Le Tissier*	*Dodd*	*Dowie*	*Maddison*	*Benali**	*Banger*
								Ref: K Cooper	City start brightly with the ball on the floor. The penalty is for Moore's push on Rennie. By reverting to the long ball, City play into Saints' hands and waste Wegerle's skills. Oggy is axed for the first time in nine years. Williams pops up to net after Flowers can't hold Ndlovu's shot.											
38	A	ASTON VILLA		9	D	0-0	0-0		Gould	Borrows	Babb	Atherton	Gynn	Rennie	McGrath	Hurst	Quinn	Wegerle*	Williams J	Jenkinson
	10/4		***38,543***	*2*	51				*Bosnich*	*Barrett*	*Staunton*	*Teale*	*McGrath*	*Richardson*	*Houghton*	*Parker*	*Saunders*	*Atkinson*	*Yorke**	*Daley*
								Ref: A Gunn	Villa lose their grip on the title by slipping up at home, whilst Man Utd score a very late winner to leapfrog over them. City set out to defend and Atherton and Babb are outstanding and Gould has only one save to make. Villa have the possession but Coventry have the determination.											
39	H	MANCHESTER U		10	L	0-1	0-1		Gould	Borrows	Babb	Atherton	Gynn	Rennie	McGrath*	Hurst	Quinn !	Wegerle	Williams J	Jenkinson
	12/4		**24,410**	*1*	51			*Irwin 40*	*Schmeichel*	*Parker*	*Irwin*	*Bruce*	*Sharpe*	*Pallister*	*Cantona**	*Ince*	*McClair*	*Hughes*	*Giggs*	*Robson*
								Ref: R Gifford	United tighten their grip on the title with a fortuitous win, thanks to Irwin's stunning long-range drive. Wegerle hits the post before mayhem descends and Schmeichel tumbles to the floor after a clash with Mick Quinn, who is shown a red card. TV pictures later exonerate Quinn.											
40	A	LIVERPOOL		12	L	0-4	0-2		Gould	Borrows*	Babb	Atherton	Gynn	Rennie	Ndlovu^	Hurst	Quinn	Wegerle	Williams J	Pearce/Jenkinson
	17/4		*33,328*	*8*	51			*Walters 16, 33, 50p, Burrows 75*	*James*	*Jones*	*Burrows*	*Nicol*	*Wright*	*Whelan*	*Stewart**	*Hutchison*	*Rush*	*Barnes*	*Walters*	*Rosenthal*
								Ref: T Ward	City fans regret chanting 'Villa reject' at Mark Walters, as he nets a hat-trick. His second is a delicious inch-perfect chip from 30 yards, and his penalty is for Pearce's clumsy lunge at Stewart. City have their moments, with Leigh Jenkinson hitting the bar, but Burrows' hard shot ends it.											
41	A	CHELSEA		13	L	1-2	0-1	Quinn 57	Gould	Fleming*	Babb	Atherton	Busst	Rennie	Gynn^	Hurst	Quinn	Wegerle	Williams J	Borrows/**Boland**
	1/5		*14,186*	*8*	51			*Spencer 14, Cascarino 71*	*Kharine*	*Clarke*	*Lee*	*Townsend*	*Johnsen*	*Spackman*	*Barnard*	*Spencer**	*Cascarino*	*Hall*	*Wise*	*Hopkin*
								Ref: R Groves	David Webb has pulled Chelsea out of their slump, but City's run continues in this end of season game with nothing at stake. Quinn celebrates being captain with a lovely lobbed effort after Kharine had punched out. Cascarino nabs the winner: he has scored against City for three teams.											
42	H	LEEDS		15	D	3-3	2-1	Williams 5, Quinn 39, Ndlovu 73	Gould	Borrows	Babb	Atherton	McGrath	Rennie	Jenkinson*	Hurst	Quinn	Ndlovu	Williams J	Wegerle
	8/5		19,571	*17*	52			*Wallace 6, 89, 90*	*Beeney*	*Wallace Ray*	*Dorigo*	*Batty*	*Newsome*	*Whyte !*	*Shutt**	*Wallace Rod*	*Chapman*	*Hodge*	*Tinkler^*	*Rocastle/Kerr*
	Home		Away					Ref: K Morton	The fans say farewell to the Spion Kop, which is demolished after the game. Liverpool boss Graeme Souness is rumoured to be watching Ndlovu. Nuddy turns on his finest performance, scoring one and making two. The game is tossed away to the 10 men after Whyte was sent off.											
Average	14,950		19,395																	

Coca-Cola Cup					F-A	H-T	Scorers, Times, and Referees	1	2	3	4	5	6	7	8	9	10	11	subs used
2:1	H	SCARBOROUGH	2	W	2-0	0-0	Borrows 72p, Ndlovu 74	Ogrizovic	Borrows	Sansom	Atherton	Pearce	Ndlovu	McGrath	Hurst	Babb	Gallacher	Williams J	
23/9		5,989	*3:8*					*Evans*	*Thompson*	*Mudd*	*Lee*	*Hirst*	*Curran*	*Ashdjian*	*Murphy*	*Mooney*	*Foreman^*	*Jules**	*Himsworth/Mockler*
							Ref: A Smith	Phil Babb makes his first start as a striker, as City make heavy weather of Scarborough. It is the first ever game between the clubs and Borrows breaks the deadlock after Hurst's corner is handled by Foreman. Ndlovu scores a tasty second with some wizardry and Gallacher goes close.											
2:2	A	SCARBOROUGH	3	L	0-3	0-0		Ogrizovic	Borrows	Sansom	Atherton	Pearce	Smith	McGrath	Babb	Rosario*	Gallacher	Williams J	Fleming
7/10		*2,633*	*3:7*				*Mooney 72, Foreman 89, Hirst 90*	*Ford*	*Thompson*	*Mudd*	*Lee*	*Hirst*	*Curran*	*Ashdjian**	*Himsworth*	*Mooney*	*Foreman*	*Jules*	*Wheeler*
							Ref: R Hart (City lose 2-3 on aggregate)	Another disastrous cup exit, to lowly Scarborough, after 20 minutes of madness. Early chances are spurned and warnings go unheeded until Mooney capitalises on Babb's loose ball. Foreman levels a minute from time and incredibly Lee Hirst's header wins the tie in the 93rd minute.											

FA Cup																			
3	A	NORWICH	10	L	0-1	0-0		Ogrizovic	Borrows	Babb	Atherton	Pearce	Ndlovu	McGrath*	Williams J	Rosario	Quinn^	Gallacher	Busst/Gynn
13/1		*15,301*	*1*				*Beckford 46*	*Gunn*	*Culverhouse*	*Bowen*	*Butterworth*	*Polston*	*Megson**	*Crook*	*Beckford*	*Sutton*	*Fox*	*Phillips*	*Goss*
							Ref: K Hackett	Beckford has made only six starts and scored once since his £925,000 move from Port Vale but scrambles the winner for the leaders. City play five strikers but miss Robson and Hurst in midfield and fade after the goal. Gould is banished from the bench after verbals with the linesman.											

		Home					Away					
	P	W	D	L	F	A	W	D	L	F	A	Pts
1 Manchester U	42	14	5	2	39	14	10	7	4	28	17	84
2 Aston Villa	42	13	5	3	36	16	8	6	7	21	24	74
3 Norwich	42	13	6	2	31	19	8	3	10	30	46	72
4 Blackburn	42	13	4	4	38	18	7	7	7	30	28	71
5 QP Rangers	42	11	5	5	41	32	6	7	8	22	23	63
6 Liverpool	42	13	4	4	41	18	3	7	11	21	37	59
7 Sheffield Wed	42	9	8	4	34	26	6	6	9	21	25	59
8 Tottenham	42	11	5	5	40	25	5	8	10	20	41	59
9 Manchester C	42	7	8	6	30	25	8	4	9	26	26	57
10 Arsenal	42	8	8	7	25	20	7	5	9	15	18	56
11 Chelsea	42	9	7	5	29	22	5	7	9	22	32	56
12 Wimbledon	42	9	4	8	32	23	5	8	8	24	32	54
13 Everton	42	7	6	8	26	27	8	2	11	27	28	53
14 Sheffield Utd	42	10	6	5	33	19	4	4	13	21	34	52
15 COVENTRY	42	7	4	10	29	28	6	9	6	23	29	52
16 Ipswich	42	8	9	4	29	22	4	7	10	21	33	52
17 Leeds	42	12	8	1	40	17	0	7	14	17	45	51
18 Southampton	42	10	6	5	30	21	3	5	13	24	40	50
19 Oldham	42	10	6	5	43	30	3	4	14	20	44	49
20 Crys Palace	42	6	9	6	27	25	5	7	9	21	36	49
21 Middlesboro	42	8	5	8	33	27	3	6	12	21	48	44
22 Nott'm Forest	42	6	4	11	17	25	4	6	11	24	37	40
	924	214	132	118	723	499	118	132	214	499	723	1256

Odds & ends

Double wins: (4) Tottenham, Sheffield Wed, Oldham, Middlesbrough.
Double losses: (5) QP Rangers, Chelsea, Manchester C, Arsenal, Manchester U.

Won from behind: (1) Blackburn.
Lost from in front: (2) Manchester C (h), Sheffield U (h).

High spots: Winning the first four away games, a club record.
The Liverpool and Villa home wins.
Winning at championship-chasing Blackburn.
Mick Quinn's arrival and his glut of goals.
Leading the Premiership after three games.

Low spots: Winning only one of last 11 games to slump from 5th to 16th.
The embarrassment at Scarborough.

Red cards: City – Quinn (Manchester U h).
Red cards: Opponents – Bradshaw (Sheff U a), Redknapp (Liverpool h), Whyte (Leeds h).

Player of the Year: Peter Atherton.
Ever-presents: (0).
Hat-tricks: (0).
Opposing hat-tricks: (2) Walters (Aston Villa), Wallace (Leeds).
Leading scorer: (17) Mick Quinn.

	Appearances						Goals			
	Lge	*Sub*	LC	*Sub*	FAC	*Sub*	**Lge**	LC	FAC	**Tot**
Atherton, Peter	**39**		2		1					
Babb, Phil	**27**	*7*	2		1					
Billing, Peter	**3**									
Boland, Willie		*1*								
Borrows, Brian	**36**	*2*	2		1		**2**	1		**3**
Busst, David	**10**					*1*				
Fleming, Terry	**8**	*3*		*1*						
Flynn, Sean	**4**	*3*								
Gallacher, Kevin	**19**	*1*	2		1		**6**			**6**
Gould, Jonathan	**9**									
Greenman, Chris	**1**	*1*								
Gynn, Michael	**18**	*2*				*1*	**2**			**2**
Hurst, Lee	**35**		1				**2**			**2**
Jenkinson, Leigh	**2**	*3*								
McGrath, Lloyd	**20**	*5*	2		1					
Middleton, Craig	**1**									
Ndlovu, Peter	**27**	*5*	1		1		**7**	1		**8**
Ogrizovic, Steve	**33**		2		1					
Pearce, Andy	**21**	*3*	2		1		**1**			**1**
Quinn, Mick	**26**				1		**17**			**17**
Rennie, David	**9**									
Robson, Stewart	**14**	*1*								
Rosario, Robert	**28**		1		1		**4**			**4**
Rowland, Keith (loan)		*2*								
Sansom, Kenny	**21**		2							
Sheridan, Tony	**1**									
Smith, David	**6**		1				**1**			**1**
Wegerle, Roy	**5**	*1*								
Williams, John	**38**	*3*	2		1		**8**			**8**
Williams, Paul A (loan)	**1**	*1*								
(own-goals)							**2**			**2**
30 players used	**462**	***44***	**22**	***1***	**11**		**52**	**2**		**54**

No		Date	Att	Pos	Pt	F-A	H-T	Scorers, Times, and Referees	SQUAD	NUMBERS	IN	USE								subs used
1	A	ARSENAL			W	3-0	1-0	Quinn 34p, 62, 65	Gould	Flynn	Sheridan	Rennie	Babb	Atherton	Williams J	Robson*	Quinn	Wegerle	Ndlovu	**Morgan**
		14/8	*24,897*		3				*Seaman*	*Dixon*	*Winterburn*	*Jensen^*	*Linighan*	*Adams*	*Limpar*	*Davis*	*Wright*	*Campbell*	*Merson**	*McGoldrick/Keown*
								Ref: A Wilkie	Double Cup winners Arsenal open their new stand, but City wreck their party with Quinn registering the club's first Premiership hat-trick. Robson's serious injury after 10 minutes adds to Lee Hurst's training injury, and does not bode well. Lee Dixon fouls Ndlovu for the penalty.											
2	H	NEWCASTLE			W	2-1	0-1	Ndlovu 58, Harford 85	Gould	Flynn	Morgan^	Rennie	Babb	Atherton	Williams J	Sheridan*	Quinn	Wegerle	Ndlovu	**Harford/Wil'ms PR**
		18/8	15,763		6			*Atherton 22 (og)*	*Srnicek !*	*Venison*	*Beresford*	*Bracewell*	*Scott*	*Watson*	*Lee*	*Clark*	*Cole*	*O'Brien*	*Papa'siliou**	*Wright*
								Ref: I Borrett	City leave it late to beat 10 men Newcastle in a thrilling game. Atherton deflects O'Brien's weak free-kick past Gould. Srnicek is sent off for a foul on Wegerle but Quinn blasts the penalty. Ndlovu equalises and Harford breaks the Magpies resolve eleven minutes after coming on.											
3	H	WEST HAM		5	D	1-1	0-1	Wegerle 57	Gould	Flynn	Morgan	Rennie	Babb	Atherton	Williams J^	Sheridan*	Quinn	Wegerle	Ndlovu	Boland/Williams PR
		21/8	12,864	*19*	7			*Gordon 44*	*Miklosko*	*Breacker*	*Dicks*	*Allen M*	*Foster*	*Potts*	*Rowland*	*Butler*	*Morley*	*Allen C*	*Gordon*	
								Ref: S Lodge	Newly promoted West Ham gain their first point and are unlucky not to win. City rarely get going and fall behind when Gould fails to hold Breacker's shot and Gordon nips in. Wegerle scores his first goal for the club but too many players have off days. Butler hits the post late on.											
4	A	OLDHAM		9	D	3-3	1-1	Williams J 9, Ndlovu 74, Wegerle 84p	Gould	Borrows	Morgan*	Rennie	Babb	Atherton	Williams J	McGrath	Quinn^	Wegerle	Ndlovu	Williams PR/Boland
		24/8	*10,817*	*14*	8			*Bernard 38, Ritchie 49p, Olney 63*	*Gerrard*	*Fleming*	*Pointon*	*Henry*	*Jobson*	*Redmond*	*Halle*	*Milligan*	*Olney*	*Ritchie*	*Bernard*	
								Ref: P Foakes	A roller-coaster game with City coming back from the dead to earn a draw and almost snatch a win. Ndlovu's switch to attack midway through the second half is decisive. He unsettles the Oldham defence, scores one and is fouled by Fleming for the penalty. Gould criticises the officials.											
5	A	MANCHESTER C		7	D	1-1	0-1	Wegerle 85	Gould	Booty*	Williams PR	Rennie	Busst	Atherton	Williams J	Boland	McGrath	Wegerle	Ndlovu	Jenkinson
		27/8	*21,537*	*20*	9			*Sheron 34*	*Coton*	*Flitcroft*	*Phelan*	*McMahon*	*Curle*	*Vonk*	*White*	*Groenendijk*	*Sheron*	*Quinn*	*Holden*	
								Ref: P Don	Peter Reid has been sacked after four games and Brian Horton is the new Man City boss. Manchester have the greater possession but City, with seven players injured, make the better chances. Boland and Booty make good full debuts but Jenkinson doesn't touch the ball in seven minutes.											
6	H	LIVERPOOL		4	W	1-0	1-0	Babb 21	Gould	McGrath	Morgan	Rennie	Babb	Atherton	Williams J*	Boland	Quinn^	Wegerle	Ndlovu	Williams PR/Sheridan
		1/9	16,735	*3*	12				*Grobbelaar*	*Jones !*	*Burrows**	*Nicol*	*Wright*	*Ruddock*	*Whelan*	*Molby*	*Clough*	*Rush*	*McManam'n*	*Walters*
								Ref: K Burge	Two incidents stand out in this absorbing game. Babb scores his first City goal when he springs the offside trap from Boland's free-kick. 20 minutes from time Rob Jones gets a red card after fouls on Ndlovu and Wegerle. Jonnie Gould, watched by Scotland, makes three good saves.											
7	A	ASTON VILLA		4	D	0-0	0-0		Ogrizovic	McGrath	Morgan	Rennie	Babb	Atherton	Williams J*	Boland	Quinn	Wegerle^	Ndlovu	Williams PR/Sheridan
		11/9	*31,181*	*5*	13				*Spink*	*Barrett*	*Staunton*	*Richardson*	*McGrath*	*Teale*	*Cowans*	*Townsend*	*Saunders*	*Atkinson*	*Whitting'm**	*Houghton*
								Ref: M Bodenham	City retain the only unbeaten run in the Premiership, thanks to a committed rearguard action which thwarts Villa's strikeforce. Phil Babb and Peter Atherton are superb and Oggy, in for the flu victim Gould, has a commanding game. John Gayle joins from Birmingham for £100,000.											
8	H	CHELSEA		7	D	1-1	0-1	Morgan 49	Ogrizovic	McGrath	Morgan	Rennie	Babb	Atherton	Williams J*	Boland	Quinn	Wegerle	Ndlovu	Sheridan
		18/9	13,586	*14*	14			*Peacock 36*	*Kharine*	*Clarke*	*Sinclair*	*Dow*	*Kjeldbjerg*	*Donaghy*	*Newton*	*Hoddle*	*Shipperley**	*Peacock*	*Wise*	*Spencer*
								Ref: P Durkin	City's fifth comeback of the season makes it the best start since 1937. Glen Hoddle is Chelsea's new player-manager. This is his first game against City since the 1987 Cup final and he is majestic. A draw is a fair result but City had chances to win as Wegerle and Ndlovu dazzled.											
9	H	LEEDS		10	L	0-2	0-1		Ogrizovic	Booty*	Morgan^	Rennie	Babb	Atherton	**Kruszynski**	Boland	Quinn	Wegerle	**Gayle**	Williams J/Sheridan
		25/9	13,933	*4*	14			*Wallace 20, 48*	*Beeney*	*Kelly*	*Dorigo*	*Wetherall*	*Fairclough*	*Newsome*	*Strachan*	*McAllister*	*Deane*	*Wallace*	*Speed*	
								Ref: K Cooper	Rod Wallace hasn't scored all season but he loves playing City and gets his second brace in two seasons to end the unbeaten run. Ndlovu is on international duty and John Williams is dropped, so City lack width. Gordon Strachan runs the game and Leeds look title challengers again.											
10	A	NORWICH		11	L	0-1	0-1		Ogrizovic	Morgan	Williams PR	Sheridan*	Babb	Atherton	Williams J	Boland	Quinn^	Wegerle	Jenkinson	Flynn/Kruszynski
		2/10	*16,239*	*4*	14			*Fox 45*	*Gunn*	*Culverhouse*	*Bowen*	*Megson*	*Newman*	*Polston*	*Fox*	*Goss*	*Sutton*	*Ekoku*	*Crook*	
								Ref: D Gallagher	Norwich look jaded after a UEFA trip to Arnhem in midweek but have too much in their locker for City. Oggy is back to his best, thwarting Ekoku, last week's four-goal hero against Everton, and Megson. He can't stop Fox scoring an injury-time goal after outwitting Paul Williams.											

No	Venue	Opponent / Date	Att	Pos	Pts	Res	FT	HT	Scorers, Times, Referees												Subs
11	H	SOUTHAMPTON		13		D	1-1	0-0	Babb 88	Gould	Busst*	Morgan	McGrath	Babb	Atherton	Williams J^	Boland	Quinn	Wegerle	Ndlovu	Jenkinson/Flynn
		16/10	**9,837**	*21*	15				*Charlton 57*	*Flowers*	*Kenna*	*Charlton*	*Reid*	*Moore*	*Monkou*	*Allen*	*Maddison*	*Dowie*	*Moody*	*Adams*	
									Ref: J Worrall	Gould is on the verge of buying Craig Burley from Chelsea, and on this performance City need someone. Phil Babb's late equaliser is barely deserved after a pitiful display which rarely puts the Saints under pressure. Booty has gone to Crewe for free and Harford needs back surgery.											
12	A	QP RANGERS		13		L	**1-5**	0-3	Ndlovu 76 *[Barker 88]*	Gould	Borrows	Morgan^	McGrath	Babb	Atherton	Flynn	Boland	Quinn	Ndlovu	Jenkinson*	Wegerle/Williams PR
		23/10	*12,979*	*5*	15				*Ferdinand 15, Allen 30, 45, Impey 75,*	*Stejskal*	*Bardsley*	*Wilson*	*Wilkins*	*Peacock*	*McDonald*	*Impey**	*Barker*	*Ferdinand*	*Allen*	*Sinclair*	*Holloway*
									Ref: G Ashby	Gould dramatically resigns after this drubbing by a sublime Rangers team, inspired by Ferdinand and Bradley Allen. Sinclair and Impey make the bullets and City's defence collapses embarrassingly. The reason for Gould's departure is, he insists, is that he has been told to sell Ndlovu.											
13	H	SHEFFIELD UTD		13		D	0-0	0-0		Ogrizovic	Borrows	Morgan	McGrath	Babb	Rennie	Flynn	Boland	Quinn	Wegerle*	Ndlovu	Williams J
		31/10	10,439	*18*	16					*Tracey*	*Bradshaw*	*Ward*	*Falconer**	*Tuttle*	*Hoyland*	*Hodges*	*Rogers*	*Littlejohn*	*Hartfield*	*Whitehouse*	*Cork*
									Ref: A Gunn	The threatened demo supporting Gould is a damp squib, as is the game. Neal calls for the bickering to stop - it's affecting the players. Julian Darby is signed from Bolton and Arsenal are allegedly ready to bid £3 million for Ndlovu. United are nine games without a win and in trouble.											
14	H	EVERTON		13		W	2-1	1-0	Quinn 27, 49	Ogrizovic	Borrows	Morgan	McGrath	Babb	Rennie	Flynn*	Boland	Quinn	Wegerle	Ndlovu	**Darby**
		6/11	11,550	*12*	19				*Rideout 70*	*Southall*	*Holmes*	*Hinchcliffe*	*Ebbrell*	*Watson*	*Ablett*	*Ward**	*Horne*	*Cottee*	*Rideout*	*Beagrie*	*Barlow*
									Ref: A Wilkie	Borrows is back from the wilderness and stars, setting up the first goal and marking Peter Beagrie. City's nerves fray after their second goal and Rideout pulls one back, only for Tony Cottee's penalty seven minutes from time to hit a post. City then survive to give Neal his first win.											
15	A	SHEFFIELD WED		11		D	0-0	0-0		Ogrizovic	Borrows	Morgan	McGrath*	Babb	Rennie	Flynn	Boland	Quinn	Williams J	Ndlovu	Atherton
		20/11	*23,379*	*17*	20					*Pressman*	*Nilsson*	*Worthington*	*Palmer*	*Pearce*	*Walker*	*Waddle*	*Hyde*	*Jones*	*Jemson**	*Sinton*	*Francis*
									Ref: G Poll	Five days after his testimonial game McGrath is stretchered off with ligament trouble which will end his career. It is a nothing game but Quinn misses two good chances. 39-year-old Trevor Francis makes his final Owls appearance but makes no difference. Babb plays for Rep of Ireland.											
16	A	BLACKBURN		11		L	1-2	0-1	Ndlovu 62	Ogrizovic	Borrows	Morgan	Atherton	Babb	Rennie*	**Marsden**	Boland	Quinn	Williams J	Ndlovu	Flynn
		23/11	*15,136*	*2*	20				*Shearer 32, 63*	*Flowers*	*May*	*Wright*	*Batty*	*Berg*	*Marker*	*Ripley**	*Sherwood*	*Shearer*	*Newell*	*Le Saux*	*Gallacher*
									Ref: K Burge	Blackburn fail to make their domination count and City almost grab a point but Ndlovu can't repeat his earlier great finish. Shearer is given too much room for both his goals: he has scored eleven in his last eight starts. Phil Neal is given the manager's job and Mick Brown is his deputy.											
17	H	MANCHESTER U		15		L	0-1	0-0		Ogrizovic	Atherton	Morgan	Darby	Babb	Rennie	Flynn	Boland*	Quinn^	Wegerle	Ndlovu	Marsden/Williams J
		27/11	**17,009**	*1*	20				*Cantona 60*	*Schmeichel*	*Parker*	*Irwin*	*Ince*	*Pallister*	*Bruce*	*Giggs*	*Ferguson*	*Cantona*	*Hughes*	*Sharpe*	
									Ref: S Lodge	The league leaders are lucky to leave with three points and have Schmeichel to thank for doing so. The great Dane makes four wonder saves, including a last-minute save from Marsden which defied belief. Midfielder Marsden, on loan from Huddersfield, is creating a good impression.											
18	H	ARSENAL		13		W	1-0	0-0	Quinn 79	Ogrizovic	Atherton	Morgan	Darby	Babb	Rennie	Flynn	Boland	Quinn	Wegerle	Ndlovu	
		4/12	12,632	*5*	23					*Seaman*	*Dixon*	*Winterburn*	*Selley*	*Keown*	*Adams^*	*McGoldrick**	*Davis*	*Wright*	*Smith*	*Merson*	*Campbell/Bould*
									Ref: R Hart	Another excellent performance sees off Arsenal, who had previously lost only one away game. But for David Seaman, the margin would have been greater. Flynn gives the Arsenal left flank a torrid time and sets up Quinn's opportunistic goal to complete the double over the Gunners.											
19	A	WEST HAM		16		L	2-3	1-2	Darby 41, 77	Ogrizovic	Atherton	Morgan	Darby	Babb	Rennie	Flynn	Boland^	Quinn	Wegerle*	Ndlovu	Williams J/Marsden
		11/12	*17,243*	*9*	23				*Breacker 11, Butler 40, Morley 59p*	*Miklosko*	*Breacker*	*Burrows*	*Bishop**	*Gale*	*Potts*	*Marsh*	*Butler*	*Morley*	*Chapman*	*Holmes*	*Allen M*
									Ref: K Cooper	An excellent match with new-look Hammers causing City big problems. The visitors' only start playing when it's 0-2, but Darby's goalscoring feats ensure City are in with a chance. Williams appears to be tripped in the area but the ref waves play on. Ndlovu fouls Marsh for the penalty.											
20	H	OLDHAM		16		D	1-1	1-0	Wegerle 29	Ogrizovic	Borrows	Morgan	Darby	Babb	Atherton	Flynn	Marsden	Quinn*	Wegerle	Ndlovu	Williams J
		18/12	11,792	*18*	24				*Bernard 50*	*Hallworth*	*Fleming*	*Pointon*	*Halle*	*Pedersen*	*Redmond*	*Bernard*	*Milligan*	*Adams*	*Sharp*	*Holden**	*Ritchie*
									Ref: D Gallagher	A poor relegation battle leaves City fans wondering how they can play so badly against the lesser teams. Quinn's misses are embarrassing and Oggy misses Holden's driven corner for Paul Bernard to head in. Harford and Hurst are out for the season. The gate is boosted by free tickets.											
21	A	WIMBLEDON		15		W	2-1	1-1	Ndlovu 26, Williams J 71	Ogrizovic	Borrows	Morgan	Darby	Babb	Atherton	Flynn	Marsden	Williams J	Wegerle	Ndlovu	
		26/12	***4,739***	*12*	27				*Holdsworth 38*	*Segers*	*Barton*	*McAllister*	*Jones*	*Scales*	*Fitzgerald*	*Ardley*	*Earle*	*Fashanu*	*Holdsworth*	*Fear**	*Dobbs^/Clarke*
									Ref: M Bodenham	John Williams returns for the axed Quinn and scores after dispossessing Scales and makes the other goal for Ndlovu with a fine pass. City are under the cosh in the first half but the Dons peter out badly. Vinnie Jones' 50-yard effort that almost catches Oggy unawares is all they offer.											

No	Date			Att	Pos	Pt		F-A	H-T	Scorers, Times, and Referees	SQUAD	NUMBERS	IN	USE								subs used
22		A	TOTTENHAM		13		W	2-1	1-1	Babb 25, Wegerle 77	Ogrizovic	Borrows	Morgan	Darby	Babb	Atherton	Flynn	Marsden	Williams J*	Wegerle	Ndlovu	Quinn
	1/1			*26,015*	*12*	30				*Caskey 43*	*Thorstvedt*	*Kerslake*	*Edinburgh*	*Samways*	*Calderwood*	*Sedgley*	*Caskey*	*Barmby*	*Anderton*	*Dozzell*	*Hazard**	*Campbell*
										Ref: T Holbrook	City's second win in the capital in a week is fully deserved. Under Phil Neal they are playing a more attractive brand of football. Wegerle and Marsden are flourishing. Marsden and Ndlovu combine to set up Wegerle for the winner after City had increasingly exposed Spurs' failings.											
23		H	SWINDON		12		D	1-1	0-0	Wegerle 73	Ogrizovic	Borrows	Morgan	Darby	Babb	Atherton	Flynn	Marsden	Williams J*	Wegerle	Ndlovu	Quinn
	3/1			15,869	*22*	31				*Mutch 89*	*Hammond*	*Summerbee*	*Bodin*	*Fenwick*	*Taylor*	*Whitbread*	*Moncur*	*Horlock*	*Maskell**	*Mutch*	*Ling*	*Scott*
										Ref: B Hill	Sky TV show City dominate bottom of the table Swindon in a superb match but they are robbed by Mutch's late goal. Chris Marsden is the star again but City are prevaricating and his loan period is over. John Gorman's side are lucky to survive the woodwork being struck three times.											
24		A	SOUTHAMPTON		13		L	0-1	0-1		Ogrizovic	Borrows	Williams PR	Darby	Babb	Atherton	Flynn	Rennie	Quinn	Williams J*	Ndlovu	Jenkinson
	15/1			*12,397*	*20*	31				*Le Tissier 44p*	*Beasant*	*Kenna*	*Charlton*	*Widdrington*	*Wood*	*Monkou*	*Allen*	*Maddison*	*Dowie*	*Le Tissier*	*Dodd*	
										Ref: P Don	Saints have dispensed with boss Branfoot and are searching for a replacement. City have a long injury list but perform dismally in this defeat. Le Tissier's penalty is for Paul Williams' kamikaze tackle on Dowie. City have a strong penalty appeal turned down for a foul on P Williams.											
25		H	QP RANGERS		14		L	0-1	0-1		Ogrizovic	Borrows	Morgan	Darby	Babb	Atherton	Flynn	Rennie*	Quinn	Williams J	Ndlovu	**Robertson**
	22/1			12,065	*8*	31				*White 25*	*Stejskal*	*Bardsley*	*Wilson*	*Wilkins**	*Peacock*	*Yates*	*Holloway*	*Barker*	*Penrice*	*White*	*Sinclair*	*Meaker*
										Ref: A Wilkie	City would not take a risk on Marsden's fitness and he has signed for Wolves. Robertson, a £250,000 signing from Rangers, is the alternative sub, coming on for 14 minutes. Borrows has fractured his jaw and plays in a protective mask. White wins a poor game with a smart finish.											
26		H	IPSWICH		12		W	1-0	1-0	Flynn 5	Ogrizovic	Borrows	Morgan	Darby	Babb	Atherton	Flynn	Rennie	Gayle	Williams J*	Ndlovu	Quinn
	2/2			11,244	*13*	34					*Forrest*	*Youds*	*Thompson*	*Stockwell*	*Wark*	*Linighan*	*Williams*	*Johnson^*	*Marshall*	*Guentchev**	*Slater*	*Kiwomya/Palmer*
										Ref: D Allison	Just how Ipswich have lost only once in 15 games, and beaten Spurs 3-0 last week, is baffling. They look a very poor side, but City struggle to win despite a superb header from Sean Flynn. Quinn is axed but comes on and misses a penalty after Eddie Youds bodychecks Peter Ndlovu.											
27		A	SWINDON		12		L	1-3	0-2	Darby 53	Ogrizovic	Borrows	Morgan	Darby	Babb	Atherton	Flynn	Rennie	Gayle*	Williams J^	Ndlovu	Quinn/Robertson
	5/2			*14,640*	*22*	34				*Fjortoft 8, 35p, 79p*	*Hammond*	*Summerbee*	*Nijholt*	*Kilcline*	*Taylor*	*Whitbread*	*Moncur*	*Horlock*	*Fjortoft*	*Scott*	*Ling**	*Bodin*
										Ref: K Burge	Fjortoft scored his first goal in 21 games for Swindon last week and follows it up with a hat-trick. Two are penalties, harshly given for fouls by Atherton, on Moncur and Fjortoft. Brian Kilcline made the first goal with a header that was blocked. Swindon's fourth win of a dismal season.											
28		A	SHEFFIELD UTD		13		D	0-0	0-0		Ogrizovic	Borrows	Morgan	Darby	Babb	Atherton	Flynn	Rennie	Quinn	Williams J	Ndlovu	
	12/2			*15,394*	*21*	35					*Tracey*	*Gage*	*Nilsen*	*Kamara*	*Tuttle*	*Gayle*	*Hodges*	*Ward**	*Scott*	*Flo*	*Whitehouse*	*Littlejohn*
										Ref: J Worrall	The press are linking Ndlovu and Babb with moves to Borussia Dortmund and Villa respectively. Quinn is recalled and misses three golden chances. John Williams nearly wins the game with a sinuous dribble and shot that Kelly just saves. With one win in eleven, Utd are in trouble.											
29		H	MANCHESTER C		11		W	**4-0**	0-0	Rennie 53, Quinn 75, Williams 87, [Ndlovu 90]	Ogrizovic	Borrows	Morgan	Darby	Babb	Atherton	Flynn	Rennie	Quinn*	Williams J	Ndlovu	Jenkinson
	19/2			11,739	*20*	38					*Coton*	*Edghill*	*Phelan*	*McMahon*	*Kernaghan*	*Vonk*	*Rocastle*	*Lomas^*	*Sheron*	*Shutt*	*Griffiths**	*Mike/Simpson*
										Ref: G Ashby	Two wins in twenty games have dragged Brian Horton's team into the relegation mire, and they look certs for the drop. Everything clicks for City with Quinn, Ndlovu and Williams all scoring their first goals of the year. David Rennie bags his first City goal and shines in midfield.											
30		A	NEWCASTLE		11		L	0-4	0-0		Ogrizovic	Borrows	Morgan	Darby	Babb*	Atherton	Flynn^	Rennie	Jenkinson	Williams J	Ndlovu	Busst/Robertson
	23/2			*32,216*	*5*	38				*Cole 49, 70, 77, Mathie 86*	*Srnicek*	*Watson*	*Elliott*	*Lee**	*Neilson*	*Appleby*	*Fox*	*Clark*	*Cole*	*Beardsley*	*Sellars^*	*Robinson/Mathie*
										Ref: R Hart	Newcastle recover from three defeats in a row to give City a thrashing after an even first half. Cole's three goals are down to defensive lapses in a game beamed back to a subdued Highfield Road. Babb's absence in the second half is significant. Mathie scores a minute after coming on.											
31		A	LIVERPOOL		11		L	0-1	0-1		Ogrizovic	Borrows	Morgan	Darby	Rennie	Atherton	Flynn*	Boland	Quinn	Williams J	Ndlovu	**Pickering**
	26/2			*38,547*	*5*	38				*Rush 2*	*James*	*Jones*	*Dicks*	*Redknapp*	*Wright*	*Ruddock*	*McManam'n*	*Whelan*	*Walters**	*Rush*	*Barnes*	*Clough*
										Ref: D Elleray	Roy Evans celebrates his first home game as Liverpool manager with an easy win, though City have chances to draw. Morgan hits the post in the last minute. The Reds miss chances when they are on top, but City fail to take advantage of their slow back four. Robson needs another op.											

No	Venue / Date	Opponent / Att	Pos	Res / Pts	F-A	H-T	Scorers, Times, and Referees	1	2	3	4	5	6	7	8	9	10	11	subs used
32	H	ASTON VILLA	12	L	0-1	0-1		Ogrizovic	Borrows	Morgan	Darby	Babb	Atherton	Flynn	Rennie	Quinn	Williams J	Ndlovu	
	6/3	14,323	*5*	38			*Daley 20*	*Bosnich*	*Barrett*	*Cox*	*Richardson*	*Ehiogu*	*Teale*	*Parker*	*Townsend*	*Saunders*	*Fenton*	*Daley*	
							Ref: K Hackett	City's bête-noire, Hackett, denies them two clear penalty claims, as they throw caution to the wind in a bid to rescue the game after a toothless first 75 minutes. Villa are in the Coca-Cola Cup final but are nothing special. Neal warns Sandy Robertson to work harder in the English game.											
33	A	LEEDS	13	L	0-1	0-0		Ogrizovic	Borrows	Morgan	Darby	Babb	Atherton	Flynn*	Boland	Quinn	Williams J^	Ndlovu	Jenkinson/Pickering
	19/3	*30,023*	*5*	38			*Wallace 54*	*Lukic*	*Kelly*	*Dorigo*	*Wetherall*	*Fairclough*	*Newsome*	*Strachan*	*McAllister*	*Deane*	*Wallace*	*Speed*	
							Ref: A Wilkie	Four games without a goal or a point means City are looking over their shoulders. Oggy is their hero again, keeping the score down in a poor performance on a dreadful pitch. City have rejected a £1.5 million Newcastle bid for Phil Babb, but financial pressure may mean he has to go.											
34	H	NORWICH	12	W	2-1	1-0	Flynn 28, Quinn 70	Ogrizovic	Borrows	Morgan	Darby	Babb	Atherton	Williams J*	Rennie	Quinn	Flynn	Ndlovu	Boland
	26/3	13,515	*9*	41			*Eadie 46*	*Gunn*	*Culverhouse*	*Bowen*	*Megson*	*Polston**	*Butterworth*	*Adams*	*Goss*	*Sutton*	*Eadie*	*Crook*	*Woodthorpe*
							Ref: D Frampton	City's midweek bid to re-sign Rosario failed, so Neal throws Flynn up front and it works. He scores the first after Gunn failed to hold Ndlovu's shot and brings the best out of the rotund Quinn. Hot prospect Eadie equalises, but Quinn defeats the draw experts after fine work by Ndlovu.											
35	H	WIMBLEDON	13	L	1-2	0-2	Ndlovu 64	Ogrizovic	Borrows	Morgan	Darby	Babb	Atherton	Williams J*	Rennie	Quinn	Flynn	Ndlovu	Jenkinson
	2/4	11,312	*8*	41			*Castledine 32, Holdsworth 40*	*Segers*	*Barton*	*Elkins*	*Castledine*	*Scales*	*Blackwell*	*Gayle*	*Earle*	*Fashanu**	*Holdsworth*	*Fear*	*Blissett*
							Ref: M Bodenham	The Crazy gang are heading for a top six finish and frighten City's defence to death. Both their goals are from corners and Dean Holdsworth's is his 19th of the season. Ndlovu's stunning run and left-footer sparks a late rally, but the Dons deserve their win. Babb wins another Eire cap.											
36	A	IPSWICH	12	W	2-0	0-0	Flynn 55, Ndlovu 66	Ogrizovic	Borrows	Morgan	Darby	Babb	Atherton	Boland	Rennie	Ndlovu	Flynn	Jenkinson	
	4/4	*12,633*	*15*	44				*Baker*	*Youds**	*Johnson*	*Stockwell*	*Linighan*	*Whelan*	*Williams*	*Mason*	*Palmer*	*Guentchev*	*Slater*	*Durrant*
							Ref: R Gifford	Quinn is unhappy at being axed but his stand-in Flynn scores a good goal and Ndlovu buries a dismal Ipswich, who have won only two in 16. It's City's first win at Portman Road in 17 visits since 1970 and increases the pressure on manager John Lyall. Wegerle has an injury setback.											
37	H	TOTTENHAM	12	W	1-0	0-0	Ndlovu 62p	Ogrizovic	Borrows*	Morgan	Pickering	Babb	Atherton	Boland	Rennie	Ndlovu	Flynn	Jenkinson	McGrath
	9/4	14,487	*18*	47				*Thorstvedt*	*Kerslake*	*Campbell**	*Samways*	*Scott*	*Mabbutt*	*Sedgley*	*Howells^*	*Anderton*	*Sheringham*	*Barmby*	*Rosenthal/Dozzell*
							Ref: M Reed	An excellent City performance, lacking only in goals. A snow storm gives a winter feel as Pickering makes his full debut, but he is replaced by McGrath making his final appearance. Scott fouls Ndlovu, who scores from the resulting penalty. The Zimbabwean hits the bar near the end.											
38	H	SHEFFIELD WED	12	D	1-1	1-1	Ndlovu 25p	Ogrizovic	Borrows	Morgan	Darby	Babb	Atherton	Boland	Rennie	Ndlovu	Flynn	Jenkinson	
	16/4	13,052	*6*	48			*Jones 43*	*Pressman*	*Nilsson^*	*Worthington*	*Palmer*	*Pearce*	*Walker*	*Jones*	*Hyde*	*Bright*	*Bart-W'ms**	*Sheridan*	*Watson/Coleman*
							Ref: R Hart	With little at stake this is a surprisingly bright game, with Ndlovu starring and winning his battle with England defender Des Walker. Nilsson concedes the penalty by fouling Ndlovu but the Owls reply with a stunning 25-yard free-kick by Ryan Jones. Woods is on loan to Shrewsbury.											
39	A	EVERTON	12	D	0-0	0-0		Ogrizovic	Borrows	Morgan	Darby	Babb	Atherton	Boland	Rennie	Ndlovu	Flynn	Jenkinson*	Pickering
	23/4	*23,352*	*18*	49				*Southall*	*Jackson*	*Hinchcliffe*	*Ebbrell*	*Watson*	*Unsworth*	*Stuart*	*Horne**	*Cottee*	*Angell*	*Limpar*	*Preki*
							Ref: R Dilkes	Neither keeper has much to do in a dour game which Everton desperately need to win to avoid relegation. City's defence, with Babb superb, is rock solid, but up front Ndlovu and Flynn are held by Watson and rookie Unsworth. Babb looks set to go and Wegerle may be fit for USA 94.											
40	H	BLACKBURN	12	W	2-1	1-1	Darby 11, 55	Ogrizovic	Borrows	Morgan	Darby	Babb	Atherton	Boland	Rennie	Ndlovu	Flynn	Jenkinson	
	2/5	16,646	*2*	52			*Le Saux 29*	*Flowers*	*May*	*Wright*	*Morrison^*	*Hendry*	*Berg*	*Atkins**	*Sherwood*	*Shearer*	*Wilcox*	*Le Saux*	*Makel/Marker*
							Ref: P Don	Blackburn's title hopes are extinguished by City in a gripping game covered by Sky TV. Darby is the hero with two well-taken goals but Ndlovu dazzles with his speed and skill and gives Morrison a torrid time. Rovers' large away following takes defeat well and applauds City.											
41	A	CHELSEA	10	W	2-1	2-1	Ndlovu 32, Morgan 34	Gould	Borrows	Morgan	Darby	Babb	Atherton	Boland	Rennie	Ndlovu	Flynn	Jenkinson	
	4/5	*8,923*	*14*	55			*Cascarino 43*	*Kharine*	*Clarke*	*Sinclair*	*Hopkin**	*Johnsen*	*Duberry*	*Burley*	*Newton*	*Cascarino*	*Fleck*	*Barnard*	*Donaghy*
							Ref: I Borrett	Ndlovu's delicious chip is another candidate for Goal of the Month and Steve Morgan's 25-yard free-kick leaves Kharine standing. Chelsea are preoccupied with their Wembley appointment next week and show little fight against a confident and pressing City, who are unbeaten in six.											
42	A	MANCHESTER U	11	D	0-0	0-0		Ogrizovic	Borrows	Morgan	Darby	Babb	Atherton	Boland	Rennie	Ndlovu	Flynn	Jenkinson	
	8/5	***44,717***	*1*	56				*Walsh*	*Neville*	*Irwin*	*Robson*	*Pallister*	*Bruce**	*McKee^*	*McClair*	*Cantona*	*Dublin*	*Sharpe*	*Parker/Keane*
	Home	Away					Ref: S Lodge	An afternoon to remember as United pick up the Premiership trophy at the end of a forgettable game played at three-quarter pace. Bryan Robson says his farewells to the United hordes and the double awaits next week at Wembley. Eric Cantona is accused by Babb of stamping.											
Average	13,352	20,809																	

Coca-Cola Cup					F-A	H-T	Scorers, Times, and Referees	SQUAD	NUMBERS	IN	USE								subs used
2:1	H	WYCOMBE	7	W	3-0	2-0	Morgan 14, 41, Quinn 66	Ogrizovic	Booty	Morgan	Rennie	Babb	Atherton	Williams J*	Boland	Quinn^	Wegerle	Ndlovu	Gayle/Williams PR
22/9		9,656	*3:6*					*Hyde*	*Cousins*	*Potter*	*Crossley*	*Evans*	*Ryan*	*Carroll*	*Langford^*	*Thompson**	*Scott*	*Guppy*	*Hayrettin/Hemmings*
							Ref: T Lunt	City look set for an easy passage after a comfortable win in their first ever game with Wycombe. Steve Morgan, a summer signing from Plymouth, scores two and Quinn ends his goal drought. Midfielder Detsi Kruszynski joins for a month and City bungle their free-ticket offer.											
2:2	A	WYCOMBE	11	L	2-4	0-1	Morgan 111, Babb 117	Ogrizovic	Flynn*	Morgan	Rennie	Babb	Atherton	Kruszynski	Boland	Gayle	Wegerle	Williams J^	Jenkinson/Busst
5/10		*5,933*	*3:4*		*aet*		*Ryan 31, Scott 63, Evans 87, Cousins 92*	*Hyde*	*Cousins*	*Crossley*	*Kerr*	*Evans*	*Ryan*	*Carroll*	*Hayrettin**	*Hemmings^*	*Scott*	*Guppy*	*Hutch'n/Moussaddik*
							Ref: J Brandwood (City win 6-5 on aggregate)	It's Wycombe's debut league season and they almost get their first big scalp after leading 4-3 on aggregate two minutes into extra-time. Gould rings the changes and Quinn is axed. City are outplayed and outfought but survive a torrid night with the two late goals saving their blushes.											
3	A	OLDHAM	13	L	0-2	0-1		Ogrizovic	Borrows	Williams PR*	McGrath	Babb	Rennie	Flynn	Boland	Ndlovu^	Wegerle !	Morgan	Gayle/Quinn
26/10		*10,071*	*20*				*Beckford 18, Sharp 62*	*Gerrard*	*Makin*	*Fleming*	*Milligan*	*Redmond*	*Halle*	*Bernard*	*Brennan*	*Sharp*	*Beckford*	*Holden*	
							Ref: K Cooper	Phil Neal is pleased with the team's performance in his first match as caretaker boss, but the wretched cup form continues. Wegerle is sent off after 25 minutes for verbal abuse of a linesman and City, with Ndlovu lacking support, never look like coming back. Latics to play Tranmere.											

FA Cup																			
3	A	NEWCASTLE	12	L	0-2	0-1		Ogrizovic	Borrows	Morgan	Darby	Babb	Atherton	Ndlovu	Flynn	Williams J	Wegerle*	Williams PR^	Quinn/Rennie
8/1		*35,444*	*5*				*Cole 21, Beardsley 76*	*Hooper*	*Elliott*	*Beresford*	*Robinson*	*Scott*	*Howie*	*Lee*	*Clark*	*Cole*	*Beardsley*	*Sellars**	*Watson*
							Ref: P Foakes	Newcastle outclass City from the first moments and should have won by a mile. Andy Cole scores his 29th goal of the season after Beardsley's shot cannoned off a post and Beardsley scores after a dazzling run from his own half. Wegerle injures knee ligaments and will be out for a time.											

		Home						Away					
		P	W	D	L	F	A	W	D	L	F	A	Pts
1	Manchester U	42	14	6	1	39	13	13	5	3	41	25	92
2	Blackburn	42	14	5	2	31	11	11	4	6	32	25	84
3	Newcastle	42	14	4	3	51	14	9	4	8	31	27	77
4	Arsenal	42	10	8	3	25	15	8	9	4	28	13	71
5	Leeds	42	13	6	2	37	18	5	10	6	28	21	70
6	Wimbledon	42	12	5	4	35	21	6	6	9	21	32	65
7	Sheffield Wed	42	10	7	4	48	24	6	9	6	28	30	64
8	Liverpool	42	12	4	5	33	23	5	5	11	26	32	60
9	QP Rangers	42	8	7	6	32	29	8	5	8	30	32	60
10	Aston Villa	42	8	5	8	23	18	7	7	7	23	32	57
11	COVENTRY	42	9	7	5	23	17	5	7	9	20	28	56
12	Norwich	42	4	9	8	26	29	8	8	5	39	32	53
13	West Ham	42	6	7	8	26	31	7	6	8	21	27	52
14	Chelsea	42	11	5	5	31	20	2	7	12	18	33	51
15	Tottenham	42	4	8	9	29	33	7	4	10	25	26	45
16	Manchester C	42	6	10	5	24	22	3	8	10	14	27	45
17	Everton	42	8	4	9	26	30	4	4	13	16	33	44
18	Southampton	42	9	2	10	30	31	3	5	13	19	35	43
19	Ipswich	42	5	8	8	21	32	4	8	9	14	26	43
20	Sheffield Utd	42	6	10	5	24	23	2	8	11	18	37	42
21	Oldham	42	5	8	8	24	33	4	5	12	18	35	40
22	Swindon	42	4	7	10	25	45	1	8	12	22	55	30
		924	192	142	128	663	532	128	142	192	532	663	1244

Odds & ends

Double wins: (3) Arsenal, Tottenham, Ipswich.
Double losses: (2) Leeds, QP Rangers.

Won from behind: (1) Newcastle.
Lost from in front: (0).

High spots: Quinn's opening day hat-trick at Highbury.
Eight-game unbeaten start - best start since 1937.
Seven game unbeaten end to season.
Ending Blackburn's title hopes.
Holding champions United at Old Trafford.
Winning the Daily Mail Fair Play league.

Low spots: Sudden departure of Gould after QPR defeat.
Defeat at Wycombe, despite going through on aggregate.
Passive defeat at Oldham in Coca-Cola Cup.

Red cards: City – Wegerle (Oldham LC a).
Red cards: Opponents – Srnicek (Newcastle h), Jones (Liverpool h).

Player of the Year: Phil Babb.
Ever-presents: (0).
Hat-tricks: (1) Mick Quinn.
Opposing hat-tricks: (2) Fjortoft (Swindon), Cole (Newcastle).
Leading scorer: (11) Peter Ndlovu.

	Appearances						Goals			
	Lge	*Sub*	LC	*Sub*	FAC	*Sub*	**Lge**	LC	FAC	**Tot**
Atherton, Peter	**39**	*1*	2		1					
Babb, Phil	**40**		3		1		**3**	1		**4**
Boland, Willie	**24**	*3*	3							
Booty, Martyn	**2**		1							
Borrows, Brian	**29**		1		1					
Busst, David	**2**	*1*		*1*						
Darby, Julian	**25**	*1*			1		**5**			**5**
Flynn, Sean	**33**	*3*	2		1		**3**			**3**
Gayle, John	**3**		1	*2*						
Gould, Jonathan	**9**									
Harford, Mick		*1*					**1**			**1**
Jenkinson, Leigh	**10**	*6*		*1*						
Kruszynski, Detsi	**1**	*1*	1							
Marsden, Chris (loan)	**5**	*2*								
McGrath, Lloyd	**10**	*1*	1							
Morgan, Steve	**39**	*1*	3		1		**2**	3		**5**
Ndlovu, Peter	**40**		2		1		**11**			**11**
Ogrizovic, Steve	**33**		3		1					
Pickering, Ally	**1**	*3*								
Quinn, Mick	**28**	*4*	1	*1*		*1*	**8**	1		**9**
Rennie, David	**34**		3			*1*	**1**			**1**
Robertson, Sandy		*3*								
Robson, Stewart	**1**									
Sheridan, Tony	**4**	*4*								
Wegerle, Roy	**20**	*1*	3		1		**6**			**6**
Williams, John	**27**	*5*	2		1		**3**			**3**
Williams, Paul R	**3**	*6*	1	*1*	1					
27 players used	**462**	***47***	**33**	***6***	**11**	***2***	**43**	**5**		**48**

No	Date		Att	Pos	Pt	F-A	H-T	Scorers, Times, and Referees	SQUAD	NUMBERS	IN	USE								subs used
1	H	WIMBLEDON			D	1-1	0-0	Busst 70	Ogrizovic	Borrows	Morgan	Darby	Busst	Babb	Boland^	Rennie	Quinn	Flynn	Jenkinson*	**Cook**/Wegerle
	20/8		11,005		1			*Castledine 55*	*Segers*	*Barton*	*Elkins*	*Jones*	*Scales*	*Fitzgerald*	*Gayle*	*Castledine*	*Harford^*	*Holdsworth*	*Talboys**	*Ardley/Blissett*
								Ref: R Gifford	The East stand is open, Atherton has gone to Sheff Wed for a cut-price £800,000 and Harford returns as a Wimbledon player. It is hyped as the start of City's new era but the Dons are the wrong team to start any era with and a small crowd are restless. Busst saves it with a diving header.											
2	A	NEWCASTLE			L	0-4	0-3		Ogrizovic	Borrows	Morgan	Darby	Busst	Rennie	Flynn*	Cook	Quinn	Wegerle	Jenkinson^	Pickering/Boland
	24/8		*34,163*		1			*Lee 21, 34, Watson 26, Cole 73*	*Srnicek*	*Hottiger*	*Beresford*	*Venison*	*Peacock*	*Albert*	*Lee*	*Watson^*	*Cole*	*Fox*	*Sellars**	*Elliott/Mathie*
								Ref: P Danson	Babb has a hamstring injury. City fans glimpse what life might be without him, and it's frightening. Newcastle, even without Beardsley, romp home as City's defence has an off day. US World Cup star Cobi Jones awaits his work permit and Gary Gillespie re-joins on a month's loan.											
3	A	BLACKBURN		20	L	0-4	0-0		Ogrizovic	Borrows	Morgan	Darby	Busst	Babb	Flynn*	Rennie	Quinn !	Wegerle	Cook	Williams J
	27/8		*21,657*	*2*	1			*Sutton 67, 74, 88, Wilcox 77*	*Flowers*	*Warhurst*	*Le Saux*	*Slater*	*Hendry*	*Gale**	*Ripley^*	*Sherwood*	*Shearer*	*Sutton*	*Wilcox*	*Pearce/Atkins*
								Ref: G Poll	Mick Quinn's red card in the 65th minute for swearing at the ref precipitates a City collapse. Despite Babb's marking job on Alan Shearer, £5 million striker Chris Sutton hits a hat-trick. For an hour City match Rovers in an entertaining match. New signing Paul Cook hits the crossbar.											
4	H	ASTON VILLA		22	L	0-1	0-1		Ogrizovic	Borrows	Morgan	Darby	Busst	Babb	Boland	Rennie*	Flynn	Wegerle	Cook	Williams J
	29/8		12,218	*9*	1			*Yorke 3*	*Bosnich*	*Barrett*	*King*	*Richardson*	*Ehiogu*	*McGrath*	*Yorke*	*Townsend*	*Fashanu*	*Saunders*	*Staunton*	
								Ref: P Durkin	This defeat makes it the worst City start for 70 years and they are bottom for the first time in 20 years. A poor game is decided by an early error by Rennie who can do little right. Babb will sign for Liverpool and City are linked to Joachim Bjorklund, Liam Daish and Dean Richards.											
5	A	QP RANGERS		20	D	2-2	1-2	Cook 27, Dublin 84	Ogrizovic	Pickering	Morgan	Rennie	Busst	Darby	Flynn	Cook*	**Dublin**	Wegerle	Jenkinson^	Boland/Williams J
	10/9		*11,398*	*13*	2			*Penrice 35, 37*	*Roberts*	*Bardsley*	*Brevett*	*Barker*	*McDonald*	*Yates*	*Impey*	*Holloway*	*Ferdinand*	*Penrice**	*Sinclair*	*Gallen*
								Ref: J Worrall	Desperate City win a hard-earned point with a late header from new £2 million signing Dion Dublin. Les Ferdinand is on top of his game and could have bagged a hat-trick, but Penrice again scores two against City. A defender to replace Babb is essential and Phil Neal scours Europe.											
6	H	LEEDS		18	W	2-1	0-0	Dublin 50, Cook 83p	Ogrizovic	Pickering	Morgan	Boland	Busst	Rennie	**Jones**	Darby	Dublin	Flynn	Cook	
	17/9		15,383	*6*	5			*Speed 85*	*Lukic*	*Kelly*	*Worthington*	*McAllister*	*Wetherall**	*Palmer*	*Strachan*	*Whelan*	*Wallace*	*Masinga^*	*Speed*	*Fairclough/Pemb'rt'n*
								Ref: B Hill	Cobi Jones finally makes his debut and earns the penalty when his mazy run is ended by Chris Fairclough's trip. Dublin celebrates being made skipper with a glancing header and City notch their first win. Leeds are fresh from defeating Man United, but don't match City for passion.											
7	H	SOUTHAMPTON		19	L	1-3	1-1	Dublin 2	Ogrizovic	Pickering	Morgan	Boland^	Busst	Rennie*	Jones	Darby	Dublin	Flynn	Cook	Gillespie/Wegerle
	24/9		11,798	*13*	5			*Dowie 19, 55, Ekelund 82*	*Grobbelaar*	*Kenna*	*Charlton*	*Magilton*	*Monkou*	*Charlton*	*Le Tissier*	*Maddison*	*Dowie*	*Ekelund*	*Allen*	
								Ref: K Morton	Ndlovu's knee op is taking time to heal and he hasn't played all season. The new star, Dublin, chips Grobbelaar for a goal that will later feature in Bruce's match-rigging case. Saints are in charge and City are undone by the magic of Le Tissier and the speed of Danish debutant Ekelund.											
8	A	LEICESTER		21	D	2-2	1-1	Wegerle 11, Dublin 73	Ogrizovic	Pickering	Morgan	Darby	Busst	Gillespie !	Flynn	Cook	Dublin	Wegerle*	Jones	Borrows
	3/10		*19,372*		6			*Roberts 45, 85*	*Poole*	*Grayson*	*Lewis**	*Draper*	*Willis !*	*Mohan*	*Carr*	*Blake*	*Joachim*	*Roberts*	*Philpot*	*Smith*
								Ref: K Cooper	Sky TV cover an all-action derby and see Gillespie, in his first full game for 11 years, and Willis sent off for innocuous first-half offences. Leicester come back twice. Neal and Leicester boss Little are fuming, but Neal is also unhappy at Leicester's late goal which looked offside.											
9	H	IPSWICH		17	W	2-0	1-0	Wark 45 (og), Cook 75p	Ogrizovic	Pickering	Morgan	Darby	Busst	Rennie	Flynn	Cook	Dublin	Wegerle	Jones*	Ndlovu
	10/10		**9,509**		9				*Forrest*	*Yallop*	*Johnson*	*Sedgley*	*Wark*	*Linighan*	*Williams*	*Slater**	*Palmer*	*Kiwomya*	*Thomsen*	*Cotterell*
								Ref: R Hart	Sky TV cameras are present again but it's far from compulsive viewing. City are good value against a woeful Ipswich. Veteran Wark scores a spectacular header to stop a cross reaching Dublin and Cook wraps it up after Wegerle is fouled by Linighan. Forrest keeps the score down.											
10	A	EVERTON		14	W	2-0	2-0	Dublin 8, Wegerle 17	Ogrizovic	Pickering	Morgan	Darby	Busst	Rennie	Flynn	Cook	Dublin	Wegerle	Jones	
	15/10		*28,219*	*22*	12				*Southall*	*Jackson*	*Burrows*	*Parkinson**	*Unsworth*	*Ablett*	*Samways*	*Horne*	*Ferguson*	*Amokachi*	*Durrant*	*Stuart*
								Ref: D Elleray	Everton haven't won a game and Mike Walker's tenure looks slim. Dublin, whom the Everton board rejected a year ago, resulting in Kendall's resignation, scores the inevitable goal. The Toffees much-vaunted strikeforce of Ferguson and Amokachi are contained by Busst and Rennie.											

No	Venue	Opponent / Att	Pos	Res / Pts	F-A	H-T	Scorers, Times, and Referees	1	2	3	4	5	6	7	8	9	10	11	subs used
11	A	ARSENAL	15	L	1-2	0-2	Wegerle 81p	Ogrizovic	Pickering	Morgan^	Darby	Busst	**Pressley**	Flynn	Rennie	Dublin	Wegerle	Jones*	Ndlovu/Borrows
23/10		*31,725*	*9*	12			*Wright 13, 32*	*Seaman*	*Dixon*	*Winterburn*	*Parlour*	*Bould*	*Keown*	*Selley*	*Campbell*	*Wright**	*Smith*	*Schwarz*	*McGoldrick*
							Ref: A Wilkie	Steven Pressley, a £630,000 signing from Rangers, has a nightmare. He is booked and hands Ian Wright a goal on a plate. The Arsenal striker limps off at half-time after scoring twice to break a club record of scoring in ten games in a row. Winterburn blocks Dublin for the penalty.											
12	H	MANCHESTER C	13	W	1-0	0-0	Dublin 86	Ogrizovic	Pickering	Borrows	Darby	Busst	Rennie	Flynn	Cook	Dublin	Wegerle	Ndlovu	
29/10		15,802	*9*	15				*Tracey*	*Hill*	*Phelan*	*Lomas*	*Vonk*	*Brightwell I*	*Summerbee*	*Flitcroft*	*Quinn*	*Walsh*	*Beagrie*	
							Ref: M Bodenham	Man City, with nine goals in two games, play like the home side and pin Coventry back for long periods. They defend well and snatch a late victory when Ndlovu beats his man and Dublin slots home the cross. Stewart Robson has one final operation to attempt to solve his injury jinx.											
13	H	CRYS PALACE	14	L	1-4	1-2	Dublin 23	Ogrizovic	Pickering*	Borrows	Darby	Busst	Rennie	Flynn^	Boland	Dublin	Wegerle	Ndlovu	Morgan/Jones
2/11		10,729	*11*	15			*Preece 18, 49, Salako 20, Newman 80*	*Martyn*	*Patterson*	*Gordon*	*Southgate*	*Coleman*	*Shaw*	*Humphrey*	*Newman*	*Armstrong*	*Preece*	*Salako*	
							Ref: P Jones	Newly promoted Palace slaughter City with a slick performance. Salako is the architect, scoring with a header and crossing for two more goals. Poor old Pickering is eventually withdrawn to avoid more embarrassment. It's the worst display of the season and City's progress is halted.											
14	A	CHELSEA	15	D	2-2	1-0	Dublin 45, Ndlovu 77	Ogrizovic	Borrows	Morgan	Darby	Busst	Pressley	Jones	Cook	Dublin	Wegerle	Ndlovu	
6/11		*17,090*	*8*	16			*Spencer 46, Kjeldbjerg 69*	*Hitchcock*	*Barness*	*Myers*	*Spackman*	*Johnsen*	*Kjeldbjerg*	*Rocastle**	*Hopkin*	*Shipperley*	*Spencer*	*Newton*	*Burley*
							Ref: S Lodge	A confident City respond to Neal's harsh words after the Palace defeat and are unlucky not to win all three points. Spencer's goal deflects off Borrows and City finish the stronger with Dublin hitting the bar and Darby going close. John Williams is sent off whilst on loan to Notts Co.											
15	H	NORWICH	13	W	1-0	0-0	Jones 62	Ogrizovic	Borrows	Morgan	Darby	Busst	Pressley	Jones	Cook	Dublin	Flynn	Ndlovu	
19/11		11,891	*9*	19				*Gunn*	*Polston*	*Bowen*	*Crook*	*Newsome*	*Prior*	*Eadie*	*Milligan*	*Robins^*	*Newman*	*Adams**	*Sutch/Goss*
							Ref: G Willard	Cobi Jones scores his first goal to clinch a deserved win against the draw specialists. A poor first hour is followed by an exciting finale, despite the absence of the injured Wegerle. Mick Quinn has gone on loan to Plymouth and Ndlovu has become the club's most capped international.											
16	A	WEST HAM	10	W	1-0	0-0	Busst 58	Ogrizovic	Borrows	Morgan	Darby	Busst	Pressley	Jones	Cook	Dublin*	Flynn	Ndlovu	Jenkinson
26/11		*17,251*	*17*	22				*Miklosko*	*Brown*	*Dicks*	*Bishop**	*Whitbread*	*Potts*	*Moncur*	*Marsh*	*Cottee*	*Morley*	*Holmes*	*Rush*
							Ref: M Reed	Traffic problems cause City to arrive late and delay the kick-off. City win well, defending solidly and breaking fast. Busst, for some reason up in attack, heads home Jones' cross to clinch it. Cottee, the man who could never stop scoring against City, has a header well saved by Oggy.											
17	H	LIVERPOOL	10	D	1-1	0-1	Flynn 58	Ogrizovic	Borrows	Morgan	Darby	Busst*	Pressley	Jones	Cook	Flynn	Ndlovu	Jenkinson	Pickering
3/12		21,032	*4*	23			*Rush 2*	*James*	*Bjornebye**	*Harkness*	*Scales*	*Ruddock*	*Babb*	*McManam'n*	*Redknapp*	*Rush*	*Fowler*	*Thomas*	*Walters*
							Ref: K Burge	With Wegerle and Dublin injured it's a makeshift attack but Flynn earns his corn with a headed goal. Liverpool had threatened to submerge City in the first half but Neal's half-time words sparked a revival which almost won the game. Phil Babb gets a muted reception on his return.											
18	A	WIMBLEDON	12	L	0-2	0-2		Ogrizovic	Borrows	Morgan	Darby	Busst	Pressley	Jones	Cook	Flynn	Wegerle*	Ndlovu	Williams J
10/12		*7,349*	*16*	23			*Leonhardsen 4, Harford 17*	*Segers*	*Cunningham*	*Kimble*	*Barton*	*Thorn*	*Fitzgerald*	*Ekoku*	*Leonhardsen*	*Harford**	*Holdsworth^*	*Elkins*	*Clarke/Goodman*
							Ref: R Dilkes	A ragged team performance on Oggy's 400th league appearance is punished by a Harford-inspired Dons. He flicks on for Leonhardsen and then beats Oggy with a low shot. City never threaten and even Cook's weak penalty, for a foul on Ndlovu, is saved by Segers. Dion is missed.											
19	H	NEWCASTLE	12	D	0-0	0-0		Ogrizovic	Borrows	Morgan	Darby	Busst	Pressley	Jones	Cook	Flynn	Wegerle*	Ndlovu	Boland
17/12		17,237	*3*	24				*Srnicek*	*Hottiger*	*Beresford*	*Venison*	*Howey*	*Peacock*	*Fox*	*Watson*	*Cole*	*Beardsley**	*Kitson*	*Clark*
							Ref: P Danson	Newcastle have gone off the boil after their excellent start to the season but they still look title candidates. Oggy keeps City in the game with three great saves and a penalty save from the disappointing Cole, after a Pressley foul eight minutes from time. Mike Marsh is on wanted list.											
20	H	NOTT'M FOREST	12	D	0-0	0-0		Ogrizovic	Borrows	Morgan	Darby	Busst*	Pressley	Jones	Cook	Flynn	Wegerle^	Ndlovu	Pickering/Quinn
26/12		19,116	*5*	25				*Crossley*	*Lyttle*	*Pearce*	*Stone*	*Chettle*	*Cooper*	*Phillips**	*Gemmill^*	*Collymore*	*Bohinen*	*Woan*	*Haaland/McGregor*
							Ref: A Wilkie	Forest are fresh from ending Man United's long unbeaten home run but are held in a mediocre game of few chances. Pearce blasts over a 20th-minute penalty after Morgan fouls the tricky Bohinen. Captain Borrows is City's star, moving to centre-half when Busst limps off early on.											
21	A	SHEFFIELD WED	16	L	**1-5**	1-3	Ndlovu 17p *[Whittingham 57, 64]*	Ogrizovic	Borrows*	Morgan	Darby	Gillespie	Pressley	Jones	Cook	Flynn	Wegerle	Ndlovu^	Pickering/Quinn
28/12		*26,056*	*13*	25			*Bright 14, 45, Waddle 38,*	*Pressman*	*Atherton*	*Nolan*	*Bart-Will'ms*	*Pearce*	*Walker*	*Sheridan*	*Hyde*	*Bright^*	*Whittingham*	*Ingesson**	*Waddle/Watson*
							Ref: K Morton	Wednesday are rampant against a woeful Coventry whose injury list grows longer and even Oggy has an off day. Ndlovu scores when Pressman brings down Flynn but Cook misses from the spot after Quinn is fouled by Walker. Quinn fires the rebound wide. Dublin is sorely missed.											

No	Date		Att	Pos	Pt	F-A	H-T	Scorers, Times, and Referees	SQUAD	NUMBERS	IN	USE								subs used
22	H	TOTTENHAM		17	L	0-4	0-1	*[Sheringham 81]*	Ogrizovic	Pickering	Borrows	**Marsh**	Morgan	Darby	Jones	Cook^	Flynn	Wegerle*	Williams PR	Quinn/**Hall**
	31/12		19,965	*6*	25			*Darby 7 (og), Barmby 67, Anderton 77,*	*Walker*	*Austin*	*Campbell*	*Popescu**	*Calderwood*	*Mabbutt*	*Anderton*	*Barmby^*	*Klinsmann*	*Sheringham*	*Howells*	*Rosenthal/Neth'cott*
								Ref: G Ashby	Gerry Francis has taken over from Ardiles and transformed Spurs' team of all-stars. They are unbeaten in eight and demolish City's makeshift and fragile defence. Marsh, signed yesterday from West Ham for £450,000, can do little to thwart Klinsmann, Anderton and Sheringham.											
23	A	MANCHESTER U		17	L	0-2	0-1		Ogrizovic	Pickering	Williams PR	Marsh	Morgan	Pressley !	Flynn^	Cook	Dublin	Wegerle*	Jenkinson	Darby/Jones
	3/1		**43,130**	*2*	25			*Scholes 29, Cantona 49p*	*Walsh*	*Neville G*	*Irwin*	*Keane**	*Pallister*	*Bruce*	*Gillespie*	*Butt*	*Cantona*	*Scholes*	*Giggs*	*McClair*
								Ref: G Willard	Dion returns to a stirring reception from the Old Trafford faithful and brightens City's play. The title contenders are hard to stop. Scholes and Cantona are United's matchmakers, Cantona from a penalty after Pressley fouls Scholes and gets red carded. This was the Sky TV fixture.											
24	A	MANCHESTER C		17	D	0-0	0-0		Ogrizovic	Borrows	Williams PR	Darby	Morgan	Pressley	Flynn	Marsh	Dublin	Ndlovu	Jenkinson	
	14/1		*20,632*	*11*	26				*Dibble*	*Summerbee*	*Phelan*	*Brightwell D**	*Curle*	*Kernaghan*	*Gaudino*	*Flitcroft*	*Rosler*	*Walsh*	*Beagrie*	*Simpson*
								Ref: D Gallagher	Eight games without a goal from open play is why City are sliding towards the relegation zone and they rarely look like ending the run here. They do have two good penalty appeals turned down and deserve the point. The fickle Maine Road fans are calling for Brian Horton's head.											
25	H	ARSENAL		19	L	0-1	0-0		Ogrizovic	Pickering	Williams PR	Darby*	Borrows	Rennie	Marsh	Cook	Dublin	Wegerle	Jenkinson	Jones
	21/1		14,557	*11*	26			*Hartson 78*	*Seaman*	*Dixon*	*Morrow*	*Keown*	*Bould*	*Linighan*	*Hillier**	*Campbell*	*Wright^*	*Hartson*	*Schwarz*	*Parlour/Kiwomya*
								Ref: J Worrall	Arsenal are a club in disarray after bung allegations against manager Graham and a cup defeat at home to Millwall, but they leave Highfield Road with a win and City in trouble. Hartson's deflected goal, in only his second game for the Gunners, makes it nine games without a win.											
26	A	NORWICH		19	D	2-2	1-1	Dublin 22, Jenkinson 76	Ogrizovic	Pickering	Williams PR	Darby*	Borrows	Rennie	Marsh	Cook	Dublin	Ndlovu	Jenkinson	Wegerle
	25/1		*14,024*	*9*	27			*Adams 32p, Ward 55*	*Tracey*	*Prior*	*Bowen*	*Adams*	*Newsome*	*Polston*	*Sutch**	*Newman*	*Ward*	*Sheron*	*Milligan*	*Eadie*
								Ref: P Don	Jenkinson's first City goal gives them a deserved equaliser after two soft goals are conceded. The ball strikes Cook's arm for the penalty and Rennie's missed header lets in Ward. On-loan Tracey plays his only Norwich league game. The clubs will meet again in the Cup on Saturday.											
27	H	CHELSEA		20	D	2-2	2-2	Flynn 26, Burley 36 (og)	Ogrizovic	Pickering	Morgan	Marsh	Borrows	Pressley	Flynn	Rennie	Dublin	Ndlovu	Jenkinson*	Wegerle
	4/2		13,423	*12*	28			*Stein 14, Spencer 33p*	*Kharine*	*Clarke**	*Minto*	*Spackman*	*Johnsen*	*Sinclair*	*Burley*	*Peacock*	*Stein^*	*Spencer*	*Wise*	*Rocastle/Furlong*
								Ref: R Hart	Eleven games without a win and City are in the four-team drop zone. Oggy drops Minto's shot for Stein to score and Pressley gives away yet another penalty when fouling Clarke. Before he limps off, Leigh Jenkinson's crosses are headed past the dodgy Kharine by Flynn and Burley.											
28	A	CRYS PALACE		17	W	2-0	0-0	Jones 75, Dublin 85	Ogrizovic	Pickering	Morgan	Marsh	Borrows	Pressley	Flynn*	Rennie	Dublin	Jones	Ndlovu	Darby
	11/2		*11,871*	*18*	31				*Martyn*	*Patterson*	*Gordon*	*Southgate*	*Coleman*	*Shaw*	*Bowry**	*Pitcher*	*Dowie*	*Ndah*	*Salako*	*Preece*
								Ref: M Bodenham	City's first win in twelve can't stop Phil Neal from getting the sack and Big Ron takes over. It's a dreadful game in driving rain and City soak up the pressure before Jones and Dublin snatch late goals. What happened to the Palace side which easily won at Highfield Road in November?											
29	H	WEST HAM		14	W	2-0	1-0	Ndlovu 25, Marsh 67	Ogrizovic	Pickering	Morgan	**Richardson**	Borrows	Rennie	Flynn	Cook	Dublin	Marsh	Ndlovu	
	18/2		17,563	*20*	34				*Miklosko*	*Breacker*	*Dicks*	*Allen*	*Martin**	*Potts*	*Moncur*	*Williamson*	*Cottee*	*Hutchison*	*Holmes^*	*Rieper/Boere*
								Ref: R Dilkes	Atkinson's arrival adds 5,000 to the gate and he gets a standing ovation. £300,000 new signing Kevin Richardson is an instant success and two excellent goals round off a memorable day. West Ham have more possession but lack a cutting edge. Mark Hateley is tipped to be Ron's No.2.											
30	H	LEICESTER		12	W	**4-2**	2-0	Flynn 18, 76, Marsh 27, Ndlovu 87	Ogrizovic	Pickering	Morgan	Richardson	Borrows	Rennie	Flynn	Cook	Dublin	Marsh	Ndlovu	
	25/2		20,650	*22*	37			*Lowe 64, Roberts 74*	*Poole*	*Grayson*	*Lewis*	*Galloway*	*Willis*	*Hill*	*Parker*	*Draper*	*Robins*	*Roberts*	*Lowe*	
								Ref: R Gifford	A rip-roaring derby. City stroll into a two-goal lead with constructive and incisive football, but Leicester force their way back into the game with a determined second-half display. Two late goals finish off the visitors' resistance. Three City wins in a row, and Leicester going down.											
31	A	SOUTHAMPTON		12	D	0-0	0-0		Gould	Pickering	**Burrows**	Richardson	Borrows	Rennie	Flynn	Cook	Dublin	Marsh	Ndlovu	
	4/3		*14,505*	*18*	38				*Grobbelaar*	*Kenna*	*Benali*	*Dodd*	*Monkou*	*Hall*	*Le Tissier*	*Magilton*	*Shipperley*	*Maddison*	*Heaney**	*Maskell*
								Ref: K Morton	Jonathan Gould is the hero in only his second game since his father left the club eighteen months ago. He makes several outstanding saves to deny the Saints and keep them in the relegation zone; it's their 14th draw. £1 million signing from Everton, David Burrows, has a quiet debut.											

No	Venue	Opponent	Att	Pos	Res/Pts	F-A	H-T	Scorers, Times, Referees	1	2	3	4	5	6	7	8	9	10	11	Subs used
32	A	ASTON VILLA		12	D	0-0	0-0		Gould	Pickering	Burrows	Richardson	Borrows	Rennie	Flynn	Boland	Dublin	Ndlovu	Cook	
	6/3		*26,186*	*11*	39				*Bosnich*	*Charles*	*Staunton*	*Teale*	*Ehiogu*	*McGrath*	*Yorke*	*Houghton^*	*Saunders*	*Johnson**	*Taylor*	*Fenton/Carr*
								Ref: G Poll	Big Ron gets a tumultuous reception from the Villa fans but the game doesn't live up to the hype. Villa force the pace, especially after half-time, but lack the cutting edge against City's solid defence. Paul McGrath is awesome and Ndlovu, as usual, gets little change out of him.											
33	H	BLACKBURN		12	D	1-1	1-0	Dublin 30	Gould	Pickering	Burrows	Richardson	Borrows	Rennie	Flynn	Boland	Dublin	Marsh*	Ndlovu	Pressley
	11/3		18,556	*1*	40			*Shearer 87*	*Flowers*	*Pearce*	*Le Saux*	*Atkins**	*Hendry*	*Berg*	*Ripley*	*Sherwood*	*Shearer*	*Sutton^*	*Warhurst*	*Slater/Newell*
								Ref: T Holbrook	The Premiership leaders grab a late equaliser when Shearer beats Gould in the air and heads home Le Saux's cross. City dominate the first half with Marsh and Richardson in great form. Dalglish's Rovers, with a narrow lead over Man U, turn to the long ball game and get their reward.											
34	A	LIVERPOOL		9	W	3-2	2-0	Ndlovu 20, 35p, 85	Gould	Pickering	Burrows	Richardson	Borrows	Rennie	Boland	Cook	Dublin	Marsh	Ndlovu	
	14/3		*27,183*	*4*	43			*Molby 76p, Burrows 90 (og)*	*James*	*Jones*	*Bjornebye**	*Thomas*	*Ruddock*	*Scales*	*McManam'n*	*Redknapp*	*Rush*	*Fowler*	*Molby*	*Walters*
								Ref: M Reed	Ndlovu finally realises all his potential with a superb hat-trick to stun the Kop. It's the first by a visiting player since Allcock of Norwich in 1962 and Peter's first ever. One is a penalty, as James clips Marsh's heels. Pool are Coca-Cola finalists and have lost only twice in 25 games.											
35	A	LEEDS		10	L	0-3	0-1		Gould	Pickering	Burrows*	Richardson	Borrows	Rennie	Boland^	Cook	Flynn	Marsh	Ndlovu	Morgan/Williams J
	18/3		*29,179*	*6*	43			*Yeboah 39, Gould 50 (og), Wallace 56*	*Lukic*	*Kelly*	*Dorigo*	*McAllister*	*Radebe**	*Palmer*	*Tinkler*	*Wallace*	*Yeboah*	*Deane*	*Speed*	*Couzens*
								Ref: R Hart	The nine-game run ends with a below-par display and Leeds are easy winners on Big Ron's birthday. Yeboah is hot and scores his sixth in six games. Gould boobs and palms in Kelly's cross. Mick Quinn is loaned to Watford and John Filan is signed from Cambridge for £200,000.											
36	H	QP RANGERS		12	L	0-1	0-0		Ogrizovic	Pickering	Burrows	Richardson	Pressley	Rennie	Flynn*	Cook	Dublin	Marsh	Ndlovu	Robertson
	1/4		15,751	*9*	43			*Sinclair 85*	*Roberts*	*Brevett*	*Wilson*	*Barker*	*McDonald*	*Ready*	*Impey*	*Holloway!*	*Dichio*	*Gallen*	*Sinclair*	
								Ref: P Danson	Strachan has been appointed as Ron's No.2 and more performances like this will see him playing. The honeymoon is over and City are awful. QPR are down to 10 men from the 21st minute when Holloway is sent off for two yellow cards. They win the game with Sinclair's great shot.											
37	H	SHEFFIELD WED		12	W	2-0	1-0	Dublin 3, Ndlovu 88	Ogrizovic	Pickering	Burrows	Richardson	Borrows	Pressley	**Strachan^**	Cook	Dublin	Wegerle*	Ndlovu	Williams J/Hall
	15/4		15,753	*11*	46				*Woods*	*Atherton*	*Nolan*	*Petrescu**	*Pearce*	*Walker*	*Sheridan*	*Hyde*	*Hirst*	*Whittingham*	*Ingesson^*	*Waddle/Bart-W'ms*
								Ref: G Willard	The bottom of the table is squeezing up with seven points separating eleven clubs and this nervous victory is vital. Strachan adds stability but tires and City cling onto the lead that Dublin's power-header had given them. At the death Ndlovu produces a great run and finish to clinch it.											
38	A	NOTT'M FOREST		15	L	0-2	0-2		Ogrizovic	Pickering	Burrows	Richardson	Borrows	Pressley	Marsh^	Cook*	Dublin	Williams J	Ndlovu	Hall/Wegerle
	17/4		*26,253*	*3*	46			*Woan 9, Collymore 42*	*Crossley*	*Lyttle*	*Pearce*	*Stone*	*Chettle*	*Cooper*	*Phillips*	*Bohinen*	*Collymore*	*Roy**	*Woan^*	*Lee/McGregor*
								Ref: P Durkin	Forest have the game won by half-time against an out-of-touch City, who only start performing after the break. Collymore and Brian Roy are devastating and cause City lots of problems including the second goal headed home by Collymore. Burrows is booked and will miss one game.											
39	H	MANCHESTER U		15	L	2-3	1-1	Ndlovu 39, Pressley 72	Gould	Borrows	Hall	Richardson	Pressley	Rennie	Strachan	Cook	Dublin	Wegerle	Ndlovu	
	1/5		**21,858**	*2*	46			*Scholes 32, Cole 55, 79*	*Schmeichel*	*Neville G*	*Irwin*	*McClair*	*Pallister*	*May*	*Butt*	*Scholes**	*Hughes*	*Cole*	*Sharpe*	*Beckham*
								Ref: P Don	United start the game eight points behind leaders Blackburn with two games in hand. They are lucky to beat the gallant Sky Blues. City twice come from behind only to lose a game of stunning intensity when Richardson's mistake lets in Cole to score. Ndlovu scores with a cheeky flick											
40	A	IPSWICH		18	L	0-2	0-0		Gould	Borrows	Burrows	Richardson	Pressley*	Rennie	Strachan	Hall	Dublin	Ndlovu	Cook	Jones
	6/5		*12,893*	*22*	46			*Marshall 52, Pressley 62 (og)*	*Wright*	*Stockwell*	*Yallop*	*Mason*	*Wark*	*Linighan^*	*Williams*	*Tanner**	*Marshall*	*Mathie*	*Thomsen*	*Norfolk/Chapman*
								Ref: M Reed	Ipswich are already relegated and have lost 12 of their last 14 games, but they have more to offer than a woeful City who are back in deep trouble. Oggy has broken a leg in a friendly but Gould's confidence is fragile. He boobs for the first. Pressley and he screw up for the second.											
41	A	TOTTENHAM		15	W	3-1	1-0	Ndlovu 32, 62p, Dublin 67	**Filan**	Pickering	Burrows	Richardson	Borrows	Rennie	Strachan	Darby	Dublin	Wegerle*	Ndlovu	Jones
	9/5		*24,124*	*7*	49			*Anderton 83*	*Walker*	*Campbell**	*Edinburgh*	*Howells*	*Calderwood*	*Mabbutt*	*Anderton*	*Barmby*	*Klinsmann*	*Sheringham*	*McMahon*	*Nethercott*
								Ref: A Wilkie	Strachan and Ndlovu are the stars of a stunning victory which guarantees safety and steals the glory from Jurgen Klinnsman's White Hart Lane farewell. Ndlovu heads in Strachan's cross. Strachan is felled by Edinburgh and Ndlovu scores from the spot. Strachan sets up Dublin's hook.											
42	H	EVERTON		16	D	0-0	0-0		Filan	Pickering	Burrows	Richardson	Borrows	Rennie	Strachan	Darby	Dublin	Ndlovu	Jenkinson	
	14/5		21,787	*15*	50				*Southall*	*Barrett*	*Ablett*	*Parkinson*	*Jackson*	*Unsworth*	*Samways**	*Ebbrell*	*Stuart*	*Amokachi*	*Limpar*	*Ferguson*
	Home		Away					Ref: P Jones	With both sides safe, the game has an end-of-term feel but the ground is full. Many chances are created, notably Limpar's bar-shuddering drive and Southall's wonder save from Peter Ndlovu. The Zimbabwean finishes the season on a high note, with a fascinating duel with Earl Barrett.											
Average	15,980		22,107																	

Coca-Cola Cup					F-A	H-T	Scorers, Times, and Referees	SQUAD	NUMBERS	IN	USE								subs used
2:1	A	WREXHAM	18	W	2-1	1-1	Darby 37, Flynn 77	Ogrizovic	Pickering	Morgan	Boland	Busst	Rennie	Jones	Darby	Dublin	Flynn	Cook	
20/9		5,286	2:8				*Jones 43*	*Marriott*	*Jones*	*Hardy*	*Brammer*	*Humes*	*Hunter*	*Bennett*	*Owen*	*Connolly*	*Watkin*	*Durkan*	
							Ref: E Lomas	Wrexham have lost only once this season and give City a run for their money on a wet night. The early home pressure is soaked up and the outstanding Julian Darby hits them on the break. Despite a quick equaliser, Wrexham fade and Flynn heads the winner from Pickering's cross.											
2:2	H	WREXHAM	21	W	3-2	1-0	Dublin 17, 59, Wegerle 63	Ogrizovic	Pickering	Morgan	Darby	Busst	Gillespie	Flynn	Cook !	Dublin	Wegerle	Jones	
5/10		8,615	*1:13*				*Cross 49, Bennett 73p*	*Marriott*	*Jones*	*Hardy*	*Hughes**	*Hunter*	*Pejic*	*Bennett*	*Owen*	*Connolly*	*Cross*	*Durkan*	*Watkin*
							Ref: K Burge (City win 5-3 on aggregate)	Wrexham refuse to lie down in an entertaining tie and have thrown everyone forward when Roy Wegerle nets. After umpteen corners a header hits Cook on the arm, the Robins get a penalty and Paul Cook gets an unlucky red card. Dublin makes it six goals in six games since his move.											
3	A	BLACKBURN	15	L	0-2	0-0		Ogrizovic	Pickering	Borrows	Darby	Busst	Rennie	Flynn*	Cook	Dublin	Wegerle	Ndlovu	Jones
26/10		*14,538*	*4*				*Shearer 55, 63*	*Flowers*	*Berg*	*Le Saux*	*Warhurst*	*Hendry*	*Gale*	*Ripley*	*Atkins*	*Shearer*	*Sutton*	*Wilcox*	
							Ref: D Gallagher	It is four years since City went beyond Round 3 in this competition. After an even first half Shearer wrecks this season's dreams. Ndlovu gets his first start of the season and Wegerle is in devastating form. Gale blatantly fouls Dublin but ref Gallagher turns down the penalty appeals.											

FA Cup																			
3	H	WEST BROM	17	D	1-1	0-0	Wegerle 52p	Ogrizovic	Borrows	Williams PR	Marsh	Morgan	Pressley	Flynn	Cook	Dublin	Wegerle*	Jenkinson	Darby
7/1		16,563	*1:17*				*Ashcroft 85p*	*Naylor*	*Parsley*	*Edwards*	*Bradley*	*Mardon*	*Raven*	*Donovan*	*Ashcroft*	*Rees**	*Hunt*	*Hamilton*	*Smith*
							Ref: P Durkin	4,000 Albion fans make this sound like a home game and their side earn a deserved replay with Ashcroft's late penalty. Pressley is the villain again, the third penalty he has conceded in three weeks and his seventh booking in eleven games. Dublin is hauled down for City's penalty.											
3R	A	WEST BROM	17	W	2-1	0-0	Dublin 82, Ndlovu 84	Ogrizovic	Borrows	Williams PR	Darby	Morgan	Rennie	Marsh	Cook !	Dublin	Ndlovu	Jenkinson*	Wegerle
18/1		*23,230*	*1:16*				*Raven 49*	*Naylor*	*O'Regan*	*Edwards*	*Bradley !*	*Mardon*	*Raven**	*Donovan*	*Ashcroft*	*Rees^*	*Hunt*	*Hamilton*	*Smith/Taylor*
							Ref: P Durkin	It looks bleak for City as Cook is sent off after 15 minutes for foul language, but they hold on for half an hour. Four minutes after Raven's goal Bradley is sent off and City seize their chance. Dublin's glorious looping header and Ndlovu's goal of the month settle this enthralling replay.											
4	H	NORWICH	19	D	0-0	0-0		Ogrizovic	Pickering	Morgan*	Rennie	Borrows	Pressley	Marsh	Cook	Dublin	Ndlovu	Jenkinson	Wegerle
28/1		15,122	*9*					*Tracey**	*Ullathorne*	*Bowen*	*Adams*	*Newsome*	*Polston*	*Sutch*	*Newman^*	*Eadie*	*Sheron"*	*Milligan*	*M'shll/Akinb'/Cureton*
							Ref: G Willard	Phil Neal demands to be judged when all his players are fit, and that time is now. A poor game improves after the break and Marshall, on for the injured Tracey, keeps the Canaries in the hunt. Dublin and Ndlovu are thwarted by a 19-year-old keeper as Wegerle returns to top form.											
4R	A	NORWICH	20	L	1-3	1-1	Ndlovu 32	Ogrizovic	Pickering	Morgan	Rennie	Borrows	Pressley	Flynn	Marsh	Dublin^	Wegerle*	Ndlovu	Jones/Darby
8/2		*14,673*	*10*		*aet*		*Sheron 8, 108, Eadie 103*	*Marshall*	*Ullathorne*	*Bowen*	*Adams^*	*Newsome*	*Polston*	*Sutch*	*Crook**	*Eadie*	*Sheron*	*Milligan*	*Goss/Akinbiyi*
							Ref: G Willard	City match the Canaries in every department but finishing and pay for missed chances. The influential Wegerle and Dublin limp off and City's hopes are cruelly ended by the razor sharp Sheron and Eadie. Ndlovu scores with a rare header but Andy Marshall is again in sparkling form.											

		Home						Away					
	P	W	D	L	F	A	W	D	L	F	A	Pts
1 Blackburn	42	17	2	2	54	21	10	6	5	26	18	89
2 Manchester U	42	16	4	1	42	4	10	6	5	35	24	88
3 Nott'm Forest	42	12	6	3	36	18	10	5	6	36	25	77
4 Liverpool	42	13	5	3	38	13	8	6	7	27	24	74
5 Leeds	42	13	5	3	35	15	7	8	6	24	23	73
6 Newcastle	42	14	6	1	46	20	6	6	9	21	27	72
7 Tottenham	42	10	5	6	32	25	6	9	6	34	33	62
8 QP Rangers	42	11	3	7	36	26	6	6	9	25	33	60
9 Wimbledon	42	9	5	7	26	26	6	6	9	22	39	56
10 Southampton	42	8	9	4	33	27	4	9	8	28	36	54
11 Chelsea	42	7	7	7	25	22	6	8	7	25	33	54
12 Arsenal	42	6	9	6	27	21	7	3	11	25	28	51
13 Sheffield Wed	42	7	7	7	26	26	6	5	10	23	31	51
14 West Ham	42	9	6	6	28	19	4	5	12	16	29	50
15 Everton	42	8	9	4	31	23	3	8	10	13	28	50
16 COVENTRY	42	7	7	7	23	25	5	7	9	21	37	50
17 Manchester C	42	8	7	6	37	28	4	6	11	16	36	49
18 Aston Villa	42	6	9	6	27	24	5	6	10	24	32	48
19 Crys Palace	42	6	6	9	16	23	5	6	10	18	26	45
20 Norwich	42	8	8	5	27	21	2	5	14	10	33	43
21 Leicester	42	5	6	10	28	37	1	5	15	17	43	29
22 Ipswich	42	5	3	13	24	34	2	3	16	12	59	27
	924	205	134	123	697	498	123	134	205	498	697	1252

Odds & ends

Double wins: (1) West Ham.
Double losses: (2) Manchester U, Arsenal.

Won from behind: (1) West Brom FAC (a).
Lost from in front: (1) Southampton (h).

High spots: Eight-game unbeaten run in the spring.
Ndlovu's hat-trick in Anfield victory - the first by a visiting player in 33 years.
The win at Tottenham to assure safety.

Low spots: 11 games without a win in mid-season.
The mini-slump after safety looked assured.
More cup misery.

Red cards: City – Quinn (Blackburn a), Cook (Wrexham LC h), Gillespie (Leicester a), Pressley (Manchester U a), Cook (West Brom FAC a).
Red cards: Opponents – Willis (Leicester a), Holloway (QPR a), Bradley (West Brom FAC a).

Player of the Year: Brian Borrows.
Ever-presents: (0).
Hat-tricks: (1) Peter Ndlovu.
Opposing hat-tricks: (1) Sutton (Blackburn).
Leading scorer: (16) Dion Dublin.

	Appearances						Goals			
	Lge	*Sub*	LC	*Sub*	FAC	*Sub*	Lge	LC	FAC	Tot
Babb, Phil	**3**									
Boland, Willie	**9**	*3*	1							
Borrows, Brian	**33**	*2*	1		4					
Burrows, David	**11**									
Busst, David	**20**		3				**2**			**2**
Cook, Paul	**33**	*1*	3		3		**3**			**3**
Darby, Julian	**27**	*2*	3		1	*2*		1		**1**
Dublin, Dion	**31**		3		4		**13**	2	1	**16**
Filan, John	**2**									
Flynn, Sean	**32**		3		2		**4**	1		**5**
Gillespie, Gary	**2**	*1*	1							
Gould, Jonathan	**7**									
Hall, Marcus	**2**	*3*								
Jenkinson, Leigh	**10**	*1*			3		**1**			**1**
Jones, Cobi	**16**	*5*	2	*1*		*1*	**2**			**2**
Marsh, Mike	**15**				4		**2**			**2**
Morgan, Steve	**26**	*2*	2		4					
Ndlovu, Peter	**28**	*2*	1		3		**11**		2	**13**
Ogrizovic, Steve	**33**		3		4					
Pickering, Ally	**27**	*4*	3		2					
Pressley, Steven	**18**	*1*			3		**1**			**1**
Quinn, Mick	**3**	*3*								
Rennie, David	**28**		2		3					
Richardson, Kevin	**14**									
Robertson, Sandy		*1*								
Strachan, Gordon	**5**									
Wegerle, Roy	**21**	*5*	2		2	*2*	**3**	1	1	**5**
Williams, John	**1**	*6*								
Williams, Paul R	**5**				2					
(own-goals)							**2**			**2**
29 players used	**462**	***42***	**33**	***1***	**44**	***5***	**44**	**5**	**4**	**53**

F.A. CARLING PREMIERSHIP

Manager: Ron Atkinson

SEASON 1995-96

No	Date	Opponent	Att	Pos	Pt	F-A	H-T	Scorers, Times, and Referees	SQUAD	NUMBERS	IN	USE								subs used
1	A	NEWCASTLE			L	0-3	0-1		Filan	Borrows	Hall*	Burrows	**Williams PD**	Rennie	**Telfer**	Richardson	Dublin	Ndlovu	**Salako**	Pickering
	19/8		*36,485*		0			*Lee 8, Beardsley 81p, Ferdinand 83*	*Hislop*	*Barton*	*Beresford*	*Clark*	*Peacock*	*Howey*	*Gillespie*	*Lee*	*Ferdinand*	*Beardsley*	*Ginola**	*Fox*
								Ref: R Dilkes	Ferdinand, Ginola, Barton and Hislop make their debuts for the Geordies in an exciting game not as one-sided as the scoreline suggests. It is 1-0 until the last ten minutes, when Beardsley scores after Borrows fouls him. Lee's pass finds City chasing the game and Ferdinand seals it.											
2	H	MANCHESTER C			W	2-1	1-0	Telfer 12, Dublin 86	Filan	Pickering	Hall	Richardson	Williams PD	Borrows	Telfer	**Isaias**	Dublin	Ndlovu	Salako	
	23/8		16,568		3			*Rosler 81*	*Immel*	*Edghill*	*Phelan*	*Lomas**	*Symons*	*Brightwell I^*	*Summerbee*	*Flitcroft*	*Rosler*	*Walsh*	*Kinkladze*	*Quinn/Kernaghan*
								Ref: P Alcock	The Brazilian Isaias is unveiled and inspires City to an excellent first half. Telfer's goal from Pickering's cross threatens to open the floodgates but Dublin and Ndlovu are wasteful. Man City claw their way back with Rosler's goal, but Dion's header from Salako's cross clinches the win.											
3	H	ARSENAL		11	D	0-0	0-0		Filan	Pickering	Burrows	Richardson	Williams PD	Borrows	Telfer	Isaias	Dublin	Ndlovu	Salako	
	26/8		20,081	*7*	4				*Seaman*	*Dixon**	*Winterburn*	*Keown*	*Bould*	*Adams*	*Parlour^*	*Platt*	*Wright*	*Bergkamp*	*Merson*	*Jensen/Helder*
								Ref: S Dunn	The Gunners arrived suitably hyped with big signings Bergkamp and Platt. City's new signings have started well, especially John Salako, who sets up a stream of chances. Peter Ndlovu wastes many, being denied by Seaman, but also blatantly pushed by Adams in an entertaining game.											
4	A	CHELSEA		10	D	2-2	1-2	Isaias 45, Ndlovu 54	Filan	Pickering	Burrows	Richardson	Williams PD	Borrows	Telfer	Isaias	Dublin	Ndlovu	Salako	
	30/8		*22,718*	*15*	5			*Wise 6, Hughes 11*	*Kharine*	*Clarke*	*Minto*	*Gullit*	*Johnsen*	*Sinclair*	*Lee*	*Peacock*	*Hughes*	*Spencer*	*Wise**	*Burley*
								Ref: G Willard	Glen Hoddle's signing of Ruud Gullit is the most exciting in the Premier League and the Dutchman's pass for Hughes' goal is sheer class. City make it hard but inspired by Salako, back in the England squad, they roar back with Isaias' first goal and a Nuddy special in a gripping game.											
5	H	NOTT'M FOREST		11	D	1-1	1-1	Dublin 10	Filan	Pickering	Burrows	Richardson	Williams PD	Borrows	Telfer	Isaias	Dublin	Ndlovu	Salako	
	9/9		17,238	*8*	6			*Roy 23*	*Crossley*	*Lyttle*	*Pearce*	*Stone*	*Chettle*	*Cooper*	*Phillips*	*Bohinen**	*Campbell^*	*Roy*	*Woan*	*Gemmill/Silenzi*
								Ref: P Jones	Forest are fortunate to leave Highfield Road with their 18-match unbeaten run intact. Only a dreadful mistake by Paul Williams lets in Roy to score. Dion had netted with a header from the edge of the area, with Crossley off his line. £1.8 million Italian signing Silenzi has a quiet debut.											
6	A	MIDDLESBROUGH		14	L	1-2	0-0	Isaias 47	Filan	Pickering	Hall	Richardson	Williams PD	Borrows	Telfer	Isaias	Dublin*	Ndlovu	Salako	**Barnwell**
	16/9		*27,882*	*10*	6			*Vickers 58, Fjortoft 78*	*Walsh*	*Cox*	*Morris*	*Vickers*	*Pearson*	*Whyte*	*Barmby*	*Pollock*	*Fjortoft*	*Mustoe*	*Hignett*	
								Ref: G Poll	After two clean-sheets for Boro at the new Riverside Stadium, Isaias becomes the first opposing player to score there. Dion's departure with a knee injury affects City, and Boro wrest the initiative away. Atkinson is angered by City's capitulation. John Williams goes to Wycombe.											
7	A	BLACKBURN		16	L	**1-5**	1-2	Ndlovu 34	Filan	Pickering	Hall	Richardson	Williams PD	Borrows	Telfer	Isaias	Salako	Ndlovu	Cook*	**Christie**
	23/9		*24,382*	*13*	6			*Shearer 8, 60, 67, Hendry 23, Pearce 75*	*Flowers*	*Berg*	*Le Saux**	*Batty*	*Hendry*	*Pearce*	*Kenna*	*Sherwood*	*Shearer*	*Sutton*	*Newell*	*Makel*
								Ref: K Cooper	In their new purple and gold away kit, City crumble after an even first half. Ndlovu causes problems to the home defence and Flowers fouls him, only for Nuddy to hit the post from the spot, his first ever miss. He atones later but it's Shearer's day. His first is his 100th for Blackburn.											
8	H	ASTON VILLA		18	L	0-3	0-1		Filan	Pickering*	Hall	Busst	Williams PD	Borrows	Telfer	Richardson	Ndlovu	Isaias	Salako	Strachan
	30/9		21,004	*2*	6			*Yorke 1, Milosevic 84, 87*	*Bosnich*	*Charles*	*Wright*	*Draper*	*Ehiogu*	*Southgate*	*Taylor*	*Townsend*	*Milosevic*	*Yorke*	*Staunton*	
								Ref: A Wilkie	The old enemy sting City after 13 seconds when Yorke heads the fastest ever goal by a visiting player. The Sky Blues, playing a 3-5-2 formation, are denied by an imperious Bosnich and then destroyed by Milosevic in the last six minutes. Blackburn bid £3 million for Telfer.											
9	A	LIVERPOOL		17	D	0-0	0-0		Filan	Pickering	Borrows	Richardson	Busst	Williams PD	Telfer	Boland	**Lamptey**	Ndlovu	Salako	
	14/10		*39,079*	*5*	7				*James*	*Jones**	*Harkness*	*Babb*	*Wright*	*Ruddock*	*McManam'n*	*Redknapp*	*Collymore^*	*Fowler*	*Barnes*	*McAteer/Rush*
								Ref: P Danson	A much improved performance as City become the first side to leave Anfield with a point. Despite the Reds having the major share of the game City create some good chances. Lamptey blasts the best of them over the bar. £8.5 million Stan Collymore is substituted after a poor showing.											
10	H	SHEFFIELD WED		17	L	0-1	0-1		Filan	Pickering	Borrows	Richardson	Busst	Williams PD	Strachan	Telfer	Lamptey*	Ndlovu	Salako	Hall
	21/10		14,002	*12*	7			*Whittingham 16*	*Pressman*	*Nolan*	*Briscoe^*	*Pembridge*	*Atherton*	*Walker*	*Waddle**	*Ingesson*	*Bright*	*Whittingham*	*Sinton*	*Hyde/Williams*
								Ref: J Winter	This is the eleventh league game Dublin has missed since he joined City, and they haven't won any of them. The Ndlovu-Lamptey combo isn't working and both miss chances despite the presence of Gordon Strachan. Salako and Telfer have faded and Guy Whittingham's goal is enough.											

11	A	LEEDS	19	L	1-3	1-2	Dublin 12	Filan	Pickering	Hall	Richardson	Busst	Rennie	Telfer	Williams PD	Dublin	Ndlovu*	Salako	Lamptey
	28/10	*30,025*	*8*	7			*McAllister 39, 43, 90p*	*Lukic*	*Kelly*	*Pemberton*	*Palmer*	*Wetherall*	*Jobson*	*Whelan^*	*McAllister*	*Deane**	*Yeboah*	*Speed*	*Couzens/Sharp*
							Ref: G Ashby	This is not as one-sided as the score suggests. City take an early lead through the restored Dublin but endure bad luck and dodgy refereeing. McAllister's hat-trick consists of a deflected shot that John Filan had covered, a swerving free-kick and a penalty for Marcus Hall's handball.											
12	H	TOTTENHAM	19	L	2-3	1-2	Dublin 7, Williams P 48	Filan	Borrows*	Hall	Richardson	Busst	Rennie	Telfer	Williams PD	Dublin	Lamptey^	Salako	Pickering/Isaias
	4/11	17,567	*9*	7			*Fox 20, Sheringham 25, Howells 46*	*Walker*	*Austin*	*Wilson*	*Howells*	*Campbell*	*Mabbutt*	*Fox*	*Dozzell*	*Armstrong*	*Sheringham*	*Rosenthal**	*Calderwood*
							Ref: J Winter	Spurs gain revenge for the cup defeat but it's not a classic. Dion Dublin's early lead is squandered by poor marking and sloppy defending. Sheringham is the star, setting up £4.2 million Ruel Fox and scoring with a deft chip. Howells scores a third and Spurs soak up the pressure.											
13	A	QP RANGERS	19	D	1-1	0-1	Dublin 75	Ogrizovic	**Shaw**	Hall	Richardson	Williams PD	Rennie	Telfer*	Isaias	Dublin	Ndlovu	Salako	Strachan
	19/11	***11,189***	*16*	8			*Barker 37*	*Sommer*	*Ready*	*Brevett^*	*Barker*	*Yates*	*Maddix*	*Impey*	*Zelic*	*Dichio*	*Gallen*	*Sinclair**	*Wilkins/Challis*
							Ref: M Bodenham	A fighting display earns a late equaliser when Salako crosses for Dublin to head home. Telfer's poor clearance sets up Barker's goal and David Rennie has one of his off days but Oggy, returned from his broken leg, saves his blushes. £1 million debut boy Shaw marks dangerous Sinclair.											
14	H	MANCHESTER U	20	L	0-4	0-1		Ogrizovic	Shaw	Hall	Richardson	Williams PD	Rennie	Strachan	Isaias*	Dublin	Ndlovu	Salako	Cook
	22/11	**23,344**	*2*	8			*Irwin 28, McClair 47, 76, Beckham 57*	*Schmeichel*	*Neville G**	*Irwin*	*Beckham*	*Pallister*	*Bruce"*	*McClair*	*Butt^*	*Cantona*	*Cole*	*Giggs*	*Neville P/Sharpe/May*
							Ref: K Burge	City are given a drubbing by the masters in a one-sided game. The summer hopes have disappeared and relegation looks a strong bet. The game is over two minutes into the second half, when Giggs wonderfully sets up Brian McClair's first. Julian Darby joins West Brom for £200,000.											
15	H	WIMBLEDON	19	D	3-3	1-2	Heald 14 (og), Dublin 67, Rennie 83	Ogrizovic	Shaw !	Hall	Richardson	Williams PD !	Rennie	Telfer	Cook^	Dublin	Ndlovu	Salako*	Pickering/Isaias
	25/11	**12,496**	*16*	9			*Jones 28p, Goodman 42, Leonh'dson 58*	*Heald*	*Perry*	*Kimble*	*Jones*	*Pearce*	*Thorn*	*Goodman**	*Earle*	*Harford"*	*Ekoku*	*Leonhardsen*	*C'ham^/Clarke/Gayle*
							Ref: R Hart	Incidents and excitement compensate for the inadequacies of two struggling sides. City come back from 1-3 down with only nine men. Paul Williams goes after 27 minutes for handball which gives a penalty and Shaw after 80 for two yellows. The Dons haven't won in 10, City in 13.											
16	A	SHEFFIELD WED	20	L	3-4	2-2	Dublin 18, 36, 56 *[Bright 71]*	Ogrizovic	Pickering	Hall	Richardson	Shaw	Rennie*	Telfer	Williams PD	Dublin	Ndlovu	Salako	Strachan
	4/12	*16,229*	*14*	9			*Whittingham 25, Hirst 38, Degryse 61,*	*Pressman*	*Nolan*	*Briscoe*	*Nicol*	*Atherton*	*Walker*	*Waddle**	*Degryse*	*Bright*	*Hirst*	*Whitingham*	*Hyde*
							Ref: M Reed	With Busst, Boland and Wood ordered off in the reserves, City have picked up six red cards in 17 days. Dion is superb and gives City the lead three times only for a profligate defence to throw it away. Only Oggy emerges with any credit. It is City's worst run without a win since 1919.											
17	H	BLACKBURN	19	W	**5-0**	1-0	Busst 40, Dublin 60, Rennie 64, [Ndlovu 74, Salako 88]	Ogrizovic	Pickering	Hall	Busst	**Whyte**	Rennie	Telfer	Richardson	Dublin	Ndlovu	Salako	
	9/12	13,409	*11*	12				*Flowers*	*Berg*	*Le Saux*	*Batty*	*Marker*	*Sutton*	*Ripley*	*Sherwood*	*Shearer*	*Newell**	*Bohinen^*	*Warhurst/McKinley*
							Ref: S Dunn	On a snowbound pitch only one side wants to play and the champions are slaughtered. On loan Chris Whyte plays in a solid back three and the long losing run is over. Both clubs are competing for £3 million Chris Coleman and it's clear who needs him most. An orange ball is used.											
18	A	ASTON VILLA	19	L	1-4	0-1	Dublin 54	Filan	Shaw	Hall	Richardson !	Busst	Williams PD	Telfer	Ndlovu*	Dublin	**Whelan**	Salako^	Pickering/Rennie
	16/12	*28,486*	*4*	12			*Johnson 12, Milosevic 48, 63, 80*	*Bosnich**	*Charles*	*Wright*	*Southgate*	*Ehiogu*	*McGrath "*	*Taylor*	*Draper*	*Milosevic*	*Yorke^*	*Johnson*	*Spink/T'send/Scim'ca*
							Ref: P Alcock	Williams and Shaw return from suspension and the goals start leaking again. Once Richardson is sent off for two yellow cards just before the break City are dead. Dublin's goal offers a glimmer but the deadly Milosevic scores his first goals at Villa Park, and five in all against City.											
19	H	EVERTON	19	W	2-1	0-0	Busst 48, Whelan 84	Ogrizovic	Pickering*	Hall	Richardson	Busst	Shaw	Telfer	Williams PD	Dublin	Whelan	Salako	Rennie
	23/12	16,638	*12*	15			*Rideout 67*	*Southall*	*Jackson*	*Unsworth*	*Ebbrell*	*Watson*	*Short*	*Kanchelskis*	*Parkinson*	*Amokachi*	*Stuart*	*Limpar**	*Rideout*
							Ref: S Lodge	Noel Whelan, City's £2 million signing from Leeds celebrates his home debut with a late wonder goal after Rideout cancels out Busst's header. Oggy, back from suspension, keeps City in the game with a string of saves before an exciting finale results in the third win of the season.											
20	A	BOLTON	17	W	2-1	1-1	Whelan 44, Salako 90p	Ogrizovic	Pickering	Hall	Boland	Busst	Shaw	Telfer	Williams PD	Dublin	Whelan	Salako	
	30/12	*16,678*	*20*	18			*McGinlay 14*	*Branagan*	*Green*	*Phillips*	*Curcic*	*Fairclough*	*Taggart*	*Sneekes*	*Todd*	*McGinlay*	*Blake*	*Sellars*	
							Ref: A Wilkie	Bolton, back in the top flight after 15 years, have lost eight out of ten and look doomed. Keith Branagan has a brain-storm in the last minute and upends Whelan for Salako to score from the spot. City deserve to win in a stirring climax to a frantic relegation game in a blustery wind.											
21	H	SOUTHAMPTON	17	D	1-1	0-0	Whelan 83	Ogrizovic	Pickering	Hall	Richardson	Busst	Shaw	Telfer*	Williams PD	Dublin	Whelan	Salako	Lamptey
	1/1	16,822	*16*	19			*Heaney 64*	*Beasant*	*Dodd*	*Charlton**	*Neilson*	*Hall*	*Monkou*	*Venison*	*Magilton*	*Shipperley*	*Maddison*	*Heaney*	*Benali*
							Ref: K Cooper	The Saints easily contain the Sky Blues in a poor game until Whelan's wonder goal wins a vital point. His run starts on the half-way line and takes him past the whole defence before a toe-poke sends it past Beasant. The ref blows for time two minutes early and has to restart the game.											

No	Date		Att	Pos	Pt	F-A	H-T	Scorers, Times, and Referees	SQUAD	NUMBERS	IN	USE								subs used
22	H	NEWCASTLE		17	L	0-1	0-1		Ogrizovic	Pickering	Hall	Richardson	Busst	Shaw	Telfer*	Williams PD	Dublin	Whelan	Salako	Ndlovu
	14/1		20,532	*1*	19			*Watson 44*	*Srnicek*	*Barton*	*Beresford*	*Clark*	*Peacock*	*Albert*	*Watson*	*Lee*	*Ferdinand*	*Beardsley*	*Ginola*	
								Ref: P Jones	Despite going out of the FA Cup at home to Chelsea the Magpies are nine points clear at the top of the table. Sky TV viewers see a mediocre game won after Salako lost control the ball on the edge of the box, allowing Watson to steam through. Pickering does a good job on Ginola.											
23	A	MANCHESTER C		17	D	1-1	0-0	Dublin 66	Ogrizovic	Pickering	Hall	Richardson	Shaw	Borrows	Ndlovu	Telfer	Dublin	Whelan	Salako	
	20/1		*25,710*	*18*	20			*Rosler 55*	*Immel*	*Summerbee*	*Brightwell I*	*Brown*	*Symons*	*Curle*	*Lomas**	*Flitcroft*	*Rosler*	*Quinn*	*Kinkladze*	*Phillips*
								Ref: R Hart	A poor game that only warms up in the last 20 minutes. Brian Borrows returns for the suspended Busst but in-form Paul Williams is injured. Alan Ball's nightmare first season in charge is lightened only by Kinkladze who has a quiet game. Dane Ronnie Ekelund is on loan at City.											
24	A	WEST HAM		18	L	2-3	0-0	Dublin 64, Whelan 82	Ogrizovic	Pickering	Hall	Richardson*	Shaw	Borrows	Telfer	Williams PD^	Dublin	Whelan	Salako	Ndlovu/Strachan
	31/1		*18,884*	*14*	20			*Rieper 46, Cottee 60, Dowie 86*	*Miklosko*	*Brown*	*Dicks*	*Bishop*	*Rieper*	*Potts*	*Moncur**	*Williamson*	*Dowie*	*Cottee^*	*Hughes*	*Whitbread/Lampard*
								Ref: G Poll	A dreadful first half by City, who only pick up once they are two goals down. They fight back well but concede a sloppy third to the ubiquitous Dowie. West Ham pull out of the drop zone but City look marooned after this dire display. Lamptey is sent off in the African Nations Cup.											
25	A	ARSENAL		18	D	1-1	1-1	Whelan 23	Ogrizovic	Borrows	Hall	Richardson	Busst	Shaw	Strachan*	Telfer	Dublin	Whelan	Salako	Ndlovu
	3/2		*35,623*	*9*	21			*Bergkamp 24*	*Seaman*	*Dixon*	*Winterburn*	*Clarke*	*Marshall*	*Linighan*	*Jensen**	*Merson*	*Wright*	*Bergkamp*	*Helder*	*Hughes*
								Ref: S Dunn	An entertaining game which either team could have won. City start like a train and should have led before Noel Whelan's arrogant chip from Richardson's pass beats Seaman. Bergkamp replies immediately, but Oggy saves Wright's second-half penalty when Hall brings him down.											
26	H	CHELSEA		17	W	1-0	1-0	Whelan 43	Ogrizovic	Pickering	Borrows	Richardson	Busst	Shaw	Salako	Telfer	Dublin	Whelan	Ndlovu*	Williams PD
	10/2		20,629	*10*	24				*Hitchcock*	*Petrescu*	*Phelan*	*Lee*	*Clarke*	*Sinclair**	*Gullit*	*Peacock*	*Furlong*	*Spencer^*	*Newton*	*Johnsen/Wise*
								Ref: R Dilkes (B Coddington)	Hoddle's team arrive unbeaten in eight and are beaten by Whelan's delicate chip for his seventh goal in ten games. City miss more chances and have to thank Oggy for a brilliant stop from Peacock's shot. Busst and Shaw win plaudits too. Crewe's Neil Lennon is set to sign for £750,000.											
27	H	MIDDLESBROUGH		17	D	0-0	0-0		Ogrizovic	Pickering^	Burrows	Richardson	**Daish**	Shaw	Telfer*	**Jess**	Dublin	Whelan	Salako	Busst/Lamptey
	24/2		17,979	*13*	25				*Walsh*	*Cox*	*Fleming*	*Vickers*	*Whyte*	*Whelan*	*Barmby*	*Pollock*	*Fjortoft*	*Mustoe*	*Kavanagh*	
								Ref: P Durkin	City parade new signings Eoin Jess and Liam Daish in a very poor game not helped by the rapidly deteriorating pitch. Boro arrive after eight straight defeats and have fallen from 4th place but City never look like breaking down a stern rearguard and muster only one shot on target.											
28	H	WEST HAM		16	D	2-2	2-2	Salako 7, Whelan 15	Ogrizovic	Borrows	Burrows*	Richardson	Daish	Shaw	Salako	Jess	Dublin	Whelan	Ndlovu	Williams PD
	2/3		17,448	*11*	26			*Cottee 2, Rieper 19*	*Miklosko*	*Potts*	*Dicks*	*Bishop*	*Rieper*	*Bilic*	*Hughes*	*Williamson*	*Dowie*	*Cottee**	*Rowland*	*Harkes*
								Ref: M Bodenham	A vast improvement from last week but City fail to capitalise on their territorial advantage. Cottee equals Ian Rush's record of 14 goals against City and opens the floodgates. Salako finishes off a good move between Jess and Whelan and Noel chips Ludek Miklosko after Dion's nod on.											
29	A	EVERTON		15	D	2-2	1-2	Daish 38, Williams P 85	Ogrizovic	Borrows	Shaw	Williams PD	Daish	Busst	Telfer^	Jess	Dublin	Whelan*	Salako	Ndlovu/Strachan
	9/3		*34,517*	*7*	27			*Ferguson 17, 25*	*Southall*	*Hottiger*	*Hinchcliffe*	*Ebbrell*	*Unsworth*	*Short^*	*Kanchelskis*	*Parkinson**	*Ferguson*	*Stuart*	*Grant*	*Amokachi/O'Connor*
								Ref: P Danson	A game of two halves. City look beaten at half-time, 0-2 down with Whelan off injured and Duncan Ferguson in deadly form. The second half is a different matter and headers from Liam Daish and Paul Williams earn a deserved point. Ndlovu's header should have won it but goes wide.											
30	H	BOLTON		16	L	0-2	0-0		Ogrizovic	Borrows	Burrows	Williams PD	Daish	Shaw	Salako	Jess	Dublin	Whelan	Ndlovu*	Strachan
	16/3		17,168	*20*	27			*Stubbs 66, 70*	*Branagan*	*Green*	*Phillips*	*Bergsson*	*Fairclough*	*Coleman*	*Curcic*	*Stubbs*	*Paatelainen*	*Blake**	*Sellars*	*De Freitas*
								Ref: K Burge	Bolton continue their mini revival with a crucial win against a nervous and desperate City. The Sky Blues look the better side but lack punch and make crucial errors which allow Alan Stubbs to score twice. Only Williams does himself justice. Paul Cook goes to Tranmere on loan.											
31	A	SOUTHAMPTON		18	L	0-1	0-1		Ogrizovic	Borrows	Burrows	Richardson	Daish	Shaw	Jess	Williams PD	Dublin	Whelan	Salako*	Ndlovu
	25/3		*14,461*	*17*	27			*Dodd 2*	*Beasant*	*Dodd*	*Charlton*	*Magilton*	*Neilson*	*Monkou*	*Le Tissier*	*Venison*	*Shipperley*	*Watson**	*Heaney*	*Warren*
								Ref: S Lodge	An important relegation battle is live on Sky TV and Dodd's header from Le Tissier's corner is enough to win it. City go close on a number of occasions but Andy Gray accuses Coventry of lacking commitment in a heated confrontation with Ron. Saints end a run of four straight defeats.											

No	Venue/Date	Opponent/Att	Pos	Res/Pts	F-A	H-T	Scorers, Times, and Referees	1	2	3	4	5	6	7	8	9	10	11	subs used
32	A	TOTTENHAM	19	L	1-3	1-0	Dublin 21	Ogrizovic	Borrows	Burrows^	Richardson	Daish	Shaw	Jess*	Williams PD	Dublin	Whelan	Ndlovu	Strachan/Salako
	30/3	*26,808*	*6*	27			*Sheringham 51, Fox 52, 65*	*Walker*	*Austin*	*Wilson*	*Howells*	*Campbell*	*Nethercott*	*Fox*	*Dozzell*	*Armstrong*	*Sheringham*	*Sinton*	
							Ref: R Hart	A sad result after City take the lead with a super volley from Dublin. At that stage they look in control but everything falls apart as Spurs rattle in three in 15 minutes and City are in big trouble. Richard Shaw played on with a fractured cheekbone and Burrows' hamstring flares up again.											
33	H	LIVERPOOL	18	W	1-0	1-0	Whelan 18	Ogrizovic	Pickering	Borrows*	Richardson	Daish	Busst	Telfer	Williams PD	Dublin	Whelan	Ndlovu^	Salako/Jess
	6/4	23,037	*3*	30				*James*	*McAteer*	*Jones^*	*Scales*	*Matteo*	*Harkness**	*McManam'n*	*Redknapp*	*Collymore*	*Fowler*	*Barnes*	*Thomas/Rush*
							Ref: P Jones	The escape act starts here with an impressive win over the title contenders, who had beaten Newcastle 4-3 in the game of the season three days earlier. Whelan scores with an acrobatic finish and there's no shortage of commitment, although Salako goes too far and breaks Harkness's leg.											
34	A	MANCHESTER U	19	L	0-1	0-0		Ogrizovic	Pickering	Salako	Richardson	Daish	Busst*	Telfer^	Williams PD	Dublin	Whelan	Ndlovu	Boland/Jess
	8/4	***50,322***	*1*	30			*Cantona 47*	*Schmeichel*	*Irwin*	*Sharpe*	*Beckham*	*May*	*Neville G*	*McClair*	*Butt*	*Cantona*	*Cole*	*Giggs*	
							Ref: D Gallagher	David Busst's sickening injury casts a massive shadow over the game. His right leg crumples as he collides with Irwin at the far post in the second minute and it takes nine minutes to remove him from the pitch. The players are visibly affected and Cantona's goal wins a tight game.											
35	H	QP RANGERS	18	W	1-0	0-0	Jess 69	Ogrizovic	Pickering	Hall	Richardson	Daish	Rennie*	Strachan	Williams PD	Dublin	Whelan	Ndlovu	Jess
	13/4	22,906	*19*	33				*Sommer*	*Bardsley*	*Brevett*	*Barker*	*Yates*	*McDonald*	*Impey !*	*Holloway*	*Hateley**	*Gallen*	*Sinclair*	*Wilkins*
							Ref: K Cooper	A pulse-raising exercise in brinkmanship sees substitute Jess snatch a vital goal. The nerves are evident in the first half and Rangers hit the woodwork twice. Impey is sent off after a clash with Hall. Old boy Mark Hateley looks past it and Richard Shaw plays with a protective mask.											
36	A	NOTT'M FOREST	17	D	0-0	0-0		Ogrizovic	Pickering	Hall	Richardson	Daish	Williams PD	Strachan*	Jess	Dublin	Whelan	Ndlovu	Salako
	17/4	*24,629*	*9*	34				*Crossley*	*Haaland*	*Pearce*	*Stone*	*Chettle*	*Cooper*	*Bart-Will'ms*	*Gemmill**	*Campbell^*	*Lee*	*Woan*	*Phillips/Howe*
							Ref: M Read	City edge out of the bottom three roared on by 4,500 fans. Forest have chances galore in the first half but City finish the game stronger and Whelan hits the woodwork. Jess has his best game yet, controlling midfield when City are in the ascendancy and forcing Crossley to tip over.											
37	A	WIMBLEDON	16	W	2-0	0-0	Ndlovu 51, 89	Ogrizovic	Pickering	Hall	Shaw	Dublin	Burrows	Salako	Telfer	Jess	Whelan	Ndlovu	
	27/4	*15,796*	*14*	37				*Sullivan*	*Cunningham*	*Kimble*	*Jones*	*Reeves*	*Perry*	*Gayle**	*Earle*	*Holdsworth*	*Ekoku*	*Clarke^*	*Goodman/Harford*
							Ref: S Dunn	This tremendous win might have been enough to ensure safety but Saints and Man City also win away and City are just ahead on goal-difference with one game left. Over 6,000 fans travel to see Ndlovu settle the nerves just after the break. Dion plays a blinder in defence.											
38	H	LEEDS	16	D	0-0	0-0		Ogrizovic	Pickering	Burrows	Hall	Daish	Shaw	Telfer	Jess	Dublin	Whelan	Salako	
	5/5	22,757	*13*	38				*Lukic*	*Kelly*	*Worthington*	*Palmer*	*Wetherall*	*Radebe*	*Tinkler*	*McAllister*	*Masinga*	*Wallace*	*Gray**	*Couzens*
	Home	Away					Ref: D Elleray	With Man City two down at half-time City think a point is enough but the other Sky Blues draw level and it's a nerve-racking last few minutes until the score is confirmed and City are safe again. They have the better of the first half but a draw is fair. Fighting on the pitch does not help.											
Average	18,505	26,311																	

Coca-Cola Cup					F-A	H-T	Scorers, Times, and Referees	SQUAD	NUMBERS	IN	USE								subs used
2:1	H	HULL	14	W	2-0	2-0	Richardson 24, Lamptey 35	Gould	Pickering	Hall	Richardson	Williams PD	Borrows	Telfer	Isaias	Lamptey	Ndlovu	Salako	
20/9		8,915	*2:20*					*Wilson*	*Lowthorpe*	*Lawford*	*Humphries**	*Dewhurst !*	*Abbott*	*Williams*	*Fewings"*	*Mason^*	*Windass*	*Mann*	*Hobson/Gordon/Fettis*
							Ref: R Poulain	Ghanaian Nii Lamptey makes his bow for the injured Dublin and grabs a useful goal against poor Hull. Richardson scores his first goal when a poor clearance lands at his feet. Dewhurst is sent off after 42 minutes for appearing to tread on Lamptey's head, but City fail to take advantage.											
2:2	A	HULL	18	W	1-0	1-0	Lamptey 10	Filan	Borrows	Hall	Richardson	Busst	Williams PD	Strachan	Telfer	Lamptey	Ndlovu*	Salako	Christie
4/10		*6,929*	*2:23*					*Wilson*	*Lowthorpe*	*Lawford*	*Hobson*	*Humphries*	*Abbott*	*Williams**	*Fewings"*	*Brown^*	*Windass*	*Mann*	*P'cock/Gordon/Mas'n*
							Ref: S Lodge (City win 3-0 on aggregate)	The early goal ends the tie but City fail to take advantage of the poor opposition and chances go begging. Lamptey scores a wonderful goal, beating two men before driving firmly in, but he is often caught offside by poor positioning. Ron wants to buy Richard Jobson for £750,000.											
3	H	TOTTENHAM	17	W	3-2	0-2	Ndlovu 55p, Busst 61, Salako 76	Filan	Borrows*	Hall	Richardson	Busst	Williams PD	Strachan^	Telfer	Lamptey	Ndlovu	Salako	Pickering/Dublin
25/10		18,267	*9*				*Armstrong 2, Busst 20 (og)*	*Walker*	*Austin*	*Wilson*	*Howells*	*Calderw'd**	*Mabbutt*	*McMahon*	*Campbell*	*Armstrong*	*Sheringham*	*Rosenthal*	*Dozzell*
							Ref: S Dunn	A stunning comeback after City looked dead and buried at half-time. Calderwood's handball gives Ndlovu a penalty and Dublin's arrival as sub sparks more action. Spurs are so busy watching Dion at a free-kick that Busst ghosts in. Salako wins it after Dion's header is saved. Magic!											
4	A	WOLVES	19	L	1-2	0-2	Williams 67	Ogrizovic !	Pickering^	Hall	Richardson	Williams PD	Rennie	Telfer	Isaias*	Dublin	Ndlovu	Strachan	Gould/Lamptey
29/11		*24,628*	*1:20*				*Venus 32, Ferguson 33*	*Stowell*	*Rankine*	*Thompson*	*Ferguson*	*Law*	*Richards*	*Venus*	*Goodman*	*Bull*	*Atkins*	*Birch*	
							Ref: S Lodge	City's season of woe continues as Oggy is sent off for handball outside the area and within a minute they are two down to an average Wolves team. A Williams header offers hope but the late siege never happens and Atkinson's three-year unbeaten record in this competition is ended.											

FA Cup																			
3	A	PLYMOUTH	17	W	3-1	0-1	Pickering 53, Salako 55, Telfer 58	Ogrizovic	Pickering	Hall	Richardson	Busst !	Shaw	Telfer	Williams PD	Dublin	Whelan	Salako	
6/1		*17,721*	*2:4*				*Baird 19*	*Blackwell*	*Billy*	*Williams*	*Logan*	*Heathcote*	*Hill*	*Baird**	*Mauge^*	*Littlejohn*	*Evans*	*Leadbitter*	*Twiddy/Saunders*
							Ref: G Willard	A rousing cup-tie full of action. City look down and out when Busst is sent off for a professional foul on Mickey Evans after 18 minutes and Plymouth take the lead from the resulting free-kick. City fight back with three goals in five minutes in a much-improved second-half display.											
4	H	MANCHESTER C	18	D	2-2	1-1	Whelan 2, Dublin 90	Ogrizovic	Borrows	Hall	Richardson	Busst	Shaw	Strachan	Telfer*	Dublin	Whelan	Salako	Ndlovu
7/2		18,775	*17*				*Busst 33 (og), Flitcroft 81*	*Immel*	*Summerbee*	*Brightwell I*	*Brown*	*Symons*	*Curle*	*Lomas*	*Flitcroft*	*Rosler*	*Clough*	*Kinkladze*	
							Ref: G Ashby	On the eve of his 39th birthday Strachan sets up the late equaliser and shines with his never-say-die approach. A promising start tails off badly with neither side getting a grip and Flitcroft's goal after Dublin's poor clearance looks to be the winner. Dion keeps his feet to earn a replay.											
4R	A	MANCHESTER C	17	L	1-2	0-1	Dublin 85	Ogrizovic	Pickering	Burrows	Richardson	Busst	Shaw	Strachan	Telfer*	Dublin	Whelan	Salako	Lamptey
14/2		*22,419*	*18*				*Clough 20, Quinn 46*	*Immel*	*Summerbee*	*Brown*	*Lomas*	*Symons*	*Curle**	*Clough*	*Flitcroft*	*Rosler*	*Quinn*	*Kinkladze*	*Creaney*
							Ref: K Cooper	David Burrows returns after a six-month lay-off and performs well. City are unlucky to lose but Whelan lets them down with a bad miss at 0-0. Dublin also misses and Nii Lamptey hits a post. Man City take their two chances and go through to a Manchester derby in the 5th round.											

		Home					Away					
	P	W	D	L	F	A	W	D	L	F	A	Pts
1 Manchester U	38	15	4	0	36	9	10	3	6	37	26	82
2 Newcastle	38	17	1	1	38	9	7	5	7	28	28	78
3 Liverpool	38	14	4	1	46	13	6	7	6	24	21	71
4 Aston Villa	38	11	5	3	32	15	7	4	8	20	20	63
5 Arsenal	38	10	7	2	30	16	7	5	7	19	16	63
6 Everton	38	10	5	4	35	19	7	5	7	29	25	61
7 Blackburn	38	14	2	3	44	19	4	5	10	17	28	61
8 Tottenham	38	9	5	5	26	19	7	8	4	24	19	61
9 Nott'm Forest	38	11	6	2	29	17	4	7	8	21	37	58
10 West Ham	38	9	5	5	25	21	5	4	10	18	31	51
11 Chelsea	38	7	7	5	30	22	5	7	7	16	22	50
12 Middlesbrough	38	8	3	8	27	27	3	7	9	8	23	43
13 Leeds	38	8	3	8	21	21	4	4	11	19	36	43
14 Wimbledon	38	5	6	8	27	33	5	5	9	28	37	41
15 Sheffield Wed	38	7	5	7	30	31	3	5	11	18	30	40
16 COVENTRY	38	6	7	6	21	23	2	7	10	21	37	38
17 Southampton	38	7	7	5	21	18	2	4	13	13	34	38
18 Manchester C	38	7	7	5	21	19	2	4	13	12	39	38
19 QP Rangers	38	6	5	8	25	26	3	1	15	13	31	33
20 Bolton	38	5	4	10	16	31	3	1	15	23	40	29
	760	186	98	96	580	408	96	98	186	408	580	1042

Odds & ends

Double wins: (0).
Double losses (5) Aston Villa, Sheff Wed, Tottenham, Manchester U, Newcastle.

Won from behind (3) Bolton (a), Plymouth FAC (a), Tottenham LC (h).
Lost from in front (5) Midlesbrough (a), Leeds (a), Tottenham (h), Sheffield Wed (a), Tottenham (a).

High spots: Blackburn home victory - biggest home win for seven years.
Avoiding relegation with only one defeat in last six games.
The Coca-Cola Cup win over Tottenham after being 0-2 down.

Low spots: 14 League games without a win - the worst run since 1919.
The Coca-Cola Cup exit at Molineux.

Red cards: City – Williams and Shaw (Wimbledon h), Ogrizovic (Wolves LC a), Richardson (A Villa a), Busst (Plymouth FAC a).
Red cards: Opponents – Impey (QP Rangers h), Dewhurst (Hull LC h).

Player of the Year: Paul Williams.
Ever-presents: (0).
Hat-tricks: (1) Dion Dublin.
Opposing hat-tricks: (3) Shearer (Blackburn), McAllister (Leeds), Milosevic (Aston Villa).
Leading scorer: (16) Dion Dublin.

	Appearances						Goals			
	Lge	*Sub*	LC	*Sub*	FAC	*Sub*	**Lge**	LC	FAC	**Tot**
Barnwell, Jamie		*1*								
Boland, Willie	**2**	*1*								
Borrows, Brian	**21**		3		1					
Burrows, David	**11**				1					
Busst, David	**16**	*1*	2		3		**2**	1		**3**
Christie, Iyssden		*1*		*1*						
Cook, Paul	**2**	*1*								
Daish, Liam	**11**						**1**			**1**
Dublin, Dion	**34**		1	*1*	3		**14**		2	**16**
Filan, John	**13**		2							
Gould, Jonathan			1	*1*						
Hall, Marcus	**24**	*1*	4		2					
Isaias, Marques	**9**	*2*	2				**2**			**2**
Jess, Eoin	**9**	*3*					**1**			**1**
Lamptey, Nii	**3**	*3*	3	*1*		*1*		2		**2**
Ndlovu, Peter	**27**	*5*	4			*1*	**5**	1		**6**
Ogrizovic, Steve	**25**		1		3					
Pickering, Ally	**26**	*4*	2	*1*	2				1	**1**
Rennie, David	**9**	*2*	1				**2**			**2**
Richardson, Kevin	**33**		4		3			1		**1**
Salako, John	**34**	*3*	3		3		**3**	1	1	**5**
Shaw, Richard	**21**				3					
Strachan, Gordon	**5**	*7*	3		2					
Telfer, Paul	**31**		4		3		**1**		1	**2**
Whelan, Noel	**21**				3		**8**		1	**9**
Whyte, Chris (loan)	**1**									
Williams, Paul D	**30**	*2*	4		1		**2**	1		**3**
(own-goals)							**1**			**1**
27 players used	**418**	*37*	**44**	*5*	**33**	*2*	**42**	**7**	**6**	**55**

No Date			Att	Pos	Pt	F-A	H-T	Scorers, Times, and Referees	SQUAD	NUMBERS	IN	USE								subs used
1	H	NOTT'M FOREST			L	0-3	0-2		Ogrizovic	Borrows	Burrows	Richardson	Daish	Williams	Salako	**McAllister**	Dublin	Whelan^	**O'Neill***	Jess/**Ducros**
17/8			19,459		0			*Campbell 13, 36, 47*	*Crossley*	*Cooper*	*Pearce*	*Stone**	*Chettle*	*Jerkan*	*Bt-Williams*	*Haaland*	*Campbell*	*Saunders^*	*Woan*	*Gemmill/McGregor*
								Ref: A Wilkie	£3 million signing Gary McAllister cannot help City fulfil the expectations in this dreadful defeat. Forest are all over City and Campbell could have secured his hat-trick in the first half hour. Michael O'Neill is substituted after 45 minutes of his debut and Noel Whelan needs an X-ray.											
2	A	WEST HAM			D	1-1	1-0	McAllister 12	Ogrizovic	**Genaux***	Burrows	Jess^	Daish	Shaw	Telfer	McAllister	Dublin	Ducros	Salako	Borrows/Williams
21/8			*21,580*		1			*Rieper 74*	*Miklosko*	*Breacker**	*Dicks*	*Williamson*	*Bilic*	*Rieper*	*Slater*	*Lazaridis*	*Jones^*	*Dowie*	*Hughes*	*Futre/Bowen*
								Ref: S Dunn	Atkinson makes five changes after Saturday's defeat and sees a big improvement. City lead for an hour, thanks to McAllister's header from Ducros's super cross. West Ham turn the heat up after the break with Futre enjoying a lively first taste of English football. Reiper volleys in.											
3	A	CHELSEA		19	L	0-2	0-1		Ogrizovic	Genaux	Burrows	Jess*	Daish !	Shaw	Telfer	McAllister	Dublin	Whelan^	Salako	Williams/Ducros
24/8			*25,024*	*2*	1			*Leboeuf 29, Vialli 74*	*Kharine*	*Petrescu*	*Myers^*	*Johnsen*	*Leboeuf*	*Clarke*	*Morris**	*Di Matteo*	*Vialli*	*Hughes M*	*Wise*	*Burley/Minto*
								Ref: P Danson	An exciting game is spoilt by the incompetent officials who fail to see Dan Petrescu's blatant handball which leads to the first goal. Liam Daish is sent off for protesting and Ron and Gordon will face disciplinary action. City's ten men fight hard but fall to Vialli's first goal in England.											
4	H	LIVERPOOL		20	L	0-1	0-0		Ogrizovic	Genaux	Burrows	Jess	Daish*	Shaw	Borrows	McAllister	Dublin	Whelan^	Salako	Ducros/Isaias
4/9			22,949	*3*	1			*Babb 68*	*James*	*McAteer*	*Bjornebye*	*Matteo*	*Wright*	*Babb*	*McManam'n*	*Thomas*	*Collymore*	*Fowler*	*Barnes*	
								Ref: G Poll	A patchy game is won by old boy Babb, who scores his first Liverpool goal after McAllister plays him onside at a corner. Gary McAllister has replaced Dublin as skipper and both Dion and Whelan look shadows of last season. Only Salako looks in form. A pedantic referee books seven.											
5	A	MIDDLESBROUGH		20	L	0-4	0-2		Ogrizovic	Borrows	Burrows	Jess*	Williams	Shaw	Telfer	McAllister	Dublin	Whelan^	Salako	Strachan/Ducros
7/9			*29,811*	*7*	1			*Ravenelli 3, 73, Juninho 28, 80*	*Miller*	*Cox*	*Fleming*	*Vickers*	*Whyte*	*Whelan*	*Emerson*	*Mustoe*	*Ravanelli*	*Barmby*	*Juninho*	
								Ref: G Barber	Another abysmal result sets the alarm bells ringing. Boro's foreign imports take City apart and Fabricio Ravanelli, playing in red boots, has scored six in five games. The Brazilians Juninho and Emerson earn Bryan Robson's men an easy win but are assisted by City's woeful defence.											
6	H	LEEDS		18	W	2-1	0-1	Salako 57, Whelan 65	Ogrizovic	Borrows	Hall	Richardson	Burrows	Shaw	Telfer	McAllister	Dublin	Whelan	Salako	
14/9			17,298	*12*	4			*Couzens 1*	*Martyn*	*Kelly*	*Harte*	*Palmer*	*Wetherall*	*Jobson*	*Couzens**	*Wallace*	*Rush*	*Hateley*	*Gray^*	*Ford/Blunt*
								Ref: G Willard	George Graham is the new boss at Leeds, replacing the sacked Howard Wilkinson. Couzens scores after 51 seconds and it takes City almost an hour to pull level, after a dazzling run by man of the match John Salako. Whelan grabs the winner against his old club from Dublin's header.											
7	A	SUNDERLAND		18	L	0-1	0-0		Ogrizovic	Borrows	Burrows	Richardson	Daish*	Shaw^	Telfer	McAllister	Dublin	Whelan	Salako	Hall/Jess
21/9			*19,459*	*10*	4			*Agnew 51*	*Coton*	*Hall*	*Scott*	*Bracewell*	*Ball*	*Melville*	*Gray*	*Ord*	*Stewart*	*Quinn**	*Agnew*	*Russell*
								Ref: M Riley	This is City's last appearance at Roker Park. The game is a dreadful advert for the Premier League. Agnew's winner is the first home goal since mid-April and rescues the game. The pressure is on Atkinson after a dreadful start. Belgian Genaux is out for two months with a groin injury.											
8	H	BLACKBURN		19	D	0-0	0-0		Ogrizovic	Borrows	Hall	Richardson	Daish	Burrows	Telfer	McAllister	Dublin	Whelan	Salako	
28/9			17,032	*20*	5				*Flowers*	*Marker*	*Croft*	*Sherwood*	*Hendry*	*Coleman**	*Donis*	*Bohinen*	*Sutton*	*Gallacher^*	*Wilcox"*	*Ripley/Fenton/McKinlay*
								Ref: J Winter	This is the first relegation battle of the season. Neither side look good enough. Ray Harford is under pressure with Rovers winless in eight, and his team rarely threaten. Kevin Gallacher makes his first visit since leaving City four years ago. City are booed off to fans' chants of 'rubbish'.											
9	H	SOUTHAMPTON		19	D	1-1	0-1	Dublin 90	Ogrizovic	Borrows^	Hall	Richardson	Daish	Burrows*	Telfer	McAllister	Jess"	Whelan	Salako	Williams/Ndlovu/Dublin
13/10			15,477	*18*	6			*Le Tissier 17*	*Moss*	*Dodd*	*Charlton*	*Neilson*	*Dryden*	*Lundekvam*	*Le Tissier*	*Magilton**	*Shipperley"*	*Watson^*	*Slater*	*Oakley/Ostenstad/Berkovic*
								Ref: P Durkin	Another dog-fight, but a more exciting one. Dublin is dropped but comes on after 67 minutes to grab a late equaliser, his first goal of the season. Le Tissier's goal is magnificent. He takes advantage of sloppy play by Borrows and Oggy and hits a 30-yard screamer past the static keeper.											
10	A	ARSENAL		19	D	0-0	0-0		Ogrizovic"	Telfer	Williams*	Richardson	Daish	Shaw	Jess^	McAllister	Dublin	Whelan	Salako	Ndlovu/Burrows/Filan
19/10			*38,140*	*1*	7				*Seaman*	*Dixon*	*Winterburn*	*Keown*	*Bould*	*Adams*	*Platt*	*Vieira*	*Wright*	*Hartson**	*Merson*	*Bergkamp*
								Ref: P Jones	Brave Oggy, playing his 450th league game for City, is carried off seven minutes from time after a clash with the petulant Wright. It is an ill-tempered match with ugly incidents on the pitch and in the tunnel. City earn a point though Arsenal, under Wenger for the first time, stay top.											

No Date	Venue	Opponent Att	Pos	Res Pts	F-A	H-T	Scorers, Times, and Referees	1	2	3	4	5	6	7	8	9	10	11	subs used
11	H	SHEFFIELD WED	19	D	0-0	0-0		Ogrizovic	Williams	Salako	Richardson	Daish	Shaw	Telfer	McAllister	Dublin	Whelan	Ndlovu	
26/10		17,269	*8*	8				*Pressman*	*Atherton*	*Nolan*	*Pembridge*	*Newsome*	*Walker*	*Blinker^*	*Hyde*	*Booth*	*Carbone"*	*Trustfull**	*Humphreys/Oakes/Whit'ham*
							Ref: K Burge	Another predictable draw, City's fifth in a row. The vultures are circling above beleaguered Atkinson. Ndlovu has his first start of the season but can't improve the scoring record. Strachan is angry at rumours linking him to the vacant Hibs job. Ukrainian Alex Evtushok comes on trial.											
12	A	EVERTON	18	D	1-1	0-1	McAllister 68	Ogrizovic	Borrows*	Shaw	Richardson	Daish	Williams	Telfer	McAllister	Dublin	Whelan^	Salako	Ndlovu/Strachan
4/11		*31,477*	*9*	9			*Stuart 45p*	*Southall*	*Barrett*	*Hinchcliffe*	*Short*	*Watson*	*Unsworth**	*Kanchelskis*	*Parkinson^*	*Barmby*	*Stuart*	*Speed*	*Branch/Grant*
							Ref: G Poll	Big Ron moves upstairs and Strachan takes over team matters after an exciting draw. Everton parade £5.75 million Barmby on Sky TV and are stronger early on. Richardson is unlucky to concede a penalty for handball after Oggy fails to hold a cross. McAllister saves it with a screamer.											
13	A	WIMBLEDON	18	D	2-2	0-1	Whelan 56, Dublin 70	Ogrizovic	Shaw	Burrows	Jess	Daish	Williams	Ndlovu	McAllister	Dublin	Whelan	Salako	
16/11		***10,307***	*4*	10			*Earle 45, Gayle 54*	*Sullivan*	*Cunningham*	*Thatcher*	*Jones*	*Blackwell*	*Perry*	*Ardley^*	*Earle*	*Ekoku**	*Gayle*	*Leonhardsen*	*Holdsworth/Fear*
							Ref: M Bodenham	The sixth league draw in a row is a club record, and it is thanks to Oggy. The 39-year-old keeps City in the game with a string of saves until Whelan, with a nonchalant side-foot volley from outside the area, and Dublin rescue a point. Huckerby signs from Newcastle for £1 million.											
14	H	ASTON VILLA	18	L	1-2	0-1	Dublin 75	Ogrizovic	Shaw^	Burrows*	Jess	Daish	Williams	Ndlovu"	McAllister	Dublin	Whelan	Salako	Borrows/Telfer/**Huckerby**
23/11		21,335	*8*	10			*Joachim 29, Staunton 85*	*Oakes*	*Nelson*	*Wright*	*Draper"*	*Ehiogu*	*Southgate*	*Townsend*	*Curcic**	*Joachim^*	*Johnson*	*Staunton*	*Taylor/Scimeca/Milosevic*
							Ref: P Durkin	City are unlucky to lose a thrilling game to a Staunton thunderbolt after Huckerby, with his first touch, creates Dublin's equaliser. Joachim's is a freak goal, when Oggy fails to hold a harmless through ball. Tempers boil over at the end and Townsend and Whelan are lucky not to see red.											
15	A	DERBY	19	L	1-2	1-1	Dublin 43	Ogrizovic	Telfer	Shaw	Jess	Daish	Williams	Huckerby	McAllister	Dublin	Whelan	Salako*	Strachan
30/11		*18,042*	*9*	10			*Asanovic 12p, Ward 79*	*Hoult*	*Rowett*	*Laursen*	*Yates*	*McGrath**	*Stimac*	*Flynn*	*Powell D*	*Ward*	*Sturridge*	*Asanovic^*	*Dailly/Carsley*
							Ref: M Riley	Newly promoted Derby move from the Baseball Ground next summer. Ashley Ward is their star, fouled by Shaw for the penalty and pouncing for the winner. Dublin heads in from Salako's corner and misses three good chances. Strachan is rumoured to want Wimbledon's Chris Perry.											
16	H	TOTTENHAM	20	L	1-2	0-1	Whelan 60	Ogrizovic	Borrows*	Shaw	Jess^	Daish	Williams	Huckerby	McAllister	Dublin	Whelan	Salako	Genaux/Telfer
7/12		19,656	*10*	10			*Sheringham 29, Sinton 75*	*Walker*	*Carr*	*Wilson*	*Howells*	*Calderwood*	*Campbell*	*Fox*	*Neilson**	*Iverson*	*Sheringham*	*Sinton*	*Dozzell*
							Ref: G Willard	Scotland's assistant manager, Alex Miller, is Strachan's No 2 but he cannot stop City losing once more after they had equalised. It is ten games without a win and things look bleak. There is no lack of spirit but City need a bit of luck. 'Crisis' club Spurs win after four defeats in a row.											
17	H	NEWCASTLE	19	W	2-1	2-0	Huckerby 6, McAllister 31	Ogrizovic	Telfer	Shaw	Williams	Daish	Dublin	Richardson	McAllister	Huckerby^	Whelan*	Salako	Jess/Borrows
17/12		22,092	*4*	13			*Shearer 61*	*Srnicek*	*Watson*	*Elliott*	*Lee*	*Peacock*	*Howey*	*Gillespie*	*Beardsley*	*Shearer*	*Ferdinand*	*Ginola*	
							Ref: P Jones	Newcastle's team of stars is rocked by their old boy Huckerby, who scores from Richardson's delicious pass and then makes McAllister's goal. City had not scored in the first-half at home all season but fully deserve this win. Dublin plays at the back and shackles Shearer and Ferdinand.											
18	A	LEICESTER	17	W	2-0	1-0	Dublin 11, 72	Ogrizovic	Telfer	Shaw	Williams	Daish	Dublin	Richardson	McAllister	Huckerby*	Whelan	Salako	Jess
21/12		*20.038*	*13*	16				*Keller*	*Grayson*	*Kamark*	*Izzet*	*Hill**	*Prior*	*Lennon*	*Taylor*	*Claridge*	*Marshall*	*Heskey*	*Parker*
							Ref: G Barber	Defender Dublin is the hero, heading in McAllister set pieces to give City their first away win. City weather Leicester's storm aided by another fine display from Oggy. Suddenly the confidence is flowing and City look a useful side with Gary McAllister playing like an international.											
19	A	LEEDS	15	W	3-1	3-1	Huckerby 30, Dublin 38, McAllister 40p	Ogrizovic	Telfer	Shaw	Williams	Daish	Dublin	Richardson	McAllister	Huckerby*	Whelan !	Salako	Jess
26/12		*36,465*	*14*	19			*Deane 9*	*Martyn*	*Kelly*	*Halle*	*Palmer*	*Wetherall^*	*Beesley**	*Jackson*	*Radebe*	*Rush*	*Deane*	*Bowyer*	*Dorigo/Yeboah*
							Ref: M Bodenham	City score three goals in eleven minutes, giving them their first win at Leeds in 20 years. Huckerby's goal is special and he is fouled by Palmer for the penalty, City's first for a year. Gary Kelly's spot-kick is saved by Oggy. Leeds old boy Noel Whelan is sent off for two yellow cards.											
20	H	MIDDLESBROUGH	14	W	**3-0**	1-0	Huckerby 29, McAllister 64p, Cox 85 (og)	Ogrizovic	Telfer	Shaw	Williams	Daish	Dublin	Richardson	McAllister	Huckerby	Whelan	Salako	
28/12		20,605	*17*	22				*Walsh*	*Liddle*	*Morris^*	*Blackmore*	*Cox*	*Vickers*	*Emerson*	*Hignett**	*Ravanelli*	*Beck*	*Juninho*	*Campbell/Fjortoft*
							Ref: S Lodge	Boro's stars don't look too keen on a bone-hard pitch and City celebrate Oggy's record-breaking 544th appearance with their fourth win in a row. No defender has been able to cope with Huckerby's speed and strength, but today he scores with his head. His influence is immeasurable.											
21	H	SUNDERLAND	12	D	2-2	2-2	Dublin 10, Daish 28	Ogrizovic	Telfer	Shaw	Williams	Daish	Dublin !	Richardson	McAllister	Huckerby	Whelan*	Salako	Borrows
1/1		17,671	*11*	23			*Bridges 6, Agnew 18p*	*Perez*	*Hall*	*Kubicki*	*Bracewell*	*Ord*	*Melville*	*Gray*	*Mullin*	*Bridges*	*Kelly*	*Agnew*	
							Ref: G Poll	On an icy pitch City are unchanged for the fifth time, but their winning run is ended. They twice come from behind with headed goals from Dublin and Daish, who made up for his rash challenge on Mullin for the penalty. Dublin is sent off after 40 minutes for kicking out at Bridges.											

No	Date		Att	Pos	Pt	F-A	H-T	Scorers, Times, and Referees	SQUAD	NUMBERS	IN	USE								subs used
22	A	BLACKBURN		15	L	0-4	0-3		Ogrizovic	Telfer	Shaw	Williams	Daish	Borrows	Richardson	McAllister	Dublin !	Huckerby	Salako*	Jess
	11/1		*24,055*	*14*	23			*Sutton 17, 34, Gallacher 30, Donis 76*	*Flowers*	*Kenna*	*Le Saux*	*Sherwood^*	*Hendry*	*Berg*	*Flicroft*	*Bohinen*	*Sutton*	*Gallacher**	*Wilcox*	*Donis/Fenton*
								Ref: P Durkin	With Whelan suspended, Dublin reverts to being a striker and is sent off, for the second game running, for a bad challenge on Berg after 20 minutes. Strachan is manager of the month, but it is the kiss of death. Rovers run City ragged and the Sky Blues don't manage a shot on target.											
23	H	MANCHESTER U		16	L	0-2	0-0		Ogrizovic	Telfer	Shaw	Richardson	Borrows	Williams	Jess*	McAllister	Huckerby	Whelan	Salako	Hall
	18/1		**23,080**	*1*	23			*Giggs 60, Solskjaer 79*	*Schmeichel*	*Neville G*	*Irwin*	*Keane*	*Johnsen**	*Pallister*	*Poborsky*	*Scholes*	*Cantona*	*Solskjaer*	*Giggs*	*Casper*
								Ref: S Dunn	United are unbeaten in twelve and are looking favourites for the Premiership. City work hard but rarely trouble Schmeichel. Darren Huckerby is denied a penalty when Neville appears to foul him. United take control and Ryan Giggs curls in a beauty. Liam Daish is injured in training.											
24	A	NOTT'M FOREST		14	W	1-0	0-0	Huckerby 51	Ogrizovic	Telfer	Shaw	Richardson	Borrows	Williams	Jess	McAllister	Huckerby*	Whelan	Hall	Ndlovu
	29/1		*22,619*	*17*	26				*Crossley*	*Lyttle*	*Pearce*	*Haaland*	*Chettle*	*Cooper*	*Bt-Williams*	*Phillips^*	*Campbell*	*Clough**	*Woan*	*Lee/Guinan*
								Ref: A Wilkie	Dublin has started a six-match ban but City finally manage to win a game without him. A six-pointer is settled by Huckerby's far-post header. Forest's caretaker boss Stuart Pearce is having a hard time. City have sold Genaux to Udinese for £800,000 and bought Breen for £2.5 million.											
25	A	SHEFFIELD WED		15	D	0-0	0-0		Ogrizovic	Telfer	Shaw	Richardson	**Breen**	Williams	Jess	McAllister	Huckerby	Whelan*	Hall	Ndlovu
	1/2		*21,793*	*8*	27				*Pressman*	*Nicol*	*Nolan*	*Atherton*	*Stefanovic*	*Walker*	*Pembridge*	*Hyde*	*Booth*	*Hirst^*	*Whitingh'm**	*Blinker/Trustfull*
								Ref: M Bodenham	David Pleat's Wednesday have lost only once in 17 games, so City set out to soak up the pressure and catch them on the break. The chances to attack are few and far between, but Wednesday rarely trouble Oggy. It is a disciplined performance, with new boy Gary Breen in good form.											
26	A	ASTON VILLA		16	L	1-2	0-1	Staunton 78 (og)	Ogrizovic	Telfer	Shaw	Richardson^	Breen	Williams	Jess*	McAllister	Huckerby	Whelan	Hall	Ndlovu/Strachan
	19/2		*30,409*	*5*	27			*Yorke 43, 75*	*Bosnich*	*Nelson*	*Wright*	*Draper*	*Ehiogu*	*Southgate*	*Townsend*	*Taylor*	*Milosevic*	*Yorke*	*Staunton*	
								Ref: K Burge	Cup fever grips Coventry, but Villa bring City down to earth. Dreams of ending the Villa hoodoo are shattered. Dwight Yorke looks in deadly form and scores twice. Staunton's header over Bosnich makes for a lively finale, but City deserve nothing from a negative, spiritless display.											
27	H	EVERTON		16	D	0-0	0-0		Ogrizovic	Telfer	Shaw	Richardson	Breen	Williams	Ndlovu*	McAllister	Dublin	Huckerby	Hall	Whelan
	22/2		19,452	*10*	28				*Gerrard*	*Barrett*	*Phelan*	*Short*	*Watson*	*Unsworth*	*Stuart*	*Thomsen*	*Ferguson*	*Barmby*	*Speed*	
								Ref: J Winter	Dublin and Ndlovu return but can't spark a poor game, littered with wasted chances. Short hits the post in the first half but City have the better opportunities after the break, with Huckerby failing to score from three one-on-one's. With rivals also losing, it's a missed chance to pull away.											
28	A	MANCHESTER U		16	L	1-3	0-2	Huckerby 86	Ogrizovic	Shaw	**Evtushok***	Whelan	Breen	Williams	Jess	McAllister	Dublin	Huckerby	Hall^	Ndlovu/Telfer
	1/3		***55,230***	*1*	28			*Breen 4 (og), Jess 5 (og), Poborsky 47*	*Schmeichel*	*Neville G*	*Irwin**	*Poborsky*	*May*	*Pallister*	*Beckham"*	*Cruyff*	*Cantona*	*Cole*	*Giggs^*	*Neville P/Johnsen/McClair*
								Ref: G Barber	United have one eye on a Champions League tie with Porto and haven't lost in 16 league games. Within five minutes Breen strokes the ball past Oggy and Cole's shot cannons in off Jess. Evtushok is substituted after 30 minutes of his debut. Huckerby's is surely the goal of the game.											
29	H	WIMBLEDON		16	D	1-1	1-1	Dublin 37	Ogrizovic	Telfer	Dublin	Richardson	Breen	Williams	Jess	McAllister	Huckerby	Whelan	Shaw	
	3/3		**15,266**	*6*	29			*Ekoku 32*	*Heald*	*Cunningham*	*Kimble*	*McAllister*	*Blackwell*	*Perry*	*Ardley*	*Earle*	*Ekoku^*	*Gayle**	*Castledine*	*Harford/Holdsworth*
								Ref: D Elleray	The Dons are having their best ever season and are still in both cup competitions, but they are fortunate to escape with a point. The first half is City's best 45 minutes of the season but they are stunned by Ekoku's classy goal. City have 28 efforts on goal but only Dion's header counts.											
30	H	LEICESTER		16	D	0-0	0-0		Ogrizovic	Telfer*	Evtushok	Richardson	Breen	Dublin	Jess"	McAllister	Huckerby	Whelan	Shaw	Salako^/Ndlovu/Borrows
	8/3		19,199	*10*	30				*Keller*	*Grayson*	*Guppy*	*Watts*	*Elliott*	*Walsh*	*Lennon*	*Parker*	*Robins^*	*Heskey**	*Izzet*	*Taylor/Lawrence*
								Ref: P Alcock	Martin O'Neill's Leicester play a Coca-Cola semi-final in three days, but look a dour bunch. They stop City from playing and look the stronger side at the finish. Salako returns after injury as sub but after 25 minutes is replaced by Ndlovu. City are booed off. It gets tighter at the bottom.											
31	A	NEWCASTLE		16	L	0-4	0-2	*[Elliott 87]*	Ogrizovic	Shaw	Evtushok*	Richardson"	Breen	Dublin	Telfer	McAllister	Huckerby^	Jess	Hall	Borrows !/Ndlovu/Boland
	15/3		*36,571*	*4*	30			*Watson 12, Lee 45, Beardsley 76p,*	*Hislop*	*Watson*	*Elliott*	*Batty*	*Peacock*	*Albert*	*Barton*	*Lee^*	*Asprilla**	*Beardsley*	*Ginola"*	*Gillespie/Clark/Crawford*
								Ref: G Ashby	Shearer and Ferdinand are out, but City can't improve their record of one win in eleven. They are under the cosh from the start with Asprilla the architect, setting up the first, fouled by Dublin for the penalty, and causing Brian Borrows to become the first City substitute to be sent off.											

No Date	H/A	Opponent / Att	Pos	Res / Pts	F-A	H-T	Scorers, Times, and Referees	1	2	3	4	5	6	7	8	9	10	11	subs used
32	H	WEST HAM	18	L	1-3	1-2	Rieper 9 (og)	Ogrizovic	Telfer	Shaw	Richardson	Breen	Dublin	Williams	McAllister	Huckerby	Whelan^	Hall*	Ndlovu/Burrows
22/3		22,290	*14*	30			*Hartson 27, 49, Ferdinand 34*	*Miklosko*	*Breacker**	*Dicks*	*Potts*	*Bilic*	*Rieper*	*Moncur*	*Ferdinand^*	*Hartson*	*Kitson*	*Bishop"*	*Rowlan/Dowie/Porfirio*
							Ref: M Reed	A devastating result and a poor performance against fellow strugglers. City started well, but as soon as the impressive Hartson equalised their confidence evaporated. The defensive failings, with Dublin at sea for once, are brutally exposed. With a tough run-in, the omens are not good.											
33	A	LIVERPOOL	17	W	2-1	0-0	Whelan 70, Dublin 90	Ogrizovic	Shaw	Burrows	Richardson	Williams	Dublin	Whelan	McAllister	Huckerby^	Jess*	Ndlovu	Hall/Strachan
6/4		*40,079*	*3*	33			*Fowler 50*	*James*	*McAteer*	*Bjornebye**	*Matteo*	*Kvarme*	*Harkness*	*McManam'n*	*Redknapp*	*Collymore*	*Fowler*	*Barnes*	*Berger*
							Ref: P Danson	An unbelievable win after 90 minutes under the Red cosh is arguably the best result in 30 years. City go into the game bottom and leap three places. Fowler's goal is in Strachan's words 'world-class'. McAllister's corners bemuse James and Dublin's 92nd-minute goal is stunning.											
34	H	CHELSEA	15	W	3-1	0-1	Dublin 49, Williams 51, Whelan 58	Ogrizovic	Telfer	Borrows	Strachan^	Williams	Shaw	Whelan	McAllister	Dublin	Ndlovu*	Burrows	Huckerby/Richardson
9/4		19,889	*7*	36			*Hughes P 43*	*Grodas*	*Burley*	*Minto*	*Sinclair*	*Leboeuf*	*Clarke*	*Newton*	*Di Matteo*	*Zola*	*Hughes M^*	*Hughes P**	*Vialli/Granville*
							Ref: D Gallagher	40-year-old Strachan starts for the first time this season and is inspirational. Chelsea arrive as FA Cup favourites and leave a bedraggled rabble. Chelsea haven't packed their away kit and have to wear City's red and black away kit. Three goals in nine minutes push City closer to safety.											
35	A	SOUTHAMPTON	15	D	2-2	0-1	Ndlovu 62, Whelan 74	Ogrizovic	Telfer	Borrows	Shaw	Williams	Burrows*	Whelan	McAllister	Dublin	Huckerby^	Ndlovu	Strachan/Richardson
19/4		*15,251*	*19*	37			*Evans 27, Ostenstad 47*	*Taylor*	*Van Gobbel*	*Benali*	*Magilton*	*Dodd*	*Lundekvam*	*Oakley*	*Berkovic**	*Ostenstad*	*Evans*	*Slater*	*Neilson*
							Ref: P Jones	Gordon Strachan starts on the bench and the City are two down when he comes off it to inspire another fightback. For an hour Saints dominate and City's defensive frailty returns. When Peter Ndlovu and Noel Whelan score, City look like world beaters and could have snatched a win.											
36	H	ARSENAL	15	D	1-1	1-1	Dublin 2	Ogrizovic	Telfer	Borrows	Strachan^	Williams	Shaw	Whelan	McAllister	Dublin*	Ndlovu	Burrows	Huckerby/Richardson
21/4		20,004	*2*	38			*Wright 19p*	*Seaman*	*Dixon**	*Winterburn*	*Keown*	*Bould*	*Adams*	*Platt*	*Vieira*	*Wright*	*Bergkamp*	*Merson^*	*Parlour/Anelka*
							Ref: K Burge	The Premiership looks out of Arsenal's grasp but second place is up for grabs. Dion Dublin gets the perfect start with a perfect finish from McAllister's deflected pass. Oggy drops the ball and has to foul Wright, who scores from the spot. Both sides waste chances in an even game.											
37	H	DERBY	18	L	1-2	0-0	McAllister 59p	Ogrizovic	Telfer	Borrows*	Strachan^	Williams	Shaw	Whelan	McAllister	Dublin	Ndlovu"	Burrows	Breen/Jess/Huckerby
3/5		22,854	*10*	38			*Rowett 49, Sturridge 67*	*Poom*	*Carsley**	*Powell C*	*Rowett*	*Laursen*	*Dailly*	*v d Laan^*	*Powell D*	*Ward*	*Sturridge*	*Trollope*	*Yates/Willems*
							Ref: R Dilkes	With Sunderland, Southampton and West Ham winning, this result is disastrous and City are in dire trouble. They need to rely on others losing now. This was never going to be a showpiece, there being too much at stake. McAllister's penalty after Dublin is fouled gives short-lived hope.											
38	A	TOTTENHAM	17	W	2-1	2-1	Dublin 13, Williams 39	Ogrizovic	Telfer	Burrows	Richardson	Williams	Shaw	Whelan*	McAllister	Dublin	Huckerby	Ndlovu	Jess
11/5		*33,029*	*10*	41			*McVeigh 44*	*Baardsen*	*Carr*	*Edinburgh*	*Scales*	*Vega*	*Campbell*	*Fox*	*Dozzell*	*McVeigh**	*Sheringham*	*Sinton^*	*Fenn/Clapham*
	Home	Away					Ref: M Bodenham	The obituaries have been written but the corpse refuses to lie down. This is the greatest escape of all time. Sunderland lose and Boro draw and with City's game kicking off late the last quarter of an hour is nail-biting. Ogrizovic, the ultimate hero, makes two super saves to seal the win.											
Average	19,625	27,862																	

Coca-Cola Cup					F-A	H-T	Scorers, Times, and Referees	SQUAD	NUMBERS	IN	USE								subs used
2:1	H	BIRMINGHAM	18	D	1-1	0-1	Daish 88	Ogrizovic	Borrows	Burrows	Richardson	Daish	Shaw	Telfer	McAllister	Dublin	Whelan	Salako	
	18/9	11,823 *1:14*					*Furlong 38*	*Bennett*	*Poole*	*Ablett*	*Castle^*	*Breen*	*Bruce*	*Bowen**	*Horne*	*Furlong*	*Newell*	*Legg*	*Devlin/Tait*
							Ref: S Dunn	City enjoy the majority of the possession and chances but are thwarted by Blues' defence and Ian Bennett in particular. Old boy Paul Furlong scores with a deflected goal and it looks likely to end the scoring until Daish's volley near the end thwarts Trevor Francis' expensive team.											
2:2	A	BIRMINGHAM	18	W	1-0	0-0	McAllister 62	Ogrizovic	Borrows	Hall	Richardson	Daish !	Burrows	Telfer	McAllister	Dublin	Whelan	Salako	
	24/9	*15,281 1:17*						*Bennett*	*Edwards*	*Ablett*	*Castle*	*Breen*	*Bruce*	*Devlin*	*Horne*	*Furlong*	*Newell*	*Donowa**	*Bowen*
							Ref: P Alcock (City win 2-1 on aggregate)	City go through after McAllister's free-kick takes a slight deflection off Furlong and beats Bennett. Fifteen minutes from time Blues old boy Daish is sent off for the second time this season for two yellows. City notch their first away win on Sky TV. Breen impresses City's bosses.											
3	A	GILLINGHAM	19	D	2-2	2-0	Telfer 25, 27	Ogrizovic	Borrows	Hall	Richardson	Williams	Shaw	Telfer	McAllister	Dublin	Whelan	Salako	
	22/10	*10,603 2:15*					*Onuora 58, Ratcliffe 75*	*Stannard*	*Smith*	*Morris*	*Hess'thaler*	*Harris*	*Bryant*	*Bailey**	*Ratcliffe*	*Onuora*	*Butler*	*Chapman*	*Puttnam*
							Ref: P Durkin	This enthralling cup-tie is delayed for 15 minutes because of crowd congestion. City totally dominate the first half and Salako creates Telfer's two goals. Tony Pulis's team switch to a direct approach and it pays off. Onuora heads in and Ratcliffe's long-range screamer earns the replay.											
3R	H	GILLINGHAM	18	L	0-1	0-0		Ogrizovic	Borrows	Shaw	Richardson	Daish	Williams	Telfer*	McAllister	Jess^	Whelan	Salako	Strachan/Dublin
	13/11	12,639 *2:18*					*Smith 71*	*Stannard*	*Smith*	*Harris*	*Hess'thaler*	*Green*	*Bryant*	*Bailey*	*Ratcliffe*	*Onuora*	*Butler*	*Armstrong*	
							Ref: R Dilkes	Strachan's first game in charge brings an embarrassing cup exit. Gillingham are ordinary but deserve their win. City make no impact in attack and look suspect at the back. This is Gillingham's first ever win over a top division side. Dave Busst is forced to retire after 13 leg operations.											

FA Cup																			
3	H	WOKING	16	D	1-1	0-0	Jess 75	Ogrizovic	Telfer	Shaw	Richardson	Borrows	Williams	Jess	McAllister	Huckerby	Whelan	Salako	
	25/1	16,011 *VC:6*					*Thompson 89*	*Batty*	*Howard*	*Taylor*	*Foster*	*Brown*	*Jones*	*Thompson*	*Wye S*	*Steele*	*Hunter**	*Walker*	*Hay*
							Ref: M Riley	Neutrals would have thought Woking to be the Premiership side. They should have buried labouring City. Even after Jess drives a low shot the non-leaguers fight back. Woking push men forward until Thompson sticks out a toe to grab the headlines by forcing a replay. Woking's day!											
3R	A	WOKING	15	W	2-1	1-1	Whelan 11, Foster 78 (og)	Ogrizovic	Telfer	Shaw	Richardson	Borrows	Williams	Jess^	McAllister	Huckerby*	Whelan	Hall	Ndlovu/Strachan
	4/2	*6,000 VC:6*					*Steele 36*	*Batty*	*Howard*	*Taylor*	*Foster*	*Brown*	*Jones*	*Thompson*	*Wye S*	*Steele*	*Hay**	*Walker*	*Hunter*
							Ref: M Riley	City almost slip on the banana skin at Kingfield Stadium, despite Whelan early goal. Geoff Chapple's team are deservedly back in it before half-time, thanks to Walker's dazzling display. The second half is end to end, but Foster scores as he tries to head McAllister's cross clear.											
4	A	BLACKBURN	15	W	2-1	2-1	Jess 28, Huckerby 44	Ogrizovic	Telfer	Shaw	Richardson	Borrows	Williams	Jess	McAllister	Huckerby*	Whelan	Hall	Ndlovu
	15/2	*21,123 13*					*Sherwood 1*	*Flowers*	*Kenna*	*Le Saux*	*Sherwood*	*Hendry*	*Berg*	*Flicroft**	*McKinlay*	*Sutton*	*Gallacher*	*Wilcox*	*Warhurst*
							Ref: S Lodge	A goal down after 49 seconds, City stage a stirring comeback to win a highly entertaining tie and reach the 5th Round for the first time since 1987. A massive following roars them on. Oggy tops it all by saving Sutton's 64th minute penalty, after Borrows fouled Kevin Gallacher.											
5	A	DERBY	16	L	2-3	2-2	Huckerby 5, Whelan 13	Ogrizovic	Telfer	Shaw	Richardson	Dublin	Williams	Jess*	McAllister	Huckerby	Whelan	Hall	Ndlovu
	26/2	*18,003 13*					*Ward 16, Van der Laan 40, Sturridge 87*	*Hoult*	*Carsley*	*Trollope*	*Rowett*	*Laursen*	*Dailly*	*v d Laan*	*Powell D*	*Ward*	*Sturridge*	*Asanovic*	
							Ref: P Danson	City throw away a two-goal lead and are beaten by a late Dean Sturridge goal in a thrilling tie on a boggy pitch. Huckerby and Whelan run Derby's defence - missing Stimac, Poom and McGrath - ragged in the first half. But once the Rams are level they look the more likely to win.											

		P	W	D	L	F	A	W	D	L	F	A	Pts
			Home					Away					
1	Manchester U	38	12	5	2	38	17	9	7	3	38	27	75
2	Newcastle	38	13	3	3	54	20	6	8	5	19	20	68
3	Arsenal	38	10	5	4	36	18	9	6	4	26	14	68
4	Liverpool	38	10	6	3	38	19	9	5	5	24	18	68
5	Aston Villa	38	11	5	3	27	13	6	5	8	20	21	61
6	Chelsea	38	9	8	2	33	22	7	3	9	25	33	59
7	Sheffield Wed	38	8	10	1	25	16	6	5	8	25	35	57
8	Wimbledon	38	9	6	4	28	21	6	5	8	21	25	56
9	Leicester	38	7	5	7	22	26	5	6	8	24	28	47
10	Tottenham	38	8	4	7	19	17	5	3	11	25	34	46
11	Leeds	38	7	7	5	15	13	4	6	9	13	25	46
12	Derby	38	8	6	5	25	22	3	7	9	20	36	46
13	Blackburn	38	8	4	7	28	23	1	11	7	14	20	42
14	West Ham	38	7	6	6	27	25	3	6	10	12	23	42
15	Everton	38	7	4	8	24	22	3	8	8	20	35	42
16	Southampton	38	6	7	6	32	24	4	4	11	18	32	41
17	COVENTRY	38	4	8	7	19	23	5	6	8	19	31	41
18	Sunderland	38	7	6	6	20	18	3	4	12	15	35	40
19	Middlesbro*	38	8	5	6	34	25	2	7	10	17	35	39
20	Nott'm Forest	38	3	9	7	15	27	3	7	9	16	32	34
		760	162	119	99	559	411	99	119	162	411	559	1018

* deducted 3 points

Odds & ends

Double wins: (1) Leeds.
Double losses: (3) Aston Villa, Manchester U, Derby.

Won from behind: (5) Leeds (h&a), Liverpool (a), Chelsea (h), Blackburn FAC.
Lost from in front: (2) West Ham (h), Derby FAC (a).

High spots: The Greatest Escape at Spurs on the final day.
The amazing injury-time win at Anfield.
Four successive wins over Christmas.

Low spots: Ten games without a win in the autumn.
Held at home by Woking.
Beaten at home by Gillingham in Strachan's first match as manager.
Losing to Derby in the FA Cup after leading 2-0.

Red cards: City – Daish (Chelsea a), Daish (Birmingham LC a), Whelan (Leeds a), Dublin (Sund' h), Dublin (Blackburn a), Borrows (Newcastle a).

Player of the Year: Dion Dublin.
Ever-presents: (2) Steve Ogrizovic, Gary McAllister.
Hat-tricks: (0).
Opposing hat-tricks: Campbell (Nott'm Forest).
Leading scorer: (13) Dion Dublin.

	Appearances						Goals			
	Lge	*Sub*	LC	*Sub*	FAC	*Sub*	Lge	LC	FAC	Tot
Boland, Willie		*1*								
Borrows, Brian	**16**	*7*	4		3					
Breen, Gary	**8**	*1*								
Burrows, David	**17**	*1*	2							
Daish, Liam	**20**		3				**1**	1		**2**
Dublin, Dion	**33**	*1*	3	*1*	1		**13**			**13**
Ducros, Andrew	**1**	*4*								
Evtushok, Alex	**3**									
Filan, John		*1*								
Genaux, Regis	**3**	*1*								
Hall, Marcus	**10**	*3*	2		3					
Huckerby, Darren	**21**	*4*			4		**5**		2	**7**
Isaias, Marques		*1*								
Jess, Eoin	**19**	*8*	1		4				2	**2**
McAllister, Gary	**38**		4		4		**6**	1		**7**
Ndlovu, Peter	**10**	*10*				*3*	**1**			**1**
O'Neill, Michael	**1**									
Ogrizovic, Steve	**38**		4		4					
Richardson, Kevin	**25**	*3*	4		4					
Salako, John	**23**	*1*	4		1		**1**			**1**
Shaw, Richard	**35**		3		4					
Strachan, Gordon	**3**	*6*		*1*		*1*				
Telfer, Paul	**31**	*3*	4		4			2		**2**
Whelan, Noel	**34**	*1*	4		4		**6**		2	**8**
Williams, Paul D	**29**	*3*	2		4		**2**			**2**
(own-goals)							**3**		1	**4**
25 players used	**418**	***60***	**44**	***2***	**44**	***4***	**38**	**4**	**7**	**49**

F.A. CARLING PREMIERSHIP

Manager: Gordon Strachan

SEASON 1997-98

No	Date		Att	Pos	Pt	F-A	H-T		SQUAD	NUMBERS	IN	USE								subs used
1	H	CHELSEA			W	3-2	1-1	Dublin 41, 82, 88	Ogrizovic	Breen^	Burrows	**Soltvedt**	Williams	Shaw	Telfer	McAllister	Dublin	Huckerby*	Salako	**Lightbourne**/Boland
	9/8		22,691		3			*Sinclair 39, Flo 71*	*De Goey*	*Petrescu*	*Le Saux*	*Sinclair*	*Leboeuf*	*Clarke*	*Poyet*	*Di Matteo^*	*Hughes**	*Zola*	*Wise*	*Flo/Morris*
								Ref: P Durkin	City are outplayed for long periods in the sweltering weather but refuse to lie down. They capitalise on Chelsea's sloppiness in glorious fashion with Dublin exposing Leboeuf's defensive frailties and grabbing the first home hat-trick for nine years. Breen looks out of position at full back.											
2	A	ARSENAL			L	0-2	0-1		Ogrizovic	Breen	Burrows	Soltvedt^	Williams	Shaw	Telfer	McAllister	Dublin	Huckerby*	Salako	Lightbourne/Boland
	11/8		*37,324*		3			*Wright 29, 47*	*Seaman*	*Garde*	*Winterburn*	*Vieira*	*Grimandi*	*Marshall*	*Parlour*	*Petit**	*Wright*	*Bergkamp*	*Overmars^*	*Platt/Hughes*
								Ref: K Burge	On a hot and humid night the impressive Gunners outplay City but win courtesy of two errors. Oggy spills a shot and Shaw's back-pass stops short. Ian Wright pounces on both errors and stands one goal behind Cliff Bastin's goalscoring record. Arsenal look potential title contenders.											
3	H	BOLTON		10	D	2-2	2-0	Telfer 8, Huckerby 20	Ogrizovic	Breen	Burrows	Soltvedt*	Williams	Shaw	Telfer	Richardson	Dublin	Huckerby	Salako	Boland
	23/8		16,640	*8*	4			*Blake 69, 76*	*Branagan*	*Cox**	*Elliott*	*Pollock*	*Bergsson*	*Taggart*	*Thompson*	*Frandsen*	*Blake*	*McGinlay^*	*Sellars*	*Phillips/Beardsley*
								Ref: M Riley	The proverbial game of two halves. City should have been five up at the break but by the end Bolton deserved a point. Telfer is impressive, as is Richardson, in for the injured McAllister. Nathan Blake punishes casual defending after new-boy Peter Beardsley makes his debut as a sub.											
4	H	WEST HAM		11	D	1-1	1-0	Huckerby 38	Ogrizovic	Breen	Burrows	Soltvedt*	Williams	Shaw	Telfer	Richardson	Dublin	Huckerby^	Salako	Boland/Lightbourne
	27/8		18,291	*5*	5			*Kitson 61*	*Miklosko*	*Breacker*	*Laziridis*	*Ferdinand*	*Reiper*	*Unsworth*	*Berkovic*	*Lomas*	*Hartson*	*Kitson**	*Moncur*	*Dowie*
								Ref: N Barry	The points are deservedly shared in an intriguing clash. City finish the first half very strongly after Huckerby scores from close range. West Ham then turn up the heat, with Laziridis giving Breen a hard time and Kitson getting on the end of a rebound. Richardson is again City's star.											
5	A	MANCHESTER U		12	L	0-3	0-1		Ogrizovic	**Nilsson**	Burrows	Hall	Williams	Shaw	Telfer	Richardson	Dublin	Huckerby	Salako	
	30/8		***55,074***	*1*	5			*Cole 2, Keane 72, Poborsky 90*	*Schmeichel*	*Neville G*	*Neville P*	*Keane*	*Pallister*	*Berg*	*Beckham*	*Butt*	*Cole**	*Sheringham*	*Giggs*	*Poborsky*
								Ref: G Ashby	Strachan is impressed with the team's performance and the scoreline is harsh on them. Cole's goal is a deflection and City could have been level at half-time. Nilsson makes a promising debut, marking Giggs and getting forward. United are off colour but have yet to concede a goal.											
6	H	SOUTHAMPTON		8	W	1-0	0-0	Soltvedt 65	Ogrizovic	Nilsson	Burrows	Soltvedt	Williams	Shaw	Telfer	McAllister	Dublin	Huckerby	Salako	
	13/9		18,666	*20*	8				*Jones*	*Dodd*	*Todd*	*Richardson*	*Monkou*	*Lundekvam*	*Bowen*	*Oakley*	*Ostenstad**	*Evans*	*Hughes^*	*Davies/Neilson*
								Ref: U Rennie	McAllister returns after injury and has an excellent first half. Richardson has a quiet Saints debut after his midweek move. City deservedly win on Oggy's 40th bithday. Soltvedt breaks the deadlock with a fine finish. Roland Nilsson is outstanding but Williams picks up his fifth booking.											
7	A	SHEFFIELD WED		11	D	0-0	0-0		Ogrizovic	Nilsson	Burrows	Soltvedt*	Williams	Shaw	Telfer	McAllister	Dublin	Salako	Hall	Boland
	20/9		*21,087*	*19*	9				*Pressman^*	*Nolan*	*Nicol*	*Atherton**	*Newsome*	*Walker*	*Magilton"*	*Whittingh'm*	*Hirst*	*Di Canio*	*Pembridge*	*Collins/Clarke/Oakes*
								Ref: G Willard	The Owls' poor start continues and they are lucky to leave with a point after John Salako, playing up front, misses five good chances. Peter Atherton and Kevin Pressman limp off early on and Wednesday never get going. Strachan's post-match comments about Salako are ominous.											
8	H	CRYS PALACE		12	D	1-1	1-1	Dublin 8	Ogrizovic	Nilsson	Burrows	Hall	Williams	Shaw	Telfer	McAllister	Dublin	Ducros^	**Shilton***	Boland/Lightbourne
	24/9		**15,910**	*11*	10			*Fullarton 9*	*Miller*	*Muscat*	*Gordon*	*Edworthy*	*Hreidarsson*	*Linighan*	*Lombardo**	*Roberts*	*Shipperley*	*Freedman^*	*Fullarton*	*McKenzie/Veart*
								Ref: G Barber	Injuries and suspension mean that Sam Shilton, son of Peter, makes his debut and Ducros gets a rare game. City let workmanlike Palace off the hook after Dion's goal. Coppell is resigned to losing his assistant Wilkins to Fulham, and dreams of having money to compete at the top level											
9	A	BLACKBURN		12	D	0-0	0-0		Ogrizovic	Nilsson	Burrows	Boland	Breen	Shaw	Telfer*	McAllister	Dublin !	Huckerby^	Hall	O'Neill/Lightbourne
	28/9		*19,086*	*5*	11				*Flowers*	*Valery**	*Kenna*	*Sherwood*	*Hendry*	*Henchoz*	*Gallacher*	*Flitcroft*	*Sutton*	*Dahlin^*	*Wilcox !*	*Duff/Bohinen*
								Ref: P Jones	Oggy equals George Curtis's record league appearances of 487 and City end a miserable run at Ewood. The game is overshadowed by the two red cards. Dublin goes after 42 minutes for elbowing Colin Hendry. Jason Wilcox goes after 70 minutes for lashing out at Michael O'Neill.											
10	H	LEEDS		12	D	0-0	0-0		Ogrizovic	Nilsson	Burrows	Soltvedt	Breen	Shaw	Boland	McAllister	Dublin	Salako	O'Neill*	Ducros^/**Haworth**
	4/10		17,771	*7*	12				*Martyn*	*Halle*	*Robertson*	*Haaland*	*Radebe*	*Wetherall*	*Kelly*	*Hopkin*	*Hasselb'nk**	*Wallace*	*Ribeiro*	*Lilley*
								Ref: A Wilkie	Six games unbeaten at home is the best start for almost twenty years. Leeds are tough opposition but Breen handles the threat of Hasselbaink and Wallace superbly. O'Neill is stretchered off with a dislocated shoulder after 24 minutes and Ducros his substitute is later substituted.											

No	Venue	Opponent / Date	Att	Pos	Res / Pts	F-A	H-T	Scorers, Times, and Referees	1	2	3	4	5	6	7	8	9	10	11	Subs used
11	A	BARNSLEY		15	L	0-2	0-1		Ogrizovic	Nilsson	Burrows	Boland	Breen	Shaw	Salako	McAllister	Haworth	Lightb'rne*	Hall	**Johansen**
		20/10	*17,463*	*19*	12			*Ward 11, Redfearn 66p*	*Watson*	*Eaden*	*Barnard*	*Bullock^*	*Sheridan*	*De Zeeuw*	*Thompson*	*Redfearn*	*Ward*	*Liddell**	*Krizan*	*Hristov/Moses*
								Ref: P Alcock	Barnsley had lost six in a row but are 'up for it' against a lacklustre City. Ashley Ward scores the first and, just as City appear to be getting on top, Neil Redfearn scores a penalty after David Burrows fouls Bullock. David Watson keeps the Tykes in the match with a string of fine saves.											
12	H	EVERTON		15	D	0-0	0-0		Ogrizovic	Nilsson	Burrows	Soltvedt	Williams	Shaw	Salako*	McAllister	Haworth	Huckerby	Hall	Johansen
		25/10	18,755	*16*	13				*Southall*	*Barrett*	*Hinchcliffe*	*Williamson*	*Watson*	*Short*	*Stuart*	*Oster*	*Ferguson*	*Cad'mart'n**	*Speed*	*Barmby*
								Ref: S Lodge	Breen is away on international duty and Williams returns. Everton have tightened things up after the cup game and Oggy has to pull off some good stops. Noel Whelan, yet to play after pre-season injuries, will be out until Christmas. Strachan is angry with the FA about Dublin's ban.											
13	A	WIMBLEDON		12	W	2-1	2-1	Huckerby 17, Dublin 22	Ogrizovic	Telfer	Burrows	Williams	Breen	Shaw	Soltvedt	McAllister	Dublin	Huckerby	Hall	
		1/11	***11,201***	*10*	16			*Cort 28*	*Sullivan*	*Cunningh'm"*	*Thatcher*	*Jones*	*Blackwell*	*Perry*	*Hughes C^*	*Earle*	*Ekoku**	*Cort*	*Hughes M*	*Gayle/Clarke/Ardley*
								Ref: U Rennie	Dublin and Huckerby are reunited and give the side a real potent look. Both goals are opportunistic, the second after Neil Sullivan fails to clear properly. City soak up the pressure in the second half and break out three times to go close. Gary McAllister plays an outstanding second half.											
14	H	NEWCASTLE		10	D	2-2	1-1	Dublin 4, 82	Ogrizovic	Nilsson	Burrows	Williams	Breen	Shaw	Telfer	McAllister	Dublin	Huckerby*	Hall	Haworth
		8/11	22,670	*9*	17			*Barnes 31, Lee 87*	*Given*	*Watson*	*Pistone*	*Batty**	*Peacock*	*Albert*	*Gillespie*	*Lee*	*Barnes*	*Ketsbaia*	*Beresford*	*Barton*
								Ref: P Durkin	Dublin reappears from behind the goal-line to surprise Shay Given and score the first. A superb second half climaxes with Dublin scoring what looks like the winner, only for the defence to back off allowing Lee to score a shock equaliser. Gordon Strachan has signed a six-year contract.											
15	A	DERBY		12	L	1-3	0-3	Huckerby 71	Ogrizovic	Nilsson	Burrows	Williams^	Breen	Shaw	Telfer	McAllister	Dublin	Haworth*	Hall	Huckerby/Boland
		22/11	*29,351*	*5*	17			*Baiano 3, Eranio 30p, Wanchope 39*	*Poom*	*Kozluk*	*Powell C*	*Carsley*	*Laursen**	*Dailly*	*Eranio*	*Rowett*	*Wanchope*	*Sturridge*	*Baiano^*	*Powell D/Hunt*
								Ref: D Elleray	City's first game at Pride Park, where Derby are unbeaten, is effectively over by half-time. Francisco Baiano scores one, and is brought down by Burrows for the penalty before Wanchope races away for the third. Strachan has contretemps with ref Elleray over his handling of the game.											
16	H	LEICESTER		15	L	0-2	0-1		Ogrizovic	Nilsson	Hall	Boland^	Breen	Shaw	Telfer	McAllister*	Dublin	Huckerby	Williams	Soltvedt/Haworth
		29/11	18,332	*6*	17			*Fenton 32, Elliott 75p*	*Keller*	*Kaamark*	*Guppy*	*Prior*	*Elliott*	*Walsh*	*Lennon*	*Izzet*	*Marshall*	*Fenton*	*Savage*	
								Ref: M Bodenham	City's home record goes, with the first defeat at home by Leicester for 21 years. City lack the guile needed to break down battling Leicester for whom Elliott is outstanding, and who scores from the spot after Shaw brings down Izzet. McAllister is carried off with a serious looking injury.											
17	A	ASTON VILLA		16	L	0-3	0-1		Ogrizovic	Nilsson	Burrows	Williams !	Breen !	Shaw	Telfer"	Soltvedt	Dublin	Huckerby^	Whelan*	Hall/Haworth/**Strachan**
		6/12	*33,250*	*11*	17			*Collymore 21, Hendrie 71, Joachim 85*	*Bosnich*	*Charles*	*Wright*	*Southgate*	*Ehiogu*	*Staunton*	*Grayson*	*Draper*	*Milosevic^*	*Collymore"*	*Yorke**	*Hendrie/Joachim/Curcic*
								Ref: G Barber	The nightmare at Villa Park continues as Stan Collymore scores his first home goal. City have two players sent off for only the second time in their history - Williams for two bookings and Breen for pushing Charles in the last minute. Two Villa substitutes scoring is a unique event.											
18	H	TOTTENHAM		14	W	4-0	1-0	Huckerby 42, 84, Breen 63, Hall 87	**Hedman**	Nilsson	Burrows	Whelan^	Breen	Shaw	Telfer	McAllister*	Dublin	Huckerby	Hall	Soltvedt/O'Neill
		13/12	19,490	*18*	20				*Walker*	*Carr*	*Wilson^*	*Neilson*	*Mabbutt*	*Calderwood*	*Fox*	*Anderton**	*Ferdinand*	*Ginola*	*Sinton"*	*Iverson/Edinburgh/Clemence*
								Ref: S Dunn	Spurs are in the relegation zone after three defeats in a row and new boss Gross has a tough job on. Once the second goal goes in the visitors fall apart and City notch their biggest win for two years. Oggy is axed for only the second time in 13 years and Hedman finally makes his bow.											
19	A	LIVERPOOL		16	L	0-1	0-1		Hedman	Nilsson	Hall	**Boateng**	Dublin	Shaw	Telfer	Soltvedt*	Haworth^	Huckerby	Whelan	Strachan/Ducros
		20/12	*39,707*	*5*	20			*Owen 14*	*James*	*McAteer*	*Harkness*	*Redknapp*	*Matteo*	*Kvarme*	*McManam'n*	*Carragher*	*Fowler*	*Owen*	*Leonhardsen*	
								Ref: P Alcock	City lose at Anfield for the first time in four years. A poor game is brightened by the form of new signing Boateng. Three City defenders are suspended and Dublin plays for the first time this season in defence. McManaman superbly sets up the goal for super boy Michael Owen.											
20	A	WEST HAM		17	L	0-1	0-1		Hedman	Nilsson	Hall	Boateng !	Dublin	Shaw	Telfer	O'Neill*	Whelan	Huckerby	Shilton	Lightbourne
		26/12	*24,532*	*8*	20			*Kitson 17*	*Forrest*	*Impey*	*Laziridis*	*Ferdinand*	*Pearce*	*Unsworth*	*Berkovic**	*Lomas*	*Hartson*	*Kitson*	*Lampard*	*Potts*
								Ref: G Poll	A makeshift side struggles to make any impact on a West Ham team that has lost only once at home. George Boateng's over-eagerness earns him two yellow cards and City's fourth dismissal of the season. Romanian Moldovan signs from Grasshoppers of Zurich for £3.25 million.											
21	H	MANCHESTER U		14	W	3-2	1-1	Whelan 12, Dublin 86p, Huckerby 88	Hedman	Nilsson	Burrows	Boateng*	Williams	Shaw	Telfer	Whelan	Dublin	Huckerby	Hall^	Boland/Soltvedt
		28/12	**23,055**	*1*	23			*Solskjaer 30, Sheringham 47*	*Pilkington*	*Neville G*	*Johnson**	*Scholes*	*Pallister*	*Berg*	*Beckham*	*Sheringham*	*Cole*	*Solskjaer^*	*Giggs*	*Curtis/Butt*
								Ref: N Barry	An amazing comeback gives City their first win over United for nine years. Dublin scores City's first penalty of the season after Henning Berg fouls Huckerby. Huckerby snatches it with a spectacular twisting run for BBC's goal of the month. United's season goes downhill from here.											

No	Date			Att	Pos	Pt		F-A	H-T	Scorers, Times, and Referees	SQUAD	NUMBERS	IN	USE								subs used
22		A	CHELSEA		17		L	1-3	1-0	Telfer 30	Hedman	Shaw	Burrows	Boland	Breen	Williams	Telfer	Whelan	Dublin	Huckerby	Salako*	**Moldovan**
	10/1			*34,647*	*2*	23				*Nicholls 65, 70, Di Matteo 78*	*De Goey*	*Clarke*	*Le Saux*	*Lambourde*	*Leboeuf*	*Duberry*	*Wise*	*Di Matteo*	*Hughes*	*Zola^*	*Granville**	*Nicholls/Gullit*
										Ref: M Reed	City lose an exciting game after looking in control. They sit back too deep, although the game was there to be won, and Chelsea surge forward. Shaw is exposed at right-back and Graham Le Saux's crosses make the first two goals for sub Mark Nicholls. Moldovan has a muted debut.											
23		H	ARSENAL		16		D	2-2	1-0	Whelan 21, Dublin 66p	Hedman	Nilsson	Burrows	Boateng	Breen	Williams !	Telfer	Soltvedt	Dublin	Huckerby	Whelan	
	17/1			22,777	*5*	24				*Bergkamp 50, Anelka 57*	*Seaman*	*Dixon*	*Winterburn*	*Keown**	*Bould*	*Upson*	*Parlour*	*Vieira !*	*Anelka*	*Bergkamp*	*Petit^*	*Grimandi/BoaMorte*
										Ref: S Lodge	City put on their best 45 minutes of the season and should have been home and dry by the break. Paul Williams has a stinker. His back-pass is too weak and Bergkamp equalises. Then the Dutchman dives and Williams goes. Justice is done by Dublin after Vieira handles and is sent off.											
24		A	BOLTON		13		W	5-1	1-1	Whelan 26, Huckerby 58, 65,	Hedman	Nilsson	Burrows	Boateng"	Breen	Shaw^	Telfer	Soltvedt	Dublin	Huckerby*	Whelan	Moldovan/Hall/Strachan
	31/1			*25,000*	*19*	27				*Sellars 21* [Dublin 73, 79]	*Branagan*	*Cox*	*Phillips*	*Pollock**	*Fairclough*	*Todd*	*Frandsen*	*Sheridan*	*Blake*	*Taylor^*	*Sellars*	*Beardsley/Holdsworth*
										Ref: D Gallagher	City take their time to get going in their first visit to the Reebok and Whelan's brilliant effort keeps them level. After the break City run riot and the Dublin-Huckerby partnership gives City their biggest away win since 1959. Poor Bolton fall apart and look good bets for relegation.											
25		H	SHEFFIELD WED		12		W	1-0	0-0	Dublin 74p	Hedman	Nilsson	Burrows	Boateng	Breen	Shaw	Telfer	Soltvedt*	Dublin	Huckerby	Hall	Strachan
	7/2			18,371	*14*	30					*Pressman*	*Nolan*	*Hinchcliffe*	*Atherton*	*Newsome*	*Walker*	*Rudi**	*Hyde"*	*Carbone*	*Di Canio*	*Pembridge^*	*Whit'gh'm/Mayrleb/Magilton*
										Ref: G Ashby	Dublin celebrates his call-up to the England squad with his third penalty in successive home league games after Newsome hauls him down. He has however rejected City's offer of a new contract and could leave soon. Huckerby and Hall are in B squad. John Salako is on the transfer list.											
26		A	SOUTHAMPTON		10		W	2-1	2-0	Whelan 14, Huckerby 29	Hedman	Nilsson	Burrows	Strachan*	Breen	Dublin	Whelan	Soltvedt	Moldovan	Huckerby	Hall	Boland
	18/2			*15,091*	*12*	33				*Le Tissier 80p*	*Jones*	*Dodd*	*Todd^*	*Palmer*	*Monkou*	*Lundekvam*	*Oakley*	*Richardson"*	*Ostenstad*	*Hirst*	*Williams**	*Le Tissier/Spedding/Hughes*
										Ref: P Alcock	An excellent first-half showing gives City their first win at the Dell for ten years. Noel Whelan scores the first and sets Huckerby on his way to chipping the keeper from 25 yards. Le Tissier's late penalty, after Nilsson had fouled him, sets up a close finish but City deserve their win.											
27		H	BARNSLEY		10		W	1-0	0-0	Dublin 89p	Hedman	Nilsson	Burrows	Boateng	Breen	Dublin	Telfer	Soltvedt^	Moldovan*	Huckerby	Whelan	Hall/Strachan
	21/2			20,262	*20*	36					*Watson*	*Eaden*	*Jones*	*Bullock^*	*Moses*	*Markstedt*	*Bosancic*	*Redfearn*	*Ward*	*Fjortoft**	*Sheridan"*	*Hendrie/Marcelle/Hristov*
										Ref: A Wilkie	A late and dubious penalty given when Dublin falls under pressure from Markstedt is typical of the bad luck the Tykes have had in their first ever season in the top flight. They battle hard but do not create a chance. Lightbourne joins Stoke for £425,000 after being on loan to Fulham.											
28		A	CRYS PALACE		10		W	3-0	2-0	Telfer 1, Moldovan 40, Dublin 77	Hedman	Nilsson	Hall	Boateng	Breen	Dublin	Telfer	Soltvedt*	Moldovan	Huckerby	Whelan	Strachan
	28/2			*21,810*	*20*	39					*Miller*	*Smith*	*Gordon*	*Edworthy*	*Hreidarsson*	*Ismael*	*Fullarton*	*Roberts*	*Dyer^*	*Brolin"*	*Rodger**	*Jansen/Bent/McKenzie*
										Ref: D Elleray	Telfer's goal after 45 seconds is the fastest City goal since 1991. Palace haven't won at home all season and when Moldovan rounds the keeper it is as good as over. Seven wins in a row is a new club record and Dublin's goal makes him the club's leading scorer in the top flight era.											
29		A	NEWCASTLE		10		D	0-0	0-0		Ogrizovic	Nilsson	Burrows	Boateng	Breen	Dublin	Telfer^	Soltvedt	Moldovan*	Huckerby	Whelan	Haworth/Strachan
	14/3			*36,767*	*15*	40					*Given*	*Pistone*	*Pearce**	*Batty*	*Howey*	*Albert^*	*Ketsbaia*	*Lee*	*Shearer*	*Andersson*	*Speed*	*Dabizas/Barton*
										Ref: P Jones	A poor game with few chances. Dublin does a fine marking job on Shearer. Moldovan misses two good chances and Oggy makes two super saves. McAllister has an operation on cruciate ligaments and will miss the World Cup. Telfer in Scotland B squad and Salako goes to Bolton.											
30		H	DERBY		9		W	1-0	1-0	Huckerby 44	Ogrizovic	Nilsson	Burrows	Boateng	Breen	Shaw	Telfer	Soltvedt	Dublin	Huckerby	Whelan	
	28/3			18,700	*7*	43					*Hoult*	*Delap*	*Powell C*	*Dailly*	*Laursen*	*Stimac*	*Carsley^*	*Bohinen*	*Wanchope*	*Baiano"*	*Powell D**	*Burton/Rowett/Solis*
										Ref: K Burge	City bounce back from the Cup defeat and deserve a bigger win. Just days after signing a new four-year deal, Huckerby scores with a close-range volley and causes mayhem in the Derby defence. Ray Clarke, City's man in Europe who found Boateng, has unearthed Belgian Clement.											
31		A	LEICESTER		10		D	1-1	0-0	Whelan 80	Ogrizovic	Nilsson	Burrows	Boateng	Breen	Shaw	Telfer	Soltvedt	Dublin	Huckerby	Whelan	
	4/4			*21,137*	*12*	44				*Wilson 78*	*Keller*	*Savage*	*Guppy*	*Prior^*	*Elliott*	*Kaamark*	*Zagorakis*	*Lennon*	*Heskey*	*Cottee**	*Izzet*	*Fenton/Wilson*
										Ref: G Barber	On the eve of receiving his PFA merit award Oggy has a blinder, making three world-class saves as Leicester threaten to run riot. Wilson's goal looks to have won it, but Whelan pounces from a breakaway. Dublin and Huckerby are short-listed for PFA awards. City are unbeaten in nine.											

No	Venue	Opponent / Date	Att	Pos	Res / Pts	F-A	H-T	Scorers, Times, and Referees	1	2	3	4	5	6	7	8	9	10	11	Subs used
32	H	ASTON VILLA		11	L	1-2	0-1	Whelan 59	Ogrizovic	Nilsson	Burrows	Boateng*	Breen	Shaw	Telfer	Soltvedt^	Dublin	Huckerby	Whelan	Hall/Moldovan
		11/4	22,790	*8*	44			*Yorke 5, 48*	*Bosnich*	*Grayson*	*Wright*	*Southgate*	*Ehiogu*	*Staunton*	*Joachim*	*Hendrie*	*Milosevic**	*Yorke*	*Taylor*	*Scimeca*
								Ref: D Gallagher	Europe talk looks ambitious as Villa, with new manager Gregory, end City's run and gain revenge for the Cup. City's first home defeat since December as Yorke scores twice. Whelan looks the man most likely to save it, scoring with a curling 20-yarder and almost grabbing a second.											
33	A	TOTTENHAM		10	D	1-1	0-0	Dublin 87	Ogrizovic	Nilsson	Burrows	Strachan"	Breen	Shaw	Telfer	Whelan	Dublin	Moldovan*	Hall^	Huckerby/Soltvedt/Boland
		13/4	*33,463*	*17*	45			*Berti 68*	*Walker*	*Carr*	*Neilson*	*Berti*	*Vega*	*Campbell*	*Fox*	*Saib**	*Armstrong^*	*Klinsmann*	*Ginola*	*Calderwood/Ferdinand*
								Ref: M Riley	Spurs are desperate for points to avoid relegation and deserve to win a drab game. Berti breaks the deadlock with a rising header from a corner, but Dion pops up unmarked to slide home with the first chance of the game and intensify Spurs' anxiety. Oggy's 500th league game for City.											
34	H	LIVERPOOL		11	D	1-1	0-1	Dublin 47p	Ogrizovic	Nilsson	Burrows	Boland*	Breen	Shaw	Whelan	Soltvedt	Dublin	Huckerby	Hall	Williams
		19/4	22,724	*3*	46			*Owen 33*	*Friedel*	*Jones*	*Bjornebye*	*Redknapp**	*Matteo*	*Babb*	*McManam'n*	*Ince*	*Owen*	*Murphy*	*Leonhardsen*	*Riedle*
								Ref: N Barry	An excellent game which ebbed and flowed. Liverpool are out of the title race but Owen is bubbling. He scores a goal out of nothing and against the run of play. City are rewarded when Babb fouls Huckerby, and Dublin, with a new approach, scores his sixth penalty since Xmas.											
35	A	LEEDS		10	D	3-3	2-2	Huckerby 20, 34, 62	Ogrizovic	Nilsson	Hall	Boland	Breen	Shaw	Telfer	Soltvedt*	Dublin	Huckerby	Whelan	Williams
		25/4	*36,522*	*5*	47			*Hasselbaink 16, 28, Kewell 75*	*Martyn*	*Kelly*	*Harte^*	*Halle*	*Wetherall*	*Hiden*	*Bowyer*	*Haaland*	*Hasselbaink*	*Wallace**	*Kewell*	*Hopkin/Robertson*
								Ref: M Reed	A thriller at Elland Road with Darren Huckerby taking the individual honours with a superb hat-trick. All three are made by his fantastic speed, to which Leeds have no answer. Jimmy Floyd Hasselbaink is not far behind, scoring from a narrow angle and then from a curling free-kick.											
36	H	WIMBLEDON		11	D	0-0	0-0		Hedman	Nilsson	Burrows	Boland	Breen	Shaw	Telfer	Soltvedt*	Dublin	Huckerby	Whelan	Moldovan
		29/4	17,947	*13*	48				*Sullivan*	*Thatcher*	*Kimble*	*Roberts*	*Blackwell**	*Perry*	*Hughes M*	*Ardley*	*Euell^*	*Leaburn*	*Kennedy"*	*McAllister/Ekoku/Fear*
								Ref: J Winter	Wimbledon need one point to be mathematically safe and grind one out in the worst home game of the season. Neither side look like scoring, with City finding it difficult to break down the Dons' rearguard in which Chris Perry is outstanding. Magnus Hedman is back in place of Oggy.											
37	H	BLACKBURN		11	W	2-0	2-0	Dublin 19p, Boateng 34	Hedman	Nilsson	Burrows	Boateng^	Breen	Shaw	Telfer	Soltvedt	Dublin	Huckerby*	Whelan	Moldovan/Boland
		2/5	18,792	*6*	51				*Filan*	*Valery**	*Croft*	*Flitcroft*	*Hendry*	*Henchoz*	*Kenna*	*McKinlay^*	*Sutton*	*Gallacher*	*Wilcox*	*Duff/Dahlin*
								Ref: S Lodge	A fine game to bring the curtain down on the home programme. Valery handles for Dublin to score from the spot. Sub keeper Tim Flowers is ordered off from the bench for foul language. Boateng nets the goal his efforts deserve with a close-range shot after good work by Soltvedt.											
38	A	EVERTON		11	D	1-1	0-1	Dublin 89	Hedman	Nilsson	Burrows	Boateng	Breen*	Shaw	Telfer"	Soltvedt	Dublin	Huckerby^	Whelan	Williams/Haworth/Hall
		10/5	*40,109*	*17*	52			*Farrelly 7*	*Myrhe*	*O'Kane*	*Ball*	*Short*	*Watson*	*Tiler*	*Farrelly^*	*Hutchison*	*Ferguson*	*Madar**	*Barmby*	*Cadamarteri/McCann*
		Home	Away					Ref: P Alcock	In a tense and nail-biting atmosphere Everton need to win to stay up. Everton lead comfortably until Williams fouls Cadermateri for a dubious penalty six minutes from time, but Hedman saves Barmby's shot. Dublin's header makes Everton sweat but they survive on goal-difference.											
Average		19,718	29,085																	

Coca-Cola Cup						F-A	H-T	Scorers, Times, and Referees	SQUAD	NUMBERS	IN	USE								subs used
2:1	A	BLACKPOOL		8	L	0-1	0-0		Ogrizovic	Nilsson	Burrows	Soltvedt*	Williams	Shaw	Telfer^	McAllister	Lightbourne	Johansen	Salako	Hall/Breen
		16/9	*5,884*	*2:14*				*Linighan 76*	*Banks*	*Bryan*	*Bradshaw*	*Bonner*	*Linighan*	*Lydiate*	*Philpott*	*Mellon*	*Quinn*	*Preece**	*Ellis*	*Malkin*
								Ref: T Heilbron	The game is spoiled by heavy wind and rain and there is little football. Blackpool have most of the chances and Linighan's header gives them a narrow lead. Dublin and Huckerby's injuries give Johansen and Lightbourne, who complains of a laser beam, an opportunity they fail to take.											
2:2	H	BLACKPOOL		12	W	3-1	0-1	McAllister 61p, 89p, Dublin 70	Ogrizovic	Breen	Burrows	Boland	Williams^	Shaw	O'Neill	McAllister	Dublin	Lightbo'rne*	Hall	Ducros/Soltvedt
		1/10	9,605	*2:7*				*Linighan 36*	*Banks*	*Bryan*	*Bradshaw*	*Clarkson*	*Linighan*	*Lydiate*	*Bonner*	*Mellon*	*Ellis*	*Preece*	*Philpott*	
								Ref: M Reed (City win 3-2 on aggregate)	Injury-hit City are lucky to win after a dire first half saw them 0-2 down on aggregate. Superb McAllister lifts City and they pull it round thanks to two penalties. Bryan fouls Dublin for the first and needlessly handles for the second. Dublin's flying header is his 50th goal for City.											
3	H	EVERTON		12	W	4-1	2-1	Hall 6, Salako 33, 59, Haworth 62	Ogrizovic	Nilsson	Burrows	Williams	Breen	Shaw	Salako*	McAllister	Haworth	Lightbourne	Hall	Boland
		15/10	10,114	*18*				*Barmby 16*	*Gerrard*	*Short*	*Hinchcliffe*	*Williamson**	*Watson*	*Bilic*	*Stuart*	*Oster*	*Ferguson^*	*Barmby*	*Speed*	*Ball/Cadamarteri*
								Ref: S Dunn	City run a poor Everton side ragged for their biggest win for almost two years. Marcus Hall scores a stunning goal, his first at senior level. Salako's second is a delicious chip and Haworth's is a stunning right-footer. Howard Kendall has a row with his players on the pitch at the end.											
4	A	ARSENAL		10	L	0-1	0-0		Ogrizovic	Nilsson	Burrows	Williams	Breen	Shaw	Telfer	McAllister	Dublin	Haworth*	Hall	Huckerby
		18/11	*30,199*	*2*		*aet*		*Bergkamp 99*	*Manninger*	*Dixon*	*Mendez^*	*Keown*	*Bould*	*Upson*	*Parlour*	*Platt*	*Anelka**	*Bergkamp*	*Hughes*	*Wreh/Marshall*
								Ref: G Ashby	City put up a good performance against an under-strength Gunners but lack punch up front. In extra-time Huckerby hits the post and fluffs a one-on-one with the keeper. Bergkamp in a similar situation is deadly. Strachan's number two, Alex Miller, becomes manager of Aberdeen.											

FA Cup																				
3	A	LIVERPOOL		14	W	3-1	1-1	Huckerby 45, Dublin 62, Telfer 87	Hedman	Shaw	Burrows	Boateng	Breen	Williams	Telfer	Whelan	Dublin	Huckerby	Hall	
		3/1	*33,888*	*4*				*Redknapp 7*	*James*	*McAteer*	*Harkness*	*Redknapp*	*Matteo*	*Kvarme^*	*McManam'n*	*Ince*	*Fowler*	*Riedle*	*Leonh'rds'n**	*Berger/Murphy*
								Ref: M Riley	Huckerby is the hero of an outstanding win. He equalises Redknapp's free-kick with a dazzling solo run and cool finish. He runs the Reds ragged after the break. Dublin scores after James saves his shot and Telfer scores after he hits the post. 4,000 City fans can't believe their eyes											
4	H	DERBY		16	W	2-0	2-0	Dublin 38, 45	Hedman	Nilsson	Burrows	Boateng"	Breen	Shaw	Telfer	Soltvedt	Dublin	Huckerby^	Whelan*	Hall/Moldovan/Strachan
		24/1	22,816	*6*					*Poom*	*Eranio*	*Powell C*	*Yates*	*Stimac*	*Laursen*	*Carsley"*	*Baiano**	*Wanchope*	*Burton^*	*Powell D*	*Willems/Dailly/Rowett*
								Ref: M Bodenham	Dublin is having a golden spell and Glenn Hoddle sees him score two to give City their first home FA Cup win over top flight opposition since 1984. Derby get frustrated and cut up rough with three bookings and Baiano is withdrawn for his own good. Record gate receipts of £365,000.											
5	A	ASTON VILLA		12	W	1-0	0-0	Moldovan 72	Hedman	Nilsson	Burrows	Strachan^	Breen	Shaw*	Boateng	Soltvedt	Dublin	Huckerby	Hall	Moldovan/Boland
		14/2	*36,979*	*13*					*Bosnich*	*Scimeca*	*Wright*	*Grayson*	*Ehiogu*	*Southgate*	*Hendrie*	*Draper**	*Joachim*	*Collymore*	*Staunton*	*Byfield*
								Ref: G Willard	Despite being without the suspended Telfer and Whelan, City win for the first time ever at Villa Park in an emotional day. 7,000 City fans roar them home with Moldovan grabbing the goal after Soltvedt misses three chances. Boateng is immense, as is Dion, who is switched to the back.											
QF	H	SHEFFIELD UTD		10	D	1-1	1-1	Dublin 32p	Ogrizovic	Nilsson	Burrows	Boateng	Breen	Dublin	Telfer	Strachan*	Moldovan^	Huckerby	Whelan	Soltvedt/Hall
		7/3	23,084	*1:5*				*Marcello 45*	*Kelly*	*Short^*	*Quinn*	*Marker*	*Holdsworth*	*Sandford*	*Borbokis*	*Ford*	*Taylor*	*Marcello**	*Stuart*	*Beard/Katchouro*
								Ref: S Dunn	City let the Blades off the hook after dominating the game. Dublin's penalty is his fifth in six home games and is awarded when Marker fouls Strachan. Dublin's clearance is hammered home by Marcello. In the dying minutes Oggy races back to save from Katchouro after a bad error.											
QF	A	SHEFFIELD UTD		10	L	1-1	1-0	Telfer 10	Ogrizovic	Nilsson	Burrows	Boateng	Breen	Dublin	Telfer	Soltvedt^	Moldovan*	Huckerby	Whelan	Haworth/Strachan
R		17/3	*29,034*	*1:5*				*Holdsworth 89*	*Kelly*	*Short**	*Nilsen*	*Marker^*	*Holdsworth*	*Sandford*	*Borbokis*	*Ford*	*Taylor*	*Marcello"*	*Quinn*	*Katchouro/Dellas/Morris*
								Ref: S Dunn (City lose 1-3 on pens)	A marvellous game in which City fail to find an all-important second goal after Telfer's low drive. They miss good chances, including an open goal for Moldovan and pay for it when Holdsworth hooks home. Extra-time is a stalemate and penalties send the fortuitous Blades through.											

		Home						Away				
	P	W	D	L	F	A	W	D	L	F	A	Pts
1 Arsenal	38	15	2	2	43	10	8	7	4	25	23	78
2 Manchester U	38	13	4	2	42	9	10	4	5	31	17	77
3 Liverpool	38	13	2	4	42	16	5	9	5	26	26	65
4 Chelsea	38	13	2	4	37	14	7	1	11	34	29	63
5 Leeds	38	9	5	5	31	21	8	3	8	26	25	59
6 Blackburn	38	11	4	4	40	26	5	6	8	17	26	58
7 Aston Villa	38	9	3	7	26	24	8	3	8	23	24	57
8 West Ham	38	13	4	2	40	18	3	4	12	16	39	56
9 Derby	38	12	3	4	33	18	4	4	11	19	31	55
10 Leicester	38	6	10	3	21	15	7	4	8	30	26	53
11 COVENTRY	38	8	9	2	26	17	4	7	8	20	27	52
12 Southampton	38	10	1	8	28	23	4	5	10	22	32	48
13 Newcastle	38	8	5	6	22	20	3	6	10	13	24	44
14 Tottenham	38	7	8	4	23	22	4	3	12	21	34	44
15 Wimbledon	38	5	6	8	18	25	5	8	6	16	21	44
16 Sheffield Wed	38	9	5	5	30	26	3	3	13	22	41	44
17 Everton	38	7	5	7	25	27	2	8	9	16	29	40
18 Bolton	38	7	8	4	25	22	2	5	12	16	39	40
19 Barnsley	38	7	4	8	25	35	3	1	15	12	47	35
20 Crys Palace	38	2	5	12	15	39	6	4	9	22	32	33
	760	184	95	101	592	427	101	95	184	427	592	1045

Odds & ends

Double wins: (1) Southampton.
Double losses: (1) Aston Villa.

Won from behind: (5) Chelsea (h), Manchester U (h), Bolton (a) Liverpool FAC (a), Blackpool LC (h).
Lost from in front: (1) Chelsea (a).

High spots: FA Cup run, especially the win at Villa Park.
Not having to suffer a relegation battle.
The form of Dublin, joint leading Premiership scorer, and Huckerby.
The improved media coverage given to City.
The 13-game unbeaten run.

Low spots: The penalty shoot-out defeat at Bramall Lane.
The poor disciplinary record - five red cards.
Dublin not being selected for England's World Cup 22.

Red cards: City – Dublin (Blackburn a), Williams and Breen (A Villa a), Boateng (West Ham a), Williams (Arsenal h).
Red cards: Opponents – Wilcox (Blackburn a), Vieira (Arsenal h), Flowers (Blackburn (h).

Player of the Year: Dion Dublin.
Ever-presents: (0).
Hat-tricks: (2) Dion Dublin, Darren Huckerby.
Opposing hat-tricks: (0).
Leading scorer: (23) Dion Dublin.

	Appearances						Goals			
	Lge	*Sub*	LC	*Sub*	FAC	*Sub*	Lge	LC	FAC	Tot
Boateng, George	**14**				5		**1**			**1**
Boland, Willie	**8**	*11*	1	*1*		*1*				
Breen, Gary	**30**		3	*1*	5		**1**			**1**
Burrows, David	**33**		4		5					
Dublin, Dion	**36**		2		5		**18**	1	4	**23**
Ducros, Andrew	**1**	*2*		*1*						
Hall, Marcus	**20**	*5*	3	*1*	2	*2*	**1**	1		**2**
Haworth, Simon	**4**	*6*	2			*1*		1		**1**
Hedman, Magnus	**14**				3					
Huckerby, Darren	**32**	*2*		*1*	5		**14**		1	**15**
Johansen, Martin		*2*	1							
Lightbourne, Kyle	**1**	*6*	3							
McAllister, Gary	**14**		4					2		**2**
Moldovan, Viorel	**5**	*5*			2	*2*	**1**		1	**2**
Nilsson, Roland	**32**		3		4					
O'Neill, Michael	**2**	*2*	1							
Ogrizovic, Steve	**24**		4		2					
Richardson, Kevin	**3**									
Salako, John	**11**		2					2		**2**
Shaw, Richard	**33**		4		3					
Shilton, Sam	**2**									
Soltvedt, Trond-Egil	**26**	*4*	1	*1*	3	*1*	**1**			**1**
Strachan, Gavin	**2**	*7*			2	*2*				
Telfer, Paul	**33**		2		4		**3**		2	**5**
Whelan, Noel	**21**				4		**6**			**6**
Williams, Paul D	**17**	*3*	4		1					
26 players used	**418**	***55***	**44**	***6***	**55**	***9***	**46**	**7**	**8**	**61**

No	Date		Att	Pos	Pt	F-A	H-T	Scorers, Times, and Referees	SQUAD	NUMBERS	IN	USE								subs used
1	H	CHELSEA			W	2-1	2-1	Huckerby 11, Dublin 16	Hedman	Nilsson	Burrows	Boateng^	Williams	Shaw	Telfer	Soltvedt	Dublin	Huckerby	Whelan*	Hall M/**Hall P**
	15/8		23,042		3			_Poyet 37_	_De Goey_	_Ferrer_	_Le Saux_	_Wise_	_Desailly_	_Leboeuf_	_Poyet_	_Di Matteo^_	_Vialli*_	_Casiraghi_	_Babayaro_	_Flo/Zola_
								Ref: G Barber	France's World Cup-winning defenders are ripped apart by City's speed and height in a fascinating duel in the sun. Dublin nods on for Huckerby to chip in the first, and Dion's header from Whelan's free-kick makes it four defeats in a row at Coventry for Gianluca Vialli's boys.											
2	A	NOTT'M FOREST			L	0-1	0-0		Hedman	Nilsson*	Burrows	Boateng	Breen	Shaw	Telfer	Soltvedt^	Dublin	Huckerby	Whelan	**Wallemme**/Hall P
	22/8		_22,546_		3			_Stone 51_	_Beasant_	_Bonalair_	_Rogers_	_Thomas*_	_Chettle_	_Armstrong_	_Stone_	_Gemmill_	_Darcheville^_	_Freedman_	_Hodges_	_Johnson/Harewood_
								Ref: K Burge	Newly promoted Forest, under Bassett, are lucky to win after the Sky Blues dominate the game but miss a hatful of chances. Wallemme and Shaw's language difficulties are at fault for the goal. Croatian Robert Jarni will sign for Real Madrid this week, giving City a £750,000 profit.											
3	H	WEST HAM		10	D	0-0	0-0		Hedman	Shaw	Burrows	Boateng	Breen	Wallemme^	Telfer	Soltvedt*	Dublin	Huckerby	Whelan	Hall P/**Edworthy**
	29/8		20,818	_8_	4				_Hislop_	_Impey_	_Lazaridis_	_Margas_	_Ruddock_	_Ferdinand_	_Lampard_	_Lomas*_	_Hartson_	_Wright_	_Berkovic_	_Moncur_
								Ref: N Barry	Redknapp's team dominate a physical first half, with Hartson and Ian Wright reunited for the first time, but City finish stronger. Wallemme is superb as is Ferdinand who marks Huckerby well. Penalty appeals are turned down when Hartson handles and Telfer forces Hislop to save.											
4	A	LIVERPOOL		16	L	0-2	0-1		Hedman	Nilsson^	Burrows	Boateng	Breen	Wallemme	Telfer	Soltvedt*	Dublin	Huckerby	Hall P"	Edworthy/Shaw/Shilton
	9/9		_41,771_	_1_	4			_Berger 26, Redknapp 48_	_Friedel_	_Heggem_	_Staunton_	_Ince_	_Carragher_	_Babb_	_McMan'm'n_	_Redknapp_	_Owen_	_Riedle_	_Berger_	
								Ref: D Gallagher	Liverpool, under joint managers Evans and Houllier, are unbeaten and are rarely troubled by the Sky Blues, despite Dublin winning the aerial battle. But for stout defending and missed chances, it could have been a bigger scoreline. Redknapp's shot deflects in off Riedle for the second.											
5	A	MANCHESTER U		19	L	0-2	0-1		Hedman	Shaw	Burrows	Boateng	Breen	Wallemme	Edworthy	**Quinn**	Dublin	Huckerby*	Telfer	Hall P
	12/9		**_55,193_**	_5_	4			_Yorke 20, Johnsen 47_	_Schmeichel_	_Neville G_	_Neville P_	_Keane_	_Johnsen"_	_Staam_	_Beckham^_	_Scholes_	_Yorke_	_Solskjaer_	_Giggs*_	_Blomqvist/Butt/Berg_
								Ref: U Rennie	The warning signs are clear with no goals for 434 minutes and it's almost no contest. The disappointing Huckerby is pulled off and City await the return of McAllister from injury. Quinn makes a bright debut but City are outclassed. £12m Yorke makes it three in two games for United.											
6	H	NEWCASTLE		19	L	**1-5**	1-3	Whelan 5 _[Glass 59]_	Hedman	Edworthy	Burrows	Boateng	Breen	Wallemme	Whelan	Quinn	Dublin	Haworth	Hall P*	Shilton
	19/9		22,639	_9_	4			_Dabizas 14, Shearer 43, 89, Speed 44,_	_Given_	_Watson_	_Charvet_	_Lee_	_Dabizas_	_Pearce_	_Gillespie^_	_Solano*_	_Shearer_	_Guivarc'h"_	_Glass_	_Speed/Barton/Dalglish_
								Ref: R Harris	Ruud Gullit's Newcastle, fresh from a European game in Belgrade, are flattered by the scoreline but take their chances clinically. Shearer is at his predatory best and Glass scores a fine individual goal. Whelan, in for Telfer – injured playing head tennis in the bath – scores with a header.											
7	A	CHARLTON		19	D	1-1	0-0	Whelan 69	Hedman	Nilsson	Burrows*	Boateng	Breen	Shaw	Telfer	Quinn	Dublin	Whelan	Shilton^	Edworthy/Hall P
	26/9		_20,043_	_14_	5			_Hunt 75_	_Ilic_	_Mills_	_Powell_	_Redfearn_	_Rufus_	_Youds_	_Newton*_	_Kinsella_	_Hunt_	_Mendonca^_	_Mortimer_	_Jones K/Jones S_
								Ref: J Winter	Edworthy, on for the injured Burrows, and out of position, slips and lets in Hunt, whom manager Curbishley is about to sub. It is two points thrown away after man of the match Whelan's brave header looked enough to win it. £2m left-winger Steve Froggatt will sign from Wolves.											
8	H	ASTON VILLA		19	L	1-2	0-2	Soltvedt 70	Hedman	Nilsson	Edworthy	Boateng	Breen^	Shaw	Telfer	Quinn*	Dublin	Whelan	**Froggatt**	Soltvedt/Wallemme
	3/10		22,650	_1_	5			_Taylor 29, 40_	_Bosnich_	_Charles^_	_Wright_	_Barry_	_Southgate_	_Ehiogu_	_Hendrie_	_Taylor_	_Merson*_	_Collymore_	_Thompson_	_Joachim/Grayson_
								Ref: S Lodge	Unbeaten Villa are buzzing and helped by a dreadful mistake by the linesman for their second goal, with Merson and Taylor offside. City make a game of it after the break but Bosnich is superb with only Soltvedt able to breach Villa's defence. Leeds want Strachan as their new boss.											
9	H	SHEFFIELD WED		19	W	1-0	0-0	Dublin 75	Hedman	Nilsson	Edworthy	Boateng	Breen	Shaw	Telfer*	McAllister	Dublin	Whelan	Froggatt	Huckerby
	18/10		**16,003**	_15_	8				_Pressman_	_Atherton_	_Briscoe_	_Jonk_	_Thome_	_Walker_	_Alexand'rs'n_	_Sommer_	_Carbone*_	_Booth_	_Humphreys_	_Whittingham_
								Ref: D Elleray	Sky viewers get few thrills but it's a vital win and McAllister's return from injury is welcome. Whelan is the star again, setting up numerous chances, including the cross for Dublin's winner, his first goal since the opening day. Unsettled Wallemme wants a move back to France.											
10	A	SOUTHAMPTON		18	L	1-2	0-2	Dublin 61	Hedman	Nilsson^	Burrows*	Boateng"	Breen	Shaw	Whelan	McAllister	Dublin	Huckerby	Froggatt	Edworthy/Telfer/Soltvedt
	24/10		_15,152_	_20_	8			_Le Tissier 24, Ostenstaad 45_	_Jones_	_Hiley_	_Benali_	_Howells*_	_Monkou_	_Lundekvam_	_Ripley_	_Hughes M_	_Ostenstaad"_	_Le Tissier_	_Oakley^_	_Palmer/Bridge/Beattie_
								Ref: R Harris	Le Tissier is at his best in the first half with a far-post header and a teasing cross for Ostenstaad to score. City give themselves a mountain to climb and, although Froggatt's crosses cause havoc, Dublin's super header from 17 yards is the only reward. Blackburn bid £6.75m for Dion.											

No	Venue	Opponent	Att	Pos	Pts	F-A	H-T	Scorers, Times, and Referees												Subs used
11	H	ARSENAL		19	L	0-1	0-0		Hedman	Nilsson	Hall M	Boateng*	Breen	Shaw	Telfer	McAllister^	Whelan	Huckerby"	Froggatt	**Clement**/Soltvedt/Hall P
31/10			23,039	*3*	8			*Anelka 64*	*Seaman*	*Dixon*	*Winterburn*	*Vieira*	*Keown*	*Bould*	*Parlour*	*Petit*	*Anelka*	*Ljungberg**	*Overmars^*	*Boa Morte/Hughes*
								Ref: U Rennie	After the Luton disaster, City regain some pride with a battling performance but the poaching Anelka is on the spot when Hedman fails to hold Overmars' shot. Vieira is a colossus for Arsenal. The game is overshadowed by the death of a security guard hit by the Arsenal team coach.											
12	A	BLACKBURN		17	W	2-1	0-0	Huckerby 53, Whelan 74	Hedman	Nilsson	Edworthy	Clement	Breen*	Shaw	Telfer	McAllister^	Whelan	Huckerby	Froggatt	Williams/Boateng
7/11			*23,779*	*18*	11			*Sherwood 73*	*Flowers*	*Kenna*	*Davidson*	*Sherwood*	*Peacock^*	*Henchoz*	*Johnson*	*Dailly*	*Sutton**	*Blake*	*Duff*	*Davies/Marcolin*
								Ref: P Durkin	Dion has gone to Villa but the arrival of his replacement Andreas Lund sparks City's strikers. Whelan is devastating, with a stunning winner and hitting the bar twice. Belgian Clement has an impressive full debut. Blackburn boss Roy Hodgson is only two games away from the sack.											
13	H	EVERTON		15	W	3-0	1-0	Froggatt 16, Huckerby 49, Whelan 90	Hedman	Nilsson	Edworthy	Clement	Williams	Shaw	Telfer	McAllister	Whelan	Huckerby	Froggatt	
15/11			19,279	*17*	14				*Myhre*	*Cleland^*	*Ball*	*Short*	*Materazzi*	*Unsworth*	*Grant*	*Hutchison*	*Ferguson*	*Bakayoko**	*Collins*	*Cadamarteri/Milligan*
								Ref: G Poll	The Lund deal is off and Rune Lange is a new target but the players respond with a super show for Sky TV. All three goals are terrific, with Froggatt's scorcher the goal of the month. The winger then sets up Huckerby's rocket, and Whelan's tops an awesome individual display.											
14	A	MIDDLESBROUGH		16	L	0-2	0-0		Hedman	Nilsson	Edworthy	Clement	Williams	Shaw	Telfer	McAllister^	Whelan	Huckerby*	Froggatt	**Jackson**/Boateng
21/11			*34,293*	*7*	14			*Gordon 66, Ricard 83*	*Schwarzer*	*Stockdale*	*Gordon*	*Cooper*	*Vickers*	*Festa**	*Summerbell*	*Townsend*	*Ricard*	*Deane*	*Beck*	*Maddison*
								Ref: G Willard	A disappointing performance and only good defending by Shaw and Nilsson averts a bigger defeat. Gordon's 25-yard effort ends City's feeble efforts and Ricard's goal, although he handles, is the icing on the cake. With Lange rejecting terms, City have Celtic's Darren Jackson on loan.											
15	H	LEICESTER		17	D	1-1	0-0	Huckerby 78	Hedman	Nilsson	Edworthy	Clement*	Williams	Shaw	Telfer	McAllister	Soltvedt	Huckerby	Froggatt	Boateng
28/11			19,887	*13*	15			*Heskey 88*	*Keller*	*Sinclair !*	*Ullathorne*	*Lennon*	*Walsh*	*Elliott*	*Impey*	*Izzet*	*Heskey*	*Fenton**	*Guppy*	*Savage*
								Ref: M Riley	Soltvedt is no replacement for the injured Whelan but City blow it against ten-man Leicester. Huckerby's rare header looks enough until Hedman's poor punch falls to Heskey. Frank Sinclair is harshly sent off for two yellow cards. Paul Hall turns down a move to Port Vale.											
16	A	WIMBLEDON		17	L	1-2	0-0	McAllister 54p	Hedman	Nilsson*	Edworthy	Boateng	Williams	Shaw	Telfer	McAllister	Whelan	Huckerby	Froggatt	Breen
5/12			***11,717***	*8*	15			*Euell 71, 83*	*Sullivan*	*Cunningh'm*	*Thatcher*	*Ardley*	*Blackwell*	*Perry*	*Hughes M*	*Earle*	*Ekoku*	*Gayle**	*Euell*	*Ainsworth*
								Ref: S Dunn	City are dominant for the first half but after the penalty, when Perry brings down Huckerby, they sit back. Jason Euell twice springs the offside trap and finishes well. Strachan is upset with the referee who ignores Thatcher's handball. Nilsson's late neck injury looks serious but is not.											
17	A	LEEDS		17	L	0-2	0-1		Hedman	Nilsson	Edworthy	Clement*	Williams	Shaw	Boateng^	McAllister	Whelan	Soltvedt	Froggatt	Jackson/Hall P
14/12			*31,802*	*3*	15			*Hopkin 40, Bowyer 90*	*Martyn*	*Bowyer*	*Harte*	*Molenaar*	*Woodgate*	*Radebe**	*Batty^*	*Hopkin*	*Hasselbaink*	*Smith*	*Kewell*	*Halle/McPhail*
								Ref: G Poll	Batty is back in O'Leary's Leeds fold and Huckerby and Telfer are suspended. Leeds have fewer chances than City but are deadly. Hopkin taps in the first after the poor Boateng's error, and Bowyer hits home the loose ball after Hedman saves well from Hasselbaink. City to buy Aloisi.											
18	H	DERBY		17	D	1-1	1-0	Whelan 17	Hedman	Nilsson	Edworthy*	Soltvedt	Williams	Shaw	Telfer^	McAllister"	Whelan	Huckerby	Froggatt	Breen/Boateng/**Aloisi**
20/12			16,602	*12*	16			*Carsley 50*	*Poom*	*Delap*	*Dorigo"*	*Laursen*	*Carbonari*	*Prior*	*Powell*	*Bohinen*	*Wanchope*	*Sturridge^*	*Harper**	*Carsley/Elliott/Hunt*
								Ref: U Rennie	The Sky Blues fail to make their first-half domination count with missed chances galore and three fair penalty claims rejected. Boss Jim Smith reorganised and Derby fought their way back but didn't deserve a point. Whelan's goal from Froggatt's cross is reward for another good display.											
19	H	TOTTENHAM		17	D	1-1	0-1	Aloisi 81	Ogrizovic	Nilsson	Edworthy^	Soltvedt	Williams*	Shaw	Boateng	McAllister	Whelan	Huckerby"	Froggatt	Breen/Aloisi/Shilton
26/12			**23,091**	*13*	17			*Campbell 18*	*Walker*	*Carr*	*Sinton*	*Nielsen*	*Campbell*	*Young*	*Fox*	*Anderton*	*Ferdinand^*	*Armstrong*	*Ginola**	*Clemence/Iversen*
								Ref: K Burge	Hedman's migraine gives 41-year-old Oggy his first game of the season but he can't stop Campbell's sloppy goal. Whelan's luck is out with two efforts hitting the woodwork but Aloisi is an instant hero 16 minutes after coming on. Walker saves George Graham's team from defeat.											
20	A	WEST HAM		17	L	0-2	0-1		Ogrizovic	Nilsson	Edworthy^	Soltvedt	Breen	Shaw	Boateng	McAllister	Whelan	Aloisi*	Froggatt	Huckerby/Telfer
28/12			*25,662*	*6*	17			*Wright 7, Hartson 68*	*Hislop*	*Sinclair*	*Lazaridis*	*Pearce*	*Ferdinand*	*Dicks*	*Berkovic**	*Lomas*	*Hartson*	*Wright^*	*Lampard*	*Potts/Omoyinmi*
								Ref: P Durkin	The travelling fans are unhappy with another away defeat and boo McAllister. The bruising Hartson muscled past Breen to set up Wright and the ex-Arsenal man repaid the favour for the second. Strachan is adamant that three penalty claims are valid but a defeat was all City deserved.											
21	H	NOTT'M FOREST		17	W	**4-0**	1-0	Huckerby 45, 46, 75, Telfer 55	Hedman	Nilsson	Burrows^	Soltvedt	Williams	Shaw	Telfer	McAllister"	Aloisi*	Huckerby	Whelan	Jackson/Shilton/Quinn
9/1			17,158	*20*	20				*Beasant*	*Lyttle*	*Armstrong**	*Hjelde*	*Chettle*	*Doig*	*Johnson*	*Gemmill"*	*V Hooijdonk*	*Stone*	*Bt-Willi'ms^*	*Freedman/Woan/Quashie*
								Ref: P Jones	Caretaker Mickey Adams is keeping the seat warm for Big Ron after Bassett's sacking but Huckerby and Co are irresistible. Darren scores his second hat-trick in successive games. The third goal is a candidate for goal of the season as five or six players are beaten by his dazzling run.											

F.A. CARLING PREMIERSHIP

Manager: Gordon Strachan

SEASON 1998-99

No	Date		Att	Pos	Pt	F-A	H-T	Scorers, Times, and Referees	SQUAD	NUMBERS	IN	USE								subs used
22	A	CHELSEA		17	L	1-2	1-1	Huckerby 9	Hedman	Nilsson	Burrows	Soltvedt	Williams	Shaw	Telfer	McAllister*	Huckerby	Boateng	Froggatt	Aloisi
	16/1		*34,869*	*1*	20			*Leboeuf 45, Di Matteo 90*	*De Goey*	*Ferrer**	*Le Saux*	*Wise*	*Lambourde*	*Leboeuf*	*Petrescu*	*Di Matteo*	*Vialli*	*Zola*	*Babayaro*	*Goldbaek*
								Ref: J Winter	The Sky Blues give their best display of the season and deserve something from a battling display. The game is spoilt by ugly shenanigans, resulting in Strachan being dismissed from the pitch-side. Vialli's team's goals both come in stoppage time, overturning Huckerby's neat chip.											
23	H	LIVERPOOL		16	W	2-1	0-0	Boateng 60, Whelan 72	Hedman	Nilsson*	Burrows	Soltvedt	Williams	Shaw	Boateng	McAllister	Whelan	Huckerby	Froggatt	Breen
	30/1		23,057	*6*	23			*McManaman 86*	*James*	*Heggem*	*Bjornebye*	*Matteo*	*Staunton"*	*Song**	*Berger^*	*Redknapp*	*Owen*	*Fowler*	*Ince*	*McManaman/Riedle/Gerrard*
								Ref: M Riley	Hard work and concentration are the keys to a battling victory over the resurgent Reds. Debut boy Rigobert Song is led a merry dance by Huck but it is Boateng, finally back to his best, with a header, and Whelan, who Strachan thinks should play for England, who clinch the points.											
24	A	TOTTENHAM		16	D	0-0	0-0		Hedman	Nilsson	Breen"	Soltvedt^	Williams*	Shaw	Telfer	McAllister	Whelan	Huckerby	Froggatt	**Konjic**/Clement/Aloisi
	6/2		*34,376*	*11*	24				*Walker*	*Carr*	*Taricco^*	*Nielsen*	*Campbell*	*Young*	*Anderton*	*Freund*	*Ferdinand*	*Iversen**	*Sinton*	*Armstrong/Sherwood*
								Ref: S Lodge	A resilient defensive display thwarts Spurs and edges City closer to safety. Breen and Telfer are in for the suspended Burrows and Boateng, and £2m Bosnian defender Mo Konjic gets his first outing as a sub. Huckerby misses two chances but George Graham's boys miss a few more.											
25	A	NEWCASTLE		17	L	1-4	1-1	Whelan 18	Hedman	Nilsson	Burrows	Soltvedt*	Konjic	Shaw	Boateng	McAllister	Whelan	Huckerby^	Froggatt	Clement/Aloisi
	17/2		36,352	*10*	24			*Shearer 19, 75, Speed 55, Saha 58*	*Given*	*Charvet*	*Domi*	*Hamann*	*Dabizas*	*Howey*	*Solano*	*Speed"*	*Shearer*	*Saha^*	*Glass**	*Brady/Ketsbaia/Barton*
								Ref: S Dunn	An even first half is forgotten after the break as Gullit's team up the tempo. Shearer has now scored 15 goals against the Sky Blues and tonight gives Konjic a torrid time. Speed's goal is made by Shearer and Saha heads in from Solano's corner. Huckerby is unhappy at being taken off.											
26	H	MANCHESTER U		18	L	0-1	0-0		Hedman	Nilsson	Burrows^	Telfer	Williams	Shaw	Boateng	McAllister	Whelan*	Huckerby	Froggatt	Aloisi/Soltvedt
	20/2		22,594	*1*	24			*Giggs 78*	*Schmeichel*	*Neville G*	*Irwin*	*Keane*	*Johnsen*	*Staam**	*Beckham*	*Scholes*	*Yorke"*	*Cole^*	*Giggs*	*Berg/Solskjaer/Neville P*
								Ref: D Gallagher	After matching Fergie's boys blow for blow, one lapse of concentration costs them dearly. Saints and Charlton win and City are back in the drop-zone. Shaw and Williams are awesome against the 40-goal Cole/Yorke combo. Peter Schmeichel defies them with two world-class saves.											
27	A	ASTON VILLA		17	W	4-1	1-0	Aloisi 24, 72, Boateng 50, 83	Hedman	Nilsson	Burrows	Telfer	Williams	Shaw	Boateng	McAllister	Aloisi	Huckerby*	Froggatt	**McSheffrey**
	27/2		*38,799*	*4*	27			*Dublin 54p*	*Oakes*	*Watson^*	*Wright*	*Grayson*	*Southgate*	*Scimeca*	*Merson*	*Taylor**	*Dublin*	*Joachim*	*Hendrie*	*Draper"/Barry/Collymore*
								Ref: U Rennie	City's first ever league win at Villa is a very special one. Gregory's men are outclassed and even a pumped up Dublin makes no difference. Boateng's display will earn him a big move to Villa. Aloisi's left foot does the rest. 16-year old McSheffrey is City's youngest ever player.											
28	H	CHARLTON		15	W	2-1	0-0	Whelan 66, Soltvedt 85	Hedman	Nilsson	Burrows	Telfer	Williams	Shaw	Whelan	McAllister	Aloisi !	Huckerby*	Froggatt	Soltvedt
	6/3		20,255	*17*	30			*Hunt 55*	*Royce*	*Robinson^*	*Powell*	*Mills*	*Brown*	*Tiler*	*Redfearn**	*Kinsella*	*Hunt"*	*Pringle*	*Jones K*	*Barnes/Barness/Mortimer*
								Ref: J Winter	A goal down and reduced to ten men, after the provoked Aloisi sees red for cuffing Mills, the Sky Blues come back to win a scrappy game. Whelan, roared on by a noisy crowd, ploughed through the mud for the first. Soltvedt clinches it with a left-foot volley deflected in off Mills.											
29	H	BLACKBURN		15	D	1-1	1-0	Aloisi 22	Hedman	Nilsson	Burrows	Telfer	Konjic*	Shaw	Boateng	McAllister^	Whelan	Aloisi	Froggatt	Clement/Huckerby
	13/3		19,694	*18*	31			*Wilcox 67*	*Filan*	*McAteer*	*Davidson*	*Marcolin*	*Taylor*	*Henchoz*	*Dunn^*	*Ward*	*Sutton*	*Jansen**	*Wilcox*	*Duff/Johnson*
								Ref: S Dunn	A desperate relegation battle sees Brian Kidd's patched up side grab a point with Wilcox's clinical finish. Aloisi scores a stunning goal but misses a much easier chance. Sutton's late tackle on Konjic prompts a pitched battle. City accuse Villa of an illegal approach to Boateng.											
30	A	ARSENAL		15	L	0-2	0-1		Hedman	Nilsson*	Burrows	Soltvedt^	Konjic	Shaw	Telfer	McAllister	Quinn	Huckerby	Froggatt	Edworthy/**Gioacchini**
	20/3		*38,074*	*2*	31			*Parlour 16, Overmars 80*	*Seaman*	*Dixon**	*Winterburn*	*Vieira*	*Adams*	*Keown*	*Parlour*	*Petit*	*Anelka^*	*Bergkamp*	*Overmars"*	*Ljungberg/Kanu/Diawara*
								Ref: P Alcock	With Aloisi and Whelan suspended, City play five across midfield to thwart Wenger's men but lack punch up front. Kanu's introduction creates gaps which Overmars exploits. On-loan striker Gioacchini from Venice gets 15 minutes of fame. Nilsson breaks two ribs and punctures a lung.											
31	A	SHEFFIELD WED		15	W	2-1	1-0	McAllister 18p, Whelan 83	Hedman	Breen	Edworthy	Telfer	Williams	Shaw	Boateng	McAllister*	Whelan	Huckerby	Froggatt	Clement
	3/4		*28,136*	*14*	34			*Rudi 50*	*Srnicek*	*Atherton*	*Briscoe*	*Jonk"*	*Thome*	*Walker**	*Alexand'rs'n*	*Carbone*	*Cresswell*	*Humphreys^*	*Rudi*	*Newsome/Sonner/Scott*
								Ref: K Burge	City snatch a vital win to take them four points away from the drop-zone. Huckerby is brought down by Srnicek for the penalty but City have to withstand strong Owls pressure after Rudi's goal before Whelan's late goal condemns Danny Wilson's team to their fifth defeat on the trot.											

No	Date	Opponent / Att	Pos	Res / Pts	F-A	H-T	Scorers, Times, and Referees	1	2	3	4	5	6	7	8	9	10	11	subs used
32	H	SOUTHAMPTON	15	W	1-0	0-0	Boateng 63	Hedman	Breen	Burrows	Soltvedt	Williams	Shaw	Boateng	McAllister	Whelan	Huckerby*	Telfer	Gioacchini
	5/4	21,404	*19*	37				*Moss*	*Hiley*	*Colleter*	*Dodd*	*Monkou*	*Lundekvam*	*Hughes D"*	*Marsden*	*Hughes M*	*Beattie^*	*Bridge**	*Le Tissier/Pahars/Kachloul*
							Ref: U Rennie	The out-of-form Boateng, visibly unsettled by transfer talk, snatches the winner after Moss fails to hold Soltvedt's header. Dave Jones' team are in the bottom three and need a soccer miracle. Referee Rennie upsets everyone with his fussy handling. Gary Breen is resigned to leaving.											
33	A	EVERTON	15	L	0-2	0-1		Hedman	Breen	Burrows	Soltvedt	Williams	Shaw	Telfer*	McAllister	Whelan	Huckerby	Boateng	Aloisi
	11/4	*32,341*	*16*	37			*Campbell 28, 87*	*Myhre*	*Short*	*Ball*	*Dacourt*	*Watson*	*Materazzi !*	*Weir*	*Gemmill*	*Campbell*	*Jeffers**	*Barmby*	*Grant*
							Ref: R Harris	Everton are fighting for their lives and deserve the win. Materazzi gets his third red card of the season for two fouls on Huckerby in a rough game. Campbell, his goals apart, is anonymous but has 9 in 14 against City. Jeffers looks more dangerous and Hedman twice saves from him.											
34	H	MIDDLESBROUGH	16	L	1-2	0-0	McAllister 72	Hedman	Breen*	Burrows	Soltvedt	Williams	Shaw	Whelan	McAllister	Aloisi	Huckerby	Boateng	Clement
	17/4	19,228	*7*	37			*Kinder 64, Gordon 82*	*Schwarzer*	*Baker*	*Gordon*	*Cooper*	*Vickers*	*Pallister**	*Maddison*	*Townsend*	*Ricard^*	*Deane*	*O'Neill*	*Kinder"/Armstrong/Mustoe*
							Ref: P Jones	Hedman is injured in the second minute but gamely plays on with little to save. City are dominant but Schwarzer plays a blinder to keep them out. With the fans shouting for Hedman to be subbed he is flat-footed for Boro's goals. Strachan argues that Hedman was happy to continue.											
35	A	LEICESTER	16	L	0-1	0-1		Hedman	Breen	Burrows	Clement"	Williams	Shaw	Telfer*	Quinn	Aloisi^	Huckerby	Boateng	Hall M/Gioacchini/Soltvedt
	24/4	*20,224*	*11*	37			*Marshall 45*	*Keller*	*Impey*	*Guppy*	*Sinclair*	*Elliott*	*Kaamark*	*Lennon"*	*Marshall^*	*Heskey*	*Cottee**	*Savage*	*C'mbell/Fenton/Gunnl'gs'n*
							Ref: G Barber	Whelan and McAllister are suspended and City spend most of a dismal game soaking up Leicester pressure. Guppy's crosses cause them big problems and Marshall's stoppage-time header is from one of them. Boateng is unhappy playing wide. Four points are still needed for safety.											
36	H	WIMBLEDON	16	W	2-1	2-0	Huckerby 16, Whelan 28	Hedman	Edworthy	Burrows*	Soltvedt	Breen	Shaw	Boateng	McAllister	Whelan	Huckerby	Telfer	Hall M
	1/5	21,198	*13*	40			*Hartson 73*	*Sullivan*	*Jupp*	*Thatcher*	*Earle*	*Blackwell*	*Cunningh'm*	*Hughes C**	*Euell*	*Hartson*	*Gayle*	*Kennedy*	*Leaburn*
							Ref: G Poll	Huckerby ends his 14-game goal drought by beating the offside trap and City are on top of a good game for over an hour. When the Dons start their aerial bombardment, Hartson's goal exposes the nerve ends but it's a fair result. Kinnear's heart-attack means Mick Harford is in charge.											
37	A	DERBY	16	D	0-0	0-0		Hedman	Edworthy	Hall M	Soltvedt	Breen	Shaw	Boateng	McAllister	Whelan	Huckerby*	Telfer	Aloisi
	8/5	*32,450*	*7*	41				*Poom*	*Delap"*	*Schnoor*	*Laursen*	*Carbonari*	*Prior*	*Powell*	*Eranio**	*Wanchope*	*Sturridge*	*Beck^*	*Murray/Baiano/Harper*
							Ref: P Alcock	A point is enough for safety in a poor game. Beck and Wanchope miss first-half chances and after the break City improve. In the last minute Paulo Wanchope misses when the ball gets stuck between his legs. Huckerby's 100th offside of the season wins him the Premiership award!											
38	H	LEEDS	15	D	2-2	0-1	Aloisi 63, Telfer 71	Hedman	Nilsson	Burrows*	Soltvedt	Breen^	Shaw	Boateng	McAllister	Whelan	Huckerby"	Telfer	Edworthy/Williams/Aloisi
	16/5	23,049	*4*	42			*Wijnhard 41, Hopkin 90*	*Robinson*	*Haaland**	*Granville"*	*Batty*	*Wetherall*	*Radebe*	*Jones*	*McPhail*	*Hasselbaink*	*Wijnhard*	*Ribeiro^*	*Hopkin/Kewell/Harte*
	Home	Away					Ref: S Lodge	Hopkin's goal is 20 seconds after the end of stoppage time and wrecks an excellent Sky Blues performance. There are chances galore at both ends but City are dominant after the break. Aloisi's header and Telfer's wicked shot are put into the shade by Nilsson's emotional farewell.											
Average	20,773	30,399																	

Worthington Cup		Att	Pos	Res	F-A	H-T	Scorers, Times, and Referees	SQUAD	NUMBERS	IN USE									subs used
2:1 H	SOUTHEND		19	W	1-0	0-0	Hall P 64	Hedman	Shaw*	Burrows	Boateng	Breen	Wallemme"	Telfer	Clement^	Dublin	Huckerby	Hall P	Shilton/Soltvedt/Williams
16/9		6,631	*3:8*					*Margetson*	*Hails*	*Stimpson*	*Morley*	*Newman*	*Coleman*	*Maher*	*Gooding*	*Burns*	*Whyte**	*Jones*	*Fitzpatrick*
							Ref: C Foy	The eight hour goal drought is over but the Sky Blues are far from convincing against Alvin Martin's Southend. Belgian Clement makes a quiet first start and another newcomer, Paul Hall, grabs the goal. Whelan is back in favour after his involvement in off-field fisticuffs.											
2:2 A	SOUTHEND		19	W	4-0	3-0	Boateng 6, Dublin 27, Whelan 45, [Soltvedt 83]	Hedman	Shaw	Burrows	Boateng"	Williams*	Wallemme	Boland	Quinn^	Dublin	Whelan	Shilton	Clement/Strachan/Soltvedt
22/9		*6,292*	*3:10*					*Margetson*	*Hails*	*Stimpson*	*Morley*	*Newman*	*Coleman*	*Maher*	*Gooding*	*Fitzpatrick**	*Whyte*	*Clarke*	*Dublin*
							Ref: G Poll (City win 5-0 on aggregate)	A weakened side is weaker when Breen misses the bus and Williams clashes heads with Burrows. City are too strong for a poor Southend team and clinically punish defensive slackness. Shilton, making a rare appearance, creates two goals and Clement looks comfy at centre-half.											
3 A	LUTON		18	L	0-2	0-0		Hedman	**Brightwell**	Hall M	Boateng	Breen	Shaw	Telfer	McAllister	Whelan	Huckerby	Hall P*	Soltvedt
27/10		*9,051*	*2:4*				*Gray 50, Davis S 77*	*Davis K*	*Alexander*	*Thomas*	*McKinnon*	*Davis S*	*Johnson*	*Evers*	*Spring*	*Douglas**	*Gray*	*McGowan*	*Fotiades*
							Ref: C Wilkes	Lennie Lawrence's Luton outclass and outfight a woeful Coventry side who don't get a shot on target. An embarrassed Strachan admits they were so bad that he didn't know who to take off. Dublin refuses to play with a big transfer looming and is fined £40,000 – but later quashed.											

FA Cup		Att	Pos	Res	F-A	H-T	Scorers, Times, and Referees												subs used
3 H	MACCLESFIELD		17	W	7-0	3-0	Froggatt 28, Whelan 36, Payne 45 (og), [Huckerby 60, 71, 89, Boateng 88]	Hedman	Nilsson"	Burrows^	Soltvedt	Williams	Shaw	Boateng	McAllister	Whelan*	Huckerby	Froggatt	Aloisi/Shilton/Telfer
2/1		14,206	*2:23*					*Price*	*Hitchin*	*Howarth*	*Wood^*	*Sodje"*	*Payne*	*Askey*	*Sedgemore*	*Matias**	*Tomlinson*	*Davies*	*Whittaker/Lonergan?Durkan*
							Ref: G Willard	Poor league form is forgotten as City equal their Cup scoring record in their biggest home win for 35 years. McAllister's display wins over the boo-boys and Huckerby's pace destroys Sammy McIlroy's Silkmen after a nervous first 25 minutes. After the break it's one-way traffic.											
4 A	LEICESTER		17	W	3-0	1-0	Whelan 16, Telfer 90, Froggatt 90	Hedman	Edworthy	Burrows	Soltvedt	Williams	Shaw	Boateng !	McAllister *	Whelan	Huckerby^	Froggatt	Clement/Telfer
23/1		*21,207*	*12*					*Keller*	*Sinclair*	*Ullathorne^*	*Zagorakis**	*Walsh*	*Elliott*	*Impey*	*Lennon*	*Heskey*	*Izzet*	*Guppy*	*Parker/Taggart*
							Ref: A Wilkie	Stout defending and a string of fine saves deny Martin O'Neill's team's onslaught after Whelan's delightful chip. Then, down to ten men, City survive an Elliott penalty and, with an equaliser looking certain, two breakaways result in late goals. Lady Luck smiles on the Sky Blues.											
5 A	EVERTON		16	L	1-2	0-1	McAllister 84	Hedman	Nilsson	Burrows	Clement^	Breen	Shaw	Boateng*	McAllister	Whelan	Huckerby	Froggatt"	Telfer/Soltvedt/Aloisi
13/2		*33,907*	*17*				*Jeffers 20, Oster 78*	*Myhre*	*Ward**	*Ball*	*Dacourt*	*Watson*	*Dunne*	*Oster"*	*Grant*	*Hutchison*	*Jeffers^*	*Barmby*	*O'Kane/Cada'teri/Bakayoko*
							Ref: U Rennie	City fans' Wembley dreams are dashed as the team barely compete in one of their worst displays of the season. 18-year-old Francis Jeffers robs Shaw to score and Oster wraps it up. Everton had scored only three home goals all season. Huckerby is tamed by the 37-year-old Dave Watson.											

		Home					Away					
	P	W	D	L	F	A	W	D	L	F	A	Pts
1 Manchester U	38	14	4	1	45	18	8	9	2	35	19	79
2 Arsenal	38	14	5	0	34	5	8	7	4	25	12	78
3 Chelsea	38	12	6	1	29	13	8	9	2	28	17	75
4 Leeds	38	12	5	2	32	9	6	8	5	30	25	67
5 West Ham	38	11	3	5	32	26	5	6	8	14	27	57
6 Aston Villa	38	10	3	6	33	28	5	7	7	18	18	55
7 Liverpool	38	10	5	4	44	24	5	4	10	24	25	54
8 Derby	38	8	7	4	22	19	5	6	8	18	26	52
9 Middlesbro	38	7	9	3	25	18	5	6	8	23	36	51
10 Leicester	38	7	6	6	25	25	5	7	7	15	21	49
11 Tottenham	38	7	7	5	28	26	4	7	8	19	24	47
12 Sheffield Wed	38	7	5	7	20	15	6	2	11	21	27	46
13 Newcastle	38	7	6	6	26	25	4	7	8	22	29	46
14 Everton	38	6	8	5	22	12	5	2	12	20	35	43
15 COVENTRY	38	8	6	5	26	21	3	3	13	13	30	42
16 Wimbledon	38	7	7	5	22	21	3	5	11	18	42	42
17 Southampton	38	9	4	6	29	26	2	4	13	8	38	41
18 Charlton	38	4	7	8	20	20	4	5	10	21	36	36
19 Blackburn	38	6	5	8	21	24	1	9	9	17	28	35
20 Nott'm Forest	38	3	7	9	18	31	4	2	13	17	38	30
	760	169	115	96	553	406	96	115	169	406	553	1025

Odds & ends

Double wins: (1) Sheffield Wed.
Double losses: (4) Newcastle, Arsenal, Manchester U, Middlesbrough.

Won from behind: (1) Charlton (h).
Lost from in front: (4) Newcastle (h), Wimbledon (a), Chelsea (a), Newcastle (a).

High spots: Wins at Villa and Leicester.
Huckerby's back-to-back hat-tricks.
Record equalling Cup win

Low spots: Poor away form.
Disappointing form of Boateng and Huckerby.
FA Cup exit at Everton after high expectations.
Embarrassing League Cup exit at Luton.
Disappointment at Stamford Bridge after great display.

Red cards: City – Boateng (Leicester a, FAC), Aloisi (Charlton h).
Red cards: Opponents – Sinclair (Leicester h), Materazzi (Everton a).

Player of the year: Richard Shaw.
Ever-presents: (0).
Hat-tricks: (2) Darren Huckerby.
Opposing hat-tricks: (0).
Leading scorer: (13) Noel Whelan.

	Appearances						**Goals**			
	Lge	*Sub*	LC	*Sub*	FAC	*Sub*	**Lge**	LC	FAC	**Tot**
Aloisi, John	**7**	*9*				*2*	**5**			**5**
Boateng, George	**29**	*4*	3		3		**4**	1	1	**6**
Boland Willie			1							
Breen, Gary	**21**	*4*	2		1					
Brightwell, Ian			1							
Burrows, David	**23**		2		3					
Clement, Phillipe	**6**	*6*	1	*1*	1	*1*				
Dublin, Dion	**10**		2				**3**	1		**4**
Edworthy, Marc	**16**	*6*			1					
Froggatt, Steve	**23**				3		**1**		2	**3**
Gioacchini, Stef (loan)		*3*								
Hall, Marcus	**2**	*3*	1							
Hall, Paul	**2**	*7*	2					1		**1**
Haworth, Simon	**1**									
Hedman, Magnus	**36**		3		3					
Huckerby, Darren	**31**	*3*	2		3		**9**		3	**12**
Jackson, Darren (loan)		*3*								
Konjic, Mohammed	**3**	*1*								
McAllister, Gary	**29**		1		3		**3**		1	**4**
McSheffrey, Gary		*1*								
Nilsson, Roland	**28**				2					
Ogrizovic, Steve	**2**									
Quinn, Barry	**6**	*1*	1							
Shaw, Richard	**36**	*1*	3		3					
Shilton, Sam	**1**	*4*	1	*1*		*1*				
Soltvedt, Trond-Egil	**21**	*6*		*3*	2	*1*	**2**	1		**3**
Strachan, Gavin				*1*						
Telfer, Paul	**30**	*2*	2			*3*	**2**		1	**3**
Wallemme, Jean-Guy	**4**	*2*	2							
Whelan, Noel	**31**		2		3		**10**	1	2	**13**
Williams, Paul	**20**	*2*	1	*1*	2					
(own-goals)									1	**1**
31 players used	**418**	***68***	**33**	***7***	**33**	***8***	**39**	**5**	**11**	**55**

F.A. CARLING PREMIERSHIP

Manager: Gordon Strachan

SEASON 1999-2000

No	Date	Att	Pos	Pt	F-A	H-T	Scorers, Times, and Referees	SQUAD	NUMBERS	IN	USE								subs used
1	H SOUTHAMPTON			L	0-1	0-0		Hedman	Edworthy	Burrows	**Chippo^**	Williams	Shaw	Telfer	McAllister	Whelan	Huckerby*	**Hadji**	Aloisi/Froggatt
	7/8	19,602		0			*Ostenstaad 85*	*Jones*	*Dodd*	*Benali*	*Marsden*	*Lundekvam*	*Richards*	*Hughes M*	*Le Tissier**	*Ostenstaad*	*Pahars*	*Kachloul^*	*Ripley/Beresford*
							Ref: P Jones	Dave Jones' Saints grab their first opening day win for 11 years to deflate the Moroccans' debut day. Hadji is at the heart of everything but too many chances go begging. Noel Whelan is in trouble for saying he wants to play for Leeds, and Saints are on the verge of signing Soltvedt.											
2	A LEICESTER			L	0-1	0-1		Hedman	Edworthy	Burrows !	Chippo	Williams	Shaw	Telfer	McAllister	Whelan	Hadji	Froggatt*	Aloisi
	11/8	*19,196*		0			*Izzet 24p*	*Flowers*	*Impey*	*Guppy*	*Sinclair*	*Elliott*	*Taggart^*	*Savage*	*Lennon*	*Marshall**	*Cottee*	*Izzet*	*Campbell/Gilchrist*
							Ref: N Barry	Huckerby has gone to Leeds for £5.5million. City start brightly but the harsh penalty against Edworthy for fouling Lennon knocks them back. Burrows sees the first red card of his career after 69 minutes for an elbow on Savage. The defence looks good but who is going to score goals?											
3	A WIMBLEDON		16	D	1-1	0-0	McAllister 90p	Hedman	Breen	Burrows	Chippo	Williams	Shaw	Telfer	McAllister	Whelan	Aloisi	Hadji*	Froggatt
	14/8	**10,635**	*10*	1			*Cort 67*	*Sullivan*	*Cunningham*	*Thatcher*	*Roberts"*	*Blackwell*	*Pedersen*	*Cort*	*Earle**	*Hartson*	*Gayle*	*Andersen^*	*Euell/Hughes M/Ardley*
							Ref: M Halsey	Egil 'Drillo' Olsen's men try to defend at 1-0 and in injury-time Pedersen brings down Aloisi to give City a goal at last. They deserve the point for a spirited display with Chippo starring. It's the smallest Premiership gate for two years on a wet day. Strikers galore are linked with City.											
4	H DERBY		12	W	2-0	1-0	Keane 43, 67	Hedman	Edworthy	Burrows	Chippo	Williams	Shaw	Telfer*	McAllister	Whelan	**Keane^**	Hadji"	Froggatt/Strachan/Aloisi
	21/8	**17,658**	*19*	4				*Poom*	*Borbokis*	*Delap*	*Laursen*	*Carbonari*	*Prior*	*Eranio^*	*Powell*	*Sturridge"*	*Burton**	*Johnson*	*Beck/Bohinen/Harper*
							Ref: J Winter	At £6 million Robbie Keane is the most expensive teenager ever and it's a dream start with two poacher's goals celebrated with his trademark cartwheel. He's the first debut double-scorer since Mick Quinn in 1992. Jim Smith's Derby have little to offer and City's backline looks solid.											
5	H MANCHESTER U		16	L	1-2	0-0	Aloisi 79	Hedman	Breen"	Edworthy	Chippo	Williams	Shaw	Hadji^	McAllister	Whelan*	Keane	Froggatt	Telfer/Aloisi/Konjic
	25/8	22,022	*1*	4			*Scholes 62, Yorke 75*	*V d Gouw*	*Neville P"*	*Irwin*	*Keane*	*Stam*	*Berg*	*Beckham*	*Butt^*	*Yorke*	*Sheringh'm**	*Giggs*	*Scholes/Solskjaer/Curtis*
							Ref: A Wilkie	City are a match for the European champions until Scholes enters the fray on the hour and his shot is deflected in by Breen. Beckham's wonder cross makes a second before Keane creates for Aloisi's angled shot. Froggatt misses a good chance and Whelan goes off with an ankle injury.											
6	A SUNDERLAND		16	D	1-1	1-0	Keane 33	Hedman	Breen	Edworthy	Chippo !	Williams	Shaw	Hadji*	McAllister	Aloisi^	Keane	Froggatt	Telfer/McSheffrey
	29/8	*39,427*	*12*	5			*Phillips 72*	*Sorensen*	*Makin*	*Gray*	*Rae*	*Butler*	*Bould*	*Summerbee*	*Schwarz*	*Quinn*	*Phillips*	*McCann**	*Oster*
							Ref: S Lodge	Keane stuns the Stadium of Light in City's first ever visit after being set up by first-half hero Chippo. After the break it's all Sunderland and Peter Reid's men are saved by Phillips' volley. Chippo turns villain with two yellow cards and is sent off three minutes from time. A fair result.											
7	H LEEDS		17	L	3-4	2-3	McAllister 2p, Aloisi 17, Chippo 54	Hedman	Quinn"	Edworthy	Chippo	Williams	Shaw	Hadji	McAllister	Aloisi*	Keane	Froggatt^	Hall M/Strachan/McSheff'
	11/9	21,528	*4*	5			*B'yer 7, Huck' 25, Harte 33p, Brid's 80*	*Martyn*	*Mills*	*Harte^*	*Batty*	*Radebe*	*Duberry**	*Hopkin*	*Bowyer*	*Bridges*	*Huckerby*	*Kewell*	*Kelly/Woodgate*
							Ref: S Dunn	City are twice in front but Hedman flusters and gives Leeds two, including Huck's predictable goal on his return. Chippo hits a volley from the edge of the box and O'Leary's men win it as Kewell hits the post but the offside Bridges scores. Lineswoman Wendy Toms upsets Strachan.											
8	A TOTTENHAM		17	L	2-3	0-1	Keane 54, Chippo 74	Hedman	Edworthy	Burrows^	Williams	Konjic	Shaw	Chippo	McAllister	Hadji	Keane	Froggatt*	Hall M/Hall P
	19/9	*35,224*	*9*	5			*Iversen 7, Armstrong 49, Leon'dsen 51*	*Walker*	*Carr*	*Taricco*	*Freund*	*Young*	*Perry*	*Leonhards'n*	*Sherwood*	*Armstrong^*	*Iversen*	*Ginola**	*Dominguez/Nielsen*
							Ref: A D'Urso	City's defensive frailty is exposed again but a late fightback makes the scoreline respectable. Iversen scores one and makes the others and a thrashing looks on. Keane scores another wonder goal made by star man Edworthy. Loan signing Carlton Palmer can't get registered in time.											
9	H WEST HAM		15	W	1-0	1-0	Hadji 36	Hedman	Edworthy	Hall M	**Palmer**	Konjic	Shaw	Telfer	McAllister^	Hadji	Keane	Chippo*	Williams/McSheffrey
	25/9	19,985	*9*	8				*Hislop*	*Sinclair*	*Keller**	*Lomas*	*Stimac*	*Potts*	*Foe*	*Lampard*	*Wanchope*	*Di Canio*	*Moncur !*	*Newton*
							Ref: D Elleray	Harry Redknapp's boys are out of luck despite having the lion's share of a scrappy second half. Hedman is back to his best, foiling Wanchope who also misses good chances. Hadji's header gives City their first home win over West Ham since 1995. Moncur gets two yellows and is off.											
10	A EVERTON		14	D	1-1	1-1	McAllister 12	Hedman	Edworthy	Hall M	Palmer	Konjic*	Shaw	Telfer	McAllister	Hadji	Keane	Chippo	Williams
	2/10	*34,839*	*6*	9			*Jeffers 2*	*Gerrard*	*Ball*	*Dunne^*	*Xavier*	*Gough*	*Weir*	*Barmby**	*Hutchison*	*Campbell*	*Jeffers*	*Collins*	*Cadamarteri/Gemmill*
							Ref: N Barry	Palmer stars as City survive a torrid first half to dominate the second but Keane has a knock and is below par. Walter Smith's men have a hangover from their win over Liverpool but it's their best start for 20 years. Hadji confides he is playing with steak in his boot for a foot injury.											

No	H/A	Opponent	Pos	Res	F-A	H-T	Scorers, Times, Referees	1	2	3	4	5	6	7	8	9	10	11	subs used
11	H	NEWCASTLE	13	W	4-1	3-0	Palmer 13, Williams 21, Keane 39, [Hadji 90]	Hedman	Edworthy*	Hall M	Palmer	Williams	Shaw	Telfer	McAllister^	Hadji	Keane	Chippo	Froggatt/**Roussel**
16/10		23,022	*19*	12			*Domi 81*	*Given*	*Barton !*	*Domi*	*Lee*	*Hughes*	*Dabizas*	*Solano*	*Dyer*	*Shearer*	*Gallacher*	*Speed*	
							Ref: A Wiley	Hedman's early saves keep City in the game and they go ahead against the run of play. Williams' 25-yarder could have gone anywhere and Given boobs for Keane's fifth goal in eight. Bobby Robson is fuming that Barton sees red for a forearm smash on Chippo after 30 minutes.											
12	A	SHEFFIELD WED	13	D	0-0	0-0		Hedman	Telfer	Hall M	Palmer	Williams	Shaw	Chippo*	McAllister	Hadji	Keane	Froggatt	Roussel
23/10		*23,296*	*20*	13				*Srnicek*	*Atherton*	*Hinchcliffe**	*Jonk*	*Thome*	*Walker*	*Alexand'son*	*Sonner*	*Booth^*	*De Bilde*	*Rudi*	*Briscoe/Sibon*
							Ref: M Riley	Danny Wilson's Owls have only one win, but go close to another but for Hedman, linked with Newcastle, who makes some key saves. On-loan Belgian striker Roussel looks useful but City's best chance falls to Palmer who heads wide. Noel Whelan needs an operation on his ankle.											
13	H	WATFORD	13	W	**4-0**	2-0	Keane 17, Froggatt 33, Hadji 49, [McAllister 62p]	Hedman	Telfer	Hall M	Palmer	Williams	Shaw	Hadji	McAllister	Roussel	Keane	Froggatt	
31/10		21,697	*19*	16				*Chamberlain*	*Lyttle*	*Easton*	*Gibbs*	*Palmer*	*Panayi**	*Miller^*	*Hyde*	*Wooter*	*Smith"*	*Johnson*	*Ngonge/Ward/Gudmundson*
							Ref: P Durkin	Sky TV record City scoring four for the second successive home game for the first time since 1966. Graham Taylor's injury-hit team are out of their depth and Keane is at his best. Roussel makes the first, Keane's one-two with Froggatt makes it two, and Palmer handles for the penalty.											
14	A	BRADFORD C	13	D	1-1	1-1	McAllister 1	Hedman	Telfer	Hall M	Palmer	Williams	Shaw	Chippo	McAllister	Hadji	Keane	Froggatt	
6/11		*17,587*	*17*	17			*Mills 43*	*Clarke*	*Halle^*	*Sharpe*	*McCall*	*Wetherall*	*O'Brien*	*Redfearn*	*Windass*	*Saunders**	*Mills*	*Blake"*	*Beagrie/Lawrence/Rankin*
							Ref: B Knight	Two points dropped in their first visit to Bradford since 1960. McAllister scores City's fastest ever Premiership goal but Lee Mills replies after fouling Hall. Paul Jewell's team are fighters but short on class. The dazzling Keane unluckily hits the post. Froggatt gets surprise England call.											
15	H	ASTON VILLA	11	W	2-1	1-1	Roussel 8, Keane 65	Hedman	Telfer	Hall M	Palmer	Williams	Breen	Hadji	McAllister	Roussel*	Keane	Chippo^	Whelan/Burrows
22/11		20,174	*13*	20			*Dublin 41*	*James*	*Delaney**	*Wright*	*Taylor*	*Calderwood*	*Southgate*	*Stone*	*Boateng*	*Dublin*	*Joachim^*	*Hendrie*	*Watson/Vassell*
							Ref: G Barber	Sky dub City the entertainers after their first home win over Villa since 1992. Keane, who the beleagured John Gregory refused to pay over the odds for, rubs salt in the wound with a sparkling display and goal. Eight games unbeaten with Carlton Palmer, now signed, a major influence.											
16	H	LEICESTER	12	L	0-1	0-0		Hedman	Telfer	Burrows^	Palmer	Williams	Breen	Hadji	McAllister	Roussel*	Keane	Chippo	Whelan/Froggatt
27/11		22,016	*5*	20			*Heskey 60*	*Flowers*	*Impey*	*Guppy*	*Sinclair*	*Elliott*	*Taggart*	*Savage*	*Lennon*	*Heskey*	*Cottee*	*Izzet*	
							Ref: S Lodge	Martin O'Neill's no-nonsense team do the double over City for the first time since 1952. The still-unfit Whelan replaces the concussed Roussel early on and Burrows is badly injured. Heskey's goal is made from nothing and although City dominate the last half hour, the Foxes hang on.											
17	A	SOUTHAMPTON	11	D	0-0	0-0		Hedman	Telfer	Froggatt	Palmer	Williams	Breen	Hadji	McAllister	Roussel*	Keane	Chippo	Whelan
4/12		*15,168*	*16*	21				*Jones*	*Tessem*	*Colleter*	*Dodd*	*Richards*	*Benali*	*Ripley*	*Oakley*	*Beattie*	*Pahars**	*Kachloul*	*Davies*
							Ref: J Winter	City are relieved with a point with Hedman again a hero, saving late chances from Beattie and Davies. Edworthy, Shaw, Konjic, Burrows and Hall are all injured and the defence is wobbly. Dean Richards heads against the bar while Paul Jones tips Hadji's vicious shot onto the bar.											
18	A	LIVERPOOL	13	L	0-2	0-1		Hedman	Telfer	Froggatt	Palmer	Williams	Breen	Hadji^	McAllister	Whelan*	Keane	Chippo	Roussel/**Normann**
18/12		*44,024*	*5*	21			*Owen 45, Camara 74*	*Westerveld*	*Gerrard*	*Matteo*	*Carragher*	*Hyppia*	*Henchoz*	*Thompson**	*Hamann*	*Owen*	*Camara^*	*Berger*	*Smicer"/Heggem/Murphy*
							Ref: A D'Urso	On the 40th anniversary of Shankly's first game as manager City don't spoil the party. Two minutes stoppage time is displayed but Owen's goal is four minutes later. Camara's strike is quality. Whelan is sharper but misses a good chance at 0-0. Normann impresses for 15 minutes.											
19	H	ARSENAL	13	W	3-2	2-0	McAllister 7, Hadji 41, Keane 71	Hedman	Telfer	Froggatt	Palmer	Williams	Breen	Chippo^	McAllister	Roussel	Keane*	Hadji	Whelan/**Gustafsson**
26/12		22,750	*4*	24			*Ljungberg 67, Suker 86*	*Seaman*	*Dixon*	*Winterburn*	*Grimandi**	*Adams*	*Keown*	*Ljungberg*	*Petit*	*Kanu*	*Henry*	*Overmars*	*Suker*
							Ref: R Harris	City turn on the style for Sky and wreck Wenger's Xmas. City control midfield where Vieira is missing, suspended. McAllister's shot takes a deflection whilst Hadji's is a superb bender. Keane wins it with a delicate chip past Adams and Seaman, and more chances go begging.											
20	H	CHELSEA	13	D	2-2	0-0	Roussel 54, Keane 82	Hedman	Telfer	Froggatt	Palmer	Williams	Breen	Chippo	McAllister	Roussel*	Keane	Hadji	Whelan
4/1		20,152	*7*	25			*Flo 55, 83*	*De Goey*	*Ferrer*	*Babayaro*	*Desch'mps^*	*Thome*	*Desailly*	*Di Matteo"*	*Poyet**	*Flo*	*Zola*	*Wise*	*Petrescu/Morris/Sutton*
							Ref: P Durkin	Twice Chelsea catch City cold within a minute of scoring and level the scores. Vialli's men are up for a fight and concede 21 fouls but avoid defeat on the ground for the first time in five years. Cedric Roussel is proving to be a diamond up front and Sky TV have another cracker.											
21	H	WIMBLEDON	12	W	2-0	0-0	McAllister 56p, Keane 74	Hedman	Telfer	Froggatt	Palmer	Williams	Breen	**Eustace**	McAllister	Roussel*	Keane	Whelan	Normann
15/1		19,005	*14*	28				*Sullivan*	*Cunningham*	*Kimble*	*Earle*	*Hreidarsson*	*Andersen*	*Andresen*	*Euell*	*Cort*	*Francis^*	*Ardley**	*Badir/Gray*
							Ref: S Bennett	Numerous chances go begging until Kimble's handball resulted in a penalty. The Dons under Olsen look a sorry bunch and don't have a shot on target. Williams is a rock in his 150th City appearance, whilst evergreen McAllister plays out of his skin alongside the impressive Eustace.											

No	Date		Att	Pos	Pt	F-A	H-T	Scorers, Times, and Referees	SQUAD	NUMBERS	IN USE									subs used
22	A	DERBY		12	D	0-0	0-0		Hedman	Telfer	Froggatt	Eustace^	Williams	Breen	Strachan*	McAllister	Roussel	Keane	Whelan	Quinn/Gustafsson
	22/1		*28,381*	*16*	29				*Poom*	*Delap*	*Scnoor*	*Laursen*	*Carbonari*	*Elliott**	*Burley*	*Johnson*	*Strupar*	*Burton^*	*Bohinen*	*Kinkladze/Christie*
								Ref: G Barber	Thirteen away games without a win and no sign of a win here with a makeshift side. The Moroccans are away and Palmer is suspended. City deny a £10m bid from Inter for Keane but sign Roussel for £1.2m. Burton and Froggatt both hit woodwork. Jim Smith is happy with a point.											
23	A	MANCHESTER U		12	L	2-3	0-1	Roussel 65, 90	Hedman	Gustafsson	Shaw	Palmer	Williams	Breen	Telfer*	McAllister	Roussel	Keane	Froggatt	Eustace
	5/2		***61,380***	*1*	29			*Cole 39, 54, Scholes 77*	*Bosnich*	*Neville G*	*Neville P*	*Keane*	*Stam*	*Silvestre*	*Beckham*	*Scholes*	*Cole*	*Shering'm^*	*Solskjaer**	*Butt/Cruyff*
								Ref: A Wilkie	The crowd is the largest at a City league game since 1937 and a Premiership record. Roussel is the first City player to score two on the ground, both made by Eustace. Cole's two ensure United go six points clear. Hadji and Chippo fly in too late to play. Gustafsson's first start is great.											
24	H	SUNDERLAND		12	W	3-2	3-0	Keane 3, Hadji 13, Roussel 18	Hedman	Gustafsson	Froggatt*	Eustace	Breen	Shaw	Chippo^	McAllister	Roussel	Keane	Hadji	Quinn/Normann
	12/2		22,099	*6*	32			*Phillips 54, Rae 88*	*Sorensen*	*Makin*	*Williams**	*McCann^*	*Butler*	*Craddock*	*Summ'bee"*	*Schwarz*	*Quinn*	*Phillips*	*Kilbane*	*Holloway/Roy/Rae*
								Ref: P Alcock	Sunderland are blown away in a scintillating first half and resort to bully-boy tactics including a vicious career-ending tackle on Froggatt by Summerbee. Hadji is awesome and has a hand in all three goals. Reid's men rally, Kilbane hits the post in the 90th minute and hearts stop.											
25	A	MIDDLESBROUGH		12	L	0-2	0-2		Hedman	Gustafs'n*	Burrows^	Palmer	Williams	Shaw	Chippo	McAllister	Roussel"	Keane	Hadji	Eustace/Breen/Quinn
	19/2		*32,798*	*14*	32			*Festa 8, Ricard 20*	*Schwarzer*	*Fleming*	*Ziege*	*Festa*	*Pallister*	*Cooper*	*Summerbell*	*Ince*	*Ricard*	*Campbell*	*Juninho**	*Maddison*
								Ref: G Barber	The woeful away form continues as Boro win only their second game in 14 to ease pressure on Bryan Robson. Burrows and Palmer don't look fit in an abject City display with only three goal attempts. Injured Froggatt is out of England squad. Strachan admits he picked the wrong team.											
26	H	TOTTENHAM		13	L	0-1	0-0		Hedman	Shaw	Burrows	Eustace	Williams*	Breen	Chippo	McAllister	Whelan^	Keane	Hadji	Quinn/Normann
	26/2		23,073	*9*	32			*Armstrong 82*	*Walker*	*Carr*	*Taricco^*	*Freund*	*Campbell*	*Perry*	*Anderton*	*Sherwood*	*Armstrong*	*Ginola*	*Leonhardsen*	*Clemence/Young*
								Ref: P Durkin	There is a minute's silence for the late Stanley Matthews. Injury-hit City are closed down by George Graham's team who snatch an undeserved victory thanks to Hedman's boob. Keane is well-marked by Sol Campbell. New signings Colin Hendry and Ysrael Zuniga wait in the wings.											
27	A	LEEDS		14	L	0-3	0-2		Hedman	Quinn*	Burrows	Eustace	**Hendry**	Breen	Chippo	McAllister	Roussel	**Zuniga^**	Whelan	Shaw/Normann
	5/3		*38,710*	*2*	32			*Kewell 5, Bridges 42, Wilcox 85*	*Martyn*	*Kelly*	*Harte*	*Bakke*	*Radebe*	*Woodgate**	*McPhail*	*Bowyer"*	*Bridges^*	*Kewell*	*Wilcox*	*Haaland/Huckerby/Jones*
								Ref: J Winter	Another poor away display and Leeds coast it. O'Leary's men are in the middle of a UEFA Cup-tie with Roma and have the game won by half-time. Strachan gambles with Zuniga, for the injured Keane, but he is out of his depth. Late sub Huckerby sets up the third for bored Leeds.											
28	A	ASTON VILLA		14	L	0-1	0-1		Hedman	Gustaffson	Froggatt	Eustace^	Hendry	Shaw	Chippo	McAllister	Roussel	Keane*	Hadji	Whelan/Burrows
	11/3		*33,177*	*7*	32			*Ehiogu 45*	*Enckelman*	*Delaney*	*Wright*	*Barry*	*Ehiogu*	*Southgate*	*Taylor*	*Boateng*	*Carbone*	*Joachim^*	*Merson**	*Stone/Walker*
								Ref: U Rennie	Four games, no goals, no points and no sign of any here. Too many basic mistakes cost City dearly. Ehiogu heads in Merson's free-kick at the far post and it's as good as over. Gregory's men, with only one defeat in 20 games, look more likely to add more. Palmer is out for the season.											
29	H	EVERTON		14	W	1-0	0-0	McAllister 86	Hedman	Gustaffson	Burrows	Eustace*	Hendry	Shaw	Chippo	McAllister	Roussel	Whelan	Hadji	Zuniga
	15/3		18,513	*8*	35				*Gerrard*	*Dunne*	*Collins*	*Xavier*	*Gough*	*Weir*	*Barmby"*	*Hughes S^*	*Hughes M*	*Moore**	*Pembridge*	*Cada'teri/Unsw'th/Gemmill*
								Ref: M Halsey	After 8 hours and 38 minutes, McAllister ends the goal drought and seals a vital win. There's sheer relief after an anxious game which City deservedly won. It's Jurassic park with four over-34s and both sides have long injury lists. Mark Hughes debuts for Walter Smith's team.											
30	H	BRADFORD C		12	W	**4-0**	2-0	Roussel 7, Whelan 21, Eustace 85p,	Hedman	Gustaffson	Quinn	Eustace	Hendry	Shaw	Chippo	McAllister*	Roussel^	Whelan	Hadji	Telfer/Zuniga
	18/3		19,194	*18*	38			[Zuniga 86]	*Davison*	*Halle^*	*Jacobs"*	*McCall*	*Wetherall*	*O'Brien*	*Lawrence*	*Whalley**	*Windass*	*Saunders*	*Beagrie*	*Cadete/Blake/Sharpe*
								Ref: S Lodge	Any slight fears about relegation are gone as a woeful Bradford side are swept away. Eustace crowns a great display by scoring his first league goal from the spot after Zuniga is felled by Lee Sharpe but has to fight Chippo for the right. Zuniga also scores his first with a super volley.											
31	A	ARSENAL		14	L	0-3	0-0		Ogrizovic	Gustaffson*	Froggatt	Eustace	Hendry	Shaw	Chippo	McAllister	Roussel	Whelan	Hadji^	Telfer/Normann
	26/3		*38,027*	*4*	38			*Henry 50, Grimandi 79, Kanu 80*	*Seaman*	*Dixon*	*Winterburn*	*Vieira*	*Luzhny*	*Grimandi*	*Parlour*	*Petit*	*Henry^*	*Bergkamp**	*Overmars"*	*Kanu/Ljungberg/Suker*
								Ref: B Knight	42-year old Oggy plays his first game for 15 months because of Hedman's back injury and saves City from a hammering. Arsenal have just reached the UEFA semi-final and are slow to warm up, then it's one way traffic. Strachan has a new six-year contract. Telfer in Scotland squad.											

No	Venue / Date	Opponent / Att	Pos	Res / Pts	FT	HT	Scorers, Times, and Referees	1	2	3	4	5	6	7	8	9	10	11	Subs used
32	H	LIVERPOOL	14	L	0-3	0-2		Ogrizovic	Telfer	Froggatt	Eustace^	Hendry	Shaw	Chippo	McAllister	Roussel	Whelan*	Hadji	Keane/Quinn
	1/4	**23,084**	*3*	38			*Owen 23, 38, Heskey 78*	*Westerveld*	*Carragher*	*Matteo*	*Gerrard**	*Hyppia*	*Henchoz"*	*Thompson*	*Hamann*	*Heskey*	*Owen^*	*Berger*	*Murphy/Camara/Song*
							Ref: M Reed	Oggy makes his 600th first-team appearance but can't stop the impressive Reds who are chasing a Champions League spot. Michael Owen is unstoppable and bemuses City's defence who barely compete. Heskey heads his first Pool goal and but for Oggy it would have been more.											
33	A	CHELSEA	14	L	1-2	1-0	McAllister 18	Hedman	Telfer	Froggatt	Quinn	Hendry	Shaw	Chippo	McAllister	Whelan*	Keane	Hadji^	Zuniga/Burrows
	12/4	*32,316*	*4*	38			*Hendry 53 (og), Zola 58*	*De Goey*	*Petrescu*	*Harley*	*Wise*	*Thome*	*Leboeuf*	*Poyet^*	*Morris*	*Flo**	*Zola*	*Di Matteo"*	*Weah/Ambros'ti/Dalla Bona*
							Ref: G Poll	City take the lead in a downpour. Hendry and Whelan create it for Macca. Two substitutions swing the game with, first, Hendry turning in Ambrosetti's cross, then George Weah making the winner. Vialli's Chelsea, captained by Jody Morris for the night, are in the FA Cup final.											
34	H	MIDDLESBROUGH	14	W	2-1	1-0	Ince 32(og), Keane 61	Hedman	Telfer	Froggatt	Eustace	Hendry	Breen	Hadji	McAllister	Whelan	Keane	Chippo*	Burrows
	15/4	19,430	*13*	41			*Ziege 64p*	*Schwarzer*	*Fleming^*	*Ziege*	*Ince*	*Festa*	*Vickers*	*Mustoe*	*Summ'bell**	*Ricard*	*Deane*	*Campbell"*	*Juninho/Stamp/Stockdale*
							Ref: N Barry	Eustace's battle with Ince livens up a dire first half. Boro have lost only one in seven and only start playing when two down. Keane makes the first, which ricochets off Ince, and the second is vintage Robbie after Whelan's through-ball. Eustace fouls Andy Campbell for the penalty.											
35	A	WEST HAM	14	L	**0-5**	0-2	*[Kanoute 83]*	Hedman	Telfer	Burrows	Quinn"	Hendry^	Breen	Eustace	McAllister	Whelan	Keane	Normann*	Roussel/Shaw/**Betts**
	22/4	*24,719*	*8*	41			*Carrick 7, Margas 14, Di Canio 50, 66,*	*Feuer*	*Sinclair*	*Minto**	*Ferdinand*	*Stimac*	*Margas*	*Carrick*	*Lampard*	*Wanchope*	*Kanoute*	*Di Canio*	*Newton*
							Ref: A D'Urso	Redknapp's men inflict the biggest league defeat since 1992. Without Hadji and Chippo, City are ripped apart by Di Canio who makes three and scores two. Hendry goes off with serious facial injuries. Normann's first start in a 3-5-2 formation is a disaster. Chants of 'Strachan out'.											
36	A	NEWCASTLE	14	L	0-2	0-0		Hedman	Shaw	Telfer	Chippo	Williams	Breen	Hadji	McAllister	Roussel*	Keane^	Whelan"	Eustace/Zuniga/Betts
	29/4	*36,408*	*12*	41			*Shearer 78p, Gavilan 84*	*Given*	*Barton*	*Pistone*	*Lee"*	*Hughes*	*Dabizas*	*Gavilan^*	*Speed*	*Shearer*	*Dyer*	*Domi**	*Ketsbaia/McClen/Griffin*
							Ref: P Jones	City comfortably hold Bobby Robson's team until an inexplicable penalty – Whelan adjudged to have handled. Shearer scores his 299th goal and Gavilan wraps it up with a sweet angled shot. Quinn has broken his leg on his Irish debut. Out of contract McAllister is linked to Liverpool.											
37	H	SHEFFIELD WED	14	W	4-1	1-0	McAllister 38, 70, Zuniga 67, Hadji 80	Ogrizovic	Breen	Telfer	Chippo*	Williams	Shaw	Hadji	McAllister	Zuniga	Keane	Whelan	Eustace
	6/5	19,920	*19*	44			*De Bilde 81*	*Pressman*	*Nolan*	*Hinchcliffe*	*Jonk*	*Atherton*	*Walker**	*Alexand'sn^*	*Horne"*	*Booth*	*De Bilde*	*Quinn*	*Haslam/Sibon/Sonner*
							Ref: S Bennett	Peter Shreeve's Owls are relegated. McAllister is the architect of a fine win in the new strip with two goals and a shot that hits the crossbar for Zuniga to head in. Hadji is dazzling with five goal attempts in the first half. Oggy does a double lap of honour after his farewell game.											
38	A	WATFORD	14	L	0-1	0-1		Hedman	Breen	Telfer	Chippo	Williams^	Shaw	Hadji	McAllister	Zuniga*	Keane	Whelan	Normann"/Gustafs'n/Quinn
	14/5	*18,977*	*20*	44			*Helguson 44*	*Day*	*Cox**	*Ward*	*Palmer*	*Page*	*Robinson*	*Bonnot*	*Helguson*	*Smith*	*Mooney*	*Perpetuini*	*Gibbs*
Average	Home 20,785	Away 30,752					Ref: U Rennie	The away record is woeful. No wins for the first time ever, 22 games without a win and nine defeats in a row. Graham Taylor's relegated team show more grit and fight than City in a carnival atmosphere. City's large following are stunned by Helguson's overhead kick for the only goal.											

Worthington Cup	Att			F-A	H-T	Scorers, Times, and Referees	SQUAD	NUMBERS	IN USE									subs used
2:1 A TRANMERE	17	L		1-5	1-0	McAllister 7	**Nuzzo**	Breen^	Burrows !	Strachan	Williams	Shaw	Edworthy	McAllister	McSheff'y*	Eustace	Froggatt	Hall P/Konjic
14/9	*6,759 1:23*					*Taylor 50, 90, Kelly 58, 63, 80*	*Achterberg*	*Allen*	*Roberts*	*Henry**	*Challinor*	*Yates*	*Parkinson*	*Morgan*	*Kelly*	*Taylor*	*Mahon*	*Thompson*
						Ref: U Rennie	After being in control for 45 minutes City lose the plot with some awful defending and direct football from John Aldridge's team. Burrows gets a red card in his first game back following a ban, after tangling with Mahon. Their biggest League Cup defeat since 1965 and no excuses.											
2:2 H TRANMERE	17	W		3-1	3-1	McAllister 21, Chippo 44, 45	Kirkland	Edworthy	Hall M	Palmer	Konjic	Shaw	Telfer	McAllister	Hadji	McSheff'y*	Chippo	Eustace
22/9	12,429 *1:24*					*Taylor 22*	*Achterberg*	*Hill*	*Roberts*	*Allen*	*Challinor*	*Yates*	*Thompson*	*Morgan*	*Kelly*	*Taylor**	*Mahon*	*Parkinson*
						Ref: T Jones (City lose 4-6 on aggregate)	City look capable of pulling back the deficit but in the end it's too big a job and they fall at the first hurdle for the first time since 1992. 13 attempts on goal and 10 corners are not enough but Chippo's 25-yarder deserves to win any game. Strange decisions from the ref don't help.											

FA Cup	Att			F-A	H-T	Scorers, Times, and Referees												subs used
3 A NORWICH	11	W		3-1	0-0	Whelan 58, Roussel 76, Eustace 84	Hedman	Telfer	Froggatt	Palmer	Williams*	Breen	Hadji	McAllister	Whelan*	Keane	Chippo	Eustace/Roussel
11/12	*15,702 1:14*					*Llewelyn 66*	*Marshall*	*Sutch*	*Fugelstad*	*Anselin^*	*Fleming*	*Jackson*	*De Blasiis*	*Russell*	*Roberts*	*Dalglish**	*Llewelyn*	*Forbes/Kenton*
						Ref: P Alcock	A thrilling second half makes up for a dull first. Marshall concedes two soft goals and Eustace's first senior goal means two subs score for the first time. The rusty Whelan gets stick from some fans and is lucky not to be sent off for using an elbow. Bruce Rioch's team deserve a replay.											
4 H BURNLEY	13	W		3-0	1-0	Chippo 11, 69, Whelan 75	Hedman	Telfer^	Froggatt	Palmer"	Williams	Breen	Hadji	McAllister	Roussel*	Keane	Chippo	Whelan/Gustaffson/Eustace
8/1	22,770 *2:6*						*Crichton*	*West**	*Armstrong*	*Mellon*	*Davis*	*Thomas*	*Mullin*	*Cook*	*Cooke*	*Payton*	*Little*	*Branch*
						Ref: S Lodge	Newly energised by Ramadan, Chippo is the hero as City make heavy weather of Stan Ternent's brave boys. City deserve it on their first-half display but 4,000 noisy Burnley fans will disagree. It is Chippo and Hadji's last game for a month while they play in the African Nations Cup.											
5 H CHARLTON	12	L		2-3	2-2	Roussel 15, 21	Hedman	Telfer	Froggatt	Palmer	Williams*	Breen	Eustace^	McAllister	Roussel	Keane	Normann"	Shaw/Gustafsson/**Delorge**
29/1	22,842 *1:1*					*Robinson 40, Newton 45, Hunt 88*	*Kiely*	*Shields*	*Powell*	*Stuart^*	*Rufus*	*Brown*	*Newton*	*Kinsella**	*Hunt*	*Pringle*	*Robinson"*	*Todd/Salako/Konchesky*
						Ref: D Gallagher	City's Wembley dream is over after Curbishley's men come from two down. City relax and Charlton's wingers rip them apart. The limping Williams is exposed, as is Froggatt, and despite City having more chances it's Charlton day. The Div 1 leaders are unbeaten in 9 away games.											

		Home						Away					
	P	W	D	L	F	A	W	D	L	F	A	Pts
1 Manchester U	38	15	4	0	59	16	13	3	3	38	29	91
2 Arsenal	38	14	3	2	42	17	8	4	7	31	26	73
3 Leeds	38	12	2	5	29	18	9	4	6	29	25	69
4 Liverpool	38	11	4	4	28	13	8	6	5	23	17	67
5 Chelsea	38	12	5	2	35	12	6	6	7	18	22	65
6 Aston Villa	38	8	8	3	23	12	7	5	7	23	23	58
7 Sunderland	38	10	6	3	28	17	6	4	9	29	39	58
8 Leicester	38	10	3	6	31	24	6	4	9	24	31	55
9 West Ham	38	11	5	3	32	23	4	5	10	20	30	55
10 Tottenham	38	10	3	6	40	26	5	5	9	17	23	53
11 Newcastle	38	10	5	4	42	20	4	5	10	21	34	52
12 Middlesbro	38	8	5	6	23	26	6	5	8	23	26	52
13 Everton	38	7	9	3	36	21	5	5	9	22	28	50
14 COVENTRY	38	12	1	6	38	22	0	7	12	9	32	44
15 Southampton	38	8	4	7	26	22	4	4	11	19	40	44
16 Derby	38	6	3	10	22	25	3	8	8	22	32	38
17 Bradford C	38	6	8	5	26	29	3	1	15	12	39	36
18 Wimbledon	38	6	7	6	30	28	1	5	13	16	46	33
19 Sheffield Wed	38	6	3	10	21	23	2	4	13	17	47	31
20 Watford	38	5	4	10	24	30	1	2	16	11	46	24
	760	187	92	101	635	424	101	92	187	424	635	1048

Odds & ends

Double wins: (0).
Double losses: (5) Leicester, Manchester U, Leeds, Tottenham, Liverpool.

Won from behind: (0).
Lost from in front: (4) Leeds (h), Chelsea (a), Tranmere LC (a), Charlton FAC (h).

High spots: The dramatic arrival of Robbie Keane.
The excellent home form and some stunning football.
The win over Arsenal at Christmas.
The Sunderland home win – one of the best 45 minutes in the elite era.

Low spots: The worst away record in the club's history.
The Tranmere Worthington Cup debacle.
The Charlton FA Cup exit.

Red cards: City – Burrows (Leic'ter a; Tranmere a LC), Chippo (Sund'nd a).
Red cards: Opponents – Moncur (West Ham h), Barton (Newcastle h).

Player of the Year: Gary McAllister.
Ever-presents: (1) Gary McAllister.
Hat-tricks: (0).
Opposing hat-tricks: (1) David Kelly (Tranmere).
Leading scorer: (13) Gary McAllister.

	Appearances						Goals			
	Lge	*Sub*	LC	*Sub*	FAC	*Sub*	Lge	LC	FAC	Tot
Aloisi, John	3	*4*					2			2
Betts, Robert		*2*								
Breen, Gary	20	*1*	1		3					
Burrows, David	11	*4*	1							
Chippo, Youssef	33		1		2		2	2	2	6
Delorge, Laurent						*1*				
Edworthy, Marc	10		2							
Eustace, John	12	*4*	1	*1*	1	*2*	1		1	2
Froggatt, Steve	21	*5*	1		3		1			1
Gustafsson, Tomas	7	*3*				*2*				
Hadji, Moustapha	33		1		2		6			6
Hall, Marcus	7	*2*	1							
Hall, Paul		*1*		*1*						
Hedman, Magnus	35				3					
Hendry, Colin	9									
Huckerby, Darren	1									
Keane, Robbie	30	*1*			3		12			12
Kirkland, Chris			1							
Konjic, Mo	3	*1*	1	*1*						
McAllister, Gary	38		2		3		11	2		13
McSheffrey, Gary		*3*	2							
Normann, Runar	1	*7*			1					
Nuzzo, Rafaele (loan)			1							
Ogrizovic, Steve	3									
Palmer, Carlton	15		1		3		1			1
Quinn, Barry	5	*6*								
Roussel, Cedric	18	*4*			2	*1*	6		3	9
Shaw, Richard	27	*2*	2			*1*				
Strachan, Gavin	1	*2*	1							
Telfer, Paul	26	*4*	1		3					
Whelan, Noel	20	*6*			1	*1*	1		2	3
Williams, Paul	26	*2*	1		3		1			1
Zuniga, Ysrael	3	*4*					2			2
(own-goals)							1			1
33 players used	**418**	***68***	**22**	***3***	**33**	***8***	**47**	**4**	**8**	**59**

No	Date		Att	Pos	Pt	F-A	H-T	Scorers, Times, and Referees	SQUAD	NUMBERS	IN	USE								subs used
1	H	MIDDLESBROUGH			L	1-3	1-1	Eustace 40	Hedman	Breen^	Hall	Palmer	Hendry	Williams	**Thomps'n** !	Eustace*	Roussel	**Bellamy**	Chippo	Telfer/Aloisi
	19/8		20,623		0			*Job 19, Boksic 59, 63*	*Schwarzer*	*Fleming*	*O'Neill*	*Cooper*	*Pallister*	*Vickers*	*Job^*	*Karembeu*	*Boksic**	*Deane*	*Ince*	*Whelan/Okon*
								Ref: B Knight	Hendry is booed after two errors let in debut-boy Boksic to grab the points for Bryan Robson's team. After a strong first half City wilt in the hot sun and Tommo is the first City league debutant to see red after 70 minutes for two yellows. Only Palmer and Eustace look the part.											
2	A	SOUTHAMPTON			W	2-1	1-0	Bellamy 20p, Roussel 62	Hedman	Edworthy	Hall	Palmer	Williams	Shaw	Telfer	Eustace	Roussel	Bellamy*	Chippo	Zuniga
	23/8		***14,801***		3			*Tessem 52*	*Jones*	*Dodd*	*Bridge*	*Marsden^*	*Lundekvam*	*Khalej*	*Draper*	*Oakley*	*Davies**	*Rosler*	*Kachloul"*	*Pahars/Tessem/Beattie*
								Ref: P Taylor	A deserved win in a scrappy game ends the dire away run after 508 days against Hoddle's men. In the new black kit the defence looks tighter and the work-rate is high. El Khalej fouls Eustace for the spot-kick and Roussel heads in Telfer's corner on City's last league visit to the Dell.											
3	A	MANCHESTER C		4	W	2-1	2-0	Edghill 24 (og), Bellamy 45	Hedman	Edworthy	Hall	Palmer	Williams	Shaw	Telfer	Eustace	Roussel	Bellamy	Chippo*	Thompson
	26/8		*34,140*	*16*	6			*Horlock 75*	*Weaver*	*Edghill**	*Tiatto*	*Haaland*	*Howey*	*Prior*	*Wiekens*	*Horlock*	*Weah*	*Wanchope*	*Kennedy^*	*Grant/Dickov*
								Ref: A D'Urso	Royle's newly promoted team have just hit four past Sunderland. Edghill is the villain with a headed back-pass that beats Weaver, then letting Bellamy skin him. He's booed then subbed. City hang on for their first league win at the ground since 1986 despite Weah's strong presence.											
4	H	NEWCASTLE		9	L	0-2	0-1		Hedman	Edworthy	Hall	Palmer	Williams	Shaw	Telfer	Eustace*	Roussel	Bellamy^	Chippo	Hadji/Aloisi
	6/9		22,102	*1*	6			*Shearer 30p, Gallacher 58*	*Given*	*Charvet*	*Domi**	*Lee*	*Hughes*	*Goma*	*Dyer*	*Speed*	*Shearer*	*Cordone"*	*Glass^*	*Griffin/Gallacher/Kerr*
								Ref: A Wiley	City are stunning until Charvet's dive gives Shearer his 200th league goal and 14th against the Sky Blues. Hall's clearance ricochets into Gallacher's path and the ex-City man clinches the win. Robson's Newcastle look solid but City are out of luck. Unhappy Hendry could be off.											
5	H	LEEDS		9	D	0-0	0-0		Hedman	Edworthy	Hall	Palmer	Williams	Shaw	Hadji	Chippo	Roussel	Bellamy*	Telfer^	Zuniga/Eustace
	9/9		20,363	*6*	7				*Martyn*	*Kelly*	*Harte*	*Dacourt*	*Duberry*	*Radebe*	*Bowyer*	*McPhail*	*Bridges*	*Smith*	*Huckerby**	*Wilcox*
								Ref: P Durkin	Hadji captains the side for the first time in a defence-dominated game. The midfield duels between Bowyer and Palmer, and Dacourt and Chippo, are niggly. City match Leeds for quality and Eustace blasts the best chance over. Leeds head for Barcelona this week but don't ease up.											
6	A	ARSENAL		12	L	1-2	0-1	Hadji 80	Hedman	Edworthy"	Hall	Palmer	Williams	Shaw	Hadji	Chippo	Roussel	Bellamy^	Telfer*	Eustace/Zuniga/Breen
	16/9		*37,794*	*2*	7			*Wiltord 24, Vernazza 72*	*Seaman*	*Luzhny*	*Silvinho*	*Grimandi*	*Adams*	*Keown*	*Parlour^*	*Ljungberg*	*Wiltord**	*Bergkamp"*	*Pires*	*Henry/Vernazza/Kanu*
								Ref: M Dean	Wenger's Arsenal dominate for 75 minutes. Hadji scores City's first at Highbury for five years with a stunning free-kick and Hall hits the bar at the death. Wiltord is yards offside and Vernazza's first Arsenal goal is a tap in after Hedman's save. Roussel accuses Keown of elbowing.											
7	H	WEST HAM		17	L	0-3	0-2		Hedman	Edworthy	Hall"	Palmer	Williams	Shaw	Thompson*	Chippo	Zuniga^	Bellamy	Hadji	Eustace/Aloisi/Breen
	23/9		20,132	*18*	7			*Di Canio 38, Cole 40, Lampard 69*	*Hislop*	*Sinclair^*	*Winterburn*	*Ferdinand**	*Stimac*	*Pearce S*	*Lampard*	*Lomas*	*Kanoute"*	*Di Canio*	*Cole*	*Carrick/Potts/Diawara*
								Ref: N Barry	Strachan says it's the worst in his 5½ years at the club and the team are booed off. West Ham are in control throughout with their slick passing and Di Canio's silky skills. City barely have a goal attempt and Redknapp's men get their first win of the season. City in hunt for Lee Carsley.											
8	A	CHARLTON		16	D	2-2	1-0	Aloisi 41, Bellamy 70p	Hedman	Edworthy	Hall	Palmer	Williams	Shaw	Telfer	Eustace	Aloisi*	Bellamy	Chippo	Roussel
	30/9		*20,043*	*7*	8			*Hunt 59, Johansson 88*	*Kiely*	*Konchesky"*	*Powell*	*Kinsella*	*Rufus*	*Brown*	*Stuart*	*Jensen*	*Hunt^*	*Johansson*	*Robinson**	*Salako/Lisbie/Shields*
								Ref: R Styles	A much-improved City are well on top until Hunt follows up after Jensen's shot hits the bar. Bellamy restores the lead after Rufus handles a Telfer corner. Johansson's scissor-kick after Shaw's poor clearance makes it seven goals in eight. Curbishley's men are buzzing but lucky.											
9	H	TOTTENHAM		13	W	2-1	2-0	Aloisi 12, Eustace 25	**Kirkland**	Telfer	Edworthy	Palmer !	Breen	Shaw	Eustace	Chippo	Aloisi*	Bellamy^	Hadji	Roussel/Hendry
	14/10		21,430	*11*				*Rebrov 53*	*Walker*	*Carr*	*Thatcher*	*Freund**	*Vega*	*Perry*	*Anderton*	*Sherwood*	*Ferdinand*	*Rebrov*	*Leonh'ds'n^*	*Iversen/Dominguez*
								Ref: P Jones	19-year-old Kirkland's impressive league debut earns the first home win. Aloisi's screamer and Eustace's clinical goal from Bellamy's pass put City on top. City weather the storm after Palmer's red card for retaliation on Perry with Breen, in for the suspended Williams, supreme.											
10	A	CHELSEA		15	L	**1-6**	0-2	Roussel 88 *[Flo 67]*	Kirkland !	Telfer	Edworthy	Palmer	Breen	Williams	Eustace^	Chippo	Aloisi*	Bellamy"	Hadji	**Miller**/Shaw/Roussel
	21/10		*34,646*	*10*				*Hasselbaink 24p, 42, 52, 58, Zola 48,*	*De Goey*	*Melchiot*	*Babayaro"*	*Ferrer**	*Desailly*	*Leboeuf*	*Poyet*	*Wise*	*Hasselbaink*	*Zola*	*Dalla Bona^*	*Flo/Jokanovic/Bogarde*
								Ref: S Lodge	Kirkland's dismissal for 'fouling' Jimmy Floyd is a travesty and is later overturned. On-loan keeper Alan Miller's protection is woeful and new boss Ranieri's team let rip for City's biggest defeat since 1991. The Dutchman is the first to score four against them since Ian Rush in '84.											

No	H/A	Opponent	Pos	Res	F-A	H-T	Scorers, Times, and Referees	1	2	3	4	5	6	7	8	9	10	11	Subs used
11	A	SUNDERLAND	16	L	0-1	0-0		Kirkland	Telfer	**Guerrero"**	Shaw	Williams	Breen	Chippo	Quinn^	Aloisi*	Bellamy	Hadji	Roussel/Eustace/Thompson
28/10		*44,526*	*9*				*Thome 52*	*Sorensen*	*Makin*	*Gray*	*Hutchison*	*Thome*	*Craddock*	*Rae*	*Williams*	*Quinn**	*Phillips*	*Arca*	*Dichio*
							Ref: A Wiley	City, playing 3-5-2, shake off the Chelsea defeat and even Peter Reid says they deserve a point. Thome's far-post header makes it six unbeaten for the Wearsiders. Bellamy's perfectly good goal is disallowed. The suspended Palmer wants to be a manager. Roussel is told to sharpen up.											
12	H	MANCHESTER U	17	L	1-2	0-2	Zuniga 65	Kirkland	Edworthy	Guerrero	Shaw	Williams	Breen	Thompson"	Quinn^	**Bothroyd***	Hadji	Chippo	Zuniga/Eustace/Telfer
4/11		21,077	*1*				*Cole 27, Beckham 37*	*Barthez*	*Neville P*	*Irwin*	*Keane*	*Brown*	*Neville G*	*Beckham*	*Scholes**	*Cole*	*Sher'gh'm^*	*Giggs*	*Solskjaer/Yorke*
							Ref: G Poll	City are in awe of Ferguson's United. A gutsier display after the break and a header from Zuniga give them brief hope. Beckham superbly crosses for Cole and bends a free-kick past a flimsy wall and an unsighted Kirkland. Roy Keane and the disrespectful Eustace have a tiff.											
13	A	LIVERPOOL	17	L	1-4	0-1	Thompson 56 *[Heskey 82, 87]*	Kirkland	Breen	Guerrero^	Palmer	Williams	Shaw	Thompson	Strachan"	Bellamy	Hadji	Chippo*	Roussel/Edworthy/Eustace
12/11		*43,701*	*3*				*McAllister 12, Gerrard 51,*	*Westerveld*	*Babbel*	*Traore*	*Gerrard^*	*Hyppia*	*Henchoz*	*Barmby*	*McAllister*	*Heskey*	*Owen**	*Smicer"*	*Murphy/Carragher/Ziege*
							Ref: M Riley	The script is written for McAllister who scores his first goal and makes two more. But for Kirkland's keeping and Owen's misses it could have been ten. Even so, City have the worst goal-difference in the league. David Thompson's goal is a 30-yard stunner and Bellamy also goes close.											
14	H	IPSWICH	17	L	0-1	0-0		Kirkland	Breen	Edworthy	Telfer	Williams	Konjic	Thompson	Chippo	Roussel*	Bellamy	Hadji	Aloisi
20/11		19,327	*5*				*Wilnis 90*	*Wright R*	*Wilnis*	*Hreidarsson*	*Magilton*	*Venus*	*McGreal^*	*Wright J**	*Holland*	*Stewart*	*Scowcroft*	*Clapham*	*Reuser/Bramble*
							Ref: D Elleray	Sky viewers see City slump to a fifth defeat in a row, the worst run since 1991. Wilnis's header from Reuser's cross a minute into stoppage time gives Burley's 'tractor boys' the win. Thompson shines and hits the bar but the team are booed off. Strachan gets a vote of confidence.											
15	H	ASTON VILLA	17	D	1-1	0-1	Hadji 83	Kirkland	Breen	Edworthy	Telfer	Williams	Konjic	Thompson	Chippo*	Roussel^	Zuniga"	Hadji	Eustace/Aloisi/Palmer
25/11		21,455	*6*				*Dublin 8*	*James*	*Stone*	*Wright*	*Alpay*	*Southgate*	*Barry*	*Taylor**	*Boateng*	*Dublin*	*Merson*	*Hendrie*	*Delaney*
							Ref: J Winter	Dublin ends his goal drought as expected with a tap in from Taylor's cross. Zuniga, in for the dropped Bellamy, makes no headway and it is Hadji, pushed up front, who grabs a deserved equaliser from Aloisi's flick. Konjic ties up Dublin and City finish strongly. Palmer is on the list.											
16	A	BRADFORD C	18	L	1-2	0-0	Aloisi 64	Kirkland	Breen	Quinn	Palmer	Williams	Konjic*	Telfer	Eustace	Aloisi	Hadji	Thompson^	Chippo/Bellamy
2/12		*15,532*	*20*				*Collymore 80, Beagrie 83*	*Clarke*	*Nolan*	*Myers**	*O'Brien*	*Molenaar*	*Atherton*	*Carbone*	*McCall*	*Windass*	*Collymore*	*McKinlay*	*Beagrie*
							Ref: M Dean	The situation is dire. City are in the bottom three for the first time since Feb 1999. Chances are squandered before the influential Hadji sets up Aloisi for a sweet left-footer. Jim Jeffries' inspired substitute, Peter Beagrie, swings the game although Collymore looks offside for the first.											
17	H	LEICESTER	17	W	1-0	1-0	Bellamy 40	Hedman	Breen	Quinn	**Carsley**	Williams	Konjic	Thompson	Telfer^	Aloisi*	Hadji	Bellamy	Roussel/Palmer
10/12		**17,275**	*4*					*Royce*	*Sinclair^*	*Davidson*	*Rowett*	*Elliott*	*Gilchrist*	*Savage*	*Izzet**	*Akinbiyi*	*Eadie*	*Oakes*	*Benjamin/Impey*
							Ref: S Dunn	High flying Foxes under new manager Peter Taylor are brought to earth. Bellamy heads in their ninth attempt on goal – from Telfer's cross – for his first home goal. New midfielder Carsley makes a solid debut. City hang on in the last ten minutes but deserve the win for the hard work.											
18	A	DERBY	18	L	0-1	0-1		Hedman	Breen	Quinn	Carsley	Williams^	Konjic	Thompson"	Telfer	Aloisi*	Hadji	Bellamy	Roussel/Chippo/Eustace
16/12		*27,869*	*17*				*Christie 8*	*Poom*	*Martin**	*Johnson*	*Riggott*	*Carbonari*	*West*	*Eranio^*	*Burley*	*Christie"*	*Delap*	*Powell*	*Burton/Murray/Morris*
							Ref: M Messias	Another six-pointer is lost and despite dominating for long periods City have few chances in a scrappy game. Hedman saves Burley's shot with his legs but Christie fires home. Palmer and Hendry are on loan to Watford and Bolton. Leicester's Elliott is charged with elbowing Bellamy.											
19	H	SOUTHAMPTON	18	D	1-1	1-0	Thompson 33	Kirkland	Breen	Quinn	Carsley	Williams	Konjic	Thompson"	Telfer	Roussel*	Hadji	Bellamy^	Chippo/Zuniga/Eustace
22/12		18,082	*15*				*Tessem 51*	*Jones*	*Khalej*	*Bridge*	*Marsden*	*Lundekvam*	*Richards*	*Tessem*	*Gibbens**	*Beattie*	*Kachloul*	*Draper*	*Davies*
							Ref: A Wiley	A dreadful game with fellow strugglers. City fail to take chances and crucially lose concentration for the unmarked Tessem to head in. Tommo wastes eight corners but scores from a 35-yard free-kick which bounces awkwardly in front of Jones. The 100th league game between the clubs.											
20	A	EVERTON	18	W	2-1	0-0	Hadji 69, Breen 87	Kirkland	Breen	Quinn	Carsley	Williams	Konjic*	Thompson	Telfer	Zuniga"	Hadji	Bellamy^	Edworthy/Chippo/Aloisi
26/12		*35,794*	*14*				*Gemmill 85*	*Myhre*	*Watson*	*Naysmith*	*Gravesen*	*Weir*	*Ball*	*Gemmill*	*Pembridge^*	*Ferguson*	*Cadamart"*	*Tal**	*Unsworth/Nyarko/Moore*
							Ref: N Barry	A passionate display earns a vital win. Scott Gemmill's fierce shot cancels out Hadji's header and it looks like a draw until Breen heads in Thompson's free-kick for his first goal for three years. Breen shackles Duncan Ferguson and Kirkland is hit by a missile. Konjic injured again.											
21	A	MIDDLESBROUGH	17	D	1-1	1-0	Whelan 41(og)	Kirkland	Edworthy	Quinn	Carsley	Williams	Breen	Thompson	Telfer	Zuniga*	Hadji	Bellamy^	Aloisi/Chippo
30/12		*30,499*	*18*				*Boksic 86*	*Schwarzer*	*Fleming*	*O'Neill*	*Ehiogu*	*Festa*	*Cooper**	*Karembeu^*	*Ince*	*Ricard*	*Whelan"*	*Okon*	*Vickers/Boksic/Deane*
							Ref: D Gallagher	A spectacular own-goal by Whelan on his birthday looks to have given City the points until Boksic fires in from a narrow angle for his first home goal. Boro are unbeaten under Terry Venables and City gain their first point in four visits to the Riverside and their first goal since 1995.											

No	Date			Att	Pos	Pt	F-A	H-T	Scorers, Times, and Referees	SQUAD NUMBERS IN USE											subs used
22		H	MANCHESTER C		17	D	1-1	0-0	Edworthy 72	Kirkland	Edworthy	Quinn^	Carsley	Williams	Breen	Thompson	Telfer	Zuniga*	Hadji	Bellamy"	Aloisi/Eustace/Chippo
	1/1			21,991	*19*				*Wanchope 54*	*Weaver*	*Edghill**	*Granville*	*Dunne*	*Morrison*	*Howey*	*Bishop^*	*Haaland*	*Wanchope*	*Huckerby**	*Tiatto*	*Goater/Wright-Phillips*
									Ref: B Knight	Another case of two points lost as the lack of fire-power continues. Eighteen shots and twelve corners only produce Edworthy's first ever goal after Weaver's boob. Huckerby gives Quinn a skinning but Williams is his nemesis. An unbeaten Christmas but six points is not enough.											
23		A	NEWCASTLE		18	L	1-3	0-1	Thompson 79	Hedman	Edworthy	Quinn	Carsley	Williams	Breen	Thompson	Eustace	Aloisi*	Bellamy	Telfer	Bothroyd
	13/1			*50,159*	*7*				*Speed 4, Ameobi 58, Dyer 67*	*Harper*	*Barton*	*Quinn*	*Speed*	*Hughes*	*Goma*	*Solano*	*Acuna*	*Ameobi*	*Dyer*	*Bassedas**	*Glass*
									Ref: J Winter	Kirkland pulls a hamstring in the warm-up and Hedman gets his chance. City miss seven good chances with Bellamy and Aloisi the culprits and Robson's Newcastle take their chances with Dyer superb. Tommo scores direct from a corner. City are without a win here since 1988.											
24		H	EVERTON		19	L	1-3	0-3	Carsley 86p *[Campbell 31]*	Kirkland	Edworthy	Quinn	Carsley	Konjic*	Breen	Thompson	Eustace	Zuniga"	Hadji	Telfer^	Palmer/Chippo/Aloisi
	20/1			19,172	*15*				*Gemmill 8, Cadamarteri 15,*	*Myhre*	*Cleland^*	*Unsworth*	*Gemmill*	*Watson*	*Ball*	*Alexand'n**	*Pembridge*	*Campbell*	*Cadamarteri*	*Tal*	*Jevons/Clarke*
									Ref: P Durkin	It's twenty years since City were 0-3 down at half-time at home and they are dire. A gutless and incompetent display; Strachan needs protection at the end. Everton have 14 players out injured and haven't won in seven but coast home. Konjic is so at sea he is subbed after 26 minutes.											
25		A	LEEDS		19	L	0-1	0-0		Hedman	Quinn*	Hall	Shaw	Williams	Breen	Thompson"	Carsley^	Bellamy	Hadji	Eustace	Telfer/Chippo/Bothroyd
	31/1			*36,555*	*10*				*Keane 69*	*Martyn*	*Mills*	*Harte*	*Batty*	*Ferdinand*	*Radebe*	*Bowyer*	*Bakke*	*Viduka*	*Keane*	*Wilcox*	
									Ref: R Harris	City work hard in a dour game but lack any cutting edge. Old boy Keane predictably nets with an overhead kick when a draw looked on. Nine bookings are not a true reflection of the game. City's 3-5-2 format looks solid but John Hartson is still needed and insuring him is a problem.											
26		H	ARSENAL		19	L	0-1	0-0		Hedman	Quinn*	Hall	Carsley	Williams	Shaw	Thompson*	Eustace	Roussel	Hadji	Bellamy	Bothroyd
	3/2			22,034	*2*				*Bergkamp 77*	*Seaman*	*Dixon*	*Cole*	*Vieira*	*Adams*	*Stepanovs*	*Lauren**	*Parlour*	*Wiltord*	*Bergkamp*	*Pires^*	*Grimandi/Vivas*
									Ref: M Dean	A standing ovation for a brave show in which City match Wenger's Gunners but they desperately need points. Bergkamp's glancing header from Wiltord's cross is enough, though Bellamy and Eustace rue misses. Eustace roughs up Vieira and the rusty Roussel is set to join Wolves.											
27		A	WEST HAM		19	D	1-1	0-0	Dailly 89 (og)	Hedman	Quinn^	Hall	Carsley*	Breen	Shaw	Thompson	Eustace	**Hartson**	Bellamy"	Hadji	Chippo/Bothroyd/Edworthy
	12/2			*22,586*	*14*				*Cole 82*	*Forrest*	*Schemmel*	*Winterburn*	*Tihinen*	*Dailly*	*Pearce S*	*Lampard*	*Carrick*	*Kanoute*	*Di Canio*	*Cole*	
									Ref: D Gallagher	Hartson has signed on a pay-as-you-play basis and has a goal disallowed and a strong penalty appeal rejected on his debut. Redknapp's men looked to have won the Sky game when prodigy Joe Cole scores. But Thompson's free-kick spins off Dailly's shoulder for a precious point.											
28		H	CHARLTON		19	D	2-2	1-1	Bellamy 8, Hartson 66	Hedman	Edworthy	Hall	Carsley	Breen	Shaw	Thompson	Quinn	Hartson	Bellamy	Chippo*	Aloisi
	24/2			19,478	*8*				*Rufus 21, Johansson 46*	*Ilic*	*Fish*	*Powell*	*Kinsella**	*Rufus*	*Todd*	*Kishishev*	*Jensen^*	*Svensson*	*Johansson"*	*Stuart*	*Newton/Konchesky/Lisbie*
									Ref: M Halsey	An opportunity missed as Derby and Man City win. The dodgy Ilic spills Quinn's shot and it's 1-0 but Hedman's flapping causes the equaliser. John Hartson's untidy goal is deserved but not enough. Alan Curbishley's hard working Charlton are having their best season since the 1950s.											
29		H	CHELSEA		19	D	0-0	0-0		Kirkland	Quinn	Hall	Carsley*	Breen	Shaw	Thompson	Eustace	Hartson	Bellamy	Hadji^	Chippo/Aloisi
	3/3			21,708	*10*					*Cudicini*	*Ferrer*	*Le Saux*	*Wise*	*Desailly**	*Leboeuf*	*Poyet"*	*Jokanovic*	*Hasselbaink*	*Gudjohns'n^*	*Gronkjaer*	*Terry/Zola/Stanic*
									Ref: S Bennett	Kirkland replaces the dropped Hedman, and pulls off a string of fine saves. Cudicini is also in great form and saves well from Hadji and Thompson. Ranieri's Chelsea are still without an away win and haven't won at Coventry since 1992. Roland Nilsson is back as a coach.											
30		A	TOTTENHAM		19	L	0-3	0-2		Kirkland	Quinn	Hall	Carsley	Breen	Shaw	Thompson*	Eustace^	Hartson	Hadji	Bellamy	Telfer/Chippo"/Edworthy
	17/3			*35,606*	*11*				*Iversen 28, Ferdinand 34, Rebrov 58*	*Sullivan*	*Iversen*	*Young*	*Perry*	*Campbell*	*Doherty*	*Freund*	*King*	*Ferdinand*	*Rebrov*	*Clemence*	
									Ref: G Poll (sub P Taylor 45)	Playing wide on the left, Bellamy has a blistering first 25 minutes and creates three good chances. Spurs, who sacked George Graham in the week, score with their first attack and it's all over. Woeful defending from set pieces create the first two goals and it's beginning to look bleak.											
31		H	DERBY		19	W	2-0	1-0	Hadji 44, Hartson 49	Kirkland	Quinn	Hall	Carsley	Breen	Shaw	Eustace	Telfer	Hartson	Hadji !	Bellamy*	Chippo
	31/3			19,622	*16*					*Oakes**	*Delap*	*Johnson*	*Mawene*	*Carbonari*	*Higginboth'*	*Burley"*	*Gudjohns'n^*	*Burton*	*Christie*	*Powell*	*Poom/Kinkladze/Murray*
									Ref: D Elleray	Hartson lifts City 'from the dead' and adds to his three Welsh goals in two games with a superb header from Telfer's corner. Hadji heads the first but sees red on 72 minutes after spitting at Higginbotham. Jim Smith's Derby are poor and it's City's first league win since Boxing Day.											

No	Venue	Opponent	Pos	Res	F-A	H-T	Scorers, Times, and Referees	1	2	3	4	5	6	7	8	9	10	11	Subs used
32	A	LEICESTER	18	W	**3-1**	2-1	Bellamy 1, Carsley 18, Hartson 50	Kirkland	Quinn	Hall	Carsley	Breen	Shaw	Eustace*	Telfer	Hartson	Hadji^	Bellamy	Chippo/Williams
	7/4	19,545	*10*				*Akinbiyi 8*	*Royce*	*Impey*	*Davidson^*	*Rowett*	*Elliott**	*Taggart*	*Marshall*	*Izzet"*	*Akinbiyi*	*Gunnlaug'n*	*Lewis*	*Oakes/Guppy/Benjamin*
							Ref: G Barber	A battling performance, aided by the confidence of a 49-second goal from Hadji's cross. It's five defeats in a row for Taylor's Foxes and they are never in this game. Carsley heads in Quinn's cross, Hartson heads home Telfer's corner – three goals for the first time and a derby double.											
33	A	MANCHESTER U	19	L	2-4	2-2	Hartson 11, 33	Kirkland	Quinn	Hall	Carsley	Breen	Shaw	Eustace^	Telfer*	Hartson	Thompson	Bellamy	Chippo/Williams
	14/4	***67,637***	*1*				*Yorke 13, 28, Giggs 81, Scholes 87*	*Goram**	*Neville G*	*Silvestre*	*Keane*	*Brown*	*Staam*	*Scholes*	*Butt^*	*Cole"*	*Yorke*	*Giggs*	*V d Gouw/Beck'm/Solskjaer*
							Ref: M Riley	Hartson destroys on-loan Goram in his only United appearance but it's in vain. Persistent United end City's brave action with two late goals, the second a stunning 30-yard Scholes shot. Middlesbrough's shock win at Highbury means United are champs and City are five points adrift.											
34	H	SUNDERLAND	18	W	1-0	1-0	Hartson 21	Kirkland	Quinn	Hall	Carsley	Breen	Shaw	Eustace*	Telfer	Hartson	Bothroyd	Bellamy	Thompson
	16/4	20,934	*7*					*Sorensen*	*Williams*	*McCartney*	*Schwarz^*	*Thome*	*Varga !*	*Arca**	*McCann*	*Hutchison"*	*Phillips*	*Kilbane*	*Craddock/Thirlwell/Quinn*
							Ref: D Gallagher	An inability to add to Hartson's well-worked headed goal means it is a nail-biting finish with Sunderland throwing everything at City. Captain Breen stands firm, though, and it's three wins out of four. Clumsy Varga is off for two yellows. Boro lose and the gap narrows to two points.											
35	A	IPSWICH	18	L	0-2	0-1		Kirkland	Quinn"	Hall	Carsley^	Breen	Shaw	Eustace	Telfer	Hartson	Bothroyd*	Bellamy	Zuniga/Edworthy/Williams
	21/4	*24,612*	*3*				*Reuser 20, Wright J 56*	*Branagan*	*Makin*	*Hreidarsson*	*Magilton*	*Bramble*	*McGreal*	*Wright J*	*Holland*	*Stewart^*	*Armstrong*	*Reuser**	*Clapham/Naylor*
							Ref: G Barber	Burley's Ipswich are heading for Europe and too good for City who lack their recent passion. Their passing is poor and Bellamy, heavily booed by the home fans, misses a golden chance at 0-1. Quinn struggles against the tricky Reuser and Breen boobs for the second goal.											
36	H	LIVERPOOL	19	L	0-2	0-0		Kirkland	Quinn	Hall	Telfer	Breen	Williams	Chippo	Eustace	Hartson	Hadji	Bellamy*	Zuniga
	28/4	**23,063**	*5*				*Hyppia 84, McAllister 86*	*Westerveld*	*Babbel*	*Carragher*	*Hamann*	*Hyppia*	*Henchoz*	*Murphy*	*McAllister*	*Heskey"*	*Fowler**	*Berger^*	*Owen/Ziege/Biscan*
							Ref: S Bennett	The dead-ball master McAllister returns to haunt the Sky Blues. After Hyppia heads in his corner he bends in a free-kick to help Houllier's Reds towards a Champions League place. Williams and Eustace rue their misses in a battling display on Hadji's return from suspension.											
37	A	ASTON VILLA	19	L	2-3	2-0	Hadji 17, 25	Kirkland	Quinn	Hall^	Carsley	Breen	Williams	Eustace	Telfer*	Hartson	Hadji	Bellamy	Edworthy/Zuniga
	5/5	*39,761*	*8*				*Vassell 61, Angel 81, Merson 85*	*James*	*Delaney*	*Wright*	*Boateng^*	*Southgate*	*Barry*	*Merson*	*Taylor*	*Dublin*	*Vassell"*	*Staunton**	*Ginola/Hendrie/Angel*
							Ref: M Riley	Ultimately the result is immaterial but City beggar belief to throw away a two-goal lead with woeful defending and naïve tactics. Telfer's broken leg after 37 minutes and Ginola's introduction are crucial. Hadji's header and volley are forgotten in the tears as relegation is a reality.											
38	H	BRADFORD C	19	D	0-0	0-0		Kirkland	Edworthy	Quinn	Carsley	Williams*	Shaw	Chippo^	Strachan"	Hartson	Zuniga	Hadji	**Davenport**/Bothroyd/Betts
	19/5	20,299	*20*					*Davison*	*Nolan^*	*Jacobs*	*Halle*	*McCall*	*Myers*	*Blake**	*Locke*	*Ward*	*Carbone*	*Whalley*	*Grant/Kerr*
	Home	Away					Ref: A Wiley	Everyone is glad to see the end of this desperate end to a miserable season. With nothing to play for there is little entertainment against Jim Jeffries' side. Carbone, McCall, Zuniga and debutant Davenport shine. A planned lap of honour is aborted as fans jeers. A sad end to an era.											
Average	20,535	33,463																	

Worthington Cup	Att		F-A	H-T	Scorers, Times, and Referees												subs used
2:1 A PRESTON	12	W	3-1	2-0	Zuniga 4, Hall 45, Strachan 85p	Hedman	Edworthy	Hall	Palmer	Williams !	Shaw	Hadji	Eustace	Zuniga^	Bellamy"	Chippo*	Strachan/Aloisi/Breen
19/9	*10,770 1:6*				*Alexander 48p*	*Lucas*	*Alexander*	*Edwards*	*Appleton*	*Gregan*	*Murdock*	*Cartwright*	*Rankine*	*McBride*	*Basham*	*McKenna*	
					Ref: J Winter	City's first League Cup meeting with David Moyes' team is tough. The home side raise their game after the break and score when Williams handles. Soon after, Williams is off for two yellows and in trouble for kicking the scoreboard. A foul on Aloisi restores the two-goal cushion.											
2:2 H PRESTON	17	W	4-1	3-0	Aloisi 6, 25, 55p, Eustace 17	Hedman*	Edworthy	Hall	Eustace	Williams^	Shaw	Telfer	Chippo	Aloisi"	Bellamy	Hadji	Kirkland/Breen/Bothroyd
27/9	*7,416 1:5*				*Rankine 46*	*Lonergan*	*Alexander*	*Edwards*	*Gregan*	*Jackson*	*Murdock^*	*Cartwright**	*Rankine*	*Robinson*	*Basham"*	*Anderson*	*Barry-Murphy/Kidd/Eyres*
					Ref: C Foy (City win 7-2 on aggregate)	16-year-old Lonergan is Preston's youngest player since the 70s and can do nothing about City's blistering start. Bellamy makes the first and third, and Hadji the second, before Hedman goes off with a chest injury. Murdock fouls Aloisi for the penalty but Strachan demands more.											
3 A SOUTHAMPTON	16	W	1-0	0-0	Eustace 119	Kirkland	Quinn	Guerrero	Shaw	Williams	Breen	Hadji	Eustace	Roussel*	Zuniga^	Chippo	Thompson/Strachan
1/11	*11,809 18*		*aet*			*Jones*	*Oakley*	*Bridge*	*Tessem**	*Lundekvam*	*Dodd*	*Davies*	*Draper*	*Beattie*	*Pahars*	*Kachloul^*	*Khalej/Bleidelis*
					Ref: S Dunn	Roussel has a goal ruled out and is carried off in a neck brace. Chances fall to Davies, Zuniga and Pahars, and Kirkland pulls off some good saves in a scrappy game. Eustace scores from 12 yards after Saints fail to clear. City have a striker crisis and Mo Konjic pleads to get a game.											
4 A IPSWICH	17	L	1-2	0-1	Bellamy 53p	Kirkland	Breen	Quinn	Telfer	Williams	Konjic	Thompson	Eustace	Aloisi	Bellamy	Chippo*	Hadji
28/11	*19,563 3*				*Bramble 5, Johnson 65*	*Branagan*	*Wilnis*	*Hreidarsson*	*Wright J*	*Bramble*	*Scales*	*Reuser**	*Holland^*	*Johnson*	*Scowcroft*	*Clapham*	*Stewart/Croft*
					Ref: P Durkin	City are punished for Chippo's early mistake when he gifts the ball to Bramble. They have their share of chances but fail to make them count and Ipswich deservedly go through to the last eight. Wilnis fouls Chippo for the penalty but then Chippo boobs again and Johnson wraps it up.											

FA Cup																	
3 A SWINDON	17	W	2-0	1-0	Bellamy 4, Hadji 64	Kirkland	Edworthy	Quinn	Carsley	Williams	Breen	Thompson	Telfer	Bellamy	Hadji	Chippo	
6/1	*14,445 2:20*					*Griemink*	*Hall*	*Davies^*	*Cowe*	*Reeves*	*Dryden*	*Duke*	*Whitley**	*Alexander"*	*Invincible*	*Woan*	*O'Halloran/Williams/Young*
					Ref: S Bennett	An easy victory in a dull game which City should have won by a bigger margin. Yet again chances go begging. Bellamy profits from Davies' back-pass and Hadji has a tap-in. Andy King's team are poor, with Australian prodigy Invincible continually offside. City on trail for Hartson.											
4 A MANCHESTER C	19	L	0-1	0-0		Hedman	Edworthy*	Hall	Shaw	Williams	Breen	Quinn	Carsley	Bellamy	Bothroyd	Eustace	Telfer
27/1	*24,637 18*				*Goater 90*	*Weaver*	*Dunne^*	*Ritchie**	*Grant*	*Morrison*	*Prior*	*Whitley*	*Haaland*	*Wanchope"*	*Huckerby*	*Granville*	*Charvet/Wiekens/Goater*
					Ref: D Elleray	City restore some pride against Royle's team and look set for a replay until Goater heads in Grant's corner in the 93rd minute. Hall and Shaw return in a 3-5-2 line-up but it's Strachan's earliest Cup exit as boss. Eustace hits the post and misses a sitter. City fans cause trouble at the end.											